Education Psychology and Content Area Reading:
Adapted for Stage II New Pathways to Teaching in New Jersey

Second Custom Edition

Taken from:
Educational Psychology, Twelfth Edition
by Anita Woolfolk

Content Area Reading: Teaching and Learning in an Age of Multiple Literacies,
by Maureen McLaughlin

Creating Literacy Instruction: For All Students, Eighth Edition
by Thomas G. Gunning

The Adolescent: Development, Relationships, and Culture, Thirteenth Edition
by Kim Gale Dolgin

Adolescent Portraits: Identity, Relationships, and Challenges, Seventh Edition
by Andrew Garrod, Lisa Smulyan, Sally I. Powers, and Robert Kilkenny

Adolescent Portraits: Identity, Relationships, and Challenges, Sixth Edition
by Andrew Garrod, Lisa Smulyan, Sally I. Powers, and Robert Kilkenny

Cover Art: *The Little Town*, by Peter Arvidson.

Taken from:

Educational Psychology, Twelfth Edition
by Anita Woolfolk
Copyright © 2013, 2010, 2005, 2001, 1997 by Pearson Education, Inc.
Upper Saddle River, New Jersey 07458

Content Area Reading: Teaching and Learning in an Age of Multiple Literacies,
by Maureen McLaughlin
Copyright © 2010 by Pearson Education, Inc.
Boston, Massachusetts 02116

Creating Literacy Instruction: For All Students, Eighth Edition
by Thomas G. Gunning
Copyright © 2013, 2008, 2005 by Pearson Education, Inc.
Upper Saddle River, New Jersey 07458

The Adolescent: Development, Relationships, and Culture, Thirteenth Edition
by Kim Gale Dolgin
Copyright © 2011, 2008, 2005 by Pearson Education, Inc.
Published by Allyn & Bacon
Boston, Massachusetts 02116

Adolescent Portraits: Identity, Relationships, and Challenges, Seventh Edition
by Andrew Garrod, Lisa Smulyan, Sally I. Powers, and Robert Kilkenny
Copyright © 2012, 2008, 2005 by Pearson Education, Inc.
Boston, Massachusetts 02116

Adolescent Portraits: Identity, Relationships, and Challenges, Sixth Edition
by Andrew Garrod, Lisa Smulyan, Sally I. Powers, and Robert Kilkenny
Copyright © 2008, 2005, 2002, 1999, 1995, 1992 by Pearson Education, Inc.
Published by Allyn & Bacon

This special edition published in cooperation with Pearson Learning Solutions.

All trademarks, service marks, registered trademarks, and registered service marks are the property of their respective owners and are used herein for identification purposes only.

Pearson Learning Solutions, 501 Boylston Street, Suite 900, Boston, MA 02116
A Pearson Education Company
www.pearsoned.com

Printed in the United States of America

1 2 3 4 5 6 7 8 9 10 VOCR 17 16 15 14 13 12

000200010271692045

MC

ISBN 10: 1-256-84171-4
ISBN 13: 978-1-256-84171-5

OVERVIEW OF EDUCATION PSYCHOLOGY AND SELECTED TOPICS ON ADOLESCENCE

Introduction

Welcome to the beginning of an exciting career in teaching. This book was specifically designed for the New Pathways to Teaching in New Jersey Teacher Candidates. We are so pleased to welcome you into our program and hope that your experience will be positive and rewarding.

This book will provide an introduction to Educational Psychology, which is a critical element in the understanding of children, adolescents and young adults. We have also incorporated two additional chapters into this book relating to the traits of an adolescent as additional information to the chapters devoted to child development; one on Adolescent Society, Culture and Subculture and one on Social Development: The Changing Nature of Friendship and Romance. In addition, we have included 3 case studies for you to ponder and discuss. We have also created an interesting assignment related to eating disorders, substance abuse, self-esteem and juvenile delinquency. In this assignment, you will be asked to research one of these topics and report your findings to your colleagues.

This focus on adolescence will prepare some of you to teach in a middle school environment. However, we believe that it is very important for all teachers to understand the development and characteristics of children, adolescents and young adults. If you teach in an elementary school, some of the children in 4th and 5th grades are approaching adolescence and it is important to understand their needs and issues during that sensitive time in their lives. If you are teaching in a secondary school, as you already know, many of your students will be going through adolescence and you will need to be prepared for the challenges of that transition. Therefore, a clear understanding of human development will help you create an environment that will promote both the educational and emotional needs of your students.

Best of luck to you during this important year and in your teaching career. May you find happiness, fulfillment and joy in your classrooms and in your professional endeavors!

Many thanks to The Curriculum Committee of New Pathways to Teaching in New Jersey for all of their hard work!

Dr. Fran Levin
Academic Director of NPTNJ

Brief Contents

Part 1
STUDENTS

Chapter 1, 2, 4–6 taken from chapters 2–6 of *Educational Psychology*, Twelfth Edition by Anita Woolfolk

Chapter 3 taken from chapter 14 of *The Adolescent: Development, Relationships, and Culture*, Thirteenth Edition by Kim Gale Dolgin

chapter one
COGNITIVE DEVELOPMENT

WHAT WOULD YOU DO?

▶ **TEACHERS' CASEBOOK:** Symbols and Cymbals

The district curriculum guide calls for a unit on poetry, including lessons on *symbolism* in poems. You are concerned that many of your 4th grade students may not be ready to understand this abstract concept. To test the waters, you ask a few students what a *symbol* is.

"It's sorta like a big metal thing that you bang together." Tracy waves her hands like a drum major.

"Yeah," Sean adds, "My sister plays one in the high school band."

You realize they are on the wrong track here, so you try again. "I was thinking of a different kind of symbol, like a ring as a symbol of marriage or a heart as a symbol of love, or …"

You are met with blank stares.

Trevor ventures, "You mean like the Olympic torch?"

"And what does that symbolize, Trevor?" you ask.

"Like I said, a torch." Trevor wonders how you could be so dense.

CRITICAL THINKING

- What do these students' reactions tell you about children's thinking?
- How would you approach this unit?
- What more would you do to "listen" to your students' thinking so you could match your teaching to their level of thinking?
- How would you give your students concrete experiences with symbolism?
- How will you decide if the students are not developmentally ready for this material?

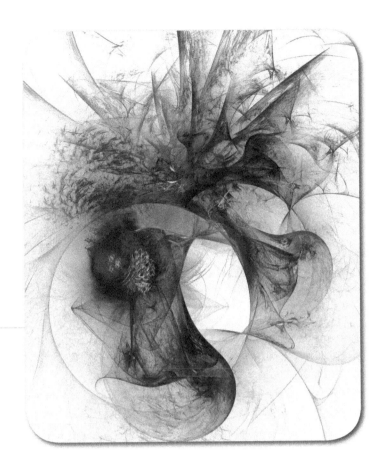

OVERVIEW AND OBJECTIVES

What is going on with Trevor? In this chapter, you will find out. We begin with a definition of development and examine three questions about development that psychologists have debated for many years: nature versus nurture, continuity versus discontinuity, and critical versus sensitive periods for development. Next we look at general principles of human development that most psychologists affirm. To understand cognitive development, we begin by studying how the brain works and then explore the ideas of two of the most influential cognitive developmental theorists, Jean Piaget and Lev Vygotsky. Piaget's ideas have implications for teachers about how their students think and what they can learn. We will consider criticisms of his ideas as well. The work of Lev Vygotsky, a Russian psychologist, highlights the important role teachers and parents play in the cognitive development of the child. Vygotsky's theory is becoming more and more influential in the field of child development. By the time you have completed this chapter, you should be able to:

Objective 1.1:   Provide a definition of development that takes into account three agreed-upon principles.

Objective 1.2:   Discuss three continuing debates about development, along with current consensus on these questions.

Objective 1.3:   Summarize some current research on the physical development of the brain and possible implications for teaching.

Objective 1.4:   Explain how the principles and stages presented in Piaget's theory of cognitive development influence current educational research and practice.

Objective 1.5:   Explain how the principles presented in Vygotsky's theory of development influence current educational research and practice.

A DEFINITION OF DEVELOPMENT

In the next few chapters, as we explore how children develop, we will encounter some surprising situations.

- Leah, a 5-year-old, is certain that rolling out a ball of clay into a snake creates more clay.
- A 9-year-old child in Geneva, Switzerland, firmly insists that it is impossible to be Swiss and Genevan at the same time: "I'm already Swiss. I can't also be Genevan."
- Jamal, a very bright elementary school student, cannot answer the question "How would life be different if people did not sleep?" because he insists, "People HAVE TO SLEEP!"
- A young girl who once said her *feet* hurt, suddenly begins to refer to her *foots,* and then describes her *footses,* before she finally returns to talking about her *feet.*
- A 2-year-old brings his own mother to comfort a friend who is crying, even though the friend's mother is available, too.

What explains these interesting events? You will soon find out, because you are entering the world of child and adolescent development.

The term **development** in its most general psychological sense refers to certain changes that occur in human beings (or animals) between conception and death. The term is not applied to all changes, but rather to those that appear in orderly ways and remain for a reasonably long period of time. A temporary change caused by a brief illness, for example, is not considered a part of development. Human development can be divided into a number of different aspects. **Physical development**, as you might guess, deals with changes in the body. **Personal development** is the term generally used for changes in an individual's personality. **Social development** refers to changes in the way an individual relates to others. And **cognitive development** refers to changes in thinking, reasoning, and decision making.

Many changes during development are simply matters of growth and **maturation**. Maturation refers to changes that occur naturally and spontaneously and that are, to a large extent, genetically programmed. Such changes emerge over time and are relatively unaffected by environment, except in cases of malnutrition or severe illness. Much of a person's physical development falls into this category. Other changes are brought about through learning, as individuals interact with their environment. Such changes make up a large part of a person's social development. But what about the development of thinking and personality? Most psychologists agree that in these areas, both maturation and interaction with the environment (or *nature* and *nurture,* as they are sometimes called) are important, but they disagree about the amount of emphasis to place on each one. Nature versus nurture is one of three continuing discussions in theories of development.

Three Questions Across the Theories

Because there are many different approaches to research and theory, there are some continuing debates about key questions surrounding development.

WHAT IS THE SOURCE OF DEVELOPMENT? NATURE VERSUS NURTURE. Which is more important in development, the "nature" of an individual (heredity, genes, biological processes, maturation, etc.) or the "nurture" of environmental contexts (education, parenting, culture, social policies, etc.)? This debate has raged for at least 2,000 years and has accumulated many labels along the way, including "heredity versus environment," "biology versus culture," "maturation versus learning," and "innate versus acquired abilities." In earlier centuries, philosophers, poets, religious leaders, and politicians argued the question. Today scientists bring new tools to the discussion as they can map genes or trace the effects of drugs on brain activity, for example (Gottlieb, Wahlsten, & Lickliter, 2006). Even in scientific explanations, the pendulum has swung back and forth between nature and nurture (Cairns & Cairns, 2006; Overton, 2006).

Today the environment is seen as critical to development, but so are biological factors and individual differences. In fact, some psychologists assert that behaviors are determined 100% by biology and 100% by environment—they can't be separated (Miller, 2011). Current views emphasize complex **coactions** (joint actions) of nature and nurture. For example, a child born with a very easy-going, calm disposition will likely elicit different reactions from parents, playmates, and teachers than a child who is often upset and difficult to soothe; this shows that individuals are active in constructing their own environments. But environments shape individuals as well—if not, what good would education be? So today, the either/or debates about nature and nurture are of less interest to educational and developmental psychologists. As a pioneering developmental psychologist said over 100 years ago, the more exciting questions involve understanding how "both causes work together" (Baldwin, 1895, p. 77).

WHAT IS THE SHAPE OF DEVELOPMENT? CONTINUITY VERSUS DISCONTINUITY.
Is human development a continuous process of increasing abilities, or are there leaps to new stages when abilities actually change? A continuous process would be like gradual improvement in your running endurance through systematic exercise. A discontinuous change (also called *qualitative*) would be like many of the changes in humans during puberty, such as the ability to reproduce—an entirely different ability. Qualitative changes are contrasted with purely quantitative change, such as the adolescent growing taller.

You can think of continuous or quantitative change like walking up a ramp to go higher and higher: Progress is steady. A discontinuous or qualitative change is more like walking up stairs: There are level periods, and then you ascend the next step all at once. Piaget's theory of cognitive development, described in the next section, is an example of *qualitative*, discontinuous change in children's thinking abilities. But other explanations of cognitive development based on learning theories emphasize gradual, continuous, *quantitative* change.

TIMING: IS IT TOO LATE? CRITICAL VERSUS SENSITIVE PERIODS.   Are there critical periods during which certain abilities, such as language, need to develop? If those opportunities are missed, can the child still "catch up"? These are questions about timing and development. Many earlier psychologists, particularly those influenced by Freud, believed that early childhood experiences were critical, especially for emotional/social and cognitive development. But does early toilet training really set all of us on a particular life path? Probably not. More recent research shows that later experiences are powerful, too, and can change the direction of development (Kagan & Herschkowitz, 2005). Most psychologists today talk about **sensitive periods**—not critical periods. There are times when a person is especially ready for or responsive to certain experiences.

BEWARE OF EITHER/OR.   As you might imagine, these debates about development proved too complicated to be settled by splitting alternatives into either/or possibilities (Griffins & Gray, 2005). Today, most psychologists view human development, learning, and motivation as a set of interacting and coacting contexts, from the inner biological structures and processes that influence development such as genes, cells, nutrition, and disease, to the external factors of families, neighborhoods, social relationships, educational and health institutions, public policies, time periods, historical events, and so on. So the effects of a childhood disease on the cognitive development of a child born in the 16th century to a poor family and treated by bloodletting or leeches will be quite different than the effect of the same disease on a child born in 2012 to a wealthy family and given

Development Orderly, adaptive changes we go through between conception and death and remain for a reasonably long period of time.

Physical development Changes in body structure and function over time.

Personal development Changes in personality that take place as one grows.

Social development Changes over time in the ways we relate to others.

Cognitive development Gradual orderly changes by which mental processes become more complex and sophisticated.

Maturation Genetically programmed, naturally occurring changes over time.

Coactions Joint actions of individual biology and the environment—each shapes and influences the other.

Sensitive periods Times when a person is especially ready for or responsive to certain experiences.

the best treatment available for that time period. Throughout the rest of this book, we will try to make sense of development, learning, motivation, and teaching without falling into the *either/or trap*.

General Principles of Development

Although there is disagreement about exactly how development takes place, there are a few general principles almost all theorists would support.

1. **People develop at different rates.** In your own classroom, you will have a whole range of examples of different developmental rates. Some students will be larger, better coordinated, or more mature in their thinking and social relationships. Others will be much slower to mature in these areas. Except in rare cases of very rapid or very slow development, such differences are normal and should be expected in any large group of students.
2. **Development is relatively orderly.** People develop abilities in a logical order. In infancy, they sit before they walk, babble before they talk, and see the world through their own eyes before they can begin to imagine how others see it. In school, they will master addition before algebra, Harry Potter before Shakespeare, and so on. But "orderly" does not necessarily mean linear or predictable—people might advance, stay the same for a period of time, or even go backwards.
3. **Development takes place gradually.** Very rarely do changes appear overnight. A student who cannot manipulate a pencil or answer a hypothetical question may well develop this ability, but the change is likely to take time.

THE BRAIN AND COGNITIVE DEVELOPMENT

If you have taken an introductory psychology class, you have read about the brain and nervous system. You probably remember that there are several different areas of the brain and that certain areas are involved in particular functions. For example, the feathery looking *cerebellum* coordinates and orchestrates balance and smooth, skilled movements—from the graceful gestures of the dancer to the everyday action of eating without stabbing yourself in the nose with a fork. The cerebellum may also play a role in higher cognitive functions such as learning. The *hippocampus* is critical in recalling new information and recent experiences, while the *amygdala* directs emotions. The *thalamus* is involved in our ability to learn new information, *particularly* if it is verbal. Figure 1.1 shows the various regions of the brain.

Advances in brain imaging techniques have allowed scientists remarkable access to the functioning brain. For example, **functional magnetic resonance imaging (fMRI)** shows how

Functional magnetic resonance imaging (fMRI) An MRI is an imaging technique that uses a magnetic field along with radio waves and a computer to create detailed pictures of the inside of the body. A functional MRI uses the MRI to measure the tiny changes that take place in the brain during brain activity.

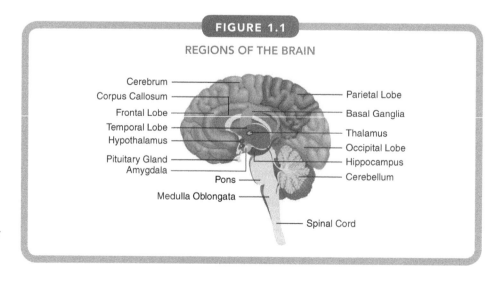

FIGURE 1.1

REGIONS OF THE BRAIN

Cerebrum
Corpus Callosum
Frontal Lobe
Temporal Lobe
Hypothalamus
Pituitary Gland
Amygdala
Pons
Medulla Oblongata
Parietal Lobe
Basal Ganglia
Thalamus
Occipital Lobe
Hippocampus
Cerebellum
Spinal Cord

blood flows within the brain when children or adults do different cognitive tasks. **Event-related potential (ERP)** measurements assess electrical activity of the brain through the skull or scalp as people perform activities such as reading or learning vocabulary words. **Positron emission tomography (PET)** scans can track brain activity under different conditions.

Let's begin our look at the brain by examining its tiny components—neurons, synapses, and glial cells.

The Developing Brain: Neurons

A newborn baby's brain weighs about one pound, barely one third of the weight of an adult brain. But this infant brain has billions of **neurons**, the specialized nerve cells that accumulate and transmit information (in the form of electrical activity) in the brain and other parts of the nervous system. Neurons are a grayish color, so they sometimes are called the *gray matter* of the brain. One neuron has the information processing capacity of a small computer. That means the processing power of one 3-pound human brain is likely greater than all the computers in the world. Of course, computers do many things, like calculate square roots of large numbers, much faster than humans can (Anderson, 2010). These incredibly important neuron cells are tiny—about 30,000 could fit on the head of a pin (Sprenger, 2010). Scientists once believed that all the neurons a person would ever have were present at birth, but now we know that the production of new neurons, **neurogenesis**, continues into adulthood (Johnson, 2003).

Neuron cells send out long arm- and branch-like fibers called *axons* and *dendrites* to connect with other neuron cells. The fiber ends from different neurons don't actually touch—there are tiny spaces between them, about one billionth of a meter in length, called **synapses**. Neurons share information by releasing chemicals that jump across the synapses. Axons transmit information out to muscles, glands, or other neurons; dendrites receive information and transmit it to the neuron cells themselves. Figure 1.2 shows these components of the neuron system (Anderson, 2010).

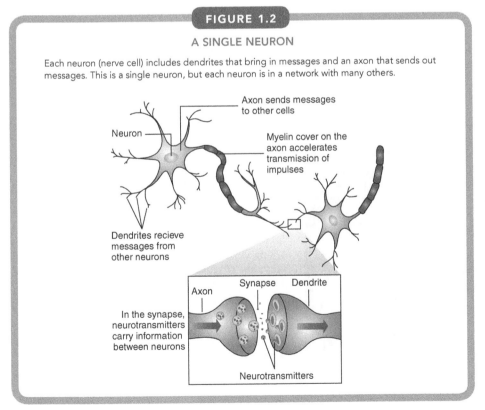

FIGURE 1.2

A SINGLE NEURON

Each neuron (nerve cell) includes dendrites that bring in messages and an axon that sends out messages. This is a single neuron, but each neuron is in a network with many others.

Axon sends messages to other cells

Neuron

Myelin cover on the axon accelerates transmission of impulses

Dendrites recieve messages from other neurons

In the synapse, neurotransmitters carry information between neurons

Axon   Synapse   Dendrite

Neurotransmitters

Event-related potential (ERP) Measurements that assess electrical activity of the brain through the skull or scalp.

Positron emission tomography (PET) A method of localizing and measuring brain activity using computer-assisted motion pictures of the brain.

Neurons Nerve cells that store and transfer information.

Neurogenesis The production of new neurons.

Synapses The tiny space between neurons—chemical messages are sent across these gaps.

At birth, each of the child's 100 to 200 billion neurons has about 2,500 synapses. However, the fibers that reach out from the neurons and the synapses between the fiber ends increase during the first years of life, perhaps into adolescence or longer. By ages 2 to 3, each neuron has around 15,000 synapses; children this age have many more synapses than they will have as adults. In fact, they are *oversupplied* with the neurons and synapses that they will need to adapt to their environments. However, only those neurons that are used will survive, and unused neurons will be "pruned." This pruning is necessary and supports cognitive development. Researchers have found that some developmental disabilities are associated with a gene defect that interferes with pruning (Bransford, Brown, & Cocking, 2000; Cook & Cook, 2009).

Two kinds of overproduction and pruning processes take place. One is called *experience-expectant* because synapses are overproduced in certain parts of the brain during specific developmental periods, awaiting (expecting) stimulation. For example, during the first months of life, the brain expects visual and auditory stimulation. If a normal range of sights and sounds occurs, then the visual and auditory areas of the brain develop. But children who are born completely deaf receive no auditory stimulation and, as a result, the auditory processing area of their brains becomes devoted to processing visual information. Similarly, the visual processing area of the brain for children blind from birth becomes devoted to auditory processing (Nelson, 2001; Neville, 2007).

Experience-expectant overproduction and pruning processes are responsible for general development in large areas of the brain and may explain why adults have difficulty with pronunciations that are not part of their native language. For example, the distinction between the sounds of *r* and *l* is important in English but not in Japanese, so by about 10 months, Japanese infants lose the ability to discriminate between *r* and *l*—*those neurons are pruned away.* As a result, Japanese adults learning these sounds require intense instruction and practice (Bransford et al., 2000; Hinton, Miyamoto, & Della-Chiesa, 2008).

The second kind of synaptic overproduction and pruning is called *experience-dependent*. Here, synaptic connections are formed based on the individual's experiences. New synapses are formed in response to neural activity in very localized areas of the brain when the individual is not successful in processing information. Again, more synapses are produced than will be kept after "pruning." Experience-dependent processes are involved in individual learning, such as mastering unfamiliar sound pronunciations in a second language you are studying.

Stimulating environments may help in the pruning process in early life (experience-expectant period) and also may support increased synapse development in adulthood (experience-dependent period) (Cook & Cook, 2009). In fact, animal studies have shown that rats raised in stimulating environments (with toys, tasks for learning, other rats, and human handling) develop and retain 25% more synapses than rats who are raised with little stimulation. Even though the research with rats may not apply directly to humans, it is clear that extreme deprivation can have negative effects on human brain development. But extra stimulation will not necessarily improve development for young children who are getting adequate or typical amounts (Byrnes & Fox, 1998; Kolb & Whishaw, 1998). So spending money on expensive toys or baby education programs probably offers more stimulation than is necessary. Pots and pans, blocks and books, sand and water all provide excellent stimulation—especially if accompanied by caring conversations with parents or teachers.

Look back at Figure 1.2. It appears that there is nothing between the neurons but air. Actually, this

SUPPORTING BRAIN DEVELOPMENT Studies of the brain indicate that stimulating environments and meaningful interactions with parents and teachers likely support better brain development.

is wrong. The spaces are filled with **glial cells**, the *white matter* of the brain. There are trillions of these cells—they greatly outnumber neurons. Glial cells appear to have many functions such as fighting infections, controlling blood flow and communication among neurons, and providing the *myelin* coating (see Figure 1.2) around axon fibers (Ormrod, 2011). **Myelination**, the coating of axon neuron fibers with an insulating fatty glial covering, influences thinking and learning. This process is something like coating bare electrical wires with rubber or plastic. This myelin coating makes message transmission faster and more efficient. Myelination happens quickly in the early years, but continues gradually into adolescence, with the child's brain doubling in volume in the first year of life and doubling again around puberty (Anderson, 2010).

The Developing Brain: Cerebral Cortex

Let's move from the neuron level to the brain itself. The outer 1/8-inch-thick covering is the cerebral cortex—the largest area of the brain. It is a thin sheet of neurons, but it is almost 3 square feet in area for adults. To get all that area in your head, the sheet is crumpled together with many folds and wrinkles (Anderson, 2010). In humans, this area of the brain is much larger than it is in lower animals. The cerebral cortex accounts for about 85% of the brain's weight in adulthood and contains the greatest number of neurons. The cerebral cortex allows the greatest human accomplishments, such as complex problem solving and language.

The cortex is the last part of the brain to develop, so it is believed to be more susceptible to environmental influences than other areas of the brain (Gluck, Mercado, & Myers, 2008; Schacter, Gilbert, & Wenger, 2009). Parts of the cortex mature at different rates. The region of the cortex that controls physical motor movement matures first, then the areas that control complex senses such as vision and hearing, and last, the frontal lobe that controls higher-order thinking processes. The temporal lobes of the cortex that play major roles in emotions, judgment, and language do not develop fully until the high school years and maybe later.

Different areas of the cortex seem to have distinct functions, as shown in Figure 1.3. Even though different functions are found in particular areas of the brain, these specialized functions are quite specific and elementary. To accomplish more complex functions

---

FIGURE 1.3

A VIEW OF THE CEREBRAL CORTEX

This is a simple representation of the left side of the human brain, showing the cerebral cortex. The cortex is divided into different areas, or lobes, each having a variety of regions with different functions. A few of the major functions are indicated here.

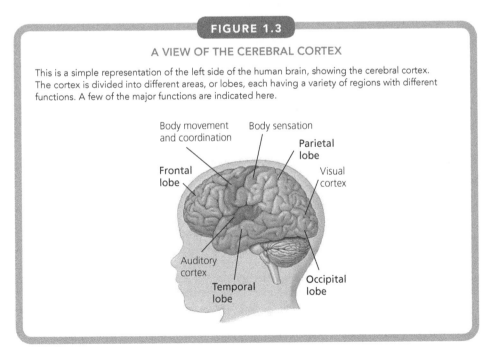

Glial cells The *white matter* of the brain. These cells greatly outnumber neurons and appear to have many functions such as fighting infections, controlling blood flow and communication among neurons, and providing the *myelin* coating around axon fibers.

Myelination The process by which neural fibers are coated with a fatty sheath called *myelin* that makes message transfer more efficient.

such as speaking or reading, the various areas of the cortex must communicate and work together (Anderson, 2010; Byrnes & Fox, 1998).

Another aspect of brain functioning that has implications for cognitive development is **lateralization**, or the specialization of the two hemispheres of the brain. We know that each half of the brain controls the opposite side of the body. Damage to the right side of the brain will affect movement of the left side of the body and vice versa. In addition, certain areas of the brain affect particular behaviors. For most of us, the left hemisphere of the brain is a major factor in language processing, and the right hemisphere handles much of our spatial-visual information and emotions (nonverbal information). For some left-handed people, the relationship may be reversed, but for most left-handers, and for females on average, there is less hemispheric specialization altogether (Anderson, 2010; O'Boyle & Gill, 1998). The brains of young children show more **plasticity** (adaptability) because they are not as specialized or lateralized as the brains of older children and adults. Young children with damage to the left side of the brain are somewhat able to overcome the damage, which allows language development to proceed. Different areas of the brain take over the functions of the damaged area. But in older children and adults, this compensation is less likely to occur after damage to the left brain hemisphere.

These differences in performance by the brain's hemispheres, however, are more relative than absolute; one hemisphere is just more efficient than the other in performing certain functions. Language is processed "differently, but simultaneously" by the left and right hemispheres (Alferink & Farmer-Dougan, 2010, p. 44). Nearly any task, particularly the complex skills and abilities that concern teachers, requires simultaneous participation of many different areas of the brain in constant communication with each other. For example, the right side of the brain is better at figuring out the meaning of a story, but the left side is where grammar and syntax are understood, so both sides of the brain have to work together in reading. Remember, no mental activity is exclusively the work of a single part of the brain—so there is no such thing as a "right-brained student" unless that individual has had the left hemisphere removed—a rare and radical treatment for some forms of epilepsy.

Adolescent Development and the Brain

The brain continues to develop throughout childhood and adolescence. During adolescence, changes in the brain increase individuals' abilities to control their behavior in both low-stress and high-stress situations, to be more purposeful and organized, and to inhibit impulsive behavior (Wigfield et al., 2006). But these abilities are not fully developed until the early 20s, so adolescents may "seem" like adults, at least in low-stress situations, but their brains are not fully developed. They often have trouble avoiding risks and controlling impulses. This is why adolescents' brains have been described as "high horse power, poor steering" (Organization for Economic Cooperation and Development [OECD], 2007, p. 6). One explanation looks to differences in the pace of development for two key systems involved in making sound decisions about risky behaviors and controlling impulsive behavior—the limbic system and the prefrontal cortex of the brain (Casey, Getz, & Galvan, 2008). The limbic system develops earlier; it is involved with emotions and reward-seeking/novelty/risk-taking/sensation-seeking behaviors. The prefrontal lobe takes more time to develop; it is involved with judgment and decision making.

As the limbic system matures, adolescents become more responsive to pleasure seeking and emotional stimulation. In fact, adolescents appear to need more intense emotional stimulation than either children or adults, so these young people are set up for taking risks and seeking thrills. Risk taking and novelty seeking can be positive factors for adolescent development as young people courageously try new ideas and behaviors—and learning is stimulated (McAnarney, 2008). But their less mature prefrontal lobe is not yet good at saying, "Whoa—that thrill is too risky!" So in emotional situations, thrill seeking wins out over caution, at least until the prefrontal lobe catches up and becomes more integrated with the limbic system toward the end of adolescence. Then risks can be evaluated in terms of long-term consequences, not immediate thrills (Casey et al., 2008; Steinberg, 2008). In addition, there are individual differences: Some adolescents are more prone than others to engage in risky behaviors.

Lateralization The specialization of the two hemispheres (sides) of the brain cortex.

Plasticity The brain's tendency to remain somewhat adaptable or flexible.

Teachers can take advantage of their adolescent students' intensity by helping them devote their energy and passion to areas such as politics, the environment, or social causes (Price, 2005) or by guiding them to explore emotional connections with characters in history or literature. Connections to family, school, community, and positive belief systems help adolescents "put the brakes" on reckless and dangerous behaviors (McAnarney, 2008).

Other changes in the neurological system during adolescence affect sleep; teenagers need about 9 hours of sleep per night, but many students' biological clocks are reset so it is difficult for them to fall asleep before midnight. Yet in many school districts, high school begins by 7:30, so 9 hours of sleep are impossible to get and students are continually sleep deprived. Classes that keep students in their seats, taking notes for the full period may literally "put the students to sleep." With no time for breakfast and little for lunch, these students' nutritional needs are often deprived as well (Sprenger, 2005).

Putting It All Altogether: How the Brain Works

What is your conception of the brain? Is the brain a culture-free container that holds knowledge the same way for everyone? Is the brain like a library of facts or a computer filled with information? Do you wake up in the morning, download what you need for the day, and then go merrily on your way? Is the brain like a pipe that transfers information from one person to another—a teacher to a student, for example? Kurt Fischer (2009) offers a different view, based on neuroscience research. Knowing is actively constructing understandings and actions. Knowledge is based in our activities:

> When animals and people do things in their worlds, they shape their behavior. Based on brain research, we know that likewise they literally shape the anatomy and physiology of their brains (and bodies). When we actively control our experience, that experience sculpts the way that our brains work, changing neurons, synapses, and brain activity. (p. 5)

Cultural differences in brain activity provide examples of how interactions in the world shape the brain. For example, in one study, when Chinese speakers added and compared Arabic numbers, they showed brain activity in the motor (movement) areas of their brains, whereas English speakers performing the same tasks had activity in the language areas of their brains (Tang et al., 2006). One explanation is that Chinese children are taught arithmetic using an abacus—a calculation tool that involves movement and spatial positions. As adults, these children retain a kind of visual-motor sense of numbers (Varma, McCandliss, & Schwartz, 2008). There also are cultural differences in how languages affect reading. For example, when they read, native Chinese speakers activate additional parts of their brain associated with spatial information processing, probably because the language characters used in written Chinese are pictures. But Chinese speakers also activate these spatial areas of the brain when they read English, demonstrating that reading proficiency can be reached through different neural pathways (Hinton, Miyamoto, & Della-Chiesa, 2008).

So the brain is ever changing, shaped by activity, culture, and context. We build knowledge as we do things, as we manipulate objects and ideas mentally and physically. What are the implications of this for teaching? Many publications for parents and teachers have useful ideas about the brain and education, but beware of suggestions that oversimplify. As you will see next, the jury still is out on many of these "brain-based" programs.

Neuroscience, Learning, and Teaching

There are many popular neuromyths about the brain, as you can see in Table 1.1 on the next page. We have to be careful about what we encounter in the media.

We know teaching can change the organization and structure of the brain. For example, individuals who are deaf and use sign language have different patterns of electrical activity in their brains than people who are deaf and do not use sign language (Varma, McCandliss, & Schwartz, 2008).

INSTRUCTION AND BRAIN DEVELOPMENT. Several studies have shown differences in brain activity associated with instruction. For example, the intensive instruction and practice provided to rehabilitate stroke victims can help them regain functioning by forming new connections and using new areas of the brain (Bransford, Brown, & Cocking, 2000;

TABLE 1.1 • **Myths About the Brain**

COMMON MYTHS	TRUTH
1. You use only 10 percent of your brain.	1. Use all your brain. That is why strokes are so devastating.
2. Listening to Mozart will make children smarter.	2. Listening won't, but learning to play a musical instrument is associated with increased cognitive achievement.
3. Some people are more "right brained," and others are more "left brained."	3. It takes both sides of your brain to do most things.
4. A young child's brain can only manage to learn one language at a time.	4. Children all over the world can and do learn two languages at once.
5. You can't change your brain.	5. Our brains are changing all the time.
6. Damage to the brain is permanent.	6. Most people recover well from minor brain injuries.
7. Playing games like Sudoku keeps your brain from aging.	7. Playing Sudoku makes you better at playing Sudoku and similar games. Physical exercise is a better bet to prevent decline.
8. The human brain is the biggest brain.	8. Sperm whales have brains 5 times heavier than those of humans.
9. Alcoholic beverages kill brain cells.	9. Heavy drinking does not kill brain cells but it can damage the nerve ends called dentrites and this causes problems with communicating messages in the brain. This damage is mostly reversible.
10. The adolescent's brain is the same as that of an adult.	10. There are critical differences between adolescents' and adults' brains: Adolescents' brains have "high horsepower, but poor steering" (Fischer, 2009).

Source: Adapted from Aamodt, S., & Wang, S. (2008); Fischer, K. W. (2009); Freeman, S. (2011); OECD (2007).

McKinley, 2011). In another example, Margarete Delazer and her colleagues (2005) compared students' brain activity as they learned new arithmetic operations, either by just memorizing the answers or by learning an algorithm strategy. Using functional magnetic resonance imaging (fMRI), the researchers found that students who simply memorized answers showed greater activity in the area of the brain that specializes in retrieving verbal information, whereas the students who used a strategy showed greater activity in the visual-spatial processing portion of the brain.

Bennett Shaywitz and his colleagues (2004) reported a dramatic demonstration of brain changes in children following instruction. The researchers studied 28 children ages 6 to 9 who were good readers and 49 children who were poor readers. Again, fMRIs showed differences in the brain activity of the two groups. The poor readers underused parts of their brains' left hemisphere and sometimes overused their right hemispheres. After over 100 hours of intensive instruction in letter–sound combinations, reading ability improved; the brains of the poor readers started to function more like those of the good readers and continued this functioning a year later. Poor readers who received the standard school remediation did not show the brain function changes.

In another dramatic example of how teaching can affect brain development, Fischer (2009) describes two children who each had one brain hemisphere removed as a treatment for severe epilepsy. Nico's right hemisphere was removed when he was 3, and his parents were told he would never have good visual-spatial skills. With strong and constant support and teaching, Nico grew up to be a skilled artist! Brooke's left hemisphere was removed when he was 11. His parents were told he would lose his ability to talk. Again, with strong support, he regained enough speaking and reading ability to finish high school and attend community college.

THE BRAIN AND LEARNING TO READ. Brain imaging research is revealing interesting differences among skilled and less skilled readers as they learn new vocabulary. For example, one imaging study showed that less skilled readers had trouble establishing high-quality representations of new vo-cabulary words in their brains, as indi-cated by *event-related potential (ERP)* measurements of electrical activity of the brain. When they encountered the new word later, less skilled readers' brains of-ten didn't recognize that they had seen the word before, even though they had learned the words in an earlier lesson. If words you have learned seem unfamiliar later, you can see how it would be hard to understand what you read (Balass, Nelson, & Perfetti, 2010).

Reading is not innate or automatic—every brain has to be taught to read (Frey & Fisher, 2010). Reading is a complex integration of the systems in the brain that recognize sounds, written symbols, meanings, and sequences, and then con-nect with what the reader already knows. This has to happen quickly and auto-matically (Wolf et al., 2009). Will brain research help us teach reading more ef-fectively? Judith Willis (2009), a neuro-biologist who became a science teacher,

BRAIN RESEARCH AND READING Brain research may help us understand why strategies for teaching reading are or are not effective.

cautions that "Neuroimaging and the other brain monitoring systems used for reading research offer *suggestive* rather than completely empirical links between how the brain learns and metabolizes oxygen or glucose, conducts electricity, or changes its cellular density" (p. 333).

Although the strategies for teaching reading that are consistent with brain research are not completely new, the research may help us understand *why* these strat-egies work. What are some strategies suggested? Use multiple approaches that teach sounds, spelling, meanings, sequencing, and vocabulary through reading, writing, dis-cussing, explaining, drawing, and modeling. Different students may learn in different ways, but all need practice in literacy.

EMOTIONS, LEARNING, AND THE BRAIN. Finally, another clear connection between the brain and classroom learning is in the area of emotions and stress. Let's step inside a high school math classroom described by Hinton, Miyamoto, and Della-Chiesa (2008, p. 91) for an example:

> Patricia, a high school student, struggles with mathematics. The last few times she an-swered a mathematics question she got it wrong and felt terribly embarrassed, which formed an association between mathematics . . . and negative emotions. . . . Her teacher had just asked her to come to the blackboard to solve a problem. This caused an immedi-ate transfer of this emotionally-charged association to the amygdala, which elicits fear. Meanwhile, a slower, cortically-driven cognitive appraisal of the situation is occurring: she remembers her difficulty completing her mathematics homework last night, notices the problem on the board contains complicated graphs, and realizes that the boy she has a crush on is watching her from a front-row seat. These various thoughts converge to a cog-nitive confirmation that this is a threatening situation, which reinforces her progressing fear response and disrupts her ability to concentrate on solving the mathematics problem.

In Chapter 8, you will see that anxiety interferes with learning, whereas challenge, interest, and curiosity can support learning. If students feel unsafe and anxious, they are not likely to be able to focus attention on academics (Sylvester, 2003). But if students are not challenged or interested, learning suffers too. Keeping the level of challenge and support "just right" is a challenge for teachers. And helping students learn to regulate their own emotions and motivation is an important goal for education (see Chapter 7).

POINT/COUNTERPOINT: Brain-Based Education

Educators are hearing more and more about brain-based education, the importance of early stimulation for brain development, the "Mozart effect," and right- and left-brain activities. In fact, based on some research findings that listening to 10 minutes of Mozart can briefly improve spatial reasoning (Rauscher & Shaw, 1998; Steele, Bass, & Crook, 1999), a former governor of Georgia established a program to give a Mozart CD to every newborn. The scientists who had done the work couldn't believe how their research had been "applied" (Katzir & Pare-Blagoev, 2006). In fact, the governor apparently had confused experiments on infant brain development with studies of adults (Pinker, 2002). Are there clear educational implications from the neuroscience research on the brain?

POINT ▶ **No, the implications are not clear.** John Bruer, president of the James S. McDonnell Foundation, has written articles that are critical of the brain-based education craze (Bruer, 1999, 2002). He notes that many so-called applications of brain research begin with solid science, but then move to unwarranted speculation, and end in a sort of appealing folk tale about the brain and learning. He suggests that for each claim, the educator should ask, "Where does the science end and the speculation begin?" For example, one claim that Bruer questions is the notion of right-brain, left-brain learning.

"Right brain versus left brain" is one of those popular ideas that will not die. Speculations about the educational significance of brain laterality have been circulating in the education literature for 30 years. Although repeatedly criticized and dismissed by psychologists and brain scientists, the speculation continues. David Sousa devotes a chapter of How the Brain Learns to explaining brain laterality and presents classroom strategies that teachers might use to ensure that both hemispheres are involved in learning. . . . Now let's consider the brain sciences and how or whether they offer support for some of the particular teaching strategies Sousa recommends. To involve the right hemisphere in learning, Sousa writes, teachers should encourage students to generate and use mental imagery. . . . What brain scientists currently know about spatial reasoning and mental imagery provides counter examples to such simplistic claims as these. Such claims

arise out of a folk theory about brain laterality, not a neuroscientific one. . . . Different brain areas are specialized for different tasks, but that specialization occurs at a finer level of analysis than "using visual imagery." Using visual imagery may be a useful learning strategy, but if it is useful it is not because it involves an otherwise underutilized right hemisphere in learning. (Bruer, 1999, 653–654)

Ten years later, Kurt Fischer (2009), President of the International Mind, Brain, and Education Society, lamented:

Expectations for neuroscience and genetics to shape educational practice and policy have exploded far beyond what is merited by the state of the emerging field of MBE [mind body education] and the level of knowledge about how brains and genetics function . . . Many neuromyths " have entered popular discourse — beliefs about how the brain and body work that are widely accepted but blatantly wrong" (OECD, 2007b). Most of what is put forward as "brain based education" builds on these scientifically inaccurate myths: The one small way that neuroscience relates to most brain-based education is that the students have brains. There is no grounding for these claims in the young field of neuroscience.

No teacher doubts that the brain is important in learning. As Steven Pinker (2002), professor of psychology at Harvard University, observed, does anyone really think learning takes place somewhere else like the pancreas? But knowing that learning affects the brain does not tell us how to teach. All learning affects

Simply put, learning will be more effective "if educators help to minimize stress and fear at school, teach students emotional regulation strategies, and provide a positive learning environment that is motivating to students" (Hinton, Miyamoto, & Della-Chiesa, 2008).

As you can imagine, based on these and other amazing research results, educators have looked for applications of neuroscience research for their instruction. This has led to vigorous debate between the enthusiastic educational advocates of brain-based education and the skeptical neuroscience researchers who caution that studies of the brain do not really address major educational questions. See the *Point/Counterpoint* for a slice of this debate.

STOP & THINK As a teacher, you don't want to fall for overly simplistic "brain-based" teaching slogans. But obviously the brain and learning are intimately related—this is not a surprise. So how can you be a savvy, "neuroscientific" teacher (Murphy & Benton, 2010)?

Lessons for Teachers: General Principles

What can we learn from neuroscience? Here are some general teaching implications drawn from Driscoll (2005), Murphy and Benton (2010), Sprenger (2010), and Wolfe (2010):

the brain. ". . . this should be obvious, but nowadays any banality about learning can be dressed up in neurospeak and treated like a great revelation of science" (2002, p. 86). Virtually all of the so-called best practices for brain-based education are simple restatements of good teaching based on understandings of how people learn, not how their brain works. For example, we have known for over 100 years that it is more effective to learn in many shorter practice sessions as opposed to one long cramming session. To tie that fact to building more dendrites does not give teachers new strategies (Alferink & Farmer-Dougan, 2010). Finally, Richard Haier and Rex Jung (2008) look to the future: "Someday, we believe that our educational system will be informed by neuroscience knowledge, especially concerning intelligence, but how we get from here to there remains unclear" (p. 177).

COUNTERPOINT ▶ **Yes, teaching should be brain-based.** Articles in popular magazines such as *Newsweek* assert, " . . . it's naive to say that brain discoveries have no consequences for understanding how humans learn" (Begley, 2007). Do scientists agree? In their article on "Applying Cognitive Neuroscience Research to Education" in the *Educational Psychologist*, Tami Katzir and Juliana Paré-Blagoev (2006) concluded, "When applied correctly, brain science may serve as a vehicle for advancing the application of our understanding of learning and development. . . . Brain research can challenge common-sense views about teaching and learning by suggesting additional systems that are involved in particular tasks and activities" (p. 70). A number of universities, including Harvard, Cambridge, Dartmouth, the University of Texas at Arlington, University of Southern California, Beijing Normal University, Southeast University in Nanjing, and Johns Hopkins, have established training programs for educators in brain-education studies (Fischer, 2009; Wolfe, 2010).

Brain research is leading to much better understandings about learning disabilities. For example, neuroscience studies of people with reading disabilities have found that these individuals may have trouble with sounds and sound patterns or with retrieving the names of very familiar letters, so there may be different bases for the reading disabilities (Katzir & Paré-Blagoev, 2006).

There are examples of applying knowledge of brain research to education. A reading improvement product called *FastForword* was developed by two neuroscientists, Dr. Michael Merzenich and Dr. Paula Tallal and is already in use today in classrooms around the country (see http://www.scilearn.com/results/success-stories/index.php). It specifically uses discoveries in neural plasticity to change the brain's ability to read the printed word (Tallal & Miller, 2003).

In his Presidential address for the First Conference of the International Mind, Brain, and Education Society, Kurt Fischer, a developmental psychologist and Harvard professor, noted:

> The primary goal of the emerging field of Mind, Brain, and Education is to join biology, cognitive science, development, and education in order to create a sound grounding of education in research. The growing, worldwide movement needs to avoid the myths and distortions of popular conceptions of brain and genetics and build on the best integration of research with practice, creating a strong infrastructure that joins scientists with educators to study effective learning and teaching in educational settings. (2009, p. 3–16)

Fischer makes the point that we can go from understanding how the brain works to understanding cognitive processes, and then to developing educational practices. But jumping directly from knowledge about the brain to educational practices probably involves too much speculation.

Beware of Either/Or. Schools should not be run on curriculums based solely on the biology of the brain. However, to ignore what we do know about the brain would be equally irresponsible. Brain-based learning offers some direction for educators who want more purposeful, informed teaching. At the very least, the neuroscience research is helping us to understand why effective teaching strategies, such as distributed practice, work.

Resources: Podcast on understanding the brain: http://www.oecd.org/document/60/0,3343,en_2649_35845581_38811388_1_1_1_1,00.html

1. The brain can place some limits on learning in the form of brain anomalies in neural wiring or structure, but learning can occur through alternate pathways in the brain (as Nico and Brooke demonstrate). Thus, there are multiple ways both to teach and to learn a skill, depending on the student.

2. Many cognitive functions are differentiated—they are associated with different parts of the brain. Thus, learners are likely to have preferred modes of processing (visual or verbal, for example) as well as varying capabilities in these modes. Using a range of modalities for instruction and activities that draw on different senses may support learning—for example, using maps and songs to teach geography. Assessment should be differentiated, too.

3. The brain is relatively plastic, so enriched, active environments and flexible instructional strategies are likely to support cognitive development in young children and learning in adults.

4. Some learning disorders may have a neurological basis; neurological testing may assist in diagnosing and treating these disorders, as well as in evaluating the effects of various treatments.

5. The brain can change, but it takes time, so teachers must be consistent, patient, and compassionate in teaching and reteaching in different ways, as Nico's and Brooke's parents and teachers could tell you.
6. Learning from real life problems and concrete experiences helps students construct knowledge and also gives them multiple pathways for learning and retrieving information.
7. The brain seeks meaningful patterns and connections with existing networks, so teachers should tie new information to what students already understand and help them form new connections. Information that is not linked to existing knowledge will be easily forgotten.
8. It takes a long time to build and consolidate knowledge. Numerous visits in different contexts over time (not all at once) help to form strong, multiple connections.
9. Large, general concepts should be emphasized over small specific facts so students can build enduring, useful knowledge categories and associations that are not constantly changing.
10. Stories should be used in teaching. Stories engage many areas of the brain—memories, experiences, feelings, and beliefs. Stories also are organized and have a sequence—beginning, middle, end—so they are easier to remember than unrelated or unorganized information.

For the rest of the chapter, we turn from the brain and cognitive development to examine several major theories of cognitive development, the first offered by a biologist turned psychologist, Jean Piaget.

PIAGET'S THEORY OF COGNITIVE DEVELOPMENT

Swiss psychologist Jean Piaget was a real prodigy. In fact, in his teens, he published so many scientific papers on mollusks (marine animals such as oysters, clams, octopuses, snails, and squid) that he was offered a job as the curator of the mollusk collection at the Museum of Natural History in Geneva. He told the museum officials that he wanted to finish high school first. For a while, Piaget worked in Alfred Binet's laboratory in Paris developing intelligence tests for children. The reasons children gave for their wrong answers fascinated him, and this prompted him to study the thinking behind their answers—this question intrigued him for the rest of his life (Green & Piel, 2010). He continued to write until his death at the age of 84 (Miller, 2011).

During his long career, Piaget devised a model describing how humans go about making sense of their world by gathering and organizing information (Piaget, 1954, 1963, 1970a, 1970b). We will examine Piaget's ideas closely, because they provide an explanation of the development of thinking from infancy to adulthood.

STOP & THINK Can you be in Pittsburgh, Pennsylvania, and the United States all at the same time? Is this a difficult question for you? How long did it take you to answer? •

According to Piaget (1954), certain ways of thinking that are quite simple for an adult, such as the Pittsburgh question above, are not so simple for a child. For example, do you remember the 9-year-old child at the beginning of the chapter who was asked if he could be a Genevan? He answered, *"No, that's not possible. I'm already Swiss, I can't also be Genevan"* (Piaget, 1965/1995, p. 252). Imagine teaching this student geography. The student has trouble with classifying one concept (Geneva) as a subset of another (Switzerland). There are other differences between adult and child thinking. Children's concepts of time may be different from

STUDYING CHILDREN'S THINKING Jean Piaget was a Swiss psychologist whose insightful descriptions of children's thinking changed the way we understand cognitive development.

your own. They may think, for example, that they will some day catch up to a sibling in age, or they may confuse the past and the future. Let's examine why.

Influences on Development

Cognitive development is much more than the addition of new facts and ideas to an existing store of information. According to Piaget, our thinking processes change radically, though slowly, from birth to maturity because we constantly strive to make sense of the world. Piaget identified four factors—biological maturation, activity, social experiences, and equilibration—that interact to influence changes in thinking (Piaget, 1970a). Let's briefly examine the first three factors. We'll return to a discussion of equilibration in the next section.

One of the most important influences on the way we make sense of the world is *maturation*, the unfolding of the biological changes that are genetically programmed. Parents and teachers have little impact on this aspect of cognitive development, except to be sure that children get the nourishment and care they need to be healthy.

Activity is another influence. With physical maturation comes the increasing ability to act on the environment and learn from it. When a young child's coordination is reasonably developed, for example, the child can discover principles about balance by experimenting with a seesaw. Thus, as we act on the environment—as we explore, test, observe, and eventually organize information—we are likely to alter our thinking processes at the same time.

As we develop, we are also interacting with the people around us. According to Piaget, our cognitive development is influenced by *social transmission*, or learning from others. Without social transmission, we would need to reinvent all the knowledge already offered by our culture. The amount people can learn from social transmission varies according to their stage of cognitive development.

Maturation, activity, and social transmission all work together to influence cognitive development. How do we respond to these influences?

Basic Tendencies in Thinking

As a result of his early research in biology, Piaget concluded that all species inherit two basic tendencies, or "invariant functions." The first of these tendencies is toward **organization**—the combining, arranging, recombining, and rearranging of behaviors and thoughts into coherent systems. The second tendency is toward **adaptation**, or adjusting to the environment.

ORGANIZATION.   People are born with a tendency to organize their thinking processes into psychological structures. These psychological structures are our systems for understanding and interacting with the world. Simple structures are continually combined and coordinated to become more sophisticated and thus more effective. Very young infants, for example, can either look at an object or grasp it when it comes in contact with their hands. They cannot coordinate looking and grasping at the same time. As they develop, however, infants organize these two separate behavioral structures into a coordinated higher-level structure of looking at, reaching for, and grasping the object. They can, of course, still use each structure separately (Flavell, Miller, & Miller, 2002; Miller, 2011).

Piaget gave a special name to these structures: **schemes**. In his theory, schemes are the basic building blocks of thinking. They are organized systems of actions or thought that allow us to mentally represent or "think about" the objects and events in our world. Schemes can be very small and specific, for example, the sucking-through-a-straw scheme or the recognizing-a-rose scheme. Or they can be larger and more general, for example, the drinking scheme or the gardening scheme. As a person's thinking processes become more organized and new schemes develop, behavior also becomes more sophisticated and better suited to the environment.

ADAPTATION.   In addition to the tendency to organize psychological structures, people also inherit the tendency to adapt to their environment. Two basic processes are involved in adaptation: assimilation and accommodation.

Organization Ongoing process of arranging information and experiences into mental systems or categories.

Adaptation Adjustment to the environment.

Schemes Mental systems or categories of perception and experience.

Assimilation takes place when we use our existing schemes to make sense of events in our world. Assimilation involves trying to understand something new by fitting it into what we already know. At times, we may have to distort the new information to make it fit. For example, the first time many children see a raccoon, they call it a "kitty." They try to match the new experience with an existing scheme for identifying animals.

Accommodation occurs when we must change existing schemes to respond to a new situation. If data cannot be made to fit any existing schemes, then more appropriate structures must be developed. We adjust our thinking to fit the new information, instead of adjusting the information to fit our thinking. Children demonstrate accommodation when they add the scheme for recognizing raccoons to their other systems for identifying animals.

People adapt to their increasingly complex environments by using existing schemes whenever these schemes work (assimilation) and by modifying and adding to their schemes when something new is needed (accommodation). In fact, both processes are required most of the time. Even using an established pattern such as sucking through a straw requires some accommodation if the straw is of a different size or length than the type you are used to. If you have tried drinking juice from box packages, you know that you have to add a new skill to your sucking-through-a-straw scheme—don't squeeze the box or you will shoot juice through the straw, straight up into the air and into your lap. Whenever new experiences are assimilated into an existing scheme, the scheme is enlarged and changed somewhat, so assimilation involves some accommodation (Mascolo & Fischer, 2005).

There are also times when neither assimilation nor accommodation is used. If people encounter something that is too unfamiliar, they may ignore it. Experience is filtered to fit the kind of thinking a person is doing at a given time. For example, if you overhear a conversation in a foreign language, you probably will not try to make sense of the exchange unless you have some knowledge of the language.

EQUILIBRATION. According to Piaget, organizing, assimilating, and accommodating can be viewed as a kind of complex balancing act. In his theory, the actual changes in thinking take place through the process of **equilibration**—the act of searching for a balance. Piaget assumed that people continually test the adequacy of their thinking processes in order to achieve that balance. Briefly, the process of equilibration works like this: If we apply a particular scheme to an event or situation and the scheme works, then equilibrium exists. If the scheme does not produce a satisfying result, then **disequilibrium** exists, and we become uncomfortable. This motivates us to keep searching for a solution through assimilation and accommodation, and thus our thinking changes and moves ahead. Of course, the level of disequilibrium must be just right or optimal—too little and we aren't interested in changing, too much and we may be discouraged or anxious and not change.

Four Stages of Cognitive Development

Now we turn to the actual differences that Piaget hypothesized for children as they grow. Piaget believed that all people pass through the same four stages in exactly the same order. The stages are generally associated with specific ages, as shown in Table 1.2, but these are only general guidelines, not labels for all children of a certain age. Piaget noted that individuals may go through long periods of transition between stages and that a person may show characteristics of one stage in one situation, but traits of a higher or lower stage in other situations. Therefore, remember that knowing a student's age is never a guarantee you will know how the child thinks (Orlando & Machado, 1996).

INFANCY: THE SENSORIMOTOR STAGE. The earliest period is called the **sensorimotor** stage, because the child's thinking involves seeing, hearing, moving, touching, tasting, and so on. During this period, infants develop **object permanence**, the understanding that objects exist in the environment whether they perceive them or not. This is the beginning of the important ability to construct a mental representation. As most parents discover, before infants develop object permanence, it is relatively easy to take something away from them. The trick is to distract them and remove the object while they are not looking—"out of sight, out of mind." The older infant who searches for the ball that has

Assimilation Fitting new information into existing schemes.

Accommodation Altering existing schemes or creating new ones in response to new information.

Equilibration Search for mental balance between cognitive schemes and information from the environment.

Disequilibrium In Piaget's theory, the "out-of-balance" state that occurs when a person realizes that his or her current ways of thinking are not working to solve a problem or understand a situation.

Sensorimotor Involving the senses and motor activity.

Object permanence The understanding that objects have a separate, permanent existence.

TABLE 1.2 • **Piaget's Stages of Cognitive Development**

STAGE	APPROXIMATE AGE	CHARACTERISTICS
Sensorimotor	0–2 years	Learns through reflexes, senses, and movement—actions on the environment. Begins to imitate others and remember events; shifts to symbolic thinking. Comes to understand that objects do not cease to exist when they are out of sight—object permanence. Moves from reflexive actions to intentional activity.
Preoperational	Begins about the time the child starts talking, to about 7 years old	Develops language and begins to use symbols to represent objects. Has difficulty with past and future—thinks in the present. Can think through operations logically in one direction. Has difficulties understanding the point of view of another person.
Concrete operational	Begins about first grade, to early adolescence, around 11 years old	Can think logically about concrete (hands-on) problems. Understands conservation and organizes things into categories and in series. Can reverse thinking to mentally "undo" actions. Understands past, present, and future.
Formal operational	Adolescence to adulthood	Can think hypothetically and deductively. Thinking becomes more scientific. Solves abstract problems in logical fashion. Can consider multiple perspectives and develops concerns about social issues, personal identity, and justice.

rolled out of sight is indicating an understanding that objects still exist even when they are not in view (Moore & Meltzoff, 2004). Some researchers suggest that infants as young as 3 to 4 months may know that an object still exists, but they do not have either the memory skills to "hold on" to the location of the object or the motor skills to coordinate a search (Baillargeon, 1999; Flavell et al., 2002).

A second major accomplishment in the sensorimotor period is the beginning of logical, **goal-directed actions**. Think of the familiar clear plastic container baby toy with a lid and several colorful items inside that can be dumped out and replaced. A 6-month-old baby is likely to become frustrated trying to get to the toys inside. An older child who has mastered the basics of the sensorimotor stage will probably be able to deal with the toy in an orderly fashion by building a "container toy" scheme: (1) get the lid off, (2) turn the container upside down, (3) shake if the items jam, and (4) watch the items fall. Separate lower-level schemes have been organized into a higher-level scheme to achieve a goal.

The child is soon able to reverse this action by refilling the container. Learning to reverse actions is a basic accomplishment of the sensorimotor stage. As we will soon see, however, learning to reverse thinking—that is, learning to imagine the reverse of a sequence of actions—takes much longer.

EARLY CHILDHOOD TO THE EARLY ELEMENTARY YEARS: THE PREOPERATIONAL STAGE. By the end of the sensorimotor stage, the child can use many action schemes. However, as long as these schemes remain tied to physical actions, they are of no use in recalling the past, keeping track of information, or planning. For this, children need what Piaget called **operations**, or actions that are carried out and reversed mentally rather than physically. At the **preoperational** stage the child is moving toward mastery, but has not yet mastered these mental operations (so thinking is preoperational).

Goal-directed actions Deliberate actions toward a goal.

Operations Actions a person carries out by thinking them through instead of literally performing the actions.

Preoperational The stage before a child masters logical mental operations.

"I can't tell you 'cause I'm wearin' my mittens."

Family Circus © 2002 Bil Keane, Inc.
King Features Syndicate

According to Piaget, the first type of thinking that is separate from action involves making action schemes symbolic. The ability to form and use symbols—words, gestures, signs, images, and so on—is thus a major accomplishment of the preoperational period and moves children closer to mastering the mental operations of the next stage. This ability to work with symbols to represent an object that is not present, such as using the word *horse* or a picture of a horse or even pretending to ride a broomstick horse, is called the **semiotic function**. In fact, the child's earliest use of symbols is in pretending. Children who are not yet able to talk will often use action symbols—pretending to drink from an empty cup or touching a comb to their hair, showing that they know what each object is for. This behavior also shows that their schemes are becoming more general and less tied to specific actions. The eating scheme, for example, can be used in playing house. During the preoperational stage, there is also rapid development of that very important symbol system, language. Between the ages of 2 and 4, most children enlarge their vocabulary from about 200 to 2,000 words.

As the child moves through the preoperational stage, the developing ability to think about objects in symbolic form remains somewhat limited to thinking in one direction only, or using one-way logic. It is very difficult for the child to "think backwards," or imagine how to reverse the steps in a task. **Reversible thinking** is involved in many tasks that are difficult for the preoperational child, such as the conservation of matter.

Conservation is the principle that the amount or number of something remains the same even if the arrangement or appearance is changed, as long as nothing is added and nothing is taken away. You know that if you tear a piece of paper into several pieces, you will still have the same amount of paper. To prove this, you know that you can reverse the process by taping the pieces back together. Here is a classic example of difficulty with conservation. Leah, a 5-year-old, is shown two identical glasses, both short and wide in shape. Both have exactly the same amount of colored water in them. She agrees that the amounts are "the same." The experimenter then pours the water from one of the glasses into a taller, narrower glass and asks, "Now, does one glass have more water, or are they the same?" Leah responds that the tall glass has more because "It goes up more here" (she points to higher level on taller glass).

Piaget's explanation for Leah's answer is that she is focusing, or *centering*, attention on the dimension of height. She has difficulty considering more than one aspect of the situation at a time, or **decentering**. The preoperational child cannot understand that decreased diameter compensates for increased height, because this would require taking into account two dimensions at once. Thus, children at the preoperational stage have trouble freeing themselves from their own immediate perceptions of how the world appears.

This brings us to another important characteristic of the preoperational stage. Preoperational children, according to Piaget, have a tendency to be **egocentric**, to see the world and the experiences of others from their own viewpoint. The concept of egocentrism, as Piaget intended it, does not mean selfish; it simply means children often assume that everyone else shares their feelings, reactions, and perspectives. For example, if a little girl at this stage is afraid of dogs, she may assume that all children share this fear. The 2-year-old at the beginning of this chapter who brought his own mother to comfort a distressed friend—even though the friend's mother was available—was simply seeing the situation through his own eyes. Very young children center on their own perceptions and on the way the situation appears to them. This is one reason it is difficult for preoperational children to understand that *your* right hand is not on the same side as theirs when you are facing them.

Research has shown that young children are not totally egocentric in every situation, however. Children as young as 2 describe more details about a situation to a parent who was not present than they provide to a parent who experienced the situation with them. So young children do seem quite able to take the needs and different perspectives of

Semiotic function The ability to use symbols—language, pictures, signs, or gestures—to represent actions or objects mentally.

Reversible thinking Thinking backward, from the end to the beginning.

Conservation Principle that some characteristics of an object remain the same despite changes in appearance.

Decentering Focusing on more than one aspect at a time.

Egocentric Assuming that others experience the world the way you do.

GUIDELINES — FAMILY AND COMMUNITY PARTNERSHIPS

Helping Families Care for Preoperational Children

Encourage families to use concrete props and visual aids whenever possible.
Examples

1. When they use words such as *part, whole,* or *one half,* encourage families to demonstrate using objects in the house such as cutting an apple or pizza into parts.
2. Let children add and subtract with sticks, rocks, or colored chips. This technique also is helpful for early concrete-operational students.

Make instructions relatively short—not too many steps at once. Use actions as well as words.
Examples

1. When giving instructions such as how to feed a pet, first model the process, then ask the child to try it.
2. Explain a game by acting out one of the parts.

Help children develop their ability to see the world from someone else's point of view.
Examples

1. Ask children to imagine "how your sister felt when you broke her toy."

2. Be clear about rules for sharing or use of material. Help children understand the value of the rules and develop empathy by asking them to think about how they would like to be treated. Avoid long lectures on "sharing" or being "nice."

Give children a great deal of hands-on practice with the skills that serve as building blocks for more complex skills such as reading comprehension or collaboration.
Examples

1. Provide cut-out letters or letter magnets for the refrigerator to build words.
2. Do activities that require measuring and simple calculations—cooking, dividing a batch of popcorn equally.

Provide a wide range of experiences in order to build a foundation for concept learning and language.
Examples

1. Take trips to zoos, gardens, theaters, and concerts; encourage storytelling.
2. Give children words to describe what they are doing, hearing, seeing, touching, tasting, and smelling.

---

others into account, at least in certain situations (Flavell et al., 2002). And in fairness to young children, even adults can make assumptions that others feel or think like they do. For example, have you ever gotten a gift that the giver loved but was clearly inappropriate for you? The *Family and Community Partnerships Guidelines* give ideas for working with preoperational thinkers and for guiding families in supporting the cognitive development of their children.

LATER ELEMENTARY TO THE MIDDLE SCHOOL YEARS: THE CONCRETE-OPERA-TIONAL STAGE. Piaget coined the term **concrete operations** to describe this stage of "hands-on" thinking. The basic characteristics of the stage are the recognition of the logical stability of the physical world; the realization that elements can be changed or transformed and still conserve many of their original characteristics; and the understanding that these changes can be reversed.

Look at Figure 1.4, on the next page to see examples of the different tasks given to children to assess conservation and the approximate age ranges when most children can solve these problems. According to Piaget, the ability to solve conservation problems depends on having an understanding of three basic aspects of reasoning: identity, compensation, and reversibility. With a complete mastery of **identity**, the student knows that if nothing is added or taken away, the material remains the same. With an understanding of **compensation**, the student knows that an apparent change in one direction can be compensated for by a change in another direction. That is, if the glass is narrower, the liquid will rise higher in the glass. And with an understanding of reversibility, the student can mentally cancel out the change that has been made. Leah apparently knew it was the same water (identity), but lacked compensation and reversibility, so she was still moving toward conservation.

Concrete operations Mental tasks tied to concrete objects and situations.

Identity Principle that a person or object remains the same over time.

Compensation The principle that changes in one dimension can be offset by changes in another.

FIGURE 1.4

SOME PIAGETIAN CONSERVATION TASKS

In addition to the tasks shown here, other tasks involve the conservation of number, length, weight, and volume. These tasks are all achieved over the concrete-operational period.

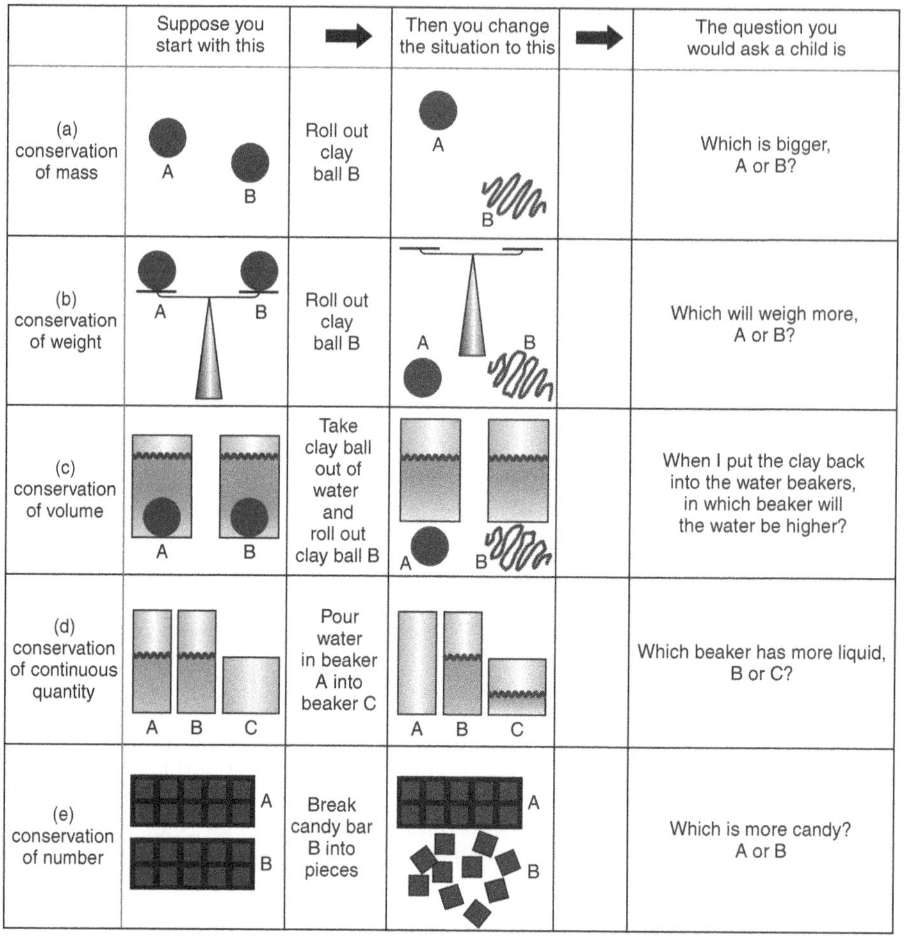

Source: Woolfolk, A., & Perry, N. E. ., Child Development, © 2012 by Pearson Education, Inc. Reproduced by permission of Pearson Education, Inc. All rights reserved.

Classification Grouping objects into categories.

Reversibility A characteristic of Piagetian logical operations—the ability to think through a series of steps, then mentally reverse the steps and return to the starting point; also called *reversible thinking.*

Another important operation mastered at this stage is **classification**. Classification depends on a student's abilities to focus on a single characteristic of objects in a set (for example, color) and group the objects according to that characteristic. More advanced classification at this stage involves recognizing that one class fits into another. A city can be in a particular state or province and also in a particular country, as you probably knew when I asked you earlier about Pittsburgh, Pennsylvania, USA. As children apply this advanced classification to locations, they often become fascinated with "complete" addresses such as Lee Jary, 5116 Forest Hill Drive, Richmond Hill, Ontario, Canada, North America, Northern Hemisphere, Earth, Solar System, Milky Way, Universe.

Classification is also related to **reversibility**. The ability to reverse a process mentally allows the concrete-operational student to see that there is more than one way to classify a group of objects. The student understands, for example, that buttons can be classified by color, and then reclassified by size or by the number of holes.

Seriation is the process of making an orderly arrangement from large to small or vice versa. This understanding of sequential relationships permits a student to construct a logical series in which A < B < C (A is less than B is less than C) and so on. Unlike the preoperational child, the concrete-operational child can grasp the notion that B can be larger than A but still smaller than C.

With the abilities to handle operations such as conservation, classification, and seriation, the student at the concrete-operational stage has finally developed a complete and very logical system of thinking. However, this system of thinking is still tied to physical reality. The logic is based on concrete situations that can be organized, classified, or manipulated. Thus, children at this stage can imagine several different arrangements for the furniture in their rooms. They do not have to solve the problem strictly through trial and error by actually moving the furniture. However, the concrete-operational child is not yet able to reason about hypothetical, abstract problems that involve the coordination of many factors at once. This kind of coordination is part of Piaget's next and final stage of cognitive development.

In any grade you teach, knowledge of concrete-operational thinking will be helpful (see the *Guidelines*). In the early grades, the students are moving toward this logical system of thought. In the middle grades, it is in full flower, ready to be applied and extended

Seriation Arranging objects in sequential order according to one aspect, such as size, weight, or volume.

GUIDELINES

Teaching the Concrete-Operational Child

Continue to use concrete props and visual aids, especially when dealing with sophisticated material.
Examples
1. Use time lines in history and three-dimensional models in science.
2. Use diagrams to illustrate hierarchical relationships such as branches of government and the agencies under each branch.

Continue to give students a chance to manipulate and test objects.
Examples
1. Set up simple scientific experiments such as the following involving the relationship between fire and oxygen. What happens to a flame when you blow on it from a distance? (If you don't blow it out, the flame gets larger briefly, because it has more oxygen to burn.) What happens when you cover the flame with a jar?
2. Have students make candles by dipping wicks in wax, weave cloth on a simple loom, bake bread, set type by hand, or do other craft work that illustrates the daily occupations of people in the colonial period.

Make sure presentations and readings are brief and well organized.
Examples
1. Assign stories or books with short, logical chapters, moving to longer reading assignments only when students are ready.
2. Break up a presentation, giving students an opportunity to practice the first steps before introducing the next steps.

Use familiar examples to explain more complex ideas.
Examples
1. Compare students' lives with those of characters in a story. After reading *Island of the Blue Dolphins* (the true story of a girl who grew up alone on a deserted island), ask, "Have you ever had to stay alone for a long time? How did you feel?"
2. Teach the concept of area by having students measure two school rooms that are different sizes.

Give opportunities to classify and group objects and ideas on increasingly complex levels.
Examples
1. Give students slips of paper with individual sentences written on each paper and ask the students to group the sentences into paragraphs.
2. Compare the systems of the human body to other kinds of systems: the brain to a computer, the heart to a pump. Break down stories into components, from the broad to the specific: author, story, characters, plot, theme, place, time.

Present problems that require logical, analytical thinking.
Examples
1. Discuss open-ended questions that stimulate thinking: "Are the brain and the mind the same thing?" "How should the city deal with stray animals?" "What is the largest number?"
2. Use sports photos or pictures of crisis situations (Red Cross helping in disasters, victims of poverty or war, senior citizens who need assistance) to stimulate problem-solving discussions.

by your teaching. Students in high school and even adults still commonly use concrete-operational thinking, especially in areas that are new or unfamiliar.

HIGH SCHOOL AND COLLEGE: FORMAL OPERATIONS.

Some students remain at the concrete-operational stage throughout their school years, even throughout life. However, new experiences, usually those that take place in school, eventually present most students with problems that they cannot solve using concrete operations.

STOP & THINK You are packing for a long trip, but want to pack light. How many different three-piece outfits (slacks, shirt, jacket) will you have if you include three shirts, three slacks, and three jackets (assuming of course that they all go together in fashion perfection)? Time yourself to see how long it takes to arrive at the answer. •

What happens when a number of variables interact, as in a laboratory experiment or the question above? Then a mental system for controlling sets of variables and working through a set of possibilities is needed. These are the abilities Piaget called **formal operations**.

At the level of formal operations, the focus of thinking can shift from what is to what might be. Situations do not have to be experienced to be imagined. You met Jamal at the beginning of this chapter. Even though he is a bright elementary school student, he could not answer the question, "How would life be different if people did not have to sleep?" because he insisted, "People HAVE TO SLEEP!" In contrast, the adolescent who has mastered formal operations can consider contrary-to-fact questions. In answering, the adolescent demonstrates the hallmark of formal operations—**hypothetico-deductive reasoning**. The formal-operational thinker can consider a hypothetical situation (people do not sleep) and reason *deductively* (from the general assumption to specific implications, such as longer workdays, more money spent on energy and lighting, smaller houses without bedrooms, or new entertainment industries). Formal operations also include *inductive* reasoning, or using specific observations to identify general principles. For example, the economist observes many specific changes in the stock market and attempts to identify general principles about economic cycles from this information.

Abstract formal-operational thinking is necessary for success in many advanced high school and college courses. For example, most math is concerned with hypothetical situations, assumptions, and givens: "Let $x = 10$," or "Assume $x2 + y2 = z2$," or "Given two sides and an adjacent angle … " Work in social studies and literature requires abstract thinking, too: "What did Wilson mean when he called World War I the 'war to end all wars'?" "What are some metaphors for hope and despair in Shakespeare's sonnets?" "What symbols of old age does T. S. Eliot use in *The Waste Land?*" "How do animals symbolize human character traits in Aesop's fables?"

The organized, scientific thinking of formal operations requires that students systematically generate different possibilities for a given situation. For example, if asked, "How many different shirt/slacks/jacket outfits can you make using three of each kind of clothing?" the child using formal operations can systematically identify the 27 possible combinations. (Did you get it right?) A concrete-operational thinker might name just a few combinations, using each piece of clothing only once. The underlying system of combinations is not yet available.

Another characteristic of this stage is **adolescent egocentrism**. Unlike egocentric young children, adolescents do not deny that other people may have different perceptions and beliefs; the adolescents just become very focused on their own ideas. They spend much time examining their own beliefs and attitudes. This leads to what Elkind (1981) calls the sense of an *imaginary audience*—the feeling that everyone is watching. Thus, adolescents believe that others are analyzing them: "Everyone noticed that I wore this shirt twice this week." "The whole class thought my answer was dumb!" You can see that social blunders or imperfections in appearance can be devastating if "everybody is watching." Luckily, this feeling of being "on stage" seems to peak in early adolescence by age 14 or 15, although in unfamiliar situations we all may feel our mistakes are being noticed.

Connect and Extend to PRAXIS II™

Reasoning (II, A1)
Be able to distinguish between inductive and deductive reasoning. Explain the role that each plays in the learning of concepts.

Formal operations Mental tasks involving abstract thinking and coordination of a number of variables.

Hypothetico-deductive reasoning A formal-operations problem-solving strategy in which an individual begins by identifying all the factors that might affect a problem and then deduces and systematically evaluates specific solutions.

Adolescent egocentrism Assumption that everyone else shares one's thoughts, feelings, and concerns.

The ability to think hypothetically, consider alternatives, identify all possible combinations, and analyze their own thinking has some interesting consequences for adolescents. Because they can think about worlds that do not exist, they often become interested in science fiction. Because they can reason from general principles to specific actions, they often are critical of people whose actions seem to contradict their principles. Adolescents can deduce the set of "best" possibilities and imagine ideal worlds (or ideal parents and teachers, for that matter). This explains why many students at this age develop interests in utopias, political causes, and social issues. They want to design better worlds, and their thinking allows them to do so. Adolescents also can imagine many possible futures for themselves and may try to decide which is best. Feelings about any of these ideals may be strong.

PLAYING FOR AN IMAGINARY AUDIENCE Adolescents may seem "alone in a crowd." They can become very focused on their own ideas and feel everyone is noticing their every mistake.

DO WE ALL REACH THE FOURTH STAGE? Most psychologists agree that there is a level of thinking more sophisticated than concrete operations. But there is a debate about how universal formal-operational thinking actually is, even among adults. The first three stages of Piaget's theory are forced on most people by physical realities. Objects really are permanent. The amount of water doesn't change when it is poured into another glass. Formal operations, however, are not so closely tied to the physical environment. Being able to use formal operations may be the result of practice in solving hypothetical problems and using formal scientific reasoning—abilities that are valued and taught in literate cultures, particularly in college. Even so, only about 30% to 40% of high school students can perform Piaget's formal-operational tasks (Meece & Daniels, 2008). The *Guidelines* will help you support the development of formal operations in your students.

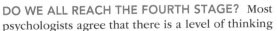

GUIDELINES

Helping Students to Use Formal Operations

Continue to use concrete-operational teaching strategies and materials.

Examples

1. Use visual aids such as charts and illustrations as well as somewhat more sophisticated graphs and diagrams, especially when the material is new.
2. Compare the experiences of characters in stories to students' experiences.

Give students the opportunity to explore many hypothetical questions.

Examples

1. Have students write position papers, then exchange these papers with the opposing side and debate topical social issues such as the environment, the economy, and national health insurance.
2. Ask students to write about their personal vision of a utopia; write a description of a universe that has no sex differences; write a description of Earth after humans are extinct.

Give students opportunities to solve problems and reason scientifically.

Examples

1. Set up group discussions in which students design experiments to answer questions.
2. Ask students to justify two different positions on animal rights, with logical arguments for each position.

Whenever possible, teach broad concepts, not just facts, using materials and ideas relevant to the students' lives (Delpit, 1995).

Examples

1. When discussing the Civil War, consider racism or other issues that have divided the United States since then.
2. When teaching about poetry, let students find lyrics from popular songs that illustrate poetic devices, and talk about how these devices do or don't work well to communicate the meanings and feelings the songwriters intended.

Piaget himself (1974) suggested that most adults might only be able to use formal-operational thought in a few areas where they have the greatest experience or interest. Taking a college class fosters formal-operational abilities in that subject, but not necessarily in others (Lehman & Nisbett, 1990). So expect many students in your middle-school or high-school classes to have trouble thinking hypothetically, especially when they are learning something new. Sometimes, students find shortcuts for dealing with problems that are beyond their grasp; they may memorize formulas or lists of steps. These systems may be helpful for passing tests, but real understanding will take place only if students are able to go beyond this superficial use of memorization.

Information Processing, Neo-Piagetian, and Neuroscience Views of Cognitive Development

There are explanations for why children have trouble with conservation and other Piagetian tasks. These explanations focus on the development of information processing skills, such as attention, memory capacity, and learning strategies. As children mature and their brains develop, they are better able to focus their attention, process information more quickly, hold more information in memory, and use thinking strategies more easily and flexibly. Siegler (2000) proposes that as children grow older, they develop progressively better rules and strategies for solving problems and thinking logically. Teachers can help students develop their capacities for formal thinking by putting them in situations that challenge their thinking and reveal the shortcomings of their logic. Siegler's approach is called *rule assessment* because it focuses on understanding, challenging, and changing the rules that students use for thinking.

Some developmental psychologists have formulated **neo-Piagetian theories** that retain Piaget's insights about children's construction of knowledge and the general trends in children's thinking, but add findings from information processing theories about the role of attention, memory, and strategies. For example, Robbie Case (1992, 1998) devised an explanation of cognitive development suggesting that children develop in stages within specific domains such as numerical concepts, spatial concepts, social tasks, storytelling, reasoning about physical objects, and motor development. As children practice using the schemes in a particular domain (for example, using counting schemes in the number concept area), accomplishing the schemes requires less attention. The schemes become more automatic because the child does not have to "think so hard." This frees up mental resources and memory to do more, so the child is able to combine simple schemes into more complex ones and invent new schemes when needed (assimilation and accommodation in action).

Kurt Fischer (2009) connected cognitive development in different domains to research on the brain. He also examined development in different domains such as reading or math. You may remember Nico and Brooke, the remarkable children we met earlier in the chapter who each had one side of their brain removed to treat severe epilepsy, yet both still developed other pathways in their brains to recover lost spatial and verbal abilities. We have seen that one of the implications of research on the brain is that there are multiple pathways for learning.

Fischer has found, however, that even though their brains follow different pathways as they master skills in speaking, reading, and mathematics, children's growth patterns show a similar series of spurts and they go through predictable levels of development. When learning a new skill, children move through three tiers—from *actions* to *representations* to *abstractions*. Within each tier, the pattern is moving from accomplishing a single action to mapping or coordinating two actions together such as coordinating addition and multiplication in math, to creating whole systems of understanding. At the level of abstractions, they finally move to constructing explanatory principles. This may remind you of sensorimotor, concrete operations, and formal operations in Piaget's theory. Look at Table 1.3, which shows the movement through the tiers of *actions* to *representations* to *abstractions*.

For each skill level, the brain reorganizes itself, too. Table 1.3 shows this progression between birth and 30 years old for the skill of arithmetic operations: addition, subtraction, multiplication, and division. Notice the column that says "emergence of optimal level."

Neo-Piagetian theories More recent theories that integrate findings about attention, memory, and strategy use with Piaget's insights about children's thinking and the construction of knowledge.

TABLE 1.3 • **A Pattern of Cognitive Development over 30 Years**

As children develop skills in speaking, reading, and mathematics, their growth patterns show a similar series of spurts. In learning a new skill, children move from *actions* to *representations* to *abstractions*.

TIERS	LEVELS	AGE OF EMERGENCE OF OPTIMAL LEVEL	AGE OF FUNCTIONAL LEVEL
		23–25 yrs	30–45 yrs
	Ab4. Principles	18–20	23–40
Abstraction	Ab3. Systems	14–16	17–30
	Ab2. Mappings	10–12	13–20
	Rp4./Ab1. Single Abstraction	6–7	7–12
Representations	Rp3 Systems	3½–4½	4–8
	Rp2 Mappings	2	2–5
	Sm4./Rp1. Single Representations	11–13 mos	11–24 mos
Actions	Sm3. Systems	7–8	7–13
	Sm2. Mappings	3–4	3–9
	Sm1. Single Actions		

Source: Fischer, K. W. (2009). Mind, brain, and education: Building a scientific groundwork for learning and teaching. Mind, Brain, and Education, 3, 2–16.

This column shows the ages at which the skills will develop if the individuals have *quality support and the chance to practice*. The age the skill emerges without support and practice is shown in the last column. Support and practice are keys in another explanation of cognitive development we will discuss soon—Vygotsky's theory.

Some Limitations of Piaget's Theory

Although most psychologists agree with Piaget's insightful descriptions of *how* children think, many disagree with his explanations of *why* thinking develops as it does.

THE TROUBLE WITH STAGES. Some psychologists have questioned the existence of four separate stages of thinking, even though they agree that children do go through the changes that Piaget described (Mascolo & Fischer, 2005; Miller, 2011). One problem with the stage model is the lack of consistency in children's thinking. For example, children can conserve number (the number of blocks does not change when they are rearranged) a year or two before they can conserve weight (a ball of clay does not change when you flatten it). Why can't they use conservation consistently in every situation? In fairness, we should note that in his later work, even Piaget put less emphasis on stages of cognitive development and gave more attention to how thinking *changes* through equilibration (Miller, 2011).

Another problem with the idea of separate stages is that the processes may be more continuous than they seem. Changes may seem like discontinuous, qualitative leaps when we look across longer time periods. The 3-year-old persistently searching for a lost toy seems qualitatively different from the infant who doesn't seem to miss a toy or search when the toy rolls under a sofa. But if we watched a developing child very closely and observed moment-to-moment or hour-to-hour changes, we might see that indeed there are gradual, continuous changes. Rather than appearing all at once, the knowledge that a hidden toy still exists may be a product of the older child's more fully developed memory: He knows that the toy is under the sofa because he remembers seeing it roll there, whereas the infant can't hold on to that memory. The longer you require children to wait before searching—the longer you make them remember the object—the older they have to be to succeed (Siegler & Alibali, 2005).

CHILD EXPERTS One limitation of Piaget's theory appears to be the underestimation of young children's cognitive abilities. For instance, his theory does not explain how these young girls can play chess at the same level as many adults could.

Change can be both continuous and discontinuous, as described by a branch of mathematics called *catastrophe theory*. Changes that appear suddenly, like the collapse of a bridge, are preceded by many slowly developing changes such as gradual, continuous corrosion of the metal structures. Similarly, gradually developing changes in children can lead to large changes in abilities that seem abrupt (Dawson-Tunik, Fischer, & Stein, 2004; Siegler & Alibali, 2005).

UNDERESTIMATING CHILDREN'S ABILITIES. It now appears that Piaget underestimated the cognitive abilities of children, particularly younger ones. The problems he gave young children may have been too difficult and the directions too confusing. His subjects may have understood more than they could demonstrate when solving these problems. For example, work by Gelman and her colleagues (Gelman, 2000; Gelman & Cordes, 2001) shows that preschool children know much more about the concept of number than Piaget thought, even if they sometimes make mistakes or get confused. As long as preschoolers work with only 3 or 4 objects at a time, they can tell that the number remains the same, even if the objects are spread far apart or clumped close together. Mirjam Ebersbach (2009) demonstrated that most of the German kindergartners in her study considered all three dimensions—width, height, and length—when they estimated the volume of a wooden block (actually, how many small cubes it would take to make bigger blocks of different sizes). In other words, we may be born with a greater store of cognitive tools than Piaget suggested. Some basic understandings or core knowledge, such as the permanence of objects or the sense of number, may be part of our evolutionary equipment, ready for use in our cognitive development (Geary & Bjorklund, 2000; Woodward & Needham, 2009).

Piaget's theory does not explain how even young children can perform at an advanced level in certain areas where they have highly developed knowledge and expertise. An expert 9-year-old chess player may think abstractly about chess moves, whereas a novice 20-year-old player may have to resort to more concrete strategies to plan and remember moves (Siegler, 1998).

Finally, Piaget argued that the development of cognitive operations such as conservation or abstract thinking cannot be accelerated. He believed that children had to be developmentally ready to learn. Quite a bit of research, however, has shown that with effective instruction, children can learn to perform cognitive operations such as conservation. They do not have to naturally discover these ways of thinking on their own. Knowledge and experience in a situation affect the kind of thinking that students can do (Brainerd, 2003).

COGNITIVE DEVELOPMENT AND CULTURE. One final criticism of Piaget's theory is that it overlooks the important effects of the child's cultural and social group. Research across different cultures has generally confirmed that although Piaget was accurate about the sequence of the stages in children's thinking, the age ranges for the stages vary. Western children typically move to the next stage about 2 to 3 years earlier than children in non-Western societies. But careful research has shown that these differences across cultures depend on the subject or domain tested and whether the culture values and teaches knowledge in that domain. For example, children in Brazil who sell candy in the streets instead of attending school appear to fail a certain kind of Piagetian task—class inclusion (Are there more daisies, more tulips, or more flowers in the picture?). But when the tasks are phrased within concepts they understand—selling candy—then these children perform better than Brazilian children the same age who attend school (Saxe, 1999). When a culture or context emphasizes a cognitive ability, children growing up in that culture tend to acquire that ability sooner. In a study that compared Chinese 1st-, 3rd-, and 5th-grade students to American students in the same grades, the Chinese students mastered a Piagetian task that involved distance, time, and speed relationships about 2 years ahead of American students, most likely because the Chinese education system puts more emphasis on math and science in the early grades (Zhou, Peverly, Beohm, & Chongde, 2001).

Even concrete operations such as classification may develop differently in different cultures. For example, when individuals from the Kpelle people of Africa were asked to sort 20 objects, they created groups that made sense to them—a hoe with a potato, a knife with an orange. The experimenter could not get the Kpelle to change their categories; they said this way of sorting is how a wise man would do it. Finally, the experimenter asked in desperation, "Well, how would a fool do it?" Then the subjects promptly created the four neat classification piles the experimenter had expected—food, tools, and so on (Rogoff & Morelli, 1989).

There is another increasingly influential view of cognitive development. Proposed years ago by Lev Vygotsky and recently rediscovered, this theory ties cognitive development to culture.

VYGOTSKY'S SOCIOCULTURAL PERSPECTIVE

Psychologists today recognize that culture shapes cognitive development by determining what and how the child will learn about the world—the content and processes of thinking. For example, young Zinacanteco Indian girls of southern Mexico learn complicated ways of weaving cloth through informal instruction by adults in their communities. Cultures that prize cooperation and sharing teach these abilities early, whereas cultures that encourage competition nurture competitive skills in their children (Bakerman et al., 1990; Ceci & Roazzi, 1994). The stages observed by Piaget are not necessarily "natural" for all children because to some extent they reflect the expectations and activities of Western cultures, as the Kpelle people described above have taught us (Kozulin, 2003; Rogoff, 2003).

A major spokesperson for this **sociocultural theory** (also called *sociohistoric*) was a Russian psychologist who died almost 80 years ago. Lev Semenovich Vygotsky was only 38 when he died of tuberculosis, but during his brief life he produced over 100 books and articles. Some of the translations now available are Vygotsky (e.g., 1978, 1986, 1987a, 1987b, 1987c, 1993, 1997). Vygotsky began studying learning and development to improve his own teaching. He went on to write about language and thought, the psychology of art, learning and development, and educating students with special needs. His work was banned in Russia for many years because he referenced Western psychologists. But in the past 40 years, with the rediscovery of his writings, Vygotsky's ideas have become major influences in psychology and education and have provided alternatives to many of Piaget's theories (Gredler, 2009; Kozulin, 2003; Van Der Veer, 2007; Wink & Putney, 2002).

Vygotsky believed that human activities take place in cultural settings and that they cannot be understood apart from these settings. One of his key ideas was that our specific mental structures and processes can be traced to our interactions with others. These social interactions are more than simple influences on cognitive development—they actually create our cognitive structures and thinking processes (Palincsar, 1998). In fact, "Vygotsky conceptualized development as the transformation of socially shared activities into internalized processes" (John-Steiner & Mahn, 1996, p. 192). We will examine three themes in Vygotsky's writings that explain how social processes form learning and thinking: the social sources of individual thinking; the role of cultural tools in learning and development, especially the tool of language; and the zone of proximal development (Driscoll, 2005; Wertsch & Tulviste, 1992).

The Social Sources of Individual Thinking

Vygotsky assumed that

> Every function in a child's cultural development appears twice: first, on the social level and later on the individual level; first between people (interpsychological) and then

SOCIOCULTURAL THEORY Lev Vygotsky elaborated the sociocultural theory of development. His ideas about language, culture, and cognitive development have become major influences in the fields of psychology and education.

Sociocultural theory Emphasizes role in development of cooperative dialogues between children and more knowledgeable members of society. Children learn the culture of their community (ways of thinking and behaving) through these interactions.

inside the child (intrapsychological). This applies equally to voluntary attention, to logical memory, and to the formation of concepts. All the higher functions originate as actual relations between human individuals. (1978, p. 57)

In other words, higher mental processes, such as directing your own attention and thinking through problems, first are *co-constructed* during shared activities between the child and another person. Then these **co-constructed processes** are internalized by the child and become part of that child's cognitive development (Gredler, 2009). For example, children first use language in activities with others, to regulate the behavior of the others ("No nap!" or "I wanna cookie."). Later, however, the child can regulate her own behavior using private speech ("careful—don't spill"), as you will see in a later section. So, for Vygotsky, social interaction was more than influence; it was the origin of higher mental processes such as problem solving. Consider this example:

> A six-year-old has lost a toy and asks her father for help. The father asks her where she last saw the toy; the child says "I can't remember." He asks a series of questions—did you have it in your room? Outside? Next door? To each question, the child answers, "no." When he says "in the car?" she says "I think so" and goes to retrieve the toy. (Tharp & Gallimore, 1988, p. 14)

Who remembered? The answer is really neither the father nor the daughter, but the two together. The remembering and problem solving were co-constructed—between people—in the interaction. But the child (and the father) may have internalized strategies to use next time something is lost. At some point, the child will be able to function independently to solve this kind of problem. So, like the strategy for finding the toy, higher functions appear first between a child and a "teacher" before they exist within the individual child (Kozulin, 1990; 2003).

Here is another example of the social sources of individual thinking. Richard Anderson and his colleagues (2001) studied how 4th graders in small-group classroom discussions *appropriate* (take for themselves and use) argument stratagems that occur in the discussions. An *argument stratagem* is a particular form such as "I think [POSITION] because [REASON]," where the student fills in the position and the reason. For example, a student might say, "I think that the wolves should be left alone because they are not hurting anyone." Another strategy form is "If [ACTION], then [BAD CONSEQUENCE]," as in "If they don't trap the wolves, then the wolves will eat the cows." Other forms manage participation, for example, "What do you think [NAME]?" or "Let [NAME] talk."

Anderson's research identified 13 forms of talk and argument that helped to manage the discussion, get everyone to participate, present and defend positions, and handle confusion. The researchers found that the use of these different forms of talking and thinking *snowballed*: Once a useful argument was employed by one student, it spread to other students and the argument stratagem form appeared more and more in the discussions. Open discussions—students asking and answering each other's questions—were better than teacher-dominated discussion for the development of these argument forms. Over time, these ways of presenting, attacking, and defending positions could be internalized as mental reasoning and decision making for the individual students.

Both Piaget and Vygotsky emphasized the importance of social interactions in cognitive development, but Piaget saw a different role for interaction. He believed that interaction encouraged development by creating disequilibrium—that is, cognitive conflict motivated change. Thus, Piaget believed that the most helpful interactions were those between peers, because peers are on an equal basis and can challenge each other's thinking. Vygotsky, on the other hand, suggested that children's cognitive development is fostered by interactions with people who are more capable or advanced in their thinking—people such as parents and teachers (Moshman, 1997; Palinscar, 1998). Of course, students can learn from both adults and peers, and today, computers can play a role in supporting communication across distances or in different languages.

Cultural Tools and Cognitive Development

Vygotsky believed that **cultural tools**, including technical tools (such as printing presses, plows, rulers, abacuses, graph paper—today, we would add mobile devices, computers,

Co-constructed process A social process in which people interact and negotiate (usually verbally) to create an understanding or to solve a problem. The final product is shaped by all participants.

Cultural tools The real tools (computers, scales, etc.) and symbol systems (numbers, language, graphs) that allow people in a society to communicate, think, solve problems, and create knowledge.

the Internet, real-time translators for mobile devices and chats, search engines, digital organizers and calendars, assistive technologies for students with learning challenges...) and psychological tools (signs and symbol systems such as numbers and mathematical systems, Braille and sign language, maps, works of art, codes, and language) play very important roles in cognitive development. For example, as long as the culture provides only Roman numerals for representing quantity, certain ways of thinking mathematically—from long division to calculus—are difficult or impossible. But if a number system has a zero, fractions, positive and negative values, and an infinite quantity of numbers, then much more is possible. The number system is a psychological tool that supports learning and cognitive development—it changes the thinking process. This symbol system is passed from adult to child and from child to child through formal and informal interactions and teachings.

TECHNICAL TOOLS IN A DIGITAL AGE. The use of technical tools such as calculators and spell checkers has been somewhat controversial in education. Technology is increasingly "checking up" on us. I rely on the spell checker in my word processing program to protect me from embarrassment. But I also read student papers with spelling replacements that must have come from decisions made by the word processing program—without a "sense check" by the writer. Is student learning harmed or helped by these technology supports? Just because students learned mathematics in the past with paper-and-pencil procedures and practice does not mean that this is the best way to learn. For example, in the Third International Mathematics and Science Study (TIMSS, 1998), on every test at the advanced level, students who said that they used calculators in their daily math coursework performed much better than students who rarely or never used calculators. In fact, the research on calculators over the past decade has found that rather than eroding basic skills, calculator use has positive effects on students' problem-solving skills and attitudes toward math (Waits & Demana, 2000).

PSYCHOLOGICAL TOOLS. Vygotsky believed that all higher-order mental processes such as reasoning and problem solving are *mediated* by (accomplished through and with the help of) psychological tools. These tools allow children to transform their thinking by enabling them to gain greater and greater mastery of their own cognitive processes; thus they advance their own development as they use the tools. In fact, Vygotsky believed the essence of cognitive development is mastering the use of psychological tools such as language to accomplish the kind of advanced thinking and problem solving that could not be accomplished without those tools (Gredler, 2009; Karpov & Haywood, 1998). The process is something like this: As children engage in activities with adults or more capable peers, they exchange ideas and ways of thinking about or representing concepts—drawing maps, for example, as a way to represent spaces and places. Children internalize these co-created ideas. Thus, children's knowledge, ideas, attitudes, and values develop through appropriating or "taking for themselves" the ways of acting and thinking provided by both their culture and other members of their group (Wertsch, 2007).

In this exchange of signs and symbols and explanations, children begin to develop a "cultural tool kit" to make sense of and learn about their world (Wertsch, 1991). The kit is filled with technical tools such as graphing calculators or rulers directed toward the external world and psychological tools for acting mentally such as concepts, problem-solving strategies, and (as we saw earlier) argument strategems. Children do not just receive the tools, however. They transform the tools as they construct their own representations, symbols, patterns, and understandings. As we learned from Piaget, children's constructions of meaning are not the same as those of adults. In the exchange of signs and symbols such as language, children create their own understandings (a raccoon is a "kitty"). These understandings are gradually changed (a raccoon is a raccoon) as the children continue to engage in social activities and try to make sense of their world (John-Steiner & Mahn, 1996; Wertsch, 1991). In Vygotsky's theory, language is the most important symbol system in the tool kit, and it is the one that helps to fill the kit with other tools.

The Role of Language and Private Speech

Language is critical for cognitive development because it provides a way to express ideas and ask questions, the categories and concepts for thinking, and the links between the past and the future. Language frees us from the immediate situation to think about what was and what might be (Das, 1995; Driscoll, 2005). Vygotsky thought that:

> the specifically human capacity for language enables children to provide for auxiliary tools in the solution of difficult tasks, to overcome impulsive action, to plan a solution to a problem prior to its execution, and to master their own behavior. (1978, p. 28)

Vygotsky placed more emphasis than Piaget on the role of learning and language in cognitive development. He believed that "thinking depends on speech, on the means of thinking, and on the child's socio-cultural experience" (Vygotsky, 1987a, p. 120). In fact, Vygotsky believed that language in the form of private speech (talking to yourself) guides cognitive development.

PRIVATE SPEECH: VYGOTSKY'S AND PIAGET'S VIEWS COMPARED. If you have spent much time around young children, you know that they often talk to themselves as they play. This can happen when the child is alone or, even more often, in a group of children—each child talks enthusiastically, without any real interaction or conversation. Piaget called this the **collective monologue** and he labeled all of the children's self-directed talk "egocentric speech." He assumed that this egocentric speech is another indication that young children can't see the world through the eyes of others, so they chat away without taking into account the needs or interests of their listeners. As they mature, and especially as they have disagreements with peers, Piaget believed, children develop *socialized speech*. They learn to listen and exchange (or argue) ideas.

Vygotsky had very different ideas about young children's **private speech**. Rather than being a sign of cognitive immaturity, Vygotsky suggested that these mutterings play an important role in cognitive development because they move children in stages toward self-regulation: the ability to plan, monitor, and guide your own thinking and problem solving. First the child's behavior is regulated by others using language and other signs such as gestures. For example, the parent says, "No!" when the child reaches toward a candle flame. Next, the child learns to regulate the behavior of others using the same language tools. The child says "No!" to another child who is trying to take away a toy, often even imitating the parent's voice tone. The child also begins to use private speech to regulate her own behavior, saying "no" quietly to herself as she is tempted to touch the flame. Finally, the child learns to regulate her own behavior by using silent inner speech (Karpov & Haywood, 1998).

For example, in any preschool room you might hear 4- or 5-year-olds saying, "No, it won't fit. Try it here. Turn. Turn. Maybe this one!" while they do puzzles. Around the age of 7, children's self-directed speech goes underground, changing from spoken to whispered speech and then to silent lip movements. Finally, the children just "think" the guiding words. The use of private speech peaks at around age 9 and then decreases, although one study found that some students from ages 11 to 17 still spontaneously muttered to themselves during problem solving (McCafferty, 2004; Winsler, Carlton, & Barry, 2000; Winsler & Naglieri, 2003). Vygotsky called this inner speech "an internal plane of verbal thinking" (Vygotsky, 1934/1987c, p. 279)—a critical accomplishment on the road to higher-order thinking.

This series of steps from spoken words to silent inner speech is another example of how higher mental functions first appear between people as they communicate and regulate each other's behavior, and then emerge again within the individual as cognitive processes. Through this fundamental process, the child is using language to accomplish important cognitive activities such as directing attention, solving problems, planning, forming concepts, and gaining self-control. Research supports Vygotsky's ideas (Berk & Spuhl, 1995; Emerson & Miyake, 2003). Children and adults tend to use more private speech when they are confused, having difficulties, or making mistakes (Duncan & Cheyne, 1999). Have you ever thought to yourself something like, "Let's see, the first step is" or "Where did I use my glasses last?" or "If I read to the end of this page, then I can . . . "? You were using inner speech to remind, cue, encourage, or guide yourself.

Collective monologue Form of speech in which children in a group talk but do not really interact or communicate.

Private speech Children's self-talk, which guides their thinking and action. Eventually, these verbalizations are internalized as silent inner speech.

TABLE 1.4 • **Differences between Piaget's and Vygotsky's Theories of Egocentric or Private Speech**

	PIAGET	VYGOTSKY
	Represents an inability to take the perspective of another and engage in reciprocal communication.	Represents externalized thought; its function is to communicate with the self for the purpose of self-guidance and self-direction.
Course of Development	Declines with age.	Increases at younger ages and then gradually loses its audible quality to become internal verbal thought.
Relationship to Social Speech	Negative; least socially and cognitively mature children use more egocentric speech.	Positive; private speech develops out of social interaction with others.
Relationship to Environmental Contexts		Increases with task difficulty. Private speech serves a helpful self-guiding function in situations where more cognitive effort is needed to reach a solution.

Source: From "Development of Private Speech among Low-Income Appalachian Children," by L. E. Berk and R. A. Garvin, 1984, Developmental Psychology, 20, p. 272. Copyright © 1984 by the American Psychological Association. Adapted with permission.

This internal verbal thinking is not stable until about age 12, so children in elementary school may need to continue talking through problems and explaining their reasoning in order to develop their abilities to control their thinking (Gredler, 2009). Because private speech helps students regulate their thinking, it makes sense to allow, and even encourage, students to use private speech in school. Teachers' insisting on total silence when young students are working on difficult problems may make the work even harder for them. Take note when muttering increases in your class—this could be a sign that students need help.

Table 1.4 contrasts Piaget's and Vygotsky's theories of private speech. We should note that Piaget accepted many of Vygotsky's arguments and came to agree that language could be used in both egocentric and problem-solving ways (Piaget, 1962).

The Zone of Proximal Development

According to Vygotsky, at any given point in development, there are certain problems that a child is on the verge of being able to solve. The child just needs some structure, clues, reminders, help with remembering details or steps, encouragement to keep trying, and so on. Some problems, of course, are beyond the child's capabilities, even if every step is explained clearly. The **zone of proximal development (ZPD)** is the area between the child's current development level "as determined by independent problem solving" and the level of development that the child could achieve "through adult guidance or in collaboration with more capable peers" (Vygotsky, 1978, p. 86). It is a dynamic and changing space as student and teacher interact and understandings are exchanged. This is the area where instruction can succeed. Kathleen Berger (2012) called this area the "magic middle"—somewhere between what the student already knows and what the student isn't ready to learn.

PRIVATE SPEECH AND THE ZONE. We can see how Vygotsky's beliefs about the role of private speech in cognitive development fit with the notion of the zone of proximal development. Often, an adult uses verbal prompts and structuring to help a child solve a problem or accomplish a task. We will see later that this type of support has been called *scaffolding*. This support can be gradually reduced as the child takes over the guidance, perhaps first by giving the prompts as private speech and finally as inner speech. Let's move forward to a future day in the life of the girl in the example on page 30 who had lost her toy and listen to her *thoughts* when she realizes that a schoolbook is missing. They might sound something like this:

"Where's my math book? Used it in class. Thought I put it in my book bag after class. Dropped my bag on the bus. That dope Larry kicked my stuff, so maybe..."

Zone of proximal development Phase at which a child can master a task if given appropriate help and support.

The girl can now systematically search for ideas about the lost book without help from anyone else.

THE ROLE OF LEARNING AND DEVELOPMENT. Piaget defined *development* as the active construction of knowledge and *learning* as the passive formation of associations (Siegler, 2000). He was interested in knowledge construction and believed that cognitive development has to come before learning—the child had to be cognitively "ready" to learn. He said that "learning is subordinated to development and not vice-versa" (Piaget, 1964, p. 17). Students can memorize, for example, that Geneva is in Switzerland, but still insist that they cannot be Genevan and Swiss at the same time. True understanding will take place only when the child has developed the operation of *class inclusion*—that one category can be included within another. But as we saw earlier, research has not supported Piaget's position on the need for cognitive development to precede learning (Brainerd, 2003).

In contrast, Vygotsky believed that learning is an active process that does not have to wait for readiness. In fact, "properly organized learning results in mental development and sets in motion a variety of developmental processes that would be impossible apart from learning" (Vygotsky, 1978, p. 90). He saw learning as a tool in development—learning pulls development up to higher levels and social interaction is a key in learning (Glassman, 2001; Wink & Putney, 2002). Vygotsky's belief that learning pulls development to higher levels means that other people, including teachers, play a significant role in cognitive development.

Limitations of Vygotsky's Theory

Vygotsky's theory added important considerations by highlighting the role of culture and social processes in cognitive development, but he may have gone too far. As we have seen in this chapter, we may be born with a greater store of cognitive tools than either Piaget or Vygotsky suggested. Some basic understandings, such as the idea that adding increases quantity, may be part of our biological predispositions, ready for use to guide our cognitive development. Young children appear to figure out much about the world before they have the chance to learn from either their culture or teachers (Schunk, 2008; Woodward & Needham, 2009). Also, Vygotsky did not detail the cognitive processes underlying developmental changes—for example, *which* cognitive processes allow students to engage in more advanced and independent participation in social activities? The major limitation of Vygotsky's theory, however, is that it consists mostly of general ideas; Vygotsky died before he could expand and elaborate on his ideas and pursue his research. His students continued to investigate his ideas, but much of that work was suppressed by Stalin's regime until the 1950s and 1960s (Gredler, 2005, 2009; Kozulin, 1990, 2003). A final limitation might be that Vygotsky did not have time to detail the applications of his theories for teaching, even though he was very interested in instruction. So, most of the applications described today have been created by others—and we don't even know if Vygotsky would agree with them.

IMPLICATIONS OF PIAGET'S AND VYGOTSKY'S THEORIES FOR TEACHERS

Piaget did not make specific educational recommendations and Vygotsky did not have enough time to develop a complete set of applications. But we can glean some guidance from both men.

Piaget: What Can We Learn?

Piaget was more interested in understanding children's thinking than in guiding teachers. He did express some general ideas about educational philosophy, however. He believed that the main goal of education should be to help children learn how to learn, and that education should "form not furnish" the minds of students (Piaget, 1969, p. 70). Piaget has taught us that we can learn a great deal about how children think by listening carefully and by paying close attention to their ways of solving problems. If we understand children's thinking, we will be better able to match teaching methods to children's current knowledge and abilities; in other words, we will be better able to differentiate instruction.

Even though Piaget did not design programs of education based on his ideas, his influence on current educational practice is huge (Hindi & Perry, 2007). For example, the National Association for the Education of Young Children has guidelines for developmentally appropriate practice (DAP) that incorporate Piaget's findings (Bredekamp, 2011; Bredekamp & Copple, 1997).

UNDERSTANDING AND BUILDING ON STUDENTS' THINKING. The students in any class will vary greatly in both their level of cognitive development and their academic knowledge. As a teacher, how can you determine whether students are having trouble because they lack the necessary thinking abilities or because they simply have not learned the basic facts? To do this, Case (1985b) suggests you observe your students carefully as they try to solve the problems you have presented. What kind of logic do they use? Do they focus on only one aspect of the situation? Are they fooled by appearances? Do they suggest solutions systematically or by guessing and forgetting what they have already tried? Ask your students how they tried to solve the problem. Listen to their strategies. What kind of thinking is behind repeated mistakes or problems? Students are the best sources of information about their own thinking (Confrey, 1990a).

ACTIVE LEARNING The ability to manipulate concrete objects helps children understand abstract relationships such as the connection between symbols and quantity.

An important implication of Piaget's theory for teaching is what Hunt years ago (1961) called "the problem of the match." Students must be neither bored by work that is too simple nor left behind by teaching they cannot understand. According to Hunt, disequilibrium must be kept "just right" to encourage growth. Setting up situations that lead to unexpected results can help create an appropriate level of disequilibrium. When students experience some conflict between what they think should happen (a piece of wood should sink because it is big) and what actually happens (it floats!), they may rethink the situation, and new knowledge may develop.

Many materials and lessons can be understood at several levels and can be "just right" for a range of cognitive abilities. Classics such as *Alice in Wonderland*, myths, and fairy tales can be enjoyed at both concrete and symbolic levels. It is also possible for a group of students to be introduced to a topic together, and then work individually on follow-up activities matched to their learning needs. Using multi-level lessons is called *differentiated instruction* (Hipsky, 2011; Tomlinson, 2005b). We will look at this approach more closely in Chapter 11.

ACTIVITY AND CONSTRUCTING KNOWLEDGE. Piaget's fundamental insight was that individuals construct their own understanding; learning is a constructive process. At every level of cognitive development, you will also want to see that students are actively engaged in the learning process. In Piaget's words:

> Knowledge is not a copy of reality. To know an object, to know an event, is not simply to look at it and make a mental copy or image of it. To know an object is to act on it. To know is to modify, to transform the object, and to understand the process of this transformation, and as a consequence to understand the way the object is constructed. (Piaget, 1964, p. 8)

This active experience, even at the earliest school levels, should not be limited to the physical manipulation of objects. It should also include mental manipulation of ideas that arise out of class projects or experiments (Gredler, 2005, 2009). For example, after a social studies lesson on different jobs, a primary-grade teacher might show students a picture of a woman and ask, "What could this person be?" After answers such as "teacher," "doctor," "secretary," "lawyer," "saleswoman," and so on, the teacher could suggest, "How about a daughter?" Answers such as "sister," "mother," "aunt," and "granddaughter" may follow. This should help the children switch dimensions in their classification and center on another aspect of the situation. Next, the teacher might suggest "American," "jogger," or "blonde." With older children, hierarchical classification might be involved: It is a picture of a woman, who is a human being; a human being is a primate, which is a mammal, which is an animal, which is a life form.

Connect and Extend to PRAXIS II™

Implications of Piaget's Theory (I, A2)
The music, physical education, and art teachers in a rural, pre-K-to-8 school district work with students who characterize several of Piaget's stages. How should these three teachers adjust their teaching from level to level over the course of a week?

SCAFFOLDING LEARNING According to Vygotsky, much of children's learning is assisted or mediated by teachers or parents and tools in their environment, and most of this guidance is communicated through language.

All students need to interact with teachers and peers in order to test their thinking, to be challenged, to receive feedback, and to watch how others work out problems. Disequilibrium is often set in motion quite naturally when the teacher or another student suggests a new way of thinking about something. As a general rule, students should act on, manipulate, observe, and then talk and/or write about (to the teacher and each other) what they have experienced. Concrete experiences provide the raw materials for thinking. Communicating with others makes students use, test, and sometimes change their thinking strategies.

Vygotsky: What Can We Learn?

Like Piaget, Vygotsky believed that the main goal of education was the development of higher mental functions, not simply filling students' memories with facts. So Vygotsky probably would oppose educational curricula that are an inch deep and a mile wide or seem like "trivial pursuit." As an example of this trivial pursuit curriculum, Margaret Gredler (2009) described a set of materials for a 9-week science unit that had 61 glossary terms such as *aqueous solution, hydrogen bonding,* and *fractional crystallization*—many terms described with only one or two sentences.

There are at least three ways that higher mental functions can be developed through cultural tools and passed from one individual to another: *imitative* learning (where one person tries to imitate the other), *instructed* learning (where learners internalize the instructions of the teacher and use these instructions to self-regulate), and *collaborative* learning (where a group of peers strives to understand each other and learning occurs in the process) (Tomasello, Kruger, & Ratner, 1993). Vygotsky was most concerned with the second type, *instructed* learning through direct teaching or by structuring experiences that encourage another's learning, but his theory supports learning through *imitation* or *collaboration* as well. Thus, Vygotsky's ideas are relevant for educators who teach directly, intentionally use modeling to teach, or create collaborative learning environments (Das, 1995; Wink & Putney, 2002). That pretty much includes all of us.

Connect and Extend to PRAXIS II™

Implications of Vygotsky's Theory (I, A2)
Make a list of scaffolding techniques that would be appropriate with different instructional levels and content areas. Think of scaffolding techniques that others have used when you learned things outside of school (e.g., sports, hobbies).

THE ROLE OF ADULTS AND PEERS. Vygotsky believed the child is not alone in the world "discovering" the cognitive operations of conservation or classification. This discovery is assisted or mediated by family members, teachers, peers, and even software tools (Puntambekar & Hubscher, 2005). Most of this guidance is communicated through language, at least in Western cultures. In some cultures, observing a skilled performance, not talking about it, guides the child's learning (Rogoff, 1990). Some people have called this adult assistance **scaffolding**, taken from Wood, Bruner, and Ross (1976). The idea is that children use the help for support while they build a firm understanding that will eventually allow them to solve the problems on their own. Actually, when Wood and his colleagues introduced the term *scaffolding*, they were talking about how teachers set up or structure learning environments, but Vygotsky's theory implies more dynamic exchanges between student and teacher that allow the teacher to support students in the parts of the task they cannot do alone—the interactions of assisted learning, as you will see next (Schunk, 2008).

ASSISTED LEARNING. Vygotsky's theory suggests that teachers need to do more than just arrange the environment so that students can discover on their own. Children cannot and should not be expected to reinvent or rediscover knowledge already available in their cultures. Rather, they should be guided and assisted in their learning (Karpov & Haywood, 1998).

Assisted learning, or guided participation, requires first learning from the student what is needed; then giving information, prompts, reminders, and encouragement at the right time and in the right amounts; and gradually allowing the students to do more and more on their own. Teachers can assist learning by adapting materials or problems to students' current levels; demonstrating skills or thought processes; walking students

Scaffolding Support for learning and problem solving. The support would be clues, reminders, encouragement, breaking the problem down into steps, providing an example or anything else that allows the student to grow in independence as a learner.

TABLE 1.5 • **Strategies to Provide Scaffolding**

- Model the thought process for the students: Think out loud as you solve the problem or outline an essay, for example.
- Provide organizers or starters such as *who, what, why, how, what next?*
- Do part of the problem.
- Give hints and cues.
- Encourage students to set short-term goals and take small steps.
- Connect new learning to students' interests or prior learning.
- Use graphic organizers: timelines, charts, tables, categories, checklists, and graphs.
- Simplify the task, clarify the purpose, and give clear directions
- Teach key vocabulary and provide examples.

Sources: Adapted from http://projects.coe.uga.edu/epltt/index.php?title=Scaffolding#Sharing_a_Specific_Goal
http://condor.admin.ccny.cuny.edu/~group4/
http://k6educators.about.com/od/helpfornewteachers/a/scaffoldingtech.htm

through the steps of a complicated problem; doing part of the problem (for example, in algebra, the students set up the equation and the teacher does the calculations or vice versa); giving detailed feedback and allowing revisions; or asking questions that refocus students' attention (Rosenshine & Meister, 1992). Cognitive apprenticeships (Chapter 10) are examples. Look at Table 1.5 for examples of strategies that can be used in any lesson.

Reaching Every Student: Teaching in the "Magic Middle"

Both Piaget and Vygotsky probably would agree that students need to be taught in the magic middle (Berger, 2012) or the place of the "match" (Hunt, 1961)—where they are neither bored nor frustrated. Students should be put in situations where they have to reach to understand, but where support from other students or the teacher is also available. Sometimes the best teacher is another student who has just figured out how to solve the problem, because this student is probably operating in the learner's *zone of proximal development*.

Assisted learning Providing strategic help in the initial stages of learning, gradually diminishing as students gain independence.

GUIDELINES

Applying Vygotsky's Ideas in Teaching

Tailor scaffolding to the needs of students.
Examples

1. When students are beginning new tasks or topics, provide models, prompts, sentence starters, coaching, and feedback. As the students grow in competence, give less support and more opportunities for independent work.
2. Give students choices about the level of difficulty or degree of independence in projects; encourage them to challenge themselves, but to seek help when they are really stuck.

Make sure students have access to powerful tools that support thinking.
Examples

1. Teach students to use learning and organizational strategies, research tools, language tools (wikis, dictionaries, or computer searches), spreadsheets, and word-processing programs.
2. Model the use of tools; show students how you use an appointment book or electronic notebook to make plans and manage time, for example.

Build on the students' cultural funds of knowledge (Gonzales, Moll, & Amanti, 2005; Moll et al., 1992).
Examples

1. Identify family knowledge by having students interview each other's families about their work and home knowledge (agriculture, economics, manufacturing, household management, medicine and illness, religion, child care, cooking, etc.).
2. Tie assignments to these funds of knowledge and use community experts to evaluate assignments.

Capitalize on dialogue and group learning.
Examples

1. Experiment with peer tutoring; teach students how to ask good questions and give helpful explanations.
2. Experiment with cooperative learning strategies described in Chapter 7.

For more information about Vygotsky and his theories, see http://tip. psychology.org/vygotsky.html

Connect and Extend to PRAXIS II™

Distinctions Between Piaget's and Vygotsky's Theories (I, A2)
Consider how two teachers—one based in Vygotskian theory and one based in Piagetian theory—might differ in their concepts of learning and teaching and the instructional techniques that they might prefer.

Having a student work with someone who is just a bit better at the activity would be a good idea because both students benefit in the exchange of explanations, elaborations, and questions. In addition, students should be encouraged to use language to organize their thinking and to talk about what they are trying to accomplish. Dialogue and discussion are important avenues to learning (Karpov & Bransford, 1995; Kozulin & Presseisen, 1995; Wink & Putney, 2002). The *Guidelines* on the previous page gave more ideas for applying Vygotsky's insights.

Cognitive Development: Lessons for Teachers

In spite of cross-cultural differences in cognitive development and the different theories of development, there are some convergences. Piaget, Vygotsky, and more recent researchers studying cognitive development and the brain probably would agree with the following big ideas:

1. Cognitive development requires both physical and social stimulation.
2. To develop thinking, children have to be mentally, physically, and linguistically active. They need to experiment, talk, describe, reflect, write, and solve problems. But they also benefit from teaching, guidance, questions, explanations, demonstrations, and challenges to their thinking.
3. Teaching students what they already know is boring. Trying to teach what the student isn't ready to learn is frustrating and ineffective.
4. Challenge with support will keep students engaged but not fearful.

▼ SUMMARY

A Definition of Development (pp. 4–6)

What are the different kinds of development? Human development can be divided into physical development (changes in the body), personal development (changes in an individual's personality), social development (changes in the way an individual relates to others), and cognitive development (changes in thinking).

What are three questions about development and three general principles? For decades, psychologists and the public have debated whether development is shaped more by nature or nurture, whether change is a continuous process or involves qualitative differences or stages, and whether there are critical times for the development of certain abilities. We know today that these simple either/or distinctions cannot capture the complexities of human development where coactions and interactions are the rule. Theorists generally agree that people develop at different rates, that development is an orderly process, and that development takes place gradually.

The Brain and Cognitive Development (pp. 6–16)

What part of the brain is associated with higher mental functions? The cortex is a crumpled sheet of neurons that serves three major functions: receiving signals from sense organs (such as visual or auditory signals), controlling voluntary movement, and forming connections. The part of the cortex that controls physical motor movement develops or matures first, then the areas that control complex senses such as vision and hearing, and last, the frontal lobe, which controls higher-order thinking processes.

What is lateralization and why is it important? Lateralization is the specialization of the two sides, or hemispheres, of the brain. For most people, the left hemisphere is the major factor in language, and the right hemisphere is prominent in spatial and visual

processing. Even though certain functions are associated with particular parts of the brain, the various parts and systems of the brain work together to learn and perform complex activities such as reading and constructing understanding.

What are some implications for teachers? Recent advances in both methods and findings in the neurosciences provide exciting information about brain activity during learning and brain activity differences among people with varying abilities and challenges and from different cultures. There are some basic implications for teaching based on these findings, but many of the strategies offered by "brain-based" advocates are simply good teaching. Perhaps we now know more about why these strategies work.

Piaget's Theory of Cognitive Development (pp. 16–29)

What are the main influences on cognitive development? Piaget's theory of cognitive development is based on the assumption that people try to make sense of the world and actively create knowledge through direct experiences with objects, people, and ideas. Maturation, activity, social transmission, and the need for equilibrium all influence the way thinking processes and knowledge develop. In response to these influences, thinking processes and knowledge develop through changes in the organization of thought (the development of schemes) and through adaptation—including the complementary processes of assimilation (incorporating into existing schemes) and accommodation (changing existing schemes).

What is a scheme? Schemes are the basic building blocks of thinking. They are organized systems of actions or thought that allow us to mentally represent or "think about" the objects and events in our world. Schemes may be very small and specific (grasping, recognizing a square), or they may be larger and more general (using a map in a new city). People adapt to their environment as they increase and organize their schemes.

As children move from sensorimotor to formal-operational thinking, what are the major changes? Piaget believed that young people pass through four stages as they develop: sensorimotor, preoperational, concrete-operational, and formal-operational. In the sensorimotor stage, infants explore the world through their senses and motor activity, and work toward mastering object permanence and performing goal-directed activities. In the preoperational stage, symbolic thinking and logical operations begin. Children in the stage of concrete operations can think logically about tangible situations and can demonstrate conservation, reversibility, classification, and seriation. The ability to perform hypothetico-deductive reasoning, coordinate a set of variables, and imagine other worlds marks the stage of formal operations.

How do neo-Piagetian and information processing views explain changes in children's thinking over time? Information processing theories focus on attention, memory capacity, learning strategies, and other processing skills to explain how children develop rules and strategies for making sense of the world and solving problems. Neo-Piagetian approaches also look at attention, memory, and strategies and at how thinking develops in different domains such as numbers or spatial relations. Research in neuroscience suggests that when learning a new skill, children move through three tiers—from *actions* to *representations* to *abstractions*. Within each tier, the pattern is moving from accomplishing a single action to mapping or coordinating two actions together such as coordinating addition and multiplication in math, to creating whole systems of understanding.

What are some limitations of Piaget's theory? Piaget's theory has been criticized because children and adults often think in ways that are inconsistent with the notion of invariant stages. It also appears that Piaget underestimated children's cognitive abilities; he insisted that children could not be taught the operations of the next stage, but had to develop them on their own. Alternative explanations place greater emphasis on students' developing information processing skills and ways teachers can enhance their development. Piaget's work is also criticized for overlooking cultural factors in child development.

Vygotsky's Sociocultural Perspective (pp. 29–34)

According to Vygotsky, what are three main influences on cognitive development? Vygotsky believed that human activities must be understood in their cultural settings. He believed that our specific mental structures and processes can be traced to our interactions with others; that the tools of the culture, especially the tool of language, are key factors in development; and that the zone of proximal development is the area where learning and development are possible.

What are psychological tools and why are they important? Psychological tools are signs and symbol systems such as numbers and mathematical systems, codes, and language that support learning and cognitive development—they change the thinking process by enabling and shaping thinking. Many of these tools are passed from adult to child through formal and informal interactions and teachings.

Explain how interpsychological development becomes intrapsychological development. Higher mental processes appear first between people as they are co-constructed during shared activities. As children engage in activities with adults or more capable peers, they exchange ideas and ways of thinking about or representing concepts. Children internalize these co-created ideas. Thus children's knowledge, ideas, attitudes, and values develop through appropriating, or "taking for themselves," the ways of acting and thinking provided by their culture and by the more capable members of their group.

What are the differences between Piaget's and Vygotsky's perspectives on private speech and its role in development? Vygotsky's sociocultural view asserts that cognitive development hinges on social interaction and the development of language. As an example, Vygotsky describes the role of children's self-directed talk in guiding and monitoring thinking and problem solving, whereas Piaget suggests that private speech is an indication of the child's egocentrism. Vygotsky, more than Piaget, emphasized the significant role played by adults and more able peers in children's learning. This adult assistance provides early support while students build the understanding necessary to solve problems on their own later.

What is a student's zone of proximal development? At any given point in development, there are certain problems that a child is on the verge of being able to solve and others that are beyond the child's capabilities. The zone of proximal development is the area where the child cannot solve a problem alone, but can be successful under adult guidance or in collaboration with a more advanced peer.

What are two criticisms or limitations of Vygotsky's theory? Vygotsky may have overemphasized the role of social interaction in cognitive development—children figure out quite a bit on their own. Also, because he died so young, Vygotsky was not able to develop and elaborate on his theories. His students and others since have taken up that work.

Implications of Piaget's and Vygotsky's Theories for Teachers (pp. 34–38)

What is the "problem of the match" described by Hunt? The "problem of the match" is that students must be neither bored by work that is too simple nor left behind by teaching they cannot understand. According to Hunt, disequilibrium must be carefully balanced to encourage growth. Situations that lead to errors can help create an appropriate level of disequilibrium.

What is active learning? Why is Piaget's theory of cognitive development consistent with active learning? Piaget's fundamental insight was that individuals construct their own understanding; learning is a constructive process. At every level of cognitive development, students must be able to incorporate information into their own schemes. To do this, they must act on the information in some way. This active experience, even at the earliest school levels, should include both physical manipulation of objects and mental manipulation of ideas. As a general rule, students should act, manipulate, observe, and then talk and/or write about what they have experienced. Concrete experiences provide the raw materials for thinking. Communicating with others makes students use, test, and sometimes change their thinking abilities.

What is assisted learning, and what role does scaffolding play? Assisted learning, or guided participation in the classroom, requires scaffolding—understanding the students' needs, giving information, prompts, reminders, and encouragement at the right time and in the right amounts, and then gradually allowing the students to do more and more on their own. Teachers can assist learning by adapting materials or problems to students' current levels, demonstrating skills or thought processes, walking students through the steps of a complicated problem, doing part of the problem, giving detailed feedback and allowing revisions, or asking questions that refocus students' attention.

▼ KEY TERMS

Accommodation (18)
Adaptation (17)
Adolescent egocentrism (24)
Assimilation (18)
Assisted learning (36)
Classification (22)
Co-constructed process (30)
Coactions (5)
Cognitive development (4)
Collective monologue (32)
Compensation (21)
Concrete operations (21)
Conservation (20)
Cultural tools (30)
Decentering (20)
Development (4)
Disequilibrium (18)
Egocentric (20)

Equilibration (18)
Event-related potential (ERP) (7)
Formal operations (24)
Functional magnetic resonance imaging
   (fMRI) (6)
Glial cells (9)
Goal-directed actions (19)
Hypothetico-deductive reasoning (24)
Identity (21)
Lateralization (10)
Maturation (4)
Myelination (9)
Neo-Piagetian theories (26)
Neurogenesis (7)
Neurons (7)
Object permanence (18)
Operations (19)
Organization (17)

Personal development (4)
Physical development (4)
Plasticity (10)
Positron emission tomography (PET) (7)
Preoperational (19)
Private speech (32)
Reversibility (22)
Reversible thinking (20)
Scaffolding (36)
Schemes (17)
Semiotic function (20)
Sensitive periods (5)
Sensorimotor (18)
Seriation (23)
Social development (4)
Sociocultural theory (29)
Synapses (7)
Zone of proximal development (33)

▼ CONNECT AND EXTEND TO LICENSURE

MULTIPLE-CHOICE QUESTIONS

1. Mr. Winstel was worried about his former star student, Ramon. As the seventh grade year progressed, Ramon was frequently being called into the principal's office for skateboard stunts that broke school rules and bordered on dangerous. Recently, Ramon's parents contacted Mr. Winstel to alert him to the fact Ramon had been skipping school to hang out with some older boys in the neighborhood. Which of the following answers would typically best describe what is happening with Ramon?

   A. Ramon's culture demands that boys of his age begin to engage in behaviors which reflect fearlessness.

   B. Ramon's limbic system is maturing but his prefrontal lobe has not yet caught up.

   C. Ramon is engaging in deviant behaviors as a cry for attention from his parents.

   D. Ramon is undergoing a period of synaptic pruning which causes adolescents to engage in risk taking behavior.

2. Miss McClintock discovered that five of the children in her class were developmentally advanced. All of the students' language skills were exploding! While many of the students still had trouble sharing, a few appeared to understand that by sharing everyone could be happy. Finally, there was even one child who could solve conservation problems. According to Piagetian theory, in what stage are the students in Miss McClintock' class?

   A. Formal Operations

   B. Concrete Operations

   C. Preoperational

   D. Sensorimotor

3. In introducing students to persuasive advertising methods, which of the following approaches would be most apt to lead to student retention?

   A. Determine what students already know about the topic and connect new information to their prior knowledge.

   B. Have students initially watch several commercials and take notes.

   C. Lecture students on the major persuasive techniques and have a quiz to assess learning.

   D. Have students form groups to research persuasive techniques.

4. Research studies involving the brain and learning indicate all but which one of the following statements is true?

   A. There is no such thing as "left brain" and "right brain" thinking.

   B. The production of new neurons continues into adulthood.

   C. Using different modalities for instruction and activities that draw on different senses may support learning.

   D. Pruning can damage heavily used cognitive pathways.

CONSTRUCTED-RESPONSE QUESTIONS

Case

Mr. Gething remembered that when planning for instruction students should be neither bored nor frustrated. Although this made sense to him, he was unsure how he would compensate for the diverse group of students he had in his second period language arts class. There were students who had difficulty with the English language and other students who planned to participate in the school's annual Shakespearean play. He knew that by grouping students of mixed ability, he could occasionally draw upon the talents of his knowledgeable students to assist the less advanced students. He also understood that without guidelines, students may not accomplish anything.

5. Explain the theory of learning Mr. Gething is initially drawing upon and the individual credited with it.

6. What is term for the assistance the more knowledgeable class members may provide to the less advanced students in order for them to succeed? List some strategies these students might use to assist their peers.

▼ WHAT WOULD THEY DO?

TEACHERS' CASEBOOK: Symbols and Cymbals

Here is how several expert teachers said they would help their students understand abstract concepts.

LINDA GLISSON AND SUE MIDDLETON • 5th Grade Team Teachers
St. James Episcopal Day School, Baton Rouge, LA

To begin the lesson, I would have the students use a dictionary to define the word *symbolism* (root word—*symbol*) to discover that it means "something that stands for or represents something else." I would then give them a brief "across the curriculum" exercise in ways they incorporate symbols and symbolism into their thinking every day. For example (social studies, American history): The American flag is just a piece of cloth. Why then do we recite a pledge to it? Stand at attention when it passes in a parade? What does it stand for? (English, literature—fables and fairy tales): What does the wolf usually represent (stand for)? The lion? The lamb? (Art): What color stands for a glorious summer day? Evil? Goodness and purity? I would continue with math symbols, scientific symbols, and music symbols and lead the students toward contributing other examples such as symbols representing holidays. I would then tell them about their own examples of symbolism that I had recorded. The students' participation in and enthusiasm for the exercises would serve to determine whether they were ready for the material.

DR. NANCY SHEEHAN-MELZACK • Art and Music Teacher
Snug Harbor Community School, Quincy, MA

Even very young children can recognize symbols if the symbol is presented first and the explanation required second. A drawing of an octagon on a pole has always elicited the answer, "A stop sign," whenever I have shown it. Children recognize symbols, but the teacher needs to work from their concrete knowledge to the more abstract concept, and there are a great many symbols in their daily life on which one can draw. Children as young as 1st graders can recognize traffic sign shapes, letters of the alphabet, and numbers, and further recognize that they stand for directions, sounds, and how many. When they talk about these very common symbols, they can also realize they all use them for the same meaning.

VALERIE A. CHILCOAT • 5th/6th Grade Advanced Academics
Glenmount School, Baltimore, MD

Concrete examples of symbolism must come from the students' own world. Street signs, especially those with pictures and not words, are a great example. These concrete symbols, however, are not exactly the same as symbolism used in poetry. The link has to be made from the concrete to the abstract. Silly poetry is one way to do this. It is motivating to the students to read or listen to, and it can provide many examples of one thing acting as another. This strategy can also be used in lower grades to simply expose children to poetry containing symbolism.

KAREN BOYARSKY • 5th Grade Teacher
Walter C. Black Elementary School, Hightstown, NJ

You can tell a lot about students' thinking simply by interpreting their reactions. Knowing how to interpret students' reactions is just as important as any other assessment tool you might use. In this case, it is clear that the students are confused about the concept of symbolism. This is a difficult concept even for many 5th graders to understand and should be approached slowly. One approach to this topic would be to present students with pictures of familiar symbols, such as McDonald's Golden Arches, the Nike Swoosh, or the Target logo. Students could attempt to explain what each of these symbols mean. A discussion about why manufacturers choose to use symbols instead of words would follow. Another approach would be to have the students interpret comparisons that use *like* or *as*. For example, "Sue is as pretty as a flower." The teacher would guide the student to see that the author is using a flower to symbolize Sue's looks..

chapter two
THE SELF, SOCIAL, AND MORAL DEVELOPMENT

You have seen it before, but this year the situation in your middle-school classroom seems especially vicious. A clique of popular girls has made life miserable for several of their former friends—who are now "rejects." The discarded friends have committed the social sins of not fitting in—they wear the wrong clothes or aren't pretty enough or aren't interested in boys yet. To keep the status distinctions clear between themselves and "the others," the popular girls spread gossip about their former friends, often disclosing the intimate secrets revealed when the "out" girls and the "in" girls were *best* friends—only a few months ago. Today, you discover that Stephanie, one of the rejected girls, has written a long, heart-baring e-mail to her former best friend Alison, asking why Alison is "acting so mean." The now-popular Alison forwarded the e-mail to the entire school and Stephanie is humiliated. She has been absent for three days since the incident.

CRITICAL THINKING

- How would you respond to each of the girls?
- What—if anything—would you say to your other students?
- Are there ways you can address the issues raised by this situation in your classes?
- Reflecting on your years in school, were your experiences more like those of Alison or Stephanie?

OVERVIEW AND OBJECTIVES

Schooling involves more than cognitive development. As you think back on your years in school, what stands out—highlights of academic knowledge or memories of feelings, friendships, and fears? In this chapter, we examine the latter, which comprise personal, social, and moral development.

We begin by looking at a basic aspect of development that affects all the others—physical changes as students mature. Then we explore Urie Bronfenbrenner's bioecological theory and use it as a framework for examining the three major influences on children's personal and social development: families, peers, and teachers. Families today have gone through many transitions, and these changes affect the roles of teachers. Next, we explore ideas about how we come to understand ourselves by looking at self-concept and identity, including racial-ethnic identity. Erikson's theory of psychosocial development provides a lens for viewing these developments. Finally, we consider moral development. What factors determine our views about morality? What can teachers do to foster such personal qualities as honesty and cooperation? Why do students cheat in their academic work, and what can be done?

By the time you have completed this chapter, you should be able to:

Objective 2.1: Describe general trends and group differences in physical development through childhood and adolescence.

Objective 2.2: Discuss how the components of Bronfenbrenner's bioecological model influence development.

Objective 2.3: Discuss the relationship between parenting styles and children's development.

Objective 2.4: Describe general trends and group differences in the development of self-concept and identity.

Objective 2.5: Explain how positive peer relations (friendships) and negative peer relations (aggression) affect children's social development.

Objective 2.6: Explain current theories of moral development.

PHYSICAL DEVELOPMENT

This chapter is about personal and social development, but we begin with a kind of development that is a basic concern of all individuals and families—physical development.

STOP & THINK How tall are you? What grade were you in when you reached that height? Were you one of the tallest or shortest students in your middle or high school, or were you about average? Did you know students who were teased because of something about their physical appearance? How important was your physical development to your feelings about yourself? •

Physical and Motor Development

For most children, at least in the early years, growing up means getting bigger and stronger, and becoming more coordinated. It also can be a frightening, disappointing, exciting, and puzzling time.

YOUNG CHILDREN. Preschool children are very active. Their *gross-motor* (large muscle) skills improve greatly during these early years. Between ages 2 and about 4 or 5, preschoolers' muscles grow stronger, their brains develop to better integrate information about movements, their balance improves, and their center of gravity moves lower, so they are able to run, jump, climb, and hop. By age 2, most children stop "toddling." Their awkward, wide-legged gait becomes smooth and rhythmic—they have perfected walking. During their third year, most children learn to run, throw, and jump, but these activities are not well controlled until age 4 or 5. Most of these movements develop naturally if the child has normal physical abilities and the opportunity to play. Children with physical problems, however, may need special training to develop these skills. And because they can't always judge when to stop, many preschoolers need interludes of rest scheduled after periods of physical exertion (Darcey & Travers, 2006; Thomas & Thomas, 2008).

Fine-motor skills such as tying shoes or fastening buttons, which require the coordination of small movements, also improve greatly during the preschool years. Children should be given the chance to work with large paintbrushes, fat pencils and crayons, large pieces of drawing paper, large Legos, and soft clay or playdough to accommodate their current skills. During this time, children will begin to develop a lifelong preference for their right or left hand. By age 5, about 90% of students prefer their right hand for most skilled work, and 10% or so prefer their left hand, with more boys than girls being left-handed (Feldman, 2004; Hill & Khanem, 2009). This is a genetically based preference, so don't try to make children switch.

ELEMENTARY SCHOOL YEARS. During the elementary-school years, physical development is fairly steady for most children. They become taller, leaner, and stronger, so they are better able to master sports and games. There is tremendous variation among children, however. A particular child can be much larger or smaller than average and still be perfectly healthy. Because children at this age are very aware of physical differences but are not the most tactful people, you may overhear comments such as "You're too little to be in fifth grade. What's wrong with you?" or "How come you're so fat?"

Throughout elementary school, many of the girls are likely to be as large as or larger than the boys in their classes. Between the ages of 11 and 14, girls are, on average, taller and heavier than boys of the same age. This size discrepancy can give girls an advantage in physical activities, but some girls may feel conflict over this and, as a result, downplay their physical abilities (Woolfolk & Perry, 2012).

THE ADOLESCENT YEARS. Puberty marks the beginning of sexual maturity. It is not a single event, but a series of changes involving almost every part of the body. The sex differences in physical development observed during the later elementary years become even more pronounced at the beginning of puberty. But these changes take time. The earliest visible signs of puberty in girls are the growth of nipples and budding of their breasts at around age 10 for European American and Canadian adolescents. At about the same time, boys' testes and scrotum begin to grow larger. On average, between ages 12 and 13, girls have their first menstrual period (called **menarche**) and boys have their first sperm ejaculation (called **spermarche**). Boys develop facial hair over the next several years, reaching their final beard potential by about age 18 or 19—with some exceptions who take longer to develop their final facial hair. Less welcome changes in puberty are increases in skin oiliness, skin acne, and body odor.

STUDENTS COME IN ALL SIZES The physical changes of adolescence have significant effects on the individual's identity. Psychologists have been particularly interested in the academic, social, and emotional differences they have found between adolescents who mature early and those who mature later.

Girls reach their final height by age 15 or 16, several years ahead of boys, so there is a time in middle school, as in late elementary school, when many girls are taller than their male classmates. Most boys continue growing until about age 19, but both boys and girls can continue to grow slightly until about age 25 (Thomas & Thomas, 2008; Wigfield, Byrnes, & Eccles, 2006). The ages for reaching maximum height are a bit younger for African American and Latino/a adolescents and a bit older for Asian Americans.

EARLY AND LATER MATURING. Psychologists have been particularly interested in the academic, social, and emotional differences they have found between adolescents who mature early and those who mature later. For girls, maturing way ahead of classmates can be a definite disadvantage. Being larger and more "developed" than everyone else your age is not a valued characteristic for girls in many cultures (Jones, 2004). Early maturation is associated with emotional difficulties such as depression, anxiety, and eating disorders, especially in societies that define thinness as attractive (Steinberg, 2005). Other problems for early maturing girls are lower achievement in school, drug and alcohol abuse, unplanned pregnancy, suicide, and greater risk of breast cancer in later life. Around the world, early menarche has been related to bulimia and alcohol use in Finland, suicide and alcohol use in Norway, and depression and anxiety in Australia (Mendle et al., 2007). In addition, researchers have found a correlation between age at menarche and adult **body mass index (BMI**, a measure of body fat); the younger the girl was when she had her first period, the greater her adult BMI, on average (Harris et al., 2008). Later-maturing girls seem to have fewer problems, but they may worry that something is wrong with them, so adult reassurance and support is important.

Early maturity in males is associated with popularity. The early maturer's taller, broad-shouldered body type fits the cultural stereotype for the male ideal; late-maturing boys may experience lower self-esteem because they are smaller and less muscular than the "ideal" for men. In fact, there is some evidence that the standards regarding physical appearance have increased (Harter, 2006). Even so, recent research points to more disadvantages than advantages for early maturation in boys (Westling, Andrews, Hampson, & Peterson, 2008). Early maturing boys tend to engage in more delinquent behavior—and this is true for White, African American, and Mexican American boys (Cota-Robles, Neiss, & Rowe, 2002). They also appear to be at greater risk for depression and for abusing alcohol and cigarettes (Westling et al., 2008).

Connect and Extend to PRAXIS II™

Human Development (I, A2)
Explain how development in one domain (e.g., physical, emotional) can affect development in other domains.

Puberty The physiological changes during adolescence that lead to the ability to reproduce.

Menarche The first menstrual period in girls.

Spermarche The first sperm ejaculation for boys.

Body mass index (BMI) A measure of body fat that evaluates weight in relation to height.

GUIDELINES

Dealing with Physical Differences in the Classroom

Address students' physical differences in ways that do not call unnecessary attention to the variations.
Examples

1. Try to seat smaller students so they can see and participate in class activities, but avoid seating arrangements that are obviously based on height.
2. Balance sports and games that rely on size and strength with games that reflect cognitive, artistic, social, or musical abilities, such as charades or drawing games.
3. Don't use, and don't allow students to use nicknames based on physical traits.
4. Make sure there is a good supply of left-handed scissors for preschool classes.

Help students obtain factual information on differences in physical development.
Examples

1. Set up science projects on sex differences in growth rates.
2. Have readings available that focus on differences between early and late maturers. Make sure that you present the positives and the negatives of each.

3. Find out the school policy on sex education and on informal guidance for students. Some schools, for example, encourage teachers to talk to girls who are upset about their first menstrual period, while other schools expect teachers to send the girls to talk to the school nurse (if your school still has one—budget cuts have eliminated many).
4. Give the students models in literature or in their community of accomplished and caring individuals who do not fit the culture's ideal physical stereotypes.

Accept that concerns about appearance and the opposite sex will occupy much time and energy for adolescents.
Examples

1. Allow some time at the end of class for socializing.
2. Deal with some of these issues in curriculum-related materials.

For more information about accommodations for physical differences in your classroom, see http://dos.claremontmckenna.edu/PhysicalLearningDiff.asp

Boys who mature late may have a more difficult time initially. However, some studies show that in adulthood, males who matured later tend to be more creative, tolerant, and perceptive. Perhaps the trials and anxieties of maturing late teach some boys to be better problem solvers (Brooks-Gunn, 1988; Steinberg, 2005). All adolescents can benefit from knowing that there is a very wide range for timing and rates in "normal" maturation and that there are advantages for both early and late maturers. The *Guidelines* give ideas for dealing with physical differences in the classroom.

Play, Recess, and Physical Activity

Maria Montessori once noted, "Play is children's work," and Piaget and Vygotsky would agree. More recently, the American Academy of Pediatrics stated, "Play is essential to development because it contributes to the cognitive, physical, social, and emotional well-being of children and youth" (Ginsburg, 2007, p. 182). The brain develops with stimulation, and play provides some of that stimulation at every age. In fact, some neuroscientists suggest that play might help in the important process of pruning brain synapses during childhood (Pellis, 2006). Other psychologists believe play allows children to experiment safely as they learn about their environment, try out new behaviors, solve problems, and adapt to new situations (Pellegrini, Dupuis, & Smith, 2007). Babies in the sensorimotor stage learn by exploring, sucking, pounding, shaking, throwing—acting on their environments. Preoperational preschoolers love make-believe play and use pretending to form symbols, explore language, and interact with others. They are beginning to play simple games with predictable rules. Elementary-school-age children also like fantasy, but are beginning to play more complex games and sports, and thus learn cooperation, fairness, negotiation, and winning and losing as well as developing more sophisticated language. As children grow into adolescents, play continues to be part of their physical and social development (Woolfolk & Perry, 2012).

PHYSICAL EXERCISE AND RECESS. There are good, academic reasons for encouraging children to exercise. Phillip Tomporowski and his colleagues (2008) reviewed the research on physical activity and cognitive development and concluded that "systematic exercise programs may actually enhance the development of specific types of mental processing known to be important for meeting challenges encountered both in academics and throughout the lifespan" (p. 127). Other researchers note that students in Asian countries, who consistently outperform U.S. students on international reading, science, and mathematics tests, have more frequent recess breaks throughout the school day. One study of 11,000 students who were 8 and 9 years old found that students who had daily recess of 15 minutes or longer every day were better behaved in class than students who had little or no recess. This was true even after controlling for student gender and ethnicity, public or private school setting, and class size (Barros, Silver, & Stein, 2009). These recess breaks may be especially important for students with attention-deficit hyperactive disorders (ADHD). In fact, if more breaks were provided, there might be fewer students, especially boys, diagnosed with ADHD (Pellegrini & Bohn, 2005).

Schools have a role in promoting physical activity. This can be especially important for students living in poverty and children with disabilities. Unfortunately, recess time is being cut to allow for more academic time focused on test preparation (Ginsburg, 2007; Pellegrini & Bohn, 2005). But the federal government has recognized the value of physical activity. In 2004, the United States Congress passed a law that requires educational agencies that receive federal aid, which covers most schools, to have a wellness policy. Different agencies, including the American Heart Association, recommend that as part of a wellness program, all children and youth should have a minimum of 30 minutes per day of moderate to vigorous physical activity (McKenzie & Kahan, 2008). One reason for concern about physical activity for children is the increase in childhood obesity, as you will see next.

Challenges in Physical Development

Physical development is public—everyone sees how tall, short, heavy, thin, muscular, or coordinated you are. As students move into adolescence, they feel "on stage," as if everyone is evaluating them; and physical development is part of what is being evaluated. So there are psychological consequences to physical development too (Thomas & Thomas, 2008).

OBESITY. If you have seen the news lately, you know that obesity is a growing problem in America, especially for children. In fact, since 1971, the incidence of childhood obesity has doubled in every age group from ages 2 to 19 (Centers for Disease Control, 2009). Obesity usually is defined as being more than 20% heavier than average compared to others of the same age, sex, and body build. Table 2.1 shows how the trend is increasing.

TABLE 2.1 • **The Increase in Childhood Obesity**

The data below are from the National Health and Nutrition Examination Survey (NHANES) completed by the National Center for Health Statistics.

PREVALENCE OF OVERWEIGHT AMONG U.S. CHILDREN AND ADOLESCENTS (AGED 2–19 YEARS)

	SURVEY PERIODS			
	1971–1974	1976–1980	1988–1994	2007–2008
Ages 2 through 5	5%	5%	7.2%	10.4%
Ages 6 through 11	4%	6.5%	11.3%	19.6%
Ages 12 through 19	6.1%	5%	10.5%	18.1%

Source: Centers for Disease Control and Prevention. http://www.cdc.gov/obesity/childhood/data.html

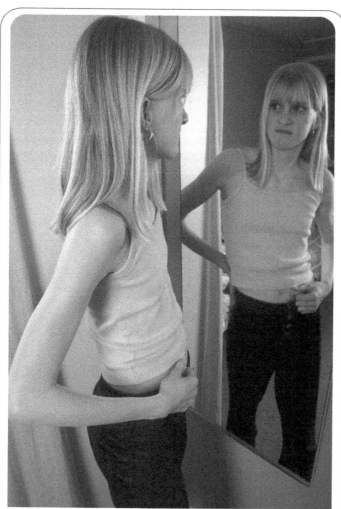

DON'T TURN AWAY FROM ME Students with anorexia usually require professional help—don't ignore the warning signs. A teacher may be the person who begins the chain of help for students with these tragic problems.

The consequences of obesity are serious for children and adolescents: diabetes, strain on bones and joints, respiratory problems, and a greater chance of heart problems as adults. Playing with friends or participating in sports can be affected negatively. In addition, children with obesity often are the targets of cruel teasing. Like everything else involving children's development, there probably are many interacting causes for this increase in obesity rates including poor diet, genetic factors, increased hours sitting in front of televisions and playing video games, and lack of exercise (Woolfolk & Perry, 2012). There is another challenge in physical development for many children that involves not too much weight, but too little.

EATING DISORDERS. Adolescents going through the changes of puberty are very concerned about their bodies. This has always been true, but today, the emphasis on fitness and appearance makes adolescents even more likely to worry about how their bodies "measure up." Both boys and girls can become dissatisfied with their bodies during adolescence because they don't match the cultural ideals in magazines and films. For girls, it also appears that conversations with friends about appearance can make dissatisfactions worse (Jones, 2004). For some, the concern becomes excessive. One consequence is eating disorders such as **bulimia** (binge eating) and **anorexia nervosa** (self-starvation), both of which are more common in females than in males. Bulimics often binge, eating an entire gallon of ice cream or a whole cake. Then, to avoid gaining weight, they force themselves to vomit or they use strong laxatives to purge themselves of the extra calories. Bulimics tend to maintain a normal weight, but the purging can permanently damage their digestive systems.

Anorexia is an even more dangerous disorder, for anorexics either refuse to eat or eat practically nothing while often exercising obsessively. In the process, they may lose 20% to 25% of their body weight, and some (about 20%) literally starve themselves to death. Anorexic students become very thin, and may appear pale, have brittle fingernails, and develop fine dark hairs all over their bodies. They are easily chilled because they have so little fat to insulate their bodies. They often are depressed, insecure, moody, and lonely. Girls may stop having their menstrual period. These eating disorders often begin in adolescence and are becoming more common— about 1% of adolescents (mostly, but not all girls) become anorexic (Rice & Dolgin, 2002). These students usually require professional help. Don't ignore the warning signs—less than one-third of people with eating disorders actually receive treatment (Stice & Shaw, 2004). A teacher may be the person who begins the chain of help for students with these tragic problems. The *Guidelines* give a few ideas for supporting positive body images in adolescents.

People certainly are more than physical bodies. The rest of this chapter is about personal and moral development, beginning with a theoretical frame to put that development in context.

Bulimia Eating disorder characterized by overeating, then getting rid of the food by self-induced vomiting or laxatives.

Anorexia nervosa Eating disorder characterized by very limited food intake.

GUIDELINES

Supporting Positive Body Images

Listen to adolescents talk about their health.
Examples

1. If they mention wanting to lose weight, seize the opportunity to talk about healthy weight, body image, and cultural influences on youth.
2. It they mention diets they or their friends are trying, provide them with nutritionally sound information about myths, misinformation, and dangers related to fad diets.
3. In general, be attentive. An adolescent may make a brief comment that could serve as a terrific entrance into a valuable conversation about body image.

Ask questions.
Examples

1. Are you concerned about your weight (or shape or size) at all? Do you think your friends are concerned about their weight? Do you or your friends talk a lot about your weight?
2. Do you know that diets are the worst way to lose or maintain weight? Have you ever dieted? Why?

3. Do you know that eating only low-fat or fat-free foods is NOT healthy eating? Do you know that you need fat in your diet, and that without it you can have all kinds of health problems?

Make available resources for adolescents who have body image issues.
Examples

1. Have accurate, youth-oriented resources available to read, look up on the Internet, or find in a library.
2. Encourage youth to continue conversations about these issues with you, their parents, a health professional, a trusted teacher, or a caring, knowledgeable adult.
3. Deal with some of these issues in curriculum-related materials.

For more information about adolescents and body image, see
http://www.epi.umn.edu/let/pubs/img/adol_ch13.pdf

Source: Adapted from Story, M., & Stang, J. (2005). Nutrition needs of adolescents. In J. S. M. Story (Ed.), Guidelines for adolescent nutritional services. Minneapolis, MN: University of Minnesota, pp. 158–159.

BRONFENBRENNER: THE SOCIAL CONTEXT FOR DEVELOPMENT

We put the developing person in context by exploring the work of Urie Bronfenbrenner (1917–2005), who was born in Moscow, Russia, but moved with his family to the United States when he was 6. Bronfenbrenner completed a double major in psychology and music at Cornell in 1938 and a Ph.D. in psychology from the University of Michigan, in 1942. Over his long career in psychology he worked as a clinical psychologist in the U.S. Army and as a professor at the University of Michigan and at Cornell. He also helped to found the Head Start early childhood program.

The Importance of Context and the Bioecological Model

Educational and developmental psychologists are increasingly interested in the role of context. **Context** is the total situation that surrounds and interacts with an individual's thoughts, feelings, and actions to shape development and learning. There are contextual effects both internal and external to the developing individual. For example, hormone levels within the body are contexts for developing organs, including the brain, as well as for adolescents' self-concepts during puberty. In this book, however, we focus on the contexts outside the person. Children grow up in families and are members of particular ethnic, language, religious, and economic communities. They live in neighborhoods, attend schools, and are members of classes, teams, or glee clubs. The social and educational programs, along with the policies of governments affect their lives. These contexts influence the development of behaviors, beliefs, and knowledge by providing resources, supports, incentives and punishments, expectations, teachers, models, tools—all the building blocks of learning and development (Dodge, 2011; Lerner, Theokas, & Bobek, 2005).

Context Internal and external circumstances and situations that interact with the individual's thoughts, feelings, and actions to shape development and learning.

Contexts also affect how actions are interpreted. For example, if a stranger approaches a 7-month-old infant, the baby is likely to cry if the setting is unfamiliar, but she may not cry if the stranger is in her home. Adults are more likely to help a stranger in need in small towns as opposed to larger cities (Kagan & Herschkowitz, 2005). Think about a hearing a telephone ring. Is it 3:00 in the afternoon or 3:00 in the morning? Did you just call someone and leave a message asking for a return call? Has the phone been ringing off the hook, or is this the first call in days? Did you just sit down to dinner? The meaning of the ring and the feelings you have will vary, depending on the context.

Urie Bronfenbrenner's **bioecological model** of development (Bronfenbrenner, 1989; Bronfenbrenner & Morris, 2006) recognizes that the physical and social contexts in which we develop are ecosystems because they are constantly interacting with and influencing each other. Look at Figure 2.1. Every person lives within a microsystem, inside a mesosystem, embedded in an exosystem, all of which are a part of the macrosystem—like a set of Russian painted dolls, nested one inside the other. In addition, all development occurs in and is influenced by the time period—the chronosystem.

In the microsystem are the person's immediate relationships and activities. For a child, the microsystem might be the immediate family, friends, or teachers and the activities of play and school. Relationships in the microsystem are reciprocal—they flow in both directions. The child affects the parent and the parent influences the child, for example. The mesosystem is the set of interactions and relationships among all the elements of the microsystem—the family members interacting with each other or with the teacher. Again, all relationships are reciprocal—the teacher influences the parents and the parents affect the teacher, and

Bioecological model
Bronfenbrenner's theory describing the nested social and cultural contexts that shape development. Every person develops within a *microsystem*, inside a *mesosystem*, embedded in an *exosystem*, all of which are a part of the *macrosystem* of the culture. All development occurs in and is influenced by the time period—the *chronosystem*.

FIGURE 2.1

URIE BRONFENBRENNER'S BIOECOLOGICAL MODEL OF HUMAN DEVELOPMENT

Every person develops within a *microsystem* (family, friends, school activities, teacher, etc.) inside a *mesosystem* (the interactions among all the microsystem elements), embedded in an *exosystem* (social settings that affect the child, even though the child is not a direct member—community resources, parents' work place, etc.); all are part of the *macrosystem* (the larger society with its laws, customs, values, etc.). All development occurs in and is influenced by the time period—the *chronosystem*.

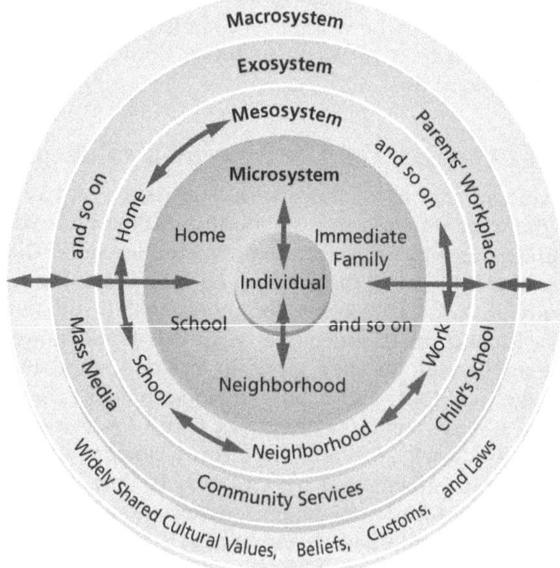

these interactions affect the child. The exosystem includes all the social settings that affect the child, even though the child is not a direct member of these systems. Examples are the teachers' relations with administrators and the school board; the parents' jobs; the community resources for health, employment, or recreation; or the family's religious affiliation. The macrosystem is the larger society—its values, laws, conventions, and traditions.

Families

The first context for child development is the mother's womb. Scientists are learning more about the effects of this first environment—the role of the expectant mother's level of stress, nutrition, smoking, alcohol and drug intake, exercise, and general health in her infant's development. Clearly, the influence of the family begins before birth, but many new influences follow (Woolfolk & Perry, 2012).

FAMILY STRUCTURE. In the United States, the proportion of children growing up in a home with just one parent has doubled since the 1970s. About 10% of children have parents who never married, and most of these children (89%) live with their mothers. In fact, projections are that only about half of all children will grow up with two parents who

FAMILIES CAN BE MANY TYPES Only about 25% of all U.S. households are made up of a married husband and wife living with their biological children. Families also can include grandparents, adopted children, foster children, stepchildren, two moms or two dads, blended families, single parents, and many other possibilities.

stay married (Amato, 2006; Schoen & Canulas-Romo, 2006). Increasingly, children today may be part of **blended families**, with stepbrothers or stepsisters who move in and out of their lives. Some children live with an aunt, with grandparents, with one parent, in foster or adoptive homes, or with an older brother or sister. In some cultures such as Asian, Latin American, or African, children are more likely to grow up in **extended families**, with grandparents, aunts, uncles, and cousins living in the same household or at least in daily contact with each other. In addition, there are several million gay and lesbian parents in the United States (estimates are hard to determine because some parents conceal details about their sexual orientation to protect their children from bias and prejudice). Thus the best advice is to avoid the phrases "your parents" and "your mother and father" and instead to speak of "your family" when talking to students.

No matter who is doing the parenting, research has identified characteristic differences in parents' styles.

PARENTING STYLES. One well-known description of **parenting styles** is based on the research of Diane Baumrind (1991, 1996). Her early work focused on a careful longitudinal study of 100 (mostly European American, middle-class) preschool children. Through observation of children and parents and interviews with parents, Baumrind and the other researchers who built on her findings identified four parenting styles based on the parents' high or low levels of warmth and control:

- *Authoritative parents* (high warmth, high control) set clear limits, enforce rules, and expect mature behavior. But they are warm with their children. They listen to concerns, give reasons for rules, and allow more democratic decision making. There is less strict punishment and more guidance. Parents help children think through the consequences of their actions (Hoffman, 2001).
- *Authoritarian parents* (low warmth, high control) seem cold and controlling in their interactions with their children. The children are expected to be mature and to do what the parent says, "Because I said so!" There is not much talk about emotions. Punishments are strict, but not abusive. The parents love their children, but they are not openly affectionate.
- *Permissive parents* (high warmth, low control) are warm and nurturing, but they have few rules or consequences for their children and expect little in the way of mature behavior because "They're just kids."
- *Rejecting/Neglecting/Uninvolved parents* (low warmth, low control) don't seem to care at all and can't be bothered with controlling, communicating, or teaching their children.

Authoritarian, authoritative, and permissive parents love their children and are trying to do their best—they simply have different ideas about the best ways to parent. In broad strokes, there are differences in children's feelings and behavior associated with these three parenting styles. At least in European American, middle-class families, children of *authoritative* parents are more likely to do well in school, be happy with themselves, and relate well to others. Children of *authoritarian* parents are more likely to feel guilty or depressed, and children of *permissive* parents may have trouble interacting with peers— they are used to having their way (Berger, 2006; Spera, 2005).

Of course, the extreme of permissiveness becomes indulgence. Indulgent parents cater to their children's every whim—perhaps it is easier than being the adult who must make unpopular decisions. Both indulgent and rejecting/neglecting/uninvolved parenting styles can be harmful. For example, when 3,407 9th- through 12th-grade European American students described their parents' styles and their peer-group orientation, students, especially girls, who characterized their parents as uninvolved were more likely to be oriented toward "partyers" and "druggies" who did not endorse adult values (Durbin, Darling, Steinberg, & Brown, 1993).

CULTURE AND PARENTING. Much of the work on parenting styles has focused on European American middle-class families. But cultures differ in parenting styles. Research indicates that higher control, more authoritarian parenting is linked to better grades

Blended families Parents, children, and stepchildren merged into families through remarriages.

Extended families Different family members—grandparents, aunts, uncles, cousins, etc.—living in the same household or at least in daily contact with the children in the family.

Parenting styles The ways of interacting with and disciplining children.

Connect and Extend to PRAXIS II™

Families (I, B6)
Understand the influence of families, their culture, and values on student learning.

for Asian and African American students (Glasgow, Dornbusch, Troyer, Steinberg, & Ritter, 1997). Parenting that is strict and directive, with clear rules and consequences, combined with high levels of warmth and emotional support, is associated with higher academic achievement and greater emotional maturity for inner-city children (Garner & Spears, 2000; Jarrett, 1995). Differences in cultural values and in the danger level of some urban neighborhoods may make tighter parental control appropriate, and even necessary (Smetana, 2000). In addition, in cultures that have a greater respect for elders and a more group-centered rather than individualist philosophy, it may be a misreading of the parents' actions to perceive their demand for obedience as "authoritarian" (Lamb & Lewis, 2005; Nucci, 2001). In fact, research by Ruth Chao (2001; Chao & Tseng, 2002) has challenged Baumrind's conclusions for Asian families. Chao finds that an alternative parenting style of *chiao shun* (a Chinese term that Chao translates as "training") better characterizes parenting in Asian and Asian American families.

Research with Latino parents also questions whether studies of parenting styles based on European American families are helpful in understanding Latino families. Using a carefully designed observation system, Melanie Domenech Rodríguez and her colleagues included a third dimension of parenting—giving children more or less autonomy (freedom to make decisions). They found that almost all of the Latino parents they studied could be characterized as *protective* (high on warmth, high on control/demand, and low on granting autonomy) or *authoritative* (high on all three—warmth, control/demand, and granting autonomy). Also, these Latino parents tended to be more demanding and less likely to grant autonomy to their female children (Domenech Rodríguez, Donovick, & Crowley, 2009).

Whatever the structure of the families you work with, here are some *Family and Community Partnership Guidelines* for making connections.

STUDYING CULTURAL DIFFERENCES IN PARENTING The results of Ruth Chao's studies of Asian American parenting styles have challenged models of parenting based on European American parents and children. She is also studying whether serving as a translator or "language broker" for parents who do not speak English has an impact on the child's psychological well-being and relationship with the parents.

GUIDELINES — FAMILY AND COMMUNITY PARTNERSHIPS

Connecting with Families

1. Work with families to co-create methods for family involvement. Offer a range of possible participation methods. Make sure the plans are realistic and fit the lives of the families you are dealing with.

2. Remember that some students' families have had negative experiences with schools or may fear or mistrust schools and teachers. Find other places to collaborate: before or after ball games, or at a local church or recreation center. Go where families go; don't always expect them to come to school.

3. Maintain regular home–school contact through telephone calls or notes. If a family has no telephone, identify a contact person (relative or friend) who can take messages. If literacy is a problem, use pictures, symbols, and codes for written communication.

4. Make all communications positive, emphasizing growth, progress, and accomplishments.

5. With the families, design family–student celebrations of the student's efforts and successes (a movie, special meal, trip to the park or library, going out for ice cream or pizza).

6. On a regular basis, send home a note in word or picture form that describes the student's progress. Ask families to indicate how they celebrated the success and to return the note.

7. Follow up with a telephone call to discuss progress, answer questions, solicit family suggestions, and express appreciation for the families' contributions.

8. Make sure families feel welcome if they visit the classroom.

For more information on family school partnerships, see http://www.gse.harvard.edu/hfrp/projects/family.html

Source: From "Effects of Parent Involvement in Isolation or in Combination with Peer Tutoring on Student Self-Concept and Mathematics Achievement," by J. Fantuzzo, G. Davis, and M. Ginsburg, Journal of Educational Psychology, 87, pp. 272–281. Copyright © 1995 by the American Psychological Association. Adapted with permission of the APA.

ATTACHMENT. The emotional bond that forms between people is called **attachment**. The first attachment is between the child and parents or other caregivers. The quality of this bond appears to have implications for forming relationships throughout life (Thompson & Raikes, 2003). Children who form what are called secure attachments with caregivers receive comfort when needed and are more confident to explore their world, perhaps because they know they can count on the caregiver. Children who form insecure or disorganized attachments can be fearful, sad, anxious, clinging, rejecting, or angry in interactions with the caregivers. Some research indicates that authoritarian parenting styles are related to forming insecure attachments, but as we saw above, many factors influence the effects of parenting styles (Roeser, Peck, & Nasir, 2006).

The quality of attachment has implications for teachers. For example, in preschools, children who have formed secure attachments with parents/caregivers are less dependent on teachers and interact with other children appropriately. Secure attachment is positively related to achievement test scores, teacher assessments of social competence throughout the school years, and even to lower dropout rates (Roeser, Peck, & Nasir, 2006). As we will see later, researchers are currently examining students' attachment to teachers and schools as a positive force in their lives.

DIVORCE. The divorce rate in the United States is one of the highest in the world. Some analysts estimate that between 40% and 50% of first-time marriages that took place in the 1990s will end in divorce—and the divorce rate is even higher for second and third marriages (Amato, 2001; Schoen & Canulas-Romo, 2006). And as too many of us know from experiences in our own families, separation and divorce are stressful events for all participants, even under the best circumstances. The actual separation of the parents may have been preceded by years of conflict in the home or may come as a shock to all, including friends and children. During the divorce itself, conflict may increase as property and custody rights are being negotiated. After the divorce, more changes may disrupt the child's life as the custodial parent moves to a new neighborhood or works longer hours. For the child, this can mean leaving behind important friendships in the old neighborhood or school, just when support is needed the most. Even in those rare cases where there are few conflicts, ample resources, and the continuing support of friends and extended family, divorce is never easy for anyone. However it can be a better alternative for children than growing up in a home filled with conflict and discord. "Destructive conflict in any type of family undermines the well-being of parents and children" (Hetherington, 2006, p. 232).

The first two years after the divorce seem to be the most difficult period for both boys and girls and especially hard for young adolescents (ages 10–14). Recent research also indicates that divorce is harder on boys than girls, maybe because mothers still tend to get custody of children, which leaves boys without a male role model in the house (Fuller-Thomson & Dalton, 2011). Children may have problems in school or just skip school, lose or gain an unusual amount of weight, have trouble sleeping, or experience other difficulties. However, adjustment to divorce is an individual matter; some children respond with increased responsibility, maturity, and coping skills (Amato, 2006; Amato, Loomis, & Booth, 1995; APA, 2004). Over time, about 75% to 80% of children in divorced families adapt and become reasonably well adjusted (Hetherington & Kelly, 2003). See the *Guidelines* for ideas about how to help students dealing with divorce.

Peers

Children also develop within peer groups. Rubin and his colleagues (2005) distinguish between two kinds of peer groups: cliques and crowds. *Cliques* are relatively small, friendship-based groups (typically between 3 and a dozen members). Cliques are more evident in middle childhood. *Crowds* are less intimate, more loosely organized groups in which members may or may not interact with one another.

Attachment Forming an emotional bond with another person, initially a parent or family member.

STOP & THINK Think back to high school—did you have friends in any of these groups: normals, populars, brains, jocks, partyers, druggies, others? What were the main "crowds" at your school? How did your friends influence you? •

GUIDELINES

Helping Children of Divorce

Take note of any sudden changes in behavior that might indicate problems at home.
Examples

1. Be alert to physical symptoms such as repeated headaches or stomach pains, rapid weight gain or loss, fatigue or excess energy.
2. Be aware of signs of emotional distress such as moodiness, temper tantrums, difficulty in paying attention or concentrating.
3. Let parents know about the students' signs of stress.

Talk individually to students about their attitude or behavior changes. This gives you a chance to find out about unusual stress such as divorce.
Examples

1. Be a good listener. Students may have no other adult willing to hear their concerns.
2. Let students know you are available to talk, and let the student set the agenda.

Watch your language to make sure you avoid stereotypes about "happy" (two-parent) homes.
Examples

1. Simply say "your families" instead of "your mothers and fathers" when addressing the class.
2. Avoid statements such as "We need volunteers for room mother" or "Your father can help you."

Help students maintain self-esteem.
Examples

1. Recognize a job well done.
2. Make sure the student understands the assignment and can handle the workload. This is not the time to pile on new and very difficult work.

3. The student may be angry with his or her parents, but may direct the anger at teachers. Don't take the student's anger personally.

Find out what resources are available at your school.
Examples

1. Talk to the school psychologist, guidance counselor, social worker, or principal about students who seem to need outside help.
2. Consider establishing a discussion group, led by a trained adult, for students whose parents are going through a divorce.

Be sensitive to both parents' rights to information.
Examples

1. When parents have joint custody, both are entitled to receive information and attend parent–teacher conferences.
2. The noncustodial parent may still be concerned about the child's school progress. Check with your principal about state laws regarding the noncustodial parent's rights.

Be aware of long-term problems for students moving between two households.
Examples

1. Books, assignments, and gym clothes may be left at one parent's house when the student is currently on visitation with the other parent.
2. Parents may not show up for their turn to pick up their child at school or may miss a parent–teacher conference because the note never got home.

For ideas about helping children understand divorce, see
http://muextension.missouri.edu/xplor/hesguide/humanrel/gh6600.htm

CROWDS.   Adolescents are more likely to affiliate with larger crowds that provide them with an identity (e.g., Terrice is a jock, Lou's a brain, Olivia is a druggie). Laurence Steinberg and his colleagues have identified peer groups or crowds such as "jocks," "brains," "populars," and "druggies" that share common behaviors and attitudes (Durbin, Darling, Steinberg, & Brown, 1993; Steinberg, 1996, 1998). Based on a three-year study that surveyed 20,000 students in nine high schools in Wisconsin and California, Steinberg found that peers provide incentives for certain activities and ridicule others, which creates a school culture that affects the way the teachers behave. One in every five students Steinberg studied said that their friends made fun of people who tried to do well in school. Steinberg concluded that about 40% of the students were just going through the motions of learning. About 90% had copied someone else's homework and 66% had cheated on a test within the last year. Steinberg claims that this lack of investment is due in part to peer pressure because for many adolescents, "peers—not parents—are the chief determinants of how intensely they are invested in school and how much effort they devote to their education" (1998, p. 331). Let's look more closely at these powerful peer influences.

DRESS CODES AND MORE Peer cultures may set "rules" for how to dress and behave and in so doing determine which activities, music, or other students are in or out of favor.

PEER CULTURES. Different crowds or groups of students who have a set of "rules"—how to dress, talk, style their hair, and interact with others—are called **peer cultures**. The group determines which activities, music, or other students are in or out of favor. For example, when Jessica, a popular high school student, was asked to explain the rules that her group lives by, she had no trouble:

OK. No. 1: clothes. You cannot wear jeans any day but Friday, and you cannot wear a ponytail or sneakers more than once a week. Monday is fancy day—like black pants or maybe you bust out with a skirt. You have to remind people how cute you are in case they forgot over the weekend. No. 2: parties. Of course we sit down and discuss which ones we're going to because there is no point in getting all dressed up for a party that's going to be lame. (Talbot, 2002, p. 28)

These peer cultures encourage conformity to the group rules. When another girl in Jessica's group wore jeans on Monday, Jessica confronted her: "Why are you wearing jeans today? Did you forget it was Monday?" (Talbot, 2002, p. 28). Jessica explained that the group had to suspend this "rebel" several times, not allowing her to sit with them at lunch.

To understand the power of peers, we have to look at situations where the values and interests of parents clash with those of peers, and then see whose influence dominates. In these comparisons, peers usually win in matters of style and socializing. Parents and teachers still are influential in matters of morality, career choice, and religion (Harris, 1998). Also, not all aspects of peer cultures are bad or cruel. The norms in some groups are positive and support achievement in school.

CLIQUES AND FRIENDSHIPS. Friendships are central to students' lives. When there has been a falling-out or an argument, when rumors are started and pacts are made to ostracize someone (as with Alison and Stephanie at the beginning of the chapter), the results can be devastating. Beyond the immediate trauma of being "in" or "out" of the clique, peer relationships influence students' motivation and achievement in school (A. Ryan, 2001). In one study, 6th grade students without friends showed lower levels of academic achievement and fewer positive social behaviors and were more emotionally distressed, even two years later, than students with at least one friend (Wentzel, Barry, & Caldwell, 2004). The characteristics of friends and the quality of the friendships matter, too. Having stable, supportive relationships with friends who are socially competent and mature enhances social development, especially during difficult times such as parents' divorce or transition to new schools (Hartup & Stevens, 1999). Children who are rejected by their peers are less likely to participate in classroom learning activities, so their achievement suffers; they are more likely to drop out of school as adolescents and may even evidence more problems as adults. For example, rejected aggressive students are more likely to commit crimes as they grow older (Buhs, Ladd, & Herald, 2006; Coie & Dodge, 1998; Fredricks, Blumenthal, & Paris, 2004).

POPULARITY. What does it mean to be popular? We could answer this question by observing students or by using ratings from parents or teachers. But the most common way to assess popularity is to ask the students themselves two questions: Is this child liked? and What is this child like? Based on answers to these questions, we can identify four categories of children (see Table 2.2).

As you can see in Table 2.2, *popular* (highly rated) children may behave in positive or negative ways. *Rejected* children probably merit their low ratings because they are aggressive, immature, socially unskilled, or withdrawn. *Controversial* children get mixed reviews; they display both positive and negative social behaviors. Finally, *neglected* children are almost invisible—their peers simply do not mention them—but there is no consistent evidence that neglected children are anxious or withdrawn (Rubin et al., 2005).

Peer cultures Groups of children or adolescents with their own rules and norms, particularly about such things as dress, appearance, music, language, social values, and behavior.

TABLE 2.2 • **What Does It Take to Be Popular?**

POPULAR CHILDREN
Popular prosocial children: These children are both academically and socially competent. They do well in school and communicate well with peers. When they disagree with other children, they respond appropriately and have effective strategies for working things out. *Popular antisocial children:* This subgroup of children often includes boys who are aggressive. They may be athletic, and other children tend to think they are "cool" in the ways they bully other children and defy adult authority.
REJECTED CHILDREN
Rejected aggressive children: High rates of conflict and hyperactivity/impulsivity characterize the behaviors of this subgroup. These children have poor perspective-taking skills and self-control. They often misunderstand the intentions of others, assign blame, and act aggressively on their angry or hurt feelings. *Rejected withdrawn children:* These children are timid and withdrawn, often the targets of bullies. They are often socially awkward and withdraw from social interactions to avoid being scorned or attacked.
CONTROVERSIAL CHILDREN
As the descriptor implies, these children have both positive and negative social qualities and, as a result, their social status can change over time. They can be hostile and disruptive in some situations and then engage in positive prosocial behaviors in others. These children have friends and are generally happy with their peer relationships.
NEGLECTED CHILDREN
Perhaps surprisingly, most of these children are well adjusted and they are not less socially competent than other children. Peers tend to view them as shy, but they don't report being lonely or unhappy about their social lives. Apparently they don't experience the extreme social anxiety and wariness that withdrawn children do.

Source: Woolfolk, A., & Perry, N. E. (2012). Child and adolescent development. *Columbus, OH: Pearson, P. 416.*

WHO IS LIKELY TO HAVE PROBLEMS WITH PEERS? Children and adolescents are not always tolerant of differences. New students who are physically, intellectually, ethnically, racially, economically, or linguistically different may be rejected in classes with established cliques or crowds. Students who are aggressive, withdrawn, and inattentive-hyperactive are more likely to be rejected. But classroom context matters too, especially for aggressive or withdrawn students. In classrooms where the general level of aggression is high, being aggressive is less likely to lead to peer rejection. And in classrooms where solitary play and work are more common, being withdrawn is not as likely to lead to rejection. Thus, part of being rejected is just being too different from the norm. Also, being more attractive or engaging in prosocial behaviors such as sharing, cooperating, and friendly interactions are associated with peer acceptance, no matter what the classroom context. Many aggressive and withdrawn students lack these social skills; inattentive-hyperactive students often misread social cues or have trouble controlling impulses, so their social skills suffer, too (Coplan, Prakash, O'Neil, & Armer, 2004; Stormshak, Bierman, Bruschi, Dodge, & Coie, 1999). A teacher should be aware of how each student gets along with the group. Are there outcasts? Careful adult intervention can often correct such problems, especially at the late elementary and middle-school levels, as we will see next (Pearl, Leung, Acker, Farmer, & Rodkin, 2007).

Reaching Every Student: Teacher Support

Because they are the main adults in students' lives for many hours each week, teachers have opportunities to play a significant role in students' personal and social development. For students facing emotional or interpersonal problems, teachers are sometimes the best source of help. When students have chaotic and unpredictable home lives, they need a caring, predictable structure in school. They need teachers who set clear limits, are consistent, enforce rules firmly but not punitively, respect students, and show genuine concern. Being liked by teachers can offset the negative effects of peer rejection in middle school. And students who have few friends, but are not rejected—simply ignored by other students—can remain well adjusted academically and socially when they are liked and supported by teachers.

As a teacher, you can be available to your students if they want to talk about their personal problems without requiring them to do so. One of my student teachers gave a boy in her class a journal entitled "Very Hard Thoughts" so that he could write about his parents' divorce. Sometimes he talked to her about the journal entries, but at other times, he just recorded his feelings. The student teacher was very careful to respect the boy's privacy about his writings.

ACADEMIC AND PERSONAL CARING. When researchers ask students to describe a "good teacher," three qualities are consistently at the center of their descriptions. Good teachers have positive interpersonal relationships—they care about their students. Second, good teachers keep the classroom organized and maintain authority without being rigid or "mean." Finally, good teachers are good motivators—they can make learning fun by being creative and innovative so students learn something. It appears that authoritative teaching strategies, like authoritative approaches to parenting, lead to positive relationships with students and enhance motivation for learning (Noguera, 2005; Woolfolk Hoy & Weinstein, 2006). We will look at motivation in Chapter 9 and at management in Chapter 10, so for now let's focus on caring and teaching.

For nearly two decades, research has documented the value and importance of positive relationships with teachers for students at every grade level (Davis, 2003). Teachers' behaviors that communicate liking and respect, such as eye contact, relaxed body posture, and smiling, are associated with students' liking of teachers, interest in courses, and motivation to achieve (Woolfolk & Perry, 2012). For example, one of my doctoral graduates studied middle-school mathematics classes and found that students' perceptions of their teachers' affective support and caring were related to the effort they invested in learning math (Sakiz, Pape, & Woolfolk Hoy, 2008). Tamera Murdock and Angela Miller (2003) found that 8th grade students' perceptions that their teachers cared about them were significantly related to the students' academic motivation, even after taking into account the motivational influences of parents and peers.

Students define caring in two ways. One is *academic caring*—setting high, but reasonable expectations and helping students reach those goals. The second is *personal caring*—being patient, respectful, humorous, willing to listen, interested in students' issues and personal problems. For higher-achieving students, academic caring is especially important, but for students who are placed at risk and often alienated from school, personal caring is critical (Cothran & Ennis, 2000; Woolfolk Hoy & Weinstein, 2006). In fact, in one study in a Texas high school, the Mexican and Mexican American students saw teacher caring as a prerequisite for their own caring about school; in other words, they needed to be *cared for* before they could *care about* school (Valenzuela, 1999). Unfortunately, in the same school, the mostly non-Latino teachers expected the students to care about school before they would invest their caring in the students. And for many teachers, caring about school meant behaving in more "middle-class" ways.

These contrasting student and teacher views can lead to a downward spiral of mistrust. Students withhold their cooperation until teachers "earn it" with their authentic caring. Teachers withhold caring until students "earn it" with respect for authority and cooperation. Marginalized students expect unfair treatment and behave defensively when they sense any unfairness. Teachers get tough and punish. Students feel correct about their mistrusting and become more guarded and defiant. Teachers feel correct in mistrusting and become more controlling and punitive, and on it goes (Woolfolk Hoy & Weinstein, 2006).

Of course, students need both academic and personal caring. Katz (1999) interviewed eight Latino immigrant students in a middle school and concluded:

> High expectations without caring can result in setting goals that are impossible for the student to reach without adult support and assistance. On the other hand, caring without high expectations can turn dangerously into paternalism in which teachers feel sorry for "underprivileged" youth but never challenge them academically. High expectations and caring in tandem, however, can make a powerful difference in students' lives. (p. 814)

In short, caring means not giving up on students in addition to demonstrating and teaching kindness in the classroom (Davis, 2003).

Teachers and Child Abuse

Certainly, one critical way to care about students is to protect their welfare and intervene in cases of abuse. Although accurate information about the number of abused children in the United States is difficult to find because many cases go unreported, every year about 3,000,000 cases of abuse and neglect are reported and 900,000 are confirmed. That means a child is abused or neglected every 35 seconds (Children's Defense Fund, 2010; U.S. Department of Health and Human Services, 2007). Of course, parents are not the only people who abuse children. Siblings, other relatives, and even teachers have been responsible for the physical and sexual abuse of children.

As part of your responsibilities as a teacher, you must alert your principal, school psychologist, or school social worker if you suspect abuse. In all 50 states, the District of Columbia, and the U.S. territories, the law requires certain professionals, often including teachers, to report suspected cases of child abuse. The legal definition of *abuse* has been broadened in many states to include neglect and failure to provide proper care and supervision. Be sure that you understand the laws in your state or province on this important issue, as well as your own moral responsibility. At least four children die of abuse or neglect each day in the United States, in many cases because no one would "get involved" (Children's Defense Fund, 2011). Even children who survive abuse pay a great price. In school alone, physically abused children are more likely to be aggressive in the classroom and are retained in grades and referred for special education services more often than children who were not abused (Roeser, Peck, & Nasir, 2006). What should you look for as indicators of abuse? Table 2.3 on the next page lists possible indicators.

Society and Media

All of the students you will teach grew up in a world of media, mobility, and machines. An astounding percentage, over 70% in 2010, had a television in their own bedroom. Many had computers and cell phones, even from early ages (Rideout, Foehr, & Roberts, 2010; Turkle, 2011). Each year their use of technology increases (Nielsen, 2010). In 2010, 75% of children ages 12 to 17 had cell phones. Figure 2.2 shows the different technologies that 12- and 17-year-olds use daily to keep in touch with friends.

A recent Nielsen Report documented that teens are sending or receiving an average of 3,339 text messages per month—over 100 per day (Nielsen, 2010). When do they have time

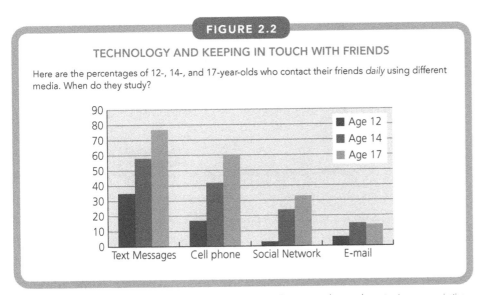

FIGURE 2.2

TECHNOLOGY AND KEEPING IN TOUCH WITH FRIENDS

Here are the percentages of 12-, 14-, and 17-year-olds who contact their friends *daily* using different media. When do they study?

Source: Based on data from Lenhart, A. (2010). Teens, cell phones and /texting: Text messages become the centerpiece communication. Washington, D.C.: Pew Research Center.

TABLE 2.3 • **Indicators of Child Abuse**

The following are some of the signs of abuse. Not every child with these signs is abused, but these indicators should be investigated. To learn about who must report child abuse, see http://www.childwelfare.gov/systemwide/laws_policies/statutes/manda.cfm

	PHYSICAL INDICATORS	BEHAVIORAL INDICATORS
Physical Abuse	• Unexplained bruises and welts (in various stages of healing), marks in the shape of belt buckles or electrical cords, human bite marks, puncture marks, bald spots, regularly appearing after absences or weekends • Unexplained burns, especially cigarette burns, burns in the shape of irons, rope burns, or immersion-burns (sock-like or glove-like) • Unexplained fractures, lacerations, or abrasions in various stages of healing • Injuries attributed to the child being "clumsy" or "accident-prone"	• Awkward movements, complains of soreness • Self-destructive • Withdrawn and aggressive—behavioral extremes • Uncomfortable with physical contact • Arrives at school early or stays late, as if afraid • Chronic runaway (adolescents) • Wears high neck, long sleeved clothing, not matching weather, to cover body • Frequent absences
Physical Neglect	• Abandonment • Unattended physical problems or medical needs • Constnt fatigue, lack of energy • Little or no supervision • Often hungry, dressed inappropriately for weather, poor hygiene • Lice, distended stomach, emaciation	• Falls asleep in class • Steals food, begs from classmates • Reports that no caretaker is at home • Frequently absent or tardy, or stays as long as possible at school • Self-destructive • Trouble with the law
Sexual Abuse	• Difficulty walking or sitting • Pain or itching in genital area • Torn, stained, or bloodied underclothing • Bruises or bleeding in external genitalia • Venereal disease, especially in pre-teens • Frequent urinary or yeast infections • Pregnancy	• Doesn't want to change for gym, PE • Withdrawn, chronic depression • Role reversal, overly concerned for siblings • Promiscuity, excessive seductiveness • Peer problems, lack of involvement • Massive weight change • Suicide attempts (especially adolescents) • Inappropriate sex play or premature understanding of sex, frequent masturbation, sexual play with dolls or stuffed animals • Sudden school difficulties

Source: Adapted from several state and national child abuse prevention Web sites:
U.S. Department of Health and Human Services: http://www.childwelfare.gov/pubs/usermanuals/sexabuse/sexabusec.cfm;
Pennsylvania:
http://www.pa-fsa.org/about_child_abuse__neglect/indicators_of_child_abuse.aspx;
New Jersey:
http://www.state.nj.us/dcf/abuse/indicators/.

for anything else? And these texts demand immediate attention. One high school sopho- more told Sherry Turkle (2011) that within his circle of friends, texts had to be answered as soon as possible, within 10 minutes, maximum. As he noted, "Texting is pressure" (p. 266). This pressure means that peers and even parents are always present—their messages demanding a response, even if the student is in class and must text in secret under the desk or with hands inside a backpack. Students and adults are spending more time with technology and less with each other. But these instant, superficial communications via cell phones, computers, iPads, and other electronic communication devices are not necessarily ties that bind students in deep relationships; instead, they are ties that preoccupy and dis- tract (Turkle, 2011). What will it be like to teach students who send and receive over 100 text messages a day, and who can't focus on your class when a Facebook posting appears? These are questions you will have to answer when you step into a classroom.

IDENTITY AND SELF-CONCEPT

What is identity? Is identity different from self-concept or self-esteem? How do we come to understand other people and ourselves? In this section we look at the development of identity and sense of self. You will see patterns similar to those noted in Chapter 1 for cog- nitive development. Children's understandings of themselves are concrete at first. Early views of self and friends are based on immediate behaviors and appearances. Children assume that others share their feelings and perceptions. Their thinking about themselves and others is simple, segmented, and rule-bound, not flexible or integrated into organized systems. In time, children are able to think abstractly about internal processes—beliefs, intentions, values, and motivations. With these developments in thinking, then, children can incorporate more abstract qualities into their knowledge of self, others, and situations (Harter, 2003; Woolfolk & Perry, 2012).

In this section you will encounter the term *identity* along with several *self-* terms: *self-concept, self-esteem,* and *self-worth.* The distinctions among these terms are not always sharp, and there is disagreement even among psycholo- gists about what each term means (Roeser, Peck, & Nasir, 2006). In general, *identity* is a broader concept than the *self-* terms. Identity includes people's general sense of themselves along with all their beliefs and attitudes. Identity integrates all the different aspects and roles of the self (Wigfield et al., 2006). But it is common for researchers to use *self-concept* and *identity* interchange- ably. To make matters easier, I will, too. We begin our consideration of identity/ self-concept with the framework of Erik Erikson.

Erik Erikson proposed a theory of psychoso- cial development that describes tasks to be accomplished at different stages of life.

Erikson: Stages of Psychosocial Development

Like Piaget, Erik Erikson did not start his career as a psychologist. He skipped college, travelled around Europe, and ended up teaching in Vienna, where he studied psychoanalysis with Anna Freud, the daughter of Sigmund Freud. Soon after completing his training, he had to flee from the Nazis. He was denied citizenship in Denmark, so he moved to his second choice—New York City. Even though he had never attended college, on the basis of his groundbreak- ing work, he became a distinguished University Professor at Harvard. Later in his career he worked with the original Dr. Spock—Benjamin Spock, the widely read pediatrician whose books guided many baby boomers' parents, mine included (Green & Piel, 2010; Miller, 2011).

Erikson offered a basic framework for understanding the needs of young people in relation to the society in which they grow, learn, and later make their contribu- tions. Erikson's **psychosocial** theory emphasizes the emergence of the self, the search for identity, the individual's relationships with others, and the role of culture throughout life.

Like Piaget, Erikson regarded development as a passage through an interdependent series of stages, each with its particular goals, concerns, accomplishments, and dangers,

Psychosocial Describing the relation of the individual's emotional needs to the social environment.

TABLE 2.4 • **Erikson's Eight Stages of Psychosocial Development**

STAGES	APPROXIMATE AGE	IMPORTANT EVENT	DESCRIPTION
1. Basic trust versus basic mistrust	Birth to 12–18 months	Feeding	The infant must form a first loving, trusting relationship with the caregiver or develop a sense of mistrust.
2. Autonomy versus shame/doubt	18 months to 3 years	Toilet training	The child's energies are directed toward the development of physical skills, including walking, grasping, controlling the sphincter. The child learns control but may develop shame and doubt if not handled well.
3. Initiative versus guilt	3 to 6 years	Independence	The child continues to become more assertive and to take more initiative but may be too forceful, which can lead to guilt feelings.
4. Industry versus inferiority	6 to 12 years	School	The child must deal with demands to learn new skills or risk a sense of inferiority, failure, and incompetence.
5. Identity versus role confusion	Adolescence	Peer relationships	The teenager must achieve identity in occupation, gender roles, politics, and religion.
6. Intimacy versus isolation	Young adulthood	Love relationships	The young adult must develop intimate relationships or suffer feelings of isolation.
7. Generativity versus stagnation	Middle adulthood	Parenting/Mentoring	Each adult must find some way to satisfy and support the next generation.
8. Ego integrity versus despair	Late adulthood	Reflection on and acceptance of one's life	The culmination is a sense of acceptance of oneself and a sense of fulfillment.

Source: Lefton, Lester A., Psychology, 5th Edition, © 1994. Reprinted by permission of Pearson Education, Inc. Upper Saddle River, NJ.

as shown in Table 2.4 above. At each stage, Erikson suggests that the individual faces a **developmental crisis**. Each crisis can be resolved by embracing an extreme position or by the healthier and more productive stance of finding a balance between the extreme responses. The way in which the individual resolves each crisis influences resolution of future crises and has a lasting effect on that person's self-image and view of society. We will look briefly at all eight stages in Erikson's theory—or, as he called them, the "eight ages of man."

THE PRESCHOOL YEARS: TRUST, AUTONOMY, AND INITIATIVE. Erikson identifies trust versus mistrust as the basic conflict of infancy. According to Erikson, the infant will develop a sense of trust if its needs for food and care are met with comforting regularity and responsiveness from caregivers. In this first year, infants are in Piaget's sensorimotor stage and are just beginning to learn that they are separate from the world around them. This realization is part of what makes trust so important: Infants must trust the aspects of their world that are beyond their control (Miller, 2011; Posada et al., 2002). Having a secure

Developmental crisis A specific conflict whose resolution prepares the way for the next stage.

attachment (described earlier in this chapter) helps young children develop trust and also learn when mistrust is appropriate—either extreme of complete trust or mistrust is dysfunctional.

Erikson's second stage, **autonomy** *versus shame and doubt*, marks the beginning of self-control and self-confidence as young children begin to assume responsibilities for self-care such as feeding, toileting, and dressing. During this period, parents must tread a fine line in being protective—but not overprotective. If parents do not reinforce their children's efforts to master basic motor and cognitive skills, children may begin to feel shame; they may learn to doubt their abilities to manage the world. Erikson believes that children who experience too much doubt at this stage will lack confidence in their own abilities throughout life. Of course, some doubt is appropriate if the task is too difficult or dangerous—again the need for balance.

For Erikson, the next stage of **initiative** *versus guilt* "adds to autonomy the quality of undertaking, planning, and attacking a task for the sake of being active and on the move" (Erikson, 1963, p. 255). The challenge of this period is to maintain a balance between zest for activity and an understanding that not every impulse can be acted on. Again, adults must tread a fine line, this time in providing supervision without interference. If children are not allowed to do things on their own, a sense of guilt may develop; they may come to believe that what they want to do is always "wrong." The *Guidelines* on the next page suggest ways of encouraging initiative.

DEVELOPING INITIATIVE Children need opportunities to learn things for themselves in order to develop a sense of initiative.

THE ELEMENTARY AND MIDDLE SCHOOL YEARS: INDUSTRY VERSUS INFERIORITY. Let's set the stage for the next phase. Between the ages of 5 and 7, when most children start school, cognitive development is proceeding rapidly. Children can process more information faster and their memory spans are increasing. They are moving from preoperational to concrete-operational thinking. As these internal changes progress, the children are spending hours every weekday in the new physical and social world of school. They must now reestablish Erikson's stages of psychosocial development in the unfamiliar school setting. They must learn to trust new adults, act autonomously in this more complex situation, and initiate actions in ways that fit the new rules of school.

The next psychosocial challenge for the school years is what Erikson calls **industry** *versus inferiority*. Students are beginning to see the relationship between perseverance and the pleasure of a job completed. In modern societies, children's ability to move between the worlds of home, neighborhood, and school, and to cope with academics, group activities, and friends will lead to a growing sense of competence. Difficulty with these challenges can result in feelings of inferiority. Children must master new skills and work toward new goals, at the same time they are being compared to others and risking failure.

The skills and concepts children learn in preschool and the early grades are critical. They set students on pathways toward achievement or failure for the rest of their school years (Paris, Morrison, & Miller, 2006). In fact, Entwisle and Alexander (1998) claim, "How well students do in the primary grades matters more for their future success than does their school performance at any other time" (p. 354). Because schools tend to reflect middle-class values and norms, making the transition to school and meeting the challenge of *industry versus inferiority* may be especially difficult for children who differ economically or culturally. The *Guidelines* on the next page give ideas for encouraging industry.

After elementary school, in the transition to middle school, students confront an increased focus on grades and performance as well as more competition on all fronts— academic, social, and athletic. Just when they are eager to make decisions and assume more independence, students encounter more rules, required courses, and assignments. They

Connect and Extend to PRAXIS II™

Erikson's Psychosocial Theory of Development (I, A1, 2)
The school population spans four stages of Erikson's theory. Identify the major crisis of each of these stages. How can teachers support positive resolution of each of these stages? What are implications for negative resolution of these crises?

Autonomy Independence.

Initiative Willingness to begin new activities and explore new directions.

Industry Eagerness to engage in productive work.

GUIDELINES

Encouraging Initiative and Industry

Encourage children to make and to act on choices.
Examples
1. Have a free-choice time when children can select an activity or game.
2. As much as possible, avoid interrupting children who are very involved in what they are doing.
3. When children suggest an activity, try to follow their suggestions or incorporate their ideas into ongoing activities.
4. Offer positive choices: Instead of saying, "You can't have the cookies now," ask, "Would you like the cookies after lunch or after naptime?"

Make sure that each child has a chance to experience success.
Examples
1. When introducing a new game or skill, teach it in small steps.
2. Avoid competitive games when the range of abilities in the class is great.

Encourage make-believe with a wide variety of roles.
Examples
1. Have costumes and props that go along with stories the children enjoy. Encourage the children to act out the stories or make up new adventures for favorite characters.
2. Monitor the children's play to be sure no one monopolizes playing "teacher," "Mommy," "Daddy," or other heroes.

Be tolerant of accidents and mistakes, especially when children are attempting to do something on their own.
Examples
1. Use cups and pitchers that make it easy to pour and hard to spill.
2. Recognize the attempt, even if the product is unsatisfactory.
3. If mistakes are made, show students how to clean up, repair, or redo.

4. If a student consistently behaves in ways that are highly unusual or unacceptable, seek guidance from the school counselor or psychologist. The best time to help children deal with psychosocial problems is at an early age.

Make sure that students have opportunities to set and work toward realistic goals.
Examples
1. Begin with short assignments, then move on to longer ones. Monitor student progress by setting up progress checkpoints.
2. Teach students to set reasonable goals. Write down goals and have students keep a journal of progress toward these goals.

Give students a chance to show their independence and responsibility.
Examples
1. Tolerate honest mistakes.
2. Delegate to students tasks such as watering class plants, collecting and distributing materials, monitoring the computer lab, grading homework, keeping records of forms returned, and so on.

Provide support to students who seem discouraged.
Examples
1. Use individual charts and contracts that show student progress.
2. Keep samples of earlier work so students can see their improvements.
3. Have awards for most improved, most helpful, most hardworking.

---

change from a close connection with one teacher all year to more impersonal relations with numerous teachers in many different subjects across the year. They also go from being the most mature and highest status students in a small, familiar elementary school to being the "babies" in a large, impersonal middle school (Murdock, Hale, & Weber, 2001; Rudolph, Lambert, Clark, & Kurlakowsky, 2001; Wigfield, Eccles, MacIver, Rueman, & Midgley, 1991). In this demanding context, they face the next challenge—identity.

ADOLESCENCE: THE SEARCH FOR IDENTITY. As students move into adolescence, they are developing capabilities for abstract thinking and understanding the perspectives of others. Even greater physical changes are taking place as the students approach puberty. So, with developing minds and bodies, young adolescents must confront the central issue of constructing an **identity** that will provide a firm basis for adulthood. The individual has been developing a sense of self since infancy. But adolescence marks the first time that a conscious effort is made to answer the now-pressing question: "Who am I?" The conflict

Identity The complex answer to the question: "Who am I?"

defining this stage is *identity* versus *role confusion*. Identity refers to the organization of the individual's drives, abilities, beliefs, and history into a consistent image of self. It involves deliberate choices and decisions, particularly about work, values, ideology, and commitments to people and ideas (Miller, 2011; Penuel & Wertsch, 1995). If adolescents fail to integrate all these aspects and choices, or if they feel unable to choose at all, role confusion threatens.

STOP & THINK Have you decided on your career? What alternatives did you consider? Who or what was influential in shaping your decision? •

James Marcia (1991, 1994, 1999) expanded on Erikson's theory of identity formation. Specifically, he focused on two essential processes in achieving a mature identity: exploration and commitment. **Exploration** refers to the process by which adolescents consider and try out alternative beliefs, values, and behaviors in an effort to determine which will give them the most satisfaction. **Commitment** refers to individuals' choices concerning political and religious beliefs, for example, usually as a consequence of exploring the options. Then, Marcia identified four categories of identity status that arise from four patterns of exploration and commitment.

CONSTRUCTING AN IDENTITY With developing minds and bodies, young adolescents must confront the central issue of developing an identity that will provide a firm basis for adulthood. With adolescence comes a pressing question: "Who am I?"

The first, **identity achievement**, means that after *exploring* the realistic options, the individual has made choices and is *committed* to pursuing them. It appears that few students achieve this status by the end of high school; students who attend college may take even longer to decide. It is not uncommon for the explorations to continue into the early 20s. About 80% of students change their majors at least once (just ask my mom). And some adults may achieve a firm identity at one period in their lives, only to reject that identity and achieve a new one later. So identity, once achieved, may not be unchanging for everyone (Adams, Berzonsky, & Keating, 2006; Kroger, 2000; Nurmi, 2004).

Adolescents in the midst of struggling with choices are experiencing what Erikson called a **moratorium**. Erikson used the term *moratorium* to describe exploration with a delay in commitment to personal and occupational choices. This delay is very common, and probably healthy, for modern adolescents. Erikson believed that adolescents in complex societies have an identity crisis during moratorium. Today, the period is no longer referred to as a *crisis* because, for most people, the experience is a gradual exploration rather than a traumatic upheaval (Grotevant, 1998; Wigfield, Byrnes, & Eccles, 2006). Both identity-achieved and moratorium statuses are considered healthy.

Identity foreclosure is commitment without exploration. Foreclosed adolescents have not experimented with different identities or explored a range of options, but simply have committed themselves to the goals, values, and lifestyles of others—usually their parents, but sometimes cults or extremist groups. Foreclosed adolescents tend to be rigid, intolerant, dogmatic, and defensive (Frank, Pirsch, & Wright, 1990).

Identity diffusion occurs when individuals do not explore any options or commit to any actions. They reach no conclusions about who they are or what they want to do with their lives. Adolescents experiencing identity diffusion may be apathetic and withdrawn, with little hope for the future, or they may be openly rebellious. These adolescents often go along with the crowd, so they are more likely to abuse drugs (Archer & Waterman, 1990; Kroger, 2000).

Schools that give adolescents experiences with community service, real-world work, internships, and mentoring help to foster identity formation (Cooper, 1998). See the *Guidelines* on the next page for other ideas about supporting identity formation.

Exploration In Marcia's theory of identity statuses, the process by which adolescents consider and try out alternative beliefs, values, and behaviors in an effort to determine which will give them the most satisfaction.

Commitment In Marcia's theory of identity statuses, individuals' choices concerning political and religious beliefs, for example, usually as a consequence of exploring the options.

Identity achievement Strong sense of commitment to life choices after free consideration of alternatives.

Moratorium Identity crisis; suspension of choices because of struggle.

Identity foreclosure Acceptance of parental life choices without consideration of options.

Identity diffusion Uncenteredness; confusion about who one is and what one wants.

GUIDELINES

Supporting Identity Formation

Give students many models for career choices and other adult roles.
Examples

1. Point out models from literature and history. Have a calendar with the birthdays of eminent women, minority leaders, or people who made a little-known contribution to the subject you are teaching. Briefly discuss the person's accomplishments on his or her birthday.

2. Invite guest speakers to describe how and why they chose their professions. Make sure all kinds of work and workers are represented.

Help students find resources for working out personal problems.
Examples

1. Encourage them to talk to school counselors.
2. Discuss potential outside services.

Be tolerant of teenage fads as long as they don't offend others or interfere with learning.
Examples

1. Discuss the fads of earlier eras (neon hair, powdered wigs, love beads).
2. Don't impose strict dress or hair codes.

Give students realistic feedback about their work and support for improving. Adolescents may need many "second chances."
Examples

1. When students misbehave or perform poorly, make sure they understand the consequences of their behavior—the effects on themselves and others.

2. Give students model answers or show them other students' completed projects from previous years so they can compare their work to good examples.

3. Never use a student's work as a "bad" example. Create negative examples from multiple sources including mistakes you have made.

4. Because students are "trying on" roles, keep the roles separate from the person. Criticize the behavior without criticizing the student.

For more ideas about working with adolescents using Erikson's theory, see http://www.cde.ca.gov/ls/cg/pp/documents/erikson.pdf

IDENTITY AND TECHNOLOGY. Some scholars of technology have speculated that establishing a separate identity is complicated for adolescents today because they are constantly connected to others. Parents often give a cell phone to their children somewhere between the ages of 9 and 13, or even earlier, with the specific requirement that the children always answer a call from the parent. Sherry Turkle (2011) calls this happy recipient of a new cell phone a "tethered child," now able to participate in activities such as spending time at a mall or on the beach that would not have been allowed without the safety tether of the phone. But the price paid is that these children never navigate social and physical landscapes completely alone—parents and friends always are a speed dial away. The chance to solve problems, experience autonomy, and handle situations on your own is the basis for achieving identity and mature judgment. The tethered child is never alone. Texting means the tether is even shorter. The high school students Turkle interviewed talked about the "big mistake" of teaching their parents to text or IM. A friend of mine is a physician at a university heath center. She describes undergraduate patients who respond to her question, "What are your health concerns today?" with the answer, "My mom is on the phone—she'll tell you" and then the college student hands a cell phone to the doctor. Constant connectivity complicates achieving a separate identity and autonomy.

Connectivity also "offers new possibilities for experimenting with identity, particularly in adolescence, the sense of a free space, what Eric Erikson called the *moratorium*" (Turkle, 2011, p. 152). On Second Life or The Sims Online or other life simulations sites, adolescents can create whole new identities and keep multiple personalities "alive." Some people even talk about their "life mix," a mash up of what they live online and what they live in real life. For some adolescents, the boundaries may be unclear and easily crossed. Is the profile adolescents create on Facebook the "real" person, or as one high school senior described, the identity that you "mold" to present to the world? But with world-wide access to the self-presentation, a critical question arises, "How will the self I present be judged by others?" For connected and tethered adolescents today, Elkind's imaginary audience (discussed in Chapter 1) is now a real online audience. The consequences are not all positive, as another senior agonized:

> You have to know that everything you put up will be perused very carefully. And that makes it necessary for you to obsess over what you do put up and how you portray yourself. . . And when you have to think about what you come across as, that's just another way that. . . . you are thinking of yourself in a bad way. (Turkle, 2011, p. 184)

BEYOND THE SCHOOL YEARS. The crises of Erikson's stages of adulthood all involve the quality of human relations. **Intimacy** *versus isolation* refers to a willingness to relate to another person on a deep level, to have a relationship based on more than mutual need. Someone who has not achieved a sufficiently strong sense of identity tends to fear being overwhelmed or swallowed up by another person and may retreat into isolation. **Generativity** *versus stagnation* extends the ability to care for another person and involves concern and guidance for both the next generation and future generations. Productivity and creativity are essential features. Achieving **integrity** *versus despair* means consolidating your sense of self and fully accepting its unique and now unalterable history.

Erikson's work helped start the life-span development approach, and his theories have been especially useful in understanding adolescence and developing concepts of self. But feminists have criticized his notion that identity precedes intimacy, because their research indicates that for women, identity achievement is fused with achieving intimacy (Miller, 2011). And, as you will see next, recent research has focused on identity issues not fully explored by Erikson—racial and ethnic identity.

Racial-Ethnic Identity

As early as 1903, W.E.B. DuBois wrote about the "double consciousness" of African Americans. In essence, African Americans, like other ethnic or racial groups, are conscious of their ethnic identity as they negotiate being members of the larger culture as well. Ethnic minority students have to "sift through two sets of cultural values and identity options" to achieve a firm identity, so they may need more time to explore possibilities—a longer moratorium in Erikson's terms (Markstrom-Adams, 1992, p. 177). But the exploration is important; some psychologists consider ethnic identity a "master status," one that dominates all other identity concerns when judging the self (Charmaraman & Grossman, 2010; Herman, 2004).

ETHNIC IDENTITIES: OUTCOME AND PROCESS. Jean Phinney (1990, 2003) describes four outcomes for ethnic minority youth in their search for identity. They can try *assimilation*, fully adopting the values and behaviors of the majority culture and rejecting their ethnic culture. At the opposite end, they can be *separated*, associating only with members of their ethnic culture. A third possibility is *marginality*, living in the majority culture, but feeling alienated and uncomfortable in it and disconnected from the minority culture as well. The final alternative is *biculturalism* (sometimes called *integration*), maintaining ties to both cultures. And there are at least three ways to be bicultural. You could alternate between the two cultures, being fully "majority" in your behavior in one situation and fully "minority" in other situations. Or you could blend the two cultures by finding values and behaviors that are common to both and acting on them. Finally, you could fuse the two cultures by truly merging them into a new and complete whole (Phinney & Devich-Nevarro, 1997).

No matter what your identity outcome is, having strong positive feelings about your own ethnic group seems to be important for good mental health (Steinberg, 2005). In fact, Amy Marks and her colleagues (2011) determined that bicultural adolescents who form strong, positive multiethnic identities have higher self-esteem, fewer mental health problems, and higher academic achievement than peers with a single ethnic identity or an undeveloped multiethnic identity.

Intimacy Forming close, enduring relationships with others.

Generativity Sense of concern for future generations.

Integrity Sense of self-acceptance and fulfillment.

KNOWING YOURSELF When majority adolescents are knowledgeable and secure about their own heritage, they are also more respectful of the heritage of others.

Some psychologists have used Marcia's identity statuses to understand the process of forming an ethnic identity. Children may begin with an unexamined ethnic identity, either because they have not explored at all (diffusion) or because they have accepted the identity encouraged by others (foreclosure). Many European American adolescents could fit the unexamined category. A period of ethnic identity exploration (moratorium) might be followed by a resolution of the conflict (identity achieved).

RACIAL IDENTITY: OUTCOME AND PROCESS. William Cross (1991; Cross & Cross, 2007; DeCuir-Gunby, 2009) devised a framework that specifically addresses African American racial identity. The process he calls **nigrescence** has five stages:

- *Pre-encounter:* At this stage, Cross says that an African American's attitude may range from ignoring race to feeling neutral about race, to actually being anti-Black. African Americans at this stage may adopt certain beliefs of White Americans, including the tendency to see "Whiteness" as superior. Some level of self-hate is a possible consequence. At the pre-encounter stage, people value other aspects of their identity, such as religion, profession, or social status.

- *Encounter:* This stage is often triggered by encounters with overt, covert, or institutional racism. For instance, when an African American is followed around in an upscale store, is assaulted by police, or sees news reports about such assaults, then his or her eyes are opened to the reality that race matters in society. The African American becomes attuned to his or her Blackness.

- *Immersion/Emersion:* Cross sees this as a transition—an in-between state that may cause people to be anxious about "becoming the 'right kind' of Black person" (Cross, 1991, p. 202). In response to encounters with discrimination, the individuals fill their lives with symbols of Blackness; they buy books about Black experiences and socialize mainly with other African Americans, for example. They are eager to understand their racial heritage more deeply.

- *Internalization:* Individuals are firmly connected to and secure in their sense of racial identity. They don't worry about what friends or outsiders think—they are confident in their own standards of Blackness.

- *Internalization-Commitment:* This stage is very closely connected with internalization. The main difference is a person's continued interest in and commitment to Black affairs. Such individuals chart their lives to connect to their Black racial identity; for example, a painter dedicates his life to painting Black images or a researcher dedicates her life to studying African American educational experiences.

Determining a racial identity may be even more complicated for biracial or multiracial adolescents. The parent they live with, the make-up of their neighborhood, their appearance, and experiences of discrimination or support can influence these adolescents' decisions about racial identity. Some psychologists think that these challenges help multiracial youth develop stronger and more complex identities, but other researchers argue that the challenges present an extra burden in an already tough process (Herman, 2004). Perhaps the outcome depends in part on the support adolescents receive in facing the challenges.

Nigrescence The process of developing a Black identity.

Racial and ethnic pride A positive self-concept about one's racial or ethnic heritage.

RACIAL AND ETHNIC PRIDE. For all students, pride in family and community is part of the foundation of a stable identity. Special efforts to encourage **racial and ethnic pride** are particularly important, so that students examining their identities do not get the message that differences are deficits (Spencer & Markstrom-Adams, 1990). In one study, researchers found that African American preschool students whose homes were rich with African American culture had more factual knowledge and better problem-solving skills. Parents who encouraged their children to be proud of their heritage reported fewer behavior problems with their children (Caughy, O'Campo, Randolph, & Nickerson, 2002). In other research, positive racial identity was found to be related to higher self-esteem and fewer emotional problems for both African American and White adolescents (DuBois, Burk-Braxton, Swenson, Tevendale, & Hardesty, 2002).

Each of us has an ethnic heritage. Janet Helms (1995) has written about stages in White identity development. Richard Milner (2003) has pointed to the importance of racial identity development and awareness, especially in teaching. When majority adolescents are knowledgeable and secure about their own heritage, they are also more respectful of the heritage of others. Thus, exploring the racial and ethnic roots of all students should foster both pride in self and acceptance of others (Rotherham-Borus, 1994).

In the next sections we move from overarching considerations of identity to more specific conceptions of self. In educational psychology, much research is focused on self-concept and self-esteem.

Self-Concept

The term *self-concept* is part of our everyday conversations. We talk about people who have a "low" self-concept or individuals whose self-concept is not "strong," as if self-concept were the oil level in a car or your abdominal muscles. These actually are misuses of the term. In psychology, **self-concept** generally refers to individuals' knowledge and beliefs about themselves—their ideas, feelings, attitudes, and expectations (Harter, 2006; Pajares & Schunk, 2001). We could consider self-concept to be our attempt to explain ourselves to ourselves, to build a scheme (in Piaget's terms) that organizes our impressions, feelings, and beliefs about ourselves. But this model or scheme is not permanent, unified, or unchanging. Our self-perceptions vary from situation to situation and from one phase of our lives to another.

THE STRUCTURE OF SELF-CONCEPT.   A student's overall self-concept is based on other, more specific concepts, including academic and nonacademic self-concepts. Herbert Marsh (2006) and his colleagues have identified up to 17 different self-concepts in nonacademic areas (e.g., physical appearance, popularity, trustworthiness, relations with parents, emotional stability) and academic areas (verbal, mathematics, problem solving, art, computers). For adolescents, both their overall academic self-concept (how quickly they learn or how well they do in school in general) and their subject-specific self-concept (how good they are in math) may influence their actions and motivation. For example, Martin Brunner and his colleagues (2010) suggest "students' educational aspirations (e.g., whether to go on to higher education) are driven by general academic self-concept, whereas the training program or college major chosen is influenced by the profile of subject-specific academic self-concepts" (p. 977). For adults, however, the separate, specific self-concepts are not necessarily integrated into an overall self-concept, so self-concept probably is more situation-specific in adults (Marsh & Ayotte, 2003; Marsh, Craven, & Martin, 2006; Schunk, Pintrich, & Meece, 2008).

HOW SELF-CONCEPT DEVELOPS.   The self-concept evolves through constant self-evaluation in different situations. Children and adolescents are continually asking themselves, in effect, "How am I doing?" They gauge the verbal and nonverbal reactions of significant people—parents and other family members in the early years, and friends, schoolmates, and teachers later—to make judgments (Harter, 1998, 2006).

Younger children tend to have positive and optimistic views of themselves. In one study, over 80% of the 1st graders surveyed thought they were the best students in their class (Stipek, 1981). With more experience in school, children make self-concept appraisals based on their own improvement. Researchers followed 60 students in New Zealand from the time they started school until the middle of their third year (Chapman, Tunmer, & Prochnow, 2000). In the first 2 months of school, differences in reading self-concept

Self-concept Individuals' knowledge and beliefs about themselves—their ideas, feelings, attitudes, and expectations.

began to develop, based on the ease or difficulty students had learning to read. Students who entered school with good knowledge about sounds and letters learned to read more easily and developed more positive reading self-concepts. Over time, differences in the reading performance of students with high and low reading self-concepts grew even greater. Thus, the children's early experiences with the important school task of reading had a strong impact on their self-concept.

As they mature, students become more realistic, but many are not accurate judges of their own abilities (Paris & Cunningham, 1996). In fact, some students suffer from "illusions of incompetence"—they seriously underestimate their own competence (Phillips & Zimmerman, 1990). As we have seen, during the middle-school years, students grow more self-conscious. At this age, self-concepts are tied to physical appearance and social acceptance as well as school achievement, so these years can be exceedingly difficult for students such as Stephanie, described at the opening of this chapter (Wigfield, Eccles, & Pintrich, 1996).

Both self and other comparisons shape self-concepts, at least in Western cultures. Students' self-concepts in math are shaped by how their math performance compares to their performance history. They also compare themselves to other math students (Altermatt, Pomerantz, Ruble, Frey, & Greulich, 2002; Schunk et al., 2008). Students who are strong in math in an average school feel better about their math skills than do students of equal ability in high-achieving schools. Marsh (1990; Marsh et al., 2008) calls this the "Big-Fish-Little-Pond Effect (BFLP)." Research that surveyed 265,180 15-year-old students in 10,221 schools across 41 countries around the world found the BFLP effect in every one of these countries (Seaton, Marsh, & Craven, 2009). Participation in a gifted and talented program seems to have a "Little-Fish-in-a-Big-Pond" effect: Students who participate in gifted programs, compared to similar students who remain in regular classes, tend to show declines in academic self-concepts over time, but no changes in nonacademic self-concepts (Marsh & Craven, 2002; Preckel, Goetz, & Frenzel, 2010).

SELF-CONCEPT AND ACHIEVEMENT. Many psychologists consider self-concept to be the foundation of both social and emotional development. Research has linked self-concept to a wide range of accomplishments—from performance in competitive sports to job satisfaction to pride, enjoyment, and achievement in school (Byrne, 2002; Marsh & Hau, 2003; Goetz, Cronjaeger, Frenzel, Ludtke, & Hall, 2010; Möller & Pohlmann, 2010). Some evidence for the link between self-concept and school achievement is that performance in academic subjects is correlated with specific self-concepts in those areas, but not with social or physical self-concepts. For example, in one study, math self-concept correlated .77 with math test scores, .59 with grades, and .51 with coursework selection (Marsh et al., 2006; O'Mara, Marsh, Craven, & Debus, 2006).

CHOICES SHAPE FUTURES The courses selected in high school put students on a path toward the future, so self-concepts about particular academic subjects can be life-changing influences.

That last correlation of math self-concept with course selection points to an important way self-concept affects learning in school. Think back to high school. When you had a chance to choose courses, did you pick your worst subjects—those where you felt least capable? Probably not. Herbert Marsh and Alexander Yeung (1997) examined how 246 boys in early high school in Sydney, Australia, chose their courses. Academic self-concept for a particular subject (mathematics, science, etc.) was the most important predictor of course selection—more important than previous grades in the subject or overall self-concept. The courses selected in high school put students on a path toward the future, so self-concepts about particular academic subjects can be life-changing influences.

Unfortunately, heavy emphasis on grade point averages (GPAs) for admission to some colleges can affect course choice as well, especially if students avoid classes to protect their GPAs because they see themselves as "no good" in math, science, world languages, or other challenging classes. Of course, we know from Chapter 1 that correlation is not cause—higher self-concept probably can encourage higher achievement but high achievement likely also leads to higher self-concept, so the causes work in both directions (Pinxten, De Fraine, Van Damme & D'Haenens, 2010).

Self-Esteem

STOP & THINK How strongly do you agree or disagree with the following statements?
  On the whole, I am satisfied with myself.
  I feel that I have a number of good qualities.
  I wish I could have more respect for myself.
  At times, I think that I am no good at all.
  I certainly feel useless at times.
  I take a positive attitude toward myself. •

These *Stop & Think* questions are taken from a widely used measure of self-esteem (Hagborg, 1993; Rosenberg, 1979). **Self-esteem** is an affective reaction—an overall judgment of self-worth that includes feeling confident and proud of yourself as a person. If people judge themselves positively—if they "like what they see"—we say that they have high self-esteem (Schunk, Pintrich, & Meece, 2008). Can you see the judgments of self-worth in the *Stop & Think* questions?

The terms *self-concept* and *self-esteem* are often used interchangeably, even though they have distinct meanings. Self-concept is a cognitive structure, a belief about who you are—for example, the belief that you are a good athlete. Self-esteem is an overall, general feeling of self-worth that incorporates your self-concepts in all areas of your life, so it is the "summary judgment" about your worth as a person (O'Mara, Marsh, Craven, & Debus, 2006). As you can see in the *Stop & Think* items above, the questions are pretty general; no specific areas such as academics or appearance are targeted. Self-esteem is influenced by whether the culture around you values your particular characteristics and capabilities (Bandura, 1997; Schunk et al., 2008). Some writers use *self-concept* and *self-esteem* interchangeably. But there is a conceptual difference—thinking versus valuing.

Do schools affect self-esteem: Is school important? As you can see from the *Point/Counterpoint* on the next page the school's role in student self-esteem has been hotly debated.

Over 100 years ago, William James (1890) suggested that self-esteem is determined by how successful we are in accomplishing tasks or reaching goals we value. If a skill or accomplishment is not important, incompetence in that area doesn't threaten self-esteem. Students must have legitimate success with tasks that matter to them. The reasons individuals give for their successes or failures also are important. In order to build self-esteem, students must attribute their successes to their own actions, not to luck or to special assistance.

Connect and Extend to PRAXIS II™

Self-Esteem (I, A2)
Understand the bidirectional effects of school life and self-esteem on each other. What can teachers do to enhance students' self-esteem?

Sex Differences in Self-Concept and Self-Esteem

Do girls and boys differ in their self-concepts? A study followed 761 middle-class, primarily European American students from 1st grade through high school (Jacobs, Lanza, Osgood, Eccles, & Wigfield, 2002). It is difficult to get longitudinal data, so this is a valuable study. In 1st grade, girls and boys had comparable perceptions of their own abilities in language arts, but boys felt significantly more competent in math and sports. Competence beliefs declined for both boys and girls across the grades, but boys fell faster in math, so that by high school, math competence beliefs were about the same for boys and girls. In language arts, boys' competence ratings fell more sharply than those of girls after 1st grade, but both leveled off during high school. In sports, competence ratings for both boys and girls dropped, but boys remained significantly more confident in their competence in sports throughout the entire 12 years.

Other studies have also found that girls tend to see themselves as more able than boys in reading and close friendships; boys are more confident about their abilities in math and athletics. Of course, some of these differences in self-confidence may reflect actual differences in achievement—girls tend to be better readers than boys, for example. As we have seen, many self-beliefs are reciprocally related to achievement—each affects the other (Eccles, Wigfield, & Schiefele, 1998; Pinxten, De Fraine, Van Damme & D'Haenens, 2010). When these results are examined together with Marsh and Yeung's (1997) findings

Self-esteem The value each of us places on our own characteristics, abilities, and behaviors.

POINT/COUNTERPOINT: What Should Schools Do to Encourage Students' Self-Esteem?

More than 2,000 books about how to increase self-esteem have been published. Schools and mental health facilities continue to develop self-esteem programs (Slater, 2002). The attempts to improve students' self-esteem have taken three main forms: personal development activities such as sensitivity training; self-esteem programs where the curriculum focuses directly on improving self-esteem; and structural changes in schools that place greater emphasis on cooperation, student participation, community involvement, and ethnic pride. Are these efforts valuable?

POINT

▶ **The self-esteem movement has problems.** Some people have accused schools of developing programs where the main objective is "to dole out a huge heaping of praise, regardless of actual accomplishments" (Slater, 2002, p. 45). But Erik Erikson (1980) warned years ago: "Children cannot be fooled by empty praise and condescending encouragement. They may have to accept artificial bolstering of their self-esteem in lieu of something better...." Erikson went on to explain that a strong and positive identity comes only from "wholehearted and consistent recognition of real accomplishment, that is, achievement that has meaning in their culture" (p. 95).

Frank Pajares and Dale Schunk (2002) point to another problem. "[W]hen what is communicated to children from an early age is that nothing matters quite as much as how they feel or how confident they should be, one can rest assured that the world will sooner or later teach a lesson in humility that may not easily be learned. An obsession with one's sense of self is responsible for an alarming increase in depression and other mental difficulties" (p. 16). Sensitivity training and self-esteem courses assume that we encourage self-esteem by changing the individual's beliefs, making the young person work harder against the odds. But what if the student's environment is truly unsafe, debilitating, and unsupportive? Some people have overcome tremendous problems, but to expect everyone to do so "ignores the fact that having positive self-esteem is almost impossible for many young people, given the deplorable conditions under which they are forced to live by the inequities in our society" (Beane, 1991, p. 27).

Worse yet, some psychologists are now contending that low self-esteem is not a problem, whereas high self-esteem may be. For example, they contend, people with high self-esteem are more willing to inflict pain and punishment on others (Baumeister, Campbell, Krueger, & Vohs, 2003; Slater, 2002). In addition, high self-esteem does not seem to predict academic learning. In a large study of adolescents, global self-esteem did not correlate with any of the nine academic outcomes measured (Marsh et al., 2006). And when people set self-esteem as a main goal, they may pursue that goal in ways that are harmful over the long run. They may, for example, avoid constructive criticisms or challenging tasks (Crocker & Park, 2004). Psychologist Lauren Slater (2002) in her article, "The Trouble with Self-Esteem" suggests that we rethink self-esteem and move toward honest self-appraisal that will lead to self-control. She suggests, "Maybe self-control should replace self-esteem as a primary peg to reach for" (p. 47).

COUNTERPOINT

▶ **The self-esteem movement has promise.** A study that followed 322 6th grade students for two years found that students' satisfaction with school, their sense that classes were interesting and teachers cared, and teacher feedback and evaluations influenced students' self-esteem. In physical education, teachers' opinions were especially powerful in shaping students' conceptions of their athletic abilities (Hoge, Smit, & Hanson, 1990). Being placed in a low-ability group or being held back in school seems to have a negative impact on students' self-esteem, but learning in collaborative and cooperative settings seems to have a positive effect (Covington, 1992; Deci & Ryan, 1985). Interestingly, special programs such as "Student of the Month" or admission to advanced math classes had little effect on self-esteem. (Relate the latter to the "Big-Fish-Little-Pond Effect.")

Beyond the "feel-good psychology" of some aspects of the self-esteem movement is a basic truth: Self-esteem is a basic right of all humans. We deserve to respect ourselves, and schools should not undermine this right (Beane, 1991). If we view self-esteem accurately as a product of our thinking and our actions—our values, ideas, and beliefs as well as our interactions with others—then we see a significant role for the school. Practices that allow authentic participation, cooperation, problem solving, and accomplishment should replace policies that damage self-esteem, such as tracking and competitive grading.

Beyond Either/Or. Another possibility is to refocus on more specific self-concepts, because self-concepts in specific areas such as math are related to learning in math (O'Mara et al., 2006). Because self-concept and achievement probably affect each other, the researcher concluded:

In summary, whereas the optimal way to improve self-concept over the short-term is to focus interventions directly on self-concept enhancement, interventions that combine direct self-concept enhancement in concert with performance enhancement, coupled with appropriate feedback and praise, are likely to be advantageous when the goals of the intervention are to improve both self-concept and performance. (Marsh et al., 2006, p. 198)

that academic self-concept influences course selection, it seems that many students make decisions about courses that forever limit their future options.

For most ethnic groups (except African Americans), males are more confident about their abilities in math and science. Unfortunately, there are no long-term studies of other ethnic groups, so these patterns may be limited to European Americans.

Teachers' feedback, grading practices, evaluations, and communication of caring for students can make a difference in how students feel about their abilities in particular subjects. But the greatest increases in self-esteem come when students grow more competent in areas they value—including the social areas that become so important in adolescence. Thus, a teacher's greatest challenge is to help students achieve important understandings and skills.

UNDERSTANDING OTHERS AND MORAL DEVELOPMENT

As we seek our own identity and form images of ourselves, we are also learning about right and wrong. One aspect of moral development is understanding the "significant others" around us. How do we learn to interpret what others are thinking and feeling?

Theory of Mind and Intention

By the time they are 2 or 3 years old, children are beginning to develop a **theory of mind**, an understanding that other people are people too, with their own minds, thoughts, feelings, beliefs, desires, and perceptions (Astington & Dack, 2008; Flavell, Miller, & Miller, 2002; Miller, 2009). Children need a theory of mind to make sense of other people's behavior. Why is Sarah crying? Does she feel sad because no one will play with her? Children also need a theory of mind to understand that beliefs can differ from reality and that people can have different views. As you will see in Chapter 4, one explanation for autism is that children with this condition lack a theory of mind to help them understand their own or other people's emotions and behaviors.

Around the age of 2, children have a sense of intention, at least of their own intentions. They will announce, "I wanna peanut butter sandwich." As children develop a theory of mind, they also are able to understand that other people have intentions of their own. Older preschoolers who get along well with their peers are able to separate intentional from unintentional actions and to react accordingly. For example, they will not get angry when another child accidentally knocks over their block tower. But aggressive children have more trouble assessing intention. They are likely to attack anyone who topples their tower, even accidentally (Dodge & Pettit, 2003). As children mature, they are more able to assess and consider the intentions of others.

With a developing theory of mind, children are increasingly able to understand that other people have different feelings and experiences, and therefore may have a different viewpoint or perspective. This **perspective-taking ability** develops over time until it is quite sophisticated in adults. Being able to understand how others might think and feel is important in fostering cooperation and moral development, reducing prejudice, resolving conflicts, and encouraging positive social behaviors in general (Gehlbach, 2004). Some coaching in perspective-taking from the teacher might help if children mistreat peers and the mistreatment is not part of a deeper emotional or behavioral disorder (Woolfolk & Perry, 2012).

Moral Development

Along with a more advanced theory of mind and an understanding of intention, children also are developing a sense of right and wrong. In this section we focus on children's **moral reasoning**, their thinking about right and wrong and their active construction of moral judgments. Some of the earliest moral issues in classrooms involve dividing and sharing materials, or **distributive justice** (Damon, 1994). For young children (ages 5 to 6), fair distribution is based on equality; thus, teachers often hear, "Keshawn got more than I did—that's not fair!" In the next few years, children come to recognize that some people

Theory of mind An understanding that other people are people too, with their own minds, thoughts, feelings, beliefs, desires, and perceptions.

Perspective-taking ability Understanding that others have different feelings and experiences.

Moral reasoning The thinking process involved in judgments about questions of right and wrong.

Distributive justice Beliefs about how to divide materials or privileges fairly among members of a group; follows a sequence of development from equality to merit to benevolence.

should get more based on merit—they worked harder or performed better. Finally, around age 8, children are able to take need into account and to reason based on benevolence; they can understand that some students may get more time or resources from the teacher because those students have special needs.

Another area that involves moral development is an understanding of rules. If you have spent time with young children, you know that there is a period when you can say, "Eating in front of the TV is not allowed!" and get away with it. For young children, rules simply exist. Piaget (1965) called this the state of **moral realism**. At this stage, the child of 5 or 6 believes that rules about conduct or rules about how to play a game are absolute and can't be changed. If a rule is broken, the child believes that the punishment should be determined by how much damage is done, not by the intention of the child or by other circumstances. So, accidentally breaking three cups is worse than intentionally breaking one, and in the child's eyes, the punishment for the three-cup offense should be greater.

As children interact with others and see that different people have different rules, there is a gradual shift to a **morality of cooperation**. Children come to understand that people make rules and people can change them. When rules are broken, both the damage done and the intention of the offender are taken into account.

KOHLBERG'S THEORIES OF MORAL DEVELOPMENT. Lawrence Kohlberg's (1963, 1975, 1981) theory of moral development is based in part on Piaget's ideas, described earlier.

- -

STOP & THINK A man's wife is dying. There is one drug that could save her, but it is very expensive, and the druggist who invented it will not sell it at a price low enough for the man to buy it. Finally, the man becomes desperate and considers stealing the drug for his wife. What should he do, and why? •

- -

Kohlberg evaluated the moral reasoning of both children and adults by presenting them with **moral dilemmas**, or hypothetical situations like the one above in which people must make difficult decisions and give their reasons. Based on their reasoning, Kohlberg proposed a detailed sequence of stages of moral reasoning, or judgments about right and wrong. He divided moral development into three levels: (1) *preconventional*, where judgment is based solely on a person's own needs and perceptions; (2) *conventional*, where the expectations of society and laws are taken into account; and (3) *postconventional*, where judgments are based on abstract, more personal principles of justice that are not necessarily defined by society's laws. Each of these three levels is further divided into two stages:

Preconventional Level

- Stage 1: *Obedience Orientation*—Obey rules to avoid punishments and bad consequences.
- Stage 2: *Rewards/Exchange Orientation*—Right and wrong is determined by personal needs and wants—"If I want it, it is right."

Conventional Level

- Stage 3: *Being Nice/Relationships Orientation*—Being good means being nice and pleasing others.
- Stage 4: *Law and Order Orientation*—Laws and authorities must be obeyed; the social system must be maintained.

Postconventional (Principled) Level

- Stage 5: *Social Contract Orientation*—The moral choice is determined by socially agreed upon standards—"the greatest good for the greatest number."

Moral realism Stage of development wherein children see rules as absolute.

Morality of cooperation Stage of development wherein children realize that people make rules and people can change them.

Moral dilemma Situations in which no choice is clearly and indisputably right.

- Stage 6: *Universal Ethical Principles Orientation*—There are universal principles of human dignity and social justice that individuals should uphold, no matter what the law or other people say.

Moral reasoning is related to both cognitive and emotional development. As we have seen, abstract thinking becomes increasingly important in the higher stages of moral development, as children move from decisions based on absolute rules to those based on abstract principles such as justice and mercy. The ability to see another's perspective, to judge intentions, and use formal-operational thinking to imagine alternative bases for laws and rules also enters into judgments at the higher stages.

CRITICISMS OF KOHLBERG'S THEORY. Even though there is evidence that the different levels of reasoning identified by Kohlberg do form a hierarchy, with each stage being an advancement in reasoning over the previous one (Boom, Brugman, & van der Heijden, 2001), his stage theory has been criticized. First, in reality, the stages do not seem to be separate, sequenced, and consistent. People often give reasons for moral choices that reflect several different stages simultaneously. Or a person's choices in one instance may fit one stage and his or her decisions in a different situation may reflect another stage. When asked to reason about helping someone else versus meeting their own needs, both children and adolescents reason at higher levels than when they are asked to reason about breaking the law or risking punishment (Arnold, 2000; Eisenberg et al., 1987; Sobesky, 1983).

Second, in everyday life, making moral choices involves more than reasoning. Emotions, competing goals, relationships, and practical considerations all affect choices. People may be able to reason at higher levels, but they may make choices at lower levels based on these other factors (Carpendale, 2000). Kohlberg emphasized cognitive reasoning about morality, but overlooked other aspects of moral maturity, such as character and virtue, that operate to solve moral problems in everyday life (Walker & Pitts, 1998).

GENDER DIFFERENCES: THE MORALITY OF CARING. One of the most hotly debated criticisms of Kohlberg's theory is that the stages are biased in favor of Western male values that emphasize individualism. His stages do not represent the way moral reasoning develops either in women or in other cultures, because the stage theory was based on a longitudinal study of American men only (Gilligan, 1982; Gilligan & Attanucci, 1988).

Carol Gilligan (1982) has proposed a different sequence of moral development, an "ethic of care." Gilligan suggests that individuals move from a focus on self-interest to moral reasoning based on commitment to specific individuals and relationships, and then to the highest level of morality based on the principles of responsibility and care for all people (which is a bit like Kohlberg's stage 3). If women never reach what Kohlberg considers the higher stages of justice, are they morally immature?

Some research supports this ethic of care and indicates that it is more typical of women's orientation to moral problem solving, especially when they reason about personal and real-life issues (Garmon, Basinger, Gregg, & Gibbs, 1996). However, a meta-analysis that combined the results of 113 studies found only small differences in moral orientation in line with Gilligan's theory (Jaffee & Hyde, 2000). The meta-analysis suggests both men and women use care to reason about interpersonal dilemmas and justice to reason about societal dilemmas. Moral reasoning was more strongly influenced by the context and content of the dilemma than by the gender of the reasoner. Even though men and women both seem to value caring and justice, there is some evidence that in everyday life, women feel more guilty about violating caring norms (being inconsiderate or untrustworthy) and men feel more guilty when they show violent behaviors (fighting or damaging property) (Williams & Bybee, 1994).

Caring for students and helping students learn to care has become a theme for many educators. For example, Nel Noddings (1995) urged that "themes of care" be used to organize the curriculum. Possible themes include "Caring for Self," "Caring for Family and Friends," and "Caring for Strangers and the World." Using the theme of "Caring for Strangers and the World," there could be units on crime, war, poverty, tolerance, ecology, or technology. The events after the massive tornado destruction in the Midwestern United States or

TABLE 2.5 **Using "Caring for Strangers and the World" as a Teaching Theme**

As part of a unit on "Caring for Strangers and the World," high-school students examine the issue of crime in several classes. In every class, the study of aspects of crime would be continually tied to the theme of caring and to discussions of safety, responsibility, trust in each other and in the community, and commitment to a safer future.

SUBJECT	ELEMENTS
Mathematics	Statistics: Gather data on the location and rates of crimes, ages of offenders, and costs of crime to society. Is there a correlation between severity of punishment and incidence of crime? What is the actual cost of a criminal trial?
English and Social Studies	Read *Oliver Twist*. Relate the characters to their social and historical context. What factors contributed to crime in 19th century England? Read popular mysteries. Are they literature? Are they accurate depictions of the criminal justice system?
Science	Genetics: Are criminal tendencies heritable? Are there sex differences in aggressive behavior? Are women less competent than men in moral reasoning (and why did some social scientists think so)? How would you test this hypothesis?
Arts	Is graffiti art really art?

Source: Based on "Teaching Themes of Care," by Nel Noddings, Phi Delta Kappan, 76, pp. 675–679.

earthquakes in Haiti and Japan that left thousands homeless might be a starting point for these units. Table 2.5 shows how a focus on crime and caring for strangers could be integrated into several high school classes.

Moral Judgments, Social Conventions, and Personal Choices

STOP & THINK

1. If there were no law against it, would it be OK to blind someone?
2. If there were no rule against it, would it be OK to chew gum in class?
3. Who should decide your favorite vegetable or how to style your hair? •

We probably could agree that it is wrong to blind someone, wrong to break class rules, and wrong to dictate food preferences or hairstyles for other people—but it is a different kind of "wrong" in each case. The first question is about actions that are inherently immoral. The answer to the question is concerned with conceptions of justice, fairness, human rights, and human welfare. Even young children know that it is not OK to hurt other people or steal from them—law or no law. But some rules, like no gum chewing in question 2, are **social conventions**—agreed-upon rules and ways of doing things in a particular situation. Students (mostly) avoid chewing gum when the class rules (conventions) say so. It is not inherently immoral to chew gum—it is just against the rules. Some classes—in college, for example—work well using different rules. And it is not immoral to dislike lima beans (at least I hope not) or to wear your hair long if you are a male; these are *personal choices*—individual preferences and private issues.

Other criticisms of Kohlberg's stages are that they mix up moral judgments with decisions about social conventions and also overlook personal choice. Larry Nucci (2001) offers an explanation of moral development that covers all three domains or areas: *moral judgments, social conventions,* and *personal choice.* Children's thinking and reasoning develops across all domains, but the pace of development may not be the same in every area.

Social conventions Agreed-upon rules and ways of doing things in a particular situation.

MORAL VERSUS CONVENTIONAL DOMAINS. For teachers, the most common "right and wrong" situations involve the moral and conventional domains. In the moral domain, beginning with a few basic ideas about right and wrong ("It is wrong to hurt others"), children move through the following stages: a sense that justice means equal treatment for all; an appreciation of equity and special needs; a more abstract integration of equity and equality along with a sense of caring in social relations; and finally, a sense as adults that morality involves beneficence and fairness and that moral principles are independent of the norms of any particular group.

In the *conventional domain*, children begin by believing that the regularities they see are real and right—for example, men have short hair and women have longer hair, so that is the way it should be. As they mature, children see the exceptions (men with pony tails, women with very short cuts) and realize that conventions are arbitrary. Next, children understand that rules, even though they are arbitrary, are made to maintain order and that people in charge make the rules. As students move through adolescence, they swing from understanding conventions as the appropriate ways to operate in a social system to viewing them as nothing but society's standards that have become set because they are widely applied and seldom challenged. Finally, adults realize that conventions are useful in coordinating social life, but changeable, too. So, compared to young children, older adolescents and adults generally are more accepting of others who think differently about conventions and customs.

IMPLICATIONS FOR TEACHERS. Nucci (2001) offers several suggestions for creating a moral atmosphere in your classroom. First, it is important to establish a community of mutual respect and warmth with a fair and consistent application of the rules. Without that kind of community, all your attempts to create a moral climate will be undermined. Second, teachers' responses to students should be appropriate to the domain of the behavior—moral or conventional. For example, here are some responses to moral issues (Nucci, 2001, p. 146):

1. When an act is inherently hurtful or unjust, emphasize the harm done to others: "John, that really hurt Jamal."
2. Encourage perspective-taking: "Chris, how would you feel if someone stole from you?"

In contrast, here are two responses to rules or conventional issues:

3. Restate the rule: "Lisa, you are not allowed to be out of your seat during announcements."
4. Command: "Howie, stop swearing!"

In all four cases, the teacher's response fits the domain. To create an inappropriate response, just switch responses 1 or 2 with 3 or 4. For example, "Lisa, how would you feel if other people got out of their seat during announcements?" Lisa might feel just fine. And it is a weak response to a moral transgression to say, "John, it is against the rules to hit." It is more than against the rules—it hurts and it is wrong.

In the third domain—personal—children must sort out what decisions and actions are their personal choices and what decisions are outside personal choice. This process is the foundation for developing moral concepts related to individual rights, fairness, and democracy. Here, diverse cultures may have very different understandings about individual choice, privacy, and the role of individuality in the larger society.

Diversity in Moral Reasoning

There are a number of broad cultural distinctions that might influence moral reasoning. Some cultures can be considered more traditional, with greater emphasis on customs and rituals that change slowly over time. In contrast, traditions and customs tend to change more rapidly in modern cultures. Nucci (2001) suggests that in more traditional cultures, customs may become "moralized." For example, not wearing head coverings in some cultures may seem to be in the conventional domain to outsiders, but is closer to the moral domain for members of the culture, especially when religious beliefs are involved.

CREATING MORAL CLIMATES Educators can create a moral climate in their schools and classrooms by promoting and reinforcing a community of mutual respect.

Consider the findings of one study described by Nucci that asked devout Hindus to rate 35 behaviors that violated community norms. An eldest son eating chicken a day after his father's death was considered the worst violation and beating a disobedient wife was the least offensive. What seems like a convention (eating chicken) is a moral issue because the Hindus believed that the son's behavior would prevent his father from receiving salvation—a terrible and eternal fate. So, to understand what is convention and what is moral, we need to know about the beliefs of the culture.

In cultures that are more family-centered or group-oriented (often called *collectivist cultures*), the highest moral value might involve putting the opinions of the group before decisions based on individual conscience. Research has found that children's reasoning about moral, conventional, and personal domains is similar across cultures. Even in societies such as China that encourage deference to authority, Chinese children agree with Western children that adults have no right to dictate how children spend their free time. And people without authority, including children, should be obeyed when what they want you to do is fair and just, but disobeyed when what they dictate is immoral or unjust (Helwig, Arnold, Tan, & Boyd, 2003; Kim, 1998).

In the last years of his life, Kohlberg was studying moral behavior in schools. We turn to that topic now.

Moral Behavior: Aggression, and Cheating

Three important influences on moral behavior are modeling, internalization, and self-concept. First, children who have been consistently exposed to caring, generous adult models will tend to be more concerned for the rights and feelings of others (Eisenberg & Fabes, 1998; Woolfolk & Perry, 2012). Second, most theories of moral behavior assume that young children's moral behavior is first controlled by others through direct instruction, supervision, rewards and punishments, and correction. But in time, children **internalize** the moral rules and principles of the authority figures who have guided them; that is, children adopt the external standards as their own. If children are given reasons they can understand when they are corrected—particularly reasons that highlight the effects of actions on others—then they are more likely to internalize moral principles. They learn to behave morally even when "no one is watching" (Hoffman, 2000).

Finally, we must integrate moral beliefs and values into our total sense of who we are, our self-concept.

> The tendency for a person to behave morally is largely dependent on the extent to which moral beliefs and values are integrated in the personality, and in one's sense of self. The influence our moral beliefs have on our lives, therefore, is contingent on the personal importance that we as individuals attach to them—we must identify and respect them as our own. (Arnold, 2000, p. 372)

AGGRESSION. Aggression should not be confused with assertiveness, which means affirming or maintaining a legitimate right. Saying, "You are sitting in my chair!" is assertive. Pushing the invader out of the chair is aggressive. There are several forms of aggression. The most common form is **instrumental aggression**, which is intended to gain an object or privilege, such as shoving to get a chair or snatching a book from another student. The intent is to get what you want, not to hurt the other child, but the hurt may happen

Connect and Extend to PRAXIS II™

Moral Development (I, A2)
Moral issues can have an important impact on the classroom. Identify major issues related to moral development and explain what a teacher can do to appropriately address these issues.

Internalize Process whereby children adopt external standards as their own.

Instrumental aggression Strong actions aimed at claiming an object, place, or privilege—not intended to harm, but may lead to harm.

anyway. A second kind is **hostile aggression**—inflicting intentional harm. Hostile aggression can take the form of either **overt aggression**, such as threats or physical attacks (as in, "I'm gonna beat you up!"), or **relational aggression**, which involves threatening or damaging social relationships (as in, "I'm never going to speak to you again!"). Boys are more likely to use overt aggression and girls, like Alison in the opening case, are more likely to use relational aggression, especially in middle school and beyond (Ostrov & Godleski, 2010). A final kind of hostile aggression is a growing concern today, **cyber aggression**—using e-mail, Twitter, Facebook, or other social media to spread rumors, make threats, or otherwise terrorize peers, as Stephanie's "friends" did in the case at the beginning of this chapter.

Aggressive students tend to believe that violence will be rewarded, and they use aggression to get what they want. They are more likely to believe that violent retaliation is acceptable: "It's OK to shove people when you're mad" (Egan, Monson, & Perry, 1998). Seeing violent acts go unpunished probably affirms and encourages these beliefs. In addition, some children, particularly boys, have difficulty reading the intentions of others (Dodge & Pettit, 2003; Zelli, Dodge, Lochman, & Laird, 1999). They assume another child "did it on purpose" when their block tower is toppled, they are pushed on the bus, or some other mistake is made. Retaliation follows and the cycle of aggression continues.

Children with more serious conduct problems often are identified during elementary school. But the problems are not new behaviors—usually they are behaviors the students have not outgrown from their early years (Petitclerc, Boivin, Dionne, Zoccolillo & Tremblay, 2009). So waiting for children to "outgrow" aggressive behaviors does not work. For example, one study in Finland asked teachers to rate students' aggression by answering "never," "sometimes," or "often" to statements such as "hurts another child when angry." Teacher-rated aggression when students were age 8 predicted school adjustment problems in early adolescence and long-term unemployment in adulthood (Kokko & Pulkkinen, 2000). Similar results were found in a study conducted in Canada, New Zealand, and the United States. Boys (but not girls) who were often physically aggressive in elementary school were at risk for continuing violent and nonviolent forms of delinquency through adolescence (Broidy et al., 2003).

It is clear that helping children handle aggression can make a lasting difference in their lives. One of the best approaches for preventing problems with aggression later in life is to intervene early. For example, one study found that aggressive children whose teachers taught them conflict management strategies were diverted from a life path of aggression and violence (Aber, Brown, & Jones, 2003). Sandra Graham (1996) has successfully experimented with approaches that help aggressive 5th and 6th grade boys become better judges of others' intentions. Strategies include engaging in role-play, participating in group discussions of personal experiences, interpreting social cues from photographs, playing pantomime games, making videos, and writing endings to unfinished stories. The boys in the 12-session training group showed clear improvement in reading the intentions of others and responding with less aggression.

RELATIONAL AGGRESSION. Insults, gossip, exclusion, taunts—all are forms of relational aggression, sometimes called *social aggression* because the intent is to harm social connections. After 2nd or 3rd grade, girls tend to engage in relational aggression more than boys, possibly because as girls become aware of gender stereotypes, they push their overt aggression underground into verbal, not physical, attacks. Relational aggression can be even more damaging than overt physical aggression—both to the victim and the aggressor. Victims, like Stephanie in the chapter opening, often are devastated. Teachers and other students may view relational aggressors as even more problematic than physical aggressors (Crick, Casas, & Mosher, 1997; Ostrov & Godleski, 2010). As early as preschool, children need to learn how to negotiate social relations without resorting to any kind of aggression. Interviews with adolescents reveal how much they count on their teachers and other adults in the school to protect them (Garbarino & deLara, 2002). We will examine more specific classroom strategies, especially strategies for handling bullying, in Chapter 10, *Creating Learning Environments*.

Hostile aggression Bold, direct action that is intended to hurt someone else; unprovoked attack.

Overt aggression A form of hostile aggression that involves physical attack.

Relational aggression A form of hostile aggression that involves verbal attacks and other actions meant to harm social relationships.

Cyber aggression Using e-mail, Twitter, Facebook, or other social media to spread rumors, make threats, or otherwise terrorize peers.

MEDIA, MODELING, AND AGGRESSION. Modeling plays an important role in the expression of aggression (Bandura, Ross, & Ross, 1963). Children who grow up in homes filled with harsh punishment and family violence are more likely to use aggression to solve their own problems (Patterson, 1997).

One very real source of aggressive models is found in almost every home in America—television. From ages 6 to 11, children spend an average of 28 hours a week watching television—more time than any other activity except sleep (Rideout, Foehr, & Roberts, 2010). With all this viewing, the possible influence of television violence is a real concern because in the United States, 82% of TV programs have at least some violence. The rate for children's programs is especially high—an average of 32 violent acts per hour, with cartoons being the worst. And in over 70% of the violent scenes, the violence goes unpunished (Kirsh, 2005; Mediascope, 1996). Does watching violent TV increase aggression? A panel of experts assembled by the U.S. Surgeon General to study media and violence reached a strong and clear conclusion: "Research on violent television and films, video games, and music reveals unequivocal evidence that media violence increases the likelihood of aggressive and violent behavior in both immediate and long-term contexts" (Anderson et al., 2003, p. 81).

You can reduce the negative effects of TV violence by stressing three points with your students: (1) most people do not behave in the aggressive ways shown on television; (2) the violent acts on TV are not real, but are created by special effects and stunts; and (3) there are better ways to resolve conflicts, and these are the ways most real people use to solve their problems (Huesmann et al., 2003). Also, avoid using TV viewing as a reward or punishment because that makes television even more attractive to children (Slaby et al., 1995). But television is not the only source of violent models. Students growing up in the inner cities see gang violence. Newspapers, magazines, and the radio are filled with stories of murders, rapes, and robberies. Many popular films are also filled with graphic depictions of violence, often performed by the "hero" who saves the day. And what about those video games?

VIDEO GAMES AND AGGRESSIVE BEHAVIOR. Recently researchers reviewed 130 reports based on over 130,000 participants from Western countries such as the United States, Australia, Germany, Italy, the Netherlands, Portugal, and the United Kingdom, as well as from Japan (Anderson et al., 2010). They found that playing violent video games is a causal factor for increased aggressive thoughts, feelings, and actions, along with decreased feelings of empathy. Culture and gender had very little impact on how susceptible players were to the effects of these games. But playing positive video games can increase prosocial behaviors, so it is not that games themselves are bad. It appears that we learn what we play, but there are few prosocial games and many violent ones. So an important issue facing teachers, parents, and our whole society is determining what we should do to limit the risks to children. The *Guidelines* give some ideas for dealing with aggression and encouraging cooperation.

MODELS OF AGGRESSION One very real source of aggressive models is television programming with a high degree of violent content.

CHEATING. About 80% to 90% of high school and college students cheat at some point in school. In fact, the rates of academic cheating have been rising for the past 30 years, perhaps in response to increased pressures and high-stakes testing (Murdock & Anderman, 2006).

There are some individual differences in cheating. Most studies of adolescent and college-age students find that males are more likely to cheat than females and lower-achieving students are more likely to cheat than higher achievers. Students focusing on performance goals (making good grades, looking smart) as opposed to learning goals, and

GUIDELINES

Dealing with Aggression and Encouraging Cooperation

Present yourself as a nonaggressive model.
Examples
1. Do not use threats of aggression to win obedience.
2. When problems arise, model nonviolent conflict-resolution strategies.

Ensure that your classroom has enough space and appropriate materials for every student.
Examples
1. Prevent overcrowding.
2. Make sure prized toys or resources are plentiful.
3. Remove or confiscate materials that encourage personal aggression, such as toy guns.
4. Avoid highly competitive activities and evaluations.

Make sure students do not profit from aggressive behaviors.
Examples
1. Comfort the victim of aggression and ignore the aggressor.
2. Use reasonable punishment, especially with older students.

Teach directly about positive social behaviors.
Examples
1. Incorporate lessons on social ethics/morality through reading selections and discussions.

2. Discuss the effects of antisocial actions such as stealing, bullying, and spreading rumors.
3. Provide models and encouragement—role-play appropriate conflict resolution.
4. Build self-esteem by building skills and knowledge.
5. Seek help for students who seem especially isolated and victimized.

Provide opportunities for learning tolerance and cooperation.
Examples
1. Emphasize the similarities among people rather than the differences.
2. Set up group projects that encourage cooperation.

For more ideas, see the National Youth Violence Prevention Resource Center: http://www.safeyouth.gov/Resources/Prevention/Pages/PreventionHome.aspx

---

students with a low sense of academic self-efficacy (a belief that they probably can't do well in school) are more likely to cheat. Finally, students who are impulsive may be more likely to cheat. (Anderman, Cupp, & Lane, 2009; Murdock & Anderman, 2006).

But cheating is not all about individual differences—the situation plays a role as well. In one study, the level of cheating decreased when students moved from math classes that emphasized competition and grades to classes that emphasized understanding and mastery (Anderman & Midgley, 2004). Students are less likely to cheat when they view their teacher as credible. If students trust the teacher as a credible source, they may be more likely to value the content being taught and therefore want to actually learn it (Anderman, Cupp, & Lane, 2009). In addition, students also are particularly likely to cheat when they are behind or "cramming for tests" or when they believe that their teachers do not care about them. For example, Erica had this perspective:

> I am a high school honors student, and I think there are different degrees of cheating. I'm a dedicated student, but when my history teacher bombards me with 50 questions due tomorrow or when a teacher gives me a fill-in-the-blanks worksheet on a night when I have swim practice, church, aerobics—and other homework—I'm going to copy from a friend! . . . Since I only do this when I need to, it isn't a habit. Every kid does this when they're in a pinch. (Jensen et al., 2002, p. 210)

Tamera Murdock and Eric Anderman (2006) have proposed a model for integrating what we know about cheating and doing research to learn more. They suggest that in deciding to cheat, students ask three questions: What is my goal? Can I do this? What are the costs? See Table 2.6 on the next page for some example answers to these questions that might be associated with decisions about whether to cheat, and some example strategies to support *not* cheating.

TABLE 2.6 • **When Do Students Cheat?**

Tamera Murdock and Eric Anderman have developed a model of academic cheating based on the answers to three questions.

QUESTIONS	LESS LIKELY TO CHEAT: EXAMPLE ANSWERS	MORE LIKELY TO CHEAT: EXAMPLE ANSWERS	WHAT CAN THE TEACHER DO? EXAMPLE STRATEGIES
What is my goal?	The goal is to learn, get smarter, and be the best I can be. It is my goal.	The goal is to look good, outperform others. The goal is imposed on me.	Communicate that the point of the class is to learn—everyone can get better.
Can I do it?	I can do it with reasonable effort.	I doubt my ability to do it.	Build students' confidence by helping them take small but successful steps. Point out students' past accomplishments.
What are the costs?	I will get caught and punished if I cheat. I will feel morally wrong or dishonored if I cheat.	I probably won't get caught and punished if I cheat. Everyone does it, so it can't be wrong. The pressure is too great—I can't fail. I have to cheat.	Make mistakes an opportunity to learn. Take the pressure out of assignments with the chance to revise. Monitor to prevent cheating and follow through with reasonable penalties.

Source: Adapted from Murdock and Anderman (2006).

The implications for teachers are straightforward. To prevent cheating, try to avoid putting students in high-pressure situations. Make sure they are well prepared for tests, projects, and assignments so they can do reasonably well without cheating. Be a trustworthy and credible source of information. Focus on learning and not on grades. Encourage collaboration on assignments and experiment with open-book, collaborative, or take-home tests. I often tell my students what concepts will be on the test and encourage them to discuss the concepts and their applications before the test. You might also make extra help available for those who need it. Be clear about your policies in regard to cheating, and enforce them consistently. Help students to resist temptation by monitoring them carefully during testing.

PERSONAL/SOCIAL DEVELOPMENT: LESSONS FOR TEACHERS

Certainly both Erikson and Bronfenbrenner stress that individuals are influenced by their social and cultural contexts. For example, here are a few big ideas:

1. Students whose parents are divorcing can benefit from authoritative teachers who are both warm and clear about requirements.
2. For all students, self-concepts are increasingly differentiated over time—they may feel competent in one subject, but not in others, or very capable as friends or family members, but not good about work in school.
3. For all students, it is a challenge to forge a meaningful identity that integrates their decisions about career, religion, ethnicity, gender roles, and connection to society. Teachers are in a position to support this quest.

4. Being rejected by peers is harmful for all students. Many students need guidance in developing social skills, in more accurately reading the intentions of others, in resolving conflicts, and in coping with aggression. Again, teachers can provide guidance.

5. When working under high pressure, with unreasonable workloads, and with little chance of being caught, many students will cheat. It is up to teachers and schools to avoid these conditions.

▼ SUMMARY

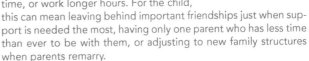

Physical Development (pp. 44–49)

Describe the changes in physical development of children in the preschool, elementary, and secondary grades. During the preschool years, there is rapid development of children's gross- and fine-motor skills. Physical development continues throughout the elementary-school years, with girls often ahead of boys in size. With adolescence comes puberty and emotional struggles to cope with all the related changes.

What are some of the consequences of early and late maturation for boys and girls? Females mature about two years ahead of males. Early-maturing boys are more likely to enjoy high social status; they tend to be popular and to be leaders. But they also tend to engage in more delinquent behavior—this is true for White, African American, and Mexican American boys. Early maturation is not generally beneficial for girls.

What is the role of recess and physical activity in development? Play supports brain development, language, and social development. Children release tensions, learn to solve problems, adapt to new situations, cooperate, and negotiate. The increase in childhood obesity is linked to inactivity and increased time spent watching TV and playing passive games such as video and Internet games.

What are some of the signs of eating disorders? Anorexic students may appear pale, have brittle fingernails, and have fine dark hairs developing all over their bodies. They are easily chilled because they have so little fat to insulate their bodies. They often are depressed, insecure, moody, and lonely. Girls may stop having their menstrual period.

Bronfenbrenner: The Social Context for Development (pp. 49–61)

Describe Bronfenbrenner's bioecological model of development. This model takes into account both the biological aspects internal to the individual and the nested social and cultural contexts that shape development. Every person develops within a microsystem (immediate relationships and activities) inside a mesosystem (relationships among microsystems), embedded in an exosystem (larger social settings such as communities); all of these are part of the macrosystem (culture). In addition, all development occurs in and is influenced by the time period—the chronosystem.

What are some aspects of the family that affect students in school? Students probably have experienced different parenting styles, and these styles can influence their social adjustment. At least in European American, middle-class families, children of authoritative parents are more likely to be happy with themselves and relate well to others, whereas children of authoritarian parents are more likely to feel guilty or depressed, and children of permissive parents may have trouble interacting with peers. But cultures also differ in parenting styles. Research indicates that higher-control parenting is linked to better grades for Asian and African American students.

How does divorce affect students? During the divorce itself, conflict may increase as property and custody rights are being decided. After the divorce, the custodial parent may have to move to a less expensive home, go to work for the first time, or work longer hours. For the child, this can mean leaving behind important friendships just when support is needed the most, having only one parent who has less time than ever to be with them, or adjusting to new family structures when parents remarry.

Why are peer relationships important? Peer relationships play a significant role in healthy personal and social development. There is strong evidence that adults who had close friends as children have higher self-esteem and are more capable of maintaining intimate relationships than adults who had lonely childhoods. Adults who were rejected as children tend to have more problems, such as dropping out of school or committing crimes.

What are peer cultures? Groups of students develop their own norms for appearance and social behavior. Group loyalties can lead to rejection for some students, leaving them upset and unhappy.

How can teachers' academic and personal caring affect students? Students value caring in teachers. Caring can be expressed as support for academic learning and as concern for personal problems. For higher-achieving and higher socioeconomic status students, academic caring may be more important, but for students who are alienated from school, personal caring may be more important.

What are some signs of child abuse? Signs of abuse or neglect include unexplained bruises, burns, bites, or other injuries and fatigue, depression, frequent absences, poor hygiene, inappropriate clothing, problems with peers, and many others. Teachers must report suspected cases of child abuse, and can be instrumental in helping students cope with other risks as well.

Self-Concept and Identity (pp. 61–73)

What are Erikson's stages of psychosocial development? Erikson's emphasis on the relationship between society and the individual is a psychosocial theory of development—a theory that connects personal development (psycho) to the social environment (social). Erikson believed that people go through eight life stages, each of which involves a central crisis. Adequate resolution of each crisis leads to greater personal and social competence and a stronger foundation for solving future crises. In the first two stages, an infant must develop a sense of trust over mistrust and a sense of autonomy over shame and doubt. In early childhood, the focus of the third stage is on developing initiative and avoiding feelings of guilt. In the child's elementary school years, the fourth stage involves achieving a sense of industry and avoiding feelings of inferiority. In the fifth stage, identity versus role confusion, adolescents consciously attempt to solidify their identity. According to Marcia, these efforts may lead to identity diffusion, foreclosure, moratorium, or achievement. Erikson's three stages of adulthood involve struggles to achieve intimacy, generativity, and integrity.

Describe the formation of ethnic and racial identities. Ethnic and racial minority students are confronted with the challenge of forming an identity while living in two worlds—the values, beliefs, and behaviors of their group and those of the larger culture. Most explanations for identity development describe stages moving from being unaware of differences between minority group and majority cultures, to different ways of negotiating the differences, and finally to an integration of cultures.

How does self-concept change as children develop? Self-concept (definition of self) becomes increasingly complex, differentiated, and abstract as we mature. Self-concept evolves through constant self-reflection, social interaction, and experiences in and out of school. Students develop a self-concept by comparing themselves to personal (internal) standards and social (external) standards. High self-esteem is related to better overall school experience, both academically and socially. Gender and ethnic stereotypes are significant factors as well.

Distinguish between self-concept and self-esteem. Both self-concept and self-esteem are beliefs about the self. Self-concept is our attempt to build a scheme that organizes our impressions, feelings, and attitudes about ourselves. But this model is not permanent. Self-perceptions vary from situation to situation and from one phase of our lives to another. Self-esteem is an evaluation of your self-worth. If people evaluate their worth positively, we say that they have high self-esteem. Self-concept and self-esteem are often used interchangeably, even though they have distinct meanings. Self-concept is a cognitive structure and self-esteem is an affective evaluation.

Are there differences in self-concepts for girls and boys? From 1st to 12th grade, competence beliefs decline for both boys and girls in math, language arts, and sports. By high school, boys and girls express about the same competence in math, girls are higher in language arts, and boys are higher in sports. In terms of general self-esteem, both boys and girls report declines in the transition to middle school, but boys' self-esteem goes up in high school while girls' self-esteem stays down.

Understanding Others and Moral Development (pp. 73–82)

What is a theory of mind and why is it important? A theory of mind is an understanding that other people are people too, with their own minds, thoughts, feelings, beliefs, desires, and perceptions. Children need a theory of mind to make sense of other people's behavior. As children develop a theory of mind, they also are able to understand that other people have intentions of their own.

How do perspective-taking skills change as students mature? An understanding of intentions develops as children mature, but aggressive students often have trouble understanding the intentions of others. Social perspective-taking also changes as we mature. Young children believe that everyone has the same thoughts and feelings they do. Later, they learn that others have separate identities and therefore separate feelings and perspectives on events.

What are the key differences among the preconventional, conventional, and postconventional levels of moral reasoning? Kohlberg's theory of moral development includes three levels: (1) a preconventional level, where judgments are based on self-interest; (2) a conventional level, where judgments are based on traditional family values and social expectations; and (3) a postconventional level, where judgments are based on more abstract and personal ethical principles. Critics suggest that Kohlberg's view does not account for possible cultural differences in moral reasoning or differences between moral reasoning and moral behavior.

Describe Gilligan's levels of moral reasoning. Carol Gilligan has suggested that because Kohlberg's stage theory was based on a longitudinal study of men only, it is very possible that the moral reasoning of women and the stages of women's development were not adequately represented. She has proposed an "ethic of care." Gilligan believes that individuals move from a focus on self-interest to moral reasoning based on commitment to specific individuals and relationships, and then to the highest level of morality based on the principles of responsibility and care for all people. Women are somewhat more likely to use a care orientation, but studies also show that both men and women can use both orientations.

How does thinking in the moral and conventional domains change over time? Beliefs about morality move from the young child's sense that justice means equal treatment for all to the adult's understanding that morality involves beneficence and fairness and that moral principles are independent of the norms of any particular group. In thinking about social conventions, children begin by believing that the regularities they see are real and right. After going through several stages, adults realize that conventions are useful in coordinating social life, but changeable too.

What influences moral behavior? Adults first control young children's moral behavior through direct instruction, supervision, rewards and punishments, and correction. A second important influence on the development of moral behavior is modeling. Children who have been consistently exposed to caring, generous adult models will tend to be more concerned for the rights and feelings of others.

What are the different types of aggression? Peer aggression can be instrumental (intended to gain an object or privilege), or hostile (intended to inflict harm). Hostile aggression can be either overt threats or physical attacks, or relational aggression, which involves threatening or damaging social relationships. Boys are more likely to use overt aggression and girls are more likely to use relational aggression. Today the many social media applications and sites provide other avenues for relational aggression.

How does ever-present media affect aggression and empathy? The world and the media provide many negative models of behavior. In time, children internalize the moral rules and principles of the authority figures who have guided them. If children are given reasons—particularly reasons that highlight the effects of actions on others—they can understand when they are corrected and then they are more likely to internalize moral principles. Some schools have adopted programs to increase students' capacity to care for others.

Why do students cheat? In schools, cheating is a common behavior problem that involves moral issues. The decision to cheat is based on three questions: What is my goal? Can I do this? What are the costs? Cheating is caused by both individual and situational factors, but if the pressure is great enough and the chance of getting caught is slim, many students will cheat.

▼ KEY TERMS

Anorexia nervosa (48)
Attachment (54)
Autonomy (63)
Bioecological model (50)
Blended families (52)
Body mass index (BMI) (45)
Bulimia (48)
Commitment (65)
Context (49)
Cyber aggression (79)
Developmental crisis (62)
Distributive justice (73)
Exploration (65)
Extended families (52)
Generativity (67)
Hostile aggression (79)

Identity (64)
Identity achievement (65)
Identity diffusion (65)
Identity foreclosure (65)
Industry (63)
Initiative (63)
Instrumental aggression (78)
Integrity (67)
Internalize (78)
Intimacy (67)
Menarche (45)
Moral dilemmas (74)
Moral realism (74)
Moral reasoning (73)
Morality of cooperation (74)
Moratorium (65)

Nigrescence (68)
Overt aggression (79)
Parenting styles (52)
Peer cultures (56)
Perspective-taking ability (73)
Psychosocial (61)
Puberty (45)
Racial and ethnic pride (68)
Relational aggression (79)
Self-concept (69)
Self-esteem (71)
Social conventions (76)
Spermarche (45)
Theory of mind (73)

▼ CONNECT AND EXTEND TO LICENSURE

MULTIPLE-CHOICE QUESTIONS

1. While several school districts limit the amount of time devoted to recess and play, the National Association for the Education of Young Children has recommended that children engage in play activities for all but which one of the following reasons?

    A. Play increases competence which children need to successfully navigate their world.

    B. Play engages many senses and children learn best when the whole self is involved.

    C. Children learn to appreciate that others have their own point of view through play.

    D. Play increases children's anxiety which prepares them for later challenges they may face.

2. Authoritative teaching strategies are associated with what students identify as "good teachers." Identify which one of the following educators is demonstrating authoritative techniques in the classroom.

    A. When Marcus failed to take his seat upon entering the room, Miss Thomas reminded him of the class rules and consequences.

    B. Paulo, a shy new student to the class, was forced by Mr. Hall on his first day in his new school to give a speech about his past experiences in Guatemala.

    C. Dina was allowed by her teacher to skip recess and play inside by herself because she did not have any friends.

    D. Mr. Krall allowed the students to have two free days at the beginning of the year in which to become acquainted with their peers in the classroom.

3. When a new student arrives in Ms. Taylor's class, she understands that they may initially have adjustment issues. In addition to pairing new students up with a partner to assist them in navigating Central Middle School, she also makes sure she addresses their psychosocial needs. Which one of the following strategies would be appropriate for a new student in Ms. Taylor's middle-school class?

    A. Allow the student to plan what they would like to do during their day at school.

    B. Encourage the student to take responsibility for their own personal needs.

    C. Provide support so that new students can feel a sense of competence and success.

    D. Let students know that the relationships they make in middle school are important to their emotional well-being and happiness later in life.

4. Research suggests that a majority of students cheat at one point in their academic career. Which one of the following is not a recommendation to reduce cheating in the classroom?

    A. Clear guidelines on what constitutes cheating accompanied by consequences which when imposed will deter other students due to their severity.

    B. Reduce the focus on grades and provide the material for students with which they must be familiar.

    C. Encourage collaboration with peers on assignments in order to provide support necessary and decrease anxiety.

    D. Ensure students are well prepared for assignments and tests.

CONSTRUCTED-RESPONSE QUESTIONS

Case

Suzanne Wilson entered Ms. Sullivan's class in the fall without any friends. While many of the third graders engaged in collaborative games on the playground, Suzanne would stand on the periphery and the other students did not include her. In class she appeared to be more typical of a younger child, sucking her thumb when she became upset and refusing to share during group activities. By December, Ms. Sullivan decided that steps should be taken to intervene. Mr. and Mrs. Wilson were called in for a parent meeting. When the Wilsons arrived, Suzanne was with them. What then transpired was shocking to Ms. Sullivan. Suzanne refused to allow her parents to talk with her teacher in private. Yelling above the crying and screaming, the Wilsons apologized and suggested they return on another day when Suzanne was feeling more agreeable.

1. Identify and explain the parenting style the Wilsons practice.

2. What strategies should Ms. Sullivan employ to assist Suzanne in her emotional development?

▼ WHAT WOULD THEY DO?

TEACHERS' CASEBOOK: Mean Girls

Here is how several expert teachers said they would address the situation with Alison and the clique of "mean girls."

THOMAS NAISMITH • Science Teacher Grades 7–12
Slocum Independent School District, Elkhart, TX

To bring civility to this classroom, I would address the situation in two stages. First, I would meet individually with the two girls involved in the most recent incident. I would make it very clear to Alison that her behavior was totally inappropriate and that such behavior was far beneath her. I would suggest to her that I was sure that it was just a temporary lapse of good judgment on her part and that I was sure that such an incident would not occur again. I would also ask her to play a role in helping to stop some of the other inappropriate behavior that was occurring in my classroom.

I would explain to Stephanie that she did not need to be embarrassed, because her classmates would appreciate the fact that she had made an effort to restore an old "friendship." I would comment on her positive qualities, explain that she should feel good about herself, and suggest that she seek the companionship of students who are open to her friendship.

The second step would be to address the class as a whole. I would be nonspecific in my comments, but I would make it very clear that the gossip and other "ugly" behavior would need to stop. I would explain that our classroom is a mini-society and that every member has the responsibility of treating others appropriately. I would further explain that they did not have to be "friends" with everyone, but should treat everyone with respect and dignity.

JACALYN D. WALKER • 8th Grade Science Teacher
Treasure Mountain Middle School, Park City, UT

Never work in a vacuum. This is especially important in a middle school or junior high school. Work with your school counselor, other grade level teachers, and parents. If you are doing this, you will have several options for dealing with this problem. You cannot fake caring about 12-, 13-, and 14-year-olds. They can spot a fake. You must be working with this age group because you truly like them as people. You appreciate their humor and their abilities. With a caring, trusting, and respectful relationship, students will be open to your help and guidance. Parents are often not involved in the classroom at these grade levels, but there are great programs available to get parents involved.

NANCY SCHAEFER • Grades 9–12
Cincinnati Hills Christian Academy High School, Cincinnati, OH

I would first make a phone call to Stephanie's home. Under the guise of calling about assignments because of the days she has missed, I would talk to one of her parents or guardians. My first goal would be to find out if the parents are aware of the situation. Sometimes girls like Stephanie are too embarrassed to tell their parents the whole story or even any of the real story. If the parents did not know the entire story, I might try to get Stephanie on the phone and help her tell her parents. Letting the adults around her know what has happened can relieve some of the shame she might be feeling.

I would then work with Stephanie and one or more of her parents to plan Stephanie's transition back to school. A school counselor might also be involved in this conversation. The adults would help Stephanie come up with a plan for how to handle possible difficult situations: face-to-face encounters with Alison, encounters with other old "friends," mean messages she might receive during the school day, or comments made to her by other students. We would help her think through these situations and practice how she could respond. I could talk to Stephanie's teachers to work on rearranging groups or seating to move the girls away from each other or to foster other friendships for Stephanie. Since almost everyone has stories about unfaithful friends, Stephanie might benefit from talking with a freshman or sophomore about that person's experiences and how they made new friends. Finally, I would try to arrange a brief and supervised meeting between Stephanie and Alison. Allowing an encounter to happen in a controlled environment would provide Stephanie an outlet to voice her hurt, without her having to resort to inappropriate actions.

During all of this, I would want to make sure that someone was also working with Alison, to prevent the escalation of events. This may be an administrator responsible for discipline, if school rules were violated, the school counselor, or another teacher with a good relationship with Alison. I would encourage the involvement of Alison's parents, especially if this were not the first vicious episode..

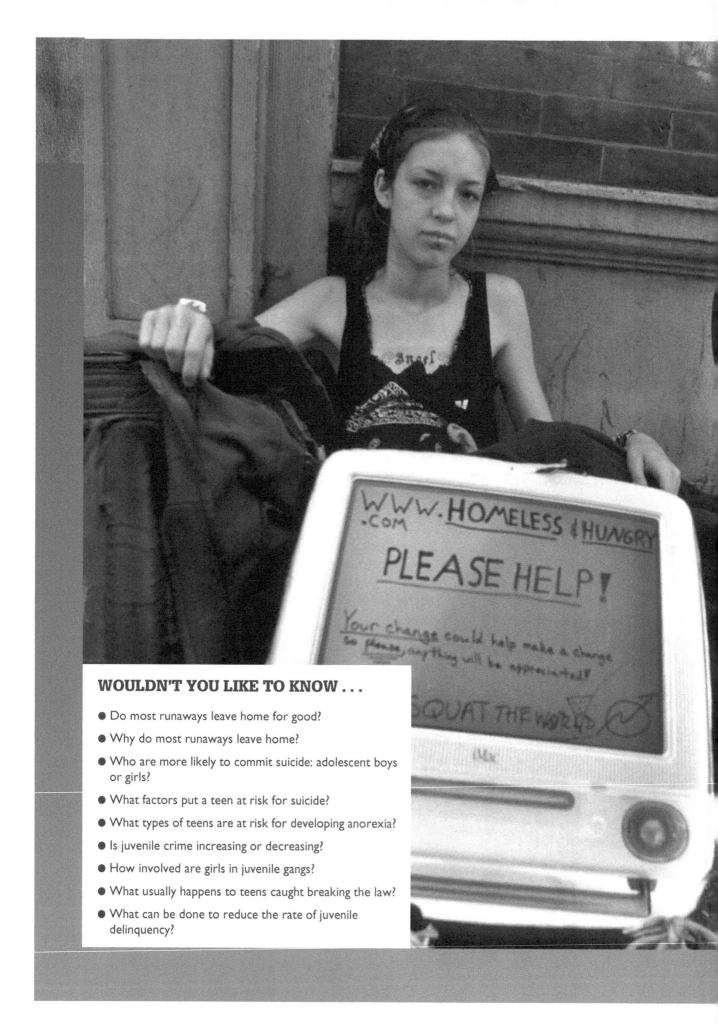

WOULDN'T YOU LIKE TO KNOW . . .

- Do most runaways leave home for good?
- Why do most runaways leave home?
- Who are more likely to commit suicide: adolescent boys or girls?
- What factors put a teen at risk for suicide?
- What types of teens are at risk for developing anorexia?
- Is juvenile crime increasing or decreasing?
- How involved are girls in juvenile gangs?
- What usually happens to teens caught breaking the law?
- What can be done to reduce the rate of juvenile delinquency?

Adolescent Stress and Alienation

Sometimes, adolescents who are angry or unhappy turn outward, expressing pent-up emotions through various forms of acting-out behavior: truancy, aggression, promiscuity, theft, or assault. Sometimes the anger or unhappiness turns against the self, which can result in depression or self-harm. For the most part, these distressed youths feel alienated from family and school; they do not function in the mainstream of adolescent or adult society. Their actions are an expression of their feelings of alienation, which they have found difficult to deal with in socially approved ways (Calabrese & Adams, 1990).

In this chapter, we discuss several manifestations of disturbed, acting-out behavior: running away, depression, suicide, eating disorders, and juvenile delinquency. Although these problems are quite different from one another, they stem from many of the same fundamental causes. There is a growing understanding that although the expressions of disturbance may vary, the root causes are often the same. Furthermore, adolescent problem behaviors—whether they involve substance abuse, pregnancy, delinquency, suicide, or dropping out—tend to *cluster*. In other words, teenagers who engage in one of these activities tend to engage in several of them (Ozer, Park, Paul, et al., 2003).

Clustering occurs for two reasons. The first is common causation. Family discord, association with deviant peers, poverty, and school failure all contribute to a host of behavioral problems (and, therefore, are mentioned multiple times throughout this and other chapters). The second reason for clustering is that one problem can directly trigger another. For example, the stresses caused by running away can lead a youth to substance abuse, promiscuity, and criminal activity.

Running Away

Running away from home is more common than most persons imagine. National estimates indicate that the number of adolescents who run away from home each year ranges from 1 to 2 million (Hammer, Finkelhor, & Sedlak, 2002). It is believed that one in seven adolescents will run away at least once before his or her eighteenth birthday (Sedlak, Finkelhor, Hammer, et al., 2002). Caucasian teenagers are more likely to flee home than their Latino or African American peers (Tyler & Bersani, 2008). Adolescents raised in single-parent or blended family homes are many times as likely to run away than those being raised by both of their biological parents (Sanchez, Waller, & Greene, 2006). A minority of adolescents who run away are running from foster care, group homes, or residential treatment facilities. Runaways are likely to have been victimized either at home or at school (Tyler & Bersani, 2008), and they are more likely to be female than male (Sanchez,

Waller, & Greene, 2006). Teens who leave home are more likely to come from urban rather than rural or suburban areas and to be from the Western half of the country.

Most runaways are 16 or older, but one-third are 15 or younger (Snyder & Sickmund, 2006). These young teenagers find it particularly hard to cope with life on the street—even more so than their older counterparts. Young teens' small size leaves them especially vulnerable to victimization and makes it impossible for them to find legitimate work. They are unlikely to take advantage of social services (shelters, food banks, etc.) because they are afraid they will be turned over to their parents.

Classes of Runaways

There are many reasons for running away and many typologies that classify runaways based upon their motivation for leaving home. However, there are two primary classes of runaways: *intent runaways* and *transient runaways*. Intent runaways are those who really mean to flee. They want to be gone—if not forever, then for a long time. Transient runaways are those who leave more at the spur of the moment and do not intend to stay away for more than a few hours or a day or two. These teens often leave home because they are afraid: perhaps they think that their parents will beat them for getting failing grades, or maybe they have violated their curfew and are terrified to return home. Other teens are angry, perhaps over having been denied permission to do something or having been disciplined.

The reason it is worthwhile at the outset of this discussion to distinguish these two groups is that about *half* of all runaways—the transient runaways—return home within two days (Finkelhor, Hotaling, & Sedlak, 1990). The vast majority run to friends' or relatives' houses, and often their parents know where they are (Snyder & Sickmund, 2006). The fact that an adolescent would take the rather extreme measure of running away for even a short time does not speak particularly well of his or her family's dynamics, and it is quite possible that this behavior is an early warning of more serious problems to come. Still, transient running is a far less serious and less risky behavior than intent running with no plans of returning.

> **ANSWERS WOULDN'T YOU LIKE TO KNOW . . .**
> Do most runaways leave home for good?
>
> No. About half stay away for only a day or two and go to a friend's or relative's house. Most of the more intent runaways, who are gone for long periods of time, eventually go home as well.

PERSONAL ISSUES PREVENTING TEENS FROM RUNNING AND FINDING THEM WHEN THEY DO

Most teens do not run away on the spur of the moment with the intent of staying away. Rather, their leaving is a dramatic move that they have usually considered for some time. This means that an alert parent or teacher who is aware of the warning signs might be able to speak with the adolescent and head off the behavior.

The most direct and obvious sign of planning to run is that the teen will have begun to accumulate the resources he or she will need to live on the street. He or she may be hoarding money or have packed a suitcase or backpack. In addition, he or she may gather personal mementos, such as photos of close friends.

Some runaways hint at or even directly state their intent to leave home. They sometimes confide their plans to friends. Hints, direct statements, and rumors reported by others should be taken seriously.

Other possible signs are less specific to running away but signal trouble. Changes in behavior, rebelliousness, a need for solitude, switching friends, and truancy often indicate that a problem is brewing and is worth looking into.

If an adolescent has disappeared and is believed to have run away from home, the Office of Juvenile Justice and Delinquency Prevention (1998) recommends the following actions:

1. Check with persons who may know the teenager's whereabouts: friends, neighbors, and so on.
2. Check locations that the adolescent frequents to see if he or she is there.
3. Examine the youth's bedroom and school locker for clues (such as notes or maps) as to where he or she may have gone.
4. Check past telephone bills for unexplained long-distance calls the youth may have made.
5. Examine the adolescent's e-mail account.
6. Call the police and make a report. Ask the police to put out a "Be on the lookout" alert.
7. Disseminate the news that the youth is missing, including a photo of him or her.
8. Contact national runaway help hotlines and the National Center for Missing and Exploited Children to see if the child has been in contact with them.

So, keeping in mind that a full 50 percent of runaways are gone only a night or two, let us examine the more serious intent runaways.

Reasons for Running Away

Rotheram-Borus and her colleagues (1996) have identified six reasons for youths' running away:

- Deserted by their parents as a result of parental death or divorce
- Thrown out of their homes by their parents
- Left home because their parents could not cope with their homosexuality
- Left home after having been sexually abused by their parent(s)
- Left home or thrown out because they have substance abuse problems
- Left home or thrown out because they have long-standing mental health problems

It is widely agreed that the most common thread running through the backgrounds of intent runaways is that they come from dysfunctional homes. They have a history of having been sexually or physically abused, neglected, and rejected by their parents. Their parents constantly fight and are frequently substance abusers (Baron, 1999; Terrell, 1997). Some estimates have suggested that as many as 70 percent of runaways have been abused in some way (Jencks, 1994).

Most adolescents, then, have been *pushed out* of their homes. They flee from what they perceive to be an intolerable situation. The majority of intent runaway adolescents say that they tried to make their family situation work but failed in their attempt (Schaffner, 1998). Other teens are **throwaways;** that is, their parents have actively encouraged them to leave or have actually thrown them out of their homes (Gullotta, 2003). Only a relatively small number of youths are pulled toward a glamorous vision of life on the street.

Runaway girls generally view their parents as controlling and punitive of their behavior in the home, whereas many runaway boys report minimal family control and supervision, which leads to outside forces, such as peers, becoming causal agents in running away. Thus, low levels of control allow boys opportunities to leave. Many parents of runaways are so absorbed with their own problems that they have little time to consider their children. Such youths report they are not wanted by their parents.

Given their poor family relationships, it is not surprising that most adolescents who run away exhibit a

throwaways adolescents who have been told to leave home.

host of problem behaviors before they leave home (e.g., Robert, Pauzé, & Fournier, 2005). They often commit delinquent acts, do not get along well with peers, and are anxious or depressed. Many have experienced difficulties in school. Children who are slow learners, left back to repeat grades, or ostracized by school personnel seek to escape the school environment that rejects them. An examination of the prevalence of arithmetic and reading difficulties in 16- to 21-year-old clients of a shelter for runaway and homeless street youths found that 52 percent had reading disabilities, 29 percent had trouble with arithmetic and written work, and only 20 percent were normal achievers (Barwick & Siegel, 1996).

Throwaways

One of the largest studies of runaways to date, the NISMART study (Hammer, Finkelhor, & Sedlak, 2002), found that not all runaways had, in fact, run away. Forty-four percent had been thrown out of their homes or asked to leave by their parents, and a large number of other teens had left voluntarily but then were not permitted to return when they wanted to. As noted earlier, these youths are more properly called *throwaways*.

What motivates a family to sever all ties with an adolescent child? Sometimes, the parents are distressed at their child's incorrigible behavior, whether it is substance abuse, promiscuity, delinquency, or the like. Sometimes, the child has a long-standing mental illness, such as conduct disorder, that makes him or her difficult to live with. Sometimes, the child has engaged in incest with a sibling or with one of the parents (Gullotta, 2003). Regardless of the reason, the parents of a throwaway are not making a good, mature decision when they decide to abandon their child. If the family had been strong and healthy, the child's behaviors either would not have occurred or would have been dealt with in a more proactive, healing manner. Shutting the door in a child's face may reduce the parents' problems, but it will only exacerbate the child's.

Another reason that parents ask their children to leave home is dire poverty. Some parents simply cannot afford to feed and clothe all their children. In these cases, the parents will sometimes ask the older children to fend for themselves so that the parents can concentrate on caring for the younger ones (Shinn & Weitzman, 1996). Similarly, some youths are on the street because they have outgrown foster care and been discharged with no means of support (National Coalition of the Homeless, 2008).

Life on the Street

Adolescents who have run away quickly find that life on the street is extremely difficult. Homeless youths are likely to be victimized by others. One study found that 43 percent of the street-living adolescent boys and 39 percent of the adolescent girls they sampled had been assaulted with a weapon (Whitbeck & Simons, 1990). Boys were more often robbed and beaten whereas girls were more commonly sexually assaulted.

The most common way that runaway teens support themselves is to get money from friends or relatives (Benoit-Bryan, 2008). However, in order to get enough money for food, clothes, and shelter, adolescents who have been on the street for more than a few days are usually forced to turn to drug dealing, shoplifting, and theft (Terrell, 1997). Significant numbers engage in prostitution, taking money for sex, or in so-called **survival sex,** swapping sexual favors for food or shelter. An estimated 75 percent of hard-core street youths engage in some form of crime and 25 to 50 percent engage in either prostitution or survival sex (Greene, Ennet, & Ringwalt, 1999; Kipke, O'Connor, Palmer, et al., 1995; Kipke, Palmer, LaFrance, et al., 1997). Even so, street youths often go hungry (Antoniades & Tarasuk, 1998).

Engaging in these activities causes runaways to associate with deviant individuals who draw them further into unhealthy lifestyles. The fact that many hard-core runaways use drugs and engage in sex with multiple partners, usually without condoms, puts them at high risk for contracting human immunodeficiency virus (HIV), which causes acquired immune deficiency syndrome (AIDS) (Booth, Zhang, & Kwiatkowski, 1999). It also leads to extremely high pregnancy rates: homeless adolescent girls are more than 10 times as likely to become pregnant as their at-home peers (Thompson, Bender, Lewis, et al., 2008). Homeless youths are subject to high rates of psychological problems, as well. They experience low self-esteem and depression, engage in various forms of self-injurious behavior, and are at high risk for suicide (Molnar, Shade, Kral, et al. 1999; Yoder, 1999). One study of homeless youths in Los Angeles found that two-thirds were clinically depressed; in comparison, about 7 percent of the overall adolescent population is depressed (Unger, Kipke, Simon, et al., 1997). Most studies report an attempted suicide rate of between 20 and 40 percent (Kidd, 2003). The mortality rate of street youths is estimated to be 40 times as high as that of at-home adolescents (Shaw & Dorling, 1998).

> **ANSWERS WOULDN'T YOU LIKE TO KNOW . . .**
> Why do most runaways leave home?
>
> Most intent runaways leave home because of intolerable conditions, such as abuse. Almost half of runaways, however, are told to leave or are thrown out by their parents.

Help for Runaways

Runaway youths need a variety of services to help with their many problems. These services include but are not limited to short-term emergency shelters where they can find temporary food and shelter; medical, including psychological, care; access to social workers who can try to reunite them with their families if that is appropriate or help them make arrangements to live on their own; educational programs so that they can attend class and graduate from high school; long-term, stable residential placements; and job training and placement. Unfortunately, the services available to runaway and throwaway youths are, at the current time, inadequate.

Worldwide Scope

Homeless youths are not just an American phenomenon. An estimated 100 million children and adolescents are homeless across the globe. Like their American counterparts, these children and adolescents suffer from malnutrition, self-destructive behaviors, and substance abuse. They eat out of garbage cans and steal or prostitute themselves to survive. Most of these children are from families living deep in poverty. Some have run away, some have been abandoned, and some have lost parents to death.

Le Roux and Smith (1998) blame the increase in the numbers of street children on a combination of industrialization/urbanization and drought with its resulting famine. Urbanization breaks down the traditional extended family structure in rural communities, leaving mothers and fathers to care for children

on their own. Famine destroys villages, kills parents, and forces families to make difficult choices when there is simply not enough food to feed them all. In some locales, AIDS has decimated the adult population, leaving large numbers of children and teens to fend for themselves.

Depression and Suicide

Depression

Depression would be an important enough topic to cover in some depth even if it were not related to suicide. Clinical depression is a serious condition that can make a person's life miserable—even unbearable—and trigger a host of other problems. When people are depressed, they feel both helpless—that there is nothing they can do to improve their terrible situation—and hopeless—that their situation will never change for the better. They feel sad and are self-critical; they also believe that others are critical of them. Depressed individuals feel overwhelmed at having to make even simple decisions. They often neglect their appearance and may act out their frustrations in an aggressive fashion (American Psychiatric Association, 2000).

Depression is quite common during adolescence: between 15 and 20 percent of teenagers have been clinically depressed at least once by the time they

survival sex swapping sexual favors for food or shelter.

depression a serious psychological disorder marked by sadness, helplessness, and hopelessness.

Homeless youths around the world sleep on the streets, eat out of garbage cans, and steal or prostitute themselves to survive.

enter young adulthood (Lewinsohn & Essau, 2002). Furthermore, episodes of depression are frequently recurrent, with each bout usually lasting seven to nine months. About two-thirds of adolescents who are clinically depressed have at least one other psychological disorder, as well—often substance abuse.

Depression runs in families. Depressed adolescents are three times more likely to have a close family member with depression than adolescents who are not depressed. The families of depressed youths are also more likely to be filled with discord, and divorce is more common. Depressed teen parents often have a history of overprotecting them (Nilzon & Palmérus, 1997).

Depression is equally common in boys and girls during childhood. However, girls' depression rates increase during adolescence whereas boys' rates do not (Wade, Cairney, & Pevalin, 2002), so that by adulthood, women are twice as likely as men to experience depression (Graber & Sontag, 2009). Depression in boys and girls is typically triggered by different events. Girls are more likely than boys to become depressed because of problems with social relationships. For example, whereas unpopular girls are more likely to be depressed than popular girls, this relationship is not true for boys (Oldenburg & Kerns, 1997). Girls are also more likely to feel others' pain and to become depressed because of the stresses that those they care about are experiencing (Eberhart, Shih, Hammen, et al., 2006). Also, when boys have a problem, they tend to cope with it through denial and avoidance; that is, they try to distract themselves and not think about it. Girls, conversely, tend to ruminate on their problems. This latter coping strategy is more likely to lead to depression whenever it is used (U.S. Department of Health and Human Services, 1999). Girls who experience depression are more likely than boys to have that depression continue into adulthood (Gjerde & Westenberg, 1998). (For other suggestions as to why adolescent girls have higher depression rates than adolescent boys, see the Personal Issues box on p. 360.)

Most kinds of stress increase the likelihood of depression. For example, students who do poorly in school are at heightened risk. It follows, then, that students with attention-deficit hyperactivity disorder, learning disabilities, and conduct disorder are especially vulnerable. Loss of a loved one—whether a family member, close friend, boyfriend, or girlfriend—can also trigger depression, as can traumas such as assault (National Institute of Mental Health, 2000).

Some question remains as to whether depression in adolescents is the same condition as depression in adults. Although many commonalities have been identified, there are a few differences in how the disorder is manifested in the two age groups. For example, adolescents are more likely to have physical ailments as part of their depression than are adults, but they are less likely to be tired or to lose their appetite

(Carlson & Kashini, 1988). In addition, some antidepressants that relieve symptoms in adults have much less effect on adolescents (Birmaher, Ryan, Williamson, et al., 1996). To some, these variations suggest a possible difference in the biological foundations of the disorders.

There are two links that tie depression to suicide. First, as mentioned before, depressed youths are at significantly increased risk for suicide (Birmaher, Arbelaez, & Brent, 2002). Second, there is concern that one of the most common treatments for depression—prescription SSRIs (selective serotonin reuptake inhibitors), which include antidepressants such as Prozac—can trigger suicidal thoughts and behavior in adolescents. This is a real cause for alarm: in 2002, American physicians wrote nearly 11 million prescriptions for SSRIs for youths younger than age 17 (Hampton, 2004). Concern grew to the point that in October 2004, the U.S. Food and Drug Administration issued a "black box" warning, stating that these medications put minors at increased risk for suicide and that they should be used with extreme caution in this population. (A number of European countries had previously restricted the use of SSRI antidepressants to adult patients.) The government's panelists determined that using these drugs doubled the risk of suicidal thoughts and behaviors in depressed adolescents who were using them.

Not all researchers are convinced that the dangers outweigh the benefits, however. For example, Vasa, Carlino, and Pine (2006) believe that the suicidal link has been exaggerated; they agree that the risk does double, but they note that the increase is from 2 to 4 percent and so is still small. In addition, they point out that the suicide risk of adolescents who are on psychotropic medications and are under treatment is still much less than that of untreated depressed adolescents. They also point to an inverse negative correlation between the number of prescriptions for these medications and the adolescent suicide rate in any given geographical region, a negative relationship that weakens the argument for a strong causal relationship between taking SSRIs and adolescent suicide. This linkage is under great scrutiny right now, and more will be known in a few years.

Suicide

Suicide is an important topic because it is the third-leading cause of adolescent death (behind accidents and homicides) (Anderson & Smith, 2003). In 2007, 15 percent of American adolescents had seriously considered suicide and 11 percent had gone so far as to make a suicide plan (Centers for Disease Control, 2008). The incidence of suicide among children, especially those younger than 13, is rare (Brent, Baugher, Bridge, et al., 1999) because adolescents are more

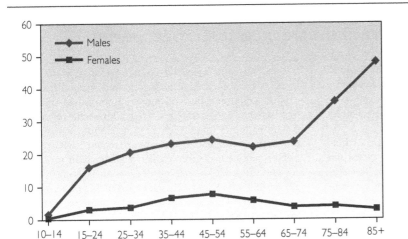

FIGURE 3.1 SUICIDE MORTALITY
BY SEX AND AGE GROUP: 2002

Source: Data from Centers for Disease Control (2004c).

likely than children to have a psychological disorder, which is a significant risk factor for suicide. Also, adolescents have more mature cognitive skills than children and can thus make more effective suicide plans (Shaffer, Gould, Fisher, et al., 1996).

Contrary to popular belief, the suicide mortality rate increases with age, reaching a peak in males older than 85 and in females ages 45 to 54 (Centers for Disease Control, 2004c). Teens are *not* more likely to commit suicide than older persons. Figure 3.1 shows these trends. As Figure 3.2 indicates, the suicide rate in the 15- to 24-year-old age group tripled from 1950 to 1995—from about 4.5 deaths per 100,000 adolescents to more than 13. Since then, the adolescent suicide rate has declined to about 10 deaths per 100,000 (U.S. Bureau of the Census, 2008).

Only a small percentage of people who attempt suicide succeed in killing themselves. Estimates of the ratio of adolescent suicide attempts to fatalities vary from 100 to 1 to 350 to 1 (Seroczynski, Jacquez, &

Cole, 2003). About 4,500 young people between ages 15 and 24 successfully commit suicide each year (Centers for Disease Control, 2008). Girls are about twice as likely as boys to attempt suicide, but 85 percent of successful suicides are committed by boys (Anderson & Smith, 2003). One of the reasons males succeed more often is that they frequently use more violent means—hanging, jumping from heights, single-vehicle automobile accidents, or shooting or stabbing themselves—whereas females more often use passive and less dangerous methods, such as taking pills. Females more often make multiple threats but less often really want to kill themselves or actually do it (Peck & Warner, 1995).

Suicide rates also vary by race and ethnicity. Native American adolescents have the highest suicide rate—four times that of Caucasian adolescents. Caucasian adolescents have a higher suicide rate than African American adolescents, and African Americans have a higher rate than Hispanic Americans (National Adolescent Health Information Center, 2006).

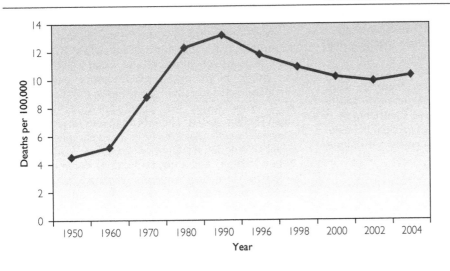

FIGURE 3.2
ADOLESCENT SUICIDE
RATES: 1950 TO 2004

Source: Data from U.S. Bureau
of the Census (2008).

PERSONAL ISSUES WHY ARE ADOLESCENT GIRLS MORE LIKELY TO BE DEPRESSED THAN ADOLESCENT BOYS?

During childhood, boys and girls are equally likely to be depressed, but by adulthood, women are twice as likely to be depressed as men. It is thus during adolescence that this gender difference in the rates of depression first emerges. But why?

An obvious explanation would seem to be the hormonal fluctuations associated with women's menstrual cycle. Evidence for this hypothesis is weak, however (Seroczynski, Jacquez, & Cole, 2003). A second explanation for this difference has to do with gender differences in body satisfaction. Both males and females become less satisfied with their bodies during adolescence, but females' dissatisfaction increases more than males'. Since discontent with one's physique is associated with depression, this could account for the higher depression rate in adolescent females (Kostanski & Gullone, 1998).

Perhaps the most intriguing explanation has come from work linking biological and societal factors. Petersen and her colleagues (1993) noted that depression rates were highest when adolescents made the transition to middle school on or about the time they were experiencing puberty. Because girls hit puberty about two years earlier than boys, in most communities, girls are more likely than boys to begin middle school and to begin experiencing pubertal change at the same time. Experiencing these two significant stressors at once could be overwhelming. It is therefore likely that a confluence of factors—those described here and the social issues described in the body of the text—work together to contribute to girls' higher depression rates.

ANSWERS WOULDN'T YOU LIKE TO KNOW . . .

Who are more likely to commit suicide: adolescent boys or girls?

Girls are much more likely to attempt suicide, but boys are much more likely to succeed.

Causes and Motives of Suicide

Why do adolescents attempt to take their own lives? What are their motives? Many people are surprised to learn that 90 percent of persons who commit suicide have one or more psychological disorders. Most commonly, they are depressed, but they also are likely to have a substance abuse problem or an anxiety disorder. In fact, the two best predictors of suicide are clinical depression and a previous suicide attempt (U.S. Department of Health and Human Services, 1999).

To put this in context, remember that although psychological disorders have a biological component, they are primarily caused by negative experiences and stressors in the environment. Thus, there are some commonalities in the backgrounds of most youths who commit suicide. In particular, a significant body of empirical literature suggests that suicidal behavior in the teenage years is largely associated with family processes (Koopmans, 1995).

Family Relationships

Impaired family relationships are the second common factor observed in suicidal youth. Studies have indicated that many different aspects of family life can be implicated in suicide ideation, attempts, and comple-

tions (e.g., Bridge, Goldstein, & Brent, 2006). For example, parental psychopathology and substance abuse are correlated with attempted and completed adolescent suicide (Brent, 1995); in addition, suicidal behavior runs in families, and this appears to be at least in part from genetic causes (Brent & Mann, 2005). Poor parent-child relationships clearly contribute to adolescent suicidal behavior (e.g., Yuen, Andrade, Nahulu, et al., 1996); the degree to which the child gets along and communicates with his or her father seems especially important (Gould, Fisher, Parides, et al., 1996). Parents who fail to monitor their children also put their children at increased risk (King, Schwab-Stone, Flisher, et al., 2001). Adolescents from one-parent homes are more likely to attempt and commit suicide than adolescents from intact families (Weitoft, Hjern, Haglund, et al., 2003), in part because of lessened monitoring and in part because of poorer parent-child relationships.

All of these factors sum to an absence of any warm, parental figure with whom to identify, with a resulting sense of emotional and social isolation.

Those who attempt suicide often state that they do not feel close to any adult. Many times, they have trouble communicating with significant others around them (Stivers, 1988). There is no one to turn to when they need to talk. Lack of closeness to parents leads to a lack of emotional support when it is needed (Dukes & Lorch, 1989). One study found three common characteristics of college students who had thoughts of suicide (Dukes & Lorch, 1989). They had poor relationships with parents, poor relationships with peers, and a sense of personal helplessness regarding their future. When social integration is high, suicide rates for all age groups are lower (Lester, 1991).

PERSONAL ISSUES PREVENTING SUICIDE

Recognize the Precipitating Conditions

- The loss of a close friend or family member through death or relocation
- Other significant loss, such as a loss of job, home, status, and so on
- Substance abuse
- Depression
- A long-standing but recently exacerbated problem
- Feelings of worthlessness
- Social isolation

Recognize the Signs That Suicide May Be Imminent

- Depression that disappears for no reason
- Declining school or work performance
- Lack of interest in formerly enjoyed activities
- Deteriorating physical appearance
- Self-abusive, self-injurious behavior
- Explicit or veiled statements that the person is going to die or go away
- Preparation of a will or verbal statements giving away possessions
- Sentimental visits to favorite places
- Acquisition of lethal means, such as a gun, pills, poison, and so on

What You Can Do

- Do *not* ignore these signs. Speak to your friend. You will *not* encourage someone to commit suicide by asking about his or her problems or whether he or she has contemplated suicide.
- Listen to what your friend has to say. Be empathic and sympathetic. Do *not* belittle or trivialize his or her problems.
- Let your friend know that you care.
- Try to diminish feelings of hopelessness by helping your friend brainstorm solutions to his or her problem.
- Do *not* leave your friend alone if you believe that he or she is suicidal.
- Get rid of any means the person has to kill himself or herself. Ask to hold the means until you have had more time to try to help.
- Get help. Encourage your friend to speak to a counselor or call a crisis hotline. Let your friend know that you will not abandon him or her if he or she speaks to someone else.
- If you cannot get your friend to contact someone with training in this area, make the contact yourself.

ANSWERS WOULDN'T YOU LIKE TO KNOW . . .

What factors put a teen at risk for suicide?

Most, but not all, teens who commit suicide are depressed. Many of them use drugs or alcohol, and many have a history of sexual abuse. Suicide is often triggered by the loss of someone or something important in the teen's life.

The background of social isolation makes these adolescents particularly vulnerable to the loss of a love object, which may trigger the suicide attempt. The loss of a parent in childhood makes any subsequent loss of a family member, peer, boyfriend, or girlfriend particularly hard to accept (Agerbo, Nordentoft, & Mortensen, 2002). Many studies have found that loss and low family support are good predictors of an adolescent's suicide attempt (e.g., Morano, Cisler, & Lemerond, 1993).

Other Psychological Correlates

The risk of suicide among adolescents, especially males, increases with alcohol and drug abuse (Brent, Baugher, Bridge, et al., 1999). Under the influence of drugs or alcohol, adolescents are more likely to act on impulse or to overdose and kill themselves without intending to do so. Other psychological problems—conduct disorder, post-traumatic stress syndrome, anxiety disorders, and eating disorders—also increase the likelihood of suicidal behavior (Bridge, Goldstein, & Brent, 2006).

A disproportionate number of adolescents who commit suicide have a history of sexual abuse (Pompili, Mancinelli, Girardi, et al., 2004).

Sexual Orientation

Gay and lesbian teens are more likely to attempt and actually complete suicide than heterosexual teens (Lester, 2006). As many as 30 percent of homosexual adolescents attempt suicide (Safren & Heimberg, 1999). These youths have the same risk factors as their straight peers: substance abuse, depression, loss, family discord, and so on. The rates among homosexual teens are higher because, as a group, they face the additional stressors of acknowledging their sexual orientation, of experiencing negative reactions by parents and friends, and of being victimized by hate-motivated individuals (Garland & Zigler, 1993; Savin-Williams, 1994).

Copycat Suicides

Copycat suicide is a real phenomenon (U.S. Department of Health and Human Services, 1999). Knowing someone who commits suicide not only increases one's feelings of loss, but also disinhibits one's own restraints about suicide. One person's suicide, in effect, "gives permission" for others to commit suicide, too. This is especially true if the suicide is well publicized and results in extensive media coverage (Stack, 2003). In fact, fictional accounts of suicides presented on television or in movies can trigger copycat attempts (Gould, 2001).

Unsuccessful Attempts

Sometimes, attempted suicide is a cry for help to get attention or sympathy or an attempt to manipulate other people. Attempted suicide is not necessarily an effort to die but rather a communication to others in an effort to improve one's life. These attempts that seem destined to fail—for example, an overdose of pills taken 10 minutes before a parent is due home from work—are called **suicide gestures.** As a matter of fact, desired changes in one's life situation as a result of attempted suicide may be accomplished. However, many suicidal gestures for help misfire and lead to death.

RESEARCH HIGHLIGHT A RAPID RISE IN SELF-INJURIOUS BEHAVIOR

An unfortunate behavior appears to be gaining ground with adolescents: self-injurious, or self-mutilating, behavior. Self-injurious behavior is defined as behavior that intentionally causes harm to the body for purposes not socially sanctioned (e.g., not for cosmetic purposes, such as body piercing) and without the apparent intent to commit suicide (Alderman, 1997). Self-injury most often takes the form of cutting with a knife or razor blade, but it also includes burning, picking at wounds, swallowing sharp objects, biting, inserting sharp objects into one's body cavities, scratching oneself, punching hard objects, and purposefully falling down stairs (Burrows, 1992; Styer, 2006).

There is not a great deal of research on the prevalence of self-mutilation in the adolescent population. The relatively few studies that have been conducted have yielded results ranging from 14 to 39 percent for the general, nonclinical population and 40 to 61 percent in clinical, inpatient samples (cited in Nock & Prinstein, 2005). In some but not all of these studies girls have been found to self-injure more than boys (e.g., Kirkcaldy, Richardson-Vejlgaard, & Siefen, 2009, who also found that middle children were more likely than eldest or youngest children to self-injure). The behavior is so newly widespread in persons without other forms of psychopathology that it is not included in the American Psychological Association's *Diagnostic and Statistical Manual*, although some clinicians are calling for its inclusion in the next edition.

What motivates self-injurious behavior? It is closely linked to adolescent depression (e.g., Briere & Gil, 1998), borderline personality disorder (Sansone, Gaither, & Songer, 2002), suicide attempts (Jacobson & Gould, 2007), and eating disorders (Paul, Schroeter, Dahme, et al., 2002), but clearly many adolescents who have not been diagnosed with full-blown psychological disorders are injuring themselves. Adolescents who have been sexually abused have high rates of self-harm (Zlotnick, Shea,

Pearlstein, et al., 1996). In general, self-harm seems to be a response to high levels of stress and unhappiness. Therefore, any adolescent who is coping with substantial problems—for example, homeless youth (Tyler, Whitbeck, Hoyt, et al., 2003)—are at heightened risk.

Why has this behavior surfaced now? We can only speculate. It might be because body piercing "opened the door" to the practice. We know that it, like suicide, is a copycat phenomenon, spreading once it has been identified in a community or given publicity (Yates, 2004).

Self-mutilation can help an adolescent deal with overwhelming stress in multiple ways (Suyemoto, 1998). First, it can be used to express one's pain in a visible form to oneself and to others. Second, it can be a means of achieving control over emotions that would otherwise be devastating. Nock and Prinstein (2005) found evidence for both of these motivations—cries for help and emotional control—but reported that the majority of the self-injurers they studied did so to "stop feeling bad" or "to become numb." These effects last for at least 24 hours (Kamphuis, Ruyling, & Reijntjes, 2007). Most self-mutilators feel little or no pain when they injure themselves (Zila & Kiselica, 2001) because they have elevated endogenous endorphin levels (Sher & Stanley, 2008).

Fortunately, a variety of therapies have proven effective in helping self-mutilators stop their harmful behavior. Yaryura-Tobias, Neziroglu, and Kaplan (1995), for example, had success with an exposure then response prevention technique. This is an approach most commonly used to treat obsessive-compulsive disorder. Clients are monitored when they desire to injure themselves and are not permitted to do so; eventually, the urge diminishes and the habit is broken. Other forms of behavior modification and cognitive therapy can also be beneficial (reviewed by Zila & Kiselica, 2001). Most therapists use a multipronged approach (Suyemoto & MacDonald, 1995).

IN THEIR OWN WORDS

"I feel out of control. I reach for my car keys, press one deep in the pale flesh of my forearm, and slowly drag it across my skin. As the metal carves through my arm, the tension increases to an almost unbearable level. When I finally pull the key away, I am rushed with a tremendous feeling of relief. My breathing slows and my muscles relax. All the tension I felt before is completely relieved and I sink into an almost catatonic calm.

"I don't do it to mutilate myself; I do it to hurt myself. I think that is the most misunderstood aspect of self-injury. It's not a cry for help; it's not a suicide attempt. It is a way to deal with stress, a coping mechanism no different from drinking or cigarette smoking. It's a way to overwhelm emotional pain with physical pain. The relief is temporary but instant; it pours over you like warm rain and you feel nothing but quiet euphoria. It's a drugless high."

IN THEIR OWN WORDS

"A year and a half ago, a friend of mine killed herself. We had known each other since seventh grade, and she and I became closer during college. Carrie was always a troubled girl, but no one knew the extent of her pain until it was too late. She had always been dramatic and a little eccentric, and people knew she loved attention. About a year before she killed herself, she became strangely morbid. She would talk about what her funeral would be like, who would come, who would be sorry, etc. She also became fairly promiscuous, sleeping with boyfriends of girls she knew casually. When we would be out, she would burn herself with cigarettes. Because her behavior was exhibitory, we all figured she was just doing it for attention.

"Apparently, Carrie had been diagnosed with depression. Little did we know she had stopped taking her medication a week before she killed herself. That week, she prepared herself. She apologized to our friend for not picking her for kickball in fourth grade. The next day, she got up, went for a run with her dog (her favorite thing to do), returned, and hung herself in her barn with her dog's leash.

"Not only was her suicide very sad, but I have realized how selfish it was, too. Not only did she leave behind two younger siblings (one of whom found her), but she left all her friends a mess. Her mother is now a chain smoker and drinks regularly."

Contrary to common opinion, suicide attempts in a great majority of cases are considered in advance and weighed rationally against other alternatives. The attempter may have tried other means: rebellion, running away from home, lying, stealing, or other attention-getting devices. Having tried these methods and failed, the person turns to suicide attempts. Most adolescents who attempt suicide talk about it first. If others are alerted in time, if they pay attention to these developments and take them seriously

suicide gestures suicide attempts that seem destined to fail and that really are cries for help rather than true attempts.

Adolescent suicide is particularly difficult for the family and friends who are left behind. They may suffer from loss and emptiness as well as from feelings of responsibility for not recognizing the problem.

enough to try to remedy the situation, a death may be prevented (Ghang & Jin, 1996).

Survivors

Adolescent suicide is particularly devastating for family and peers who are left behind. Survivors typically experience fear, rage, guilt, and depression, as well as shock, disbelief, and numbness. They feel responsible for not recognizing the signals that might have been given and preventing the suicide, and they feel angry at the victim for deserting them. Feelings of loss and emptiness and a sense of disbelief are often followed by bouts of self-doubt and recrimination. Recovering from the loss may take one to two years, depending on the survivor's personality and the events surrounding the suicide. Intense feelings have to be worked through as survivors come to terms with the loss (Baugher, 1999).

Eating Disorders

Societal stereotypes of physical attractiveness cause most adolescent girls to desire to be slim. In fact, it has become the norm for girls to begin dieting in early adolescence if not before (Tyrka, Graber, & Brooks-Gunn, 2000). Sometimes the desire to be thin is carried to such an extreme that an eating disorder develops. No longer a rarity, eating disorders are the third most common chronic illness among adolescent girls (Rosen, 2003). Two of these disorders are discussed here: anorexia nervosa and bulimia.

Anorexia Nervosa

Anorexia nervosa is a life-threatening emotional disorder characterized by an obsession with food and weight. It is sometimes referred to as the *starvation sickness* or *dieter's disease*. In order to be diagnosed as anorexic, an individual must be at least 15 percent under normal body weight for his or her height and build. In addition, an individual must show an excessive fear of gaining weight and becoming fat; he or she must have a distorted body image such that he or she does not perceive himself or herself as being underweight. Furthermore, a female must experience *amenorrhea*, or the absence of menstrual cycling (American Psychiatric Association, 2000). It is not uncommon for anorexics to be clinically depressed (Kennedy, Kaplan, Garfinkel, et al., 1994) and to exhibit obsessive-compulsive traits (Fisher, Fornari, Waldbaum, et al., 2002). Some anorexics also engage in binging and purging behaviors.

Anorexia is also associated with numerous medical conditions: slow heartbeat, cardiac arrest (potentially a cause of death), low blood pressure, dehydration, hypothermia, electrolyte abnormalities, metabolic changes, constipation, and abdominal distress (Becker, Grinspoon, Klibanski, et al., 1999). Once the illness has progressed, anorexics become thin and emaciated in appearance. They feel cold, even in warm weather. The body grows fine silky hair (lanugo) to conserve body heat. A potassium deficiency may cause malfunction of the kidneys. Researchers have also found brain abnormalities coupled with impaired mental and memory performance in anorexic girls, a result of the malnutrition they suffer (e.g., Seed, Dixon, McClusky, et al., 2000).

Although some anorexics have only one bout with the condition, between 30 and 40 percent relapse (Herzog, Dorer, Keel, et al., 1999). Ultimately, more than 10 percent of anorexics die because of medical problems associated with malnutrition (Reijonen, Pratt, Patel, et al., 2003). Their obsession with dieting is frequently combined with a compulsion to exercise (Davis, 1999). Hunger and fatigue are usually denied, and any attempt to interfere with their eating and exercising regimen is angrily resisted. Anorexics are very difficult to treat (Woodside, 2005).

Anorexia is less common among African American than Caucasian girls, even though African American girls tend to be heavier (Walcott, Pratt, & Patel, 2003). Anorexia is also much less common in males. Those males who do develop the disorder are often athletes, dancers, or models who have reason to control their weight (Rolls, Federoff, & Guthrie, 1991). Wrestlers, body builders, and long-distance runners are especially at risk (Garner, Rosen, & Barry, 1998). Some 90 to 95 percent of anorexics are female, usually between the ages of 12 to 18. The disorder became more common through the 1970s and 1980s, but the prevalence has leveled off at about 0.3 percent in adolescent and young adult females (Hoek, 2006). Although it is most common in middle- and upper-middle class adolescent girls, it has been known to occur among individuals from all economic classes and a wide variety of age groups.

ANSWERS WOULDN'T YOU LIKE TO KNOW . . .

What types of teens are at risk for developing anorexia?

Early adolescent Caucasian girls who are perfectionists and who have controlling, overly protective parents are at the highest risk for developing anorexia.

Much of the recent research into the cause of anorexia has focused on anorexics' relationships with their families. Families with anorexic daughters are often described as noncohesive and unsupportive (Tyrka, Graber, & Brooks-Gunn, 2000). They raise their daughters to be full of guilty feelings (Berghold & Lock, 2002), and mothers transfer their own excessive concerns about weight and attractiveness to their daughters (Hirokane, Tokomura, Nanri, et al., 2005). In other words, girls are more likely to diet if their mothers do as well, and they are more likely to engage in extreme weight-loss measures if their mothers are dissatisfied with their own bodies (Benedikt, Wertheim, & Love, 1998; Hill & Pallin, 1998). Eating disorders have also been linked to sexual abuse (Fornari & Dancyger, 2003).

Some of this research is longitudinal, and so it is possible to say that impaired family relationships are a strong predictor of disordered eating symptoms—stronger even than being overweight (Archibald, Graber, & Brooks-Gunn, 1999). This association between disordered family relationships and anorexia holds true in early adolescence but not in middle and late adolescence (Archibald, Linver, Graber, et al., 2002).

The fact that anorexia nervosa appears at puberty after the development of sexual characteristics suggests that sexual conflict is a central issue in the illness. Apparently, anxiety develops over feminine physiological changes. The girl's developing body demands that she comes to terms with her female sexual identification. She has the task of integrating her new body image with her concept of female sexual and gender roles. If she cannot accept her female sexual identity, she may seek to repress her physical development to a stage of prepubertal development. She then actually distorts her body through extreme weight loss and takes on a slim, masculine appearance. She may become severely emaciated in appearance, removing all outward signs of her secondary sex characteristics. In addition, she stops menstruating. These efforts represent the girl's desperate attempt to halt her sexual development. Instead of progressing forward through adolescence, she regresses to a prepubertal stage of development and delays the maturation process.

Anorexics have a pervasive sense of inadequacy and distorted body images and this often leads to depression. They have low self-esteem (Surgenor, Maguire, Russell, et al., 2007), reflecting negative attitudes about their physical attractiveness (Canals, Carbajo, Fernandez, et al., 1996). Anorexics are often described as compliant, self-doubting, dependent, perfectionistic, and anxious (McVey, Pepler, Davis, et al., 2002). They are not very attuned to their body's internal signals of hunger (Wonderlich, Lilenfeld, Riso, et al., 2005). Adolescents with anorexia nervosa rarely look at themselves and, even when forced to, rarely perceive their body images accurately. They view their bodies with disgust, which is a projection of how they actually feel about themselves.

What are the various forms of treatment for anorexia nervosa? Medical treatment involves monitoring the physical condition of the anorexic and trying to return her weight to the safe range. Behavior modification uses rewards and deprivation, contingent on eating behavior and weight gain. Family therapy seeks to solve underlying family interaction

anorexia nervosa an eating disorder characterized by an obsession with food and with being thin.

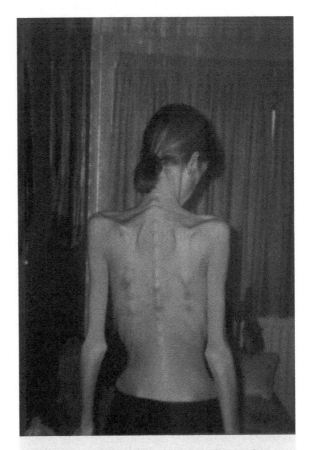

Individuals with anorexia go way beyond becoming slim. They have distorted body images and lose weight to the point that they do considerable damage to their health.

problems and to improve relationships with the anorexic (Dare, Eisler, Russell, et al., 1990). Individual counseling can be used to help the individual resolve her emotional conflicts. One review found that family therapy was most effective overall (Le Grange & Lock, 2005). The goals are to eliminate the anorexic symptoms and to enable the patient to feel and act as an independent person who likes herself, is confident about her capabilities, and is in control of her life. Accomplishing these goals may require lengthy therapy (Lask, Waugh, & Gordo, 1997).

Bulimia

Bulimia is the binge-purge syndrome. The name comes from the Greek *bous limos*, which means "ox hunger" (Ieit, 1985). The first cases of bulimia that appeared in the literature were in connection with anorexia nervosa (Vandereycken, 1994). Originally, bulimia was diagnosed as a subtype of anorexia; however, bulimia is now designated a separate eating disorder (American Psychiatric Association, 2000).

In order to be diagnosed with bulimia, an individual must (1) participate in repeated episodes of binge eating over which he or she has no control; (2) engage in excessive compensatory behaviors to avoid gaining weight, such as fasting, vomiting, and abusing laxatives; and (3) unduly allow his or her weight to influence self-esteem. Moreover, the binging must occur at least twice per week over a period of at least three months (American Psychiatric Association, 2000).

Bulimia is characterized by a compulsive and rapid consumption of large quantities of high-calorie food in a short period of time (Holleran, Pascale, & Fraley, 1988). One study of the frequency and duration of binging episodes among bulimic clients in an outpatient setting revealed an average of 13.7 hours spent in binge eating each week (Mitchell, Pyle, & Eckert, 1981). Binging and purging may occur many times daily. Caloric consumption can range from 1,200 to 11,500 calories per episode, with carbohydrates as the primary food. Many bulimic individuals report losing the ability to perceive a sense of fullness. Episodes usually take place secretly, often in the afternoon or evening and sometimes at night. Induced vomiting is the usual aftermath of binge-eating episodes. Bulimics use laxatives, diuretics, enemas, amphetamines, compulsive exercising, or fasting to offset the huge food intake.

Bulimics are unhappy with the appearance of their bodies and yearn to attain the thin shape glamorized by society (Ruuska, Kaltiala-Heino, Rantanen, et al., 2005). However, they lack control over eating. The bu-

limic feels driven to consume food and, because of a concern about body size, to purge afterward. Binges usually follow periods of stress and are accompanied by anxiety, depressed mood, and self-deprecating thoughts during and after the episode (Davis & Jamieson, 2005; Wegner, Smyth, Crosby, et al., 2002).

Who develops bulimia? It is more common, by far, in girls than boys; only about 10 percent of bulimics are male (Nye & Johnson, 1999). Bulimia tends to develop in middle to late adolescence and lasts into the twenties, which is a somewhat later age range than for anorexia (Reijonen, Pratt, Patel, et al., 2003). Girls from lower-income families are relatively more likely to develop bulimia than girls from upper-income families (Gard & Freeman, 1996).

Bulimics wish to be perfect, yet they have a poor self-image, are shy, and lack assertiveness (Bardone, Vohs, Abramson, et al., 2000). Like anorexics, they are often perfectionistic and unsatisfied with the way they look. They believe themselves to be unattractive (Young, Clopton, & Bleckley, 2004). They feel pressured by others to be thin.

Because of unrealistic standards, compulsive dieting, and the drive for perfection, pressure builds up, which is relieved through lapses of control during binge-purge episodes. This is followed by feelings of shame and guilt, which contribute to a sense of low self-esteem and depression. Bulimics are often difficult to treat because they resist seeking help or sabotage their treatment.

The families of bulimics are somewhat different from those of anorexics. Whereas the families of anorexics tend to be overprotective, repressed, and enmeshed, the families of bulimics are better described as chaotic, stressful, disengaged (Tyrka, Graber, & Brooks-Gunn, 2000) and to exhibit poor communication (Moreno, Selby, Aved, et al., 2000). Even so, the parents of bulimics are typically intrusive about their daughter's weight and appearance (Rorty, Yager, Rossotto, et al., 2000).

Some of the most promising treatment programs involve cognitive-behavioral approaches that help clients identify unrealistic and self-defeating cognitions and assumptions (Phillips, Greydanus, Pratt, et al., 2003). Correcting these irrational beliefs is an essential step toward changing the bulimic's behavior. Family therapy has also been found useful (e.g., Paulson-Karlsson, Engstron, & Nevonen, 2009). Therapists have found that antidepressants can reduce binging and purging behaviors (Freeman, 1998).

Many individuals find it difficult to distinguish between anorexia nervosa and bulimia. To help clarify the differences, Table 3.1 provides a point-by-point comparison of these two disorders.

TABLE 3.1 COMPARISON OF ANOREXIA NERVOSA AND BULIMIA

CHARACTERISTIC	ANOREXIA NERVOSA	BULIMIA
Weight	Emaciated	Near normal
Prevalence	1% of adolescent girls	2% to 3% of adolescent girls
Age of Onset	Teens	Late teens, early twenties
Race/Ethnicity	Primarily Caucasian	No racial/ethnic differences
Eating Behavior	Barely eats	Periodically consumes large quantities and then purges
Personality	Dependent, anxious, perfectionistic	Moody, impulsive, unable to tolerate frustration
Emotional State	Denial	Guilt and shame
Desire to Change	No desire to change	Great desire to change
Behavior Motivation	Desire for control and rejection of femininity	Desire to be perceived as attractive
Family Background	Enmeshed and repressed	Conflicted and stress filled
Treatment Success	Very difficult to treat	Somewhat easier to treat

Juvenile Delinquency

The term *juvenile delinquency* refers to the violation of the law by a juvenile, which in most states means anyone younger than 18. The legal term **juvenile delinquent** was established for young lawbreakers so that they could avoid the disgrace and stigma of being classified in legal records as criminals and to separate underage people and treat them differently from adult criminals. Most are tried in juvenile courts where the intent is to rehabilitate them.

A young person may be labeled a *delinquent* for breaking any of a number of laws, ranging from murder to truancy from school. Violations of laws that apply only to minors—for instance, underage drinking, curfew violations, and truancy—are called **status crimes.** Because laws are inconsistent, a particular action may be considered delinquent in one community but not in another. Furthermore, law enforcement officials differ in the method and the extent to which they enforce the law. In some communities, the police may simply talk to adolescents who are accused of minor crimes; in others, the police refer youths to their parents; and in still others, they may arrest them and refer them to juvenile courts. As with adults, many crimes adolescents commit are never discovered or, if discovered, are not reported or prosecuted. Most statistics, therefore, understate the extent of juvenile crime (Flannery, Hussey, Biebelhausen, et al., 2003).

Incidence of Delinquency

According to the Office of Juvenile Justice and Delinquency Prevention, in 2006, juveniles were responsible for 15 percent of all violent crime arrests and 29 percent of all property crime arrests in the United States (Snyder & Sickmund, 2006). As Figure 3.3 indicates, juveniles contribute most to the total incidence rates of arson, vandalism, and motor vehicle theft; they are less involved in murder and aggravated assault. The rate at which juveniles commit violent crimes remained fairly constant between the mid-1970s and the mid-1980s but then rose sharply between 1985 and 1993. Since then, the juvenile violent crime rate has dropped and is, in fact, now lower than it has been since 1980 (see Figure 3.4, p. 105).

This trend also holds true for the juvenile homicide rate in particular. As a result of the increasing societal attention paid to killings by youths, there is the widespread misconception that the adolescent homicide rate has continued to rise. Instead, the juvenile homicide rate has dropped dramatically since

bulimia an eating disorder characterized by binge-eating episodes and purging.

juvenile delinquent a juvenile who violates the law.

status crimes violations of laws that apply only to minors, such as underage drinking, violating curfews, and truancy.

Many youths engage in status crimes, such as underage drinking.

FIGURE 3.3 ARRESTS INVOLVING JUVENILES BY TYPE OF CRIME: 2006

Source: Data from Snyder & Sickmund (2006).

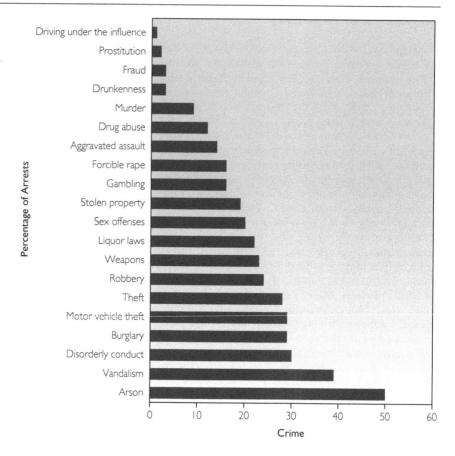

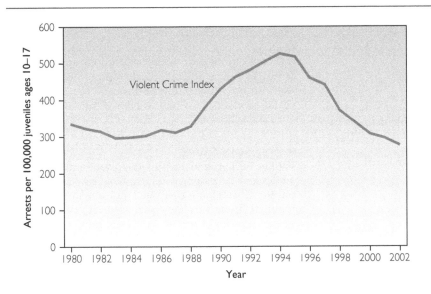

FIGURE 3.4 JUVENILE CRIME
RATE: 1980–2002

Source: Data from Snyder (2004).

it peaked in 1993. Most of this drop has resulted from a decrease in the use of firearms. Juvenile murders committed with other types of weapons have remained nearly constant, unfortunately. Still, the 2003 juvenile murder rate was at a 30-year low (Snyder & Sickmund, 2006).

African American youths are more likely to commit murder than their White counterparts. The vast majority of adolescents who murder kill someone of their own race or ethnic group, which means African American adolescents are also far more likely to be the victims of homicide than White youths. Adolescent males are considerably more likely than females to murder and to be murdered (Fox & Zawitz, 2006).

Teenagers are two and a half times more likely than adults to be the victims of violent crimes. Teens are more likely to be the victims of property crimes, too. Crimes with juvenile victims are committed both by adults and by other teenagers. In fact, only about one in four juvenile homicide victims is killed by another adolescent (Synder & Sickmund, 2006).

Currently, girls account for about 25 percent of all juvenile arrests. However, for many years, the girls' arrest rate has been climbing faster than that for boys, and so the gap continues to narrow. In addition, boys who are involved in the juvenile justice system are likely to be referred for violations of the law, whereas girls are more likely to be referred for truancy, runaway behaviors, and social/personal problems. Boys tend to engage in a broad range of serious delinquent behaviors, whereas the behaviors of girls tend to be more narrowly constrained (Lahey, Van Hulle, Waldman, et al., 2006). For example, girls are more likely to restrict assaults to family

members than to acquaintances or strangers; the reverse is true for boys (Roe-Sepowitz, 2009).

Adolescents are more likely to commit crimes and to be victimized when away from school than when at school. On school days, most crimes involving juveniles occur during the hours after school lets out, between 3 P.M. and 6 P.M. On weekends and holidays, most juvenile crime occurs between 8 P.M. and 10 P.M. This suggests that providing after-school programs would reduce crime more than enforcing curfews (Snyder & Sickmund, 2006).

Causes of Delinquency

Antisocial behavior usually begins early in life (Tolan, Guerra, & Kendall, 1995). Much research has been dedicated to trying to determine its cause. In general, the causes of delinquency may be grouped into three major categories:

- *Environmental causes* include elements in the adolescent's neighborhood and community.
- *Interpersonal causes* refer to the influences of family, friends, siblings, and peers.
- *Personal causes* refer to personality traits and biological predispositions to antisocial behavior found within the delinquent.

ANSWERS WOULDN'T YOU LIKE TO KNOW . . .

Is juvenile crime increasing or decreasing?

Juvenile crime has been decreasing since the mid-1990s. This is true for both violent and nonviolent offenses.

Also, as Bronfenbrenner (1979) explained in his ecological analysis of behavior, these three types of factors interact with one another in synergistic ways; they are not independent.

Environmental Causes

The most important environmental factors that have been investigated in relation to juvenile delinquency are the following:

- Poverty
- Living in a high-crime area
- The presence of gangs
- The availability of drugs
- Having substandard schools
- Living in a fragmented, noncohesive neighborhood
- Exposure to media violence
- Rapid social change

Many of these factors, of course, typically co-occur. That is why youths raised in impoverished areas are more likely to commit delinquent acts and to participate in violent offenses than middle-class youths (Farrington, 2009). Keep in mind, though, that some middle-class adolescents do get involved in crime, and that many poor teenagers do not.

What distinguishes those poverty-stricken teens who become delinquents from those who do not? This is where the interrelations among the different types of risk factors come into play. Chung and his colleagues (Chung, Hawkins, Gilchrist, et al., 2002) tried to answer this question by looking broadly at the lives of poor children and seeing who later became delinquent. They found, for example, that adolescents who avoided becoming delinquent had different temperaments, were closer to their parents, were more closely monitored by their parents, were less involved with antisocial peers, did better in school, and lived in neighborhoods in which drugs were not as ubiquitous than did those adolescents who began to break the law. Furthermore, the circumstances of those youths who were delinquent only for a short time differed along many of the same dimensions, to a lesser degree, than those youth who were chronically delinquent. In a similar study, Fergusson, Swin-Campbell, and Horwood (2004) found that only those lower-income youth who were physically disciplined by their parents, lacked maternal care, frequently missed school, and associated with delinquent peers got into trouble themselves.

Other research has shown that some school environments foster antisocial attitudes and behaviors. In particular, *disorganized schools*—in which rules are only sporadically enforced, there are problems with overcrowding, and after-school programs are unavailable—are the ones most prone to promote delinquency (Flannery, Hussey, Biebelhausen, et al., 2003).

Today's adolescents are also living in a period of rapid cultural change, which tends to foster delinquency. Values that once were commonly accepted are now questioned. Social institutions such as the family that once offered security and protection may exert an upsetting influence instead. The specter of social, economic, and political unrest stimulates anxieties and rebellion.

Interpersonal Causes

Family background has an important influence on adolescent development and adjustment and hence on social conduct. Disrupted homes and strained family relationships have been associated with delinquent behavior. Lack of family cohesion and angry family relationships are particularly important correlates of delinquency (Bischof, Stiph, & Whitney, 1995). Parents who model aggression or who reinforce the violent behavior that they observe in their children are most likely to have delinquent children (Patterson, DeBarysne, & Ramsey, 1989). Poor parental monitoring and inconsistent discipline are also associated with children's aggression and antisocial behavior (Herrenkohl, Hawkins, Chun, et al., 2001). Parents who physically abuse their children or their spouses model aggression most acutely, and so it is little wonder that their children are often aggressive (Flannery, Huff, & Manos, 1998).

One of the strongest predictors of criminal behavior by a teenager is that a close relative has also been involved in criminal activity (e.g., Odgers, Milne, Caspi, et al., 2007). Farrington and his colleagues (2001) provide six mechanisms for this association: (1) intergenerational continuities in exposure to the risk factors of poverty, toxic neighborhoods, and so on; (2) self-selection, so that antisocial individuals choose other antisocial individuals as friends; (3) shared genetic tendencies; (4) modeling and social learning within the home; (5) poor parenting practices by the antisocial parent; (6) labeling and bias by the authorities against known criminal families.

An adolescent's peers also have a large influence upon whether he or she becomes involved in delinquency. Adolescents become delinquent in part because they are socialized into it, both intentionally and unintentionally, by peers. For example, Coie and Miller-Johnson (2001) found that boys who were both aggressive and rejected by their peers were the ones who were most likely to become delinquent at a later age. Youths who have a high degree of peer orientation—with the wrong peers—are also more likely to have a high level of delinquency involvement (Elliott & Menard, 1996). For example, teens who begin to associate with antisocial youth—who join a gang, for example—show increased amounts of antisocial activity (Gatti, Tremblay, Vitraro, et al., 2005). Even so,

Involvement in school and community organizations, such as the teen club shown here, is often a deterrent to delinquent activity.

close association with deviant peers usually occurs only after there are both established negative family interactions and a history of rejection by mainstream peers. In other words, peers can exacerbate and encourage delinquency in youths who are already unhappy and poorly adjusted.

Personal Causes

There have also been efforts to determine whether certain personality factors predispose adolescents to delinquency. No single personality type can be associated with delinquency, but it is known that those who become delinquent are more likely to be socially assertive, defiant, ambivalent to authority, resentful, hostile, and impulsive or lacking in self-control (Caspi, Lynan, Moffitt, et al., 1993; Feldman & Weinberger, 1994). Self-control tends to be associated with an entire constellation of personality and behavioral traits, each of which by itself is negatively related to delinquency. Namely, these traits are (1) ability to delay gratification, (2) persistence, (3) caution, (4) ability to set long-term goals, (5) awareness of the importance of academic skills, and (6) sensitivity to others' feelings (Gottfredson & Hirshi, 1990).

Some delinquents consistently exhibit low self-esteem and a negative self-image. Others maintain high self-esteem through denial of their problems and by failure to admit the incongruity between their behaviors and their self-perceptions. Such adolescents become adept at denial. They refuse to accept responsibility for their actions and continually blame other people or circumstances for getting them into trouble. In many cases, delinquents have a psychological disorder such as ODD, conduct disorder, or ADHD (see the Research Highlight box).

Research has studied the extent to which delinquency is related to alcohol or drug use (Watts & Wright, 1990). Several studies have found that drinking is strongly associated with serious delinquency, especially when other factors are present, such as previous arrests, association with criminals or drug users, or heroin use by the adolescent. Furthermore, there is a strong relationship between adolescents who are raised by substance-abusing parents and juvenile delinquency. Adolescents from substance-abusing homes have been found to suffer from low self-esteem, depression, anger, and a variety of acting-out behaviors (McGaha & Leoni, 1995).

School performance is also an important factor in delinquency (Maguin & Loeber, 1996). In particular, a lack of school success—poor grades, classroom misconduct, and an inability to adjust to the school program and to get along with administrators, teachers, and parents—is associated with delinquency (Huizinga & Jakob-Chien, 1998). Delinquent youths have also been found to score lower on social cognitive skills than nondelinquent youths (Edwards, 1996).

Delinquents experience greater conflict in all relationships, which reduces the quality and stability of friendships. Lochman and Dodge (1994), for example, found that aggressive adolescents are more likely than nonaggressive adolescents to perceive others as being hostile. If a person interprets others' behavior as threatening, then he or she will more likely behave aggressively.

Although most delinquency is believed to have environmental causes, in some cases, organic or biological factors may be directly or indirectly influential. It has been found, for example, that some juvenile delinquents show evidence of a maturational lag in the development of the frontal lobe system of the brain (Chretien & Persinger, 2000). It is not that their cognition is impaired; rather, these juveniles cannot act on the basis of the knowledge they have or think through the consequences of their actions.

Other researchers have emphasized the role of biological influences in delinquency, as well. There is some evidence to show that tendencies toward delinquency may be inherited, although it is often difficult to determine whether family influences are rooted in the environment in which a child is raised or their genetic inheritance (Rowe, Rodgers, & Meseck-Bushey, 1992). It is true that certain personality characteristics, such as temperament, are genetically influenced, so that a child may have a predisposition to behave poorly. If the parents do not know how to cope, psychological disturbance in the adolescent may result.

High levels of testosterone and low levels of the neurotransmitter serotonin are also associated with aggressive behavior (Flannery, Hussey, Biebelhausen, et al., 2003). Furthermore, some research has linked these chemical imbalances with criminal activity. These chemicals likely work in conjunction with environmental and situational inputs; for example, having a low level of serotonin might make one less prone to feel happy and content, opening the door for destructive behavior.

Juvenile Gangs

During the 1980s and 1990s, youth gangs again surfaced as a major crime problem in the United States. News stories about violent crimes committed by youth gang members—crimes that often seemed to involve random victims—appeared frequently in the mass media. What does research say about youth gang crime today?

According to the most recent National Youth Gang Survey (Egley & O'Donnell, 2009), there are about 27,000 youth gangs in the United States. This figure is lower than in the mid-1990s, but higher than earlier this century: gang membership, which had been falling has been rising for the past seven or eight years. About 25 percent more police jurisdictions now report gang problems than in 2002. Gangs are most common in large cities; suburbs are the next most likely location, followed by small cities. Rural areas are least likely to have a gang problem (National Youth Gang Center, 2009).

A large body of research has characterized the typical gang member as a lower-income, minority male adolescent who does not get along with his family (Duke, Martinez, & Stein, 1997). In 2006, about 45 percent of all gang members were Latino and one-third were African American (National Youth Gang Center, 2009). Although the number of gang members who are female has held constant at about 6 to 7 percent for quite some time, more gangs have female members and there are more all-female gangs. Because gang

RESEARCH HIGHLIGHT CONDUCT DISORDER, ODD, AND ADHD

Conduct disorder is the psychological disorder most associated with juvenile delinquency. It can be described as a chronic behavior pattern in which the individual violates age-appropriate societal norms and tramples on others' rights. These long-standing disruptive behaviors impair the adolescent's ability to function in social, occupational, and academic settings.

In order to be diagnosed with conduct disorder, an individual must exhibit at least three different disruptive symptoms. The *Diagnostic and Statistical Manual of Mental Disorders* (4th ed., revised.) clusters these symptoms in four broad groups:

1. Aggression toward people or animals (e.g., hitting or threatening classmates, throwing rocks at others' pets)
2. Destruction of property (e.g., vandalism, arson, graffiti)
3. Theft and/or deceitfulness (e.g., lying, conning, cheating, stealing)
4. Serious rule violations (e.g., repeated truancy, staying out all night) (American Psychiatric Association, 2000)

These symptoms may appear prior to adolescence or after it has begun.

Adolescents with conduct disorder often have poor social skills and don't know how to get along with others. They aren't good at handling frustration and can explode with anger. They are likely to begin using drugs at an early age and to be sexually precocious (Altepeter & Korger, 1999).

Conduct disorder is similar to both **oppositional defiant disorder (ODD)** and **attention-deficit hyperactivity disorder (ADHD)** in that persons with these disorders behave disruptively. But conduct disorder is different from both, as well. Persons with ODD are less likely to actually hurt others than are those with conduct disorder. Individuals with ODD argue and get angry. They blame others and may be defensive or disobedient, especially when interacting with authority figures. Youths with ODD go out of their way to annoy their teachers and parents but are less likely to pester peers. Individuals with ADHD often exhibit low frustration tolerance and poor impulse control, and so they may verbally or physically attack others when aroused. These antisocial behaviors, however, are more by-products of their other symptoms than symptoms in themselves. Still, meta-analyses indicate a strong linkage between delinquency and ADHD (e.g., Pratt, Cullen, Blevins, et al., 2002).

Inner-city males comprise the largest group of street gang members. They join gangs for a variety of emotional and social needs, including companionship, protection, and excitement.

membership is satisfying and profitable, many members do not want to quit as they get older: more than 60 percent of gang members are 18 or older.

Why do some individuals join gangs whereas others with similar backgrounds reject them? One theory says that a self-selection process is involved, such that youths who are already dysfunctional join gangs. A competing theory claims that normal adolescents join gangs and are then coerced into deviant behavior by their gang mates. These theories are not mutually exclusive, and both postulates appear correct: adolescents who elect to join gangs are troubled to start with, but their level of delinquency increases once they join a gang. In particular, adolescents who join gangs often have poor relationships with their parents and unresolved ethnic identities (Duke, Martinez, & Stein, 1997). They engage in antisocial activities to raise money, to gain status and approval, to bond with their gang peers, and to protect themselves.

It is generally accepted that gang membership is a primarily male activity. It appears that when girls do join gangs, they are kept more-or-less on the periphery; one role they do play is to serve as sex partners for the male gang members. Some self-report data, though, place the number of female gang members much higher

(as high as 38 percent) (Snyder & Sickmund, 2006) than the usually cited government statistics. Regardless, the conclusion remains that female gang members are less likely than male members to engage in violent activities and to be arrested, but they are as likely to engage in criminal activity (Egley, Howell, & Major, 2006). In addition, girls tend both to join and leave gangs at younger ages than boys. Finally, girls, even more than boys, join gangs to fulfill a need for connections and relationships.

Youths who are members of gangs are more likely than nonmembers to steal, to commit assaults, to carry weapons, and to kill. Gang members are also more likely to be involved in an early pregnancy, to use drugs, to be assaulted, to be injured in a drive-by shooting, and to be killed at an early age (Flannery, Huff, & Manos, 1998). Thus, for some youths, joining a gang is a last-ditch effort to improve their lives that backfires.

The Juvenile Justice System

Each state determines its own process for handling juvenile delinquents. Although this process varies among states, each system consists of three distinct

---

ANSWERS WOULDN'T YOU LIKE TO KNOW . . .

How involved are girls in juvenile gangs?

As many as one-third of gangs contain female members, but fewer than 10% of gang members are female.

---

conduct disorder a psychological order typified by aggressive, hurtful, deceitful behavior.

oppositional defiant disorder (ODD) a psychological disorder that causes a person to get angry and argue, blame and annoy others, and disobey authority figures.

attention-deficit hyperactivity disorder (ADHD) a behavioral disorder characterized by impulsivity, an inability to pay attention, and an inability to sit still.

ANSWERS WOULDN'T YOU LIKE TO KNOW . . .

What usually happens to teens caught breaking the law?

When the police catch a teenager doing something illegal, they usually let him or her go after delivering a warning or contacting his or her parents or school officials. The teen is not usually sent through the criminal justice system. If a teen is arrested, tried, and found guilty by the courts, the most likely outcome is probation.

---

entities: the police, the juvenile court, and the correctional system.

The Police

The first contact any adolescent has with the juvenile justice system is the local police department. Charged with maintaining and enforcing the law, the police screen cases that may go before the courts. When offenses are discovered, the police may take any one of several actions: (1) ignore the offenses; (2) let the juvenile go with a warning; (3) report the problem to parents; (4) refer the case to the school, a social welfare agency, clinic, or counseling or guidance center; (5) take the juvenile into custody for questioning, to be held or reprimanded by a juvenile officer; or (6) after investigation, arrest the juvenile and turn the matter over to juvenile court. If arrested and awaiting trial, the juvenile may be released with or without bail or kept in a special detention center.

One problem is that in the beginning of the process, police exercise a good deal of discretion; this opens the door to bias and inconsistency. Some police officers enforce the law differentially. An individual officer may arrest adolescents who come from the "wrong section" of town or have the wrong color skin but may release adolescents who come from well-to-do families or are neatly dressed. Some officers are far harder on juveniles than are other officers. One of the reasons adolescent offenders become bitter toward the police is because of perceived unfair and discriminatory treatment or harassment.

Many communities hire juvenile officers who are specialists in dealing with youths. Such officers go far beyond law enforcement functions and strive to assist adolescents and their families in solving problems. Some large cities have separate juvenile bureaus with four basic functions:

1. To protect juveniles

2. To prevent juvenile delinquency

3. To investigate cases of juveniles who are delinquents or involved as accessories by association with adult criminals

4. To dispose of juvenile cases

Police in many communities now go far beyond law enforcement, from sponsoring boys' and girls' clubs to offering drug education programs and safety education in local schools.

RESEARCH HIGHLIGHT THE CASE THAT CHANGED JUVENILE COURT

Prior to the 1900s, the legal system treated juveniles as adults. If arrested, they appeared in adult courts; if sentenced, they went to adult prisons. Reformers working at the turn of the twentieth century were effective in changing this policy. They argued that minors could and should be rehabilitated rather than punished. The courts, they claimed, should assume the role of *parens patriae* and act in the best interests of the child. Although this was a noble intent, in practice it meant that juveniles were treated inconsistently and that their constitutional rights were often violated.

The case that changed the system involved a 15-year-old boy named Gerald Gault. In 1964, Gerald was arrested and detained by the police after a neighbor complained that he had made obscene phone calls to her. The police failed to notify Gerald's parents of his arrest. Neither Gerald's father nor the complainant was present at the hearing.

Witnesses were neither sworn in nor cross-examined, and no official record was kept of the proceedings. The judge ordered that Gerald be sent to a juvenile detention center until his twenty-first birthday, a six-year sentence. In contrast, the maximum penalty that an adult could have received for the same offense would have been a $50 fine and two months in jail.

The case was appealed in the Arizona Supreme Court, but the appeal was denied. When presented to the U.S. Supreme Court in 1967, the Court found in Gerald's favor in a narrow 5 to 4 ruling. It decreed that minors are entitled to due process as outlined in the Bill of Rights and the Fourteenth Amendment. Since that time, even though juvenile court remains separate from adult court, minors are guaranteed the same judicial rights as adults; for example, they have the right to an attorney, they may cross-examine witnesses, and they cannot be made to incriminate themselves.

The Juvenile Court

Even if a juvenile's case is remanded to juvenile court, there are several possible outcomes. First, the case may be dismissed (e.g., for lack of evidence). Second, the case can be handled informally in private hearings. These private hearings often occur in the judge's chambers. The judge can choose to let the juvenile go without penalty or can assign specific conditions that the juvenile must follow for a set period of time. These conditions often include obeying a curfew, regularly attending school, meeting with a counselor, and victim restitution. If the juvenile agrees to the conditions and follows them, then all is well. If he or she does not, the case is reopened and the third option, a formal hearing in juvenile court, is invoked. (Of course, some cases immediately are assigned a formal hearing.) The best juvenile court systems hire judges or magistrates with special qualifications for juvenile court work, who understand not only the law but also child psychology and social problems.

A fourth option exists in many states as well: the juvenile might be transferred to adult criminal court. This usually occurs only if the crime was especially violent or if the juvenile was a repeat offender.

The Correctional System

The majority of juvenile offenders brought to court, especially those charged for the first time, are placed on probation, given suspended sentences, and/or ordered to get help from the proper medical, psychological, or social service agency. The purpose of the court is not just to punish but also to ensure proper treatment and rehabilitation of the delinquent. Thus, the judge often must make thoughtful decisions regarding the best treatment.

The backbone of the correctional procedure is the probation system, whereby the juvenile is placed under the care of a probation officer to whom she or he must report and who strives to regulate and guide his or her conduct. About two-thirds of convicted delinquents are placed on probation (Snyder & Sickmund, 2006).

Probation based entirely on threat of punishment is poor rehabilitation, and so most juveniles placed on probation are also required to attend counseling sessions and make restitution to their victims. Studies show that juvenile offenders who are placed on probation have lower rearrest rates and generally better records than those detained in juvenile facilities. However, this occurs in part because the most serious offenders—those least likely to be rehabilitated—are not placed on probation in the first place.

Most juvenile correction systems include detention centers. Many of these are reception and diagnostic centers that place juveniles under temporary restraint while awaiting a hearing. If hearings have already been held, the individuals are placed in the center for further diagnosis and evaluation before more permanent action is taken. About one-tenth of adolescents in detention centers are not delinquents (Snyder & Sickmund, 2006). They are juveniles in need of supervision (JINS) who are wards of the court because their parents cannot, will not, or should not care for them. Some of the parents are ill or deceased; others have neglected, rejected, or abused the juveniles to the point that they have been taken out of the home. Some adolescents in detention facilities have run away from home. Many are awaiting disposition by the court. Critics charge that overcrowded detention centers are no place for these juveniles. They have done nothing wrong—indeed, they have been victimized—and they are mixed in with juveniles who may have committed serious assaults or even homicides. Similarly, one can question the wisdom of mixing the comparatively innocuous status offenders with more seriously criminal peers, as the potential for intimidation, harassment, and even inappropriate modeling seems substantial.

If a juvenile is sentenced to be held in a facility, there are a number of options. These include detention centers, long-term secure training schools, group homes, shelters, boots camps, and wilderness/ranch camps. About 30 percent of incarcerated juveniles are held in private, rather than public, facilities. The majority of incarcerated youths are in either detention centers or secure training schools (Snyder & Sickmund, 2006).

The system has been improved greatly by the use of *token economies*, which place the emphasis on a 24-hour positive learning environment (Miller, Cosgrove, & Doke, 1990). In this system, students earn points for good behavior, with points convertible to money that can be used to purchase goods or privileges. Money can be spent for room rental, for fines for misconduct, in the commissary or snack bar, or for recreation. Students earn points for academic accomplishments and schoolwork, for proper social behavior, for doing chores or other jobs, or for social development. Under this system, adolescents make great gains in academic achievement; on-the-job training; or eliminating assaultive, disruptive, and antisocial behavior.

One of the criticisms of these correctional institutions is that once the juveniles are released to the community, they often come under the same influences and face many of the same problems that led to detention in the first place. One suggestion has been to use more halfway houses and group homes where youths may live, going from there to school or to work. In this way, some control can be maintained over the

parens patriae the philosophy that the juvenile court is to act in the best interests of the child.

Of all the options available in the juvenile correction system, sending a youth to an adult prison is the worst way to rehabilitate him or her.

adolescents until they have learned self-direction. One of the most important needs is to prepare youths for employment after discharge.

Only a small number of juvenile delinquents end up serving time in adult prisons. In 2003, 1 percent of persons admitted to adult prisons were younger than 18 (Snyder & Sickmund, 2006). This percentage climbed greatly in the 1990s, peaking in 1996, and has consistently dropped since then. The vast majority of adolescents incarcerated in adult facilities have committed serious person offenses, such as assault or homicide.

It is good that this number is so small, since sending adolescents to adult prisons is the worst way to rehabilitate them. A percentage of inmates of a prison population are violent individuals who prefer antisocial behavior, have no regard for the interests of others, and show little or no remorse. They contrast with adolescents, who are young and still developing. In spite of this, the average sentence for a juvenile is greater than for an adult who has committed the same crime (Cullen & Wright, 2002).

Once in prison, youths have no adequate adult male or female role models with whom they can have significant relationships. Furthermore, once they have a prison record, their chances of finding a useful life are jeopardized. They learn that fear, bribery, cheating, and violence are acceptable ways of dealing with problems. In addition, many prisoners are harassed and bullied by fellow prisoners, who may use them in any number of ways, includ-

ing for homosexual activities. If adolescents were not antagonistic toward authority and the system on arrival in prison, they soon become so.

Counseling and therapy, both individually and in groups, are important parts of any comprehensive program of treatment and correction of juvenile offenders. Individual therapy on a one-to-one basis is time consuming, with too few professionals and too many delinquents, but it can be effective. Some therapists believe that group therapy reaches a juvenile sooner than individual therapy because the delinquent feels less anxious and defensive in the group situation. Group therapy is sometimes offered to both juvenile offenders and their parents, in which case it becomes similar to other types of family therapy. Work with parents is especially important in correcting family situations that contribute to the delinquency in the first place.

The Restorative Justice Movement

A new approach to juvenile justice has gained momentum during the past 20 years: the **restorative justice movement.** This approach tries to balance the needs of the victim (for reparation and confrontation), the community at large (for security and protection), and the juvenile perpetrator (to learn skills so he or she has alternatives to crime). To be sure, offenders are held accountable for their crimes: they are expected to understand the harm they have caused, to accept responsibility for that harm, and to repair the damage they have caused. In theory, by meeting with their victim and making restitution and by having opportunities for education, counseling, and community service, offenders become not only more morally mature but gain a feeling of integration into the community and the desire and skills to become productive members of that community (Okimoto, Wenzel, & Feather, 2009).

The restorative justice approach is not without its critics (see Cullen & Wright, 2002). For example, it is unclear how such an approach could be implemented in the case of a serious crime, such as rape or murder, in which the victim might be understandably unwilling to confront the offender. Also, what happens if an offender promises to cooperate and then does not? What if he or she goes through the program and then commits additional offenses? To date, research on the effectiveness of the restorative justice approach has

been mixed. More time will be needed to tell whether restorative justice is more effective than other rehabilitative approaches.

ANSWERS WOULDN'T YOU LIKE TO KNOW . . .
What can be done to reduce the rate of juvenile delinquency?
Programs that build life skills, create hope for the future, provide mentors, and instill prosocial values can and do reduce juvenile delinquency.

restorative justice movement an approach to juvenile justice that addresses the needs of the victim, the community, and the perpetrator; it focuses on restitution for the victim and personal development for the offender.

SUMMARY

1. Alienated adolescents feel estranged from family, friends, and school. They turn away from the mainstream youth and adult society and express their feelings through various types of acting-out or self-destructive behavior, including running away, depression, suicide, eating disorders, and juvenile delinquency.

2. Adolescents run away from home for a number of reasons. Most runaways come from dysfunctional families. Runaways may also have problems with delinquency, academics, and peer relationships.

3. About half of all runaways, called *transient runaways,* are gone only for a night or two. *Intent runaways* are generally more serious about leaving home and are gone for longer periods of time.

4. About half of intent runaways did not leave home voluntarily; rather, they were thrown out by their parents because of poverty, their own misbehavior, or family disintegration.

5. The consequences of running away may be disastrous. Runaways are likely to be victimized by others. They must often resort to drug dealing, theft, and prostitution to earn money for food and shelter. Because of unsafe sex practices and intravenous drug use, many are at risk for HIV and AIDS.

6. Assistance to runaway youths is inadequate. More emergency shelters, more comprehensive services, stable residential placements, and transitional programs for older adolescents are all needed.

7. Adolescent homelessness is a worldwide, rather than a national, problem.

8. Between 15 and 20 percent of adolescents will experience major clinical depression before they are out of their teens. Adolescent girls are twice as likely to suffer from depression as adolescent boys, and girls' depression is more often triggered by social factors.

Teenagers who have suffered a personal loss or who are having trouble at school are at heightened risk for depression.

9. Suicide is the third leading cause of death among adolescents (after accidents and homicide). Girls are more likely to attempt suicide than boys, but boys are more likely to succeed because they use more violent means.

10. Most adolescents who commit suicide are clinically depressed or are substance abusers.

11. Adolescents who commit suicide often have dysfunctional family backgrounds. In addition, these youths often lack impulse control. Because of the extra stresses they experience, gay and lesbian teens are especially likely to attempt or commit suicide.

12. Adolescent suicide is especially hard on survivors, who suffer fear, rage, guilt, and depression.

13. Anorexia nervosa is a life-threatening emotional disorder characterized by an obsession with food and weight. Symptoms include constant preoccupation with food and dieting; body image disturbances; excessive weight loss; amenorrhea; hyperactivity; moodiness; isolation; and strong feelings of insecurity, helplessness, depression, and loneliness. Anorexia is also associated with numerous medical conditions.

14. Anorexia is found primarily in teenage girls and usually appears at puberty. Anorexics often have disturbed relationships with their parents.

15. Bulimia is a binge-purge syndrome characterized by compulsive and rapid consumption of large quantities of high-calorie food, followed by efforts to purge the food.

16. Bulimics are unhappy with the appearance of their bodies, yet they are impulsive, lack control over eating, and are anxious and depressed with low self-es-

teem. Bulimics usually come from families that are characterized by strife and conflict.

17. Juvenile delinquency is the violation of the law by anyone under legal age. From the mid-1980s to the mid-1990s, the juvenile crime rate rose sharply. It has since been declining. Boys are more likely to commit offenses than girls, but girls' rates are rising faster than boys' rates.

18. The causes of delinquency may be grouped into three major categories: environmental, interpersonal, and personal.

19. Environmental factors leading to delinquency include poverty, living in a gang-infested neighborhood, and attending substandard schools. Not all delinquents are poor, however.

20. Interpersonal factors leading to delinquency include coming from an abusive, dysfunctional family and associating with deviant peers.

21. Personal factors leading to delinquency include poor self-control, psychological disorders, substance abuse, poor academic performance, and low social-cognitive skills.

22. Individuals may be predisposed to antisocial behavior because of maturation lags in the brain, genetic endowment, and biochemical imbalances.

23. Adolescents often organize themselves into juvenile gangs for protection, companionship, excitement, or status. Such gangs are a problem because they force members to engage in antisocial and illegal acts that they would not participate in if acting on their own. Dysfunctional youths are more prone to join gangs than psychologically healthy youths; after they join, youths are more likely to engage in deviant activities than they were before.

24. The juvenile justice system consists of the police, the juvenile court, and the correctional system (including the probation system, detention centers, training schools, ranches, forestry camps, farms, halfway houses, group homes, treatment centers, and prisons).

25. The newest approach to juvenile rehabilitation is the restorative justice approach. This model addresses the needs of the victim, the offender, and the community and incorporates both rehabilitation and punishment.

KEY TERMS

anorexia nervosa 100

attention-deficit hyperactivity disorder (ADHD) 108

bulimia 102

conduct disorder 108

depression 93

juvenile delinquent 103

oppositional defiant disorder (ODD) 108

parens patriae 110

restorative justice movement 112

status crimes 103

suicide gestures 98

survival sex 93

throwaways 92

THOUGHT QUESTIONS

Personal Reflection

1. Do you know an adolescent who ran away from home? What were the circumstances?
2. Have you or someone you've been close to battled with depression? Was there a specific cause? How were you or how was he or she helped?
3. Have you ever known anyone who had an eating disorder? Describe the person and explain why you think he or she became that way.
4. Did you commit any status or criminal offenses when you were younger? Why? Were you ever caught? What happened, and how did the consequences affect you?
5. Have you known a juvenile offender who was sent to a training school or correctional institution who became a productive, law-abiding citizen? What factors made the difference?

Group Discussion

6. Should runaways be forced to return home? When should they? When should they not?
7. To what do you attribute gender differences in depression rates? Can anything be done about it?
8. Have you known an adolescent who committed suicide? What were the circumstances? What crisis intervention steps did your school take (if any)?
9. How do you account for the fact that the percentage of those younger than 18 who are arrested is decreasing?
10. Why do far greater number of males than females become delinquent? What factors may be exerting an influence?
11. Why do some adolescents who are brought up in crime-prone neighborhoods not become delinquent?
12. What should parents do if their adolescent is running around with a group whose members are known to be delinquent?
13. How can society decrease the appeal of joining a gang? How can we discourage youths from doing so?
14. What is your opinion of the juvenile justice system? How could it be improved? What do you think is needed to reform known juvenile offenders?

Debate Questions

15. Parents whose children run away from home for more than a day or two should be required to receive counseling.
16. Most teens occasionally have suicidal thoughts. They shouldn't be taken seriously.
17. The media contributes greatly to eating disorders and should be held responsible for them to some degree.
18. Schools should take an active role in preventing delinquency.
19. Delinquents who have been diagnosed with conduct disorder should be treated differently by the system than delinquents who do not have this disorder.

SUGGESTED READING

Al-Rawashdeh, A. (2009). *Runaway Youth: Psychosocial Characteristics*. Saarbrücken, Germany: VDM.

Bartol, C. R., and Bartol, A. M. (2008). *Juvenile Delinquency and Antisocial Behavior: A Developmental Perspective*. Upper Saddle River, NJ: Prentice Hall.

Berman, A. L., Jobes, D. A., and Silverman, M. M. (2005). *Adolescent Suicide: Assessment and Intervention*. Washington, DC: American Psychological Association.

Heibrun, K., Goldstein, N. E. S., and Redding, R. E. (Eds.). (2005). *Juvenile Delinquency: Prevention, Assessment, and Intervention*. New York: Oxford University Press.

Howell, J. C. (2003). *Preventing and Reducing Juvenile Delinquency: A Comprehensive Framework*. Thousand Oaks, CA: Sage.

Jackson, R. K., and McBride, W. D. (2000). *Understanding Street Gangs*. Belmont, CA: Wadsworth.

Kalodner, C. R. (2003). *Too Fat or Too Thin? A Reference Guide to Eating Disorders*. Westport, CT: Greenwood.

Koplewicz, H. (2003). *More Than Moody: Recognizing and Treating Adolescent Depression*. New York: Perigee.

Nixon, M. K., & Heath, N. L. (Eds.). (2009). *Self-injury in Youth: The Essential Guide to Assessment and Intervention*. New York: Routledge.

Noel-Hoeksema, S., and Hilt, L. M. (Eds.). (2008). *Handbook of Depression in Adolescents*. New York: Routledge.

USEFUL WEB SITES

Anorexia Nervosa and Related Eating Disorders (AN-RED)
www.anred.com

This site, which is especially clearly written, contains information on the three most well-known eating disorders (anorexia, bulimia, and obesity) as well as information on less common disorders.

National Center for Missing and Exploited Children
http://missingkids.org

The site of this private, nonprofit organization has separate information sections for professionals and parents. It details the steps to take to report a missing adolescent and what to do if someone you love is missing. It also has an FAQs page and a newsroom.

National Eating Disorder Association (NEDA)
www.edap.org/p.asp?webpage_10=294

Click on the button at the top of the page, labeled "Eating Disorder Information." This site is especially useful for those interested in information about eating disorders in males and body image.

National Strategy for Suicide Prevention
www.mentalhealth.org/suicideprevention/default.asp

This site, administered by the U.S. Department of Health and Human Services, contains facts, information about prevention programs, databases, and a newsroom.

Office of Juvenile Justice and Delinquency Prevention
www.ojjdp.ncjrs.org

This federal agency has an extensive Web site filed with the most current facts, statistics, and reports available on all aspects of juvenile delinquency.

chapter four
LEARNER DIFFERENCES AND LEARNING NEEDS

▶ **TEACHERS' CASEBOOK:** Including Every Student

It is a new school year and your district has had a change in policy. "Special Education" programs have been discontinued and ALL students will now be included in general education classrooms full time. You knew that you were going to have students with a wide range of abilities, social skills, and motivation for learning in your classroom, but now you also have a student with severe asthma, a fairly high functioning student with Asperser's syndrome, a student with severe learning disabilities, and two students who are on medication for ADHD. It is not clear what resources will be available to you, but even so, you want to face this challenge with confidence and a sense of efficacy for teaching all students.

CRITICAL THINKING

- How will you design a standards-based curriculum that will allow all of the students to learn to their fullest potential and demonstrate proficiency toward the standards?

- What can you do to address the specific problems of your students who have been identified with special needs?

- How will you remain confident in you new situation?

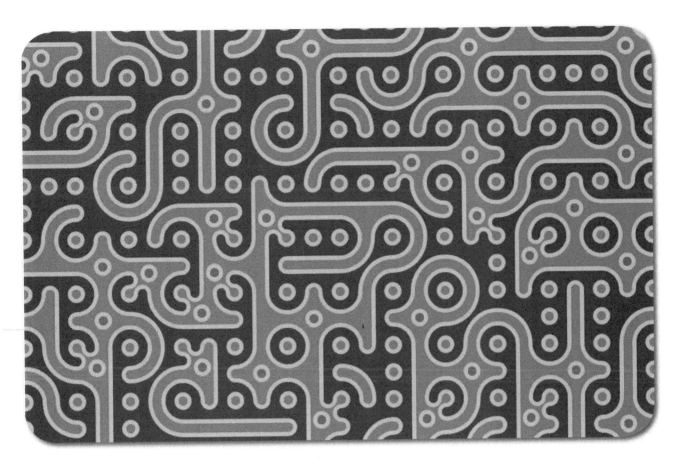

OVERVIEW AND OBJECTIVES

To answer the critical thinking questions, you need an understanding of individual differences. So far, we have talked little about individuals. We have discussed principles of development that apply to everyone—stages, processes, conflicts, and tasks. Our development as human beings is similar in many ways, but not in every way. Even among members of the same family, there are marked contrasts in appearance, interests, abilities, and temperament, and these differences have important implications for teaching. We will spend some time analyzing the concepts of intelligence and learning styles because these terms are so often misunderstood. You probably will have at least one student with special needs in your class, whatever grade you teach, so in this chapter we also explore both common and less frequently occurring learning problems that students may have. As we discuss each problem area, we will consider how a teacher might recognize problems, seek help, and plan instruction, including using the approach of response to intervention. By the time you have completed this chapter, you should be able to:

Objective 4.1: Describe current hierarchical theories and multiple theories of intelligence.

Objective 4.2: Explain how intelligence is measured, and discuss what these measurements tell teachers.

Objective 4.3: Discuss the values and limitations of considering students' learning styles.

Objective 4.4: Discuss the implications of the IDEA and Section 504 protections for contemporary education.

Objective 4.5: Understand the special educational needs of students with learning challenges.

Objective 4.6: Recognize the special educational needs of students who are gifted and talented.

INTELLIGENCE

Because the concept of intelligence is so important, so controversial, and so often misunderstood in education, we will spend quite a few pages discussing it. But before we begin, let's examine the practice of labeling people based on differences such as intelligence, ability, or disability.

Language and Labels

Every child is a distinctive collection of talents, abilities, and limitations. But some students also have learning disabilities, communication disorders, emotional or behavioral disorders, intellectual disabilities, physical disabilities, impaired vision or difficulties hearing, autism spectrum disorders, traumatic brain injury, or some combination of these challenges. Others have remarkable gifts and talents. Even though we will use terms like these throughout the chapter, a caution is in order: *Labeling students is a controversial issue.*

A label does not tell which methods to use with individual students. For example, few specific "treatments" automatically follow from a "diagnosis" of behavioral disorder; many different teaching strategies and materials are appropriate. Further, the labels can become self-fulfilling prophecies. Everyone—teachers, parents, classmates, and even the students themselves—may see a label as a stigma that cannot be changed. Finally, labels are mistaken for explanations, as in, "Santiago gets into fights because he has a behavior disorder." "How do you know he has a behavior disorder?" "Because he gets into fights." (Friend, 2011).

On the other hand, some educators argue that for younger students, at least, being labeled as "special needs" protects the child. For example, if classmates know a student has intellectual disabilities (once called *mental retardation*), they will be more willing to accept his or her behaviors. Of course, diagnostic labels still open doors to some programs, useful information, adaptive technology and equipment, or financial assistance. Labels probably both stigmatize and help students.

DISABILITIES AND HANDICAPS. A **disability** is just what the word implies—an inability to do something specific such as pronounce words or see or walk. A **handicap** is a disadvantage in certain situations. Some disabilities lead to handicaps, but not in all contexts. For example, being blind (a visual disability) is a handicap if you want to drive a car, but not when you are composing music or talking on the telephone. Stephen Hawking, the greatest living physicist, has Lou Gehrig's disease and no longer can walk or talk. He once said that he is lucky that he became a theoretical physicist "because it is all in the mind. So my disability has not been a serious handicap." It is important that we do not create *handicaps* for people by the way we react to their *disabilities*. Some educators have suggested that we drop the word *handicap* altogether because the source of the word is demeaning. *Handicap* came from the phrase "cap-in-hand," used to describe people with disabilities who once were forced to beg just to survive (Hardman, Drew, & Egan, 2005).

We can think of all human characteristics as being on a continuum, for instance, from very acute hearing to complete deafness. We all fall somewhere on that continuum, and our position on the continuum changes over our lifetimes. As we age, for example, there are likely to be changes in hearing, vision, and even some aspects of intellectual ability, as you will see later in this chapter.

Disability The inability to do something specific such as walk or hear.

Handicap A disadvantage in a particular situation, sometimes caused by a disability.

When speaking about a person with a disability, it is important that we avoid the language of pity, as in "confined to a wheelchair" or "victim of AIDS." Wheelchairs are not confining. They allow people to get around. Using "victim of" or "suffering with" makes the person seem powerless. On their resources Web site, the United Spinal Association offers a free pdf booklet with many ideas about disability. Every teacher should read it. See Figure 4.1 for an example.

Another way of showing respect to individuals with disabilities is to use "person-first" language, discussed next.

PERSON-FIRST LANGUAGE. Because everyone has a range of abilities, it makes sense to avoid labels such as "emotionally disturbed student" or "at-risk student." Describing a complex person with one or two words implies that the condition labeled is the most important aspect of the person. Actually, the individual has many characteristics and abilities, and to focus on the disability is to misrepresent the individual. An alternative is "person-first" language or speaking of "students with a behavior disorder" or "students placed at risk." Here, the emphasis is on the students first.

Students with learning disabilities	NOT	Learning disabled students
Students receiving special education	NOT	Special education students
A person with epilepsy	NOT	An epileptic
A child with a physical disability	NOT	A crippled child
Children diagnosed with autism	NOT	Autistic children or autistics

POSSIBLE BIASES IN THE APPLICATION OF LABELS. Even though there are many good tests and careful procedures for identifying students with disabilities and using labels properly, racial and ethnic minority students are overrepresented in the disability categories and underrepresented in gifted programs. For example, based on their actual

---

FIGURE 4.1

DISABILITY ETIQUETTE

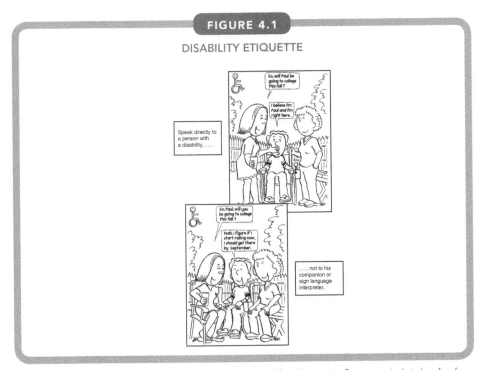

Source: Reprinted from "Disability Etiquette" © Permission granted by United Spinal Association. Go to www.unitedspinal.org for a free download of the full publication. Illustrations by Yvette Silver.

LABELS MAY PROMOTE FALSE STEREOTYPES When labels take precedence over individual characteristics, the labels themselves constitute a handicap. Stereotypes about people who use wheelchairs might interfere with recognition of this young girl's other characteristics and her individuality.

numbers in schools, African American students are about twice as likely to be identified as having a mental health condition and three times as likely to be identified as having an intellectual disability. And these students are more likely than White or Asian students to be placed outside of the general education system for most of their school day. The opposite is true for Latina/o and Asian students; they are less likely to be diagnosed in almost all categories except hearing impairments. Gifted programs have only about 8% each of African American and Latina/o students, even though these students comprise about 13% and 20% of the school population, respectively (U.S. Department of Education, 2007).

For almost four decades, educators have struggled to understand the causes of these over- and under-representations. Explanations include the higher poverty rates among African American and Latina/o families, which lead to poorer prenatal care, nutrition, and health care; systematic biases in teachers' attitudes, curriculum, instruction, and the referral process itself; and teachers' lack of preparation for working effectively with ethnic minority students (Friend, 2011). To deal with the referral problem, educators have recommended gathering more information about a student before a formal referral is made. How long has the student been in the United States? What about proficiency with English? Are there unusual stressors such as being homeless? Does the curriculum build on the student's funds of cultural knowledge (Chapter 5)? Is the classroom culturally compatible (Chapter 6) and engaging (Chapter 9)? Is the teacher knowledgeable about and respectful of the student's culture? Can the student's abilities be assessed through alternative approaches such as creativity tests and portfolios or performances (Chapter 12)? Having more knowledge about the student and his or her circumstances outside of school should help teachers make better decisions about what programs are appropriate (Gonzales, Brusca-Vega, & Yawkey, 1997; National Alliance of Black School Educators, 2002).

Intelligence is widely used in placement decisions and as a label in life in general. Let us begin with a basic question...

What Does Intelligence Mean?

- -

STOP & THINK Who was the most intelligent person in your high school? Write down a name and the first 4 or 5 words that come to mind when you see that person in your mind's eye. What made you pick this individual? •

- -

The idea that people vary in what we call **intelligence** has been with us for a long time. Plato discussed similar variations over 2,000 years ago. Most early theories about the nature of intelligence involved one or more of the following three themes: (1) the capacity to learn; (2) the total knowledge a person has acquired; and (3) the ability to adapt successfully to new situations and to the environment in general. A recent definition captures these elements and stresses higher-order thinking: "the ability to reason deductively or inductively, think abstractly, use analogies, synthesize information, and apply it to new domains" (Kanazawa, 2010, p. 281).

INTELLIGENCE: ONE ABILITY OR MANY? There are moderate to high correlations among scores on *all* mental tests. In fact, this consistent finding "is arguably both the best established and the most striking phenomenon in the psychological study of intelligence" (van der Mass et al., 2006, p. 855). Because of these persistent intercorrelations, some psychologists believe intelligence is a basic ability that affects performance on all cognitively oriented tasks, from solving mathematical problems to analyzing poetry to taking history essay examinations. What could explain these results? Charles Spearman (1927) suggested mental energy, which he called g, was used to perform any mental test. Spearman added that each test also requires some specific abilities as well—so ability to do any mental task is based on g + task-specific abilities. Today, psychologists generally agree that we can mathematically compute a common factor (g) across cognitive tests, but this computed factor is simply an indication or measure of **general intelligence**—it is not general intelligence itself (Kanazawa, 2010). Just having an overall mathematical indicator of intelligence isn't much help in understanding specific human abilities, so the notion of g does not have much explanatory power (Blair, 2006).

Raymond Cattell and John Horn's theory of fluid and crystallized intelligence is more helpful in providing explanations (Cattell, 1963; Horn, 1998; Kanazawa, 2010). **Fluid intelligence** is the mental efficiency and reasoning ability included in Kanazawa's definition of intelligence, quoted above. The neurophysiological underpinnings of fluid intelligence may be related to changes in brain volume, myelinization (coating of neural fibers that makes processing faster), the density of dopamine receptors, or processing abilities in the prefrontal lobe of the brain such as selective attention and especially *working memory* (Waterhouse, 2006), an aspect of brain functioning we will explore in Chapter 8. This aspect of intelligence increases until late adolescence (about age 22) because it is grounded in brain development, and then declines gradually with age. Fluid intelligence is sensitive to injuries and diseases.

In contrast, **crystallized intelligence** is the ability to apply the problem-solving methods appropriate in your cultural context—the "application to new domains" part of Kanazawa's definition of intelligence. Crystallized intelligence can increase throughout the life span because it includes learned skills and knowledge such as reading, facts, and how to hail a cab, make a quilt, or design a unit on symbolism in poetry. By investing fluid intelligence in solving problems, we develop our crystallized intelligence, but many tasks in life such as mathematical reasoning draw on both fluid and crystallized intelligence (Ferrer & McArdle, 2004; Finkel, Reynolds, McArdle, Gatz, & Pederson, 2003; Hunt, 2000).

The most widely accepted psychometric view today is that intelligence, like self-concept, has many facets and is a hierarchy of abilities, with general ability at the top and

Intelligence Ability or abilities to acquire and use knowledge for solving problems and adapting to the world.

General intelligence (g) A general factor in cognitive ability that is related in varying degrees to performance on all mental tests.

Fluid intelligence Mental efficiency, nonverbal abilities grounded in brain development.

Crystallized intelligence Ability to apply culturally approved problem-solving methods.

more specific abilities at lower levels of the hierarchy (Carroll, 1997; Sternberg, 2000). John Carroll (1997) identifies one general ability, a few broad abilities (such as fluid and crystallized abilities, learning and memory, visual and auditory perception, and processing speed), and at least 70 specific abilities such as language development, memory span, and simple reaction time. General ability may be related to the maturation and functioning of the frontal lobe of the brain, while specific abilities may be connected to other parts of the brain (Byrnes & Fox, 1998).

Multiple Intelligences

Connect and Extend to PRAXIS II™

Multiple Intelligences (I, B1)
Many teachers erroneously assume that they must address each of the 8 intelligences in each lesson they design. What are some of the realistic implications of the theory for classroom instruction?

While Howard Gardner was a developmental psychologist doing research with two very different groups—artistically gifted students at Harvard's Project Zero and patients with brain injuries at Boston's Veterans Administration Medical Center—he started thinking about a new theory of intelligence. Time and time again at the VA Medical Center, Gardner observed brain-injured patients who were lost spatially, but could do all kinds of verbal tasks, and other patients who had the opposite set of abilities and problems. He also worked with young children at Project Zero who could draw expertly but not craft a good sentence, and vice versa. Gardner concluded that there are several separate mental abilities, and developed his now-famous **theory of multiple intelligences** that describes at least eight separate intelligences (1983, 2003, 2009).

WHAT ARE THESE INTELLIGENCES? The eight intelligences in multiple intelligence (MI) theory are linguistic (verbal), musical, spatial, logical-mathematical, bodily-kinesthetic (movement), interpersonal (understanding others), intrapersonal (understanding self), and naturalist (observing and understanding natural and human-made patterns and systems). Gardner stresses that there may be more kinds of intelligence—eight is not a magic number. Recently, he has speculated that there may be a spiritual intelligence and an existential intelligence—the abilities to contemplate big questions about the meaning of life (Gardner, 2009). As Gardner witnessed firsthand in his early research with veterans and students, individuals may excel in one of these eight areas, but have no remarkable abilities, or may even have problems, in the other seven. Table 4.1 summarizes these eight intelligences.

Gardner believes that intelligence has a biological base. An intelligence is a "biopsychological potential to process information in certain ways in order to solve problems or create products that are valued in at least one culture or community" (Gardner, 2009, p. 5). Varying cultures and eras of history place different values on the eight intelligences. A naturalist intelligence is critical in farming cultures, whereas verbal and mathematical intelligences are important in technological cultures. In fact, Gardner suggests what industrialized cultures usually label as "intelligence" is just a combination of linguistic and logical mathematical skills, especially those taught in modern, secular schools (2009).

CRITICS OF MI THEORY. Gardner's MI theory has not received wide acceptance in the scientific community, even though many educators have embraced it. Lynn Waterhouse (2006) concluded that there have been no published studies that validate multiple intelligences theory. The eight intelligences are not independent; there are correlations among the abilities. In fact, logical-mathematical and spatial intelligences are highly correlated (Sattler, 2001). So, these "separate abilities" may not be so separate after all. Evidence linking musical and spatial abilities has prompted Gardner to consider that there may be connections among the intelligences (Gardner, 1998). In addition, some critics suggest that several intelligences are really talents (bodily-kinesthetic skill, musical ability) or personality traits (interpersonal ability). Other "intelligences" are not new at all. Many researchers have identified verbal and spatial abilities as elements of intelligence. Daniel Willingham (2004) has been even more blunt. "In the end, Gardner's theory is not that helpful. For scientists the theory is almost certainly incorrect. For educators, the daring applications forwarded by others in Gardner's name (and of which he disapproves) are unlikely to help students" (p. 24).

Theory of multiple intelligences In Gardner's theory of intelligence, a person's eight separate abilities: logical-mathematical, linguistic, musical, spatial, bodily-kinesthetic, interpersonal, intrapersonal, and naturalist.

TABLE 4.1 • **Eight Intelligences**

Howard Gardner's theory of multiple intelligences suggests that there are eight kinds of human abilities. An individual might have strengths or weaknesses in one or several areas.

INTELLIGENCE	END STATES	CORE COMPONENTS
Logical-mathematical	Scientist, Mathematician	Sensitivity to, and capacity to discern, logical or numerical patterns; ability to handle long chains of reasoning.
Linguistic	Poet, Journalist	Sensitivity to the sounds, rhythms, and meanings of words; sensitivity to the different functions of language.
Musical	Composer, Violinist	Abilities to produce and appreciate rhythm, pitch, and timbre; appreciation of the forms of musical expressiveness.
Spatial	Navigator, Sculptor	Capacities to perceive the visual-spatial world accurately and to perform transformations on one's initial perceptions.
Bodily-kinesthetic	Dancer, Athlete	Abilities to control one's body movements and to handle objects skillfully.
Interpersonal	Therapist, Salesman	Capacities to discern and respond appropriately to the moods, temperaments, motivations, and desires of other people.
Intrapersonal	Person with detailed, accurate self-knowledge	Access to one's own feelings and the ability to discriminate among them and draw on them to guide behavior; knowledge of one's own strengths, weaknesses, desires, and intelligence.
Naturalist	Botanist, Farmer, Hunter	Abilities to recognize plants and animals, to make distinctions in the natural world, to understand systems and define categories (perhaps even categories of intelligence).

Source: From "Multiple Intelligences Go to School," by H. Gardner and T. Hatch, Educational Researcher, 18(8), p. 6. Copyright © 1989 by the American Educational Research Association. Reproduced by permission of the publisher. Also Educational Information and Transformation, edited by J. Kane. Published by Prentice Hall. Copyright © 2002 by Prentice Hall. Reprinted by permission of Pearson Education, Inc., Upper Saddle River, NJ.

So there is not yet strong research evidence that adopting a multiple intelligences approach will enhance learning. In one of the few carefully designed evaluations, Callahan, Tomlinson, and Plucker (1997) found no significant gains in either achievement or self-concept for students who participated in START, a multiple intelligences approach to identifying and promoting talent in students who were at risk of failing.

GARDNER RESPONDS. In response to these criticisms, defenders of MI theory say that the critics have a very narrow view of intelligence and research about intelligence. Gardner based his theory on a set of criteria that integrated a wide range of research in psychology:

- Potential isolation by brain damage
- The existence of prodigies and other exceptional individuals who are experts in some areas and average or below in others
- An identifiable core operation or set of operations
- A distinctive developmental trajectory, culminating in expert performances

- An evolutionary history and evolutionary plausibility
- Support from experimental psychological tasks
- Evidence from psychometric findings
- Susceptibility to encoding in a symbol system (Gardner, 2009, p. 5)

Gardner's supporters believe newer research methods that look at dynamic models and study intelligence in cultural contexts will support MI theory (Chen, 2004; Gardner & Moran, 2006). In addition, Gardner (2003, 2009) also has responded to critics by identifying a number of myths, misconceptions, and misuses related to multiple intelligences theory and schooling. For example, he stresses that an intelligence is not the same as a sensory system—there is no "auditory intelligence" or "visual intelligence." Intelligences are not the same as learning styles. (Gardner doesn't believe that people actually have consistent learning styles.) Another misconception is that multiple intelligences theory disproves the idea of general intelligence. Gardner does not deny the existence of a general ability, but he does question how useful general intelligence is as an explanation for human achievements. Stay tuned for more developments.

MULTIPLE INTELLIGENCES GO TO SCHOOL. First let's consider a few misuses of MI theory in schools. Gardner particularly deplored an educational project in Australia that proclaimed different ethnic groups had certain specific intelligences but lacked others. Gardner went on television in Australia to call this program what it really was— "pseudoscience" and "veiled racism" (2009, p. 7). The project was cancelled. Another misuse is that some teachers embrace a simplistic version of Gardner's theory. They include every "intelligence" in every lesson, no matter how inappropriate.

A better way to use the theory is to focus on six Entry Points—narrative, logical-quantitative, aesthetic, experiential, interpersonal, and existential/foundational—in designing a curriculum (Gardner, 1991). For example, to teach about evolution, teachers might use the Entry Points as follows (Kornhaber, Fierros, & Veenema, 2004):

Narrative: Provide rich stories about Darwin's voyage to the Galapagos Islands or traditional folktales about the different plants and animals.

Logical-quantitative: Examine Darwin's attempts to map the distributions of the species or pose logical problems about what would happen to the ecosystem if one species disappeared.

Aesthetic: Examine Darwin's drawings of the species he studied on the Galapagos Islands.

Experiential: Do laboratory activities such as breeding fruit flies or completing virtual simulations of evolutionary processes.

Interpersonal: Form research teams or hold debates.

Existential/foundational: Consider questions about why species die out or what the purpose is for variation in species.

Multiple Intelligences: Lessons for Teachers

After 20 years of work on his multiple intelligences theory, Gardner believes two lessons are most important for teachers (2009). First, teachers should take the individual differences among students seriously and differentiate their instruction to connect with each student. Much of this book will help you do just that. Second, any discipline, skill, or concept should be taught in several appropriate ways (but not eight ways every time). Anything worth knowing has different representations and multiple connections to various ways of thinking. And understandings can be expressed in words, images, movements, tables, charts, numbers, equations, poetry, and on and on. These two big ideas should *guide* educational interventions, but Gardner stresses that his theory is not itself an educational intervention. The MI theory expands our thinking about abilities and avenues for teaching, but learning is still hard work, even if there are multiple paths to knowledge.

Intelligence as a Process

As you can see, the theories of Spearman, Cattell and Horn, Carroll, and Gardner tend to describe how individuals differ in the *content* of intelligence—different abilities. Work in cognitive psychology has emphasized instead the *information processing* that is common to all people. How do humans gather and use information to solve problems and behave intelligently? New views of intelligence are emerging from this work. The debates in the 2006 issue of *Behavioral and Brain Sciences* emphasized working memory capacity, the abilities to focus attention and inhibit impulses, and emotional self-regulation as aspects of fluid cognitive abilities.

Robert Sternberg's (1985, 2004; Stemler, Sternberg, Grigorenko, Jarvin, & Sharpes, 2009) **triarchic theory of successful intelligence** is a cognitive process approach to understanding intelligence. Sternberg uses the term *successful intelligence* to stress that intelligence is more than what is tested by mental abilities measures: Intelligence is about life success based on your own definition of success in your cultural context.

WHAT'S SMART? There has been considerable controversy over the meaning of intelligence, whether there is more than one way to be "smart," and how we should measure intelligence.

Sternberg believes the processes involved in intelligence are universal for humans. These processes are defined in terms of components—elementary information processes that are classified by the functions they serve and by how general they are. There are at least three different functions served. The first function—higher-order planning, strategy selection, and monitoring—is performed by *metacomponents* (sometimes called *executive processes*). A second function—implementing the strategies selected—is handled by *performance components*, such as taking notes to focus attention in class. The third function—gaining new knowledge—is performed by *knowledge-acquisition components*, such as separating relevant from irrelevant information as you try to understand a new concept. Some processes are specific; that is, they are necessary for only one kind of task, such as solving analogies. Other processes, such as monitoring progress and switching strategies, are very general and may be necessary in almost every cognitive task. This may help to explain the persistent correlations among all types of mental tests. People who are effective in selecting good problem-solving strategies, monitoring progress, and moving to a new approach when the first one fails are more likely to be successful on all types of tests.

Applying *metacomponents*, *performance components*, and *knowledge-acquisition components* allows individuals to solve problems in different situations and to develop three kinds of successful intelligence: analytic, creative, and practical. *Analytic intelligence* involves applying these components to situations with relatively familiar problems. *Creative intelligence* is necessary to cope successfully with new experiences in two ways: (1) using **insight**, or the ability to deal effectively with novel situations and find new solutions, and (2) using **automaticity**, the ability to become efficient and automatic in thinking and problem solving—the ability to quickly make the new solutions part of your cognitive tool kit, so to speak.

The third part of the triarchic theory, *practical intelligence*, highlights the importance of choosing an environment in which you can succeed, adapting to that environment, and reshaping it if necessary. People who are successful often seek situations in which their abilities will be valued, then work hard to capitalize on those abilities and compensate for any weaknesses. Thus, intelligence in this third sense involves practical matters

Triarchic theory of successful intelligence A three-part description of the mental abilities (thinking processes, coping with new experiences, and adapting to context) that lead to more or less intelligent behavior.

Insight The ability to deal effectively with novel situations.

Automaticity The result of learning to perform a behavior or thinking process so thoroughly that the performance is automatic and does not require effort.

TAKING AN INDIVIDUAL IQ TEST. This girl is completing a task like one she would encounter on the WISC-IV intelligence test. This assessment is conducted by a highly trained adult and takes an hour or two to complete, depending on how many subtests are given. Individual intelligence tests are more accurate and reliable than group tests.

such as career choice or social skills. In a field study in Voronezh, Russia, Elena Grigorenko and Robert Sternberg (2001) found that adults with higher practical and analytical intelligence coped better both mentally and physically with the stresses caused by rapid changes in that part of the world.

In recent years, Sternberg has added the concept of "wisdom" to his explanation of successful intelligence to create the *WICS theory* (Wisdom, Intelligence, Creativity Synthesized). According to WICS theory, the goal of education is to help citizens use: "(a) creativity to generate new ideas and problems as well as possible solutions to the problems, (b) analytical intelligence to evaluate the quality of these solutions, (c) practical intelligence to implement decisions and persuade others of their value, and (d) wisdom to ensure that these decisions help achieve a common good over the long and short terms" (Grigorenko et al., 2009, p. 965).

Even though there are many theories of intelligence, teachers, students, and parents are most familiar with intelligence as a number or score on an IQ test.

Measuring Intelligence

STOP & THINK How are an inch and a mile alike? What does *obstreperous* mean? Repeat these numbers backwards: 8 5 7 3 0 2 1 9 7. In what two ways is a lamp better than a candle? •

These items, taken from Sattler (2001, p. 222), are similar to the verbal questions from a common individual intelligence test for children. Another part of the test asks the child to copy a design using blocks, find the missing part of a picture, or select from several pictures the two that go together. Even though psychologists do not agree about what intelligence is, they do agree that intelligence, as measured by standardized tests, is related to learning in school. Why is this so? It has to do in part with the way intelligence tests were first developed.

BINET'S DILEMMA. In 1904, Alfred Binet was confronted with the following problem by the minister of public instruction in Paris: How can students who will need special instruction and extra help be identified early in their school careers, before they fail in regular classes? Binet was also a political activist and very concerned about the rights of children. He believed that having an objective measure of learning ability could protect students living in poverty who might be forced to leave school because they were the victims of discrimination and assumed to be slow learners.

Binet and his collaborator Theodore Simon wanted to measure not merely school achievement, but also the intellectual skills students needed to do well in school. After trying many different tests and eliminating items that did not discriminate between successful and unsuccessful students, Binet and Simon finally identified 58 tests, several for each age group from 3 to 13. Binet's tests allowed the examiner to determine a **mental age** for a child. A child who succeeded on the items passed by most 6-year-olds, for example, was considered to have a mental age of 6, whether the child was actually 4, 5, 6, 7, or 8 years old.

Mental age In intelligence testing, a performance that represents average abilities for that age group.

GUIDELINES

Interpreting IQ Scores

Check to see if the score is based on an individual or a group test. Be wary of group test scores.
Examples

1. Individual tests include the Wechsler Scales (WPPSI–III, WISC-IV, WAIS-IV), the Stanford-Binet, the McCarthy Scales of Children's Abilities, the Woodcock-Johnson Psycho-Educational Battery, the Naglieri Nonverbal Ability Test—Individual, and the Kaufman Assessment Battery for Children.

2. Group tests include the Otis-Lennon School Abilities Tests, Slosson Intelligence Test, Raven Progressive Matrices, Naglieri Nonverbal Ability Test—Multiform, Differential Abilities Scales, and Wide Range Intelligence Test.

Remember that IQ tests are only estimates of general aptitude for learning.
Examples

1. Ignore small differences in scores among students.

2. Bear in mind that even an individual student's scores may change over time for many reasons, including measurement error.

3. Be aware that a total score is usually an average of scores on several kinds of questions. A score in the middle or average range may mean that the student performed at the average on every kind of question or that the student did quite well in some areas (for example, on verbal tasks) and rather poorly in other areas (for example, on quantitative tasks).

Remember that IQ scores reflect a student's past experiences and learning.
Examples

1. Consider these scores to be predictors of school abilities, not measures of innate intellectual abilities.

2. If a student is doing well in your class, do not change your opinion or lower your expectations just because one score seems low.

3. Be wary of IQ scores for minority students and for students whose first language was not English. Even scores on "culture-free" tests are lower for students placed at risk.

4. Remember that both adaptive skills and scores on IQ tests are used to determine intellectual abilities and disabilities.

For more about interpreting IQ scores, see
http://www.wilderdom.com/personality/L2-1UnderstandingIQ.html

---

The concept of **intelligence quotient**, or **IQ**, was added after Binet's test was brought to the United States and revised at Stanford University to give us the Stanford-Binet test. An IQ score was computed by comparing the mental-age score to the person's actual chronological age. The formula was

$$\text{Intelligence Quotient} = \text{Mental Age/Chronological Age} \times 100$$

The early Stanford-Binet test has been revised five times, most recently in 2003 (Roid, 2003). The practice of computing a mental age has proved to be problematic because IQ scores calculated on the basis of mental age do not have the same meaning as children get older. To cope with this problem, the concept of deviation IQ was introduced. The **deviation IQ** score is a number that tells exactly how much above or below the average a person scored on the test, compared to others in the same age group, as you will see in the next section.

WHAT DOES AN IQ SCORE MEAN? Most intelligence tests are designed so that they have certain statistical characteristics. For example, the average score is 100; 50% of the people from the general population who take the tests will score 100 or below, and 50% will score above 100. About 68% of the general population will earn IQ scores between 85 and 115. Only about 16% will receive scores below 85, and only 16% will score above 115. Note, however, that these figures hold true for White, native-born Americans whose first language is Standard English. Whether IQ tests should even be used with ethnic minority-group students is hotly debated.

GROUP VERSUS INDIVIDUAL IQ TESTS. The Stanford-Binet is an individual intelligence test. It has to be administered to one student at a time by a trained psychologist and it takes about two hours. Most of the questions are asked orally and do not require reading or writing. A student usually pays closer attention and is more motivated to do well when working directly with an adult. The *Guidelines* will help you interpret IQ scores realistically.

Connect and Extend to PRAXIS II™

Intelligence Testing (II, C1,4)
The public often misunderstands intelligence testing. Be prepared to respond to questions about the appropriate uses of intelligence tests. What are some inappropriate uses of these tests?

Intelligence quotient (IQ) Score comparing mental and chronological ages.

Deviation IQ Score based on a statistical comparison of an individual's performance with the average performance of others in that age group.

Psychologists also have developed group tests that can be given to whole classes or schools. Compared to an individual test, a group test is much less likely to yield an accurate picture of any one person's abilities. When students take tests in a group, they may do poorly because they do not understand the instructions, because they have trouble reading, because their pencils break or they lose their place on the answer sheet, because other students distract them, or because the answer format confuses them (Sattler, 2001). As a teacher, you should be very wary of IQ scores based on group tests.

THE FLYNN EFFECT: ARE WE GETTING SMARTER? Ever since IQ tests were introduced in the early 1900s, scores in 20 different industrialized countries and in some more traditional cultures have been rising (Daley, Whaley, Sigman, Espinosa, & Neumann, 2003). In fact, in a generation, the average score goes up about 18 points on standardized IQ tests—maybe you really are smarter than your parents! This is called the **Flynn effect** after James Flynn, a political scientist who documented the phenomenon. Some explanations include better nutrition and medical care for children and parents, increasing complexity in the environment that stimulates thinking, smaller families who give more attention to their children, increased literacy of parents, more and better schooling, and better preparation for taking tests. One result of the Flynn effect is that the norms used to determine scores (you will read more about norms in Chapter 12) have to be continually revised. In other words, to keep a score of 100 as the average, the test questions have to be made more difficult. This increasing difficulty has implications for any program that uses IQ scores as part of its entrance requirements. For example, some "average" students of the previous generation might be identified today as having intellectual disabilities because the test questions are harder (Kanaya, Scullin, & Ceci, 2003).

INTELLIGENCE AND ACHIEVEMENT. Scoring higher on IQ tests is related to school achievement for children in all ethnic groups. But standard IQ tests measure only analytic IQ, not practical or creative IQs. Elena Grigorenko and her colleagues (2009) used the usual standardized test scores and GPA to predict middle-school students' achievement in high school, but also included tests of students' abilities to manage their own learning and motivation, along with measures of practical and creative intelligence. Using this broader picture of students' abilities, the researchers were able to make better predictions, not only of achievement in high school but also of the rate of growth. So IQ test scores can provide some prediction of achievement, but if measures of self-regulated learning skills, practical intelligence, and creativity are included, more accurate predictions are likely.

But what about life after school? Do people who score high on IQ tests achieve more in life? Here the answer is less clear because life success and education are intertwined. High school graduates earn over $200,000 more than non-graduates in their lifetime; college graduates earn over $1,100,000 more; grads with doctoral degrees earn $2,400,000 more; and graduates with professional degrees (physicians, lawyers, etc.), over $3,400,000 more in their lifetime (Cheeseman Day & Burger, 2002). People with higher intelligence test scores tend to complete more years of school and to have higher-status jobs. However, when the number of years of education is held constant, the correlation decreases between IQ scores, income, and success in later life. Just as Grigorenko et al. (2009) found, other factors such as self-regulation, motivation, social skills, and luck may make the difference in life achievement (Goleman, 1995; Neisser et al., 1996).

Gender Differences in Intelligence

From infancy through the preschool years, most studies find few differences between boys and girls in overall mental and motor development or in specific abilities. During the school years and beyond, psychologists find no differences in general intelligence on the standard measures—these tests have been designed and standardized to minimize sex differences. However, scores on some tests of specific abilities show sex differences. Also, the scores of males tend to be slightly more variable in general, so there are more males than

Flynn effect Because of better health, smaller families, increased complexity in the environment, and more and better schooling, IQ test scores are steadily rising.

females with very high and very low scores on tests (Halpern et al., 2007; Lindberg, Hyde, Peterson, & Linn, 2010). In addition, there are more boys diagnosed with learning disabilities, ADHD, and autism. Diane Halpern and her colleagues (2007) summarize the research:

> By the end of grade school and beyond, females perform better on assessments of verbal abilities when assessments are heavily weighted with writing and the language-usage items cover topics with which females are familiar; sex differences favoring females are much larger in these conditions than when assessments of verbal abilities do not include writing. In contrast, males excel on certain visuospatial-ability measures. (p. 40)

There is a caution, however. In most studies of sex differences, race and ethnicity are not taken into account. For example, when ethnic groups are studied separately, there may be very small differences in mathematics performance favoring White males in high school and college, but slight differences favoring females among ethnic minority students. Also, there seem to be small differences in complex problem-solving skills favoring boys in high school, perhaps because problem solving is taught more in physics classes than in math, and boys are more likely than girls to take physics—another reason to encourage all students to get a good background in science (Lindberg et al., 2010).

Several recent international *meta-analyses* (analyses that combine data from many different studies on the same topic) have found few differences in mathematics achievement for boys and girls. For example, Sara Lindberg and her colleagues analyzed data from 242 studies that included 1.3 million elementary through high school students. Overall, they found that in the United States and some other nations, girls' and boys' performance in mathematics is comparable, but there are some differences by nations—girls scored higher than boys in several countries such as Russia, Bahrain, and Mexico, and boys' scores were higher in other countries such as Switzerland, the Netherlands, and African nations (Else-Quest, Hyde, & Linn, 2010; Lindberg et al., 2010). Also, the International Comparisons in Fourth-Grade Reading Literacy (Mullis, Martin, Gonzalez, & Kennedy, 2003) revealed that in 34 countries, 4th grade boys scored below girls in reading literacy. Finally, girls in general tend to get higher grades than boys in mathematics classes.

Males on average are better on tests that require mental rotation of a figure in space, prediction of the trajectories of moving objects, and navigating. Some researchers argue that evolution has favored these skills in males (Buss, 1995; Geary, 1995, 1999), but others relate these skills to males' more active play styles, their greater experience with video games, and their participation in athletics (Else-Quest et al., 2010; Stumpf, 1995). Some educational psychologists believe that spatial skills are neglected in school curriculums and that even a small amount of instruction can make a big difference for students (Uttal, Hand, & Newcombe, 2009). The cross-cultural comparisons suggest that much of the difference in mathematics scores comes from learning, not biology. And studies showing that adults rated a math paper attributed to "John T. McKay" a full point higher on a 5-point scale than the same paper attributed to "Joan T. McKay" suggests that discrimination and stereotyped expectations play a role as well (Angier & Chang, 2005).

Lindberg and her colleagues sum it up well: "Overall, it is clear that in the United States and some other nations, girls have reached parity with boys in mathematics performance. It is crucial that this information be made widely known to counteract stereotypes about female math inferiority held by gatekeepers such as parents and teachers and by students themselves" (2010, p. 1134). I agree that combating these stereotypes is critical. Melanie Steffens and her colleagues (2010) in Germany found that by age 9, girls already had developed implicit (out of awareness) math-gender stereotypes; the girls associated men with mathematics. These implicit beliefs grew stronger into adolescence, predicted girls' achievement in math, and affected their decisions to take elective math courses.

HEREDITY OR ENVIRONMENT? Nowhere has the nature-versus-nurture debate raged so hard as in the area of intelligence. Should intelligence be seen as a potential, limited by our genetic makeup? Or does intelligence simply refer to an individual's current level of intellectual functioning, as influenced by experience and education?

Beware of either/or comparisons: It is impossible to separate intelligence "in the genes" from intelligence "due to experience." Today, most psychologists believe that differences in intelligence are the result of both heredity and environment, probably in about equal proportions for children (Petrill & Wilkerson, 2000). And environmental influences include everything from the health of a child's mother during pregnancy to the amount of lead in the child's home to the quality of teaching a child receives. For example, Japanese and Chinese students know much more mathematics than American students, but their intelligence test scores are quite similar. This superiority in math probably is related to differences in the way mathematics is taught and studied in the three countries and to the self-motivation skills of many Asian students (Baron, 1998; Stevenson & Stigler, 1992).

BEING SMART ABOUT IQ TESTS. We saw that intelligence tests originally were developed, in part, to protect the rights of children from poorer families who might be denied an education on the false grounds that they weren't able to learn. We also saw that intelligence tests predict school success equally accurately for students of different races and income levels. Even so, these tests can never be free of cultural content, so they always will have some biases built in. Keep this in mind when you see your students' scores on any test. Finally, remember that the results of every assessment for every student should be used to support that student's learning and development and to identify effective practices, not to deny the student access to resources or appropriate teaching. For all adults caring for children—parents, teachers, administrators, counselors, medical workers—it is especially important to realize that cognitive skills, like any other skills, are always improvable. *Intelligence is a current state of affairs, affected by past experiences and open to future changes.*

Now that you have a sense of what intelligence means, let's consider another kind of individual difference that often is misunderstood and misused in education—learning styles.

LEARNING AND THINKING STYLES

For many years, researchers have examined individual differences in "styles"—cognitive styles, learning styles, problem-solving styles, thinking styles, decision-making styles . . . the list goes on. Li-fang Zhang and Robert Sternberg (2005) organize the work on individual styles into three traditions. *Cognitive-centered* styles assess the ways people process information, for example, by being reflective or impulsive in responding (Kagan, 1976). *Personality-centered* styles assess more stable personality traits such as being extroverted versus being introverted or relying on thinking versus feeling (Myers & McCaulley, 1988). *Activity-centered* styles assess a combination of cognition and personality traits that affect how people approach activities, so these styles may be of special interest to teachers.

One theme in activity-centered approaches is the differences between surface and deep approaches to processing information in learning situations (Snow, Corno, & Jackson, 1996). Students who take a surface-processing approach focus on memorizing the learning materials, not understanding them. These students tend to be motivated by rewards, grades, external standards, and the desire to be evaluated positively by others. Individuals who have a deep-processing approach see the learning activities as a means for understanding some underlying concepts or meanings. They tend to learn for the sake of learning and are less concerned about how their performance is evaluated. Of course, the situation can encourage deep or surface processing, but there is evidence that individuals have tendencies to approach learning situations in characteristic ways (Biggs, 2001; Coffield, Moseley, Hall, & Ecclestone, 2004; Tait & Entwistle, 1998).

Learning Styles/Preferences

Here is another "style" term. You may have heard about **learning styles** or used the phrase yourself. Learning style usually is defined as the way a person approaches learning and studying. But beware—some conceptions of learning styles have little research support; others are based on solid studies. First—the cautions.

Connect and Extend to PRAXIS II™

Learning/Cognitive Styles (I, B1) Familiarize yourself with the major issues involved with learning and cognitive styles, and understand their implications for classroom practice.

Learning styles Characteristic approaches to learning and studying.

LEARNER DIFFERENCES AND LEARNING NEEDS **131**

CAUTIONS ABOUT LEARNING STYLES. Since the late 1970s, a great deal has been written about differences in students' "learning styles" (Dunn & Dunn, 1978, 1987; Dunn & Griggs, 2003; Gregorc, 1982; Keefe, 1982). But I believe **learning preferences** is a more accurate label because most of the research describes preferences for particular learning environments—for example, where, when, with whom, or with what lighting, food, or music you like to study. There are a number of instruments for assessing students' learning preferences—The Learning Style Inventory (Dunn, Dunn, & Price, 1989), Learning Styles Inventory (Revised) (Kolb, 1985), and the Learning Style Profile (Keefe & Monk, 1986).

Are these useful tools? Tests of learning style have been strongly criticized (Pashler, McDaniel, Rohrer, & Bjork, 2009). In fact, in an extensive examination of learning styles instruments, researchers at the Learning Skills Research Centre in England concluded, "with regard to work by Dunn and Dunn, Gregorc, and Riding, our examination of the re- liability and validity of their learning style instruments strongly suggests that they should not be used in education or business" (Coffield, et al., 2004, p. 127). Most researchers are skeptical about the value of learning preferences. "The reason researchers roll their eyes at learning styles research is the utter failure to find that assessing children's learn- ing styles and matching to instructional methods has any effect on their learning (Stahl, 2002, p. 99). In fact, an experimental study had college students self-assess their learning style as auditory, visual, or kinesthetic and then taught the students in keeping with their professed style (Kratzig & Arbuthnott, 2006). Matching learning with teaching styles did not improve learning. When the researchers examined how people identified their own learning styles, they concluded that people's judgments represented preferences rather than superior skills in using auditory, visual, or kinesthetic modalities. If college students have trouble identifying their own learning style, think about 4th or 9th graders!

In summary, the most recent review of learning styles research ends with these words: "The contrast between the enormous popularity of the learning-styles approach within education and the lack of credible evidence for its utility is, in our opinion, striking and disturbing. If classification of students' learning styles has practical utility, it remains to be demonstrated" (Pashler et al., 2009, p. 117).

So why are these ideas so popular? Part of the answer is that many thriving commercial companies are making large profits by providing advice to teachers, tu- tors, and managers about learning styles based on "inflated claims and sweeping conclusions which go beyond the current knowledge base" (Coffield et al., 2004, p. 127). Money talks.

THE VALUE OF CONSIDERING LEARNING STYLES. There is one learning styles dis- tinction that has research support. Richard Mayer (e.g., Mayer & Massa, 2003) has been studying the distinction between visual and verbal learners, with a focus on learning from computer-based multimedia. Here, the assessment of learning styles is carefully done and more valid than assessments based on many of the commercial inventories. Mayer is find- ing that there is a visualizer–verbalizer dimension and that it has three facets: *cognitive spatial ability* (low or high), *cognitive style* (visualizer versus verbalizer), and *learning preference* (visual learner versus verbal learner), as shown in Table 4.2. So the picture is more complex than simply being a visual or a verbal learner. A student might have a preference for learning with pictures, but low spatial ability could make using pictures for learning less effective. To complicate matters even more, spatial abilities may be important for learning from static pictures, but less important for learning from animation—so the type of learning materials matters too (Hoeffler & Leutner, 2011). These differences can be reliably measured, but research has not identified the effects of teaching to these styles; certainly, presenting information in multiple modalities might be useful.

So before you try to accommodate all your students' learning styles, remember that students, especially younger ones, may not be the best judges of how they should learn. Preference for a particular style does not guarantee that using the style will be effective. Sometimes students, particularly poorer students, prefer what is easy and comfortable; real learning can be hard and uncomfortable. In some cases, students prefer to learn in a certain way because they have no alternatives; it is the only way they know how to approach the task. These students may benefit from developing new—and perhaps more

Learning preferences Preferred ways of studying and learning, such as using pictures instead of text, working with other people versus alone, learning in structured or in unstructured situations, and so on.

TABLE 4.2 • **Three Facets of the Visualizer-Verbalizer Dimension**

There are three dimensions to visual versus verbal learning: ability, style, and preference. Individuals can be high or low on any or all of these dimensions.

FACET	TYPES OF LEARNERS	DEFINITION
Cognitive Ability	High spatial ability	Good abilities to create, remember, and manipulate images and spatial information
	Low spatial ability	Poor abilities to create, remember, and manipulate images and spatial information
Cognitive Style	Visualizer	Thinks using images and visual information
	Verbalizer	Thinks using words and verbal information
Learning Preference	Visual learner	Prefers instruction using pictures
	Verbal learner	Prefers instruction using words

Source: From R. E. Mayer & L. J. Massa (2003). "Three Facets of Visual and Verbal Learners: Cognitive Ability, Cognitive Style and Learning Preference." Journal of Educational Psychology, 95 (4), p. 838 .

effective—ways to learn. Learning styles probably are a minor factor in learning; factors such as teaching strategies and social connections in classrooms likely play much larger roles (Kratzig & Arbuthnott, 2006).

Beyond Either/Or

Even though much of the work on matching learning styles and preferences to teaching is suspect, with unreliable measures and inflated claims, there is some value in thinking about learning styles. First, by helping students think about how they learn, you can develop thoughtful self-monitoring and self-awareness. In upcoming chapters, we will look at the value of such self-knowledge for learning and motivation. Second, looking at individual students' approaches to learning might help teachers appreciate, accept, and accommodate student differences and differentiate instruction (Coffield et al., 2004; Rosenfeld & Rosenfeld, 2004).

Schools can make available learning options, such as having quiet, private corners as well as large tables for working; comfortable cushions as well as straight chairs; brightly lighted desks along with darker areas; headphones for listening to music as well as earplugs; structured as well as open-ended assignments; and information available from visuals, podcasts, and DVDs as well as books. Will making these alterations lead to greater learning? Here the answer is not clear. Very bright students appear to need less structure and to prefer quiet, solitary learning (Torrance, 1986) and the visual–verbal distinction seems to be valid. If nothing else, some accommodation of student preferences may make your classroom more inviting and student-friendly and communicate to your students that you care about them as individuals.

Thus far, we have focused mostly on the varying abilities and styles of students. For the rest of the chapter, we will consider factors that can interfere with learning. It is important for all teachers to be aware of these issues because laws and policy changes over the past 40 years have expanded teachers' responsibilities in working with all students.

INDIVIDUAL DIFFERENCES AND THE LAW

STOP & THINK Have you ever had the experience of being the only one in a group who had trouble doing something? How would you feel if every day in school you faced the same kind of difficulty, while everyone else seemed to find the work easier than you? What kind of support and teaching would you need to keep trying? •

IDEA

Since 1975, in the United States, a series of laws, beginning with PL 94-142 (the Education of the Handicapped Act), has led to revolutionary changes in the education of children with disabilities. The legislation, now called the **Individuals with Disabilities Education Improvement Act (IDEA)** or sometimes **IDEIA**, was revised in 1990, 1997, and 2004. At the most general level, the law now requires states to provide a **free, appropriate public education (FAPE)** for all students with disabilities who participate in special education. There are no exceptions—the law requires **zero reject**. This policy also applies to students with communicable diseases such as AIDS. The expenses of meeting the special needs of these students are considered a public responsibility. Every state in the United States has a *child find* system to alert and educate the public about services for children with disabilities and to distribute useful information.

The definition of *disability* is specific in IDEA. The 13 categories of disabilities covered are listed in Table 4.3, along with the numbers of students in each category. About 13% of all students, ages 6 through 21, receive special education services under IDEA (National Center for Education Statistics, 2009). Most of these students spend some of their school day in general education classes. Table 4.3 also indicates the percentage of

TABLE 4.3 • **Students Ages 6–21 Served Under IDEA**

There are 13 categories of students served under IDEA. Below are the number of students in each category in 2008–2009 and the percentage of students in each category who are taught in general education classrooms at least 40% of their school day.

DISABILITY	NUMBER OF STUDENTS IN 2008–2009	PERCENTAGE OF THESE STUDENTS WHO SPEND AT LEAST 40% OF THE DAY IN GENERAL EDUCATION CLASSES
Specific learning disabilities	2,522,735	90
Speech/language impairments	1,121,496	92
Other health impairments (not orthopedic)	648,112	84
Intellectual disability (mental retardation)	475,713	44
Emotional disturbances	417,872	58
Autism spectrum disorders	292,638	54
Multiple disabilities	123,924	30
Developmental delay	96,853	83
Hearing impairments	70,682	71
Orthopedic impairments	62,332	68
Visual impairments	25,975	76
Traumatic brain injury	24,857	68
Deaf-blind	1,735	47
Total	5,884,924	

Source: Individual with Disabilities Education (IDEA) Act Data, Data Accountability Center, 2008. Available online https://www.ideadata.org/arc_toc10.asp#partbCC

Individuals with Disabilities Education Improvement Act (IDEA) Latest amendment of PL 94-142; guarantees a free public education to all children regardless of disability.

Free, appropriate public education (FAPE) Public funding to support appropriate educational programs for all students, no matter what their needs.

Zero reject A basic principle of IDEA specifying that no student with a disability, no matter what kind or how severe, can be denied a free public education.

ACCESS TO PUBLIC EDUCATION The Individuals with Disabilities Education Act (IDEA) guarantees a free and appropriate public education to all students regardless of disability.

these students who are taught in general education classes for at least 40% of their school day. You can see that no matter what grade or subject you teach, you will work with students with special needs.

Before we look at the different categories, let's examine the requirements in IDEA. There are three major points of interest to parents and teachers: the concept of "least restrictive placement"; the individualized education program (IEP); and the protection of the rights of both students with disabilities and their parents.

LEAST RESTRICTIVE ENVIRONMENT. IDEA requires states to develop procedures for educating each child in the **least restrictive environment**, a setting that is as close to the general education class setting as possible. Over the years, recommended approaches to achieve this have moved from **mainstreaming** (including children with special needs in a few regular education classes as convenient), to **integration** (fitting the child into existing class structures), to **inclusion** (restructuring educational settings to promote belonging for all students) (Avramidis, Bayliss, & Burden, 2000). Even though the IDEA legislation does not use the word *inclusion*, today the least restrictive environment is assumed to be inclusion as much as possible. In the end, successful inclusion probably depends on teachers being knowledgeable and well prepared, getting the support they need to teach, and being committed to inclusion. However, an emphasis on standardized testing may interfere with good teaching for included students (Friend, 2011; Idol, 2006; Kemp & Carter, 2006).

INDIVIDUALIZED EDUCATION PROGRAM. The drafters of the laws recognized that each student is unique and may need a specially tailored program to make progress. The **Individualized Education Program**, or **IEP**, is an agreement between parents and the school about the services that will be provided to the student. The IEP is written by a team that includes the student's parents or guardians, a general education teacher who works with the student, a special education teacher, a representative of the school district (often the principal), a qualified person who can interpret the student's evaluation results (often a school psychologist), and (if appropriate) the student. For students 16 and older, the team may include representatives from outside agencies who are providing services to help the student make transitions to life and support services after school. If the school and parents agree, the team could add other people who have special knowledge of the child (for example, a therapist). The program usually is updated each year. The IEP must state in writing:

1. The student's present level of academic achievement and functional performance (sometimes referred to as *PLAAFP*).
2. Annual goals—measurable performance goals for the year. Students with significant needs or multiple disabilities may also have *short-term objectives* or *benchmarks* to make sure progress is continuous. The plan must tell how progress toward these goals and objectives will be measured. Parents must get progress reports at least as often as report cards are sent home for all students.
3. A statement of specific special education and related services to be provided to the student and details of when and where those services will be initiated. This statement can include descriptions of supplementary aids and assistive technologies (for example, using speech recognition software such as *Dragon®* to dictate answers or compose essays, or writing using a computer).
4. An explanation of how much of the student's program WILL NOT be in regular classroom and school settings.

Least restrictive environment (LRE) Educating each child with peers in the regular classroom to the greatest extent possible.

Mainstreaming Teaching children with disabilities in regular classes for part or all of their school day.

Integration Fitting the child with special needs into existing class structures.

Inclusion The integration of all students, including those with severe disabilities, into regular classes.

Individualized Education Program (IEP) Annually revised program for an exceptional student, detailing present achievement level, goals, and strategies, drawn up by teachers, parents, specialists, and (if possible) the student.

GUIDELINES — FAMILY AND COMMUNITY PARTNERSHIPS

Productive Conferences

Plan and prepare for a productive conference.
Examples
1. Have a clear purpose and gather the needed information. If you want to discuss student progress, have work samples available.
2. Send home a list of questions, and ask families to bring the information to the conference. Sample questions from Friend and Bursuck (2002) are:
   - What is your child's favorite class activity?
   - Does your child have worries about any class activities? If so, what are they?
   - What are your priorities for your child's education this year?
   - What questions do you have about your child's education in my class this year?
   - How could we at school help make this the most successful year ever for your child?
   - Are there any topics you want to discuss at the conference that I might need to prepare for? If so, please let me know.
   - Would you like other individuals to participate in the conference? If so, please give me a list of their names.
   - Is there particular school information you would like me to have available? If so, please let me know.

During the conference, create and maintain an atmosphere of collaboration and respect.
Examples
1. Arrange the room for private conversation. Put a sign on your door to avoid interruptions. Meet around a conference table for better collaboration. Have tissues available.
2. Address families as "Mr." and "Ms.," not "Mom" and "Dad" or "Grandma." Use students' names.
3. Listen to families' concerns and build on their suggestions for their children.

After the conference, keep good records and follow up on decisions.
Examples
1. Make notes to yourself and keep them organized.
2. Summarize any actions or decisions in writing and send a copy to the family and any other teachers or professionals involved.
3. Communicate with families on other occasions, especially when there is good news to share.

For more information about parent conferences, see: http://content.scholastic.com/browse/home.jsp *and search using "parent teacher conference."*

---

5. A statement about how the student will participate in state and district-wide assessments, particularly those required by the No Child Left Behind accountability procedures.
6. Beginning at age 14 and by age 16, a statement of needed transitional services to move the student toward further education or work in adult life. (Friend, 2011; Rosenberg, Westling, & McLeskey, 2011)

Figure 4.2 on the next page is an example of an individual transition planning (ITP) form for employment.

THE RIGHTS OF STUDENTS AND FAMILIES. Several stipulations in IDEA protect the rights of parents and students. Schools must have procedures for maintaining the confidentiality of student records. Testing practices must not discriminate against students from different cultural backgrounds. Parents have the right to see all records relating to the testing, placement, and teaching of their child. If they wish, parents may obtain an independent evaluation of their child. Parents may bring an advocate or representative to the meeting at which the IEP is developed. Students whose parents are unavailable must be assigned a surrogate parent to participate in the planning. Parents must receive written notice (in their native language) before any evaluation or change in placement is made. Finally, parents have the right to challenge the program developed for their child, and are protected by due process of law. Because teachers often have conferences with these families, I have provided some *Guidelines* to make the meetings more effective, but be aware that guidelines apply to meetings with all your students and their parents.

Connect and Extend to PRAXIS II™

Individual Education Programs (IEP) (I, B3)
When you sign an IEP, you are signing an important educational and legal document. Be sure that you can explain the purpose of an IEP, identify its components, and describe the kind of information that can be contained in one.

FIGURE 4.2

EXAMPLE OF A TRANSITION PLANNING FORM

This ITP was developed for a student who is moving toward work in a grocery store. The plan describes the needed services so the student can transition into supported employment.

ILLUSTRATIVE TRANSITION PLANNING FORM IN THE AREA OF EMPLOYMENT

Student: *Robert Brown*
Meeting Date: *January 20, 2003*
Graduation Date: *June, 2004*

IEP/Transition Planning Team Members: *Robert Brown (student), Mrs. Brown (parent), Jill Green (teacher), Mike Weatherby (Vocational Education), Dick Rose (Rehabilitation), Susan Marr (Developmental Disabilities Agency)*

TRANSITION PLANNING AREA: *Employment*

Student Preferences and Desired Postschool Goals: *Robert would like to work in a grocery store as a produce stocker.*

Present Levels of Performance: *Robert has held several work experience placements in local grocery stores (see attached placement summaries). He requires a self-management checklist using symbols to complete assigned work tasks. His rate of task completion is below the expected employer levels.*

Need Transition Services: *Robert will require job placement, training, and follow-along services from an employment specialist. In addition, he needs bus training to get to his job.*

ANNUAL GOAL: *Robert will work Monday through Friday from 1:00 to 4:00 p.m. at Smith's Food Center as a produce stocker, completing all assigned tasks without assistance from the employment specialist on ten consecutive weekly performance probes.*

Activities	Person	Completion Date
1. Place Robert on the state supported employment waiting list.	Susan Marr	May 1, 2003
2. Obtain a monthly bus pass.	Mrs. Brown	February 1, 2003
3. Schedule Robert for employee orientation training.		February 16, 2003

Source: McDonnell, John J.; Hardman, Michael L.; McDonnell Andrea P., Introduction to Persons With Moderate and Severe Disabilities: Educational and Social Issues, 2nd Edition, © 2003. Reprinted by permission of Pearson Education Inc., Upper Saddle River, NJ.

Section 504 Protections

Not all students who need special accommodations in school are covered by IDEA or are eligible for the services provided by the law. But these students' educational needs may be covered by other legislation. As a consequence of the civil rights movement in the 1960s and 1970s, the federal government passed the Vocational Rehabilitation Act of 1973. **Section 504** of that law prevents discrimination against people with disabilities in any program that receives federal money, such as public schools.

Through Section 504, all school-age children are ensured an equal opportunity to participate in school activities. The definition of *disability* is broad in Section 504. If a student has a condition that substantially limits participation in school, then the school still must develop a plan for giving that student access to education, even though the school gets no extra funds. To get assistance through Section 504, students must be assessed, often by a team, and a plan developed. Unlike IDEA, however, there are fewer rules about how this must happen, so individual schools design their own procedures (Friend, 2011). Look at Table 4.4 to see an example of the kinds of accommodations that might be made for a student. Many of these ideas seem to be "just good teaching." But I have been surprised to see how many teachers won't let students use calculators or audio recorders because "they should learn to do it like everyone else!" Two major groups are considered for Section 504 accommodations: students with medical or health needs (such as diabetes, drug addiction or alcoholism, severe allergies, communicable diseases, or temporary disabilities resulting from accidents) and students with attention-deficit hyperactivity disorder, if they are not already covered by IDEA.

The **Americans with Disabilities Act of 1990 (ADA)** prohibits discrimination against persons with disabilities in employment, transportation, public access, local government, and telecommunications. This comprehensive legislation extends the protections of Section 504 beyond the school and workplace to libraries, local and state government, restaurants, hotels, theaters, stores, public transportation, and many other settings.

TABLE 4.4 • **Examples of Accommodations Under Section 504**

The types of accommodations that can be written into a Section 504 plan are almost without limit. Some accommodations may relate to physical changes in the learning environment (for example, air filters are installed to remove allergens). However, many students who have Section 504 plans have functional impairments related to their learning or behavior, and their needs are somewhat similar to those of students with disabilities. The following is a sample of instructional accommodations that could be incorporated into a Section 504 plan:

- Seat the student nearest to where the teacher does most of his/her instruction.
- Have the student sit next to a peer who can help as needed.
- Seat the student away from the distractions of doorways or windows.
- Fold assignments in half so that the student is less overwhelmed by the quantity of work.
- Make directions telegraphic, that is, concise and clear.
- Allow use of a calculator or tape recorder.
- Use voice recognition software on the computer for written assignments.
- Mark right answers instead of wrong answers.
- Send a set of textbooks to be left at home so that the student does not have to remember to bring books from school.
- Provide books on tape so that the student can listen to assignments instead of reading them.

If you review these items, you can see that many of them just make good instructional sense. They are effective instructional practices that help learners with special needs succeed in your classroom.

Source: From Marilyn Friend & William D. Bursuck, Including Students with Special Needs: A Practical Guide for Classroom Teachers, 3e. Published by Allyn and Bacon, Boston, MA. Copyright © 2002 by Pearson Education. Adapted by permission of the publisher.

Section 504 A part of civil rights law that prevents discrimination against people with disabilities in programs that receive federal funds, such as public schools.

Americans with Disabilities Act of 1990 (ADA) Federal legislation prohibiting discrimination against persons with disabilities in employment, transportation, public access, local government, and telecommunications.

STUDENTS WITH LEARNING CHALLENGES

Before we look at some of the learning challenges children face, let's overview recent work on the neuroscience of learning difficulties. With all of the new technology, the amount of research on the brain and learning disabilities has grown exponentially.

Neuroscience and Learning Challenges

One of the early explanations for learning disabilities was minimal brain dysfunction. We now know that there are many other factors involved in the learning challenges children face, but certainly injuries or diseases of the brain can lead to disabilities in language, mathematics, attention, or behavior. In addition, there is some evidence that intensive teaching interventions can lead to changes in brain functioning (Simos et al., 2007). Studies of the brains of students with learning disabilities and with attention deficit disorders show some differences in structure and activity compared to those of students without problems. For example, people with attention disorders may have some areas of the brain that are smaller. The flow of blood appears to be lower than typical in the cerebellum and frontal lobes and the levels of electrical activity are different in certain brain areas, compared to people without attention deficits (Barkley, 2006). Elementary school students with specific language disabilities appear to have immature auditory systems—their brains process basic auditory information in a way similar to the brains of children 3 to 4 years younger (Goswami, 2004). The implications of these brain differences for instruction are still being worked out. It is difficult to determine exactly which came first, the learning problems or the brain differences (Friend, 2011).

Quite a bit of research on learning problems has focused on working memory, partly because working memory capacity is a good predictor of a range of cognitive skills including language understanding, reading and mathematics abilities, and fluid intelligence (Bayliss, Jarrold, Baddeley, Gunn, & Leigh, 2005). In addition, some studies indicate that children who have learning disabilities in reading and mathematics problem solving have considerable difficulties with working memory (Siegel, 2003; Swanson & Saez, 2003). Specifically, some research shows that children with learning disabilities have problems using the system of working memory that holds verbal and auditory information while you work with it. Because children with learning disabilities have trouble holding on to words and sounds, it is difficult for them to put the words together to comprehend the meaning of a sentence or to figure out what a math story problem is really asking about.

An even more serious problem may be difficulties retrieving needed information from long-term memory, so it is hard for these children to simultaneously hold on to information (such as the result from the first two figures multiplied in an algebra problem) while they have to transform new incoming information, such as the next numbers to add. Important bits of information keep getting lost. Finally, children with learning disabilities in arithmetic and problem solving seem to have problems holding visual–spatial information such as number lines or quantity comparisons in working memory, so creating mental representations of "less than" and "greater than" problems is challenging (D'Amico & Guarnera, 2005).

As you saw in Table 4.3, almost one-half of all students receiving some kind of special education services in the public schools are diagnosed as having learning disabilities—by far the largest category of students with disabilities. We begin our exploration of learning challenges with these students.

Students with Learning Disabilities

How do you explain a student who struggles to read, write, spell, or learn math, even though he or she does not have intellectual disabilities, emotional problems, or educational disadvantages and has normal vision, hearing, and language capabilities? The student probably has a **learning disability**, but there is no fully agreed-upon definition of this term. One text on learning disabilities describes eight definitions (Hallahan et al., 2005), including the definition used in IDEA: "a disorder in one or more of the basic

Learning disability Problem with acquisition and use of language; may show up as difficulty with reading, writing, reasoning, or math.

psychological processes involved in understanding or using language, spoken or written, that may manifest itself in imperfect ability to listen, think, speak, read, write, spell, or do mathematical calculation" (p. 15). Most definitions agree that students with learning disabilities perform significantly below what would be expected, given their other abilities.

Most educational psychologists believe there are both physiological and environmental bases for learning disabilities, such as brain injury, exposure to toxins before birth from mothers who smoked or drank while pregnant, poor nutrition, lead-based paint in the home, or even poor instruction (Smith, 2004). Genetics plays a role as well. If parents have a learning disability, their children have a 30% to 50% chance of having a learning disability too (Friend, 2011).

STUDENT CHARACTERISTICS. Students with learning disabilities are not all alike. The most common characteristics are specific difficulties in one or more academic areas; poor coordination; problems paying attention; hyperactivity and impulsivity; problems organizing and interpreting visual and auditory information; seeming lack of motivation; and difficulties making and keeping friends (Hallahan & Kauffman, 2006; Rosenberg et al., 2011). As you can see, many students with other disabilities (such as attention-deficit hyperactive disorder) and many normal students may have some of the same characteristics. To complicate the situation even more, not all students with learning disabilities will have these problems, and very few will have all of these characteristics. One student may be 3 years behind in reading but above grade level in math, while another student may have the opposite strengths and weaknesses and a third may have problems with organizing and studying that affect almost all subject areas.

Most students with learning disabilities have difficulties reading. Table 4.5 lists some of the most common problems, although these problems are not always signs of learning disabilities. For English-speaking students, these difficulties appear to be *phonemic awareness*—problems with relating sounds to letters that make up words, making spelling hard as well (Lyon, Shaywitz, & Shaywitz, 2003; Willcutt et al., 2001). For Chinese

TABLE 4.5 • **Reading Problems of Students with Learning Disabilities**

Do any of your students show these signs? They could be indications of learning disabilities.

ANXIETY AROUND READING
• Reluctant to read • Cries or acts out to avoid reading • Seems tense when reading

DIFFICULTY RECOGNIZING WORDS OR LETTERS
• Inserts an incorrect word, substitutes or skips words • Reverses letters or numbers—48 for 24, for example • Mispronounces words—"cape" for "cope" • Mixes up order of words in sentences: "I can bikes ride" for "I can ride bikes." • Reads very slowly and with little fluency—starts and stops often

POOR VOCABULARY SKILLS
• Can't read new vocabulary words • Has limited vocabulary

DIFFICULTY WITH UNDERSTANDING OR REMEMBERING WHAT WAS READ
• Can't recall basic facts from the reading • Can't make inferences or identify the main idea

Source: Based on information from Smith, D. D., & Tyler, N. C. (2010). Introduction to Special Education: Making a Difference (7th ed.). Columbus, OH: Merrill, and Helpguide.org. http://www.helpguide.org/mental/learning_disabilities.htm

speakers, reading disabilities seem to be related to *morphological awareness* or the ability to combine morphemes into words. Morphemes are the smallest units of meaning that make sense alone. For example, *books* has two morphemes: "book" and "s"—the "s" has meaning because it makes "book" plural. Recognizing units of meaning in Chinese characters is helpful in learning the language (Shu, McBride-Chang, Wu, & Liu, 2006).

Math, both computation and problem solving, is the second most common problem area for students with learning disabilities. Whereas English-speaking students with reading disabilities have trouble associating sounds with letters, students with some math disabilities have difficulty automatically associating numerals (1, 2, 3, etc.) with the correct magnitude—how many is 28, for example. So, before young students learn math computations, some may need extra practice to become automatic in associating numerals with the quantities they represent (Rubinsten & Henik, 2006).

The writing of some students with learning disabilities is virtually unreadable, and their spoken language can be halting and disorganized, as you can see in Figure 4.3. Students with learning disabilities often lack effective ways of approaching academic

FIGURE 4.3

WRITING SAMPLE FROM A STUDENT WITH LD

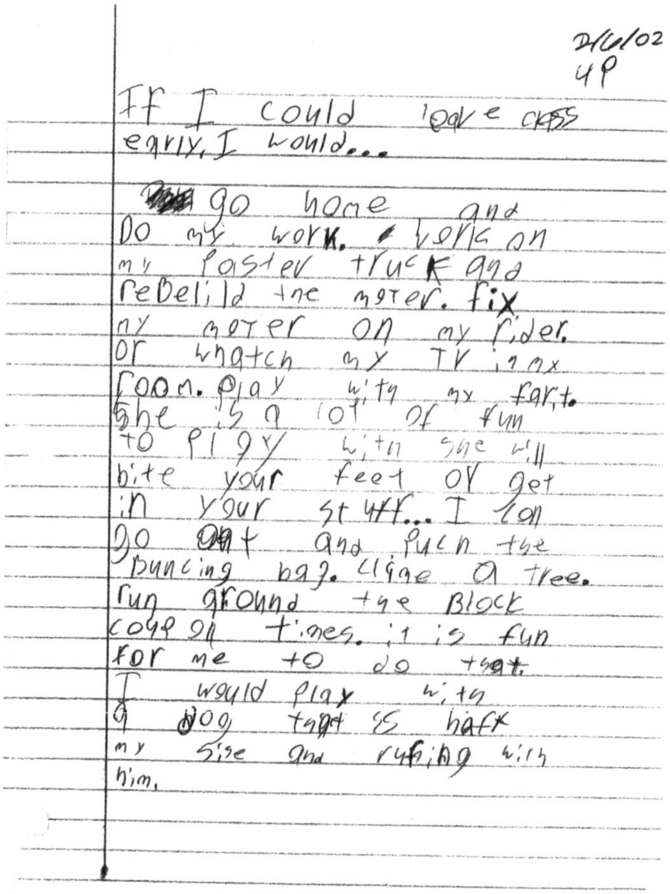

Source: From Friend, Marilyn, Special Education: Contemporary Perspectives for School Professionals, 2e. Published by Allyn and Bacon, Boston, MA. Copyright 2008 by Pearson Education. Adapted by permission of the publisher.

tasks. They don't know how to focus on the relevant information, get organized, apply learning strategies and study skills, change strategies when the one being used isn't working, or evaluate their learning. They tend to be passive learners, in part because they don't know how to learn—they have failed so often. Working independently is especially trying, so homework and seatwork are often left incomplete (Hallahan et al., 2005).

TEACHING STUDENTS WITH LEARNING DISABILITIES. Early diagnosis is important so that students with learning disabilities do not become terribly frustrated and discouraged. The students themselves do not understand why they are having such trouble, and they may become victims of **learned helplessness**. This condition was first identified in learning experiments with animals. The animals were put in situations in which they received punishment (electric shocks) that they could not control. Later, when the situation was changed and they could have escaped the shocks or turned them off, the animals didn't even bother trying (Seligman, 1975). They had learned to be helpless victims. Students with learning disabilities may also come to believe that they cannot control or improve their own learning. This is a powerful belief. The students never exert the effort to discover that they can make a difference in their own learning, so they remain passive and helpless.

Students with learning disabilities may also try to compensate for their problems and develop bad learning habits in the process, or they may begin avoiding certain subjects out of fear of not being able to handle the work. To prevent these things from happening, teachers should refer the students to the appropriate professionals in the school as early as possible.

Two general approaches, preferably used together, are highly effective for students with learning disabilities (Friend, 2011). The first is *direct instruction*, described in Chapter 14. The basics of this approach are clear explanations and demonstrations of new material, teaching in small steps with practice after each step, immediate feedback, and teacher guidance and support. The second general approach is *strategy instruction*, described in Chapter 9. Strategies are specific rules for focusing attention and accomplishing tasks, such as **TREE** for supporting elementary students' persuasive writing.

Topic sentence: Tell what you believe.
Reasons: Tell 3 or more reasons why you believe this. Will your readers believe this?
Ending: Wrap it up!
Examine: Check for all 3 parts.

These strategies have to be taught using good direct instruction—explanation, examples, and practice with feedback. See Chapter 11 for more details about these two approaches.

Here are some other general strategies for working with students with learning disabilities. In the preschool and elementary years, keep verbal instructions short and simple; have students repeat directions back to you to be sure they understand; give multiple examples and repeat main points several times; allow more practice than usual, especially when the material is new. Many of these strategies are useful in secondary grades as well. In addition, directly teach older students self-monitoring strategies, such as cueing students to ask, "Was I paying attention?" Teach students to use external memory strategies such as note taking, and devices such as assignment books, to-do lists, or electronic calendars (Hardman, Drew, & Egan, 2005). In every grade, connect new material to knowledge students already have. You may be thinking that these are good ideas for many students who need more support and direct teaching of study skills. You are right.

Students with Hyperactivity and Attention Disorders

STOP & THINK If a student is struggling with time management and organization issues, what kind of accommodations would you provide? •

You probably have heard of and may even have used the term *hyperactivity*. The notion is a modern one; there were no "hyperactive children" 50 to 60 years ago.

Learned helplessness The expectation, based on previous experiences with a lack of control, that all of one's efforts will lead to failure.

Such children, like Mark Twain's Huckleberry Finn, were seen as rebellious, lazy, or "fidgety" (Nylund, 2000). Today, attention-deficit hyperactive disorder (ADHD) is common. Not too long ago, I opened the newspaper and saw the headline, "ADHD diagnoses soar in 4 years." The Centers for Disease Control now puts the number of children in the United States diagnosed with ADHD as 1 in 10 (Wechsler, 2010). But the United States is not alone. A report from the 2nd International Congress on ADHD (Thome & Reddy, 2009) noted evidence is increasing that ADHD is a worldwide problem and that people with ADHD have striking and consistent characteristics in every culture. The rates in different countries vary from 4% to 10% worldwide (Fabiano et al., 2009; Gerwe et al., 2009). Closer to home, many student teachers in my program have classes that include 5 or 6 students diagnosed as "hyperactive," and in one class, there are 10 students with that diagnosis. Even closer, several of my immediate family members have ADHD.

Connect and Extend to PRAXIS II™

ADHD (I, B2)
A new student's parent calls you to tell you that a neurologist has diagnosed her child with ADHD. What typical behaviors can you expect from the student? What can you do to support that student's development?

DEFINITIONS. Actually, hyperactivity is not one particular condition, but two kinds of problems that may or may not occur together—attention disorders and impulsive-hyperactivity problems. About half the children diagnosed in the United States have both conditions. Today, most psychologists agree that the main problem for children labeled hyperactive is directing and maintaining attention, not simply controlling their physical activity. The American Psychiatric Association (APA) has established a diagnostic category called **attention-deficit hyperactivity disorder (ADHD)** to identify children with this problem. APA defines ADHD as "a pervasive pattern of inattention, impulsivity and/or hyperactivity that is more frequent and severe than is typically observed in individuals at a comparable level of development" (American Psychiatric Association, DSM-IV-TR, 2000, p. 78). Some of the indicators listed in the DSM-IV-TR are:

- **Inattention:** Doesn't pay close attention to class activities, details of work, teacher directions, class discussions; can't organize work, notebooks, desk, assignments; easily distracted and forgetful.
- **Hyperactivity:** fidgets, and squirms; can't stay in assigned seat; can't move slowly, seems driven by a motor to go fast; talks excessively.
- **Impulsivity:** Blurts out answers; has trouble waiting for a turn; interrupts.

All children show some of these behaviors some of the time, but children with ADHD are likely to have some of these symptoms before age 7, the symptoms occur across many settings (not just school), and the symptoms lead to problems learning and getting along with others. ADHD usually is diagnosed in elementary school, but research suggests that problems with attention and hyperactivity may begin to show up as early as 3 years old (Friedman-Weieneth, Harvey, Youngswirth, & Goldstein, 2007). Even though about 2 to 3 times more boys than girls are identified as hyperactive, the gap appears to be narrowing. Girls have the same symptoms as boys, but tend to show the symptoms in less obvious ways, so they may not be identified as often and thus may miss getting appropriate support (Friend, 2011).

Just a few years ago, most psychologists thought that ADHD diminished as children entered adolescence, but now there is evidence that the problems can persist into adulthood for at least half of those with ADHD (Hirvikoski et al., 2011). Adolescence—with the increased stresses of puberty, transition to middle or high school, more demanding academic work, and more engrossing social relationships—can be an especially difficult time for students with ADHD (Taylor, 1998). When children diagnosed with ADHD become adults, about 30% have no more symptoms, 25% have persistent behavioral problems such as drug use or criminal behaviors, and around 25% develop major depression (Rosenberg et al., 2011).

Attention-deficit hyperactivity disorder (ADHD) Current term for disruptive behavior disorders marked by overactivity, excessive difficulty sustaining attention, or impulsiveness.

TREATING ADHD WITH DRUGS. Today, there is an increasing reliance on drug therapy for ADHD, but there is controversy about this approach, as you can see in the *Point/Counterpoint.*

POINT/COUNTERPOINT: Pills or Skills for Children With ADHD?

About 3% of school-age children in the United States (ages 6 to 18) take some kind of medication for ADHD. Should children with ADHD be given drugs?

POINT

▶ **Yes, drugs are helpful in ADHD.** Ritalin and other prescribed drugs such as Adderall, Focalin, Dexadrine, Vyvanse, and Cylert are stimulants, but in particular dosages, they tend to have paradoxical effects on many children with ADHD. Short-term effects include possible improvements in social behaviors such as cooperation, attention, and compliance. Research suggests that about 70% to 80% of children with ADHD are more manageable and better able to benefit from educational and social interventions when on medication (Hutchinson, 2009). In fact, both stimulants such as Adderall and Ritalin and nonstimulant treatments such as Strattera appear to have some helpful effects for many children and adolescents with ADHD (Kratchovil, 2009). Positive results also have been reported with Buspar, usually used to treat anxiety, and even some supplements such as pycnogenol (Trebaticka et al., 2009). There is also some evidence that Strattera might have positive effects on working memory, planning, and inhibition—at least for the Chinese children studied (Yang et al., 2009). German researchers studying the effects of longer-acting, once-a-day Concerta concluded that the transition from short-acting stimulants to Concerta was "associated with significant improvements in daily functioning in several areas of life, severity of disease, and in quality of life" (Gerwe et al., 2009, p. 185).

COUNTERPOINT

▶ **No, drugs should not be the first treatment tried with ADHD.** Many children experience negative side effects when taking these drugs, such as increased heart rate and higher blood pressure, interference with growth rate, insomnia, weight loss, and nausea (Smith & Tyler, 2010). For most children, these side effects are mild and can be controlled by adjusting the dosage. However, little is known about the long-term effects of drug therapy. A new drug called Strattera is not a stimulant, but may lead to increased thoughts of suicide. As a parent or teacher, you need to keep up with the research on treatments for ADHD.

Many studies have concluded that the improvements in behavior from the drugs *seldom* lead to improvements in academic learning or peer relationships, two areas where children with ADHD have great problems. Because children appear to improve dramatically in their behavior, parents and teachers, relieved to see change, may assume the problem has been cured. It hasn't. The children still need special help in learning, especially interventions focused on how to make *connections* among elements in readings or presentations in order to build coherent, accurate representations of the information (Bailey et al., 2009; Doggett, 2004; Purdie, Hattie, & Caroll, 2002).

Beware of Either/Or. The bottom line is that even if students in your class are on medication, it is critical that they also learn the academic and social skills they will need to succeed. They need to learn how and when to apply learning strategies and study skills. Also, they need to be encouraged to persist when challenged by difficult tasks and to see themselves as having control over their learning and behavior. Medication alone will not make this happen, but it may help. For learning to occur, medication needs to be paired with other effective interventions.

ALTERNATIVES/ADDITIONS TO DRUG TREATMENTS. Gregory A. Fabiano and his colleagues (2009) identified 174 studies conducted between 1967 and 2006 that included almost 3,000 participants in behavioral treatments for ADHD; all studies met rigorous standards of quality research. Behavioral treatments involve the application of methods derived from behavioral learning theories such as contingency management, time-out, shaping, self-regulation, and modeling. The researchers then compared treated with untreated groups or individuals before and after one or more different kinds of treatments. Their conclusion? Findings were clear and impressive. "Based on these results, there is strong and consistent evidence that behavioral treatments are effective for treating ADHD" (p. 129). In an interview, Gregory Fabiano said, "Our results suggest that efforts should be redirected from debating the effectiveness of behavioral interventions to dissemination, enhancing and improving the use of these programs in community, school and mental health settings." Researchers working with adults in Sweden also found that behavioral methods stressing a balance between accepting and changing ADHD symptoms and behaviors proved effective (Hirvikoski et al., 2011).

In sum, one large study in Australia concluded what you might guess—we should attack the problem on all fronts:

> Multimodal approaches to intervention have been found to be most effective in terms of lasting change. For most, but not all children and adolescents, treatment with psychostimulants has beneficial effects, provided that it is accompanied by remedial tuition, counseling, and behavior management by parents/teachers, as required. Thus, advice from several different professions may be necessary. (van Kraayenoord, Rice, Carroll, Fritz, Dillon, & Hill, 2001, p. 7)

Even if students in your class are on medication, it is critical that they also learn the academic and social skills they will need to survive. Again, this will not happen by itself, even if behavior improves with medication (Purdie et al., 2002).

Lessons for Teachers: Learning Disabilities and ADHD

Long assignments may overwhelm students with learning disabilities and attention deficits, so give them a few problems or paragraphs at a time with clear consequences for completion. Another promising approach combines instruction in learning and memory strategies with motivational training. The goal is to help students develop the "skill and will" to improve their achievement. They are also taught to monitor their own behavior and encouraged to be persistent and to see themselves as "in control" (Pfiffner, Barkley, & DuPaul, 2006).

The notion of being in control is part of a therapy strategy for dealing with ADHD, one that stresses personal agency. Rather than treating the problem child, David Nylund's (2000) SMART approach enlists the child's strengths to conquer his or her problems—to put the child in control. New metaphors for the situation are developed. Rather than seeing the problems as inside the child, Nylund helps everyone see ADHD, Trouble, Boredom, and other enemies of learning as outside the child—demons to be conquered or unruly spirits to be enlisted in the service of what the child wants to accomplish. The focus is on solutions. The steps of the **SMART** approach are:

Separating the problem of ADHD from the child
Mapping the influence of ADHD on the child and family
Attending to the exceptions to the ADHD story
Reclaiming special abilities of children diagnosed with ADHD
Telling and celebrating the new story. (Nylund, 2000, p. xix)

As a teacher, you can look for times when the student is engaged—even short times. What is different about these times? Discover the student's strengths and allow yourself to be amazed by them. Make changes in your teaching that support the changes the student is trying to make. Nylund gives the following example: Chris (age 9) and his teacher, Ms. Baker, became partners in putting Chris in control of his concentration in school. Ms. Baker moved Chris's seat to the front of the room. The two designed a subtle signal to get Chris back on track, and Chris organized his messy desk. These sound like some of the Section 504 accommodations in Table 4.4. When Chris's concentration improved, Chris received an award at a party given in his honor. Chris described how he was learning to listen in class: "You just have to have a strong mind and tell ADHD and Boredom not to bother you" (Nylund, 2000, p. 166). Students with ADHD have some suggestions, too, as you can see in Table 4.6 taken from Nylund (2000, pp. 202–203).

Students with Communication Disorders

Students with communication disorders who are between the ages of 6 and 21 are the second largest group served by special education. These students may have language disorders, speech disorders, or both. They make up about 19% of students receiving services. Communication disorders can arise from many sources, because so many different aspects of the individual are involved in learning language and using speech. A child with a hearing impairment will not learn to speak normally. Injuries can cause neurological problems that interfere with speech or language. Children who are not listened to, or whose perception of the world is distorted by emotional problems, will reflect these problems

TABLE 4.6 • **Students with ADHD Give Teachers Advice**

Students with ADHD make these recommendations for their teachers (Nylund, 2000):

- Use lots of pictures (visual clues) to help me learn.
- Recognize cultural and racial identity.
- Know when to bend the rules.
- Notice when I am doing well.
- Don't tell the other kids that I am taking Ritalin.
- Offer us choices.
- Don't just lecture—it's boring!
- Realize that I am intelligent.
- Let me walk around the classroom.
- Don't give tons of homework.
- More recess!
- Be patient.

in their language development. Because speaking involves movements, any impairment of the motor functions involved with speech can cause language disorders. And because language development and thinking are so interwoven, any problems in cognitive functioning can affect ability to use language.

SPEECH DISORDERS. Students who cannot produce sounds effectively for speaking are considered to have a **speech disorder**. About 5% of school age children have some form of speech impairment. Articulation problems and fluency disorders (stuttering) are the two most common problems.

Articulation disorders include distorting a sound like a lisp (*thumtimes* for *sometimes*), substituting one sound for another (*shairp* for *chair*), adding a sound (*chuch air* for *chair*), or omitting sounds (*chai* for *chair*) (Rosenberg et al., 2011). Keep in mind, however, that most children are 6 to 8 years old before they can successfully pronounce all English sounds in normal conversation. The sounds of the consonants *l, r, y, s, v,* and *z* and the consonant blends *sh, ch, ng, zh,* and *th* are the last to be mastered (Friend, 2011). Also, there are dialect differences based on geography that do not represent articulation problems. A child in your class who is from New England might say "ideer" for "idea," but have no speech impairment.

Stuttering generally appears between the ages of 3 and 4. Causes of stuttering are unknown, but might include emotional or neurological problems or learned behavior. If stuttering continues more than a year or so, the child should be referred to a speech therapist. Early intervention can make a big difference (Hardman et al., 2005). When you are working with a student who stutters, speak to the child often, privately, and without hurrying, interrupting, or finishing the child's words and sentences. Pause often, especially after the child finishes speaking—communicate that it is OK to take time to think before you speak. Notice when the stuttering is more and less frequent. Avoid pressuring the child to speak quickly. In class discussions, call on her or him early in the discussion so tension won't build up, and ask a question that can be answered with few words. Speak frankly about the stuttering, but assure the student it is nothing to be ashamed of—many successful people, including kings, have shared the challenge and learned to improve (Friend, 2011; Rosenberg et al. 2011).

Voicing problems, a third type of speech impairment, include speaking with an inappropriate pitch, quality, or loudness, or in a monotone. A student with any of these problems should be referred to a speech therapist. Recognizing the problem is the first step. Be alert for students whose pronunciation, loudness, voice quality, speech fluency, expressive range, or rate is very different from that of their peers. Pay attention also to students who seldom speak. Are they simply shy, or do they have difficulties with language?

LANGUAGE DISORDERS. Language differences are not necessarily language disorders. Students with language disorders are markedly deficient in their ability to understand or express language, compared with other students of their own age and cultural group

Speech disorder Inability to produce sounds effectively for speaking.

Articulation disorders Any of a variety of pronunciation difficulties, such as the substitution, distortion, or omission of sounds.

Voicing problems Inappropriate pitch, quality, loudness, or intonation.

TABLE 4.7 • **Encouraging Language Development**

- Talk about things that interest children.
- Follow the children's lead. Reply to their initiations and comments. Share their excitement.
- Don't ask too many questions. If you must, use questions such as *how did/do...*, *why did/do...*, and *what happened...* that result in longer explanatory answers.
- Encourage children to ask questions. Respond openly and honestly. If you don't want to answer a question, say so and explain why. (*I don't think I want to answer that question; it's very personal.*)
- Use a pleasant tone of voice. You need not be a comedian, but you can be light and humorous. Children love it when adults are a little silly.
- Don't be judgmental or make fun of children's language. If you are overly critical of children's language or try to catch and correct all errors, they will stop talking to you.
- Allow enough time for children to respond.
- Treat children with courtesy by not interrupting when they are talking.
- Include children in family and classroom discussions. Encourage participation and listen to their ideas.
- Be accepting of children and of their language. Hugs and acceptance can go a long way.
- Provide opportunities for children to use language and to have that language work for them to accomplish their goals.

Source: Adapted from information in Owens, Robert E. Jr. Language Disorders: A Functional Approach to Assessment and Intervention, 5e. Published by Allyn and Bacon, Boston, MA. Copyright © 2010 by Pearson Education. Adapted by permission of the publisher.

(Owens, 2012). Students who seldom speak, who use few words or very short sentences, or who rely only on gestures to communicate should be referred to a qualified school professional for observation or testing. Table 4.7 gives ideas for promoting language development for all students.

Students with Emotional or Behavioral Difficulties

Students with **emotional and behavioral disorders** can be among the most difficult to teach in a regular class, and they are a source of concern for many prospective teachers (Avramidis, Bayliss, & Burden, 2000). The future is not bright for students with emotional and behavioral disorders who do not get appropriate help. About one-third of these students are arrested during their school years and half are unemployed 3 to 5 years after leaving school (Rosenberg et al., 2011), so early intervention is really important.

Professionals in education define behavioral disorders as behaviors that deviate so much from the norm that they interfere with the child's own growth and development and/or the lives of others. The language in IDEA describes *emotional disturbances* (*ED*) that involve inappropriate behaviors, unhappiness or depression, fears and anxieties, and trouble with relationships. The American Psychological Association and the medical community refer to these behavioral difficulties as *mental disorders* (Friend, 2011). Table 4.8 describes a few of the specific disorders covered by the Diagnostic and Statistical Manual of Mental Disorders (4th edition, revised), also called the DSM-IV-TR.

However they are defined, what you will observe as a teacher are students who are aggressive, anxious, withdrawn, or depressed and who often have difficulty following rules, paying attention, or interacting with others. There are over 400,000 students with emotional disturbances in the United States, making this the 5th largest group receiving services. This number has increased about 20% since 1991–1992. As with learning disabilities and ADHD, there are more boys than girls diagnosed with these disorders—at least 3 times as many boys as girls identified. One troubling fact is that African American students are overrepresented in this category. They make up about 13% of the population, but about 26% of the students identified with emotional and behavioral disorders.

The range of possible emotional and behavioral disorders is wide. And students with other disabilities—learning disabilities, intellectual disabilities, or ADHD, for example—may also have emotional or behavioral problems as they struggle in school. Methods from applied behavioral analysis and direct teaching of self-regulation skills (Chapter 8)

Emotional and behavioral disorders Behaviors or emotions that deviate so much from the norm that they interfere with the child's own growth and development and/or the lives of others—inappropriate behaviors, unhappiness or depression, fears and anxieties, and trouble with relationships.

TABLE 4.8 • **Examples of Emotional and Behavioral Disorders from the *Diagnostic and Statistical Manual of Mental Disorders***

The definition of emotional and behavior disorders in IDEA is general: It does not list particular conditions. However, in the medical community many specific disorders have been identified, and these are included in the *Diagnostic and Statistical Manual of Mental Disorders* (fourth edition, text revision) (*DSM-IV-TR*). Instead of being called emotional and behavior disorders, they are referred to as mental disorders. The following list, although not complete, includes examples of mental disorders listed in that publication that educators would consider emotional and behavior disorders:

- **Anxiety disorders.** Anxiety disorders occur when students experience an overwhelming sense of fear or dread. One example is obsessive-compulsive disorder (OCD) in which students cannot stop themselves from worrying excessively about a specific concern, for example, germs. Other examples include phobias (fear of specific items, such as spiders, or fear of certain activities, such as going to school) and posttraumatic stress disorder (PTSD) in which students re-live in nightmares or flashbacks a traumatic event that they witnessed.
- **Disruptive behavior disorders.** This category includes three types of disorders:
  - *Attention deficit-hyperactivity disorder*. . . is characterized by inattention, a high level of activity and impulsivity, or a combination of these. Note, though, that it often is not considered a disability.
  - *Oppositional defiant disorder* (ODD) is diagnosed when students are defiant with adults and vindictive or blaming with peers to an excessive degree over a long period of time.
  - *Conduct disorders* are diagnosed when students fight, bully, display cruelty to animals or people, or otherwise repeatedly break serious rules.
- **Eating disorders.** The most common eating disorder is anorexia nervosa in which students believe they are overweight and refuse to eat, even when they are near starvation.
- **Mood disorders.** Also called affective disorders, this group includes depression . . . and bipolar disorder, also called manic depression, in which students' moods swing from extreme highs (manic) to extreme lows (depression).
- **Tic disorders.** Tics are involuntary, rapid, stereotyped movements of specific muscle groups. Students with tics may blink their eyes or repeatedly sniff. The most well known tic disorder is Tourette syndrome, a disorder that ranges from mild to severe and includes both facial or other physical tics as well as vocal tics, often "barking" or profanity.

Source: From Friend, Marilyn. Special Education: Contemporary Perspectives for School Professionals, 2e. Published by Allyn and Bacon, Boston, MA. Copyright © 2008 by Pearson Education. Reprinted by permission of the publisher.

are two useful approaches. Another possibility that has proved helpful for these students is to provide structure, organizational tools, and choices. Here are some ideas from Terri Swanson (2005):

- Structure the environment by minimizing visual and auditory stimulation, establishing clear visual boundaries between areas where different behaviors are expected, or organizing supplies in easy-to-use holders.
- Structure schedules by posting monthly and daily schedules, having clear starting and ending signals and clear procedures for turning in work.
- Structure activities by color-coding subject folders (blue for math, etc.), posting verbal instructions with visual prompts, or putting all materials needed for an activity in a "Science box."
- Structure rules and routines, for example, giving students a script to use in asking other students to play a game with them, writing rules out in a positive way, or preparing students for changes in routines such as spring break by reviewing pictures of what will be happening over the break.
- Offer choices by providing a short list of alternatives for completing assignments or projects.

Because students with emotional and behavioral disorders frequently break rules and push the limits, teachers often find themselves disciplining them. Be aware that there

GUIDELINES

Disciplining Students with Emotional Problems

Be careful not to violate due process rights of students—students and parents must know the behaviors expected and the consequences for misbehavior.

Examples

1. Communicate expectations clearly and in writing.
2. Ask parents and students to sign a copy of the classroom rules.
3. Post rules and consequences in class and on a class Web page.

Be very careful with severe punishments that remove students from class for a long time. These constitute a change in the child's educational program (IEP) and require due process.

Examples

1. Always follow due process for suspensions of more than 10 days.
2. Be aware of possible due process requirements for prolonged periods of time-out (in-school suspension).

Punishments for students with severe emotional problems must serve a clear educational purpose.

Examples

1. Give a rationale for punishment or correction that ties an action to a student's learning or the learning of others in the class.
2. Use written behavior contracts that include a rationale.

Make sure the rule and the punishment are reasonable.

Examples

1. Consider the student's age and physical condition.
2. Does the punishment match the offense and the way others in the class are treated?

3. Do other teachers handle similar situations in the same way?
4. Try less intrusive punishments first. Be patient. Move to more severe actions only when less severe procedures fail.

Keep good records and work collaboratively so all involved are informed.

Examples

1. Document the punishment of all students in a journal or log. List what precipitated the punishment, what procedures were used, how long the punishment lasted, the results, modifications to the punishment, and new results.
2. Note meetings with families, special education teachers, and the principal.
3. Make any changes involving management plans with families and other teachers.

Always use positive consequences in conjunction with negative ones.

Examples

1. If students lose points for breaking rules, give them ways to regain points through positive behavior.
2. Recognize genuine accomplishment and small steps—DON'T say, "Well, it's about time you . . ."

For more information on disciplining students with disabilities, see:
http://www.nasponline.org/communications/spawareness/effdiscipfs.pdf

---

have been court rulings on disciplining students with serious emotional problems (Yell, 1990). The *Guidelines* may help when you are faced with these situations.

Let's consider an area where teachers may be able to detect problems and make a difference—suicide.

SUICIDE. Of course, not every student with emotional or behavioral problems will consider suicide, but depression often is associated with suicide. Up to 10% of adolescents have attempted suicide at some point, but even more have considered it. Native Americans and students living in rural communities are more likely to commit suicide. There are several general risk factors, and they seem to apply to both male and female African American, Latino, and White adolescents: depression and substance abuse, history of suicide in the family, being under stress, tendency to be impulsive or perfectionistic, belief that a person goes to a better place after dying, and family rejection or conflict. Having more than one of these risk factors is especially dangerous (Friend, 2011; Steinberg, 2005). In addition, there is concern today that some drugs prescribed for depression or ADHD may increase the risk of suicide in adolescents.

Suicide often comes as a response to life problems—problems that parents and teachers sometimes dismiss. There are many warning signs that trouble is brewing. Watch for changes in eating or sleeping habits, weight, grades, disposition, activity level, or interest in friends or activities that were once fun. Students at risk sometimes suddenly give away prized possessions such as iPads, books, clothing, or pets. They may seem depressed or hyperactive and may say things like "Nothing matters anymore," "I shouldn't be here," "If I died, people might love me more," "You won't have to worry about me anymore," or "I wonder what dying is like." They may start missing school or quit doing work. It is especially dangerous if the student not only talks about suicide but also has a plan for carrying it out.

If you suspect that there is a problem, talk to the student directly, ask about his or her concerns. One feeling shared by many people who attempt suicide is that no one cared enough to ask. Ask about specifics, and take the student seriously. You may need to become an advocate for the student with administrators, parents, or other adults who dismiss the warning signs. Also, be aware that teenage suicides often occur in clusters. After one student acts or when stories about a suicide are reported in the media, other teens are more likely to copy the suicide (Lewinsohn, Rohde, & Seeley, 1994; Rice & Dolgin, 2002). Table 4.9 lists common myths and facts about suicide.

DRUG ABUSE. Although drug abuse is not always associated with emotional or behavioral problems and people without these challenges may abuse drugs, many adolescents with emotional problems also abuse drugs. Abusing drugs is especially dangerous for African American males. In one study that followed a sample of adolescents from ages 19 to 27, about 33% of the African American young men who abused drugs died by age 27, compared to 3% for White males. The death rate for both African American and White females who abused drugs was 1% (Clark, Martin, & Cornelius, 2008).

TABLE 4.9 • **Myths and Facts about Suicide**

Myth:	People who talk about suicide don't kill themselves, they are just trying to get attention.
Fact:	People who die by suicide usually talk about it first. They are in pain and oftentimes reach out for help because they do not know what to do and have lost hope. Always take talk about suicide seriously. Always.
Myth:	Only certain types of people commit suicide.
Fact:	All types of people commit suicide—male and female, young and old, rich and poor, country people and city people. It happens in every racial, ethnic, and religious group.
Myth:	You should never ask people who are suicidal if they are thinking about suicide or if they have thought about a method, because just talking about it will give them the idea.
Fact:	Asking people if they are thinking about suicide does not give them the idea for suicide. And it is important to talk about suicide with people who are suicidal because you will learn more about their mindset and intentions, and allow them to diffuse some of the tension that is causing their suicidal feelings.
Myth:	Most people who kill themselves really want to die.
Fact:	The vast majority of people who are suicidal do not want to die. They are in pain, and they want to stop the pain. Suicide is often intended as a cry for help.
Myth:	Young people never think about suicide, they have their entire life ahead of them.
Fact:	Suicide is the third leading cause of death for young people ages 15–24. Sometimes children under 10 die by suicide.

Source: Adapted from information by Kevin Caruso, Suicide Myths, Suicide.org. Available online at http://www.suicide.org/suicide-myths.html

TABLE 4.10 • **Percentage of Students in the United States Grades 8 through 12 Who Reported Using These Drugs in the Past 30 Days**

DRUG	8TH GRADE	10TH GRADE	12TH GRADE	SIGNIFICANT INCREASE OVER ALL GRADES 2009–2010
Any illicit drug	9.5	18.5	23.8	
Marijuana	8.0	16.7	21.4	yes
Inhalants	3.6	2.0	1.4	
LSD	.6	.7	.8	
Ecstasy	1.1	1.9	1.4	yes
Cocaine	.6	.9	1.3	
Heroin	0.4	.4	.4	
Amphetamines	1.8	3.3	3.3	
Been drunk	5.0	14.7	26.8	
Cigarettes	7.1	13.6	19.2	
Smokeless tobacco	4.1	7.5	8.5	

Source: Drawn from data in Johnston, L. D., O'Malley, P. M., Bachman, J. G., & Schulenberg, J. E. (2011). Monitoring the Future National Results on Adolescent Drug Use: Overview of Key Findings, 2010. Ann Arbor: Institute for Social Research, The University of Michigan. Available online at http://www.monitoringthefuture.org/

Modern society makes growing up a very confusing process. Notice the messages from films and billboards. "Beautiful," popular, happy people drink alcohol and smoke cigarettes, with little concern for their health. Males are encouraged to "drink like a man!" We have over-the-counter drugs for almost every common ailment, and constant ads from drug companies broadcast the benefits of new prescription medications. Coffee or an "energy drink" wakes us up, and a pill helps us sleep. And then we tell students to "say no!" to drugs.

For many reasons, not just because of these contradictory messages, drug use has become a problem for students. Accurate statistics are hard to find, but estimates from the *Monitoring the Future* survey by researchers at the University of Michigan (Johnston, O'Malley, Bachman, & Schulenberg, 2011) indicate that 9.5% of 8th graders, 18.5% of 10th graders, and 23.8% of 12th graders reported using an illicit drug *in the past 30 days*, with marijuana being the most popular (see Table 4.10). In fact, marijuana use increased among teens from 2008 through 2010—the last data available when I wrote this chapter, with about 1% of 8th graders, 3% of 10th graders, and 6% of 12th graders reporting they use marijuana *daily*. Patterns of use for other drugs are inconsistent—use of ecstasy, cigarettes, and heroin is increasing for older students, but use of alcohol, cocaine, Vicodin, and sedatives is down. Use of many other drugs has leveled off—LSD, PCP, crack cocaine, OxyContin, methamphetamine, cough and cold medicines taken to get high, several so-called "club drugs" (Rohypnol, GHB, and ketamine), and anabolic steroids. Younger adolescents are more likely to use inhalants (glues, paint thinners, nail polish remover, aerosol sprays, etc.). They are inexpensive and available. And students don't realize that they are risking injury or death when they use inhalants.

Remarkably, about 15% of high school boys and 2% of girls have used some form of spit or other type of smokeless tobacco. The use of smokeless tobacco can cause cancers of the mouth, throat, larynx, esophagus, stomach, and pancreas; receding gums and gum disease (leading finally to tooth loss, pre-cancerous spots in the mouth), nicotine addiction, and possibly to heart disease and stroke (American Cancer Society, 2010).

PREVENTION. We should distinguish between experimentation and abuse. Many students try something at a party, but do not become regular users. Providing information or "scare" tactics such as the DARE drug prevention program seems to have little positive effect and may even encourage curiosity and experimentation (Dusenbury & Falco, 1995; Tobler & Stratton, 1997).

So what is more effective? Adam Fletcher and his colleagues analyzed research on school programs around the world. One overwhelmingly frequent finding was that after taking into account students' prior drug use and personal characteristics, "disengagement from school and poor teacher–student relations were associated with subsequent drug use and other risky health behaviors" (Fletcher, Bonell, & Hargreaves, 2008, p. 217). For example, the researchers describe one study that found, for young adolescents, being disconnected with school predicted their drug use 2 to 4 years later. One implication is that engaging adolescents in schools, forming positive relationships, and connecting the students to caring adults and peers is critical in creating a protective environment.

Students with Intellectual Disabilities

A word about terms. **Intellectual disability** is a more current name for *mental retardation*. You may also have heard the terms *cognitive impairment, general learning disability*, or *cognitive disability*. Intellectual disability is the preferred name, because the term *mental retardation* is considered offensive and stigmatizing; however, mental retardation still is used in the IDEA definitions and in many schools. In 2007, the American Association on Mental Retardation changed its name to the American Association on Intellectual and Developmental Disabilities (AAIDD) to reflect this rejection of the term *mental retardation*. The AAIDD definition of *intellectual disability* is "a disability characterized by significant limitations in both intellectual functioning and adaptive behavior as expressed in conceptual, social, and practical adaptive skills. This disability originates before age 18" (AAIDD.org).

Intellectual function is usually measured by IQ tests, with a score below 70 being one of the indicators. But an IQ score below the 70 range is not enough to diagnose a child as having intellectual disabilities. There must also be problems with adaptive behavior, day-to-day independent living, and social functioning. This caution is especially important when interpreting the scores of students from different cultures. Defining disability based on test scores alone can create what some critics call "the 6-hour retarded child"—students who are seen as disabled only for the part of the day they attend school.

Only about 1% of the population fit the AAIDD's definition of disability in both intellectual functioning and adaptive behavior. For years, this group was further divided into mild (IQ 50–69), moderate (IQ 35–49), severe (IQ 20–34), and profound levels (IQ below 20). Many school districts still use this system, and so does the World Health Organization. However, the IQ ranges are not perfect predictors of individuals' abilities to function, so the AAIDD now recommends a classification scheme based on the amount of support that a person requires to function at his or her highest level. Support varies from intermittent (e.g., as needed during stressful times), to limited (consistent support, but time-limited such as employment training), to extensive (daily care such as living in a group home), to pervasive (constant high-intensity care for all aspects of living) (Taylor, Richards, & Brady, 2005).

As a regular teacher, you may not have contact with children needing extensive or pervasive support unless your school is participating in a full inclusion program, but you probably will work with children needing intermittent or limited support. In the early grades, these students may simply learn more slowly than their peers. They need more time and more practice to learn, and they may have difficulty transferring learning from one setting to another or putting small skills together to accomplish a more complex task. They often have difficulties with metacognitive skills and executive functioning required to plan, monitor, and redirect attention and learning strategies (Simon, 2010), so very

Intellectual disabilities/Mental retardation Significantly below-average intellectual and adaptive social behavior, evident before age 18.

GUIDELINES

Teaching Students with Intellectual Disabilities

1. Develop specific learning objectives based on an analysis of each student's learning strengths and weaknesses. No matter what a student knows, he or she is ready to learn the next step.

2. Work on practical skills and concepts based on the demands of adult life.

3. Analyze the task the student will be learning—identify the specific steps involved in successful completion—don't overlook any steps in your planning.

4. State and present objectives simply.

5. Present material in small, logical steps. Practice extensively before going on to the next step. Use resources such as computer drill and practice exercises in class or have volunteers and family members continue guiding practice outside class.

6. Do not skip steps. Students with average intelligence can form conceptual bridges from one step to the next and make metacognitive judgments about how they are doing, but children with below-average intelligence need every step and bridge made explicit. Make connections for the student. Do not expect him or her to "see" the connections.

7. Be prepared to present the same idea in many different ways using different representations (verbal, visual, hands-on, etc.).

8. Go back to a simpler level if you see the student is not following.

9. Be especially careful to motivate the student and maintain attention. Allow and encourage different ways of expressing understanding—written, drawings, oral responses, gestures, etc.

10. Find materials that do not insult the student. A middle school boy may need the low vocabulary of "See Spot run," but will be insulted by the age of the characters and the content of the story.

11. Focus on a few target behaviors or skills so you and the student have a chance to experience success. Everyone needs positive reinforcement.

12. Be aware that students with below-average intelligence must overlearn, repeat, and practice more than children of average intelligence. They must be taught how to study, and they must frequently review and practice their newly acquired skills in different settings.

13. Pay close attention to social relations. Simply including students with below-average intelligence in a regular class will not guarantee that they will be accepted or that they will make and keep friends.

14. Establish peer tutoring programs and train all students in the class to serve as tutors and as tutees—see Chapter 10 for specifics.

For more information, see: http://www.aaidd.org/

---

structured and complete teaching and guidance makes sense. The *Guidelines* list more suggestions.

Learning goals for many students with intellectual disabilities who are between the ages of 9 and 13 include basic reading, writing, and arithmetic; learning about the local environment; social behavior; and personal interests. In middle and senior high school, the emphasis is on vocational and domestic skills, literacy for living (reading signs, labels, and newspaper ads; completing a job application), job-related behaviors such as courtesy and punctuality; health self-care; and citizenship skills. Today, there is a growing emphasis on **transition programming**—preparing the student to live and work in the community. As you saw earlier in the chapter, the law requires that schools design an IEP, or individualized educational program, for every child with disabilities. An ITP, or individualized transition plan, may be part of the IEP for students with intellectual disabilities (Friend, 2011).

Students with Health and Sensory Impairments

Some health impairments you may encounter are cerebral palsy, seizure disorders, asthma, HIV/AIDS, diabetes, visual impairments, and hearing impairments.

CEREBRAL PALSY AND MULTIPLE DISABILITIES. Damage to the brain before or during birth or during infancy can cause a child to have difficulty coordinating his or her body movements. The problem may be very mild, so the child simply appears a bit clumsy, or so severe that voluntary movement is practically impossible. The most common form of **cerebral palsy** is characterized by **spasticity** (overly tight or tense muscles). Many children

Transition programming Gradual preparation of students with special needs to move from high school into further education or training, employment, or community involvement.

Cerebral palsy Condition involving a range of motor or coordination difficulties due to brain damage.

Spasticity Overly tight or tense muscles, characteristic of some forms of cerebral palsy.

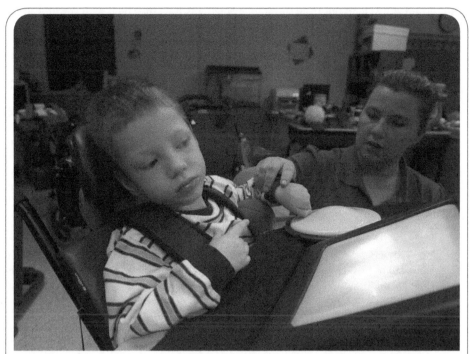

INSTRUCTIONAL ACCOMMODATIONS Physical and instructional accommodations can enable students with many kinds of disabilities to participate in general education classrooms. A specially designed desk enables this young child with cerebral palsy to work independently in class.

with cerebral palsy also have secondary handicaps. In the classroom, these secondary handicaps are the greatest concern—and these are generally what the regular teacher can help with most. For example, many children with cerebral palsy also have visual impairments or speech problems, and about 50% to 60% have mild to severe intellectual disabilities. But many students with cerebral palsy are average to well above average in measured intelligence (Pellegrino, 2002).

SEIZURE DISORDERS (EPILEPSY). A seizure is a cluster of behaviors that occurs in response to abnormal neurochemical activities in the brain (Hardman, Drew, & Egan, 2005). People with **epilepsy** have recurrent seizures, but not all seizures are the result of epilepsy; temporary conditions such as high fevers, infections, or withdrawal from drugs can also trigger seizures. Seizures take many forms and differ with regard to the length, frequency, and movements involved.

Most **generalized seizures** (once called *grand mal*) are accompanied by uncontrolled jerking movements that ordinarily last two to five minutes, possible loss of bowel or bladder control, and irregular breathing, followed by a deep sleep or coma. On regaining consciousness, the student may be very weary, confused, and in need of extra sleep. Most seizures can be controlled by medication. If a student has a seizure accompanied by convulsions in class, the teacher must take action so the student will not be injured. The major danger to a student having such a seizure is being injured from striking a hard surface during the violent jerking.

If a student has a seizure, stay calm and reassure the rest of the class. Do not try to restrain the child's movements; you can't stop the seizure once it starts. Lower the child gently to the floor, away from furniture or walls. Move hard objects away. Loosen scarves, ties, or anything that might make breathing difficult. Turn the child's head gently to the side, and put a soft coat or blanket under his or her head. Never put anything in the student's mouth—it is NOT true that people having seizures can swallow their tongues. Don't attempt artificial respiration unless the student does not start breathing again after

Epilepsy   Disorder marked by seizures and caused by abnormal electrical discharges in the brain.

Generalized seizure   A seizure involving a large portion of the brain.

the seizure stops. Find out from the student's parents how they deal with seizures. If one seizure follows another and the student does not regain consciousness in between, if the student is pregnant or has a medical ID that does not say "epilepsy, seizure disorder," if there are signs of injury, or if the seizure goes on for more than 5 minutes, get medical help right away (Friend, 2011).

Not all seizures are dramatic. Sometimes the student just loses contact briefly. The student may stare, fail to respond to questions, drop objects, and miss what has been happening for 1 to 30 seconds. These were once called *petit mal*, but they are now referred to as **absence seizures** and can easily go undetected. If a child in your class appears to daydream frequently, does not seem to know what is going on at times, or cannot remember what has just happened when you ask, you should consult the school psychologist or nurse. The major problem for students with absence seizures is that they miss the continuity of the class interaction—these seizures can occur as often as 100 times a day. If their seizures are frequent, students will find the lessons confusing. Question these students to be sure they are understanding and following the lesson. Be prepared to repeat yourself periodically.

OTHER SERIOUS HEALTH CONCERNS: ASTHMA, HIV/AIDS, AND DIABETES. There are many other health problems that affect students' learning, in great part because the students miss school, leading to lost instructional time and missed opportunities for friendships. Asthma is a chronic lung condition affecting 5 to 6 million children in America; it is more common for students in poverty. You probably have heard quite a bit about HIV/AIDS, a chronic illness in children that often can be controlled with medication. Luckily, we are making great progress in preventing HIV infection in children in the United States.

Type 2 diabetes is a chronic condition that affects the way the body metabolizes sugar (glucose). This condition needs to be taken seriously because it can affect almost every major organ in the body, including the heart, blood vessels, nerves, eyes, and kidneys (Mayo Clinic, 2009). For most children, this disease can be managed, or prevented altogether, by eating healthy foods, being physically active, and maintaining a healthy body weight. When diet and exercise modifications are not enough, children will need medications, such as insulin, to manage their blood sugar (Rosenberg et al., 2011; Werts, Culatta, & Tompkins, 2007).

With all health conditions, teachers need to talk to parents to find out how the problems are handled, what the signs are that a dangerous situation might be developing, and what resources are available for the student. Keep records of any incidents—they may be useful in the student's medical diagnosis and treatment.

STUDENTS WITH VISION IMPAIRMENTS. In the United States, only about 1 child in 1,000 has a visual impairment so serious that special educational services are needed. Most members of this group needing special services are classified as having **low vision**. This means they can read with the aid of a magnifying glass or large-print books. A small group of students, about 1 in every 2,500, is **educationally blind**. These students must use hearing and touch as their predominant learning channels (Kirk, Gallagher, & Anastasiow, 1993).

Students who have difficulty seeing often hold books either very close to or very far from their eyes. They may squint, rub their eyes frequently, or complain that their eyes burn or itch. The eyes may actually be swollen, red, or encrusted. Students with vision problems may misread material on the whiteboard or chalkboard, describe their vision as being blurred, be very sensitive to light, or hold their heads at an odd angle. They may become irritable when they have to do deskwork or lose interest if they have to follow an activity that is taking place across the room (Hunt & Marshall, 2002). Any of these signs should be reported to a qualified school professional.

Special materials and equipment that help these students to function in regular classrooms include large-print books; software that converts printed material to speech or to Braille; personal organizers that have talking appointment books or address books; special calculators; an abacus; three-dimensional maps, charts, and models; and special

Absence seizure A seizure involving only a small part of the brain that causes a child to lose contact briefly.

Low vision Vision limited to close objects.

Educationally blind Needing Braille materials in order to learn.

measuring devices. For students with visual problems, the quality of the print is often more important than the size, so watch out for hard-to-read handouts and blurry copies.

The arrangement of the room is also an issue. Students with visual problems need to know where things are, so consistency matters—a place for everything and everything in its place. Leave plenty of space for moving around the room, and make sure to monitor possible obstacles and safety hazards such as trash cans in aisles and open cabinet doors. If you rearrange the room, give students with visual problems a chance to learn the new layout. Also make sure these students have a buddy for fire drills or other emergencies (Friend & Bursuck, 2002).

STUDENTS WHO ARE DEAF. You will hear the term *hearing impaired* to describe these students, but the deaf community and researchers object to this label, so I will use their preferred terms, *deaf* and *hard of hearing*. The number of deaf students has been declining over the past three decades, but when the problem does occur, the consequences for learning are serious (Hunt & Marshall, 2002). Signs of hearing problems are turning one ear toward the speaker, favoring one ear in conversation, or misunderstanding conversation when the speaker's face cannot be seen. Other indications include not following directions, seeming distracted or confused at times, frequently asking people to repeat what they have said, mispronouncing new words or names, and being reluctant to participate in class discussions. Take note particularly of students who have frequent earaches, sinus infections, or allergies.

In the past, educators have debated whether oral or manual approaches are better for children who are deaf or hard of hearing. Oral approaches involve speech reading (also called *lip reading*) and training students to use whatever limited hearing they may have. Manual approaches include sign language and finger spelling. Research indicates that children who learn some manual method of communicating perform better in academic subjects and are more socially mature than students who are exposed only to oral methods. Today, the trend is to combine both approaches (Hallahan & Kauffman, 2006).

Another perspective suggests that people who are deaf are part of a different culture with a different language, values, social institutions, and literature. Hunt and Marshall (2002) quote one deaf professional: "How would women like to be referred to as male-impaired, or whites like to be called black-impaired? I'm not impaired; I'm deaf!" (p. 348). From this perspective, a goal is to help deaf children become bilingual and bicultural, to enable them to function effectively in both cultures. Technological innovations and the many avenues of communication through e-mail and the Internet have expanded communication possibilities for all people.

Autism Spectrum Disorders and Asperger Syndrome

You may be familiar with the term *autism*. In 1990 **autism** was added to the IDEA list of disabilities qualifying for special services. It is defined as "a developmental disability significantly affecting verbal and nonverbal communication and social interaction, generally evident before age three, that adversely affect the child's educational performance" (34 Federal Code of Regulations § 300.7). I will use the term preferred by professionals in the field, **autism spectrum disorders** to emphasize that autism includes a range of disorders from mild to major. You might also hear the term **pervasive developmental disorder (PDD)**, especially if you are talking with medical professionals. Estimates of the number of children with autism vary greatly, but are increasing dramatically. IDEA places the number on the autism spectrum at .25% of all children, ages 3 to 21. The most recent report from the Centers for Disease Control is 1 in every 310 girls and 1 in every 70 boys (CDC, 2010). Other estimates range as high a 1% of all children, ages 3 to 17 (Friend, 2011).

From early on, children with autism spectrum disorders may have difficulties in social relations. They do not form connections with others, avoid eye contact, or don't share feelings such as enjoyment or interest in others. Communication is impaired. About half of these students are nonverbal; they have no or very few language skills. Others make up their own language. They may obsessively insist on regularity and sameness in their environments—change is very disturbing. They may repeat behaviors or gestures and have restricted interests, watching the same DVD over and over, for example. They

Autism/Autism spectrum disorders Developmental disability significantly affecting verbal and nonverbal communication and social interaction, generally evident before age 3 and ranging from mild to major.

Pervasive developmental disorder (PDD) A term favored by the medical community to describe autism spectrum disorders.

SOME FACES OF ASPERGER SYNDROME In his book, *The Genesis of Artistic Creativity: Asperger Syndrome and the Arts,* Michael Fitzgerald (2005) speculates that the famous musicians Beethoven and Mozart, and the artists van Gogh and Warhol display behaviors associated with Asperger syndrome.

may be very sensitive to light, sound, touch, or other sensory information—sounds may be painful, for example, or the slight flickering of fluorescent lights may seem like constant bursts, causing severe headaches. They may be able to memorize words or steps in problem solving, but not use them appropriately or become very confused when the situation changes or questions are asked in a different way (Franklin, 2007; Friend, 2011; Matson, Matson, & Rivet, 2007).

Asperger syndrome is one of the disabilities included in the autism spectrum. Children with Asperger syndrome have many of the characteristics described above, but they have the greatest trouble with social relations. Language is less affected. Their speech may be fluent but unusual, mixing up pronouns of "I" and "you," for example. Many students with autism also have moderate to severe intellectual disabilities, but those with Asperger syndrome usually have average to above average intelligence (Friend, 2011).

THEORY OF MIND. One current explanation for autism and Asperger syndrome is that children with these disorders lack a theory of mind (Miller, 2009). We examined this concept briefly in Chapter 2—theory of mind is an understanding that you and other people have minds, thoughts, and emotions. Students with autism have difficulty explaining their own behaviors, appreciating that other people might have different feelings, and predicting how behaviors might affect emotions. So, for example, a student may not understand why classmates are bored by his constant repetition of stories or obscure facts about topics he finds fascinating. Or the student may stand too close or too far away when interacting, not realizing that she is making other people uncomfortable (Friend, 2011; Harris, 2006).

INTERVENTIONS. Early and intense interventions that focus on communications and social relations are particularly important for children with autism spectrum disorders. Without interventions, behaviors such as poor eye contact and odd-seeming mannerisms tend to increase over time (Matson et al., 2007). As they move into elementary school, some of these students will be in inclusive settings, others will be in specialized classes, and many will be in some combination of these two. Collaboration among teachers and the family is particularly important. Strategies such as providing smaller classes, offering structured environments, finding a class "buddy" to give support, maintaining a safe "home base" for times of stress, ensuring consistency in instruction and transition routines, implementing assistive technologies, and using visuals may be part of a collaborative plan (Friend, 2011; Harrower & Dunlap, 2001). Through adolescence and the transition to adulthood, instruction and guidance in life, work, and social skills are important educational goals.

Response to Intervention (RTI)

One of the problems for students with serious learning problems is that they have to struggle through the early grades, often falling farther and farther behind, until they are identified, assessed, qualified for an IDEA category, receive an individualized educational program (IEP), and finally get appropriate help. This has been called the "wait to fail" model. The reauthorization of IDEA in 2004 gave educators a new option for assessing and educating students who might have serious learning problems. The process is called **response to intervention** or **RTI**. The main goal of RTI is to make sure students get appropriate research-based instruction and support as soon as possible, in kindergarten if they need it, before they have fallen too far behind. A second goal is to make sure teachers are systematic in documenting the interventions they have tried with these students and describing how well each intervention worked. In addition, instead of using the discrepancy between IQ scores and student achievement to identify students with learning disabilities, educators can now use RTI criteria to determine who needs more intensive learning support (Klinger & Orosco, 2010). However, this last use of RTI has been criticized for not being a valid or reliable way of assessing students with learning disabilities because it does not provide a comprehensive and thorough picture of the student's strengths and weaknesses, including documenting other problems that might be present (Reynolds & Shaywitz, 2009).

RESPONSE TO INTERVENTION (RTI) One of the main goals of the response to intervention (RTI) process is to identify students who may have learning difficulties as early as possible so that they don't fall too far behind before problems are recognized. A second goal is to document what works and what doesn't with each student for planning.

One common way of reaching these RTI goals is to use a three-tiered system (sometimes a fourth tier is added). The first tier is to use a strong, well-researched way of teaching all students (we will look at these kinds of approaches in Chapter 14). Students who are struggling in the tier 1 curriculum, as identified by ongoing quality classroom assessments, are moved to the second tier and receive extra support and additional small-group instruction. If some students still make limited progress, they move to the third tier for additional one-to-one intensive help and perhaps a special needs assessment (Buffum, Mattos, & Weber, 2010). The approach has at least two advantages—students get extra help right away and the information gained based on their responses to the different interventions can be used for IEP planning, if the students reach the third stage of RTI. For more information on RTI, go to the Web site for the National Center on Response to Intervention (http://www.rti4success.org/).

We end the chapter with another group that has special needs, but is not covered by IDEA or Section 504—highly intelligent or talented students.

STUDENTS WHO ARE GIFTED AND TALENTED

Consider this situation, a true story.

> Latoya was already an advanced reader when she entered 1st grade in a large urban school district. Her teacher noticed the challenging chapter books Latoya brought to school and read with little effort. After administering a reading assessment, the school's reading consultant confirmed that Latoya was reading at the 5th grade level. Latoya's parents reported with pride that she had started to read independently when she was 3 years old and "had read every book she could get her hands on." (Reis et al., 2002)

In her struggling urban school, Latoya received no particular accommodations, and by 5th grade, she was still reading at just above the 5th grade level. Her 5th grade teacher had no idea that Latoya had ever been an advanced reader.

Response to intervention (RTI) A process to make sure students get appropriate research-based instruction and support as soon as possible and that teachers are systematic in documenting what interventions they have tried with these students so this information can be used in planning.

Here is another true story:

> Alex Wade's field is linguistics. In his search for the perfect language—and "annoyed," he says, with Esperanto—he has created 10 languages and 30 or 40 alphabets, including one language without verbs, just for the challenge. He's taking courses at the University of Nevada, Reno, in Basque, linguistics, and microbiology (because he also has a talent for science). . . . Alex is 13. (Kronholz, 2011)

Latoya and Alex are not alone. They are part of a group with special needs that is often overlooked by the schools: **gifted and talented students**. There is growing recognition that gifted students are being poorly served by most public schools. A national study found that more than one-half of all gifted students do not achieve in school at a level equal to their ability (Tomlinson-Keasey, 1990). Yet a survey of the states in 2008 by the National Association for Gifted Children (NAGC) found that at least a dozen states would not allow students to start kindergarten early, even if they were reading at a high level. At least 30 states allow only 11th and 12th graders to take college courses. What would that mean for students like Latoya and Alex (Kronholz, 2011)?

Who Are These Students?

There are many definitions of *gifted* because individuals can have many different gifts. Remember that Gardner (2003) identified eight separate "intelligences" and Sternberg (1997) suggests a triarchic model. Renzulli and Reis (2003) have a different three-part conception of giftedness: above-average general ability, a high level of creativity, and a high level of task commitment or motivation to achieve. The No Child Left Behind Act (2002) defines gifted students as those "who give evidence of high achievement capability in areas such as intellectual, creative, artistic, or leadership capacity, or in specific academic fields, and who need services or activities not ordinarily provided by the school in order to fully develop those capabilities" (p. 544). The College of William and Mary's Center for Gifted Education makes additional distinctions based on measured IQ: gifted learners score above 130 on IQ tests, the highly gifted score above 145, the exceptionally gifted above 160, and the profoundly gifted above 175 (Kronholz, 2011).

Truly gifted children are not the students who simply learn quickly with little effort. The work of gifted students is original, extremely advanced for their age, and potentially of lasting importance. These children may read fluently with little instruction by age 3 or 4. They may play a musical instrument like a skillful adult, turn a visit to the grocery store into a mathematical puzzle, and become fascinated with algebra when their friends are having trouble with simple addition (Winner, 2000). Recent conceptions widen the view of giftedness to include attention to the children's culture, language, and special needs (Association for the Gifted, 2001). These newer conceptions are more likely to identify children like Latoya.

What do we know about these remarkable individuals? A classic study of the characteristics of the academically and intellectually gifted was started decades ago by Lewis Terman and colleagues (1925, 1947, 1959; Holahan & Sears, 1995). This huge project followed the lives of 1,528 gifted males and females and continued until 2010. The subjects all had IQ scores in the top 1% of the population (140 or above on the Stanford-Binet individual test of intelligence). They were identified on the basis of these test scores and teacher recommendations.

Terman and colleagues found that these gifted children were larger, stronger, and healthier than the norm. They often walked sooner and were more athletic. They were more emotionally stable than their peers and became better-adjusted adults than the average individual. They had lower rates of delinquency, emotional difficulty, divorce, drug problems, and so on. Of course, the teachers in Terman's study who made the nominations may have selected students who were better adjusted initially. And remember, Terman's study just tells about academically gifted students. There are many other kinds of gifts.

Gifted and talented students Very bright, creative, and talented students.

WHAT IS THE ORIGIN OF THESE GIFTS? Studies of prodigies and geniuses in many fields document that deep and prolonged practice is necessary to achieve at the highest levels. For example, it took Newton 20 years to move from his first ideas to his ultimate contribution (Howe, Davidson, & Sloboda, 1998; Winner, 2000). I remember listening to the early reports of Bloom's study of world-class concert pianists, sculptors, Olympic swimmers, research neurologists, mathematicians, and tennis champions, (1982). To study talent in tennis, Bloom's research team had interviewed the top tennis players in the world, their coaches, parents, siblings, and friends. One coach said that he would make a suggestion, and a few days later the young athlete would have mastered the move. Then the parents told how the child had practiced that move for hours on end after getting the coach's tip. So, focused, intense practice plays a role. Also, the families of prodigies tend to be child-centered and to devote hours to supporting the development of their child's gifts. Bloom's research team described tremendous sacrifices made by families: rising before dawn to drive their child to a swimming coach or piano teacher in another city, working two jobs, or even moving the whole family to another part of the country to find the best

ORIGINS OF GIFTEDNESS For years, researchers have debated the nature/ nurture question about people with extraordinary abilities and talents. Studies of prodigies and geniuses in many fields document that deep and prolonged practice is necessary to achieve at the highest levels.

teachers or coaches. The children responded to the family's sacrifices by working harder and the families responded to the child's hard work by sacrificing more—an upward spiral of investment and achievement.

But hard work will never make me a world-class tennis player or a Newton. There is a role for nature as well. The children studied by Bloom showed early and clear talent in the areas they later developed. As children, great sculptors were constantly drawing and great mathematicians were fascinated with dials, gears, and gauges. Parents' investments in their children came after the children showed early high-level achievement (Winner, 2000, 2003). Recent research suggests that gifted children, at least those with extraordinary abilities in mathematics, music, and visual arts, may have unusual brain organization—which can have both advantages and disadvantages. Giftedness in mathematics, music, and visual arts appears to be associated with superior visual-spatial abilities and enhanced development of the right side of the brain. Children with these gifts are also more likely not to have right-hand dominance and to have language related-problems. These brain differences are evidence that "gifted children, child prodigies, and savants are not made from scratch but are born with unusual brains that enable rapid learning in a particular domain" (Winner, 2000, p. 160).

WHAT PROBLEMS DO THE GIFTED FACE? In spite of Bloom's and Terman's findings, it would be incorrect to say that every gifted student is superior in adjustment and emotional health. In fact, gifted adolescents, especially girls, are more likely to be depressed, and both girls and boys may be bored, frustrated, and isolated. Schoolmates may be consumed with baseball or worried about failing math, while the gifted child is fascinated with Mozart, focused on a social issue, or totally absorbed in computers, drama, or geology. Gifted children may be impatient with friends, parents, and even teachers who do not share their interests or abilities (Woolfolk & Perry, 2012). One researcher asked 13,000 gifted students in 7 states to name one word for their experiences. The most commonly used word was "waiting." "Waiting for teachers to move ahead, waiting for classmates to catch up, waiting to learn something new—always waiting" (Kronholz, 2011, p. 3).

Because their language is well developed, gifted students may be seen as show-offs when they are simply expressing themselves. They are sensitive to the expectations and feelings of others, so these students may be very vulnerable to criticisms and taunts. Because they are goal directed and focused, they may seem stubborn and uncooperative. Their keen sense of humor can be used as a weapon against teachers and other students

(Hardman, Drew, & Egan, 2005; Robinson & Clinkenbeard, 1998). Adjustment problems seem to be greatest for the most gifted, those in the highest range of academic ability (e.g., above 180 IQ). The chance of any teacher encountering a student in this highest IQ range is only about 1 in 80 over an entire 40-year career—but what if such a student walks into your class (Kronholz, 2011)?

Identifying Gifted Students

Identifying gifted children is not always easy, and teaching them well may be even more challenging. Many parents provide early educational experiences for their children. In middle and high school, some very able students deliberately earn lower grades, making their abilities even harder to recognize. Girls are especially likely to hide their abilities (Woolfolk & Perry, 2012).

RECOGNIZING GIFTS AND TALENTS. Here are a few questions to guide identification, suggested by Marilyn Friend (2011). Who can easily manipulate abstract symbol systems such as mathematics? Who can concentrate for long periods of time on personal interests? Who remembers easily? Who developed language and reading early, like Latoya described at the beginning of this section? Who is curious and has many interests? Whose work is original and creative? Certainly Alex's interests and creativity in inventing languages, described earlier, fit these last two critieria. These students may also prefer to work alone, have a keen sense of justice and fairness, be energetic and intense, form strong commitments to friends—often older students—and struggle with perfectionism.

Group achievement and intelligence tests tend to underestimate the IQs of very bright children. Group tests may be appropriate for screening, but they are not appropriate for making placement decisions. There is some evidence that using individual IQ tests such as the WISC-IV, which include evaluations of verbal comprehension and working memory, are the best predictors of achievement in reading and math for gifted students (Rowe, Kingsley, & Thompson, 2010). Many psychologists recommend a case study approach. This means gathering many kinds of information about the student in different contexts: test scores, grades, examples of work, projects and portfolios, letters or ratings from community or church members, self-ratings, nominations from teachers or peers, and so on (Renzulli & Reis, 2003). Especially for recognizing artistic talent, experts in the field can be called in to judge the merits of a child's creations. Science projects, exhibitions, performances, auditions, and interviews are all possibilities. Creativity tests and tests of self-regulation skills may identify some children not picked up by other measures, particularly minority students who may be at a disadvantage on the other types of tests (Grigorenko, et al., 2009). Remember, students with remarkable abilities in one area may have much less impressive abilities in others. In fact, there may be up to 180,000 students in American schools who are gifted *and* learning disabled. In addition, there are two other groups who are underrepresented in gifted education programs: girls and students living in poverty (Stormont, Stebbins, & Holliday, 2001). See Table 4.11 for ideas about identifying and supporting these students.

Teaching Gifted Students

Some educators believe that gifted students should be *accelerated*—moved quickly through the grades or through particular subjects. Other educators prefer *enrichment*—giving the students additional, more sophisticated, and more thought-provoking work, but keeping them with their age-mates in school. Actually, both may be appropriate (Torrance, 1986). One way of doing this is through *curriculum compacting*—assessing students' knowledge of the material in the instructional unit, then teaching only for those goals not yet reached (Reis & Renzulli, 2004). Using curriculum compacting, teachers may be able to eliminate about half of the usual curriculum content for some gifted students without any loss of learning. The time saved can be used for learning goals that include enrichment, sophistication, and novelty (Werts et al., 2007).

ACCELERATION. Many people object to acceleration, but most careful studies indicate that truly gifted students who begin primary, elementary, middle, or high school, college,

TABLE 4.11 • **Recognizing and Supporting All Students with Gifts and Talents**

Recognizing Gifted Students with Learning Disabilities. Here are some ideas for supporting gifted students with learning disabilities (McCoach, Kehle, Bray, & Siegle, 2001):
• Identify these students by looking longitudinally at achievement. • Remediate skill deficits, but also identify and develop talents and strengths. • Provide emotional support; it is important for all students, but especially for this group. • Help students learn to compensate directly for their learning problems, and assist them in "tuning in" to their own strengths and difficulties.
Recognizing Gifts in Girls. As young girls develop their identities in adolescence, they often reject being labeled as gifted—being accepted and popular and "fitting in" may become more important than achievement (Basow & Rubin, 1999; Stormont et al., 2001). How can teachers reach girls who are gifted?
• Notice when girls' test scores seem to decline in middle or high school. • Encourage assertiveness, achievement, high goals, and demanding work from all students. • Provide models of achievement through speakers, internships, or readings. • Look for and support gifts in arenas other than academic achievement.
Recognizing Gifted Students Who Live in Poverty. Health problems, lack of resources, homelessness, fears about safety and survival, frequent moves, and responsibilities for the care of other family members all make achievement in school more difficult. To identify students with gifts:
• Use alternative assessment, teacher nomination, and creativity tests. • Be sensitive to cultural differences in values about cooperative or solitary achievement (Ford, 2000). • Use multicultural strategies to encourage both achievement and the development of racial identities.

or even graduate school early do as well as, and usually better than, nongifted students who are progressing at the normal pace. Social and emotional adjustment does not appear to be impaired. Gifted students tend to prefer the company of older playmates (Davis, Rimm, & Siegle, 2011). In fact, Colangelo, Assouline, and Gross (2004) collected the research on the many benefits of acceleration and published two volumes called *A Nation Deceived: How Schools Hold Back America's Brightest Children*. These publications from the University of Iowa make a powerful case for acceleration.

An alternative to skipping grades is to accelerate students in one or two particular subjects or to allow concurrent enrollment in advanced placement or college courses, but keep them with peers for the rest of the time (Robinson & Clinkenbeard, 1998). For students who are extremely advanced intellectually (for example, those scoring 160 or higher on an individual intelligence test), the only practical solution likely is to accelerate their education (Davis, Rimm, & Siegle, 2011; Kronholz, 2011).

METHODS AND STRATEGIES. Teaching methods for gifted students should encourage abstract thinking (formal-operational thought), creativity, reading of high-level and original texts, and independence, not just the learning of greater quantities of facts. One approach that *does not* seem promising with gifted students is cooperative learning in mixed-ability groups. Gifted students tend to learn more when they work in groups with other high-ability peers (Fuchs, Fuchs, Hamlett, & Karns, 1998; Robinson & Clinkenbeard, 1998). In fact, students in gifted programs appear to be less bored when they are ability grouped with others like themselves. An interesting tradeoff for gifted students is that their academic self-concepts tend to decrease when they are grouped with other high-ability students—an example of the "Little-Fish-in-a-Big-Pond" effect described in Chapter 3 (Preckel, Goetz, & Frenzel, 2010).

In working with gifted and talented students, a teacher must be imaginative, flexible, tolerant, and unthreatened by the capabilities of these students. The teacher must ask: What do these children need most? What are they ready to learn? Who can help me to challenge them? Challenge and support are critical for all students. But challenging students who know more than anyone else in the school about history or music or science or math can be a challenge! Answers might come from faculty members at nearby colleges, retired professionals, books, museums, the Internet, or older students. Strategies might be as simple as letting the child do math with the next grade. Other options are summer institutes; courses at nearby colleges; classes with local artists, musicians, or dancers; independent research projects; selected classes in high school for younger students; honors classes; and special-interest clubs (Rosenberg, Westling, & McLeskey, 2011).

In the midst of providing challenge, don't forget the support. We all have seen the ugly sights of parents, coaches, or teachers forcing the joy out of their talented students by demanding practice and perfection beyond the child's interest. Just as we should not force children to stop investing in their talent ("Oh, Michelangelo, quit fooling with those sketches and go outside and play"), we also should avoid destroying intrinsic motivation with heavy doses of pressure and external rewards.

This has been a brief, selective look at the needs of children. If you decide that students in your class might benefit from special services of any kind, the first step is making a referral. How would you begin? Table 4.12 guides you through the referral process. In Chapter 11, when we discuss differentiated teaching, we will look at more ways to reach all your students.

TABLE 4.12 • **Making a Referral**

1. Contact the student's parents. It is very important that you discuss the student's problems with the parents *before* you refer.
2. Before making a referral, check *all* the student's school records. Has the student ever:

   - had a psychological evaluation?
   - qualified for special services?
   - been included in other special programs (e.g., for disadvantaged children; speech or language therapy)?
   - scored far below average on standardized tests?
   - been retained?

   Do the records indicate:

   - good progress in some areas, poor progress in others?
   - any physical or medical problem?
   - that the student is taking medication?

3. Talk to the student's other teachers and professional support personnel about your concern for the student. Have other teachers also had difficulty with the student? Have they found ways of dealing successfully with the student? Document the strategies that you have used in your class to meet the student's educational needs. Your documentation will be useful as evidence that will be helpful to or be required by the committee of professionals who will evaluate the student. Demonstrate your concern by keeping written records. Your notes should include items such as:

   - exactly what you are concerned about
   - why you are concerned about it
   - dates, places, and times you have observed the problem
   - precisely what you have done to try to resolve the problem
   - who, if anyone, helped you devise the plans or strategies you have used
   - evidence that the strategies have been successful or unsuccessful

Remember that you should refer a student only if you can make a convincing case that the student may have a handicapping condition and probably cannot be served appropriately without special education. Referral for special education begins a time-consuming, costly, and stressful process that is potentially damaging to the student and has many legal ramifications.

▼ SUMMARY

Intelligence (pp. 118–130)

What are the advantages of and problems with labels? Labels and diagnostic classifications can easily become both stigmas and self-fulfilling prophecies, but they can also open doors to special programs and help teachers develop appropriate instructional strategies.

What is person-first language? "Person-first" language ("students with intellectual disabilities," "students placed at risk," etc.) is an alternative to labels that describe a complex person with one or two words, implying that the condition labeled is the most important aspect of the person. With person-first language, the emphasis is on the students first, not on the special challenges they face.

Distinguish between a disability and a handicap. A disability is an inability to do something specific such as see or walk. A handicap is a disadvantage in certain situations. Some disabilities lead to handicaps, but not in all contexts. Teachers must avoid imposing handicaps on disabled learners.

What is g? Spearman suggested there is one mental attribute, which he called g or general intelligence, that is used to perform any mental test, but that each test also requires some specific abilities in addition to g. A current version of the general plus specific abilities theory is Carroll's work identifying a few broad abilities (such as learning and memory, visual perception, verbal fluency) and at least 70 specific abilities. Fluid and crystallized intelligence are two of the broad abilities identified in most research.

What is Gardner's view of intelligence and his position on g? Gardner contends that an intelligence is a biological and psychological potential to solve problems and create outcomes that are valued by a culture. These intelligences are realized to a greater or lesser extent as a consequence of the experiential, cultural, and motivational factors in a person's environment. The intelligences are: linguistic, musical, spatial, logical-mathematical, bodily-kinesthetic, interpersonal, intrapersonal, naturalist, and perhaps existential. Gardner does not deny the existence of g, but questions how useful g is as an explanation for human achievements.

What are the elements in Sternberg's theory of intelligence? Sternberg's triarchic theory of intelligence is a cognitive process approach to understanding intelligence: Analytic/componential intelligence involves mental processes that are defined in terms of components: metacomponents, performance components, and knowledge-acquisition components. Creative/experiential intelligence involves coping with new experiences through insight and automaticity. Practical/contextual intelligence involves choosing to live and work in a context where success is likely, adapting to that context, and reshaping it if necessary. Practical intelligence is made up mostly of action-oriented tacit knowledge learned during everyday life.

How is intelligence measured, and what does an IQ score mean? Intelligence is measured through individual tests (Stanford-Binet, Wechsler, etc.) and group tests (Otis-Lennon School Abilities Tests, Slosson Intelligence Test, Raven Progressive Matrices, Naglieri Nonverbal Ability Test—Multiform, Differential Abilities Scales, Wide Range Intelligence Test, etc.). Compared to an individual test, a group test is much less likely to yield an accurate picture of any one person's abilities. The average score is 100. About 68% of

the general population will earn IQ scores between 85 and 115. Only about 16% of the population will receive scores below 85 or above 115. These figures hold true for White, native-born Americans whose first language is Standard English. Intelligence predicts success in school, but is less predictive of success in life when level of education is taken into account.

What is the Flynn effect and what are its implications? Since the early 1900s, IQ scores have been rising. To keep 100 as the average for IQ test scores, questions have to be made more difficult. This increasing difficulty has implications for any program that uses IQ scores as part of the entrance requirements. For example, students who were not identified as having learning problems a generation ago might be identified as having intellectual disabilities now because the test questions are harder.

Are there sex differences in cognitive abilities? Girls seem to be better on verbal tests, especially when writing is involved. Males seem to be superior on tasks that require mental rotation of objects. The scores of males tend to be more variable in general, so there are more males than females with very high and very low scores on tests. Research on the causes of these differences has been inconclusive, except to indicate that academic socialization and teachers' treatment of male and female students in mathematics classes may play a role.

Learning and Thinking Styles (pp. 130–132)

Distinguish between learning styles and learning preferences. Learning styles are the characteristic ways a person approaches learning and studying. Learning preferences are individual preferences for particular learning modes and environments. Even though learning styles and learning preferences are not related to intelligence or effort, they can affect school performance.

Should teachers match instruction to individual learning styles? Results of some research indicate that students learn more when they study in their preferred setting and manner, but most research does not show a benefit. Many students would do better to develop new—and perhaps more effective—ways to learn.

What learning style distinctions are the most well supported by research? One distinction that is repeatedly found in research is deep versus surface processing. Individuals who have a deep-processing approach see the learning activities as a means for understanding some underlying concepts or meanings. Students who take a surface-processing approach focus on memorizing the learning materials, not understanding them. A second is Mayer's visualizer–verbalizer dimension that has three facets: cognitive spatial ability (low or high), cognitive style (a visualizer versus a verbalizer), and learning preference (a verbal learner versus a visual learner).

Individual Differences and the Law (pp. 132–137)

Describe the main legal requirements that pertain to students with disabilities. Beginning with Public Law 94-142 (1975) and continuing with many reauthorizations including IDEA, the Individuals with Disabilities Education Act (2004), the requirements for teaching students with disabilities have been spelled out. Each learner or student with special needs (zero reject) should be educated in the least restrictive environment according to an individualized education program (IEP). The laws also protect the rights of students with special needs and their parents. In addition, Section 504 of the Vocational Rehabilitation Act of 1973 prevents discrimination against people with disabilities in any program that receives federal money, such as public schools. Through Section 504, all school-age children are ensured an equal opportunity to participate in school activities. The definition of disability is broad in Section 504 and in the Americans with Disabilities Act.

Students with Learning Challenges (pp. 138–157)

What does research in neuroscience tell us about learning problems? Studies of the brains of students with learning disabilities and with attention deficit disorders show some differences in structure and activity compared to those of students without problems. Students with learning disabilities have problems in using the system of working memory that holds verbal and auditory information while you work with it. Because children with learning disabilities have trouble holding on to words and sounds, it is difficult for them to put the words together to comprehend the meaning of a sentence or to figure out what a math story problem is really asking about. There also may be difficulties retrieving needed information from long-term memory while transforming new incoming information, such as the next numbers to add. Important bits of information keep getting lost.

What is a learning disability? Specific learning disabilities are disorders in one or more of the basic psychological processes involved in understanding or using spoken or written language. Listening, speaking, reading, writing, reasoning, or mathematical abilities might be affected. These disorders are intrinsic to the individual, presumed to be the result of central nervous system dysfunction, and may occur across the life span. Students with learning disabilities may become victims of learned helplessness when they come to believe that they cannot control or improve their own learning and therefore cannot succeed. A focus on learning strategies often helps students with learning disabilities.

What is ADHD and how is it handled in school? Attention-deficit hyperactivity disorder (ADHD) is the term used to describe individuals of any age with hyperactivity and attention difficulties. Use of medication to address ADHD is controversial, but currently on the rise. For many students there are negative side effects. In addition, little is known about the long-term effects of drug therapy. There also is no evidence that the drugs lead to improvement in academic learning or peer relationships. Approaches that combine motivational training with instruction in learning and memory strategies and behavior modification seem effective. The SMART approach that focuses on the abilities of children is another possibility.

What are the most common communication disorders? Common communication disorders include speech impairments (articulation disorders, stuttering, and voicing problems) and oral language disorders. If these problems are addressed early, great progress is possible.

What are the best approaches for students with emotional and behavioral disorders? Methods from applied behavioral analysis and direct teaching of social skills are two useful approaches. Students also may respond to structure and organization in the environment, schedules, activities, and rules.

What are some warning signs of potential suicide? Students at risk of suicide may show changes in eating or sleeping habits, weight, grades, disposition, activity level, or interest in friends. They sometimes suddenly give away prized possessions such as iPods, CDs, clothing, or pets. They may seem depressed or hyperactive and may start missing school or quit doing work. It is especially dangerous if the student not only talks about suicide, but also has a plan for carrying it out.

What defines intellectual disabilities? Before age 18, students must score below about 70 on a standard measure of intelligence and must have problems with adaptive behavior, day-to-day independent living, and social functioning. The AAIDD now recommends a classification scheme based on the amount of support that a person requires to function at his or her highest level. Support varies from intermittent (e.g., as needed during stressful times), to limited (consistent support, but time limited such as employment training), to extensive (daily care such as living in a group home), to pervasive (constant high-intensity care for all aspects of living).

How can schools accommodate the needs of students with physical disabilities? If the school has the necessary architectural features, such as ramps, elevators, and accessible rest rooms, and if teachers allow for the physical limitations of students, little needs to be done to alter the usual educational program. Identifying a peer to help with movements and transitions can be useful.

How would you handle a seizure in class? Do not restrain the child's movements. Lower the child gently to the floor, away from furniture or walls. Move hard objects away. Turn the child's head gently to the side, put a soft coat or blanket under the student's head, and loosen any tight clothing. Never put anything in the student's mouth. Find out from the student's parents how they deal with seizures. If one seizure follows another and the student does not regain consciousness in between, if the student is pregnant, or if the seizure goes on for more than 5 minutes, get medical help right away.

What are some signs of visual and hearing impairments? Holding books very close or far away, squinting, rubbing eyes, misreading the chalkboard, and holding the head at an odd angle are possible signs of visual problems. Signs of hearing problems are turning one ear toward the speaker, favoring one ear in conversation, or misunderstanding conversation when the speaker's face cannot be seen. Other indications include not following directions, seeming distracted or confused at times, frequently asking people to repeat what they have said, mispronouncing new words or names, and being reluctant to participate in class discussions.

How does autism differ from Asperger syndrome? Asperger syndrome is one of the autism spectrum disorders. Many students with autism also have moderate-to-severe intellectual disabilities, but those with Asperger syndrome usually have average-to-above-average intelligence and better language abilities than other children with autism.

What is Response to Intervention (RTI)? RTI is an approach to supporting students with learning problems as early as possible, not waiting for years to assess, identify, and plan a program. One RTI process is a three-tiered system. The first tier is to use a strong, well-researched way of teaching all students. Students who do not do well with these methods are moved to the second tier and receive extra support and additional small-group instruction. If some students still make limited progress, they move to the third tier for one-to-one intensive help and perhaps a special needs assessment.

Students Who Are Gifted and Talented (pp. 157–162)

What are the characteristics of gifted students? Gifted students learn easily and rapidly and retain what they have learned; use common sense and practical knowledge; know about many things that the other children don't; use a large number of words easily and accurately; recognize relations and comprehend meaning; are alert and keenly observant and respond quickly; are persistent and highly motivated on some tasks; and are creative or make interesting connections. Teachers should make special efforts to support underrepresented gifted students—girls, students who also have learning disabilities, and children living in poverty.

Is acceleration a useful approach with gifted students? Many people object to acceleration, but most careful studies indicate that truly gifted students who are accelerated do as well as and usually better than nongifted students who are progressing at the normal pace. Gifted students tend to prefer the company of older playmates and may be bored if kept with children their own age. Skipping grades may not be the best solution for a particular student, but for students who are extremely advanced intellectually (with a score of 160 or higher on an individual intelligence test), the only practical solution may be to accelerate their education.

▼ KEY TERMS

Absence seizure (154)
Americans with Disabilities Act of 1990 (ADA) (137)
Articulation disorders (145)
Attention-deficit hyperactivity disorder (ADHD) (142)
Autism/Autism spectrum disorders (155)
Automaticity (125)
Cerebral palsy (152)
Crystallized intelligence (121)
Deviation IQ (127)
Disability (118)
Educationally blind (154)
Emotional and behavioral disorders (146)
Epilepsy (153)
Fluid intelligence (121)
Flynn effect (128)

Free, appropriate public education (FAPE) (133)
General intelligence (g) (121)
Generalized seizure (153)
Gifted and talented students (158)
Handicap (118)
Inclusion (134)
Individualized Education Program (IEP) (134)
Individuals with Disabilities Education Improvement Act (IDEA) (133)
Insight (125)
Integration (134)
Intellectual disabilities/Mental retardation (151)
Intelligence (121)
Intelligence quotient (IQ) (127)
Learned helplessness (141)
Learning disability (138)

Learning preferences (131)
Learning styles (130)
Least restrictive environment (LRE) (134)
Low vision (154)
Mainstreaming (134)
Mental age (126)
Pervasive developmental disorder (PDD) (155)
Response to intervention (RTI) (157)
Section 504 (137)
Spasticity (152)
Speech disorder (145)
Theory of multiple intelligences (122)
Transition programming (152)
Triarchic theory of successful intelligence (125)
Voicing problems (145)
Zero reject (133)

▼ CONNECT AND EXTEND TO LICENSURE

MULTIPLE-CHOICE QUESTIONS

1. African American students are more likely to be identified for special education services and placed outside of the general education system than Caucasian students. All but which one of the following are attempts to explain this overrepresentation?

   A. High poverty rates which lead to poor prenatal care, nutrition, and health care.

   B. Teachers who are unprepared to work with ethnic minority students.

   C. Biases in teachers' attitudes and the curriculum.

   D. African American students comprise 80% of the gifted and talented population.

2. Developmental psychologist Howard Gardner's multiple intelligences theory continues to impact classrooms today in the United States based upon its reflection of which current classroom strategy?

   A. Differentiated instruction

   B. Sternberg's triarchic theory of successful intelligence

   C. Mainstreaming

   D. Response to Intervention (RTI)

3. When a student has been identified as needing special education services, the Individuals with Disabilities Education Act mandates all but which one of the following?

   A. Accommodations must be made during state standardized testing of all students receiving special education services.

   B. The law requires states to provide a free, appropriate public education (FAPE) for all students with disabilities who participate in special education.

   C. States are required to develop procedures for educating children in the least restrictive environment

   D. Students receiving special education services must have an Individualized Education Program.

4. Several students in Mr. Collins' kindergarten class appear to have deficits in their abilities. The school is unable to assess the children and begin providing special education services until next year. Which one of the following solutions would be the best?

   A. Mr. Collins should contact the parents of the students who need services and encourage them to work with their children at home.

   B. The school should wait until next year to begin services.

   C. Mr. Collins should begin Response to Intervention.

   D. The students in question should be sent to a school which specializes in special education services.

CONSTRUCTED-RESPONSE QUESTIONS

Case

Many beginning teachers become overwhelmed when they discover they have numerous students in their class with special needs. First year teacher Paige Morris was no exception. Of her twenty-five students, seven were identified as needing special education services. While Paige was certified in special education and elementary education, she felt ill-equipped to write and implement so many Individualized Education Plans. To make matters more concerning, three of her students were identified as ADHD. Miss Morris began to imagine herself trying to control a chaotic classroom without the tools she needed to succeed.

5. List the parts of an Individualized Education Program which must be in writing. Identify the aspect(s) of the IEP for which Paige is responsible.

6. Which parts of each child's program would assist Miss Morris in better understanding her students before they begin the school year?

▼ WHAT WOULD THEY DO?

TEACHERS' CASEBOOK: Including Every Student

Here is how several expert teachers said they would work with students with a wide range of abilities.

BARBARA PRESLEY • Transition/Work Study Coordinator—High School Level

B.E.S.T.T. Program (Baldwinsville Exceptional Student Training and Transition Program) C.W. Baker High School, Baldwinsville, NY

As a transition coordinator, it is my responsibility to link the special education standards to transition. Therefore, connecting work and tasks assigned at work sites to classroom standards was done in conjunction with classroom teachers. All requisite work skills and behaviors were reinforced in the classroom. Classroom instructional topics were integrated at each work site and reinforced by Job Coaches while students were at their work site. Job Coaches, teachers, and the transition coordinator communicate daily through goal books. Success breeds confidence for adults and students. For special needs students, the importance of linking and aligning classroom education with community education cannot be overstated.

JENNIFER PINCOSKI • Learning Resource Teacher: K–12

Lee County School District, Fort Myers, FL

One of the most important considerations when setting up the classroom is how to group students to maximize learning. Students should be assessed early on to provide the teacher with information on individual learning styles, interests, strengths, and needs; teachers who are prepared with this knowledge will be better able to group students appropriately.

Learning groups should be fluid, meaning that they will change often, depending on objectives and circumstances. Students may be grouped in a variety of ways, including: heterogeneously (a student with strengths in a skill area can assist a student who struggles), homogeneously by skill deficit (to provide interventions), by learning styles, and by areas of interest.

Part of the process of understanding students' needs also includes research. There are numerous resources available for teachers to educate themselves on support strategies for students with ADHD, Autism Spectrum Disorders, learning disabilities, and health impairments. These resources can include staff members on campus (counselor, nurse, special education teacher, etc.), as well as community advocacy groups, scholarly journals and literature (accessible at the local library), and, of course, the Internet.

Ultimately, the best way to support students is to learn about their strengths and challenges, and use this information to assist in the physical and educational organization of the classroom community.

JESSICA N. MAHTABAN • 8th Grade Math

Woodrow Wilson Middle School, Clifton, NJ

It is vital for me to become very familiar with all of the students' IEPs and to discuss the modifications that need to take place in the classroom with the special education teacher. Once everything has been reviewed, I can begin to construct the curriculum, which must accommodate all my students. Differentiated instruction will be integrated into the curriculum. Portfolios will be the major source of assessment for my students. Each student learns differently and at different a pace, which is why the portfolio would be the best assessment, since they show the individual growth of each student. Frequent contact with parents is the key component for helping each student succeed in the classroom and beyond.

AUREN ROLLINS • 1st Grade Teacher

Boulevard Elementary School, Shaker Heights, OH

Meeting the individual needs of all students is a challenging but essential part of teaching! In this situation, I would create differentiated learning centers, where students could work on curricular components in skill-based groups. The opportunity to work with smaller groups of students whose abilities are similar would allow me to differentiate the curriculum to best meet their academic needs. Groupings would need to be fluid and flexible to ensure that the students were continually being challenged by the curriculum. At each learning center, I would provide a variety of materials and literature related to the subject matter that are designed to meet the wide range of learning styles presented by the students. Additionally, I would allow the students working in the centers to choose which of the provided materials they would like to use to support their learning. Giving the students choices will help with student motivation. I would even consider enlisting their input as to which materials they would like in each center. Finally, I would enlist willing and able parent or community volunteers to assist me in managing the students at the learning centers. The combination of small, skill-based groups, engaging learning materials, and choice will allow students to tackle the curriculum to their fullest potential.

LINDA SPARKS • 1st Grade
John F. Kennedy School, Billerica MA

Most of our classes are inclusion classes, with limited resources for additional help. At the beginning of the year, I go through all of the records, IEPs, and 504 plans and write down my questions, concerns, and specific information that will help the student. Next, we all meet as a team with the teachers from the previous year and specialists who work with the students. I have found this very helpful in setting up a plan for the students in my class. Then, I don't spend time re-evaluating students in areas where team members already know how students can be most successful. I am given the resources needed to start the year, and we continue to meet throughout the year as additional resources are needed. We are also fortunate to have a volunteer program through the senior center, parent community, and local businesses. These adult volunteers commit to a specific number of hours a week, are trained by school staff for specific skills the students will need help with, and begin to implement these skills with the students.

PAUL DRAGIN • ESL Grades 9–12
Columbus East High School, Columbus OH

This situation has become the norm—at least in public schools in large urban areas. The special needs students who have been identified should have an IEP (Individualized Education Plan) that addresses specifics pertaining to the student's cognitive and/or behavioral issues. This would guide my instructional deviation to help ensure that I am providing the curriculum in a format that is more easily comprehended by those who may have challenges that are greater than mainstream students. The medical issue concerning the student with asthma is something that requires a greater sensitivity to ensure that I am alert to any possible medical emergency that may occur in the classroom. Confidence in this trying situation comes from attempting various strategies with the students and discovering, through trial and error, which are most effective at meeting their diverse educational needs.

PAULA COLEMERE • Special Education Teacher—
English, History
McClintock High School, Tempe, AZ

It is every teacher's dream to have a room full of eager learners who are all on grade level. In my experience, this never happens! In any classroom, there are students who are below, at, or above grade level in their abilities. First, teachers need to know that fair doesn't mean equal. If I assign a five-paragraph essay to the class, but a student with a learning disability in writing struggles to write that much, I could either extend the due date or modify it to a three-paragraph essay. If the student is really low ability, I may only require a solid paragraph. Likewise, I would challenge the brightest students to go deeper. I would make sure my students knew I believed in them and would build their confidence in their abilities. Proximity is huge in classroom management; by constantly moving around the classroom, I can prompt my students to stay on task or to remind them of appropriate classroom behavior. This is done very quietly and privately. I also give a great deal of positive reinforcement as I walk around and point out all of the right things students are doing. The positive messages must outnumber negative messages.

chapter five

LANGUAGE DEVELOPMENT, LANGUAGE DIVERSITY, AND IMMIGRANT EDUCATION

▶ **TEACHERS' CASEBOOK:** Cultures Clash in the Classroom

Your high school classes this year are about equally divided among three groups—African Americans, Asians, and Latinos/as. Students from each of the three groups seem to stick together, rarely making friends with students from "outside." When you ask students to select partners for projects, the divisions are usually on ethnic lines. At times, there are insults exchanged between the groups, and the atmosphere of the class is becoming tense. Often the Asian or Latino students communicate in their native language—one you don't understand—and you assume that the joke is on you because of the looks and laughs directed your way. You realize that you are having trouble establishing positive relationships with many of the students whose language, culture, and background are very different from yours, and many other students, picking up on your discomfort, shy away from them too.

CRITICAL THINKING

- What is the real problem here?
- How would you help the students (and yourself) to feel more comfortable with each other?
- What are your first goals in working on this problem?
- How will these issues affect the grade levels you will teach?

OVERVIEW AND OBJECTIVES

Virtually all developed countries, and many developing ones, are becoming more diverse. Multiple languages fill many classrooms. For a range of reasons, including unrest across the globe, families are immigrating to find a better, safer life—and their children will likely be in your classrooms. In this new chapter of our book, we look at how the over 6,000 natural languages in the world developed, what role culture plays, the stages in language development, and the emergence of literacy. Next we consider diversity in language development and dual language development. But language diversity is more than bilingualism. Because all of us speak at least one dialect, we examine what teachers need to know about dialects and genderlects—a new term for me—along with the role of schools in second (or third) language learning. Finally we turn to the critical issue for you—how to become a capable and confident teacher of immigrant students and second language learners. What is the role of bilingual education and sheltered instruction? Do the emotions and concerns of these students affect their learning? How can you identify English language learners with special talents or special needs? By the time you have completed this chapter, you should be able to:

Objective 5.1: Understand how language develops and know how to support emergent literacy.

Objective 5.2: Discuss what happens when children develop two languages.

Objective 5.3: Address whether dialect differences affect learning and discuss what teachers can do.

Objective 5.4: Discuss whether English immersion or bilingual instruction is better for English language learners.

Objective 5.5: Explain who are the Generation 1.5 students and describe their learning characteristics.

Objective 5.6: Define sheltered instruction and explain how it works.

Objective 5.7: Discuss how teachers can recognize special learning needs and talents when they do not speak their students' first language.

THE DEVELOPMENT OF LANGUAGE

All children in every culture master the complicated system of their native language, unless severe deprivation or physical problems interfere. This knowledge is remarkable. To have a conversation, children must coordinate sounds, meanings, words and sequences of words, volume, voice tone, inflection, and turn-taking rules. Yet, by about age 4, most children have a vocabulary of thousands of words and knowledge of the grammar rules for basic conversations (Colledge et al., 2002).

What Develops? Language and Cultural Differences

There are over 6,000 natural languages in the world (Tomasello, 2006). In general, cultures develop words for the concepts that are important to them. For example, how many different shades of green can you name? Mint, olive, emerald, teal, sea foam, chrome, turquoise, chartreuse, lime, apple . . . An oil painting artist can add cobalt titanate green, cinnabar green, phthalo yellow green, viridian green, and many others. English-speaking countries have over 3,000 words for colors. In contrast, the Himba people of Namibia and a tribe of hunter-gatherer people in Papua New Guinea who speak Berinmo have five words for colors, even though they can recognize many color variations. But whether there are few or many color terms, children gradually acquire the color categories that are appropriate for their culture (Roberson, Davidoff, Davies, & Shapiro, 2004).

Languages change over time to reflect changing cultural needs and values. The Shoshoni Native Americans have one word that means, "to make a crunching sound walking on the sand." This word was valuable in the past to communicate about hunting, but today new words describing technical tools have been added to the Shoshoni language, as the group's life moves away from nomadic hunting. To hear hundreds of new 21st century tool words, listen to techies talk about computers (Price & Crapo, 2002).

THE PUZZLE OF LANGUAGE. It is likely that many factors— biological, cultural, and experiential—play a role in language development. To master a language, children must be able to (a) read the intentions of others so they can acquire the words, phrases, and concepts of their language and also (b) find patterns in the ways other people use these words and phrases to construct the grammar of their language (Tomasello, 2006). The important point is that children learn language as they develop other cognitive abilities by actively trying to make sense of what they hear and by looking for patterns and making up rules to put together the jigsaw puzzle of language.

In this process, humans may have built-in biases, rules, and constraints about language that restrict the number of possibilities considered. For example, young children seem to have a constraint specifying that a new label refers to a whole object, not just a part. Another built-in bias leads children to assume that the label refers to a class of similar objects. So the child learning about the rabbit is equipped naturally to assume that "rabbit" refers to the whole animal (not just its ears) and that other similar-looking animals are also rabbits (Jaswal & Markman, 2001; Markman, 1992). Reward and correction play a role in helping children learn correct language use, but the child's thinking in putting together the parts of this complicated system is very important (Waxman & Lidz, 2006).

Expressive vocabulary The words a person can speak.

Receptive vocabulary The words a person can understand in spoken or written words.

When and How Does Language Develop?

Table 5.1 shows the milestones of language development, ages 2 to 6, in Western cultures, along with ideas for encouraging development.

SOUNDS AND PRONUNCIATION. By about age 5, most children have mastered the sounds of their native language, but a few sounds may remain unconquered. You saw in the previous chapter that the sounds of the consonants *l, r, y, s, v,* and *z* and the consonant blends *sh, ch, ng, zh,* and *th* are the last to be mastered (Friend, 2011). Young children may understand and be able to use many words, but prefer to use the words they can pronounce easily. As children learn to hear differences in the sounds of language, they enjoy rhymes, songs, and general sound silliness. They like stories by Dr. Seuss partly because of the sounds, as is evidenced by the book titles—*All Aboard the Circus McGurkus* or *Wet Pet, Dry Pet, Your Pet, My Pet.* The young son of a friend of mine wanted to name his new baby sister Brontosaurus "just because it's fun to say."

THE DEVELOPMENT OF LANGUAGE The important point is that children learn language as they develop other cognitive abilities by actively trying to make sense of what they hear and by looking for patterns and making up rules to put together the jigsaw puzzle of language.

VOCABULARY AND MEANING. As you can see in Table 5.1, children between ages 2 and 3 can use about 450 words (**expressive vocabulary**) even though they can understand many more (**receptive vocabulary**). By age 6, children's expressive vocabularies will grow to about 2,600 words and their receptive vocabularies will be an impressive 20,000 plus words

TABLE 5.1 • **Milestones in Early Childhood Language and Ways to Encourage Development**

AGE RANGE	MILESTONE	STRATEGIES TO ENCOURAGE DEVELOPMENT
Between 2 and 3	Identifies body parts; calls self "me" instead of name; combines nouns and verbs; has a 450-word vocabulary; uses short sentences; matches 3–4 colors; knows *big* and *little*; likes to hear same story repeated; forms some plurals; answers "where" questions	• Help the child listen and follow instructions by playing simple games • Repeat new words over and over • Describe what you are doing, planning, thinking • Have the child deliver simple messages for you • Show the child you understand what he or she says by answering, smiling, and nodding your head • Expand what the child says. Child: "more juice." You say, "Chris wants more juice."
Between 3 and 4	Can tell a story; sentence length of 4–5 words; vocabulary about 1,000 words; knows last name, name of street, several nursery rhymes	• Talk about how objects are the same or different • Help the child to tell stories using books and pictures • Encourage play with other children Talk about places you've been or will be going
Between 4 and 5	Sentence length of 4–5 words; uses past tense; vocabulary of about 1,500 words; identifies colors, shapes; asks many questions like "why?" and "who?"	• Help the child sort objects and things (e.g., things to eat, animals) • Teach the child how to use the telephone • Let the child help you plan activities • Continue talking about the child's interests • Let the child tell and make up stories for you
Between 5 and 6 At every age	Sentence length of 5–6 words; average 6-year-old has vocabulary of about 10,000 words; defines objects by their use; knows spatial relations (like "on top" and "far") and opposites; knows address; understands *same* and *different*; uses all types of sentences	• Praise children when they talk about feelings, thoughts, hopes, fears • Sing songs, rhymes • Talk with them as you would an adult • Listen and show your pleasure when the child talks to you • Carry on conversations with the child • Ask questions to get the child to think and talk • Read books to the child every day, increasing in length as the child develops

Source: Reprinted from LDOnLine.org with thanks to the Learning Disabilities Association of America.

"WHEN I SAY 'RUNNED', YOU KNOW I MEAN 'RAN'. LET'S NOT QUIBBLE."

Copyright © 2000 Sydney Harris. Reprinted with permission of Sydney Harris.

(Otto, 2010). Some researchers estimate that students in the early grades learn up to 20 words a day (Bloom, 2002). In the early elementary years, some children may have trouble with abstract words such as *justice* or *economy*. They also may not understand the subjunctive case ("If I were a butterfly") because they lack the cognitive ability to reason about things that are not true ("But you aren't a butterfly"). They may interpret all statements literally and thus misunderstand sarcasm or metaphor. For example, fables are understood concretely simply as stories instead of as moral lessons. Many children are in their preadolescent years before they are able to distinguish being kidded from being taunted, or before they know that a sarcastic remark is not meant to be taken literally. But by adolescence, students are able to use their developing cognitive abilities to learn abstract word meanings and to use poetic, figurative language (Owens, 2012).

Young children begin to elaborate their simple language by adding plurals; endings for verbs such as *-ed* and *-ing*; small words like *and, but*, and *in*; articles (*a, the*); and possessives (*the girl's hair*). A classic study by Jean Berko (1958) demonstrated that children could even apply these rules to make words that they had never encountered plural, possessive, or past tense. For example, when shown a picture of a single "wug," the preschool children in the study could answer correctly "wugs" when the researcher said, "Now there is another one. There are two of them. There are two _____." In the process of figuring out the rules governing these aspects of language, children make some very interesting mistakes.

GRAMMAR AND SYNTAX.   For a brief time, children may use irregular forms of particular words properly, as if they are saying what they have heard. Then, as they begin to learn rules, they **overregularize** words by applying the rules to everything. Children who once said, "Our car is broken" begin to insist, "Our car is broked." A child who once talked about her *feet* may discover the *-s* for plurals and refer to her *foots* or *feets*, then learn about *-es* for plurals (*horses, kisses*) and describe her *footses*, before she finally returns to talking about her *feet* (Flavell et al., 2002). Parents often wonder why their child seems to be "regressing." Actually, these "mistakes" show how logical and rational children can be as they try to assimilate new words into existing schemes. Apparently these overregularizations happen in all languages, including American Sign Language. Because most languages have many irregular words, accommodation is necessary in mastering language. According to Joshua Hartshore and Michael Ullman (2006), girls tend to overregularize verb tenses more than boys, so they are more likely to say *holded* instead of *held*. The researchers speculate that because girls may have better memory for words, they have better access to similar words (*folded, molded, scolded*) and generalize to *holded*.

Early on, children master the basics of **syntax** (word order) in their native language, but overregularizing plays a role in mastering syntax too. For example, because the usual order in English is subject–verb–object, preschoolers just mastering the rules of language have trouble with sentences in any other order. If 4-year-old Justin hears a statement in the passive voice, like "The truck was bumped by the car," he probably thinks the truck did the bumping to the car because "truck" came first in the sentence. Interestingly, however, in languages where the passive voice is more important, such as the South African language Sesotho, children use this construction much earlier, as young as 3 or 4 (Demuth, 1990). So in talking with young children, in English at least, it is generally better to use direct language. By early elementary school, many children can understand the meaning of passive sentences, but they do not use such constructions in their normal conversations, unless the passive construction is common in their culture.

PRAGMATICS: USING LANGUAGE IN SOCIAL SITUATIONS.   **Pragmatics** involves the appropriate use of language to communicate in social situations—how to enter a conversation, tell a joke, interrupt, keep a conversation going, or adjust your language for the listener. Children show an understanding of pragmatics when they talk in simpler sentences to younger children or command their pets to "Come here!" in louder, deeper voices, or provide more detail when describing an event to a parent who was absent from the event (Flavell et al., 2002; Rice, 1989). So even young children seem quite able to fit their language to the situation, at least with familiar people.

Overregularize To apply a rule of syntax or grammar in situations where the rule does not apply, e.g., "the bike was broked."

Syntax The order of words in phrases or sentences.

Pragmatics The rules for when and how to use language to be an effective communicator in a particular culture.

Rules for the appropriate use of language vary across cultures. For example, Shirley Brice Heath (1989) spent many hours observing White middle-class families and African American families who were poor. She found that the adults asked different kinds of questions and encouraged different kinds of "talk." White adults asked test-like questions with right answers, such as "How many cars are there?" or "Which car is bigger?" These questions seemed odd to African American children whose families don't ask about what they already know. The African American child might wonder, "Why would my aunt ask me how many cars? She can see there are 3." Instead, African American families encouraged rich storytelling and also teasing that hones their children's quick wit and assertive responses.

METALINGUISTIC AWARENESS.   Around the age of 5, students begin to develop **metalinguistic awareness**. This means their understanding about language and how it works becomes explicit. They have knowledge about language itself. They are ready to study and extend the rules that have been implicit—understood but not consciously expressed. This process continues throughout life, as we all become better able to use language. Learning to read and write, which begins with *emergent literacy*, encourages metalinguistic awareness.

Emergent Literacy

Today, in most languages, reading is a cornerstone of learning, and the foundation for reading is built in early childhood. Because young children vary greatly in their knowledge and skills related to reading, research has expanded to study what supports these emerging literacy skills (often called **emergent literacy**). Look at Figure 5.1, which shows a 6-year-old's story and grocery list, to see some emerging literacy skills.

FIGURE 5.1

A STORY AND A GROCERY LIST

This child knows quite a bit about reading and writing—letters make words that communicate meaning, writing goes from left to right and lists go down the page, and stories look different than shopping lists.

Emergent writing samples provided by Kalla Terpenning, who just turned 6.

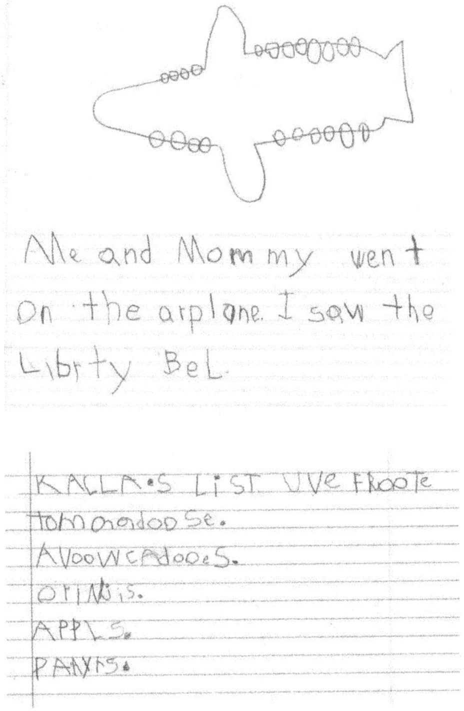

Me and Mommy went
On the airplane. I saw the
Librty Bel.

KALLA'S LIST UVE FROOTe
TOMOroidooSe.
AVooWCADooeS.
OriNJis.
APPLS.
PAYRS.

Metalinguistic awareness
Understanding about one's own use of language.

Emergent literacy The skills and knowledge, usually developed in the preschool years, that are the foundation for the development of reading and writing.

Source: Woolfolk, Anita; Perry, Nancy E., Child and Adolescent Development, 1st Edition, © 2012. Reprinted by permission of Pearson Education, Inc., Upper Saddle River, NJ.

What are the most important skills that help literacy emerge? Here, the answers are not certain, but research has identified two broad categories of skills that are important for later reading: (1) skills related to understanding sounds and codes such as knowing that letters have names, that sounds are associated with letters, and that words are made up of sounds; and (2) oral language skills such as expressive and receptive vocabulary, knowledge of syntax, and the ability to understand and tell stories, for example (Dickinson et al., 2003; Storch & Whitehurst, 2002).

Some educators have emphasized decoding skills, others oral language, but a study by the National Institute of Child Health and Human Development (NICHD) Early Childhood Research Network (2005b) that followed over 1,000 children from age 3 through 3rd grade found that oral language skills at age 4½ predicted word decoding in 1st grade and reading comprehension in 3rd grade. The NICHD researchers concluded, "most recent investigations find that preschool oral language skills [for example, size of vocabulary, ability to use syntax, ability to understand and tell stories] play an important role along side code skills in predicting reading in the transition to school" (p. 439). Because this was not an experimental design, we cannot be sure that early decoding and oral language skills cause later reading achievement. But the results of this study suggest that decoding and oral language skills are likely an important part of the puzzle; these skills often support each other. *Beware of either/or choices* between emphasizing decoding versus oral language—both are important.

INSIDE-OUT AND OUTSIDE-IN SKILLS.   One way to think about emergent literacy that captures both code and oral language skills for emergent literacy is the notion of **inside-out skills** and **outside-in skills** and processes, described in Table 5.2. This model, developed by Grover Whitehurst and Christopher Lonigan (1998) includes two interdependent sets of skills and processes.

> A reader must decode units of print into units of sound and units of sound into units of language. This is an inside-out process. However, being able to say a written word or series of written words is only a part of reading. The fluent reader must understand those auditory derivations, which involves placing them in the correct conceptual and contextual framework. This is an outside-in process. (p. 855)

For example, to understand even a simple sentence in print, such as "She ordered a camera from Amazon?" the reader must know about letters, sounds, grammar, and punctuation. The reader also has to remember the first words as he is reading the last ones. But these inside-out skills are not enough. To understand, the reader needs to have conceptual knowledge—what is a camera? What does it mean to order? Is this the Amazon River or Amazon online? Why the question mark? Who is asking? How does this sentence fit in the context of the story? Answering these questions takes outside-in skills and knowledge.

BUILDING A FOUNDATION.   What builds this foundation of emergent literacy skills? Two related activities are critical: (1) conversations with adults that develop knowledge about language and (2) joint reading, using books as supports for talk about sounds, words, pictures, and concepts (NICHD Early Childhood Research Network, 2005a). Especially in the early years, the children's home experiences are central in the development of language and literacy (Burgess, Hecht & Lonigan, 2002; Sénéchal & LeFevre, 2002). In homes that promote literacy, parents and other adults value reading as a source of pleasure, and there are books and other printed materials everywhere. Parents read to their children, take them to bookstores and libraries, limit the amount of television everyone watches, and encourage literacy-related play such as setting up a pretend school or writing "letters" (Pressley, 1996; Snow, 1993; Whitehurst et al., 1994). Childcare workers and teachers can help. In a study that followed almost 300 low-income children from kindergarten to 5th grade, researchers found that the more families were involved with the school, the better their children's literacy development. School involvement was especially valuable when mothers had less education themselves (Dearing, Kreider, Simpkins, & Weiss, 2006).

Inside-out skills The emergent literacy skills of knowledge of graphemes, phonological awareness, syntactic awareness, phoneme-grapheme correspondence, and emergent writing.

Outside-in skills The emergent literacy skills of language, narrative, conventions of print, and emergent reading.

TABLE 5.2 • **Components of Emergent Literacy**

COMPONENT	BRIEF DEFINITION	EXAMPLE
Outside-in Processes		
Language	Semantic, syntactic, and conceptual knowledge	A child reads the word "bat" and connects the meaning to knowledge of baseball or flying mammals.
Narrative	Understanding and producing narrative	A child can tell a story, understands that books have stories.
Conventions of print	Knowledge of standard print formats	The child understands that print is read from left-to-right and front-to-back in English; understands the difference between pictures and print or the cover and the inside of the book.
Emergent reading	Pretending to read	Child takes a favorite book and retells the "story," often by using pictures as cues.
Inside-out Processes		
Knowledge of graphemes	Letter-name knowledge	A child can recognize letters and name letters.
Phonological awareness	Detection of rhyme; manipulation of syllables; manipulation of individual phonemes	A child can tell you words that rhyme with "hat." A child can clap as she says sounds in a word *cat*: /k/ /ă/ /t/
Syntactic awareness	Repair grammatical errors	A child says, "No! you say I *went* to the zoo, not I *goed* to the zoo."
Phoneme-grapheme correspondence	Letter-sound knowledge	The child can answer the question, "What sounds do these letters make?"
Emergent writing	Phonetic spelling	The child writes "eenuf," or "hambrgr."
Other Factors	Emergent literacy also depends on other factors such as short-term memory for sounds and sequences, the ability to recognize and name lists of letters, motivation, and interest.	

Source: Woolfolk, Anita; Perry, Nancy E., Child and Adolescent Development, 1st Edition, © 2012. Reprinted by permission of Pearson Education, Inc., Upper Saddle River, NJ.

Emergent Literacy and Bilingual Children

Emergent literacy skills are critical for school readiness, regardless of the child's language or languages (Hammer, Farkas, & Maczuga, 2010). Most school programs expect all children to learn to read in English. According to new research by Carol Hammer and her colleagues, this emphasis on reading only in English may not be necessary. In fact, one key factor may facilitate literacy development—growth in receptive language. You probably remember that *receptive* language is made up of the words and language structures you understand, even if you do not use them in your *expressive* language, the words and structures you actually use when you talk.

In one study, Hammer followed 88 children for two years in a Head Start program (Hammer, Lawrence, & Miccio, 2007). The mothers of all the children spoke the Puerto Rican dialect of Spanish. There actually were two groups of students—those who had been expected to speak both English and Spanish from birth and those who were not expected to learn English until they started Head Start at age 3. The researchers found that it was not a particular score on any test, but *growth in receptive language* in general during the program that predicted early reading outcomes—and it did not matter if the students spoke English and Spanish from birth or if they just started speaking English in school. They concluded "that growth in children's English receptive language abilities during Head Start, as opposed to the level of English they had achieved by the end of Head Start, positively predicted the children's emergent reading abilities in English and

GUIDELINES

Supporting Language and Promoting Literacy

FOR FAMILIES

Read with your children.
Examples

1. Help children understand that books contain stories, that they can visit the stories as often as they like, that the pictures in the books go along with the story meaning, and that the words are always the same when they visit the story—that's reading! (Hulit & Howard, 2006)
2. Have a night-time reading ritual.

Choose appropriate books and stories.
Examples

1. Choose books with simple plots and clear illustrations.
2. Make sure illustrations precede the text related to the illustration. This helps children learn to predict what is coming next.
3. Ensure that language is repetitive, rhythmic, and natural.

FOR TEACHERS

Use stories as a springboard for conversations.
Examples

1. Retell stories you have read with your students.
2. Talk about the words, activities, and objects in the books. Do the students have anything like these in their home or classroom?

Identify and build on strengths the families already have (Delpit, 2003).
Examples

1. What are the histories, stories, and skills of family members? Students can draw or write about these.
2. Show respect for the student's language by celebrating poems or songs from the language.

Provide home activities to be shared with family members.
Examples

1. Encourage family members to work with children to read and follow simple recipes, play language games, keep diaries or journals for the family, and visit the library. Get feedback from families or students about the activities.
2. Give families feedback sheets and ask them to help evaluate the child's schoolwork.

3. Provide lists of good children's literature available locally—work with libraries, clubs, and churches to identify sources.

FOR SCHOOL COUNSELORS AND ADMINISTRATORS

Communicate with families about the goals and activities of your program.
Examples

1. Have someone from the school district, the community, or even an older student translate into the language of the child's family any material you plan to send home.
2. At the beginning of school, send home a description of the goals to be achieved in your class—make sure it is in a clear and readable format.
3. As you start each unit, send home a newsletter describing what students will be studying—give suggestions for home activities that support the learning.

Involve families in decisions about curriculum.
Examples

1. Have planning workshops at times family members can attend—provide child care for younger siblings, but let children and families work together on projects.
2. Invite parents to come to class to read to students, take dictation of stories, tell stories, record or bind books, and demonstrate skills.

Make it easier for families to come to school.
Examples

1. Provide babysitting for younger children while families meet with teachers.
2. Consider transportation needs of families—can they get to school?

For more information on Family Literacy Partnerships, see http://www.famlit.org/

Source: Hulit, Lloyd M.; Howard, Merle R., Born to Talk: An Introduction to Speech and Language Development, 4th edition, © 2006. Reprinted by permission of Pearson Education, Inc., Upper Saddle River, NJ.

the children's ability to identify letters and words in English. This was the case regardless of the level of the children's prior exposure to English" (p. 243). In addition, growth in Spanish language abilities predicted reading performance in Spanish.

One implication is that teachers and parents should focus on continuing language development and not worry about rushing children into speaking English exclusively. As Hammer and her colleagues note, "If bilingual children's language growth is progressing well in either Spanish or English during the preschool years, positive early English and Spanish reading outcomes result in kindergarten" (p. 244). These findings are consistent with the recommendations of the Society for Research in Child Development: "Investing in dual-language instead of English-only programs and encouraging pre-kindergarten attendance can improve learning opportunities for Hispanic children and increase their chances of success" (SRCD, 2009, p. 1). The *Guidelines* give some ideas.

This brings us to a very important topic for teachers today—diversity in language development.

DIVERSITY IN LANGUAGE DEVELOPMENT

Many children learn two languages simultaneously while they are growing up. In fact, the United States is "one of the few countries in the world that takes pride in the fact that we speak only one language" (Noguera, 2005, p. 13).

Dual Language Development

If you mastered your own first language, then added a second or third language, you are an example of *additive bilingualism*—you kept your first language and added another. But if you lost your first language when you added a second one, you experienced *subtractive bilingualism* (Norbert, 2005). If family members and the community value a child's first language, he or she is more likely to keep that language when a second one is learned. But if a child experiences discrimination against the first language, he or she may leave the first language behind as proficiency is gained in a new language (Hamers & Blanc, 2000; Montrul, 2010). Immigrants are more likely to experience discrimination and therefore "subtract" their first language.

If they are exposed to two languages from birth, **bilingual** children (children who speak two languages) reach the language milestones in both languages on the same schedule as **monolingual** children (children learning only one language). Initially, bilingual children may have a larger vocabulary in the language that they are learning from the person with whom they spend the most time or have the closest bond, so a child who stays home all day with a Chinese-speaking parent will likely use more Chinese words. But over time, these children can become fully and equally bilingual if the dual language exposure (a) begins early in life (before age 5), (b) occurs across a wide and rich range of contexts, and (c) is systematic, consistent, and sustained in the home and community (Petitto, 2009; Petitto & Kovelman, 2002). Another requirement is that the second language must provide more than 25% of the child's language input; with less exposure, the child is unlikely to learn the second language (Pearson et al., 1997). Bilingual children may mix vocabularies of the two languages when they speak, but this is not necessarily a sign that they are confused because their bilingual parents often intentionally mix vocabularies as well, selecting the word that best expresses their intent (Creese, 2009). So, with consistent and sustained engagement in two languages, children can be fully bilingual.

Recent research on the brain and bilingualism shows that people who learn two languages before about age 5 process both languages in the same way as those who learn only one language and use the same parts of their brains (mostly in the left hemisphere). In contrast, people who learn a second language later have to use both hemispheres of their brain as well as the frontal lobe and working memory. They have to apply more cognitive effort. As Laura-Ann Petitto (2009) notes, "*Later* bilingual exposure does *change* the typical pattern of the brain's neural organization for language processing, but early bilingual exposure does not" (p. 191).

SECOND LANGUAGE LEARNING. What if you didn't learn two languages as you were growing up? When and how should you learn a second language? To answer that question, you have to remember the distinction between **critical periods** for learning (if learning doesn't happen then, it never will) and **sensitive periods,** times when we are especially responsive to learning. There is no critical period that limits the possibility of language learning by adults (Marinova-Todd, Marshall, & Snow, 2000). In fact, older children go through the stages of language learning faster than young children. Adults have more learning strategies and greater knowledge of language in general to bring to bear in mastering a

Connect and Extend to PRAXIS II™

Bilingual Issues (IV, B4)
Identify the major issues related to the debate over bilingual education. Explain the major approaches to bilingual education, and describe steps that a teacher can take to promote the learning and language acquisition of non–English-speaking students.

Bilingual Speaking two languages and dealing appropriately with the two different cultures.

Monolingual Speaking only one language.

Critical periods If learning doesn't happen during these periods, it never will.

Sensitive periods Times when we are especially responsive to learning certain things.

second language (Diaz-Rico & Weed, 2002). But recent research on the brain and bilingualism suggests *"there is most definitely a 'sensitive period' for optimal bilingual language and reading exposure and mastery.* Age of first bilingual exposure predicts how strong a reader a bilingual child can and will become in each of their two languages" (Petitto, 2009, p. 192).

Even though there is no *critical* period for learning a language, there appears to be a critical period for learning accurate language pronunciation. The earlier people learn a second language, the more their pronunciation is near native. This is because from birth to about 4 months, infants can discriminate all the basic sound building blocks from any of the world's 6,000 or so languages. But after about 14 months they lose this capability and hone in on the sounds of the language they are learning. For children learning two languages at once, however, this developmental window seems to stay open longer, so these children can continue to differentiate sounds past 14 months (Petitto, 2009).

After adolescence it is almost impossible to learn a new language without speaking with an accent (Anderson & Graham, 1994). Even if a child overhears a language, without actually learning it formally, this can improve later learning. After studying college students learning Spanish, Terry Au and colleagues concluded that "Although waiting until adulthood to learn a language almost guarantees a bad accent, having overheard the target language during childhood seems to lessen this predicament substantially" (Au, Knightly, Jun, & Oh, 2002, p. 242). So the best time to acquire two languages on your own through exposure (and to learn native pronunciation for both languages) is early childhood (Au, Oh, Knightly, Jun, & Romo, 2008).

BENEFITS OF BILINGUALISM. There is no cognitive penalty for children who learn and speak two languages. In fact, there are benefits. Higher degrees of bilingualism are correlated with increased cognitive abilities in such areas as concept formation, creativity, theory of mind, cognitive flexibility, and understanding that printed words are symbols for language. In addition, these children have more advanced *metalinguistic* understanding of how language works; for example, they are more likely to notice grammar errors. Even more impressive, children from monolingual English-speaking families who attended bilingual schools and learned Spanish had better phoneme awareness and reading comprehension than their peers who were educated in an English-only program. Looking at all this research, Petitto (2009) concluded that "early bilingualism offers no disadvantages; on the contrary, young bilinguals may be afforded a linguistic and a reading advantage…. Moreover, learning to read in two languages may afford an advantage to children from monolingual homes in key phoneme awareness skills vital to reading success" (p. 193).

Heritage language The language spoken in the student's home or by members of the family.

These conclusions hold as long as there is no stigma attached to being bilingual and as long as children are not expected to abandon their first language in order to learn the second (Bialystok, 2001; Bialystok, Majumder, & Martin, 2003; Galambos & Goldin-Meadow, 1990; Hamers & Blanc, 2000). Laura Petitto and Ioulia Kovelman (2003) suggest that perhaps humans evolved to speak multiple languages because this would have survival value, so maybe the "contemporary pockets of civilization where one language is spoken are the aberrant deviation; in other words, perhaps our brains were neurologically set to be multilingual" (p. 14). In addition, speaking two languages is an asset when graduates enter the business world (Mears, 1998).

LANGUAGE LOSS. Even though the advantages of bilingualism seem clear, many children and adults are losing their heritage language (Montrul, 2010). **Heritage language** is the language spoken in a student's home or by older relatives when the larger society outside the home speaks a different language

DIVERSITY IN LANGUAGE DEVELOPMENT Higher degrees of bilingualism are correlated with increased cognitive abilities in such areas as concept formation, creativity, theory of mind, cognitive flexibility, and understanding that printed words are symbols for language.

(English in the United States). Often students who lose their heritage language were born in a new country after their parents or grandparents immigrated, so the students never lived in the country where everyone spoke their heritage language. In a large survey of 8th and 9th grade first- and second-generation children of immigrants in Miami and San Diego, Portes and Hao (1998) found that only 16% had retained the ability to speak their heritage language well. And 72% said they preferred to speak English. The languages of Native Americans are disappearing as well. Only about one-third still exist and 9 out of 10 of those are no longer spoken by the children (Krauss, 1992). Two Chinese American college students interviewed by Wong and Xiao (2010) expressed concerns this way:

> One of my biggest fears is that later on having kids and them not being able to speak Chinese, because my level of Chinese is not at the same level of my parents, and so I'm scared that it will get lost. (p. 161)
>
> My heritage language is definitely Toishan (Taishan), but even so, my parents don't always speak it fluently, so . . . I know somewhere down the line, I'm probably the last one to even speak it . . . and I feel like it is not my heritage anymore. (p. 165)

Rather than losing one language to gain another, the goal should be **balanced bilingualism**—being equally fluent in both languages (Gonzalez, 1999). Students' home language connects them to extended family and important cultural traditions, but outside their homes, English connects them to academic, social, and economic opportunities (Borrero & Yeh, 2010).

In many countries there are schools that focus on retaining heritage languages and cultures. Students attend these schools afternoons, weekends, or summers in addition to their regular public school. In Great Britain, these institutions are called *supplementary* or *complementary* schools. In Australia they are called *community language* or *ethnic schools*. In the United States and Canada, the name often is *heritage language schools* (Creese, 2009). Look at Table 5.3 for a sampling of these schools and their missions.

Balanced bilingualism Adding a second language capability without losing your heritage language.

TABLE 5.3 • **Schools That Support Heritage Languages in the United States and Canada**

LANGUAGE	SCHOOL	DESCRIPTION
German	German Heritage Language School, Halifax Nova Scotia http://www.german-language-school.ca/	Offers classes for adults and children. Lessons once a week for two hours on Thursday afternoons. German language skills (reading, writing, speaking, listening).
Chinese	Reidmount Saturday School, Markam, Ontario http://www.rhls.ca/	A co-educational Saturday school that offers Chinese (Mandarin and Cantonese), Chinese History, English (grammar and writing), Mathematics, Science, Communications, and Drawing for students from junior kindergarten to Grade 11.
Chinese	Chinese Heritage School, Monmouth Junction, NJ http://www.chsnj2000.org/	In addition to the regular language class, they also emphasize verbal conversation, Chinese Culture and family values. Their intention is to create a fun environment where children are motivated to study Chinese language, and feel proud to be Chinese.
Many languages	The Alliance for the Advancement of Heritage Languages in America http://www.cal.org/heritage/index.html	The mission of the Alliance is to promote the maintenance and development of heritage languages for the benefit of individuals, communities, and society.
Spanish	Grupo Educa http://www.elgrupoeduca.org/	Grupo Educa's mission is to enhance the Spanish language opportunities for children with a pre-existing knowledge of Spanish. Founded in June 2003 by a group of Southern California parents looking to expose their preschool-aged children to a dual-English/Spanish education.
Arabic and Hindi	Arabic and Hindi Heritage Language Classes, UCLA, Los Angeles http://www.international.ucla.edu/languages/programs/article.asp?parentid=105146	Intensive 5-week courses are for high school students who speak Hindi or Arabic at home and want to develop literacy and a deeper understanding of historical and contemporary South Asian culture. The project-based curriculum uses culturally relevant themes as a vehicle for listening, writing, speaking, and reading tasks.

Here are some ideas for learning about heritage schools in your area, suggested by Angela Creese (2009), a professor of educational linguistics at the University of Birmingham, United Kingdom:

- Find out which complementary/heritage schools are located in your area and make contact with them.
- When your students attend complementary/heritage schools, attend their awards ceremonies and presentations. Show your commitment to their bilingual and multicultural projects.
- Find out if teachers work in both the complementary/heritage and mainstream school sectors—ask them to undertake professional development workshops for other teachers in school.
- Ask a lead teacher of a complementary/heritage school to give an assembly.
- Encourage small-scale research and/or practical projects that would harness the potential links between complementary and mainstream schooling. (p. 272)

Signed Languages

People who can communicate in both a spoken and a signed language or in two different signed languages are considered bilingual (Petitto, 2009). There are a number of other parallels between spoken languages and the many signed languages used around the world, such as American Sign Language (ASL), Signed English (USA, Ireland, New Zealand, Australia, Great Britain), Lingua de Signos Nicaraguense (Nicaraguan Sign Language), Warlpiri Sign Language (Australia Aboriginal), and Langue des Signes Quebecoise (LSQ) or Quebec Sign Language. Each of these languages is distinct and not simply a derived version of a spoken language. For example, people using Quebec Sign Language and French Sign Language cannot understand each other, even though the French spoken language is common to both countries.

Both spoken and signed languages have large vocabularies and complex grammars. Laura Ann Petitto and Iugio Kovelman (2003) suggest that the same mechanisms for language acquisition are used for both spoken and signed languages. In addition, the milestones for signed language are the same as for spoken language. For example, children "say" their first words at about the same time, around 12 months, with both spoken and signed languages (Bloom, 2002). In fact, research with children learning a signed and a spoken language from infancy demonstrates that "being exposed to two languages from birth—and, in particular, being exposed to a signed and a spoken language from birth—does not cause a child to be language delayed or confused" (Petittto & Kovelman, 2003, p. 16). As with two spoken languages, children can become balanced bilinguals in a spoken and a signed language.

In the 1970s, language researchers were able to study the birth of a new socially shared signed language when Nicaragua established its first school for the deaf. The students came using their own unique invented sign languages. Over the years, a new language emerged that was based on the students' own sign languages. As the children developed the new Lingua de Signos Nicaraguense (Nicaraguan Sign Language), it became more systematic. The vocabulary expanded and the grammar grew more complex. New students learned the developing Nicaraguan Sign Language as their native language (Hoff, 2006; Senghaus & Coppola, 2001).

What Is Involved in Being Bilingual?

In the United States from 1995 to 2005 there was almost a 100% increase in the number of students who speak Asian languages and a 65% increase in the number of Spanish-speaking students. In fact, the United States has the 5th largest Spanish-speaking population in the world (Lessow-Hurley, 2005). The states with the largest number of English learners are Texas, California, Florida, New York, and Illinois, but numbers are surging in the Midwest, South, Nevada, and Oregon (Peregoy & Boyle, 2009). With these increased numbers come many misconceptions about bilingualism, as you can see in Table 5.4.

TABLE 5.4 • **Myths and Misconceptions about Being Bilingual**

In the table below, L1 means the original language and L2 means the second language.

MYTH	TRUTH
Learning a second language (L2) takes little time and effort.	Learning English as a second language takes 2–3 years for oral and 5–7 years for academic language use.
All language skills (listening, speaking, reading, writing) transfer from L1 to L2.	Reading is the skill that transfers most readily.
Code-switching is an indication of a language disorder.	Code-switching indicates high-level language skills in both L1 and L2.
All bilinguals easily maintain both languages.	It takes great effort and attention to maintain high-level skills in both languages.
Children do not lose their first language.	Loss of L1 and underdevelopment of L2 are problems for second language learners (semilingual in L1 and L2).
Exposure to English is sufficient for L2 learning.	To learn L2, students need to have a reason to communicate, access to English speakers, interaction, support, feedback, and time.
To learn English, students' parents need to speak only English at home.	Children need to use both languages in many contexts.
Reading in L1 is detrimental to learning English.	Literacy-rich environments in either L1 or L2 support development of necessary prereading skills.
Language disorders must be identified by tests in English.	Children must be tested in both L1 and L2 to determine language disorders.

Source: Brice, Alejandro E., The Hispanic Child: Speech, Language, Culture and Education, 1st Edition, © 2002. Reprinted by permission of Pearson Education, Inc., Upper Saddle River, NJ.

What does it really mean to be bilingual? Some definitions of *bilingualism* focus exclusively on a language-based meaning: Bilingual people, or bilinguals, speak two languages. Other definitions are more rigorous and define bilinguals as "adults who had early, intensive, and maintained dual language exposure and who use their two languages in their adult daily life" (Petitto, 2009, p. 186). But being bilingual and bicultural also means mastering the knowledge necessary to communicate in two cultures as well as dealing with potential discrimination (Borrero & Yeh, 2010). Consider these two students:

> A 9th-grade boy, who recently arrived in California from Mexico: "There is so much discrimination and hate. Even from other kids from Mexico who have been here longer. They don't treat us like brothers. They hate even more. It makes them feel more like natives. They want to be American. They don't want to speak Spanish to us; they already know English and how to act. If they are with us, other people will treat them more like wetbacks, so they try to avoid us." (Olsen, 1988, p. 36)
>
> Over 20 years later, a Chinese American college student is conflicted: 'Because I was born here, my parents . . . think that English is the language of the world, (but) I tell my mom that Mandarin is important, and she doesn't think so. She's kind of stuck in the old ways . . . like America is the only way to make money . . . I feel that as a Chinese American . . . second generation, I'm the first one to actually not follow what was followed before." (Wong & Xiao, 2010, p. 168)

The experiences of these two students show that you must also be able to move back and forth between two cultures and two languages while still maintaining a sense of your own identity, so bilingualism requires biculturalism as well (Lee, Wong, & Alvarez, 2008). Being a successful bilingual student has one more requirement—learning *academic language*.

TABLE 5.5 • **Common Errors and Accomplishments as Students Learn a Second Language**

LANGUAGE STAGE	COMMON ERRORS AND LIMITATIONS	ACCOMPLISHMENTS
During the first year of learning the language	• No speech at all • Only understands one word at a time • Mispronounces words • Leaves out words • One or two word responses • Relies heavily on context	• Uses pantomiming, gestures, pointing to communicate • Can use "yes," "no," or single words
During the second year of learning the language	• Basic pronunciation and grammar mistakes • Limited vocabulary	• Uses whole sentences • Good comprehension (in context) • Uses language to function well socially
During the third year and beyond of learning the language	• Some errors with complex grammar	• Can tell whole stories • Good comprehension • Beginning to understand and use academic language • Larger vocabulary

Source: Based on information from Miranda, T. Z. (2008). Bilingual Education for All Students: Still Standing after All These Years. In L. S. Verplaetse & N. Migliacci (Eds.), *Inclusive Pedagogy for English Language Learners: A Handbook of Research-Informed Practices* (pp. 257–275). New York: Erlbaum.

Contextualized and Academic Language

Proficiency in a second language has two separate aspects: face-to-face communication (known as *basic* or *contextualized language skills*) and academic uses of language such as reading and doing grammar exercises (known as *academic English*) (Fillmore & Snow, 2000; Garcia, 2002). **Academic language** is the entire range of language used in elementary, secondary, and university level schools. Academic language includes the general words and concepts used in many subjects such as *analyze, evaluate,* or *summarize,* as well as words and strategies specific to disciplines such as *angle, factor the equation,* or *derivative* in math, a *factor* in statistics, or a *derivative* in finance (you see how complicated this gets when the same word has two very different meanings in different fields). Academic language is associated with abstract, higher-order, complex concepts (Vogt, Echevarria, & Short, 2010).

It takes about 2 to 3 years in a good-quality program for children who are learning a new language to be able to use basic or contextualized language face to face in conversations. The stages for basic second language learning are shown in Table 5.5.

Mastering academic language skills such as reading texts in the new language takes much longer than three years—more like 5 to 10 years, depending on how much academic knowledge the student already had in his or her native language. So children who seem to "know" a second language in conversation may still have great difficulty with complex schoolwork in that language (Bialystok, 2001; Verplaetse & Migliacci, 2008). Here is how one Spanish-speaking international student, who went on to earn a doctoral degree and teach at a university, described her struggles with texts in college:

I could not understand why I was doing so poorly. After all, my grammar and spelling were excellent. It took me a long time to realize that the way text is organized in English is considerably different from the way text is organized in a romance language, Spanish. The process involved a different set of rhetorical rules which were grounded in cultural

Academic language The entire range of language used in elementary, secondary, and university-level schools including words, concepts, strategies, and processes from academic subjects.

GUIDELINES

Promoting Language Learning

Provide structures, frameworks, scaffolds, and strategies.
Examples

1. "Think aloud" as you solve a problem by building on and clarifying the input of students.
2. Use visual organizers, story maps, or other aids to help students organize and relate information.

Teach relevant background knowledge and key vocabulary concepts.
Examples

1. Informally assess students' current background knowledge. Directly teach needed information, if missing.
2. Focus on key vocabulary words and use those words consistently.

Give focused and useful feedback.
Examples

1. Focus feedback on meaning, not grammar, syntax, or pronunciation.
2. Give frequent, brief, clear feedback—use words from the student's first language when you can.
3. Make sure to let students know when they are successful.
4. Break assignments and activities into smaller, "bite-sized pieces" with feedback after each "bite."

Keeps students involved and engaged.
Examples

1. Use small-group and pairs work.
2. Create situations where students talk at length.
3. Challenge students with clear higher-order questions—allow time to think and write out answers, maybe in pairs.

Show authentic respect for students' culture and language.
Examples

1. Learn about your students' personal and language background: What languages are spoken at home? When did the family arrive? How long have they lived in the United States? What schooling did they receive in other countries?
2. Learn about the students' religious background, food preferences and restrictions, and family customs; then incorporate students' experiences into writing and language arts activities.
3. Learn some key words in the students' languages.
4. View diversity as an asset; reject cultural deficit notions.

Sources: Adapted from Peregoy, S. F., &. Boyle, O. F. (2009). Reading, Writing, and Learning in ESL: A Resource Book for Teaching K–12 English Learners (5th ed.). Boston: Allyn & Bacon/Pearson; Echevarria, J., & Graves, A. (2011). Content Instruction: Teaching English Learners with Diverse Abilities (4th ed.). Columbus, OH: Pearson; and Gersten, R. (1996b). Literacy Instruction for Language-Minority Students: The Transition Years. The Elementary School Journal, 96, 217–220.

ways of being. I had never heard of the thesis statement, organizational rules, cohesion, coherence, or other features of discourse. (Sotillo, 2002, p. 280)

One 10th grader from Mexico described how her teacher helped her master academic language:

What I really love about my ESL teacher is that she explains how to organize our thoughts and how to write in school ways. She also teaches us what to do to be good, critical readers. That is so helpful in my other classes and I know it will be good for life. (Walqui, 2008, p. 111).

The *Guidelines* above give ideas for promoting language learning, but also keep cultural differences in mind as you teach. There are many ways that cultural differences might interfere with developing academic English and content understanding. For example, many Asian students come from a culture that believes asking the teacher questions is rude and inappropriate because questioning implies that the teacher has done a poor job of instruction. In Asian classrooms this might cause the teacher to lose face in front of the students—an entirely unacceptable situation. Thus teachers need to ask themselves why their English learners are not asking questions. For another example, class discussion may be considered a waste of time in cultures in which the teacher is viewed as the source of authoritative knowledge. How would students learn from other students who are not authorities? So beliefs about learning shaped by culture and previous experiences in different kinds of classrooms may explain why English learners seem quiet and reluctant to speak in class. English language learners also may think that their teachers are not very good because they do not explain everything. They also may strongly prefer memorization as a learning strategy if memorization was emphasized in their previous schools (thanks to Dr. Alan Hirvela at Ohio State University for pointing out these possible cultural differences in beliefs about schools and teachers).

We turn to other language teaching issues next, as we consider dialects.

DIALECT DIFFERENCES IN THE CLASSROOM

Communication is at the heart of teaching, but as we have seen in this chapter, culture affects communication. In this section, we will examine two kinds of language differences—dialect differences and genderlects.

Dialects

STOP & THINK When you want a soft drink, what do you call it? Do you think people in other parts of the United States use the same term? •

Growing up in Texas, we always asked, "Do you want a *coke?*" If the answer was yes, the next question was, "What kind—Coca-Cola, root beer, 7-Up, orange?" When I moved to New Jersey, I had to ask for a *soda*—if I asked for a coke, then that is just what I got. Twenty years later, at our moving-to-Ohio party, my colleague who had grown up in Columbus, Ohio, said, "You are going to have to learn to speak Midwestern and ask for a '*bottlapop.*'" Different regions have different ways of speaking—both in their accents and in their word usage.

A **dialect** is any variety of a language spoken by a particular group. Eugene Garcia (2002) defines a dialect as "a regional variation of language characterized by distinct grammar, vocabulary, and pronunciation" (p. 218). The dialect is part of the group's collective identity. Actually, every person reading this book speaks at least one dialect, maybe more, because there is no one absolute standard English. The English language has several dialects, for example, Australian, Canadian, British, and American. Within each of these dialects are variations. A few examples of dialects of American English are Southern, Bostonian, Cajun, and African American Vernacular (Garcia, 2002).

Dialects differ in their rules about pronunciation, grammar, and vocabulary, but it is important to remember that these differences are not errors. Each dialect is logical, complex, and rule-governed. An example of this is the use of the double negative. In many versions of American English, the double negative construction, such as "I don't have no more," is incorrect. But in many dialects, such as some varieties of African American Vernacular English, and in other languages (for instance, Russian, French, Spanish, and Hungarian), the double negative is part of the grammatical rules. To say "I don't want anything" in Spanish, you must literally say, "I don't want nothing," or "No quiero nada."

DIALECTS AND PRONUNCIATION.   Dialects also differ is pronunciation, which can lead to spelling problems. In some varieties of African American Vernacular English and in Southern dialects, for instance, there is less attention paid to pronouncing the ends of words. A lack of attention to final consonants, such as *s*, can lead to failure to indicate possession, third-person singular verbs, and plurals in the standard way. So *John's book* might be *John book*, and the singular and plural will sound the same for words such as *thinks*, *wasps*, and *lists*. When endings are not pronounced, there are more *homonyms* (words that sound alike but have different meanings) in the student's speech than the unknowing teacher may expect; *spent* and *spend* might sound alike, for example. Even without the confusions caused by dialect differences, there are many homonyms in English. Usually, special attention is given to words such as these when they come up in spelling lessons. If teachers are aware of the special homonyms in student dialects, they can teach these differences directly. Table 5.6 gives some other examples of dialect differences.

Dialect Any variety of a language spoken by a particular group.

TABLE 5.6 • **A Few Examples of Dialect Differences in African American English and Spanish Influenced English**

AREA OF LANGUAGE	STANDARD ENGLISH	AFRICAN AMERICAN ENGLISH
Sounds: Final consonants dropped	Hand, picked	Han, pick
Noun plurals	Two puppies	Two puppy
Noun possessives	Mama's house	Mama house
Past tense	John came.	John come.
Use of *being* verb	John is sick.	John sick.
Use of *bin* for remote past	She has been running for a long time.	She bin running.
Multiple negation	I don't ever have any problems.	I don't never have no problems.
AREA OF LANGUAGE	STANDARD ENGLISH	SPANISH INFLUENCED ENGLISH
Sounds: Alternate *ch* and *sh* sounds	Chair, snow	Share, chow
Sounds: Final consonants dropped	Start, least	Star, leas
Reflexive pronouns	Himself, themselves	Hisself, theirselves
Borrow for *lend*	Lend me a pencil.	Borrow me a pencil.
Barely for *recently*	They recently graduated from high school.	They barely graduated from high school.
Multiple negation	I don't have any pain.	I don't have no pain.
Using words from Spanish	15-year-old girl's coming out party	quinceñera

Source: Brice, Alejandro E.; Brice, Roanne, Language Development: Monolingual and Bilingual Acquisition, 1st Edition, © 2009. Reprinted by permission of Pearson Education, Inc., Upper Saddle River, NJ.

DIALECTS AND TEACHING. How can teachers cope with linguistic diversity in the classroom? First, they can be sensitive to their own possible negative stereotypes about children who speak a different dialect. Second, teachers can ensure comprehension by repeating instructions using different words and by asking students to paraphrase instructions or give examples. The best teaching approach seems to be to focus on understanding the students and accepting their language as a valid and correct system, but to teach the alternative forms of English (or whatever the dominant language is in your country) that are used in more formal work settings and writing so that the students will have access to a range of opportunities. For example, Lisa Delpit (1995) describes Martha Demientieff, a Native Alaskan teacher of Athabaskan children in a small village. The teacher's goal is for her students to become fluent in both their dialect, which she calls "Heritage English," and the "Formal English" of employers and others outside the village. She explains to her students that people outside the village will judge them by the way they talk and write. She goes on to explain:

> We have to feel sorry for them because they have only one way to talk. We're going to learn two ways to say things. One will be our Heritage way. The other will be Formal English. Then when we go to get jobs, we'll be able to talk like those people who only

DIALECT DIFFERENCES IN THE CLASSROOM Teachers should accept their linguistically diverse students' languages as valid and correct systems, but also teach the dominant language used in more formal work settings and writing so that the students will have access to a range of opportunities.

know and can only listen to one way. Maybe after we get the jobs we can help them to learn how it feels to have another language, like ours, that feels so good. We'll talk like them when we have to, but we'll always know our way is best. (p. 41)

Moving between two speech forms is called **code-switching**—something we all have learned to do. Sometimes, the code is formal speech for educational or professional communication. At other times, the code is informal for talk among friends and family. And occasionally, the codes are different dialects. Even young children recognize variations in codes. Delpit (1995) describes the reaction of one of her 1st grade students to her very first reading lesson. After she carefully recited the memorized introduction from the teacher's manual, a student raised his hand and asked, "Teacher, how come you talkin' like a white person? You talkin' just like my momma talk when she get on the phone."

Learning the alternative versions of a language is easy for most children, as long as they have good models, clear instruction, and opportunities for authentic practice.

Genderlects

If you had to guess what **genderlects** are, based on what you know about dialects, you probably would figure out that genderlects are different ways of talking for males and females. There are some small differences between boys and girls—girls tend to be slightly more talkative and affiliative in their speech (affiliative speech is talk intended to establish and maintain relationships). But much of the research has been conducted with White, middle-class children and the results do not necessarily hold for other groups and cultures. For example, some research reports that girls are more likely to cooperate and to talk about caring, whereas boys are more competitive and talk about rights and justice. But other studies have found that African American girls in one study were just as likely as boys to compete and talk about their rights in conversations (Leaper & Smith, 2004).

As with most aspects of language, there are cultural differences in genderlects. Interrupting is a good example. In America, boys interrupt more often than girls, but in Africa, the Caribbean, South America, and Eastern Europe, females interrupt males much more often than they do in America. And in Thailand, Hawaii, Japan, and Antigua, the style of speaking for boys and girls is overlapping—this overlapping talk is not interruption but cooperative turn taking (Owens, 2005).

TEACHING IMMIGRANT STUDENTS AND ENGLISH LANGUAGE LEARNERS

Felipe Vargas is a 5th grader who came with his family from Mexico to the United States more than three years ago so his father could take a job in a chicken-processing plant. Many Mexicans have come to work at the plant, and now there is a Spanish-speaking church, a Mexican grocery, and a Mexican bar and restaurant in the little northern Georgia town where they live. Felipe's mother, who takes care of the home and children, speaks no English, but his father and his older brother, Enrique, both speak a little. Enrique was 15 when the family came to this country. He left school after one year in an ESOL program, and went to work in the chicken plant. He is proud to be contributing to the family, but dreams of being a car mechanic; he spends all his free time fixing cars for neighbors

Code-switching Moving between two speech forms.

Genderlects Different ways of talking for males and females.

and earns a little extra money that way. Felipe's oldest sister is 15 now, and, like him, spent two years in an ESOL program before transitioning to regular English-speaking classes. Her parents have chosen a husband for her from "back home," and she plans to leave school as soon as she turns 16, although she would rather not marry the man her parents have chosen. His two younger sisters are 8 and 4; the youngest is in a special Head Start class to learn English, and the other is repeating 2nd grade because she is having a hard time learning to read.

Felipe gets mostly Cs in school. He still struggles a bit with reading his textbooks, but he has many Anglo friends in his class and has no trouble talking English with them; in fact, he translates for his parents when they come to school for parent conferences, which they do whenever his father can get off

TEACHING IMMIGRANT STUDENTS AND ENGLISH LANGUAGE LEARNERS Most educational psychologists believe that no culture is deficient, but rather that there may be incompatibilities between the student's home culture and the expectations of the school.

work. Math is his real talent; he consistently gets As on his tests, and he is in the highest "math group," so he goes to another teacher for math. That teacher calls him "Phillip" and tells him he could be an accountant or maybe an engineer when he grows up. Felipe likes this idea, but his father says that college would cost too much money and reminds him that the family plans to go back to Mexico someday, when they have saved enough to buy a small farm, which is his father's dream.

There are so many students like Felipe and his siblings in America schools today. For the remainder of this chapter we explore ways of teaching these students so that their dreams of college and careers can come true wherever they finally live.

Immigrants and Refugees

In 2003, 12% of the people living in the United States were born in another country. Many of these children, like Felipe Vargas and his siblings, will be immigrants. **Immigrants** are people who voluntarily leave their country to become permanent residents in a new place. People from Mexico, like Felipe's family, are the largest U.S. immigrant group (Okagaki, 2006). **Refugees** are a special group of immigrants who also relocate voluntarily, but they are fleeing their home country because it is not safe. The United States requires that individuals seeking refugee status have "a well-founded fear of persecution on account of race, religion, nationality, membership in a particular social group, or political opinion" (U.S. Citizenship and Immigration Services, 2011). Since 1975, more than 3,000,000 refugees have permanently resettled in the United States, half of them children (Refugee Council USA, 2011).

In earlier decades, these new immigrants were expected to assimilate—that is, to enter the cultural **melting pot** and become like those who had arrived earlier. For years, the goal of American schools was to be the fire under the melting pot. Immigrant children who spoke different languages and had diverse religious and cultural heritages were expected to come to the schools, master English, and learn to become mainstream Americans. Of course, most schools were designed to serve European American middle-class children, so it was the immigrant children who were expected to do the adapting and changing—rather than the schools. *Involuntary immigrants*, descendants of the slaves forced to migrate to the United States, often were not welcome at all in the cultural melting pot.

Immigrants People who voluntarily leave their country to become permanent residents in a new place.

Refugees A special group of immigrants who also relocate voluntarily, but who are fleeing their home country because it is not safe.

Melting pot A metaphor for the absorption and assimilation of immigrants into the mainstream of society so that ethnic differences vanish.

In the 1960s and 1970s, some educators suggested that immigrants, students of color, and poor students had problems in school because they were "culturally disadvantaged" or "culturally handicapped." The assumption of this **cultural deficit model** was that the students' home culture was inferior because it had not prepared them to fit into the schools. Today, educational psychologists reject the idea of cultural deficits. They believe that no culture is deficient, but rather that there may be incompatibilities between the student's home culture and the expectations of the school (Gallimore & Goldenberg, 2001). Also, there is an increasing sense among many ethnic groups that they do not want to assimilate completely into mainstream American society. Rather, they want to maintain their culture and identity while still being a respected part of the larger society. Multiculturalism is the goal—more like a salad bowl filled with many ingredients instead of the prior melting pot idea (Banks, 1997, 2006; Stinson, 2006).

In past decades, most U.S. immigrants were concentrated in large urban areas and in California, Texas, Arizona, and New York. But today there are "New Ellis Islands" in many other cities and towns, particularly in the Midwestern states. Given the challenges of teaching students who have a range English speaking abilities coupled with the demands of accountability testing, it is clear that teachers everywhere are under pressure (Garcia & Tyler, 2010). And there is not much help--less than 1% of elementary and secondary school teachers are prepared to teach English as a Second Language (Aud et al., 2010).

Classrooms Today

English language learners are the fastest growing segment of the United States population. From 1994 to 2004, there was a 125% increase in students with limited English proficiency in Ohio where I teach (Newman, Samimy, & Romstedt, 2010). In 2008, nearly 21% of school-age children in the United States spoke a language other than English at home—almost three times as many as in 1979 (Aud et al., 2010). There are projections that by 2030, about 40% of the students in pre-kindergarten through high school will speak limited English (Guglielmi, 2008). By some estimates, Latinos alone will comprise about one quarter of the U.S. population by 2050 (U.S. Census Bureau, 2011). These changes are not limited to the United States. By 2031, it is projected that one in three Canadians will belong to a visible minority and one in four will be foreign born, so it is likely that the number of people who speak languages other than the official English and French will increase in Canada as well (Freisen, 2010). In fact, all the developed countries have many immigrant students. For example, more than half of the students under age 12 in the Amsterdam schools are from immigrant families (Crul & Holdaway, 2009).

Because immigrant families tend to live in particular neighborhoods, the schools in these communities generally have the largest number of immigrants and **English language learner (ELL)** students. Some of these students may not even be able to read and write in their native language. Clearly, schools serving these students need extra resources to hire and train native-language speaking teachers and aides, provide smaller classes, and purchase well-designed materials to teach complex academic subjects to students with limited English language skills (Crul & Holdaway, 2009). As you can guess, these extra resources are not always available.

FOUR STUDENT PROFILES. Following are four general profiles of English learners in today's classrooms (Echevarria & Graves, 2011).

- *Balanced bilinguals.* These students speak, read, and write well both in their first language and in English. They have the academic knowledge needed to continue learning in both languages and the skills and attitudes to do so. These students may not present difficult teaching challenges, but they do need to maintain their skills in both languages and cultures.
- *Monolingual/literate students.* These students are literate in their native language (at or above grade level when working in their native language), but speak limited English.

Cultural deficit model A model that explains the school achievement problems of ethnic minority students by assuming that their culture is inadequate and does not prepare them to succeed in school.

English language learners (ELLs) Students who are learning English when their primary or heritage language is not English.

The teaching challenge here is to help the students develop English and continue to learn academic subjects.

- *Monolingual/preliterate students.* These students are not literate. They may not read or write in their native language or they may have very limited literacy skills. Some have never have attended school. In addition, they speak limited English. These students require the greatest support in learning both academic subjects and language.
- *Limited bilingual.* These students can converse well in both languages, but for some reason they have trouble learning academically. There may be underlying challenges such as learning disabilities or emotional problems. Further testing often is helpful to diagnose problems.

These student profiles are related to the distinction we encountered earlier in the chapter between contextualized conversational language and academic language. You may remember that it takes from 2 to 3 years to develop good conversational language, but 5 to 10 years to master academic language. *Conversational* skills include, for example, using appropriate vocabulary and sentences, asking and answering questions, starting and stopping conversations, listening, and understanding and using idioms.

Academic language includes reading and writing fluency; grammar and syntax; knowledge of specialized vocabulary; following written and oral directions; collaborating with other students on assignments; understanding different types of texts and forms of writing such as fiction, poetry, math problems, science charts and graphs, and timelines in history; and study skills such as outlining, summarizing, and reading comprehension (Echevarria & Graves, 2011). So to be successful in learning content, English language learners must put together an understanding of language with knowledge of terms, concepts, and conventions specific to a particular subject such as mathematics or biology. Figure 5.2 shows all the different domains of language that must come together for learning.

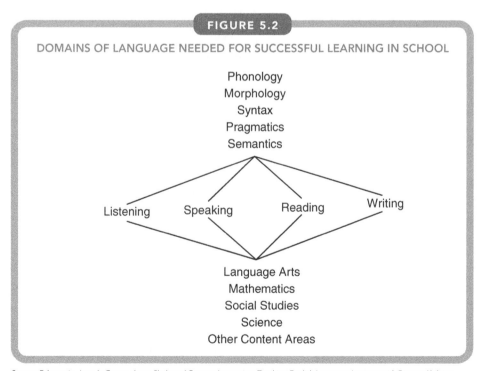

FIGURE 5.2

DOMAINS OF LANGUAGE NEEDED FOR SUCCESSFUL LEARNING IN SCHOOL

Phonology
Morphology
Syntax
Pragmatics
Semantics

Listening   Speaking   Reading   Writing

Language Arts
Mathematics
Social Studies
Science
Other Content Areas

Source: Echevarria, Jana J.; Graves, Anne, Sheltered Content Instruction: Teaching English Language Learners with Diverse Abilities, Coursesmart ETextbook, 4th Edition, © 2011. Reprinted by permission of Pearson Education, Inc., Upper Saddle River, NJ.

If you teach at a school with many English language learners, there probably will be school personnel who do formal assessments to provide appropriate placements for these students.

Generation 1.5: Students in Two Worlds

- -

STOP & THINK Imagine you are this person:

You came to the United States at about the age of one. Your family was undocumented. You have a younger brother and sister who were born in the United States and are legal citizens, but you are not. Your parents and older siblings worked hard, often two jobs, so that the younger children could get a good education. You attended kindergarten, elementary, and high school in your family's new community in the United States. You graduated from high school with good grades and hoped to attend college, but soon discovered you did not qualify for scholarship support and would have to pay international student tuition, which you cannot afford. Even as a hardworking and promising student, you cannot legally work, vote, or drive in many states, in spite of the fact that you have lived virtually all your life in the United States and speak fluent English. •

- -

If you were this student, you would be a member of a large group, often called **Generation 1.5** because their characteristics, educational experiences, and language fluencies are somewhere in between those of students born in the United States and students who are recent immigrants (Gonzalez, 2010). They were not born in the United States, but have lived here most of their lives because they came with their families when they were young. The language spoken in their homes may not be English, but they often speak fluent conversational English, even if their academic English is not as well developed. Actually, there are several kinds of Generation 1.5 students, described by Dubarry and Lima (2003).

- Students from United States territories such as Puerto Rico, sometimes called "in-migrants."
- U.S.-born children of immigrants who live in close-knit communities where the heritage language is maintained by the residents for family and business life.
- Children who are sent by their often-wealthy parents to live with older siblings in order to receive education in United States, sometimes called "parachute children."
- Children of families who move back and forth between different countries.
- Immigrants who speak other "Englishes" such as English from Jamaica, East India, or Singapore.

These students may share several characteristics and challenges. They may not have developed strong literacy skills in the language used at home because their schooling was not in that language. They may have acquired much of their English through listening to and speaking with friends or older siblings, watching television, or listening to music. They have been called "ear learners" because they have built their knowledge of English on the language they have heard in their environment. But what they hear is often colloquial language or slang, so they may have trouble learning how to read and write accurately in English. Many of us know if the grammar is correct in what we hear or read because we have heard (mostly) accurate grammar all our lives—our ears have taught us well. But for many Generation 1.5 students, their ear learning has given them an imperfect, even inaccurate conception of English grammar. Because they are "ear learners," they may use incorrect verb or noun forms, mispronounce plurals, or mix up words that sound very similar, for example, *confident* and *confidence*. They rely on context, gestures, facial cues, and intonations to make sense of language, so reading is more difficult and proofreading is hard because they cannot "hear" mistakes. Complex academic reading and writing assignments are very challenging (Harklau, Losey, & Siegal, 1999; Reid & Byrd 1998; Roberge, 2002). In contrast, many of my international graduate students who learned English mostly as "eye learners" through reading, writing, and vocabulary and grammar exercises can write well, but they have

Generation 1.5 Students whose characteristics, educational experiences, and language fluencies are somewhere in between those of students born in the United States and students who are recent immigrants.

more difficulty with oral interactions. Knowing what kind of students you have and how they first learned English should help you understand the mistakes they make and the challenges they face.

Bilingual Education and English Learners

There are several terms associated with bilingual education. In the United States, students who are just learning English sometimes are called **limited-English-proficient** or **LEP**. More often, as we have seen, these students are called English language learners (ELLs), because their primary or heritage language is not English. **English as a Second Language (ESL)** is the name given to the *classes* devoted to teaching these students English. Limited proficiency in English often means lower academic achievement and poorer job prospects. So one issue around diversity in language development is how we should teach these students.

TWO APPROACHES TO ENGLISH LANGUAGE LEARNING. Virtually everyone agrees that all citizens should learn the official language of their country. But when and how should instruction in that language begin? Is it better to teach English language learners to read first in their native language or should they begin reading instruction in English? Do these children need some oral lessons in English before reading instruction can be effective? Should other subjects, such as mathematics and social studies, be taught in the primary (home) language until the children are fluent in English? As you can see in the *Point/Counterpoint* on the next page, debates about this question have raged for quite a while.

RESEARCH ON BILINGUAL EDUCATION. There are strong advantages for simultaneous bilingual learning. Remember Petitto's (2009) finding that monolingual English speakers who participated in a bilingual program excelled in the skills needed for reading in both languages. When the National Literacy Panel on Language—Minority Children and Youth reviewed studies of English-only *immersion* versus native language *maintenance* programs, they found that the students in the native language maintenance programs performed better on many different measured outcomes (Francis, Lesaux, & August, 2006). In a study that directly compared immersion and maintenance programs in 128 classrooms in Texas and California, Lee Branum-Martin and his colleagues (2010) found that the amount of teaching conducted in English and Spanish could not be predicted by type of program—there were many local variations. Some English immersion teachers used quite a bit of Spanish and some Spanish language maintenance programs taught quite a bit in English. Another finding was that Spanish language maintenance programs had a positive impact on English performance.

A study funded by the U.S. Department of Education (Gersten et al., 2007) identified five major recommendations for English learners, summarized here (Peregoy & Boyle, 2009).

1. Begin instruction with a formative assessment (see Chapter 12) of reading to determine exactly what the English learners know and what they are ready to learn, and to identify students who will need more help in reading.
2. Use small-group interventions to focus instruction on the areas of need identified in the assessments.
3. Target teaching essential vocabulary for the content in your curriculum as well as common words, phrases, and expressions used class.
4. Directly teach academic English—develop the students' abilities to read texts, write academic assignments, and use formal language and argument.
5. Make wide use of peer-assisted learning, particularly work in pairs, to complete academic tasks.

BILINGUALISM FOR ALL: TWO-WAY IMMERSION. Students in the United States need to master both conversational and academic English to achieve at high levels, but they

Limited-English-proficient (LEP) A term also used for students who are learning English when their primary or heritage language is not English—not the preferred term because of the negative connotations.

English as a Second Language (ESL) The classes devoted to teaching ELL students English.

POINT/COUNTERPOINT: What Is the Best Way to Teach English Language Learners?

There are two basic positions on this question, which have given rise to two contrasting teaching approaches: one that focuses on *immersion* in English-only teaching to make the transition to English as quickly as possible. The other approach attempts to *maintain or improve* the native language and use that language as the primary teaching language until English skills are more fully developed.

▶ POINT

Structured English Immersion is the best approach for ELL students. Proponents of the *immersion/fast transition* approach believe that English ought to be introduced as early and as intensively as possible; they argue that valuable learning time is lost if students are taught in their native language. Advocates cite the successes of the Canadian Immersion program as evidence that language immersion works (Baker, 1998). In an article for educational administrators, Kevin Clark claims: "These programs have the potential to accelerate ELLs' English language development and linguistic preparation for grade-level academic content" (2009, p. 42). Many schools today follow this line of thinking and offer **Structured English Immersion** or SEI. There are different perspectives on SEI, but usually it is defined as having two basic features: (1) teachers use English as much as possible in instruction, and (2) the level of the students' abilities in the class determines how teachers use and teach English: English use and teaching must be appropriate for student abilities (Ramirez, Yuen, & Ramey, 1991). There are at least three reasons why schools adopt this approach (Clark, 2009):

1. Some states have mandated this immersion by law and have limited the amount of teaching that can be done in the child's native language.

2. The accountability tests that all school districts in the United States must administer are in English. Schools where students don't score well on these tests face penalties, so getting the test takers to achieve English proficiency as fast as possible benefits the schools.

3. Schools are concerned that ELL students who do not get intensive and continuing English instruction may learn adequate conversational English but never develop the academic English needed for achievement in secondary schools and beyond.

Immersion in a language is the best way to learn a new language and is the basis for many language-learning programs around the world (Clark, 2009).

▶ COUNTERPOINT

Students' native language should be maintained. Teaching *in* English and hoping students will figure it out is not the same as *teaching* English. Proponents of *native-language maintenance instruction* raise four important issues (Gersten, 1996b; Goldenberg, 1996; Hakuta & Garcia, 1989).

1. Deep learning in the first language supports second language learning. For example, research on a large national sample that followed 8th graders for 12 years found that for Latino students, proficiency in the first language of Spanish predicted reading ability in English and English reading ability predicted achievement in school and in careers (Guglielmi, 2008). The metacognitive strategies and knowledge developed when students learn to read in their first language are transferred to reading in a second language as well (van Gelderen, Schoonen, Stoel, de Glopper, & Hulstijn, 2007). So maintaining and increasing proficiency in the first language is important. The learning strategies and academic content (math, science, history, etc.) that students learn in their native language are not forgotten when they learn English.

2. Children who are forced to try to learn math or science in an unfamiliar language are bound to have trouble. What if you had been forced to learn fractions or biology in a second language that you had studied for only a semester? Some psychologists believe students taught by this approach may become **semilingual**; that is, they are not proficient in either language. Being semilingual may be one reason the dropout rate is so high for low-SES Latino students (Ovando & Collier, 1998).

3. If the first language is neglected and the entire emphasis is on English, students may get the message that their home languages (and therefore, their families and cultures) are second class.

4. Years ago, Kenji Hakuta cited a "paradoxical attitude of admiration and pride for school-attained bilingualism on the one hand and scorn and shame for home-brewed immigrant bilingualism on the other" (1986, p. 229). Ironically, by the time students have mastered academic English and let their home language deteriorate, they reach secondary school and are encouraged to learn a "second" language. Sometimes native speakers of Spanish are encouraged to learn French or German, so they risk becoming semilingual in three languages (Miranda, 2008).

Beyond Either/Or. It is difficult to separate politics from practice in the debate about bilingual education. It is clear that high-quality bilingual education programs can have positive results. Students improve in the subjects that were taught in their native language, in their mastery of English, and in self-esteem as well (Crawford, 1997; Francis, Lesaux, & August, 2006). English as a second language (ESL) programs seem to have positive effects on reading comprehension (Proctor, August, Carlo, & Snow, 2006). But attention today is shifting from debate about general approaches to a focus on effective teaching strategies. As you will see many times in this book, a combination of clarity of learning goals and direct instruction in needed skills—including learning strategies and tactics, teacher- or peer-guided practice leading to independent practice, authentic and engaging tasks, opportunities for interaction and conversation that are academically focused, and warm encouragement from the teacher— seems to be effective (Chamot & O'Malley, 1996; Gersten, 1996b; Goldenberg, 1996).

should not sacrifice their native language in the process. The goal of schools should be balanced bilingualism. One approach to reaching this goal is to create two-way immersion classes that mix students who are learning a second language with students who are native speakers. The objective is for both groups to become fluent in both languages (Peregoy & Boyle, 2009; Sheets, 2005). My daughter spent a summer in such a program in Quebec and was ahead in every French class after that.

For truly effective education for ELLs, we will need many bilingual teachers. If you have a competence in another language, you might want to develop it fully for your teaching. Because there is only one qualified teacher for every 100 English language learners (Hawkins, 2004), promoting language learning is a responsibility for most teachers. Figure 5.3 shows teaching strategies that will support language and literacy development across the grade levels.

When students exit an immersion or a bilingual program with some English skills, they are not finished learning. The next phase for many students is sheltered instruction.

Sheltered Instruction

The challenge for most teachers working with immigrant and ELL students is to teach the subject matter and develop students' English language skills at the same time.

FIGURE 5.3

TEACHING STRATEGIES FOR PROMOTING LEARNING AND LANGUAGE ACQUISITION

Effective teaching for students in bilingual and ESL classrooms combines many strategies—direct instruction, mediation, coaching, feedback, modeling, encouragement, challenge, and authentic activities—many opportunities to read, write, and talk.

Strategies \ Grade Level	K	1	2	3	4	5	6	7	8	9	10	11	12
Alphabet books	→								→				
Assessment													
Formal					→								→
Informal	→												→
Dialogue journals	→												→
Drawing	→												→
Experiments	→												→
Invented spelling	→						→						
Labeling	→												→
Language experience	→												→
Name charts	→	→											
Play centers	→	→											
Reading aloud	→											→	
Shared reading	→			→									
Wall charts	→	→											
Word recognition													
Sight words	→	→											
Phonics	→			→									
Context	→											→	
Dictionary	→											→	

Source: Peregoy, Suzanne F.; Boyle, Owen F., Reading, Writing and Learning in ESL: A Resource Book for Teaching K-12 English Learners, 5th edition, © 2009. Reprinted by permission of Pearson Education, Inc., Upper Saddle River, NJ.

Structured English immersion (SEI) An environment that teaches English rapidly by maximizing instruction in English and using English at a level appropriate to the abilities of the ELLs in the class.

Semilingual A lack of proficiency in any language; speaking one or more languages inadequately.

Sheltered instruction Approach to teaching that improves English language skills while teaching content to ELL students by putting the words and concepts of the content into context to make the content more understandable.

Sheltered Instruction Observation Protocol or SIOP® An observational system to check that each element of sheltered instruction is present for a teacher.

Sheltered instruction is one approach that has proved successful in reaching both goals. Sheltered instruction teaches content to ELL students by putting the words and concepts of the content into context to make the content more understandable. Strategies include simplifying and controlling language, giving attention to the relevant grammar and forms of English—helping students "crack the code," using visuals and gestures, and including real-life supports and examples. In addition, there is an emphasis on student talk and discussion instead of the teacher doing all the talking. In order to be clearer about what good sheltered instruction looks like, Jana Echevarría and her colleagues (2008) identified eight key elements: preparation, building background, comprehensibility, strategies, interaction, practice and application, lesson delivery, and review and assessment. Then the researchers developed an observational system to check that each element was included in teaching. The system is called the **Sheltered Instruction Observation Protocol or SIOP®**. Figure 5.4 gives some examples of what each element of SIOP® might include.

FIGURE 5.4

SOME EXAMPLES OF THE SHELTERED INSTRUCTION OBSERVATION PROTOCOL OR SIOP®

The SIOP® has 30 characteristics or areas to assess during observation. Each characteristic is rated from 4 (Highly Evident) to 0 (Not Evident) or NA (Not Applicable). These ratings are converted into a score.

Observer: _____   Teacher:_____

Date: _____   School: _____

Grade: _____   ESL level: _____

Class: _____   Lesson: Multi-day Single-day (circle one)

Directions: Circle the number that best reflects what you observe in a sheltered lesson. You may give a score from 0–4. Cite under "Comments" specific examples of the behaviors observed. Total Score: ☐ % Score ☐ Tape #:_____

	Highly Evident		Somewhat Evident		Not Evident	NA
Preparation	4	3	2	1	0	
1. **Content objectives** clearly defined, displayed, and reviewed with students	☐	☐	☐	☐	☐	☐
2. **Language objectives** clearly defined, displayed, and reviewed with students	☐	☐	☐	☐	☐	☐
3. **Content concepts** appropriate for age and educational background level of students	☐	☐	☐	☐	☐	☐
4. **Supplementary materials** used to a high degree, making the lesson clear and meaningful (e.g., computer programs, graphs, models, visuals)	☐	☐	☐	☐	☐	☐
5. **Adaptation of content** (e.g., text, assignment) to all levels of student proficiency	☐	☐	☐	☐	☐	☐
6. **Meaningful activities** that integrate lesson concepts (e.g., interviews, letter writing, simulations, models) with language practice opportunities for reading. writing, listening, and/or speaking	☐	☐	☐	☐	☐	☐

Comments:

Building Background						
7. **Concepts explicitly linked** to students' background experiences	☐	☐	☐	☐	☐	☐
8. **Links explicitly made** between past learning and new concepts	☐	☐	☐	☐	☐	☐
9. **Key vocabulary emphasized** (e.g., introduced, written, repeated, and highlighted for students to see)						

Comments:

	Highly Evident		Somewhat Evident		Not Evident	NA

Comprehensible

10. **Speech** appropriate for students' proficiency level (e.g., slower rate, enunciation and simple sentence structure for beginners) ☐ ☐ ☐ ☐ ☐ ☐ / ☐ ☐ ☐ ☐ ☐ ☐

11. **Clear explanation** of academic tasks ☐ ☐ ☐ ☐ ☐ ☐

12. A variety of techniques used to make **content concepts** clear (e.g., modeling, visuals, hands-on activities, demonstration, gestures, body language)
Comments:

Strategies

13. Ample opportunities for students to use **learning strategies** ☐ ☐ ☐ ☐ ☐ ☐

14. **Scaffolding techniques** consistently used assisting and supporting student understanding (e.g., think-alouds) ☐ ☐ ☐ ☐ ☐ ☐

15. A variety of questions or tasks that promote **higher-order thinking skills** (e.g., literal, analytical, and interpretive questions) ☐ ☐ ☐ ☐ ☐ ☐
Comments:

Interaction

16. Frequent opportunities for **interaction** and discussion between teacher/student and among students, which encourage elaborated responses about lesson concepts ☐ ☐ ☐ ☐ ☐ ☐

17. **Grouping configurations** support language and content objectives of the lesson ☐ ☐ ☐ ☐ ☐ ☐

18. Sufficient **wait time for student response** consistently provided ☐ ☐ ☐ ☐ ☐ ☐

19. Ample opportunities for students to **clarify key concepts in L1** as needed with aide, peer, or L1 text
Comments:

Practice/Application

20. **Hands-on materials and/or manipulatives** provided for students to practice using new content knowledge ☐ ☐ ☐ ☐ ☐ ☐

21. Activities provided for students to **apply content and language knowledge** in the classroom ☐ ☐ ☐ ☐ ☐ ☐

22. Activities integrate all **language skills** (i.e., reading, listening, and speaking) ☐ ☐ ☐ ☐ ☐ ☐
Comments:

Lesson Delivery

23. **Content objectives** clearly supported by lesson delivery ☐ ☐ ☐ ☐ ☐ ☐

24. **Language objectives** clearly supported by lesson delivery ☐ ☐ ☐ ☐ ☐ ☐

25. **Students engaged** approximately 90–100% of the period ☐ ☐ ☐ ☐ ☐ ☐

26. **Pacing** of the lesson appropriate to the students' ability level ☐ ☐ ☐ ☐ ☐ ☐
Comments:

Review/Assessment

27. Comprehensive **review of key vocabulary** ☐ ☐ ☐ ☐ ☐ ☐

28. Comprehensive **review of key content concepts** ☐ ☐ ☐ ☐ ☐

29. Regular **feedback provided** to students on their output (e.g., language, content, work) ☐ ☐ ☐ ☐ ☐ ☐

30. **Assessment of student comprehension** and learning of all lesson objectives (e.g., spot checking, group response) throughout the lesson ☐ ☐ ☐ ☐ ☐ ☐
Comments:

Source: Echevarria, Jana J.; Graves, Anne, Sheltered Content Instruction: Teaching English Language Learners with Diverse Abilities, Coursesmart ETextbook, 4th Edition, © 2011. Reprinted by permission of Pearson Education, Inc., Upper Saddle River, NJ.

What might this look like? Here is an activity for a 7th grade language arts class in which students are learning the literary process of comparing and contrasting characters in stories (Vogt, Echevarria, & Short, 2010). In the same lesson, students also are learning some vocabulary specific to language arts content (*character traits*) as well as academic vocabulary used in many subjects (*compare, contrast*). Finally, the students are practicing higher order thinking skills by considering questions about situational behaviors and characters' traits such as, "Do people always act the same? Are shy people shy in every situation? Do motives affect behavior? Do traits affect behavior—always the same way?" The students have already read two stories, "Seventh Grade" by Gary Soto and "The Special Powers of Blossom Culp" by Richard Peck. To learn vocabulary about traits, the students explore a long list of traits, from "able" and "active" to "worried" and "young." They also complete a semantic feature analysis (SFA) of the main characters in the two stories—an example is shown in Figure 5.5.

Using the SFA, students can compare their analyses, look for patterns, and discuss their conclusions. They can work in pairs to write comparison-and-contrast essays so they have more opportunities to communicate. All of these activities involve English language learners in thinking, reading, speaking, and writing as they learn new content concepts, academic vocabulary, and comprehension strategies.

Affective and Emotional/Social Considerations

STOP & THINK You walk into one of your education classes. The instructor moves to the lectern and says:

> Mina-san, ohayō gozaimasu. Kyō wa, kyō iku shinrigaku no jū gyō ja arimasen. Kyō wa, nihon no bangō , ichi kara jū made benkyō -oshimasu. Soshite, kono kyōshitsu wa Amerika no kyōshitsu ja arimasen. Ima wa Nihon no kyōshitsu desu. Nihon no kyōshitsu dewa, shinakerebanaranai koto wa mittsu mo arimasu. Tatsu, rei, suwaru. Mina-san, tatte kudasai. Doshite tatteimasen ka? Wakarimasen ka?

The class continues in the same way until you are handed the "test" and told to "Do your best—this is 20% of your grade." You can't believe it! What would you do?

FIGURE 5.5

SEMANTIC FEATURE ANALYSIS OF CHARACTERS IN TWO SHORT STORIES

	confident	shy	eccentric	compassionate	easily embarrassed	cruel
Seventh Grade						
Victor	−	+	−	+	+	−
Teresa	+	−	−	+	NE	−
Michael	+	−	+	+	−	−
Mr. Bueller	+	−	−	+	−	−
The Special Powers of Blossom Culp						
Blossom	+	−	+	−	−	−
Blossom's Mama	+	−	+	−	−	−
Letty	+	−	−	−	NE	+
Miss Cartwright	+	NE	−	+	−	−

GUIDELINES

Providing Emotional Support and Increasing Self-Esteem for English Language Learners

Create learning activities that promote success in reading and writing.

Examples

1. Have weekly individual conferences with younger students and record their retelling of a story. Let students edit and revise the dictation and read it to a partner.
2. Do interactive journals with older students—collect each week and write back.

Make sure students have plenty of time to practice and get careful, targeted corrections.

Examples

1. Point out privately what is correct, almost correct, and wrong in written work.
2. Be sensitive about public oral corrections and build on what is correct, but do not accept clearly incorrect answers.

Connect teaching to relevant knowledge from students' lives.

Examples

1. Ask students to survey family members about favorite films— use film characters to discuss elements of literature—plot, point of view, etc.
2. Have students create construction firms and plan projects to learn math concepts.

Actively involve learners.

Examples

1. Use timelines in history compared to personal timelines based on family history.
2. Do projects in science based on animals or farming for rural students.

Use different grouping strategies.

Examples

1. Try pairs for writing stories and practicing oral presentations.
2. Create small teams to research recent immigrant groups' culture and language.

Provide native language support.

Examples

1. Learn and use as much of the students' language as possible—if they can learn, so can you.
2. Find Internet translation sources and local native speaking volunteers.
3. Bring native language magazines and books into the classroom.

Involve family and community members.

Examples

1. Bring in storytellers, local business owners, artists, craftspeople.
2. Create a Welcome Center for your class.

Hold high expectations for all students, and communicate these expectations clearly.

Examples

1. Keep scrapbooks of previous students who have gone on to careers or college.
2. Don't accept mediocre work.
3. Be a model of respect for diversity and an enemy of bigotry.

Source: Echevarria, Jana J.; Graves, Anne, Sheltered Content Instruction: Teaching English Language Learners with Diverse Abilities, Coursesmart ETextbook, 4th Edition, © 2011. Reprinted by permission of Pearson Education, Inc., Upper Saddle River, NJ.

Does this seem impossible? Actually, one of my doctoral students (Yough, 2010) designed this lesson (without the test) so his educational psychology class would experience how it feels to have important content taught in a language you don't speak (assuming your Japanese is a bit rusty!). Research on ELL students shows that they may experience severe challenges and stress in school. They may feel that they don't belong, and that others are making fun of them, or just ignoring them. Everyone else seems to know the rules and the right words. It takes courage and persistence to keep trying to communicate; it is easier to say as little as possible. So the practice in communicating that these students desperately need just doesn't happen.

What can teachers do to support students' courage and persistence in communicating? The first step is to create a classroom community that is caring and respectful. We explore strategies for creating classroom community in Chapter 13. Echevarria and Graves (2011) suggest additional steps to provide emotional support and increase self-esteem for ELL students, as you can see in the *Guidelines*.

Another problem is related to cultural differences. As we saw earlier, students who immigrate to the United States in their middle or high school years may have experienced very different educational systems and educational values "back home." They may have been very successful in those systems, perhaps by excelling in the memorizing required by the curriculum. When they encounter a different approach to education, suddenly they may struggle and feel as if they know little or nothing. As a teacher, you need to learn the strengths of these students and acknowledge their abilities—and build on their knowledge. We turn to that topic next.

Working with Families: Using the Tools of the Culture

Luis Moll and his colleagues wanted a better way to teach the children of working-class Mexican American families in the barrio schools of Tucson, Arizona (Moll et al., 1992). Rather than adopt a model of remediating the students' deficits, Moll decided to identify and build on the tools and cultural **funds of knowledge** of their families. By interviewing the families, the researchers identified their extensive knowledge about agriculture, economics, medicine, household management, mechanics, science, and religion. When teachers based their assignments on these funds of knowledge, students were more engaged and teachers were educated about their students' lives. For example, by participating in a Funds of Knowledge project, one teacher realized that she always had thought about her students in terms of deficits and problems—poor achievement, alienation, family troubles, and poverty. But then she got to know the families by focusing on their resources, not their limitations. She also learned that her students' actions often were misinterpreted:

> Strong family values and responsibility are characteristics of the families I visited. . . . My students were expected to participate in household chores such as cleaning house, car maintenance, food preparation, washing dishes, and caring for younger siblings. I learned what this insight meant when one of my students was unable to attend school drama and chorus rehearsals one day. In my journal entry detailing this project, I noted the following incident:
>
> -Wednesday (11/25/92) The music teacher commented (to me), "You know, Leticia has missed two chorus rehearsals." Before I could answer, the school drama teacher stepped in to add, "Oh, she's very irresponsible." She had signed up to be in the Drama Club and had only been to two meetings. I said "Wait a minute. . . ." I then told her how Leticia's younger brother was being hospitalized for a series of operations, and when the mother had to leave, she left Leticia in charge of caring for her two younger siblings. In fact, her missing after-school rehearsals was an act of responsibility, obedience and loyalty to her family. (Gonzales et al., 1993)

By engaging with students' families, this teacher learned about the valuable cognitive resources in the community, and her respect for her students and their families increased. Moll's work also was the basis for the Welcome Center project in a prekindergarten through 5th grade elementary school in the Southwest. Within four years the school had gone from 12% to 43% Latino/a, with most of these students recently arrived immigrants. The Welcome Center was a "social and instructional space where recent immigrant families in the school would come to trade a variety of expertise, meet each other, gather information about their children's education, and share general information on practical matters" (DaSilva Iddings, 2009, p. 207). The Center was a bright, comfortable, informal space with a small kitchen, picnic tables, computer and printer, books and magazines in Spanish and English, math manipulatives, showcases for children's work, and other welcoming features. Fifth graders offered homework assistance after school at the center. Spanish-speaking families taught classes in Spanish, cooking, and dancing for community members. English literacy activities were provided for adults and children learning together. The center produced many success stories—teachers who connected with students' families and came to appreciate the value of their students' language and culture, immigrant families who moved toward citizenship, and others who opened businesses and restaurants. Connections with families may be especially important for the success of immigrant students. The *Family and Community Partnerships Guidelines* have more ideas.

Funds of knowledge Knowledge that families and community members have acquired in many areas of work, home, and religious life that can become the basis for teaching.

GUIDELINES —FAMILY AND COMMUNITY PARTNERSHIPS

Welcoming All Families

Make sure communication with families is understandable.
Examples
1. Use the families' home languages wherever possible.
2. Use oral forms of communication—phone calls or home visits—whenever possible.

Balance positive and negative messages.
Examples
1. Send home notes or descriptions about their child's accomplishments or acts of kindness.
2. Explain disciplinary actions as ways of helping children succeed.

Establish systems for welcoming new families.
Examples
1. Assign more experienced "buddy" parents to communicate with new families.
2. Connect with multilingual media in your community to make announcements about school.

Make sure messages get through.
Examples
1. Establish telephone trees or texting networks.
2. Set the expectation that there will be a weekly note sent home so parents can ask their children about it.
3. Establish a class newsletter or Web site and incorporate multiple languages.

SPECIAL CHALLENGES: ENGLISH LANGUAGE LEARNERS WITH DISABILITIES AND SPECIAL GIFTS

If you remember the four profiles of ELLs described earlier, you know that one type of student may have learning disabilities, but it is very difficult to tell because the student's language is limited. English language learners with disabilities are difficult to diagnose—expert assessment is necessary (Garcia & Tyler, 2010). Sometimes students are inappropriately placed in special education just because they have problems with English, but other times, students who would benefit from special services are denied placement because their problems are assumed to be simply language learning issues (USDE, 2004). In addition, students with special talents and gifts may be difficult to recognize.

English Language Learners with Disabilities

As a teacher, one of your decisions will be whether to refer a struggling ELL student for testing. Of course, the first step is to use the best teaching approaches, incorporating sheltered instruction to develop both subject matter learning and English language development. But if progress seems much slower than usual, you might ask the following questions, suggested by George De George (2008): What is the student's educational background, and what is the background of his or her family? When did the student come to the United States? Being born in the United States but speaking another language at home or immigrating when very young actually can make learning in the early grades more difficult. Students who immigrate after successfully learning in their home country schools have literacy skills to build on. They know some academic content and they know they can learn in school. In contrast, the children who speak another language at home and have never been to school have no oral English to use as they learn the letters and sounds of written English. Bilingual instruction is the best strategy here.

Other questions to ask when considering a referral are: Were there any problems or complications during the mother's pregnancy? Has the child experienced any serious injuries or illnesses? Has the child moved around a great deal? Has the child had adequate opportunities to learn in a good bilingual or ESL program? Have the teachers who worked with the child been trained in teaching English as a second language? Is the student making progress, even if he or she is behind others the same age? Does the student have any talents or special skills to build on? These questions will help you determine if the student's difficulties are due to lack of learning opportunities, inadequate teaching, or a disability. No matter what the diagnosis—attention and appropriate teaching are needed. Students who have difficulties with English are much more likely to drop out of school (USDE, 2004).

Reaching Every Student: Recognizing Giftedness in Bilingual Students

Because they may be struggling with academic English, even though they are very knowledgeable, bilingual students may be overlooked for gifted and talented programs.

TABLE 5.7 • **Identifying Bilingual Students with Gifts and Talents**

Here are some ideas for identifying bilingual students with gifts and talents. Watch for students who:

_____ Learn English quickly
_____ Take risks in trying to communicate in English
_____ Practice English skills by themselves
_____ Initiate conversations with native English speakers
_____ Do not frustrate easily
_____ Are curious about new words or phrases and practice them
_____ Question word meanings; for example, "How can a bat be an animal and also something you use to hit a ball?"
_____ Look for similarities between words in their native language and English
_____ Are able to modify their language for less capable English speakers
_____ Use English to demonstrate leadership skills; for example, use English to resolve disagreements and to facilitate cooperative learning groups
_____ Prefer to work independently or with students whose level of English proficiency is higher than theirs
_____ Are able to express abstract verbal concepts with a limited English vocabulary
_____ Are able to use English in a creative way; for example, can make puns, poems, jokes, or original stories in English
_____ Become easily bored with routine tasks or drill work
_____ Have a great deal of curiosity
_____ Are persistent; stick to a task
_____ Are independent and self-sufficient
_____ Have a long attention span
_____ Become absorbed with self-selected problems, topics, and issues
_____ Retain, easily recall, and use new information
_____ Demonstrate social maturity, especially in the home or community

Source: Castellano, Jaime A.; Diaz, Eva, Reaching New Horizons: Gifted and Talented Education for Culturally and Linguistically Diverse Students, 1st Edition, © 2002. Reprinted by permission of Pearson Education, Inc., Upper Saddle River, NJ.

A 10th grade boy from Mexico, in the United States for two years, told an interviewer in Spanish:

> High school is hard for me because my English is so limited. …There are times when I feel a lot of pressure because I want to say something, but I don't know how to say it. There are many times when the teacher is asking questions, I know the answer, but I am afraid that people might laugh at me. (Walqui, 2008, p. 104)

This student might well be gifted. To identify gifted bilingual students, you can use a case study or portfolio approach in order to collect a variety of evidence, including interviews with parents and peers, formal and informal assessments, samples of student work and performances, and student self-assessments. The checklist in Table 5.7, from Castellano and Diaz (2002), is a useful guide.

▼ SUMMARY

The Development of Language (pp. 170–177)

How are humans predisposed to develop language? What roles do culture and learning play? Cultures create words for the concepts that are important to them. Children develop language as they build on other cognitive abilities by actively trying to make sense of what they hear, looking for patterns, and making up rules. In this process, built-in biases and rules may limit the search and guide the pattern recognition. Reward and correction play a role in helping children learn correct language use, but the child's thought processes are very important.

What are the elements of language? By age 5, most children have mastered almost all the sounds of their native language. In terms of vocabulary, we understand more words than we use. By age 6, children understand up to 20,000 words and use about 2,600 words. Understanding of words that express abstract ideas and hypothetical situations comes later as cognitive abilities develop. As children develop an understanding of grammar, they may apply new rules too widely, saying "broked" for "broken," for example. Understanding the passive voice in syntax develops after understanding active voice.

What are pragmatics and metalinguistic awareness? Pragmatics is knowledge about how to use language—when, where, how, and to whom to speak. Metalinguistic awareness, knowledge about your own use of language and how language works, begins around age 5 or 6 and grows throughout life.

What are the most important skills that help literacy emerge? Research has identified two broad categories of skills that are important for later reading: (1) understanding sounds and codes such as knowing that letters have names, that sounds are associated with letters, and that words are made up of sounds; and (2) oral language skills such as expressive and receptive vocabulary, knowledge of syntax, and the ability to understand and tell stories. One way to think about emergent literacy that captures both code and oral language skills for emergent literacy is the notion of inside-out skills (the ability to decode units of print into units of sound and units of sound into units of language) and outside-in skills and processes (the ability to understand those auditory derivations, which involves placing them in the correct conceptual and contextual framework). For bilingual Spanish-speaking students, growth in receptive language in Spanish or English predicts early reading outcomes. Parents and teachers can support emerging literacy by reading with children, retelling stories and talking about them, and limiting time spent watching television.

Diversity in Language Development (pp. 177–184)

What is involved in learning two languages? Children can learn two languages at once if they have adequate opportunities in both languages. There are cognitive advantages to learning more than one language, so it is valuable to retain your heritage language even as you learn another. The best time to learn accurate pronunciation is early childhood, but people of any age can learn a new language. Having overheard a language as a child can improve one's ability to learn that language as an adult. Even though the advantages of bilingualism seem clear, many children and adults are losing their heritage language. Rather than losing one language to gain another, the goal should be balanced bilingualism—being equally fluent in both languages. People who can communicate in both a spoken and a signed language or in two different signed languages are considered bilingual.

What does it mean to be truly bilingual? Some definitions of bilingualism focus exclusively on a language-based meaning: Bilingual people, or bilinguals, speak two languages. Other definitions are more rigorous and define bilinguals as adults who use their two languages effectively in their adult daily life, which includes being bicultural as well—moving back and forth between two cultures and two languages while still maintaining a sense of identity. Proficiency in a second language has two separate aspects: face-to-face communication (*contextualized language skills*) that take about two to three years in a good program to develop, and academic uses of language such as reading and doing grammar exercises (known as *academic English*) that take about 5 to 10 years to develop. Bilingual students also often struggle with social adjustment problems relating to biculturalism.

How do cultural differences affect bilingual students? Cultural differences might interfere with developing academic English and content understanding. For example, many Asian students come from a culture that believes asking the teacher questions is rude and inappropriate because questioning implies that the teacher has done a poor job of instruction. Thus teachers need to ask themselves why their English language learners are not asking questions. So beliefs about learning shaped by culture and previous experiences in different kinds of classrooms may explain why ELLs seem quiet and reluctant to speak in class. These students may also think that their teachers are not very good because the teachers do not explain everything. They also may strongly prefer memorization as a learning strategy if memorization was emphasized in their previous schools.

Dialect Differences in the Classroom (pp. 184–196)

What is a dialect? A dialect is any variety of a language spoken by a particular group. The dialect is part of the group's collective identity. Every person reading this book speaks at least one dialect, maybe more, because there is no one absolute standard English. Dialects differ in their rules about pronunciation, grammar, and vocabulary, but it is important to remember that these differences are not errors. Each dialect is logical, complex, and rule-governed. There are even some differences in how men and women talk, called genderlects.

How should teachers take dialects into account? Teachers can be sensitive to their own possible negative stereotypes about children who speak a different dialect. Teachers also can ensure comprehension by repeating instructions using different words and by asking students to paraphrase instructions or give examples. The best teaching approach seems to be to focus on understanding the students and to accept their language as a valid and correct system, but to teach the alternative forms of English (or whatever the dominant language is in your country) that are used in more formal work settings and writing so that the students will have access to a range of opportunities.

Teaching Immigrant Students and English language Learners (pp. 196–199)

Distinguish between the terms *immigrant* and *refugee*. Immigrants are people who voluntarily leave their country to become permanent residents in a new place. Refugees are a special group of immigrants who also relocate voluntarily, but they are fleeing their home country because it is not safe.

Distinguish between the "melting pot" and multiculturalism. Statistics point to increasing cultural diversity in American society. Old views—that minority group members and immigrants should lose their cultural distinctiveness and assimilate completely in the American "melting pot" or be regarded as culturally deficient—are being replaced by new emphases on multiculturalism, equal educational opportunity, and the celebration of cultural diversity.

What are four general profiles of English Language Learners? *Balanced bilinguals* speak, read, and write well both in their first language and in English. *Monolingual/literate students* are literate in their native language (at or above grade level when working in their native language), but speak limited English. *Monolingual/preliterate students* are not literate. They may not read or write in their native language or they may have very limited literacy skills. *Limited bilingual* students can converse well in both languages, but for some reason they have trouble learning academically. There may be underlying challenges such as learning disabilities or emotional problems.

What is Gen 1.5? Generation 1.5 are students whose characteristics, educational experiences, and language fluencies are somewhere in between those of students born in the United States and students who are recent immigrants. They were not born in the United States, but have lived here most of their lives because they came with their families when they were young. The language spoken in their homes may not be English, but they often speak fluent conversational English, even if their academic English is not as well developed. They may tend to be "ear learners" who have mastered language by listening to and interacting with the language models around them.

What are the names related to English learners? English learners sometimes are called *limited-English-proficient* or *LEP*. More often, these students are called *English language learners (ELLs)*, because their primary or heritage language is not English. *English as a Second Language (ESL)* is the name given to the classes devoted to teaching these students English. Limited proficiency in English often means lower academic achievement and poorer job prospects. So one issue around diversity in language development is how we should teach these students.

What is bilingual education? Although there is much debate about the best way to help bilingual students master English, studies show it is best if they are not forced to abandon their first language. The more proficient students are in their first language, the faster they will master the second.

What is sheltered instruction? Sheltered instruction is one approach that has proved successful in teaching English and academic content. Sheltered instruction teaches content to ELLs by putting the words and concepts of the content into context to make the content more understandable. Strategies include simplifying and controlling language, giving attention to the relevant grammar and forms of English—helping students "crack the code," using visuals and gestures, and including real life supports and examples. In addition, there is an emphasis on student talk and discussion instead of the teacher doing all the talking. There are affective and emotional considerations for English language learners. They may experience severe challenges and stress in school. They may feel that they don't belong, that others are making fun of them, or just ignoring them. Building on students' funds of cultural knowledge is one way to make classrooms more supportive and teaching more effective.

Special Challenges: English Language Learners with Disabilities and Special Gifts (pp. 199–201)

How do teachers deal with the special needs of English language learners? As a teacher, one of your decisions will be whether to refer a struggling ELL student for testing. Of course, the first step is to use the best teaching approaches, incorporating sheltered instruction to develop both subject matter learning and English language development. But if progress seems much slower than usual, you might refer the student for observation or testing. No matter what the diagnosis—attention and appropriate teaching are needed. Students who have difficulties with English are much more likely to drop out of school. And because language differences can mask giftedness, teachers should make special efforts to identify bilingual students and English language learners who have gifts and talents.

▼ KEY TERMS

Academic language (182)
Balanced bilingualism (179)
Bilingual (177)
Code-switching (186)
Critical periods (177)
Cultural deficit model (188)
Dialect (184)
Emergent literacy (173)
English as a Second Language (ESL) (191)
English language learners (ELLs) (188)
Expressive vocabulary (170)

Funds of knowledge (198)
Genderlects (186)
Generation 1.5 (190)
Heritage language (178)
Immigrants (187)
Inside-out skills (174)
Limited-English-proficient (LEP) (191)
Melting pot (187)
Metalinguistic awareness (173)
Monolingual (177)
Outside-in skills (174)

Overregularize (172)
Pragmatics (172)
Receptive vocabulary (170)
Refugees (187)
Semilingual (192)
Sensitive periods (177)
Sheltered instruction (194)
Sheltered Instruction Observation Protocol or SIOP (194)
Structured English Immersion (SEI) (192)
Syntax (172)

▼ CONNECT AND EXTEND TO LICENSURE

MULTIPLE-CHOICE QUESTIONS

1. During the 1960s and 1970s, it was suggested by some educators that students of color and students living in poverty were culturally disadvantaged. The cultural deficit model implied students' home cultures were inferior because they failed to prepare them to fit into school. What is the current idea held by educational psychologists with respect to mismatches between students' home environments and school?

   A. There may be incompatibilities between the student's home culture and the expectations of the school.

   B. Deficits between the home culture and school can be compensated through special education services.

   C. Historically the gap between the home environment and the school environment is inconsequential.

   D. There is an increasing sense that ethnic groups should want to assimilate completely into mainstream American society.

2. Ms. Carney decided to visit the Mexican families of her ELL students to gain a better understanding of their backgrounds and culture. Drawing upon the research of Luis Moll and current best practice, what do you think Ms. Carney decided to do with the new information she gained from her family visits?

   A. She shared it with her supervisors and continued to remediate the students' deficits.

   B. She made notations about the information she gathered in her students' cumulative files.

   C. She decided to identify and build on the tools and cultural funds of knowledge of her students' families.

   D. She decided to not share the information as her supervisors may not have approved of her family visits.

3. Once Mr. Heney learned that his Asian ELL students consider it rude to ask the teacher questions because questioning implies that the teacher has done a poor job of teaching, he could generalize to which one of the following assumptions?

   A. If his English Language Learners are not asking questions he needs to ask them why.

   B. He should always quiz his Asian students as they may not be able to understand.

   C. Asian students are always very polite but their silence can mean they do not respect him as a teacher.

   D. Mr. Heney cannot make any generalizations about culture and learning.

4. One important way in which a teacher can motivate students is to show an interest in their lives. All but which one of the following are appropriate motivational strategies that demonstrate an interest in the lives of students from diverse backgrounds?

   A. Incorporate students' traditions into writing and language arts activities.

   B. Show respect for students' diversity by learning some key words in their language.

   C. Ask students to write a three-page essay in English about their family.

   D. Inquire about students' past experiences in their native country.

CONSTRUCTED-RESPONSE QUESTIONS

Case

Nick Takis was delighted that his portfolio had helped him land his first teaching job in Texas. Although he had never been to that state, he was excited about the prospect of his own classroom. When he arrived for his two week induction period in August his sunny mood began to wane. He learned that several of the students in his class were not fluent in English. To prepare for the challenge ahead, he drew upon what one of his favorite professors always suggested, "Break big projects down to bite size, and make sure you have all the information you need to make decisions."

5. What are the four general profiles of English learners in today's classroom with which Nick should familiarize himself?

6. What tips could you offer Nick Takis that would help him to promote language learning in his class?

▼ WHAT WOULD THEY DO?

TEACHERS' CASEBOOK: Cultures Clash in the Classroom

Here is how several expert teachers said they would establish positive relationships with the class described at the beginning of the chapter that included African American, Asian, and Latino/a students who did not get along.

JENNIFER PINCOSKI • Learning Resource Teacher: K–12
Lee County School District, Fort Myers, FL

The teacher has difficulty connecting with his/her students because the cultures are so different and the groups don't understand each other. The teacher's discomfort is evident, which is problematic because as the classroom leader, a teacher's attitude and behavior set the tone for everyone. Establishment of an inclusive and accepting learning environment starts at the top. It is important to model understanding and acceptance by respecting students as individuals, celebrating their differ ences, and showing a genuine interest in their lives.

This is a good opportunity to get to know students on a more personal level. After assigning a quiet, independent task, the teacher can use this time to have brief conferences with each student one on one. Conferences should focus on becoming acquainted with the students, learning about their interests, and discussing goals. Not only does this help develop positive relationships, it also provides important information that can be used to plan future lessons and activities.

Furthermore, in an effort to get students from different cultures to interact, the teacher may need to change the physical arrangement of the room and/or reassign seats. Rather than allowing students to choose their own groups, the teacher could either assign groups randomly or purposefully group students according to strengths, interests, learning styles, etc. Groups should change frequently, and assignments should be thoughtfully designed to complement students' individual characteristics.

LAUREN ROLLINS • 1st Grade Teacher
Boulevard Elementary School, Shaker Heights, OH

At the beginning of each school year, I set aside a significant amount of time to get to know my students, for them to get to know each other, and for them to get to know me. This is an integral part of building a classroom community. Familiarization with each group's culture is mandatory to achieve a successful outcome. It is also important that the groups of students learn to have mutual respect for each other. This is so important that it is worth suspending the curriculum until these goals are met. One activity would be to invite the students to share their backgrounds and cultures in a "show and tell" situation. Another activity would be to create "compliment charts" for each other. The students would write compliments, positive statements, and qualities that they like about each other on the charts. At the end of the activity, each student will walk away feeling respected and appreciated. It is a "feel good" activity and a big step toward respecting and appreciating the members of the classroom.

LINDA SPARKS • 1st Grade
John F. Kennedy School, Billerica, MA

Students are very quick to pick up on what a person thinks about them or how someone feels about them. I have not had this specific incident happen in my class as I am in an elementary school. But, I believe this can happen at any level, especially when the teacher feels uncomfortable in the setting. Students pick right up on how a teacher feels about them. They need to be respected in order to learn to be respectful, while building their trust and confidence. Once that trust is earned, the students are more willing to participate in activities in the classroom. I would have to do some flexible grouping as simple as "If you have green sneakers on, move to the left corner." They are not moving because they are of a specific ethnic group. I always have a jar with these quirky questions to move kids around, especially when I am changing desks. This also will maximize instruction because now they want their group to beat out their friends' group. When this happens, students will begin to get along socially while academic needs are being met.

PAULA COLEMERE • Special Education Teacher—English, History
McClintock High School, Tempe, AZ

My first goal is always to create a safe learning environment for my students. With underlying issues based on racial divisions in a class, it would be difficult for students to come to class prepared to learn. The hostility needs to be erased in this class. To work toward this goal, I would have the class do a team building activity. This activity would be built to show students that no matter how they look, they are much more alike than different. There is an activity I have done where students walk to the center line if they have ever experienced something. It starts simple, but gets deeper. For example, the facilitator might say, "Go to the center line if you know someone who has been murdered." Sadly, many students have experienced this and they will see they are not alone. Following this activity, I would have a discussion with the students about leaving our differences at the door. This is a teachable moment, as we will come across people throughout our lives that we don't like or who are different from us, but we have to find a way to make the relationship work to hold a job.

chapter six
CULTURE AND DIVERSITY

▶ **TEACHERS' CASEBOOK:** White Girls Club

You teach in a fairly homogeneous primary school. In fact, most of your kindergarten–first grade students are middle- or upper middle-class and white. In January, a new student came to your school—the daughter of an African American professor who recently arrived to teach at the nearby college. After a few weeks, you notice that the new student is not being included in many activities. She sits alone in the library and plays alone at recess. No one sits with her at lunch, and at recess she is the last to be chosen for any team. This is troubling enough, but then one day you overhear two of your higher achieving girls talking about their "White Girls Club."

CRITICAL THINKING

- Would you investigate to learn more about this "Club"? How?
- If you found that your students had created a club that excluded nonwhite students, what would you do?
- If you teach older students, what can you do about student groups that define themselves by who *cannot* be members? ·

OVERVIEW AND OBJECTIVES

The cultural composition of American classrooms is changing. The same can be said for classrooms in many countries today. In a talk to the American Educational Research Association, Frank Pajares, one of the wisest educational psychologists I know, said, "The critical questions in education involve matters that cannot be settled by universal prescription. They demand attention to the cultural forces that shape our lives" (Pajares, 2000, p. 5). I believe he is right. In this chapter, we examine the many cultures that form the fabric of our society. We begin by considering some statistics about diversity in schools, and then meet four individuals whose stories bring the statistics to life—you met another one, Felipe, in Chapter 5. Next, we trace the schools' responses to different ethnic and cultural groups. With a broad conception of culture as a basis, we then examine three important dimensions of every student's identity: social class, race/ethnicity, and gender. Then, we turn to a consideration of multicultural education, a general process of school reform that incorporates and embraces diversity, and we look at approaches to creating culturally compatible and resilient classrooms. The last section presents three general principles for teaching every student. By the time you have completed this chapter, you should be able to:

Objective 6.1: Describe how social class, ethnicity, and race influence teaching and learning in a diverse society.

Objective 6.2: Explain the meaning of *stereotype threat,* and examine its possible effects on student achievement.

Objective 6.3: Describe the development of gender identity and the role of gender in teaching.

Objective 6.4: Define multicultural education.

Objective 6.5: Apply research on diversity to the creation of culturally compatible classrooms.

Connect and Extend to PRAXIS II™

The Larger Community (IV, B1,3)
Familiarize yourself with the predicted changes in the U.S. population over the next several decades. How are those changes likely to affect education? What can schools and teachers do to adjust positively to those changes?

Culture The knowledge, values, attitudes, and traditions that guide the behavior of a group of people and allow them to solve the problems of living in their environment.

TODAY'S DIVERSE CLASSROOMS

In this text we take a broad interpretation of cultural diversity, so we will examine social class, race, ethnicity, and gender as aspects of diversity. We begin with a look at the meaning of culture. Many people associate this concept with the "cultural events" section of the newspaper—art galleries, museums, Shakespeare festivals, classical music concerts, and so on. Culture has a much broader meaning; it embraces the whole way of life of a group of people.

American Cultural Diversity

There are many definitions of **culture**. Most include some or all of the following: the knowledge, skills, rules, norms, practices, traditions, self-definitions, institutions (educational, legal, communal, religious, political, etc.), language, and values that shape and guide beliefs and behavior in a particular group of people as well as the art, literature, folklore, and artifacts produced and passed down to the next generation (Cohen, 2009, 2010; Pai & Alder, 2001). The group constructs a culture—a program for living—and communicates the program to members. Groups can be defined along regional, ethnic, religious, racial, gender, social class, or other lines. Each of us is a member of many groups, so we all are influenced by many different cultures. Sometimes, the influences are incompatible or even contradictory. For example, if you are a feminist but also a Roman Catholic, you may have trouble reconciling the two different cultures' beliefs about the ordination of women as priests. Your personal belief will be based, in part, on how strongly you identify with each group.

There are many different cultures within every modern country. In the United States, students growing up in a small rural town in the Great Plains are part of a cultural group that is very different from that of students in a large Northeastern urban center or students in a Texas suburb. Within those small towns in the Great Plains, the son or daughter of a convenience store clerk grows up in a different culture from the child of the town doctor or dentist. Individuals of African, Asian, Hispanic, Native American, or European descent have distinctive histories and traditions. Everyone living within a particular country shares many common experiences and values, especially because of the influence of the mass media. But other aspects of their lives are shaped by differing cultural backgrounds.

Culture has been compared to an iceberg. One-third of the iceberg is visible; the rest is hidden and unknown. The visible signs of culture, such as costumes and marriage traditions, reflect only a small portion of the differences among cultures, as you can see in Figure 6.1.

Many of the differences are "below the surface." They are implicit, unstated, even unconscious biases and beliefs (Sheets, 2005). Cultures differ in rules for conducting interpersonal relationships, for example. In some groups, listeners give a slight affirmative nod of the head and perhaps an occasional "uh huh" to indicate they are listening carefully. But members of other cultures listen without giving acknowledgment, or with eyes downcast, as a sign of respect. In some cultures, high-status individuals initiate conversations and ask the questions, and low-status individuals only respond. In other cultures, the pattern is reversed.

Cultural influences are widespread and pervasive. Some psychologists even suggest that culture defines intelligence. For example, physical grace is essential in Balinese social life, so the ability to master physical movements is a mark of intelligence in that culture. Manipulating words and numbers is important in Western societies, so in these cultures such skills are indicators of intelligence (Gardner, 1983). Even symptoms of psychological disorders are affected by culture. In industrialized cultures where cleanliness

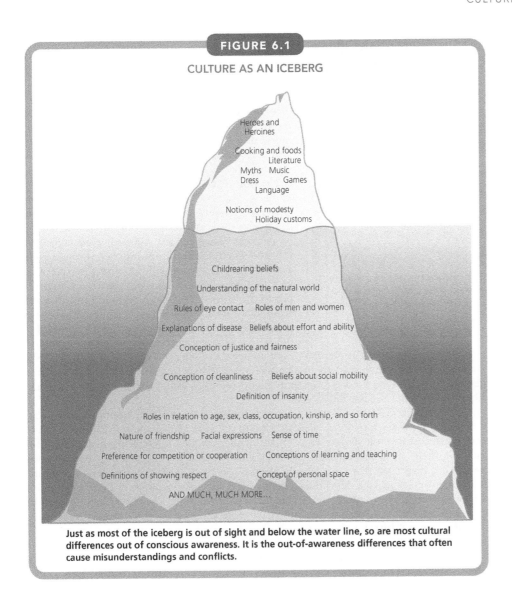

FIGURE 6.1

CULTURE AS AN ICEBERG

Heroes and Heroines

Cooking and foods
Literature
Myths   Music
Dress   Games
Language

Notions of modesty
Holiday customs

Childrearing beliefs

Understanding of the natural world

Rules of eye contact   Roles of men and women

Explanations of disease   Beliefs about effort and ability

Conception of justice and fairness

Conception of cleanliness   Beliefs about social mobility

Definition of insanity

Roles in relation to age, sex, class, occupation, kinship, and so forth

Nature of friendship   Facial expressions   Sense of time

Preference for competition or cooperation   Conceptions of learning and teaching

Definitions of showing respect   Concept of personal space

AND MUCH, MUCH MORE…

Just as most of the iceberg is out of sight and below the water line, so are most cultural differences out of conscious awareness. It is the out-of-awareness differences that often cause misunderstandings and conflicts.

is emphasized, people with obsessive-compulsive disorders often become obsessed with cleaning their hands, whereas in Bali, where social networks are emphasized, people with obsessive-compulsive disorders often become obsessed with knowing all the details about the lives of their friends and family—their social network (Lemelson, 2003).

Let's get more specific about cultural diversity by meeting some students.

Meet Four More Students

Classrooms are becoming more diverse. But teachers do not work with statistics; they work with students—unique individuals, such as Felipe Vargas, the 5th grader you met in Chapter 5. Nancy Knapp from the University of Georgia invites us to meet four more individuals. These students are not specific people; they are composites of the characteristics of real people Nancy has known and taught. The names and schools are fictional, but the lives are very real.

Ternice Mattox is a 7th grader who lives with her mother and three younger siblings in a large city in the Northeast. Her mother works the 7:00–3:00 shift at a dry-cleaning plant and then cleans offices some nights and weekends to make ends meet, so Ternice gets her

JUST ONE CULTURE? Definitions of *culture* apply to regional, ethnic, religious, racial, gender, social class, and other areas of difference. Each of us is a member of many groups, so we all are influenced by many different cultures.

brothers and sister up and ready for school every day, feeds them dinner when they get home, and makes sure they do their homework at night; she has been doing this since she was 10.

School hasn't ever been very hard for Ternice; in elementary school she usually got Bs, even though a lot of the teachers said she talked too much. But she never really liked school until last year. Her 6th grade English teacher seemed to want students to talk. She had them reading stories about real people, like you could meet any day downtown. In class, she got people talking about what the characters should do and why the authors wrote the stories the way they did. Best of all, she let you write about whatever you wanted, even your own life; and she didn't count off for every mistake right away, but let you work with her and with the other kids until you had a final copy you could be really proud of. In that class, Ternice found out that she really liked to write, and her teacher said she was good at it; one of her stories even got published in the school newspaper. Ternice talked and wrote so much in that class that Anthony Bailey got on her about why she was "actin' so white." She got mad and told him that acting foolish was worse than acting white, but it still bothered her. She and Anthony kind of go together, and she likes him a lot; she has "Ternice and 'Tone" written all over her notebooks.

Her English class this year is not nearly as good. Her teacher from last year wants her to take some tests, to see if she can get into the gifted program, but Ternice is not so sure about that. Even if she got in, she's afraid she wouldn't know anyone; almost all the kids in "gifted" are white, and the few black kids are from another part of town. Besides, her friends might not like it, especially Anthony; at her school, "brains" don't go around with "regulars," and vice versa. Her mama wants her to try, and says there's no telling where she can go from there, but Ternice doesn't want to go anywhere that's away from all her friends. Still, she wishes she could have more classes like her English class last year.

Benjamin Whittaker lives in a suburb of Colorado Springs with his father, the vice president at a local bank and member of the board of a local hospital. His mother and father are divorced, but Ben still sees his mom every two weeks for the weekend. His older sister is in her second year of college, taking a pre-veterinary course. Ben started high school this year; he's taking algebra, world history, French, English, and freshman chemistry. His course schedule was his father's idea, especially the freshman chemistry. Ben feels completely out of his league in that class, but his father insisted that if he was going to get into pre-med in college, he had to get a jump-start on science. Ben's mother says medicine is where the money is, and she knows Ben can do it, if he just gets focused.

Ben's not so sure. He has never been a star student like his sister, and he really struggled at the beginning of middle school. He just couldn't get the hang of taking notes; either he couldn't figure out what was most important, so he'd try to write down everything the teachers said, or he'd get distracted by something, and miss whole sections of the lecture. He also had a hard time keeping track of his assignments, and when he did remember to do them, his notebooks and backpack were such a mess that sometimes he'd lose them before he got them turned in. At the end of the first semester, his homeroom teacher suggested he be evaluated for ADHD, and his family doctor put him on a trial dose of Ritalin, which seemed to help. With some additional coaching on organizational skills, Ben gradually improved and finished 8th grade with a solid B average. He still takes Ritalin on school days, but not on the weekends, which is when he does most of his artwork.

Art is what Ben really loves; since he was a little boy he has been drawing people and animals and whole scenes out of his imagination. Sometimes when he's working on a drawing, he loses all track of time; his mom calls it being "zoned in," and teases him that he'd forget to eat if she didn't come up and get him. Lately, he's been experimenting with the graphics program on his computer, and he's even drawn a few panels of his own Web comic. He's only shown it to some friends, but they thought it was pretty funny. It's weird, he never has trouble focusing on his art, but even with the Ritalin, he's having more and more trouble focusing on his schoolwork this year. He's worried his grades won't be very good; he may even flunk chemistry. Ben knows he could do better if he took a lighter load, especially if he could move out of the advanced track and take some art courses; but his parents say art is nice for a hobby, but it's no way to make a living.

Davy Walker is a 2nd grader who is worried he will be held back this year, but he's afraid to ask his teacher about it. He doesn't really like asking questions, anyway, because everyone looks at you, and sometimes they laugh if you ask a dumb one. The problem is, he just can't seem to catch on to reading the way most of the other kids do. He can read some of the words if he has enough time, especially if no one is listening to him, but he hates it when the teacher has them take turns reading aloud. Everyone else seems to read so much better and faster that he just freezes up and makes stupid mistakes.

His teacher had a conference with his mom and dad last fall, and told them he needed to read more at home. His parents own a family restaurant in the small town in Oregon where they live, and his mom and dad both work pretty long hours there; even his older sister helps out some on weekends. His mom tried for a while to get him to read to her when she put him to bed at night, but it didn't work out very well. He got sick of the baby books that were all he could read, and when she got him to try something harder, it went so slowly that she got impatient and quit. Davy was just as glad. When he grows up, he's going to run the restaurant for his dad. He can already clear tables and stack the dishes in the big dishwasher, and sometimes his dad lets him help run the cash register and make change. When he's older, he'll learn to take orders and work the grill. Davy doesn't see what reading has to do with running a good restaurant.

Jessie Kinkaid is a junior at Red Falls High School in Wisconsin. She lives with her mother, who works as a doctor's receptionist, in a small house in town. Her father owns the Ford car dealership, and lives just outside of town with his second wife and Jessie's 3-year-old half-brother, so she sees him pretty often.

Jessie is in the vocational track at school and mostly makes Cs, with a few Ds. Once in a while, she fails a course, but she'll have enough credits to graduate by the end of next year, which is all she really cares about. Her home economics teacher says she has a real flair for cooking, and wants Jessie to bring up her grades so she can apply to chef's school. Jessie likes to cook and knows she's good at it, but doesn't see any point in going to more school. She's only graduating to please her parents; she knows what she's going to do with her life. After graduation she's going to get a job in town some- where for a couple years to save up some money, and then she'll marry Walter Aiken. She and Walt have been going together since she was a freshman and he was a junior. Walt started this year at UW-Platteville to get a degree in animal science, and they plan to wait until he is finished before they get married. Then they'll move into the small house on the Aiken's farm until Walt's dad is ready to retire, probably in another three or four years. Then Walt will take over the farm, and they'll move into the big house; Jessie hopes they'll have at least one child by then.

So Jessie doesn't see any point in worrying about her grades, as long as she graduates. Her father agrees it would be foolish to waste time and money on extra schooling she'll never use. Jessie's mother, who left school at 17 to marry, is the one urging Jessie to think about going on. She says she just wants Jessie to "keep all her options open."

Felipe, Ternice, Ben, Davy, and Jessie are just five students, and there are millions more—unique collections of abilities and experiences. They speak different languages, have different ethnic and racial backgrounds, and live in different kinds of communities. Some come from families in poverty, others from families with power and privilege—but all face challenges in their education. For the remainder of the chapter we will look at the dimensions of cultural differences in schools today.

STOP & THINK Take a quick break from reading and turn on the television. (Don't do this if you won't come back to reading until next Tuesday!) Find a channel with commercials. (I know, it is harder to find one without.) Listen to about 15 commercials. For each one, is the voice or the character in the ad old or young? Economically privileged or poor? Male or a female? What is the character's ethnicity or race? Do a quick tally of how many instances you observe in each category. •

Connect and Extend to PRAXIS II™

Cultural and Gender Differences in the Classroom (III, B)
What are the sources of possible miscommunication between students and teachers in the classroom because of cultural or gender differences? Identify steps a teacher can take to minimize such problems.

Cautions: Interpreting Cultural Differences

Before we discuss cultural differences, two cautions are necessary. First, we will consider social class, ethnicity, race, and gender separately, because much of the available research focuses on only one of these variables. Of course, real children are not just African American, or middle class, or male; they are complex beings and members of many groups, just like the five students you met earlier.

The second caution is that group membership is not destiny. Just knowing a student is a member of a particular cultural group does not define what that student is like. People are individuals. For example, if a student in your class consistently arrives late, it may be that the student has a job before school, must walk a long distance, is responsible for getting younger siblings to school like Ternice, or even that he or she dreads school, much like Jessie.

CULTURAL CONFLICTS AND COMPATIBILITIES. The differences between cultures may be very obvious, tip-of-the iceberg characteristics such as holiday customs and dress, or they may be very subtle, below-the-surface differences such as how to get your turn in conversations. When subtle cultural differences meet, misunderstandings and conflicts are common. These conflicts can happen when the values and competencies of the dominant, mainstream culture are used to determine what is considered "normal" or appropriate behavior in schools. In these cases, children who have been socialized in a different culture may be perceived as acting inappropriately, not following the rules, or being rude and disrespectful.

Rosa Hernandez Sheets (2005) describes a 5-year-old Mexican American girl who tried to bring a bread roll, part of her school cafeteria lunch, home to give to her little brother every day. Her parents were proud of her for sharing, but the school officials made her throw the roll away, because it was against school rules to take food from the cafeteria. The girl was conflicted about following school rules versus honoring her family's cultural values. The teacher in this case solved the problem by talking to the cafeteria cook, putting the roll in a plastic bag, and placing the bag in the girl's backpack to be taken home after school.

Not all cultural differences lead to clashes in school, however. For example, compared to other ethnic groups, Asian Americans have the highest graduation rates from high school, college, and graduate school—so sometimes they are labeled as "model minorities" (Lee, 2006). Is this fair?

DANGERS IN STEREOTYPING. There are dangers in stereotyping both Asians and Asian Americans as model students—quiet, hardworking, and passive. Acting on these stereotypes can reinforce conformity and stifle assertiveness. Stacey Lee (2006) describes another stereotype confronting Asian Americans. They are seen as perpetual foreigners. No matter how many decades their families have lived in America, even 4th- or 5th-generation Asian American students are not seen as "real" Americans. In fact, Lee's research shows that teachers tend to refer to these students as "Asian," not "Asian American" or "American." That would be like calling me a German student because my great-grandfather came to Wisconsin from Germany. I was born in Texas and my knowledge of German culture is limited to my grandmother's recipe for pfefferneuse—excellent, by the way. Too often, students take these stereotypes to heart and feel "foreign" even in the country of their birth—America. One high school student told Lee (2004), "Watching MTV affected the way I acted very much. I wanted to be more Americanized. I changed my hair color. I got colored contact lenses" (p. 44). Later in this chapter, we will explore ways to make classrooms compatible with the home cultures of students. First, however, we need to examine some of the effects of cultural conflicts and discrimination on student achievement.

ECONOMIC AND SOCIAL CLASS DIFFERENCES

Even though most researchers would agree that social class is one of the most meaningful cultural dimensions in people's lives, those same researchers have great difficulty defining *social class* (Liu et al., 2004). Different terms are used—social class, socioeconomic status (SES), economic background, wealth, poverty, or privilege. Some people consider only economic differences; others add considerations of power, influence, mobility, control over resources, and prestige.

Social Class and SES

In modern societies, levels of wealth, power, and prestige are not always consistent. Some people—for instance, university professors—are members of professions that are reasonably high in terms of social status, but provide little wealth or power (believe me). Other people have political power even though they are not wealthy, or they may be members of the social register in a town, even though their family money is long gone. Most people are generally aware of their social class—that is, they perceive that some groups are above them in social class and some are below. They may even show a kind of "*classism*" (like racism or sexism), believing that they are "better" than members of lower social classes and avoiding association with them. For example, in an ethnographic study (see Chapter 1 if you don't remember what *ethnographic* means), Marissa, a member of the most popular and privileged clique in her high school, described the "grits"—the least popular group:

> Grits are poor. I think they mostly live in the country. We—[quickly correcting herself] some of my friends call them hicks or rednecks. I guess most live on the Hill—that's over on the west side of town. It's the slums. Grits smoke, do drugs, dress grungy. They have those hick accents. They usually get bad grades. They don't like school so I think they drop out a lot. They don't really fit in. They are troublemakers. I don't see them much; they aren't in any of my classes. (Brantlinger, 2004, pp. 109–110)

In addition to social class, there is another way of thinking about differences that is commonly used in research. Sociologists and psychologists combine variations in wealth, power, control over resources, and prestige into an index called **socioeconomic status,** or **SES**. In contrast to social class, most people are not conscious of their SES designation. SES is usually ascribed to people by researchers; different formulas for determining SES might lead to different assignments (Liu et al., 2004; Sirin, 2005). No single variable, not even income, is an effective measure of SES. Most researchers identify four general levels of SES: upper, middle, working, and lower. The main characteristics of these four levels are summarized in Table 6.1 on the next page. As you watched the commercials in the *Stop & Think* activity, how many people did you see who appeared to be in the lower-class SES?

Poverty and School Achievement

You saw in Chapter 1 that about 1 in 5 Americans under the age of 18 lives below the poverty level—$22,050 annual income for a family of four. That is 21% of all children in the United States. In fact, 9% of all children live in extreme poverty ($11,025 annual income). More than half of all poor children live in eight states (California, Texas, New York, Florida, Illinois, Georgia, Ohio, and Michigan). For a while, there were improvements. In 2000, the number of families in poverty was the lowest in 21 years—about 6.2 million (U.S. Census Bureau, September 25, 2001), but rates have been rising again since then to over 15 million. It is likely that 40% of all American children will live in poverty at some time in their lives (Koppelman, 2011).

In 2008, the absolute number of children living in poverty was similar for non-Hispanic White children (4.9 million), Latina/o children (5.6 million), and African American children (4.5 million). But the rate of poverty is higher for African American, Latino, and Native American children—35% of African American, 34% of Native American, and 31% of Latino children lived in poverty in 2008, whereas 13% of Asian and 11% of non-Hispanic White children were poor (National Poverty Center, 2011). African American and Latino families headed by single women have the highest poverty rate—about 50% (Moore, Redd, Burkhauser, Mbwana, & Collins, 2009). Contrary to many stereotypes, more poor

Connect and Extend to PRAXIS II™

Economic Conditions/ Socioeconomic Status (SES) (IV, B2) Be aware of the possible effects of socioeconomic status on student achievement. Consider what steps teachers can take to minimize those effects.

Socioeconomic status (SES) Relative standing in the society based on income, power, background, and prestige.

TABLE 6.1 • **Selected Characteristics of Different Social Classes**

	UPPER CLASS	MIDDLE CLASS	WORKING CLASS	LOWER CLASS
Income	$200,000+	$110,000–$200,000 (1/2) $50,000–$110,000 (1/2)	$25,000–$50,000	Below $25,000
Occupation	Corporate, professional, family money	White-collar, skilled blue-collar	Blue-collar	Minimum wage, unskilled labor
Education	Prestigious colleges and graduate schools	High school, college, or professional school	High school	High school or less
Home ownership	At least one home	Usually own home	About half own a home	Uncommon
Health coverage	Full	Usually	Limited	Uncommon
Neighborhoods	Exclusive or comfortable	Comfortable	Modest	Deteriorating
Afford children's college	Easily	Usually	Seldom	Uncommon
Political power	National, state, local	State or local	Limited	No

Source: Information from Macionis, J. J. (2010). Sociology (13th ed). Upper Saddle River, NJ: Pearson and Macionis, personal communication, 4/2/2010.

children live in suburban and rural areas than in central cities. But poverty rates are high in urban schools. In the 100 largest public school districts across the country, 56% of the students qualified for free and reduced-price lunches in 2008–2009, based on their low family income (NCES, 2011).

The average correlation between SES and achievement tests is moderate, about .30 to .40 (Sackett, Kuncel, Arneson, Cooper, & Waters, 2009; Sirin, 2005). In general, high-SES students of all ethnic groups show higher average levels of achievement on test scores and stay in school longer than low-SES students (Berliner, 2005; Gutman, Sameroff, & Cole, 2003). Poor children are at least twice as likely as non-poor children to be kept back in school. And the longer the child is in poverty, the stronger the impact is on achievement. For example, even when we take into account parents' education, the chance that children will be retained in grades or placed in special education classes increases by 2% to 3% for every year the children live in poverty (Ackerman, Brown, & Izard, 2004; Bronfenbrenner, McClelland, Wethington, Moen, & Ceci, 1996).

What are the effects of low socioeconomic status that might explain the lower school achievement of these students? No single cause is to blame (Evans, 2004). Poor health care for mother and child, dangerous or unhealthy home environments, limited resources, family stress, interruptions in schooling, exposure to violence, overcrowding, homelessness, discrimination, and other factors lead to school failures, low-paying jobs—and another generation born into poverty. Evans (2004), Jensen (2009), and McLoyd (1998) describe other possible explanations. Let's take a closer look at each of them.

HEALTH, ENVIRONMENT, AND STRESS. The negative effects of poverty begin even before a child is born. Families in poverty have less access to good prenatal and infant health care and nutrition. Over half of all adolescent mothers receive no prenatal care at all. Poor mothers and adolescent mothers are more likely to have premature babies, and prematurity is associated with many cognitive and learning problems. Children in poverty are more likely to be exposed to both legal drugs (nicotine, alcohol) and illegal drugs (cocaine, heroin) before birth. Children whose mothers take drugs during pregnancy can have problems with organization, attention, and language skills.

In the early years, children in poverty experience higher levels of stress hormones than children in middle-class and wealthy families. High levels of these hormones can interfere with the flow of blood in the brain as well as the development of synaptic connections (Shonkoff, 2006). In addition, stress hormones can deplete the body's supply of tryptophan (Richell, Deakin, & Anderson, 2005), an amino acid that calms impulsive and violent behaviors (Hudley & Novak, 2007). Poor children are four times as likely to experience stress due to evictions, lack of food, overcrowding, or utility disconnections. Increased stress is related to increased school absences, decreased attention and concentration, problems with memory and thinking, reduced motivation and effort, increased depression, and reduced neurogenesis (growth of new brain cells) (Jensen, 2009). As they grow, poor children breathe more polluted air and drink more contaminated water (Evans, 2004). They are at least twice as likely as non-poor children to suffer lead poisoning, which is associated with lower school achievement and long-term neurological impairment (McLoyd, 1998).

LOW EXPECTATIONS—LOW ACADEMIC SELF-CONCEPT. Because poor students may wear older clothes, speak in a dialect, or be less familiar with books and school activities, teachers and other students may assume that these students are not bright. The teacher may avoid calling on them, assuming they don't know the answer, set lower standards, and accept poor work. Thus, low expectations become institutionalized and the educational resources provided to these children are inadequate (Borman & Overman, 2004). Low expectations, along with a lower-quality educational experience, can lead to a sense of learned helplessness, described in Chapter 4. Low-SES children, particularly those who also encounter racial discrimination, may decide that school is a dead end. Without a high school diploma, these students find few rewards awaiting them in the work world. Many available jobs barely pay a living wage.

PEER INFLUENCES AND RESISTANCE CULTURES. Some researchers have suggested that low-SES students may become part of a **resistance culture**. To members of this culture, making it in school means selling out and trying to act "middle class." In order to maintain

Resistance culture Group values and beliefs about refusing to adopt the behaviors and attitudes of the majority culture.

WEALTH AND SCHOOL SUCCESS Wealthy students of all ethnic groups seem to show higher average levels of school success than poor students, who are also at least twice as likely to be kept back in school. The resources available to these groups of students are starkly different.

SUMMER SETBACKS. Children in poverty lose ground academically during the summers while middle- and upper-class families provide many educational experiences over the summer for their children. One study suggests that the four summer vacations between 2nd and 6th grade account for 80% of the achievement differences between poor and advantaged students.

their identity and their status within the group, low-SES students must reject the behaviors that would make them successful in school—studying, cooperating with teachers, even coming to class (Bennett, 2011; Ogbu, 1987, 1997). John Ogbu linked identification with a resistance culture to poor Latino American, Native American, and African American groups, but similar reactions have been noted for poor White students both in the United States and in England and high school students in Papua New Guinea (Woolfolk Hoy, Demerath, & Pape, 2002). This is not to say that all low-SES students resist achievement. Adolescents whose parents value academic achievement tend to select friends who also share those values (Berndt & Keefe, 1995). Many young people are high achievers in spite of either their economic situation or negative peer influences (O'Connor, 1997). And we should not forget that some aspects of schooling—competitive grading, public reprimands, stressful testing and assignments, and repetitive work that is too hard or too easy—can encourage resistance in all students (Okagaki, 2001). To focus solely on students' resistance is a way of blaming students for their lower achievement; instead, educators should focus on making school an inclusive place that does not invite resistance (Stinson, 2006).

HOME ENVIRONMENT AND RESOURCES. Families in poverty seldom have access to high-quality preschool care for their young children, the kind of care that enhances cognitive and social development (Duncan & Brooks-Gunn, 2000; Vandell, 2004). Poor children read less and spend more time watching television; they have less access to books, computers, libraries, trips, and museums (Evans, 2004; Kim & Guryan, 2010). Again, not all low-income families lack resources. Many families provide rich learning environments for their children. When parents of any SES level support and encourage their children—by reading to them, providing books and educational toys, taking the children to the library, making time and space for learning—the children tend to become better, more enthusiastic readers (Peng & Lee, 1992).

Home and neighborhood resources seem to have the greatest impact on children's achievement when school is not in session—during the summer or before students enter school.

SUMMER SETBACKS. Over the past decade, evidence has been mounting that students in poverty begin school about 6 months behind in reading skills compared to students from wealthier homes, but the difference between the groups grows to almost 3 years by 6th grade. One explanation for this growing gap is that the children from poorer homes, and especially those whose first language in not English, lose ground over the summer. Even though both groups make comparable achievement gains during the school year, every summer vacation creates about a 3-month reading achievement gap between poor and advantaged children (Kim & Guryan, 2010). One study suggested that the 4 summer vacations between 2nd and 6th grade accounted for 80% of the achievement differences between poor and advantaged students (Allington & McGill-Frazen, 2003, 2008). This truly is a case of the rich getting richer. Wealthier children have greater access to books all the time, but especially over the summer. They read more, and the more children read, the better readers they become—volume of reading matters.

POINT/COUNTERPOINT: Is Tracking an Effective Strategy?

Tracking students into different classes or strands (college prep, vocational, remedial, gifted, etc.) has been standard procedure in many schools for a long time, but does it work? Critics say tracking is harmful, whereas supporters claim it is useful, even though it presents challenges.

POINT ▶ Tracking is harmful and should be eliminated.

According to Tom Loveless, writing in the April 1999 issue of *Educational Leadership*, "Prominent researchers and prestigious national reports have argued that tracking stands in the way of equal educational opportunity" (p. 28).

Loveless goes on to cite the work of Braddock and Slavin (1993); Carnegie Council on Adolescent Development (1995); Oakes (1985); and Wheelock (1992)—all of whom make the argument against tracking. What is the basis for these claims? Surprisingly, the evidence is not clear or direct. For example, a few well-done and carefully designed studies found that tracking increases the gap between high and low achievers by depressing the achievement of low-track students and boosting the achievement of high-track students (Gamoran, 1987; Kerckhoff, 1986). And Gamoran also found that the achievement gap between low- and high-track students is greater than the gap between students who drop out of school and students who graduate. Because low-income students and students of color are overrepresented in the lower tracks, they suffer the greatest harm from tracking and should benefit the most from the elimination of tracking (Oakes, 1990b; Oakes & Wells, 2002). Is this likely? In an interview with Marge Scherer (1993), Jonathan Kozol described the cruel predictive side of tracking:

> [T]racking is so utterly predictive. The little girl who gets shoved into the low reading group in 2nd grade is very likely to be the child who is urged to take cosmetology instead of algebra in the 8th grade, and most likely to be in vocational courses, not college courses, in the 10th grade, if she hasn't dropped out by then. (p. 8)

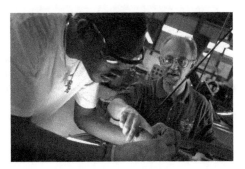

COUNTERPOINT ▶ Eliminating tracking will hurt many students.

Researchers who have looked closely at tracking believe that tracking may be harmful for some students some of the time, but not for all students and not all of the time. First, as most people agree, tracking seems to have positive effects for the high-track students. Gifted programs, honors classes, and advanced placement classes seem to work (Fuchs, Fuchs, Hamlett, & Karns, 1998; Robinson & Clinkenbeard, 1998). No one, especially parents, wants to eliminate the positive effects of these programs. And the chance of being assigned to a high track is 10% greater for African American students (Gamoran & Mare, 1989), so detracking could be a special disservice to these students.

What would happen if schools were detracked? Loveless (1999) identifies some possible hidden costs. First, results of a large national study suggest that when low-track 10th graders are assigned to heterogeneous classes rather than low tracks, they gain about 5 percentage points in achievement. So far, so good. But average students lose 2 percentage points when put into heterogeneous classes and high-ability students lose about 5 points.

> The achievement gap is indeed narrowed, but apparently at the expense of students in regular and high tracks, representing about 70% of 10th graders in the United States. (Loveless, 1999, p. 29)

Another consequence of detracking is bright flight—the withdrawal of the brightest students from the schools. Both African American and White parents distrust mixed-ability classes to meet the needs of their children (Public Agenda Foundation, 1994).

Beware of Either/Or. In some classes, using a mixed-ability structure seems to hinder the achievement of all students. For example, students in heterogeneous algebra classes don't learn as much as students in tracked classes—whatever the ability level of the students (Epstein & MacIver, 1992). And a meta-analysis of student self-esteem found that students in low-track classes did *not* have lower self-esteem than students in heterogeneous classes (Kulik & Kulik, 1997).

So what is the answer? As usual, it is more complicated than simply detracking versus tracking. Careful attention to every student's achievement may mean different answers at different times.

TRACKING: POOR TEACHING. A final explanation for the lower achievement of many low-SES students is that these students experience **tracking** and therefore have a different academic socialization; that is, they are actually taught differently (Oakes, 1990b). If they are tracked into "low-ability," "general," "practical," or "vocational" classes, they may be taught to memorize and be passive. Middle-class students are more likely to be encouraged to think and be creative in their classes. Is tracking a problem? Read the *Point/Counterpoint* for the arguments.

Even if they are not tracked, low-income students are more likely to attend schools with inadequate resources and less-effective teachers (Evans, 2004). For example, in

Tracking Assignment to different classes and academic experiences based on achievement.

GUIDELINES

Teaching Students Who Live in Poverty

Educate yourself about the effects of poverty on student learning.
Examples
1. Read articles from good journals.
2. Seek reliable sources such as Eric Jensen's (2009), *Teaching with Poverty in Mind: What Being Poor Does to Kids' Brains and What Schools Can Do about It.*

Set and maintain high expectations.
Examples
1. Guard against feeling sorry for students, excusing poor work, and expecting less. Replace pity with empathy based on solid knowledge of your students.
2. Communicate to students that they can succeed with good effort.
3. Provide constructive criticism because you believe your students can do quality work.
4. Add challenging subjects and AP classes.

Develop caring relationships with your students.
Examples
1. Use inclusive language—"our class," "our projects," "our school," "our efforts."
2. Talk to students outside class. Make a point to identify their interests and abilities.
3. Attend sports or other events where your students participate.
4. Create a class welcome center for families (see Chapter 5).

Build learning and self-regulation skills as part of the curriculum.
Examples
1. Teach students how to organize work, focus attention, or seek appropriate help.
2. Include conflict management and social problem-solving skills in lessons.

Notice health problems.
Examples
1. Notice who seems to be absent or tardy often.
2. Check to see whether some students struggle to hear the class discussions. Can they see from the back of the room?
3. Model healthy eating and physical activity.

Assess student knowledge, start where they are, but don't stay there (Milner, 2010).
Examples
1. Use short ungraded assessments that target the learning objectives for each unit.
2. Differentiate instruction (Chapter 14) based on results.

Many examples adapted from Jensen, E. (2009). Teaching with Poverty in Mind: What Being Poor Does to Kids' Brains and What Schools Can do About It. Alexandria, VA: Association for Supervision and Curriculum Development.

high-poverty schools, over 50% of math teachers and over 60% of science teachers are inexperienced or teaching outside their subject expertise—they were not trained for the subjects they are teaching (Jensen, 2009). When low-SES students receive a substandard education, this gives them inferior academic skills and limits their life chances, beginning with not preparing them for higher education (Anyon, 1980; Knapp & Woolverton, 2003). See the *Guidelines* for a few ideas about quality teaching for students who live in poverty.

ETHNICITY AND RACE IN TEACHING AND LEARNING

The United States truly is a diverse society. By the year 2023, almost two-thirds of the school-age population will be African American, Asian, Latina/Latino, or from other ethnic groups (Children's Defense Fund, 2010). Before we look at the research on ethnicity and race, let's clarify some terms.

Terms: Ethnicity and Race

Ethnicity usually refers to a group's shared common cultural characteristics such as history, homeland, language, traditions, or religion. We all have some ethnic heritage, whether our background is Italian, Ukrainian, Hmong, Chinese, Japanese, Navajo, Hawaiian, Puerto Rican, Cuban, Hungarian, German, African, or Irish—to name only a few.

Ethnicity A cultural heritage shared by a group of people.

Race, on the other hand, is defined as "a category composed of men and women who share biologically transmitted traits that are defined as socially significant," such as skin color or hair texture (Macionis, 2003, p. 354). In effect, race is a label people apply to themselves and to others based on appearances. There are no biologically pure races. For any two humans chosen at random, an average of only .012% (about one-hundredth of one percent) of the alphabetic sequence of their genetic codes is different due to race (Myers, 2005). Today many psychologists emphasize that ethnicity and race are socially constructed ideas. Still, race is a powerful construct. At the individual level, race is part of our identity—how we understand ourselves and interact with others. At the group level, race is involved with economic and political structures (Omi & Winant, 1994).

Sociologists sometimes use the term **minority group** to label a group of people that receives unequal or discriminatory treatment. Strictly speaking, however, the term refers to a numerical minority compared to the total population. Referring to particular racial or ethnic groups as minorities is technically incorrect in some situations, because in certain places, such as Chicago or Mississippi, the "minority" group—African Americans—is actually the majority. This practice of referring to people as minorities because of their racial or ethnic heritage has been criticized because it is misleading and has negative historical connotations (Milner, 2010).

Ethnic and Racial Differences in School Achievement

A major concern in schools is that some ethnic groups consistently achieve below the average for all students (Matthews, Kizzie, Rowley, & Cortina, 2010; Uline & Johnson, 2005). This pattern of results tends to hold for all standardized achievement tests, but the gaps have been narrowing over the past four to five decades (Raudenbush, 2009). For example, as you can see in Figure 6.2 on the next page, on the National Assessment of Educational Progress in mathematics, the gap between scores of White and African American 4th graders has narrowed from 34 points in 1996 to 26 points in 2009. The gap between White and Hispanic 4th graders has narrowed from 25 in 1996 to 21 in 2009 (NCES, 2009).

Proponents of this notion of an "achievement gap" have been criticized for taking a narrow view, assuming that the scores of White, middle-class students are the norm that all other students must be compared to and measured by. Multicultural scholar H. Richard Milner (2010) reminds teachers that "people of color may experience a different type of 'normal' life and that excellence can and does emerge in multiple and varied forms: people of color from all walks of life are successful" (p. 9). He suggests that we think about other kinds of "gaps," such as teacher education and quality gaps, affordable housing gaps, challenging curriculum gaps, health care and nutrition gaps, school funding gaps, and quality childcare gaps—all culminating in *opportunity gaps* for many students of color.

Opportunity gaps lead to education completion gaps. Across all the United States in 2007, about 80% of White students graduated from high school, compared to 60% of African American students, 62% of Latino/a students, 91% of Asian/Pacific Islanders, and 61% of Native Americans. But again, these are averages across all the states. If we look state by state, we see some interesting differences. For example, Nevada had the lowest overall completion rate (52%), whereas Iowa, Nebraska, Vermont, and Wisconsin all had rates above 86%. In the other states, completion rates for White students ranged from 66% in South Carolina to 94% in Wisconsin; for African Americans from 51% in Florida and South Carolina to 100% in New Hampshire; Latino/a students from 44% in South Carolina to over 90% in West Virginia and Vermont; and Asian American students from 77% in Hawaii to 100% in Arkansas, Delaware, Idaho, Illinois, Maine, Missouri, Montana, New Hampshire, New Jersey, North Dakota, Oklahoma, South Dakota, and West Virginia (NCES, 2009).

Although there still are consistent differences among ethnic groups on tests of cognitive abilities, most researchers agree that the reasons for these differences are mainly the legacy of discrimination, the product of cultural mismatches and language differences, or a result of growing up in poverty. Because many students from ethnic groups are also

Race A socially constructed category based on appearances and ancestry.

Minority group A group of people who have been socially disadvantaged—not always a minority in actual numbers.

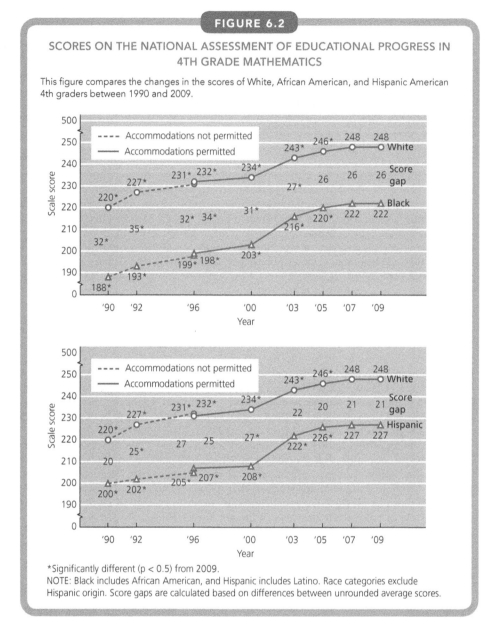

FIGURE 6.2

SCORES ON THE NATIONAL ASSESSMENT OF EDUCATIONAL PROGRESS IN 4TH GRADE MATHEMATICS

This figure compares the changes in the scores of White, African American, and Hispanic American 4th graders between 1990 and 2009.

*Significantly different (p < 0.5) from 2009.
NOTE: Black includes African American, and Hispanic includes Latino. Race categories exclude Hispanic origin. Score gaps are calculated based on differences between unrounded average scores.

Source: National Assessment of Educational Progress (2011). National Report Card. Available online at http://nces.ed.gov/nationsreportcard/pubs/main2009/2010451.asp Downloaded May 4, 2011.

economically disadvantaged, it is important to separate the effects of these two sets of influences on school achievement (Roberts, Mohammed, & Vaughn, 2010). For example, a recent study found that learning and self-regulation skills (such as attentiveness, persistence, organization, learning independence) explained the literacy development of African American boys from kindergarten to 5th grade, even after taking into account the effects of the boys' SES, home environment, and problem behaviors (Matthews, Kizzie, Rowley, & Cortina, 2010). So early development of these learning skills can help to close the opportunity gap, at least for African American boys, and probably for others.

Rather than focusing on achievement gaps, many educators have called for more research on the successes of African American and Latino/a students. Berry (2005) studied two middle-school-aged African American boys who were successful in mathematics. In the lives of those students, Berry found support and high expectations from family and teachers; positive math experiences in preschool and elementary school; connections to church and athletic extracurricular activities; and positive identities as math students. Berry encouraged educators and researchers "to focus on the success stories of those African American men and boys who are successful to identify the strengths, skills, and other significant factors it takes to foster success" (p. 61).

One final theme characterized the successful African American boys—their families had prepared them to understand and deal with discrimination, our next topic.

The Legacy of Discrimination

When we considered explanations for why low-SES students have trouble in school, we listed the limited educational opportunities and low expectations/biases of teachers and fellow students. This has been the experience of many ethnic minority students as well. For example, in some areas of the South in 1924, Black students attended their own separate schools for only 6 months out of the year because they were expected to work in the fields the other 6 months. White students continued in their separate schools a full 9 months. The highest grade available for the Black students was 8th (Raudenbush, 2009).

STOP & THINK Legal segregation came to an end in 1954. Take a moment to imagine you were living back then and the child described below was your own. What would you do?

[In] the city of Topeka, Kansas, a minister walked hand in hand with his seven-year-old daughter to an elementary school four blocks from their home. Linda Brown wanted to enroll in the 2nd grade, but the school refused to admit her. Instead, public school officials required her to attend another school two miles away. This meant that she had to walk six blocks to a bus stop, where she sometimes waited half an hour for the bus. In bad weather, Linda Brown would be soaking wet by the time the bus came; one day she became so cold at the bus stop that she walked back home. Why, she asked her parents, could she not attend the school only four blocks away? (Macionis, 2003, p. 353) •

Her parents' answer to this question, with the help of other concerned families, was to file a suit challenging the school policy. You know the outcome of the 1954 *Brown* v. *the Board of Education of Topeka* ruling. "Separate but equal" schools for Black children were declared inherently unequal. Even though segregation in schools became illegal nearly 60 years ago, about two-thirds of all African American students still attend schools where students of color make up at least 50% of the student body. Segregation in housing and neighborhoods persists, and some areas have drawn school boundary lines deliberately to separate school enrollments along racial lines (Kantor & Lowe, 1995; Ladson-Billings, 2004).

Years of research on the effects of desegregation have mostly shown that legally mandated integration is not a quick solution to the detrimental effects of centuries of racial inequality. In part because White students left integrated schools as the number of students of color increased, many urban schools today are more segregated than they were before the Supreme Court ordered busing and other desegregation measures. The schools in Los Angeles, Miami, Baltimore, Chicago, Dallas, Memphis, Houston, and Detroit have fewer than 11% non-Hispanic White students. And in almost 90% of the schools that have mostly African American and Latina/o students, at least half of the students live in poverty, so racial segregation becomes economic segregation as well (Ladson-Billings, 2004; Orfield & Frankenberg, 2005; Raudenbush, 2009).

Too often, even in integrated schools, minority-group students are resegregated in low-ability tracks. Simply putting people in the same building does not mean that they will come to respect each other or even that they will experience the same quality of education (Ladson-Billings, 2004; Pettigrew, 1998).

LINDA BROWN Nine-year-old Linda Brown, the plaintiff in *Brown* v. *Board of Education of Topeka.*

Doonesbury   BY GARRY TRUDEAU

Connect and Extend to PRAXIS II™

Racial Bias (IV, B4)
Describe the possible effects of racial discrimination and bias on minority students. What can teachers and schools do to address the lingering effects of this discrimination?

WHAT IS PREJUDICE? The word *prejudice* is closely related to the word *prejudge*. **Prejudice** is a rigid and irrational generalization—a prejudgment—about an entire category of people. Prejudice is made up of beliefs, emotions, and tendencies toward particular actions. For example, you are prejudiced against people who are overweight if you think they are lazy (belief), feel disgusted (emotion), and refuse to date them (action) (Myers, 2010). Prejudice can be positive or negative; that is, you can have positive as well as negative irrational beliefs about a group, but the term usually refers to negative attitudes. Targets of prejudice can be based on race, ethnicity, religion, politics, geographic location, language, sexual orientation, gender, or appearance.

Racial prejudice is pervasive, and racism is not confined to one group (Clark, Anderson, Clark, & Williams, 1999). Blatant prejudice has decreased in the past four decades. For example, in 1970, over 50% of Americans agreed that it was all right to keep minorities out of their neighborhoods. By 1995, the number had dropped to about 10% (Myers, 2005). But subtle, below-the-surface racism continues. In response to several police shootings of unarmed Black men, researchers created a videogame that showed a series of White or Black men holding either a gun or a non-weapon such as a flashlight or wallet. Participants in the research were told to "shoot" whenever the person in the videogame held a weapon. Race was not mentioned. Nevertheless, participants shot armed targets more quickly and more frequently when those targets were Black, rather than White, but decided not to shoot unarmed targets more quickly and more frequently when they were White (Greenwald, Oakes, & Hoffman, 2003). When the participants in another study were actual police officers, they were more likely to mistakenly shoot unarmed Black suspects compared with unarmed White suspects (Plant & Peruche, 2005). Besides this obvious threat to well-being for those who are targets of prejudice, research in psychology shows that prejudice against individuals can undermine their mental and physical health, educational achievement, and success on the job (McKown, 2005).

THE DEVELOPMENT OF PREJUDICE. Prejudice starts early. By about age 6, over half the White children in a United States sample and 85% of students in a Canadian sample had significant pro-White, anti-Black biases. Two popular beliefs are that young children are innocently colorblind and that they will not develop biases unless their parents teach them to be prejudiced. Although these beliefs are appealing, they are not supported by research. Even without direct coaching from their parents, many young children develop racial prejudice. Current explanations of the development of prejudice combine personal, social, and societal factors (Katz, 2003; McKown, 2005).

One source of prejudice is the human tendency to divide the social world into two categories—us and them, or the in-group and the out-group. These divisions may be made on the basis of race, religion, sex, age, ethnicity, or even athletic team membership. We tend to see members of the out-group as inferior to and different from us, but similar to each other—"they all look alike" (Aboud, 2003; Lambert, 1995). Also, those who have more (more money, more social status, more prestige) may justify their privilege by assuming that they deserve to "have" because they are superior to the "have-nots." This can lead to blaming the victims: People who live in poverty or women who are raped are seen as causing their problems by their behavior—"they got what they deserved." Emotions play a part as well. When things go wrong, we look for someone or some whole group

Prejudice Prejudgment or irrational generalization about an entire category of people.

to blame. For example, after the tragic events of 9/11, some people vented their anger by attacking innocent Arab Americans (Myers, 2010).

But prejudice is more than a tendency to form in-groups, a self-justification, or an emotional reaction—it is also a set of cultural values. Children learn about valued traits and characteristics from their families, friends, teachers, and the world around them. Think back to your analysis of commercials—did you observe many women or people of color? For years, most of the models presented in books, films, television, and advertising were European Americans. People of different ethnic and racial backgrounds were seldom the "heroes" (Ward, 2004). This is changing. In 2002, the Oscar awards for best actress and best actor went to African Americans, but Denzel Washington won for his portrayal of a villain. In 2005, Jamie Fox won an Oscar for his remarkable portrayal of Ray Charles—a hero. And of course, at the time I am writing, Barack Obama is President of the United States.

- -

STOP & THINK List 3 traits most characteristic of:
College freshmen
Politicians
Athletes
Buddhists
Members of the National Rifle Association •

- -

Prejudice is difficult to combat because it can be part of our thinking processes. You saw in Chapter 1 that children develop schemas—organized bodies of knowledge—about objects, events, and actions. We have schemas that organize our knowledge about people we know, and all our daily activities. We can also form schemas about groups of people. When I asked you to list the traits most characteristic of college freshmen, politicians, athletes, Buddhists, and members of the National Rifle Association, you probably could generate a list. That list would show that you have a **stereotype**—a schema—that organizes what you know (and believe) about the group.

As with any schema, we use our stereotypes to make sense of the world. Having a schema allows you to process information more quickly and efficiently, but it also allows you to distort information to make it fit your schema better (Macrae, Milne, & Bodenhausen, 1994). This is the danger in racial, ethnic, and gender stereotypes. We notice information that confirms or agrees with our stereotype—our schema—and miss or dismiss information that does not fit. For example, if a juror has a negative stereotype of Asian Americans and is listening to evidence in the trial of an Asian American, the juror may interpret the evidence more negatively. The juror may actually forget testimony in favor of the defendant, and remember more damaging testimony instead. Information that fits the stereotype is even processed more quickly (Anderson, Klatzky, & Murray, 1990; Baron, 1998).

CONTINUING DISCRIMINATION.   Prejudice consists of beliefs and feelings (usually negative) about an entire category of people. The third element of prejudice is a tendency to act, called *discrimination*. **Discrimination** is unequal treatment of particular categories of people. Clearly, many Americans face prejudice and discrimination in subtle or blatant ways every day. For example, Latinos, African Americans, and Native Americans make up about 35% of the U.S. population, but only 17% of the House of Representatives and 5% of the Senate (Koppelman, 2011). In the 2007–2008 school year, less than 4% of the doctorates awarded went to Latino students, 6% to African Americans, and .4% to Native Americans. In contrast, 27% of the doctorates were awarded to non-residents of the United States (NCES, 2010). Less than 9% of the scientists, engineers, and mathematicians in the United States are either African American or Hispanic American. Even though their attitudes toward science and math are more favorable than those of White students, Black and Hispanic students begin to lose out in science and math as early as elementary school. They are chosen less often for gifted classes and acceleration or enrichment programs. They are more likely to be tracked into "basic skills" classes. As they progress through middle school, high school, and college, their paths take them farther and farther out of

Stereotype Schema that organizes knowledge or perceptions about a category.

Discrimination Treating or acting unfairly toward particular categories of people.

the pipeline that produces our scientists. If they do persist and become scientists or engineers, they, along with women, will still be paid less than White employees for the same work (Mendoza & Johnson, 2000; National Science Foundation, 2011).

The families of racial and ethnic minority students often have to be vigilant about discrimination to protect their children. They may teach their children to notice and resist possible discrimination. Teachers may unintentionally offend these families if they are not sensitive to possible messages of discrimination. Carol Orange (2005) described a teacher who sent home a holiday worksheet that featured an alphabetical list of all the students in the class. Three students' names were not in the typed list, but were handwritten, out of order, and on the side of the sheet. Two of these students were Latino and one was African American. The mother of the African American student was very upset that her son was truly "marginalized" (written in the margins) on the list. These three students were added to the class (and hence, the list) later in the year, after the list was set up, but the teacher could have avoided this insult (unintended on her part) by redoing the list to give every student a place—a small but important symbol that she valued each one of them.

There is another problem caused by stereotypes and prejudice that can undermine academic achievement—stereotype threat.

Stereotype Threat

Stereotype threat is an "apprehensiveness about confirming a stereotype" (Aronson, 2002, p. 282). The basic idea is that when individuals are in situations in which a stereotype applies, they bear an extra emotional and cognitive burden—the possibility of confirming the stereotype, either in the eyes of others or in their own eyes. Thus, when girls are asked to solve complicated mathematics problems, for example, they are at risk of confirming widely held stereotypes that girls are inferior to boys in mathematics. It is not necessary that the individual believe the stereotype. All that matters is that the person is aware of the stereotype and cares about performing well enough to disprove its unflattering implications (Aronson, Lustina, Good, Keough, Steele, & Brown, 1999; Huguet & Régner, 2007). What are the results of stereotype threat? Recent research provides answers that should interest all teachers.

SHORT-TERM EFFECTS: TEST PERFORMANCE. One review of the research on women, math, and stereotype threat concluded that very subtle clues that might activate anxiety, such as asking test takers to indicate their gender on an answer sheet before taking a math test, tend to lower math scores for women, especially when tests are difficult, the women are moderately identified with the math field, and being female is an important part of their identity. The differences are small on average—something like a female with average math ability scoring 450 instead of the expected average of 500 on an SAT- or GRE-type test. One study estimated that removing stereotype threat might mean an additional 6% of women getting a passing score on a high-stakes calculus test (Nguyen & Ryan, 2008; Wout, Dasco, Jackson, & Spencer, 2008). In other studies, girls in high school and college have scored below boys on a math test when stereotype threats are present, but the same as boys when these threats are not present (Smith & Hung, 2008). Just telling the girls that the math test they are about to take does not reveal gender differences is enough to eliminate any differences in scores.

In a series of experiments, Joshua Aronson, Claude Steele, and their colleagues demonstrated that when African American or Latino college students are put in situations that induce stereotype threat, their performance suffers (Aronson, 2002; Aronson & Steele, 2005; Okagaki, 2006). For example, African American and White undergraduate subjects in an experiment at Stanford University were told that the test they were about to take would precisely measure their verbal ability. A similar group of subjects was told that the purpose of the test was to understand the psychology of verbal problem solving and not to assess individual ability. As shown in Figure 6.3, when the test was presented as diagnostic of verbal ability, the African American students solved about half as many problems as the White students. In the non-threat situation, the two groups solved about the same number of problems.

All groups, not just minority-group students, can be susceptible to stereotype threat. In another study, the subjects were White male college students who were very strong in mathematics. One group was told that the test they were taking would help experimenters

Stereotype threat The extra emotional and cognitive burden that your performance in an academic situation might confirm a stereotype that others hold about you.

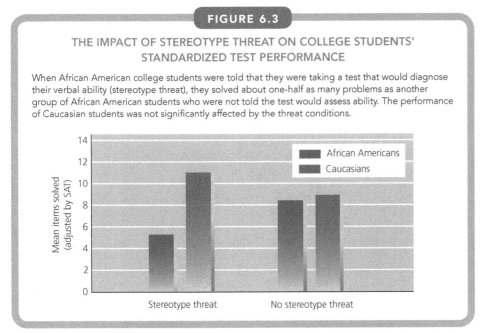

FIGURE 6.3

THE IMPACT OF STEREOTYPE THREAT ON COLLEGE STUDENTS'
STANDARDIZED TEST PERFORMANCE

When African American college students were told that they were taking a test that would diagnose their verbal ability (stereotype threat), they solved about one-half as many problems as another group of African American students who were not told the test would assess ability. The performance of Caucasian students was not significantly affected by the threat conditions.

Source: Adapted from "The Effect of Stereotype Threat on the Standardized Test Performance of College Students," by J. Aronson, C. M. Steele, M. F. Salinas, & M. J. Lustina in Readings About the Social Animal, *10th ed. Worth Publishers. Reprinted by permission of Joshua Aronson, Ph.D.*

determine why Asian students performed so much better than Whites on that particular test. Another group just took the test. The group that faced the stereotype threat of confirming that "Asians are better in math" scored significantly lower on the test (Aronson et al., 1999). The individuals most vulnerable to stereotype threat are those who care the most and who are most deeply invested in high performance (Ryan & Ryan, 2005). The pressures of No Child Left Behind testing are likely to increase vulnerability.

Why does stereotype threat affect test performance? Anxiety is part of a model developed by Katherine Ryan and Allison Ryan (2005) to explain the links between stereotype threat and lower math performance for women and African Americans. When these students are in situations that evoke stereotype threats, such as high-pressure tests, they tend to adopt performance-avoidance goals. We will examine this kind of goal more deeply in Chapter 12, but the short version is that setting performance-avoidance goals means the students want to avoid looking dumb. Students who set these kinds of self-protective goals don't persist or use effective strategies. They tend to adopt self-handicapping strategies such as not trying or procrastinating—they just want to survive without looking stupid. But because they put off studying or didn't try, they are anxious and unprepared during the test. Ryan and Ryan sum up their model:

> Concerns about fulfilling a negative stereotype (females and Blacks do not do well in math) bring about a performance-avoid goal orientation towards the test-taking situation for students who are invested in doing well on the test. A performance-avoid goal will lead to an increase in the worry component of test anxiety, make self-efficacy vulnerable, and [lead] to cognitive disorganization or diminishment. (2005, p. 60)

Two other related explanations are that stereotype threat reduces working memory capacity—so students can't hold as much in their minds (Okagaki, 2006), and that it also decreases interest and engagement in the task—why get absorbed in something that will make you look incompetent? (Smith, Sansone, & White, 2007).

LONG-TERM EFFECTS: DISIDENTIFICATION. If students continue to adopt performance-avoidance goals and develop self-defeating strategies to avoid looking stupid, they may withdraw, claim to not care, exert little effort, or even drop out of school—they psychologically disengage from success and claim "math is for nerds" or "school is for losers." Once students define academics as "uncool," it is unlikely they will exert the effort needed for real learning. There is some evidence that Black male students are more likely than Black female students and White students to disidentify with academics—that is, to separate their sense of self-esteem from their academic achievement (Cokley, 2002; Major & Schmader, 1998; Steele, 1992). Other studies have questioned this disidentification connection, however. Historically, education has been valued among African American communities (Walker, 1996). One study found that African American adolescents who had strong Afrocentric beliefs also had higher achievement goals and self-esteem than adolescents who identified with the larger White culture (Spencer, Noll, Stoltzfus, & Harpalani, 2001).

The message for teachers is to help all students see academic achievement as part of their ethnic, racial, and gender identity.

COMBATING STEREOTYPE THREAT. Aronson, Fried, and Good (2002) demonstrated the powerful effects of changing beliefs about intelligence. African American and White undergraduates were asked to write letters to "at-risk" middle-school students to encourage them to persist in school. Some of the undergraduates were given evidence that intelligence is improvable and encouraged to communicate this information to their pen pals. Others were given information about multiple intelligences, but not told that these multiple abilities can be improved. The middle-school students were not real, but the process of writing persuasive letters about improving intelligence proved powerful. The African American college students—and the White students to a lesser extent—who were encouraged to believe that intelligence can be improved had higher grade-point averages and reported greater enjoyment of and engagement in school when contacted at the end of the next school quarter. Changing their beliefs about the improvability of intelligence also led to higher year-end math achievement scores for middle-school girls (Good, Aronson, & Inzlicht, 2003). So, believing that intelligence can be improved might inoculate students against stereotype threat. In another study, reframing a threatening test as a "challenge" that "sharpens the mind" decreased the impact of stereotype threat for 4th to 6th grade African American students and for Princeton University students from high schools that rarely send students to Ivy League schools (Alter, Aaronson, Darley, Rodriguez, & Ruble, 2009).

In Chapter 9, we will discuss test anxiety and how to overcome the negative effects of anxiety. Many of these strategies are also appropriate for helping students resist stereotype threat.

GENDER IN TEACHING AND LEARNING

In this section, we examine the development of two related identities—sexual identity and gender-role identity. We particularly focus on how men and women are socialized and the role of teachers in providing an equitable education for both sexes.

Sex and Gender

The word *gender* usually refers to traits and behaviors that a particular culture judges to be appropriate for men and for women. In contrast, *sex* refers to biological differences (Brannon, 2002; Deaux, 1993). An individual's identity in terms of gender and sex has three components: gender identity, sexual orientation, and gender-role behaviors (Patterson, 1995; Ruble, Martin, & Berenbaum, 2006). **Gender identity** is a person's self-identification as male or female. *Gender-role behaviors* are those behaviors and characteristics that the culture associates with each gender, and *sexual orientation* involves the person's choice of a sexual partner.

Relations among these three elements are complex. For example, a woman may identify herself as a female (gender identity), but behave in ways that are not consistent with the gender role (play football or wrestle), and may be heterosexual, bisexual, or homosexual in her sexual orientation. So **sexual identity** is a complicated construction of beliefs, attitudes, and behaviors. Erikson and many other earlier psychologists thought

Gender identity The sense of self as male or female as well as the beliefs one has about gender roles and attributes.

Sexual identity A complex combination of beliefs about gender roles and sexual orientation.

that identifying your gender identity was straightforward; you simply realized that you were male or female and acted accordingly. But today, we know that some people experience conflicts about their gender. For example, transsexuals often report feeling trapped in the wrong body; they experience themselves as female, but their biological sex is male, or vice versa (Ruble et al., 2006; Yarhouse, 2001).

SEXUAL ORIENTATION. During adolescence, about 8% of boys and 6% of girls report engaging in some same-sex activity or feeling strong attractions to individuals of their own sex. Males are more likely than females to experiment with same-sex partners as adolescents, but females are more likely to experiment later, often in college. Fewer adolescents actually have a homosexual or bisexual orientation—about 4% of adolescents identify themselves as gay (males who choose male partners), lesbian (females who choose female partners), or bisexual (people who have partners of both sexes). This number increases to between 5% to 13% for adults (Savin-Williams, 2006).

Scientists debate the origins of homosexuality. Most of the research has been with men, so less is known about women. Evidence so far suggests that both biological and social factors are involved. For example, sexual orientation is more similar for identical twins than for fraternal twins, but not all identical twins have the same sexual orientation (Ruble et al., 2006).

There are quite a few models describing the development of sexual orientation as part of identity. Generally, the models include the following or similar stages (Yarhouse, 2001):

• *Feeling different*—Beginning around age 6, the child may be less interested in the activities of other children who are the same sex. Some children may find this difference troubling and fear being "found out." Others do not experience these anxieties.
• *Feeling confused*—In adolescence, as they feel attractions for peers of the same sex, students may be confused, upset, lonely, and unsure of what to do. They may lack role models and may try to change themselves by becoming involved in activities and dating patterns that fit heterosexual stereotypes.
• *Acceptance*—As young adults, many individuals sort through sexual orientation issues and identify themselves as gay, lesbian, or bisexual. They may or may not make their sexual orientation public, but might share the information with a few friends.

The problem with phase models of identity development is that the identity achieved is assumed to be final. Actually, newer models emphasize that sexual orientation can be flexible, complex, and multifaceted; it can change over the lifetime. For example, people may have dated or married opposite-sex partners at one point in their lives, but have same-sex attractions or partners later in their lives, or vice versa (Garnets, 2002).

Parents and teachers are seldom the first people to hear about the adolescent's sexual identity concerns. But if a student does seek your counsel, Table 6.2 on the next page provides some ideas for reaching out.

Gender Roles

Gender roles are expectations about how males and females should behave—about what is masculine and what is feminine. Gender roles vary by culture, time, and place. What was expected of women in the United States in the 1700s definitely has changed, even though women generally still are the primary caregivers and in charge of the home.

When and how do children develop gender roles? As early as age 2, children are aware of gender differences—they know whether they are girls or boys and that mommies are girls and daddies are boys. By age 3 or so, they realize that their sex cannot be changed; they will always be male or female. Biology plays a part in gender role development. Very early, hormones affect activity level and aggression, with boys tending to prefer active, rough, noisy play. Play styles lead young children to prefer same-sex play partners with similar styles, so by age 4, children spend three times as much play time with same-sex playmates as with opposite-sex playmates; by age 6, the ratio is 11 to 1 (Benenson, 1993; Hines, 2004; Maccoby, 1998).

TABLE 6.2 • **Reaching Out to Help Students Struggling with Sexual Identity**

These ideas come from the *Attic Speakers Bureau*, a program of The Attic Youth Center, where trained peer educators reach out to youth and youth-service providers in schools, organizations, and health-care facilities.

REACHING OUT
If a lesbian, gay, bisexual, or transgender youth or a youth questioning his or her own sexual orientation should come to you directly for assistance, remember the following simple, 5-point plan: LISTEN It seems obvious, but the best thing that you can do in the beginning is allow that individual to vent and express what is going on in his or her life. AFFIRM Tell them, "You are not alone." This is crucial. A lot of l/g/b/t/q youth feel isolated and lack peers with whom they can discuss issues around sexual orientation. Letting them know that there are others dealing with the same issues is invaluable. This statement is also important because it does not involve a judgment call on your part. REFER You do not have to be the expert. A referral to someone who is trained to deal with these issues is a gift you are giving to that student, not a dismissal of responsibility. ADDRESS Deal with harassers—do not overlook issues of verbal or physical harassment around sexual orientation. It is important to create and maintain an environment where all youth feel comfortable and welcome. FOLLOW-UP Be sure to check in with the individual to see if the situation has improved and if there is anything further you may be able to do. There are also some things that you as an individual can do to better serve l/g/b/t/q youth and youth dealing with issues around sexual orientation: • Work on your own sense of comfort around issues of sexual orientation and sexuality. • Get training on how to present information on sexual orientation effectively. • Dispel myths around sexual orientation by knowing facts and sharing that information. • Work on setting aside your own personal biases to better serve students dealing with issues around sexual orientation and sexuality.

Source: From Figure 3. Copyright © The Attic Speakers Bureau and Carrie E. Jacobs, Ph.D. Reprinted with permission.

But biology is not the whole story; boys and girls may be treated differently, too. Researchers have found that boys are given more freedom to roam the neighborhood and are allowed to tackle potentially dangerous activities earlier, such as crossing the street alone. Thus, independence and initiative seem to be encouraged more in boys than in girls. In fact, parents, peers, and teachers may reward behaviors that seem gender appropriate—gentle kindness in girls and strong assertiveness in boys (Brannon, 2002).

And then there are the toys! Walk through any store's toy section and see what is offered to girls and boys. Dolls and kitchen sets for girls and toy weapons for boys have been with us for decades. But we cannot blame the toy makers alone. Adults buying for children favor gender-typed toys; fathers also tend to discourage young sons from playing with "girl's" toys (Brannon, 2002).

Through their interactions with family, peers, teachers, toys, and the environment in general, children begin to form **gender schemas**, or organized networks of knowledge about what it means to be male or female. Gender schemas help children make sense of the world and guide their behavior (see Figure 6.4). So a young girl whose schema for "girls" includes "girls play with dolls and not with trucks" or "girls can't be scientists" will pay attention to, remember, and interact more with dolls than trucks, and she may avoid science activities (Golombok et al., 2006; Leaper, 2002; Liben & Signorella, 1993). Of course, these are averages, and individuals do not always fit the average. An individual girl might decide, for example, that the gender schema "trucks are for boys" doesn't matter to her. She plays with the truck if it interests her (Liben & Bigler, 2002).

By age 4, children have an initial sense of gender roles, and by 5 or so, they have developed a gender schema that describes what clothes, games, toys, behaviors, and careers are "right" for boys and girls—and these ideas can be quite rigid (Brannon, 2002). Even in this era of great progress toward equal opportunity, a preschool girl is more likely to

Gender schemas Organized cognitive structures that include gender-related information that influences how children think and behave.

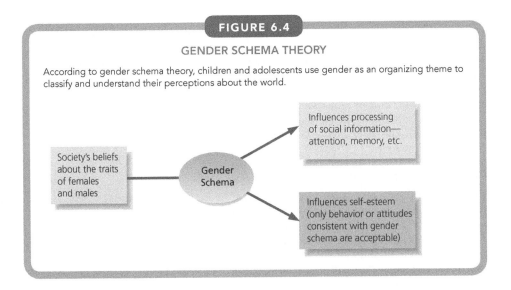

FIGURE 6.4

GENDER SCHEMA THEORY

According to gender schema theory, children and adolescents use gender as an organizing theme to classify and understand their perceptions about the world.

tell you she wants to become a nurse than to say she wants to be an engineer. After she had given a lecture on the dangers of sex stereotyping in schools, a colleague of mine brought her young daughter to her college class. The students asked the little girl, "What do you want to be when you grow up?" The child immediately replied, "A doctor," and her professor/mother beamed with pride. Then the girl whispered to the students in the front row, "I really want to be a nurse, but my Mommy won't let me." Actually, this is a common reaction for young children. Preschoolers tend to have more stereotyped notions of sex roles than older children, and all ages seem to have more rigid and traditional ideas about male occupations than about what occupations females should pursue (Woolfolk & Perry, 2012). Later, as adolescents go through puberty, they may become even more focused on behaving in "masculine" or "feminine" ways, as defined by their peer culture. So many factors, from biology to cultural norms, play a role in gender role development. Beware of either/or explanations.

While I was proofreading this very page for a previous edition, riding cross-country on a train, the conductor stopped beside my seat. He said, "I'm sorry, dear, for interrupting your homework, but do you have a ticket?" I had to smile at his (I'm sure unintended) sexism. I doubt that he made the same comment to the man across the aisle who was writing on his legal pad. Like racial discrimination, messages of sexism can be subtle, and they can appear in classrooms.

Gender Bias in Curriculum Materials

Unfortunately, schools often foster **gender biases** in a number of ways. Publishers have established guidelines to prevent gender bias in teaching materials, but it still makes sense to check them for stereotypes. For example, even though children's books now have an equal number of males and females as central characters, there still are more males in the titles and the illustrations, and the characters (especially the boys) continue to behave in stereotypic ways. Boys are more aggressive and argumentative, and girls are more expressive and affectionate. Girl characters sometimes cross gender roles to be more active, but boy characters seldom show "feminine" expressive traits (Brannon, 2002; Evans & Davies, 2000). Also, video learning packages, virtual worlds, social media sites, and sources such as YouTube have not been carefully screened like most texts for gender, racial, ethnic, economic, religious, or age stereotypes and biases, and they can be sources of stereotyped messages (Henry, 2011). DVDs, computer programs, and testing materials often feature boys more than girls and include other biases. One look at the body builds of males and females in video combat games shows what unreal and unhealthy body images they promote.

Gender biases Different views of males and females, often favoring one gender over the other.

Another "text" that students read long before they arrive in your classroom is television. A content analysis of television commercials found that White male characters were more prominent than any other group (did you find that when you took the "commercial break" in the *Stop & Think* activity earlier?). Even when only the actor's voice could be heard, men were 10 times more likely to narrate commercials. And the same pattern of men as the "voice of authority" on television occurred in the United Kingdom, Europe, Australia, and Asia. Women were more likely than men to be shown as dependent on men and often were depicted at home (Brannon, 2002). So, both before and after going to school, students are likely to encounter texts that overrepresent males.

Connect and Extend to PRAXIS II™

Gender Bias (IV, B4)
There has been much debate in the news media over possible gender bias in schools. What can you as a teacher do to reduce or eliminate gender bias and its effects?

Gender Bias in Teaching

There has been quite a bit of research on teachers' treatment of male and female students. You should know, however, that most of these studies have focused on White students, so the results reported in this section hold mostly for White male and female students.

Many studies describe what seem like biases favoring boys. One of the best-documented findings of the past 30 years is that teachers have more overall interactions with boys than with girls; however, this includes more negative interactions with boys, but not more positive interactions (Jones & Dindia, 2004). This is true from preschool to college. Teachers ask more questions of males, give males more feedback (praise, criticism, and correction), and offer more specific and valuable comments to boys. The effect of these differences is that from preschool through college, girls, on the average, receive 1,800 fewer hours of attention and instruction than boys (Sadker, Sadker, & Klein, 1991). Of course, these differences are not evenly distributed. Some boys, generally high-achieving White students, receive more than their share, whereas high-achieving girls receive the least teacher attention.

Not all biases in school favor boys. In the past 10 years in North America, Western Europe, Australia, and some Asian countries, there have been questions about whether schools are serving boys well. This concern is fueled by data from many countries that seem to show underachievement in boys. For example, data from a U.S. government survey shows the average 11th grade boy writes at the level of an average 8th grade girl (Younger & Warrington, 2006). More dramatic accusations include that schools are trying to destroy "boys' culture" and force "feminine, frilly content" on boys.

GENDER-SPECIFIC TEACHING? Good teaching is good teaching; regardless of the gender of the students, the goal should be successful learning for everyone.

Discrimination against girls has ended, the argument runs. Indeed, thanks to feminism, girls have special treatment and special programs. Now, what about the boys? It is boys who are slower to learn to read, more likely to drop out of school, more likely to be disciplined, more likely to be in programs for children with special needs. In school it is girls who are doing better, boys who are in trouble—and special programs for boys that are needed. (Connell, 1996, p. 207)

One explanation for why boys struggle in school is that the expectations of schooling do not fit the way boys learn (Gurian & Henley, 2001), particularly African American boys (Stinson, 2006). Another suggestion is that boys sabotage their own learning by resisting school expectations and rules to "display their masculinity and get respect" (Kleinfield, 2005, p. B6). Critics of the schools suggest that boys need smaller classes, more discussions, better discipline, mentoring programs, and more men in their schools—90% of elementary teachers are female (Svoboda, 2001).

GUIDELINES

Avoiding Gender Bias in Teaching

Check to see if textbooks and other materials you are using present an honest view of the options open to both males and females.

Examples

1. Identify whether both males and females are portrayed in traditional and nontraditional roles at work, at leisure, and at home.

2. Discuss your analyses with students, and ask them to help you find sex-role biases in other materials—magazine advertising, TV programs, news reporting, for example.

Watch for any unintended biases in your own classroom practices.

Examples

1. Monitor whether you group students by sex for certain activities. Is the grouping appropriate?

2. Monitor whether you call on one sex or the other for certain answers—boys for math and girls for poetry, for example.

3. Monitor your metaphors. Don't ask students to "tackle the problem."

Look for ways in which your school may be limiting the options open to male or female students.

Examples

1. Find out what advice guidance counselors give to students in course and career decisions.

2. Look into whether there is a good sports program for both girls and boys.

3. See if girls are encouraged to take advanced placement courses in science and mathematics and if boys are encouraged in English and foreign language classes.

Use gender-free language as much as possible.

Examples

1. Make sure you speak of "law-enforcement officer" and "mail carrier" instead of "policeman" and "mailman."

2. Be sure you name a committee "head" instead of a "chairman."

Provide role models.

Examples

1. Assign articles in professional journals written by female research scientists or mathematicians.

2. Have recent female graduates who are majoring in science, math, engineering, or other technical fields come to class to talk about college.

3. Create electronic mentoring programs for both male and female students to connect them with adults working in areas of interest to the students.

Make sure all students have a chance to do complex, technical work.

Examples

1. Experiment with same-sex lab groups so girls do not always end up as the secretaries, boys as the technicians.

2. Rotate jobs in groups or randomly assign responsibilities.

What if you witness gender bias as a student teacher? See this site for ideas: http://www.tolerance.org/teach/magazine/features.jsp?p=0&is=36&ar=563#

A current suggestion for making schools more effective for both boys and girls is single-sex classrooms. A few years ago, the *New York Times Magazine* had a cover story about that topic (Weil, 2008). The research on this approach from around the world suggests that teaching boys and girls in separate classes can have positive effects on student learning, motivation, and engagement, but only if certain demanding conditions are met. Teachers must realize that there are no boy- or girl-specific teaching strategies—good teaching is good teaching. Regrouping students by sex does not make teaching easier; in fact, it can make class management more difficult. To succeed, both teachers and students must understand that the goal of their single-sex classrooms is better learning for everyone in an atmosphere that supports more open discussions with less concern about making impressions on peers (Younger & Warrington, 2006). The *Guidelines* provide additional ideas about avoiding gender bias for all students in your classes.

We have dealt with a wide range of differences in this chapter. How can teachers provide an appropriate education for all of their students? One answer is multicultural education with culturally compatible classrooms.

Connect and Extend to PRAXIS II™

Multicultural Education (III, B)
Know the major dimensions of
multicultural education. Describe
how these dimensions influence
each other.

MULTICULTURAL EDUCATION: CREATING CULTURALLY COMPATIBLE CLASSROOMS

Multicultural education is

[a] process of comprehensive school reform and basic education for all students. It challenges and rejects racism and other forms of discrimination in schools and society and accepts and affirms the pluralism (ethnic, racial, linguistic, religious, economic, and gender, among others) that students, their communities, and their teachers reflect. (Nieto & Bode, 2008, p. 44)

James Banks (2006) suggests that multicultural education has five dimensions: *content integration, the knowledge construction process, prejudice reduction, an empowering school culture and social structure,* and an *equity pedagogy,* as shown in Figure 6.5. Many people are familiar only with the dimension of *content integration,* or using examples and content from a variety of cultures when teaching a subject. And because they believe that multicultural education is simply a change in content, some teachers assume that it is irrelevant for subjects such as science and mathematics. But if you consider the other four dimensions—helping students understand how knowledge is constructed, reducing prejudice, creating social structures in schools that support learning and development for all students, and using equity pedagogy or teaching methods that reach all students—then you will see that this view of multicultural education is relevant to all subjects and all students.

An examination of the alternative approaches to multicultural education is beyond the scope of an educational psychology text, but be aware that there is no general agreement about the "best" approach. Many educators have suggested that culturally relevant pedagogy should be an element in multicultural education reform.

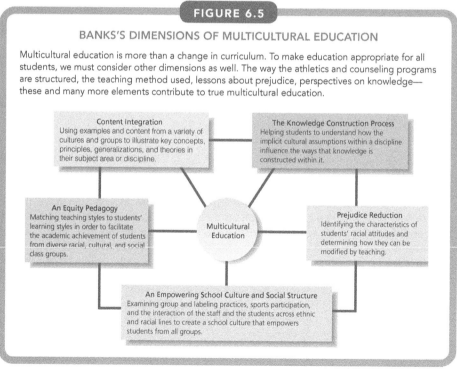

FIGURE 6.5

BANKS'S DIMENSIONS OF MULTICULTURAL EDUCATION

Multicultural education is more than a change in curriculum. To make education appropriate for all students, we must consider other dimensions as well. The way the athletics and counseling programs are structured, the teaching method used, lessons about prejudice, perspectives on knowledge—these and many more elements contribute to true multicultural education.

Content Integration
Using examples and content from a variety of cultures and groups to illustrate key concepts, principles, generalizations, and theories in their subject area or discipline.

The Knowledge Construction Process
Helping students to understand how the implicit cultural assumptions within a discipline influence the ways that knowledge is constructed within it.

An Equity Pedagogy
Matching teaching styles to students' learning styles in order to facilitate the academic achievement of students from diverse racial, cultural, and social class groups.

Multicultural Education

Prejudice Reduction
Identifying the characteristics of students' racial attitudes and determining how they can be modified by teaching.

An Empowering School Culture and Social Structure
Examining group and labeling practices, sports participation, and the interaction of the staff and the students across ethnic and racial lines to create a school culture that empowers students from all groups.

Source: Reprinted with the permission of James A. Banks from James A. Banks, An Introduction to Multicultural Education (4th edition). Boston: Allyn and Bacon, page 32.

Multicultural education
Education that promotes equity in the schooling of all students.

Culturally Relevant Pedagogy

Several researchers have focused on teachers who are especially successful with students of color and students in poverty (Delpit, 1995; Ladson-Billings, 1994, 1995; Moll, Amanti, Neff, & Gonzalez, 1992; Siddle Walker, 2001). The work of Gloria Ladson-Billings (1990, 1992, 1995) is a good example. For three years, she studied excellent teachers in a California school district that served an African American community. In order to select the teachers, she asked parents and principals for nominations. Parents nominated teachers who respected them, created enthusiasm for learning in their children, and understood their children's need to operate successfully in two different worlds—the home community and the White world beyond. Principals nominated teachers who had few discipline referrals, high attendance rates, and high standardized test scores. Ladson-Billings was able to examine in depth 8 of the 9 teachers who were nominated by *both* parents and principals.

Based on her research, Ladson-Billings developed a conception of teaching excellence. She uses the term **culturally relevant pedagogy** to describe teaching that rests on three propositions.

1. *Students must experience academic success.* "Despite the current social inequities and hostile classroom environments, students must develop their academic skills. The ways those skills are developed may vary, but all students need literacy, numeracy, technological, social, and political skills in order to be active participants in a democracy" (Ladson-Billings, 1995, p. 160).
2. *Students must develop/maintain their cultural competence.* As they become more academically skilled, students still retain their cultural competence. "Culturally relevant teachers utilize students' culture as a vehicle for learning" (Ladson-Billings, 1995, p. 161). For example, one teacher used rap music to teach about literal and figurative meaning, rhyme, alliteration, and onomatopoeia in poetry. Another brought in a community expert known for her sweet potato pies to work with students. Follow-up lessons included investigations of George Washington Carver's sweet potato research, numerical analyses of taste tests, marketing plans for selling pies, and research on the educational preparation needed to become a chef.
3. *Students must develop a critical consciousness to challenge the status quo.* In addition to developing academic skills while retaining cultural competence, excellent teachers help students "develop a broader sociopolitical consciousness that allows them to critique the social norms, values, mores, and institutions that produce and maintain social inequities" (Ladson-Billings, 1995, p. 162). For example, in one school, students were upset that their textbooks were out of date. They mobilized to investigate the funding formulas that allowed middle-class students to have newer books, wrote letters to the newspaper editor to challenge these inequities, and updated their texts with current information from other sources.

Ladson-Billings (1995) noted that many people have said her three principles "are just good teaching." She agrees that she is describing good teaching, but questions "why so little of it seems to be occurring in classrooms populated by African American students" (p. 159). Geneva Gay (2000) uses the term *culturally responsive teaching* to describe a similar approach that uses the "cultural knowledge, prior experiences, frames of reference, and performance styles of ethnically diverse students to make learning encounters more relevant to and effective for them. It teaches to and through the strengths of these students. It is culturally validating and affirming" (p. 29).

Lisa Delpit (2003) describes three steps for teaching students of color that are consistent with culturally relevant pedagogy: (1) Teachers must be convinced of the inherent intellectual capability, humanity, and spiritual character of their students—they must believe in the children. There are many examples around the country of schools where low-income African American students are reading well above grade level and doing advanced math. When scores are low, the fault is not in the students, but in their education. (2) Teachers must fight the foolishness that high test scores or scripted lessons are evidence of good learning and good teaching. Successful instruction is "constant, rigorous, integrated across disciplines, connected to students' lived cultures, connected to their intellectual

Culturally relevant pedagogy Excellent teaching for students of color that includes academic success, developing/maintaining cultural competence, and developing a critical consciousness to challenge the status quo.

legacies, engaging, and designed for critical thinking and problem solving that is useful beyond the classroom" (p. 18). (3) Teachers must learn who their students are and the legacies they bring. Then, students can explore their own intellectual legacies and understand the important reasons for academic, social, physical, and moral excellence—not just to "get a job" but also "for our community, for your ancestors, for your descendents" (p. 19).

Michael Pressley and his colleagues (2004) did a case study of a very successful K–12 school for African American students. The characteristics of effective teaching at the school are shown in Table 6.3.

In the past, discussions of teaching low-income students from racial, ethnic, or language minority groups have focused on remediating problems or overcoming perceived deficits. But thinking today emphasizes teaching to the strengths and the resilience of these students.

TABLE 6.3 • **Research-Based Characteristics of Schools and Teachers Associated with Academic Achievement for African American Students**

CHARACTERISTICS OF SCHOOLS	CHARACTERISTICS OF EFFECTIVE TEACHING	OTHER CHARACTERISTICS
Strong administrative leadership	Dedicated teachers who are accountable to produce results	Much total academic time: A very long functional school day/week, including before-school-hours to after-school-hours interactions and tutoring, good use of almost every minute of every class hour, and summer school for students who need it
Frequent evaluation of student progress	Much teacher scaffolding, encouraging student self-regulation	Students who help one another with academics
Emphasis on academics	Curriculum and instruction emphasizing understanding	Strong family–school connections
Safe and orderly environment	Mentoring, especially with regard to college admissions	Donors and visibly supportive, successful alumni
High expectations for student achievement including selective recruitment/retention of students, with the school weeding out students who are not using the opportunity well in favor of students who will (i.e., weeding out misbehaving students, students not meeting academic standards)	Intentional, massive, and frequent attempts to motivate students, including use of the following mechanisms: Positive expectations Visible care by teachers and administrators Praise of specific accomplishments Generally positive atmosphere, encouragement of effort attributions Cooperative learning experiences Tangible rewards for achievements	Motivational mechanisms not often encountered in schools: Extreme community celebrations of academic achievements Encouragement of a possible self as college graduate and successful professional Discouragement of negative possible selves Development of informed pride in African American heritage and life

(Continued)

CHARACTERISTICS OF SCHOOLS	CHARACTERISTICS OF EFFECTIVE TEACHING	OTHER CHARACTERISTICS
Excellent classroom management in most classrooms, resulting in/including a high proportion of academic time on task.	Teachers who provide strong instructional supports for academic achievement (e.g., study guides, test expectations made apparent, informative, feedback on homework and before exams).	Many extracurricular and curricular-enrichment activities—almost all academically oriented or intended to increase commitment to academic pursuits.
		An attractive school building loaded with resources to support academic pursuits

Source: Adapted from Pressley, Raphael, DiBella, & Gallagher, 2004, pp. 234–235.

Fostering Resilience

In any given week, 12% to 15% of school-age children who have urgent needs for social and emotional support do not receive the help they need. Community and mental health services often don't reach the students who are at the highest risk. But many children at risk for academic failure not only survive—they thrive. They are resilient students. What can we learn from these students? What can teachers and schools do to encourage **resilience**?

RESILIENT STUDENTS. Students who seem able to thrive in spite of serious challenges are actively engaged in school. They have good interpersonal skills, confidence in their own ability to learn, positive attitudes toward school, pride in their ethnicity, and high expectations (Borman & Overman, 2004; Lee, 2005). Also, students who have high intelligence or valued talents are more protected from risks. Being easy-going and optimistic is associated with resilience as well. Factors outside the student—interpersonal relationships and social support—matter, too. It helps to have a warm relationship with a parent who has high expectations and supports learning by organizing space and time at home for study. But even without such a parent, a strong bond with someone competent—a grandparent, aunt, uncle, teacher, mentor, or other caring adult—can serve the same supportive function. Involvement in school, community, or religious activities can provide more connections to concerned adults and also teach lessons in social skills and leadership (Berk, 2005).

RESILIENT CLASSROOMS. You can't choose personalities or parents for your students. And if you could, stresses can build up for even the most resilient students. Beth Doll and her colleagues (2005) suggest that we have to change classrooms instead of kids because "alternative strategies will be more enduring and most successful when they are integrated into naturally occurring systems of support [like schools] that surround children" (p. 3). In addition, there is some evidence that changes in classrooms—such as reducing class size, creating an orderly and safe environment, and forming supportive relationships with teachers—have a greater impact on the academic achievement of African American students compared to Latino and White students (Borman & Overman, 2004). So how can you create a classroom that supports resilience?

In formulating their suggestions for characteristics of resilient classrooms, Doll and her colleagues (2005) drew on research in education and psychology on best practices for children in poverty and children with disabilities. There are two strands of elements that bind students to their classroom community: self-agency and connected relationships.

Resilience The ability to adapt successfully in spite of difficult circumstances and threats to development.

PROMOTING RESILIENCE Stresses can build up for even the most resilient students. How can you create a classroom community that supports resilience? One important factor is having connected relationships.

SELF-AGENCY STRAND

- **Academic self-efficacy,** a belief in your own ability to learn, is one of the most consistent predictors of academic achievement. As you will see in Chapter 8, self-efficacy emerges when students tackle challenging, meaningful tasks with the support needed to be successful and observe other students doing the same thing. Accurate and encouraging feedback from teachers also helps.
- **Behavioral self-control,** or student self-regulation, is essential for a safe and orderly learning environment. Chapters 8 and 10 will give you ideas for helping students develop self-control.
- **Academic self-determination,** which includes making choices, setting goals, and following through, is the third element in the self-agency strand. As you will see in Chapter 9, students who are self-determined are more motivated and committed to learning.

RELATIONSHIP STRAND

- **Caring teacher–student relationships** are consistently associated with better school performance, especially for students who face serious challenges. We saw the power of caring teachers in Chapter 2 and we will continue to see the value of these relationships throughout this text.
- **Effective peer relations,** as we saw in Chapter 2, also are critical in connecting students to school.
- **Effective home–school relationships** are the final element in building a caring, connected network for students. In the School Development program, James Comer has found that when parents stay involved, their children's grades and test scores improve (Comer, Haynes, & Joyner, 1996). The *Family and Community Partnerships Guidelines* give some ideas for connecting with families.

Diversity in Learning

Over two decades ago Roland Tharp (1989) outlined several dimensions of classrooms that reflect the diversity of the students and can be tailored to better fit their backgrounds: social organization, cultural values, learning preferences, and sociolinguistics. His advice is still relevant today.

GUIDELINES — FAMILY AND COMMUNITY PARTNERSHIPS

Building Learning Communities

Joyce Epstein (1995) describes six types of family/school/community partnerships. The following guidelines are based on her six categories.

Parenting partnerships: Help all families establish home environments to support children as students.
Examples

1. Offer workshops, videos, courses, family literacy fairs, and other informational programs to help parents cope with parenting situations that they identify as important.
2. Establish family support programs to assist with nutrition, health, and social services.
3. Find ways to help families share information with the school about the child's cultural background, talents, and needs—learn from the families.

Communication: Design effective forms for school-to-home and home-to-school communication.
Examples

1. Make sure communications fit the needs of families. Provide translations, visual support, large print—whatever is needed to make communication effective.
2. Visit families in their neighborhoods after gaining their permission. Don't expect family members to come to school until a trusting relationship is established.
3. Balance messages about problems with communications of accomplishments and positive information.

Volunteering: Recruit and organize parent help and support.
Examples

1. Do an annual postcard survey to identify family talents, interests, times available, and suggestions for improvements.
2. Establish a structure (telephone tree, etc.) to keep all families informed. Make sure families without telephones are included.
3. If possible, set aside a room for volunteer meetings and projects.

Learning at home: Provide information and ideas for families about how to help children with schoolwork and learning activities.
Examples

1. Provide assignment schedules, homework policies, and tips on how to help with schoolwork without doing the work.
2. Get family input into curriculum planning—have idea and activity exchanges.
3. Send home learning packets and enjoyable learning activities, especially over holidays and summers.

Decision-making partnerships: Include families in school decisions, developing family and community leaders and representatives.
Examples

1. Create family advisory committees for the school with parent representatives.
2. Make sure all families are in a network with their representative.

Community partnerships: Identify and integrate resources and services from the community to strengthen school programs, family practices, and student learning and development.
Examples

1. Have students and parents research existing resources—build a database.
2. Identify service projects for students—explore service learning.
3. Identify community members who are school alumni and get them involved in school programs.

For more ideas on partnerships with parents, see http://www.projectappleseed.org/chklst.html

Source: Excerpt from pp. 704–705, "School/Family/Community Partnerships: Caring for Children We Share," by J. L. Epstein, Phi Delta Kappan, 76, pp. 701–712. Copyright © 1995 by Phi Delta Kappan. Reprinted with permission of Phi Delta Kappan and the author.

SOCIAL ORGANIZATION. "A central task of educational design is to make the organization of teaching, learning, and performance compatible with the social structures in which students are most productive, engaged, and likely to learn" (Tharp, 1989, p. 350). Social structure or social organization in this context means the ways people interact to accomplish a particular goal. For example, the social organization of Hawaiian society depends heavily on collaboration and cooperation. Children play together in groups of friends and siblings, with older children often caring for the younger ones. When cooperative work groups of four or five boys and girls were established in Hawaiian classrooms, student learning and participation improved (Okagaki, 2001, 2006). The teacher worked intensively with one group while the children in the remaining groups helped each other. But when the same structure was tried in a Navajo classroom, students would not work together. These children are socialized to be more solitary and not to play with children of the opposite sex. By setting up same-sex working groups of only two or three Navajo students, teachers encouraged them to help each other. If you have students from several cultures, you may need to provide choices and variety in grouping structures.

CULTURAL VALUES AND LEARNING PREFERENCES.   Results of some research suggest that Hispanic American students are more oriented toward family and group loyalty. This may mean that these students prefer cooperative activities and dislike being made to compete with fellow students (Garcia, 1992; Vasquez, 1990). Four values shared by many Latina/o students are:

Familismo—tightly knit families. Discussing family problems or business may be seen as disloyal.
Simpatia—value of interpersonal harmony. Assertively voicing personal opinions or arguing may be seen as inappropriate.
Respecto—respect for people in authority, for example, teachers and government officials.
Personalismo—valuing of close interpersonal relationships; discomfort with distant, cold, professional relationships. (Dingfelder, 2005)

The learning styles of African Americans may be inconsistent with teaching approaches in most schools. Some of the characteristics of this learning style are a visual/global approach rather than a verbal/analytic approach; a preference for reasoning by inference rather than by formal logic; a focus on people and relationships; a preference for energetic involvement in several activities simultaneously rather than routine, step-by-step learning; a tendency to approximate numbers, space and time; and a greater dependence on nonverbal communication. Students of color who identify with their traditional cultures tend to respond better to open-ended questions with more than one answer, as opposed to single, right-answer questions. Questions that focus on meaning or the "big picture" may be more productive than questions that focus on details (Bennett, 2011; Gay, 2000; Sheets, 2005).

Native Americans also appear to have a more global, visual style of learning. For example, Navajo students prefer hearing a story all the way through to the end before discussing parts of the story. Teachers who stop reading to ask comprehension questions seem odd to these students and interrupt their learning process (Tharp, 1989). Also, these students sometimes show strong preferences for learning privately, through trial and error, rather than having their mistakes made public (Vasquez, 1990).

There has been little research on the learning styles of Asian Americans, perhaps because they are viewed as a "model minority," as you saw earlier. Some educators suggest that Asian children tend to value teacher approval and to work well in structured, quiet learning environments where there are clear goals and social support (Manning & Baruth, 1996). Other research suggests that there are clear and deep differences in Asian and Western styles of learning. Students from Asian cultures tend be more interdependent and to value learning with others, which might explain some of their success in school. Western values emphasize independence and individual learning, which might explain some of the United States' successes in science, technology, and innovation (Chang et al., 2011). But, as you saw earlier, there are dangers in stereotyping any group, especially in terms of cultural learning styles.

CAUTIONS (AGAIN) ABOUT LEARNING STYLES RESEARCH.   In considering this research on learning styles, you should keep two points in mind. First, the validity of some of the learning styles research has been strongly questioned, as we saw in the previous chapter. Second, there is a heated debate today about whether identifying ethnic group differences in learning styles and preferences is a dangerous, racist, sexist exercise. In our society, we are quick to move from the notion of "difference" to the idea of "deficits" and stereotypes (Gordon, 1991; O'Neil, 1990). I have included the information about learning style differences because I believe that, used sensibly, this information can help you better understand your students. But, it is dangerous and incorrect to assume that every individual in a group shares the same learning style (Sheets, 2005). The best advice for teachers is to be sensitive to individual differences in all your students and to make available alternative paths to learning. Never prejudge how a student will learn best based on assumptions about the student's ethnicity or race. Get to know the individual.

SOCIOLINGUISTICS.   **Sociolinguistics** is the study of "the courtesies and conventions of conversation across cultures" (Tharp, 1989, p. 351). Knowledge of sociolinguistics will help you understand why communication sometimes breaks down in classrooms. The classroom is a special setting for communicating; it has its own set of rules for when, how, to whom, about what subject, and in what manner to use language. Sometimes, the sociolinguistic skills of students do not fit the expectations of teachers or counselors, as we saw earlier.

In order to be successful, students must know the communication rules; that is, they must understand the **pragmatics** of the classroom—when, where, and how to communicate. This is not such an easy task. As class activities change, rules change. Sometimes you have to raise your hand (during the teacher's presentation), but sometimes you don't (during story time on the rug). Sometimes it is good to ask a question (during discussion), but other times it isn't so good (when the teacher is reprimanding you). These differing activity rules are called **participation structures,** and they define appropriate participation for each class activity. Most classrooms have many different participation structures. To be competent communicators in the classroom, students sometimes have to read very subtle, nonverbal cues telling them which participation structures are currently in effect. For example, when the teacher moves to the white board, students should look up and be ready for instructions.

SOURCES OF MISUNDERSTANDINGS.   Some children are simply better than others at reading the classroom situation because the participation structures of the school match the structures they have learned at home. The communication rules for most school situations are similar to those in middle-class homes, so children from these homes often appear to be more competent communicators. They know the unwritten rules. Students who are not White and middle class may not know the rules. For example, researchers found that Pueblo Indian students participated twice as much in classes where teachers waited longer to react. Waiting longer also helps girls to participate more freely in math and science classes (Grossman & Grossman, 1994). Students from different cultural backgrounds may have learned participation structures that conflict with the behaviors expected in school. For example, one study found that the home conversation style of Hawaiian children is to chime in with contributions to a story. In school, however, this overlapping style is viewed as "interrupting." When the teachers learned about these differences and made their reading groups more like their students' home conversation groups, the young Hawaiian children in their classes improved in reading (Au, 1980; Tharp, 1989).

It seems that even students who speak the same language as their teachers may still have trouble communicating, and thus learning school subjects. What can teachers do? Especially in the early grades, you should make communication rules for activities clear and explicit. Do not assume students know what to do. Use cues to signal students when changes occur. Explain and demonstrate appropriate behavior. I have seen teachers show young children how to use their "inside voice," "six-inch voice," or "whisper voice." One teacher said and then demonstrated, "If you have to interrupt me while I'm working with other children, stand quietly beside me until I can help you." Be consistent in responding to students. If students are supposed to raise their hands, don't call on those who break the rules. In these ways you will teach students how to learn in school.

Lessons for Teachers: Teaching Every Student

The goal of this chapter is to give you a sense of the diversity in today's and tomorrow's schools and to help you meet the challenges of teaching in a multicultural classroom. How will you understand and build on all the cultures of your students? How will you deal with many different languages? Here are three general teaching principles to guide you in finding answers to these questions.

Sociolinguistics The study of the formal and informal rules for how, when, about what, to whom, and how long to speak in conversations within cultural groups.

Pragmatics The rules for when and how to use language to be an effective communicator in a particular culture.

Participation structures The formal and informal rules for how to take part in a given activity.

REACHING EVERY STUDENT Know your students, respect your students, teach your students.

KNOW YOUR STUDENTS. We must learn who our students are and understand the legacies they bring (Delpit, 2003). Nothing you read in a chapter on cultural differences will teach you enough to understand the lives of all your students. If you can take other courses in college or read about other cultures, I encourage you to do it. But reading and studying are not enough. You should get to know your students' families and communities. Elba Reyes, a successful bilingual teacher for children with special needs, describes her approach:

Usually I find that if you really want to know a parent, you get to know them on their own turf. This is key to developing trust and understanding the parents' perspective. First, get to know the community. Learn where the local grocery store is and what the children do after school. Then schedule a home visit at a time that is convenient for the parents. The home environment is not usually as ladened with failure. I sometimes observed the child being successful in the home, for example, riding a bicycle or helping with dinner. (Bos & Reyes, 1996, p. 349)

Try to spend time with students and parents on projects outside school. Ask parents to help in class or to speak to your students about their jobs, their hobbies, or the history and heritage of their ethnic group. In the elementary grades, don't wait until a student is in trouble to have the first meeting with a family member. Watch for and listen to the ways that your students interact in large and small groups. Have students write to you, and write back to them. Eat lunch with one or two students. Spend some nonteaching time with them.

RESPECT YOUR STUDENTS. From knowledge ought to come respect for your students' learning strengths—for the struggles they face and the obstacles they have overcome. We must believe in our students (Delpit, 2003). For a child, genuine acceptance is a necessary condition for developing self-esteem. Sometimes the self-image and occupational aspirations of minority children actually decline in their early years in public school, probably because of the emphasis on majority culture values, accomplishments, and history. By presenting the accomplishments of particular members of an ethnic group or by bringing that group's culture into the classroom (in the form of literature, art, music, or any cultural knowledge), teachers can help students maintain a sense of pride in their cultural group. This integration of culture must be more than the "tokenism" of sampling ethnic foods or wearing costumes. Students should learn about the socially and intellectually important contributions of the various groups. There are many excellent references that provide background information, history, and teaching strategies for different groups of students (e.g., Banks, 2002; Gay, 2000; Irvine & Armento, 2001; Ladson-Billings, 1995).

TEACH YOUR STUDENTS. The most important thing you can do for your students is teach them to read, write, speak, compute, think, and create—through constant, rigorous, culturally connected instruction (Delpit, 2003). Too often, goals for low-SES or minority-group students have focused exclusively on basic skills. Students are taught words and sounds, but the meaning of the story is supposed to come later. Knapp, Turnbull, and Shields (1990, p. 5) make these suggestions:

- Focus on meaning and understanding from beginning to end—for example, by orienting instruction toward comprehending reading passages, communicating important ideas in written text, or understanding the concepts underlying number facts.
- Balance routine skill learning with novel and complex tasks from the earliest stages of learning.

GUIDELINES

Culturally Relevant Teaching

Experiment with different grouping arrangements to encourage social harmony and cooperation.
Examples

1. Try "study buddies" and pairs.
2. Organize heterogeneous groups of four or five.
3. Establish larger teams for older students.

Provide a range of ways to learn material to accommodate a range of learning styles.
Examples

1. Give students verbal materials at different reading levels.
2. Offer visual materials—charts, diagrams, and models.
3. Provide tapes for listening and viewing.
4. Set up activities and projects.

Teach classroom procedures directly, even ways of doing things that you thought everyone would know.
Examples

1. Tell students how to get the teacher's attention.
2. Explain when and how to interrupt the teacher if students need help.
3. Show which materials students can take and which require permission.
4. Demonstrate acceptable ways to disagree with or challenge another student.

Learn the meaning of different behaviors for your students.
Examples

1. Ask students how they feel when you correct or praise them. What gives them this message?

2. Talk to family and community members and other teachers to discover the meaning of expressions, gestures, or other responses that are unfamiliar to you.

Emphasize meaning in teaching.
Examples

1. Make sure students understand what they read.
2. Try storytelling and other modes that don't require written materials.
3. Use examples that relate abstract concepts to everyday experiences; for instance, relate negative numbers to being overdrawn in your checkbook.

Get to know the customs, traditions, and values of your students.
Examples

1. Use holidays as a chance to discuss the origins and meaning of traditions.
2. Analyze different traditions for common themes.
3. Attend community fairs and festivals.

Help students detect racist and sexist messages.
Examples

1. Analyze curriculum materials for biases.
2. Make students "bias detectives," reporting comments from the media.
3. Discuss the ways that students communicate biased messages about each other and decide what should be done when this happens.
4. Discuss expressions of prejudice such as anti-Semitism.

- Provide context for skill learning that establishes clear reasons for needing to learn the skills.
- Influence attitudes and beliefs about the academic content areas as well as skills and knowledge.
- Eliminate unnecessary redundancy in the curriculum (e.g., repeating instruction in the same mathematics skills year after year).

And finally, teach students directly about how to be students. In the early grades, this could mean directly teaching the courtesies and conventions of the classroom: how to get a turn to speak, how and when to interrupt the teacher, how to whisper, how to get help in a small group, how to give an explanation that is helpful. In the later grades, it may mean teaching the study skills that fit your subject. You can ask students to learn "how we do it in school" without violating principle number two above—respect your students. Ways of asking questions around the kitchen table at home may be different from ways of asking questions in school, but students can learn both ways, without deciding that either way is superior. And you can expand ways of doing it in school to include more possibilities. The *Guidelines* give more ideas.

▼ SUMMARY

Today's Diverse Classrooms (pp. 208–212)

What is culture? There are many conceptions of culture, but most include the knowledge, skills, rules, traditions, beliefs, and values that guide behavior in a particular group of people: Culture is a program for living. Everyone is a member of many cultural groups, defined in terms of geographic region, nationality, ethnicity, race, gender, social class, and religion. Membership in a particular group does not determine behavior or values, but makes certain values and kinds of behavior more likely. Wide variations exist within each group. You met four individuals, Ternice, Benjamin, Davy, and Jessie, who embody that diversity.

Economic and Social Class Differences (pp. 213–218)

What is SES, and how does it differ from social class? Social class reflects a group's prestige and power in a society. Most people are aware of the social class that they share with similar peers. Socioeconomic status (SES) is a term used by sociologists for variations in wealth, power, control over resources, and prestige. Socioeconomic status is determined by several factors—not just income—and often overpowers other cultural differences. No single variable is an effective measure of SES, but most researchers identify four general levels of SES: upper, middle, working, and lower classes. The main characteristics of these four levels are summarized in Table 6.1.

What is the relationship between SES and school achievement? Socioeconomic status and academic achievement are moderately correlated. High-SES students of all ethnic groups show higher average levels of achievement on test scores and stay in school longer than low-SES students. The longer the child is in poverty, the stronger the impact is on achievement. Why is there a correlation between SES and school achievement? Low-SES students may suffer from inadequate health care, teachers' lowered expectations of them, low self-esteem, learned helplessness, participation in resistance cultures, school tracking, understimulating home environments, and summer setbacks. This last striking finding is that low-SES children lose academic ground outside school over the summer, whereas higher-SES children continue to advance.

Ethnicity and Race in Teaching and Learning (pp. 218–226)

Distinguish between ethnicity and race. Ethnicity (culturally transmitted behavior) and race (biologically transmitted physical traits) are socially significant categories people use to describe themselves and others. Minority groups (either numerically or historically unempowered) are rapidly increasing in population.

How can differences in ethnicity of teachers and students affect school performance? Conflicts can arise from differences between teachers and students in culture-based beliefs, values, and expectations. Cultural conflicts are usually about below-the-surface differences, because when subtle cultural differences meet, misunderstandings are common. Students in some cultures learn attitudes and behaviors that are more consistent with school expectations. Differences among ethnic groups in cognitive and academic abilities are largely the legacy of racial segregation and continuing prejudice and discrimination.

Distinguish among *prejudice*, *discrimination*, and *stereotype threat*. Prejudice is a rigid and irrational generalization—a

prejudgment or attitude—about an entire category of people. Prejudice may target people in particular racial, ethnic, religious, political, geographic, or language groups, or it may be directed toward the gender or sexual orientation of the individual. Discrimination is unequal treatment of or actions toward particular categories of people. Stereotype threat is the extra emotional and cognitive burden that your performance in an academic situation might confirm a stereotype that others hold about you. It is not necessary that the individual even believe the stereotype. All that matters is that the person is aware of the stereotype and cares about performing well enough to disprove its unflattering implications. In the short run, the fear that you might confirm a negative stereotype can induce test anxiety and undermine performance. Over time, experiencing stereotype threat may lead to disidentification with schooling and academic achievement.

Gender in Teaching and Learning (pp. 226–231)

What are the stages of achieving a sexual orientation for gay and lesbian youth? Stages of achieving a sexual orientation for gay and lesbian students can also follow a pattern from discomfort to confusion to acceptance. Some researchers contend that sexual identity is not always permanent and can change over the years.

What are gender roles and how do they develop? Gender role is the image each individual has of himself or herself as masculine or feminine in characteristics—a part of self-concept. Biology (hormones) plays a role, as does the differential behavior of parents and teachers toward male and female children. Through their interactions with family, peers, teachers, and the environment in general, children begin to form gender schemas, or organized networks of knowledge about what it means to be male or female.

How are gender biases communicated? In children's books, there are more males in the titles and the illustrations, and the characters (especially the boys) continue to behave in stereotypic ways. Girl characters sometimes cross gender roles to be more active, but boy characters seldom show "feminine" expressive traits. Some overrepresentation of gender exists in television commercials too. Teachers interact more with boys in both positive and negative ways. Lately some educators have claimed that schools are not supportive of boys, and same-sex classrooms have been suggested as an answer. The research on the value of these classrooms is mixed.

Multicultural Education: Creating Culturally Compatible Classrooms (pp. 232–241)

What is multicultural education? Multicultural education is a field of study designed to increase educational equity for all students. According to the multicultural ideal, America should be transformed into a society that values diversity. James Banks suggests that multicultural education has five dimensions: integrating content, helping students understand how knowledge is influenced by beliefs, reducing prejudice, creating social structures in schools that support learning and development for all students, and using teaching methods that reach all students.

What is culturally relevant pedagogy? "Culturally relevant pedagogy is an approach to teaching that uses the cultural knowledge, prior experiences, frames of reference, and learning styles of ethnically diverse students to make learning encounters more relevant and effective for them. It teaches to and through the strengths of these students" (Gay, 2000). Gloria Ladson-Billings (1995, 2004) describes culturally relevant teaching that rests on three propositions: Students must experience academic success, develop/maintain their cultural competence, and develop a critical consciousness to challenge the status quo.

What are the elements of a resilient classroom? There are two strands of elements that bind students to their classroom community. One strand emphasizes the self-agency of students—their capacity to set and pursue goals. This includes academic self-efficacy, self-control, and self-determination. The second strand emphasizes caring and connected relationships with the teacher, peers, and the home.

▼ KEY TERMS

Culturally relevant pedagogy (233)
Culture (208)
Discrimination (223)
Ethnicity (218)
Gender biases (229)
Gender identity (226)
Gender schemas (228)

Minority group (219)
Multicultural education (232)
Participation structures (239)
Pragmatics (239)
Prejudice (222)
Race (219)
Resilience (235)

Resistance culture (215)
Sexual identity (226)
Socioeconomic status (SES) (213)
Sociolinguistics (239)
Stereotype (223)
Stereotype threat (224)
Tracking (217)

▼ CONNECT AND EXTEND TO LICENSURE

MULTIPLE-CHOICE QUESTIONS

1. Socioeconomic status and school achievement are often correlated. Which one of the following statements is not true regarding the relationship between SES and levels of achievement?
   A. The longer a child lives in poverty, the greater the impact is on achievement.
   B. Poor children are no more likely to be kept back in school than non-poor children.
   C. High-SES students of all ethnic groups generally show higher levels of achievement on test scores and stay in school longer than low-SES students.
   D. More poor children live in suburban and rural areas than in central cities.

2. Educators often believe students are not bright based upon inadequate resources at home. This inadequacy manifests itself as a lack of familiarity with school related activities. When this occurs, what is the likely outcome?
   A. These students work harder to prove themselves to their teachers.
   B. Teachers may have low expectations which negatively impact future academic success.
   C. The students will perform poorly because they will never catch up with their peers.
   D. Teachers understand that not all students will be able to academically achieve.

3. Damon, an African American student in Diane Collins' math class, pushed his math test away from him after a few minutes and proclaimed, "This is stupid. I don't know why we even have to do this." What should Ms. Collins consider?
   A. She should consider sending Damon to the Principal's office for insubordination.

   B. She might have made the test too difficult for her African American students so she should make an easier test next time.
   C. Damon may be exhibiting performance-avoidance goals because he doesn't want to look dumb.
   D. Damon's high self-efficacy has caused him to determine that testing is a waste of his time.

4. In an effort to avoid gender bias in his fourth grade classroom, Mr. Bonner used gender-free language, provided positive role models, and ensured all students had opportunities to engage in various activities by rotating classroom jobs and activities. His school was also experimenting with single-sex classrooms. Next year, Mr. Bonner thought he might opt to teach in one of those classrooms. All but which of the following are true concerning single-sex classrooms?
   A. There are positive effects on learning, motivation, and engagement if certain conditions are met.
   B. Teaching is not easier when regrouping students by sex.
   C. Teachers must realize there are specific boy and girl teaching strategies.
   D. There is often less concern about making impressions on peers.

CONSTRUCTED-RESPONSE QUESTIONS

Case

Paulo Nzambi moved from his home in Angola to the United States in the fifth grade. While his English and schooling were adequate, his teacher Katie Wyant worried about his social adjustment. His quiet demeanor and soft voice were, in many ways, the opposite of his male peers. Paulo appeared hesitant when interacting with her as if he was unsure about how to behave. As the year progressed, Katie noticed he had not made any progress in adjusting to the classroom. She decided she needed to be proactive in finding a solution.

5. In order to acquire a better understanding of Paulo and make school a more positive experience, what three types of relationships would assist Paulo as well as Miss Wyant?
6. What aspects of culturally relevant teaching might Katie Wyant employ to assist Paulo Nzambi in his transition to an American classroom?

▼ WHAT WOULD THEY DO?
TEACHERS' CASEBOOK: White Girls Club

Here is how some expert teachers responded to the situation described at the beginning of the chapter about the "White Girls Club."

JENNIFER PINCOSKI • Learning Resource Teacher: K–12
Lee County School District, Fort Myers, FL

All teachers feel the pressure of high-stakes testing and meeting academic standards, and unfortunately, this leaves little time to provide character education and team-building activities. Even kindergarten classrooms have sacrificed social skills/ friendship lessons for additional academic instruction, even though many students come to school not knowing how to appropriately interact with peers.

In the face of No Child Left Behind and Race to the Top mandates, briefly suspending content instruction to teach kindness and build a respectful classroom community may sound like a waste of valuable academic time. However, teachers who establish a positive learning environment where students feel safe and valued ultimately spend less time redirecting and correcting misbehaviors. Students who feel accepted and appreciated will demonstrate longer time on task and greater interest in learning than those who don't.

In this case, the entire class could benefit from lessons on diversity, respect, and tolerance. School counselors are a great resource for these types of activities, and are often available to teach or co-teach the lessons.

In the long run, a proactive approach is far more efficient than a reactive one. Taking the time to build rapport and establish a sense of community will preserve hours of instruction that would have been lost to peer conflict, off-task behaviors, and non-compliance.

LAUREN ROLLINS • 1st Grade Teacher
Boulevard Elementary School, Shaker Heights, OH

Discrimination of any kind will not be tolerated in my classroom! I would attack this unfortunate situation through a variety of different approaches—whole-class instruction, private small-group discussions, and one-on-one meetings with my new student and her parents. I would start my whole-class lesson by passing out candy (or some other desired object—stickers, pencils, etc.) to one chosen group of people—only boys, students with brown eyes, etc. I would purposely choose a group that excluded the girls who have formed the "White Girls Club." This activity would spark a conversation with the class about how unfair it is that one group of students got to do something that another group did not. We would talk about how the excluded group felt by this slight and why it is important not to discriminate against people for any reason. I would also include a read-aloud of a children's book that supported this topic. I would stop throughout my reading to discuss the feelings of the different characters in the book. Next, I would meet privately with the girls who have formed the club. I would remind them that excluding people from a group is unacceptable and will not be tolerated by me. Either everyone gets to play, or no one does. Lastly, I would meet with my new student and her parents. I would ask her to give me the names of a few students in my class with whom she would be interested in building a relationship. I would encourage her parents to set up one-on-one play dates for their daughter outside of school with the hope of them building relationships.

LINDA SPARKS • Grade 1
John F. Kennedy School, Billerica MA

We begin each year setting up classroom rules and expectations. We write them down and all students sign the "contract." It is then posted in a visible place in the classroom. Throughout the year we will go over the rules. The first one always states that we treat others the way we want to be treated. We have had these "clubs" pop up, from "only boys can play a sport at recess" to "the way a child looks." When I notice a change in classroom climate, I always begin with a generalized scenario (e.g., out at recess, the principal noticed that only the boys were playing basketball but some of the girls were watching and wanting to play). We would then brainstorm a list of what the principal could do to help let the girls play. It is amazing the wonderful ideas that come up when the student is not being put on the spot, but rather the whole class is getting the chance to share their thoughts. I find that starting this way, students will start to think of specific times when this has happened to them and how it was resolved. It is amazing how quickly these "clubs" or "groups" disappear once the lesson has been presented. We have a few programs we use in our school for teaching tolerance. We have Second Step in which scenarios are presented and students role play the scene. This is one of their favorites. Another is a bucket filler, where students can be caught doing something good either by another student or by a staff member. The person who catches them fills out a bucket-filling slip and it gets put into a big silver bucket. No one wants to be a bucket dipper by making people feel sad or left out. No matter what the age, clubs can quickly dissipate when the students are the ones who are given the chance to resolve the problem.

PAULA COLEMERE • Special Education Teacher—English, History
McClintock High School, Tempe, AZ

In one of my favorite lessons for the beginning of the year I give each student five mixed beans and have students choose which is the "best" one. We then discuss why they chose the bean as the best and discuss the differences in beans before connecting to people. After the discussion, we role play different scenarios that deal with diversity; this is a good lesson because it addresses self-esteem in addition to diversity. While all students can use a boost to self-esteem, it would hopefully help the new girl to feel better about the situation. This lesson can be tailored to younger or older students. Since these students are young, I would hope this would be a gentle way for the girls in the "club" to see that what they have been doing is wrong. My next step would be to conference with the girls and mediate if necessary.

PAUL DRAGIN • ESL Grades 9–12
Columbus East High School, Columbus OH

Based on the observations, I would not hesitate to act quickly in this situation of exclusion. Based on the age group of the students, I would attack this problem two ways initially. I would spend classroom time talking about building community and present some scenarios and videos about how it feels to be excluded or left out. With children at this impressionable age, this troubling dilemma may leave an indelible mark on some if handled in such a way that they internalize the feelings that the excluded student is inevitably confronted with being the "other." I would contact the parents of the girls who made the "White girls club" comment and let them know what I overheard and witnessed regarding the new student. Hopefully, this could turn an unfortunate situation into a great learning opportunity that would stick with the students whenever they are confronted with someone racially, ethnically, or culturally different from them.

JESSICA N. MAHTABAN • 8th Grade Math
Woodrow Wilson Middle School, Clifton, NJ

My immediate response would be to investigate the "club." I could talk to each girl individually and ask why she started the club as well as why they felt it was important to exclude people from their club. Also, I must make sure the parents, administration, and counselors are aware of the situation as well.

It is my job to explain to my students as best I can that it's not polite to exclude anyone. I would give them different scenarios about exclusion and ask for them to reflect on their personal feelings for each scenario. We would discuss in groups as well as the whole class about the scenarios and their feelings. Problem solving together would be the best approach to finding various solutions to problems as well as figuring out who can help them in different situations. Hopefully, by the end of these lessons each student will understand that our classroom is a family, and that, as a family, we celebrate differences—not segregate.

BARBARA PRESLEY • Transition/Work Study Coordinator—High School Level, B.E.S.T.T. Program (Baldwinsville Exceptional Student Training and Transition Program)
C.W. Baker High School, Baldwinsville, NY

Eliminating bias can only be achieved through exposure, knowledge, and experience. In my work with severely disabled students, I found that special needs students' peers were less judgmental and exclusionary when they were given the opportunity to interact with our students. I would definitely find out about any "club" that has the potential to be destructive. We created situations where the skills and aptitudes of our special needs students were spotlighted; they then invited typical peers to join them. Almost everyone wants to share in a success, so our students' peers joined in and the prejudice and malice diminished.

SARA VINCENT • Special Education
Langley High School, McLean, VA

Discrimination and racism often occur because of ignorance. The best solution to minimize discrimination is educating individuals about diverse cultures. The teacher can invite the new student's family into the classroom to talk about their backgrounds and experiences, or she can have the entire class complete a project on family history. Once the other students in the classroom learn more about the new student's culture, they will be more likely to accept her differences and understand that she is not much different from them. In addition, the teacher can have the new student be team leader at recess or in the classroom so that she will not be picked last. This will help her gain confidence in befriending her peers. While the teacher attempts to focus on positive aspects of educating her students, she should make the administration aware of the "White Girls Club" situation. Administrators should intervene and bring attention to the situation if the troubling behaviors of the other girls continue.

Part 2
LEARNING AND MOTIVATION

Chapter 7–9 taken from chapters 10–12 of *Educational Psychology*, Twelfth Edition by Anita Woolfolk

chapter seven
THE LEARNING SCIENCES AND CONSTRUCTIVISM

▶ **TEACHERS' CASEBOOK:** Learning to Cooperate

You want to use cooperative learning with your middle-school students. Many students have worked in groups, but few seem to have participated in true cooperative learning. When you surveyed the class members about their experiences, most rolled their eyes and groaned. You take it that their experiences have not been very positive. These students have a wide range of abilities, including some who are truly gifted and talented, several who are just learning English, and a few who are very shy; and then there are others who would take over and dominate every discussion if you let them. You believe that collaboration is a crucial 21st century skill for all students and that learning together can deepen understanding as students question, explain, and build on each other's thinking. No matter what, you want the experience of learning together to build your students' confidence and your sense of efficacy as a teacher, so you want authentic successes.

CRITICAL THINKING

- How would you begin to introduce cooperative learning to your students?
- What tasks will you choose to start?
- How will you establish groups?
- What will you watch and listen for to be sure the students are making the most of the experience?

OVERVIEW AND OBJECTIVES

For past chapters, we have analyzed different aspects of learning. We considered behavioral, information processing, and cognitive science explanations of what and how people learn. We have examined complex cognitive processes such as metacognitive skills and problem solving. These explanations of learning focus on the individual and what is happening in his or her "head." In this chapter, we expand our investigation of learning to include insights from a relatively recent interdisciplinary approach called the *learning sciences*. This approach brings together work in many fields that study learning, including educational psychology, computer science, neuroscience, and anthropology. One of the foundations of the learning sciences is constructivism, a broad perspective that calls attention to two critical aspects of learning: social and cultural factors. In this chapter, we examine the role of other people and the cultural context in learning. Sociocultural constructivist theories have roots in cognitive perspectives, but have moved well beyond these early explanations. We will explore a number of teaching strategies and approaches that are consistent with cognitive perspectives—inquiry, problem-based learning, cooperative learning, cognitive apprenticeships, and service learning. Finally, we will examine learning in this digital age, including the considerations about learning in technology-rich environments.

By the time you have completed this chapter, you should be able to:

Objective 7.1:   Describe the collaborative approach that led to the interdisciplinary field of learning sciences.

Objective 7.2:   Explain different perspectives on constructivism as a theory of learning and teaching.

Objective 7.3:   Identify the common elements in most contemporary constructivist theories.

Objective 7.4:   Apply constructivist principles to classroom practice.

Objective 7.5:   Evaluate the use of community-based activities/service learning.

Objective 7.6:   Describe positive and negative influences of technology on the learning and development of children and adolescents.

THE LEARNING SCIENCES

In previous chapters, psychologists were responsible for most of the theory and research we discussed. But many other people have also studied learning: Today, there are multiple perspectives included in the learning sciences.

What Are the Learning Sciences?

The interdisciplinary field of the **learning sciences** encompasses research in psychology, education, computer science, philosophy, sociology, anthropology, neuroscience, and other fields that study learning. You already have explored some of the foundations of the learning sciences, including the make-up of working memory and the role of cognitive load in learning; how information is represented in complex structures such as schemas; what experts know and how their knowledge is different from that of novices; metacognition; problem solving; thinking and reasoning; and how knowledge transfers (or doesn't transfer) from the classroom to the world beyond.

No matter what their focus, all knowledge workers in the learning sciences are interested in how deep knowledge in subjects like science, mathematics, and literacy is actually acquired and applied in the real world of scientists and mathematicians and writers. In the *Cambridge Handbook of Learning Sciences*, R. Keith Sawyer (2006) contrasts what it takes for deep learning to occur with traditional classroom practices that have dominated schooling in many countries for decades. Look at Table 7.1 to see the differences.

Basic Assumptions of the Learning Sciences

Even though the different fields in the learning sciences approach their study from varying perspectives, there is growing agreement about some basic assumptions (Sawyer, 2006):

- **Experts have deep conceptual knowledge.** Experts know many facts and procedures, but just learning facts and procedures will not make you an expert. Experts have deep conceptual understanding that allows them to put their knowledge into action; they are able to apply and modify their knowledge to fit each situation. Experts' deep conceptual knowledge generates problem finding and problem solving.
- **Learning comes from the learner.** Better instruction alone will not transfer deep understandings from teachers to students. Learning is more than receiving and processing information transmitted by teachers or texts. Rather, students must actively participate in their own personal construction of knowledge. We are knowledge inventors, not copy machines (de Koek, Sleegers, & Voeten, 2004).
- **Schools must create effective learning environments.** It is the job of the school to create environments where students are active in constructing their own deep understandings so they can reason about real-world problems and transfer their learning from school to their lives beyond the school walls.
- **Prior knowledge is key.** Students come into our classrooms filled with knowledge and beliefs about how the world works. Some of these preconceptions are right, some are part right, and some are wrong. If teaching does not begin with what the students "know," then the students will learn what it takes to pass the test, but their knowledge and beliefs about the world will not change.

Learning sciences An interdisciplinary science of learning, based on research in psychology, education, computer science, philosophy, sociology, anthropology, neuroscience, and other fields that study learning.

250

TABLE 7.1 • **How Deep Learning Contrasts with Learning in Traditional Classrooms**

LEARNING IN TRADITIONAL CLASSROOMS	BUT FINDINGS FROM COGNITIVE SCIENCE SHOW THAT DEEP LEARNING REQUIRES THAT:
Class material is not related to what students already know. Example: Teacher says, "Igneous rocks are . . .	Learners relate new understandings to what they already know and believe. Example: Teacher says, "Have any of you seen granite counter tops on TV home shows or maybe you have one in your house? What do they look like . . .?"
Class material presented and learned as disconnected bits of knowledge. "The definition of metamorphic rocks is. . . ."	Learners integrate and interconnect their knowledge in expanding conceptual systems. "We already have learned about two kinds of rocks. We also learned last week about how the earth has changed over the centuries, with some ocean floors becoming land areas. Today we will learn about how marble and diamonds. . . . "
Lessons involve memorizing facts and doing procedures without understanding how or why. "To divide fractions, invert and multiply . . ."	Learners search for patterns and recognize or invent underlying principles. "Remind me what it means to divide. . . . Ok, so ¾ divided by ½ means how many sets of what are in. . . .?
Learners have trouble understanding ideas that are not straight from the textbook or explained in the same way. "What does your textbook say about . . ."	Learners evaluate new ideas, even if not in the text, and integrate them into their thinking. "On TV yesterday there was a story about a new drug that is effective in curing one out of 8 cases of. . . . What is the probability of a cure?"
Authorities and experts are the source of unchanging and accurate facts and procedures. "Scientists agree. . . ."	Learners understand that knowledge is socially constructed by people, so ideas require critical examination. "Here is an excerpt from the Presidential debates last week. Let's think about how you would determine what statements are more supported by evidence . . .?"
Learners simply memorize everything instead of thinking about the purpose of learning and the best strategies for that purpose. "This will be on the test."	Learners think about why they are learning, monitor their understanding, and reflect on their own learning processes. "How could you use this concept in your own life? How can you tell if you are understanding it?"

Source: Based on Sawyer, K. (2006). The new science of learning. In R. K. Sawyer (Ed.). The Cambridge handbook of the learning sciences (p. 4). New York: The Cambridge University Press. New York: Oxford University Press.

- **Reflection is necessary to develop deep conceptual knowledge.** Students need to express and perform the knowledge they are developing through writing, conversations, drawings, projects, skits, portfolios, reports, and so on. But the performance is not enough. To develop deep conceptual knowledge, students need to reflect—thoughtfully analyze their own work and progress.

Embodied Cognition

Recently a new theme has emerged in the cognitive and learning sciences—**embodied cognition.** This is awareness that "the way we think about and represent information reflects the fact that we need to interact with the world" (Ashcraft & Radvansky, 2010, p. 32).

Embodied cognition Theory stating that cognitive processes develop from real-time, goal-directed interactions between humans and their environment.

These interactions occur through our senses and bodies, and the way our bodies interact with the world to achieve our goals affects our thinking. In other words, our cognitive processes have deep roots in the interactions of our bodies with the real world—what develops cognitively depends on our sensorimotor engagement with the world. In this view of cognition, the body, not the mind, is primary, but the body needs the mind to successfully interact in the world. In some ways, this perspective is similar to Piaget's idea that thinking emerges early on from the infant's sensorimotor interaction in the world. Instead of being just simple conduits for outside world sounds and images, our senses and motor responses are central to how we think. So we have to understand how our physical body interacts with the world in order to understand our mind (Wilson, 2002).

Actually, it appears that humans are capable of both real-time, situation-by-situation, adaptive, ever-changing interactions (where the *mind is serving the body* to succeed, for example, driving in traffic or doing a jigsaw puzzle) and abstract thinking using symbols and representations developed in earlier times to solve current problems (where *the body—brain control system—is serving the mind*, for example, *in using images or analogies to learn a new language*). Humans' ability to mentally represent and manipulate symbols that are not present in real time is critical. In fact, Margret Wilson (2002) suggests:

> This takeover by the mind, and the concomitant ability to mentally represent what is distant in time or space, may have been one of the driving forces behind the runaway train of human intelligence that separated us from other hominids. (p. 635)

In educational psychology, these fundamental assumptions of the learning sciences and embodied cognition all lead to the conclusion that thinking is constructive. In the next section we look at both cognitive and social constructivism—topics you will hear about repeatedly in your preparation for teaching.

COGNITIVE AND SOCIAL CONSTRUCTIVISM

Consider this situation:

> A young child who has never been to the hospital is in her bed in the pediatric wing. The nurse at the station down the hall calls over the intercom above the bed, "Hi Chelsea, how are you doing? Do you need anything?" The girl looks puzzled and does not answer. The nurse repeats the question with the same result. Finally, the nurse says emphatically, "Chelsea, are you there? Say something!" The little girl responds tentatively, "Hello wall—I'm here."

Chelsea encountered a new situation—a talking wall. The wall is persistent. It sounds like a grown-up wall. She shouldn't talk to strangers, but she is not sure about walls. She uses what she knows and what the situation provides to construct meaning and to act.

Here is another example of constructing meaning. This time, Kate and her 9-year-old son Ethan co-construct understandings as they buy groceries:

Ethan: (running to get a shopping cart) Do we need the big one?

Kate: We might—better too big than not big enough. Here is our list—where do we go first?

Ethan: We need ice cream for the party! (Ethan heads toward frozen foods)

Kate: Whoa! What happened to the ice cream carton you left out on the kitchen counter?

Ethan: It melted and it wasn't out that long. I promise!

Kate: Right and we may be in this store a while, so let's start with things that won't melt while we are shopping—I usually buy produce first.

Ethan: What's "produce"?

Kate: Things that grow—fruits and vegetables "produced" by farmers.

Ethan: OK, the list says cucumbers. Here they are. Wait there are two kinds. Which do you want? The little ones say "local." What's local?

Kate: Local means from around here—close to us, close to our "location." Hmmm.— the big ones are 75 cents *each* and these smaller ones are $1.15 *a pound*. How would you decide which is a better deal?.

Ethan: I guess bigger is better, right? Or is local better?

Kate: Well, I wonder if they cost the same for the amount you get—per pound. How could you figure that out?

Ethan: I don't know—the price for a pound isn't on the big ones, just the price each.

Kate: When the doctor wants to know how many pounds you weigh, she puts you on a scale. What if you weighed a big cucumber over there on that food scale?

Ethan: OK—it weighs ½ a pound.

Kate: So half a pound costs 75 cents—what would a whole pound cost—that's 2 halves make a whole?

Ethan: 75 cents plus 75 cents—$1.50—Gee the bigger ones are more expensive. So the smaller ones are better and they are "local"—that's good too, right?

Kate: Maybe. I like to support our local farmers. Where are the small cucumbers from—look at the tiny print on the label.

Ethan: Virginia—is that close to us?

Kate: Not really—it is about a 6-hour drive from here…

Look at the knowledge being co-constructed about planning ahead, vocabulary, math, problem solving, and even geography. Constructivist theories of learning focus on how people make meaning, both on their own like Chelsea and in interaction with others like Ethan.

Constructivist Views of Learning

Constructivism is a broad term used by philosophers, curriculum designers, psychologists, educators, and others. Ernst von Glasersfeld calls it "a vast and woolly area in contemporary psychology, epistemology, and education" (1997, p. 204). Constructivist perspectives are grounded in the research of Piaget; Vygotsky; the Gestalt psychologists; Bartlett, Bruner, and Rogoff; as well as the philosophy of John Dewey and the work in anthropology of Jean Lave, to mention just a few intellectual roots.

There is no one constructivist theory of learning, but most constructivist theories agree on two central ideas:

Central Idea 1: Learners are active in constructing their own knowledge.
Central Idea 2: Social interactions are important in this knowledge construction process (Bruning, Schraw, & Norby, 2011).

Constructivist approaches in science and mathematics education, in educational psychology and anthropology, and in computer-based education all embrace these two ideas. But even though many psychologists and educators use the term *constructivism*, they often mean very different things (Martin, 2006; McCaslin & Hickey, 2001; Phillips, 1997).

One way to organize constructivist views is to talk about two forms of constructivism: psychological and social construction (Palincsar, 1998; Phillips, 1997). We could oversimplify a bit and say that psychological constructivists focus on how individuals use information, resources, and even help from others to build and improve their mental models and problem-solving strategies—see Central Idea #1. In contrast, social constructivists view learning as increasing our abilities to participate with others in activities that are meaningful in the culture—see Central Idea #2 (Windschitl, 2002). Let's look a bit closer at each type of constructivism.

PSYCHOLOGICAL/INDIVIDUAL/COGNITIVE CONSTRUCTIVISM. Many psychological theories include some kind of constructivism because these theories embrace the idea that individuals construct their own cognitive structures as they interpret their experiences in particular situations (Palincsar, 1998). These psychological constructivists "are concerned

Constructivism View that emphasizes the active role of the learner in building understanding and making sense of information.

CONSTRUCTIVIST VIEWS Constructivist theories are based on the ideas that learners actively develop their knowledge, rather than passively receive it, in package form, from teachers or outside sources.

with how individuals build up certain elements of their cognitive or emotional apparatus" (Phillips, 1997, p. 153). Because they study individual knowledge, beliefs, self-concept, or identity, they are sometimes called *individual constructivists* or *cognitive constructivists;* they all focus on the inner psychological life of people. When Chelsea talked to the wall in the previous section, she was making meaning using her own individual knowledge and beliefs about how to respond when someone (or something) talks to you. She was using what she knew to impose intellectual structure on her world (Piaget, 1971; Windschitl, 2002). When children observe that most plants need soil to grow and then conclude that plants "eat dirt," they are using what they know about how eating supports life to make sense of plant growth (Linn & Eylon, 2006).

Using these standards, the most recent information processing theories are constructivist because they are concerned with how individuals construct internal representations (propositions, images, concepts, schemas) that can be remembered and retrieved (Mayer, 1996). The outside world is viewed as a source of input, but once the sensations are perceived and enter working memory, the important work is assumed to be happening "inside the head" of the individual (Schunk, 2012; Vera & Simon, 1993). Some psychologists, however, believe that information processing is "trivial" or "weak" constructivism because the individual's only constructive contribution is to build accurate internal representations of the outside world (Derry, 1992; Garrison, 1995; Marshall, 1996; Windschitl, 2002).

In contrast, Piaget's psychological (cognitive) constructivist perspective is less concerned with "correct" representations and more interested in meaning as it is constructed by the individual. As we saw in Chapter 1, Piaget proposed that as children develop, their thinking becomes more organized and adaptive and less tied to concrete events. Piaget's special concern was with logic and the construction of universal knowledge that cannot be learned directly from the environment—knowledge such as conservation or reversibility (Miller, 2011). Such knowledge comes from reflecting on and coordinating our own cognitions or thoughts, not from mapping external reality. Piaget saw the social environment as an important factor in development, but did not believe that social interaction was the main mechanism for changing thinking (Moshman, 1997). Some educational and developmental psychologists have referred to Piaget's kind of constructivism as **first wave constructivism** or "solo" constructivism, with its emphasis on Central Idea 1, individual meaning making (DeCorte, Greer, and Verschaffel, 1996; Paris, Byrnes, & Paris, 2001).

At the extreme end of individual constructivism is the notion of **radical constructivism.** This perspective holds that there is no reality or truth in the world, only the individual's perceptions and beliefs. Each of us constructs meaning from our own experiences, but we have no way of understanding or "knowing" the reality of others (Woods & Murphy, 2002). A difficulty with this position is that, when pushed to the extreme of relativism, all knowledge and all beliefs are equal because they are all valid individual perceptions. There are problems with this thinking for educators. First, teachers have a professional responsibility to emphasize some values, such as honesty or justice, over others, such as bigotry and deception. All perceptions and beliefs are not equal. As teachers, we ask students to work hard to learn. If learning cannot advance understanding because all understandings are equally good, then, as David Moshman (1997) notes, "we might just as well let students continue to believe whatever they believe" (p. 230). Also, it appears that some knowledge, such as

First wave constructivism A focus on the individual and psychological sources of knowing, as in Piaget's theory.

Radical constructivism Knowledge is assumed to be the individual's construction; it cannot be judged right or wrong.

counting and one-to-one correspondence, is not constructed, but universal. Knowing one-to-one correspondence is part of being human (Geary, 1995; Schunk, 2012).

VYGOTSKY'S SOCIAL CONSTRUCTIVISM.   As you also saw in Chapter 1, Vygotsky emphasized Central Idea 2 above, that social interaction, cultural tools, and activity shape individual development and learning, just as Ethan's interactions and activities in the grocery store with his mother shaped his learning about anticipating possible consequences (running out of space in the shopping cart and melted ice cream), the meaning of "produce" and "local," how to calculate price per pound, and geography (Martin, 2006). By participating in a broad range of activities with others, learners *appropriate* the outcomes produced by working together; these outcomes could include both new strategies and knowledge. **Appropriating** means being able to reason, act, and participate using cultural tools—for example, using conceptual tools such as "force" and "acceleration" to reason in physics (Mason, 2007). In psychological (cognitive) constructivism, learning means individually possessing knowledge, but in social constructivism, learning means belonging to a group and participating in the social construction of knowledge (Mason, 2007). Putting learning in social and cultural contexts is known as **second wave constructivism** (Paris, Byrnes, & Paris, 2001).

Because his theory relies heavily on social interactions and the cultural context to explain learning, most psychologists classify Vygotsky as a social constructivist (Palincsar, 1998; Prawat, 1996). However, some theorists categorize him as a psychological constructivist because he was primarily interested in development within the individual (Moshman, 1997; Phillips, 1997). In a sense, Vygotsky was both. One advantage of Vygotsky's theory of learning is that it gives us a way to consider both the psychological and the social: He bridges both camps. For example, Vygotsky's concept of the *zone of proximal development*—the area in which a child can solve a problem with the help (scaffolding) of an adult or more able peer—has been called a place where culture and cognition create each other (Cole, 1985). Culture creates cognition when the adult uses tools and practices from the culture (language, maps, computers, looms, or music) to steer the child toward goals the culture values (reading, writing, weaving, dance). Cognition creates culture as the adult and child together generate new practices and problem solutions to add to the cultural group's repertoire (Serpell, 1993). So people are both products and producers of their societies and cultures (Bandura, 2001). One way of integrating individual and social constructivism is to think of knowledge as both *individually constructed* and *socially mediated* (Windschitl, 2002).

The term **constructionism** is sometimes used to describe how public knowledge is created. Although this is not our main concern in educational psychology, it is worth a quick look.

CONSTRUCTIONISM.   Social constructionists do not focus on individual learning. Their concern is how public knowledge in disciplines such as science, math, economics, or history is constructed. Beyond this kind of academic knowledge, constructionists also are interested in how common-sense ideas, everyday beliefs, and commonly held understandings about people and the world are communicated to new members of a sociocultural group (Gergen, 1997; Phillips, 1997). Questions raised might include who determines what constitutes history, what is the proper way to behave in public, or how to get elected class president. Social constructionists believe all knowledge is socially constructed, and, more important, some people have more power than others to define what constitutes such knowledge. Relationships between and among teachers, students, families, and the community are the central issues. Collaboration to understand diverse viewpoints is encouraged, and traditional bodies of knowledge often are challenged (Gergen, 1997). The philosophies of Jacques Dierrida and Michel Foucault are important sources for constructionists. Vygotsky's theory, with its attention to the way cognition creates culture, has some elements in common with constructionism.

These different perspectives on constructivism raise some general questions, and they disagree on the answers. These questions can never be fully resolved, but different theories tend to favor different positions. Let's consider the questions.

Appropriating Being able to internalize or take for yourself knowledge and skills developed in interaction with others or with cultural tools.

Second wave constructivism A focus on the social and cultural sources of knowing, as in Vygotsky's theory.

Constructionism How public knowledge in disciplines such as science, math, economics, or history is constructed.

How Is Knowledge Constructed?

One tension among different approaches to constructivism is based on how knowledge is constructed. Moshman (1982) describes three explanations.

1. *The realities and truths of the external world direct knowledge construction.* Individuals reconstruct outside reality by building accurate mental representations such as propositional networks, concepts, cause-and-effect patterns, and condition-action production rules that reflect "the way things really are." The more the person learns, the deeper and broader his or her experience is, the closer that person's knowledge is to objective reality. Information processing holds this view of knowledge (Cobb & Bowers, 1999).

2. *Internal processes such as Piaget's organization, assimilation, and accommodation direct knowledge construction.* New knowledge is abstracted from old knowledge. Knowledge is not a mirror of reality, but rather an abstraction that grows and develops with cognitive activity. Knowledge is not true or false; it just grows more internally consistent and organized with development.

3. *Both external and internal factors direct knowledge construction.* Knowledge grows through the interactions of internal (cognitive) and external (environmental and social) factors. Vygotsky's description of cognitive development through the appropriation and use of cultural tools such as language is consistent with this view (Bruning, Schraw, & Norby, 2011). Another example is Bandura's theory of reciprocal interactions among people, behaviors, and environments described in Chapter 8 (Schunk, 2012). Table 7.2 summarizes the three general explanations about how knowledge is constructed.

TABLE 7.2 • **How Knowledge Is Constructed**

TYPE	ASSUMPTIONS ABOUT LEARNING AND KNOWLEDGE	EXAMPLE THEORIES
External Direction	Knowledge is acquired by constructing a representation of the outside world. Direct teaching, feedback, and explanation affect learning. Knowledge is accurate to the extent that it reflects the "way things really are" in the outside world.	Information processing
Internal Direction	Knowledge is constructed by transforming, organizing, and reorganizing previous knowledge. Knowledge is not a mirror of the external world, even though experience influences thinking and thinking influences knowledge. Exploration and discovery are more important than teaching.	Piaget
Both External and Internal Direction	Knowledge is constructed based on social interactions and experience. Knowledge reflects the outside world as filtered through and influenced by culture, language, beliefs, interactions with others, direct teaching, and modeling. Guided discovery, teaching, models, and coaching as well as the individual's prior knowledge, beliefs, and thinking affect learning.	Vygotsky

Knowledge: Situated or General?

A second question that cuts across many constructivist perspectives is whether knowledge is internal, general, and transferable, or bound to the time and place in which it is constructed. Psychologists who emphasize the social construction of knowledge and situated learning affirm Vygotsky's notion that learning is inherently social and embedded in a particular cultural setting (Cobb & Bowers, 1999). What is true in one time and place—such as the "fact" before Columbus's time that the earth was flat—becomes false in another time and place. Particular ideas may be useful within a specific **community of practice**, such as 15th-century navigation, but useless outside that community. What counts as new knowledge is determined in part by how well the new idea fits with current accepted practice. Over time, the current practice may be questioned and even overthrown, but until such major shifts occur, current practice will shape what is considered valuable.

Situated learning emphasizes that learning in the real world is not like studying in school. It is more like an apprenticeship where novices, with the support of an expert guide and model, take on more and more responsibility until they are able to function independently. Proponents of this view believe situated learning explains learning in factories, around the dinner table, in high school halls, in street gangs, in the business office, and on the playground.

Situated learning is often described as "enculturation," or adopting the norms, behaviors, skills, beliefs, language, and attitudes of a particular community. The community might be mathematicians or gang members or writers or students in your 8th grade class or soccer players—any group that has particular ways of thinking and doing. Knowledge is viewed not as individual cognitive structures, but rather as a creation of the community over time. The practices of the community—the ways of interacting and getting things done, as well as the tools the community has created—constitute the knowledge of that community. Learning means becoming more able to participate in those practices and use the tools (Greeno, Collins, & Resnick, 1996; Mason, 2007; Rogoff, 1998).

At the most basic level, "situated learning emphasizes the idea that much of what is learned is specific to the situation in which it is learned" (Anderson, Reder, & Simon, 1996, p. 5). Thus, some would argue, learning to do calculations in school may help students do more school calculations, but it may not help them balance a checkbook, because the skills can be applied only in the context in which they were learned—namely school (Lave, 1997; Lave & Wenger, 1991). But it also appears that knowledge and skills can be applied across contexts that were not part of the initial learning situation, as when you use your ability to read and calculate to do your income taxes, even though income tax forms were not part of your high school curriculum (Anderson, Reder, & Simon, 1996).

Learning that is situated in school does not have to be doomed or irrelevant (Bereiter, 1997). As you saw in Chapter 9, a major question in educational psychology—and education in general—concerns the transfer of knowledge from one situation to another. How can you encourage this transfer from one situation to another? Help is on the way in the next section.

Common Elements of Constructivist Student-Centered Teaching

- -

STOP & THINK What makes a lesson student centered? List the characteristics and features that put the student in the center of learning. •

- -

We have looked at some areas of disagreement among the constructivist perspectives, but what about areas of agreement? All constructivist theories assume that knowing develops as learners, like Chelsea and Ethan, try to make sense of their experiences. "Learners, therefore, are not empty vessels waiting to be filled, but rather active organisms seeking meaning" (Driscoll, 2005, p. 487). Humans construct mental models or schemas and continue to revise them to make better sense of their experiences. Again, we are knowledge inventors, not filing cabinets. Our constructions do not necessarily resemble external

Community of practice Social situation or context in which ideas are judged useful or true.

Situated learning The idea that skills and knowledge are tied to the situation in which they were learned and that they are difficult to apply in new settings.

Connect and Extend to PRAXIS II™

Student-Centered Learning (II, A3)
Many of the major initiatives to reform content-area curricula (e.g., science, mathematics) emphasize student-centered/constructivist approaches to learning. Describe the major principles of these approaches and explain how they differ from teacher-centered approaches.

reality; rather, they are our unique interpretations, like Chelsea's friendly, persistent wall. This doesn't mean that all constructions are equally useful or viable. Learners test their understandings against experience and the understandings of other people—they negotiate and co-construct meanings like Ethan did with his mother.

Constructivists share similar goals for learning. They emphasize knowledge *in use* rather than the *storing* of inert facts, concepts, and skills. Learning goals include developing abilities to find and solve ill-structured problems, critical thinking, inquiry, self-determination, and openness to multiple perspectives (Driscoll, 2005). Even though there is no single constructivist theory, many constructivist approaches recommend five conditions for learning:

1. Embed learning in complex, realistic, and relevant learning environments.
2. Provide for social negotiation and shared responsibility as a part of learning.
3. Support multiple perspectives and use multiple representations of content.
4. Nurture self-awareness and an understanding that knowledge is constructed.
5. Encourage ownership in learning. (Driscoll, 2005; Marshall, 1992)

Before we discuss particular teaching approaches, let's look more closely at these dimensions of constructivist teaching.

Complex learning environments Problems and learning situations that mimic the ill-structured nature of real life.

Social negotiation Aspect of learning process that relies on collaboration with others and respect for different perspectives.

Intersubjective attitude A commitment to build shared meaning with others by finding common ground and exchanging interpretations.

COMPLEX LEARNING ENVIRONMENTS AND AUTHENTIC TASKS.   Constructivists believe that students should not be given stripped-down, simplified problems and basic skills drills, but instead should encounter **complex learning environments** that deal with "fuzzy," ill-structured problems. The world beyond school presents few simple problems or step-by-step directions, so schools should be sure that every student has experience solving complex problems. Complex problems are not just difficult ones; rather, they have many parts. There are multiple, interacting elements in complex problems and multiple possible solutions. There is no one right way to reach a conclusion, and each solution may bring a new set of problems.

These complex problems should be embedded in authentic tasks and activities, the kinds of situations that students would face as they apply what they are learning to the real world (Needles & Knapp, 1994). Students may need support (*scaffolding*) as they work on these complex problems, with teachers helping them find resources, keeping track of their progress, breaking larger problems down into smaller ones, and so on. This aspect of constructivist approaches is consistent with situated learning in emphasizing learning in situations where the knowledge will be applied.

SOCIAL NEGOTIATION.   Many constructivists share Vygotsky's belief that higher mental processes develop through **social negotiation** and interaction, so collaboration in learning is valued. A major goal of teaching is to develop students' abilities to establish and defend their own positions while respecting the positions of others and working together to negotiate or co-construct meaning. To accomplish this exchange, students must talk and listen to each other. It is a challenge for children in cultures that are individualistic and competitive, such as the United States, to adopt what has been called an **intersubjective attitude**—a commitment to build shared meaning by finding common ground and exchanging interpretations.

MULTIPLE PERSPECTIVES AND REPRESENTATIONS OF CONTENT.   When students encounter only one model, one analogy, one way of understanding complex content, they often oversimplify

AUTHENTIC TASKS AND SOCIAL INTERACTIONS Constructivist approaches recommend that educators emphasize complex, realistic, and relevant learning environments, as well as the importance of social interactions in the learning process. For example, the students here are collaborating to create a household budget.

as they try to apply that one approach to every situation. I saw this happen in my educational psychology class when six students were presenting an example of guided discovery learning. The students' presentation was a near copy of a guided discovery demonstration I had given earlier in the semester, but with some major misconceptions. My students knew only one way to represent discovery learning. Resources for the class should have provided **multiple representations of content** using different analogies, examples, and metaphors. This idea is consistent with Jerome Bruner's (1966) **spiral curriculum,** a structure for teaching that introduces the fundamental structure of all subjects—the "big ideas"—early in the school years, then revisits the subjects in more and more complex forms over time.

UNDERSTANDING THE KNOWLEDGE CONSTRUCTION PROCESS. Constructivist approaches emphasize making students aware of their own role in constructing knowledge. The assumptions we make, our beliefs, and our experiences shape what each of us comes to "know" about the world. Different assumptions and different experiences lead to different knowledge, as we saw in Chapter 6 when we explored the role of cultural differences in shaping knowledge. If students are aware of the influences that shape their thinking, they will be more able to choose, develop, and defend positions in a self-critical way while respecting the positions of others.

STUDENT OWNERSHIP OF LEARNING. "While there are several interpretations of what [constructivist] theory means, most agree that it involves a dramatic change in the focus of teaching, putting the students' own efforts to understand at the center of the educational enterprise" (Prawat, 1992, p. 357). Student ownership does not mean that the teacher abandons responsibility for instruction. Because the design of teaching is a central issue in this book, we will spend the rest of this chapter discussing examples of *ownership of learning* and *student-centered instruction.*

APPLYING CONSTRUCTIVIST PERSPECTIVES

Even though there are many applications of constructivist views of learning, we can recognize constructivist approaches by the activities of the teacher and the students. Mark Windschitl (2002) suggests that the following activities encourage meaningful learning:

- Teachers elicit students' ideas and experiences in relation to key topics, then fashion learning situations that help students elaborate on or restructure their current knowledge.
- Students are given frequent opportunities to engage in complex, meaningful, problem-based activities.
- Teachers provide students with a variety of information resources as well as the tools (technological and conceptual) necessary to mediate learning.
- Students work collaboratively and are given support to engage in task-oriented dialogue with one another.
- Teachers make their own thinking processes explicit to learners and encourage students to do the same through dialogue, writing, drawings, or other representations.
- Students are routinely asked to apply knowledge in diverse and authentic contexts, explain ideas, interpret texts, predict phenomena, and construct arguments based on evidence, rather than focus exclusively on the acquisition of predetermined "right answers."
- Teachers encourage students' reflective and autonomous thinking in conjunction with the conditions listed above.
- Teachers employ a variety of assessment strategies to understand how students' ideas are evolving and to give feedback on the processes as well as the products of their thinking. (p. 137)

In addition, constructivist approaches include **scaffolding** to support students' developing expertise. One implication of Vygotsky's theory of cognitive development is that deep understanding requires that students grapple with problems in their zone of

Multiple representations of content Considering problems using various analogies, examples, and metaphors.

Spiral curriculum Bruner's design for teaching that introduces the fundamental structure of all subjects early in the school years, then revisits the subjects in more and more complex forms over time.

Scaffolding Teachers and students make meaningful connections between what the teacher knows and what the students know and need in order to help the students learn more.

proximal development; they need scaffolding in order to work in that zone. Here is a good definition of scaffolding that emphasizes the dynamic interactive nature of scaffolding as well as the knowledge that both teacher and student bring—both are experts on something: "Scaffolding is a powerful conception of teaching and learning in which teachers and students create meaningful connections between teachers' cultural knowledge and the everyday experience and knowledge of the student" (McCaslin & Hickey, 2001, p. 137). Look back at the grocery store conversation between Ethan and his mother at the beginning of the previous section. Notice how the mother used the melted ice cream on the kitchen counter and the scale in the doctor's office—connections to Ethan's experience and knowledge—to scaffold Ethan's understanding.

Even though there are different views of scaffolding, most educational psychologists agree on three characteristics (van de Pol, Volman, & Beishuizen, 2010):

1. **Contingency Support**: The teacher is constantly adjusting, differentiating, and tailoring responses to the student.
2. **Fading**: The teacher gradually withdraws support as the student's understanding and skills deepen.
3. **Transferring Responsibility**: Students assume more and more responsibility for their own learning.

In the next sections, we will examine three specific teaching approaches that put the student at the center and provide scaffolding: inquiry and problem-based learning, cognitive apprenticeships, and cooperative learning.

Inquiry and Problem-Based Learning

Connect and Extend to PRAXIS II™

Inquiry Learning (II, A2, 3)
Inquiry learning is a student-centered approach to learning that predates many "traditional" forms of instruction. Describe the basic structure of this approach to learning. What are its strengths and limitations? What roles does the teacher have?

John Dewey described the basic **inquiry learning** format in 1910. There have been many adaptations of this strategy, but the form usually includes the following elements (Echevarria, 2003; Lashley, Matczynski, & Rowley, 2002). The teacher presents a puzzling event, question, or problem. The students:

- formulate hypotheses to explain the event or solve the problem,
- collect data to test the hypotheses,
- draw conclusions, and
- reflect on the original problem and the thinking processes needed to solve it.

EXAMPLES OF INQUIRY. Shirley Magnusson and Annemarie Palincsar have developed a teachers' guide for planning, implementing, and assessing different phases of inquiry science units, called *Guided Inquiry Supporting Multiple Literacies or GIsML* (Hapgood, Magnusson, & Palincsar, 2004; Palincsar, Magnusson, Collins, & Cutter, 2001; Palincsar, Magnusson, Marano, Ford, & Brown, 1998). The teacher first identifies a curriculum area and some general guiding questions, puzzles, or problems. For example, the teacher chooses *communication* as the area and asks this general question: "How and why do humans and animals communicate?" Next, several specific focus questions are posed. "How do whales communicate?" "How do gorillas communicate?" The focus questions have to be carefully chosen to guide students toward important understandings. One key idea in understanding animal communication is the relationship among the animal's structures, survival functions, and habitat. Animals have specific *structures* such as large ears or echo-locators, which function to find food, attract mates, or identify predators, and these structures and functions are related to the animals' *habitats—large ears for navigating in the dark for example*. Thus, focus questions must ask about animals with different structures for communication, different functional needs for survival, and different habitats. Questions about animals with the same kinds of structures or the same habitats would not be good focus points for inquiry (Magnusson & Palincsar, 1995).

The next phase is to engage students in the inquiry, perhaps by playing different animal sounds, having students make guesses and claims about communication, and asking the students questions about their guesses and claims. Then, the students conduct both first-hand and second-hand investigations. First-hand investigations are direct experiences and experiments, for example, measuring the size of bats' eyes and ears in

Inquiry learning Approach in which the teacher presents a puzzling situation and students solve the problem by gathering data and testing their conclusions.

relation to their bodies (using pictures or videos—not real bats!). In second-hand investigations, students consult books, the Internet, interviews with experts, and other resources to find specific information or get new ideas. As part of their investigating, the students begin to identify patterns. The curved line in Figure 7.1 shows that cycles can be repeated. In fact, students might go through several cycles of investigating, identifying patterns, and reporting results before moving on to constructing explanations and making final reports. Another possible cycle is to evaluate explanations before reporting by making and then checking predictions, applying the explanation to new situations.

Inquiry teaching allows students to learn content and process at the same time. In the examples given above, students learned about how animals communicate and how structures are related to habitats. In addition, they learned the inquiry process itself—how to solve problems, evaluate solutions, and think critically.

PROBLEM-BASED LEARNING. Whereas inquiry learning grew out of practices in science, problem-based learning grew out of research on expert knowledge in medicine (Schmidt, van der Molen, te Winkel, & Wijnen, 2009). The goals of **problem-based learning** are to help students develop knowledge that is useful and flexible, not inert. Inert knowledge is information that is memorized but seldom applied (Cognition and Technology Group at Vanderbilt [CTGV], 1996; Whitehead, 1929). Other goals of problem-based learning are to enhance intrinsic motivation and skills in problem solving, collaboration, evidence-based decision making, and self-directed lifelong learning.

In problem-based learning, students are confronted with a problem that launches their inquiry as they collaborate to find solutions. The students identify and analyze the problem based on the facts from the scenario; and then they begin to generate hypotheses about solutions. As they suggest hypotheses, they identify missing information—what do they need to know to test their solutions? This launches a phase of research. Then,

Connect and Extend to PRAXIS II™

Discovery Learning (I, A1)
Many teachers, especially in mathematics and science, believe that meaningful learning in their areas is best supported by discovery learning. Be prepared to answer questions about the assumptions, techniques, strengths, and limitations of this instructional strategy.

FIGURE 7.1

A MODEL TO GUIDE TEACHER THINKING ABOUT INQUIRY-BASED SCIENCE INSTRUCTION

The straight lines show the sequence of phases in instruction and the curved lines show cycles that might be repeated during instruction.

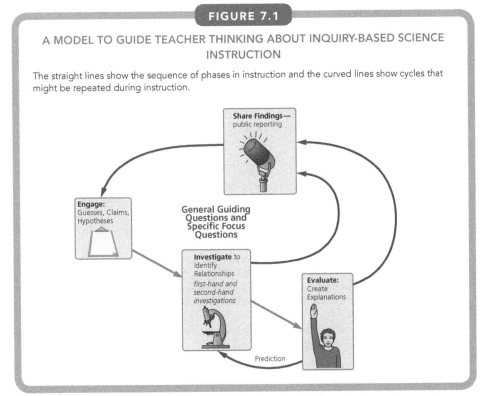

Source: Based on "Designing a Community of Practice: Principles and Practices of the GisML Community," by A. S. Palincsar, S. J. Magnusson, N. Marano, D. Ford, and N. Brown, 1998, Teaching and Teacher Education, 14, p. 12. Adapted with permission from Elsevier.

Problem-based learning
Methods that provide students with realistic problems that don't necessarily have "right" answers.

students apply their new knowledge, evaluate their problem solutions, recycle to research again if necessary, and finally reflect on the knowledge and skills they have gained. Throughout the entire process, students are not alone or unguided. Their thinking and problem solving is scaffolded by the teacher, computer software supports, models, coaching, expert hints, guides and organizational aids, or other students in the collaborative groups—so working memory is not overloaded. For example, as students work, they may have to fill in a diagram that helps them distinguish between "claims" and "reasons" in a scientific argument (Derry, Hmelo-Silver, Nagarajan, Chernobilsky, & Beitzel, 2006; Hmelo-Silver, Ravit, & Chinn, 2007).

In true problem-based learning, the problem is real and the students' actions matter. For example, during the 2010 Deepwater oil spill, many teachers used the problem as a springboard for learning. Their students researched how this spill compared to others in size, location, costliness, causes, and attempted solutions. What could be done? How do currents and tides play a role? What locations, businesses, and wildlife are in the greatest danger? What will the short-term and long-term financial and environmental impacts be? What actions can students take to play a positive role? A number of teachers blogged about using the oil spill in problem-based learning and collected resources for other teachers (see http://www.edutopia.org/blog/oil-spill-project-based-learning-resources).

Some problems are not authentic because they do not directly affect the students' lives, but they are engaging. For example, in a computer simulation called the *River of Life Challenge* (Sherwood, 2002), students meet Billy and his lab partner Suzie, who are analyzing the quality of water from a local river. Suzie is concerned that Billy's conclusions are careless and incomplete. Billy is challenged to research the issue in more depth by the *Legacy League*, a multi-ethnic group of characters who raise questions and direct Billy and Suzie to helpful resources so they can research the answers. The format for the challenge in the STAR Legacy Cycle includes six phases: encounter the challenge, generate ideas, consider multiple perspectives, research and revise your ideas, test your mettle (check your understanding), and go public about your conclusions. Undergraduate science education students who used this simulation improved their graph-reading skills as well as their conceptual understanding of several topics such as the composition of air and classes of organisms in a river ecosystem (Kumar & Sherwood, 2007).

Let's look at these phases more closely as they might take place in an upper-level science class (Klein & Harris, 2007).

1. The cycle begins with an *intriguing challenge* to the whole class. For example, in biomechanics it might be "Assume you are a living cell in a bioreactor. What things will influence how long you live?" or "Your grandmother is recovering from a broken hip. In which hand should she hold the cane to help her balance?" The question is framed in a way that makes students bring to bear their current knowledge and pre-conceptions.
2. Next, students *generate ideas* to compile what they currently know and believe using individual, small-group, or whole-group brainstorming or other activities.
3. *Multiple perspectives* are added to the process in the form of outside experts (live, on video, or from texts), Web sites, magazine or journal articles, or a CD on the subject. In the river challenge above, the Legacy League guided Billy and Suzie to explore multiple perspectives.
4. Students go deeper to *research and revise*. They consult more sources or hear class lectures, all the while revising ideas and perhaps journaling about their thinking.
5. Students *test their mettle* by getting feedback from other students or the teacher about their tentative conclusions. Some formative (ungraded) tests might check their understanding at this point.
6. Students *go public* with their final conclusions and solutions in the form of an oral presentation, poster/project, or final exam.

Project-based science is a multimedia learning environment similar to problem-based learning that focuses on K-12 grades (Krajcik & Czerniak, 2007). MyProject is a web-based science learning environment used in college (Papanikolaou & Boubouka, 2011). The teacher's role in problem-based learning is to identify engaging problems and appropriate resources, orient students to the problem by describing objectives and rationales; organize the students by helping them set goals and define tasks; support, coach, and mentor students as they gather information, craft solutions, and prepare artifacts (models, reports, videos, PowerPoints, portfolios, etc.); and support student reflection on their own learning outcomes and processes (Arends & Kilcher, 2010).

RESEARCH ON INQUIRY AND PROBLEM-BASED LEARNING.   Does using inquiry or problem-based learning activities lead to greater achievement? The debate has waged for years. Some research results say "yes." For example, using an open-ended and software-supported inquiry science approach called GenScope™ that explores genetics, students in high school science classrooms learned significantly more compared to students in traditional classrooms (Hickey et al., 1999, 2000). In a study of almost 20,000 middle-school students in a large urban district who used inquiry-based materials, those who participated in inquiry learning had significantly higher passing rates on standardized tests. African American boys especially benefited from these methods (Geier et al., 2008). Several other studies point to increases in student engagement and motivation with inquiry learning (Hmelo-Silver et al., 2007), as long as the learning is supported and students have adequate background knowledge. But not every educational psychologist agrees that problem-based learning is valuable, at least for all students, as you can see in the *Point/Counterpoint* on the next page.

Another constructivist approach that relies heavily on scaffolding is cognitive apprenticeships.

Cognitive Apprenticeships and Reciprocal Teaching

Over the centuries, apprenticeships have proved to be an effective form of education. By working alongside a master and perhaps other apprentices, young people have learned many skills, trades, and crafts. Knowledgeable guides provide models, demonstrations, and corrections, as well as a personal bond that is motivating. The performances required of the learner are real and important and grow more complex as the learner becomes more competent (Collins, 2006; Linn & Eylon, 2006; Hung, 1999). With *guided participation* in real tasks comes *participatory appropriation*—students appropriate the knowledge, skills, and values involved in doing the tasks (Rogoff, 1995, 1998). In addition, both the newcomers to learning and the old-timers contribute to the community of practice by mastering and remastering skills—and sometimes improving these skills in the process (Lave & Wenger, 1991).

Allan Collins (2006) suggests that knowledge and skills learned in school have become too separated from their use in the world beyond school. To correct this imbalance, some educators recommend that schools adopt many of the features of apprenticeships. But rather than learning to sculpt or dance or build a cabinet, apprenticeships in school would focus on cognitive objectives such as reading comprehension, writing, or mathematical problem solving. There are many **cognitive apprenticeship** models, but most share six features:

- Students observe an expert (usually the teacher) *model* the performance.
- Students get external support through *coaching* or tutoring (including hints, tailored feedback, models, and reminders).
- Students receive conceptual *scaffolding*, which is then gradually faded as the student becomes more competent and proficient.
- Students continually *articulate* their knowledge—putting into words their understanding of the processes and content being learned.
- Students *reflect* on their progress, comparing their problem solving to an expert's performance and to their own earlier performances.
- Students are required to *explore* new ways to apply what they are learning—ways that they have not practiced at the master's side.

As students learn, they are challenged to master more complex concepts and skills and to perform them in many different settings.

Cognitive apprenticeship A relationship in which a less experienced learner acquires knowledge and skills under the guidance of an expert.

POINT/COUNTERPOINT: Are Inquiry and Problem-Based Learning Effective Teaching Approaches?

Inquiry, discovery learning, and problem-based learning are very appealing, but are they effective? Specifically, does problem-based learning lead to deep understanding for most students?

POINT

▶ **Problem-Based Learning is overrated.** Paul Kirschner and his colleagues were clear and critical in their article in the *Educational Psychologist*. Even the title of the article was blunt: "Why minimal guidance during instruction does not work: An analysis of the failure of constructivist, discovery, problem-based, experiential, and inquiry-based teaching." They argued:

Although unguided or minimally guided instructional approaches are very popular and intuitively appealing, the point is made that these approaches ignore both the structures that constitute human cognitive architecture and evidence from empirical studies over the past half-century that consistently indicate that minimally guided instruction is less effective and less efficient than instructional approaches that place a strong emphasis on guidance of the student learning process. (Kirschner, Sweller, & Clark, 2006, p. 75)

These respected researchers (and others more recently) cited decades of research demonstrating that unguided discovery/inquiry and problem-based learning are ineffective, especially for students with limited prior knowledge (Kalyuga, 2011; Klahr & Nigam, 2004; Tobias, 2010). Louis Alfieri and his colleagues (2011) examined the results from 108 studies going back over 50 years and found that explicit teaching was more beneficial than unassisted discovery, especially for studies published in the most well-rated journals. Their conclusion: "unassisted discovery generally does not benefit learning" (p. 12).

But what about problem-based learning in particular? Much of the research on problem-based learning has taken place in medical schools, and results have been mixed. In one study, students learning through problem-based instruction were better at clinical skills such as problem formation and reasoning, but they were worse in their basic knowledge of science and felt less prepared in science (Albanese & Mitchell, 1993). A review of problem-based learning curricula in medical schools concluded that this approach was not effective in promoting higher levels of student knowledge (Colliver, 2000).

COUNTERPOINT

▶ **Problem-Based Learning is a powerful teaching approach.** Problem-based learning has some advantages. In another study, medical students who learned with problem-based approaches created more accurate and coherent solutions to medical problems (Hmelo, 1998). In an extensive study of a problem-based medical program in the Netherlands, Schmidt and his colleagues (2009) concluded that, compared to graduates of conventional programs, graduates of the problem-based learning program performed better in practical medical and interpersonal skills, took less time to graduate, and had small positive differences in their medical knowledge and diagnostic reasoning. MBA students who learned a concept using problem-based methods were better at explaining the concept than students who had learned the concept from lecture and discussion (Capon & Kuhn, 2004). Students who are better at self-regulation may

---

How can teaching provide cognitive apprenticeships? Mentoring in teaching is one example. Another is cross-age grouping. In the Key School, an inner-city public elementary school in Indianapolis, Indiana, students of different ages work side by side for part of every day on a "pod" designed to have many of the qualities of an apprenticeship. The pods might focus on a craft or a discipline. Examples include gardening, architecture, and "making money." Many levels of expertise are evident in the students of different ages, so students can move at a comfortable pace, but still have the model of a master available. Community volunteers, including many parents, visit to demonstrate a skill that is related to the pod topic.

Alan Schoenfeld's (1989, 1994) teaching of mathematical problem solving is another example of the cognitive apprenticeship instructional model.

COGNITIVE APPRENTICESHIPS IN READING: RECIPROCAL TEACHING. The goal of **reciprocal teaching** is to help students understand and think deeply about what they read (Palincsar, 1986; Palincsar & Brown, 1984, 1989). To accomplish this goal, students in small reading groups learn four strategies: *summarizing* the content of a passage, *asking a question* about the central point, *clarifying* the difficult parts of the material, and *predicting* what will come next. These are strategies skilled readers apply almost automatically, but poor readers seldom do—or they don't know how. To use the strategies effectively, poorer readers need direct instruction, modeling, and practice in actual reading situations.

First, the teacher introduces these strategies, perhaps focusing on one strategy each day. As the expert, the teacher explains and models each strategy and encourages

Reciprocal teaching Designed to help students understand and think deeply about what they read.

benefit more from problem-based methods (Evensen, Salisbury-Glennon, & Glenn, 2001), but using problem-based methods over time can help all students to develop self-directed learning skills.

Cindy Hmelo-Silver (2004; Hmelo-Sliver et al., 2007) reviewed the research and found good evidence that problem-based learning supports the construction of flexible knowledge and the development of problem-solving and self-directed learning skills, but there is less evidence that participating in problem-based learning is intrinsically motivating or that it teaches students to collaborate. In studies of high school economics and mathematics, recent research favors problem-based approaches for learning more complex concepts and solving multistep word problems.

Beware of Either/Or. You don't have to choose between inquiry and content-focused methods. The best approach in elementary and secondary schools may be a balance of content-focused and inquiry or problem-based methods. For example, Eva Toth, David Klahr, and Zhe Chen (2000) tested a balanced approach for teaching 4th graders how to use the controlled variable strategy in science to design good experiments. The method had three phases: (1) in small groups, students conducted exploratory experiments to identify variables that made a ball roll farther down a ramp; (2) the teacher led a discussion, explained the controlled variable strategy, and modeled good thinking about experiment design; and (3) the students designed and conducted application experiments to isolate which variables caused the ball to roll farther. The combination of inquiry, discussion, explanation, and modeling was successful in helping the students understand the concepts. Clearly scaffolding supports are key factors in successful inquiry and problem-based learning.

The difference seems to come down to completely unguided discovery versus guided, supported, and well-scaffolded inquiry. Alfieri and his colleagues (2011) concluded:

> Overall, the effects of unassisted-discovery tasks seem limited, whereas enhanced-discovery tasks requiring learners to be actively engaged and constructive seem optimal. On the basis of the current analyses, optimal approaches should include at least one of the following: (a) guided tasks that have scaffolding in place to assist learners, (b) tasks requiring learners to explain their own ideas and ensuring that these ideas are accurate by providing timely feedback, or (c) tasks that provide worked examples of how to succeed in the task. (p. 13)

student apprentices to practice. Next, the teacher and the students read a short passage silently. Then, the teacher again provides a model by summarizing, questioning, clarifying, or predicting based on the reading. Everyone reads another passage, and the students gradually begin to assume the teacher's role. The teacher becomes a member of the group, and may finally leave, as the students take over the teaching. Often, the students' first attempts are halting and incorrect. But the teacher gives clues, guidance, encouragement, support doing parts of the task (such as providing question stems), modeling, and other forms of scaffolding to help the students master these strategies. The goal is for students to learn to apply these strategies independently as they read so they can make sense of text.

APPLYING RECIPROCAL TEACHING.   Although reciprocal teaching seems to work with almost any age student, most of the research has been done with younger adolescents who can read aloud fairly accurately, but who are far below average in reading comprehension. After 20 hours of practice with this approach, many students who were in the bottom quarter of their class moved up to the average level or above on tests of reading comprehension. Palincsar has identified three guidelines for effective reciprocal teaching ("When Student Becomes Teacher," 1986):

1. *Shift gradually.* The shift from teacher to student responsibility must be gradual.
2. *Match demands to abilities.* The difficulty of the task and the responsibility must match the abilities of each student and grow as these abilities develop.

NURTURING INDEPENDENT READERS The concept of scaffolding and gradually moving the student toward independent and fluid reading comprehension is a critical component in reciprocal teaching and cognitive apprenticeships.

3. *Diagnose thinking.* Teachers should carefully observe the "teaching" of each student for clues about how the student is thinking and what kind of instruction he or she needs.

In contrast to some approaches that try to teach 40 or more strategies, an advantage of reciprocal teaching is that it focuses attention on four powerful strategies. But these strategies must be taught—not all students develop them on their own. One study of reciprocal teaching spanning over three years found that questioning was the strategy used most often, but that students had to be taught how to ask higher-level questions because most student questions were literal or superficial (Hacker & Tenent, 2002). Another advantage of reciprocal teaching is that it emphasizes practicing these four strategies in the context of actual reading—reading literature and reading texts. Finally, the idea of scaffolding and gradually moving the student toward independent and fluid reading comprehension is a critical component in reciprocal teaching and cognitive apprenticeships in general (Rosenshine & Meister, 1994).

Collaboration and Cooperation

Even with all the concern today about academic standards, performance on proficiency tests, and international comparisons of student achievement, schooling has always been about more than academic learning. Of course, academics are the prime directive, but an education also prepares students to live and work cooperatively with all kinds of people:

> Most corporations are looking for employees who are not only good at the mastery of a particular set of academic skills but who also have the ability to work harmoniously with a wide variety of coworkers as a cooperative team, to demonstrate initiative and responsibility, and to communicate effectively. (Aronson, 2000, p. 91)

For the past four decades, researchers have examined collaboration and cooperation in schools. Although there are some inconsistencies, the majority of the studies indicate that truly cooperative groups have positive effects—from preschool to college—on students' empathy, tolerance for differences, feelings of acceptance, friendships, self-confidence, awareness of the perspectives of others, higher-level reasoning, problem solving, and even school attendance (Galton, Hargreaves, & Pell, 2009; Gillies & Boyle, 2011; Solomon, Watson, & Battistich, 2001). It is even argued that cooperative learning experiences are crucial in preventing many of the social problems that plague children and adolescents (Gillies, 2003, 2004).

Connect and Extend to PRAXIS II™

Characteristics of Cooperative Learning (II, A2)
Many instructional strategies labeled as *cooperative learning* lack one or more qualities that are essential components of such techniques. List those essential qualities and explain the role of each.

Collaboration A philosophy about how to relate to others—how to learn and work.

Cooperation Way of working with others to attain a shared goal.

COLLABORATION, GROUP WORK, AND COOPERATIVE LEARNING. The terms *collaboration*, *group work*, and *cooperative learning* often are used as if they mean the same thing. Certainly there is some overlap, but there are differences as well. The distinctions between collaboration and cooperation are not always clear. Ted Panitz (1996) suggests **collaboration** is a philosophy about how to relate to others—how to learn and work. Collaboration is a way of dealing with people that respects differences, shares authority, and builds on the knowledge that is distributed among other people. **Cooperation**, on the other hand, is a way of working with others to attain a shared goal (Gillies, 2003). Collaborative learning has roots in the work of British teachers who wanted their students to respond to literature in more active ways as they learned. Cooperative learning has American roots in the work of psychologists John Dewey and Kurt Lewin. You could say that *cooperative* learning is one way to *collaborate* in schools.

Group work, on the other hand, is simply several students working together—they may or may not be cooperating. Many activities can be completed in groups. For example, students can work together to conduct a local survey. How do people feel about the plan to build a new mall that will bring more shopping and more traffic? Would the community support or oppose the building of a nuclear power plant? If students must learn 10 new definitions in a biology class, why not let them divide up the terms and definitions and teach one another? Be sure, however, that everyone in the group can handle the task. Sometimes, one or two students end up doing the work of the entire group.

Group work can be useful, but true cooperative learning requires much more than simply putting students in groups and dividing up the work. Angela O'Donnell and Jim O'Kelly, colleagues of mine from Rutgers University, describe a teacher who claimed to be using "cooperative learning" by asking students to work in pairs on a paper, each writing one part. Unfortunately, the teacher allowed no time to work together and provided no guidance or preparation in cooperative social skills. Students got a grade for their individual part and a group grade for the whole project. One student received an A for his part, but a C for the group project because his partner earned

COOPERATION: A WORTHY GOAL While academics are the key goal, education also prepares students to live and work cooperatively with all kinds of people. Studies of cooperative learning indicate its positive influence on students' empathy, tolerance, friendships, self-confidence, and even school attendance.

an F—he never turned in any work. So one student was punished with a C for a situation he could not control while the other was rewarded with a C for doing no work at all. This was not cooperative learning—it wasn't even group work (O'Donnell & O'Kelly, 1994).

BEYOND GROUPS TO COOPERATION. David and Roger Johnson (2009a), two of the founders of cooperative learning in the United States, define formal **cooperative learning** as "students working together, for one class period to several weeks, to achieve shared learning goals and complete jointly specific tasks and assignments" (p. 373). Cooperative learning has a long history in American education, moving in and out of favor over the years. Today, evolving constructivist perspectives have fueled a growing commitment to learning situations that rely on elaboration, interpretation, explanation, and argumentation— that is, cooperative learning (Webb & Palincsar, 1996, p. 844). David and Roger Johnson (2009a) note:

> From being discounted and ignored, cooperative learning has steadily progressed to being one of the dominant instructional practices throughout the world. Cooperative learning is now utilized in schools and universities throughout most of the world in every subject area and from preschool through graduate school and adult training programs. (p. 365)

Different learning theory approaches favor cooperative learning for different reasons (O'Donnell, 2002, 2006). Information processing theorists point to the value of group discussion in helping participants rehearse, elaborate, and expand their knowledge. As group members question and explain, they have to organize their knowledge, make connections, and review—all processes that support information processing and memory. Advocates of a Piagetian perspective suggest the interactions in groups can create the cognitive conflict and disequilibrium that lead an individual to question his or her understanding and try out new ideas—or, as Piaget (1985) said, "to go beyond his current state and strike out in new directions" (p. 10). Those who favor Vygotsky's theory suggest that social interaction is important for learning because higher mental functions such as reasoning, comprehension, and critical thinking originate in social interactions and are then appropriated and internalized by individuals. Students can accomplish mental tasks with social support before they can do them alone. Thus, cooperative learning provides the social support and scaffolding students need to move learning forward. To benefit from these dimensions of cooperative learning, groups must be cooperative—all members must participate. But, as any teacher or parent knows, cooperation is not automatic when students are put into groups.

Cooperative learning Situations in which elaboration, interpretation, explanation, and argumentation are integral to the activity of the group and where learning is supported by other individuals.

WHAT CAN GO WRONG: MISUSES OF GROUP LEARNING. Without careful planning and monitoring by the teacher, group interactions can hinder learning and reduce rather than improve social relations in classes (Gillies & Boyle, 2011). For example, if there is pressure in a group for conformity—perhaps because rewards are being misused or one student dominates the others—interactions can be unproductive and unreflective. Misconceptions might be reinforced, or the worst, not the best, ideas may be combined to construct a superficial or even incorrect understanding (Battistich, Solomon, & Delucci, 1993). Students who work in groups but arrive at wrong answers may be more confident that they are right—a case of "two heads are worse than one" (Puncochar & Fox, 2004). Also, the ideas of low-status students may be ignored or even ridiculed while the contributions of high-status students are accepted and reinforced, regardless of the merit of either set of ideas (Anderson, Holland, & Palincsar, 1997; Cohen, 1986). Mary McCaslin and Tom Good (1996) list several other disadvantages of group learning:

- Students often value the process or procedures over the learning. Speed and finishing early take precedence over thoughtfulness and learning.
- Rather than challenging and correcting misconceptions, students support and reinforce misunderstandings.
- Socializing and interpersonal relationships may take precedence over learning.
- Students may simply shift dependency from the teacher to the "expert" in the group—learning is still passive and what is learned can be wrong.
- Status differences may be increased rather than decreased. Some students learn to "loaf" because the group progresses with or without their contributions. Others become even more convinced that they are unable to understand without the support of the group.

The next sections examine how teachers can avoid these problems and encourage true cooperation.

Tasks for Cooperative Learning

Like so many other decisions in teaching, plans for using cooperative groups begin with a goal. What are students supposed to accomplish? Successful teachers interviewed in one study emphasized that group activities must be well planned, students need to be prepared to work in groups, and teachers' expectations for the task have to be explicitly stated (Gillies & Boyle, 2011). What is the task? Is it a true group task—one that builds on the knowledge and skills of several students—or is the task more appropriate for individuals (Cohen, 1994; O'Donnell, 2006)?

Tasks for cooperative groups may be more or less structured. Highly structured tasks include work that has specific answers—drill and practice, applying routines or procedures, answering questions from readings, computations in mathematics, and so on. Ill-structured complex tasks have multiple answers and unclear procedures, requiring problem finding and higher-order thinking. These ill-structured problems are true group tasks; that is, they are likely to require the resources (knowledge, skills, problem-solving strategies, creativity) of all the group members to accomplish, whereas individuals often can accomplish highly structured tasks just as effectively as groups. These distinctions are important because ill-structured, complex, true group tasks appear to require more and higher-quality interactions than routine tasks if learning and problem solving are to occur (Cohen, 1994; Gillies, 2004; Gillies & Boyle, 2011).

HIGHLY STRUCTURED, REVIEW, AND SKILL-BUILDING TASKS. A relatively structured task such as reviewing previously learned material for an exam might be well served by a structured technique such as STAD (Student Teams Achievement Divisions), in which teams of four students compete to determine which team's members can amass the greatest improvement over previous achievement levels (Slavin, 1995). Praise, recognition, or extrinsic rewards can enhance motivation, effort, and persistence under these conditions, and thus increase learning. Focusing the dialogue by assigning narrow roles also may help students stay engaged when the tasks involve practice or review.

ILL-STRUCTURED, CONCEPTUAL, AND PROBLEM-SOLVING TASKS. If the task is ill structured and more cognitive in nature, then an open exchange and elaborated discussion will be more helpful (Cohen, 1994; Ross & Raphael, 1990). Thus, strategies that encourage extended and productive interactions are appropriate when the goal is to develop higher-order thinking and problem solving. In these situations, a tightly structured process, competition among groups for rewards, and rigid assignment of roles are likely to inhibit the richness of the students' interactions and to interfere with progress toward the goal. Open-ended techniques such as reciprocal questioning (King, 1994), reciprocal teaching (Palincsar & Brown, 1984; Rosenshine & Meister, 1994), pair-share (Kagan, 1994), or Jigsaw (Aronson, 2000) should be more productive because, when used appropriately, they encourage more extensive interaction and elaborative thought in situations where students are being exposed to complex materials. In these instances, the use of rewards may well divert the group away from the goal of in-depth cognitive processing. When rewards are offered, the goal often becomes achieving the reward as efficiently as possible, which could mean having the highest achieving students do all the work (Webb & Palincsar, 1996).

SOCIAL SKILLS AND COMMUNICATION TASKS. When the goal of peer learning is enhanced social skills or increased intergroup understanding and appreciation of diversity, the assignment of specific roles and functions within the group might support communication (Cohen, 1994; Kagan, 1994). In these situations, it can be helpful to rotate leadership roles so that minority group students and females have the opportunity to demonstrate and develop leadership skills; in addition, all group members can experience the leadership capabilities of each individual (Miller & Harrington, 1993). Rewards probably are not necessary, and they may actually get in the way because the goal is to build community, a sense of respect, and responsibility for all team members.

Preparing Students for Cooperative Learning

David and Roger Johnson (2009a) explain five elements that define true cooperative learning groups:

- Positive interdependence
- Promotive interaction
- Individual accountability
- Collaborative and social skills
- Group processing

Group members experience *positive interdependence*. The members believe they can attain their goals only if the others in the group attain their goals as well, so they need each other for support, explanations, and guidance. *Promotive interaction* means that group members encourage and facilitate each other's efforts. They usually interact face to face and close together, not across the room, but they also could interact via digital media around the world. Even though they feel a responsibility to the group to work together and help each other, students must ultimately demonstrate learning on their own; they are held *individually accountable* for learning, often through individual tests or other assessments. *Collaborative and social skills* are necessary for effective group functioning. Often, these skills, such as giving constructive feedback, reaching consensus, and involving every member, must be taught and practiced before the groups tackle a learning task. Finally, members monitor *group processes* and relationships to make sure the group is working effectively and to learn about the dynamics of groups. They take time to ask, "How are we doing as a group? Is everyone working together? What should we do more or less of next time?"

Research in grades 8 through 12 in Australia found that students in cooperative groups that were structured to require positive interdependence and mutual helping learned more in math, science, and English than students in unstructured learning groups (Gillies, 2003). In addition, compared to students in the unstructured groups, students in the structured groups also said learning was more fun.

SETTING UP COOPERATIVE GROUPS. How large should a cooperative group be? Again, the answer depends on your learning goals. If the purpose is for the group members to review, rehearse information, or practice, 4 to 5 or 6 students is about the right size. But if the goal is to encourage each student to participate in discussions, problem solving, or computer learning, then groups of 2 to 4 members work best. Also, when setting up cooperative groups, it often makes sense to balance the number of boys and girls. Some research indicates that when there are just a few girls in a group, they tend to be left out of the discussions unless they are the most able or assertive members. By contrast, when there are only one or two boys in the group, they tend to dominate and be "interviewed" by the girls unless these boys are less able than the girls or are very shy. In some studies, but not all, of mixed-gender groups, girls avoided conflict and boys dominated discussion (O'Donnell & O'Kelly, 1994; Webb & Palincsar, 1996). Whatever the case, teachers must monitor groups to make sure everyone is contributing and learning.

If a group includes some students who are perceived as different or who are often rejected, then it makes sense to be sure that there are group members who are tolerant and kind. One successful teacher interviewed by Gillies and Boyle (2011) put it this way:

> I also try to make sure that there are one or two people in the group who have the ability to be tolerant. At least the kid in question will know that, while the other group members may not be his best friends, they won't give him a hard time. I try to put the least reactive kids in the group with the child in question. This year I've had a couple of girls who have been very good with difficult kids. They don't put up with nonsense but they don't over-react and are prepared to demonstrate some good social skills. (p. 72)

GIVING AND RECEIVING EXPLANATIONS. In practice, the effects of learning in a group vary, depending on what actually happens in the group and who is in it. If only a few people take responsibility for the work, these people will learn, but the nonparticipating members probably will not. Students who ask questions, get answers, and attempt explanations are more likely to learn than students whose questions go unasked or unanswered. In fact, there is evidence that the more a student provides elaborated, thoughtful explanations to other students in a group, the more the *explainer* learns. Giving good explanations appears to be even more important for learning than receiving explanations (O'Donnell, 2006; Webb, Farivar, & Mastergeorge, 2002). In order to explain, you have to organize the information, put it into your own words, think of examples and analogies (which connect the information to things you already know), and test your understanding by answering questions. These are excellent learning strategies (King, 1990, 2002; O'Donnell & O'Kelly, 1994).

Good explanations are relevant, timely, correct, and elaborated enough to help the listener correct misunderstandings; the best explanations tell why (Webb et al., 2002; Webb & Mastergeorge, 2003). For example, in a middle-school mathematics class, students worked in groups on the following problem:

> Find the cost of a 30-minute telephone call to the prefix 717 where the first minute costs $0.22 and each additional minute costs $0.13.

The level of explanation and help students received was significantly related to learning; the higher the level of explanation, the more learning took place. Table 7.3 shows the different levels of help. Of course, the students must pay attention to and use the help in order to learn. And the help-receiver also has responsibilities if learning is to go well. For example, if a helper says, "13 times 29," then the receiver should say, "Why is it 29?" Asking good questions and giving clear explanations are critical, and usually these skills must be taught.

ASSIGNING ROLES. Some teachers assign roles to students to encourage cooperation and full participation. Several roles are described in Table 7.4. If you use roles, be sure that they support learning. In groups that focus on social skills, roles should support listening, encouragement, and respect for differences. In groups that focus on practice, review, or mastery of basic skills, roles should support persistence, encouragement, and participation.

TABLE 7.3 • **Levels of Help in Cooperative Groups**

Students are more likely to learn if they give and get higher-level help.

LEVEL	DESCRIPTION AND EXAMPLE
Highest	
6	Verbally labeled explanation of how to solve part or all of the problem ("Multiply 13 cents by 29, because 29 minutes are left after the first minute.")
5	Numerical rule with no verbal labels for the numbers ("This is 30, so you minus 1.")
4	Numerical expression or equation ("13 times 29.")
3	Numbers to write or copy ("Put 13 on top, 29 on the bottom. Then you times it.")
2	Answer to part or all of the problem ("I got $3.77.")
1	Non-content or non-informational response ("Just do it the way she said.")
0	No response
Lowest	

Source: Adapted from Webb, N M., Troper, J. D., & Fall, R. (1995). Constructive activity and learning in collaborative small groups. Journal of Educational Psychology, 87, p. 411.

In groups that focus on higher-order problem solving or complex learning, roles should encourage thoughtful discussion, sharing of explanations and insights, probing, brainstorming, and creativity. Make sure that you don't communicate to students that the major purpose of the groups is simply to do the procedures—the roles. Roles are supports for learning, not ends in themselves (Woolfolk Hoy & Tschannen-Moran, 1999).

Often, cooperative learning strategies include group reports to the entire class. If you have been on the receiving end of these class reports, you know that they can be

TABLE 7.4 • **Possible Student Roles in Cooperative Learning Groups**

Depending on the purpose of the group and the age of the participants, having these assigned roles might help students cooperate and learn. Of course, students may have to be taught how to enact each role effectively, and roles should be rotated so students can participate in different aspects of group learning.

ROLE	DESCRIPTION
Encourager	Encourages reluctant or shy students to participate
Praiser/Cheerleader	Shows appreciation of others' contributions and recognizes accomplishments
Gate Keeper	Equalizes participation and makes sure no one dominates
Coach	Helps with the academic content, explains concepts
Question Commander	Makes sure all students' questions are asked and answered
Checker	Checks the group's understanding
Taskmaster	Keeps the group on task
Recorder	Writes down ideas, decisions, and plans
Reflector	Keeps group aware of progress (or lack of progress)
Quiet Captain	Monitors noise level
Materials Monitor	Picks up and returns materials

Source: Based on Cooperative Learning by S. Kagan. Published by Kagan Publishing, San Clemente, CA. Copyright © 1994 by Kagan Publishing.

deadly dull. To make the process more useful for the audience as well as the reporters, Annemarie Palincsar and Leslie Herrenkohl (2002) taught the class members to use *intellectual roles* as they listened to reports. These roles were based on the scientific strategies of predicting and theorizing, summarizing results, and relating predictions and theories to results. Some audience members were assigned the role of checking the reports for clear relationships between predictions and theories. Other students in the audience listened for clarity in the findings. And the rest of the students were responsible for evaluating how well the group reports linked prediction, theories, and findings. Research shows that using these roles promotes class dialogue, thinking and problem solving, and conceptual understanding (Palincsar & Herrenkohl, 2002). Table 7.5 summarizes the considerations in designing cooperative learning, based on the goals of the group.

TABLE 7.5 • **What Should You Consider in Planning and Doing Cooperative Learning?**

CONSIDERATIONS	SOCIAL SKILLS TASKS: TEAM BUILDING, COOPERATION SKILLS	STRUCTURED TASKS: REVIEW, PRACTICE FACTS, AND SKILLS	UNSTRUCTURED TASKS: CONCEPTUAL, PROBLEM SOLVING, THINKING AND REASONING
Group Size and Composition	2–5 students, common interest groups, mixed groups, random groups	2–4 students, mixed ability, high with medium and medium with low	2–4 students, select members to encourage interaction
Why Assign Roles?	to monitor participation and conflict, rotate leadership	to monitor engagement and ensure low-status students have resources to offer, i.e., Jigsaw	roles may interfere—use only to encourage interaction, divergent thinking, and extended, connected discourse, i.e., debate sides, group facilitator
Extrinsic Rewards/ Incentives	not necessary, may be helpful	to support motivation, effort, persistence	not necessary
Teacher's Role	model, encourager	model, director, coach	model facilitator
Student Skills Needed	listening, turn-taking, encouraging, managing conflict	questioning, explaining, encouraging, content knowledge, learning strategies	questioning, explaining, elaborating, probing, divergent thinking, providing rationales, synthesizing
What Supports Learning? Watch and Listen for...	modeling and practice	giving multiple, elaborated explanations, attention and practice	quantity and quality of interactions, using and connecting knowledge resources, probing, and elaboration
Potential Problems	unproductive conflict, nonparticipation	poor help-giving skills, disengaged or excluded students	disengaged or excluded students, cognitive loafing, superficial thinking, avoiding controversy
Averting Problems	simpler task, direct teaching of social skills, team building, conflict resolution skills, discuss group process	structure interdependence and individual accountability, teach helping and explaining	structure controversy, assign "thinking roles," allow adequate time
Small Start	one or two skills, i.e., listening and paraphrasing	pairs of students quizzing each other	numbered heads together

Source: From "Implications of cognitive approaches to peer learning for teacher education," by A. Woolfolk Hoy & M. Tschannen-Moran in *Cognitive perspectives on peer learning*, A. O'Donnell and A. King (Eds.), 1999, p. 278. Adapted with permission of Taylor and Francis Group, LLC, a division of Imforma plc.

TABLE 7.6 • **Question Stems to Encourage Dialogue in Reciprocal Questioning**

After participating in a lesson or studying an assignment on their own, students use these stems to develop questions, create and compare answers, and collaborate to create the best response.

What is an everyday application of ...?
How would you define .... in your own words.?
What are the advantages and disadvantages of ...?
What do you already know about ...?
Explain why .... applies to ....?
How does ..... influence ......?
What is the value of ...?
What are the reasons for ....?
What are some arguments for and against .....?
What is the your first choice about ...? Your second choice? ....? Why?
What is the best ... and why?
Compare ... and ... based only on ....
How would .... be different if ....?
Do you agree or disagree with this claim ...? What is your evidence?

Designs for Cooperation

Developing deep understandings in cooperative groups requires that all the group members *participate* in *high-quality discussions*. Discussions that support learning include talk that interprets, connects, explains, and uses evidence to support arguments. We now turn to different strategies that build in structures to support both participation and high-quality discussions.

RECIPROCAL QUESTIONING.   **Reciprocal questioning** requires no special materials or testing procedures and can be used with a wide range of ages. After a lesson or presentation by the teacher, students work in pairs or triads to ask and answer questions about the material (King, 1990, 1994, 2002). The teacher provides question stems (see Table 7.6), and then students are taught how to develop specific questions on the lesson material using the generic question stems. The students create questions, and then take turns asking and answering. This process has proved more effective than traditional discussion groups because it seems to encourage deeper thinking about the material. Questions such as those in Table 7.6, which encourage students to make connections between the lesson and previous knowledge or experience, seem to be the most helpful.

For example, using question stems like those in Table 7.6, a small group in Mr. Garcia's 9th grade world cultures class had the following discussion about the concept of culture:

Sally: In your own words, what does culture mean?

Jim: Well, Mr. Garcia said in the lesson that a culture is the knowledge and understandings shared by the members of a society. I guess it's all the things and beliefs and activities that people in a society have in common. It includes things like religion, laws, music, medical practices, stuff like that.

Sally: And dance, art, family roles.

Barry: Knowledge includes language. So, I guess cultures include language, too.

Jim: I guess so. Actually, I have a question about that: How does a culture influence the language of a society?

Barry: Well, for one thing, the language is made up of words that are important to the people of that culture. Like, the words name things that the people care about, or need, or use. And so, different cultures would have different vocabularies. Some cultures may not even have a word for *telephone,* because they don't have any. But, phones are important in our culture, so we have lots of different words for phones, like *cell phone, digital phone, desk phone, cordless phone, phone machine,* and . . .

Reciprocal questioning Students work in pairs or triads to ask and answer questions about lesson material.

Jim (laughing): I'll bet desert cultures don't have any words for *snow* or *skiing.*

Sally (turning to Barry): What's your question?

Barry: I've got a great question! You'll never be able to answer it. What would happen if there were a group somewhere without any spoken language? Maybe they were all born not being able to speak, or something like that. How would that affect their culture, or could there even be a culture?

Sally: Well, it would mean they couldn't communicate with each other.

Jim: And they wouldn't have any music! Because they wouldn't be able to sing.

Barry: But wait! Why couldn't they communicate? Maybe they would develop a nonverbal language system, you know, the way people use hand signals, or the way deaf people use sign language. (King, 2002, pp. 34–35)

JIGSAW. Elliot Aronson and his graduate students invented the **Jigsaw Classroom** when Aronson was a professor of social psychology (and I was a student) at the University of Texas at Austin. Some of my friends worked on his research team. Aronson developed the approach "as a matter of absolute necessity to help defuse a highly explosive situation" (Aronson, 2000, p. 137). The Austin schools had just been desegregated by court order. White, African American, and Hispanic students were together in classrooms for the first time. Hostility and turmoil ensued, with fistfights in corridors and classrooms. Aronson's answer was the Jigsaw Classroom.

In Jigsaw, each group member is given part of the material to be learned by the whole group. Students become "expert" on their piece. Because students have to learn and be tested on every piece of the larger "puzzle," everyone's contribution is important—the students truly are interdependent. A more recent version, Jigsaw II, adds expert groups in which the students who are responsible for the same material from each learning group confer to make sure they understand their assigned part and then plan ways to teach the information to their learning group members. Next, students return to their learning groups, bringing their expertise to the sessions. In the end, students take an individual test covering all the material and earn points for their learning team score. Teams can work for rewards or simply for recognition (Aronson, 2000; Slavin, 1995).

STRUCTURED CONTROVERSIES. Constructive conflict resolution is essential in classrooms because conflicts are inevitable and even necessary for learning. Piaget's theory tells us that developing knowledge requires cognitive conflict. David and Roger Johnson (2009b) make a powerful case for constructive intellectual conflict:

> Conflict is to student learning what the internal combustion engine is to the automobile. The internal combustion engine ignites the fuel and the air with a spark to create the energy for movement and acceleration. Just as the fuel and the air are inert without the spark, so, ideas in the classroom are inert without the spark of intellectual conflict. (p. 37)

One study of 10th graders found that students who were wrong, but for different reasons, were sometimes able to correct their misunderstandings if they argued together about their conflicting wrong answers (Schwarz, Neuman, & Biezuner, 2000). Individuals trying to exist in groups will have interpersonal conflicts, too, which also can lead to learning. In fact, research over the last 40 years demonstrates that constructive controversy in classrooms can lead to greater learning, open-mindedness, seeing the perspectives of others, creativity, motivation, engagement, and self-esteem (Johnson & Johnson, 2009b). Table 10.7 shows how academic and interpersonal conflicts can be positive forces in a learning community.

As you can see in Table 7.7, the structured part of **structured controversies** is that students work in pairs within their four-person cooperative groups to research a particular controversy, such as whether lumber companies should be allowed to cut down trees in national forests. Each pair of students researches the issue, develops a pro or con position, presents their position and evidence to the other pair, discusses the issue, and then reverses positions and argues for the other perspective. Then, the group develops a final report that summarizes the best arguments for each position and reaches a consensus (Johnson & Johnson, 2009b; O'Donnell, 2006).

Connect and Extend to PRAXIS II™

Forms of Cooperative Learning (II, A2)
STAD and Jigsaw are just two of many cooperative learning techniques, each designed for certain instructional purposes. Go to *Cooperative Learning* (http://www.utc.edu/Teaching-Resource-Center/CoopLear.html), sponsored by the University of Tennessee at Chattanooga, to learn about techniques and uses for cooperative learning.

Jigsaw Classroom A learning process in which each student is part of a group and each group member is given part of the material to be learned by the whole group. Students become "expert" on their piece and then teach it to the others in their group.

Structured controversy Students work in pairs within their four-person cooperative groups to research a particular controversy.

TABLE 7.7 • Structured Controversies: Learning from Academic and Interpersonal Conflicts

Conflict, if handled well, can support learning. Academic conflicts can lead to critical thinking and conceptual change. Conflicts of interest are unavoidable, but can be handled so no one is the loser.

ACADEMIC CONTROVERSY	CONFLICTS OF INTEREST
One person's ideas, information, theories, conclusions, and opinions are incompatible with those of another, and the two seek to reach an agreement.	The actions of one person attempting to maximize benefits prevents, blocks or interferes with another person maximizing her or his benefits.
Controversy Procedure	*Integrative (Problem-Solving) Negotiations*
Research and prepare positions	Describe wants
Present and advocate positions	Describe feelings
Refute opposing position and refute attacks on own position	Describe reasons for wants and feelings
Reverse perspectives	Take other's perspective
Synthesize and integrate best evidence and reasoning from all sides	Invent three optional agreements that maximize joint outcomes Choose one and formalize agreement

Source: From "The Three Cs of School and Classroom Management," by D. Johnson and R. Johnson. In H. J. Freiberg (Ed.), Beyond Behaviorism: Changing the Classroom Management Paradigm. Boston: Allyn and Bacon. Copyright © 1999 by Allyn & Bacon. Adapted with permission.

In addition to these approaches, Spencer Kagan (1994) has developed many cooperative learning structures designed to accomplish different kinds of academic and social tasks. The *Guidelines* on the next page give you ideas for incorporating cooperative learning in to your classes.

Reaching Every Student: Using Cooperative Learning Wisely

Cooperative learning always benefits from careful planning, but sometimes including students with special needs requires extra attention to planning and preparation. For example, cooperative structures such as scripted questioning and peer tutoring depend on a balanced interaction between the person taking the role of questioner or explainer and the student who is answering or being taught. In these interactions, you want to see and hear explaining and teaching, not just telling or giving right answers. But many students with learning disabilities have difficulties understanding new concepts, so both the explainer and the student can get frustrated, and social rejection for the student with learning disabilities might follow. Because students with learning disabilities often have problems with social relations, it is not a good idea to put them in situations where more rejection is likely. So, when you are teaching new or difficult-to-grasp concepts, cooperative learning might not be the best choice for students with learning disabilities (Kirk et al., 2006). In fact, research has found that cooperative learning in general is not always effective for students with learning disabilities (Smith, 2006).

Gifted students also may not benefit from cooperative learning when groups are mixed in ability. The pace often is too slow, the tasks too simple, and there is just too much repetition. In addition, gifted students often fall into the role of teacher or end up just doing the work quickly for the whole group. If you use mixed-ability groups and include gifted students, the challenges are to use complex tasks that allow work at different levels and keep gifted students engaged without losing the rest of the class (Smith, 2006).

Cooperative learning may be an excellent choice for English language learners (ELLs), however. The Jigsaw cooperative structure is especially helpful because all students in the group, including the ELL students, have information that the group needs, so they also must talk, explain, and interact. In fact, the Jigsaw approach was developed in response to the need to create high interdependence in diverse groups. In many classrooms today, there are 4, 5, 6, or more languages represented. Teachers can't be expected to master every heritage language spoken by all of their students every year. In these classrooms, cooperative groups can help as students work together on academic tasks. Students who speak two languages can help translate and explain lessons to others in

GUIDELINES

Using Cooperative Learning

Fit group size and composition to your learning goals.
Examples

1. For social skills and team-building goals, use groups of 2–5, common interest groups, mixed groups, or random groups.
2. For structured fact and skill-based practice and review tasks, use groups of 2–4, mixed ability such as high-middle and middle-low or high-low and middle-middle group compositions.
3. For higher-level conceptual and thinking tasks, use groups of 2–4; select members to encourage interaction.

Assign appropriate roles.
Examples

1. For social skills and team-building goals, assign roles to monitor participation and conflict; rotate leadership of the group.
2. For structured fact and skill-based practice and review tasks, assign roles to monitor engagement and insure low-status students have resources to offer, as in Jigsaw.
3. For higher-level conceptual and thinking tasks, assign roles only to encourage interaction, divergent thinking, and extended, connected discourse, as in debate teams, or group facilitator. Don't let roles get in the way of learning.

Make sure you assume a supporting role as the teacher.
Examples

1. For social skills and team-building goals, be a model and encourager.
2. For structured fact and skill-based practice and review tasks, be a model, director, or coach.
3. For higher-level conceptual and thinking tasks, be a model and facilitator.

Move around the room and monitor the groups.
Examples

1. For social skills and team-building goals, watch for listening, turn-taking, encouraging, and managing conflict.
2. For structured fact and skill-based practice and review tasks, watch for questioning, giving multiple elaborated explanations, attention, and practice.
3. For higher-level conceptual and thinking tasks, watch for questioning, explaining, elaborating, probing, divergent thinking, providing rationales, synthesizing, using and connecting knowledge sources.

Start small and simple until you and the students know how to use cooperative methods.
Examples

1. For social skills and team-building goals, try one or two skills, such as listening and paraphrasing.
2. For structured fact and skill-based practice and review tasks, try pairs of students quizzing each other.
3. For higher-level conceptual and thinking tasks, try reciprocal questioning using pairs and just a few question stems.

For more information on cooperative
learning, see: http://www.co-operation.org/
http://edtech.kennesaw.edu/intech/cooperativelearning.htm

Source: Adapted from "Implications of Cognitive Approaches to Peer Learning for Teacher Education," by A. Woolfolk Hoy and M. Tschannen-Moran, 1999. In A. O'Donnell and A. King (Eds.), Cognitive Perspectives on Peer Learning (pp. 257–284). Mahwah, NJ: Lawrence Erlbaum.

the group. Speaking in a smaller group may be less anxiety provoking for students who are learning another language; thus, ELL students may get more language practice with feedback in these groups (Smith, 2006).

Cooperative learning is only as good as its design and implementation. Cooperative methods probably are both misused and underused in schools, in part because using cooperative learning well requires time and investment in teaching students how to learn in groups (Blatchford, Baines, Rubie-Davis, Bassett, & Chowne, 2006).

Dilemmas of Constructivist Practice

Years ago, Larry Cremin (1961) observed that progressive, innovative pedagogies require infinitely skilled teachers. Today, the same could be said about constructivist teaching. We have already seen that there are many varieties of constructivism and many practices that flow from these different conceptions. We also know that all teaching today happens in a context of high-stakes testing and accountability. In these situations, constructivist teachers face many challenges. Mark Windschitl (2002) identified four teacher dilemmas of constructivism in practice, summarized in Table 7.8. The first is conceptual: How do I make sense of cognitive versus social conceptions of constructivism and reconcile these

TABLE 7.8 • **Teachers' Dilemmas of Constructivism in Practice**

Teachers face conceptual, pedagogical, cultural, and political dilemmas as they implement constructivist practices. Here are explanations of these dilemmas and some representative questions that teachers face as they confront them.

TEACHERS' DILEMMA CATEGORY	REPRESENTATIVE QUESTIONS OF CONCERN
I. *Conceptual dilemmas:* Grasping the underpinnings of cognitive and social constructivism; reconciling current beliefs about pedagogy with the beliefs necessary to support a constructivist learning environment.	Which version of constructivism is suitable as a basis for my teaching? Is my classroom supposed to be a collection of individuals working toward conceptual change or a community of learners whose development is measured by participation in authentic disciplinary practices? If certain ideas are considered correct by experts, should students internalize those ideas instead of constructing their own?
II. *Pedagogical dilemmas:* Honoring students' attempts to think for themselves while remaining faithful to accepted disciplinary ideas; developing deeper knowledge of subject matter; mastering the art of facilitation; managing new kinds of discourse and collaborative work in the classroom.	Do I base my teaching on students' existing ideas rather than on learning objectives? What skills and strategies are necessary for me to become a facilitator? How do I manage a classroom where students are talking to one another rather than to me? Should I place limits on students' construction of their own ideas? What types of assessments will capture the learning I want to foster?
III. *Cultural dilemmas:* Becoming conscious of the culture of your classroom; questioning assumptions about what kinds of activities should be valued; taking advantage of experiences, discourse patterns, and local knowledge of students with varied cultural backgrounds.	How can we contradict traditional, efficient classroom routines and generate new agreements with students about what is valued and rewarded? How do my own past images of what is proper and possible in a classroom prevent me from seeing the potential for a different kind of learning environment? How can I accommodate the worldviews of students from diverse backgrounds while at the same time transforming my own classroom culture? Can I trust students to accept responsibility for their own learning?
IV. *Political dilemmas:* Confronting issues of accountability with various stakeholders in the school community; negotiating with key others the authority and support to teach for understanding.	How can I gain the support of administrators and parents for teaching in such a radically different and unfamiliar way? Should I make use of approved curriculums that are not sensitive enough to my students' needs, or should I create my own? How can diverse problem-based experiences help students meet specific state and local standards? Will constructivist approaches adequately prepare my students for high-stakes testing for college admissions?

Source: M. Windschitl (2002). Framing constructivism in practice as the negotiation of dilemmas: An analysis of the conceptual, pedagogical, cultural, and political challenges facing teachers. Review of Educational Research, 72, p. 133. Copyright © 2002 by the American Educational Research Association. Reproduced with permission of the publisher.

different perspectives with my practice? The second dilemma is pedagogical: How do I teach in truly constructivist ways that both honor my students' attempts to think for themselves, but still insure that they learn the academic material? Third are cultural dilemmas: What activities, cultural knowledge, and ways of talking will build a community in a diverse classroom? Finally, there are political dilemmas: How can I teach for deep understanding and critical thinking, but still satisfy the accountability demands of parents and the requirements of No Child Left Behind?

SERVICE LEARNING

Service learning combines academic learning with personal and social development for secondary and college students (Woolfolk Hoy, Demerath, & Pape, 2002). A more formal definition of **service learning** is "a teaching and learning strategy that integrates meaningful

Service learning Combines academic learning with personal and social development for secondary and college students.

GUIDELINES — FAMILY AND COMMUNITY PARTNERSHIPS

Service Learning

The service should be ongoing, not just a brief project.
Examples

1. Instead of having a two-week food drive with a party for the class that collected the most, encourage a longer commitment to cook or serve food at shelters for homeless families.
2. Contact local agencies to identify real needs that your students could address or search online by zip code: http://www.volunteermatch.org/

Consider virtual volunteering. See http://www.serviceleader.org/virtual
Examples

1. Translate a document into another language.
2. Provide multimedia expertise, such as preparing a PowerPoint™, QuickTime™ or other computer-based presentation.
3. Design an agency's newsletter or brochure, or copyedit an agency's publication or proposal.
4. Proofread drafts of papers and online publications.
5. Research and write articles for brochures, newsletters, Web sites.
6. Design a logo for an agency or program, or fill other illustration needs.

Be aware of service learning projects in school. Make sure learning is at the center.
Examples

1. Have clear learning objectives for the projects.
2. Examine grade-level standards in science, history, health, literature, and other areas to see how some might be met through service projects—for example, how might concepts in biology be learned through designing a nutrition education project for senior citizens or preschool students?
3. Do students reflect over time about their experiences, keep journals, write or draw what they have learned, and include these reflections in class discussions?

Make sure the service draws on your child's talents and skills so that it is actually valuable to the recipients and he or she gains a sense of accomplishment and usefulness from applying skills to help others.
Examples

1. Youth who have artistic talents might help redecorate a game room at a senior citizens' center.
2. Individuals who are good storytellers could work with children at a day care center or in a children's clinic.
3. Students who are bilingual might help teachers translate school newsletters into the languages of fellow students' families or serve as translators at local clinics.

Design service learning opportunities so they are inclusive (Dymond, Renzaglia, & Chun, 2007).
Examples

1. Consider transportation needs for children with disabilities.
2. Link service learning projects to life skills such as social skills on the job, safety, and punctuality.
3. Encourage teachers to monitor interactions in groups for all students; be aware of how students with special needs are included.

For more ideas, see:
http://www.service-learningpartnership.org/site/PageServer

---

community service with instruction and reflection to enrich the learning experience, teach civic responsibility, and strengthen communities" (National Service Learning Clearing House, n.d.). About half of American high schools have some form of service learning (Dymond, Renzaglia, & Chun, 2007). The Alliance for Service Learning in Education Reform (1993) lists several characteristics of service learning. The activities:

- Are organized and meet actual community needs.
- Are integrated into the student's curriculum.
- Provide time to reflect and write about the service experience.
- Provide opportunities to apply newly learned academic skills and knowledge.
- Enhance both academic learning and a sense of caring for others.

Service learning activities may involve direct service (tutoring, serving meals at homeless shelters), indirect service (collecting food for shelters, raising money), or advocacy (designing and distributing posters about a food drive, writing newspaper articles) (Johnson & Notah, 1999). Service learning also could be a form of problem-based learning.

Participation in service learning can promote political and moral development for adolescents. Through service learning projects, adolescents experience their own competence and agency by working with others in need. Students see themselves as political and moral agents, rather than as merely good citizens (Youniss & Yates, 1997). In addition, service learning can help adolescents think in new ways about their relationships with people who are unlike them, and thus can lead them to become more tolerant of differences (Tierney, 1993). Finally, service learning experiences foster an "ethic of care" that can result in a growing commitment to confront difficult social problems (Rhodes, 1997). In this sense, student involvement in service learning can motivate and empower adolescents to critically reflect on their role in society (Woolfolk Hoy, Demerath, & Pape, 2002). A number of schools now have participation in service learning as a graduation requirement, but some educators question if "required" service is fair or appropriate. At least three of the school requirements have been challenged in court. but, so far, the requirements have been upheld (Johnson & Notah, 1999).

SERVICE LEARNING Community service projects can promote adolescents' moral development, feelings of competence and agency, and tolerance of differences, and encourage them to reflect critically on their roles in society.

Studies of service learning have produced mixed results. Some studies have found modest gains on measures of social responsibility, tolerance for others, empathy, attitude toward adults, and self-esteem (Solomon et al., 2001). A case study at an urban parochial high school describes a successful service learning experience program that was required for juniors and was part of a yearlong course on social justice (Youniss & Yates, 1999). In the class, students examined the moral implications of current social issues such as homelessness, poverty, exploitation of immigrant laborers, and urban violence. Students also were required to serve four times (approximately 20 hours) at an inner-city soup kitchen. The researchers concluded that students emerged from the course with "a deeper awareness of social injustice, a greater sense of commitment to confront these injustices, and heightened confidence in their abilities overall" (Yates & Youniss, 1999, p. 64).

Your students may be involved in service learning both inside and outside the school. You might share the *Family and Community Partnership Guidelines* with families and use them yourself. Many are taken from Richard Sagor (2003) and Elias and Schwab (2006).

LEARNING IN A DIGITAL WORLD

It seems that computers, smart phones, iPods, iPads, iTouches, tablets, digital readers, and interactive video games, along with iCloud, Facebook, Twitter, Google, Yahoo, ... , and other digital tools and media have changed life for everyone. Homes and schools are filled with media. For students, doing homework often involves exchanging messages with friends via e-mail, texting, or cell phones, searching the Web, and downloading resources—all the time listening to music via an iPod or watching television (Roberts, Foehr, & Rideout, 2005). Over 35% of children *ages 6 months to 3 years* have a TV in their own bedroom. There are DVD players in 95% of homes, and 27% of the children have a DVD player in their bedrooms. The television is on an average of 6 hours a day (Rideout et al. 2003; Rosen, 2010). Vandewater et al. (2005) found that the TV was on all day or most of the day in 35% of the homes they studied. In fact, children spend more time watching television than they do in any other activity except sleep.

Learning Environments and Technology

With all the technology available today, there is growing interest in *technology-rich learning environments* or TREs. These environments include virtual worlds, computer simulations that support problem-based learning such as the *River of Life Challenge* described earlier, intelligent tutoring systems, educational games, audio recordings, hand-held wireless devices, and multimedia environments—to name just a few.

There are three kinds of uses for technology in schools. First, teachers can design technology-based activities for their classrooms, for virtual learning environments, or for blended models using both in-class and virtual environments. Second, students can interact with technologies in a variety of ways, such as by using a computer or tablet to complete assignments, or by collaborating in a virtual environment with other students or teachers using interactive **cloud computing** applications. Cloud computing allows computer users online access to applications such as a Google documents or Microsoft Web Mail along with computing assets such as network-accessible data storage and processing. Finally, administrators use technology to track teacher, class, and student information in school, district, or statewide systems. You could be involved with any or all three uses of technology in your teaching.

The primary goal for integrating technology into a classroom is to support student learning. The process may seem difficult and troublesome at first, especially for teachers with few technological skills. Starting points include researching your school or district technology policies and procedures, identifying internal resources such as technology integration teams, seeking out training resources, and working with teachers who already use technology in their classes. Becoming familiar with available technological resources will help you to identify and include new technologies that will enhance your teaching. A golden rule for technology integration in any classroom is that you do not need to reinvent the wheel. Focus on identifying centers of expertise where existing resources are available to adapt and build on.

Virtual Learning Environments

Virtual Learning Environments (VLEs) is a broad term that describes many ways of learning in virtual systems. The most traditional VLE is referred to as a **Learning Management System (LMSs).** LMSs deliver e-learning using applications such as Moodle, BlackBoard, RCampus, and Desire2Learn. Learning management systems are large, complex, and costly—my university uses a system we call "Carmen" to support every course on campus. My Carmen sites have readings, discussion groups, class-built Wikis, PowerPoints, weblinks, a calendar, and many other resources. We taught classes without these assets for decades, but the learning management system has expanded our teaching and learning options. To deal with costs, some institutions use free *open-source software* to construct virtual learning environments. Tools that support open-source software include Moodle, Google Apps, Microsoft SharePoint, and PBWorks.

There are different kinds of virtual learning environments. A **Personal Learning Environment (PLE)** framework provides tools that support individualized learning in a variety of contexts and situations; the learners assume control of how and when their learning occurs. Students working in personal learning environments can download an assignment at Panera, read the material on the bus, and then post an analysis on the discussion board at 4:00 A.M. from their room—learning is asynchronous, it takes place any time and anywhere. Complex personal learning environments include tools that assess learners' knowledge and then adapt the next content to fit their needs. Tools that support PLEs include computer-based training modules, e-books, cognitive tutors, quizzes, and self-assessment tools.

A **Personal Learning Network (PLN)** is a framework in which knowledge is constructed through online peer interactions. PLNs consist of both synchronous (real time) and asynchronous technologies using interactive Web conferencing, hybrid classes, or online discussions. A PLN can be used for K–12 instructional purposes and also as a resource for professional development. Social networking tools such as Facebook, Twitter, Edutopia, and EdWeb allow the instruction to move outside the school, city, and even country to include learners with similar interests around the globe. Tools that support personal learning networks include: Web conferencing tools, such as Adobe Connect and Elluminate, instant messaging, interactive video and audio messaging, social networking, discussion boards, and blogs.

Cloud computing Allows computer users to access applications, such as a Google document or Microsoft Web Mail, as well as computing assets such as network-accessible data storage and processing to use online applications.

Virtual Learning Environments (VLE) A broad term that describes many ways of learning in virtual or online systems.

Learning Management System (LMS) Systems that deliver e-learning, provide tools and learning materials, keep records, administer assessments, and manage learning.

Personal Learning Environment (PLE) Provides tools that support individualized learning in a variety of contexts and situations.

Personal Learning Network (PLN) Framework in which knowledge is constructed through online peer interactions.

The most complex VLE is an **Immersive Virtual Learning Environment (IVLE)**. The IVLE is a simulation of a real-world environment. The purpose is to learn through enculturation, for example by being eco explorers in the rainforest or reporters covering a story about an outbreak of food poisoning in a local school (Gee, 2003; Gibson, Aldrich, & Prensky, 2006; Hamilton, 2011; Shaffer et al., 2009). Immersive Virtual Learning Environments are designed to be domain specific using realistic scenarios (Bagley & Shaffer, 2009; Shaffer et al., 2009). IVLE experiences mimic tasks required in a professional practicum, such as interviewing sources for a news story about food poisoning, following leads to identify the source of a problem, and crafting an accurate engaging article, thus blending real-world engagement in a virtual scenario. These immersive environments often include *cognitive tutors*—the technology is programmed to interact as a tutor by providing prompts after analyzing the student's response.

Massive Multi-player Online Games (MMOGs) are interactive gaming environments constructed in virtual worlds in which the learner assumes a character role of avatar. Virtual world simulations incorporating MMOGs have been used for experiential and didactic learning in the medical field for several years and quickly are gaining attention in PK–12 classrooms. The pedagogic value in good gaming design is the ability to create complex scenarios by developing lessons using modeling and problem-based learning scenarios as alternative methods of instruction (Gee, 2008). For example, Project Evoke is a game developed by the World Bank (http://www.urgentevoke.com/). As they play the game, adolescents from around the world work collectively to solve major world problems such as hunger. Stay tuned for more exciting learning worlds.

Developmentally Appropriate Computer Activities for Young Children

Digital media are appealing, but are they appropriate for preschool children? This is a hotly debated issue. Computers should not be used to do solitary drill-and-practice activities. Developmentally appropriate ways to use computers with 3- and 4-year-olds are different from the ways we use computers in kindergarten and the primary grades (http://www.kidsource.com/education/computers.children.html). With developmentally appropriate computer activities, young children can benefit cognitively without sustaining losses in creativity (Haugland & Wright, 1997). Software for children should include simple spoken directions; the activities should be open-ended and encourage discovery, exploration, problem solving, and understanding of cause and effect. Children should be able to remain in control of the activities through a variety of responses. Finally, the content should be appropriate for and respectful of diverse cultures, ages, and abilities (Fischer & Gillespie, 2003; Frost, Wortham, & Reifel, 2005). Linda Tsantis and her colleagues suggest that you ask this question about any program you are considering: "Does this software program help create learning opportunities that did not exist without it?" (Tsantis, Berwick, & Thouvebelle, 2003).

There is another important consideration—does the program's multimedia features (e.g., embedded videos, zoom-ins, music, added sounds, images) add to learning or take away from it? One danger is that programs will include attractive visuals or sound effects that actually interrupt and interfere with the development of important concepts. For example, do the sounds of a buzz saw and the thud of a falling tree in a Peter Rabbit storytelling program foster distractibility and interfere with understanding the story, plot, and characters? Maybe (Tsantis et al., 2003).

Immersive Virtual Learning Environment (IVLE) A simulation of a real-world environment that immerses students in tasks like those required in a professional practicum.

Massive Multi-player Online Games (MMOG) Interactive gaming environments constructed in virtual worlds where the learner assumes a character role of avatar.

MEDIA MULTITASKERS For older students, doing homework often involves exchanging messages with friends via e-mail or cell phones, searching the Web, and downloading resources—all the time listening to music via an iPod or watching television.

Dealing with all of this stimulation might make children better at multitasking, but also worse at deeper thought processes such as developing perspective-taking skills and understanding the plot, theme, and sequence of the story. So children learn to do several things at once, but have a superficial understanding of what they are doing (Carpenter, 2000).

Research in the Netherlands, however, demonstrated that multimedia storybooks can provide support for understanding stories and remembering linguistic information for kindergarten students from families with low educational levels who are behind in language and literacy skills (Verhallen, Bus, & de Jong, 2006). The difference in this study seemed to be that the multimedia features of the story supported understanding and memory by providing multiple pathways to meaning, giving visual and verbal representations of key story elements, focusing attention on important information, and reinforcing key ideas. This extra scaffolding may be especially important for students with limited language and literacy skills. So the bottom line is that multimedia elements should focus on meaning and not just provide attractive "bells and whistles."

Computers and Older Students

There is evidence that using computers—especially games that require multiple activities, visual attention, imagery, and fast action—supports the development of visual skills, as long as the tasks fit the student's level of ability (Subrahmanyam, Greenfield, Kraut, & Gross, 2001). But does computer use support academic learning? The answer is complex and even surprising. After reviewing hundreds of studies, including five other research reviews, Roschelle, Pea, Hoadley, Gordon, and Means (2000) concluded that there were no strong conclusions. Using computer tutorial programs appeared to improve achievement test scores for K–12 students, but simulations and enrichment programs had few effects—perhaps another example that when you teach and test specific skills, children learn the skills. More recent research reports similar results. Computers may be more useful in improving mathematics and science skills than other subjects and not very successful in improving reading (Slavin, Lake, Chambers Cheung, & Davis, 2009). Like any teaching tool, computers can be effective if used well, but just being on a computer will not automatically increase academic achievement, especially achievement as measured by standardized tests (Richtell, 2011). Roschelle and colleagues concluded that computers are more likely to increase achievement if they support the basic processes that lead to learning: active engagement, frequent interaction with feedback, authenticity and real-world connection, and productive group work (Jackson et al., 2006). See the *Guidelines* for more ideas.

DIGITALLY DISADVANTAGED? Many students have limited access to technology at home or in their communities. This split in access to technology has been called the *digital divide*.

Media/Digital Literacy

With the advent of digital media comes a new concern with literacy—media or digital literacy. Today, to be literate—that is to be able to read, write, and communicate—children have to read and write in many media, not just printed words. Films, videos, DVDs, computers, photographs, artwork, magazines, music, television, billboards, and more communicate through images and sounds. How do children read these messages? This is a new area of research and application in educational and developmental psychology (Hobbs, 2004).

As an example of practice, consider Project Look Sharp at Ithaca College, directed by Cynthia Scheibe, a developmental psychologist (http://www.ithaca.edu/looksharp/). The goal of the project is to provide materials, training, and support as teachers

GUIDELINES

Using Computers

IF YOU HAVE ONLY ONE COMPUTER IN YOUR CLASSROOM

Provide convenient access.
Examples
1. Find a central location if the computer is used to display material for the class.
2. Find a spot on the side of the room that allows seating and view of the screen, but does not crowd or disturb other students if the computer is used as a workstation for individuals or small groups.

Be prepared.
Examples
1. Check to be sure software needed for a lesson or assignment is installed and working.
2. Make sure instructions for using the software or doing the assignment are in an obvious place and clear.
3. Provide a checklist for completing assignments.

Create "trained experts" to help with computers.
Examples
1. Train student experts, and rotate experts.
2. Use adult volunteers—parents, grandparents, aunts and uncles, older siblings—anyone who cares about the students.

Develop systems for using the computer.
Examples
1. Make up a schedule to insure that all students have access to the computer and no students monopolize the time.
2. Create standard ways of saving student work.

IF YOU HAVE MORE THAN ONE COMPUTER IN YOUR CLASSROOM

Plan the arrangement of the computers to fit your instructional goals.
Examples
1. For cooperative groups, arrange so students can cluster around their group's computer.
2. For different projects at different computer stations, allow for easy rotation from station to station.

Experiment with other models for using computers.
Examples
1. Navigator Model—4 students per computer: One student is the (mouse and keyboard) driver, another is the "navigator." "Back-seat driver 1" manages the group's progress and "back-seat driver 2" serves as the timekeeper. The navigator attends a 10-minute to 20-minute training session in which the facilitator provides an overview of the basics of particular software. Navigators cannot touch the mouse. Driver roles are rotated.
2. Facilitator Model—6 students per computer: the facilitator has more experience, expertise, or training—serves as the guide or teacher.
3. Collaborative Group Model—7 students per computer: Each small group is responsible for creating some component of the whole group's final product. For example, one part of the group writes a report, another creates a map, and a third uses the computer to gather and graph census data.

NO MATTER HOW MANY COMPUTERS YOU HAVE IN YOUR CLASSROOM

Select developmentally appropriate programs that encourage learning, creativity, and social interaction.
Examples
1. Encourage two children to work together rather than having children work alone.
2. Check the implicit messages in programs. For example, some drawing programs allow children to "blow up" their projects if they don't like them, so instead of solving a problem they just destroy it. Tsantis et al. (2003) recommend a recycle metaphor instead of a "blow it up" option.
3. Look for programs that encourage discovery, exploration, problem solving, and multiple responses.

Monitor children as they work at computers.
Examples
1. Make sure computers are in areas where adults can observe them.
2. Discuss with children why some programs or Web sites are off limits.
3. Balance computer time with active play such as hands-on projects, blocks, sand, water, and art.

Keep children safe as they work at computers.
Examples
1. Teach children to shield their identity on the Internet and monitor any "friends" they may be communicating with.
2. Install filtering software to protect children from inappropriate content.

Sources: Suggestions are taken from Frost, J. L., Wortham, S. C., & Reifel, S. (2005). Play and child development (2nd ed.). Upper Saddle River, NJ: Prentice-Hall, pp. 76–80 and Tsantis, L. A., Bewick, C. J., & Thouvenelle, S. (2003, November). Examining some common myths about computer use in the early years. Beyond the Journal: Young Children on the Web (pp. 1–9).

GUIDELINES

Supporting the Development of Media Literacy

Use media to practice general observation, critical thinking, analysis, perspective-taking, and production skills.
Examples

1. Ask students to think critically about the information presented in advertising, "news" programs, and textbooks—would different people interpret the messages in differing ways?
2. Foster creativity by having students produce their own media on a topic you are studying.
3. Ask students to compare ways information might be presented in a documentary, TV news report, advertisement, public service announcement, etc.
4. Give examples of how word selection, background music, camera angles, color, etc. can be used to set a mood or bias a message.

Use media to stimulate interest in a new topic.
Examples

1. Analyze a magazine article about the topic.
2. Read sections from a novel or view film clips on the topic.

Help students identify what they already know or believe about a topic based on popular media content. Help them identify erroneous beliefs.
Examples

1. What do students "know" about space travel?
2. What have they learned about biology from advertisements?

Use media as a standard pedagogical tool.
Examples

1. Provide information about a topic through many different media sources—Internet, books, DVDs, audio recordings, online newspapers, etc.
2. Assign homework that makes use of different media.
3. Have students express opinions or attempt to persuade using different media—photographs, collages, videos, poems, songs, animated films, etc.

Analyze the effects that media had on historical events.
Examples

1. How were Native Americans portrayed in art and in films?
2. What sources of information were available 50 years ago? 100 years ago?

For more ideas, see:
http://www.ithaca.edu/looksharp/

integrate media literacy and critical thinking about media into their class lessons. Teachers participating in the project help their students become critical readers of media. One group of elementary school students studied ants in science, and then viewed the animated film, *Antz*. In the discussion after the movie, students were challenged to describe what was accurate and inaccurate in the film's portrayal of ants. What were the messages of the film? How was product placement (e.g., an ant drinking a bottle of Pepsi) used? Tests immediately and 6 months later indicated that the children performed best on the questions related to the discussion about the accuracy of the film (Scheibe, 2005). Project Look Sharp suggests these questions to guide discussion of media:

1. Who made—and who sponsored—this message, and what is their purpose?
2. Who is the target audience and how is the message specifically tailored to that audience?
3. What are the different techniques used to inform, persuade, entertain, and attract attention?
4. What messages are communicated (and/or implied) about certain people, places, events, behaviors, lifestyles, and so forth?
5. How current, accurate, and credible is the information in this message?
6. What is left out of the message that might be good to know? (p. 63)

The *Guidelines* give more ideas from Scheibe and Rogow (2004) for supporting the development of media literacy in your students.

▼ SUMMARY

The Learning Sciences (pp. 250–252)

What are some basic assumptions of the learning sciences? Key assumptions in the learning sciences are that experts develop deep conceptual knowledge, learning comes from the learner, creating learning environments is the responsibility of the school, students' prior knowledge is key, and reflection is a critical component of learning. These common assumptions enable researchers from a variety of disciplines to address the same issues of learning from a variety of perspectives.

Cognitive and Social Constructivism (pp. 252–259)

Describe two kinds of constructivism and distinguish these from constructionism. *Psychological* constructivists such as Piaget are concerned with how individuals make sense of their world, based on individual knowledge, beliefs, self-concept, or identity—also called *first wave constructivism*. *Social* constructivists such as Vygotsky believe that social interaction, cultural tools, and activity shape individual development and learning—also called *second wave constructivism*. By participating in a broad range of activities with others, learners appropriate the outcomes produced by working together; they acquire new strategies and knowledge of their world. Finally, constructionists are interested in how public knowledge in academic disciplines is constructed as well as how everyday beliefs about the world are communicated to new members of a sociocultural group.

In what ways do constructivist views differ about knowledge sources, accuracy, and generality? Constructivists debate whether knowledge is constructed by mapping external reality, by adapting and changing internal understandings, or by an interaction of external forces and internal understandings. Most psychologists believe there is a role for both internal and external factors, but differ in how much they emphasize one or the other. Also, there is discussion about whether knowledge can be constructed in one situation and applied to another or whether knowledge is situated, that is, specific and tied to the context in which it was learned. What is meant by thinking as enculturation? Enculturation is a broad and complex process of acquiring knowledge and understanding consistent with Vygotsky's theory of mediated learning. Just as our home culture taught us lessons about the use of language, the culture of a classroom can teach lessons about thinking by giving us models of good thinking; providing direct instruction in thinking processes; and encouraging practice of those thinking processes through interactions with others.

What are some common elements in most constructivist views of learning? Even though there is no single constructivist theory, many constructivist approaches recommend complex, challenging learning environments and authentic tasks; social negotiation and co-construction; multiple representations of content; understanding that knowledge is constructed; and student ownership of learning.

Applying Constructivist Perspectives (pp. 259–277)

Distinguish between inquiry methods and problem-based learning. The inquiry strategy begins when the teacher presents a puzzling event, question, or problem. The students ask questions (only yes-no questions in some kinds of inquiry) and then formulate hypotheses to explain the event or solve the problem; collect data to test the hypotheses about casual relationships; form conclusions and generalizations; and reflect on the original problem and the thinking processes needed to solve it. Problem-based learning may follow a similar path, but the learning begins with an authentic problem—one that matters to the students. The goal is to learn math or science or history or some other important subject while seeking a real solution to a real problem.

Describe six features that most cognitive apprenticeship approaches share. Students observe an expert (usually the teacher) model the performance; get external support through coaching or tutoring; and receive conceptual scaffolding, which is then gradually faded as the student becomes more competent and proficient. Students continually articulate their knowledge—putting into words their understanding of the processes and content being learned. They reflect on their progress, comparing their problem solving to an expert's performance and to their own earlier performances. Finally, students explore new ways to apply what they are learning—ways that they have not practiced at the master's side.

Describe the use of dialogue in reciprocal teaching. The goal of reciprocal teaching is to help students understand and think deeply about what they read. To accomplish this goal, students in small reading groups learn four strategies: summarizing the content of a passage, asking a question about the central point, clarifying the difficult parts of the material, and predicting what will come next. These strategies are practiced in a classroom dialogue about the readings. Teachers first take a central role, but as the discussion progresses, the students take more and more control.

What are the differences between collaboration and cooperation? One view is that collaboration is a philosophy about how to relate to others—how to learn and work. Collaboration is a way of dealing with people that respects differences, shares authority, and builds on the knowledge that is distributed among other people. Cooperation, on the other hand, is a way of working together with others to attain a shared goal.

What are the learning theory underpinnings of cooperative learning? Learning can be enhanced in cooperative groups through rehearsal and elaboration (information processing theories), creation and resolution of disequilibrium (Piaget's theory), or scaffolding of higher mental processes (Vygotsky's theory).

Describe five elements that define true cooperative learning. Students interact face-to-face and close together, not across the room. Group members experience positive interdependence—they need each other for support, explanations, and guidance. Even though they work together and help each other, members of the group must ultimately demonstrate learning on their own—they are held individually accountable for learning, often through individual tests or other assessments. If necessary, the collaborative skills important for effective group functioning, such as giving constructive feedback, reaching consensus, and involving every member, are taught and practiced before the groups tackle a learning task. Finally, members monitor group processes and relationships to make sure the group is working effectively and to learn about the dynamics of groups.

How should tasks match design in cooperative learning? A relatively structured task works well with a structured technique; extrinsic rewards can enhance motivation, effort, and persistence under these conditions; roles, especially those that focus attention on the work to be accomplished, also may be productive. On the other hand, strategies that encourage extended and productive interactions are appropriate when the goal is to develop higher-order thinking and problem solving. The use of rewards may well divert the group away from the goal of in-depth cognitive processing. When the goal of peer learning is enhanced social skills or increased intergroup understanding and appreciation of diversity, the assignment of specific roles and functions within the group might support communication. Rewards probably are not necessary and may actually get in the way because the goal is to build community, a sense of respect, and responsibility for team members.

What are some possible strategies for cooperative learning? Strategies include reciprocal questioning, Jigsaw, structured controversy, and many cooperative structures described by Spencer Kagan.

Service Learning (pp. 277–279)

What are some key characteristics of service learning? Service learning activities should be organized around and designed to meet actual community needs, and integrated into the student's curriculum. Teachers should provide time for students to reflect on and write about their service experience, offer opportunities to apply newly learned academic skills and knowledge, and strive to enhance both academic learning and a sense of caring for others. Service learning activities ought not be supplementary to students' regular activities, but instead should be an integral part of their learning.

Learning in a Digital World (pp. 279–284)

What are some possible uses of technology in education? Technology such as computers, iPods, smart phones, digital readers, and interactive gaming systems are extremely popular among young people. In fact, the many ways of communicating and interacting with others through technology may even shape the way students think about what it means to socialize. These technologies can be useful teaching tools, but they do have limitations. First, technology cannot necessarily replace the teacher when it comes to direct instruction (and not all programs are able to bring about learning). Classrooms of the future may take greater advantage of learning environments that immerse students in virtual worlds where they work alone or with others to solve problems, create projects, simulate the skills of experts, visit historical sites, tour world class museums, or play games that teach and apply academic skills. The results of research on technology-enhanced learning emphasize that technology by itself will not guarantee improvement in academic achievement—like any tool, technology must be used well by confident, competent teachers.

▼ KEY TERMS

Appropriating (255)
Cloud computing (280)
Cognitive apprenticeship (263)
Collaboration (266)
Community of practice (257)
Complex learning environments (258)
Constructionism (255)
Constructivism (253)
Cooperation (266)
Cooperative learning (267)
Embodied cognition (251)
First wave constructivism (254)

Immersive Virtual Learning Environment (IVLE) (281)
Inquiry learning (260)
Intersubjective attitude (258)
Jigsaw Classroom (274)
Learning Management System (LMS) (280)
Learning sciences (250)
Massive Multi-player Online Games (MMOG) (281)
Multiple representations of content (259)
Personal Learning Environment (PLE) (280)
Personal Learning Network (PLN) (280)

Problem-based learning (261)
Radical constructivism (254)
Reciprocal questioning (273)
Reciprocal teaching (264)
Scaffolding (259)
Second wave constructivism (255)
Service learning (277)
Situated learning (257)
Social negotiation (258)
Spiral curriculum (259)
Structured controversy (274)
Virtual Learning Environments (VLE) (280)

▼ CONNECT AND EXTEND TO LICENSURE

MULTIPLE-CHOICE QUESTIONS

1. All but which one of the following activities would be consistent with a constructivist environment?
   A. Students are given frequent opportunities to engage in complex, meaningful, problem-based activities
   B. Students work collaboratively and are given support to engage in task-oriented dialogue with one another
   C. Teachers elicit students' ideas and experiences in relationship to key topics, then fashion learning situations that assist students in elaborating on or restructuring their current knowledge
   D. Teachers employ limited assessment strategies and give feedback on products rather than processes

2. In Mr. Lawrence's classroom students are engaged in learning the art of driving. They watch Mr. Lawrence model techniques,

receive hints and feedback from him on their performance, and are encouraged to put into words the new skills they are practicing. This type of learning is best referred to as which one of the following?

    A. Reciprocal teaching

    B. Cognitive apprenticeship

    C. Cooperative learning

    D. Schema building

3. Group activities must be well planned. Students need to be prepared to work in groups, and teachers have to be explicit in stating their expectations. Which one of the following strategies is NOT an element which defines true cooperative learning?

    A. Positive interdependence and individual accountability

    B. Group processing

    C. Competition

    D. Collaborative and social skills

4. Research demonstrates that constructive controversy can lead to greater learning, open-mindedness, seeing the perspectives of others, creativity, motivation, and engagement. Which one of the following is the set up for activities that engage students in structured controversies?

    A. Students work in pairs within their four-person cooperative groups to research a particular argument.

    B. Each student is part of a group and each group member is given part of the material to be learned by the whole group. Students become experts on their piece and then teach it to the others in their group.

    C. Students intuitively understand the design that helps them think deeply about what they read.

    D. A combination of academic learning with personal and social development for secondary and college students is created.

CONSTRUCTED-RESPONSE QUESTIONS

Case

In order to infuse her class with constructivist strategies, Brenda Rhodes planned several problem-based learning scenarios. One of the scenarios required students to find a solution for their city's homeless population. Over the past few years the number of homeless individuals and families had grown alarmingly quickly. Social service agencies, shelters and businesses in the central city were struggling to deal with the challenge. Brenda believed her students would find the topic interesting and that it met the criteria for problem-based learning.

5. Does Brenda Rhodes' activity of finding a solution for the city's homeless population as a topic meet the requirements for problem-based learning? Explain your answer.

6. Identify several types of scaffolding the students might use to help them solve their problem.

▼ WHAT WOULD THEY DO?

TEACHERS' CASEBOOK: Learning to Cooperate

Here is how some practicing teachers responded to the situation described at the beginning of the chapter about the class that hated cooperative learning.

PAULA COLEMERE • Special Education Teacher—English, History
McClintock High School, Tempe, AZ

First, cooperative learning should be introduced early in the year and used in a variety of ways. Simple activities such as "think-pair-share" or "tell partner two things you learned" are basic ways of having students learn cooperatively. In addition, Socratic seminars are a great way to get students to dialogue together and gain deeper understanding of a concept. A Socratic seminar begins with the facilitator posing an open-ended question to the group. Participants are encouraged to learn through a meaningful discussion rather than memorizing bits of information. This takes practice, but if introduced early and practiced throughout the year, students will gain higher-level thinking skills. Finally, when having students do a team activity in class, groups need to be placed together thoughtfully and deliberately by the teacher. Team members need to be taught skills necessary for successful group work such as active listening and how to give and receive constructive criticism. Groups should have a variety of abilities and students should be assigned specific tasks within the group so everyone has a role and purpose.

PAUL DRAGIN • ESL Grades 9–12
Columbus East High School, Columbus OH

To introduce cooperative learning, I will begin with some exercises that require no talking, such as puzzles that can only be completed by group cooperation and sharing without any verbal communication. Each group member receives pieces that make up a puzzle; the catch is that some of the pieces belong to another group member's puzzle. By trading pieces strategically and rapidly, the goal is to be the first group to complete all puzzles. This sets the stage for a discussion about the need to work together, since each person in the group needs something that another team member has in order to complete his or her puzzle. All effective cooperative learning requires the input of each member, and without that input, the activity has no chance of reaching its full potential. The establishment of groups is open to myriad options and this is a good thing. Randomly assigning students as well as strategically assigning students to work together is an important learning opportunity for each student and better mimics real-world situations where we don't get to choose our co-workers.

JENNIFER PINCOSKI • Learning Resource Teacher, K–12
Lee County School District, Fort Myers, FL

In order to have effective groups, students need to respect each other and feel accepted by their peers. Therefore, it is important to incorporate some class-building and team-building exercises before the groups jump into academic content. The purpose of these activities is to acquaint students with one another and create a sense of community.

It will be easier to establish groups if the teacher collects information about the students first. This information can include anything from preferred learning style to favorite subject to career aspirations. It is also important to understand the students' levels of academic proficiency. Groups should be fluid, because different types of groups will accomplish different outcomes.

Teachers need to identify the objectives of an activity before creating the groups for that activity. In some situations, it might be appropriate to group students who are strong in a skill with students who have deficits in that skill. In other cases, it might be more effective to group together students with similar interests or career goals. It is up to the teacher to determine which type of group will result in the most worthwhile outcome for students.

LAUREN ROLLINS • 1st Grade
Boulevard Elementary School, Shaker Heights, OH

Group work is an important part of the curriculum and a teaching/learning method that I use with my students on a daily basis starting from the beginning of the school year. As I am getting to know my students and they are getting to know each other, cooperative learning activities are very simple and structured. These experiences allow them to build cooperative skills. Groups and the tasks for which each member is responsible are both assigned by me. As the school year progresses, I use cooperative learning to focus on specific skills, to facilitate peer tutoring, to accomplish a task, to play a game, etc. Depending on what I want the students to gain from the learning activity, groups are chosen at random, picked by the students, or selected by me. My students enjoy the opportunity to learn in these different types of groupings. As groups are working, I rotate through the classroom, making sure that the groups are on task and that each member is contributing to the learning activity. I spend a few minutes with each group to get a sense of how successfully the students are working together to accomplish the given task. I help facilitate when needed.

BARBARA PRESLEY • Transition/Work Study Coordinator—High School Level
B.E.S.T.T. Program (Baldwinsville Exceptional Student Training and Transition Program), C.W. Baker High School, Baldwinsville, NY

Throughout their high school experience, as students prepare for their life post high school, I send the youngest and newest students to "intern" with an older student who is secure and successful at their job site. The younger student is more comfortable going into a new situation with the company and support of one of their older peers. The older student gains confidence and takes pride in and ownership of the task of sharing knowledge and skills with his/her trainee. Entry-level job skills are practically universal, so each student gains from the experience.

LINDA SPARKS • 1st Grade
John F. Kennedy School, Billerica MA

I have used cooperative learning groups a lot through the years. There are so many things that can be learned and shared from working together. There is always frustration with some students, but overall it seems to work. I also try to set it up in a variety of ways, from letting them select their own groups, picking names out of a hat, passing out different topics and forming groups based on the topics. I will use assessments to organize a group as well as make sure that each student has a specific task. (Project editor, information manager, organizer, reporter, researcher, etc.) There always seems to be one student ready to take a back seat and let the others in the group do all of the work. We go over the social skills needed to work in a group. We often will post a list in the classroom of simple rules: using appropriate language, speaking quietly and respectfully while working, listening and encouraging team members, and asking for help when needed. While they work in their groups, I will walk around the class and take notes on what is being worked on. I want to make sure there are no misconceptions about the project. After the project is completed, I grade them in a variety of ways. I give a grade to each participant for his/her contribution to the project, a group grade for the project and or presentation, and a grade for group participation for the project. Students learn more when they are directly involved in what is being taught. This is yet another style of learning.

JESSICA N. MAHTABAN • 8th Grade Math
Woodrow Wilson Middle School, Clifton, NJ

The lesson would begin with a definition of cooperative learning as well as a real-world example. The first activity would be simple; it is called Numbered Heads Together (taken from Kagan in a cooperative learning class). Students number off in their teams so each teammate has a different number; then the teacher asks a question and provides think time. Students put their "heads together" to discuss the question. The teacher calls a number and the student with that number from each group shares with the class the group's answer. The activities would get more difficult as students get comfortable with cooperative learning.

In order to group students in the classroom, ideally there would be four students per group facing each other. On one side would be a high student (based on grades); next to them would be medium high student; across from this student would be a low student; and next to the low student would a medium low student. The high student would rarely interact with the low student because when paired off for activities they would only work with medium high and medium low students. Based on my 10 years of teaching experience the high student rarely has the patience to work with a low student, but the medium high and medium low students will work very well with the low student. Another method of grouping students is according to personality as well as heterogeneously.

chapter eight

SOCIAL COGNITIVE VIEWS OF LEARNING AND MOTIVATION

WHAT WOULD YOU DO?

▶ **TEACHERS' CASEBOOK:** Failure To Self-Regulate

You know that your students need to be organized and self-regulating to do well in both their current and their future classes. But many of the students just don't seem to know how take charge of their own learning. They have trouble completing larger projects—many wait until the last minute. They can't organize their work or decide what is most important. Some can't even keep up with assignments. Their book bags are disaster areas—filled with long overdue assignment sheets and class handouts from last semester crumbled in with school newsletters and permission slips for field trips. You are concerned because they will need to be much more organized and on top of their work as they progress through their education. You have so much material to cover to meet district guidelines, but many of your students are drowning in the amount of work they already have.

CRITICAL THINKING

- What organizational skills do students need to be successful in your subject or class?

- What could you do to teach these skills, while still covering the material that will be on the proficiency or achievement tests the students will have to take in the spring?

- How would you help students develop an authentic sense of efficacy for guiding their own learning?

OVERVIEW AND OBJECTIVES

In past chapters, we have analyzed different aspects of learning. We considered behavioral and information processing explanations of what and how people learn. We have examined cognitive science and complex cognitive processes such as concept learning and problem solving. These explanations of learning focus on the individual and what is happening in his or her "head." Recent perspectives have called attention to two other aspects of learning that are critical: social and cultural factors. In the previous chapter, we examined social constructivism and the interdisciplinary learning sciences. In this chapter, we look at social cognitive theory—a current view of learning and motivation that discusses dynamic interactions among many of the behavioral, personal, and cultural factors involved in learning and motivation.

Social cognitive theory has its roots in Bandura's early criticisms of behavioral views of learning. Social cognitive theory moved beyond behaviorism to focus on humans as self-directed agents who make choices and marshal resources to reach goals. Concepts such as self-efficacy and self-regulated learning are key in social cognitive theories. These concepts are important in understanding motivation as well, so this chapter provides a good path from learning to the discussion of motivation in the next chapter. We end the chapter with a look back at our tour through different models of instruction. Rather than debating the merits of each approach, we will consider the contributions of these different models of instruction, grounded in different theories of learning. Don't feel that you must choose the "best" approach—there is no such thing. Even though theorists argue about which model is best, excellent teachers don't debate. They apply all the approaches, using each one when appropriate.

By the time you have completed this chapter, you should be able to:

Objective 8.1: Define the basic principles of social cognitive theories of learning and motivation including triarchic reciprocal causality, modeling/observational learning, self-efficacy, and agency.

Objective 8.2: Discuss the roles of observation and self-efficacy in learning.

Objective 8.3: Describe important components of self-regulated learning.

Objective 8.4: Apply self-regulated learning principles to teaching.

SOCIAL COGNITIVE THEORY

In the early 1960s, Albert Bandura demonstrated that people can learn by observing both the actions of others and the consequences of those actions. Most of what is known today as *social cognitive theory* is based on the work begun by Albert Bandura in the 1950s at Stanford University. Before we talk about the theory, let's meet the man.

A Self-Directed Life: Albert Bandura

Albert Bandura's life story should be a movie. You could say he lived the American dream, except that he is from Canada. His parents were immigrants from Eastern Europe; they chose the rugged land of northern Alberta for their family farm. Bandura's parents never went to school, but they valued education. His father taught himself to read in three languages, giving young Albert a great model of self-regulated learning—a concept that figures prominently in social cognitive theory today. On the way to finishing high school, Bandura worked many jobs, including a stint as a carpenter at a furniture factory and one as a road worker on the Alaska Highway in the Yukon. He finished his undergraduate degree at the University of British Columbia in three years, even though he had to cram all his classes into the morning to have time for his afternoon jobs. Because he needed a morning class to fill one time slot, he enrolled in introductory psychology and found his future profession (Bandura, 2007, p. 46). His next stop was graduate school at the epicenter of psychological research in 1950—the University of Iowa. After earning his Ph.D. (in three years again), Bandura joined the faculty at Stanford in 1953—he was 28 years old. He is still at Stanford nearly 60 years later, and now teaches some of the children of his former students.

When I read Bandura's autobiography (see http://www.des.emory.edu/mfp/bandurabio.html for a summary with pictures), I was struck by how much his theories reflected his life as a self-directed, self-regulating learner growing up in a challenging environment. Describing his experiences in his two-teacher high school, Bandura said:

> We had to take charge of our own learning. Self-directed learning was an essential means of academic self-development, not a theoretical abstraction. The paucity of educational resources turned out to be an enabling factor that has served me well rather than an insurmountable handicapping one. The content of courses is perishable, but self-regulatory skills have lasting functional value whatever the pursuit might be. (p. 45)

In the next section we will look at the key features of Albert Bandura's work and social cognitive theory by considering four topics: moving beyond behaviorism, the concept of triarchic reciprocal causality, the power of observational learning, and the key beliefs of agency and self-efficacy.

Beyond Behaviorism

Social learning theory Theory that emphasizes learning through observation of others.

Bandura's early **social learning theory** emphasized modeling and observing others being reinforced or punished for particular behaviors. But he found basic behaviorism to be too limited. In his autobiography, Bandura (2007) describes the shortcomings of behaviorism and the need to put people in social context:

I found this behavioristic theorizing discordant with the obvious social reality that much of what we learn is through the power of social modeling. I could not imagine a culture in which its language; mores; familial customs and practices; occupational competencies; and educational, religious, and political practices were gradually shaped in each new member by rewarding and punishing consequences of their trial-and-error performances. (p. 55)

Over time, Bandura's explanations of learning included more attention to cognitive factors such as *expectations* and *beliefs* in addition to the social influences of models (Bandura, 1986, 1997, 2001). His current perspective, **social cognitive theory**, retains an emphasis on the role of other people serving as models and teachers (the *social* part of social cognitive theory), but includes thinking, believing, expecting, anticipating, self-regulating, and making comparisons and judgments (the *cognitive* part). Social cognitive theory is a *dynamic system* that explains human adaptation, learning, and motivation. The theory addresses how people develop social, emotional, cognitive, and behavioral capabilities; how people regulate their own lives; and what motivates them (Bandura, 2007; Bandura & Locke, 2003). In fact, many of the concepts from this chapter will help you understand motivation in the upcoming chapter.

ALBERT BANDURA You may remember Albert Bandura. Pictures from his famous Bobo doll experiment on observational learning are in the background. Most of what we know today as social cognitive theory is based on the work he began in the 1950s at Stanford University.

Triarchic Reciprocal Causality

I claimed that social cognitive theory describes a system. This system, called **triarchic reciprocal causality**, is the dynamic interplay among three kinds of influences: personal, environmental, and behavioral, as shown in Figure 8.1. Personal factors (beliefs, expectations, attitudes, and knowledge), the physical and social environment (resources, consequences of actions, other people, models and teachers, and physical settings), and behavior (individual actions, choices, and verbal statements) all influence and are influenced by each other.

Figure 8.1 shows the interaction of person, environment, and behavior in learning settings (Schunk, Pintrich, & Meece, 2008). External factors such as models, instructional

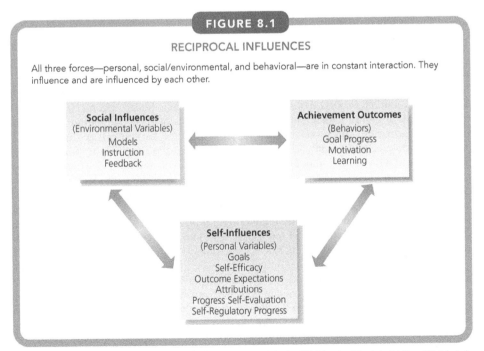

FIGURE 8.1

RECIPROCAL INFLUENCES

All three forces—personal, social/environmental, and behavioral—are in constant interaction. They influence and are influenced by each other.

Social Influences
(Environmental Variables)
Models
Instruction
Feedback

Achievement Outcomes
(Behaviors)
Goal Progress
Motivation
Learning

Self-Influences
(Personal Variables)
Goals
Self-Efficacy
Outcome Expectations
Attributions
Progress Self-Evaluation
Self-Regulatory Progress

Sources: From "Social-Self Interaction and Achievement Behavior" by D. H. Schunk, 1999, Educational Psychologist, 34, p. 221. Adapted with permission of Lawrence Erlbaum Associates, Inc. and the author.

Social cognitive theory Theory that adds concern with cognitive factors such as beliefs, self-perceptions, and expectations to social learning theory.

Triarchic reciprocal causality An explanation of behavior that emphasizes the mutual effects of the individual and the environment on each other.

strategies, or teacher feedback (elements of the environment for students) can affect student personal factors such as goals, sense of efficacy for the task (described in the next section), attributions (beliefs about causes for success and failure), and processes of self-regulation such as planning, monitoring, and controlling distractions. For example, teacher feedback can lead students to feel either more confident or more discouraged, and then the students adjust their goals accordingly. Environmental and personal factors encourage behaviors such as effort and persistence that lead to learning. But these behaviors also reciprocally impact personal factors. For example, as students achieve through increased effort (behavior), their confidence and interest increase (personal). And behaviors also affect the social environment. For example, if students do not persist or if they seem to misunderstand, teachers may change instructional strategies or learning group assignments, thus changing the learning environment for the students.

Think for a minute about the power of reciprocal causality in classrooms. If personal factors, behaviors, and the environment are in constant interaction, then cycles of events are progressive and self-perpetuating. Suppose a student who is new to the school walks into class late because he got lost in the unfamiliar building. The student has a tattoo and several visible pierced body parts. He is anxious about his first day and hopes to do better at this new school, but the teacher's initial reaction to his late entry and dramatic appearance is a bit hostile. The student feels insulted and responds in kind, so the teacher begins to form expectations about him and acts more vigilant, less trusting. The student senses the distrust. He decides that this school will be just as worthless as his previous one—and wonders why he should bother to try. The teacher sees the student's disengagement, invests less effort in teaching him, and the cycle continues. These reciprocal effects are more than hypothetical. When Trevor and Kitty Williams (2010) examined data on high school students' confidence in mathematics and achievement in mathematics in 30 different countries, they found evidence that math confidence and math achievement reciprocally influenced each other in 26 of the countries, just as Bandura would predict.

Two key elements of social cognitive theory are observational learning and self-efficacy. We will examine each of these more closely, with special emphasis on their implications for teaching.

MODELING: LEARNING BY OBSERVING OTHERS

Learning by observing others is a key element of social cognitive theory. What causes an individual to learn and perform modeled behaviors and skills? Several factors play a role. The developmental level of the observer makes a difference in learning. As children grow older, they are able to focus attention for longer periods of time, use memory strategies to retain information, and motivate themselves to practice, as you can see in Table 8.1. A second influence is the status of the model. Children are more likely to imitate the actions of others who seem competent, powerful, prestigious, and enthusiastic, so parents, teachers, older siblings, athletes, action heroes, rock stars, or film personalities may serve as models, depending on the age and interests of the child. Third, by watching others, we learn about what behaviors are appropriate for people like ourselves, so models who are seen as similar are more readily imitated (Schunk, Pintrich, & Meece, 2008). All students need to see successful, capable models who look and sound like them, no matter what their ethnicity, socioeconomic status, or gender.

Look at Table 8.1. The last three influences involve goals and expectations. If observers expect that certain actions of models will lead to particular outcomes (such as specific practice regimens leading to improved athletic performance) and the observers value those outcomes or goals, then the observers will pay attention to the models and try to reproduce their behaviors. Finally, observers are more likely to learn from models if the observers have a high level of self-efficacy—that is, if they believe they are capable of doing the actions needed to reach the goals, or at least of learning how to do so (Bandura, 1997; Schunk, Pintrich, & Meece, 2008).

TABLE 8.1 • **Factors That Affect Observational Learning**

CHARACTERISTIC	EFFECTS ON MODELING PROCESS
Developmental Status	Improvements with development include longer attention and increased capacity to process information, use strategies, compare performances with memorial representations, and adopt intrinsic motivators.
Model Prestige and Competence	Observers pay greater attention to competent, high-status models. Consequences of modeled behaviors convey information about functional value. Observers attempt to learn actions they believe they will need to perform.
Vicarious Consequences	Consequences to models convey information about behavioral appropriateness and likely outcomes of actions. Valued consequences motivate observers. Similarity in attributes or competence signals appropriateness and heightens motivation.
Outcome Expectations	Observers are more likely to perform modeled actions they believe are appropriate and will result in rewarding outcomes.
Goal Setting	Observers are likely to attend to models who demonstrate behaviors that help observers attain goals.
Self-efficacy	Observers attend to models when they believe they are capable of learning or performing the modeled behavior. Observation of similar models affects self-efficacy ("If they can do it, I can too").

Source: From Learning Theories: An Education Perspective (4th ed.), by D. H. Schunk. Published by Prentice Hall. Copyright © 2004 by Prentice Hall. Reprinted by permission of Pearson Education, Inc., Upper Saddle River, NJ.

Elements of Observational Learning

STOP & THINK Your interview for a position in the middle school is going well. The next question is: "Who are your models as teachers? Do you hear yourself saying or see yourself doing things that other teachers have done? Are there teachers from films or books that you would like to emulate?" •

Through observational learning, we learn not only *how* to perform a behavior but also what will happen to us in specific situations if we perform it. Observation can be a very efficient learning process. The first time children hold hairbrushes, cups, or tennis rackets, they usually brush, drink, or swing as well as they can, given their current muscle development and coordination. Let's take a closer look at how observational learning occurs. Bandura (1986) notes that observational learning includes four elements: paying attention, retaining information or impressions, producing behaviors, and being motivated to repeat the behaviors.

ATTENTION. In order to learn through observation, we have to pay attention. In teaching, you will have to ensure students' attention to the critical features of the lesson by making clear presentations and highlighting important points. In demonstrating a skill (for example, threading a sewing machine or operating a lathe), you may need to have students look over your shoulder as you work. Seeing your hands from the same perspective as they see their own directs their attention to the right features of the situation and makes observational learning easier.

RETENTION. In order to imitate the behavior of a model, you have to remember it. This involves mentally representing the model's actions in some way, probably as verbal steps ("Hwa-Rang, the eighth form in Tae Kwan Do karate, is a palm-heel block, then a middle riding stance punch, then . . ."), or as visual images, or both. Retention can be improved by mental rehearsal (imagining imitating the behavior) or by actual practice. In the retention phase of observational learning, practice helps us remember the elements of the desired behavior, such as the sequence of steps.

PRODUCTION.   Once we "know" how a behavior should look and remember the elements or steps, we still may not perform it smoothly. Sometimes, we need a great deal of practice, feedback, and coaching about subtle points before we can reproduce the behavior of the model. In the production phase, practice makes the behavior smoother and more expert.

MOTIVATION AND REINFORCEMENT.   Social learning theory distinguishes between acquisition and performance. We may acquire a new skill or behavior through observation, but we may not perform that behavior until there is some motivation or incentive to do so. Reinforcement can play several roles in observational learning. If we anticipate being reinforced for imitating the actions of a model, we may be more motivated to pay attention, remember, and reproduce the behaviors. In addition, reinforcement is important in maintaining learning. A person who tries a new behavior is unlikely to persist without reinforcement (Schunk, 2008). For example, if an unpopular student adopted the dress of the "in" group, but was ignored or ridiculed, it is unlikely that the imitation would continue.

Bandura identifies three forms of reinforcement that can encourage observational learning. First, of course, the observer may reproduce the behaviors of the model and receive direct reinforcement, as when a gymnast successfully executes a front flip/round-off combination and the coach/model says, "Excellent!"

But the reinforcement need not be direct—it may be **vicarious reinforcement**. The observer may simply see others reinforced for a particular behavior and then increase his or her production of that behavior. For example, if you compliment two students on the attractive illustrations in their lab reports, several other students who observe your compliments may turn in illustrated lab reports next time. Most TV ads hope for this kind of effect. People in commercials become deliriously happy when they drive a particular car or drink a specific energy drink, and the viewer is supposed to do the same; the viewer's behavior is reinforced vicariously by the actors' obvious pleasure. Punishment can also be vicarious: You may slow down on a stretch of highway after seeing several people get speeding tickets there.

The final form of reinforcement is **self-reinforcement**, or controlling your own reinforcers. This sort of reinforcement is important for both students and teachers. In fact, if one goal of education is to produce people who are capable of educating themselves, then students must learn to manage their own lives, set their own goals, and provide their own reinforcement. In adult life, rewards are sometimes vague and goals often take a long time to reach. Think about how many small steps are required to complete an education and find your first job. As a teacher, sometimes self-reinforcement is all that keeps you going. Life is filled with tasks that call for this sort of self-regulation—a topic we will address later in this chapter (Rachlin, 2004).

Social cognitive theory has some powerful implications for teaching. In this section, we will look more closely at using observational learning in teaching.

Observational Learning in Teaching

Vicarious reinforcement Increasing the chances that we will repeat a behavior by observing another person being reinforced for that behavior.

Self-reinforcement Controlling (selecting and administering) your own reinforcers.

STOP & THINK How would you incorporate observational learning into your teaching? What are the skills, attitudes, and strategies that can be modeled in teaching your subject? •

There are five possible outcomes of observational learning: directing attention, encouraging existing behaviors, changing inhibitions, teaching new behaviors and attitudes, and arousing emotions. Let's look at each of these as they occur in classrooms.

DIRECTING ATTENTION. By observing others, we not only learn about actions but also notice the objects involved in the actions. For example, in a preschool class, when one child plays enthusiastically with a toy that has been ignored for days, many other children may want to have the toy, even if they play with it in different ways or simply carry it around. This happens, in part, because the children's attention has been drawn to that particular toy.

FINE-TUNING ALREADY-LEARNED BEHAVIORS. All of us have had the experience of looking for cues from other people when we find ourselves in unfamiliar situations. Observing the behavior of others tells us which of our already-learned behaviors to use: the proper fork for eating the salad, when to leave a gathering, what kind of language is appropriate, and so on. Adopting the dress and grooming styles of TV or music idols is another example of this kind of effect.

STRENGTHENING OR WEAKENING INHIBITIONS. If class members witness one student breaking a class rule and getting away with it, they may learn that undesirable consequences do not always follow rule breaking. If the rule breaker is a well-liked, high-status class leader, the effect of the modeling may be even more pronounced. This **ripple effect** (Kounin, 1970) can work for the teacher's benefit. When the teacher deals effectively with a rule breaker, especially a class leader, the idea of breaking this rule may be inhibited for the other students viewing the interaction. This does not mean that teachers must reprimand each student who breaks a rule, but once a teacher has called for a particular action, following through is an important part of capitalizing on the ripple effect.

TEACHING NEW BEHAVIORS. Modeling has long been used, of course, to teach dance, sports, and crafts, as well as skills in subjects such as food science, chemistry, and welding. Modeling can also be applied deliberately in the classroom to teach mental skills and to broaden horizons— to teach new ways of thinking. Teachers serve as models for a vast range of behaviors, from pronouncing vocabulary words, to reacting to the seizure of a student with epilepsy, to being enthusiastic about learning. For example, a teacher might model critical thinking skills by thinking "out loud" about a student's question. Or a high school teacher concerned about girls who seem to have stereotyped ideas about careers might invite women with nontraditional jobs to speak to the class. Studies indicate that modeling can be most effective when the teacher makes use of all the elements of observational learning—attention, retention, production, and especially reinforcement and practice.

Models who are the same age as the students may be particularly effective. For example, Schunk and Hanson (1985) compared two methods for teaching subtraction to 2nd graders who had difficulties learning this skill. One group of students observed other 2nd graders learning the procedures, while another group watched a teacher's demonstration. Then, both groups participated in the same instructional program. The students who observed peer models learning not only scored higher on tests of subtraction after instruction but also gained more confidence in their own ability to learn. For students who doubt their own abilities, a good model is a low-achieving peer who keeps trying and finally masters the material (Schunk, 2004).

Connect and Extend to PRAXIS II™

Observational Learning (II, B2) Identify situations in which observational learning may be a wise approach, and describe the essential elements of effective observational learning.

Ripple effect "Contagious" spreading of behaviors through imitation.

DO AS I DO . . . Modeling has long been used to teach dance, sports, and crafts, and skills such cooking, chemistry, and welding. Modeling can also be applied deliberately in the classroom to teach mental skills and to broaden horizons—to teach new ways of thinking.

GUIDELINES

Using Observational Learning

Model behaviors and attitudes you want your students to learn.
Examples

1. Show enthusiasm for the subject you teach.
2. Be willing to demonstrate both the mental and the physical tasks you expect the students to perform. I once saw a teacher sit down in the sandbox while her 4-year-old students watched her demonstrate the difference between "playing with sand" and "throwing sand."
3. When reading to students, model good problem solving. Stop and say, "Now let me see if I remember what happened so far," or "That was a hard sentence. I'm going to read it again."
4. Model good problem solving—think out loud as you work through a difficult problem.

Use peers, especially class leaders, as models.
Examples

1. In group work, pair students who do well with those who are having difficulties.
2. Ask students to demonstrate the difference between "whispering" and "silence—no talking."

Make sure students see that positive behaviors lead to reinforcement for others.
Examples

1. Point out the connections between positive behavior and positive consequences in stories.
2. Be fair in giving reinforcement. The same rules for rewards should apply to both the students with problems and the students who do not cause trouble.

Enlist the help of class leaders in modeling behaviors for the entire class.
Examples

1. Ask a well-liked student to be friendly to an isolated, fearful student.
2. Let high-status students lead an activity when you need class cooperation or when students are likely to be reluctant at first. Popular students can model dialogues in foreign-language classes or be the first to tackle dissection procedures in biology.

For more information on observational learning,
see: http://www.readwritethink.org/lessons/lesson_view.asp?id=275

AROUSING EMOTION. Finally, through observational learning, people may develop emotional reactions to situations they have never experienced personally, such as flying or driving. A child who watches a friend fall from a swing and break an arm may become fearful of swings. After the terrible events of September 11, 2001, children may be anxious when they see airplanes flying close to the ground. News reports of shark attacks have many of us anxious about swimming in the ocean. Note that hearing and reading about a situation are also forms of observation. Some terrible examples of modeling occur with "copy-cat killings" or suicide clusters in schools. When frightening things happen to people who are similar in age or circumstances to your students, they may need to be given an opportunity to talk about their emotions.

The *Guidelines* will give you some ideas about using observational learning in the classroom.

Self-efficacy is a key element of social cognitive theory that is especially important in learning and teaching.

SELF-EFFICACY AND AGENCY

Self-efficacy A person's sense of being able to deal effectively with a particular task.

Human agency The capacity to coordinate learning skills, motivation, and emotions to reach your goals.

Bandura (1986, 1994, 1997) suggests that predictions about possible outcomes of behavior are critical for learning because they affect goals, effort, persistence, strategies, and resilience. "Will I succeed or fail? Will I be liked or laughed at?" "Will I be more accepted by teachers in this new school?" These predictions are affected by **self-efficacy**—our beliefs about our personal competence or effectiveness in a given area. Bandura (1994) defines self-efficacy as "people's beliefs about their capabilities to produce designated levels of performance that exercise influence over events that affect their lives" (p. 71).

Bandura's more recent efforts (2006) and the work of many other researchers have focused on the role of self-efficacy in **human agency**—the *exercising influence over life events* part of the definition above. Agency involves the ability to make intentional choices and action plans, design appropriate courses of action, and then motivate and regulate the execution of these plans and actions. When we discuss self-regulation later in the chapter, you will see how students and teachers can become more *agentic*—more self-directing and in charge of their own learning and motivation.

Self-Efficacy, Self-Concept, and Self-Esteem

Most people assume self-efficacy is the same as self-concept or self-esteem, but it isn't. *Self-efficacy* is future-oriented, "a context-specific assessment of competence to perform a specific task" (Pajares, 1997, p. 15). *Self-concept* is a more global construct that contains many perceptions about the self, including self-efficacy. Self-concept is developed as a result of external and internal comparisons, using other people or other aspects of the self as frames of reference. But self-efficacy focuses on your ability to successfully accomplish a particular task with no need for comparisons—the question is whether *you* can do it, not whether others would be successful. Also, self-efficacy beliefs are strong predictors of behavior, but self-concept has weaker predictive power (Anderman & Anderman, 2009; Bandura, 1997).

Self-efficacy is "context specific," which means it varies, depending on the subject or task. For example, my sense of efficacy for singing is really low, but I feel confident in my ability to read a map and navigate (except in certain cities that are hopeless). Even young students have different efficacy beliefs for different tasks. One study found that by the 1st grade, students already differentiated among their sense of efficacy for reading, for writing, and for spelling (Wilson & Trainin, 2007).

Self-efficacy is concerned with judgments of personal competence; self-esteem is concerned with judgments of self-worth. There is no direct relationship between self-esteem and self-efficacy. It is possible to feel highly efficacious in one area and still not have a high level of self-esteem, or vice versa (Valentine, DuBois, & Cooper, 2004). For example, as I confessed earlier, I have very low self-efficacy for singing, but my self-esteem is not affected, probably because my life does not require singing. But if my self-efficacy for teaching a particular class started dropping after several bad experiences, I know my self-esteem would suffer because I value teaching.

CAN I DO IT? Self-efficacy refers to the knowledge of one's own ability to successfully accomplish a particular task with no need for comparisons with others' ability—the question is "Can I do it?" not "Are others better than I am?"

Connect and Extend to PRAXIS II™

Modeling (II, B2)
Teachers often utilize modeling to teach students new behaviors. Identify the characteristics that tend to make models effective in instructional context.

Sources of Self-Efficacy

Bandura identified four sources of self-efficacy expectations: mastery experiences, physiological and emotional arousal, vicarious experiences, and social persuasion. **Mastery experiences** are our own direct experiences—usually the most powerful source of efficacy information. Successes raise efficacy beliefs, while failures lower efficacy. Level of **arousal** affects self-efficacy, depending on how the arousal is interpreted. As you face the task, are you anxious and worried (lowers efficacy) or excited and "psyched" (raises efficacy) (Bandura, 1997; Schunk, Pintrich, & Meece, 2008; Usher & Pajares, 2009)?

In **vicarious experiences**, someone else models accomplishments. The more closely the student identifies with the model, the greater the impact on self-efficacy will be. When the model performs well, the student's efficacy is enhanced, but when the model performs poorly, efficacy expectations decrease. Although mastery experiences generally are acknowledged as the most influential source of efficacy beliefs in adults, Keyser and Barling (1981) found that children (6th graders in their study) rely more on **modeling** as a source of self-efficacy information.

Social persuasion can be a "pep talk" or specific performance feedback. Social persuasion alone can't create enduring increases in self-efficacy, but a persuasive boost in self-efficacy can lead a student to make an effort, attempt new strategies, or try hard enough to succeed (Bandura, 1982). Social persuasion can counter occasional setbacks that might have instilled self-doubt and interrupted persistence. The potency of persuasion depends on the credibility, trustworthiness, and expertise of the persuader (Bandura, 1997). Table 8.2 summarizes the sources of self-efficacy.

Self-Efficacy in Learning and Teaching

STOP & THINK On a scale from 1 to 100, how confident are you that you will finish reading this chapter today? •

Let's assume your sense of efficacy is around 90 for completing this chapter. Greater efficacy leads to greater effort and persistence in the face of setbacks, so even if you are interrupted in your reading, you are likely to return to the task. I believe I can finish writing this section today, so I have resumed work on it after my computer crashed and I had to start over on several pages. Of course, that could make for a late night, because I am going to a San Francisco Giants baseball game at 7:00 tonight and may have to finish the section after the game.

Self-efficacy also influences motivation through goal setting. If we have a high sense of efficacy in a given area, we will set higher goals, be less afraid of failure, and find new strategies when old ones fail. If your sense of efficacy for reading this chapter is high, you are likely to set high goals for completing the chapter—maybe you will take some notes,

Mastery experiences Our own direct experiences—the most powerful source of efficacy information.

Arousal Physical and psychological reactions causing a person to feel alert, excited, or tense.

Vicarious experiences Accomplishments that are modeled by someone else.

Modeling Changes in behavior, thinking, or emotions that happen through observing another person—a model.

Social persuasion A "pep talk" or specific performance feedback—one source of self-efficacy.

TABLE 8.2 • **Sources of Self-Efficacy**

SOURCE	EXAMPLE
Mastery Experiences	Past successes and failures in similar situations, as perceived by the individual. To increase efficacy, the success must be attributed to the ability, effort, choices, and strategies of the individual—not to luck or extensive help from others.
Vicarious Experiences	Seeing other people like you succeed on a task or reach a goal that is similar to the one you face.
Social Persuasion	Encouragement, informational feedback, useful guidance from a trusted source.
Physiological Arousal	Positive or negative arousal—excitement and a feeling of being "psyched" and ready (increases efficacy) or a sense of anxiety and foreboding (decreases efficacy).

GUIDELINES

Encouraging Self-Efficacy

Emphasize students' progress in a particular area.
Examples

1. Return to earlier material in reviews and show how "easy" it is now.
2. Encourage students to improve projects when they have learned more.
3. Keep examples of particularly good work in portfolios.

Set learning goals for your students, and model a mastery orientation for them.
Examples

1. Recognize progress and improvement.
2. Share examples of how you have developed your abilities in a given area and provide other models of achievement who are similar to your students—no supermen or superwomen whose accomplishments seem unattainable.
3. Read stories about students who overcame physical, mental, or economic challenges.
4. Don't excuse failure because a student has problems outside school. Help the student succeed inside school.

Make specific suggestions for improvement, and revise grades when improvements are made.
Examples

1. Return work with comments noting what the students did right, what they did wrong, and why they might have made the mistakes.
2. Experiment with peer editing.
3. Show students how their revised, higher grade reflects greater competence and raises their class average.

Stress connections between past efforts and past accomplishments.
Examples

1. Have individual goal-setting and goal-review conferences with students, in which you ask students to reflect on how they solved difficult problems.
2. Confront self-defeating, failure-avoiding strategies directly.

For more information on self-efficacy, see:
http://www.emory.edu/EDUCATION/mfp/self-efficacy.html

too. If your sense of efficacy is low, however, you may avoid the reading altogether or give up easily when problems arise or you are interrupted with a better offer (Bandura, 1993, 1997; Pajares & Schunk, 2001). See the *Guidelines* for ideas about encouraging self-efficacy.

What is the most motivating level of efficacy? Should students be accurate, optimistic, or pessimistic in their predictions? There is evidence that a higher sense of self-efficacy supports motivation, even when the efficacy is an overestimation. Children and adults who are optimistic about the future are more mentally and physically healthy, less depressed, and more motivated to achieve (Flammer, 1995; Seligman, 2006). After examining almost 140 studies of motivation, Sandra Graham concluded that these qualities characterize many African Americans. She found that the African Americans studied had strong self-concepts and high expectations, even in the face of difficulties (Graham, 1994, 1995).

As you might expect, there are dangers in underestimating abilities because then students are more likely to put out a weak effort and give up easily. But there are dangers in continually overestimating performance as well. Students who think that they are better readers than they actually are may not be motivated to go back and repair misunderstandings as they read. They don't discover that they did not really understand the material until it is too late (Pintrich & Zusho, 2002).

In schools, we are particularly interested in self-efficacy for learning mathematics, writing, history, science, sports, and other subjects, as well as self-efficacy for using learning strategies and for the many other challenges that classrooms present. For example, in research with students, self-efficacy is related to writing and math performance for students from 3rd grade through high school (Fast et al., 2010; Kenney-Benson, Pomerantz, Ryan, & Patrick, 2006; Pajares, 2002), life satisfaction for adolescents (Vecchio, Gerbino, Pastorelli, Del Bove, & Caprara, 2007), use of deep processing learning strategies for college students (Prat-Sala & Redford, 2010), choice of college major (Pajares, 2002), and performance in college for older students (Elias & MacDonald, 2007). The value of self-efficacy seems to be cross-cultural. For example, self-efficacy is related to math/science goals and interests for Mexican American youth (Navarro, Flores, & Worthington, 2007), academic achievement in math for both male and female middle-school students (Kenney-Benson, Pomerantz, Ryan, & Patrick, 2006), and mathematics achievement for both Anglo and South Asian Canadian middle-school students (Klassen, 2004).

So, maybe you are thinking, sure higher self-efficacy is related to higher achievement because students who have more ability have higher self-efficacy. But these relationships between self-efficacy and achievement hold even when we take ability into account. For example, when students with the same ability in math are compared, the ones with higher self-efficacy for math perform better in math (Wigfield & Wentzel, 2007).

Research indicates that performance in school is improved and self-efficacy is increased when students (a) adopt short-term goals so it is easier to judge progress; (b) are taught to use specific learning strategies such as outlining or summarizing that help them focus attention; and (c) receive rewards based on achievement, not just engagement, because achievement rewards signal increasing competence (Graham & Weiner, 1996).

Teachers' Sense of Efficacy

Much of my own research has focused on **teachers' sense of efficacy**, defined as a teacher's belief that he or she can reach even difficult students to help them learn. This confident belief appears to be one of the few personal characteristics of teachers that predict student achievement (Tschannen-Moran & Woolfolk Hoy, 2001; Tschannen-Moran, Woolfolk Hoy, & Hoy, 1998; Woolfolk Hoy & Burke-Spero, 2005; Woolfolk Hoy, Hoy, & Davis, 2009). As with any kind of efficacy, there may be both benefits and dangers in overestimating abilities. Optimistic teachers probably set higher goals, work harder, reteach when necessary, and persist in the face of problems. But some benefits might follow from having doubts about your efficacy. The *Point/Counterpoint* looks at both sides of teachers' efficacy judgments.

It takes self-efficacy to be self-regulated. We turn to this issue next to explore how you can help your students lead a self-directed life.

Teachers' sense of efficacy A teacher's belief that he or she can reach even the most difficult students and help them learn.

TEACHER SELF-EFFICACY Research shows that teachers' sense of efficacy grows from real success with students. Experience or training that helps teachers succeed in the day-to-day tasks of teaching will contribute to their sense of efficacy.

POINT/COUNTERPOINT: Are High Levels of Teacher Efficacy Beneficial?

Based on Bandura's research on self-efficacy, we probably would assume that high sense of efficacy for teachers is a good thing. But not everyone agrees. Here is the debate.

POINT

▶ **Higher efficacy is better than lower.** The research on teachers' sense of efficacy points to many positive outcomes related to higher efficacy. With my husband and a colleague, I summarized this research (Woolfolk Hoy, Hoy, & Davis, 2009). Here are a few of the findings we identified. Teachers with a strong sense of efficacy tend be more enthusiastic and spend more time teaching in subject areas where their sense of efficacy is higher, and they tend to avoid subjects when efficacy is lower. Teachers with higher efficacy judgments tend to be more open to new ideas; more willing to experiment with new methods to better meet the needs of their students; more likely to use powerful but potentially difficult-to-manage methods such as inquiry and small-group work; and less likely to use easy-to-adopt but weaker methods such as lectures. Higher efficacy teachers are less likely to criticize students and more persistent in following up on incorrect student answers. Teachers with a higher sense of efficacy tend to select strategies that support student learning rather than those that simply cover the curriculum. Compared to low efficacy teachers, those who report a higher sense of efficacy tend to be more active in monitoring seatwork and maintaining academic focus, and they respond quickly to student misbehavior by redirecting attention without showing anger or becoming threatened. What about the students? In addition to being related to student achievement, teachers' sense of efficacy has been associated with other student outcomes such as motivation and students' own sense of efficacy.

COUNTERPOINT

▶ **There are problems with high efficacy.** In spite of the large body of literature describing positive outcomes associated with higher self-efficacy, several researchers have questioned whether higher is always better. For example, Karl Wheatley (2002, 2005) suggested that several forms of teacher self-efficacy might be problematic. One is the excessive optimism of beginning teachers that interferes with their ability to accurately judge their own effectiveness. In an analysis of students who were about to begin their student teaching, Carol Weinstein (1988) found a strong sense of "unrealistic optimism"—the tendency to believe that problems experienced by others would not happen to them. Interestingly, the unrealistic optimism was greatest for activities having to do with controlling students (e.g., maintaining discipline, and establishing and enforcing class rules). These findings are consistent with Emmer and Hickman's (1991) observations that student teachers who had trouble managing their classes still reported high levels of classroom management efficacy. Another problematic consequence of higher efficacy is resistance to acquiring new knowledge and skills and a tendency to "stick with what works"—with the ways of teaching that have provided the sense of mastery in the past. Overconfident efficacy may quickly be followed by giving up if the task proves more difficult than first thought. Wheatley (2002) believes "lower efficacy beliefs are essential for teacher learning; doubt motivates change" (p. 18).

Beyond Either/Or. It is true that persistent high efficacy perceptions in the face of poor performance (unrealistic optimism) can produce avoidance rather than action and interfere with teacher learning, but I believe that a sense of *efficacy for learning to teach* would be necessary to respond in these positive ways to the doubts described above. The challenge is to develop an authentic sense of self-efficacy—one that is accurate or just a bit optimistic.

SELF-REGULATED LEARNING

As you may remember from the beginning of this chapter, Albert Bandura said his early education in a tiny school in Canada had given him self-regulation skills that lasted a lifetime. He also noted:

> A major goal of formal education is to equip students with the intellectual tools, self-beliefs, and self-regulatory capabilities to educate themselves throughout their lifetime. The rapid pace of technological change and accelerated growth of knowledge are placing a premium on capability for self-directed learning. (Bandura, 2007, p. 10)

Today, people change jobs an average of seven times before they retire. Many of these career changes require new learning that must be self-initiated and self-directed (Martinez-Pons, 2002). Thus, one goal of teaching, as Bandura noted, should be to free students from the need for teachers, so the students can continue to learn independently throughout their lives. To continue learning independently throughout life, you must be self-regulated—what we refer to in conversations as a *self-starter*.

STOP & THINK Think about the class you are taking where you are using this textbook. On a 7-point scale—from 1 = *not at all true of me*, to 7 = *very true of me*—answer the following questions:

1. When I study for a test, I try to put together the information from class and from the book.

2. When I do homework, I try to remember what the teacher said in class so I can answer the questions correctly.

3. I know I will be able to learn the material for this class.

4. I expect to do well in this class.

5. I ask myself questions to make sure I know the material I have been studying.

6. Even when study materials are dull and uninteresting, I keep working until I finish. •

You have just answered six items from the Motivated Strategies for Learning Questionnaire (MSLQ) (Midgley, et al., 1998; Pintrich & De Groot, 1990). This questionnaire has been used in hundreds of studies to assess students' self-regulated learning and motivation. How did you do? The first two questions assess your use of *cognitive strategies*. The second two questions assess your *sense of efficacy* for this class. But the last two questions (5 and 6) specifically assess **self-regulation**, defined by Barry Zimmerman and Dale Schunk (2011) as the process we use to activate and sustain our thoughts, behaviors, and emotions in order to reach our goals. Bandura (2007) summarizes self-regulation as setting goals and mobilizing the efforts and resources needed to reach those goals. When the goals involve learning, we talk about *self-regulated learning* (Dinsmore, Alexander, & Loughlin, 2008). Self-regulated learners are "metacognitive, motived to learn, and strategic" (Perry & Rahim, 2011, p. 122).

Self-regulated learners have a combination of academic learning skills and self-control that makes learning easier, so they are more motivated; in other words, they have the skill and the will to learn (Murphy & Alexander, 2000; Schunk, 2005). Self-regulated learners transform their mental abilities, whatever they are, into academic skills and strategies (Zimmerman & Schunk, 2011). Many studies link strategy use to different measures of academic achievement, especially for middle-school and high school students (Fredricks et al., 2004). For younger students, self-regulation of attention and emotion are critical for learning and achieving in school (Valiente, Lemery-Chalfant, & Swanson, 2010).

What Influences Self-Regulation?

The concept of self-regulated learning integrates much of what is known about effective learning and motivation. As you can see from the processes described above, three factors influence skill and will: knowledge, motivation, and self-discipline or volition. In addition, there are developmental differences among students.

KNOWLEDGE. To be self-regulated learners, students need knowledge about themselves, the subject, the task, strategies for learning, and the contexts in which they will apply their learning. "Expert" students know about themselves and how they learn best. For example, they know their preferred learning approaches; what is easy and what is hard for them; how to cope with the difficult parts; what their interests and talents are; and how to use their strengths. These experts also know quite a bit about the subject being studied—and the more they know, the easier it is to learn more (Alexander, Schallert, & Reynolds, 2009). They probably understand that different learning tasks require different approaches on their part. A simple memory task, for example, might require a mnemonic strategy, whereas a complex comprehension task might be approached by means of concept maps of the key ideas. Also, these self-regulated learners know that learning is often difficult and knowledge is seldom absolute; there usually are different ways of looking at problems as well as different solutions (Greene, Muis, & Pieschl, 2010; Winne, 1995).

These expert students not only know what each task requires but also can apply the strategy needed. They can skim or read carefully. They can use memory strategies or

Self-regulation Process of activating and sustaining thoughts, behaviors, and emotions in order to reach goals.

reorganize the material. As they become more knowledgeable in a field, they apply many of these strategies automatically. In short, they have mastered a large, flexible repertoire of learning strategies. Finally, self-regulated learners think about the contexts in which they will apply their knowledge—when and where they will use their learning—so they can set motivating goals and connect present work to future accomplishments (Weinstein, 1994; Winne, 1995).

MOTIVATION. Self-regulated learners are motivated to learn (see Chapter 9). They find many tasks in school interesting because they value learning, not just performing well in the eyes of others. They believe their own intelligence and abilities are improvable. Even if they are not intrinsically motivated by a particular task, they are serious about getting the intended benefit from it. They focus their attention and other cognitive and emotional resources on the task at hand. They know why they are studying, so their actions and choices are self-determined and not controlled by others (Zimmerman, 2011). However, knowledge and motivation are not always enough. Self-regulated learners need volition or self-discipline. "Where motivation denotes commitment, volition denotes follow-through" (Corno, 1992, p. 72).

VOLITION. I am two months behind in this project. I have been writing almost all day, 6 days a week since last January. I am barely awake, but I want to keep writing because the deadline for this chapter is very near. I have knowledge and motivation, but to keep going I need a good dose of volition. **Volition** is an old-fashioned word for will-power. The more technical definition for volition is *protecting opportunities to reach goals*. Self-regulated learners know how to protect themselves from distractions—where to study, for example, so they are not interrupted. They know how to cope when they feel anxious, drowsy, or lazy (Corno, 2011; Snow, Corno, & Jackson, 1996). And they know what to do when they are tempted to stop working and have (another) cup of coffee—the temptation I'm facing now—that, and a beautiful San Francisco day that beckons me to pull weeds in the backyard (pulling weeds always looks appealing when I face a tough writing job—cleaning closets is a close second).

Volition is deliberate and effortful, but with practice it can become more automatic—a habit or a "work ethic" (Corno, 2011). William James knew this over 100 years ago. One of my favorite James quotes is about making volition a habit. He said: "do every day or two something for no other reason than that you would rather not do it, so that when the hour of dire need draws nigh, it may find you not unnerved and untrained to stand the test" (James, 1890, IV, p. 126).

Volition Will power; self-discipline; work styles that protect opportunities to reach goals by applying self-regulated learning.

Co-regulation A transitional phase during which students gradually appropriate self-regulated learning and skills through modeling, direct teaching, feedback, and coaching from teachers, parents, or peers.

Shared regulation Students working together to regulate each other through reminders, prompts, and other guidance.

DEVELOPMENT OF SELF-REGULATION. There are developmental differences in self-regulation. Self-regulation generally improves over time. In the early grades, girls may be better than boys in self-regulation (Greene, Muis, & Pieschl, 2010; Matthews, Ponitz, & Morrison, 2009).

How do students develop knowledge, motivation, and volition? Two social processes support the development of self-regulation: co-regulation and shared regulation. **Co-regulation** is a transitional phase during which students gradually appropriate self-regulated learning and skills through modeling, direct teaching, feedback, and coaching from teachers, parents, or peers. **Shared regulation** happens when students work together to regulate each other through reminders, prompts, and other guidance.

What does self-regulation look like when it has developed? Let's examine some models.

THE SKILL AND THE WILL Self-regulated learners have a combination of academic learning skills and self-control that makes learning easier; they have the *skill* and the *will* to learn.

Models of Self-Regulated Learning and Agency

Albert Bandura may have gone from high-school graduate to professor at Stanford in 6 years using his self-regulated learning knowledge and skills, but not all of your students will be Banduras with established *habits of volition*. In fact, some psychologists suggest that you think of this capacity as one of many characteristics that distinguish individuals (Snow, Corno, & Jackson, 1996). Some students are much better at it than others. How can you help more students become self-regulated learners in school? What is involved in being self-regulated?

Theoretical models of **self-regulated learning** describe how learners—like you!—set goals and mobilize the efforts and resources needed to reach those goals. There are several models of self-regulated learning, but all agree that the cognitive processes needed for self-regulated learning require effort (Greene, Muis, & Pieschl, 2010; Puustinen & Pulkkinen, 2001; Winne, 2011). Let's look at one developed by Phil Winne and Allyson Hadwin (1998), shown in Figure 8.2. This depiction of self-regulated learning has many facets, as it should when the topic at hand is how you manage your academic life.

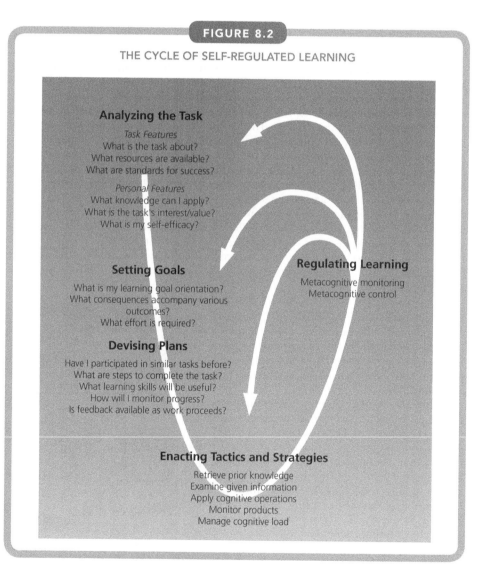

FIGURE 8.2

THE CYCLE OF SELF-REGULATED LEARNING

Analyzing the Task

Task Features
What is the task about?
What resources are available?
What are standards for success?

Personal Features
What knowledge can I apply?
What is the task's interest/value?
What is my self-efficacy?

Setting Goals

What is my learning goal orientation?
What consequences accompany various outcomes?
What effort is required?

Devising Plans

Have I participated in similar tasks before?
What are steps to complete the task?
What learning skills will be useful?
How will I monitor progress?
Is feedback available as work proceeds?

Regulating Learning

Metacognitive monitoring
Metacognitive control

Enacting Tactics and Strategies

Retrieve prior knowledge
Examine given information
Apply cognitive operations
Monitor products
Manage cognitive load

Self-regulated learning A view of learning as skills and will applied to analyzing learning tasks, setting goals and planning how to do the task, applying skills, and especially making adjustments about how learning is carried out.

Source: "The Cycle of Self-Regulated Learning" from Educational Psychology (3rd Canadian ed.) by A. E. Woolfolk, P. H. Winne, and N. E. Perry. Toronto: Pearson, 2006, p. 307, Fig 8.9. Adapted with permission of Pearson Education Canada and Philip Winne.

The model of self-regulated learning in Figure 8.2 is based on the belief that learners are *agents*. As we saw earlier, agency is the capacity to coordinate learning skills, motivation, and emotions to reach your goals. Agents are not puppets on strings held by teachers, textbook authors, or Web page designers. Instead, agents control many factors that influence how they learn. Self-regulating learners exercise agency as they engage in a cycle with four main stages: analyzing the task, setting goals and devising plans, enacting strategies and regulating learning by making needed adjustments.

1. *Analyzing the learning task.* You are familiar with this stage of self-regulated learning. What do you do when a professor announces there will be a test? You ask about conditions you believe will influence how you'll study. Is it essay or multiple-choice? Is your best friend up to date on the material to be tested and available to study with you? In general, learners examine whatever information they think is relevant in order to construct a sense of what the task is about, what resources to bring to bear, and how they feel about the work to be done—are they interested? confident? anxious? knowledgeable? clueless?

2. *Setting goals and devising plans.* Knowing conditions that influence work on tasks provides information that learners use to create goals for learning. Then, plans can be developed about how to reach those goals. What goals for studying might you set for a quiz covering only one chapter that counts just 3% toward your course grade? Would your goals change if the test covered the last six chapters and counted 30% toward your course grade? What targets are identified in these goals—repeating definitions, being able to discuss how a teacher could apply findings from key research studies described in the textbook, or critiquing theoretical positions? Choosing goals affects the shape of a learner's plans for how to study. Is practicing definitions the best approach? Is a better plan to create examples and applications of key concepts?

3. *Enacting strategies to accomplish the task.* In this phase, self-regulated learners consider what they know or need to know that will help them be successful with these strategies. They are especially alert as they enact their plan to monitor how well the plan is working. They ask themselves these questions: Is the cognitive load too great? Am I getting overwhelmed? What can I do to manage all this complex information? Is the approach I'm taking too effortful for the results I'm are achieving? Am I reaching my goals? Is my progress rate fast enough to be prepared for the test?

4. *Regulating learning.* This is metacognitive monitoring and control (see Chapter 9). In this phase, learners come to decisions about whether changes are needed in any of the three preceding phases. For example, if learning is slow, they ask these questions: Should I study with my best friend? Do I need to review some prior material that provides the foundation for the content I am now studying? Do I need to start over—identifying what the task really is and then setting new (higher, lower, different) goals?

An Individual Example of Self-Regulated Learning

Students today are faced with constant distractions. Barry Zimmerman (2002, p. 64) describes Tracy, a high-school student who is devoted to Facebook and Twitter:

> An important mid-term math exam is two weeks away, and she had begun to study while listening to popular music "to relax her." Tracy has not set any study goals for herself—instead she simply tells herself to do as well as she can on the test. She uses no specific learning strategies for condensing and memorizing important material and does not plan out her study time, so she ends up cramming for a few hours before the test. She has only vague self-evaluative standards and cannot gauge her academic preparation accurately. Tracy attributes her learning difficulties to an inherent lack of mathematical ability and is very defensive about her poor study methods. However, she does not ask for help from others because she is afraid of "looking stupid," or seek out supplementary materials from the library because she "already has too much to learn." She finds studying to be anxiety-provoking, has little self-confidence in achieving success, and sees little intrinsic value in acquiring mathematical skill.

Clearly, Tracy is unlikely to do well on the test. What would help? For an answer, let's consider Zimmerman's cycle of self-regulated learning. His cycle has three phases—*forethought, performance, reflection*—and is consistent with the Winne and Hadwin model described above. In Zimmerman's phase 1, the *forethought phase* (like Winne and Hadwin's steps 1 and 2 of analyzing the task and setting goals), Tracy needs to set clear, reasonable goals and plan a few strategies for accomplishing those goals. And Tracy's beliefs about motivation make a difference at this point, too. If Tracy had a sense of self-efficacy for applying the strategies that she planned, if she believed that using those strategies would lead to math learning and success on the test, if she saw some connections between her own interests and the math learning, and if she were trying to master the material—not just look good or avoid looking bad—then she would be on the road to self-regulated learning.

Moving from forethought to Zimmerman's *performance phase* (similar to Winne and Hadwin's step 3 of enacting the strategies) brings new challenges. Now Tracy must have a repertoire of self-control (volitional) and learning strategies, including using imagery, mnemonics, attention focusing, and other techniques such as those described in Chapters 8 and 9 (Kiewra, 2002). She also will need to self-observe, that is, monitor how things are going so she can change strategies if needed. Actual recording of time spent, problems solved, or pages written may provide clues about when or how to make the best use of study time. Turning off the music would help, too.

Finally, Tracy needs to move to Zimmerman's phase 3 of *reflection* (similar to Winne and Hadwin's step 4 of regulating learning) by looking back on her performance and reflecting on what happened. It will help her develop a sense of efficacy if she attributes successes to effort and good strategy use and avoids self-defeating actions and beliefs such as making weak efforts, pretending not to care, or assuming she is "no good at math."

Both Zimmerman's and Winne and Hadwin's models emphasize the cyclical nature of self-regulated learning: Each phase flows into the next, and the cycle continues as students encounter new learning challenges. Both models begin with being informed about the task so you can set good goals. Having a repertoire of learning strategies and tactics also is necessary in both models. And self-monitoring of progress followed by modifying plans if needed are critical to both. Notice also that the way students think about the task and their ability to do it—their *sense of efficacy for self-regulation*—is key as well (Zimmerman, 2011).

Two Classrooms

Students differ in their self-regulation knowledge and skills. But teachers must work with an entire classroom, and still "reach every student." Here are two examples of real situations where teachers did just that. The first involves writing, the second math problem solving—both complex tasks.

WRITING. Carol is a 2nd grade student described by Nancy Perry and Lynn Drummond (2002). Ms. Lynn was Carol's teacher; she characterizes Carol as "a very weak writer." Carol has difficulty finding facts and then transforming those facts into meaningful prose for a research report. Also, she has difficulty with the mechanics of writing, which, according to Ms. Lynn, "holds her back."

Over the course of the year, Ms. Lynn involved her grade 2 and 3 students in three projects about animals. Through this writing, she wanted students to learn how to: (a) do research, (b) write expository text, (c) edit and revise their writing, and (d) use the computer as a tool for researching and writing. For the first report, the class worked on one topic together (Chipmunks). They did the fact-finding and writing together, because Ms. Lynn needed to show them how to do research and write a report. Also, the class developed frameworks for working collaboratively as a community of learners. When they wrote the second report (on Penguins), Ms. Lynn offered students many more choices and encouraged them to depend more on themselves and one another. Finally, for the third report, students chose an animal, conducted a self-regulated research project, and wrote a report. Now that they knew how to do research and write a report, they could work alone or together and be successful at this complex task.

Carol worked with a student in grade 3 who was doing research on a related topic. He showed Carol how to use a table of contents, and offered advice about how to phrase ideas in her report. Also, Carol underlined words she thought were misspelled so she could check them later when she met with Ms. Lynn to edit her report. Unlike many low-achieving students who have not learned strategies for self-regulating learning, Carol was not afraid to attempt challenging tasks, and she was confident about her ability to develop as a writer. Reflecting on her progress across the school year, Carol said, "I learned a lot from when I was in grade 1 because I had a lot of trouble then."

MATH PROBLEM SOLVING. Lynn Fuchs and her colleagues (2003) assessed the value of incorporating self-regulated learning strategies into math problem-solving lessons in real classrooms. The researchers worked with 24 teachers. All of the teachers taught the same content in their 3rd grade classes. Some of these teachers (randomly chosen) taught in their usual way. Another randomly chosen group incorporated strategies to encourage problem-solving transfer—using skills and knowledge learned in the lessons to solve problems in other situations and classes. The third group of teachers added transfer and self-regulated learning strategies to their units on math problem solving. Here are a few of the transfer and self-regulated learning strategies that were taught:

- Using a key, students scored their homework and gave it to a homework collector (a peer).
- Students graphed their completion of homework on a class report.
- Students used individual thermometer graphs that were kept in folders to chart their daily scores on individual problems.
- At the beginning of each session, students inspected their previous charts and set goals to beat their previous scores.
- Students discussed with partners how they might apply problem-solving strategies outside class.
- Before some lessons, students reported to the group about how they had applied problem-solving skills outside class.

Both transfer and self-regulated learning strategies helped students learn mathematical problem solving and apply this knowledge to new problems. The addition of self-regulated learning strategies was especially effective when students were asked to solve problems that were very different from those they encountered in the lessons. Students at every achievement level as well as students with learning disabilities benefited from learning the strategies.

Technology and Self-Regulation

In the previous chapter, we saw some examples of using technology-rich environments to explore complex concepts. But to learn in these rich environments, students need metacognitive and self-regulatory skills so they won't get lost in a sea of information. If the concepts they are learning are challenging and complicated, then some scaffolding is needed to support the students' developing understandings (Azevedo, 2005; Azevedo, Johnson, Chauncey, & Graesser, 2011). For example, Roger Azevedo and his colleagues (2004) studied undergraduate students who were learning about the circulatory system using a hypermedia encyclopedia. The materials available to them included texts, diagrams, photographs, video clips, and animated examples of how the circulatory system works. There were three different learning conditions. One group of students was told just to learn all they could about the circulatory system. A second group got the same instructions, but, in addition, they had a list of 10 subgoals to guide their learning. The third group had the list of subgoals plus a self-regulation "coach," who helped them plan their learning, monitor their developing understanding, try different strategies, and handle problems when they arose. Students in all three conditions were asked to "think out loud" as they used the hypermedia materials—describing what they were thinking as they went through the materials. Students who had the support of a self-regulation coach who focused on task analysis, goal setting, using strategies, and monitoring progress developed more complete and complex mental models of the circulatory system.

GUIDELINES — FAMILY AND COMMUNITY PARTNERSHIPS

Supporting Self-Regulation at Home and in School

Emphasize the value of encouragement.
Examples

1. Teach students to encourage each other.
2. Tell families about the areas that are most challenging for their child—those that will be the most in need of encouragement.

Model self-regulation.
Examples

1. Target small steps for improving an academic skill. Tailor goals to the student's current achievement level.
2. Discuss with your students how you set goals and monitor progress.
3. Ask parents and caregivers to show their children how they set goals for the day or week, write to-do lists, or keep appointment books.

Make families a source of good strategy ideas.
Examples

1. Have short, simple materials describing a "strategy of the month" that students can practice at home.

2. Create a lending library of books about goal setting, motivation, learning, and time-management strategies for students.
3. Encourage families to help their children focus on problem-solving processes and not turn immediately to the answers at the back of the book when doing homework.

Provide self-evaluation guidelines.
Examples

1. Develop rubrics for self-evaluation with students (see Chapter 12). Model how to use them.
2. Provide record-keeping sheets for assignments early in the year; then gradually have students develop their own.
3. Encourage parents and caregivers to model self-evaluation as they focus on areas they want to improve.
4. For family conferences, have examples of materials other families have successfully used to keep track of progress.

For more ideas to share with parents and caregivers, see:
http://www.pbs.org/wholechild/parents/building.html

How could you provide this kind of self-regulation teaching and coaching for your students? Maybe peer coaches would be one way, or enlisting the help of families.

Reaching Every Student: Families and Self-Regulation

Children begin to learn self-regulation in their homes. Families can teach and support self-regulated learning through modeling, encouragement, facilitation, rewarding of goal setting, good strategy use, and other processes described in the next section (Martinez-Pons, 2002). The *Family and Community Partnerships Guidelines* give some ideas for helping students become more self-regulating.

Another Approach to Self-Regulation: Cognitive Behavior Modification

When some psychologists were studying a behavior modification approach called *self-management*—using reinforcement and punishment to manage your own behavior—Donald Meichenbaum (1977) was having success teaching impulsive students to "talk themselves through" tasks. Meichenbaum called his method *cognitive behavior modification* (Manning & Payne, 1996). **Cognitive behavior modification** focuses on self-talk to regulate behavior.

You may remember from Chapter 1 that there is a stage in cognitive development when young children seem to guide themselves through a task using private speech. They talk to themselves, often repeating the words of a parent or teacher. In cognitive behavior modification, students are taught directly how to use this **self-instruction**. Meichenbaum (1977) outlined the steps:

1. An adult model performs a task while talking to him- or herself out loud (cognitive modeling).
2. The child performs the same task under the direction of the model's instructions (overt, external guidance).

Cognitive behavior modification Procedures based on both behavioral and cognitive learning principles for changing your own behavior by using self-talk and self-instruction.

Self-instruction Talking oneself through the steps of a task.

SELF-REGULATION BEGINS AT HOME Parents can teach and support self-regulated learning through modeling, encouragement, facilitation, and rewarding of goal setting, in order to help children become more self-regulating.

3. The child performs the task while instructing him- or herself aloud (overt, self-guidance).
4. The child whispers the instructions to him- or herself as he/she goes through the task (faded, overt self-guidance).
5. The child performs the task while guiding his/her performance via private speech (covert self-instruction). (p. 32)

Brenda Manning and Beverly Payne (1996) list four skills that can increase student learning: listening, planning, working, and checking. How might cognitive self-instruction help students develop these skills? One possibility is to use personal booklets or class posters that prompt students to "talk to themselves" about these skills. For example, one 5th grade class designed a set of prompts for each of the four skills and posted the prompts around the classroom. The prompts for listening included "Does this make sense?" "Am I getting this?" "I need to ask a question now before I forget." "Pay attention!" "Can I do what he's saying to do?" Planning prompts were "Do I have everything together?" "Do I have my friends tuned out for right now?" "Let me get organized first." "What order will I do this in?" "I know this stuff!" Posters for these and the other two skills, working and checking, are shown in Figure 8.3 on the next page. Part of the power of this process is in getting students involved in thinking about and creating their own guides and prompts. Having the discussion and posting the ideas makes students more self-aware and in control of their own learning.

Actually, cognitive behavior modification as it is practiced by Meichenbaum and others has many more components than just teaching students to use self-instruction. Meichenbaum's methods also include dialogue and interaction between teacher and student, modeling, guided discovery, motivational strategies, feedback, careful matching of the task with the student's developmental level, and other principles of good teaching. The student is even involved in designing the program (Harris, 1990; Harris & Pressley, 1991). Given all this, it is no surprise that students seem to be able to generalize the skills developed with cognitive behavior modification to new learning situations (Harris, Graham, & Pressley, 1992).

Today, there are entire school intervention programs based on cognitive behavior modification. For example, the *Coping Power Program* includes training for both parents and their children, beginning in the last half of one academic year and continuing through the entire next school year. The training for students often focuses on anger and aggression. Different training sessions emphasize personal goal-setting, awareness of feelings

Connect and Extend to PRAXIS II™

Self-Regulation (II, A1)
Take a look at *The Learning Base* (http://www.allkindsofminds .org/library/challenges/ GTPSelfregulatingLearning.htm) for tips to help students develop the goals, metacognitive skills, and self-regulatory practices that can support a lifelong devotion to learning.

FIGURE 8.3

POSTERS TO REMIND STUDENTS TO "TALK THEMSELVES THROUGH" LISTENING, PLANNING, WORKING, AND CHECKING IN SCHOOL

These four posters were designed by a 5th-grade class to help them remember to use self-instruction. Some of the reminders reflect the special world of these preadolescents.

Poster 1

While Listening:
1. Does this make sense?
2. Am I getting this?
3. I need to ask a question now before I forget.
4. Pay attention.
5. Can I do what he's saying to do?

Poster 3

While Working:
1. Am I working fast enough?
2. Stop staring at my girlfriend and get back to work.
3. How much time is left?
4. Do I need to stop and start over?
5. This is hard for me, but I can manage.

Poster 2

While Planning:
1. Do I have everything together?
2. Do I have my friends tuned out for right now?
3. Let me get organized first.
4. What order will I do this in?
5. I know this stuff!

Poster 4

While Checking:
1. Did I finish everything?
2. What do I need to recheck?
3. Am I proud of this work?
4. Did I write all the words? Count them.
5. I think I finished. I organized myself. Did I daydream too much?

Source: Manning M. Lee, Payne, Beverly D., *Self-Talk for Teachers and Students: Metacognitive Strategies for Personal and Classroom Use,* 1st edition, © 1994. Reprinted by permission of Pearson Education, Inc., Upper Saddle River, NJ.

(especially anger), learning to relax and change the focus away from the angry feelings, making coping self-statements, developing organizational and study skills, seeing the perspectives of others, developing social problem-solving skills, and dealing with peer pressure by practicing how to say no (Lochman & Wells, 2003). Another similar approach is *Tools for Getting Along* (Daunic, Smith, Brank, & Penfield, 2006). Both programs have been effective in helping aggressive middle-school students to "get along" with their classmates and teachers. In addition, in psychotherapy, tools based on cognitive behavior modification have proved to be some of the most effective ways of dealing with psychological problems such as depression.

Both the *Coping Power Program* and *Tools for Getting Along* include emotional self-regulation skills. We turn to this area of self-regulation next.

Emotional Self-Regulation

Social and emotional competences and self-regulation are critical for both academic and personal development. The Collaborative for Academic, Social, and Emotional Learning (CASEL) lists five core social and emotional skills and competencies:

- **Self-awareness**—accurately assessing your feelings, interests, values, and strengths; maintaining a well-grounded sense of self-confidence
- **Self-management**—regulating your emotions to handle stress, control impulses, and persevere in overcoming obstacles; setting and monitoring progress toward personal and academic goals; expressing emotions appropriately

- **Social awareness**—taking the perspective of and empathizing with others; recognizing and appreciating individual and group similarities and differences; recognizing and using family, school, and community resources
- **Relationship skills**—establishing and maintaining healthy and rewarding relationships based on cooperation; resisting inappropriate social pressure; preventing, managing, and resolving interpersonal conflict; seeking help when needed
- **Responsible decision-making**—making decisions based on consideration of ethical standards, safety concerns, appropriate social norms, respect for others, and likely consequences of various actions; applying decision-making skills to academic and social situations; contributing to the well-being of one's school and community (http://casel.org/why-it-matters/what-is-sel/skills-competencies/)

A number of studies that followed students over several years in the United States and in Italy have found that prosocial behaviors and social competence in the early grades are related to academic achievement and popularity with peers as many as five years later (Elias & Schwab, 2006). Developing emotional self-regulation is especially important in the early years when students are learning how to learn in schools. For example, Carlos Valiente and his colleagues (2010) followed almost 300 students through kindergarten to assess the relations between effortful self-control, emotionality, and academic achievement. They found that students' anger, sadness, and shyness were negatively related to achievement and that self-control was positively related to achievement, particularly for students who showed lower levels of negative emotions. So helping students develop emotional self-regulation can set them on a good path for learning in school, and probably can help them in social relations with their peers as well. How can teachers help students develop these skills? The *Guidelines* give some ideas.

GUIDELINES

Encouraging Emotional Self-Regulation

Create a climate of trust in your classroom.
Examples
1. Avoid listening to "tattle tale" stories about students.
2. Follow through with fair consequences.
3. Avoid unnecessary comparisons and give students opportunities to improve their work.

Help students recognize and express their feelings.
Examples
1. Provide a vocabulary of emotions and note descriptions of emotions in characters or stories.
2. Be clear and descriptive about your own emotions.
3. Encourage students to write in journals about their own feelings. Protect the privacy of these writings (see trust above).

Help students recognize emotions in others.
Examples
1. For young children, "Look at Chandra's face. How do you think she feels when you say those things?"
2. For older students, use readings, analysis of characters in literature, films, or role reversals to help them identify the emotions of others.

Provide strategies for coping with emotions.
Examples
1. Discuss or practice alternatives such as stopping to think how the other person feels, seeking help, and using anger management strategies such as self-talk or leaving the scene.
2. Model strategies for students. Talk about how you handle anger, disappointment, or anxiety.

Help students recognize cultural differences in emotional expression.
Examples
1. Have students write about or discuss how they show emotions in their family.
2. Teach students to "check it out"—ask the other people how they are feeling.

For ideas about promoting emotional competence, see http://casel.org/

TEACHING TOWARD SELF-EFFICACY AND SELF-REGULATED LEARNING

STOP & THINK How are you studying right now? What goals have you set for your reading today? What is your plan for learning, and what strategies are you using right now to learn? How did you learn those strategies? •

Most teachers agree that students need to develop skills and attitudes for independent, lifelong learning (*self-regulated learning* and a *sense of efficacy for learning*). Fortunately, there is a growing body of research that offers guidance about how to design tasks and structure classroom interactions to support students' development of and engagement in self-regulated learning (Neuman & Roskos, 1997; Perry, 1998; Sinatra & Taasoobshirazi, 2011; Stoeger & Ziegler, 2011; Wharton-McDonald et al., 1997; Zimmerman & Schunk, 2011). This research indicates that students develop academically effective forms of self-regulated learning (SRL) and a sense of efficacy for learning when teachers involve them in *complex meaningful tasks* that extend over *long periods of time*, much like the constructivist activities described in Chapter 10. Also, to develop self-regulated learning and self-efficacy for learning, students need to have some *control over their learning processes and products*—they need to make choices about what to work on, where, and with whom. They also need to have *control over the difficulty* of the task—how much to read or write, at what pace, and with what level of support. And because self-monitoring and self-evaluation are key to effective SRL and a sense of efficacy, teachers can help students develop SRL by involving them in *setting criteria* for evaluating their learning processes and products, and then giving them opportunities to *reflect* on and make judgments about their progress using those standards. It helps to work in *collaboration* with peers and seek feedback from them. As you saw earlier, this has been called *shared regulation*. Throughout the entire process, teachers must *co-regulate* the task by "providing just enough and just in time information and support to facilitate students' acquisition and application of SRL" (Perry & Rahim, 2011, p. 130). Let's examine each of these more closely.

Complex Tasks

Teachers don't want to assign students tasks that are too difficult and that lead to frustration. This is especially true when students have learning difficulties or disabilities. In fact, research indicates that the most motivating and academically beneficial tasks for students are those that challenge, but don't overwhelm them (Rohrkemper & Corno, 1988; Turner, 1997); complex tasks need not be overly difficult for students.

The term *complex* refers to the design of tasks, not their level of difficulty. From a design point of view, tasks are complex when they address multiple goals and involve large chunks of meaning—for example, projects and thematic units. Furthermore, complex tasks extend over long periods of time, engage students in a variety of cognitive and metacognitive processes, and allow for the production of a wide range of products (Perry, VandeKamp, Mercer, & Nordby, 2002; Wharton-McDonald et al., 1997). For example, a study of Egyptian pyramids might result in the production of written reports, maps, diagrams, skits, and models.

Even more important, complex tasks provide students with information about their learning progress. These tasks require them to engage in deep, elaborative thinking and problem solving. In the process, students develop and refine their cognitive and metacognitive strategies. Furthermore, succeeding at such tasks increases students' self-efficacy and intrinsic motivation (McCaslin & Good, 1996; Turner, 1997). Rohrkemper and Corno (1988) advised teachers to design complex tasks that provide opportunities for students to modify the learning conditions in order to cope with challenging problems. Learning to cope with stressful situations and make adaptations is an important educational goal. Remember from Chapter 4, that according to Sternberg, one aspect of intelligence is choosing or adapting environments so that you can succeed.

Control

Teachers can share control with students by giving them choices. When students have choices (e.g., about what to produce, how to produce it, where to work, whom to work with), they are more likely to anticipate a successful outcome (increased self-efficacy) and consequently increase effort and persist when difficulty arises (Turner & Paris, 1995). Also, by involving students in making decisions, teachers invite them to take responsibility for learning by planning, setting goals, monitoring progress, and evaluating outcomes (Turner, 1997). These are qualities of highly effective, self-regulating learners.

Giving students choices creates opportunities for them to adjust the level of challenge that particular tasks present (e.g., they can choose easy or more challenging reading materials, determine the nature and amount of writing in a report, supplement writing with other expressions of learning). But what if students make poor academic choices? Highly effective, high-SRL teachers carefully consider the choices they give to students. They make sure students have the knowledge and skills they need to operate independently and make good decisions (Perry & Rahim, 2011). For example, when students are learning new skills or routines, teachers can offer choices with constraints (e.g., students must write a minimum of four sentences/paragraphs/pages, but they can choose to write more; they must demonstrate their understanding of an animal's habitat, food, and babies, but they can write, draw, or speak their knowledge).

Highly effective teachers also teach and model good decision making. For example, when students are choosing partners, teachers can ask them to consider what they need from their partner (e.g., shared interest and commitment, perhaps knowledge or skills that they need to develop). When students are making choices about how best to use their time, these teachers ask, "What can you do when you're finished? What can you do if you are waiting for my help?" Often, lists are generated and posted, so students can refer to them while they work. Finally, highly effective teachers give students feedback about the choices they make and tailor the choices they give to suit the unique characteristics of particular learners. For example, they might encourage some students to select research topics for which resources are readily available and written at a level that is accessible to the learner. Alternatively, they might encourage some students to work collaboratively versus independently to ensure they have the support and shared regulation they need to be successful.

DEVELOPING STUDENT CONTROL In order to develop self-regulated learning and self-efficacy for learning, students need to have some control over their learning processes and products; teachers can help by involving students in evaluating their learning processes, products, and progress.

Self-Evaluation

Evaluation practices that support SRL are nonthreatening. They are embedded in ongoing activities, emphasize process as well as products, focus on personal progress, and help students to interpret errors as opportunities for learning to occur. In these contexts, students enjoy and actually seek challenging tasks because the cost of participation is low (Paris & Ayres, 1994). Involving students in generating evaluation criteria and evaluating their own work also reduces the anxiety that often accompanies assessment by giving students a sense of control over the outcome. Students can judge their work in relation to a set of qualities both they and their teachers identify as "good" work. They can consider the effectiveness of their approaches to learning and alter their behaviors in ways that enhance it (Winne, 2011; Winne & Perry, 2000).

In high-SRL classrooms, there are both formal and informal opportunities for students to evaluate their learning. For example, one student teacher asked 4th- and 5th-grade students to submit reflections journals describing the games they designed with a partner or small group of collaborators for a probability and statistics unit (Perry, Phillips, & Dowler, 2004). Their journals explained their contribution to the group's process and product, and described what they learned from participating. The student teacher took these reflections into account when she evaluated the games. More informally, teachers ask students "What have you learned about yourself as a writer today?" "What do good researchers and writers do?" "What can we do that we couldn't do before?" Questions like these, posed to individuals or embedded in class discussions, prompt students' metacognition, motivation, and strategic action—the components of SRL.

Collaboration

The Committee on Increasing High School Students' Motivation to Learn (2004) concluded that when students can put their heads together, they are more receptive to challenging assignments—the very kind of complex task that develops self-regulation. The Committee added:

> Collaborative work also can help students develop skills in cooperation. Furthermore, it helps create a community of learners who have responsibility for each other's learning, rather than a competitive environment, which is alienating to many students, particularly those who do not perform as well as their classmates. (p. 51)

The most effective uses of cooperative/collaborative relationships to support SRL are those that reflect a climate of community and shared problem solving (Perry & Drummond, 2002; Perry, VandeKamp, Mercer, & Nordby, 2002). In these contexts, teachers and students actually co-regulate one another's learning (McCaslin & Good, 1996), offering support, whether working alone, in pairs, or small groups. This support is instrumental to individuals' development and use of metacognition, intrinsic motivation, and strategic action (e.g., sharing ideas, comparing strategies for solving problems, identifying everyone's area of expertise). High-SRL teachers spend time at the start of each school year teaching routines and establishing norms of participation (e.g., how to give constructive feedback and how to interpret and respond to peers' suggestions). As you will see in Chapter 10, developing useful management and learning procedures and routines takes time at the beginning of the year, but it is time well spent. Once routines and patterns of interaction are established, students can focus on learning and teachers can attend to teaching academic skills and the curriculum.

BRINGING IT ALL TOGETHER: THEORIES OF LEARNING

How can we make sense of the diversity in perspectives on learning we have explored for the last four chapters? We have considered behavioral, cognitive, constructivist (individual and social), and social cognitive explanations of what people learn and how they learn it. Table 8.3 presents a summary of several of these perspectives on learning.

TABLE 8.3 • **Four Views of Learning**

There are variations within each of these views of learning and overlaps as well, especially in constructivist views.

	BEHAVIORAL	COGNITIVE	CONSTRUCTIVIST		SOCIAL COGNITIVE
	Applied Behavioral Analysis *B. F. Skinner*	Information Processing *J. Anderson*	Individual *Jean Piaget*	Social/Situated *Lev Vygotsky*	Social Cognitive Theory *Albert Bandura*
Knowledge	Fixed body of knowledge to acquire Stimulated from outside	Fixed body of knowledge to acquire Stimulated from outside Prior knowledge influences how information is processed	Changing body of knowledge, individually constructed in social world Built on what learner brings	Socially constructed knowledge Built on what participants contribute, construct together	Changing body of knowledge, constructed in interaction with others and the environment
Learning	Acquisition of facts, skills, concepts Occurs through drill, guided practice	Acquisition of facts, skills, concepts, and strategies Occurs through the effective application of strategies	Active construction, restructuring prior knowledge Occurs through multiple opportunities and diverse processes to connect to what is already known	Collaborative construction of socially defined knowledge and values Occurs through socially constructed opportunities	Active construction of knowledge based on observation, interacting in the physical and social world, and developing agency— becoming more self-regulating
Teaching	Transmission presentation (Telling)	Transmission Guide students toward more "accurate" and complete knowledge	Challenge, guide thinking toward more complete understanding	Co-construct knowledge with students	Presenting models, demonstrating, supporting self-efficacy and self-regulation
Role of Teacher	Manager, supervisor Correct wrong answers	Teach and model effective strategies Correct misconceptions	Facilitator, guide Listen for student's current conceptions, ideas, thinking	Facilitator, guide Co-participant Co-construct different interpretation of knowledge; listen to socially constructed conceptions	Model, facilitator, motivator Model of self-regulated learning
Role of Peers	Not usually considered	Not necessary but can influence information processing	Not necessary but can stimulate thinking, raise questions	Ordinary and necessary part of process of knowledge construction	Serve as models Ordinary and necessary part of process of knowledge construction
Role of Student	Passive recipient of information Active listener, direction- follower	Active processor of information, strategy user Organizer and reorganizer of information Rememberer	Active construction (within mind) Active thinker, explainer, interpreter, questioner	Active co-construction with others and self Active thinker, explainer, interpreter, questioner Active social participant	Active co-construction with others and self Active thinker, explainer, interpreter, questioner Active social participant

Rather than debating the merits of each approach, consider their contributions to understanding learning and improving teaching. Don't feel that you must choose the "best" approach—there is no such thing. Chemists, biologists, and nutritionists rely on different theories to explain and improve health. Different views of learning can be used together to create productive learning environments for the diverse students you will teach. Behavioral theory helps us understand the role of cues in setting the stage for behaviors and the role of consequences and practice in encouraging or discouraging particular behaviors. But much of humans' lives and learning is more than behaviors. Language and higher-order thinking require complex information processing and memory—something the cognitive models help us understand. And what about the person as a creator and constructor of knowledge, not just a processor of information? Here, constructivist perspectives have much to offer. Finally, social cognitive theory highlights the important role of agency and self-direction. Life requires self-regulated learning.

I like to think of the four main learning theories in Table 8.3 as four pillars for teaching. Students must first understand and make sense of the material (constructivist); then, they must remember what they have understood (cognitive—information processing); then, they must practice and apply (behavioral) their new skills and understanding to make them more fluid and automatic—a permanent part of their repertoire. Finally, they must take charge of their own learning (social cognitive). Failure to attend to any part of the process results in lower-quality learning.

▼ SUMMARY

Social Cognitive Theory (pp. 292–294)

Distinguish between social learning and social cognitive theories. Social learning theory expanded behavioral views of reinforcement and punishment. In behavioral views, reinforcement and punishment directly affect behavior. In social learning theory, observing another person, a model, being reinforced or punished can have similar effects on the observer's behavior. Social cognitive theory expands social learning theory to include cognitive factors such as beliefs, expectations, and perceptions of self. Current social cognitive theory is a dynamic system that explains human adaptation, learning, and motivation. The theory addresses how people develop social, emotional, cognitive, and behavioral capabilities; how people regulate their own lives; and what motivates them.

What is triarchic reciprocal causality? Triarchic reciprocal causality is the dynamic interplay between three kinds of influences: personal, environmental, and behavioral. Personal factors (beliefs, expectations, attitudes, and knowledge), the physical and social environment (resources, consequences of actions, other people, models and teachers, and physical settings), and behavior (individual actions, choices, and verbal statements) all influence and are influenced by each other.

Modeling: Learning from Others (pp. 294–298)

What is modeling? Learning by observing others is a key element of social cognitive theory. Modeling is influenced by the developmental characteristics of the observer, the status and prestige of the model, the consequences of the model's actions as seen by the observer, the observer's expectations about performing the observed behaviors (will I be rewarded?), the links that the observers perceive between their goals and the models' behaviors (will doing what the model does get me what I want?), and the observer's self-efficacy (can I do it?).

What kinds of outcomes can observational learning encourage? Observational learning can lead to five possible outcomes, including

directing attention, encouraging existing behaviors, changing inhibitions, teaching new behaviors and attitudes, and arousing emotions. By directing attention, we gain insight into how others do things and what objects are involved in their actions. Encouraging or fine-tuning existing behaviors can lead to the development of good habits or make work more efficient. Observing others also has the capacity to cue us in to others' attention, which can cause us to become more or less "self-conscious" about our behavior; when others are doing something, it's easier for us to do the same. Young children in particular learn by watching and emulating others, but everyone can gain insight into how something is done well (or poorly) by observing someone else do it. Finally, observing can lead to the association of emotions with certain activities. If others are observed enjoying an activity, the observer may learn to enjoy the activity as well.

Self-Efficacy and Agency (pp. 298–303)

What is self-efficacy, and how is it different from other self-schemas? Self-efficacy is distinct from other self-schemas in that it involves judgments of capabilities specific to a particular task. Self-concept is a more global construct that contains many perceptions about the self, including self-efficacy. Compared to self-esteem, self-efficacy is concerned with judgments of personal capabilities; self-esteem is concerned with judgments of self-worth.

What are the sources of self-efficacy? Four sources are mastery experiences (direct experiences), level of arousal as you face the task, vicarious experiences (accomplishments are modeled by someone else), and social persuasion (a "pep talk" or specific performance feedback).

How does self-efficacy affect motivation? Greater efficacy leads to greater effort, persistence in the face of setbacks, higher goals, and finding new strategies when old ones fail. If sense of efficacy is low, however, people may avoid a task altogether or give up easily when problems arise.

What is teachers' sense of efficacy? One of the few personal characteristics of teachers related to student achievement is a teacher's efficacy belief that he or she can reach even difficult students to help them learn. Teachers with a high sense of efficacy work harder, persist longer, and are less likely to experience burnout. Teachers' sense of efficacy is higher in schools where the other teachers and administrators have high expectations for students and where teachers receive help from their principals in solving instructional and management problems. Efficacy grows from real success with students, so any experience or training that helps you succeed in the day-to-day tasks of teaching will give you a foundation for developing a sense of efficacy in your career. There may be some benefits to lower efficacy, if this encourages teachers to pursue professional development and improvement.

Self-Regulated Learning (pp. 303–313)

What factors are involved in self-regulated learning? One important goal of teaching is to prepare students for lifelong learning. To reach this goal, students must be self-regulated learners; that is, they must have a combination of the knowledge, motivation to learn, and volition that provides the skill and will to learn independently and effectively. Knowledge includes an understanding of self, subject, task, learning strategy, and contexts for application. Motivation to learn provides the commitment, and volition is the follow-through that combats distraction and protects persistence.

What is the self-regulated learning cycle? There are several models of self-regulated learning. Winne and Hadwin describe a four-phase model: analyzing the task, setting goals and designing plans, enacting strategies to accomplish the task, and regulating learning. Zimmerman notes three similar phases: forethought (which includes setting goals, making plans, self-efficacy, and motivation); performance (which involves self-control and self-monitoring); and reflection (which includes self-evaluation and adaptations, leading to the forethought/planning phase again).

What are some examples of teaching students to be more self-regulating? Self-regulating learners engage in four types of activities: analyzing the task, setting goals and designing plans, engaging in learning, and adjusting their approach to learning. Teaching students to be more self-regulating might take the form of providing opportunities to identify and analyze the task at hand. Students should ask themselves: What is the task? What is an ideal outcome of the task? Students may also benefit from goal-setting practice; they may ask: What are my short-term goals? What are my long-term goals? Learning strategies such as identifying important details and developing a big picture of material is the next step in the process. Finally, students need to reflect on whether they were successful and devise strategies for overcoming shortcomings in their self-regulation process. They may ask themselves: Where was I successful? Where do I need to improve in order to meet my goals in the future?

What is cognitive behavior modification? Cognitive behavior modification is a process in which self-talk is used to regulate behavior. Cognitive behavior modification may take many forms, including helping to keep students engaged in their learning or helping them deal effectively with anger and aggression. Some research has identified four skills that are particularly helpful self-talk strategies: listening, planning, working, and checking. Cognitive behavior modification can be used with students of all ages, but helping students engage in self-talk may require more adult assistance and guidance for younger children, or those who have not had opportunities to practice good self-regulation strategies.

What are the skills involved in emotional self-regulation? Emotionally self-regulating individuals are aware of their own emotions and the feelings of others—realizing that inner emotions can differ from outward expressions. They can talk about and express emotions in ways that are appropriate for their cultural group. They can feel empathy for others in distress and also cope with their own distressing emotions—they can handle stress. These individuals know that relationships are defined in part by how emotions are communicated within the relationship. All these skills come together to produce a capacity for emotional self-regulation.

Teaching Toward Self-Efficacy and Self-Regulated Learning (pp. 314–316)

How can teachers support the development of self-efficacy and self-regulated learning? Teachers should involve students in complex meaningful tasks that extend over long periods of time; provide them control over their learning processes and products—they need to make choices. They should involve students in setting criteria for evaluating their learning processes and products, and then give them opportunities to make judgments about their progress using those standards. Finally, teachers should encourage students to work collaboratively with and seek feedback from peers.

Bringing It All Together: Theories of Learning (pp. 316–318)

What is the value of the four different perspectives on learning? The behavioral, cognitive, constructivist, and social cognitive learning theories are four pillars for teaching. Students must first understand and make sense of the material (constructivist); then, they must remember what they have understood (cognitive—information processing); then, they must practice and apply (behavioral) their new skills and understanding to make them more fluid and automatic—a permanent part of their repertoire. Finally, they must take charge of their own learning (social cognitive). Failure to attend to any part of the process results in lower-quality learning.

▼ KEY TERMS

Arousal (300)
Co-regulation (305)
Cognitive behavior modification (310)
Human agency (298)
Mastery experiences (300)
Modeling (300)
Ripple effect (297)
Self-efficacy (298)

Self-instruction (310)
Self-regulated learning (306)
Self-regulation (304)
Self-reinforcement (296)
Shared regulation (305)
Social cognitive theory (293)
Social learning theory (292)
Social persuasion (300)

Teachers' sense of efficacy (302)
Triarchic reciprocal causality (293)
Vicarious experiences (300)
Vicarious reinforcement (296)
Volition (305)

▼ CONNECT AND EXTEND TO LICENSURE

MULTIPLE-CHOICE QUESTIONS

1. "I believe I will do well in this class." Chris declared to her brother. "I received a perfect score on the verbal part of the SAT, and I have always excelled in my literature classes." Chris is demonstrating which of the following?
   - A. High self-esteem
   - B. High levels of empathy
   - C. High self-efficacy in English
   - D. Low self-efficacy in English

2. Modeling is defined as changes in behavior, thinking, or emotions that happen through observing another person. Which theory and theorist is associated with learning through observation?
   - A. Behaviorist Theory, Skinner
   - B. Constructivist Theory, Piaget
   - C. Social Cognitive Theory, Bandura
   - D. Sociocultural Theory, Vygotsky

3. Miss Hutton turned around with a scowl on her face and addressed her second graders. "What do you think you're doing Johnny? Did I tell you to get out of your seat? Don't you ever let me catch you up without permission." The class sat silently with their eyes wide. When the lunch bell rang an hour later not one of the children dared to move from their seats. This is an example of which one of the following?
   - A. Self-regulation
   - B. Self-efficacy
   - C. Reciprocal causality
   - D. Vicarious learning

4. Through observational learning, one learns how to perform a behavior and also what will happen in specific situations if one performs it. Observation can be a very efficient learning process. What four elements must be met in order to learn from observation?
   - A. Attention, retention, production, and motivation/reinforcement
   - B. Attention, cognition, belief, and value
   - C. Observation, desire, developmental capability, and suitability
   - D. Observation, motivation, abstraction, and reinforcement

CONSTRUCTED-RESPONSE QUESTIONS

Case

"Marcus! Look how well you did on your spelling test!" Mr. Bonner smiled at Marcus, who beamed in response. "I knew when we started to chart your progress you would really do well. You have had three perfect scores on the last three tests. It just goes to show, you studied every night for a few minutes and your grade has gone up, up, up! I'm looking at the chart we made at the beginning of the year and I think it really helped."

"Mr. Bonner, I would like to do the same thing in math. I think if I practice every night and chart my progress, I'll get perfect grades in math too! I'll make a chart and pick out some math games I can play at home to improve.

5. How is Mr. Bonner encouraging Marcus' self-efficacy?

6. How is Marcus' response to Mr. Bonner an example of self-regulated learning?

▼ WHAT WOULD THEY DO?

TEACHERS' CASEBOOK: Failure to Self-Regulate

Here is how several expert teachers responded to the situation at the beginning of the chapter of the teacher with a class of disorganized students.

JANE W. CAMPBELL • 2nd Grade Teacher
John P. Faber Elementary School, Dunellen, NJ

To begin the year, I teach several routines that help students to become more independent and successful. First they are introduced to a homework folder labeled with the classroom number and school name. Ownership is important, so they write their own names on the label too. There are also designated sections for parent signatures, homework to be returned to school, and homework to be kept at home. Each day students put their things into the proper section. I check the students' success by walking through the room and looking at their folders. As different students become proficient, they become student helpers to help spot check other students as well. Organizing the students takes time, but once the routine is established, most students can successfully complete the task. As the routine is practiced and established, the students become successful and more self-reliant. Everyone is happy: the students, the parents, and the teacher.

CARLA S. HIGGINS • K–5 Literacy Coordinator
Legend Elementary School, Newark, OH

I don't make assumptions about my students' organizational skills. Instead, I explicitly teach them skills that work for our class and support future organization such as using a structured folder for class paperwork, frequent checkpoints, and an assignment calendar or agenda. I would include students in planning due dates by considering what it would take to complete each assignment. For longer assignments, I ask students to help create a reasonable time-line for completing steps of the project and offer frequent checks for completion of the steps. Finally, since we live in a culture where technology drives much of our communication, I would set up a Web site or e-mail reminder system to provide additional support for students and to communicate with parents to keep them involved.

MARIE HOFFMAN HURT • 8th Grade Foreign Language Teacher (German & French)
Pickerington Local Schools, Pickerington, OH

Part of being a good teacher is learning how to teach the "process" of learning alongside the required content material. In the grand scheme of teaching, content-specific learning is only a small percentage of what I teach—something I didn't expect when I started my career in education. A large part of succeeding in life (and on achievement tests!), rather than just knowing how to conjugate a French verb, is knowing the habits, routines, and learning skills that students master WHILE learning those French verbs. With this in mind, it is much easier to keep the task at hand in perspective. If a teacher focuses on fundamental strategies such as organization and planning, and inextricably links these strategies to the operation of the classroom, these concepts become second nature to the students. Students are better able to absorb and learn the content-specific material because they have the tools necessary to do so.

KELLY L. HOY • 5th Grade
The Phillips Brooks School, Menlo Park, CA

In an elementary school classroom, organizational skills are central to alleviating stress for students, teachers, and even parents. From the desk to the binder to the backpack, somehow students' paperwork mysteriously disappears. There are ways to battle the infamous "black hole" book bag or desk. Teachers should take time at the end of each period to clearly state where the assignment should be placed and each child can give a signal that his/her paper is in

the correct place. For time-sensitive projects, having different dates in which notes, drafts, and final projects are due will help students learn time management. Students can check off that they have the correct materials in assignment logs and get a teacher's initials. Periodic "book bag checks" can help students organize their book bags for homework.

PATRICIA A. SMITH • High School Math
Earl Warren High School, San Antonio, TX

In my high school mathematics classes, I spend the first two months of the school year training my students in organizational skills. All of my students are given a schedule that outlines topics of discussion, assignment due dates, and quiz and test dates. I also give each of them a "scorecard" where they keep track of their own grades. This serves as a double check for me as the teacher as well as providing a sense of ownership of earned grades to the students.

All my students have a three-ring binder with a plastic cover—their schedule fits inside the plastic cover. Early in the year, I start every class with a look at the schedule and question students on assignment due dates. In addition, I collect all assignments and tests in colored folders unique to each class section. When the students walk into my classroom and see their designated color of folder on my desk, they know that something is due. Most of my quizzes are the take-home variety. I place them on a table in the back of the room and students are responsible for locating, completing, and returning them. In fact, I put them out several days in advance and do not accept late quizzes, thereby increasing student responsibility and organization. Graded papers are also processed in the same manner, thereby perpetuating the new and orderly system and disabling the old unorganized ways.

chapter nine
MOTIVATION in LEARNING and TEACHING

▶ **TEACHERS' CASEBOOK:** Motivating Students When Resources Are Thin

It is July and you have finally gotten a teaching position. The district wasn't your first choice, but job openings were really tight, so you're pleased to have a job in your field. You are discovering that the teaching resources in your school are slim to none; the only materials available are some aging texts and the workbooks that go with them. Every idea you have suggested for software, simulation games, DVDs, field trips, or other more active teaching materials has been met with the same response, "There's no money in the budget for that." As you look over the texts and workbooks, you wonder how the students could be anything but bored by them. To make matters worse, the texts look pretty high level for your students. But the objectives in the workbooks are important. Besides, the district curriculum requires these units. Students will be tested on them in district-wide assessments next spring.

CRITICAL THINKING

- How would you arouse student curiosity and interest about the topics and tasks in the workbooks?
- How would you establish the value of learning this material?
- How would you handle the difficulty level of the texts?
- What do you need to know about motivation to solve these problems?
- What do you need to know about your students in order to motivate them?

OVERVIEW AND OBJECTIVES

Most educators agree that motivating students is one of the critical tasks of teaching. In order to learn, students must be cognitively, emotionally, and behaviorally engaged in productive class activities. We begin with the question "What is motivation?" and examine many of the answers that have been proposed, including a discussion of intrinsic and extrinsic motivation and five general theories of motivation: behavioral, humanistic, cognitive, social cognitive, and sociocultural. Next, we consider more closely several personal factors that frequently appear in discussions of motivation: needs, goal orientations, beliefs and self-perceptions, interests and curiosity, emotions, and anxiety.

How do we put all this information together in teaching? How do we create environments, situations, and relationships that encourage motivation and engagement in learning? First, we consider how the personal influences on motivation come together to support motivation to learn. Then, we examine how motivation is influenced by the academic work of the class, the value of the work, and the setting in which the work must be done. Finally, we discuss a number of strategies for developing motivation as a constant state in your classroom and as a permanent trait in your students.

By the time you have completed this chapter, you should be able to:

Objective 9.1:   Define motivation and differentiate among five theoretical explanations for learner motivation.

Objective 9.2:   Explain how learners' needs influence their motivation to learn.

Objective 9.3:   Describe the different kinds of goal orientations and their influences on motivation.

Objective 9.4:   Discuss how students' beliefs and attributions can influence motivation.

Objective 9.5:   Describe the roles of interests, curiosity, emotions, and anxiety in motivation.

Objective 9.6:   Explain how teachers can influence and encourage students' motivation to learn.

We began examining motivation in the previous chapter when we explored students' beliefs about their capabilities—their self-efficacy. We will spend another chapter on motivation because students' motivation has a direct and powerful impact on their social interactions and academic achievement in your classroom. Students with the same abilities and prior knowledge may perform quite differently, based on their motivation (Wigfield & Wentzel, 2007). So how does that work? Let's start with a basic question.

WHAT IS MOTIVATION?

Motivation is usually defined as an internal state that arouses, directs, and maintains behavior. Psychologists studying motivation have focused on five basic questions:

1. What choices do people make about their behavior? Why do some students, for example, focus on their homework and others watch television?
2. How long does it take to get started? Why do some students start their homework right away, while others procrastinate?
3. What is the intensity or level of involvement in the chosen activity? Once the backpack is opened, is the student engrossed and focused or is he just going through the motions?
4. What causes someone to persist or to give up? Will a student read the entire Shakespeare assignment or just a few pages?
5. What is the person thinking and feeling while engaged in the activity? Is the student enjoying Shakespeare, feeling competent, or worrying about an upcoming test (Graham & Weiner, 1996; Pintrich, Marx, & Boyle, 1993)?

Meeting Some Students

Many factors influence motivation and engaged learning. To get a sense of the complexity of motivation, let's step into a high-school science classroom just after the teacher has given directions for a lab activity. The student profiles are adapted from Stipek (2002).

Hopeless Geraldo won't even start the assignment—as usual. He just keeps saying, "I don't understand," or "This is too hard." When he answers your questions correctly, he "guessed" and he "doesn't really know." Geraldo spends most of his time staring into space; he is falling farther and farther behind.

Safe Sumey checks with you about every step—she wants to be perfect. You once gave her bonus points for doing an excellent color drawing of the apparatus, and now she produces a work of art for lab every time. But Sumey won't risk getting a B. If it isn't required or on the test, Sumey isn't interested in doing the work.

Satisfied Spenser, on the other hand, is interested in this project. In fact, he knows more than you do about it. Evidently he spends hours reading about chemistry and performing experiments. But his overall grade in your class is between B$^-$ and C because he never turns in homework. Spenser is satisfied with the C he can get on tests without even trying.

Defensive Daleesha doesn't have her lab manual—again, so she has to share with another student. Then she pretends to be working, but spends most of her time making fun of the assignment or trying to get answers from other students when your back is turned. She is afraid to try because if she makes an effort and fails, she fears that everyone will know she is "dumb."

Motivation An internal state that arouses, directs, and maintains behavior.

Anxious Amee is a good student in most subjects, but she freezes on science tests and "forgets" everything she knows when she has to answer questions in class. Her parents are scientists and expect her to become one too, but her prospects for this future look dim.

- -

STOP & THINK Each of these students has problems with at least one of the five areas of motivation: (1) choices, (2) getting started, (3) intensity, (4) persistence, or (5) thoughts and feelings. Can you diagnose the problems? The answers are on page 324 •

- -

Each student presents a different motivational challenge, yet you have to figure out how to motivate and teach the entire class. In the next few pages, we will look more closely at the meaning of motivation so we can better understand these students.

Intrinsic and Extrinsic Motivation

We all know how it feels to be motivated, to move energetically toward a goal or to work hard, even if we are bored by the task. What energizes and directs our behavior? The explanation could be drives, basic desires, needs, incentives, fears, goals, social pressure, self-confidence, interests, curiosity, beliefs, values, expectations, and more. Some psychologists have explained motivation in terms of personal *traits* or individual characteristics. Certain people, so the theory goes, have a strong need to achieve, a fear of tests, a curiosity about mechanical objects, or an enduring interest in art, so they work hard to achieve, avoid tests, tinker endlessly in their garages, or spend hours in art galleries. Other psychologists see motivation more as a *state*, a temporary situation. If, for example, you are reading this paragraph because you have a test tomorrow, you are motivated (at least for now) by the situation. Of course, the motivation we experience at any given time usually is a combination of trait and state. You may be studying because you value learning *and* because you are preparing for a test.

A classic distinction is made between intrinsic and extrinsic motivation. **Intrinsic motivation** is the natural human tendency to seek out and conquer challenges as we pursue personal interests and exercise our capabilities. When we are intrinsically motivated, we do not need incentives or punishments, because the activity itself is satisfying and rewarding (Anderman & Anderman, 2010; Deci & Ryan, 2002; Reiss, 2004). Satisfied Spenser studies chemistry outside school simply because he loves learning about chemistry; no one makes him do it. Intrinsic motivation is associated with many positive outcomes in school such as academic achievement, creativity, reading comprehension and enjoyment, and using deep learning strategies (Corpus, McClintic-Gilbert, & Hayenga, 2009).

In contrast, when we do something in order to earn a grade, avoid punishment, please the teacher, or for some other reason that has very little to do with the task itself, we experience **extrinsic motivation**. We are not really interested in the activity for its own sake; we care only about what it will gain us. Safe Sumey works for the grade; she has little interest in the subject itself. Extrinsic motivation has been associated with negative emotions, poor academic achievement, and maladaptive learning strategies (Corpus et al., 2009).

According to psychologists who adopt the intrinsic/extrinsic concept of motivation, it is impossible to tell just by looking if a behavior is intrinsically or extrinsically motivated. The essential difference between the two types of motivation is the student's *reason* for acting, that is, whether the **locus of causality** for the action (the location of the cause) is internal or external—inside or outside the person. Students who read or practice their backstroke or paint may be reading, swimming, or painting because they freely chose the activity based on personal interests (*internal locus of causality/intrinsic motivation*), or because someone or something else outside is influencing them (*external locus of causality/extrinsic motivation*) (Reeve, 2002; Reeve & Jang, 2006a, 2006b).

As you think about your own motivation, you probably realize that the dichotomy between intrinsic and extrinsic motivation is too either/or—too all-or-nothing. There are two explanations that avoid either/or thinking. One is that our activities fall along a continuum from fully self-determined (intrinsic motivation) to fully determined by others

Intrinsic motivation Motivation associated with activities that are their own reward.

Extrinsic motivation Motivation created by external factors such as rewards and punishments.

Locus of causality The location—internal or external—of the cause of behavior.

FOR THE MEDAL ONLY? Is this athlete motivated just by a piece of metal hanging from a ribbon, or is he also likely intrinsically motivated to achieve what he has in his sport?

Connect and Extend to PRAXIS II™

Promoting Intrinsic Motivation to Learn (I, C2, 3)
For a set of practical tips, guidelines, and suggestions for boosting and maintaining motivation to learn, go to *Increasing Student Engagement and Motivation: From Time-on-Task to Homework* (http://www.nwrel.org/request/oct00/textonly.html).

(extrinsic motivation). For example, students may freely choose to work hard on activities that they don't find particularly enjoyable because they know the activities are important in reaching a valued goal—such as spending hours studying educational psychology in order to become a good teacher. Is this intrinsic or extrinsic motivation? Actually, it is in between—the person is freely choosing to accept outside causes such as licensure requirements and then is trying to get the most benefit from the requirements. The person has *internalized an external cause* (Vansteenkiste, Lens, & Deci, 2006).

A second explanation is that intrinsic and extrinsic motivations are not two ends of a continuum. Instead, intrinsic and extrinsic tendencies are two independent possibilities, and, at any given time, we can be motivated by some aspects of each (Covington & Mueller, 2001). Teaching can create intrinsic motivation by connecting to students' interests and supporting growing competence. But you know this won't work all the time. Did you find fractions inherently interesting? Was your curiosity piqued by irregular verbs? If teachers count on intrinsic motivation to energize all their students all of the time, they will be disappointed. There are situations where incentives and external supports are necessary. Teachers must encourage and nurture intrinsic motivation, while making sure that extrinsic motivation supports learning (Anderman & Anderman, 2010; Brophy, 2003). To do this, they need to know about the factors that influence motivation.

Five General Approaches to Motivation

STOP & THINK Why are you reading this chapter? Are you curious about motivation and interested in the topic? Or is there a test in your near future? Do you need this course to earn a teaching license or to graduate? Maybe you believe that you will do well in this class, and that belief keeps you working. Perhaps it is some combination of these reasons. What motivates you to study motivation? •

Motivation is a vast and complicated subject encompassing many theories. Some theories were developed through work with animals in laboratories. Others are based on research with humans in situations that used games or puzzles. The work done in clinical or industrial psychology inspired additional theories as well. Our examination of the field will be selective; otherwise we would never finish.

STOP & THINK ANSWERS Hopeless Geraldo has trouble with getting started (2) and with a sense of despair (5); during the activity he feels defeated and helpless. Safe Sumey makes good choices (1), gets started right away (2), and persists (4). But she is not really engaged and takes little pleasure in the work (4 and 5). As long as he is following his own choices (1), Satisfied Spenser is prompt in getting started (2), engaged (3), persistent (4), and enjoys the task (5). Defensive Daleesha makes poor choices (1), procrastinates (2), avoids engagement (3), and gives up easily (4) because she is so concerned about how others will judge her (5). Anxious Amee's problems have to do with what she thinks and how she feels as she works (5). Her worry and anxiety may lead her to make poor choices (1) and procrastinate (2), which only makes her more anxious at test time. •

Reward An attractive object or event supplied as a consequence of a behavior.

Incentive An object or event that encourages or discourages behavior.

BEHAVIORAL APPROACHES TO MOTIVATION. According to the behavioral view, an understanding of student motivation begins with a careful analysis of the incentives and rewards present in the classroom. A **reward** is an attractive object or event supplied as a consequence of a particular behavior. For example, Safe Sumey was *rewarded* with bonus points when she drew an excellent diagram. An **incentive** is an object or event that encourages or discourages behavior. The promise of an A+ was an *incentive* to Sumey. Actually receiving the grade was a *reward*. Providing grades, stars, stickers, and other reinforcers for learning—or demerits for misbehavior—is an attempt to motivate students by extrinsic means of incentives, rewards, and punishments.

HUMANISTIC APPROACHES TO MOTIVATION. In the 1940s, proponents of humanistic psychology such as Carl Rogers argued that neither of the dominant schools of psychology, behavioral or Freudian, adequately explained why people act as they do. **Humanistic interpretations** of motivation emphasize such intrinsic sources of motivation as a person's needs for "self-actualization" (Maslow, 1968, 1970), the inborn "actualizing tendency" (Rogers & Freiberg, 1994), or the need for "self-determination" (Deci, Vallerand, Pelletier, & Ryan, 1991). So, from the humanistic perspective, to motivate means to encourage people's inner resources—their sense of competence, self-esteem, autonomy, and self-actualization. Maslow's theory and Deci and Ryan's self-determination theory, discussed later, are influential humanistic explanations of motivation.

COGNITIVE APPROACHES TO MOTIVATION. In cognitive theories, people are viewed as active and curious, searching for information to solve personally relevant problems. Thus, cognitive theorists emphasize intrinsic motivation. In many ways, cognitive theories of motivation also developed as a reaction to the behavioral views. Cognitive theorists believe that behavior is determined by our thinking, not simply by whether we have been rewarded or punished for the behavior in the past (Stipek, 2002). Behavior is initiated and regulated by plans (Miller, Galanter, & Pribram, 1960), goals (Locke & Latham, 2002), schemas (Ortony, Clore, & Collins, 1988), expectations (Vroom, 1964), and attributions (Weiner, 2010). We will look at goals, expectations, and attributions later in this chapter.

SOCIAL COGNITIVE THEORIES. Many influential social cognitive explanations of motivation can be characterized as **expectancy × value theories**. This means that motivation is seen as the product of two main forces: the individual's *expectation* of reaching a goal and the *value* of that goal to him or her. In other words, the important questions are, "If I try hard, can I succeed?" and "If I succeed, will the outcome be valuable or rewarding to me?" Motivation is a product of these two forces, because if either factor is zero, then there is no motivation to work toward the goal. For example, if I believe I have a good chance of making the basketball team (high expectation), and if making the team is very important to me (high value), then my motivation should be strong. But if either factor is zero (I believe I haven't a prayer of making the team, or I couldn't care less about playing basketball), then my motivation will be zero, too (Tollefson, 2000).

Jacqueline Eccles and Allan Wigfield add the element of *cost* to the expectancy × value equation. Values have to be considered in relation to the cost of pursuing them. How much energy will be required? What could I be doing instead? What are the risks if I fail? Will I look stupid (Eccles, 2009; Eccles & Wigfield, 2002)?

SOCIOCULTURAL CONCEPTIONS OF MOTIVATION. Finish this sentence: I am a/an _____. What is your identity? With what groups do you identify most strongly? **Sociocultural views of motivation** emphasize participation in communities of practice. People engage in activities to maintain their identities and their interpersonal relations within the community. Thus, students are motivated to learn if they are members of a classroom or school community that values learning. Just as we learn through socialization to speak or dress or order food in restaurants—by watching and learning from more capable members of the culture—we also learn to be students by watching and learning from members of our school community. In other words, we learn by the company we keep (Eccles, 2009; Hickey, 2003; Rogoff, Turkanis, & Bartlett, 2001). When we see ourselves as soccer players, or sculptors, or engineers, or teachers, or psychologists, we are claiming an identity within

Humanistic interpretation Approach to motivation that emphasizes personal freedom, choice, self-determination, and striving for personal growth.

Expectancy × value theories Explanations of motivation that emphasize individuals' expectations for success combined with their valuing of the goal.

Sociocultural views of motivation Perspectives that emphasize participation, identities, and interpersonal relations within communities of practice.

TABLE 9.1 • **Five Views of Motivation**

	BEHAVIORAL	HUMANISTIC	COGNITIVE	SOCIAL COGNITIVE	SOCIOCULTURAL
Source of Motivation	Extrinsic	Intrinsic	Intrinsic	Intrinsic and Extrinsic	Intrinsic
Important Influences	Reinforcers, rewards, incentives, and punishers	Need for self-esteem, self-fulfillment, and self-determination	Beliefs, attributions for success and failure, expectations	Goals, expectations, intentions, self-efficacy	Engaged participation in learning communities; maintaining identity through participation in activities of group
Key Theorists	Skinner	Maslow Deci	Weiner Graham	Locke & Latham Bandura	Lave Wenger

a group. In building an identity in the group, we move from legitimate peripheral participation to central participation. **Legitimate peripheral participation** means that beginners are genuinely involved in the work of the group, even if their abilities are undeveloped and their contributions are small. The novice weaver learns to dye wool before spinning and weaving, and the novice teacher learns to tutor one child before working with the whole group. Each task is a piece of the real work of the expert. The identities of both the novice and the expert are bound up in their participation in the community. They are motivated to learn the values and practices of the community to keep their identity as community members (Lave & Wenger, 1991; Wenger, 1998).

The behavioral, humanistic, cognitive, social cognitive, and sociocultural approaches to motivation are summarized in Table 9.1. These theories differ in their answers to the question, "What is motivation?" but each contributes in its own way toward a comprehensive understanding.

To organize the many ideas about motivation in a way that is useful for teaching, let's examine four broad areas. Most contemporary explanations of motivation include a discussion of needs, goals, beliefs, and finally, the emotional "hot" side of motivation—interests, curiosity, emotions, and anxiety (Murphy & Alexander, 2000).

NEEDS

Early research in psychology conceived of motivation in terms of trait-like needs or consistent personal characteristics. Three of the main needs studied extensively in this earlier work were the needs for *achievement, power,* and *affiliation* (Pintrich, 2003). Abraham Maslow's influential theory emphasized a hierarchy that included all these needs and more.

Maslow's Hierarchy of Needs

Maslow (1970) suggested that humans have a **hierarchy of needs** ranging from lower-level needs for survival and safety to higher-level needs for intellectual achievement and finally self-actualization. **Self-actualization** is Maslow's term for self-fulfillment, the realization of personal potential. Each of the lower needs must be met before the next higher need can be addressed.

Maslow (1968) called the four lower-level needs—for survival, then safety, followed by belonging, and then self-esteem—**deficiency needs**. When these needs are satisfied, the motivation for fulfilling them decreases. He labeled the three higher-level needs—intellectual achievement, then aesthetic appreciation, and finally self-actualization—**being needs**. When

Legitimate peripheral participation Genuine involvement in the work of the group, even if your abilities are undeveloped and contributions are small.

Hierarchy of needs Maslow's model of seven levels of human needs, from basic physiological requirements to the need for self-actualization.

Self-actualization Fulfilling one's potential.

Deficiency needs Maslow's four lower-level needs, which must be satisfied first.

Being needs Maslow's three higher-level needs, sometimes called *growth needs.*

they are met, a person's motivation does not cease; instead, it increases to seek further fulfillment. Unlike the deficiency needs, these being needs can never be completely filled. For example, the more successful you are in your efforts to develop as a teacher, the harder you are likely to strive for even greater improvement.

Maslow's theory has been criticized for the very obvious reason that people do not always appear to behave as the theory would predict. Most of us move back and forth among different types of needs and may even be motivated by many needs at the same time. Some people deny themselves safety or friendship in order to achieve knowledge, understanding, or greater self-esteem.

Criticisms aside, Maslow's theory does give us a way of looking at the whole student, whose physical, emotional, and intellectual needs are all interrelated. A child whose feelings of safety and sense of belonging are threatened by divorce may have little interest in learning how to divide fractions. If school is a fearful, unpredictable place where neither teachers nor students know where they stand, they are likely to be more concerned with security and less with learning or teaching. Belonging to a social group and maintaining self-esteem within that group, for example, are important to students. If doing what the teacher says conflicts with group rules, students may choose to ignore the teacher's wishes or even defy the teacher.

Self-determination theory is a more recent approach to motivation that focuses on human needs (Deci & Ryan, 2002; Reeve, 2009).

Self-Determination: Need for Competence, Autonomy, and Relatedness

Self-determination theory suggests that we all need to feel competent and capable in our interactions in the world, to have some choices and a sense of control over our lives, and to be connected to others—to belong to a social group. Notice that these are similar to earlier conceptions of basic needs: *competence* (achievement), *autonomy and control* (power), and *relatedness* (affiliation). Because different cultures have divergent conceptions of self, some psychologists have asked whether the needs for competence, autonomy, and relatedness are universal. In a series of studies, Hyungshim Jang and her colleagues (2009) found that experiences of competence, autonomy, and relatedness were associated with satisfying learning experiences for Korean high school students, so even in a collectivistic culture, these needs may be important.

Need for autonomy is central to self-determination because it is the desire to have our own wishes, rather than external rewards or pressures, determine our actions (Deci & Ryan, 2002; Reeve, 2009; Reeve, Deci, & Ryan, 2004). People strive to have authority in their lives, to be in charge of their own behavior. They constantly struggle against pressure from external controls such as the rules, schedules, deadlines, orders, and limits imposed by others. Sometimes, even help is rejected so that the individual can remain in command (deCharms, 1983).

SELF-DETERMINATION IN THE CLASSROOM. Classroom environments that support student self-determination and autonomy are associated with greater student interest and curiosity (even interest in homework assignments), sense of competence, creativity, conceptual learning, grades, school attendance and satisfaction, engagement, use of self-regulated learning strategies, psychological well-being, and preference for challenge. These relationships appear to hold from 1st grade through graduate school (Jang, Reeve, & Deci, 2010; Moller, Deci, & Ryan, 2006; Reeve, 2009; Shih, 2008). When students have the authority to make choices, they are more likely to believe that the work is important, even if it is not "fun." Thus, they tend to internalize educational goals and take them as their own.

In contrast to autonomy-supporting classrooms, controlling environments tend to improve performance only on rote recall tasks. When students are pressured to perform, they often seek the quickest, easiest solution. But even though controlling styles of teaching are less effective, teachers are under pressure from administrators, accountability requirements, and cultural expectations to be "in charge," along with parents' expectations

Connect and Extend to PRAXIS II™

Maslow (I, C1)
Consider how problems with satisfying Maslow's hierarchy of needs can affect student learning. Link these ideas to direct or vicarious experiences you might have had in school.

Connect and Extend to PRAXIS II™

Self-Determination (I, C3)
Understand how self-determination can boost or diminish motivation and describe practical steps that teachers can take to establish a sense of self-determination in students.

Need for autonomy The desire to have our own wishes, rather than external rewards or pressures, determine our actions.

SELF-DETERMINED STUDENTS Classroom environments that support student self-determination and autonomy are associated with greater student interest and curiosity, sense of competence, creativity, conceptual learning, and preference for challenge.

for class "discipline." In addition, students often are passive and unengaged or even defiant. Finally, some teachers equate control with useful structure or feel more comfortable with a controlling style (Reeve, 2009). Assuming you are willing to resist those pressures, how can you support student autonomy? One answer is to focus on information, not control, in your interactions with students.

INFORMATION AND CONTROL. **Cognitive evaluation theory** (Deci & Ryan, 2002) explains how students' experiences such as being praised or criticized, reminded of deadlines, assigned grades, given choices, or lectured about rules can influence their intrinsic motivation by affecting their sense of self-determination and competence. According to this theory, all events have two aspects: *controlling* and *informational*. If an event is highly controlling, that is, if it pressures students to act or feel a certain way, then students will experience less control and their intrinsic motivation will be diminished. If, on the other hand, the event provides information that increases the students' sense of competence, then intrinsic motivation will increase. Of course, if the information provided makes students feel less competent, it is likely that motivation will decrease (Pintrich, 2003). Here is an example of a more *controlling* communication:

> Your paper is due on Monday. Today, we are going to the school library. In the library, you will find information from books and Internet sites to use for your paper. Don't waste your time; don't goof off; make sure to get your work done. In the library, you may work by yourself or with a partner. (Reeve, 2009, p. 169)

This teacher may believe that he is supporting autonomy because he offered a *choice*. Contrast his message with the following statement that gives *information* about why the library visit is valuable:

> Your paper is due on Monday. As a way of helping you write a well-researched paper, we are going to where the information is—the school library. The reason we are going to the library is to find the information you need from books and Internet sites. While there, you may be tempted to goof off, but students in the past have found that a trip to the library was a crucial part of writing an excellent paper. To help you write your best possible paper, you may work in the way you wish—by yourself or with a partner. (Reeve, 2009, p. 169)

As a teacher, what can you do to support student needs for autonomy and competence? An obvious first step is to limit your controlling messages to students because controlling language (*must, ought, have* to, *should*...) can undermine student motivation (Vansteenkiste, Simons, Lens, Sheldon, & Deci, 2004). Make sure the information you provide highlights students' growing competence. The *Guidelines* give some ideas.

THE NEED FOR RELATEDNESS. The need for relatedness is the desire to establish close emotional bonds and attachments with others. When teachers and parents are responsive and demonstrate that they care about the children's interests and well-being, the children show high intrinsic motivation. Students who feel a sense of relatedness to teachers, parents, and peers are more emotionally engaged in school (Furrer & Skinner, 2003).

Cognitive evaluation theory Suggests that events affect motivation through the individual's perception of the events as controlling behavior or providing information.

GUIDELINES

Supporting Self-Determination and Autonomy

Allow and encourage students to make choices.
Examples

1. Design several different ways to meet a learning objective (e.g., a paper, a compilation of interviews, a test, a news broadcast) and let students choose one. Encourage them to explain the reasons for their choice.
2. Appoint student committees to make suggestions about streamlining procedures such as caring for class pets or distributing equipment.
3. Provide time for independent and extended projects.
4. Allow students to choose work partners as long as they focus on the task.

Help students plan actions to accomplish self-selected goals.
Examples

1. Experiment with goal cards. Students list their short- and long-term goals and then record 3 or 4 specific actions that will move them toward the goals. Goal cards are personal—like credit cards.
2. Encourage middle and high school students to set goals in each subject area, record them in a goal book or on a thumb drive, and check progress toward the goals on a regular basis.

Hold students accountable for the consequences of their choices.
Examples

1. If students choose to work with friends and do not finish a project because too much time was spent socializing, grade the project as it deserves and help the students see the connection between lost time and poor performance.
2. When students choose a topic that captures their imagination, discuss the connections between their

investment in the work and the quality of the products that follow.

Provide rationales for limits, rules, and constraints.
Examples

1. Explain reasons for rules.
2. Respect rules and constraints in your own behavior.

Acknowledge that negative emotions are valid reactions to teacher control.
Examples

1. Communicate that it is okay (and normal) to feel bored waiting for a turn, for example.
2. Communicate that sometimes important learning involves frustration, confusion, weariness.
3. Acknowledge students' perspective: "Yes, this problem is difficult." Or "I can understand why you might feel that way."

Use noncontrolling, positive feedback.
Examples

1. See poor performance or behavior as a problem to be solved, not a target of criticism.
2. Avoid controlling language, "should," "must," "have to."

For more information on self-determination theory see:
http://www.psych.rochester.edu/SDT/

Source: From 150 Ways to Increase Intrinsic Motivation in the Classroom, by James P. Raffini. Published by Allyn and Bacon, Boston, MA. Copyright © 1996 by Pearson Education and from Motivating Others: Nurturing Inner Motivational Resources by Johnmarshall Reeve. Published by Allyn and Bacon, Boston, MA. Copyright © 1996 by Pearson Education. Adapted by permission of the publisher.

All students need caring teachers, but students placed at risk have an even greater need for this kind of teacher. Positive relationships with teachers increase the likelihood that students will succeed in high school and go onto college (Stipek, 2006; Thompson, 2008; Woolfolk Hoy & Weinstein, 2006). In addition, emotional and physical problems—ranging from eating disorders to suicide—are more common among individuals who lack social relationships (Baumeister & Leary, 1995). Relatedness is similar to a sense of belonging, discussed in Chapter 3 (Osterman, 2000).

Needs: Lessons for Teachers

From infancy to old age, people want to be competent, connected, and in control. Students are more likely to participate in activities that help them grow more competent and less likely to engage in activities that hold the possibility of failure. This means that your students need appropriately challenging tasks—not too easy, but not impossible either. They also benefit from watching their competence grow, perhaps through self-monitoring systems or portfolios. To be connected, students need to feel that people in school care about them and can be trusted to help them learn.

What else matters in motivation? Many theories include goals as key elements.

GOAL ORIENTATIONS

A **goal** is an outcome or attainment an individual is striving to accomplish (Locke & Latham, 2002). When students strive to read a chapter or make a 4.0 GPA, they are involved in goal-directed behavior. In pursuing goals, students are generally aware of some current condition (I haven't even opened my book), some ideal condition (I have understood every page), and the discrepancy between the two. Goals motivate people to act in order to reduce the discrepancy between "where they are" and "where they want to be." Goal setting is usually effective for me. In addition to the routine tasks, such as eating lunch, which will happen without much attention, I often set goals for each day. For example, today I intend to finish this section, walk on the treadmill, schedule a dentist appointment, and wash another load of clothes (I know—not too exciting). Having decided to do these things, I will feel uncomfortable if I don't complete the list.

According to Locke and Latham (2002), there are four main reasons why goal setting improves performance. Goals:

1. Direct attention to the task at hand and away from distractions. Every time my mind wanders from this chapter, my goal of finishing the section helps direct my attention back to the writing.
2. Energize effort. The more challenging the goal, to a point, the greater the effort.
3. Increase persistence. When we have a clear goal, we are less likely to give up until we reach the goal: Hard goals demand effort and tight deadlines lead to faster work.
4. Promote the development of new knowledge and strategies when old strategies fall short. For example, if your goal is making an A and you don't reach that goal on your first quiz, you might try a new study approach for the next quiz, such as explaining the key points to a friend.

Types of Goals and Goal Orientations

The types of goals we set influence the amount of motivation we have to reach them. Goals that are *specific, elaborated, moderately difficult*, and *likely to be reached* in the near future tend to enhance motivation and persistence (Schunk, Pintrich, & Meece, 2008; Stipek, 2002).

Specific, elaborated goals provide clear standards for judging performance. If performance falls short, we keep going. For example, Ralph Ferretti and his colleagues (2009) gave 4th and 6th grade students either a general goal for writing a persuasive essay ("write a letter to a teacher about whether or not students should be given more out-of-class assignments…") or the general goal elaborated with specific subgoals such as:

• You need to say very clearly what your opinion or viewpoint is;
• You need to think of two or more reasons to back up your opinion;
• You need to explain why those reasons are good reasons for your opinion (p. 580)

Both students with and without learning disabilities wrote more persuasive essays when they were given specific subgoals.

Moderate difficulty provides a challenge, but not an unreasonable one. Finally, goals that can be reached *fairly soon* are not likely to be pushed aside by more immediate concerns. Groups such as Alcoholics Anonymous show they are aware of the motivating value of short-term goals when they encourage their members to stop drinking "one day at a time."

STOP & THINK On a scale from 1 (Strongly Agree) to 5 (Strongly Disagree), how would you answer these questions:

I feel really pleased in school when

___ I solve problems by working hard   ___ All the work is easy

___ I know more than the others   ___ I learn something new

___ I don't have to work hard   ___ I am the only one who gets an A

___ I keep busy   ___ I am with my friends •

___ I finish first

Goal What an individual strives to accomplish.

FOUR ACHIEVEMENT GOAL ORIENTATIONS IN SCHOOL. Goals are specific targets. **Goal orientations** are patterns of beliefs about goals related to achievement in school. Goal orientations include the reasons we pursue goals and the standards we use to evaluate progress toward those goals. For example, your target might be to make an A in this course. Are you doing so in order to *master* educational psychology—to learn all about it, or to *perform*—to look good in the eyes of your friends and family? There are four main goal orientations—mastery (learning), performance (looking good), work-avoidance, and social (Schunk, Pintrich, & Meece, 2008). In the *Stop & Think* exercise you just completed, can you tell which goal orientations are reflected in the different answers? Most of the questions were adapted from a study on students' theories about learning mathematics (Nicholls, Cobb, Wood, Yackel, & Patashnick, 1990).

The most common distinction in research on students' goals is between mastery goals (also called *task goals* or *learning goals*) and performance goals (also called *ability goals* or *ego goals*). The point of a **mastery goal** is to improve, to learn, no matter how awkward you appear. When students set mastery goals, the quality of their engagement in the task is higher—they are more invested. Students with mastery goals tend to seek challenges, persist when they encounter difficulties, and feel better about their work (Midgley, 2001). They focus on the task at hand and are not worried about how their performance "measures up" in comparison to others in the class. We often say that these people "get lost in their work." In addition, they are more likely to seek appropriate help, use deeper cognitive processing strategies, apply better study strategies, and generally approach academic tasks with confidence (Anderman & Patrick, 2012; Kaplan & Maehr, 2007).

The second kind of goal is a performance goal. Students with **performance goals** care about demonstrating their ability to others. They may be focused on getting good test scores and grades, or they may be more concerned with winning and beating other students. Students whose goal is outperforming others may do things to look smart, such as reading easy books in order to "read the most books." The evaluation of their performance by others, not what they learn, is what matters. Students with performance goals may act in ways that actually interfere with learning. For example, they may cheat or use short-cuts to get finished, work hard only on graded assignments, be upset and hide papers with low grades, choose tasks that are easy, and be very uncomfortable with assignments that have unclear evaluation criteria (Anderman & Anderman, 2010; Stipek, 2002).

"MEASURING UP" ISN'T THE POINT When students set mastery goals, the quality of their engagement in the task is higher—they are more invested. They are less worried about how their performance compares to that of others in the class.

WAIT—ARE PERFORMANCE GOALS ALWAYS BAD? Performance goals sound pretty dysfunctional, don't they? Earlier research indicated that performance goals generally were detrimental to learning, but like extrinsic motivation, a performance goal orientation may not be all bad, all of the time. In fact, some research indicates that both mastery and performance goals are associated with using active learning strategies and high self-efficacy (Midgley, Kaplan, & Middleton, 2001; Stipek, 2002). For college students, pursuing performance goals has been related to higher achievement. And, as is the case with intrinsic and extrinsic motivation, students can, and often do pursue mastery and performance goals at the same time (Anderman & Patrick, 2012).

To account for these recent findings, educational psychologists have added the distinction of approach/avoidance to the mastery/performance distinction. In other words, students may be motivated to either approach mastery or avoid misunderstanding. They may approach performance or avoid looking dumb. Table 9.2 on the next page shows examples and the effects of each kind of goal orientation. Where do you see the most problems? Do you agree that the real problems are with avoidance? Students who fear misunderstanding (mastery avoid) may be perfectionist—focused on getting it exactly

Goal orientations Patterns of beliefs about goals related to achievement in school.

Mastery goal A personal intention to improve abilities and learn, no matter how performance suffers.

Performance goal A personal intention to seem competent or perform well in the eyes of others.

TABLE 9.2 • **Goal Orientations**

Students may have either an approach or an avoidance focus for mastery and performance goal orientations.

GOAL ORIENTATION	APPROACH FOCUS	AVOIDANCE FOCUS
Mastery	*Focus:* Mastering the task, learning, understanding *Standards Used:* Self-improvement, progress, deep understanding (task-involved)	*Focus:* Avoiding misunderstanding or not mastering the task *Standards Used:* Just don't be wrong; perfectionists don't make mistakes
Performance	*Focus:* Being superior, winning, being the best *Standards Used:* Normative—getting the highest grade, winning the competition (ego-involved goal)	*Focus:* Avoiding looking stupid, avoiding losing *Standards Used:* Normative—don't be the worst, get the lowest grade, or be the slowest (ego-involved goal)

Source: From Pintrich, Paul R. and Dale H. Schunk. Motivation in Education: Theory, Research and Applications, 2e. Published by Allyn and Bacon, Boston, MA. Copyright © 2002 by Pearson Education. Adapted by permission of the publisher.

right. Students who avoid looking dumb (performance avoid) may adopt defensive, failure-avoiding strategies like Defensive Daleesha described earlier—they pretend not to care, make a show of "not really trying," or cheat (Harackiewiz, Barron, Pintrich, Elliot, & Thrash, 2002; Harackiewiz & Linnenbrink, 2005).

One final caution—performance approach goals can turn into performance avoidance goals if students are not successful in looking smart or winning. The path might lead from performance approach (trying to win), to performance avoidance (saving face and trying not to look dumb), to learned helplessness (I give up!). So teachers are wise to avoid trying to motivate using competition and social comparisons (Brophy, 2005).

BEYOND MASTERY AND PERFORMANCE. Some students don't want to learn, look smart, or avoid looking dumb; they just want to finish fast or avoid work altogether. These students try to complete assignments and activities as quickly as possible without exerting much effort (Schunk, Pintrich, & Meece, 2008). John Nicholls called these students **work-avoidant learners**—they feel successful when they don't have to try hard, when the work is easy, or when they can "goof off" (Nicholls & Miller, 1984).

A final category of goals becomes more important as students get older—**social goals**. As students move into adolescence, their social networks change to include more peers. Nonacademic activities such as athletics, dating, and "hanging out" compete with schoolwork. Social goals include a wide variety of needs and motives that have different relationships to learning—some help, but others hinder learning. For example, adolescents' goal of maintaining friendly relations can get in the way of learning when cooperative learning group members don't challenge wrong answers or misconceptions because they are afraid to hurt each other's feelings (Anderson, Holland, & Palincsar, 1997). Certainly, pursuing social goals such as having fun with friends or avoiding being labeled a "nerd" can get in the way of learning. But the goal of bringing honor to your family or team by working hard or being part of a peer group that values academics certainly can support learning (Pintrich, 2003; A. Ryan, 2001; Urdan & Maehr, 1995).

We talk about goals in separate categories, but students can and do pursue several goals at once (Bong, 2009; Darnon, Dompnier, Gillieron, & Butera, 2010). They have to coordinate their goals so they can make decisions about what to do and how to act. What if social and academic goals are incompatible? For example, if students do not see a connection between achievement in school and success in life, particularly because

Work-avoidant learners Students who don't want to learn or to look smart, but just want to avoid work.

Social goals A wide variety of needs and motives to be connected to others or part of a group.

discrimination prevents them from succeeding, then they are not likely to set academic achievement as a goal. Such anti-academic peer groups probably exist in every high school (Committee on Increasing High School Students' Engagement and Motivation to Learn, 2004; Wentzel, 1999). Sometimes, succeeding in the peer group means not achieving in school—and succeeding in the peer group is important. The need for social relationships is basic and strong for most people.

GOALS IN SOCIAL CONTEXT.   You have seen in other chapters that current thinking in educational psychology puts people in context. Goal orientation theory is no exception. The people in the situation socially construct the meaning of an activity, such as an assignment in a biology class; goals set for the activity will reflect the participants' understanding of "what they are doing." So, in a highly competitive classroom climate, students might be more likely to adopt performance goals. In contrast, in a supportive, learner-centered classroom, even a student with a lower sense of self-efficacy might be encouraged to aim for higher mastery goals. Goals are constructed as part of the triadic reciprocal interaction of person, environment, and behavior described by social cognitive theory—"interlocking perceptions of 'meaning,' 'purpose,' and 'self' in guiding and framing action, thought and emotion" (Kaplan & Maehr, 2007).

The way students perceive their class defines the *classroom goal structure*—the goals that students think are emphasized in the class (Murayama & Elliot, 2009). Lisa Fast and her colleagues (2010) found that 4th through 6th grade students had significantly higher levels of self-efficacy and mathematics achievement when they perceived their math classes as caring, challenging, and mastery oriented. So challenge, support, and a focus on learning, not looking good, seem to create a positive classroom environment.

Feedback, Goal Framing, and Goal Acceptance

Besides having specific goals and creating supportive social relationships, there are three additional factors that make goal setting in the classroom effective. The first is *feedback*. In order to be motivated by a discrepancy between "where you are" and "where you want to be," you must have an accurate sense of both your current status and how far you have to go. There is evidence that feedback emphasizing progress is the most effective. In one study, feedback to adults emphasized either that they had accomplished 75% of the standards set or that they had fallen short of the standards by 25%. When the feedback highlighted accomplishment, the subjects' self-confidence, analytic thinking, and performance were all enhanced (Bandura, 1997).

The second factor affecting motivation to pursue a goal is *goal framing*. Activities or assignments can be explained or framed as helping students' intrinsic goals, such as growing competence, self-determination, positive relationships with friends or teachers, or well-being. The alternative is portraying activities as helping students reach extrinsic goals such as working for a grade, meeting requirements, getting ready for classes next year, and so on. When activities are linked to students' intrinsic goals of becoming more competent, self-directed, and connected with others, then the students process information more deeply and persist longer to gain a conceptual (not superficial) understanding. Linking activities to the extrinsic goals of meeting someone else's standards promotes rote learning, but not deep understanding or persistence (Vansteenkiste, Lens, & Deci, 2006).

The third factor is *goal acceptance*. Commitment matters: The relationship between higher goals and better performance is strongest when people are committed to the goals (Locke & Latham, 2002). If students reject goals set by others or refuse to set their own goals, then their motivation will suffer. Generally, students are more willing to commit to the goals of others if the goals seem realistic, reasonably difficult, and meaningful—and if the goals are validated by connecting activities to students' intrinsic interests (Grolnick, Gurland, Jacob, & Decourcey, 2002).

Goals: Lessons for Teachers

Students are more likely to work toward goals that are clear, specific, reasonable, moderately challenging, and attainable within a relatively short period of time. If teachers focus on student performance, high grades, and competition, they may encourage students to set performance goals. This could undermine the students' ability to learn and become task-involved and set them on a path toward alienation from learning in school and learned helplessness (Anderman & Maehr, 1994; Brophy, 2005). Students may not yet be expert at setting their own goals or keeping these goals in mind, so encouragement and accurate feedback are necessary. If you use any reward or incentive systems, be sure the goal you set is to learn and improve in some area, not just to perform well or look smart. And be sure the goal is not too difficult. Students, like adults, are unlikely to stick with tasks or respond well to teachers who make them feel insecure or incompetent, which leads us to our next topic—the power of beliefs in motivation.

BELIEFS AND SELF-PERCEPTIONS

Thus far, we have talked about needs and goals, but there is another factor that must be considered in explaining motivation. What do students believe about learning and about themselves—their competence and the causes for success or failure? Let's start with a basic question—What do they believe about knowing?

Beliefs About Knowing: Epistemological Beliefs

What students believe about knowledge and learning (their **epistemological beliefs**) will influence their motivation and the kinds of strategies that they use.

- -

STOP & THINK How would you answer these questions taken from Chan & Sachs (2001)?

1. Which of the following is the most important thing in learning math? (a) remember what the teacher has taught you, (b) practice lots of problems, (c) understand the problems you work on.

2. Which of the following is the important thing to do in learning science? (a) faithfully do the work the teacher tells you, (b) try to see how the explanation makes sense, (c) try to remember everything you are supposed to know.

3. If you wanted to know everything there is about something, say animals, how long would you have to study it? (a) less than a year if you study hard, (b) about one or two years, (c) forever.

4. What happens when you learn more and more about something? (a) the questions get more and more complex, (b) the questions get easier and easier, (c) the questions all get answered. •

- -

Using questions like those above, researchers have identified several dimensions of epistemological beliefs (Chan & Sachs, 2001; Schommer, 1997; Schommer-Aikins, 2002; Schraw & Olafson, 2002). For example:

- **Structure of Knowledge:** Is knowledge in a field a simple set of facts or a complex structure of concepts and relationships?
- **Stability/Certainty of Knowledge:** Is knowledge fixed or does it evolve over time?
- **Ability to Learn:** Is the ability to learn fixed (based on innate ability) or changeable?
- **Speed of Learning:** Can we gain knowledge quickly or does it take time to develop knowledge?
- **Nature of Learning:** Does learning mean memorizing facts passed down from authorities and keeping the facts isolated, or does it mean developing your own integrated understandings?

Students' beliefs about knowing and learning affect the goals they set and the learning strategies they apply. For example, if you believe that knowledge should be gained quickly, you are likely to try one or two quick strategies (read the text once, spend two minutes trying to solve the word problem) and then stop. If you believe that learning means developing integrated understandings, you will process the material more deeply, connect to existing knowledge, create your own examples, or draw diagrams, and generally elaborate on the information to make it your own (Kardash & Howell, 2000; Muis &

Epistemological beliefs Beliefs about the structure, stability, and certainty of knowledge, and how knowledge is best learned.

Franco, 2009). In one study, elementary school students (grades 4 and 6) who believed that learning is understanding processed science texts more deeply than others who believed that learning is reproducing facts (Chan & Sachs, 2001). The *Stop & Think* questions you just answered were used in that study to assess the students' beliefs. The answers associated with a belief in complex, evolving knowledge that takes time to understand and grows from active learning are 1c, 2b, 3c, and 4a.

Beliefs about one dimension discussed above—ability to learn—are particularly powerful. Read on.

Beliefs About Ability

- -

STOP & THINK Rate these statements taken from Dweck (2000) on a scale from 1 (Strongly Agree) to 6 (Strongly Disagree).

_____ You have a certain amount of intelligence and you really can't do much to change it.

_____ You can learn new things, but you can't really change your basic intelligence.

_____ No matter who you are, you can change your intelligence a lot.

_____ No matter how much intelligence you have, you can always change it quite a bit. •

- -

Some of the most powerful beliefs affecting motivation in school are about ability. Adults use two basic concepts of ability (Dweck, 2002, 2006). An **entity view of ability** assumes that ability is a stable, uncontrollable trait—a characteristic of the individual that cannot be changed. According to this view, some people have more ability than others, but the amount each person has is set. An **incremental view of ability**, on the other hand, suggests that ability is unstable and controllable—"an ever-expanding repertoire of skills and knowledge" (Dweck & Bempechat, 1983, p. 144). By hard work, study, or practice, knowledge can be increased and thus ability can be improved. What is your view of ability? Look back at your answers to the *Stop & Think* questions.

Young children tend to hold an exclusively incremental view of ability. Through the early elementary grades, most students believe that effort is the same as intelligence. Smart people try hard, and trying hard makes you smart. If you fail, you aren't smart and you didn't try hard (Dweck, 2000; Stipek, 2002). At around age 11 or 12, children can differentiate among effort, ability, and performance. At about this time, they come to believe that someone who succeeds without working at all must be really smart. This is when beliefs about ability begin to influence motivation (Anderman & Anderman, 2010).

Students who hold an *entity* (unchangeable) view of intelligence tend to set performance avoid goals to avoid looking bad in the eyes of others. They seek situations where they can look smart and protect their self-esteem. Like Safe Sumey, they keep doing those things they can do well without expending too much effort or risking failure, because either one—working hard or failing—indicates (to them) low ability. To work hard but still fail would be devastating. Students with learning disabilities are more likely to hold an entity view.

In contrast, holding an *incremental* view of ability is associated with greater motivation and learning. Believing that you can improve your ability helps you focus on the *processes* of problem solving and applying good strategies, instead of on the *products* of test scores and grades (Chen & Pajares, 2010).

Teachers who hold *entity* views are quicker to form judgments about students and slower to modify their opinions when confronted with contradictory evidence (Stipek, 2002). Teachers who hold *incremental* views, in contrast, tend to set mastery goals and seek situations in which students can improve their skills, because improvement means getting smarter. Failure is not devastating; it simply indicates more work is needed. Ability is not threatened. Incremental theorists tend to set moderately difficult goals, the kind we have seen are the most motivating.

Beliefs about ability are related to other beliefs about what you can and cannot control in learning.

Entity view of ability Belief that ability is a fixed characteristic that cannot be changed.

Incremental view of ability Belief that ability is a set of skills that can be changed.

Beliefs About Causes and Control: Attribution Theory

One well-known explanation of motivation begins with the assumption that we try to make sense of our own behavior and the behavior of others by searching for explanations and causes. To understand our own successes and failures, particularly unexpected ones, we all ask, "Why?" Students ask themselves, "Why did I flunk my midterm?" or "Why did I do so well this grading period?" They may attribute their successes and failures to ability, effort, mood, knowledge, luck, help, interest, clarity of instructions, the interference of others, unfair policies, and so on. To understand the successes and failures of others, we also make attributions—that the others are smart or lucky or work hard, for example. **Attribution theories** of motivation describe how the individual's explanations, justifications, and excuses influence motivation (Anderman & Anderman, 2010).

Bernard Weiner is one of the main educational psychologists responsible for relating attribution theory to school learning (Weiner, 2000, 2010). According to Weiner, most of the attributed causes for successes or failures can be characterized in terms of three dimensions:

1. **Locus** (location of the cause—internal or external to the person). For example, attributing a great piano performance to your musical talent or hard work are internal attributions. Explaining that the performance is based on coaching from a great teacher is an external attribution.
2. **Stability** (whether the cause of the event is the same across time and in different situations). For example, talent is stable, but effort can change.
3. **Controllability** (whether the person can control the cause). For example, effort and finding a great teacher are controllable, but innate musical talent is not.

Every cause for success or failure can be categorized on these three dimensions. For instance, luck is external (locus), unstable (stability), and uncontrollable (controllability). In attribution theory, ability is usually considered stable and uncontrollable, but incremental theorists (described earlier) would argue that ability is unstable and controllable. Weiner's locus and controllability dimensions are closely related to Deci's concept of locus of causality.

Weiner believes that these three dimensions have important implications for motivation because they affect expectancy and value. The *stability* dimension, for example, seems to be closely related to expectations about the future. If students attribute their failure to stable factors such as the difficulty of the subject or an unfair teacher, they will expect to keep failing in that subject or with that teacher. But if they attribute the outcome to unstable factors such as mood or luck, they can hope for better outcomes next time. The *internal/external locus* seems to be closely related to feelings of self-esteem. If success or failure is attributed to internal factors, success will lead to pride and increased motivation, whereas failure will diminish self-esteem. The *controllability* dimension is related to emotions such as anger, pity, gratitude, or shame. If we feel responsible for our failures, we may feel guilt; if we feel responsible for successes, we may feel proud. Failing at a task we cannot control can lead to shame or anger (Weiner, 2010).

Feeling in control of your own learning seems to be related to choosing more difficult academic tasks, putting out more effort, using better strategies, and persisting longer in school work (Schunk, 2000; Weiner, 1994a, 1994b). Factors such as continuing discrimination against women, people of color, and individuals with special needs can affect these individuals' perceptions of their ability to control their lives (van Laar, 2000).

ATTRIBUTIONS IN THE CLASSROOM. People with a strong sense of **self-efficacy** (see Chapter 11) for a given task ("I'm good at math") tend to attribute their failures to lack of effort ("I should have double-checked my work"), misunderstanding directions, or just not studying enough. These are internal, controllable attributions. As a consequence, they usually focus on strategies for succeeding next time. This response often leads to achievement, pride, and a greater feeling of control. But people with a low sense of self-efficacy ("I'm terrible at math") tend to attribute their failures to lack of ability ("I'm just dumb").

The greatest motivational problems arise when students attribute failures to stable, uncontrollable causes. Such students may seem resigned to failure, depressed, helpless—what we

Connect and Extend to PRAXIS II™

Attribution Theory (I, C1)
Go to the *Encyclopedia of Psychology* (http://www.psychology.org/links/Environment_Behavior_Relationships/Motivation/) and follow its link for Attribution Theory to learn more about using principles derived from this theory to boost intrinsic motivation to learn.

Attribution theories Descriptions of how individuals' explanations, justifications, and excuses influence their motivation and behavior.

Self-efficacy Beliefs about personal competence in a particular situation.

generally call "unmotivated" (Weiner, 2000, 2010). These students respond to failure by focusing even more on their own inadequacy; their attitudes toward schoolwork may deteriorate even further. Apathy is a logical reaction to failure if students believe the causes are stable, unlikely to change, and beyond their control anyway. In addition, students who view their failures in this light are less likely to seek help; they believe nothing and no one can help, so they conceal their needs for help. This creates a downward spiral of failure and concealment—"the motivationally 'poor' children, by concealing their difficulties, become 'poorer'" (Marchland & Skinner, 2007). You can see that if a student held an entity view (ability cannot be changed) and a low sense of self-efficacy, motivation would be destroyed when failures were attributed to lack of ability ("I just can't do this and I'll never be able to learn") (Bandura, 1997; Schunk, Pintrich, & Meece, 2008; Stipek, 2002).

UNMOTIVATED? The greatest motivational problems arise when students attribute failures to uncontrollable causes and focus on their own inadequacy. Apathy is a logical reaction if students believe the causes of failure are beyond their control.

TEACHER ACTIONS AND STUDENT ATTRIBUTIONS. We also make attributions about the causes of other people's successes and failures. When a teacher assumes that student failure is attributable to forces beyond the student's control, the teacher tends to respond with sympathy and avoid giving punishments. If, however, the failures are attributed to a controllable factor such as lack of effort, the teacher's response is more likely to be irritation or anger, and reprimands may follow. These tendencies seem to be consistent across time and cultures (Weiner, 1986, 2000).

What do students make of these reactions from their teachers? Sandra Graham (1991, 1996) gives some surprising answers. There is evidence that when teachers respond to students' mistakes with pity, praise for a "good try," or unsolicited help, the students are more likely to attribute their failure to an uncontrollable cause—usually lack of ability. Does this mean that teachers should be critical and withhold help? Of course not! But it is a reminder that over-solicitous help can give unintended messages. Graham (1991) suggests that many minority group students could be the victims of well-meaning pity from teachers. Seeing the very real problems that the students face, teachers may "ease up" on requirements so the students will "experience success." But a subtle communication may accompany the pity, praise, and extra help: "You don't have the ability to do this, so I will overlook your failure." Graham says, "The pertinent question for blacks is whether their own history of academic failure makes them more likely to be the targets of sympathetic feedback from teachers and thus the recipients of low-ability cues" (1991, p. 28). This kind of benevolent feedback, even if well intended, can be a subtle form of racism.

Beliefs About Self-Worth

Whatever the label, most theorists agree that a sense of efficacy, control, or self-determination is critical if people are to feel intrinsically motivated.

LEARNED HELPLESSNESS. When people come to believe that the events and outcomes in their lives are mostly uncontrollable, they have developed **learned helplessness** (Seligman, 1975). To understand the power of learned helplessness, consider this classic experiment (Hiroto & Seligman, 1975): Subjects received either solvable or unsolvable puzzles. In the next phase of the experiment, all subjects were given a series of solvable puzzles. The subjects who struggled with unsolvable puzzles in the first phase of the experiment usually solved significantly fewer puzzles in the second phase. They had learned that they could not control the outcome, so why even try?

Learned helplessness appears to cause three types of deficits: *motivational, cognitive*, and *affective*. Students who feel hopeless, like Hopeless Geraldo described earlier,

Learned helplessness The expectation, based on previous experiences with a lack of control, that all one's efforts will lead to failure.

TABLE 9.3 • **Mastery-Oriented, Failure-Avoiding, and Failure-Accepting Students**

	ATTITUDE TOWARD FAILURE	GOALS SET	ATTRIBUTIONS	VIEW OF ABILITY	STRATEGIES
Mastery-Oriented	Low fear of failure	Learning goals: moderately difficult and challenging	Effort, use of right strategy, sufficient knowledge is cause of success	Incremental; improvable	Adaptive strategies; e.g., try another way, seek help, practice/study more
Failure-Avoiding	High fear of failure	Performance goals; very hard or very easy	Lack of ability is cause of failure	Entity; set	Self-defeating strategies; e.g., make a feeble effort, pretend not to care
Failure-Accepting	Expectation of failure; depression	Performance goals or no goals	Lack of ability is cause of failure	Entity; set	Learned helplessness; likely to give up

expect to fail, so why should they even try—thus *motivation* suffers. Because they are pessimistic about learning, these students miss opportunities to practice and improve skills and abilities, so they develop *cognitive* deficits. Finally, they often suffer from *affective* problems such as depression, anxiety, and listlessness (Alloy & Seligman, 1979). Once established, it is very difficult to reverse the effects of learned helplessness.

SELF-WORTH. What are the connections between attributions and beliefs about ability, self-efficacy, and self-worth? Covington and his colleagues suggest that these factors come together in three kinds of motivational sets: *mastery oriented, failure avoiding*, and *failure accepting*, as shown in Table 9.3 (Covington, 1992; Covington & Mueller, 2001).

Mastery-oriented students tend to value achievement and see ability as improvable (an incremental view), so they focus on mastery goals in order to increase their skills and abilities. They are not fearful of failure, because failing does not threaten their sense of competence and self-worth. This allows them to set moderately difficult goals, take risks, and cope with failure constructively. They generally attribute success to their own effort, and thus they assume responsibility for learning and have a strong sense of self-efficacy. They learn fast, have more self-confidence and energy, are more aroused, welcome concrete feedback (it does not threaten them), and are eager to learn "the rules of the game" so that they can succeed. All of these factors make for persistent, successful learning (Covington & Mueller, 2001; McClelland, 1985).

Failure-avoiding students tend to hold an entity (fixed) view of ability, so they set performance goals. They lack a strong sense of their own competence and self-worth separate from their performance. In other words, they feel only as smart as their last test grade, so they never develop a solid sense of self-efficacy. In order to feel competent, they must protect themselves (and their self-worth) from failure. If they have been generally successful, they may seek to avoid failure like Safe Sumey, simply by taking few risks and "sticking with what they know." If, on the other hand, they have experienced a good bit of failure, then they, like Defensive Daleesha, may adopt self-defeating strategies such as feeble efforts, setting very low or ridiculously high goals, or claiming not to care. Just before a test, a student might say, "I didn't study at all!" or "All I want to do is pass." Then, any grade above passing is a success. Procrastination is another example. Low grades do not imply low ability if the student can claim, "I did okay considering I didn't start the term paper until last night." All these are **self-handicapping** strategies because the students are imposing handicaps on their own achievement. Very little learning is going on.

Mastery-oriented students Students who focus on learning goals because they value achievement and see ability as improvable.

Failure-avoiding students Students who avoid failure by sticking to what they know, by not taking risks, or by claiming not to care about their performance.

Self-handicapping Students may engage in behavior that blocks their own success in order to avoid testing their true ability.

Encouraging Self-Worth

Emphasize that abilities are not set, but are always improvable.
Examples
1. Share examples of how you have improved your knowledge and skills, for example in writing, at a sport, or doing a craft.
2. Tell about your own failures that became successes when you tried new strategies or got the right help.
3. Save first drafts and finished products from students in previous classes to show how much the students improved with effort and support.

Teach directly about the difference between learning goals and performance goals.
Examples
1. Encourage students to set a small-step goal for one subject.
2. Recognize improvements often with private authentic praise.
3. Use personal best goals, not between-student competition.

Make the classroom a place where failure is just diagnostic— failure tells what needs to be improved.
Examples
1. If a student gives a wrong answer in class, say "I bet others would give that answer too. Let's examine why that is not

the best answer. This gives us a chance to dig deeper— excellent!"
2. Encourage revising, improving, polishing, and redoing with an emphasis on improvement.
3. Show students connections between their revised work and a higher grade, but emphasize their growing competence.

Encourage help seeking and help giving.
Examples
1. Teach students how to ask explicit questions about what they do not understand.
2. Recognize students who are helpful.
3. Train class experts for some ongoing needs such as technology guides or progress checkers.

_____

For more information on self-worth, see:
http://honolulu.hawaii.edu/intranet/committees/FacDevCom/guidebk/teachtip/motiv.htm

Unfortunately, failure-avoiding strategies generally lead to the very failure the students were trying to avoid. If failures continue and excuses wear thin, the students may finally decide that they are incompetent. Their sense of self-worth and self-efficacy deteriorates. They give up and thus become **failure-accepting students**. They are convinced that their problems are due to low ability. As we saw earlier, those students who attribute failure to low ability and believe ability is fixed are likely to become depressed, apathetic, and helpless. Like Hopeless Geraldo, they have little hope for change.

Teachers may be able to prevent some failure-avoiding students from becoming failure accepting by using multiple outcome measures and setting a number of goals. In this way all students have a realistic chance of succeeding on some outcome measures and reaching at least a few goals (Chen, Wu, Kee, Lin, & Shui, 2009). Also, many students may need support in aspiring to higher levels in the face of sexual or ethnic stereotypes about what they "should" want or what they "should not" be able to do well. This kind of support could make all the difference. Instead of pitying or excusing these students, teachers can teach them how to learn and then hold them accountable for their learning. This will help the students develop a sense of self-efficacy for learning and avoid learned helplessness. The *Guidelines* discuss how to encourage self-worth.

Beliefs and Attributions: Lessons for Teachers

If students believe they lack the ability to understand higher mathematics, they will probably act on this belief even if their actual abilities are well above average. These students are likely to have little motivation to tackle trigonometry or calculus, because they expect to do poorly in these areas. If students believe that failing means they are stupid, they are likely to adopt many self-handicapping, self-defeating strategies. And teachers who stress performance, grades, and competition can encourage self-handicapping without realizing they are doing so (Anderman & Anderman, 2010). Just telling students to "try harder" is not particularly effective. Students need real evidence that effort will pay off,

Failure-accepting students Students who believe their failures are due to low ability and there is little they can do about it.

that setting a higher goal will not lead to failure, that they can improve, and that abilities can be changed. They need authentic mastery experiences.

What else do we know about motivation? Feelings matter.

Interests, Curiosity, Emotions, and Anxiety

Do you remember starting school? Were you curious about what might be in store, excited about your new world, interested and challenged? Many children are. But a common concern of parents and teachers is that this curiosity and excitement about learning is replaced by a sense of drudgery and disinterest. School becomes a job you have to do—a workplace where the work is not that interesting (Wigfield & Wentzel, 2007). In fact, interest in school decreases over time from elementary to high school, with boys showing greater declines than girls. The transition to middle school is particularly linked to a decline in interest. These declines are troubling because results of research on learning in school show that interest is related to students' attention, goals, grades, and depth of learning (Dotterer, McHale, & Vrouter, 2009; Hidi & Renninger, 2006).

Tapping Interests

STOP & THINK As part of your interview for a job in a large high school, the principal asks, "How would you get students interested in learning? Could you tap their interests in your teaching?" •

There are two kinds of interests—*personal* (individual) and *situational*—the trait and state distinction again. Personal or individual interests are more long-lasting aspects of the person, such as an enduring tendency to be attracted to or to enjoy subjects such as languages, history, or mathematics, or activities such as sports, music, or films. Students with individual interests in learning in general seek new information and have more positive attitudes toward schooling. Situational interests are more short-lived aspects of the activity, text, or materials that catch and keep the student's attention. Both personal and situational interests are related to learning from texts—greater interest leads to more positive emotional responses to the material, then to greater persistence in learning, deeper processing, better remembering of the material, and higher achievement (Ainley, Hidi, & Berndorf, 2002; Hofer, 2010; Pintrich, 2003). And interests increase when students feel competent, so even if students are not initially attracted to a subject or activity, they may develop interests as they experience success (Stipek, 2002).

Ann Renninger (2009) describes a four-phase model of interest development:

situational interest triggered → situational interest maintained →
emerging individual interest → well-developed individual interest

For example, consider Julia, a graduating senior in college described by Hidi and Renninger (2006). As she waits nervously in the dentist's office, flipping through a magazine, her attention is drawn (*situational interest trigger*) to an article about a man who left his engineering job to become a facilitator in legal conflict resolution. When she is called to the dentist's chair, she is still reading the article, so she marks her place and returns to finish reading after her appointment (*situational interest maintained*). She takes notes, and, over the next weeks, searches the Internet, visits the library, and meets with her advisor to get more information about this career option (*emerging individual interest*). Four years later, Julia is enjoying her job as a facilitator as she handles more and more arbitration cases for a law firm (*well-developed, enduring individual interest*).

In the early stages of this four-phase model, emotions play a big role—feelings of excitement, pleasure, fun, and curiosity. Situational interest may be triggered by positive feelings, as when Julia started reading. Curiosity followed and helped Julia stay engaged

INTEREST AND EXCITEMENT Students' interest in and excitement about what they're learning are two of the most important factors in education.

as she learned more about becoming a facilitator. As Julia added knowledge to her curiosity and positive feelings, her personal interest emerged, and the *cycle of positive feelings, curiosity, and knowledge* continued to build enduring interest.

CATCHING AND HOLDING INTERESTS. Whenever possible, it helps to connect academic content to students' enduring individual interests. But given that the content you will teach is determined by standards in most classrooms today, it will be difficult to tailor lessons to each student's interests. You will have to rely more on triggering and maintaining situational interest. Here, the challenge is to not only *catch* but also *hold* students' interest (Pintrich, 2003). For example, Mathew Mitchell (1993) found that using computers, groups, and puzzles caught students' interest in secondary mathematics classes, but the interests did not hold. Lessons that held the students' interest over time included math activities that were related to real-life problems and active participation in laboratory activities and projects. Another source of interest is fantasy. Cordova and Lepper (1996) found that students learned more math facts during a computer exercise in which they were challenged, as captains of star ships, to navigate through space by solving math problems. The students got to name their ships, stock the (imaginary) galley with their favorite snacks, and name all the crew members after their friends. In a study of math learning with older adolescents, Durik and Harachkiewicz (2007) concluded that catching interest by using colorful learning materials with pictures was helpful for students with low initial interest in mathematics, but not for students who were already interested. For the interested students, holding interest by showing how math could be personally useful was more effective.

There are other cautions in responding to students' interests, as you can see in the *Point/Counterpoint*.

Curiosity: Novelty and Complexity

Nearly 50 years ago, psychologists suggested that individuals are naturally motivated to seek novelty, surprise, and complexity (Berlyne, 1966). Exploration probably is innate; infants must explore the world to learn about it (Bowlby, 1969). More recently, Reiss

POINT/COUNTERPOINT: Does Making Learning Fun Make for Good Learning?

When many beginning teachers are asked about how to motivate students, they often mention making learning fun. But is it necessary for learning to be fun?

▶ **Teachers should make learning fun.** When I searched "making learning fun" on Google.com, I found 10 pages of resources and references. Clearly, there is interest in making learning fun. Research shows that passages in texts that are more interesting are remembered better (Schunk, Pintrich, & Meece, 2008). For example, students who read books that interested them spent more time reading, read more words in the books, and felt more positively about reading (Guthrie & Alao, 1997).

Games and simulations can make learning more fun, too. For example, when my daughter was in the 8th grade, all the students in her grade spent three days playing a game her teachers had designed called ULTRA. Students were divided into groups and formed their own "countries." Each country had to choose a name, symbol, national flower, and bird. They wrote and sang a national anthem and elected government officials. The teachers allocated different resources to the countries. To get all the materials needed for the completion of assigned projects, the countries had to establish trade with one another. There was a monetary system and a stock market. Students had to work with their fellow citizens to complete cooperative learning assignments. Some countries "cheated" in their trades with other nations, and this allowed debate about international relations, trust, and war. Liz says she had fun—but she also learned how to work in a group without the teacher's supervision and gained a deeper understanding of world economics and international conflicts.

A highly motivating 3rd grade teacher in another study had her class set up a post office for the whole school. Each classroom in the school had an address and zip code. Students had jobs in the post office, and everyone in the school used the post office to deliver letters to students and teachers. Students designed their own stamps and set postal rates. The teacher said that the system "improves their creative writing without them knowing it" (Dolezal, Welsh, Pressley, & Vincent, 2003, p. 254).

▶ **Fun can get in the way of learning.** As far back as the early 1900s, educators warned about the dangers of focusing on fun in learning. None other than John Dewey, who wrote extensively about the role of interest in learning, cautioned that you can't make boring lessons interesting by mixing in fun like you can make bad chili good by adding some spicy hot sauce. Dewey wrote, "When things have to be made interesting, it is because interest itself is wanting. Moreover, the phrase itself is a misnomer. The thing, the object, is no more interesting than it was before" (Dewey, 1913, pp. 11–12).

There is a good deal of research now indicating that adding interest by incorporating fascinating but irrelevant details actually gets in the way of learning the important information. These "seductive details," as they have been called, divert the readers' attention from the less interesting main ideas (Harp & Mayer, 1998). For example, students who read biographies of historical figures remembered more very interesting—but unimportant—information compared to interesting main ideas (Wade, Schraw, Buxton, & Hayes, 1993).

Shannon Harp and Richard Mayer (1998) found similar results with high school science texts. These texts added emotional interest and seductive details about swimmers and golfers who are injured by lightning to a lesson on the process of lightning. They concluded that, "in the case of emotional interest versus cognitive interest, the verdict is clear. Adjuncts aimed at increasing emotional interest failed to improve understanding of scientific explanations" (p. 100). The seductive details may have disrupted students' attempts to follow the logic of the explanations and thus interfered with their comprehending the text. Harp and Mayer conclude that "the best way to help students enjoy a passage is to help them understand it" (p. 100).

(2004) listed curiosity as one of the 16 basic human motivations, and Flum and Kaplan (2006) made the case that schools should target developing an exploratory orientation in students as a major goal.

Interest and curiosity are related. Curiosity can be defined as a tendency to be interested in a wide range of areas (Pintrich, 2003). According to Renninger's (2009) four-phase model of interest described in the previous section, our individual interests begin to emerge as we raise and answer "curiosity questions" that help us organize our knowledge about a topic. In order for situational interests to develop into long-term individual interests, curiosity and the desire for exploration are necessary.

George Lowenstein (1994) suggests that curiosity arises when attention is focused on a gap in knowledge. These information gaps cause a sense of deprivation—a need to know that we call "curiosity." This idea is similar to Piaget's concept of disequilibrium, discussed in Chapter 2, and has a number of implications for teaching. First, students need some base of knowledge before they can experience gaps in that knowledge leading to curiosity. Second, students must be aware of the gaps in order for curiosity to result. In other words, they need a metacognitive awareness of what they know and don't know (Hidi, Renninger, & Krapp, 2004). Asking students to make guesses and then providing

GUIDELINES

Building on Students' Interests and Curiosity

Relate content objectives to student experiences.
Examples

1. With a teacher in another school, establish pen pals across the classes. Through writing letters, students exchange personal experiences, photos, drawings, written work, and ask and answer questions ("Have you learned cursive writing yet?" "What are you doing in math now?" "What are you reading?"). Letters can be mailed in one large mailer to save stamps or sent via email.

2. Identify classroom experts for different assignments or tasks. Who knows how to use the computer for graphics? How to search the Net? How to cook? How to use an index?

3. Have a "Switch Day" when students exchange roles with a school staff or support person. Students must research the role by interviewing their staff member, prepare for the job, dress the part for the day they take over, and then evaluate their success after the switch.

Identify student interests, hobbies, and extracurricular activities that can be incorporated into class lessons and discussions.
Examples

1. Have students design and conduct interviews and surveys to learn about each other's interests.

2. Keep the class library stocked with books that connect to students' interests and hobbies.

3. Allow choices (stories in language arts or projects in science) based on students' interests.

Support instruction with humor, personal experiences, and anecdotes that show the human side of the content.
Examples

1. Share your own hobbies, interests, and favorites.

2. Tell students there will be a surprise visitor; then dress up as the author of a story and tell about "yourself" and your writing.

Use original source material with interesting content or details.
Examples

1. Letters and diaries in history.

2. Darwin's notes in biology.

Create surprise and curiosity.
Examples

1. Have students predict what will happen in an experiment, then show them whether they were right or wrong.

2. Provide quotes from history and ask students to guess who said it.

For more information on students' interests and motivation, see: http://mathforum.org/~sarah/Discussion.Sessions/biblio.motivation.html

Source: From 150 Ways to Increase Intrinsic Motivation in the Classroom, by James P. Raffini. Published by Allyn and Bacon, Boston, MA. Copyright © 1996 by Pearson Education. Adapted by permission of the publisher. Also Motivation in Education (2nd ed.) by P. Pintrich and D. Schunk, 2002, Merrill/Prentice-Hall, pp. 298–299.

---

feedback can be helpful. Also, proper handling of mistakes can stimulate curiosity by pointing to missing knowledge. Finally, the more we learn about a topic, the more curious we may become about that subject. As Maslow (1970) predicted, fulfilling the need to know increases, not decreases, the need to know more. See the *Guidelines* for more about building interest and curiosity in the classroom.

Emotions and Anxiety

How do you feel about learning? Excited, bored, curious, fearful? Today, researchers emphasize that learning is not just about the *cold cognition* of reasoning and problem solving. Learning and information processing also are influenced by emotion, so *hot cognition* plays a role in learning as well (Pintrich, 2003). Research on emotions, learning, and motivation is expanding, in part because we know more about the brain and emotion.

NEUROSCIENCE AND EMOTION. In mammals, including humans, stimulation to a small area of the brain called the *amygdala* seems to trigger emotional reactions such as the "fight or flight" response. The responses in nonhuman animals can be strong. But human emotions are the outcome of physiological responses triggered by the brain, combined with interpretations of the situation and other information. So, hearing startling sounds during an action movie might cause a brief emotional reaction, but hearing the same sounds in the middle of the night as you are walking through a dark alley could lead to stronger and more lasting emotional reactions. Even though the amygdala plays a key role in emotions, many other brain regions are also involved. Emotions are a "constant interplay between cognitive assessments, conscious feelings, and bodily responses, with each able to influence the other" (Gluck, Mercado, & Myers, 2007, p. 418). Humans are more likely to pay attention to, learn about, and remember events, images, and readings that provoke emotional responses (Murphy & Alexander, 2000; Cowley & Underwood, 1998; Reisberg & Heuer, 1992). Emotions can affect learning by changing brain dopamine levels that influence long-term memory and by directing attention toward one aspect of the situation (Pekrun, Elliott, & Maier, 2006). Sometimes, emotions interfere with learning by taking up attention or working memory space that could be used for learning (Pekrun, Goetz, Titz, & Perry, 2002).

In teaching, we are concerned about a particular kind of emotions—those related to achievement in school. Experiences of success or failure can provoke achievement emotions such as pride, hope, boredom, anger, or shame (Pekrun, Elliot, & Maier, 2006). How can we use these findings to support learning in school?

ACHIEVEMENT EMOTIONS.   In the past, with the exception of anxiety, emotions generally were overlooked in research on learning and motivation (Linnenbrink-Garcia & Pekrun, 2011). But as you saw above, research in the neurosciences has shown that emotions are both causes and consequences of learning processes. Reinhard Pekrun and his colleagues (2006, 2010) have tested a model that relates different goal orientations to boredom and other emotions in older adolescents from the United States and Germany. The goal orientations are those we discussed earlier: mastery, performance approach, and performance avoidance.

With a *mastery goal*, students focused on an activity. They valued the activity as a way to get smarter, and they felt in control. They were not afraid of failing, so they could focus on the task at hand. The researchers found that having mastery goals predicted enjoyment in learning, hope, and pride. Students with mastery goals were less likely to feel angry or bored about learning. Boredom is a big problem in classrooms because it is associated with difficulties in paying attention, lack of intrinsic motivation, weak effort, shallow processing of information, and poor self-regulated learning (Pekrun et al., 2010)

With a *performance-approach goal*, students wanted to look good or be the best, and they focused their attention on positive outcomes. Performance-approach goals were related mostly to pride. Students with *performance-avoidance goals* focused on the fear of failing and the possibility of looking stupid. Performance-avoidance goals predicted feelings of anxiety, hopelessness, and shame. These findings are summarized in Table 9.4.

TABLE 9.4 • **How Different Achievement Goals Influence Achievement Emotions**

Different goals are associated with different emotions that can impact motivation.

GOAL ORIENTATION	STUDENT EMOTIONS
Mastery Focus on activity, controllability, positive value of activity	Increases: enjoyment of activity, pride, hope Decreases: boredom, anger
Performance-approach Focus on outcome, controllability, positive outcome value	Increases: pride
Performance-avoidance Focus on outcome, lack of controllability, negative outcome value	Increases: anxiety, hopelessness, shame

Source: *Adapted from Pekrun, R., Elliot, A. J., & Maier, M. A. (2006). Achievement goals and discrete achievement emotions: A theoretical model and prospective test. Journal of Educational Psychology, 98, 583–597.*

How can you increase positive achievement emotions and decrease boredom in the subject you teach? Students are more likely to feel bored if they believe they have little control over the learning activities and they don't value the activities. Matching challenge to the students' skill levels and giving choices can increase the students' sense of control. In addition, efforts to build student interest and show the value of the activities also help to fight boredom. And remember, achievement emotions are domain specific. The fact that students enjoy and feel proud of their work in math does not mean they will enjoy English or history (Goetz, Frenzel, Hall, & Pekrun, 2008; Pekrun et al., 2010). In addition, teachers who enjoy their subjects tend to be more enthusiastic and encourage student enjoyment, so make sure, as much as possible, that you are teaching from your own interests and passions (Brophy, 2008; Frenzel, Goetz, Lüdtke, Pekrun, & Sutton, 2009).

AROUSAL AND ANXIETY. Just as we all know how it feels to be motivated, we all know what it is like to be aroused. **Arousal** involves both psychological and physical reactions—changes in brain wave patterns, blood pressure, heart rate, and breathing rate. We feel alert, wide awake, even excited.

To understand the effects of arousal on motivation, think of two extremes. The first is late at night. You are trying for the third time to understand a required reading, but you are so sleepy. Your attention drifts as your eyelids droop. You decide to go to bed and get up early to study (a plan that you know seldom works). At the other extreme, imagine that you have a critical test tomorrow—one that determines whether you will get into the school you want. You feel tremendous pressure from everyone to do well. You know that you need a good night's sleep, but you are wide awake. In the first case, arousal is too low and in the second, too high. Psychologists have known for years that there is an optimum level of arousal for most activities (Yerkes & Dodson, 1908). Generally speaking, higher levels of arousal are helpful on simple tasks such as sorting laundry, but lower levels of arousal are better for complex tasks such as taking the SAT or GRE.

ANXIETY IN THE CLASSROOM.   At one time or another, everyone has experienced **anxiety**, or a general uneasiness, a feeling of self-doubt, and sense of tension. The effects of anxiety on school achievement are clear. Anxiety can be both a cause and an effect of school failure—students do poorly because they are anxious, and their poor performance increases their anxiety. Anxiety probably is both a *trait* and a *state*. Some students tend to be anxious in many situations (trait anxiety), but some situations are especially anxiety provoking (state anxiety) (Covington, 1992; Zeidner, 1998).

Anxiety seems to have both cognitive and affective components. The cognitive side includes worry and negative thoughts—thinking about how bad it would be to fail and worrying that you will, for example. The affective side involves physiological and emotional reactions such as sweaty palms, upset stomach, racing heartbeat, or fear (Jain & Dowson, 2009; Schunk, Pintrich, & Meece, 2008). Whenever there are pressures to perform, severe consequences for failure, and competitive comparisons among students, anxiety may be encouraged (Wigfield & Eccles, 1989). Research with school-age children shows a relationship between the quality of sleep (how quickly and how well you sleep) and anxiety. Better-quality sleep is associated with positive arousal or an "eagerness" to learn. Poor-quality sleep, on the other hand, is related to debilitating anxiety and decreased school performance. You may have discovered these relationships for yourself in your own school career (Meijer & van den Wittenboer, 2004).

HOW DOES ANXIETY INTERFERE WITH ACHIEVEMENT? Anxiety interferes with learning and test performance at three points: focusing attention, learning, and testing. When students are learning new material, they must pay attention to it. Highly anxious students evidently divide their attention between the new material and their preoccupation with how worried and nervous they are feeling. Instead of concentrating, they keep noticing the tight feelings in their chest, thinking, "I'm so tense, I'll never understand this stuff!" From the beginning, anxious students may miss much of the information they are supposed to learn because their thoughts are focused on their own worries (Cassady & Johnson, 2002).

Connect and Extend to PRAXIS II™

Test Anxiety (I, C3)
Test Taking and Anxiety (http://www.ulrc.psu.edu/studyskills/test_taking.html) provides tips and insights into addressing the problems associated with test anxiety. (And the tips might be useful for doing well on the PRAXIS II™ exam!)

Arousal Physical and psychological reactions causing a person to be alert, attentive, wide awake.

Anxiety General uneasiness, a feeling of tension.

But the problems do not end here. Even if they are paying attention, many anxious students have trouble learning material that is somewhat disorganized and difficult—material that requires them to rely on their memory. Unfortunately, much material in school could be described this way. In addition, many highly anxious students have poor study habits. Simply learning to be more relaxed will not automatically improve these students' performance; their learning strategies and study skills must be improved as well (Jain & Dowson, 2009; Naveh-Benjamin, 1991).

Finally, anxious students often know more than they can demonstrate on a test. They may lack critical test-taking skills, or they may have learned the material, but "freeze and forget" on tests (Naveh-Benjamin, McKeachie, & Lin, 1987).

Reaching Every Student: Coping with Anxiety

Some students, particularly those with learning disabilities or emotional disorders, may be especially anxious in school. When students face stressful situations such as tests, they can use three kinds of coping strategies: problem-focused self-regulating learning strategies, emotional management, and avoidance. *Problem-focused self-regulating strategies* might include planning a study schedule, borrowing good notes, or finding a protected place to study. *Emotion-focused strategies* are attempts to reduce the anxious feelings, for example, by using relaxation exercises or describing the feelings to a friend. Of course, the latter might become an *avoidance strategy*, along with going out for pizza or suddenly launching an all-out desk-cleaning attack (can't study until you get organized!). Different strategies are helpful at different points—for example, self-regulated learning before and emotion management during an exam. Different strategies fit different people and situations (Zeidner, 1995, 1998).

Teachers should help highly anxious students to set realistic goals, because these individuals often have difficulty making wise choices. They tend to select either extremely difficult or extremely easy tasks. In the first case, they are likely to fail, which will increase their sense of hopelessness and anxiety about school. In the second case, they will probably succeed on the easy tasks, but they will miss the sense of satisfaction that could encourage greater effort and ease their fears about schoolwork. Goal cards, progress charts, or goal-planning journals may help here. In addition, directly teaching students self-regulated learning strategies and supporting their self-efficacy can help them be more in control of their learning and their anxiety (Jain & Dowson, 2009).

Curiosity, Interests, and Emotions: Lessons for Teachers

Make efforts to keep the level of arousal right for the task at hand. If students are going to sleep, energize them by introducing variety, piquing their curiosity, surprising them, or giving them a brief chance to be physically active. Learn about their interests and incorporate these interests into lessons and assignments. If arousal is too great, follow the *Guidelines* for dealing with anxiety.

How can we put together all this information about motivation? How can teachers create environments, situations, and relationships that encourage motivation? We address these questions next.

MOTIVATION TO LEARN IN SCHOOL: ON TARGET

Teachers are concerned about developing a particular kind of motivation in their students—the **motivation to learn**, defined as "a student tendency to find academic activities meaningful and worthwhile and to try to derive the intended academic benefits from them" (Brophy, 1988, pp. 205–206). Motivation to learn involves more than wanting or intending to learn. It includes the quality of the student's mental efforts. For example, reading the text 11 times may indicate persistence, but motivation to learn implies more thoughtful, active study strategies, such as summarizing, elaborating the basic ideas, outlining in your own words, drawing graphs of the key relationships, and so on (Brophy, 1988).

Motivation to learn The tendency to find academic activities meaningful and worthwhile and to try to benefit from them.

GUIDELINES

Coping with Anxiety

Use competition carefully.
Examples
1. Monitor activities to make sure no students are being put under undue pressure.
2. During competitive games, make sure all students involved have a reasonable chance of succeeding.
3. Experiment with cooperative learning activities.

Avoid situations in which highly anxious students will have to perform in front of large groups.
Examples
1. Ask anxious students questions that can be answered with a simple yes or no, or some other brief reply.
2. Give anxious students practice in speaking before smaller groups.

Make sure all instructions are clear. Uncertainty can lead to anxiety.
Examples
1. Write test instructions on the board or on the test itself instead of giving them orally.
2. Check with students to make sure they understand. Ask several students how they would do the first question, exercise, or sample question on a test. Correct any misconceptions.
3. If you are using a new format or starting a new type of task, give students examples or models to show how it is done.

Avoid unnecessary time pressures.
Examples
1. Give occasional take-home tests.
2. Make sure all students can complete classroom tests within the period given.

Remove some of the pressures from major tests and exams.
Examples
1. Teach test-taking skills; give practice tests; provide study guides.
2. Avoid basing most of a report-card grade on one test.
3. Make extra-credit work available to add points to course grades.
4. Use different types of items in testing because some students have difficulty with particular formats.

Develop alternatives to written tests.
Examples
1. Try oral, open-book, or group tests.
2. Have students do projects, organize portfolios of their work, make oral presentations, or create a finished product.

Teach students self-regulation strategies (Schutz & Davis, 2000).
Examples
1. Before the test: Encourage students to see the test as an important and challenging task that they have the capabilities to prepare for. Help students stay focused on the task of getting as much information as possible about the test.
2. During the test: Remind students that the test is important (but not overly important). Encourage task focus—pick out the main idea in the question, slow down, stay relaxed.
3. After the test: Think back on what went well and what could be improved. Focus on controllable attributions—study strategies, effort, careful reading of questions, relaxation strategies.

For more information about test anxiety, see:
http://www.counselingcenter.uiuc.edu/?page_id=193

It would be wonderful if all our students came to us filled with the motivation to learn, but they don't. As teachers, we have three major goals. The first is to get students productively involved with the work of the class; in other words, to *catch* their interest and create a *state* of motivation to learn. The second and longer-term goal is to develop in our students enduring individual interests and the *trait* of being motivated to learn so they will be able to educate themselves for the rest of their lives. And finally, we want our students to be *cognitively engaged*—to think deeply about what they study. In other words, we want them to be thoughtful (Blumenfeld, Puro, & Mergendoller, 1992).

Earlier in this chapter we examined the roles of intrinsic and extrinsic motivation, attributions, goals, beliefs, self-perceptions, interests, curiosity, and emotions in motivation. Table 9.5 on the next page shows how each of these factors contributes to motivation to learn.

The central question for the remainder of the chapter is: How can teachers use their knowledge about attributions, goals, beliefs, self-perceptions, interests, and emotions to

TABLE 9.5 • **Building a Concept of Motivation to Learn**

Motivation to learn is encouraged when the following five elements come together.

SOURCE OF MOTIVATION	OPTIMUM CHARACTERISTICS OF MOTIVATION TO LEARN	CHARACTERISTICS THAT DIMINISH MOTIVATION TO LEARN
Type of Goal Set	INTRINSIC: Personal factors such as needs, interests, curiosity, enjoyment	EXTRINSIC: Environmental factors such as rewards, social pressure, punishment
Type of Involvement	LEARNING GOAL: Personal satisfaction in meeting challenges and improving; tendency to choose moderately difficult and challenging goals	PERFORMANCE GOAL: Desire for approval for performance in others' eyes; tendency to choose very easy or very difficult goals
	TASK-INVOLVED: Concerned with mastering the task	EGO-INVOLVED: Concerned with self in others' eyes
Achievement Motivation	Motivation to ACHIEVE: Mastery orientation	Motivation to AVOID FAILURE: Prone to anxiety
Likely Attributions	Successes and failures attributed to CONTROLLABLE effort and ability	Successes and failures attributed to UNCONTROLLABLE causes
Beliefs about Ability	INCREMENTAL VIEW: Belief that ability can be improved through hard work and added knowledge and skills	ENTITY VIEW: Belief that ability is a stable, uncontrollable trait

Connect and Extend to PRAXIS II™

Target (I, C1,2,3)
Describe the major features of the TARGET model and identify related strategies that are likely to boost motivation.

increase motivation to learn? To organize our discussion, we will use the TARGET model (Ames, 1992; Epstein, 1989), identifying six areas where teachers make decisions that can influence student motivation to learn.

T: task that students are asked to do
A: autonomy or authority students are allowed in working
R: recognition for accomplishments
G: grouping practices
E: evaluation procedures
T: time in the classroom

Tasks for Learning

To understand how an **academic task** can affect students' motivation, we need to analyze the task. Tasks have different values for students.

Academic tasks The work the student must accomplish, including the content covered and the mental operations required.

TASK VALUE. As you probably recall, many theories suggest that the strength of our motivation in a particular situation is determined by both our *expectation* that we can succeed and the *value* of that success to us. Perceptions of task value predict the choices students make, such as whether to enroll in advanced science classes or join the track team. Efficacy expectations predict achievement in actually doing the task—how well the students will perform in the science class or on the track team (Wigfield & Eccles, 2002b).

We can think of task value as having four components: importance, interest, utility, and cost (Eccles & Wigfield, 2002; Hulleman, Godes, Hendricks, & Harackiewicz, 2010). **Importance or attainment value** is the significance of doing well on the task; this is closely tied to the needs of the individual (the need to be well liked, athletic, etc.).

Importance/Attainment value The importance of doing well on a task; how success on the task meets personal needs.

For instance, if someone has a strong need to appear smart and believes that a high grade on a test proves you are smart, then the test has high attainment value for that person. A second component is **interest or intrinsic value**. This is simply the enjoyment one gets from the activity itself. Some people like the experience of learning. Others enjoy the feeling of hard physical effort or the challenge of solving puzzles. Tasks also can have **utility value**; that is, they help us achieve a short-term or long-term goal such as earning a degree. Finally, tasks have costs—negative consequences that might follow from doing the task such as not having time to do other things or looking awkward as you perform the task.

You can see from our discussion of task value that personal and environmental influences on motivation interact constantly. The task we ask students to accomplish is an aspect of the environment; it is external to the student. But the value of accomplishing the task is bound up with the internal needs, beliefs, and goals of the individual. Because task value has to do with choices, positive values toward academic tasks can be life-changing because choices about courses in high school and education after high school affect career and life opportunities (Durik, Vida, & Eccles, 2006).

BEYOND TASK VALUE TO GENUINE APPRECIATION. Jere Brophy (2008, p. 140) reminds teachers that there is more to value than interest or utility—there is the power of knowing: "Powerful ideas expand and enrich the quality of students' subjective lives." These ideas give us lenses for viewing the world, tools for making decisions, and frames for appreciating the beauty in words and images. An entire issue of *Theory Into Practice*, the journal I edit, is devoted to Jere's ideas about engaging students in the value and appreciation of learning (Turner, Patrick, & Meyer, 2011). One way to build appreciation is with authentic tasks.

AUTHENTIC TASKS. Recently, there has been a great deal written about the use of authentic tasks in teaching. An **authentic task** has some connection to the real-life problems and situations that students will face outside the classroom, both now and in the future. If you ask students to memorize definitions they will never use, to learn the material only because it is on the test, or to repeat work they already understand, then there can be little motivation to learn. But if the tasks are authentic, students are more likely to see the genuine utility value of the work and are also more likely to find the tasks meaningful and interesting (Pugh & Phillips, 2011). **Problem-based learning** and service learning (Chapter 10) are two examples of the use of authentic tasks in teaching. For example, a physics teacher might use skateboarding as a basis for problems and examples, knowing that skateboarding is an authentic task for many of her students (Anderman & Anderman, 2010). For younger students, compare these two teachers described by Anderman and Anderman (2010):

> Mrs. Byrnes gives her class an initial lesson on halves and quarters, divides students into groups of three, and gives each group two Twinkies and a plastic knife. She asks the students to cut one Twinkie into two equally-sized pieces, and the other Twinkie into four equally-sized pieces. Next comes the challenge–use the Twinkie pieces to determine which fraction is bigger, one-half (1/2) or three-fourths (3/4). Mrs. Byrnes then visits each group; the members must explain their work to her. When they are correct, they get to eat the Twinkies.
>
> Mr. Fletcher gives the same initial lesson on halves and quarters. He then provides each student with a worksheet with a few simple questions that are designed to help the students to learn about fractions. For these questions, the students are supposed to imagine that they have several pieces of paper, and that they cut the paper with scissors into various quantities (e.g., they cut one paper into four equal-size pieces, they cut another paper into two equal-size pieces). The students are then asked to demonstrate whether one-half (1/2) or three-fourths (3/4) is the bigger fraction. They then have to write down their answer, along with a brief explanation.

The students in Mrs. Byrnes's class were involved in a more authentic (and tasty) task involving cutting and dividing food, cooperating with others, and enjoying the fruits (or Twinkies) of their labor. They also had to figure out how to share two halves and four quarters equally among three people—advanced cooperation.

Interest or intrinsic value The enjoyment a person gets from a task.

Utility value The contribution of a task to meeting one's goals.

Authentic task Tasks that have some connection to real-life problems the students will face outside the classroom.

Problem-based learning Methods that provide students with realistic problems that don't necessarily have right answers.

Supporting Autonomy and Recognizing Accomplishment

The second area in the TARGET model involves how much choice and autonomy students are allowed. Choice and control in schools are not the norm. Children and adolescents spend literally thousands of hours in schools where other people decide what will happen. Yet we know that self-determination and a sense of internal locus of causality are critical to maintaining intrinsic motivation and student engagement (Jang, Reeve, & Deci, 2010; Reeve, Nix, & Hamm, 2003). What can teachers do to support choice without creating chaos?

SUPPORTING CHOICES. Choices should provide a range of selections that allow students to follow their interests and pick an option that is important and relevant to them (Katz & Assor, 2007). But beware of giving too many choices. Like totally unguided discovery or aimless discussions, unstructured or unguided choices can be counterproductive for learning (Garner, 1998). I know that graduate students in my classes find it disconcerting if I ask them to design a final project that will determine their grade, just as I panic when I am asked to give a talk on "whatever you want."

The alternative is *bounded choice*—giving students a range of options that set valuable tasks for them, but also allow them to follow personal interests. The balance must be just right: "too much autonomy is bewildering and too little is boring" (Guthrie et al., 1998, p. 185). Students can have input about work partners, seating arrangements, how to display work, or suggestions for class rules. But the most important kind of autonomy support teachers can provide probably is cognitive autonomy support—giving students opportunities to discuss different cognitive strategies for learning, approaches to solving problems, or positions on an issue (Stefanou, Perencevich, DiCinto, & Turner, 2004). Students also can exercise autonomy about how they receive feedback from the teacher or from classmates. Figure 9.1 describes a strategy called "Check It Out," in which students specify the skills that they want to have evaluated in a particular assignment. Over the

FIGURE 9.1

STUDENT AUTONOMY: CHECK IT OUT

Using this technique to support student autonomy, the teacher decides on a set of skills that will be developed over a unit, but the student decides which skill(s) will be evaluated on any given assignment. Over the course of the unit, all the skills have to be "checked out." This student has indicated that she wants the teacher to "check out" her creativity and verb tense.

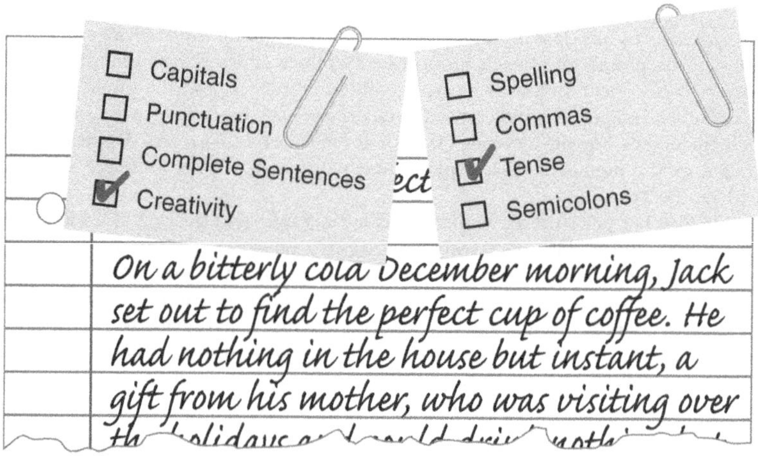

Source: From James P. Raffini, 150 Ways to Increase Intrinsic Motivation to the Classroom. Published by Allyn and Bacon, Boston, MA. Copyright © 1996 by Pearson Education. Reprinted/Adapted by permission of the publisher.

course of a unit, all the skills have to be "checked out," but students choose when each one is evaluated.

RECOGNIZING ACCOMPLISHMENT. The third TARGET area is recognition for accomplishments. Students should be recognized for improving on their own personal best, for tackling difficult tasks, for persistence, and for creativity—not just for performing better than others. Giving students rewards for activities that they already enjoy can undermine intrinsic motivation. What sort of recognition leads to engagement? One answer comes from a study by Ruth Butler (1987). Students in the 5th and 6th grades were given interesting divergent thinking tasks that were followed up by one of the following teacher responses: individual personalized comments, standardized praise ("very good"), grades, or no feedback. Interest, performance, attributions to effort, and task involvement were higher after personalized comments. Ego-involved motivation (the desire to look good or do better than others) was greater after grades and standard praise.

Grouping, Evaluation, and Time

You may remember a teacher who made you want to work hard—someone who made a subject come alive. Or you may remember how many hours you spent practicing as a member of a team, orchestra, choir, or theater troupe. If you do, then you know the motivational power of relationships with other people.

GROUPING AND GOAL STRUCTURES. Motivation can be greatly influenced by the ways we relate to the other people who are also involved in accomplishing a particular goal. Johnson and Johnson (2009a) have labeled this interpersonal factor the **goal structure** of the task. There are three goal structures: cooperative, competitive, and individualistic, as shown in Table 9.6.

When the task involves complex learning and problem-solving skills, cooperation leads to higher achievement than competition, especially for students with lower abilities. Students learn to set attainable goals and negotiate. They become more altruistic. The interaction with peers that students enjoy so much becomes a part of the learning process. The result? The need for belonging described by Maslow is more likely to be met and motivation is increased (Stipek, 2002; Webb & Palincsar, 1996). There are many

TABLE 9.6 • Different Goal Structures
Each goal structure is associated with a different relationship between the individual and the group. This relationship influences motivation to reach the goal.

	COOPERATIVE	COMPETITIVE	INDIVIDUALISTIC
Definition	Students believe their goal is attainable only if other students will also reach the goal.	Students believe they will reach their goal if and only if other students do not reach the goal.	Students believe that their own attempt to reach a goal is not related to other students' attempts to reach the goal.
Examples	Team victories—each player wins only if all the team members win: a relay race, a quilting bee, a barn raising, a symphony, a play.	Golf tournament, singles tennis match, a 100-yard dash, valedictorian, Miss America pageant.	Lowering your handicap in golf, jogging, learning a new language, enjoying a museum, losing or gaining weight, stopping smoking.

Source: Based on Learning Together and Alone: Cooperation, Competition, and Individualization (5th ed.), by D. Johnson & R. Johnson. Published by Allyn and Bacon, Boston, MA. Copyright © 1999 by Pearson Education.

Goal structure The way students relate to others who are also working toward a particular goal.

approaches to peer learning or group learning, as you saw in Chapter 8. For example, to encourage motivation with a cooperative goal structure, form reading groups based on student interests instead of abilities and change the groups every month (Anderman & Anderman, 2010).

EVALUATION.   The greater the emphasis on competitive evaluation and grading, the more students will focus on performance goals rather than mastery. And low-achieving students who have little hope of either performing well or mastering the task may simply want to get it over with (Brophy, 2005). How can teachers prevent students from simply focusing on the grade or doing the work "just to get finished"? The most obvious answer is to de-emphasize grades and to emphasize learning in the class. Students need to understand the value of the work. Instead of saying, "You will need to know this for the test," tell students how the information will be useful in solving problems they want to solve. Suggest that the lesson will answer some interesting questions. Communicate that understanding is more important than finishing. Unfortunately, many teachers do not follow this advice.

TIME.   Most experienced teachers know that there is too much work and not enough time in the school day. Even if they become engrossed in a project, students must stop and turn their attention to another class when the bell rings or when the teacher's schedule indicates it's time to move on to a new subject. Furthermore, students must progress as a group. If particular individuals can move faster or if they need more time, they may still have to follow the pace of the whole group. So scheduling often interferes with motivation by making students move faster or slower than would be appropriate or by interrupting their involvement. It is difficult to develop persistence and a sense of self-efficacy when students are not allowed to stick with a challenging activity. As a teacher, will you be able to make time for engaged and persistent learning? Some elementary classrooms have *DEAR* time—Drop Everything And Read—to give extended periods when everyone, even the teacher, reads. Some middle and high schools have *block scheduling* in which teachers work in teams to plan larger blocks of class time.

PUTTING IT ALL TOGETHER.   We can see how these motivational elements come together in real classrooms. Sara Dolezal and her colleagues observed and interviewed 3rd grade teachers in eight Catholic schools and determined if their students were low, moderate, or high in their level of motivation (Dolezal, Welsh, Pressley, & Vincent, 2003). Table 9.7 summarizes the dramatic differences in these classrooms between the use of strategies that support motivation and those that undermine it. Students in the *low-engagement* classes were restless and chatty as they faced their easy, undemanding seatwork. The classrooms were bare, unattractive, and filled with management problems. Instruction was disorganized. The class atmosphere was generally negative. The *moderately engaged* classrooms were organized to be "student friendly," with reading areas, group work areas, posters, and student artwork. The teachers were warm and caring, and they connected lessons to students' background knowledge. Management routines were smooth and organized, and the class atmosphere was positive. The teachers were good at catching student attention, but they had trouble *holding* attention, probably because the tasks were too easy. *Highly engaging* teachers had all the positive qualities of student-friendly classrooms—but they added more challenging tasks along with the support the students needed to succeed. These excellent motivators did not rely on one or two approaches to motivate their students; they applied a large repertoire of strategies from Table 9.7.

Diversity in Motivation

Because students differ in terms of language, culture, economic privilege, personality, knowledge, and experience, they will also differ in their needs, goals, interests, emotions, and beliefs. Teachers encourage motivation to learn by taking this diversity into account using TARGET—designing tasks, supporting autonomy, recognizing accomplishments, grouping, making evaluations, and managing time. Take interest, for example. Embedding

TABLE 9.7 • **Strategies That Support and Undermine Motivation in the Classroom**

A FEW STRATEGIES THAT SUPPORT MOTIVATION	
STRATEGY	EXAMPLE
Messages of accountability and high expectations	The teacher asks students to have parents review and sign some assignments.
Teacher communicates importance of work	"We need to check it for at least 1 minute, which means looking over it carefully."
Clear goals/directions	The teacher explains exactly how the students are to separate into groups and complete their nominations for their favorite book.
Connections across the curriculum	The teacher relates the concept of ratios in math to compare/contrast skills in reading.
Opportunities to learn about and practice dramatic arts	After studying about historical figures, students write and produce their own plays.
Attributions to effort	During a word game, the teacher says to a student, "Did you study last night?" The student nods. "See how it helps?"
Encouraging risk-taking	"I need a new shining face. Someone I haven't called on yet. I need a risk-taker."
Uses games and play to reinforce concept or review material	During a math lesson using balance, students spend 5 minutes weighing the favorite toy they were asked to bring in that day.
Home–school connections	As part of math science unit, a recycling activity asks families to keep a chart of everything they recycle in a week.
Multiple representations of a task	The teacher uses 4 ways to teach multiplication: "magic multipliers," sing-along multiplication facts, whole-class flash card review, "Around-the-World" game.
Positive classroom management, praise, private reprimands	"Thumbs up when you are ready to work. Table 7 has thumbs up. I like the way table 7 is waiting patiently."
Stimulating creative thought	"We are going to use our imaginations today. We are going to take a trip to an imaginary theater in our heads."
Opportunities for choice	Students can choose to use prompts for their journal writing or pick their own topic.
Teacher communicates to students that they can handle challenging tasks	"This is hard stuff and you are doing great. I know adults who have trouble with this."
Value students—communicate caring	The teacher allows a new student to sit with a buddy for the day.
A FEW STRATEGIES THAT DO NOT SUPPORT MOTIVATION TO LEARN	
Attributions to intellect rather than effort	When students remark during a lesson, "I'm stupid" or "I'm a dork," the teacher says nothing, then replies, "Let's have someone who is smart."
Teacher emphasizes competition rather than working together	The teacher conducts a poetry contest where students read poems to the class and the class members hold up cards with scores rating how well each student performed.
No scaffolding for learning a new skill	The teacher is loud and critical when students have trouble: "Just look back in the glossary and don't miss it because you are too lazy to look it up."
Ineffective/negative feedback	"Does everyone understand?" A few students say yes and the teacher moves on.
Lack of connections	On Martin Luther King Day, the teacher leads a brief discussion of King, then the remainder of the activities are about Columbus.
Easy tasks	The teacher provides easy work and "fun" activities that teach little.

A FEW STRATEGIES THAT DO NOT SUPPORT MOTIVATION TO LEARN *(continued)*	
Negative class atmosphere	"Excuse me, I said page number. If you follow and listen, you would know."
Punitive classroom management	The teacher threatens bad grades if students do not look up words in the glossary.
Work that is much too difficult	The teacher assigns independent math work that only one or two students can do.
Slow pacing	The pace is set for the slowest students—others finish and have nothing to do.
Emphasis on finishing, not learning	The teacher communicates the purpose is to finish, not learn or use the vocabulary.
Sparse, unattractive classroom	There are no decorated bulletin boards, maps, charts, or displays of student work.
Poor planning	Missing handouts force the teacher to have large instead of smaller work groups.
Public punishment	All students stand, and the teacher reads a list of those who finished the assignment and they sit down. The teacher gives public lecture on responsibility to those left standing.

Source: Adapted from "How do nine third-grade teachers motivate their students?" by S. E. Dolezal, L. M. Welsh, M. Pressley, & M. Vincent. Elementary School Journal, 2003, 103, pp. 247–248.

student writing tasks in cultural contexts is one way to catch and hold situational interest (Alderman, 2004; Bergin, 1999). When Latina/o immigrant students in middle-school classes moved from writing using worksheets and standard assignments to writing about such topics as immigration, bilingualism, and gang life—issues that were important to them and to their families—their papers got longer and the writing quality was better (Rueda & Moll, 1994).

Language is a central factor in students' connections with the school. When bilingual students are encouraged to draw on both English and their heritage language, motivation and participation can increase. Robert Jimenez (2000) found in his study of bilingual Latino/a students that successful readers viewed reading as a process of making sense; they used both of their languages to understand the material. For instance, they might look for Spanish word parts in English words to help them translate. Less-successful students had a different goal. They believed that reading just meant saying the words correctly in English. It is likely their interest and sense of efficacy for reading in English would be less, too.

Lessons for Teachers: Strategies to Encourage Motivation

Until four basic conditions are met for every student and in every classroom, no motivational strategies will succeed. First, the classroom must be relatively organized and free from constant interruptions and disruptions. (Chapter 10 will give you the information you need to make sure this requirement is met.) Second, the teacher must be a patient, supportive person who never embarrasses the students because they made mistakes. Everyone in the class should view mistakes as opportunities for learning (Clifford, 1990, 1991). Third, the work must be challenging, but reasonable. If work is too easy or too difficult, students will have little motivation to learn. They will focus on finishing, not on learning. Finally, the learning tasks must be authentic. And as we have seen, what makes a task authentic is influenced by the students' culture (Bergin, 1999; Brophy & Kher, 1986; Stipek, 1993).

Once these four basic conditions are met, the influences on students' motivation to learn in a particular situation can be summarized in four questions: Can I succeed at this task? Do I want to succeed? What do I need to do to succeed? Do I belong? (Committee on Increasing High School Students' Engagement and Motivation to Learn, 2004; Eccles & Wigfield, 1985). We want students to have confidence in their ability so they will approach learning with energy and enthusiasm. We want them to see the value of the tasks involved and work to learn, not just try to get the grade or get finished. We want students to believe that success will come when they apply good learning strategies instead of believing that their only option is to use self-defeating, failure-avoiding, face-saving strategies. When things get difficult, we want students to stay focused on the task, and not get so worried about failure that they "freeze." And we want students to feel as though they belong in school—that their teachers and classmates care about them and can be trusted.

CAN I DO IT? BUILDING CONFIDENCE AND POSITIVE EXPECTATIONS. No amount of encouragement or "cheerleading" will substitute for real accomplishment. To ensure genuine progress:

1. *Begin work at the students' level and move in small steps.* One possibility is to have very easy and very difficult questions on every test and assignment, so all students are both successful and challenged. When grades are required, make sure all the students in class have a chance to make at least a C if they work hard.
2. *Make sure learning goals are clear, specific, and possible to reach in the near future.* Break long-term projects into subgoals. If possible, give students a range of goals at different levels of difficulty and let them choose.
3. *Stress self-comparison, not comparison with others.* Give specific feedback and corrections. Tell students what they are doing right as well as what is wrong and why it is wrong. Periodically, give students a question or problem that was once hard for them but now seems easy. Point out how much they have improved.
4. *Communicate to students that academic ability is improvable* and specific to the task at hand. In other words, the fact that a student has trouble in algebra doesn't necessarily mean that geometry will be difficult. Don't undermine your efforts to stress improvement by displaying only the 100% papers on the bulletin board.
5. *Model good problem solving,* especially when you have to try several approaches. Students need to see that learning is not smooth and error-free, even for the teacher.

DO I WANT TO DO IT? SEEING THE VALUE OF LEARNING. Teachers can use intrinsic and extrinsic motivation strategies to help students see the value of the learning task.

Attainment and Intrinsic Value. To establish attainment value, we must connect the learning task with the needs of the students. It must be possible for students to meet their needs for safety, belonging, and achievement in our classes. Many students are quietly wounded by their teachers' words or school practices that embarrass, label, or demean (Olson, 2008). We must make it clear that both women and men can be high achievers in all subjects: no subjects are the territory of only one sex. It is not "unfeminine" to be strong in mathematics, car mechanics, or sports. It is not "unmasculine" to be good in literature, art, or French.

There are many strategies for encouraging intrinsic (interest) motivation. Several of the following are taken from Brophy (1988).

1. *Tie class activities to student interests* in sports, music, current events, pets, common problems or conflicts with family and friends, fads, television, and movie personalities, or other significant features of their lives (Schiefele, 1991).
2. *Arouse curiosity.* Point out puzzling discrepancies between students' beliefs and the facts. For example, Stipek (1993) describes a teacher who asked her 5th grade class if there were "people" on some of the other planets. When the students said yes, the teacher asked if people needed oxygen to breathe. Because the students had just learned this fact, they responded yes. Then the teacher told them that there is no oxygen in the atmosphere of the other planets. This surprising discrepancy between what the children knew about oxygen and what they believed about life on other planets led to a rousing discussion of the atmospheres of other planets.

3. *Make the learning task fun.* Many lessons can be taught through simulations or games (see the *Point/Counterpoint*). Used appropriately so that the activity connects with learning, these experiences can be very worthwhile and fun, too.

4. *Make use of novelty and familiarity.* Don't overuse a few teaching approaches or motivational strategies. We all need some variety. Varying the goal structures of tasks (cooperative, competitive, individualistic) can help. When the material being covered in class is abstract or unfamiliar to students, try to connect it to something they know and understand. For example, talk about the size of a large area, such as the Acropolis in Athens, in terms of football fields.

Instrumental Value. Sometimes it is difficult to encourage intrinsic motivation, and so teachers must rely on the utility or "instrumental" value of tasks. It is important to learn many skills because they will be needed in more advanced classes or for life outside school.

1. When these connections are not obvious, you should *explain the connections* to your students or ask them to explain how the material will be important in their lives (Hulleman, Godes, Hendricks, & Harackiewicz, 2010).

2. In some situations, teachers can *provide incentives and rewards* for learning. Remember, though, that giving rewards when students are already interested in the activity may undermine intrinsic motivation.

3. *Use ill-structured problems and authentic tasks* in teaching. Connect problems in school to real problems outside, such as buying your first car, making decisions about mobile phone plans, or writing a persuasive letter to a potential employer.

WHAT DO I NEED TO DO TO SUCCEED? STAYING FOCUSED ON THE TASK.

When students encounter difficulties, as they must if they are working at a challenging level, they need to keep their attention on the task. If the focus shifts to worries about performance, fear of failure, or concern with looking smart, then motivation to learn is lost.

1. *Give students frequent opportunities to respond* through questions and answers, short assignments, or demonstrations of skills and correct problems quickly. You don't want students to practice errors too long.

2. When possible, *have students create a finished product*. They will be more persistent and focused on the task when the end is in sight. For example, I often begin a house-painting project thinking I will work for just an hour and then find myself still painting hours later because I want to see the finished product.

3. *Avoid heavy emphasis on grades and competition*. An emphasis on grades forces students to focus on performance, not learning. Anxious students are especially hard hit by highly competitive evaluation.

4. *Reduce the task risk without oversimplifying it*. When tasks are risky (failure is likely and the consequences of failing are grave), student motivation suffers. For difficult, complex, or ambiguous tasks, provide students with plenty of time, support, resources, help, and the chance to revise or improve work.

5. *Model motivation to learn* for your students. Talk about your interest in the subject and how you deal with difficult learning tasks.

6. *Teach the particular learning strategies* that students will need to master the material being studied. Show students how to learn and remember so they won't be forced to fall back on self-defeating strategies or rote memory.

DO I BELONG IN THIS CLASSROOM?

This last question will take more than a page or two to address, so I have devoted a large part of Chapter 10 to the notion of creating learning communities. The support of families can be helpful as you design strategies for your students. The *Family and Community Partnerships Guidelines* give ideas for working with families.

GUIDELINES — FAMILY AND COMMUNITY PARTNERSHIPS

Motivation to Learn

Understand family goals for children.
Examples
1. In an informal setting, around coffee or snacks, meet with families individually or in small groups to listen to what their goals are for their children.
2. Mail out questionnaires or send response cards home with students, asking what skills the families believe their children most need to work on. Pick one goal for each child and develop a plan for working toward the goal both inside and outside school. Share the plan with the families and ask for feedback.

Identify student and family interests that can be related to goals.
Examples
1. Ask a member of the family to share a skill or hobby.
2. Identify "family favorites"—favorite foods, music, vacations, sports, activities, hymns, movies, games, snacks, recipes, memories. Tie class lessons to interests.

Give families a way to track progress toward goals.
Examples
1. Provide simple "progress charts" or goal cards that can be posted on the refrigerator.
2. Ask for parents' or caregivers' feedback (and mean it) about your effectiveness in helping their children.

Work with families to build confidence and positive expectations.
Examples
1. Avoid comparing one child in a family to another during conferences and discussions with family members.

2. Ask family members to highlight strong points of homework assignments. They might attach a note to assignments describing the three best aspects of the work and one element that could be improved.

Make families partners in showing the value of learning.
Examples
1. Invite family members to the class to demonstrate how they use mathematics or writing in their work.
2. Involve parents or caregivers in identifying skills and knowledge that could be applied at home and prove helpful to the family right now, for example, keeping records on service agencies, writing letters of complaint to department stores or landlords, or researching vacation destinations.

Provide resources that build skill and will for families.
Examples
1. Give family members simple strategies for helping their children improve study skills.
2. Involve older students in a "homework hotline" telephone network for helping younger students.

Have frequent celebrations of learning.
Examples
1. Invite families to a "museum" at the end of a unit on dinosaurs. Students create the museum in the auditorium, library, or cafeteria. After visiting the museum, families go to the classroom to examine their child's portfolio for the unit.
2. Place mini-exhibits of student work at local grocery stores, libraries, or community centers.

▼ SUMMARY

What Is Motivation? (pp. 324–328)

Define motivation. Motivation is an internal state that arouses, directs, and maintains behavior. The study of motivation focuses on how and why people initiate actions directed toward specific goals, how long it takes them to get started in the activity, how intensively they are involved in the activity, how persistent they are in their attempts to reach these goals, and what they are thinking and feeling along the way.

What is the difference between intrinsic and extrinsic motivation? Intrinsic motivation is the natural tendency to seek out and conquer challenges as we pursue personal interests and exercise capabilities—it is motivation to do something when we don't have

to. Extrinsic motivation is based on factors not related to the activity itself. We are not really interested in the activity for its own sake; we care only about what it will gain us.

How does locus of causality apply to motivation? The essential difference between intrinsic and extrinsic motivation is the person's reason for acting, that is, whether the locus of causality for the action is inside or outside the person. If the locus is internal, the motivation is intrinsic; if the locus is external, the motivation is extrinsic. Most motivation has elements of both. In fact, intrinsic and extrinsic motivation may be two separate tendencies—both can operate at the same time in a given situation.

What are the key factors in motivation according to a behavioral viewpoint? A humanistic viewpoint? A cognitive viewpoint? A social cognitive viewpoint? A sociocultural viewpoint? Behaviorists tend to emphasize extrinsic motivation caused by incentives, rewards, and punishment. Humanistic views stress the intrinsic motivation created by the need for personal growth, fulfillment, and self-determination. Cognitive views stress a person's active search for meaning, understanding, and competence, and the power of the individual's attributions and interpretations. Social cognitive theories take into account both the behaviorists' concern with the consequences of behavior and the cognitivists' interest in the impact of individual beliefs and expectations. Many influential social cognitive explanations of motivation can be characterized as expectancy × value theories. Sociocultural views emphasize legitimate engaged participation and identity within a community.

What are expectancy × value theories? Expectancy × value theories suggest that motivation to reach a goal is the product of our expectations for success and the value of the goal to us. If either is zero, our motivation is zero also.

What is legitimate peripheral participation? Legitimate peripheral participation means that beginners are genuinely involved in the work of the group, even if their abilities are undeveloped and their contributions are small. The identities of the novice and the expert are bound up in their participation in the community. They are motivated to learn the values and practices of the community to keep their identity as community members.

Needs (pp. 328–331)

Distinguish between deficiency needs and being needs in Maslow's theory. Maslow called four lower-level needs—survival, safety, belonging, and self-esteem—deficiency needs. When these needs are satisfied, the motivation for fulfilling them decreases. He labeled the three higher-level needs—intellectual achievement, aesthetic appreciation, and self-actualization—being needs. When they are met, a person's motivation increases to seek further fulfillment.

What are the basic needs that affect motivation, and how does self-determination affect motivation? Self-determination theory suggests that motivation is affected by the need for competence, autonomy and control, and relatedness. When students experience self-determination, they are intrinsically motivated—they are more interested in their work, have a greater sense of self-esteem, and learn more. Whether students experience self-determination depends in part on if the teacher's communications with students provide information or seek to control them. In addition, teachers must acknowledge the students' perspective, offer choices, provide rationales for limits, and treat poor performance as a problem to be solved rather than a target for criticism.

Goal Orientations (pp. 332–336)

What kinds of goals are the most motivating? Goals increase motivation if they are specific, moderately difficult, and able to be reached in the near future.

Describe mastery, performance, work-avoidant, and social goals. A mastery goal is the intention to gain knowledge and master skills, leading students to seek challenges and persist when they encounter difficulties. A performance goal is the intention to get good grades or to appear smarter or more capable than others, leading students to be preoccupied with themselves and how they appear (ego-involved learners). Students can approach or avoid these two kinds of goals—the problems are greatest with avoidance. Another kind of avoidance is evident with work-avoidant learners, who simply want to find the easiest way to handle the situation. Students with social goals can be supported or hindered in their learning, depending on the specific goal (i.e., have fun with friends or bring honor to the family).

What makes goal setting effective in the classroom? In order for goal setting to be effective in the classroom, students need accurate feedback about their progress toward goals and they must accept the goals set. Generally, students are more willing to adopt goals that seem realistic, reasonably difficult, meaningful, and validated by activities connecting them to their intrinsic interests.

Beliefs and Self-Perceptions (pp. 336–342)

What are epistemological beliefs and how do they affect motivation? Epistemological beliefs are ways of understanding how you think and learn. Individuals' epistemological beliefs can impact their approach to learning, their expectations of themselves and the work they do, and the extent to which they engage in academic tasks. Specifically, epistemological beliefs include your understanding of the structure, stability, and certainty of knowledge. A belief that knowledge can be organized into a grand scheme in which all things are related, for example, may lead students to try to connect all new knowledge with previous knowledge in a meaningful way. If the task proves excessively challenging, these students may believe the new information is not relevant to them or worth understanding.

How do beliefs about ability affect motivation? When people hold an entity theory of ability—that is, they believe that ability is fixed—they tend to set performance goals and strive to protect themselves from failure. When they believe ability is improvable (an incremental theory), however, they tend to set mastery goals and handle failure constructively.

What are the three dimensions of attributions in Weiner's theory? According to Weiner, most of the attributed causes for successes or failures can be characterized in terms of three dimensions: locus (location of the cause internal or external to the person), stability (whether the cause stays the same or can change), and responsibility (whether the person can control the cause). The greatest motivational problems arise when students attribute failures to stable, uncontrollable causes. These students may seem resigned to failure, depressed, helpless—what we generally call "unmotivated."

What is learned helplessness and what deficits does it cause? When people come to believe that the events and outcomes in their lives are mostly uncontrollable, they have developed learned helplessness, which is associated with three types of deficits: motivational, cognitive, and affective. Students who feel hopeless will be unmotivated and reluctant to attempt work. They miss opportunities to practice and improve skills and abilities, so they develop cognitive deficits and they often suffer from affective problems such as depression, anxiety, and listlessness.

How does self-worth influence motivation? Mastery-oriented students tend to value achievement and see ability as improvable, so they focus on mastery goals, take risks, and cope with failure constructively. A low sense of self-worth seems to be linked with the failure-avoiding and failure-accepting strategies intended to protect the individual from the consequences of failure. These strategies may seem to help in the short term, but are damaging to motivation and self-esteem in the long run.

Interests, Curiosity, Emotions, and Anxiety (pp. 342–348)

How do interests and emotions affect learning? Learning and information processing are influenced by emotion. Students are more likely to pay attention to, learn, and remember events, images, and readings that provoke emotional responses or that are related to their personal interests. However, there are cautions in responding to students' interests. "Seductive details," interesting bits of information that are not central to the learning, can hinder learning.

How does curiosity affect learning, and what can teachers do to stimulate curiosity in their subject area? Curiosity is the tendency toward interest in a variety of things. Students' curiosity is guided by their interests, and thus provides them with a self-driven motivation to explore new ideas and concepts. As a result, curiosity can be a powerful motivational tool that captures and maintains students' attention in school. Teachers can foster curiosity by tapping into students' interests, illustrating connections between course material and applications that may be interesting to students, and allowing students to find these connections for themselves. An example might include asking students to identify which simple machines are at work in a skateboard or rollercoaster.

What is the role of arousal in learning? There appears to be an optimum level of arousal for most activities. Generally speaking, a higher level of arousal is helpful on simple tasks, but lower levels of arousal are better for complex tasks. When arousal is too low, teachers can stimulate curiosity by pointing out gaps in knowledge or using variety in activities. Severe anxiety is an example of arousal that is too high for optimal learning.

How does anxiety interfere with learning? Anxiety can be the cause or the result of poor performance; it can interfere with attention to, learning of, and retrieval of information. Many anxious students need help in developing effective test-taking and study skills.

Motivation to Learn in School: On TARGET (pp. 348–359)

Define motivation to learn. Teachers are interested in a particular kind of motivation—student motivation to learn. Student motivation to learn is both a trait and a state. It involves taking academic work seriously, trying to get the most from it, and applying appropriate learning strategies in the process.

What does TARGET stand for? TARGET is an acronym for the six areas in which teachers make decisions that can influence student motivation to learn: the nature of the *task* that students

are asked to do, the *autonomy* students are allowed in working, how students are *recognized* for their accomplishments, *grouping* practices, *evaluation* procedures, and the scheduling of *time* in the classroom.

How do tasks affect motivation? The tasks that teachers set affect motivation. When students encounter tasks that are related to their interests, stimulate their curiosity, or are connected to real-life situations, they are more likely to be motivated to learn. Tasks can have attainment, intrinsic, or utility value for students. Attainment value is the importance to the student of succeeding. Intrinsic value is the enjoyment the student gets from the task. Utility value is determined by how much the task contributes to reaching short-term or long-term goals.

Distinguish between bounded and unbounded choices. Like totally unguided discovery or aimless discussions, unstructured or unbounded choices can be counterproductive for learning. The alternative is bounded choice—giving students a range of options that set out valuable tasks for them, but also allow them to follow personal interests. The balance must be just right so that students are not bewildered by too much choice or bored by too little room to explore.

How can recognition undermine motivation and a sense of self-efficacy? Recognition and reward in the classroom will support motivation to learn if the recognition is for personal progress rather than competitive victories. Praise and rewards should focus on students' growing competence. At times, praise can have paradoxical effects when students use the teacher's praise or criticism as cues about capabilities.

List three goal structures and distinguish among them. How students relate to their peers in the classroom is influenced by the goal structure of the activities. Goal structures can be competitive, individualistic, or cooperative. Cooperative goal structures can encourage motivation and increase learning, especially for low-achieving students.

How does the evaluative climate affect goal setting? The more competitive the grading, the more students set performance goals and focus on "looking competent," that is, they are more ego-involved. When the focus is on performing rather than learning, students often see the goal of classroom tasks as simply finishing, especially if the work is difficult.

What are some effects of time on motivation? In order to foster motivation to learn, teachers should be flexible in their use of time in the classroom. Students who are forced to move faster or slower than they should or who are interrupted as they become involved in a project are not likely to develop persistence for learning.

▼ KEY TERMS

Academic tasks (350)
Anxiety (347)
Arousal (347)
Attribution theories (338)
Authentic task (351)
Being needs (328)
Cognitive evaluation theory (330)
Deficiency needs (328)
Entity view of ability (337)
Epistemological beliefs (336)

Expectancy × value theories (327)
Extrinsic motivation (325)
Failure-accepting students (341)
Failure-avoiding students (340)
Goal (332)
Goal orientations (333)
Goal structure (353)
Hierarchy of needs (328)
Humanistic interpretation (327)
Importance/Attainment value (350)

Incentive (326)
Incremental view of ability (337)
Interest or intrinsic value (351)
Intrinsic motivation (325)
Learned helplessness (339)
Legitimate peripheral participation (328)
Locus of causality (325)
Mastery goal (333)
Mastery-oriented students (340)
Motivation (324)

▼ CONNECT AND EXTEND TO LICENSURE

MULTIPLE-CHOICE QUESTIONS

1. Miss Johnson would like for her students to be motivated to do their work without bribing them with treats or promises of extra recess time. Which one of the following is the type of motivation she should encourage in her students?
   A. Extrinsic
   B. Intrinsic
   C. Locus of control
   D. Relatedness

2. Why should educators concern themselves with Abraham Maslow's Hierarchy of Needs?
   A. The stages in students' development might determine their ability to be successful in certain subjects.
   B. Social and emotional growth can impact students in their ability to cooperate with their peers.
   C. Deficiencies in students' lives can impact their ability to succeed academically.
   D. Parenting styles determine whether students succeed academically or not.

3. Teachers who select all content for their students and insist upon students accomplishing their assignments on their own neglect which of the following aspects of self-determination?
   A. Autonomy and competence
   B. Autonomy and relatedness
   C. Relatedness and competence
   D. Autonomy, relatedness and competence

4. Which of the following is true regarding extrinsic motivation?
   A. Extrinsic motivation should be avoided at all costs because it undermines a student's intrinsic desire.
   B. Extrinsic motivation is not associated with grades and incentives.
   C. Extrinsic motivation may be necessary to initially encourage students to engage in certain activities.
   D. Extrinsic motivation is more desirable than intrinsic motivation in the classroom as educators have increased control.

CONSTRUCTED-RESPONSE QUESTIONS

Case

Stephanie Wilson had been educated in "old school methods." Her teachers insisted on straight rows of seated students who did not talk during lectures or complain about assignments. While Stephanie had been successful in this model, not all of her past classmates flourished in such a rigid environment. As a new teacher she wanted a more student friendly environment. She envisioned a classroom where students were stimulated by the activities and worked collaboratively. "I want my students to look forward to coming to school. I want them to be agents in the learning process, not just passive recipients of my curriculum." She imagined designing learning situations in which her students could all achieve. Step by step they could all learn! As her students progress, she would see when they got off the track and manage to remediate before they started to do poorly. In this way, Stephanie thought, none of her students would be failures.

5. Explain why Stephanie's plan to provide early remediation when students are struggling is a good idea.

6. How can Stephanie Wilson support self-determination and autonomy in her classroom?

▼ WHAT WOULD THEY DO?

TEACHERS' CASEBOOK: Motivating Students When Resources Are Thin

Here is how some practicing teachers responded to motivate students when resources are slim.

AIMEE FREDETTE • 2nd Grade
Fisher Elementary School, Walpole, MA

A very effective way that I use to get the children curious and interested is to pose a question to the class before the start of a lesson. This gives the children a focus for the lesson. As the year progresses, the children begin coming up with questions of their own. Another very successful way to spark interest and curiosity is the use of three-column activators, a brainstorming activity that the teacher and students do together. The students brainstorm WHAT WE THINK WE KNOW about the topic. The teacher records all responses, writing them on chart paper. Then the children brainstorm WHAT WE WANT TO KNOW about the topic. Again the teacher would record their responses. The third column, titled WHAT WE HAVE LEARNED, is added to as the theme progresses. The first two columns are referred to as the children learn about the theme.

DANIELLE HARTMAN • 2nd Grade

Claymont Elementary School, Ballwin, MO

First of all, don't get discouraged. You don't need a textbook in order to be a successful teacher. Look over the district's curriculum guides and see what the objectives are for each unit you will be teaching. Once you know the objectives, get creative. Keeping the students motivated and interested in learning is essential. By giving them choice and using a variety of teaching methods you will allow them to stay actively engaged in their learning. You will be amazed at what the students will come up with when they are given choices.

MICHAEL YASIS

L.H. Tanglen Elementary School, Minnetonka, MN

Most learning is acquired through active learning and participation. Therefore, the workbooks that focus on drill and practice, if given as the primary source of learning, most likely would bore the students. I would approach this situation by first engaging the students in a discussion to assess their prior knowledge. I would then challenge and extend their understanding of the concepts through guided discovery, building on similar examples from the "boring" workbooks. While they work on the concepts independently in their workbooks, their confidence and self-esteem will increase.

KELLY MCELROY BONIN • High School Counselor

Klein Oak High School, Spring, TX

Simply being excited to be working with the 3rd graders and showing interest and enthusiasm for the subject matter should arouse the students' interest and encourage them to learn. How many times have you heard it said, "Mrs. Energy was the best teacher I ever had. She took the most boring, difficult subject and made it fun and interesting." I have heard this so many times both as a student and as a teacher, and it proves my point. Just the fact that the teacher is excited about the material shows the students that this is important information that they need, plus they are curious about the material when they respect and like their teacher. If I felt like the difficulty level of the textbooks was too great, I would have to break the lessons down into smaller increments and use different techniques—discussion, re-teaching, group projects, etc.—to enrich the students and adapt to their level of learning. When your students are motivated, they can accomplish anything—it doesn't matter what materials are available to them, what the difficulty level of the textbook is, and so on. Kids will be motivated when their teacher truly cares about them, is passionate about the material, and makes school interesting.

PAM GASKILL • 2nd Grade

Riverside Elementary School, Dublin, OH

Teaching is inherently creative. Use your time and creativity this summer to acquaint yourself with the required objectives and think about ways in which you can make them meaningful and relevant to your students. Explore other available resources in the community, such as libraries, speakers' bureaus, and resource centers. Plan to incorporate a variety of activities such as videos, group work, field trips, projects, and speakers so that your students will remain interested and involved. Utilize materials that your students have access to from home—books, videos, artifacts, Internet printouts. It is amazing how cooperative parents can be when asked to help in specified ways. You might even make use of the old workbook pages, not in the traditional way, but for cooperative work. You can facilitate student success by pairing weaker readers with more competent readers to discuss and complete the worksheets. Stress that everyone needs to work together to learn the material. Active participation and engagement with the materials will help your students to construct their own meanings more effectively.

Part 3
TEACHING AND ASSESSING

Chapter 10–12 taken from chapters 13–15 of *Educational Psychology*, Twelfth Edition by Anita Woolfolk

Chapter 13 Case 1 and 2 taken from p. 52–66, p.160–175 of *Adolescent Portraits: Identity, Relationships, and Challenges*, Seventh Edition by Andrew Garrod, Lisa Smulyan, Sally I. Powers, and Robert Kilkenny

Chapter 13 Case 3 taken from p. 189–202 of *Adolescent Portraits: Identity, Relationships, and Challenges*, Sixth Edition by Andrew Garrod, Lisa Smulyan, Sally I. Powers, and Robert Kilkenny

Licensure appendix, glossary, and references taken from *Educational Psychology*, Twelfth Edition by Anita Woolfolk

chapter ten
CREATING LEARNING ENVIRONMENTS

▶ **TEACHERS' CASEBOOK:** Bullies and Victims

Two boys are terrorizing one of your students. These boys are larger, stronger, and older than the boy in your class, who is small for his age and shy. Unfortunately, the bullies are fairly popular, in part because they are successful athletes. There are incidents on the bus before and after school, in the gym, in the hallways, and at lunch—including intimidation, extortion of lunch money, tripping, shoving, and verbal taunts—"fag" is a favorite chant. You do not have the two bullies in any of your classes. Your student has started to miss school routinely, and when he is in class, the quality of his work is declining.

CRITICAL THINKING

- How would you handle this situation?
- Who should be involved?
- What would you do about the verbal homophobic insults?
- What would you do if the bullies were in your classes?
- What would you do if the bullies and victim were girls?

OVERVIEW AND OBJECTIVES

This chapter looks at the ways that teachers create social and physical environments for learning by examining classroom management—one of the main concerns of teachers, particularly beginning teachers. The very nature of classes, teaching, and students makes good management a critical ingredient of success, and we will investigate why this is true. Successful managers create more time for learning, involve more students, and help students to become self-managing.

A positive learning environment must be established and maintained throughout the year. One of the best ways to accomplish this is by working to prevent problems from occurring at all. But when problems arise—as they always do—an appropriate response is important. What will you do when students challenge you openly in class, when one student asks your advice on a difficult personal problem, or when another withdraws from all participation? We will examine the ways that teachers can communicate effectively with their students in these and many other situations.

By the time you have completed this chapter, you should be able to:

Objective 10.1: Relate academic learning time and student cooperation to creating and maintaining a classroom climate conducive to academic achievement and socio-emotional well-being.

Objective 10.2: Summarize the research on the roles of rules, procedures, and consequences in classroom management.

Objective 10.3: Explain how the physical environment can support or interfere with learning, and plan an appropriate arrangement for your classroom.

Objective 10.4: Identify strategies for preventing and addressing student misbehaviors, including bullying.

Objective 10.5: Characterize successful teacher–student communication.

THE NEED FOR ORGANIZATION

In study after study of the factors related to student achievement, classroom management stands out as the variable with the largest impact (Marzano & Marzano, 2003). Knowledge of and skill in classroom management are marks of expertise in teaching; and stress and exhaustion from managerial difficulties are precursors of burnout in teaching (Emmer & Stough, 2001). What is it about classrooms that makes management so critical?

Classes are particular kinds of environments. They have distinctive features that influence their inhabitants no matter how the students or the desks are organized or what the teacher believes about education (Doyle, 2006). Classrooms are *multidimensional*. They are crowded with people, tasks, and time pressures. Many individuals—all with differing goals, preferences, and abilities—must share resources, use and reuse materials without losing them, move in and out of the room, and so on. In addition, actions can have multiple effects. Calling on low-ability students may encourage their participation and thinking, but may also lead to management problems if the students are unable to answer your questions. And events occur *simultaneously*—everything happens at once and the pace is fast. Teachers have literally hundreds of exchanges with students during a single day.

In this rapid-fire existence, events are *unpredictable*. Even when plans are carefully made, a lesson can still be interrupted by a technology glitch or a loud, angry discussion right outside the classroom. Because classrooms are *public*, the way the teacher handles these unexpected intrusions is seen and judged by all. Students are always noticing if the teacher is being "fair." Is there favoritism? What happens when a rule is broken? Finally, classrooms have *histories*. The meaning of a particular teacher's or student's actions depends in part on what has happened before. The fifteenth time a student arrives late requires a different teacher response compared to the first late arrival. In addition, the history of the first few weeks of school affects life in the class for the rest of the year.

The Basic Task: Gain Their Cooperation

The basic management task for teachers is to achieve order and harmony by gaining and maintaining student cooperation in class activities (Doyle, 2006). Given the multidimensional, simultaneous, fast-paced, unpredictable, public, and historical nature of classrooms, this is quite a challenge. Gaining student cooperation means planning activities, having materials ready, making appropriate behavioral and academic demands on students, giving clear signals, accomplishing transitions smoothly, foreseeing problems and stopping them before they start, selecting and sequencing activities so that flow and interest are maintained—and much more. Also, different activities require different managerial skills. For example, a new or complicated activity may be a greater threat to classroom management than a familiar or simple activity.

Obviously, gaining the cooperation of kindergartners is not the same task as gaining the cooperation of high school seniors. During kindergarten and the first few years of elementary school, direct teaching of classroom rules and procedures is important. For children in the middle elementary years, many classroom routines have become relatively automatic, but new procedures for a particular activity may have to be taught directly, and the entire system still needs monitoring and maintenance. Toward the end of elementary school, some students begin to test and defy authority. The management challenges at

COOPERATION IS KEY Gaining student cooperation is the first task of classroom management. There are lessons, materials, time, space, and people to coordinate to keep learning on track.

this stage are to deal productively with these disruptions and to motivate students who are becoming less concerned about teachers' opinions and more interested in their social lives. By the end of high school, the challenges are to manage the curriculum, fit academic material to students' interests and abilities, and help students become more self-managing (Emmer & Evertson, 2013; Evertson & Emmer, 2013).

The Goals of Classroom Management

STOP & THINK You are interviewing for a job in a great district—it is known for innovation. The assistant principal looks at you for a moment and then asks, "What is classroom management?" How would you answer? •

The aim of **classroom management** is to maintain a positive, productive learning environment. But order for its own sake is an empty goal. It is unethical to use classroom management techniques just to keep students docile and quiet. What, then, is the point of working so hard to manage classrooms? There are at least three reasons.

ACCESS TO LEARNING. Each classroom activity has its own rules for participation. Sometimes these rules are clearly stated by the teacher, but often they are implicit and

Classroom management Techniques used to maintain a healthy learning environment, relatively free of behavior problems.

unstated. Teacher and students may not even be aware that they are following different rules for different activities (Berliner, 1983). For example, in a reading group, students may have to raise their hands to make a comment, but in a show-and-tell circle in the same class, they may simply have to catch the teacher's eye.

As we saw in Chapter 6, the rules defining who can talk, what they can talk about, when and to whom they can talk, and how long they can talk are often called **participation structures**. In order to participate successfully in a given activity, students must understand the participation structure. Some students, however, seem to come to school less able to participate than others. The participation structures they learn at home in interactions with siblings, parents, and other adults do not match the participation structures of school activities (Cazden, 2001). What can we conclude? To reach the first goal of good classroom management—giving all students access to learning—you must make sure everyone knows how to participate in class activities. The key is awareness. What are your rules and expectations? Are they understandable, given your students' cultural backgrounds and home experiences? What unspoken rules or values may be operating? Are you clearly signaling appropriate ways to participate? For some students, particularly those with behavioral and emotional challenges, direct teaching and practicing of important behaviors may be required (Emmer & Stough, 2001).

MORE TIME FOR LEARNING.   I once used a stopwatch to time the commercials during a TV quiz show. I was amazed to find that half of the program was devoted to commercials. Actually, very little quizzing took place. If you used a similar approach in classrooms, timing all the different activities throughout the day, you might be surprised by how little actual teaching takes place. Many minutes each day are lost through interruptions, disruptions, late starts, and rough transitions. Obviously, students can only learn what they encounter. Almost every study examining time and learning has found a significant relationship between time spent on content and student learning (Weinstein, Romano, & Mignano, 2011). Thus, one important goal of classroom management is to expand the sheer number of minutes available for learning. This is sometimes called **allocated time**.

Simply making more time for learning will not automatically lead to achievement. To be valuable, time must be used effectively. As you saw in the chapters on cognitive learning, the way students process information is a central factor in what they learn and remember. Basically, students will learn what they practice and think about. Time spent actively involved in specific learning tasks often is called **engaged time**, or sometimes **time on task**.

Again, however, engaged time doesn't guarantee learning. Students may be struggling with material that is too difficult or they may be using the wrong learning strategies. When students are working with a high rate of success—really learning and understanding—we call the time spent **academic learning time**. So the second goal of class management is to increase academic learning time by keeping students actively engaged in worthwhile, appropriate learning activities. Figure 10.1 shows how the 1,000+ hours of time mandated for school in most states can become only about 333 hours of quality academic learning time for a typical student.

Getting students engaged in learning early in their school careers can make a big difference. Several studies have shown that teachers' rating of students' on-task, persistent engagement in 1st grade predicts achievement test score gains and grades through 4th grade, as well as the decision to drop out of high school (Fredricks, Blumenfeld, & Paris, 2004).

MANAGEMENT FOR SELF-MANAGEMENT.   The third goal of any management system is to help students become better able to manage themselves. If teachers focus on student compliance, they will spend much of the teaching/learning time monitoring and correcting. Students come to perceive the purpose of school as just following rules, not constructing deep understanding of academic knowledge. And complex learning structures such as cooperative or problem-based learning require student *self-management*. Compliance with rules is not enough to make these learning structures work (McCaslin & Good, 1998).

Participation structures Rules defining how to participate in different activities.

Allocated time Time set aside for learning.

Engaged time/Time on task Time spent actively engaged in the learning task at hand.

Academic learning time Time when students are actually succeeding at the learning task.

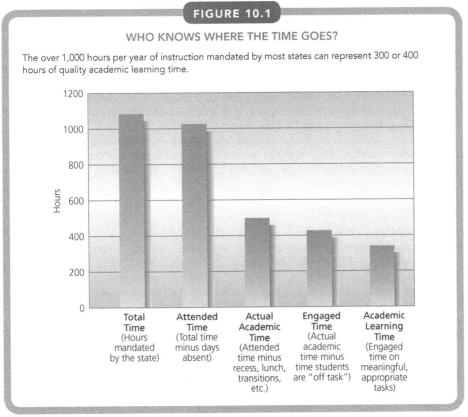

FIGURE 10.1

WHO KNOWS WHERE THE TIME GOES?

The over 1,000 hours per year of instruction mandated by most states can represent 300 or 400 hours of quality academic learning time.

Source: From Elementary Classroom Management (4th ed.), by C.S. Weinstein and A.J. Mignano, Jr., New York: McGraw-Hill. Copyright © 2007 by The McGraw-Hill Companies. Adapted with permission of the McGraw-Hill Companies, Inc.

The movement from demanding obedience to teaching self-regulation and self-control is a fundamental shift in discussions of classroom management today (Evertson & Weinstein, 2006). Tom Savage (1999) says simply, "the most fundamental purpose of discipline is the development of self-control. Academic knowledge and technological skill will be of little consequence if those who possess them lack self-control" (p. 11). Through self-control, students demonstrate responsibility—the ability to fulfil their own needs without interfering with the rights and needs of others (Glasser, 1990). Students learn self-control by making choices and dealing with the consequences, setting goals and priorities, managing time, collaborating to learn, mediating disputes and making peace, and developing trusting relations with trustworthy teachers and classmates (Bear, 2005; Rogers & Frieberg, 1994).

Encouraging **self-management** requires extra time, but teaching students how to take responsibility is an investment well worth the effort. There is good evidence for this claim. Nancy Perry and Rebecca Collie (2011) compared a preservice preparation program that instructed student teachers about how to coach their students to be self-regulated learners with other programs that did not emphasize self-regulation. The student teachers who developed self-regulation knowledge and skills were more confident, less stressed, and more engaged during their student teaching compared to other prospective teachers who did not learn how to help their students to become self-regulated. This makes sense—if you teach your students to manage their own behavior and learning, you should have fewer management problems, less stress, and more time to teach, which would support your growing sense of teacher efficacy. When elementary and secondary teachers have very effective class management systems but neglect to set student self-management as a goal, their students often find that they have trouble working independently after they graduate from these "well-managed" classes.

Self-management Management of your own behavior and acceptance of responsibility for your own actions.

CREATING A POSITIVE LEARNING ENVIRONMENT

When making plans for your class, much of what you have already learned in this book should prove helpful. You know, for example, that problems are prevented when individual variations such as those discussed in Chapters 2 through 6 are taken into account in instructional planning. Sometimes students become disruptive because the work assigned is too difficult. And students who are bored by lessons well below their ability levels may find more exciting activities to fill their time.

In one sense, teachers prevent discipline problems whenever they make an effort to motivate students. A student engaged in learning is usually not involved in a clash with the teacher or other students at the same time. All plans for motivating students are steps toward preventing problems.

Some Research Results

What else can teachers do? For several years, educational psychologists at the University of Texas at Austin studied classroom management quite thoroughly (Emmer & Stough, 2001; Emmer, Evertson, & Anderson, 1980; Emmer & Gerwels, 2006). Their general approach was to study a large number of classrooms, making frequent observations during the first weeks of school and less frequent visits later in the year. After several months, there were dramatic differences among the classes. Some had very few management problems, whereas others had many. The most and least effective teachers were identified on the basis of the quality of classroom management and student achievement later in the year.

Next, the researchers looked at their observation records of the first weeks of class to see how the effective teachers *got started*. Other comparisons were made between the teachers who ultimately had harmonious, high-achieving classes and those whose classes were fraught with problems. On the basis of these comparisons, the researchers developed management principles. They then taught these principles to a new group of teachers, and the results were quite positive. Teachers who applied the principles had fewer problems; their students spent more time learning and less time disrupting; and achievement was higher. The findings of these studies formed the basis for two books on classroom management (Emmer & Evertson, 2009, 2013; Evertson & Emmer, 2009, 2013). Many of the ideas in the following pages are from these books.

Routines and Rules Required

- -

STOP & THINK What are the three or four most important rules you will have for your classroom? •

- -

At the elementary school level, teachers must lead 20 to 30 students of varying abilities through many different activities each day. Without efficient rules and procedures, a great deal of time is wasted dealing with the same questions and issues over and over. "My pencil broke. How can I do my math?" "I'm finished with my experiment. What should I do now?" "Carlos tripped me!" "I left my homework in my locker."

At the secondary school level, teachers must meet daily with over 100 students who use dozens of materials and often change rooms. Secondary school students are also more likely to challenge teachers' authority. The effective managers studied by Emmer, Evertson, and their colleagues had planned *procedures* and *rules* for coping with these situations.

ROUTINES AND PROCEDURES.   How will materials and assignments be distributed and collected? Under what conditions can students leave the room? How will grades be determined? What are the special routines for handling equipment and supplies in science, art, or vocational classes? **Procedures** and **routines** describe how activities are accomplished in classrooms, but they are seldom written down; they are simply the ways of getting

---

Connect and Extend to PRAXIS II™

Procedures and Routines (I, C4)
Efficient procedures and routines reduce confusion and opportunities for misbehavior and they save time that can be devoted to learning tasks. Identify frequent activities or classroom events that would benefit from well-structured procedures or routines. Explain principles for establishing procedures and routines so that students are likely to observe them.

Procedures/routines Prescribed steps for an activity.

GUIDELINES

Establishing Class Routines

Determine procedures for student upkeep of desks, classroom equipment, and other facilities.
Examples

1. Set aside a cleanup time each day or once a week in self-contained classes.
2. Demonstrate and have students practice how to push chairs under the desk, take and return materials stored on shelves, sharpen pencils, use the sink or water fountain, assemble lab equipment, and so on.
3. Put a rotating monitor in charge of equipment or materials.

Decide how students will be expected to enter and leave the room.
Examples

1. Have a procedure for students to follow as soon as they enter the room. Some teachers have a standard assignment ("Have your homework out and be checking it over").
2. Inform students under what conditions they can leave the room, and make sure they understand when they need to ask for permission to do so.
3. Tell students how they should gain admission to the room if they are late.
4. Set up a policy about class dismissal. Many teachers require students to be in their seats and quiet before they can leave at the end of class. The teacher, not the bell, dismisses class.

Establish signals for getting students' attention and teach them to your students.
Examples

1. In the classroom, flick the lights on and off, sound a chord on a piano or recorder, sound a bell like the "ring bell for service" at a sales counter, move to the podium and stare silently at the class, use a phrase like "Eyes, please," take out your grade book, or move to the front of the class.
2. In the halls, raise a hand, clap once, or use some other signal to indicate "Stop."

3. On the playground, raise a hand or whistle to indicate "Line up."

Set routines for student participation in class.
Examples

1. Decide whether you will have students raise their hands for permission to speak or simply require that they wait until the speaker has finished.
2. Determine a signal to indicate that you want everyone to respond at once. Some teachers raise a cupped hand to their ear. Others preface the question with "Everyone."
3. Make sure you are clear about differences in procedures for different activities: reading group, learning center, discussion, teacher presentation, seatwork, video watching, peer learning group, library, and so forth.
4. Establish how many students at a time can be at the pencil sharpener, teacher's desk, learning center, sink, bookshelves, reading corner, or bathroom.

Determine how you will communicate, collect, and return assignments.
Examples

1. Establish a place for listing assignments. Some teachers reserve a particular corner of the board for listing assignments. Others write assignments in colored chalk. For younger students, it may be better to prepare assignment sheets or folders, color-coding them for math workbook, reading packet, and science kit.
2. Be clear about how and where assignments should be collected. Some teachers collect assignments in a box or bin; others have a student collect work while they introduce the next activity.

_____

For ideas about involving students in developing rules and procedures, see http://www.educationworld.com/a_lesson/lesson/lesson274.shtml

things done in class. Carol Weinstein and Andy Mignano (Weinstein & Novodvorsky, 2011; Weinstein, Romano, & Mignano, 2011) suggest that teachers establish routines to cover the following areas:

1. *Administrative routines,* such as taking attendance
2. *Student movement,* such as entering and leaving or going to the bathroom
3. *Housekeeping,* such as watering plants or storing personal items
4. *Lesson-running routines,* such as how to collect assignments or return homework
5. *Interactions between teacher and student,* such as how to get the teacher's attention when help is needed
6. *Talk among students,* such as giving help or socializing

You might use these six areas as a framework for planning your class routines. The *Guidelines* should help you as you plan.

Connect and Extend to PRAXIS II™

Rules (I, C4)
Fair, consistently enforced rules can have a positive effect on motivation to learn by promoting a safe and warm classroom environment. Describe how to establish and maintain effective rules. Keep in mind age-related concerns.

RULES. Unlike routines, rules are often written down and posted, because **rules** specify expected and forbidden actions in the class. They are the dos and don'ts of classroom life. In establishing rules, you should consider what kind of atmosphere you want to create. What student behaviors will help you teach effectively? What limits do the students need to guide their behavior? The rules you set should be consistent with school rules, and also in keeping with principles of learning. For example, we know from the research on small-group learning that students benefit when they explain work to peers. They learn as they teach. A rule that forbids students to help each other may be inconsistent with good learning principles. Or a rule that says, "No erasures when writing" may make students focus more on preventing mistakes than on communicating clearly in their writing (Burden, 1995; Emmer & Stough, 2001; Weinstein, Romano, & Mignano, 2011).

Rules should be positive and observable (raise your hand to be recognized). Having a few general rules that cover many specifics is better than listing all the dos and don'ts. But, if specific actions are forbidden, such as leaving the campus or smoking in the bathrooms, then a rule should make this clear (Emmer & Gerwels, 2006).

RULES FOR ELEMENTARY SCHOOL. Evertson and Emmer (2009) give four examples of general rules for elementary school classes:

1. *Respect and be polite to all people.* Give clear explanations of what you mean by "polite," including not hitting, fighting, or teasing. Examples of polite behavior include waiting your turn, saying "please" and "thank you," and not calling names. This applies to behavior toward adults (including substitute teachers) and peers.
2. *Be prompt and prepared.* This rule highlights the importance of the academic work in the class. Being prompt includes the beginning of the day as well as transitions between activities.
3. *Listen quietly while others are speaking.* This applies to the teacher and other students, in both large-class lessons and small-group discussions.
4. *Obey all school rules.* This reminds students that all school rules apply in your classroom. Then students cannot claim, for example, that they thought it was okay to chew gum or listen to an iPod in your class, even though these are against school rules, "because you never made a rule against it for us."

Whatever the rule, students need to be taught the behaviors that the rule includes and excludes. Examples, practice, and discussion will be needed before learning is complete.

As you've seen, different activities often require different rules. This can be confusing for elementary students until they have thoroughly learned all the rules. To prevent confusion, you might consider making signs that list the rules for each activity. Then, before the activity, you can post the appropriate sign as a reminder. This provides clear and consistent cues about participation structures so all students, not just the "well behaved," know what is expected. Of course, these rules must be explained and discussed before the signs can have their full effect.

RULES FOR SECONDARY SCHOOL. Emmer and Evertson (2009) suggest six examples of rules for secondary students:

1. *Bring all needed materials to class.* The teacher must specify the type of pen, pencil, paper, notebook, texts, and so on.
2. *Be in your seat and ready to work when the bell rings.* Many teachers combine this rule with a standard beginning procedure for the class, such as a warm-up exercise on the board or a requirement that students have paper with a proper heading ready when the bell rings.
3. *Respect and be polite to all people.* This covers fighting, verbal abuse, and general troublemaking. All people includes the teacher.
4. *Listen and stay seated while someone else is speaking.* This applies when the teacher or other students are talking.

Rules Statements specifying expected and forbidden behaviors; dos and don'ts.

5. *Respect other people's property.* This means property belonging to the school, the teacher, or other students.

6. *Obey all school rules.* As with the elementary class rules, this covers many behaviors and situations, so you do not have to repeat every school rule for your class. It also reminds the students that you will be monitoring them inside and outside your class. Make sure you know all the school rules. Some secondary students are very adept at convincing teachers that their misbehavior "really isn't against the rules."

These rules are more than ways to maintain order. In their study of 34 middle-school classrooms, Lindsay Matsumura and her colleagues (2008) found that having explicit rules about respecting others in the classroom predicted the number of students who participated in class discussion, so it seems clear that respect is a gateway to student engagement with the academic material and class dialogue that supports learning.

CONSEQUENCES. As soon as you decide on your rules and procedures, you must consider what you will do when a student breaks a rule or does not follow a procedure. It is too late to make this decision after the rule has been broken. For many infractions, the logical consequence is going back to "do it right." Students who run in the hall may have to return to where they started and walk properly. Incomplete papers can be redone. Materials left out should be put back. You can use **natural or logical consequences** to support social/emotional development by doing the following (Elias & Schwab, 2006):

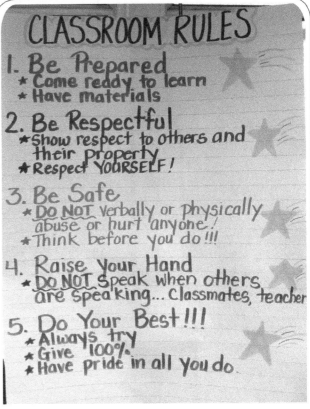

RULES PROMOTE RESPECT Classroom rules that are understood clearly by all students can help maintain a classroom environment that is respectful and more conducive to effective learning.

- Separate the deed from the doer in your response—the problem is the behavior, not the student.
- Emphasize to students that they have the power to choose their actions and thus avoid losing control.
- Encourage student reflection, self-evaluation, and problem solving—avoid teacher lecturing.
- Help students identify and give a rationale for what they could do differently next time in a similar situation.

The main point here is that decisions about penalties (and rewards) must be made early on, so students know before they break a rule or use the wrong procedure what this will mean for them. I encourage my student teachers to get a copy of the school rules and their cooperating teacher's rules, and then plan their own. Sometimes, consequences are more complicated. In their case studies of four expert elementary school teachers, Weinstein, Romano, and Mignano (2011) found that the teachers' negative consequences fell into seven categories, as shown in Table 10.1 on the next page.

WHO SETS THE RULES AND CONSEQUENCES? If you are going to involve students in setting rules or creating a constitution, you may need to wait until you have established a sense of community in your classroom. Before students can contribute meaningfully to the class rules, they need to trust the teacher and the situation (Elias & Schwab, 2006). In the first chapter, I described Ken, an expert teacher who worked with his students to establish a students' "Bill of Rights" instead of defining rules. These

Natural/logical consequences Instead of punishing, have students redo, repair, or in some way face the consequences that naturally flow from their actions.

TABLE 10.1 • Seven Categories of Penalties for Students

1. **Expressions of disappointment.** If students like and respect their teacher, then a serious, sorrowful expression of disappointment may cause students to stop and think about their behavior.
2. **Loss of privileges.** Students can lose free time. If they have not completed homework, for example, they can be required to do it during a free period or recess.
3. **Time-Out: Exclusion from the group.** Students who distract their peers or fail to cooperate can be separated from the group until they are ready to cooperate. Some teachers give a student a pass for 10 to 15 minutes. The student must go to another class or study hall, where the other students and teachers ignore the offending student for that time.
4. **Written reflections on the problem.** Students can write in journals, write essays about what they did and how it affected others, or write letters of apology—if this is appropriate. Another possibility is to ask students to describe objectively what they did; then the teacher and the student can sign and date this statement. These records are available if parents or administrators need evidence of the students' behavior.
5. **Visits to the principal's office.** Expert teachers tend to use this penalty rarely, but they do use it when the situation warrants. Some schools require students to be sent to the office for certain offenses, such as fighting. If you tell a student to go to the office and the student refuses, you might call the office saying the student has been sent. Then the student has the choice of either going to the office or facing the principal's penalty for "disappearing" on the way.
6. **Detentions.** Detentions can be very brief meetings after school, during a free period, or at lunch. The main purpose is to talk about what has happened. (In high school, detentions are often used as punishments; suspensions and expulsions are available as more extreme measures.)
7. **Contacting parents.** If problems become a repeated pattern, most teachers contact the student's family. This is done to seek support for helping the student, not to blame the parents or punish the student.

Source: From Elementary Classroom Management (4th ed.), by C.S. Weinstein and A.J. Mignano, Jr., New York: McGraw-Hill. Copyright © 2007 by The McGraw-Hill Companies. Adapted with permission of the McGraw-Hill Companies, Inc.

"rights" cover most situations that might require a "rule" and help the students move toward the goal of becoming self-managing. In a recent class, the Bill of Rights included the rights to whisper when the teacher is not talking, be treated politely, have a two-minute break between working periods, make choices about the day's schedule, have privacy and not have people take your things, and chew gum without blowing bubbles, among several others.

Developing rights and responsibilities rather than rules makes an important point to students. "Teaching children that something is wrong because there is a rule against it is not the same as teaching them that there is a rule against it because it is wrong, and helping them to understand why this is so" (Weinstein, 1999, p. 154). Students should understand that the rules are developed so that everyone can work and learn together. I might add that when Ken has had some very difficult classes, he and his students have had to establish some "laws" that protect students' rights, as you can see in Table 10.2.

Another kind of planning that affects the learning environment is designing the physical arrangement of the class furniture, materials, and learning tools.

TABLE 10.2 • Laws to Protect Our Rights

1. Follow directions the first time.
2. Speak nicely, be courteous, and respect other people, their feelings and their things. Follow the Bill of Rights.
3. Laugh at the right time for the right time.
4. Respect others' right to learn. Do not distract others. Don't be nosy. Don't yell. Remember to get quiet at countdown.
5. Talk at the right times with the right tone of voice and volume.
6. Transitions and movements are calm, quiet, careful and elegant.
7. Follow all classroom and school procedures, like: bathroom; pencil; lunch and recess; morning; dismissal; and . . .

Source: From Elementary Classroom Management (4th ed., p. 108), by C.S. Weinstein and A.J. Mignano, Jr., New York: McGraw-Hill. Copyright © 2007 by The McGraw-Hill Companies. Adapted with permission of the McGraw-Hill Companies, Inc.

Planning Spaces for Learning

STOP & THINK Think back over all the rooms in all the schools you have attended. Which ones stand out as inviting or exciting? Which ones were cold and empty? Did one teacher have a design that let students do different things in various parts of the room? •

Spaces for learning should invite and support the activities you plan for your classes, and they should respect the inhabitants of the space. This respect begins at the door for young children by helping them identify their classroom. One school that has won awards for its architecture paints each classroom door a different bright color, so young children can find their "home" (Herbert, 1998). Once inside, spaces can be created that invite quiet reading, group collaboration, or independent research. If students are to use materials, they should be able to reach them. In an interview with Marge Scherer (1999), Herb Kohl describes how he creates a positive environment in his classes.

> What I do is put up the most beautiful things I know—posters, games, puzzles, challenges—and let the children know these are provocations. These are ways of provoking them into using their minds. You have to create an environment that makes kids walk in and say, "I really want to see what's here. I would really like to look at this." (p. 9)

In terms of classroom arrangement, there are two basic ways of organizing space: personal territories and interest areas.

Connect and Extend to PRAXIS II™

Classroom Space (I, C4)
The physical organization of a class has an effect on student behavior and learning. Describe how the physical layout of classrooms can affect the learning environment. Apply principles of classroom organization to enhance learning and minimize disruption.

PERSONAL TERRITORIES. Can the physical setting influence teaching and learning in classrooms organized by territories? A front seat location does seem to increase participation for students who are predisposed to speak in class, whereas a seat in the back will make it more difficult to participate and easier to sit back and daydream (Woolfolk & Brooks, 1983). But the **action zone** where participation is greatest may be in other areas such as on one side, or near a particular learning center (Good, 1983a; Lambert, 1994). To "spread the action around," Weinstein, Romano, and Mignano (2011) suggest that teachers move around the room when possible, establish eye contact with and direct questions to students seated far away, and vary the seating so the same students are not always consigned to the back.

Horizontal rows share many of the advantages of the traditional row and column arrangements. Both are useful for independent seatwork and teacher, student, or media presentations; they encourage students to focus on the presenter and simplify housekeeping. Horizontal rows also permit students to work more easily in pairs. However, this is a poor arrangement for large-group discussion.

Clusters of four or circle arrangements are best for student interaction. Circles are especially useful for discussions but still allow for independent seatwork. Clusters permit students to talk, help one another, share materials, and work on group tasks. Both arrangements, however, are poor for whole-group presentations and may make class management more difficult.

The *fishbowl or stack* special formation, where students sit close together near the focus of attention (the back row may even be standing), should be used only for short periods of time, because it is not comfortable and can lead to discipline problems. On the other hand, the fishbowl can create a feeling of group cohesion and is helpful when the teacher wants students to watch a demonstration, brainstorm on a class problem, or see a small visual aid.

INTEREST AREAS. The design of interest areas can influence the way the areas are used by students. For example, working with a classroom teacher, Carol Weinstein (1977) was able to make changes in interest areas that helped the teacher meet her objectives of having more girls involved in the science center and having all students experiment more with a variety of manipulative materials. In a second study, changes in a library corner led to

Action zone Area of a classroom where the greatest amount of interaction takes place.

GUIDELINES

Designing Learning Spaces

Note the fixed features and plan accordingly.
Examples
1. Remember that the audiovisual center and computers need electrical outlets.
2. Keep art supplies near the sink, small-group work by a blackboard.

Create easy access to materials and a well-organized place to store them.
Examples
1. Make sure materials are easy to reach and visible to students.
2. Have enough shelves so that materials need not be stacked.

Provide students with clean, convenient surfaces for studying.
Examples
1. Put bookshelves next to the reading area, games by the game table.
2. Prevent fights by avoiding crowded work spaces.

Avoid dead spaces and "racetracks."
Examples
1. Don't have all the interest areas around the outside of the room, leaving a large dead space in the middle.
2. Avoid placing a few items of furniture right in the middle of this large space, creating a "racetrack" around the furniture.

Arrange things so you can see your students and they can see all instructional presentations.
Examples
1. Make sure you can see over partitions.
2. Design seating so that students can see instruction without moving their chairs or desks.

Make sure work areas are private and quiet.
Examples
1. Make sure there are no tables or work areas in the middle of traffic lanes; a person should not have to pass through one area to get to another.
2. Keep noisy activities as far as possible from quiet ones. Increase the feeling of privacy by placing partitions, such as bookcases or pegboards, between areas or within large areas.

Provide choices and flexibility.
Examples
1. Establish private cubicles for individual work, open tables for group work, and cushions on the floor for whole-class meetings.
2. Give students a place to keep their personal belongings. This is especially important if students don't have personal desks.

Try new arrangements; then evaluate and improve.
Examples
1. Have a "two-week arrangement"; then evaluate.
2. Enlist the aid of your students. They have to live in the room, too, and designing a classroom can be a very challenging educational experience.

For more ideas on classroom design, see http://www.edfacilities.org/rl/ classroom_design.cfm

---

more involvement in literature activities throughout the class (Morrow & Weinstein, 1986). If you design interest areas for your class, keep the *Guidelines* in mind.

Personal territories and interest areas are not mutually exclusive; many teachers use a design that combines these types of organization. Individual students' desks—their territories—are placed in the center, with interest areas in the back or around the periphery of the room. This allows the flexibility needed for both large- and small-group activities. Figure 10.2 shows an elementary classroom that combines interest area and personal territory arrangements.

Getting Started: The First Weeks of Class

Determining a room design, rules, and procedures are the first steps toward having a well-managed class, but how do effective teachers gain students' cooperation in those early critical days and weeks? One study carefully analyzed the first weeks' activities of effective and ineffective elementary teachers, and found striking differences (Emmer, Evertson, & Anderson, 1980). By the second or third week of school, students in the ineffective teachers' classrooms were more and more disruptive, and less and less on task.

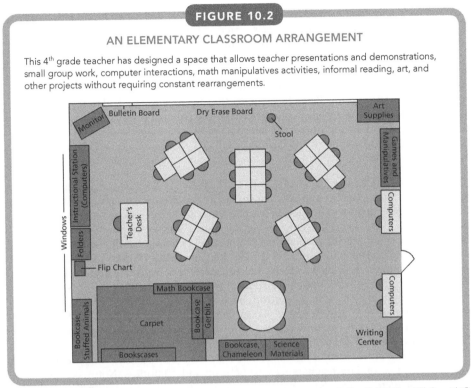

FIGURE 10.2

AN ELEMENTARY CLASSROOM ARRANGEMENT

This 4th grade teacher has designed a space that allows teacher presentations and demonstrations, small group work, computer interactions, math manipulatives activities, informal reading, art, and other projects without requiring constant rearrangements.

Source: From Elementary Classroom Management (4th ed.), by C.S. Weinstein and A.J. Mignano, Jr., New York: McGraw-Hill. Copyright © 2007 by The McGraw-Hill Companies. Adapted with permission of the McGraw-Hill Companies, Inc.

EFFECTIVE MANAGERS FOR ELEMENTARY STUDENTS. In the *effective teachers' classrooms*, the very first day was well organized. Nametags were ready. There was something interesting for each child to do right away. Materials were set up. The teachers had planned carefully to avoid any last-minute tasks that might take them away from their students. These teachers dealt with the children's pressing concerns first. "Where do I put my things?" "How do I pronounce my teacher's name?" "Can I whisper to my neighbor?" "Where is the bathroom?" The effective teachers were explicit about their expectations. They had a workable, easily understood set of rules and taught the students the most important rules right away. They taught the rules like any other subject—with lots of explanation, examples, and practice.

Throughout the first weeks, the effective managers continued to spend quite a bit of time teaching rules and procedures. Some used guided practice to teach procedures; others used rewards to shape behavior. Most taught students to respond to a bell or some other signal to gain their attention. These teachers worked with the class as a whole on enjoyable academic activities. They did not rush to get students into small groups or to start them in readers. This whole-class work gave the teachers a better opportunity to continue monitoring all students' learning of the rules and procedures. Misbehavior was stopped quickly and firmly, but not harshly.

In the *poorly managed classrooms*, the first weeks were quite different. Rules were not workable; they were either too vague or very complicated. For example, one teacher made a rule that students should "be in the right place at the right time." Students were not told what this meant, so their behavior could not be guided by the rule. Neither positive nor negative behaviors had clear, consistent consequences. After students broke a rule, ineffective managers might give a vague criticism, such as "Some of my children are too noisy," or issue a warning, but not follow through with the threatened consequence.

In the poorly managed classes, procedures for accomplishing routine tasks varied from day to day and were never taught or practiced. Instead of dealing with these obvious needs, ineffective managers spent time on procedures that could have waited. For example, one teacher had the class practice for a fire drill the first day, but left unexplained other procedures that would be needed every day. Students wandered around the classroom aimlessly and had to ask each other what they should be doing. Often the students talked to one another because they had nothing productive to do. Ineffective teachers frequently left the room. Many became absorbed in paperwork or in helping just one student. They had not made plans for how to deal with late-arriving students or interruptions. One ineffective manager tried to teach students to respond to a bell as a signal for attention, but later let the students ignore it. All in all, the first weeks in these classrooms were disorganized and filled with surprises for teachers and students alike.

EFFECTIVE MANAGERS FOR SECONDARY STUDENTS.   What about getting started in a secondary school class? It appears that many of the differences between effective and ineffective elementary school teachers are the same at the secondary level. Again, *effective managers* focus on establishing rules, procedures, and expectations on the first day of class. These standards for academic work and class behavior are clearly communicated to students and consistently enforced during the first weeks of class. Student behavior is closely monitored, and infractions of the rules are dealt with quickly. In classes with lower-ability students, work cycles are shorter; students are not required to spend long, unbroken periods on one type of activity. Instead, during each period, they are moved smoothly through several different tasks. In general, effective teachers carefully follow each student's progress, so students cannot avoid work without facing consequences (Emmer & Evertson, 1982).

With all this close monitoring and consistent enforcement of the rules, you may wonder if effective secondary teachers have to be grim and humorless. Not necessarily. The effective managers in one classic study also smiled and joked more with their students (Moskowitz & Hayman, 1976). As any experienced teacher can tell you, there is much more to smile about when the class is cooperative.

MAINTAINING A GOOD ENVIRONMENT FOR LEARNING

A good start is just that—a beginning. Effective teachers build on this beginning. They maintain their management system by preventing problems and keeping students engaged in productive learning activities. We have discussed several ways to keep students engaged. In the previous chapter on motivation, for example, we considered stimulating curiosity, relating lessons to student interests, establishing learning goals instead of performance goals, and having positive expectations. What else can teachers do?

Encouraging Engagement

- -

STOP & THINK What activities keep you completely engaged—the time just seems to disappear? What is it about those activities that keeps you focused? •

- -

Connect and Extend to PRAXIS II™

Promoting Student Engagement (I, C4)
A principle of educational psychology is that the more students are cognitively engaged in an activity, the more they are likely to learn. What tactics can teachers employ to maximize their students' cognitive engagement during learning tasks?

In general, as teacher supervision increases, students' engaged time also increases. One study found that elementary students working directly with a teacher were on task 97% of the time, whereas students working on their own were on task only 57% of the time (Frick, 1990). This does not mean that teachers should eliminate independent work for students. It simply means that this type of activity usually requires careful planning and monitoring.

When the task provides continuous cues for the student about what to do next, involvement will be greater. Activities with clear steps are likely to be more absorbing, because one step leads naturally to the next. When students have all the materials they need to complete a task, they tend to stay involved. If their curiosity is piqued, students will be motivated to continue seeking an answer. And, as you now know, students will be

GUIDELINES

Keeping Students Engaged

Make basic work requirements clear.
Examples

1. Specify and post the routine work requirements for headings, paper size, pen or pencil use, and neatness.
2. Establish and explain rules about late or incomplete work and absences. If a pattern of incomplete work begins to develop, deal with it early; speak with parents if necessary.
3. Make due dates reasonable, and stick to them unless the student has a very good excuse for lateness.

Communicate the specifics of assignments.
Examples

1. With younger students, have a routine procedure for giving assignments, such as writing them on the board in the same place each day. With older students, assignments may be dictated, posted, or given in a syllabus.
2. Remind students of upcoming assignments.
3. With complicated assignments, give students a sheet describing what to do, what resources are available, due dates, and so on. Older students should also be told your grading criteria.
4. Demonstrate how to do the assignment, do the first few questions together, or provide a sample worksheet.

Monitor work in progress.
Examples

1. When you give an assignment in class, make sure each student gets started correctly. If you check only students who raise their hands for help, you will miss those who think they know what to do but don't really understand, those who are too shy to ask for help, and those who don't plan to do the work at all.
2. Check progress periodically. In discussions, make sure everyone has a chance to respond.

Give frequent academic feedback.
Examples

1. Elementary students should get papers back the day after they are handed in.
2. Good work can be displayed in the classroom and graded papers sent home to parents each week.
3. Students of all ages can keep records of grades, projects completed, and extra credits earned.
4. For older students, break up long-term assignments into several phases, giving feedback at each point.

For more ideas, see http://trc.virginia.edu/Publications/Teaching_Concerns/TC_Topic/Engaging_Students.htm

---

more engaged if they are involved in authentic tasks—activities that have connections to real life. Also, activities are more engaging when the level of challenge is higher and when students' interests are incorporated into the tasks (Emmer & Gerwels, 2006).

Of course, teachers can't supervise every student all the time, or rely on curiosity to keep students motivated. Something else must keep students working on their own. In their study of elementary and secondary teachers, Evertson, Emmer, and their colleagues found that effective class managers at both levels had well-planned systems for encouraging students to manage their own work (Emmer & Evertson, 2009, 2013; Evertson & Emmer, 2009, 2013). The *Guidelines* are based on their findings.

Prevention Is the Best Medicine

The ideal way to manage problems, of course, is to prevent them in the first place. In a classic study, Jacob Kounin (1970) examined classroom management by comparing effective teachers, whose classes were relatively free of problems, with ineffective teachers, whose classes were continually plagued by chaos and disruption. Observing both groups in action, Kounin found that the teachers were not very different in the way they handled discipline *once problems arose*. The difference was that the successful managers were much better at preventing problems. Kounin concluded that effective classroom managers were especially skilled in four areas: "withitness," overlapping activities, group focusing, and movement management. More recent research confirms the importance of these factors (Emmer & Stough, 2001).

WITHITNESS. **Withitness** means communicating to students that you are aware of everything that is happening in the classroom—that you aren't missing anything. "With-it"

Withitness According to Kounin, awareness of everything happening in a classroom.

teachers seem to have eyes in the back of their heads. They avoid becoming absorbed by distractions or interacting with only a few students, because this encourages the rest of the class to wander. These teachers are always scanning the room, making eye contact with individual students, so the students know they are being monitored (Charles, 2011; Weinstein, Romano, & Mignano, 2011).

These teachers prevent minor disruptions from becoming major. They also know who instigated the problem, and they make sure they deal with the right people. In other words, they do not make what Kounin called *timing errors* (waiting too long before intervening) or *target errors* (blaming the wrong student and letting the real perpetrators escape responsibility for their behavior).

If two problems occur at the same time, effective managers deal with the more serious one first. For example, a teacher who tells two students to stop whispering, but ignores even a brief shoving match at the pencil sharpener communicates a lack of awareness. Students begin to believe they can get away with almost anything if they are clever.

OVERLAPPING AND GROUP FOCUS.   **Overlapping** means keeping track of and supervising several activities at the same time. For example, a teacher may have to check the work of an individual and at the same time keep a small group working by saying, "Right, go on," and stop an incident in another group with a quick "look" or reminder (Burden, 1995; Charles, 2011).

Maintaining a **group focus** means keeping as many students as possible involved in appropriate class activities and avoiding narrowing in on just one or two students. All students should have something to do during a lesson. For example, the teacher might ask everyone to write the answer to a question, and then call on individuals to respond while the other students compare their answers. Choral responses might be required while the teacher moves around the room to make sure everyone is participating. During a grammar lesson the teacher might say, "Everyone who thinks the answer is *have run,* hold up the red side of your card. If you think the answer is *has run,* hold up the green side" (Hunter, 1982). This is one way teachers can ensure that all students are involved and that everyone understands the material.

MOVEMENT MANAGEMENT.   **Movement management** means keeping lessons and the group moving at an appropriate (and flexible) pace, with smooth transitions and variety. The effective teacher avoids abrupt transitions, such as announcing a new activity before gaining the students' attention or starting a new activity in the middle of something else. In these situations, one-third of the class will be doing the new activity, many will be working on the old lesson, several will be asking other students what to do, some will be taking the opportunity to have a little fun, and most will be confused. Another transition problem Kounin noted is the slowdown, or taking too much time to start a new activity. Sometimes teachers give too many directions. Problems also arise when teachers have students work one at a time while the rest of the class waits and watches.

STUDENT SOCIAL SKILLS AS PREVENTION.   But what about the students? What can they do? When students lack social and emotional skills such as being able to share materials, read the intentions of others, or handle frustration, classroom management problems often follow. So all efforts to teach social and emotional self-regulation are steps toward preventing management problems. Over the short term, educators can teach and model these skills, and then give students feedback and practice using them in a variety of settings. Over the long term, teachers can help to change attitudes that value aggression over cooperation and compromise (Elias & Schwab, 2006).

Debra Stipek and her colleagues (1999) describe many ways teachers embed social skills lessons into school subjects and informal discussions. For example, class rules emphasize respect ("there are no stupid questions"); students learn to give "put ups" not "put downs"; the lives of historical figures provide opportunities to discuss choices and how to deal with stresses; and student conflicts become life lessons in relationships. In addition,

Overlapping Supervising several activities at once.

Group focus The ability to keep as many students as possible involved in activities.

Movement management Keeping lessons and the group moving at an appropriate (and flexible) pace, with smooth transitions and variety.

students are given a "Toolbox of Coping Skills" that contains concrete objects to be used to address problems. The Toolbox includes Post-it® notes to record student concerns and troubling situations so the incidents can be dealt with at an appropriate time. Exit and U-turn signs remind students that the best strategy may be to "exit" the situation. "Exiting to a safe place, without explanation, is taught as one appropriate face-saving, and possibly life-saving, response" (Stipek et al., 1999, p. 443). Indicators are that students do learn to use these skills.

Caring Relationships: Connections with School

All efforts directed toward building positive relationships with students and creating a classroom community are steps toward preventing management problems. Students respect teachers who maintain their authority without being rigid or harsh, who are fair and honest with them, who make sure they understand the material, who ask if something is wrong when they seem upset, and who use creative instructional practices to "make learning fun." Students also value teachers who show academic and personal caring by acting like real people (not just as teachers), sharing responsibility, minimizing the use of external controls, including everyone, searching for students' strengths, communicating effectively, and showing an interest in their students' lives and pursuits (Elias & Schwab, 2006; Wentzel, 2002; Woolfolk Hoy & Weinstein, 2006).

SCHOOL CONNECTIONS. Students who feel connected with school are happier, more engaged in school work, more self-disciplined, and less likely to be involved in dangerous behaviors such as substance abuse, violence, and early sexual activity (Freiberg, 2006; McNeely, Nonnemaker, & Blum, 2002; Pointz, Rimm-Kaufman, Grimm, & Curby, 2009). In fact, in a synthesis of 119 studies published in either English or German conducted from 1948 to 2004, Jeffrey Cornelius-White (2007) concluded that positive, warm, encouraging relationships with teachers are related to many valuable student outcomes, including higher participation in class, greater critical thinking skills, lower drop-out rates, higher self-esteem, increased motivation, less disruptive behavior, and better attendance. When Barbara Bartholomew (2008) asked a veteran special education teacher what keeps students engaged and motivated, the teacher replied without hesitation, "Students need to know that no matter what, you will never give up on them" (p. 58).

An example of respect for students and their lives comes from first-year teacher Esme Codell. "Madame Esme" (the name she preferred) had a morning ritual:

> In the morning, three things happen religiously. I say good morning, real chipper, to every single child and make sure they say good morning back. Then I collect "troubles" in a "Trouble Basket," a big green basket into which the children pantomime unburdening their home worries so they can concentrate on school. Sometimes a kid has no troubles. Sometimes a kid piles it in, and I in turn pantomime bearing the burden. This way, too, I can see what disposition the child is in when he or she enters. Finally, before they can come in, they must give me a word, which I print on a piece of tag board and keep in an envelope. It can be any word, but preferably one that they heard and don't really know or one that is personally meaningful. We go over the words when we do our private reading conferences. (Codell, 2001, p. 30)

If students perceive their schools are competitive places where they are treated differently based on race, gender, or ethnicity, then they are more likely to act out or withdraw altogether. But when

"DON'T GIVE UP ON ME" Students who feel connected with school are happier, more self-disciplined, and less likely to engage in negative behaviors. Believing that they matter and that their teachers are "on their side" helps keep students engaged and motivated.

they feel that they have choices, that the emphasis is on personal improvement and not comparisons, and that they are respected and supported by teachers, students are more likely to bond with schools (Osterman, 2000). One way of expressing respect and caring is by connecting with students' families and home lives. For example, students in China describe their teachers as high on caring. This may be because Chinese teachers spend quite a bit of time in students' homes, learning about their home life, and offering help outside school. These teachers show respect for the families and cultures of their students by their willingness to visit and to help (Jia et al., 2009; Suldo et al., 2009).

CREATING COMMUNITIES OF CARE FOR ADOLESCENTS.   The transition to high school is a particularly important time to maintain caring teacher–student relationships. Students have more teachers and fewer close relationships, just at a time when emotional, social, and academic stresses are increasing. One diverse urban school with over 2,000 students confronted this problem by creating small communities of care. These were interdisciplinary teams of students and teachers who shared common interests and participated in a Freshman Focus class during the first 9 weeks of school. The class helped students adjust to high school, get oriented to the building, and develop school skills like taking notes, social skills, and even skills for getting along with parents. The programs led to the development of positive teacher beliefs about students, supportive teacher–student relationships, and the promotion of academic and life skills (Ellerbrock & Kiefer, 2010).

DEALING WITH DISCIPLINE PROBLEMS

Being an effective manager does not mean publicly correcting every minor infraction of the rules. This kind of public attention may actually reinforce the misbehavior. The key is being aware of what is happening and knowing what is important so you can prevent problems.

Stopping Problems Quickly

Most students comply quickly when the teacher gives a *desist* (a "stop doing that") or redirects behavior. But some students are the targets of more than their share of desists. One study found that these disruptive students seldom complied with the first teacher request to stop. Often, the disruptive students responded negatively, leading to an average of 4 to 5 cycles of teacher desists and student responses before the student complied (Nelson & Roberts, 2000). Emmer and Evertson (2009) and Levin and Nolan (2000) suggest seven simple ways to stop misbehavior quickly, moving from least to most intrusive:

- *Make eye contact* with, or move closer to, the offender. Other nonverbal signals, such as pointing to the work students are supposed to be doing, might be helpful. Make sure the student actually stops the inappropriate behavior and gets back to work. If you do not, students will learn to ignore your signals.
- *Try verbal hints* such as "name-dropping" (simply insert the student's name into the lecture), asking the student a question, or making a humorous (not sarcastic) comment such as, "I must be hallucinating. I swear I heard someone shout out an answer, but that can't be because I haven't called on anyone yet!"
- *Ask students* if they are aware of the negative effects of their actions or send an "I" message, described later in the chapter.
- If they are not performing a class procedure correctly, *remind the students* of the procedure and have them follow it correctly. You may need to quietly collect a toy, comb, magazine, or note that is competing with the learning activities, while privately informing the students that their possessions will be returned after class.
- In a calm, unhostile way, ask the student to *state the correct rule or procedure* and then to follow it. Glasser (1969) proposes three questions: "What are you doing? Is it against the rules? What should you be doing?"
- *Tell the student* in a clear, assertive, and unhostile way to stop the misbehavior. (Later in the chapter, we will discuss assertive messages to students in more detail.) If students "talk back," simply repeat your statement.

GUIDELINES

Imposing Penalties

Delay the discussion of the situation until you and the students involved are calmer and more objective.
Examples

1. Say calmly to a student, "Sit there and think about what happened. I'll talk to you in a few minutes," or, "I don't like what I just saw. Talk to me during your free period today."
2. Say, "I'm really angry about what just happened. Everybody take out journals; we are going to write about this." After a few minutes of writing, the class can discuss the incident.

Impose penalties privately.
Examples

1. Make arrangements with students privately. Stand firm in enforcing arrangements.
2. Resist the temptation to "remind" students in public that they are not keeping their side of the bargain.
3. Move close to a student who must be disciplined and speak so that only the student can hear.

After imposing a penalty, reestablish a positive relationship with the student immediately.
Examples

1. Send the student on an errand or ask him or her for help.
2. Compliment the student's work or give symbolic "pat on the back" when the student's behavior warrants. Look hard for such an opportunity.

Set up a graded list of penalties that will fit many occasions.
Example

1. For not turning in homework: (1) receive reminder; (2) receive warning; (3) hand homework in before close of school day; (4) stay after school to finish work; (5) participate in a teacher–student-parent conference to develop an action plan.

Always teach problem-solving strategies along with penalties to help students learn what to do next time (Elias & Schwab, 2006).
Examples

1. Use Problem Diaries, where students record what they were feeling, identify the problem and their goal, then think of other possible ways to solve the problem and achieve the goal.
2. Try Keep Calm 5-2-5: At the first physical signs of anger, students say to themselves: "Stop. Keep Calm," then take several slow breaths, counting to 5 breathing in, 2 holding breath, and 5 breathing out.

For more ideas, see http://www.stopbullyingnow.com *or* http://www.cfchildren.org

---

- *Offer a choice.* For example, when a student continued to call out answers no matter what the teacher tried, the teacher said, "John, you have a choice. Stop calling out answers immediately and begin raising your hand to answer or move your seat to the back of the room and you and I will have a private discussion later. You decide" (Levin & Nolan, 2000, p. 177).

Many teachers prefer the use of *logical consequences*, described earlier, as opposed to penalties. For example, if one student has harmed another, you can require the offending student to make an "Apology of Action," which includes a verbal apology plus somehow repairing the damage done. This helps offenders develop empathy and social perspective taking as they think about what would be an appropriate "repair" (Elias & Schwab, 2006).

There is a caution about penalties. Never use lower achievement status (moving to a lower reading group, giving a lower grade, giving excess homework) as a punishment for breaking class rules. These actions should be done only if the benefit of the action outweighs the possible risk of harm. As Carolyn Orange (2000) notes, "Effective, caring teachers would not use low achievement status, grades, or the like as a means of discipline. This strategy is unfair and ineffective. It only serves to alienate the student" (p. 76).

If you must impose penalties, the *Guidelines,* taken from Weinstein and Novodvorsky (2011) and Weinstein, Romano, and Mignano (2011), give ideas about how to do it. The examples are taken from the actual words of the expert teachers described in their book.

Bullying and Cyber-Bullying

Bullying is a type of aggression characterized by systematic and repeated abuse of power intended to harm the victim (Merrell, Isava, Gueldner, & Ross, 2008). The line between good-natured exchanges and hostile teasing may seem thin, but a rule of thumb is that teasing someone who is less powerful or less popular or using any racial, ethnic, or religious slur should *not* be tolerated. Between 10% and 30% of children and youth are involved in bullying, and this seems to be the case around the world (Cook, Williams, Guerra, Kim, & Sadek, 2010; Guerra, Williams, & Sadek, 2011). Both bullies and victims are at risk for long-term academic, psychological, and behavioral problems (Swearer, Espelage, Vaillancourt, & Hymel, 2010).

VICTIMS.   Studies from both Europe and the United States indicate that about 10% of children are chronic victims—the constant targets of physical or verbal attacks. One kind of victim tends to have low self-esteem and to feel anxious, lonely, insecure, and unhappy. These students often are prone to crying and withdrawal; in general, when attacked, they won't defend themselves. These victims may believe that they are rejected because they have flaws that they cannot change or control—no wonder they are depressed and helpless! There is a second kind of victim—highly emotional and hot-tempered students who seem to provoke aggressive reactions from their peers. Members of this group have few friends (Pellegrini, Bartini, & Brooks, 1999).

Garbarino and deLara (2002) estimate that 160,000 children avoid school every day and thousands more drop out of school altogether because they are always afraid. Children who have been chronic victims through elementary and middle school are more depressed and more likely to attempt suicide as young adults (Graham, 1998; Hodges & Perry, 1999). And students who kill or injure others in schools are more often victims than bullies (Reinke & Herman, 2002a, 2002b). In the past years, we have seen tragic consequences when bullied students turned guns on their tormentors in schools in the United States and in Europe.

BULLYING AND TEASING.   A longitudinal study that followed a representative sample of 1st through 6th grade students for two years found that aggressive children whose teachers taught them conflict management strategies were moved away from a life path of aggression and violence (Aber, Brown, & Jones, 2003). But when teachers are silent about aggression and teasing, students may "hear" the teacher's agreement with the insult (Weinstein & Novodvorsky, 2011). Table 10.3 presents a list of dos and don'ts about teasing in schools.

Besides following these guidelines, research has shown that having a strong sense of community in your classroom is associated with more student empathy for the victims of bullying and less "blaming the victim" for being attacked (Gini, 2008). So anything you do to develop class community based on fairness and trust will be a step toward dealing with bullying. In a study of over 2,500 students in 59 schools, Nancy Guerra and her colleagues (2011) found that providing opportunities for success, promoting achievement and self-esteem, and improving teacher–student relationships also help to prevent bullying.

Unfortunately, the results are mixed on the effectiveness of many school-wide bullying prevention programs. And another discouraging finding is that administrators prefer to adopt anti-bullying programs that they heard about from colleagues rather than determine if there was any scientific evidence that the programs worked—and many don't (Swearer et al., 2010).

CHANGING ATTRIBUTIONS.   Cynthia Hudley and her colleagues (2007) at UCLA have developed a program to reduce physical aggression in elementary schools. The program,

TABLE 10.3 • **Dos and Don'ts about Teasing**

Teasing has led to some tragic situations. Talk about what to do in your class.

DO	DON'T
1. Be careful of others' feelings. 2. Use humor gently and carefully. 3. Ask whether teasing about a certain topic hurts someone's feelings. 4. Accept teasing from others if you tease. 5. Tell others if teasing about a certain topic hurts your feelings. 6. Know the difference between friendly gentle teasing and hurtful ridicule or harassment. 7. Try to read others' "body language" to see if their feelings are hurt—even when they don't tell you. 8. Help a weaker student when he or she is being ridiculed.	1. Tease someone you don't know well. 2. [If you are a boy] tease girls about sex. 3. Tease about a person's body. 4. Tease about a person's family members. 5. Tease about a topic when a student has asked you not to. 6. Tease someone who seems agitated or whom you know is having a bad day. 7. Be thin-skinned about teasing that is meant in a friendly way. 8. Swallow your feelings about teasing—tell someone in a direct and clear way what is bothering you.

Source: From Middle and Secondary Classroom Management: Lessons from Research and Practice (4th ed.), by C.S. Weinstein. Published by McGraw-Hill. Copyright © 2007 by McGraw-Hill. Adapted with permission from the McGraw-Hill Companies, Inc.

which is called BrainPower, is grounded in attribution theory, discussed in Chapter 9. The central goal of BrainPower is to teach aggressive students "to start from a presumption of accidental causes. When a social encounter with a peer results in a negative outcome (a spilled lunch tray, a bump in the lunch line, missing homework, etc.) the child will begin with the assumption that the outcome was due to accidental causes rather than intentional hostility from peers" (www.brainpowerprogram.com/index-1.html). The program also teaches accurate reading of social cues, so that students recognize when aggression against them is intentional. After students become more skillful at judging social cues, they learn and practice appropriate responses such as asking questions, being assertive—not aggressive, or seeking adult help. Two decades of research on this program shows it has been successful in changing many students' attributions and behaviors (Hudley, Graham, & Taylor, 2007).

CYBER-BULLYING.   With all the possibilities of technology come problems, too. Now bullies have new ways to torment victims using email, text messaging, Twitter, Facebook, cell phones, YouTube, Web blogs, online voting booths, and more (Weinstein & Novodvorsky, 2011). For example, when 16-year-old Denise broke up with her boyfriend, he sought revenge by posting her email address and cell phone number on Web sites and blogs devoted to sex. For months, she got embarrassing and frightening phone calls and messages (Strom & Strom, 2005). This kind of bullying is difficult to combat because the perpetrators can hide, but the damage can be long term. Table 10.4 on the next page has some ideas for dealing with cyber-bullying.

Special Problems with High School Students

Many secondary students never complete their schoolwork. Because students at this age have many assignments and teachers have many students, both teachers and students may lose track of what has and has not been turned in. It often helps to teach students how to use a daily planner—paper or electronic. In addition, teachers must keep accurate records. The most important thing is to enforce the established consequences for incomplete work. Do not pass a student because you know he or she is "bright enough" to pass. Make it clear to these students that the choice is theirs: They can do the work and pass, or they can refuse to do the work and face the consequences. You might also

Connect and Extend to PRAXIS II™

Student Misbehavior (I, C4)
Even the most well-managed classroom will have instances of student misbehavior. Explain the principles for dealing with common student misbehaviors. What strategies can teachers employ to deal fairly and effectively with those problems?

TABLE 10.4 • **Ideas for Dealing with Cyber-Bullying**

- Develop an explicit policy for acceptable in-school use of the Internet and include it in the school handbook (or your class rules). The policy should spell out what constitutes cyber-bullying and list consequences.
- Make sure that children and young people are aware that bullying will be dealt with seriously.
- Ensure that parents/guardians who express cyber-bullying concerns are taken seriously.
- Explain to students that they
    - Should never share or give out personal information, PIN numbers, phone numbers, etc.
    - Should not delete messages; they do not have to read them, but they should show them to an adult they trust. Messages can be used to take action against cyber-bullies.
    - Should not open a message from someone they don't know.
    - Should *never* reply to the message.
    - Can block the sender's message if they are being bullied through e-mail or instant messaging.
    - Can forward the messages to their Internet Service Provider.
    - Should tell an adult.
    - Should show the message to the police if it contains physical threats.
    - Should speak out against cyber-bullying.
    - Should never send messages when they are angry.
    - Should never send messages they wouldn't want others to see.
- Make parents aware of the fact that all of the major Internet Service Providers offer some form of parental controls. For example, AOL has developed "AOL Guardian," which reports with whom youngsters exchange messages and what Web sites they visit and monitors chat rooms for children 13 and under.
- Encourage parents to keep computers in a public room in the house.
- Invite members of the local police department to come to school to speak with parents and students about proper Internet use.
- Make sure ethics is included in any computer instruction given at your school.

Source: From Middle and Secondary Classroom Management: Lessons from Research and Practice *(4th ed.), by C.S. Weinstein. Published by McGraw-Hill. Copyright © 2007 by McGraw-Hill. Adapted with permission from the McGraw-Hill Companies, Inc.*

ask, in a private moment, if there is anything interfering with the student's ability to get the work done.

There is also the problem of students who continually break the same rules, always forgetting materials, for example, or getting into fights. What should you do? Seat these students away from others who might be influenced by them. Try to catch them before they break the rules, but if rules are broken, be consistent in applying established consequences. Do not accept promises to do better next time (Levin & Nolan, 2000). Teach the students how to monitor their own behavior; some of the self-regulation techniques described in Chapter 8 should be helpful. Finally, remain friendly with the students. Try to catch them in a good moment so you can talk to them about something other than their rule breaking.

A defiant, hostile student can pose serious problems. If there is an outburst, try to get out of the situation as soon as possible; everyone loses in a public power struggle. One possibility is to give the student a chance to save face and cool down by saying, "It's your choice to cooperate or not. You can take a minute to think about it." If the student complies, the two of you can talk later about controlling the outbursts. If the student refuses to cooperate, you can tell him or her to wait in the hall until you get the class started on work, then step outside for a private talk. If the student refuses to leave, send another class member for the assistant principal. Again, follow through. If the student complies before help arrives, do not let him or her off the hook. If outbursts occur frequently, you might have a conference with the counselor, family members, or other teachers. If the problem is an irreconcilable clash of personalities, the student should be transferred to another teacher. There is quite a bit of discussion today about zero tolerance for rule breaking in the schools. Is this a good idea? The *Point/Counterpoint* looks at both sides.

POINT/COUNTERPOINT: Is Zero Tolerance a Good Idea?

With the very visible violence in schools today, some districts have instituted "zero-tolerance" policies for rule breaking. One result? Two 8-year-old boys in New Jersey were suspended for making "terrorist threats." They had pointed paper guns at their classmates while playing. Do zero-tolerance policies make sense?

POINT

▶ **Zero tolerance means zero common sense.** An Internet search using keywords ["zero-tolerance" and schools] will locate a wealth of information about the policy—much of it against. For example, Oren Dorrell reported this incident in the November 2, 2009 edition of *USA Today*:

The most recent high-profile case [of zero tolerance] involved Zachary Christie, a 6-year-old who was suspended for five days on Sept. 29 after he brought a camping utensil that was part knife, fork and spoon to Downes Elementary in Newark, Del. School officials considered it a dangerous instrument and suspended the boy, adding that he couldn't return to Downes until he completed at least 45 days at an alternative school.

What does the research say? In 2006, the American Psychological Association set up a Zero Tolerance Task force to answer that question (Reynolds et al., 2008). Analyzing a decade of research, they reached the following conclusions:

- Schools are not any safer or more effective in disciplining students now than before they instituted zero tolerance.
- The higher rates of suspension caused by zero tolerance have not led to less racial bias in disciplining students.
- Zero tolerance policies can actually lead to increases in bad behavior that then lead to higher dropout rates.

In addition, zero tolerance policies can discourage students from informing teachers when the students learn that a classmate is "planning to do something dangerous." The zero tolerance rules get in the way of trusting relationships between teachers and students (Syvertsen, Flanagan, & Stout, 2009). Adolescents need both structure and support, but zero tolerance policies can create a highly structured, rigid environment that ignores the need for support. Finally, many of the popular zero-tolerance interventions such as increased security guards, hallway monitors, and the introduction of metal detectors have no apparent effect on the incidence of school bullying (Hyman et al., 2006; NCES, 2003).

COUNTERPOINT

▶ **Zero tolerance is necessary for now.** The arguments for zero tolerance focus on school safety and the responsibilities of schools and teachers to protect the students and themselves. Of course, many of the incidents reported in the news seem like overreactions to childhood pranks or worse, overzealous application of zero tolerance to innocent mistakes or lapses of memory. But how do school officials separate the innocent from the dangerous? For example, it has been widely reported that Andy Williams (the boy who killed two classmates in Santee, California) assured his friends before the shootings that he was only joking about "pulling a Columbine."

On January 13, 2003, I read a story in *USA Today* by Gregg Toppo entitled "School Violence Hits Lower Grades: Experts Who See Violent Behavior in Younger Kids Blame Parents, Prenatal Medical Problems and an Angry Society; Educators Search for Ways to Cope." The story opened with these examples: a 2nd-grader in Indiana takes off his shoe and attacks his teacher with it, a Philadelphia kindergartner hits a pregnant teacher in the stomach, and an 8-year-old in Maryland threatens to use gasoline (he knew exactly where he would pour it) to burn down his suburban elementary school. Toppo noted, "Elementary school principals and safety experts say they're seeing more violence and aggression than ever among their youngest students, pointing to what they see as an alarming rise in assaults and threats to classmates and teachers" (p. A2). Toppo cited statistics indicating that, although the incidence of school violence has decreased overall, attacks on elementary school teachers have actually increased.

Beyond Either/Or. Surely we can ask adults to use good judgment in applying rules in dangerous situations, but not feeling trapped by the rules when student actions are not intended to harm and are not dangerous.

It sometimes is useful to keep records of these incidents by logging the student's name, words and actions, date, time, place, and teacher's response. These records may help identify patterns and can prove useful in meetings with administrators, families, or special services personnel (Burden, 1995). Some teachers have students sign each entry to verify the incidents.

Fighting or destruction of property is a difficult and potentially dangerous problem. The first step is to send for help and get the names of participants and witnesses. Then, remove any students who may have gathered to watch; an audience will only make things worse. Do not try to break up a fight without help. Make sure the school office is aware of the incident; usually the school has a policy for dealing with these situations. What else can you do? The *Guidelines* on the next page for handling potentially explosive situations are taken from Weinstein and Novodvorsky (2011).

GUIDELINES

Handling Potentially Explosive Situations

Move slowly and deliberately toward the problem situation.
Examples
1. Walk slowly; then be as still as possible.
2. Establish eye-level position.

Be respectful.
Examples
1. Keep a reasonable distance.
2. Do not crowd the student. Do not get "in the student's face."
3. Speak respectfully. Use the student's name.
4. Avoid pointing or gesturing.

Be brief.
Examples
1. Avoid long-winded statements or nagging.
2. Stay with the agenda. Stay focused on the problem at hand. Do not get sidetracked.
3. Deal with less severe problems later.

Avoid power struggles.
Examples
1. Speak privately if possible.
2. Do not get drawn into "I won't, you will" arguments.
3. Don't make threats or raise your voice.

Inform the student of the expected behavior and the negative consequence as a choice or decision for the student to make. Then withdraw from the student and allow some time for the student to decide.
Examples
1. "Michael, you need to return to your desk, or I will have to send for the principal. You have a few seconds to decide." The teacher then moves away, perhaps attending to other students.
2. If Michael does not choose the appropriate behavior, deliver the negative consequences. ("You are choosing to have me call the principal.") Follow through with the consequence.

For more ideas, see: http://www.njcap.org/templated/Programs.html

Source: From Middle and Secondary Classroom Management: Lessons from Research and Practice *(4th ed.), by C.S. Weinstein. Published by McGraw-Hill. Copyright © 2007 by McGraw-Hill. Adapted with permission from the McGraw-Hill Companies, Inc.*

THE NEED FOR COMMUNICATION

STOP & THINK A student says to you, "That book you assigned is really stupid—I'm not reading it!" What do you say? •

Communication between teacher and students is essential when problems arise. Communication is more than "teacher talks—student listens." It is more than the words exchanged between individuals. We communicate in many ways. Our actions, movements, voice tone, facial expressions, and many other nonverbal behaviors send messages to our students. Many times, the messages we intend to send are not the messages our students receive.

Message Sent—Message Received

Teacher: Carl, where is your homework?

Carl: I left it in my Dad's car this morning.

Teacher: Again? You will have to bring me a note tomorrow from your father saying that you actually did the homework. No grade without the note.

Message Carl receives: I can't trust you. I need proof you did the work.

***

Teacher: Sit at every other desk. Put all your things under your desk. Jane and Laurel, you are sitting too close together. One of you move!

Message Jane and Laurel receive: I expect you two to cheat on this test.

***

A new student comes to Ms. Lincoln's kindergarten. The child is messy and un-washed. Ms. Lincoln puts her hand lightly on the girl's shoulder and says, "I'm glad you are here." Her muscles tense, and she leans away from the child.

Message student receives: I don't like you. I think you are bad.

In all interactions, a message is sent and a message is received. Sometimes teachers believe they are sending one message, but their voices, body positions, choices of words, and gestures may communicate a different message.

Students may hear the hidden message and respond to it. For example, a student may respond with hostility if she or he feels insulted by the teacher (or by another student), but may not be able to say exactly where the feeling of being insulted came from. Perhaps it was in the teacher's tone of voice, not the words actually spoken. But the teacher feels attacked for no reason. The first principle of communication is that people respond to what they think was said or meant, not necessarily to the speaker's intended message or actual words.

Students in my classes have told me about one instructor who encourages accurate communication by using the **paraphrase rule**. Before any participant, including the teacher, is allowed to respond to any other participant in a class discussion, he or she must summarize what the previous speaker said. If the summary is wrong, indicating the speaker was misunderstood, the speaker must explain again. The respondent then tries again to paraphrase. The process continues until the speaker agrees that the listener has heard the intended message.

Paraphrasing is more than a classroom exercise. It can be the first step in communicating with students. Before teachers can deal appropriately with any student problem, they must know what the real problem is. A student who says, "This book is really dumb! Why did we have to read it?" may really be saying, "The book was too difficult for me. I couldn't read it, and I feel dumb."

Diagnosis: Whose Problem Is It?

As a teacher, you may find many student behaviors unacceptable, unpleasant, or troubling. It is often difficult to stand back from these problems, take an objective look, and decide on an appropriate response. According to Thomas Gordon (1981), the key to good teacher–student relationships is determining why you are troubled by a particular behavior and who "owns" the problem. The answer to these questions is critical. If it is really the student's problem, the teacher must become a counselor and supporter, help-ing the student find his or her own solution. But if the teacher "owns" the problem, it is the teacher's responsibility to find a solution through problem solving with the student.

Diagnosing who owns the problem is not always straightforward. Let's look at three troubling situations to get some practice in this skill:

1. A student writes obscene words and draws sexually explicit illustrations in a school encyclopedia.
2. A student tells you that his parents had a bad fight and he hates his father.
3. A student quietly reads a newspaper in the back of the room.

Why are these behaviors troubling? If you cannot accept the student's behavior be-cause it has a serious effect on you as a teacher—if you are blocked from reaching your goals by the student's action—then you own the problem. It is your responsibility to con-front the student and seek a solution. A teacher-owned problem appears to be present in the first situation described above—the young pornographer—because teaching materials are damaged.

If you feel annoyed by the behavior because it is getting in the student's own way or because you are embarrassed for the child, but the behavior does not directly interfere with your teaching, then it is probably the student's problem. The student who hates his father would not prevent you from teaching, even though you might wish the student felt differently. The problem is really the student's, and he must find his own solution.

Connect and Extend to PRAXIS II™
Teacher–Student Communication (III, A)
A well-managed classroom requires a bidirectional line of communication between the teacher and students. Describe the various communication styles that teachers employ when interacting with students, and explain how those styles affect student behavior.

Paraphrase rule Policy whereby listeners must accurately summarize what a speaker has said before being allowed to respond.

The third situation is more difficult to diagnose. One argument is that the teacher is not interfered with in any way, so it is the student's problem. But teachers might find the student reading the paper distracting during a lecture, so it is their problem, and they must find a solution. In a gray area such as this, the answer probably depends on how the teacher actually experiences the student's behavior.

Having decided who owns the problem, it is time to act.

Counseling: The Student's Problem

Let's pick up the situation in which the student found the reading assignment "dumb." How might a teacher handle this positively?

Student: This book is really dumb! Why did we have to read it?

Teacher: You're pretty upset. This seemed like a worthless assignment to you. [Teacher paraphrases the student's statement, trying to hear the emotions as well as the words.]

Student: Yeah! Well, I guess it was worthless. I mean, I don't know if it was. I couldn't exactly read it.

Teacher: It was just too hard to read, and that bothers you.

Student: Sure, I felt really dumb. I know I can write a good report, but not with a book this tough.

Teacher: I think I can give you some hints that will make the book easier to understand. Can you see me after school today?

Student: Okay.

Here the teacher used **empathetic listening** to allow the student to find a solution. (As you can see, this approach relies heavily on paraphrasing.) By trying to hear the student and by avoiding the tendency to jump in too quickly with advice, solutions, criticisms, reprimands, or interrogations, the teacher keeps the communication lines open. Here are a few *unhelpful* responses the teacher might have made:

- I chose the book because it is the best example of the author's style in our library. You will need to have read it before your English II class next year. (The teacher justifies the choice; this prevents the student from admitting that this "important" assignment is too difficult.)
- Did you really read it? I bet you didn't do the work, and now you want out of the assignment. (The teacher accuses; the student hears, "The teacher doesn't trust me!" and must either defend herself or himself or accept the teacher's view.)
- Your job is to read the book, not ask me why. I know what's best. (The teacher pulls rank, and the student hears, "You can't possibly decide what is good for you!" The student can rebel or passively accept the teacher's judgment.)

Empathetic, active listening is more than a parroting of the student's words; it should capture the emotions, intent, and meaning behind them. Sokolove, Garrett, Sadker, and Sadker (1986, p. 241) have summarized the components of active listening: (1) blocking out external stimuli; (2) attending carefully to both the verbal and nonverbal messages; (3) differentiating between the intellectual and the emotional content of the message; and (4) making inferences regarding the speaker's feelings.

When students realize they really have been heard and not evaluated negatively for what they have said or felt, they begin to trust the teacher and to talk more openly. Sometimes the true problem surfaces later in the conversation.

Confrontation and Assertive Discipline

Now let's assume a student is doing something that actively interferes with teaching. The teacher decides the student must stop. The problem is the teacher's. Confrontation, not counseling, is required.

Empathetic listening Hearing the intent and emotions behind what another says and reflecting them back by paraphrasing.

"I" MESSAGES. Gordon (1981) recommends sending an **"I" message** in order to intervene and change a student's behavior. Basically, this means telling a student in a straightforward, assertive, and nonjudgmental way what she or he is doing, how it affects you as a teacher, and how you feel about it. The student is then free to change voluntarily, and often does so. Here are two "I" messages:

If you leave your book bags in the aisles,
    I might trip and hurt myself.
When you all call out, I can't concentrate
    on each answer, and I'm frustrated.

ASSERTIVE DISCIPLINE. Lee and Marlene Canter (1992; Canter, 1996) suggest other approaches for dealing with a teacher-owned problem. They call their method **assertive discipline.** Many teachers are ineffective with students because they are either wishy-washy and passive or hostile and aggressive (Charles, 2011).

EMPATHETIC LISTENING When students realize they really have been heard and not evaluated negatively for what they have said or felt, they begin to trust the teacher and to talk more openly. Sometimes the true problem surfaces later in the conversation.

Instead of telling the student directly what to do, *passive* teachers tell, or often ask, the student to *try* or to *think about* the appropriate action. The passive teacher might comment on the problem behavior without actually telling the child what to do differently: "Why are you doing that? Don't you know the rules?" or "Sam, are you disturbing the class?" Or teachers may clearly state what should happen, but never follow through with the established consequences, giving the students "one more chance" every time. Finally, teachers may ignore behavior that should receive a response or they may wait too long before responding.

A *hostile response style* involves different mistakes. Teachers may make "you" statements that condemn the student without stating clearly what the student should be doing: "You should be ashamed of the way you're behaving!" or "You never listen!" or "You are acting like a baby!" Teachers may also threaten students angrily, but follow through too seldom, perhaps because the threats are too vague—"You'll be very sorry you did that when I get through with you!"—or too severe. For example, a teacher tells a student in a physical education class that he will have to "sit on the bench for three weeks." A few days later, the team is short one member and the teacher lets the student play, never returning him to the bench to complete the three-week sentence. Often a teacher who has been passive becomes hostile and explodes when students persist in misbehaving.

In contrast with both the passive and hostile styles, an *assertive response* communicates to the students that you care too much about them and the process of learning to allow inappropriate behavior to persist. Assertive teachers clearly state what they expect. To be most effective, the teachers often look into a student's eyes when speaking and address the student by name. Assertive teachers' voices are calm, firm, and confident. They are not sidetracked by accusations such as "You just don't understand!" or "You don't like me!" Assertive teachers do not get into a debate about the fairness of the rules. They expect changes, not promises or apologies.

Not all educators believe that assertive discipline is useful. Earlier critics questioned the penalty-focused approach and emphasized that assertive discipline undermined student self-management (Render, Padilla, & Krank, 1989). John Covaleskie (1992) observed, "What helps children become moral is not knowledge of the rules, or even obedience to the rules, but discussions about the reasons for acting in certain ways" (p. 56). These critics have had an impact. More recent versions of assertive discipline focus on teaching

"I" message Clear, nonaccusatory statement of how something is affecting you.

Assertive discipline Clear, firm, unhostile response style.

students how to behave responsibly and working to establish mutual respect and trust (Charles, 2011).

CONFRONTATIONS AND NEGOTIATIONS.   If "I" messages or assertive responses fail and a student persists in misbehaving, teacher and student are in a conflict. Several pitfalls now loom. The two individuals become less able to perceive each other's behavior accurately. Research has shown that the more angry you get with another person, the more you see the other as the villain and yourself as an innocent victim. Because you feel the other person is in the wrong, and he or she feels just as strongly that the conflict is all your fault, very little mutual trust is possible. A cooperative solution to the problem is almost impossible. In fact, by the time the discussion has gone on a few minutes, the original problem is lost in a sea of charges, countercharges, and self-defense (Baron & Byrne, 2003).

There are three methods of resolving a conflict between a teacher and a student. One is for the teacher to impose a solution. This may be necessary during an emergency, as when a defiant student refuses to go to the hall to discuss a public outburst, but it is not a good solution for most conflicts. The second method is for the teacher to give in to the student's demands. You might be convinced by a particularly compelling student argument, but again, this should be used sparingly. It is generally a bad idea to be talked out of a position, unless the position was wrong in the first place. Problems arise when either the teacher or the student gives in completely.

Gordon recommends a third approach, which he calls the "no-lose method." Here, the needs of both the teacher and the student are taken into account in the solution. No one person is expected to give in completely; all participants retain respect for themselves and each other. The no-lose method is a six-step, problem-solving strategy:

1. *Define the problem.* What exactly are the behaviors involved? What does each person want? (Use active listening to help students pinpoint the real problem.)
2. *Generate many possible solutions.* Brainstorm, but remember, don't allow any evaluations of ideas yet.
3. *Evaluate each solution.* Any participant may veto any idea. If no solutions are found to be acceptable, brainstorm again.
4. *Make a decision.* Choose one solution through consensus—no voting. In the end, everyone must be satisfied with the solution.
5. *Determine how to implement the solution.* What will be needed? Who will be responsible for each task? What is the timetable?
6. *Evaluate the success of the solution.* After trying the solution for a while, ask, "Are we satisfied with our decision? How well is it working? Should we make some changes?"

Many of the conflicts in classrooms can be important learning experiences for all concerned.

Reaching Every Student: Peer Mediation and Negotiation

Handling conflict is difficult for most of us—and for young people it can be even harder. Nearly 40 years ago, a large study of more than 8,000 junior and senior high students and 500 faculty from three major cities concluded that 90% of the conflicts among students are resolved in destructive ways or are never resolved at all (DeCecco & Richards, 1974). The few studies conducted since that time have reached similar conclusions. Avoidance, force, and threats seem to be the major strategies for dealing with conflict (Johnson et al., 1995). But there are better ways—like peer mediation and negotiation strategies that teach lifelong lessons.

David Johnson and his colleagues (1995) provided conflict resolution training to 227 students in 2nd through 5th grade. Students learned a five-step negotiating strategy:

1. *Jointly define the conflict.* Separate the person from the problem and the actions involved, avoid win–lose thinking, and get both parties' goals clear.
2. *Exchange positions and interests.* Present a tentative proposal and make a case for it; listen to the other person's proposal and feelings; and stay flexible and cooperative.

3. *Reverse perspectives.* See the situation from the other person's point of view and re- verse roles and argue for that perspective.
4. *Invent at least three agreements that allow mutual gain.* Brainstorm, focus on goals, think creatively, and make sure everyone has power to invent solutions.
5. *Reach an integrative agreement.* Make sure both sets of goals are met. If all else fails, flip a coin, take turns, or call in a third party—a mediator.

In addition to learning conflict resolution, all students in Johnson and Johnson's study were trained in mediation strategies. The role of the mediator was rotated—every day the teacher chose two students to be the class mediators and to wear the mediators' T-shirts. Johnson and his colleagues found that students learned the conflict resolution and media- tion strategies and used them successfully to handle conflicts in a more productive way, both in school and at home.

Peer mediation has also been successful with older students and those with serious problems (Sanchez & Anderson, 1990). In one program, selected gang members were given mediation training, and then all members were invited to participate voluntarily in the mediation process, supervised by school counselors. Strict rules governed the proc- ess leading to written agreements signed by gang representatives. Sanchez and Anderson (1990) found that gang violence in the school was reduced to a bare minimum—"The magic of the mediation process was communication" (p. 56).

Even if you do not have formal peer mediation training in your school, you can help your students handle conflict more productively. For example, Esme Codell, the excellent first-year teacher you met earlier in this chapter, taught her 5th graders a simple four- step process and posted the steps on a bulletin board: "1. Tell person what you didn't like. 2. Tell person how it made you feel. 3. Tell person what you want in the future. 4. Person responds with what they can do. Congratulations! You are a Confident Conflict Conqueror!" (Codell, 2001, p. 23).

We have looked at quite a few perspectives on classroom management. Clearly, there is not a one-size-fits-all strategy for creating social and physical spaces for learning. What does the research tell us? Are some better than others?

Research on Management Approaches

Research provides some guidance. Emmer and Aussiker (1990) conducted a meta-analysis of three general perspectives on management: *influencing* students through listening and problem solving, as described by Gordon (1981); *group management* through class meetings and student discussion, as advocated by Glasser (1969, 1990); and *control* through rewards and punishments, as exemplified by Canter and Canter (1992). No clear conclusions could be drawn about the impact of these approaches on student behaviors. However, some evaluations have found positive effects for Freiberg's (2012; Freiberg & Lamb, 2009) Consistency Management program and for programs that use rewards and punishments (Lewis, 2001).

INTEGRATING IDEAS. In a study conducted in Australia, Ramon Lewis (2001) found that recognizing and rewarding appropriate student behaviors, talking with students about how their behavior affects others, involving students in class discipline decisions, and providing nondirective hints and descriptions about unacceptable behaviors were associated with students taking greater responsibility for their own learning. It is inter- esting that these interventions represent all three of the general approaches reviewed by Emmer and Aussiker: *influence, group management,* and *control.* In a study of over 3,000 9th grade students in Singapore, Youyan Nie and Shun Lau (2009) found that both caring and control were positively related to student engagement, so blending control, influence, caring, and group management strategies may be necessary in order to cre- ate positive learning environments. This is not always easy. Lewis also concluded that teachers sometimes find using caring, influence, and group management difficult when students are aggressive—and most in need of these positive approaches. When teachers feel threatened, it can be difficult for them to do what students need, but that may be the most important time to act positively and combine caring with control.

GUIDELINES — FAMILY AND COMMUNITY PARTNERSHIPS

Classroom Management

Make sure families know the expectations and rules of your class and school.
Examples

1. At a Family Fun Night, have your students do skits showing the rules—how to follow them and what breaking them "looks like" and "sounds like."
2. Make a poster for the refrigerator at home that describes, in a light way, the most important rules and expectations.
3. For older students, give families a list of due dates for the major assignments, along with tips about how to encourage quality work by pacing the effort—avoiding last minute panic. Some schools require family members to sign a paper indicating they are aware of the due dates.
4. Communicate in appropriate ways—use the family's first language when possible. Tailor messages to the reading level of the home.

Make families partners in recognizing good citizenship.
Examples

1. Send positive notes home when students, especially students who have had trouble with classroom management, work well in the classroom.

2. Give ideas for ways any family, even those with few economic resources, can celebrate accomplishment—a favorite food; the chance to choose a game to play; a comment to a special person such as an aunt, grandparent, or minister; the chance to read to a younger sibling.

Identify talents in the community to help build a learning environment in your class.
Examples

1. Have students write letters to carpet and furniture stores asking for donations of remnants to carpet a reading corner.
2. Find family members who can build shelves or room dividers, paint, sew, laminate manipulatives, write stories, repot plants, or network computers.
3. Contact businesses for donations of computers, printers, or other equipment.

Seek cooperation from families when behavior problems arise.
Examples

1. Talk to families over the phone or in their home. Keep good records about the problem behavior.
2. Listen to family members and solve problems with them.

COMMUNICATING WITH FAMILIES ABOUT CLASSROOM MANAGEMENT. As we have seen throughout this book, families are important partners in education. This statement applies to classroom management as well. When parents and teachers share the same expectations and support each other, they can create a more positive classroom environment and more time for learning. The *Family and Community Partnerships Guidelines* provide ideas for working with families and the community.

DIVERSITY: CULTURALLY RESPONSIVE MANAGEMENT

Research on discipline shows that African Americans and Latino/a Americans, especially males, are punished more often and more harshly than other students. These students lose time from learning as they spend more hours in detention or suspension (Gay, 2006; Monroe & Obidah, 2002; Skiba, Michael, Nardo, & Peterson, 2000). Why?

The notion that African Americans and Latino/a students are punished more because they commit more serious offenses is NOT supported by the data. Instead, these students are punished more severely for minor offenses such as rudeness or defiance—words and actions that are interpreted by teachers as meriting severe punishment. One explanation is a lack of cultural synchronization between teachers and students. "The language, style of walking, glances, and dress of black children, particularly males, have engendered fear, apprehension, and overreaction among many teachers and school administrators" (Irvine, 1990, p. 27). African American students may be disciplined for behaviors that were never intended to be disruptive or disrespectful. Teachers do their students and themselves a service if they work at becoming bicultural—helping their students to learn how to function in both mainstream and home cultures, but also learning the meaning of their students' words and actions—so they do not misinterpret and then punish their students' unintended insults (Gay, 2006).

Culturally responsive management is simply a part of the larger concept of culturally relevant teaching. Geneva Gay (2006) sums it up:

> If the classroom is a comfortable, caring, embracing, affirming, engaging, and facilitative place for students then discipline is not likely to be much of an issue. It follows then that both classroom management and school achievement can be improved for students from different ethnic, racial, social, and linguistic backgrounds by ensuring that curriculum and instruction are culturally relevant and personally meaningful for them.

I once asked a gifted educator in an urban New Jersey high school which teachers were most effective with the really tough students. He said there are two kinds: teachers who can't be intimidated or fooled and expect their students to learn, and teachers who really care about the students. When I asked, "Which kind are you?" he answered "Both!" He is an example of a "warm demander," a teacher who seems to be most effective with students placed at risk (Irvine & Armento, 2001; Irvine and Fraser, 1998). Sometimes these **warm demanders** appear harsh to outside observers (Burke-Spero, 1999; Burke-Spero & Woolfolk Hoy, 2002). Carla Monroe and Jennifer Obidah (2002) studied Ms. Simpson, an African American teacher working with her 8th grade science class. She describes herself as having high expectations for academics and behavior in her classes—so much so that she believed her students perceived her as "mean." Yet she often used humor and dialect to communicate her expectations, as in the following exchange:

Ms. Simpson [addressing the class]: If you know you're going to act the fool just come to me and say, "I'm going to act the fool at the pep rally," so I can go ahead and send you to wherever you need to go. [Class laughs.]

Ms. Simpson: I'm real serious. If you know you're having a bad day, you don't want anybody touching you, you don't want nobody saying nothing to you, somebody bump into you you're going to snap—you need to come up to me and say, "I'm going to snap and I can't go to the pep rally." [The students start to call out various comments.]

Ms. Simpson: Now, I just want to say I expect you to have the best behavior because you're the most mature students in the building . . . don't make me stop the pep rally and ask the 8th graders to leave.

Edward: We'll have silent lunch won't we? [Class laughs.]

Ms. Simpson: You don't want to dream about what you're going to have. [Class laughs.] Ok, 15 minutes for warm ups. [The students begin their warm-up assignment.]

Many African American students may be more accustomed to a directive kind of management and discipline outside of school. Their families might say, "Put down that candy" or "Go to bed," whereas White parents might ask, "Can we eat candy before dinner?" or "Isn't it time for bed?" As H. Richard Milner (2006, p. 498) says, "The question should not be which approach is right or wrong but which approach works with and connects with the students' prior knowledge and ways of knowing."

Culturally responsive management Taking cultural meanings and styles into account when developing management plans and responding to students.

Warm demanders Effective teachers with African American students who show both high expectations and great caring for their students.

▼ SUMMARY

The Need for Organization (pp. 368–371)

What are the challenges of classroom management? Classrooms are by nature multidimensional, full of simultaneous activities, fast-paced and immediate, unpredictable, public, and affected by the history of students' and teachers' actions. A teacher must juggle all these elements every day. Productive classroom activity requires students' cooperation. Maintaining cooperation is different for each age group. Young students are learning how to "go to school" and need to learn the general procedures of school. Older students need to learn the specifics required for working in different subjects. Working with adolescents requires teachers to understand the power of the adolescent peer group.

What are the goals of effective classroom management? The goals of effective classroom management are to make ample time for learning; improve the quality of time use by keeping students actively engaged; make sure participation structures are clear, straightforward, and consistently signaled; and encourage student self-management, self-control, and responsibility.

Creating a Positive Learning Environment (pp. 372–380)

Distinguish between rules and procedures. Rules are the specific dos and don'ts of classroom life. They usually are written down or posted. Procedures cover administrative tasks, student movement, housekeeping, and routines for accomplishing lessons, interactions between students and teachers, and interactions among students. Rules can be written in terms of rights and students may benefit from participating in establishing these rules. Consequences should be established for following and breaking the rules and procedures so that the teacher and the students know what will happen.

Distinguish between personal territories and interest-areas spatial arrangements. There are two basic kinds of spatial organization, territorial (the traditional classroom arrangement) and functional (dividing space into interest or work areas). Flexibility is often the key. Access to materials, convenience, privacy when needed, ease of supervision, and a willingness to reevaluate plans are important considerations in the teacher's choice of physical arrangements.

Contrast the first school week of effective and ineffective classroom managers. Effective classroom managers spent the first days of class teaching a workable, easily understood set of rules and procedures by using lots of explanation, examples, and practice. Students were occupied with organized, enjoyable activities, and they learned to function cooperatively in the group. Quick, firm, clear, and consistent responses to infractions of the rules characterized effective teachers. The teachers had planned carefully to avoid any last-minute tasks that might have taken them away from their students. These teachers dealt with the children's pressing concerns first. In contrast, for ineffective managers, procedures for accomplishing routine tasks varied from day to day and were never taught or practiced. Students talked to one another because they had nothing productive to do. Ineffective teachers frequently left the room. Many became absorbed in paperwork or in helping just one student. They had not made plans for how to deal with typical problems such as late-arriving students or interruptions.

Maintaining a Good Environment for Learning (pp. 380–384)

How can teachers encourage engagement? In general, as teacher supervision increases, students' engaged time also increases. When the task provides continuous cues for the student about what to do next, involvement will be greater. Activities with clear steps are likely to be more absorbing, because one step leads naturally to the next. Making work requirements clear and specific, providing needed materials, and monitoring activities all add to engagement.

Explain the factors identified by Kounin that prevent management problems in the classroom. To create a positive environment and prevent problems, teachers must take individual differences into account, maintain student motivation, and reinforce positive behavior. Successful problem preventers are skilled in four areas described by Kounin: "withitness," overlapping, group focusing, and movement management. When penalties have to be imposed, teachers should impose them calmly and privately. In addition to applying Kounin's ideas, teachers can prevent problems by establishing a caring classroom community and teaching students to use social skills and emotional self-regulation skills.

How do teachers help students form connections with schools? To get started on building connections, teachers should make expectations for both academic work and student behaviors clear. Respect for students' needs and rights should be at the center of class procedures. Students know that their teachers care about them when teachers try to make classes interesting, are fair and honest with them, make sure they understand the materials, and have ways to cope with students' concerns and troubles.

Dealing with Discipline Problems (pp. 384–390)

Describe seven levels of intervention in misbehavior. Teachers can first make eye contact with the student or use other nonverbal signals, then try verbal hints such as simply inserting the student's name into the lecture. Next the teacher asks if the offender is aware of the negative effects of the actions, then reminds the student of the procedure and has her or him follow it correctly. If this does not work, the teacher can ask the student to state the correct rule or procedure and then to follow it, and then move to telling the student in a clear, assertive, and unhostile way to stop the misbehavior. If this fails too, the teacher can offer a choice—stop the behavior or meet privately to work out the consequences.

What can teachers do about bullying, teasing, and cyberbullying? Teachers often underestimate the amount of peer conflict and bullying that happens in schools. Bullying involves both an imbalance of power between students and repeated attempts at harm and may take place in a variety of settings—including those in which students are not face-to-face with one another at school. Teachers can think of bullying as a form of violence and approach strategies for overcoming bullying as they would strategies to overcoming other violent acts. For example, prevention of bullying can take the form of developing a respectful classroom community and discussing conflict.

What are some challenges in secondary classrooms? Teachers working in secondary schools should be prepared to handle students who don't complete schoolwork, repeatedly break the same rule, or openly defy teachers. These students may also be experiencing new and powerful stressors. As a result, secondary students may benefit if teachers provide opportunities or point out resources for these students to seek out help and support. Teachers might also find consultation with guidance counselors and parents or caregivers helpful.

The Need for Communication (pp. 390–396)

What is meant by "empathetic listening"? Communication between teacher and student is essential when problems arise. All interactions between people, even silence or neglect, communicate some meaning. Empathetic, active listening can be a helpful response when students bring problems to teachers. Teachers must reflect back to the students what they hear them saying. This reflection is more than a parroting of words; it should capture the emotions, intent, and meaning behind them.

Distinguish among passive, hostile, and assertive response styles. The passive style can take several forms. Instead of telling the student directly what to do, the teacher simply comments on the behavior, asks the student to think about the appropriate action, or threatens but never follows through. In a hostile response style, teachers may make "you" statements that condemn the student without stating clearly what the student should be doing. An assertive response communicates to the students that the teacher cares too much about them and the process of learning to allow inappropriate behavior to persist. Assertive teachers clearly state what they expect.

What is peer mediation? Peer mediation is one good possibility for preventing violence in schools. The steps for peer mediation are: (1) Jointly define the conflict. (2) Exchange positions and interests. (3) Reverse perspectives. (4) Invent at least three agreements that allow mutual gain. (5) Reach an integrative agreement.

Diversity: Culturally Responsive Management (pp. 396–397)

What is culturally responsive management and why is it needed? African Americans and Latino/a Americans, especially males, are punished more often and more harshly than other students, but they do not commit more serious offenses. Instead, these students are punished more severely for minor offenses such as rudeness or defiance—words and actions that are interpreted by teachers as meriting severe punishment. One explanation is a lack of cultural synchronization between teachers and students. Culturally responsive management combines high expectaions for students' appropriate behavior with warmth and caring for the students as individuals.

▼ KEY TERMS

Academic learning time (370)
Action zone (377)
Allocated time (370)
Assertive discipline (393)
Classroom management (369)
Culturally responsive
    management (396)

Empathetic listening (392)
Engaged time/Time on task (370)
Group focus (382)
"I" message (393)
Movement management (382)
Natural/logical consequences (375)
Overlapping (382)

Paraphrase rule (391)
Participation structures (370)
Procedures/routines (372)
Rules (374)
Self-management (371)
Warm demanders (397)
Withitness (381)

▼ CONNECT AND EXTEND TO LICENSURE

MULTIPLE-CHOICE QUESTIONS

1. What is the aim of classroom management?
    A. To keep an orderly classroom
    B. To establish the primacy of the teacher
    C. To sustain a quiet and disciplined environment
    D. To maintain a positive productive learning environment

2. Which of the following is NOT a benefit of teaching students to be self-regulated?
    A. Students demonstrate the ability to fulfill their own needs without interfering with the rights and needs of others
    B. Teachers have fewer management problems, less stress, and more time to teach
    C. Students require increased teacher attention; therefore they learn more
    D. It requires extra time initially but leads to greater teacher self-efficacy

3. Mr. Ruiz was constantly plagued by students disrupting his English class. Determined to finally gain control, he resorted to afterschool detention, dropping letter grades, and belittling his students. When his evaluation by the principal occurred at the end of the term, he received low scores on his classroom management skills. His principal, Dr. Simon, provided feedback based upon research. Which one of the following would not be consistent with ideal ways to deal with Mr. Ruiz's problems?
    A. Teachers should begin the school year with severe consequences so students understand the teacher controls the classroom
    B. Teachers should aim to prevent classroom problems before they occur
    C. Teachers should exhibit withitness and overlapping in their activities
    D. Teachers must understand and practice movement management

4. Which of the following techniques is recommended for approaching and disciplining a student who may be prone to explosive behavior?
    A. Move swiftly and get as close to the misbehaving student as possible
    B. Ensure that there are several witnesses to the confrontation
    C. Be respectful and brief
    D. Use a loud voice to establish power

CONSTRUCTED-RESPONSE QUESTIONS
Case

It happened every day. Ginny Harding had to reprimand two boys in her class continually. Instead of feeling like a coach and mentor, Ginny started to feel like a nag. It wore on both boys and also on her. The boys were not malicious, they were just third graders being third graders. She remembered hearing an adage, one should not continue to do the same thing and expect different results. Over the next weekend Ginny decided to develop a more effective manner of handling this latest challenge.

5. List several simple ways in which Ginny Harding can quickly stop the boys from misbehaving.

6. Routines and procedures can also reduce the incidents of misbehavior by assisting students in smooth transitions from one activity to another. List several classroom operations and activities which should have an established routine or procedure.

▼ WHAT WOULD THEY DO?

TEACHERS' CASEBOOK: Bullies and Victims

Here is how some practicing teachers responded to the problems with bullies at school.

JOLITA HARPER • 3rd Grade
Preparing Academic Leaders Academy, Maple Heights, OH

I believe that the entire learning community has a clear role in preventing acts of intimidation between students, and that this is best accomplished with clear communication between all parties. Care should be taken to spread awareness between colleagues as to the nature of the situation. Classroom teachers who are alert to these instances of bullying are then able to provide an additional presence in situations, such as in hallways and the lunchroom, where this is likely to take place. Further, communication between individual classroom teachers and the victim of this bullying is essential. I would make certain to provide a sensitive ear to this student's plight as we work together to formulate alternatives toward improving the situation. Finally, in the event that the two bullying students were in my classes, I would communicate with them in such a way as to make clear the effect of their actions on others in an effort to promote empathy for their victim and, hopefully, initiate a change in their behaviors.

KEITH J. BOYLE • English Teacher, Grades 9–12
Dunellen High School, Dunellen, NJ

Errant behavior throughout the middle school may be indicative of future behavioral problems and, as many things in life, the more this misbehavior is allowed to exist, the longer it will have a chance to thrive. In this case of a child being continually bullied by two other children (gender having no bearing in this situation), the knowledge of this wrongdoing must not be ignored or isolated. I would interview both the victim and the bullies, separately, to glean as much information as possible. If this were a singular incident, I would attempt to handle it myself via contact with the pertinent parents. However, if this were a recurring problem, the administration must be made aware. Any administrator will acknowledge that to be left in the dark about a serious situation within the environs of his/her responsibility is precarious. The appropriate guidance counselor should also be involved. The gravity of abusive behavior toward fellow students must be emphasized to the offenders. Significant punitive action is integral in order to send a message to the entire community that their school is indeed a haven in which one can feel the uninhibited freedom to learn.

DAN DOYLE • History Teacher, Grade 11
St. Joseph's Academy, Hoffman, IL

As a high school teacher I'd be especially concerned about the existence of bullying among older students. While such behavior in elementary school is hurtful and damaging, it can become downright dangerous as students get older (and bigger!). I'd also be frustrated to think that, perhaps, early warning signs among these children may have been ignored or under-addressed at the elementary level, when teachers and/or parents are better positioned to get a grip on them. My first step would be to alert school personnel, particularly those who monitor hallways, the cafeteria, and other common areas, to be on the lookout for any type of bullying behavior. I'd put those responsible in communication with the guidance counselor's office; the counselor would determine whether the parents needed to be involved from there. Events in our society in recent years preclude the option of taking this sort of behavior lightly, or assuming it will take care of itself.

KELLEY CROCKETT
Meadowbrook Elementary School, Fort Worth, TX

Bullying cannot be tolerated. No school, no teacher, no administrator can afford a climate in which abusive behavior is allowed to germinate. Any incident of victimization must be immediately documented and submitted to the Principal. As well, I would schedule a conference that same day with the school counselor for my student in order to both allow another avenue of documentation and reinforce support that the problem is being aggressively addressed.

How I handle the next step depends on the administration in place but the important issue to remember is that there is a next step. The teacher must follow up with the student. Within 48 hours I would privately ask my student if there have been any further incidents. If he hesitates or acknowledges continued harassment I would direct him to write it down and I would document any questions I had asked him and his responses. I would then include his statement and my own in another report for both the Principal and the counselor.

As teachers, we hold the front line. To the children in our care we represent one of the first relationships with authority and civilize society. We can do no less than lend our voice and action to the betterment of our world.

chapter eleven
TEACHING EVERY STUDENT

WHAT WOULD YOU DO?

▶ **TEACHERS' CASEBOOK:** Reaching and Teaching Every Student

You have started a new job in a high school in your hometown. When you were in school, the students were fairly homogeneous—White, working to middle class, and English speaking. There was a "special education" class for students who had serious learning or developmental problems. But in the classes you are teaching, you find a wide range of reading levels, family incomes, and learning problems. Two of your students are virtually ready for college, whereas several others can barely read the texts—and their writing is impossible to decipher. Reading English texts is a challenge for some of your ELL students, although they seem to speak English with little trouble.

CRITICAL THINKING

- How would you differentiate instruction for these very dissimilar students?
- Do different philosophies of teaching provide different answers to this question?
- How will you grade work if you have successfully differentiated instruction?

OVERVIEW AND OBJECTIVES

Much of this text has been about learning and learners. In this chapter, we focus on teaching and teachers. Are there particular characteristics that distinguish effective from ineffective teachers? Research on whole-class teaching points to the importance of several factors that we will explore.

What else do we know about teaching? We look at how teachers plan, including how to use taxonomies of learning objectives or themes as a basis for planning.

With this foundation of knowing how to set goals and make plans, as well as an understanding of the characteristics of effective teachers, we move to a consideration of some general teacher-centered strategies: lecturing, seatwork, homework, questioning, recitation, and group discussion.

In the final section of this chapter, we will focus on how to match teaching to the needs and abilities of students through differentiated instruction, flexible grouping, and adaptive teaching. Finally we explore how teachers' beliefs about their students' abilities—teacher expectations—might influence student learning and teacher–student relationships.

By the time you have completed this chapter, you should be able to:

Objective 11.1: Identify the characteristics of effective teachers and effective classroom climates.

Objective 11.2: Develop learning objectives using Bloom's taxonomy.

Objective 11.3: Describe the processes involved in planning a lesson and differentiate among basic formats for putting plans into action.

Objective 11.4: Discuss the appropriate uses of direct instruction, homework, questioning, and group discussion.

Objective 11.5: Define differentiated instruction and adaptive teaching, and apply the approach to teaching a diverse group of students.

Objective 11.6: Explain the possible effects of teacher expectations and know how to avoid the negative implications.

Research on Teaching

This chapter is about teaching, so we will start with findings from several decades of research.

How would you go about identifying the keys to successful teaching? You might ask students, principals, college professors of education, or experienced teachers to list the characteristics of good teachers. Or you could do intensive case studies of a few classrooms over a long period. You might observe classes, rate different teachers on certain characteristics, and then see which characteristics were associated with teachers whose students either achieved the most or were the most motivated to learn. (To do this, of course, you would have to decide how to assess achievement and motivation.) You could identify teachers whose students, year after year, learned more than students working with other teachers; then you could observe the more successful teachers and note what they do. You might also train teachers to apply several different strategies to teach the same lesson and then determine which strategy led to the greatest student learning. You could videotape teachers, and then ask them to view the tapes and report what they were thinking about as they taught and what influenced their decisions while teaching, called *stimulated recall*. You might study transcripts of classroom dialogue to learn what helped students understand the material. You might use the relationships identified between teaching and learning as the basis for developing teaching approaches and testing these approaches in *design experiments*.

All of these approaches and more have been used to investigate teaching (Floden, 2001; Greeno, Collins, and Resnick, 1996; Gröschner, Seidel, & Shavelson, 2012). Let's examine some of the specific knowledge about teaching gained from these projects.

Characteristics of Effective Teachers

STOP & THINK Think about the most effective teacher you ever had—the one that you learned the most from. What were the characteristics of that person? What made that teacher so effective? •

Some of the earliest research on effective teaching focused on the personal qualities of the teachers themselves. Results revealed some lessons about three teacher characteristics: clarity, warmth, and knowledge. Recent research has focused on knowledge, so we will spend some extra time on that characteristic.

CLARITY AND ORGANIZATION. When Barak Rosenshine and Norma Furst (1973) reviewed about 50 studies of teaching, they concluded that *clarity* was the most promising teacher behavior for future research on effective teaching. Teachers who provide clear presentations and explanations tend to have students who learn more and who rate their teachers more positively (Comadena, Hunt, & Simonds, 2007; Hines, Cruickshank, & Kennedy, 1985). The clearer and less vague the teacher's explanations and instructions are, the more the students learn (Evertson & Emmer, 2009; 2012).

WARMTH AND ENTHUSIASM. As you are well aware, some teachers are much more enthusiastic than others. Some studies have found that ratings of teachers' enthusiasm for their subject are correlated with student achievement gains (Keller, Neumann, &

EFFECTIVE TEACHERS Effective teachers know how to transform their knowledge into examples, explanations, illustrations, and activities.

Fischer, 2012), whereas warmth, friendliness, and understanding seem to be the teacher traits most strongly associated with students' liking the teacher and the class in general (Hamann, Baker, McAllister, & Bauer, 2000; Madsen, 2003; Soar & Soar, 1979). But notice: These are correlational studies. The results do not tell us that teacher enthusiasm causes student learning or that warmth causes positive attitudes, only that the two variables tend to occur together. Two possible connections are that when teachers are enthusiastic, they capture and hold student attention, and that enthusiastic teachers model engagement and interest in learning. Student attention, interest, and engagement lead to learning. Of course, it is easier to be an enthusiastic teacher when your students are learning (Keller et al., 2012).

What about another important teacher characteristic—knowledge?

Knowledge for Teaching

Knowledge is the defining characteristic of expertise. **Expert teachers** have elaborate systems of knowledge for understanding problems in teaching. For example, when a beginning teacher is faced with students' wrong answers on math or history tests, all of these answers may seem about the same—wrong. But for an expert teacher, wrong answers are part of a rich system of knowledge that could include how to recognize several types of wrong answers, the misunderstanding or lack of information behind each kind of mistake, the best way to reteach and correct the misunderstanding, materials and activities that have worked in the past, and several ways to test whether the reteaching was successful. This unique kind of teacher knowledge that combines mastery of *academic content* with knowing *how to teach* the content and how to match instruction to *student differences* is called **pedagogical content knowledge** (Gess-Newsome, 2012). In addition, expert teachers have clear goals and take individual differences into account when planning for their students. These teachers are **reflective** practitioners, constantly trying to understand and improve their work with students (Hogan, Rabinowitz, & Craven, 2003).

Expert teachers Experienced, effective teachers who have developed solutions for classroom problems. Their knowledge of teaching process and content is extensive and well organized.

Pedagogical content knowledge Teacher knowledge that combines mastery of *academic content* with knowing *how to teach* the content and how to match instruction to *student differences*.

Reflective Thoughtful and inventive. Reflective teachers think back over situations to analyze what they did and why and to consider how they might improve learning for their students.

What do expert teachers know that allows them to be so successful? Lee Shulman (1987) has studied this question, and he has identified seven areas of professional knowledge. Expert teachers know:

1. The academic subjects they teach—their content knowledge is deep and interconnected.
2. General teaching strategies that apply in all subjects (such as the principles of classroom management, effective teaching, and evaluation that you will discover in this book).
3. The curriculum materials and programs appropriate for their subject and grade level.
4. Subject-specific knowledge for teaching: special ways of teaching certain students and particular concepts, such as the best ways to explain negative numbers to lower-ability students.
5. The characteristics and cultural backgrounds of learners.
6. The settings in which students learn—pairs, small groups, teams, classes, schools, and the community.
7. The goals and purposes of teaching.

This is quite a list. Obviously, one course cannot give you all the information you need to teach. In fact, a whole program of courses won't make you an expert. That takes time and experience. But studying educational psychology has added to your professional knowledge because at the heart of educational psychology is a concern with learning wherever it occurs.

Do teachers who know more about their subject have a more positive impact on their students? It depends on the subject. When Hill, Rowan, and Ball (2005) tested U.S. 1st and 3rd grade teachers' specific knowledge of the math concepts that they actually teach and their understanding of how to teach those concepts, they found that teachers with greater *content* and *pedagogical content knowledge* had students who learned more mathematics. High school students appear to learn more mathematics from teachers with degrees or significant coursework in mathematics (Wayne & Youngs, 2003). Studies in German high schools have found that math teachers with more pedagogical content knowledge have students who are more cognitively engaged and more supported in learning, and this higher quality instruction predicts higher student math achievement (Baumert et al., 2010).

When we look at teachers' knowledge of facts and concepts in other subjects, as measured by test scores and college grades, the relationship to student learning is unclear and may be indirect (Aloe & Becker, 2009). We know from Darling-Hammond and Youngs' (2002) work that the quality of teachers—as measured by whether the teachers were fully certified and have a major in their teaching field—is related to student performance. When we look at scores on teacher certification tests, there is a modest positive relationship between teachers' scores and students' achievement—the strongest evidence for this relationship is again in mathematics (Boyd, Goldhaber, Lankford, & Wyckoff, 2008).

The indirect effects are that teachers who know more may make clearer presentations and recognize student difficulties more easily. They are ready for any student questions and do not have to be evasive or vague in their answers. Thus, knowledge is necessary for effective teaching because being more knowledgeable helps teachers be *clearer*, more *organized*, and more *responsive* to student questions.

Recent Research on Teaching

A program of large-scale, longitudinal research by Robert Pianta and his colleagues (2005, 2008; Crosnoe et al., 2010; Jerome, Harme, & Pianta, 2009; Luckner & Pianta, 2011) has identified three aspects of classroom climate that are related to the development and learning of preschool and elementary school students. These three dimensions are consistent with the characteristics of teachers identified in earlier research on teaching, and they cover affective, behavioral, and cognitive dimensions, as you can see in Table 11.1. The *affective* dimension in Pianta's model is teacher *emotional support*, similar to teacher warmth and enthusiasm identified in early research. The *cognitive* dimension is instructional support, which includes concept development (activities and discussions that promote student higher-order thinking) and quality feedback that is specific and focused on the learning process. Concept development and quality feedback may be easier for teachers with greater knowledge for teaching. Pianta's third dimension is classroom organization, which includes *behavioral* concerns such as classroom and lesson management, with clear activities and routines that make more time for student learning and are really engaging—similar to the teacher characteristics of clarity and organization.

Now let's get to the specifics of teaching—the first step is planning.

TABLE 11.1 • **Dimensions of Classroom Climate**

AREA OF TEACHING	CLASSROOM CLIMATE DIMENSION	COMPONENTS	DEFINITIONS AND EXAMPLES
Affective	**Emotional Support**	*Positive Climate*	Warmth, mutual respect, positive emotional connections between teacher and students
		Negative Climate (negative predictor of learning)	Disrespect, anger, hostility
		Teacher Sensitivity	Consistency and effectiveness in responding to students' academic and emotional needs
		Regard for Students' Perspectives	Activities encourage student autonomy and emphasize students' interests, motivations, and points of view
Cognitive	**Instructional Support**	*Concept Development*	Activities and discussion promote higher-order thinking skills and cognition
		Quality of Feedback	Consistency in providing specific, process-oriented feedback and back-and-forth exchanges to extend students' learning
Behavioral	**Classroom Organization**	*Behavior Management*	Teachers' effectiveness in monitoring, preventing, and redirecting misbehavior
		Productivity	How consistently learning is maximized with clear activities and routines, teacher preparation, efficient transitions, and minimal disruptions
		Instructional Learning Formats	How well materials, modalities, and activities are used to engage students in learning

Source: Based on Brown, J. L., Jones, S. M., LaRusso, M. D., & Aber, J. L. (2010). Improving classroom quality: Teacher influences and experimental impacts of the 4Rs Program. Journal of Educational Psychology, 102, 153–167.

THE FIRST STEP: PLANNING

STOP & THINK Greta Morine-Dershimer (2006) asks which of the following are true about teacher planning:

Time is of the essence.

Plans are made to be broken.

Don't look back.

A little planning goes a long way.

You can do it yourself.

One size fits all. •

Research on Planning

When you thought about the "What Would You Do?" challenge at the beginning of this chapter, you were planning. In the past few years, educational researchers have become very interested in teachers' planning. They have interviewed teachers about how they plan, asked teachers to "think out loud" while planning or to keep journals describing their plans, and even studied teachers intensively for months at a time. What do you think they have found?

First, planning influences what students will learn, because planning transforms the available time and curriculum materials into activities, assignments, and tasks for students—*time is of the essence planning.* When a teacher decides to devote 7 hours to language arts and 15 minutes to science in a given week, the students in that class will learn more language than science. Planning done at the beginning of the year is particularly important, because many routines and patterns, such as time allocations, are established early. So, *a little planning does go a long way* in terms of what will be taught and what will be learned.

Second, teachers engage in several levels of planning—by the year, term, unit, week, and day. All the levels must be coordinated. Accomplishing the year's plan requires breaking the work into terms, the terms into units, and the units into weeks and days. For experienced teachers, unit planning seems to be the most important level, followed by weekly and then daily planning. As you gain experience in teaching, it will be easier to coordinate these levels of planning and incorporate the state and district curriculum standards as well (Morine-Dershimer, 2006).

Third, plans reduce—but do not eliminate—uncertainty in teaching. Planning must allow flexibility. There is some evidence that when teachers "overplan"—fill every minute and stick to the plan no matter what—their students do not learn as much as students whose teachers are flexible (Shavelson, 1987). So *plans are not made to be broken—but sometimes they need to be bent a bit.*

In order to plan creatively and flexibly, teachers need to have wide-ranging knowledge about students, their interests, and their abilities; the subjects being taught; alternative ways to teach and assess understanding; how to apply and adapt materials and texts; and how to pull all this knowledge together into meaningful activities. The plans of beginning teachers sometimes don't work because they lack knowledge about the students or the subject—they can't estimate how long it will take students to complete an activity, for example, or they stumble when asked for an explanation or a different example (Calderhead, 1996).

EXPERT PLANNING In planning, you can go it alone, but collaboration is better. Sharing ideas with colleagues can be one of the best experiences in teaching.

In planning, *you can do it yourself—but collaboration is better*. Working with other teachers and sharing ideas is one of the best experiences in teaching. Some educators think that a collaborative approach to planning used in Japan called *kenshu* or "mastery through study" is one reason why Japanese students do so well on international tests. A basic part of the kenshu process involves a small group of teachers developing a lesson and then videotaping one of the group members teaching the lesson. Next, all members review the tape, analyze student responses, and improve the lesson further. Other teachers try the revised lesson and more improvements follow. At the end of the school year, all the study groups may publish the results of their work. In the United States, this process is called **lesson study** (Morine-Dershimer, 2006). To learn about this approach, search the Internet using the keywords "lesson study." Then, explore some of the lesson plans available using the keywords "lesson plans," or search by subject or grade—for example, "math lesson plans" or "4th grade lesson plans."

"And then, of course, there's the possibility of being just the slightest bit too organized."

By permission of Glen Dines. From *Phi Delta Kappan*.

But even great lesson plans taken from a terrific Web site on science have to be adapted to your situation. Some of the adaptation comes before you teach and some comes after. In fact, much of what experienced teachers know about planning comes from looking back—reflecting—on what worked and what didn't, so *DO look back* on your plans and grow professionally in the process. Collaborative reflection and revising lessons are major components of the lesson study approach to planning.

Finally, there is no one model for effective planning. *One size does NOT fit all* in planning. Planning is a creative problem-solving process for experienced teachers; they know how to complete many lessons and are able to teach segments of lessons effectively. They know what to expect and how to proceed, so they don't necessarily continue to follow the detailed lesson-planning models they learned during their teacher preparation programs. Planning is more informal—"in their heads." However, many experienced teachers think it was helpful to learn this detailed system as a foundation (Clark & Peterson, 1986).

No matter how you plan, you must have a learning goal in mind. In the next section, we consider the range of goals that you might have for your students.

Objectives for Learning

We hear quite a bit today about visions, goals, outcomes, and standards. At a very general, abstract level are the grand goals society may have for graduates of public schools such as preparing them "to succeed in college and the workplace and to compete in the global economy" (USDE, Race to The Top, 2009, p. 2). But very general goals are meaningless as potential guidelines for instruction. States may turn these grand goals into *standards* and *indicators*, such as the Colorado standard that students will "Use comprehension skills such as previewing, predicting, inferring, comparing and contrasting, rereading and self-monitoring, summarizing, etc." At this level, the indicators are close to being instructional objectives (Airasian, 2005). You can find your state's standards at http://www.educationworld.com/standards/state/index.shtml.

AN EXAMPLE OF STANDARDS: TECHNOLOGY.   Here is an example of standards that relate to you—the teacher—and what you should know about technology. Two widely adopted technology standards are from the International Society for Technology in Education (ISTE) and the Partnership for 21st Century Skills. The ISTE produced the National Education Technology Standards for teachers shown below (NETS-T; http://www.iste.org/standards/nets-for-teachers/nets-for-teachers-2008.aspx):

1. **Facilitate and Inspire Student Learning and Creativity***
   Teachers use their knowledge of subject matter, teaching and learning, and technology to facilitate experiences that advance student learning, creativity, and innovation in both face-to-face and virtual environments.

Lesson study As a group, teachers develop, test, improve, and retest lessons until they are satisfied with the final version.

---

*National Educational Technology Standards for Teachers. Second edtion © 2008 ISTE ® (International Society of Technology in Education), www.iste.org. All rights reserved.

2. **Design and Develop Digital-Age Learning Experiences and Assessments**
   Teachers design, develop, and evaluate authentic learning experiences and assessment incorporating contemporary tools and resources to maximize content learning in context and to develop the knowledge, skills, and attitudes identified in the NETS•S.
3. **Model Digital-Age Work and Learning**
   Teachers exhibit knowledge, skills, and work processes representative of an innovative professional in a global and digital society.
4. **Promote and Model Digital Citizenship and Responsibility**
   Teachers understand local and global societal issues and responsibilities in an evolving digital culture and exhibit legal and ethical behavior in their professional practices.
5. **Engage in Professional Growth and Leadership**
   Teachers continuously improve their professional practice, model lifelong learning, and exhibit leadership in their school and professional community by promoting and demonstrating the effective use of digital tools and resources.

But what about your teaching? Let's move into the classroom.

CLASSROOMS: INSTRUCTIONAL OBJECTIVES. Norman Gronlund and Susan Brookhart (2009) define **instructional objectives** as intended learning outcomes. Objectives are the performances expected of students after instruction in order to demonstrate their learning. Objectives written by people with behavioral views focus on observable and measurable changes in the learner. Behavioral objectives use terms such as *list, define, add,* or *calculate.* Cognitive objectives, on the other hand, emphasize thinking and comprehension, so they are more likely to include words such as *understand, recognize, create,* or *apply.* Let's look at one well-developed method of writing specific behavioral objectives.

MAGER: START WITH THE SPECIFIC. Robert Mager (1975, 1997) developed a very influential system for writing instructional objectives. His idea is that objectives ought to describe what students will be doing when demonstrating their achievement and show how teachers will know they are doing it, so these are generally regarded as **behavioral objectives.** According to Mager, a good objective has three parts. First, it describes the intended *student behavior.* What must the student do? Second, it lists the *conditions* under which the behavior will occur: How will this behavior be recognized or tested? Third, it gives the *criteria* for acceptable performance on the test. For example, an objective in social studies might be: "Given a recent article from an online political blog [*conditions*], the student will mark each statement with an F for fact or an O for opinion [*observable student behavior*], with 75% of the statements correctly marked [*criteria*]." With this emphasis on final behavior, Mager's system requires a very explicit statement. Mager contends that often students can teach themselves if they are given well-stated objectives.

Connect and Extend to PRAXIS II™

Instructional Objectives (II, B1)
Describe the key elements of behavioral and instructional objectives. Be able to write each type of objective for a content area that you expect to teach.

Instructional objectives Clear statement of what students are intended to learn through instruction.

Behavioral objectives Instructional objectives stated in terms of observable behaviors.

Cognitive objectives Instructional objectives stated in terms of higher-level thinking operations.

GRONLUND: START WITH THE GENERAL. Gronlund and Brookhart (2009) offer a different approach, which is often used for writing **cognitive objectives.** They believe an objective should be stated first in general terms (*understand, solve, appreciate,* etc.). Then, the teacher should clarify by listing a few sample behaviors that would provide evidence that the student has attained the objective. Look at the example in Table 11.2. The goal here is comprehension of a scientific concept. A teacher could never list all the behaviors that might be involved in "comprehension," but stating an initial, general objective along with specific examples makes the purpose clear.

The most recent research on instructional objectives tends to favor approaches similar to Gronlund's. James Popham (2005a), a former proponent of very specific objectives, makes this recommendation:

> Strive to come up with a half dozen or so truly salient, broad, yet measurable instructional objectives for your own classroom. Too many small-scope, hyperspecific objectives will be of scant value to you because, if you're at all normal, you'll soon disregard [them]. On the other hand, a small number of intellectually manageable, broad, yet measurable objectives will not only prove helpful to you instructionally but will also help you answer the what-to-assess question. (pp. 104–105)

TABLE 11.2 • **A Combined Method for Creating Objectives**

GENERAL OBJECTIVE
Comprehends scientific concepts.
SPECIFIC EXAMPLES
1. Describes the concept in his or her own words. 2. Gives an example of the concept [that is new]. 3. States hypotheses based on the concept. 4. Describes how the process functions in a given situation. 5. Describes an experiment that illustrates the process.

Source: Norman E. Gronlund & Susan M. Brookhart, Gronlund's writing instructional objectives (8th ed.), Upper Saddle River, NJ: Pearson © 2009. Adapted by permission of Pearson Education, Inc.

Flexible and Creative Plans—Using Taxonomies

Connect and Extend to PRAXIS II™

Taxonomies of Educational Objectives (II, B1)
Taxonomies influence every aspect of instruction from textbook design to lesson planning. List the major objectives of each of the taxonomies, and describe the focus of each objective. Be able to incorporate these objectives into instructional objectives that you design.

STOP & THINK Think about your assignments for one of your classes. What kind of thinking is involved in doing the assignments?

Remembering facts and terms?

Understanding key ideas?

Applying information to solve problems?

Analyzing a situation, task, or problem?

Making evaluations or giving opinions?

Creating or designing something new? •

Almost 60 years ago, a group of experts in educational evaluation led by Benjamin Bloom set out to improve college and university examinations. The impact of their work has touched education at all levels around the world (Anderson & Sosniak, 1994). Bloom and his colleagues developed a **taxonomy**, or classification system, of educational objectives. Objectives were divided into three domains: *cognitive, affective,* and *psychomotor.* A handbook describing the objectives in each area was eventually published. In real life, of course, behaviors from these three domains occur simultaneously. While students are writing (psychomotor), they are also remembering or reasoning (cognitive), and they are likely to have some emotional response to the task as well (affective).

THE COGNITIVE DOMAIN.   Bloom's taxonomy of the thinking or **cognitive domain** is considered one of the most significant educational writings of the 20th century (Anderson & Sosniak, 1994). The six basic objectives in Bloom's taxonomy are *knowledge, comprehension, application, analysis, synthesis,* and *evaluation* (Bloom, Engelhart, Frost, Hill, & Krathwohl, 1956).

It is common in education to consider these objectives as a hierarchy, each skill building on those below, but this is not entirely accurate. Some subjects, such as mathematics, do not fit this structure very well (Kreitzer & Madaus, 1994). Still, you will hear many references to *lower-level* and *higher-level* objectives, with knowledge, comprehension, and application considered lower level and the other categories considered higher level. As a rough way of thinking about objectives, this can be helpful (Gronlund & Brookhart, 2009). The taxonomy of objectives can also be helpful in planning assessments because different procedures are appropriate for objectives at the various levels, as you will see in Chapter 12.

Taxonomy Classification system.

Cognitive domain In Bloom's taxonomy, memory and reasoning objectives.

In 2001, a group of educational researchers published the first major revision of the cognitive taxonomy and this is the one we use today (Anderson & Krathwohl, 2001).

1. *Remembering*: Remembering or recognizing something without necessarily understanding, using, or changing it.
2. *Understanding*: Understanding the material being communicated without necessarily relating it to anything else.
3. *Applying*: Using a general concept to solve a particular problem.
4. *Analyzing*: Breaking something down into its parts.
5. *Evaluating*: Judging the value of materials or methods as they might be applied in a particular situation.
6. *Creating*: Creating something new by combining different ideas.

The 2001 revision of Bloom's taxonomy added a new dimension—to recognize that cognitive processes must process *something*—you have to remember or understand or apply some form of knowledge. If you look at Table 11.3, you will see the result. We now have the six processes of *remembering, understanding, applying, analyzing, evaluating,* and *creating* acting on four kinds of knowledge—*factual, conceptual, procedural,* and *metacognitive.*

Consider how this revised taxonomy might suggest objectives for a social studies/language arts class. An objective that targets analyzing conceptual knowledge is:

After reading an historical account of the battle of the Alamo, students will be able to explain the author's point of view or bias.

An objective for evaluating metacognitive knowledge might be:

Students will reflect on and describe their strategies for identifying the biases of the author.

See http://projects.coe.uga.edu/epltt/index.php?title=Bloom%27s_Taxonomy for more explanations and examples.

Affective domain Objectives focusing on attitudes and feelings.

THE AFFECTIVE DOMAIN. The objectives in the taxonomy of the **affective domain**, or domain of emotional response, have not yet been revised from the original version. These

TABLE 11.3 • **A Revised Taxonomy in the Cognitive Domain**

The revised taxonomy includes cognitive processes operating on different kinds of knowledge. The verbs in the chart are examples of what might be used to create objectives.

THE KNOWLEDGE DIMENSION	THE COGNITIVE PROCESS DIMENSION					
	1. REMEMBER	2. UNDERSTAND	3. APPLY	4. ANALYZE	5. EVALUATE	6. CREATE
A. Factual Knowledge	list	summarize	classify	order	rank	combine
B. Conceptual Knowledge	describe	interpret	experiment	explain	assess	plan
C. Procedural Knowledge	tabulate	predict	calculate	differentiate	conclude	compose
D. Metacognitive Knowledge	appropriate use	execute	select strategy	change strategy	reflect	invent

Source: From Anderson, Lorin W., David R. Krathwohl, et al., A Taxonomy for Learning, Teaching, and Assessing. Published by Allyn and Bacon, Boston, MA. Copyright © 2001 by Pearson Education. Reprinted by permission of the publisher.

objectives run from least to most committed (Krathwohl, Bloom, & Masia, 1964). At the lowest level, a student would simply pay attention to a certain idea. At the highest level, the student would adopt an idea or a value and act consistently with that idea. There are five basic objectives in the affective domain:

1. *Receiving*: Being aware of or attending to something in the environment. This is the I'll-listen-to-the-concert-but-I-won't-promise-to-like-it level.
2. *Responding*: Showing some new behavior as a result of experience. At this level, a person might applaud after the concert or hum some of the music the next day.
3. *Valuing*: Showing some definite involvement or commitment. At this point, a person might choose to go to a concert instead of a film.
4. *Organization*: Integrating a new value into one's general set of values, giving it some ranking among one's general priorities. This is the level at which a person would begin to make long-range commitments to concert attendance.
5. *Characterization by value*: Acting consistently with the new value. At this highest level, a person would be firmly committed to a love of music and demonstrate it openly and consistently.

Like the basic objectives in the cognitive domain, these five objectives are very general. To write specific learning objectives, you must state what students will actually be doing when they are receiving, responding, valuing, and so on. For example, an objective for a nutrition class at the valuing level (showing involvement or commitment) might be stated: After completing the unit on food contents and labeling, at least 50% of the class will commit to the junk-food boycott project by giving up fast food for a month.

THE PSYCHOMOTOR DOMAIN.   Until recently, the **psychomotor domain**, or realm of physical ability objectives, has been mostly overlooked by teachers who were not directly involved with physical education. There are several taxonomies in this domain (e.g., Harrow, 1972; Simpson, 1972) that generally move from basic perceptions and reflex actions to skilled, creative movements. James Cangelosi (1990) provides a useful way to think about objectives in the psychomotor domain as either (1) voluntary muscle capabilities that require endurance, strength, flexibility, agility, or speed, or (2) the ability to perform a specific skill.

Objectives in the psychomotor domain should be of interest to a wide range of educators, including those in fine arts, vocational-technical education, and special education. Many other subjects, such as chemistry, physics, and biology, also require specialized movements and well-developed hand–eye coordination. Using lab equipment, the mouse on a computer, or art materials means learning new physical skills. Here are two psychomotor objectives:

Four minutes after completing a one-mile run in eight minutes or under, your heart rate will be below 120.
Use a computer mouse effectively to "drag and drop" files.

Whatever your instructional objectives are for your students, Terry TenBrink (2006, p. 57) suggests these criteria. Objectives should be:

1. Student-oriented (emphasis on what the student is expected to do).
2. Descriptive of an appropriate learning outcome (both developmentally appropriate and appropriately sequenced, with more complex objectives following prerequisite objectives).
3. Clear and understandable (not too general or too specific).
4. Observable (avoid outcomes you can't see such as "appreciating" or "realizing").

The *Guidelines* on the next page should help you if you use objectives for every lesson or even for just a few assignments.

Psychomotor domain Physical ability and coordination objectives.

GUIDELINES

Using Instructional Objectives

Avoid "word magic"—phrases that sound noble and important, but say very little, such as "Students will become deep thinkers."
Examples

1. Keep the focus on specific changes that will take place in the students' knowledge and skills.
2. Ask students to explain the meaning of the objectives. If they can't give specific examples of what you mean, the objectives are not communicating your intentions to your students.

Suit the activities to the objectives.
Examples

1. If the goal is the memorization of vocabulary, give the students memory aids and practice exercises.
2. If the goal is the ability to develop well-thought-out positions, consider position papers, debates, projects, or mock trials.

3. If you want students to become better writers, give many opportunities for writing and rewriting.

Make sure your tests are related to your objectives.
Examples

1. Write objectives and rough drafts for tests at the same time—revise these drafts of tests as the units unfold and objectives change.
2. Weight the tests according to the importance of the various objectives and the time spent on each.

For additional ideas, see
http://www.personal.psu.edu/staff/b/x/bxb11/Objectives/ or
http://edtech.tennessee.edu/~bobannon/objectives.html

Connect and Extend to PRAXIS II™

Planning Thematic Units (II, A2)
Thematic learning units that integrate two or more content areas have become common in modern classrooms. Describe the principles involved in designing these activities, and explain how student learning can be assessed.

Constructivist approach View that emphasizes the active role of the learner in building understanding and making sense of information.

Planning from a Constructivist Perspective

- - - - - - - - - - - - - -

STOP & THINK Think about the same course assignments you analyzed in the previous *Stop & Think*. What are the big ideas that run through all those assignments? What other ways could you learn about those ideas besides the assignments? •

- - - - - - - - - - - - - -

Traditionally, it has been the teacher's responsibility to do most of the planning for instruction, but new ways of planning are emerging. In **constructivist approaches**, planning is shared and negotiated. The teacher and students together make decisions about content, activities, and approaches. Rather than having specific student behaviors and skills as objectives, the teacher has overarching goals—"big ideas" or themes—that guide planning (Borich, 2011). These goals are understandings or abilities that the teacher returns to again and again. For the last decade, teaching with themes and integrated content have been major elements in planning and designing lessons and units, from kindergarten (Roskos & Neuman, 1998) through high school (Clarke & Agne, 1997). For example, Elaine Homestead and Karen McGinnis (middle-school teachers) and Elizabeth Pate (a college professor) designed a unit on "Human Interactions" that included studying racism, world hunger, pollution, and air and water quality. Students researched issues by reading textbooks and outside sources, learning to use databases, interviewing local officials, and inviting guest speakers into class. Students had to develop knowledge in science, mathematics, and social studies. They learned to write and speak persuasively, and, in the process, raised money for hunger relief in Africa (Pate, McGinnis, & Homestead, 1995).

Elementary-age students can benefit from integrated planning, too. There is no reason to work on spelling skills, then listening skills, then writing skills, and then social studies or science. All these abilities can be developed together if students work to solve authentic problems. Some topics for integrating themes with younger children are people, friendship, communications, habitats, communities, and patterns. Possibilities for older students are given in Table 11.4.

TABLE 11.4 • **Some Themes for Integrated Planning for Middle and High School Students**

Courage	Time and Space
Mystery	Groups and Institutions
Survival	Work
Human Interaction	Motion
Communities of the Future	Cause and Effect
Communication/Language	Probability and Prediction
Human Rights and Responsibilities	Change and Conservation
Identity/Coming of Age	Diversity and Variation
Interdependence	Autobiography

Sources: Based on Curriculum Development; Interdisciplinary High School Teaching by J. H. Clarke and R. M. Agne, 1997, Boston: Allyn & Bacon; and Teaching through Themes by G. Thompson, 1991, New York: Scholastic. See Thompson for resources and strategies to develop some of these themes in elementary school and Clarke and Agne for ideas at the high school level.

Let's assume you have an idea of what you want students to understand, but how do you teach to encourage understanding? You still need to decide what's happening on Monday. You need to design teaching that is appropriate for the objectives.

TEACHING APPROACHES

In this section we will provide some basic formats for putting plans into action. The first challenge is to match your teaching methods to your objectives. We begin with strategies for teaching explicit facts and concepts.

Direct Instruction

For many people, "teaching" means an instructor explaining material to students—lecture is a classic form. There was an explosion of research in the 1970s and 1980s that focused on these more traditional forms of teaching. The results of all this work identified a model of teaching that was related to improved student learning. Barak Rosenshine and Robert Stevens (1986) call this approach **direct instruction** or **explicit teaching**. Tom Good (1983a) uses the term **active teaching** to describe a similar approach.

The direct instruction model fits a specific set of circumstances because it was derived from a particular approach to research. Researchers identified the elements of direct instruction by comparing teachers whose students learned more than expected (based on entering knowledge) with teachers whose students performed at an expected or average level. The researchers focused on existing practices in American classrooms. Because the focus was on traditional forms of teaching, the research could not identify successful innovations. Effectiveness was usually defined as average improvement in standardized test scores for a whole class or school. So the results hold for large groups, but not necessarily for every student in the group. Even when the average achievement of a group improves, the achievement of some individuals may decline (Good, 1996; Shuell, 1996).

Given these conditions, you can see that direct instruction applies best to the teaching of **basic skills**—clearly structured knowledge and essential skills, such as science facts, mathematics computations, reading vocabulary, and grammar rules (Rosenshine & Stevens, 1986). These skills involve tasks that are relatively unambiguous; they can be taught step by step and evaluated by standardized tests. Franz Weinert and Andreas Helmke (1995) describe direct instruction as having the following features:

(a) the teacher's classroom management is especially effective and the rate of student interruptive behaviors is very low; (b) the teacher maintains a strong academic focus and

Connect and Extend to PRAXIS II™

Teacher-Centered Instruction (II, A3) Teacher-centered instruction is often thought of as the "traditional" approach to instruction. In what situations is this instructional format most effective? What are the basic steps involved in carrying out this form of instruction?

Direct instruction/Explicit teaching Systematic instruction for mastery of basic skills, facts, and information.

Active teaching Teaching characterized by high levels of teacher explanation, demonstration, and interaction with students.

Basic skills Clearly structured knowledge that is needed for later learning and that can be taught step by step.

uses available instructional time intensively to initiate and facilitate students' learning activities; (c) the teacher insures that as many students as possible achieve good learning progress by carefully choosing appropriate tasks, clearly presenting subject-matter information and solution strategies, continuously diagnosing each student's learning progress and learning difficulties, and providing effective help through remedial instruction. (p. 138)

To this list, Xin Ma (2012) adds moving at a brisk pace and having a warm and accepting classroom climate.

How would a teacher turn these themes into actions?

ROSENSHINE'S SIX TEACHING FUNCTIONS.   Rosenshine and his colleagues (Rosenshine, 1988; Rosenshine & Stevens, 1986) have identified six teaching functions based on the research on effective instruction. These could serve as a checklist or framework for teaching basic skills.

1. *Review and check the previous day's work.* Reteach if students misunderstood or made errors.
2. *Present new material.* Make the purpose clear, teach in small steps, and provide many examples and nonexamples of the ideas and concepts you are teaching.
3. *Provide guided practice.* Question students, give practice problems, and listen for misconceptions and misunderstandings. Reteach if necessary. Continue guided practice until students answer about 80% of the questions correctly.
4. *Give feedback and correctives based on student answers.* Reteach if necessary. (Remember, Pianta and colleagues' [2005, 2008] class climate component of instructional support included quality feedback.)
5. *Provide independent practice.* Let students apply the new learning on their own, in seatwork, cooperative groups, or homework. The success rate during independent practice should be about 95%. This means that students must be well prepared for the work by the presentation and guided practice and that assignments must not be too difficult. The point is for the students to practice until the skills become overlearned and automatic—until the students are confident. Hold students accountable for the work they do—check it.
6. *Review weekly and monthly to consolidate learning.* Include some review items as homework. Test often, and reteach material missed on the tests.

These six functions are not steps to be followed in a particular order, but all of them are elements of effective instruction. For example, feedback, review, or reteaching should occur whenever necessary and should match the abilities of the students. Also, keep in mind the age and prior knowledge of your students. The younger or the less prepared your students are, the briefer your explanations should be. Use more and shorter cycles of presentation, guided practice, feedback, and correctives.

Connect and Extend to PRAXIS II™

Advance Organizers (II, A3)
The advance organizer is an important element in many teacher-centered/expository approaches to instruction. Be able to explain the role of the advance organizer in these approaches, and identify the basic types of organizers.

Advance organizer Statement of inclusive concepts to introduce and sum up material that follows.

ADVANCE ORGANIZERS.   Teachers using direct instruction often begin with an **advance organizer**. This is an introductory statement broad enough to encompass all the information that will follow. The organizers can serve three purposes: They direct your attention to what is important in the coming material, they highlight relationships among ideas that will be presented, and they remind you of relevant information you already have.

Advance organizers fall into one of two categories, comparative and expository (Mayer, 1984). *Comparative organizers* activate (bring into working memory) already existing schemas. They remind you of what you already know, but may not realize is relevant. A comparative advance organizer for a history lesson on revolutions might be a statement that contrasts military uprisings with the physical and social changes involved in the Industrial Revolution; you could also compare the common aspects of the French, English, Mexican, Russian, Iranian, Egyptian, and American revolutions (Salomon & Perkins, 1989).

In contrast, *expository organizers* provide new knowledge that students will need in order to understand the upcoming information. In an English class, you might begin a large thematic unit on rites of passage in literature with a very broad statement of the theme and why it has been so central in literature—something like, "A central character coming of age must learn to know himself or herself, often makes some kind of journey of self-discovery, and must decide what in the society is to be accepted and what should be rejected." Such an organizer might precede reading novels such as *The Adventures of Huckleberry Finn*.

The general conclusion of research on advance organizers is that they do help students learn, especially when the material to be learned is quite unfamiliar, complex, or difficult—as long as two conditions are met (Langan-Fox, Waycott, & Albert, 2000; Morin & Miller, 1998). First, to be effective, the organizer must be understood by the students. This was demonstrated dramatically in a classic study by Dinnel and Glover (1985). They found that instructing students to paraphrase an advance organizer—which, of course, requires them to understand its meaning—increased the effectiveness of the organizer. Second, the organizer must really be an organizer: It must indicate relations among the basic concepts and terms that will be used. Concrete models, diagrams, or analogies seem to be especially good organizers (Robinson, 1998; Robinson & Kiewra, 1995).

ADVANCE ORGANZERS Advance organizers remind students of information they already know that will help them understand the new material or present key concepts they will need. This teacher is helping students bring to mind what they already know about bones in the human body before launching into the lesson.

WHY DOES DIRECT INSTRUCTION WORK?   Well-organized presentations with clear explanations, the use of advance organizers, explanatory links, and reviews can all help students perceive connections among ideas. If done well, therefore, a direct instruction lesson could be a resource that students use to construct understanding. For example, reviews and advance organizers activate prior knowledge, so the student is ready to understand. Brief, clear presentations and guided practice avoid overloading the students' information processing systems and taxing their working memories. Numerous examples and nonexamples that highlight similarities and differences give many pathways and associations for building networks of concepts. Guided practice can also give the teacher a snapshot of the students' thinking as well as their misconceptions, so these can be addressed directly as misconceptions rather than simply as "wrong answers."

Every subject, even college English or chemistry, requires some direct instruction. Noddings (1990) reminds teachers that students may need some direct instruction in how to use various manipulative materials so they can actually learn from (not just play with) the materials. Students working in cooperative groups may need guidance, modeling, and practice in how to ask questions and give explanations. And to solve difficult problems, students may need some direct instruction in possible problem-solving strategies.

Some studies have found that teachers' presentations take up one-sixth to one-fourth of all classroom time. Teacher explanation is appropriate for communicating a large amount of material to many students in a short period of time, introducing a new topic, giving background information, or motivating students to learn more on their own. Teacher presentations are therefore most appropriate for cognitive and affective objectives at the lower levels of the taxonomies described earlier: for remembering, understanding, applying, receiving, responding, and valuing (Arends, 2001; Kindsvatter, Wilen, & Ishler, 1992).

EVALUATING DIRECT INSTRUCTION.   Direct instruction, particularly when it involves extended teacher presentations or lectures, has some disadvantages. You may find that some students have trouble listening for more than a few minutes at a time and that they simply tune you out. Teacher presentations can put the students in a passive position by doing much of the cognitive work for them; this may prevent students from asking

GUIDELINES

Teaching Effectively

Use advance organizers.
Examples
1. English: Shakespeare used the social ideas of his time as a framework for his plays—Julius Caesar, Hamlet, and Macbeth deal with concepts of natural order, a nation as the human body, etc.
2. Social studies: Geography dictates economy in preindustrialized regions or nations.
3. History: Important concepts during the Renaissance were symmetry, admiration of the classical world, the centrality of the human mind.

Use a number of examples.
Examples
1. In mathematics class, ask students to point out all the examples of right angles that they can find in the room.
2. In teaching about islands and peninsulas, use maps, slides, models, postcards.

Organize your lessons carefully.
Examples
1. Provide objectives that help students focus on the purpose of the lesson.
2. Begin lessons by writing a brief outline on the board, or work on an outline with the class as part of the lesson.
3. If possible, break the presentation into clear steps or stages.
4. Review periodically.

Anticipate and plan for difficult parts in the lesson.
Examples
1. Plan a clear introduction to the lesson that tells students what they are going to learn and how they will learn it.
2. Do the exercises and anticipate student problems—consult the teachers' manual for ideas.
3. Have definitions ready for new terms, and prepare several relevant examples for concepts.
4. Think of analogies that will make ideas easier to understand.
5. Organize the lesson in a logical sequence; include checkpoints that incorporate oral or written questions or problems to make sure the students are following the explanations.

Strive for clear explanations.
Examples
1. Avoid vague words and ambiguous phrases: Steer clear of "the *somes*"—*something, someone, sometime, somehow;*

"the *not verys*"—*not very much, not very well, not very hard, not very often;* and other unspecific fillers, such as *most, not all, sort of,* and so on, *of course, as you know, I guess, in fact, or whatever,* and *more or less.*
2. Use specific (and, if possible, colorful) names instead of *it, them,* and *thing.*
3. Refrain from using pet phrases such as *you know, like,* and *Okay?*
4. Record one of your lessons to check yourself for clarity.
5. Give explanations at several levels so all students, not just the brightest, will understand.
6. Focus on one idea at a time and avoid digressions.

Make clear connections by using explanatory links such as *because, if–then,* or *therefore.*
Examples
1. "The North had an advantage in the Civil War because its economy was based on manufacturing."
2. Explanatory links are also helpful in labeling visual material such as graphs, concept maps, or illustrations.

Signal transitions from one major topic to another with phrases.
Examples
1. "The next area," "Now we will turn to," or "The second step is."
2. Outline topics, listing key points, drawing concept maps on the board, or using an overhead projector.

Communicate an enthusiasm for your subject and the day's lesson.
Examples
1. Tell students why the lesson is important. Have a better reason than "This will be on the test" or "You will need to know it next year." Emphasize the value of the learning itself.
2. Be sure to make eye contact with the students.
3. Vary your pace and volume in speaking. Use silence for emphasis.

_____

For more ideas about effective teaching, see
http://www.education.ky.gov/KDE/Instructional+Resources/Highly+Effective+Teaching+and+Learning

---

Scripted cooperation Learning strategy in which two students take turns summarizing material and criticizing the summaries.

or even thinking of questions (Freiberg & Driscoll, 2005). **Scripted cooperation** is one way of incorporating active learning into lectures. Several times during the presentation, the teacher asks students to work in pairs. One person is the summarizer and the other critiques the summary, then they switch roles for the next summary/critique. This gives

TEACHING EVERY STUDENT   419

TABLE 11.5 ● **Active Learning and Teacher Presentations**

Here are some ideas I use for keeping students cognitively engaged in lessons. They can be adapted for many ages.

Write an Answer: Pose a question, ask everyone to write a brief answer, then call on students to share what they wrote.	**Voting:** Pose two alternative explanations; ask how many agree with each (may be a good idea to ask the student to close their eyes and vote so they won't be swayed by the votes of others).
I used to think_____, but now I know_____: After a lesson, ask students to fill in the blanks, then share their results with the person beside them	**Choral Response:** Have the whole class restate in unison important facts and ideas, such as "In a right triangle, $a^2 + b^2 = c^2$"
Think-Pair-Share: Pose a question, students think of an answer on their own, then consult with a neighbor to improve the answer, then volunteers share their ideas.	**One-Minute-Write:** After a section of the lesson, students write for one minute to summarize the key points or raise a question about what is not clear to them.

students a chance to check their understanding, organize their thinking, and translate ideas into their own words. Other possibilities are described in Table 11.5.

Critics also claim that direct instruction is based on the wrong theory of learning. Teachers break material into small segments, present each segment clearly, and reinforce or correct, thus transmitting accurate understandings from teacher to student. The student is viewed as an "empty vessel" waiting to be filled with knowledge, rather than an active constructor of knowledge (Berg & Clough, 1991; Driscoll, 2005). These criticisms of direct instruction echo the criticisms of behavioral learning theories.

There is ample evidence, however, that direct instruction and explanation can help students learn actively, not passively (Leinhardt, 2001). For younger and less prepared learners, student-controlled learning without teacher direction and instruction can lead to systematic deficits in the students' knowledge. Without guidance, the understandings that students construct can be incomplete and misleading (Sweller, Kirschner, & Clark, 2007). For example, Harris and Graham (1996) describe the experiences of their daughter Leah in a whole-language/progressive education school, where the teachers successfully developed their daughter's creativity, thinking, and understanding.

> Skills, on the other hand, have been a problem for our daughter and for other children. At the end of kindergarten, when she had not made much progress in reading, her teacher said she believed Leah had a perceptual problem or a learning disability. Leah began asking what was wrong with her, because other kids were reading and she wasn't. Finally, an assessment was done. (p. 26)

The testing indicated no learning disability, strong comprehension abilities, and poor word attack skills. Luckily, Leah's parents knew how to teach word attack skills. Direct teaching of these skills helped Leah become an avid and able reader in about six weeks. Deep understanding and fluid performance—whether in reading or dance or mathematical problem solving or reading—require models of expert performance and extensive practice with feedback (Anderson, Reder, & Simon, 1995). Guided and independent practice with feedback are at the heart of the direct instruction model. See the *Guidelines* for more ideas about teaching effectively.

Seatwork and Homework

SEATWORK.   The conclusions of the limited research on **seatwork** (independent classroom-desk work) are clear; this technique is often overused. For example, a summary of research from 1975 to 2000 found that students with learning disabilities, who often have trouble improving without teacher guidance, were spending about 40% of their time on individual seatwork (Vaughn, Levy, Coleman, & Bos, 2002).

Seatwork Independent classroom work.

Seatwork should follow up a lesson and give students supervised practice. It should not be the main mode of instruction. Unfortunately, many workbook pages and worksheets do little to support the learning of important objectives. Before you assign work, ask yourself, "Does doing this work help students learn anything that matters?" Students should see the connection between the seatwork and the lesson. Tell them why they are doing the work. The objectives should be clear, all the materials that might be needed should be provided, and the work should be easy enough that students can succeed on their own. Success rates should be high—near 100%. When seatwork is too difficult, students often resort to guessing or copying just to finish.

There are several alternatives to workbooks and worksheets, such as reading silently and reading aloud to a partner; writing for a "real" audience; writing letters or journals; transcribing conversations and punctuating them properly; making up problems; working on long-term projects and reports; solving brainteasers and puzzles; and computer activities (Weinstein, Romano, & Mignano, 2011). One of my favorites is creating a group story. Two students begin a story on the computer. Then two more add a paragraph. The story grows with each new pair's addition. The students are reading and writing, editing and improving. With so many different authors, each writer may spark the creative thinking of other contributors.

Any independent work requires careful monitoring. Being available to students doing seatwork is more effective than offering students help before they ask for it. Short, frequent contacts are best (Brophy & Good, 1986). Sometimes you may be working with a small group while other students do seatwork. In these situations, it is especially important for students to know what to do if they need help. One expert teacher described by Weinstein, Romano, and Mignano (2011) taught students a rule, "Ask three, then me." Students have to consult three classmates before seeking help from the teacher. This teacher also spends time early in the year showing students how to help each other—how to ask questions and how to explain.

STOP & THINK Think back to your elementary and high school days. Do you remember any homework assignments? What sticks in your mind about those assignments? •

HOMEWORK. In contrast to the limited research on seatwork, educators have been studying the effects of homework for over 75 years (Cooper, 2004; Cooper, Robinson, & Patall, 2006; Corno, 2000; Trautwein, 2007).

To benefit from homework, students must understand the assignment. It may help to do the first few questions as a class, to clear up any misconceptions. This is especially important for students who may have no one at home to consult if they have problems with the assignment. A second way to keep students involved is to hold them accountable for completing the work correctly, not just for filling in the page. This means the work should be checked, the students given a chance to correct the errors or revise work, and the results counted toward the class grade. Expert teachers often have ways of correcting homework quickly during the first minutes of class by having students check each other's or their own work. There are other concerns about making homework effective, as you can see in the *Point/Counterpoint*.

If students get stuck on homework, they need help at home, someone who can scaffold their work without just "giving the answer" (Pressley, 1995). But many families don't know how to help (Hoover-Dempsey et al., 2001). The *Family and Community Partnerships Guidelines* on page 422 provide ideas for helping families deal with homework.

Questioning and Discussion

Teachers pose questions, students answer. This form of teaching, sometimes called *recitation,* has been with us for many years (Weinstein et al., 2011). The teacher's questions develop a framework for the subject matter involved. The pattern from the teacher's point of view consists of *initiation* (teacher asks questions), *response* (student answers), and *evaluation/reaction* (praising, correcting, probing, or expanding) or IRE (Burbules & Bruce, 2001). These steps are repeated over and over.

Connect and Extend to PRAXIS II™

Questioning (III, C)
Effective questioning skills are among the most valuable skills that a teacher can possess—and among the more difficult to develop. For guidance on asking effective questions in the classroom, read *Question Types* (http://www.unl .edu/teaching/teachquestions.html).

POINT/COUNTERPOINT: Is Homework a Valuable Use of Time?

Like so many methods in education, homework has moved in and out of favor. In the early 1900s, homework was seen as an important path to mental discipline, but by the 1940s, homework was criticized as too much drill and low-level learning. Then, in the 1950s, homework was rediscovered as a way to catch up with the Soviet Union in science and mathematics, only to be seen as putting too much pressure on students during the more laid-back 1960s. By the 1980s, homework was in again as a way to improve the standing of American children compared to students around the world (Cooper & Valentine, 2001). Today, homework is increasing in early elementary schools (Hofferth & Sandberg, 2000). Everyone has done homework—were those hours well spent?

POINT

▶ **Homework does not help students learn.** No matter how interesting an activity is, students will eventually get bored with it—so why give them work both in and out of school? They will simply grow weary of learning. And important opportunities are lost for community involvement or leisure activities that would create well-rounded citizens. When parents help with homework, they can do more harm than good—sometimes confusing their children or teaching them incorrectly. And students from poorer families often must work, so they miss doing the homework; then the learning discrepancy between the rich and poor grows even greater. Besides, the research is inconsistent about the effects of homework. For example, one study found that in-class work was better than homework in helping elementary students learn (Cooper & Valentine, 2001). In his book, *The Homework Myth: Why Our Kids Get Too Much of a Bad Thing*, Alfie Kohn (2006) suggests the schools adopt no homework as the default policy. "Changing the default to no homework would likely have two practical consequences: The number of assignments would decline and the quality of those assignments would rise. Both of these, I believe, represent significant improvements in our children's education" (p. 168).

Harris Cooper and his colleagues reviewed many studies of homework and concluded that there is little relationship between homework and learning for young students, but the relationship between homework and achievement grows progressively stronger for older students. Most of the studies involved math and reading or English homework, however, not social studies, science, or other subjects.

COUNTERPOINT

▶ **Well-planned homework can work for many students.** There is recent evidence that students in high school who do more homework (and watch less television after school) have higher grades, even when other factors such as gender, grade level, ethnicity, SES, and amount of adult supervision are taken into consideration (Cooper, Robinson, & Patall, 2006; Cooper & Valentine, 2001; Cooper, Valentine, Nye, & Kindsay, 1999). Consistent with all these findings, the National PTA makes these recommendations:

> [F]or children in grades K–2, homework is most effective when it does not exceed 10–20 minutes each day; older students, in grades 3–6, can handle 30–60 minutes a day; in junior and senior high school, the amount of homework will vary by subject. (Henderson, 1996, p. 1)

Most research examines the relationship between amount of time spent on homework (as reported by students or parents) and achievement in terms of grades or achievement tests. Another approach is to focus on effort instead of time. Students' self-reported effort on homework is consistently and positively related to student achievement (Trautwein, Schnyder, Niggli, Neuman, & Lüdtke, 2009). "High homework effort means that a student does his or her best to solve the tasks assigned. There need not be a close relationship between effort and time on homework: A student putting as much effort as possible into a homework assignment might finish in 5 min or still be working after an hour" (Trautwein & Lüdtke, 2007, p. 432). Students are more likely to put in effort if they see the homework as interesting, valuable, reasonably challenging, and not anxiety provoking—this could require some differentiated homework assignments (Dettmers, Trautwein, Ludtke, Kunter, & Baumert, 2010). So the challenge is to get students to put their best efforts into appropriate homework and not assign homework that is low quality.

Let us consider the heart of recitation, the soliciting or questioning phase. Effective questioning techniques may be among the most powerful tools that teachers employ during lessons. An essential element of contemporary learning techniques is keeping students cognitively engaged—and that is where skillful questioning strategies are especially effective. Questions play several roles in cognition. They can help students rehearse information for effective recall. They can work to identify gaps in students' knowledge base, and provoke curiosity and long-term interest. They can initiate cognitive conflict and promote the disequilibrium that results in a changed knowledge structure. They can serve as cues, tips, or reminders as an expert guides a novice in a learning experience. And students as well as teachers should learn to question effectively. I tell my students that the first step in doing a good research project is asking a good question.

GUIDELINES — FAMILY AND COMMUNITY PARTNERSHIPS

Homework

Make sure families know what students are expected to learn.
Examples

1. At the beginning of a unit, send home a list of the main objectives, examples of major assignments, key due dates, a homework "calendar," and a list of free resources available at libraries or on the Internet.

2. Provide a clear, concise description of your homework policy—how homework is counted toward class grades; consequences for late, forgotten, or missing homework, etc.

Help families find a comfortable and helpful role in their child's homework.
Examples

1. Remind families that "helping with homework" means encouraging, listening, monitoring, praising, discussing, brainstorming—not necessarily teaching and never doing the work for their child.

2. Encourage families to set aside a quiet time and place for everyone in the family to study. Make this time a regular part of the daily routine.

3. Have some homework assignments that are fun and involve the whole family—puzzles, family albums, watching a television program together and doing a "review."

4. In conferences, ask families how you could help them to support their child in completing and learning from homework. Check lists? Background reading? Web sites? Explanations of study skills?

Solicit and use suggestions from families about homework.
Examples

1. Find out what responsibilities the child has at home—how much time is available for homework.

2. Periodically, have a "homework hotline" for call-in questions and suggestions.

If no one is at home to help with homework, set up other support systems.
Examples

1. Assign study buddies who can be available over the phone.

2. If students have computers, provide lists of Internet help lines.

3. Locate free help in public libraries and make these resources known.

Take advantage of family and community "funds of knowledge" to connect homework with life in the community and life in the community with lessons in school (Moll et al., 1992).
Examples

1. Create a class lesson about how family members use math and reading in sewing and in housing construction (Epstein & Van Voorhis, 2001).

2. Design interactive homework projects that families do together to evaluate needed products for their home, for example, deciding on the best buy on shampoo or paper towels.

———————

For more ideas, see
http://www.slideshare.net/stanfreeda/unit-7-homework-strategies-parental-involvement-notes

---

For now, we will focus on teachers' questions. Many of the beginning teachers I work with are surprised to discover how valuable good questions can be and how difficult they are to create.

STOP & THINK Think back to your most recent class. What kinds of questions does your professor ask? What sort of thinking is required to answer the questions? Remembering, understanding, applying, analyzing, evaluating, or creating? How long does the professor wait for an answer? •

KINDS OF QUESTIONS. Some educators have estimated the typical teacher asks between 30 and 120 questions an hour, or about 1,500,000 questions over a teaching career (Sadker & Sadker, 2006). What are these questions like? Many can be categorized in terms of Bloom's taxonomy of objectives in the cognitive domain. Table 11.6 offers examples of questions at the different taxonomic levels.

TABLE 11.6 • **Classroom Questions for Objectives in the Cognitive Domain**

Questions can be posed that encourage thinking at every level of Bloom's taxonomy in the cognitive domain. Of course, the thinking required depends on what has gone before in the discussion.

CATEGORY	TYPE OF THINKING EXPECTED	EXAMPLES
Knowledge (Remembering)	Recalling or recognizing information as learned	Define. . . . What is the capital of . . . ? What did the text say about . . . ?
Comprehension (Understanding)	Demonstrating understanding of the materials; transforming, reorganizing, or interpreting	Explain in your own words. . . . Compare. . . What is the main idea of . . . ? Describe what you saw. . . .
Application (Applying)	Using information to solve a problem with a single correct answer	Which principle is demonstrated in . . . ? Calculate the area of. . . . Apply the rule of . . . to solve. . . .
Analysis (Analyzing)	Critical thinking; identifying reasons and motives; making inferences based on specific data; analyzing conclusions to see if supported by evidence	What influenced the writings of . . . ? Why was Washington, D.C. chosen . . . ? Which of the following are facts and which are opinions . . . ? Based on your experiment, what is the chemical . . . ?
Synthesis (Creating)	Divergent, original thinking; original plan, proposal, design, or story	What's a good name for . . . ? How could we raise money for . . . ? What would the United States be like if the South had won . . . ?
Evaluation (Evaluating)	Judging the merits of ideas, offering opinions, applying standards	Which U.S. senator is the most effective? Which painting do you believe to be better? Why? Why would you favor . . . ?

Source: Based on "Questioning Skills" by M. Sadker and D. Sadker, in J. Cooper (Ed.), CLASSROOM TEACHING SKILLS: A HANDBOOK (3rd ed.) (pp. 143–160), 1986, Boston, D. C. Heath.

Another way to categorize questioning is in terms of **convergent questions** (only one right answer) or **divergent questions** (many possible answers). Questions about concrete facts are convergent: "Who ruled England in 1540?" "Who wrote the original Peter Pan?" Questions dealing with opinions or hypotheses are divergent: "In this story, which character is most like you and why?" "In 100 years, which of the past five presidents will be most admired?"

FITTING THE QUESTIONS TO THE STUDENTS. All kinds of questions can be effective (Barden, 1995). Different patterns seem to be better for certain types of students, however. The best pattern for younger students and for lower-ability students of all ages is simple questions that allow a high percentage of correct answers, ample encouragement, help when the student does not have the correct answer, and praise. For high-ability students, the successful pattern includes harder questions at both higher and lower levels and more critical feedback (Berliner, 1987; Good, 1988).

Convergent questions Questions that have a single correct answer.

Divergent questions Questions that have no single correct answer.

Whatever their age or ability, all students should have some experience with thought-provoking questions and, if necessary, help in learning how to answer them. To master critical thinking and problem-solving skills, students must have a chance to practice those skills. They also need time to think about their answers. But classic research shows that teachers wait an average of only one second for students to answer (Rowe, 1974). When teachers learn to pose a question, then wait at least 3 to 5 seconds before calling on a student to answer, students tend to give longer answers; more students are likely to participate, ask questions, and volunteer appropriate answers; student comments involving analysis, synthesis, inference, and speculation tend to increase; and the students generally appear more confident in their answers (Berliner, 1987; Sadker & Sadker, 2006).

This seems like a simple improvement in teaching, but 5 seconds of silence is not that easy to handle. It takes practice. You might try asking students to jot down ideas or even discuss the question with another student and formulate an answer together. This makes the wait more comfortable and gives students a chance to think. Of course, if it is clear that students are lost or don't understand the question, waiting longer will not help. When your question is met with blank stares, rephrase the question or ask if anyone can clarify it. However, there is some evidence that extending wait times does not affect learning in university classes (Duell, 1994), so with advanced high-school students, you might conduct your own evaluation of wait time.

A word about selecting students to answer questions. If you call only on volunteers, then you may get the wrong idea about how well students understand the material. Also, the same people volunteer over and over again. Many expert teachers have some systematic way of making sure that they call on everyone: They pull names from a jar or check names off a list as each student speaks (Weinstein & Novodvorsky, 2011; Weinstein, Romano, & Mignano, 2011). Another possibility is to put each student's name on an index card, then shuffle the cards and go through the deck as you call on people. You can use the card to make notes about the quality of students' answers or any extra help they seem to need.

RESPONDING TO STUDENT ANSWERS. What do you do after the student answers? The most common response, occurring about 50% of the time in most classrooms, is simple acceptance—"OK" or "Uh-huh" (Sadker & Sadker, 2006). But there are better reactions, depending on whether the student's answer is correct, partially correct, or wrong. If the answer is quick, firm, and correct, simply accept the answer or ask another question. If the answer is correct but hesitant, give the student feedback about why the answer is correct: "That's right, Chris, the Senate is part of the legislative branch of government because the Senate. . . ." This allows you to explain the material again. If this student is unsure, others may be confused as well. If the answer is partially or completely wrong but the student has made an honest attempt, you should probe for more information, give clues, simplify the question, review the previous steps, or reteach the material. If the student's wrong answer is silly or careless, however, it is better simply to correct the answer and go on (Good, 1988; Rosenshine & Stevens, 1986).

John Hattie and Helen Timperley (2007) reviewed several decades of research on feedback and constructed a model to guide teachers. The model proposes three feedback questions: "Where am I going?" "How am I going?" and "Where to next?" The first question is about goals and goal clarity. The second is about progress—movement toward goals. The third question is about moving forward to improve understandings when goals are not met yet or to build on attained goals. The Hattie and Timperley model also considers the focus of the feedback on four levels: task, process, self-regulation, and self-feedback. Here are some examples (p. 90):

Task Feedback: "You need to include more about the Treaty of Versailles."
Process Feedback: "This page may make more sense if you use the strategies we talked about earlier."
Self-Regulation Feedback: "You already know the key features of the opening of an argument. Check to see whether you have incorporated them in your first paragraph."
Self-Feedback: "You are a great student." "That's an intelligent response, well done."

Hattie and Timperley argue that feedback about *process* and *self-regulation* is the most powerful because it helps students move toward deep understanding, mastery, and self-direction in learning. Feedback about self (usually praise) is common in classes, but is not effective unless the praise provides information about how effort, persistence, or self-regulation moved the student forward, as in "You are terrific—you stuck with this, revised again, and now this essay makes a powerful argument."

GROUP DISCUSSION. Group discussion is in some ways similar to the recitation strategy. A teacher may pose questions, listen to student answers, react, and probe for more information, but in a true group dialogue, the teacher does not have a

GROUP DISCUSSIONS Small group discussions allow greater student participation and exchange of ideas, but students may need help in staying focused.

dominant role. Students ask questions, answer each other's questions, and respond to each other's answers (Beck, McKeown, Worthy, Sandora, & Kucan, 1996; Burbules & Bruce, 2001; Parker & Hess, 2001).

There are many advantages to group discussions. The students are directly involved and have the chance to participate. They learn to express themselves clearly, to justify opinions, and to tolerate different views. Group discussion also gives students a chance to ask for clarification, examine their own thinking, follow personal interests, and assume responsibility by taking leadership roles in the group. Thus, group discussions help students evaluate ideas and synthesize personal viewpoints. Discussions are also useful when students are trying to understand difficult concepts that go against common sense. By thinking together, challenging each other, and suggesting and evaluating possible explanations, students are more likely to reach a genuine understanding.

Of course, there are disadvantages. Class discussions are quite unpredictable and may easily digress into exchanges of ignorance. You may have to do a good deal of preparation to ensure that participants have enough background knowledge for the discussion. Some members of the group may have great difficulty participating and may become anxious if forced to speak. And large groups are often unwieldy. In many cases, a few students will dominate the discussion while the others daydream (Arends, 2004; Freiberg & Driscoll, 2005).

Are discussions effective learning tools? In a major review of research conducted from 1964 to 2003 on the value of discussing texts for improving student comprehension, Karen Murphy and her colleagues (2009) reached some surprising conclusions. They examined a wide range of discussion formats including Instructional Conversations, Junior Great Books Shared Inquiry, Questioning the Author, Literature Circles, Book Club, and Grand Conversation—to name just a few. They found many of these approaches were very successful in increasing student talk, limiting teacher talk, and promoting students' literal interpretations of the texts they discussed. But getting students to talk more did not necessarily promote their critical thinking, reasoning, or argumentation skills. Also, discussion was more effective for students whose comprehension abilities are below average, perhaps because average and higher-ability students already have the skills to comprehend texts. A few discussion structures, such as Junior Great Books Shared Inquiry, used over a longer period of time seemed to support both comprehension of text and critical thinking. The researchers concluded, "Simply putting students into groups and encouraging them to talk is not enough to enhance comprehension and learning; it is but a step in the process" (p. 760). The *Guidelines* give some ideas for facilitating a productive group discussion.

Group discussion Conversation in which the teacher does not have the dominant role; students pose and answer their own questions.

GUIDELINES

Productive Group Discussions

Invite shy children to participate.
Examples
1. "What's your opinion, Joel?" or "Does anyone have another opinion?"
2. Don't wait until there is a deadly silence to ask shy students to reply. Most people, even those who are confident, hate to break a silence.

Direct student comments and questions back to another student.
Examples
1. "That's an unusual idea, Steve. Kim, what do you think of Steve's idea?"
2. "That's an important question, John. Maura, do you have any thoughts about how you'd answer that?"
3. Encourage students to look at and talk to one another rather than wait for your opinion.

Make sure that you understand what a student has said. If you are unsure, other students may be unsure as well.
Examples
1. Ask a second student to summarize what the first student said; then, the first student can try again to explain if the summary is incorrect.
2. "Karen, I think you're saying . . . Is that right, or have I misunderstood?"

Probe for more information.
Examples
1. "That's a strong statement. Do you have any evidence to back it up?"

2. "Did you consider any other alternatives?"
3. "Tell us how you reached that conclusion. What steps did you go through?"

Bring the discussion back to the subject.
Examples
1. "Let's see, we were discussing . . . and Sarah made one suggestion. Does anyone have a different idea?"
2. "Before we continue, let me try to summarize what has happened thus far."

Give time for thought before asking for responses.
Example
1. "How would your life be different if television had never been invented? Jot down your ideas on paper, and we will share reactions in a minute." After a minute: "Hiromi, will you tell us what you wrote?"

When a student finishes speaking, look around the room to judge reactions.
Examples
1. If other students look puzzled, ask them to describe why they are confused.
2. If students are nodding assent, ask them to give an example of what was just said.

For more ideas, see
http://www.podnetwork.org/publications/teachingexcellence/09-10/V21_N1_Takayama.pdf or http://www.extension.umn.edu/distribution/citizenship/components/00018e.html

Fitting Teaching to Your Goals

In the midst of all our discussions about methods, we have to keep in mind that the first questions should be: What should students learn? and What is worth knowing today? Then, we can match methods to goals. Deanna Kuhn (2007) said it well:

> As for direct instruction, of course it has a place. Each young student does not need to reinvent knowledge from the ground up. The challenge is to formulate what we want direct instruction to be. In doing so, it is well to keep in mind that it is students who construct meaning from such instruction and decide what it is that they will learn. (p. 112)

There is no one best way to teach. Different goals and student needs require different teaching methods. Direct instruction often leads to better performance on achievement tests, whereas the open, informal methods such as discovery learning or inquiry approaches are associated with better performance on tests of creativity, abstract thinking, and problem solving. In addition, the open methods are better for improving attitudes toward school and for stimulating curiosity, cooperation among students, and lower absence rates (Borich, 2011; Walberg, 1990). According to these conclusions, when the goals of teaching involve problem solving, creativity, understanding, and mastering processes, many approaches besides direct instruction should be effective. These guidelines are in keeping with Tom Good's conclusion that teaching should become less direct as students mature and when the goals involve affective development and problem solving or critical thinking (Good, 1983a). Every student may require direct, explicit teaching for some learning goals some of the time, but all students also need to experience more open, constructivist, student-centered teaching as well. So far, we have talked about approaches to teaching—general strategies. But in today's diverse classrooms, one size does not fit all. Within the general approach, teachers have to fit their instruction to the needs and abilities of their students—they have to differentiate instruction.

DIFFERENTIATED INSTRUCTION

Actually, the idea of adapting teaching to the abilities and needs of the learner is an ancient one. To prove it, Lyn Corno (2008, p. 161) quotes these words of Quintilian from the 5th century BC:

> Some students are slack and need to be encouraged; others work better when given a freer rein. Some respond best when there is some threat or fear; others are paralyzed by it. Some apply themselves to the task over time, and learn best; others learn best by concentration and focus in a single burst of energy. (Quintilian, trans. 1921)

Obviously Quintilian appreciated the need for fitting instruction to the student. One way to do this when teachers have many students is to use appropriate groupings.

Within-Class and Flexible Grouping

It is not unusual to have 3- to 5-year ability differences in any given classroom (Castle, Deniz, & Tortora, 2005). But even if you decided to simply forge ahead (against Quintilian's advice) and teach the same material in the same way to your entire class, you would not be alone. Differences in students' prior knowledge are a major challenge for teachers, especially in subjects that build on previous knowledge and skills such as math and science (Loveless, 1998). One answer has been ability grouping, but that also poses a number of problems.

THE PROBLEMS WITH ABILITY GROUPING. Students in many classes and schools are grouped by ability, even though there is no clear evidence that this **within-class ability grouping** is superior to other approaches. In a random sample of primary grade teachers in the United States, 63% reported using within-class ability groups for reading. Students in lower-ability groups were less likely to be asked critical comprehension questions and were given fewer opportunities to make choices about what to read (Chorzempa & Graham, 2006). For schools with lower-SES students, grouping often means that these students are segregated into lower-ability tracks. According to Paul George (2005):

> In my 3 decades of experience with this issue, when homogenous grouping is the primary strategy for organizing students in schools with significant racial and ethnic diversity in the population, the result is almost always deep, and often starkly obvious, division of students on the basis of race, ethnicity, and social class. (p. 187)

Thoughtfully constructed and well-taught ability groups in math and reading can be effective, but the point of any grouping strategy should be to provide appropriate challenge and support—that is, to reach children within their "zone of proximal development" (Vygotsky, 1997). Flexible grouping is one possible answer.

FLEXIBLE GROUPING. In **flexible grouping**, students are grouped and regrouped based on their learning needs. Assessment is continuous so that students are always working within their zone of proximal development. Arrangements might include small groups, partners, individuals, and even the whole class—depending on which grouping best supports each student's learning of the particular academic content. Flexible grouping approaches include high-level instruction and high expectations for all students, regardless of their group placement (Corno, 2008). One 5-year longitudinal study of flexible grouping in a high-needs urban elementary school found 10% to 57% increases in students who reached mastery level, depending on the subject area and grade level. Teachers received training and support in the assessment, grouping, and teaching strategies needed, and by

Differentiated instruction A flexible approach to teaching that matches content, process, and product based on student differences in readiness, interests, and learning needs.

Within-class ability grouping System of grouping in which students in a class are divided into two or three groups based on ability in an attempt to accommodate student differences.

Flexible grouping Grouping and regrouping students based on learning needs.

GUIDELINES

Using Flexible Grouping

Form and re-form groups based on accurate diagnosis of students' current performance in the subject being taught.
Examples

1. Use scores on the most recent reading assessments to establish reading groups, and rely on current math performance to form math groups.
2. Assess continuously. Change group placement frequently when students' achievement changes.

Make sure different groups get appropriately different instruction, not just the same material. Make sure teachers, methods, and pace are adjusted to fit the needs of the group.
Examples

1. Vary more than pace; fit teaching to students' interests and knowledge.
2. Assign all groups research reports, but have some be written, and others oral or PowerPoint presentations.
3. Organize and teach groups so that low-achieving students get appropriate extra instruction—not just the same material again. Make lower achieving groups smaller so students get extra attention.
4. Make sure all work is meaningful and respectful—no worksheets for lower ability groups while the higher ability groups do experiments and projects.
5. Try alternatives. For example, DeWayne Mason and Tom Good (1993) found that supplementing whole-class instruction in math with remediation and enrichment for students when they needed it worked better than dividing the class into two ability groups and teaching these groups separately.

Discourage comparisons between groups and encourage students to develop a whole-class spirit.
Examples

1. Don't seat groups together outside the context of their reading or math group.
2. Avoid naming ability groups—save the names for mixed-ability or whole-class teams.

Group by ability for one, or, at the most, two subjects.
Examples

1. Make sure there are many lessons and projects that mix members from the groups.
2. Experiment with learning strategies in which cooperation is stressed (described in Chapter 7).
3. Keep the number of groups small (two or three at most) so that you can provide as much direct teaching as possible—leaving students alone for too long leads to less learning.

For more information about classroom grouping, see these two sites: http://www.eduplace.com/science/profdev/articles/valentino.html

---

the end of the study, 95% of the teachers were using flexible grouping. The teachers in the study believed that some of the gains came because students were more focused on learning and more confident (Castle et al., 2005).

Another way to use flexible grouping is in a nongraded elementary school. Students of several ages (for example, 6, 7, and 8) are together in one class, but they are flexibly grouped within the class for instruction based on achievement, motivation, or interest in different subjects. This cross-grade grouping seems to be effective for students of all abilities as long as the grouping allows teachers to give more direct instruction to the groups. But be sensible about cross-age grouping. Mixing 3rd, 4th, and 5th graders for math or reading class based on what they are ready to learn makes sense. However, sending a large 4th grader to the 2nd grade, where he is the only older student and stands out like a sore thumb, isn't likely to work well. Also, when cross-age classes are created just because there are too few students for one grade—and not in order to better meet the students' learning needs—the results are not positive (Veenman, 1997). As we have seen repeatedly throughout this text, working at a challenging level, but one you can master with effort and support, is more likely to encourage learning and motivation.

If you ever decide to use flexible grouping in your class, the *Guidelines* should make the approach more effective (Arends, 2007; Good & Brophy, 2008).

Adaptive teaching Provides all students with challenging instruction and uses supports when needed, but removes these supports as students become able to handle more on their own.

Adaptive Teaching

Lyn Corno (2008) has developed a model of **adaptive teaching** that also addresses learner differences. In this approach, teachers see "learner variation as an opportunity for learning from teaching rather than as obstacles to be overcome" (p. 171). Adaptive teaching provides all students with challenging instruction and uses supports when needed, but removes those supports as students become able to handle more on their own. Figure 11.1 shows the continuum of support and type of instruction that matches students' needs. As shown on the far left of the figure, when students are novices in an area or have little prior knowledge and skills, the teaching is more direct and includes well-designed motivational strategies to keep them engaged. At the same time, students are taught how to apply appropriate cognitive strategies, to give them the "skills" to learn. There are short cycles of teaching, checking for understanding, and reteaching. As students develop aptitudes in the subject, teaching moves to modeling, guided practice, and coaching. By this time, students should have improved their cognitive "skills" strategies, so teaching can also focus on motivational and volitional strategies—the "will" to learn. Finally as students gain more knowledge and skills, teaching can move to guided discovery, independent study, and peer tutoring, with an emphasis on self-regulated learning—the kind of learning the students will need for the rest of their lives.

Adaptive teaching makes sure that everyone is challenged. For example, one teacher at a magnet school described how he "iced" his curriculum with some content "just beyond the reach" of even his most advanced students. He wanted to be sure all his students found some assignments difficult. He believed "everyone needs to stretch in my class" (Corno, 2008, p. 165).

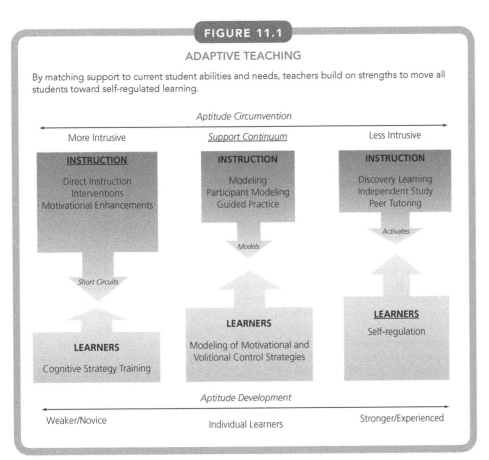

FIGURE 11.1

ADAPTIVE TEACHING

By matching support to current student abilities and needs, teachers build on strengths to move all students toward self-regulated learning.

Aptitude Circumvention

More Intrusive   *Support Continuum*   Less Intrusive

INSTRUCTION
Direct Instruction
Interventions
Motivational Enhancements

INSTRUCTION
Modeling
Participant Modeling
Guided Practice

INSTRUCTION
Discovery Learning
Independent Study
Peer Tutoring

Activates

Models

Short Circuits

LEARNERS
Self-regulation

LEARNERS
Modeling of Motivational and
Volitional Control Strategies

LEARNERS
Cognitive Strategy Training

Aptitude Development

Weaker/Novice   Individual Learners   Stronger/Experienced

Source: Based on Corno, L. (2008). On teaching adaptively. Educational Psychologist, 43(3), 161–173; and Randi, J., & Corno, L., Teaching and learner variation, in Pedagogy—Learning from Teaching, British Journal of Educational Psychology, Monograph Series II(3), pp. 47–69.

Reaching Every Student: Differentiated Instruction in Inclusive Classrooms

STOP & THINK When you think about teaching in an inclusive classroom, what are your concerns? Do you have enough training? Will you get the support you need from school administrators or specialists? Will working with the students with disabilities take time away from your other responsibilities? •

These questions are common ones, and sometimes such concerns are justified. But effective teaching for students with disabilities does not require a unique set of skills. It is a combination of good teaching practices and sensitivity to all your students. Students with disabilities need to learn the academic material, and they need to be full participants in the day-to-day life of the classroom.

To accomplish the first goal of academic learning, students with learning disabilities appear to benefit from using extended practice distributed over days and weeks and from advanced organizers such as focusing students on what they already know or stating clear objectives (Swanson, 2001).

To accomplish the second goal of integrating students with disabilities into the day-to-day life of the classroom, Marilyn Friend and William Bursuck (2002) recommend the INCLUDE strategy:

Identify the environmental, curricular, and instructional demands of your classroom.
Note students' learning strengths and needs.
Check for potential areas of student success.
Look for potential problem areas.
Use information gathered to brainstorm instructional adaptations.
Decide which adaptations to try.
Evaluate student progress.

Table 11.7 shows how the INCLUDE strategy might be applied to students with learning and behavioral disabilities.

When students have special needs, they may be referred for evaluation to child study teams, school psychologists, or teachers of students with special needs. (See Table 4.12 on page 162 for guidelines about referring students for evaluation.) The outcome of this process sometimes includes the preparation of an individualized education program or IEP, as described in Chapter 4. Figure 11.2 on page 432 is an excerpt from the IEP of a boy who had difficulty managing anger and complying with teacher requests. You may help to develop these programs for students in your classes. Well-designed programs should provide guidance for you in your planning and teaching.

Technology and Differentiation

IDEA requires that all students eligible for special education services must be considered for assistive technology. **Assistive technology** is any product, piece of equipment, or system that is used to increase, maintain, or improve the functional capabilities of individuals with disabilities (Goldman, Lawless, Pellegrino, & Plants, 2006). For students who require small steps and many repetitions to learn a new concept, computers are the perfect patient tutors, repeating steps and lessons as many times as necessary. A well-designed computer instructional program is engaging and interactive—two important qualities for students who have problems paying attention or a history of failure that has eroded motivation. For example, a math or spelling program might use images, sounds, and gamelike features to maintain the attention of a student with an attention-deficit disorder. Interactive digital media programs teach hearing people how to use sign language. Many programs do not involve sound, so students with hearing impairments can get the full benefit from the lessons. Students who have trouble reading can use programs that will "speak" a word for them if they touch the unknown word. With this immediate access to help, the students are much more likely to get the reading practice they need to prevent falling farther and farther behind. Other devices actually convert printed pages and typed texts to spoken words for students who are blind or others who benefit from hearing

Assistive technology Devices, systems, and services that support and improve the capabilities of individuals with disabilities.

TABLE 11.7 • **Making Adaptations for Students with Learning and Behavior Disabilities Using Steps in the INCLUDE Strategy**

IDENTIFY CLASSROOM DEMANDS	NOTE STUDENT STRENGTHS AND NEEDS	CHECK FOR POTENTIAL SUCCESSES/LOOK FOR POTENTIAL PROBLEMS	DECIDE ON ADAPTATIONS
Student desks in clusters of four	*Strengths* Good vocabulary skills *Needs* Difficulty attending to task	*Success* Student understands instruction if on task *Problem* Student off task—does not face instructor as she teaches	Change seating so student faces instructor
Small-group work with peers	*Strengths* Good handwriting *Needs* Oral expressive language—problem with word finding	*Success* Student acts as secretary for cooperative group *Problem* Student has difficulty expressing self in peer learning groups	Assign as secretary of group Place into compatible small group Develop social skills instruction for all students
Expect students to attend class and be on time	*Strengths* Good drawing skills *Needs* Poor time management	*Success* Student uses artistic talent in class *Problem* Student is late for class and frequently does not attend at all	Use individualized student contract for attendance and punctuality—if goals met, give student artistic responsibility in class
Textbook difficult to read	*Strengths* Good oral communication skills *Needs* Poor reading accuracy Lacks systematic strategy for reading text	*Success* Student participates well in class Good candidate for class dramatizations *Problem* Student is unable to read text for information	Provide taped textbooks Highlight student text
Lecture on women's suffrage movement to whole class	*Strengths* Very motivated and interested in class *Needs* Lack of background knowledge	*Success* Student earns points for class attendance and effort *Problem* Student lacks background knowledge to understand important information in lecture	Give student video to view before lecture Build points for attendance and working hard into grading system
Whole-class instruction on telling time to the quarter hour	*Strengths* Good coloring skills *Needs* Cannot identify numbers 7–12 Cannot count by fives	*Success* Student is able to color clock faces used in instruction *Problem* Student is unable to acquire telling time skills	Provide extra instruction on number identification and counting by fives

Source: From Including Students with Special Needs: A Practical Guide for Classroom Teachers, 3/e by Marilyn Friend & William D. Bursuck. Published by Allyn and Bacon, Boston, MA. Copyright © 2002 by Pearson Education. Adapted by permission of the publisher.

information. For the student with a learning disability whose writing can't be read, word processors produce perfect penmanship so the ideas can finally get on paper. Once the ideas are recorded, the student can reorganize and improve his or her writing without the agony of rewriting by hand (Hallahan, Kauffman, & Pullen, 2009).

With these tremendous advances in technology have come new barriers, however. Many computers have graphic interfaces. Manipulating the programs requires precise "mouse movements," as you may remember when you first learned to point and click. These maneuvers are often difficult for students with motor problems or visual impairments. And

---

FIGURE 11.2

AN EXCERPT FROM AN IEP—INDIVIDUALIZED EDUCATION PROGRAM

This IEP was developed for a 15-year-old boy to help him manage anger and comply with teacher requests.

Student: __Curt__   Age: __15__   Grade: __9__   Date: __10/12/94__

Unique Characteristics/ Needs	Special Education, Related Services, Modifications	(begin duration)	Present Levels, Objectives, Annual Goals (Objectives to include procedure, criteria, schedule)
Social Needs: ■ To learn anger management skills, especially regarding swearing ■ To learn to comply with requests Present Level: Lashes out violently when not able to complete work, uses profane language, and refuses to follow further directions from adults	1. Teacher and/or counselor consult with behavior specialists regarding techniques and programs for teaching social skills, especially anger management. 2. Provide anger management training for Curt. 3. Establish a peer group which involves role playing, etc. so Curt can see positive role models and practice newly learned anger management skills. 4. Develop a behavior plan for Curt which gives him responsibility for charting his own behavior. 5. Provide a teacher or some other adult mentor to spend time with Curt (could be talking; game play, physical activity). 6. Provide training for the mentor regarding Curt's needs/goals.	30 min., 3 x week 30 min., 2 x week 30 min., 2 x week	Goal: During the last quarter of the academic year, Curt will have 2 or fewer detentions for any reason. Objective 1: At the end of the 1st quarter, Curt will have had 10 or fewer detentions. Objective 2: At the end of 2nd quarter, Curt will have had 7 or fewer detentions. Objective 3: At the end of 3rd quarter, Curt will have had 4 or fewer detentions. Goal: Curt will manage his behavior and language in a reasonably acceptable manner as reported by faculty/peers. Objective 1: At 2 weeks, asked at end of class if Curt's behavior language was acceptable or not, 3 out of 5 teachers will say "acceptable." Objective 2: At 6 weeks, asked same question, 4 out of 6 teachers will say "acceptable." Objective 3: At 12 weeks. 6 out of 6 will say "acceptable."

Adaptations to regular program:

■ In all classes, Curt should be near front of class
■ Curt should be called on often to keep him involved and on task
■ All teachers should help Curt with study skills as trained by spelling/language specialist and resource room teacher
■ Teachers should monitor Curt's work closely in the beginning weeks/months of his program

Source: From Better IEPs, 4th ed. (p. 127) by Barbara D. Bateman. Copyright 1996, 2006 by Barbara D. Bateman. Reprinted by permission of the author and Attainment Company, Inc.

---

the information available on the Internet often is unusable for students with visual problems. Researchers are working on the problem—trying to devise ways for people to access the information nonvisually (Hallahan, Kauffman, & Pullen, 2009). For example, in 2010 the learning management system called *Canvas* was awarded the national Federation of the Blind—Nonvisual Accessibility Gold Level Certification because the system is equally accessible to blind and sighted users (NFB, 2010). One current trend is **universal design**—considering the needs of all users in the design of new tools, learning programs, or Web sites (Pisha & Coyne, 2001).

For gifted students, computers can be a connection with databases and computers in universities, museums, and research labs. Computer networks allow students to work on projects and share information with others across the country. It is also possible to have

Universal design Considering the needs of all users in the design of new tools, learning programs, or Web sites.

GUIDELINES

Teachers as Mentors

Beware of stereotypes in your thinking and teaching.
Examples

1. See every student as an individual and communicate that clearly to the student.
2. Analyze curriculum materials for biases and teach students to become bias detectors.

Take advantage of technology.
Examples

1. Use a Web program like *Eyes to the Future,* which link middle school girls with high school girls in their districts who have stayed interested in math and science as well as women who use science, math, and technology in their careers. The purpose is to help middle school girls see how their work at school relates to "real life." (http://etf.terc.edu/)
2. Establish "email pals" for students, with retired adults or successful former students as their mentors.
3. Download resources from NWREL's National Mentoring Center, especially their school-based mentoring and tutoring materials (http://www.nwrel.org/mentoring/topic_pubs. php#5).

Let students know you believe in them.
Examples

1. Set standards high and give critical feedback, but also provide support and encouragement.
2. Showcase accomplishments of former students.

Take the time to establish and maintain relationships.
Examples

1. Don't expect trust right away; you may have to earn it.
2. Stay in touch with students and keep the door open to provide guidance in the future.
3. Spend some time with students outside academics—before or after school, as part of clubs or extracurricular activities. Have some fun together. Find common interests.

If you set up a more formal mentoring system, be sure participants are trained and monitored.
Examples

1. Use materials from national mentor groups for training, for example, Elements of Effective Practice from MENTOR/ National Mentoring Partnership (http://www.mentoring.org/ start_a_program/planning_and_design/).
2. Have regular times to provide ongoing training and to deal with problems that may arise.

gifted students write programs for students and teachers. Quite a few principals around the country rely on their students to keep the technology networks in their schools working smoothly. These are just a few examples of what technology can do. Check with the resource teachers in your district to find out what is available in your school.

Mentoring Students as a Way of Differentiating Teaching

One way to make all instruction more appropriate and effective is to know your students and develop trusting relationships with them. The knowledge you gain about the students should help in adapting your teaching, and the positive relationship you establish will help students stay engaged in learning. See the *Guidelines* for ideas.

No matter how you differentiate instruction, there is one part of your teaching that should be the same for all your students—*appropriate high expectations*.

TEACHER EXPECTATIONS

Over 40 years ago, a study by Robert Rosenthal and Lenore Jacobson (1968) captured the attention of the national media in a way that few studies by psychologists have since then. The study also caused great controversy within the professional community. Debate about the meaning of the results continues (De Boer, Bosker, & van der Werf, 2010; Jussim, 2012; Jussim, Robustelli, & Cain , 2009; Rosenthal, 1995; Snow, 1995).

What did Rosenthal and Jacobson say that caused such a stir? They randomly chose several students in a number of elementary school classrooms, and then told the teachers that these students probably would make significant intellectual gains during the year. The students did indeed make larger gains than normal that year. The researchers presented data suggesting the existence of a "**Pygmalion effect**" or self-fulfilling prophecy in the classroom. A **self-fulfilling prophecy** is a groundless expectation that leads to behaviors that then make the original expectation come true (Merton, 1948). An example is a false belief that a bank is failing; this leads to a rush of patrons withdrawing money, which then causes the bank to fail as expected.

STOP & THINK When you thought about the most effective teacher you ever had, was one of the characteristics that the teacher believed in you or demanded the best from you? How did the teacher communicate that belief? •

Two Kinds of Expectation Effects

Actually, two kinds of expectation effects can occur in classrooms. In the self-fulfilling prophecy described above, the teacher's beliefs about the students' abilities have no basis in fact, but student behavior comes to match the initially inaccurate expectation. The second kind of expectation effect occurs when teachers are fairly accurate in their initial reading of students' abilities and respond to students appropriately. The problems arise when students show some improvement, but teachers do not alter their expectations to take account of the improvement. This is called a **sustaining expectation effect**, because the teacher's unchanging expectation sustains the student's achievement at the expected level. The chance to raise expectations, provide more appropriate teaching, and thus encourage greater student achievement is lost. In practice, self-fulfilling prophecy effects seem to be stronger in the early grades, and sustaining effects are more likely in the later grades (Kuklinski & Weinstein, 2001).

Sources of Expectations

There are many possible sources of teachers' expectations, including intelligence test scores (especially if they are not interpreted appropriately); gender (more behavior problems for boys and higher academic achievement for girls); notes from previous teachers; the medical or psychological reports in students' permanent files; prior knowledge about older brothers and sisters; appearance (higher expectations for attractive students); previous achievement; socioeconomic status; race and ethnicity; and the actual behaviors of the student (Van Matre, Valentine, & Cooper, 2000). Even the student's after-school activities can be a source of expectations. Teachers tend to hold higher expectations for students who participate in extracurricular activities than for students who do nothing after school. And recent research shows that some teachers may even hold expectations at the class level, that is, they have higher or lower expectations for all the students in a particular class (Rubie-Davies, 2010).

Some students are more likely than others to be the recipients of sustaining expectations. For example, withdrawn children provide little information about themselves, so teachers may sustain their expectations about these children for lack of new input (Jones & Gerig, 1994). Also, self-fulfilling prophecy effects tend to be stronger for students from lower-SES families and for African American students (De Boer, Bosker, & van der Werf, 2010). In a synthesis of over 50 studies, Harriet Tenenbaum and Martin Ruck (2007) found that teachers held higher expectation for and directed more positive questions and encouragement toward European American compared to African American and Latino/a students. The highest expectations were reserved for Asian American students. It appears that early childhood teachers may hold higher expectations for students who are more socially competent (Hinnant, O'Brien, & Ghazarian, 2009). For example, in another study of 110 students whose development was followed from age 4 to age 18, Jennifer Alvidrez and Rhona Weinstein (1999) found that teachers tended to overestimate the abilities of preschool children they rated as independent and interesting and to underestimate the abilities of children perceived as immature and anxious.

Expectations and beliefs focus attention and organize memory, so teachers may pay attention to and remember the information that fits their initial expectations (Fiske,

Pygmalion effect Exceptional progress by a student as a result of high teacher expectations for that student; named for mythological king, Pygmalion, who made a statue, then caused it to be brought to life.

Self-fulfilling prophecy A groundless expectation that is confirmed because it has been expected.

Sustaining expectation effect Student performance is maintained at a certain level because teachers don't recognize improvements.

1993; Hewstone, 1989). Even when student performance does not fit expectations, the teacher may rationalize and attribute the performance to external causes beyond the student's control. For example, a teacher may assume that the low-ability student who did well on a test must have cheated and that the high-ability student who failed must have been upset that day. In both cases, behavior that seems out of character is dismissed. It may take many instances of supposedly uncharacteristic behavior to change the teacher's beliefs about a particular student's abilities. Thus, expectations often remain in the face of contradictory evidence (Brophy, 1998).

Do Teachers' Expectations Really Affect Students' Achievement?

The answer to this question is more complicated than it might seem. There are two ways to investigate the issue. One is to give teachers unfounded expectations about their students and note if these baseless expectations have any effects. The other approach is to identify the naturally occurring expectations of teachers and study the effects of these expectations. The answer to the question of whether teacher expectations affect student learning depends in part on which approach is taken to study the question.

The original Rosenthal and Jacobson experiment used the first approach—giving teachers groundless expectations and noting the effects. A careful analysis of the results revealed that even though 1st through 6th grade students participated in the study, the self-fulfilling prophecy effects could be traced to dramatic changes in just five students in grades one and two. After reviewing the research on teacher expectations, Raudenbush (1984) concluded that these expectations have only a small effect on student IQ scores (the outcome measure used by Rosenthal and Jacobson) and only in the early years of a new school setting—in the first years of elementary school and then again in the first years of middle school.

SOURCES OF TEACHER EXPECTATIONS Students' extracurricular activities can be sources of expectations. Teachers tend to hold higher expectations for students who participate in extracurricular activities than for students who "just hang out" after school.

But what about the second approach—naturally occurring expectations? Research shows that teachers do indeed form beliefs about students' capabilities. Many of these beliefs are accurate assessments based on the best available data and are corrected as new information is collected (Jussim & Haber, 2005). But inaccuracies can make a difference. In the longitudinal study by Alvidrez and Weinstein (1999), teachers' judgments of student ability at age 4 predicted student grade-point average at age 18. The strongest predictions were for students whose abilities were *underestimated*. If teachers decide that some students are less able, and if the teachers lack effective strategies for working with lower-achieving students, then students may experience a double threat—low expectations and inadequate teaching (Good & Brophy, 2008).

Even though it is clear that teacher expectations can affect student achievement, the effects are modest on average and tend to dissipate somewhat over the years (Jussim, 2012). The power of the expectation effect depends on the age of the students (generally speaking, younger students are more susceptible) and on how differently a teacher treats high- versus low-expectation students, an issue we turn to next (Kuklinski & Weinstein, 2001). Teachers may use different instructional strategies and also have different relationships with students based on expectations.

INSTRUCTIONAL STRATEGIES.   Different grouping processes may well have a marked effect on students because different groups get different instruction (De Boer, Bosker, & van der Werf, 2010). And some teachers leave little to the imagination; they make their expectations all too clear. For example, Alloway (1984) recorded comments such as these directed to low-achieving groups:

"I'll be over to help you slow ones in a minute." "The blue group will find this hard."

GUIDELINES

Avoiding the Negative Effects of Teacher Expectations

Use information about students from tests, cumulative folders, and other teachers very carefully.
Examples
1. Avoid reading cumulative folders early in the year.
2. Be critical and objective about the reports you hear from other teachers.
3. Be flexible in your expectations—a student's label or your judgment might be wrong.

Be flexible in your use of grouping strategies.
Examples
1. Review work of students often and experiment with new groupings.
2. Use different groups for different subjects.
3. Use mixed-ability groups in cooperative exercises.

Provide both challenge and support.
Examples
1. Don't say, "This is easy, I know you can do it."
2. Offer a wide range of problems, and encourage all students to try a few of the harder ones for extra credit. Find something positive about these attempts.
3. Make sure your high expectations come with academic and emotional support for students' struggles. "Holding high standards without providing a warm environment is merely harsh. A warm environment without high standards lacks backbone" (Jussim, 2012).

Be especially careful about how you respond to low-achieving students during class discussions.
Examples
1. Give them prompts, cues, and time to answer.
2. Give ample praise for good answers.
3. Call on low achievers as often as high achievers.

Use materials that show a wide range of ethnic groups.
Examples
1. Check readers and library books. Is there ethnic diversity?
2. Ask students to research and create their own materials, based on community or family sources.

Make sure that your teaching does not reflect racial, ethnic, or sexual stereotypes or prejudice.
Examples
1. Use a checking system to be sure you call on and include all students.
2. Monitor the content of the tasks you assign. Do boys get the "hard" math problems to work at the board? Do you avoid having students with limited English give oral presentations?

Be fair in evaluation and disciplinary procedures.
Examples
1. Make sure equal offenses receive equal punishment. Find out from students in an anonymous questionnaire whether you seem to be favoring certain individuals.
2. Try to grade student work without knowing the identity of the student. Ask another teacher to give you a "second opinion" from time to time.

Communicate to all students that you believe they can learn—and mean it.
Examples
1. Return papers that do not meet standards with specific suggestions for improvements.
2. If students do not have the answers immediately, wait, probe, and then help them think through an answer.

Involve all students in learning tasks and in privileges.
Examples
1. Use some system to make sure you give each student practice in reading, speaking, and answering questions.
2. Keep track of who gets to do what job. Are some students always on the list, whereas others seldom make it?

Monitor your nonverbal behavior.
Examples
1. Do you lean away or stand farther away from some students? Do some students get smiles when they approach your desk, whereas others get only frowns?
2. Does your tone of voice vary with different students?

For more information see
http://chiron.valdosta.edu/whuitt/files/teacherexpect.html

In these remarks, the teacher not only tells the students that they lack ability, but also communicates that finishing the work, not understanding, is the goal.

Once teachers divide students into ability groups, they usually differentiate by assigning different learning activities. To the extent that teachers choose activities that challenge students and increase achievement, these differences are probably necessary. Activities become inappropriate, however, when students who are ready for more challenging work are not given the opportunity to try it because teachers believe they cannot handle it. This is an example of a *sustaining expectation effect*.

TEACHER–STUDENT INTERACTIONS. However the class is grouped and whatever the assignments are, the quantity and the quality of teacher–student interactions are likely to affect the students. Students who are expected to achieve tend to be asked more and harder questions, to be given more chances and a longer time to respond, and to be interrupted less often than students who are expected to do poorly. Teachers also give these high-expectation students cues and prompts, communicating their belief that the students can answer the question (Good & Brophy, 2008; Rosenthal, 1995). They tend to smile at these students more often and to show greater warmth through such nonverbal responses as leaning toward the students and nodding their heads as the students speak (Woolfolk & Brooks, 1983, 1985).

In contrast, with low-expectation students, teachers ask easier questions, allow less time for answering, and are less likely to give prompts. They are more likely to respond with sympathetic acceptance or even praise for inadequate answers from low-achieving students, but to criticize these same students for wrong answers. Even more disturbing, low-achieving students receive less praise than high-achieving students for similar correct answers. This inconsistent feedback can be very confusing for low-ability students. Imagine how hard it would be to learn if your wrong answers were sometimes praised, sometimes ignored, and sometimes criticized, and your right answers received little recognition (Good 1983a, 1983b; Hattie & Timperley, 2007). Even though the effects of these communications may be small each day, there can be huge effects as the expectation differences build year after year with many teachers (Trouilloud, Sarrazin, Bressoux, & Bois, 2006).

Lessons for Teachers: Communicating Appropriate Expectations

Of course, not all teachers form inappropriate expectations or act on their expectations in unconstructive ways (Babad, Inbar, & Rosenthal, 1982). The *Guidelines* may help you avoid some of these problems. But avoiding the problem may be more difficult than it seems. In general, low-expectation students also tend to be the most disruptive students. (Of course, low expectations can reinforce their desire to disrupt or misbehave.) Teachers may call on these students less, wait a shorter time for their answers, and give them less praise for right answers, partly to avoid the wrong, careless, or silly answers that can cause disruptions, delays, and digressions. The challenge is to deal with these very real threats to classroom management without communicating low expectations to some students or fostering their own low expectations of themselves. And sometimes, low expectations become part of the culture of the school—beliefs shared by teachers and administrators alike (Weinstein, Madison, & Kuklinski, 1995).

▼ SUMMARY

Research on Teaching (pp. 404–407)

What methods have been used to study teaching? For years, researchers have tried to unravel the mystery of effective teaching using classroom observation, case studies, interviews, experimentation with different methods, stimulated recall (teachers view videotapes and explain their teaching), analysis of lesson transcripts, and other approaches to study teaching in real classrooms.

What are the general characteristics of good teaching? A variety of teacher qualities are related to good teaching. Research suggests teachers who receive proper training and certification have more successful students. Although it is important, teacher knowledge of a subject is not sufficient for effective teaching. Thorough knowledge does lead to greater clarity and better organization, which are both tied to good teaching. Teachers who provide clear presentations and explanations tend to have students who learn more and who rate their teachers more positively. Teacher warmth, friendliness, and understanding seem to be the traits most strongly related to positive student attitudes about the teacher and the course in general.

What do expert teachers know? It takes time and experience to become an expert teacher. These teachers have a rich store of well-organized knowledge about the many specific situations of teaching. This includes knowledge about the subjects they teach, their students, general teaching strategies, subject-specific ways of teaching, settings for learning, curriculum materials, and the goals of education. Expert teachers also know how to be reflective practitioners—how to use their experience as a way to grow and improve in their teaching.

What does the new latest research on teaching show? A program of large-scale, longitudinal research has identified three aspects of classroom climate that are related to the development and learning of preschool and elementary school students. These three dimensions are consistent with the characteristics of teachers identified in earlier research on teaching and cover affective, behavioral, and cognitive dimensions. The *affective* dimension is teacher *emotional support*, similar to teacher warmth and enthusiasm identified in early research. The *cognitive* dimension is instructional support, which includes concept development (activities and discussions that promote student higher-order thinking) and quality feedback that is specific and focused on the learning process. The third dimension is classroom organization, which includes *behavioral* concerns such as classroom and lesson management with clear activities and routines that make more time for learning and really engage students—similar to the teacher characteristics of clarity and organization.

The First Step: Planning (pp. 408–415)

What are the levels of planning, and how do they affect teaching? Teachers engage in several levels of planning—by the year, term, unit, week, and day. All the levels must be coordinated. The plan determines how time and materials will be turned into activities for students. There is no single model of planning, but all plans should allow for flexibility. Planning is a creative problem-solving process for experienced teachers. It is more informal—"in their heads."

What is an instructional objective? An instructional objective is a clear and unambiguous description of your educational intentions for your students. Mager's influential system for writing behavioral objectives states that a good objective has three parts—the intended student behavior, the conditions under which the behavior will occur, and the criteria for acceptable performance. Gronlund's alternative approach suggests that an objective should be stated first in general terms, and then the teacher should clarify by listing sample behaviors that would provide evidence that the student has attained the objective. The most recent research on instructional objectives tends to favor approaches similar to Gronlund's.

Describe the three taxonomies of educational objectives. Bloom and others have developed taxonomies categorizing basic objectives in the cognitive, affective, and psychomotor domains. In real life, of course, behaviors from these three domains occur simultaneously. A taxonomy encourages systematic thinking about relevant objectives and ways to evaluate them. Six basic objectives are listed in the cognitive domain: remembering, understanding, applying, analyzing, evaluating, and creating, acting on four kinds of knowledge: factual, conceptual, procedural, and metacognitive. Objectives in the affective domain run from least committed to most committed. Objectives in the psychomotor domain generally move from basic perceptions and reflex actions to skilled, creative movements.

Describe constructivist planning. Planning is shared and negotiated in student-centered, or constructivist, approaches. Rather than having specific student behaviors as objectives, the teacher has overarching goals or "big ideas" that guide planning. Integrated content and teaching with themes are often part of the planning. Assessment of learning is ongoing and mutually shared by teacher and students.

Teaching Approaches (pp. 415–427)

What is direct instruction? Direct instruction is appropriate for teaching basic skills and explicit knowledge. It includes the teaching functions of review/overview, presentation, guided practice, feedback and correctives (with reteaching if necessary), independent practice, and periodic reviews. The younger or less able the students, the shorter the presentation should be, with more cycles of practice and feedback.

Distinguish between convergent and divergent and high-level versus low-level questions. Convergent questions have only one right answer. Divergent questions have many possible answers. Higher-level questions require analyzing, evaluating, and creating—students have to think for themselves. The best pattern for younger students and for lower-ability students of all ages is simple questions that allow a high percentage of correct answers, ample encouragement, help when the student does not have the correct answer, and praise. For high-ability students, the successful pattern includes harder questions at both higher and lower levels and more critical feedback. Whatever their age or ability, all students should have some experience with thought-provoking questions and, if necessary, help in learning how to answer them.

How can wait time affect student learning? When teachers pose a question and then learn to wait at least 3 to 5 seconds before calling on a student to answer, students tend to give longer answers; more students are likely to participate, ask questions, and volunteer appropriate answers; student comments involving analysis, synthesis, inference, and speculation tend to increase; and the students generally appear more confident in their answers.

What are the uses and disadvantages of group discussion? Group discussion helps students participate directly, express themselves clearly, justify opinions, and tolerate different views. Group discussion also gives students a chance to ask for clarification, examine their own thinking, follow personal interests, and assume responsibility by taking leadership roles in the group. Thus, group discussions help students evaluate ideas and synthesize personal viewpoints. However, discussions are quite unpredictable and may easily digress into exchanges of ignorance.

How can you match teaching to your goals? Different goals and student needs require different teaching methods. Direct instruction often leads to better performance on achievement tests, whereas the open, informal methods such as discovery learning or inquiry approaches are associated with better performance on tests of creativity, abstract thinking, and problem solving. In addition, the open methods are better for improving attitudes toward school and for stimulating curiosity, cooperation among students, and lower absence rates.

Differentiated Instruction (pp. 427–433)

What are the problems with ability grouping? Academic ability groupings can have disadvantages and advantages for students and teachers. Student in higher ability groups may benefit, but students in lower ability groups are less likely to be asked critical comprehension questions and are given fewer opportunities to make choices about readings and assignments. For schools with lower-SES students, grouping often means that these students are segregated even in their own classes, so ability grouping can create segregation within diverse schools.

What are the alternatives available for grouping in classes, including flexible grouping? Cross-age grouping by subject can be an effective way to deal with ability differences in a school. Within-class ability grouping, if handled sensitively and flexibly, can have positive effects, but alternatives such as cooperative learning may be better.

What is adaptive teaching? Adaptive teaching provides all students with challenging instruction and uses supports when needed, but removes those supports as students are able to handle more on their own.

What characterizes effective teaching for students with disabilities? Effective teaching for students with disabilities does not require a unique set of skills. It is a combination of good teaching practices and sensitivity to all students. Students with disabilities need to learn the academic material, and they need to be full participants in the day-to-day life of the classroom.

What resources do teachers have to work effectively with students with disabilities? When students have special needs, they may be referred for evaluation to specialists such as child study teams, school psychologists, or teachers of students with special needs. The outcome of this process sometimes includes the preparation of an individualized educational program or IEP, as described in Chapter 4, which will have teaching ideas and guidelines. In addition, differentiated instruction can improve learning for all students and developing mentoring relationships with students can help teachers connect with student abilities and needs.

Teacher Expectations (pp. 433–437)

What are some sources of teacher expectations? Sources include intelligence test scores, gender, notes from previous teachers, medical or psychological reports found in cumulative folders, ethnic background, prior knowledge about older brothers and sisters, physical characteristics, previous achievement, socioeconomic status, and the actual behaviors of the student.

What are the two kinds of expectation effects and how do they happen? The first is the self-fulfilling prophecy, in which the teacher's beliefs about the students' abilities have no basis in fact, but student behavior comes to match the initially inaccurate expectation. The second is a sustaining expectation effect, in which teachers are fairly accurate in their initial reading of students' abilities and respond to students appropriately, but they do not alter their expectations to take account of any improvement. When this happens, the teacher's unchanging expectation can sustain the student's achievement at the expected level. In practice, sustaining effects are more common than self-fulfilling prophecy effects.

What are the different avenues for communicating teacher expectations? Some teachers tend to treat students differently, depending on their own views of how well the students are likely to do. Differences in treatment toward low-expectation students may include setting less challenging tasks, focusing on lower-level learning, giving fewer choices, providing inconsistent feedback, and communicating less respect and trust. Students may behave accordingly, fulfilling teachers' predictions or staying at an expected level of achievement.

▼ KEY TERMS

Active teaching (415)
Adaptive teaching (428)
Advance organizer (416)
Affective domain (412)
Assistive technology (430)
Basic skills (415)
Behavioral objectives (410)
Cognitive domain (411)
Cognitive objectives (410)
Constructivist approach (414)

Convergent questions (423)
Differentiated instruction (427)
Direct instruction/Explicit teaching (415)
Divergent questions (423)
Expert teachers (405)
Flexible grouping (427)
Group discussion (425)
Instructional objectives (410)
Lesson study (409)
Pedagogical content knowledge (405)

Psychomotor domain (413)
Pygmalion effect (434)
Reflective (405)
Scripted cooperation (418)
Seatwork (419)
Self-fulfilling prophecy (434)
Sustaining expectation effect (434)
Taxonomy (411)
Universal design (432)
Within-class ability grouping (427)

▼ CONNECT AND EXTEND TO LICENSURE

MULTIPLE-CHOICE QUESTIONS

1. Direct instruction is best used when teachers do which one of the following.
   A. Teach basic skills
   B. Have their students explore numerous pathways to solve a mathematics problem
   C. Encourage their students to refine their creativity in art
   D. Assign critical thinking exercises

2. Homework has long been a staple of education. In order for students to gain the most from their homework experience, all but which one of the following suggestions should be followed?
   A. Establish that students understand the assignment
   B. Hold students accountable for completing the work correctly
   C. Check students' work and allow for corrections and revisions
   D. Require a parent signature to ensure collaboration with home

3. Ellen Baker knew that her new job in a middle school would require that she understand differentiated instruction. By utilizing this strategy, her students would be more apt to progress and master the concepts they needed to be successful throughout their school years. One of the techniques she decided to use involved grouping students on their learning needs. In this manner, students who had scored poorly on their fractions tests would be grouped with similar students to remediate and develop that skill. She likened this type of differentiated instruction to having students continually work in their zone of proximal development. The type of strategy Ellen Baker wants to use is referred to as which one of the following.
   A. Flexible Grouping
   B. Jigsaw
   C. Collaborative group work
   D. Peer tutoring

4. Teachers sometimes make determinations about their students' abilities based upon little evidence. When teachers expect their students will not do well, their words and actions can actually

make that expectation come true regardless of the validity. This effect is referred to as which one of the following.

A. Self-fulfilling prophecy
B. The zone of proximal development
C. Professional license
D. Supportive withdraw

CONSTRUCTED-RESPONSE QUESTIONS

Case

Although Casey Yost had done well in her college classes, she was having a difficult time with her student teaching. Her mentor teacher continually scolded her for not correctly writing her objectives and rushing through lessons. Casey didn't understand how she could both make her lessons clear and manage to cover the material necessary for the students' upcoming standardized tests. "Casey, if your students don't understand the material, it won't make a difference if you cover the material or not. Let's

review one of your objectives for the upcoming lesson. 'Students will understand fractions'. This objective is too general. How can you measure if your students 'understand'? You need to select words that correspond to specific actions that you can observe or measure. Let's try to develop a few objectives that are more specific in nature."

5. In what ways can Casey Yost avoid writing objectives that are too general?

6. In order to teach her students more effectively, list several strategies Casey can employ during instruction.

▼ WHAT WOULD THEY DO?

TEACHERS' CASEBOOK: Reaching and Teaching Every Student

Here is how some practicing teachers would differentiate instruction for the class described at the beginning of the chapter.

LOU DE LAURO • 5th Grade Language Arts
John P. Faber School, Dunellen, NJ

In your hometown you probably know a lot of people. To be successful you are going to have to use the town to help you. If you plan properly, you should be able to secure one guest a week for the entire school year. The kids will love meeting new people each week and reading with them. But you need more than a guest a week to visit your classroom. So ask the businesses in town. Maybe a business can run a fundraiser so you can purchase alternative texts for your students. Maybe the local library can introduce you to their biggest donor who might donate texts to you. Maybe you can apply for a grant with the local educational foundation to get new materials.

But you need more help. You are a teacher; you were probably a strong student who connected with your former teachers. Visit any teachers that are still teaching and get their advice on what to do. What has worked in the past may work well now, too.

Devote many hours after school to your students. Small-group instruction will help these kids. Get the two students who are practically ready for college small stipends donated by a local business so they stay after school and help you with your challenging students. I think that if you fully take advantage of your home court, this is one situation in which you can easily prevail.

MARIE HOFFMAN HURT • 8th Grade Foreign Language
Teacher (German & French)
Pickerington Local Schools, Pickerington, OH

To start, I would encourage a teacher to look beyond the general classifications of "white, working, middle class, and English speaking." Even in a class full of students who fit this demographic, there is an array of individuals. Each student learns differently and has different interests. A good teacher will recognize this and challenge students as people, not as groups. Do your best to layer as much as

you can throughout your lessons. Give students choices. Use what resources you have—in this case particularly ESL resources. Even praising students' individual characteristics and accomplishments outside the classroom sets the tone. Finally, keep in mind that you are only one person and can only give your best. Don't overwork yourself and burn out—you are no good to your students or your family if you are wiped out.

M. DENISE LUTZ • Technology Coordinator
Grandview Heights High School, Columbus, OH

Studies have shown that student success is directly related to teacher effectiveness. In today's diverse classrooms a teacher must develop effective classroom pedagogy that incorporates effective instructional strategies, uses effective classroom management strategies, and designs effective classroom curriculum to meet the needs of all learners. It is necessary to communicate learning goals for all students, track individual progress, and celebrate successes. Under the guidance of the teacher, students should learn to work collaboratively in small groups and as a cohesive class encouraging and helping one another to be successful. A teacher who establishes and maintains classroom rules and procedures while acknowledging students who do and do not follow these rules and procedures fosters this kind of environment. Consistency, trust, and authenticity will help to advance the development of effective relationships between the teacher, the home, and among class members. Effective classroom curriculum always begins with the end in mind. The teacher should have a clear picture of what mastery of content would look like for each of his or her students. Understanding the big idea and defining essential questions will guide the collection of activities and lessons that will move each student in the direction of success. The direction of success will remain the same for all students, but lessons and activities may present different paths for individuals to traverse. Today's teacher must work from day one to get to know each individual and to establish a culture of collaboration among the group.

PATRICIA A. SMITH • High School Math
Earl Warren High School, San Antonio, TX

Because this new teacher is a product of the same school system, it will be imperative to begin classroom instruction with absolutely no preconceived opinions toward any particular student. Likewise, a diverse population requires the teacher to resolve student situations discreetly and judiciously, and not publicly. The initial goals of the teacher would be to facilitate student work in a cooperative manner and engender teacher trust. Planning and organizing ice-breaker exercises the first few days of the school year could prove extremely profitable.

With a wide range of reading levels, small groups would work to the teacher's advantage. I would not suggest grouping students according to reading level at all times, but would opt to appoint a recognized student leader to orchestrate daily oral recitations. Moreover, I would select reading materials suited to all students and keep the assignments brief to avoid overwhelming struggling readers. The student leader could also design questions to gauge comprehension and give the group a follow-up spelling test. Initially, the spelling test would be composed of five to ten simple words that students could either print or write. Subsequently, as the students gain confidence and experience success, the readings could be assigned as homework and the students would be required to write a short paragraph answering a reading comprehension question.

If the teacher remains well organized, the instructional time allotted for small group interaction should not extend over 15 minutes in a single class period. Thus, the teacher would not forfeit traditional grammar lessons for the entire class but would still provide limited individualized instruction. I would also supplement SAT reading and English practice for all college bound students.

chapter twelve
CLASSROOM ASSESSMENT, GRADING, AND STANDARDIZED TESTING

▶ **TEACHERS' CASEBOOK:** Giving Meaningful Grades

Your school requires that you give letter grades to your class. You can use any method you want, as long as an A, B, C, D, or F appears for each of the subject areas on every student's report card, every grading period. Some teachers are using worksheets, quizzes, homework, and tests. Others are assigning group work and portfolios. A few teachers are individualizing standards by grading on progress and effort more than final achievement. Some are trying contract approaches and experimenting with longer-term projects, while others are relying almost completely on daily class work. Two teachers who use group work are considering giving credit toward grades for being a "good group member" or competitive bonus points for the top-scoring group. Others are planning to use improvement points for class rewards, but not for grades. Your only experience with grading was using written comments and a mastery approach that rated the students as making satisfactory or unsatisfactory progress toward particular objectives. You want a system that is reliable, fair and manageable, but also encourages learning, not just performance. And you want a system that gives the students feedback they can use to prepare for the proficiency tests required by NCLB.

CRITICAL THINKING

- What would you choose as your major graded assignments and projects?
- Would you include credit for behaviors such as group participation or effort?
- How would you put all the elements together to determine a grade for every student for every marking period?
- How would you justify your system to the principal and to the students' families, especially when the teachers in your school are using so many different criteria?
- What do you think of the wide range of criteria being used by different teachers—is this fair to students?
- How will these issues affect the grade levels you will teach?

OVERVIEW AND OBJECTIVES

As you read this chapter, you will examine assessment, testing, and grading, focusing not only on the effects they are likely to have on students, but also on practical ways to develop better methods for testing and grading.

We begin with a consideration of the basic concepts in assessment including validity and reliability. Next we examine the many types of tests teachers prepare each year and approaches to assessment that don't rely on traditional testing. Then, we explore the effects grades are likely to have on students and the very important topic of communication with students and families. How will you justify the grades you give? Finally, because standardized tests are so important today, we spend some time looking at testing, the meaning of test scores, and alternatives to traditional testing.

By the time you have completed this chapter, you should be able to:

Objective 12.1: Distinguish among evaluation, measurement, and assessment, including the functions of each.

Objective 12.2: Distinguish between norm-referenced and criterion-referenced assessments.

Objective 12.3: Describe how reliability, validity, and absence of bias are used to understand and judge assessments.

Objective 12.4: Describe two kinds of traditional classroom testing, and how authentic assessment can be used as an alternative to traditional assessments.

Objective 12.5: Describe the effects of grading on students and the types of strategies teachers can use to communicate to parents about grades.

Objective 12.6: Explain how to interpret common standardized test scores (percentile rank, stanine, grade-equivalent, scale score).

Objective 12.7: Identify some of the current issues in standardized testing.

Connect and Extend to PRAXIS II™

Types of Assessment (II, C1, 4) Understand the purposes of formative and summative assessment. Explain how teachers and students can make effective use of the information generated by each type of test.

Standardized tests Tests given, usually nationwide, under uniform conditions and scored according to uniform procedures.

Classroom assessments Classroom assessments are selected and created by teachers and can take many different forms—unit tests, essays, portfolios, projects, performances, oral presentations, etc.

BASICS OF ASSESSMENT

Would it surprise you to learn that published tests, such as college entrance exams and IQ tests, are creations of the 20th century? In the early to mid-1900s, college entrance was generally based on grades, essays, and interviews. From your own experience, you know that testing has come a long way since then—too far, say some critics. Published tests today are called **standardized tests** because they are administered, scored, and interpreted in a standard manner—same directions, time limits, and scoring for all (Popham, 2011). Standard methods of developing items, administering the test, scoring it, and reporting the scores are all implied by the term *standardized test.* The schools where you teach probably will use standardized tests, especially to meet the requirements of the No Child Left Behind (NCLB) Act. In most schools, however, teachers do not have much say in selecting these tests.

    Classroom assessments, on the other hand, are created and selected by teachers. Classroom assessments can take many different forms—unit tests, essays, portfolios, projects, performances, oral presentations—the list is long. Assessments are critical because teaching involves making many kinds of judgments—decisions based on values: "Is this software appropriate for my students?" "Will Jacob do better if he repeats the 1st grade?" "Should Emily get a B– or a C+ on the project?" This chapter is about judgments that involve measurement, testing, and grading, and all forms of assessment. We look at both classroom assessment and standardized testing, with an emphasis on the former, because teachers are responsible for classroom assessments. Before we look at either classroom or standardized assessments, let's examine some key distinctions that apply to both, beginning with the difference between measurement and assessment.

Measurement and Assessment

Measurement is quantitative—the description of an event or characteristic using numbers. Measurement tells how much, how often, or how well by providing scores, ranks, or ratings. Instead of saying, "Sarah doesn't seem to understand addition," a teacher might say, "Sarah answered only 2 of the 15 problems correctly in her addition homework." Measurement also allows a teacher to compare one student's performance on a particular task with either a specific standard or the performances of other students on the same task.

    Not all the decisions made by teachers involve measurement. Some decisions are based on information that is difficult to express numerically: student preferences, discussions with families, previous experiences, even intuition. But measurement does play a large role in many classroom decisions, and, when properly done, it can provide unbiased data for decision making.

    Increasingly, measurement specialists are using the term *assessment* to describe the process of gathering information about students' learning. **Assessment** is broader than testing and measurement because it includes all kinds of ways to sample and observe students' skills, knowledge, and abilities (Linn & Miller, 2005). Assessments can be formal, such as unit tests, or informal, such as observing who emerges as a leader in group work. Assessments can be designed by classroom teachers or by local, state, or national agencies such as school districts or the Educational Testing Service. And today, assessments can go well beyond paper-and-pencil exercises to judgments based on students' performances, portfolios, projects, or products (Popham, 2011).

FORMATIVE AND SUMMATIVE ASSESSMENT. There are two general uses or functions for assessment: formative and summative. **Formative assessment** occurs before or during instruction. The purposes of formative assessment are to guide the teacher in planning and improving instruction and to help students improve learning. In other words, formative assessment helps *form* instruction and provides feedback that is "nonevaluative, supportive, timely, and specific" (Shute, 2008, p. 153). Often students are given a formative test prior to instruction, a **pretest** that helps the teacher determine what students already know. Sometimes a test is given during instruction to see what areas of weakness remain so teaching can be directed toward the problem areas. These formative tests are not graded, so students who tend to be very anxious about "real" tests may find this low-pressure practice in test taking especially helpful.

Summative assessment occurs at the end of instruction. Its purpose is to let the teacher and the students know the level of accomplishment attained. Summative assessment, therefore, provides a summary of accomplishment. The final exam is a classic example.

SUMMATIVE ASSESSMENT The final exam is a classic example of a summative assessment. This type of assessment occurs at the end of instruction and provides a summary of accomplishment.

The distinction between formative and summative assessment is based on how the results are used. And any kind of assessment—traditional, performance, project, oral, portfolio, and so on—can be used for either formative or summative purposes. If the purpose of the assessment is to improve your teaching and help students guide their own learning, then the evaluation is *formative*. But if the purpose is to evaluate final achievement (and help determine a course grade), the assessment is *summative* (Nitko & Brookhart, 2011). In fact, the same assessment could be used as a formative evaluation at the beginning of the unit and as a summative evaluation at the end. Table 12.1 gives some examples of different uses of assessment.

The formative uses of assessment are really the most important in teaching. In fact, Popham believes "any teacher who uses tests dominantly to determine whether students get high or low grades should receive a solid F in classroom assessment" (2008, p. 256). Tests and all assessments should be used to help teachers make better instructional decisions.

TABLE 12.1 • Using Tests to Make Instructional Decisions

The best use of assessment is to plan, guide, and target instruction. Here are some decisions that can benefit from assessment results.

DECISION CATEGORY	TYPICAL ASSESSMENT STRATEGY	DECISION OPTIONS
What to teach in the first place?	Preassessment before instruction	Whether to provide instruction for specific objectives?
How long to keep teaching toward a particular instructional objective?	En route assessments of students' progress	Whether to continue or cease instruction for an objective either for an individual or for the whole class?
How effective was an instructional sequence?	Comparing students' posttest to pretest performances	Whether to retain, discard, or modify a given instructional sequence the next time it's used?

Source: From Popham, W. James, Classroom Assessment: What Teachers Need to Know, 4/e. Published by Allyn and Bacon, Boston, MA. Copyright © 2005 by Pearson Education. Adapted by permission of the publisher.

Measurement An evaluation expressed in quantitative (number) terms.

Assessment Procedures used to obtain information about student performance.

Formative assessment Ungraded testing used before or during instruction to aid in planning and diagnosis.

Pretest Formative test for assessing students' knowledge, readiness, and abilities.

Summative assessment Testing that follows instruction and assesses achievement.

Connect and Extend to PRAXIS II™

Criterion-/Norm-Referenced Tests (II, C5)
The ERIC Digest *Norm- and Criterion-Referenced Testing* (http://www.ericdigests.org/1998–1/norm.htm) describes the purposes, content, and issues related to criterion- and norm-referenced tests. Giving accurate feedback to parents is part of a teacher's job. When talking with a parent about a child's abilities, do you think the use of norm-referenced or criterion-referenced test results is more desirable?

The answers given on any type of test have no meaning by themselves; we must make some kind of comparison in order to interpret test results. There are two basic types of comparisons: In the first, a test score is compared to the scores obtained by other people who have taken the same test. (This is called a *norm-referenced comparison*.) The second type is *criterion-referenced*. Here, the score is compared to a fixed standard or minimum passing score. Actually, the same test can be interpreted either in a norm-referenced or criterion-referenced way.

NORM-REFERENCED TEST INTERPRETATIONS. In **norm-referenced testing** and grading, the people who have taken the test provide the norms for determining the meaning of a given individual's score. You can think of a *norm* as being the typical level of performance for a particular group. By comparing the individual's raw score (the actual number correct) to the norm, we can determine if the score is above, below, or around the average for that group. There are at least three types of **norm groups** (comparison groups) in education—the class or school itself, the school district, and national samples. Students in national norm groups used for large-scale assessment programs are tested one year and then the scores for that group serve as comparisons or norms every year for several years until the test is revised or renormed. The norm groups are selected so that all socioeconomic status (SES) groups are included in the sample. Because high-SES students tend to do better on many standardized tests, a high-SES school district will almost always have higher scores compared to the norm group.

Norm-referenced tests cover a wide range of general objectives. They are especially appropriate when only the top few candidates can be admitted to a program. However, norm-referenced measurement has its limitations. The results of a norm-referenced test do not tell you whether students are ready to move on to more advanced material. For instance, knowing that a student is in the top 3% of the class on a test of algebraic concepts will not tell you if he or she is ready to move on to advanced math; everyone else in the class may have a limited understanding of the algebraic concepts.

Nor are norm-referenced tests particularly appropriate for measuring affective and psychomotor objectives. To measure individuals' psychomotor learning, you need a clear description of standards. (Even the best gymnast in school performs certain exercises better than others and needs specific guidance about how to improve.) In the affective area, attitudes and values are personal; comparisons among individuals are not really appropriate. For example, how could we measure an "average" level of political values or opinions? Finally, norm-referenced tests tend to encourage competition and comparison of scores. Some students compete to be the best. Others, realizing that being the best is impossible, may compete to be the worst. Both goals have their casualties.

CRITERION-REFERENCED TEST INTERPRETATIONS. When test scores are compared, not to the scores of others, but to a given criterion or standard of performance, this is **criterion-referenced testing** or grading. To decide who should be allowed to drive a car, it is important to determine just what standard of performance works for selecting safe drivers. It does not matter how your test results compare to the results of others. If your performance on the test was in the top 10%, but you consistently ran through red lights, you would not be a good candidate for receiving a license, even though your score was high.

Criterion-referenced tests measure the mastery of very specific objectives. The results of a criterion-referenced test should tell the teacher exactly what the students can and cannot do, at least under certain conditions. For example, a criterion-referenced test would be useful in measuring the students' ability to add three-digit numbers. A test could be designed with 20 different problems, and the standard for mastery could be set at 17 correct out of 20. (The standard is often somewhat arbitrary and may be based on such things as the teacher's experience.) If two students receive scores of 7 and 11, it does not matter that one student did better than the other because neither met the standard of 17. Both need more help with addition.

In teaching basic skills, there are many instances where comparison to a preset standard is more important than comparison to the performance of others. It is not very comforting to know, as a parent, that your child is better in reading than most of

Norm-referenced testing Testing in which scores are compared with the average performance of others.

Norm group Large sample of students serving as a comparison group for scoring tests.

Criterion-referenced testing Testing in which scores are compared to a set performance standard.

the students in her class if none of the students is reading at grade level. Sometimes standards for meeting the criterion must be set at 100% correct. You would not like to have your appendix removed by a surgeon who left surgical instruments inside the body *only* 10% of the time.

Criterion-referenced tests are not appropriate for every situation, however. Many subjects cannot be broken down into a set of specific objectives. Moreover, although standards are important in criterion-referenced testing, they can often be arbitrary, as you have already seen. When deciding whether a student has mastered the addition of three-digit numbers comes down to the difference between 16 or 17 correct answers, it seems difficult to justify one particular standard over another. Finally, at times, it is valuable to know how the students in your class compare to other students at their grade level both locally and nationally. You can see that each type of test is well suited for certain situations, but each also has its limitations.

VALIDITY AND RELIABILITY The validity and reliability decisions based on tests may be affected by the extent to which the tests measure intelligence, knowledge, motivation, or differences in life experiences.

Assessing the Assessments: Reliability and Validity

One of the most common problems with the use of assessments, especially tests, is misinterpretation of results. This often happens when people believe tests are precise measurements of a student's ability. No test provides a perfect picture of a person's abilities; a test is only one small sample of behavior. Three factors are important in developing good tests and interpreting results: *reliability*, *validity*, and *absence of bias*.

RELIABILITY OF TEST SCORES. Scores are reliable if a test gives a consistent and stable "reading" of a person's ability from one occasion to the next, assuming the person's ability remains the same. A reliable thermometer works in a similar manner, giving you a reading of 100°C each time you measure the temperature of boiling water. Measuring **reliability** this way, by giving the test on two different occasions, indicates *stability* or *test-retest reliability*. If a group of people take two equivalent versions of a test and the scores on both tests are comparable, this indicates *alternate-form reliability*. Reliability can also refer to the *internal consistency* or the precision of a test. This type of reliability, known as *split-half reliability,* is calculated by comparing performance on half of the test questions with performance on the other half. If, for example, someone did quite well on all the odd-numbered items and not at all well on the even-numbered items, we could assume that the items were not very consistent or precise in measuring what they were intended to measure.

There are several ways to compute reliability, but all the possibilities give numbers between 0.0 and 1.0, like a correlation coefficient. Above .90 is considered very reliable; .80 to .90 is good, and below .80 is not very good reliability for commercially produced standardized tests such as the SAT or ACT (Haladyna, 2002). Generally speaking, longer tests are more reliable than shorter ones.

ERROR IN SCORES. All tests are imperfect estimators of the qualities or skills they are trying to measure. There are errors in every testing situation. There are sources of error related to the student such as mood, motivation, test-taking skills, or even cheating. Sometimes the errors are in your favor and you score higher than your ability might warrant; sometimes the errors go against you. There are also sources of error related to the test itself—the directions are unclear, the reading level is too high, the items are ambiguous, or the time limits are wrong.

The score each student receives always includes some amount of error. How can error be reduced? As you might guess, this returns us to the question of reliability. The

Reliability Consistency of test results.

more reliable the test scores are, the less error there will be in the score actually obtained. On standardized tests, test developers take this into consideration and make estimations of how much the students' scores would probably vary if they were tested repeatedly. This estimation is called the **standard error of measurement**. Thus, a reliable test can also be defined as one with a small standard error of measurement.

CONFIDENCE INTERVAL.   Never base an opinion of a student's ability or achievement on the exact score the student obtains. For standardized tests, many test companies now report scores using a **confidence interval**, or "standard error band," that encloses the student's actual score. This makes use of the standard error of measurement and allows a teacher to consider the range of scores that might include a student's **true score**—the score the student would get if the measurement were completely accurate and error-free.

Let us assume, for example, that two students in your class take a standardized achievement test in Spanish. The standard error of measurement for this test is 5. One student receives a score of 79 and the other, a score of 85. At first glance, these scores seem quite different. But when you consider the standard error bands around the scores, not just the scores alone, you see that the bands overlap. The first student's true score might be anywhere between 74 and 84 (that is, the actual score of 79 plus and minus the standard error of 5). The second student's true score might be anywhere between 80 and 90. Both students could have the same true score of 80, 81, 82, 83, or 84 because the score bands overlap at those numbers. It is crucial to keep in mind the idea of standard error bands when selecting students for special programs. No child should be rejected simply because the score obtained missed the cutoff by one or two points. The student's true score might well be above the cutoff point. See Figure 12.5 for a report with these score bands.

VALIDITY.   If test scores are sufficiently reliable, the next question is whether the scores are valid, or more accurately, whether the judgments and decisions based on the test scores are valid. To have **validity**, the decisions and inferences based on the test must be supported by evidence. This means that validity is judged in relation to a particular use or purpose, that is, in relation to the actual decision being made and the evidence for that decision. A particular test might be valid for one purpose, but not for another (Frisbie, 2005; Oosterhof, 2009; Popham, 2011).

There are different kinds of evidence to support a particular judgment. If the purpose of a test is to measure the skills covered in a course or unit, then we would hope to see test questions on all the important topics and not on extraneous information. If this condition is met, we would have *content-related evidence of validity*. Have you ever taken a test that dealt only with a few ideas from one lecture or just a few pages of the textbook? Then decisions based on that test (like your grade) certainly lacked content-related evidence of validity.

Some tests are designed to predict outcomes. The SATs, for example, are intended to predict performance in college. If SAT scores correlate with academic performance in college as measured by, say, grade-point average in the first year, then we have *criterion-related evidence of validity* for the use of the SAT in admissions decisions.

Most standardized tests are designed to measure some psychological characteristic or "construct" such as reasoning ability, reading comprehension, achievement motivation, intelligence, creativity, and so on. It is a bit more difficult to gather *construct-related evidence of validity*, yet this is a very important requirement—probably the most important. Construct-related evidence of validity is gathered over many years. It is indicated by a pattern of scores. For example, older children can answer more questions on intelligence tests than younger children can. This fits with our *construct* of intelligence. If the average 5-year-old answered as many questions correctly on a test as the average 13-year-old, we would doubt that the test really measured intelligence. Construct-related evidence for validity can also be demonstrated when the results of a test correlate with the results of other well-established, valid measures of the same construct.

Today, many psychologists suggest that construct validity is the broadest category and that gathering content- and criterion-related evidence is another way of determining if the test actually measures the construct it was designed to measure. Nearly 40 years ago,

Standard error of measurement Hypothetical estimate of variation in scores if testing were repeated.

Confidence interval Range of scores within which an individual's particular score is likely to fall.

True score The score the student would get if the measurement were completely accurate and error-free.

Validity Degree to which a test measures what it is intended to measure.

Sam Messick (1975) raised two important questions to consider in making any decisions about using a test: *Is the test a good measure of the characteristic it is assumed to assess? Should the test be used for the proposed purpose?* The first question is about construct validity; the second is about ethics and values.

A test must be reliable in order to be valid. For example, if an intelligence test yields different results each time it is given to the same child over the course of a few months, then, by definition, it is not reliable. Certainly, it couldn't be a valid measure of intelligence because intelligence is assumed to be fairly stable, at least over a short period of time. However, reliability will not guarantee validity. If that intelligence test gave the same score every time for a particular child, but didn't predict school achievement, speed of learning, or other characteristics associated with intelligence, then performance on the test would not be a true indicator of intelligence. The test would be reliable—but invalid. Reliability and validity are issues with all assessments, not just standardized tests. Classroom tests should yield scores that are *reliable*, that are as free from error as possible, and *valid*— accurately measure what they are supposed to.

ABSENCE OF BIAS. The third important criterion for judging assessments is absence of bias. **Assessment bias** "refers to qualities of an assessment instrument that offend or unfairly penalize a group of students because of the students' gender, ethnicity, socio-economic status, religion, or other such group-defining characteristic" (Popham, 2011, p. 111). Biases are aspects of the test such as content, language, or examples that might distort the performance of a group—either for better or for worse. For example, if a reading test used passages that described boxing or football scenarios, we might expect males on average to do better than females.

Two forms of assessment bias are *unfair penalization* and *offensiveness*. The reading assessment with heavy sports content is an example of unfair penalization—girls may be penalized for their lack of boxing or football knowledge. Offensiveness occurs when a particular group might be insulted by the content of the assessment. Offended, angry students may not perform at their best.

What about biases based on ethnicity or social class? Research on test bias shows that most standardized tests predict school achievement equally well across all groups of students (Sattler, 2001). But even so, many people believe that the tests still can be unfair to some groups. Tests may not have *procedural fairness*; that is, some groups may not have an equal opportunity to show what they know on the test. Here are a few examples:

1. The language of the test and the tester is often different from the languages of the students.
2. Answers that support middle-class values are often rewarded with more points.
3. On individually administered intelligence tests, being very verbal and talking a lot is rewarded. This favors students who feel comfortable in that particular situation.

Also, tests may not be fair because different groups have had different opportunities to learn the material tested. The questions asked tend to center on experiences and facts more familiar to the dominant culture than to minority-group students. Consider this test item for 4th graders described by Popham (2011, p. 371):

> My uncle's field is computer programming.

Look at the sentences below. In which sentence does the word *field* mean the same as it does in the boxed sentence above?

A. The softball pitcher knew how to field her position.
B. They prepared the field by spraying and plowing it.
C. I know the field I plan to enter when I finish college.
D. The doctor used a wall chart to examine my field of vision.

Items like this are included on most standardized and textbook tests. But not all families describe their work as a field of employment. If your parents work in professional fields such as computers, medicine, law, or education, the item would make sense, but what if

Assessment bias Qualities of an assessment instrument that offend or unfairly penalize a group of students because of the students' gender, SES, race, ethnicity, etc.

your parents worked at a grocery store or a car repair shop? Are these fields? Life outside class has prepared some students, but not others, for this item.

Concern about cultural bias in testing has led some psychologists to try to develop **culture-fair** or **culture-free tests**. These efforts have not been very successful. On many of the so-called culture-fair tests, the performance of students from lower-SES backgrounds and ethnic groups has been the same as or worse than their performance on the standard Wechsler and Binet Intelligence scales (Sattler, 2001). And when you think about it, how can you separate culture from cognition? Every student's learning is embedded in his or her culture and every test question emerges from some kind of cultural knowledge.

Today, most standardized tests are checked carefully for assessment bias, but teacher-made tests may have biased content as well. It makes sense to have colleagues check your tests for bias, especially when you are getting started in teaching (Popham, 2011).

With this background in the basic concepts of formative and summative assessments; norm-referenced and criterion-referenced interpretations; and attention to reliability, validity, and absence of bias, we are ready to enter the classroom, where *learning is supported by frequent assessments using cumulative questions that ask students to apply and integrate knowledge.*

CLASSROOM ASSESSMENT: TESTING

STOP & THINK Think back to your most recent test. What was the format? Did you feel that the test results were an accurate reflection of your knowledge or skills? Have you ever had to design a test? What makes a good, fair test? •

Connect and Extend to PRAXIS II™

Traditional Assessment (II C1, 2, 4) Objective and essay tests continue to have important roles in effective assessment and evaluation programs. Describe the appropriate uses of these types of tests. Identify the advantages and limitations of each.

When most people think of assessments in a classroom, they usually think of testing. As you will see shortly, teachers today have many other options, but testing is still a significant activity in most classrooms. In this section, we will examine how to evaluate the tests that accompany standard curriculum materials and show you how to write your own test questions.

Using the Tests from Textbooks

Most elementary and secondary school texts today come complete with supplemental materials such as teaching manuals and ready-made tests. Using these tests can save time, but is this good teaching practice? The answer depends on your objectives for your students, the way you teach the material, and the quality of the tests provided. If the textbook test is of high quality, matches your testing plan, and fits the instruction you actually provided for your students, then it may be the right test to use. Check the reading level of the items provided and be prepared to revise/improve them (Airasian, 2005; McMillan, 2004). Table 12.2 gives key points to consider in evaluating textbook tests.

What if there are no tests available for the material you want to cover, or the tests provided in your teachers' manuals are not appropriate for your students? Then it's time for you to create your own tests. We will consider the two major kinds of traditional tests—objective and essay.

Objective Testing

Multiple-choice questions, matching exercises, true/false statements, and short-answer or fill-in items are all types of **objective testing**. The word *objective* in relation to testing means "not open to many interpretations," or "not subjective." The scoring of these types of items is relatively straightforward compared to the scoring of essay questions because the answers are more clear-cut than essay answers.

How should you decide which item format is best for a particular test? Use the one that provides the most direct measure of the learning outcome you intended for your students (Gronlund & Waugh, 2009). In other words, if you want to see how well students can write a letter, have them write a letter, don't ask multiple-choice questions about letters. But if many different item formats will work equally well, then use multiple-choice

Culture-fair/culture-free test A test without cultural bias.

Objective testing Multiple-choice, matching, true/false, short-answer, and fill-in tests; scoring answers does not require interpretation.

TABLE 12.2 • **Key Points to Consider in Judging Textbook Tests**

1. The decision to use a textbook test or pre-made standard achievement test must come *after* a teacher identifies the objective that he or she has taught and now wants to assess.
2. Textbook and standard tests are designed for the typical classroom, but since few classrooms are typical, most teachers deviate somewhat from the text in order to accommodate their pupils' needs.
3. The more classroom instruction deviates from the textbook, the less valid the textbook tests are likely to be.
4. The main consideration in judging the adequacy of a textbook or standard achievement test is the match between its test questions and what pupils were taught in their classes:

    a. Are questions similar to the teacher's objectives and instructional emphases?
    b. Do questions require pupils to perform the behaviors they were taught?
    c. Do questions cover all or most of the important objectives taught?
    d. Is the language level and terminology appropriate for pupils?
    e. Does the number of items for each objective provide a sufficient sample of pupil performance?

Source: From Classroom Assessment: Concepts and Applications (5th ed.) by P. W. Airasian (2005). New York: McGraw-Hill, p. 161. With permission from The McGraw-Hill Companies.

questions because they are easier to score fairly and can cover many topics. Switch to other formats if writing good multiple-choice items for the material is not possible or appropriate. For example, if related concepts such as terms and definitions need to be linked, then a matching item is a better format than multiple-choice. If it is difficult to come up with several wrong answers for a multiple-choice item, try a true/false question instead. Alternatively, ask the student to supply a short answer that completes a statement (fill in the blank). Variety in objective testing can lower students' anxiety because the entire grade does not depend on one type of question that a particular student may find difficult. We will look closely at the multiple-choice format because it is the most versatile—and the most difficult to use well.

USING MULTIPLE-CHOICE TESTS.   Even though about three-fourths of education professors reject the use of multiple-choice tests in determining students' grades, about half of public school teachers endorse these tests (Banks, 2005), so you should know how to use these tests well. In fact, many schools require teachers to give students experience answering multiple-choice tests in order to prepare them for NCLB testing (McMillan, 2004). Of course, multiple-choice items can test facts, but these items can assess more than recall and recognition if they require the student to deal with new material by applying or analyzing the concept or principle being tested (Gronlund & Waugh, 2009; McMillan, 2004). For example, the following multiple-choice item is designed to assess students' ability to recognize unstated assumptions, one of the skills involved in analyzing an idea:

> An educational psychology professor states, "A z score of +1 on a test is equivalent to a percentile rank of approximately 84." Which of the following assumptions is the professor making?
>
> 1. The scores on the test range from 0 to 100.
> 2. The standard deviation of the test scores is equal to 3.4.
> 3. The distribution of scores on the test is normal. (Correct answer)
> 4. The test is valid and reliable.

If you did not know the correct answer above, don't worry. We will get to z scores later in this chapter and it will all make sense.

WRITING MULTIPLE-CHOICE QUESTIONS.   All test items require skillful construction, but good multiple-choice items are a real challenge. Some students jokingly refer to multiple-choice tests as "multiple-guess" tests—a sign that these tests are often poorly designed. Your goal in writing test items is to design them so that they measure student achievement, not test-taking and guessing skills.

GUIDELINES

Writing Objective Test Items

Make the stem clear and simple, and present only a single problem. Unessential details should be left out.

Example

Poor	Better
There are several different kinds of standard or derived scores. An IQ score is especially useful because	An advantage of an IQ score is

State the problem in the stem in positive terms. Negative language is confusing. If you must use words such as *not, no,* or *except*, underline them or type them in all capitals.

Example

Poor	Better
Which of the following is not a standard score?	Which of the following is NOT a standard score?

Do not expect students to make extremely fine discriminations among answer choices.

Example

The percentage of area in a normal curve falling between +1 and −1 standard deviations is about:

Poor		Better	
a. 66%	b. 67%	a. 14%	b. 34%
c. 68%	d. 69%.	c. 68%	d. 95%.

Make sure each alternative answer fits the grammatical form of the stem, so that no answers are obviously wrong.

Example

Poor	Better
The Stanford-Binet test yields an	The Stanford-Binet is a test of
a. IQ score.	a. intelligence.
b. reading level.	b. reading level.
c. vocational preference.	c. vocational preference.
d. mechanical aptitude.	d. mechanical aptitude.

Avoid including two distractors that have the same meaning.

If only one answer can be right and if two answers are the same, then these two must both be wrong. This narrows down the choices considerably.

Avoid using categorical words such as *always, all, only,* or *never* unless they can appear consistently in all the alternatives.

Most smart test takers know that categorical answers are usually wrong.

Avoid using the exact wording found in the textbook.

Poor students may recognize the answers without knowing what they mean.

Avoid overuse of *all of the above* and *none of the above*.

Such choices may be helpful to students who are simply guessing. In addition, using *all of the above* may trick a quick student who sees that the first alternative is correct and does not read on to discover that the others are correct, too.

Avoid obvious patterns on a test—they aid students who are guessing.

The position of the correct answer should be varied, as should its length.

The **stem** of a multiple-choice item is the part that asks the question or poses the problem. The choices that follow are called *alternatives*. The wrong answers are called **distractors** because their purpose is to distract students who have only a partial understanding of the material. If there were no good distractors, students with only a vague understanding would have no difficulty in finding the right answer. The *Guidelines* should help you write good stems and alternatives.

Stem The question part of a multiple-choice item.

Distractors Wrong answers offered as choices in a multiple-choice item.

Essay Testing

The best way to measure some learning objectives is to ask students to create answers on their own; essay questions are one way to accomplish this. The most difficult part of essay testing is judging the quality of the answers, but writing good, clear questions is not particularly easy, either. We will look at writing, administering, and grading essay tests.

We will also consider factors that can bias the scoring of essay questions and ways you can overcome these problems.

CONSTRUCTING ESSAY TESTS. Because answering takes time, true essay tests cover less material than objective tests. Thus, for efficiency, essay tests should be limited to the assessment of important, complex learning outcomes. A good essay question gives students a clear and precise task and indicates the elements to be covered in the answer. The students should know how extensive their answer needs to be and about how much time they should spend on each question. Evaluate these two essay questions from Popham (2011, pp. 183–184):

1. (High school level) You have just viewed a videotape containing three widely seen television commercials. What is the one classic propaganda technique present in all three commercials?
2. (Middle school level) Thinking back over the mathematics lesson and homework assignments you had during the past 12 weeks, what conclusions can you draw? Take no more than one page for your response.

Question 1 is pretty clear (do you agree?), but some indication of desired length would be helpful. Question 2 gives a page limit, but would you know what is being asked? What is the specific question here?

Students need ample time for answering. If more than one essay is assigned in the same class period, you may want to suggest time limits for each question. Remember, however, that time pressure increases anxiety and may prevent accurate assessment of some students. Whatever your approach, do not try to make up for the limited amount of material an essay test can cover by including a large number of questions. It would be better to plan on more frequent testing than to include more than two or three essay questions in a single class period. Combining an essay question with a number of objective items is one way to avoid the problem of limited sampling of course material (Gronlund & Waugh, 2009).

EVALUATING ESSAYS. Gronlund and Waugh (2009) offer several strategies for grading essays. When possible, a good first step is to construct a set of scoring criteria or a rubric (more on this later) and share it with students. Then, decide what type of information should be in every answer. Here is an example from TenBrink (2003, p. 326).

> *Question:* Defend or refute the following statement: Civil wars are necessary to the growth of a developing country. Cite reasons for your argument, and use examples from history to help substantiate your claim.
> *Scoring Rubric:* All answers, regardless of the position taken, should include (1) a clear statement of the position, (2) at least five logical reasons, (3) at least four examples from history that clearly substantiate the reasons given.

Once you have set your expectations for answers, you can assign points to the various parts of the essay. You might also give points for the organization of the answer and the internal consistency of the essay. You can then assign grades such as 1 to 5 or A, B, C, D, and F, and sort the papers into piles by grade. As a final step, skim the papers in each pile to see if they are comparable in quality. These techniques will help ensure fairness and accuracy in grading.

When grading essay tests that contain several questions, it makes sense to grade all responses to one question before moving on to the next. This helps prevent the quality of a student's answer to one question from influencing your reaction to the student's other answers. After you finish reading and scoring the first question, shuffle the papers so that no students end up having all their questions graded first (when you may be taking more time to give feedback or are applying stricter standards, for example) or last (when you may be tired of writing feedback or more lax in your standards). You may achieve greater objectivity if you ask students to put their names on the back of the paper, so that grading is anonymous. A final check on your fairness as a grader is to have another teacher who is equally familiar with your goals and subject matter look over a few of your tests without

NONTRADITIONAL ASSESSMENTS Alternatives to traditional testing have emerged that address what are seen as its limits, including that it emphasizes recall of facts instead of thinking and problem solving. Alternative approaches include authentic assessment, student exhibitions, and student portfolios.

knowing what grades you have assigned. This can give you valuable insights into areas of bias in your grading practices.

THE VALUE OF TRADITIONAL TESTING. Right answers are important. Even though schooling is about learning to think and solve problems, it is also about knowledge. Students must have something to think about—facts, ideas, concepts, principles, theories, explanations, arguments, images, opinions. Well-designed traditional tests can evaluate students' knowledge effectively and efficiently (Airasian, 2005). Some educators believe that traditional testing should play an even greater role than it currently does. Educational policy analysts suggest that American students, compared to students in many other developed countries, lack essential knowledge because American schools emphasize process—critical thinking, self-esteem, problem solving—more than content. In order to teach more about content, teachers will need to determine how well their students are learning the content, and traditional testing provides useful information about content learning. Tests are also valuable in motivating and guiding students' learning. There is research evidence that frequent testing encourages learning and retention. In fact, taking more frequent tests improves learning, even if there is no feedback from the test—bad teaching, but a powerful result (Roediger & Karpicke, 2006)

CRITICISMS OF TRADITIONAL TESTS. Traditional testing has been under fire since at least the 1990s. As Grant Wiggins (1991) noted then:

> We do not judge Xerox, the Boston Symphony, the Cincinnati Reds, or Dom Perignon vineyards on the basis of indirect, easy to test, and common indicators. Nor would the workers in those places likely produce quality if some generic, secure test served as the only measure of their success in meeting a standard. Demanding and getting quality, whether from students or adult workers, means framing standards in terms of the work that we undertake and value. (p. 22)

Wiggins continues to argue for assessment that makes sense, that tests knowledge as it is applied in real-world situations. Understanding cannot be measured by tests that ask students to use skills and knowledge out of context.

Your stand on traditional testing is part of your philosophy of teaching. Let's look at a few alternative approaches to classroom assessment.

AUTHENTIC CLASSROOM ASSESSMENTS

Authentic assessments ask students to apply skills and abilities as they would in real life. For example, they might use fractions to enlarge or reduce recipes. Grant Wiggins (1989) made this argument over 20 years ago:

> If tests determine what teachers actually teach and what students will study for—and they do—then the road to reform is a straight but steep one: test those capabilities and habits we think are essential, and test them in context. Make [tests] replicate, within reason, the challenges at the heart of each academic discipline. Let them be—authentic. (p. 41)

Authentic assessments
Assessment procedures that test skills and abilities as they would be applied in real-life situations.

Wiggins goes on to say that if our instructional goals for students include the abilities to write, speak, listen, create, think critically, do research, solve problems, or apply knowledge, then our tests should ask students to write, speak, listen, create, think, research, solve, and apply. How can this happen?

Many educators suggest we look to the arts and sports for analogies to solve this problem. If we think of the "test" as being the recital, exhibition, game, mock court trial, or other performance, then teaching to the test is just fine. All coaches, artists, and musicians gladly "teach" to these "tests" because performing well on these tests is the whole point of instruction. Authentic assessment asks students to perform. The performances may be thinking performances, physical performances, creative performances, or other forms. So **performance assessment** is any form of assessment that requires students to carry out an activity or produce a product in order to demonstrate learning (Airasian, 2005).

It may seem odd to talk about thinking as a performance, but there are many parallels. Serious thinking is risky, because real-life problems are not well defined. Often, the outcomes of our thinking are public—others evaluate our ideas. Like a dancer auditioning for a Broadway show, we must cope with the consequences of being evaluated. Like a potter looking at a lump of clay, a student facing a difficult problem must experiment, observe, redo, imagine, and test solutions, apply both basic skills and inventive techniques, make interpretations, decide how to communicate results to the intended audience, and often accept criticism and improve the initial solution (Eisner, 1999; Herman, 1997).

Portfolios and Exhibitions

The concern with authentic assessment has led to the development of several approaches based on the goal of performance in context. Instead of circling answers to "factual" questions about nonexistent situations, students are required to solve real problems. Facts are used in a context where they apply—for example, instead of asking students, "If you bought a toy for 69 cents and gave the clerk a dollar, how much change would you get back?" have students work in pairs with real money to role play making different purchases or set up a mock class store and have students make purchases and give change (Gronlund & Waugh, 2009, p. 151). The following is taken from the New York State Alternative Assessment in Science Project, 9–12th Grade Performance assessment (http://butterfly.ctl.sri.com/pals/tasks/9-12/Perspiration/admin.html).

Description:

Students collect data on the cooling of water in two different test tubes—one wrapped in wet newspaper and one in dry newspaper. They then identify trends in their data, make predictions, and describe how their experiment is similar to the body's perspiration. The task assesses students' abilities to make simple observations, gather and collect data, identify trends and make predictions, and demonstrate their understanding by relating the experiment to real life.

Overall Task Content Area:

Life Science

Specific Knowledge Areas:

Regulation and behavior

Performance Expectations:

- conducting investigations
- using equipment
- gathering, organizing, and representing data
- formulating conclusions from investigational data
- applying scientific principles to develop explanations and solve new problems

Students completing this "test" will use scientific knowledge to understand a real-life phenomenon—perspiration. In the process, they will have to think critically and write persuasively. Every year, most states release some of the items from past tests to the public. The Center for Technology in Learning of SRI International, a nonprofit science research

Connect and Extend to PRAXIS II™

Authentic Tests (II, C1, 2, 4)
The emphasis on student-centered learning has been accompanied by an emphasis on authentic tests. Understand the purpose, value, and advantages of these forms of assessment. Describe their characteristics and the potential problems with their use.

Performance assessments Any form of assessment that requires students to carry out an activity or produce a product in order to demonstrate learning.

institute, also provides an online resource bank of performance-based assessments linked to the National Science Education Standards. The resource is called PALS (Performance Assessment Links in Science). Go to http://butterfly.ctl.sri.com/pals/index.html; see the performance tasks for kindergarten through 12th grade. You can select tasks by standard and grade level. Each task comes with directions for students, a guide for administrators, and a scoring guide or rubric. Many also have examples of student work. The Life Science task on the previous page came from that site.

Portfolios and exhibitions are two approaches to assessment that require performance in context. With these approaches, it is difficult to tell where instruction stops and assessment starts because the two processes are interwoven (Oosterhof, 2009; Popham, 2011).

Connect and Extend to PRAXIS II™

Portfolio Assessment (II, C1, 2) For a discussion of the advantages, limitations, design, and implementation of portfolio programs, and to examine samples of portfolio checklists, go to Teachervision.com (http://www.teachervision.com/lesson-plans/lesson-4536.html).

PORTFOLIOS.   For years, photographers, artists, models, and architects have had portfolios to display their skills and show to prospective employers. A **portfolio** is a systematic collection of work, often including work in progress, revisions, student self-analyses, and reflections on what the student has learned. Written work or artistic pieces are common contents of portfolios, but student portfolios might also include letters to the portfolio readers describing each entry and its importance, graphs, diagrams, pictures or digital slideshows, PowerPoint presentations, recordings of the students reading their work, unedited and final drafts of persuasive essays or poems, lists of books read, annotated Web site addresses, peer comments, videotapes, laboratory reports, and computer programs—anything that demonstrates learning in the area being taught and assessed (Popham, 2011). There is a distinction between process portfolios and final or "best work" portfolios. The distinction is similar to the difference between formative and summative evaluation. Process portfolios document learning and show progress. Best work portfolios showcase final accomplishments (Johnson & Johnson, 2002). Table 12.3 shows some examples for both individuals and groups.

EXHIBITIONS.   An **exhibition** is a performance test that has two additional features. First, it is public, so students preparing exhibitions must take the audience into account; communication and understanding are essential. Second, an exhibition often requires many hours of preparation, because it is the culminating experience of a whole program of study. Thomas Guskey and Jane Bailey (2001) suggest that exhibits help students understand the qualities of good work and recognize those qualities in their own productions and performances. Students also benefit when they select examples of their work to exhibit and articulate their reasons for making the selections. Being able to judge quality can encourage student motivation by setting clear goals. The *Guidelines* on page 458 give some ideas for using portfolios in your teaching.

Evaluating Portfolios and Performances

Checklists, rating scales, and scoring rubrics are helpful when you assess performances, because assessments of performances, portfolios, and exhibitions are criterion-referenced, not norm-referenced. In other words, the students' products and performances are compared to established public standards, not ranked in relation to other students' work (Wiggins, 1991).

Portfolio A collection of the student's work in an area, showing growth, self-reflection, and achievement.

Exhibition A performance test or demonstration of learning that is public and usually takes an extended time to prepare.

Scoring rubrics Rules that are used to determine the quality of a student's performance.

SCORING RUBRICS.   A checklist or rating scale gives specific feedback about elements of a performance. **Scoring rubrics** are rules that are used to determine the quality of a student performance, often on a 4-point scale from "excellent" (4) to "inadequate" (1) or on a scale that assigns points to each category—10 points for excellent, 6 for good, and so on (Mabry, 1999). For example, a rubric describing excellent *delegation of responsibility* in a group research project might be:

Each student in the group can clearly explain what information is needed by the group, what information s/he is responsible for locating, and when the information is needed.

This rubric was generated using Rubistar (http://rubistar.4teachers.org/index.php), an online service for educators that allows you to select a subject area and category, then create a rubric. To get the above rubric, I chose the subject of writing—"group planning

TABLE 12.3 • **Process and Best Works Portfolios for Individuals and Groups**

Here are a few examples of how to use portfolios in different subjects.

THE PROCESS PORTFOLIO		
Subject Area	**Individual Student**	**Cooperative Group**
Science	Documentation (running records or logs) of using the scientific method to solve a series of laboratory problems	Documentation (observation checklists) of using the scientific method to solve a series of laboratory problems
Mathematics	Documentation of mathematical reasoning through double-column mathematical problem solving (computations on the left side and running commentary explaining thought processes on the right side)	Documentation of complex problem solving and use of higher-level strategies
Language Arts	Evolution of compositions from early notes through outlines, research notes, response to others' editing, and final draft	Rubrics and procedures developed to ensure high-quality peer editing
THE BEST WORKS PORTFOLIO		
Subject Area	**Individual Student**	**Cooperative Group**
Language Arts	The best compositions in a variety of styles—expository, humor/satire, creative (poetry, drama, short story), journalistic (reporting, editorial columnist, reviewer), and advertising copy	The best dramatic production, video project, TV broadcast, newspaper, advertising display
Social Studies	The best historical research paper, opinion essay on historical issue, commentary on current event, original historical theory, review of a historical biography, account of academic controversy participated in	The best community survey, paper resulting from academic controversy, oral history compilation, multidimensional analysis of historical event, press corps interview with historical figure
Fine Arts	The best creative products such as drawings, paintings, sculptures, pottery, poems, thespian performance	The best creative products such as murals, plays written and performed, inventions thought of and built

Source: From D.W. Johnson and R.T. Johnson, Meaningful Assessment: A Meaningful and Cooperative Process. Published by Allyn and Bacon, Boston, MA.

and research project"—and the category of "delegation of responsibility." The *Guidelines* on the next page give more ideas; some are taken from Goodrich (1997), Johnson and Johnson (2002), and Popham (2011).

Performance assessment requires careful judgment on the part of teachers and clear communication to students about what is good and what needs improving. In some ways, the approach is similar to the clinical method first introduced by Binet to assess intelligence: It is based on observing the student perform a variety of tasks and comparing his or her performance to a standard. Just as Binet never wanted to assign a single number to represent the child's intelligence, teachers who use authentic assessments do not try to assign one score to the student's performance. Even if rankings, ratings, and grades have to be given, these judgments are not the ultimate goals—improvement of learning is.

Connect and Extend to PRAXIS II™

Scoring Rubrics (II, C3)
Kathy Schrock's Guide for Educators (http://school.discovery.com/schrockguide/assess.html) provides information about every aspect of the use of scoring rubrics in the classroom as well as an extensive collection of rubrics that can be used or adapted by teachers.

GUIDELINES

Creating Portfolios

Involve students in selecting the pieces that will make up their portfolios.
Examples

1. During the unit or semester, ask each student to select work that fits certain criteria, such as "my most difficult problem," "my best work," "my most improved work," or "three approaches to."
2. For their final submissions, ask students to select pieces that best show how much they have learned.

Make sure the portfolios include information that shows student self-reflection and self-criticism.
Examples

1. Ask students to include a rationale for their selections.
2. Have each student write a "guide" to his or her portfolio, explaining how strengths and weaknesses are reflected in the work included.
3. Include self- and peer critiques, indicating specifically what is good and what might be improved.
4. Model self-criticism of your own productions.

Make sure the portfolios reflect the students' activities in learning.
Examples

1. Include a representative selection of projects, writings, drawings, and so forth.
2. Ask students to relate the goals of learning to the contents of their portfolios.

Be aware that portfolios can serve different functions at different times of the year.
Examples

1. Early in the year, it might hold unfinished work or "problem pieces."
2. At the end of the year, it should contain only what the student is willing to make public.

Be certain portfolios demonstrate students' growth.
Examples

1. Ask students to make a "history" of their progress along certain dimensions and to illustrate points in their growth with specific works.
2. Ask students to include descriptions of activities outside class that reflect the growth illustrated in the portfolio.

Teach students how to create and use portfolios.
Examples

1. Keep models of very well done portfolios as examples, but stress that each portfolio is an individual statement.
2. Examine your students' portfolios frequently, especially early in the year when they are just getting used to the idea. Give constructive feedback.

For more ideas about using portfolios, see http://www.teachervision.fen.com/assessment/teaching-methods/20153.html

GUIDELINES

Developing a Rubric

1. **Look at models:** Show students examples of good and not-so-good work based on composites of work not linked to individual students. Identify the characteristics that make the good ones good and the bad ones bad.
2. **List criteria:** Use the discussion of models to begin a list of what counts in quality work.
3. **Articulate gradations of quality:** Describe the best and worst levels of quality; then fill in the middle levels based on your knowledge of common problems and the discussion of not-so-good work.
4. **Practice on models:** Have students use the rubrics to evaluate the models you gave them in Step 1.
5. **Use self- and peer-assessment:** Give students their task. As they work, stop them occasionally for self- and peer-assessment.
6. **Revise:** Always give students time to revise their work based on the feedback they get in Step 5.

7. **Use teacher assessment:** In your grading, be sure to use the same rubric students used to assess their work.

Note: Step 1 may be necessary only when you are asking students to engage in a task with which they are unfamiliar. Steps 3 and 4 are useful but time consuming; you can do these on your own, especially when you've been using rubrics for a while. A class experienced in rubric-based assessment can streamline the process so that it begins with listing criteria, after which the teacher writes out the gradations of quality, checks them with the students, makes revisions, then uses the rubric for self-, peer-, and teacher assessment.

For a great explanation of using rubrics, see http://pareonline.net/getvn.asp?v=7&n=25

The article includes several links such as http://www.teach-nology.com/web_tools/rubrics/ and http://rubistar.4teachers.org/ that allow you to create and customize rubrics for your class.

It is often helpful to have students join in the development of rating scales and scoring rubrics. When students participate, they are challenged to decide what quality work looks or sounds like in a particular area. They know in advance what is expected. As students gain practice in designing and applying scoring rubrics, their work and their learning often improve. Figure 12.1 gives three alternatives—numerical, graphic, and descriptive—for rating an oral presentation.

RELIABILITY, VALIDITY, GENERALIZABILITY.   Because the teacher's personal judgment plays such a central role in evaluating performances, issues of reliability, validity, and generalizability are critical considerations. One teacher's "excellent" could be another teacher's "adequate." Research shows that when raters are experienced and scoring rubrics are well developed and refined, reliability may improve (Herman & Winters, 1994; LeMahieu, Gitomer, & Eresh, 1993). Some of this improvement in reliability occurs because a rubric focuses the raters' attention on a few dimensions of the work and gives limited scoring levels to choose from. If scorers can give only a rating of 1, 2, 3, or 4, they are more likely to agree than if they could score based on a 100-point scale. So the rubrics may achieve

---

FIGURE 12.1

THREE WAYS OF RATING AN ORAL PRESENTATION

Numerical Rating Scale

Directions:
Indicate how often the pupil performs each of these behaviors while giving an oral presentation. For each behavior circle **1** if the pupil **always** performs the behavior, **2** if the pupil **usually** performs the behavior, **3** if the pupil **seldom** performs the behavior, and **4** if the pupil **never** performs the behavior.

Physical Expression

A. Stands straight and faces audience.
    1 2 3 4
B. Changes facial expression with change in the tone of the presentation.
    1 2 3 4

Graphic Rating Scale

Directions:
Place an **X** on the line that shows how often the pupil did each of the behaviors listed while giving an oral presentation.

Physical Expression

A. Stands straight and faces audience.

    always   usually   seldom   never

B. Changes facial expression with change in the tone of the presentation.

    always   usually   seldom   never

Descriptive Rating Scale

Directions:
Place an **X** on the line at the place that best describes the pupil's performance of each behavior.

Physical Expression

A. Stands straight and faces audience.

| stands straight, always looks at audience | weaves, fidgets, eyes roam from audience to ceiling | constant, distracting movements, no eye contact with audience |

B. Changes facial expression with change in the tone of the presentation.

| matches facial expressions to content and emphasis | facial expressions usually appropriate, occasional lack of expression | no match between tone and facial expression; expression distracts |

Source: From Classroom Assessment: Concepts and applications (5th ed.) by P. W. Airasian (2005). New York: McGraw-Hill, p. 251. With permission of The McGraw-Hill Companies.

reliability not because they capture underlying agreement among raters, but because the rubrics limit options and thus limit variability in scoring (Mabry, 1999).

In terms of validity, there is some evidence that students who are classified as "master" writers on the basis of portfolio assessment are judged less capable using standard writing assessments. Which form of assessment is the best reflection of enduring qualities? It is hard to say. In addition, when rubrics are developed to assess specific tasks, the results of applying them may not predict performance on anything except very similar tasks, so we do not know whether a student's performance on a specific task will generalize to the larger area of study (Haertel, 1999; Herman & Winters, 1994; McMillan, 2004).

DIVERSITY AND BIAS IN PERFORMANCE ASSESSMENT.   Equity is an issue in all assessment and no less so with performances and portfolios. With a public performance, there could be bias effects based on a student's appearance and speech or the student's access to expensive audio, video, or graphic tools. Performance assessments have the same potential as other tests to discriminate unfairly against students who are not wealthy or who are culturally different (McDonald, 1993). And the extensive group work, peer editing, and out-of-class time devoted to portfolios means that some students may have access to greater networks of support and outright help. Many students in your classes will come from families that have sophisticated computer graphics and desktop publishing capabilities. Others may have little support from home. These differences can be sources of bias and inequity, especially in portfolios and exhibitions.

Informal Assessments

Informal assessments are ungraded (formative) assessments that gather information from multiple sources to help teachers make decisions (Banks, 2005). Early on in the unit, assessments should be formative (provide feedback, but not count toward a grade), saving the actual graded assessments for later in the unit when all students have had the chance to learn the material (Tomlinson, 2005a). Some examples of informal assessment are journals, student observations and checklists, questioning, and student self-assessment.

JOURNALS.   Journals are very flexible and widely used informal assessments. Students usually have personal or group journals and write in them on a regular basis. In their study, Michael Pressley and his colleagues (2007) found that excellent 1st grade literacy teachers used journaling for three purposes:

- As communication tools that allowed students to express their own thoughts and ideas.
- As an opportunity to apply what they have learned.
- As an outlet to encourage fluency and creative expression in language usage.

Teachers may use journals to learn about their students in order to better connect their teaching to the students' concerns and interests. But often journals focus on academic learning, usually through responses to prompts. Banks (2005) describes one high school physics teacher who asked his students to respond to these three questions in their journals:

1. How can you determine the coefficient of friction if you know only the angle of the inclined plane?
2. Compare and contrast magnetic, electronic, and gravitational fields.
3. If you were to describe the physical concept of sound to your best friend, what music would you use to demonstrate this concept?

When he read the students' journals, the teacher realized that many of the students' basic assumptions about friction, acceleration, and velocity came from personal experiences and not from scientific reasoning. His approach to teaching had to change to reach the students. The teacher never would have known to make the changes in his instruction without reading the journals (Banks, 2005).

There are many other kinds of informal assessments—keeping notes and observations about student performance, rating scales, and checklists. Every time teachers ask questions or watch students perform skills, the teachers are conducting informal assessments. Look at Table 12.4, which summarizes the possibilities and limitations of aligning different assess-

Informal assessments Ungraded (formative) assessments that gather information from multiple sources to help teachers make decisions.

ment tools with their targets. One major message in this chapter is the importance of correctly matching the type of assessment tools used to the target—to what is being assessed.

INVOLVING STUDENTS IN ASSESSMENTS.   One way to connect teaching and assessment while developing students' sense of efficacy for learning is to involve the students in the assessment process. Students can keep track of their own progress and assess their improvement. Here are other ideas, some taken from Stiggins and Chappuis (2005). Students might:

- Learn about the criteria for judging work by examining and discussing with a peer examples of good, average, and poor products or performances. Then pick a poor example and revise to improve it.
- Describe to the teacher or a peer (orally or in writing) the way they approached an assignment, the problems they encountered, the options they considered, and the final result.
- Analyze their strengths and weaknesses before starting a project, then discuss with the teacher or peers how they will use their strengths and overcome their weaknesses as they work on the project.
- In pairs, make up questions that might be on the test, explain why those are good questions, and then answer them together.

TABLE 12.4 • **Aligning Different Assessment Tools with Their Targets**

Different learning outcomes require different assessment methods.

ASSESSMENT METHOD				
Target to Be Assessed	**Selected Response**	**Essay**	**Performance Assessment**	**Personal Communication**
Knowledge Mastery	Multiple-choice, true/false, matching, and fill-in can sample mastery of elements of knowledge	Essay exercises can tap understanding of relationships among elements of knowledge	Not a good choice for this target—three other options preferred	Can ask questions, evaluate answers, and infer mastery—but a time-consuming option
Reasoning Proficiency	Can assess understanding of basic patterns of reasoning	Written descriptions of complex problem solutions can provide a window into reasoning proficiency	Can watch students solve some problems and infer about reasoning proficiency	Can ask student to "think aloud" or can ask follow-up questions to probe reasoning
Skills	Can assess mastery of the prerequisites of skillful performance—but cannot tap the skill itself	Can assess mastery of the prerequisites of skillful performance—but cannot tap the skill itself	Can observe and evaluate skills as they are being performed	Strong match when skill is oral communication proficiency; also can assess mastery of knowledge prerequisite to skillful performance
Ability to Create Products	Can assess mastery of knowledge prerequisite to the ability to create quality products—but cannot assess the quality of products themselves	Can assess mastery of knowledge prerequisite to the ability to create quality products—but cannot assess the quality of products themselves	A strong match can assess: (a) proficiency in carrying out steps in product development and (b) attributes of the product itself	Can probe procedural knowledge and knowledge of attributes of quality products—but not product quality

Source: From "Where Is Our Assessment Future and How Can We Get There?" by R. J. Stiggins. In R. W. Lissitz, W. D. Schafer (Eds.), Meaningful Assessment: A Meaningful and Cooperative Process. Published by Allyn and Bacon, Boston, MA. Copyright © 2002 by Pearson Education. Adapted by permission of the publisher.

- Look back at earlier work and analyze how they have grown by describing "I used to think . . . but now I know. . . ." After doing a few of these analyses, summarize using a frame such as: What did I know before I started? What did I learn? What do I want to learn next
- Before a major test, do a free write on these prompts "What exactly will be on the test?" "What kinds of questions will be asked (multiple-choice, essay, etc.)?" "How well will I do?" "What do I need to study to make sure I am ready?"

One last idea—the teacher arranges items on a test according to specific learning targets, and prepares a "test analysis" chart for students, with three boxes: "My strengths," "Quick review," and "Further study." After handing back the corrected test, students identify learning targets they have mastered and write them in the "My strengths" box. Next, students categorize their wrong answers as either "simple mistake" or "further study." Then, students list the simple mistakes in the "Quick review" box. Last, students write the rest of the learning targets represented by wrong answers in the "Further study" box.

No matter how you assess students, ultimately you will assign grades. We turn to that job next.

GRADING

STOP & THINK Think back on your report cards and grades over the years. Did you ever receive a grade that was lower than you expected? How did you feel about yourself, the teacher, the subject, and school in general as a result of the lower grade? What could the teacher have done to help you understand and profit from the experience? •

In determining a final grade, the teacher must make a major decision. Should a student's grade reflect the student's status in comparison with the rest of the class, or should the grade reflect the amount of material learned and how well it has been learned? In other words, should grading be *norm-referenced* or *criterion-referenced?*

Norm-Referenced versus Criterion-Referenced Grading

In **norm-referenced grading**, the major influence on a grade is the student's standing in comparison with others who also took the course. If a student studies very hard and almost everyone else does too, the student may receive a disappointing grade, perhaps a C or D. One common type of norm-referenced grading is called **grading on the curve.** How you feel about this approach probably depends on where your grades generally fall along that "curve." There is good evidence that this type of grading damages the relationships among students and between teachers and students and also diminishes motivation for most students (Krumboltz & Yeh, 1996). When you think about it, if the curve arbitrarily limits the number of good grades that can be given, then, in the game of grading, most students will be losers (Guskey & Bailey, 2001; Haladyna, 2002; Kohn, 1996b). Over 30 years ago, Benjamin Bloom (of Bloom's taxonomy) and his colleagues (1981) pointed out the fallacy of grading on the curve:

> There is nothing sacred about the normal curve. It is the distribution most appropriate to chance and random activity. Education is a purposeful activity, and we seek to have students learn what we have to teach. If we are effective in our instruction, the distribution of achievement should be very different from the normal curve. In fact, we may even insist that our educational efforts have been unsuccessful to the extent that the distribution of achievement approximates the normal distribution. (pp. 52–53)

In **criterion-referenced grading**, the grade represents a list of accomplishments. If clear objectives have been set for the course, the grade may represent a certain number of objectives met satisfactorily. When a criterion-referenced system is used, criteria for each grade generally are spelled out in advance. It is then up to the student to earn the grade she or he wants to receive. Theoretically, in this system, all students can achieve an A if

Norm-referenced grading Assessment of students' achievement in relation to one another.

Grading on the curve Norm-referenced grading that compares students' performance to an average level.

Criterion-referenced grading Assessment of each student's mastery of course objectives.

they reach the criteria. Criterion-referenced grading has the advantage of relating judgments about a student to the achievement of clearly defined instructional goals. Some school districts have developed reporting systems where report cards list objectives along with judgments about the student's attainment of each. Reporting is done at the end of each unit of instruction. The elementary school report card shown in Figure 12.2 demonstrates the relationship between assessment and the goals of the unit.

Most schools have a specified grading system, so we won't spend time here on the many possible systems. Let's consider a different question—one with research behind it. What is the effect of grades on students?

FIGURE 12.2

A CRITERION-REFERENCED REPORT CARD

This is one example of a criterion-referenced report card. Other forms are possible, but all criterion-referenced reports indicate student progress toward specific goals.

LINCOLN ELEMENTARY SCHOOL
GRADE 5

Student _____ Teacher _____ Principal __Muriel Simms__ Quarter 2 3 4

E = Excellent   S = Satisfactory   P = Making Progress   N = Needs improvement

READING PROGRAM

Materials Used: _____
_____

___ Reads with understanding
___ Is able to write about what is read
___ Completes reading group work accurately and on time
___ Shows interest in reading

Reading Skills
___ Decodes new words
___ Understands new words

Independent Reading Level
Below/At Grade Level/Above

LANGUAGE ARTS

___ Uses oral language effectively
___ Listens carefully
___ Masters weekly spelling

Writing skills
___ Understands writing as process
___ Creates a rough draft
___ Makes meaningful revisions
___ Creates edited, legible final draft

Editing skills
___ Capitalizes
___ Punctuates
___ Uses complete sentences
___ Uses paragraphs
___ Demonstrates dictionary skills

Writing skill level:
Below/At Grade Level/Above

MATHEMATICS

Problem Solving
___ Solves teacher-generated problems
___ Solves self-/student-generated problems
___ Can create story problems

Interpreting Problems
___ Uses appropriate strategies
___ Can use more than one strategy
___ Can explain strategies in written form
___ Can explain strategies orally

Math Concepts
   Understands Base Ten
Beginning/Developing/Sophisticated
   Multiplication, Basic facts
Beginning/Developing/Sophisticated
   2-Digit Multiplications
Beginning/Developing/Sophisticated
   Division
Beginning/Developing/Sophisticated
   Geometry
Beginning/Developing/Sophisticated

Overall Math Skill Level:
Beginning/Developing/Sophisticated

Attitude/Work Skills
___ Welcomes a challenge
___ Persistent
___ Takes advantage of learning from others
___ Listens to others
___ Participates in discussion

It Figures
Is working on: _____

Goals: _____
Is working on achieving goal:
_____

SOCIAL STUDIES
___ Understands subject matter
___ Shows curiosity and enthusiasm
___ Contributes to class discussions
___ Uses map skills
___ Demonstrates control of reading skills by interpreting text
Topics covered: individual cultures, Columbus–first English colonies

SCIENCE
___ Shows curiosity about scientific subject matter
___ Asks good scientific questions
___ Shows knowledge of scientific method
___ Uses knowledge of scientific method to help set up and run experiment(s)
___ Makes good scientific observations
___ Has researched scientific topic(s)
   Topic(s) _____

I Wonder
Is currently working on _____

WORKING SKILLS
___ Listens carefully
___ Follows directions
___ Works neatly and carefully
___ Checks work
___ Completes work on time
___ Uses time wisely
___ Works well independently
___ Works well in a group
___ Takes risks in learning
___ Welcomes a challenge

HOMEWORK
___ Self-selects homework
___ Completes work accurately
___ Completes work on time

PRESENTATIONS/PROJECTS
_____
_____

HUMAN RELATIONS
___ Shows courtesy
___ Respects rights of others
___ Shows self-control
___ Interacts well with peers
___ Shows a cooperative and positive attitude in class
___ Shows a cooperative attitude when asked to work with other students
___ Is willing to help other students
___ Works well with other adults (subs, student teacher, parents, etc.)

Attendance

	1st	2nd	3rd	4th
Present				
Absent				
Tardy				

Placement for next year:

Source: From Lincoln Elementary School, Grade 5, Madison, WI. Used with permission.

EFFECTS OF FEEDBACK Students often need help figuring out why their answers are incorrect; without such feedback they are likely to make the same mistakes again.

Effects of Grading on Students

When we think of grades, we often think of competition. Highly competitive classes may be particularly hard on anxious students, students who lack self-confidence, and students who are less prepared. So, although high standards and competition do tend to be generally related to increased academic learning, it is clear that a balance must be struck between high standards and a reasonable chance to succeed. Rick Stiggins and Jan Chappuis (2005) observe:

> From their very earliest school experiences, our students draw life-shaping conclusions about themselves as learners on the basis of the information we provide to them as a result of their teachers' classroom assessments. As the evidence accumulates over time, they decide if they are capable of succeeding or not. They decide whether the learning is worth the commitment it will take to attain it. They decide . . . whether to risk investing in the schooling experience. These decisions are crucial to their academic well-being. (p. 11)

It may sound as though low grades and failure should be avoided in school. But the situation is not that simple.

THE VALUE OF FAILING?   After reviewing many years of research on the effects of failure from several perspectives, Margaret Clifford (1990, 1991) concluded:

> It is time for educators to replace easy success with challenge. We must encourage students to reach beyond their intellectual grasp and allow them the privilege of learning from mistakes. There must be a tolerance for error-making in every classroom, and gradual success rather than continual success must become the yardstick by which learning is judged. (1990, p. 23)

Some level of failure may be helpful for most students, especially if teachers help the students see connections between hard work and improvement. Efforts to protect students from failure and to guarantee success may be counterproductive. Carol Tomlinson, an expert on differentiated instruction, puts it this way: "Students whose learning histories have caused them to believe that excellence can be achieved with minimal effort do not learn to expend effort, and yet perceive that high grades are an entitlement for them" (2005b, p. 266). So maybe not failure, but accurate and critical feedback can be especially important for students who are used to easy As (Shute, 2008).

RETENTION IN GRADE.   So far, we have been talking about the effects of failing a test or perhaps a course. But what about the effect of failing an entire grade—that is, of being "held back"? One study in North Carolina found that kindergarten retention had more than doubled from 1992 to 2002, with over 6% of students retained in 2002. About 10% of U.S. students ages 16–19 have been retained at least once (Wu, West, & Hughes, 2010). Retained children are more likely to be male, members of minority groups, living in poverty, and younger, and less likely to have participated in early childhood programs (Beebe-Frankenberger, Bovina, Macmillan, & Gresham, 2004; Hong & Raudenbush, 2005). Is retention a good policy? See the *Point/Counterpoint* to examine the issue.

Grades and Motivation

If you are relying on grades to motivate students, you had better think again (Smith, Smith, & De Lisi, 2001). The assessments you give should support students' motivation to learn—not their motivation to work for a good grade. But is there really a difference between working for a grade and working to learn? The answer depends in part on how a grade is determined. If you test only at a simple but detailed level of knowledge, you

POINT/COUNTERPOINT: Should Children Be Held Back?

For the last 100 years, parents and educators have debated about the value of retention versus *social promotion* (passing students on to the next grade with their peers). What does the evidence say? What are the arguments?

▶ **Yes, it just makes sense.** Retention in kindergarten for children considered "not ready" for 1st grade is a common practice. Compared to students who are relatively younger (January to August birthdays), students who are relatively older (born September to November) have higher achievement in school on average (Cobley, McKenna, Baker, & Wattie, 2009). In fact, some parents hold their son or daughter back to give the child an edge over peers in each grade thereafter or because the child was born late in the year—a practice sometimes called "academic red-shirting." In the mid-1960s, 96% of 6-year-olds were enrolled in 1st grade in the United States. By 2008, the number was 84% (Barnard-Brak, 2008). The results on academic red-shirting are mixed. Some studies have found benefits for students who have been held back by their parents, but other studies have found no benefits.

With the increased emphasis on high standards and accountability, the idea of social promotion has come under fire and retention is seen as the better way. Guanglei Hong and Stephen Raudenbush (2005) summarize this and other arguments that have been made in favor of retention:

A widely endorsed argument is that, when low-achieving students are retained in a grade, the academic status of children in a classroom will become more homogeneous, easing the teacher's task of managing instructional activities (Byrnes, 1989; also see Shepard & Smith, 1988, for a review). In particular, retaining some children in kindergarten may allow the first-grade teacher to teach at a higher level, benefiting those who would be promoted under the policy. Meanwhile, children who view grade retention as a punishment may study harder to avoid being retained in the future. Some have argued that, in comparison with the social promotion policy, repeating a grade is perhaps developmentally more appropriate and may make learning more meaningful for children who are struggling (Plummer & Graziano, 1987; Smith & Shepard, 1988). If these arguments are correct, adopting a policy of grade retention will benefit those promoted and those retained, thus boosting achievement overall. (p. 206)

▶ **No, retention is not effective.** After summarizing the arguments in favor of kindergarten retention, Hong and Raudenbush (2005) review the findings of almost a century of research. They note that even though there are a small number of studies that support the value of retention, the weight of the evidence indicates that it is not helpful and may even be harmful. Most research finds that grade retention is associated with poor long-term outcomes such as dropping out of school, higher arrest rates, fewer job opportunities, lower self-esteem (Jimerson, 1999; Jimerson, Anderson, & Whipple, 2002; Jimerson & Ferguson, 2007; Shepard & Smith, 1989). Lucy Barnard-Brak (2008) studied a national sample of 986 children who had been identified as having learning disabilities and concluded, "delayed kindergarten entrance was not associated with better academic achievement for children with learning disabilities across time" (p. 50).

The study by Hong and Raudenbush (2005) examined data on 11,843 kindergarten students who participated in a longitudinal study that followed them to the end of 1st grade. The researchers were able to compare retained and promoted students from schools that practice retention as well as promoted students from schools that practice social promotion. They found no evidence that retention improved either reading or mathematics achievement. In addition, retention did not seem to improve instruction in the 1st grade by making the class more similar in academic ability. After one year, the retained students were an average of one year behind, and evidence indicated that these children would have done better if promoted. The researchers concluded that retention "seemed to have constrained the learning potential for all but the highest-risk children" (p. 220). Another study that followed retained and promoted students for 4 years found some short-term advantages for retained students in social and behavioral skills, followed by long-term problems and vulnerabilities. The authors suggest that the "struggle-succeed-struggle" pattern may undermine academic motivation for retained students and interfere with peer relations (Wu, West, & Hughes, 2010).

Beware of Either/Or: Using Research for Children. No matter what, children who are having trouble should get help, whether they are promoted or retained. However, just covering the same material again in the same way won't solve the children's academic or social problems. As Jeannie Oakes (1999) has said, "No sensible person advocates social promotion as it is currently framed—simply passing incompetent children on to the next grade" (p. 8). The best approach may be to promote the children along with their peers, but to give them special remediation during the summer or over the next year (Mantzicopoulos & Morrison, 1992). In addition, because the inability to focus attention and self-regulate is an important aspect of readiness to learn (Blair, 2002), help should also focus on improving these skills as well. An even better approach would be to prevent the problems before they occur by providing extra resources in the early years (McCoy & Reynolds, 1999).

GUIDELINES

Using Any Grading System

Explain your grading policies to students early in the course and remind them of the policies regularly.
Examples

1. Give older students a handout describing the assignments, tests, grading criteria, and schedule.
2. Explain to younger students in a low-pressure manner how their work will be evaluated.

Base grades on clearly specified, reasonable standards.
Examples

1. Specify standards by developing a rubric with students—have anonymous examples of poor, good, and excellent work from previous classes.
2. Discuss workload and grading standards with more experienced teachers.
3. Give a few formative tests to get a sense of your students' abilities before you give a graded test.
4. Take tests yourself first to gauge the difficulty of the test and to estimate the time your students will need.

Base your grades on as much objective evidence as possible.
Examples

1. Plan in advance how and when you will test.
2. Keep a portfolio of student work. This may be useful in student or parent conferences.

Be sure students understand test directions.
Examples

1. Outline the directions on the board.
2. Ask several students to explain the directions.
3. Go over a sample question first.

Correct, return, and discuss test questions as soon as possible.
Examples

1. Have students who wrote good answers read their responses for the class; make sure they are not the same students each time.
2. Discuss why wrong answers, especially popular wrong choices, are incorrect.
3. As soon as students finish a test, give them the answers to questions and the page numbers where answers are discussed in the text.

As a rule, do not change a grade.
Examples

1. Make sure you can defend the grade in the first place.
2. DO change any clerical or calculation errors.

Guard against bias in grading.
Examples

1. Ask students to put their names on the backs of their papers.
2. Use an objective point system or model papers when grading essays.

Keep pupils informed of their standing in the class.
Examples

1. Write the distribution of scores on the board after tests.
2. Schedule periodic conferences to go over work from previous weeks.

---

may force students to choose between complex learning and a good grade. But when a grade reflects meaningful learning, working for a grade and working to learn become the same thing. As a teacher, you can use grades to motivate the kind of learning you intend students to achieve in your course. Finally, low grades generally do not encourage greater efforts. Students receiving low grades are more likely to withdraw, blame others, decide that the work is "dumb," or feel responsible for the low grade but helpless to make improvements. They give up on themselves or on school (Tomlinson, 2005b). Rather than assigning a failing grade, you might consider the work incomplete and give students support in revising or improving. Maintain high standards and give students a chance to reach them (Guskey, 2011; Guskey & Bailey, 2001).

Another effect on motivation that occurs in high schools is the race for valedictorian. Sometimes, students and families find clever ways to move ahead of the competition—but the strategies have little to do with learning. As Tom Guskey and Jane Bailey (2001) note, when a valedictorian wins by a 1/1,000 of decimal point, how meaningful is the learning behind the difference? Some high schools now name multiple valedictorians—as many as meet the highest standards of the school—because they believe that the educators' job is "not to select talent, but, rather, to develop talent" (Guskey & Bailey, 2001, p. 39).

The *Guidelines* give ideas for using any grading system in a fair and reasonable way.

Give students the benefit of the doubt. All measurement techniques involve error.
Examples
1. Unless there is a very good reason not to, give the higher grade in borderline cases.
2. If a large number of students miss the same question in the same way, revise the question for the future and consider throwing it out for that test.

Avoid reserving high grades and high praise for answers that conform to your ideas or to those in the textbook.
Examples
1. Give extra points for correct and creative answers.
2. Withhold your opinions until all sides of an issue have been explored.
3. Reinforce students for disagreeing in a rational, productive manner.
4. Give partial credit for partially correct answers.

Make sure each student has a reasonable chance to be successful, especially at the beginning of a new task.
Examples
1. Pretest students to make sure they have prerequisite abilities.
2. When appropriate, provide opportunities for students to retest to raise their grades, but make sure the retest is as difficult as the original.
3. Consider failing efforts as "incomplete" and encourage students to revise and improve.
4. Base grades more on work at the end of the unit; give ungraded work in the beginning of the unit.

Balance written and oral feedback.
Examples
1. Consider giving short, lively written comments with younger students and more extensive written comments with older students.
2. When the grade on a paper is lower than the student might have expected, be sure the reason for the lower grade is clear.
3. Tailor comments to the individual student's performance; avoid writing the same phrases over and over.
4. Note specific errors, possible reasons for errors, ideas for improvement, and work done well.

Make grades as meaningful as possible.
Examples
1. Tie grades to the mastery of important objectives.
2. Give ungraded assignments to encourage exploration.
3. Experiment with performances and portfolios.

Base grades on more than just one criterion.
Examples
1. Use essay questions as well as multiple-choice items on a test.
2. Grade oral reports and class participation.

For more thoughts about grading, see
http://teaching.berkeley.edu/bgd/grading.html

Source: General conferencing guidelines adapted from Problems in Middle and High School Teaching: A Handbook for Student Teachers and Beginning Teachers *(pp. 182–187), by A. M. Drayer, 1979, Boston: Allyn and Bacon. Copyright © 1979 by Allyn and Bacon. Adapted by permission of the author and publisher.*

Beyond Grading: Communicating with Families

No number or letter grade conveys the totality of a student's experience in a class or course. Students, families, and teachers sometimes become too focused on the end point—the grade. But communicating with families should involve more than just sending home grades. There are a number of ways to communicate with and report to families. Many teachers I know have a beginning-of-the-year newsletter or student handbook that communicates homework, behavior, and grading policies to families. Other options described by Guskey & Bailey (2001) are:

- Notes attached to report cards
- Phone calls, especially "Good News" calls
- School open houses
- Student-led conferences
- Portfolios or exhibits of student work
- Homework hotlines
- School or class Web pages
- Home visits

Conferences with parents or caregivers are often expected of teachers in elementary school and can be equally important in middle and high school. Clearly, the more skilled teachers are at communicating, the more effective they will be at conducting these conferences. Listening and problem-solving skills such as those discussed in Chapter 10 can be particularly important. When you are dealing with families or students who are angry or upset, make sure you really hear their concerns, not just their words. The atmosphere should be friendly and unrushed. Any observations about the student should be as factual as possible, based on observation or information from assignments. Information gained from a student or a parent/caregiver should be kept confidential.

One kind of information that will interest parents is their child's standardized test scores. In the next section we look at these tests.

STANDARDIZED TESTING

For as long as I can remember, educators and policy makers have been concerned about the test performance of American students. In 1983, the National Commission on Excellence in Education published *A Nation at Risk: The Imperative for Educational Reform*. According to this report, standardized test scores were at a 25-year low. More recently, politicians point to the Trends in International Mathematics and Science Study (TIMSS) data collected in 1995, 1999, 2003, and 2007 showing that the United States is behind many other developed countries in math and science test scores. These tests were repeated in Spring 2011—stay tuned for the results beginning in December of 2012 (http://timss.bc.edu/timss2011/index.html).

Part of the response to these test results has been more testing. In 2002, President Bush signed the No Child Left Behind Act that requires each state to create content standards in reading, mathematics, and science and assessments to measure student achievement linked to those standards (Linn, Baker, & Betebenner, 2002). Even though the Obama administration allowed exemptions and extensions to the strict requirements, the increase in testing and assessments will affect you, no matter what grade you teach. So teachers must be knowledgeable about testing. Understanding what standardized test scores really mean and how they can be used (or misused) is a good start. Let's look first at the results you will see from testing—the scores.

Types of Scores

STOP & THINK At your first parent conference, a mother and father are concerned about their child's percentile rank of 86. They say that they expect their child to "get close to 100 percent. We know she should be able to do that because her grade-equivalent score is half a year above her grade!" What would you say? Do they understand the meaning of these scores? •

To understand the scores from tests, you need to know some basics about different types of scores and what they tell you, but first you need to know some (easy) statistics.

MEASUREMENTS OF CENTRAL TENDENCY AND STANDARD DEVIATION. You have probably had a great deal of experience with means. A **mean** is simply the arithmetical average of a group of scores. To calculate the mean, you add the scores and divide the total by the number of scores in the distribution. The mean offers one way of measuring **central tendency**, the score that is typical or representative of the whole distribution of scores. Very high or very low scores affect the mean. Two other measures of central tendency are the median and the mode. The **median** is the middle score in a ranked list of scores, the point at which half the scores are larger and half are smaller. When there are a few very high or low scores, the median may be a better representative of the central tendency of a group than the mean. The **mode** is the score that occurs most often.

The measure of central tendency gives a score that is representative of the group of scores, but it does not tell you anything about how the scores are distributed. Two groups of scores may both have a mean of 50, but be alike in no other way. One group might contain the scores 50, 45, 55, 55, 45, 50, 50; the other group might contain the scores 100, 0, 50, 90, 10, 50, 50. In both cases, the mean, median, and mode are all 50, but the distributions are quite different.

The **standard deviation** is a measure of how widely the scores vary from the mean. The larger the standard deviation, the more spread out the scores are in the distribution. The smaller the standard deviation, the more the scores are clustered around the mean.

Connect and Extend to PRAXIS II™

Concepts of Standardized Testing (II, C5)
Be able to define norm groups, measures of central tendency, standard deviation, normal distribution, reliability, and validity, and explain their roles in standardized tests.

Mean Arithmetical average.

Central tendency Typical score for a group of scores.

Median Middle score in a group of scores.

Mode Most frequently occurring score.

Standard deviation Measure of how widely scores vary from the mean.

For example, in the distribution 50, 45, 55, 55, 45, 50, 50, the standard deviation is much smaller than in the distribution 100, 0, 50, 90, 10, 50, 50. Another way of saying this is that distributions with very small standard deviations have less **variability** in the scores.

Knowing the mean and the standard deviation of a group of scores gives you a better picture of the meaning of an individual score. For example, suppose you received a score of 78 on a test. You would be very pleased with the score if the mean of the test were 70 and the standard deviation were 4. In this case, your score would be 2 standard deviations above the mean, a score well above average.

Consider the difference if the mean of the test had remained at 70, but the standard deviation had been 20. In the second case, your score of 78 would be less than 1 standard deviation from the mean. You would be much closer to the middle of the group, with a score above average, but not high. Knowing the standard deviation tells you much more than simply knowing the **range** of scores. No matter how the majority scored on the tests, one or two students may do very well or very poorly and thus make the range very large.

THE NORMAL DISTRIBUTION.   Standard deviations are very useful in understanding test results. They are especially helpful if the results of the tests form a **normal distribution**. You may have encountered the normal distribution before. It is the bell-shaped curve, the most famous frequency distribution because it describes many naturally occurring physical and social phenomena. Many scores fall in the middle, giving the curve its bell appearance. You find fewer and fewer scores as you look out toward the end points, or *tails*, of the distribution. The normal distribution has been thoroughly analyzed by statisticians. The mean of a normal distribution is also its midpoint. Half the scores are above the mean, and half are below it. In a normal distribution, the mean, median, and mode are all the same point.

Another convenient property of the normal distribution is that the percentage of scores falling within each area of the curve is known, as you can see in Figure 12.3. A person scoring within 1 standard deviation of the mean obviously has company. Many scores pile up here. In fact, 68% of all scores are located in the area from 1 standard deviation below to 1 standard deviation above the mean. About 16% of the scores are higher than 1 standard deviation above the mean. Of this higher group, only 2% are higher than 2 standard deviations above the mean. Similarly, only about 16% of the scores are less than 1 standard deviation below the mean, and of that group only about 2% are lower than 2 standard deviations below the mean. At 2 standard deviations from the mean in either direction, the scorer has left the pack.

FIGURE 12.3

THE NORMAL DISTRIBUTION

The normal distribution or bell-shaped curve has certain predictable characteristics. For example, 68% of the scores are clustered within 1 standard deviation below to 1 standard deviation above the mean.

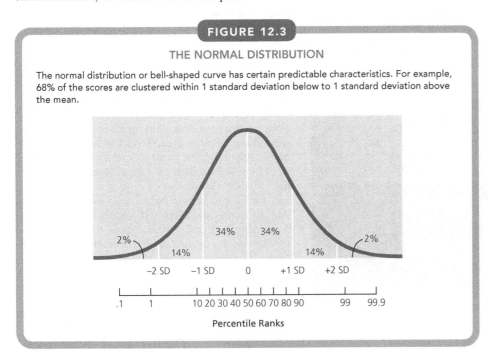

Variability Degree of difference or deviation from mean.

Range Distance between the highest and the lowest scores in a group.

Normal distribution The most commonly occurring distribution, in which scores are distributed evenly around the mean.

The SAT college entrance exam is one example of a normal distribution. The mean of the SAT is 500 and the standard deviation is 100. If you know people who made scores of 700, you know they did very well. Only about 2% of the people who take the test do that well, because only 2% of the scores are better than 2 standard deviations above the mean in a normal distribution. Your score of 78 would be in the top 2% on a test with a mean of 70 and a standard deviation of 4.

Now we are ready to look at different kinds of test scores.

PERCENTILE RANK SCORES.   Ranking is the basis for one very useful kind of score reported on standardized tests, a **percentile rank** score. In percentile ranking, each student's *raw score* (actual number correct) is compared with the raw scores of the students in the *norm group* (comparison group). The percentile rank shows the percentage of students in the norm group that scored at or below a particular raw score. If a student's score were the same as or better than three-quarters of the students in the norm group, the student would score in the *75th percentile* or have a percentile rank of 75. You can see that this does not mean that the student had a raw score of 75 correct answers or even that the student answered 75% of the questions correctly. Rather, the 75 refers to the percentage of people in the norm group whose scores on the test were equal to or below this student's score. A percentile rank of 50 means that a student has scored as well as or better than 50% of the norm group and has achieved an average score.

There is one caution in interpreting percentile scores. Differences in percentile ranks do not mean the same thing in terms of raw score points in the middle of the scale as they do at the fringes. For example, the difference between the 50th and 60th percentile might be just 2 raw points, whereas the difference on the same test between the 90th and 99th percentile could be about 10 points. So a few answers right or wrong can make a bigger difference in percentile scores if you are near the middle.

GRADE-EQUIVALENT SCORES.   **Grade-equivalent scores** are generally obtained from separate norm groups for each grade level. The average of the scores of all the 10th graders in the norm group defines the 10th grade equivalent score. Suppose the raw-score average of the 10th grade norm group is 38. Any student who attains a raw score of 38 on that test will be assigned a grade-equivalent score of 10th grade. Grade-equivalent scores are generally listed in numbers such as 8.3, 4.5, 7.6, 11.5, and so on. The whole number gives the grade. The decimals stand for tenths of a year, but they are usually interpreted as months.

Suppose a student with the grade-equivalent score of 10 is a 7th grader. Should this student be promoted immediately? Probably not. Different forms of tests are used at different grade levels, so the 7th grader may not have had to answer items that would be given to 10th graders. The high score may represent superior mastery of material at the 7th grade level rather than a capacity for doing advanced work. Even though an average 10th grader could do as well as our 7th grader on this particular test, the 10th grader would certainly know much more than this 7th grade test covered. Also, grade-equivalent score units do not mean the same thing at every grade level. For example, a 2nd grader reading at the 1st grade level would have more trouble in school than an 11th grader who reads at the 10th grade level.

Because grade-equivalent scores are misleading and are often misinterpreted, especially by parents, most educators and psychologists strongly believe *they should not be used at all*. There are several other forms of reporting available that are more appropriate.

STANDARD SCORES.   As you may remember, one problem with percentile ranks is the difficulty in making comparisons among ranks. A discrepancy of a certain number of raw-score points has a different

Percentile rank Percentage of those in the norming sample who scored at or below an individual's score.

Grade-equivalent score Measure of grade level based on comparison with norming samples from each grade.

STANDARDIZED TESTS You can tell these students are concentrating. What will their scores tell us? What do they mean?

meaning at different places on the scale. With standard scores, on the other hand, a difference of 10 points is the same everywhere on the scale.

Standard scores are based on the standard deviation. A very common standard score is called the **z score.** A z score tells how many standard deviations above or below the average a raw score is. In the example described earlier, in which you were fortunate enough to get a 78 on a test where the mean was 70 and the standard deviation was 4, your z score would be +2, or 2 standard deviations above the mean. If a person were to score 64 on this test, the score would be 1.5 standard deviation units below the mean, and the z score would be −1.5. A z score of 0 would be no standard deviations above the mean—in other words, right on the mean. Measurements similar to z scores are used when you take a bone density test. Your score will compare your bone density to that of a healthy 30-year-old. If your score is below −1, you are moving toward osteoporosis. Below −2, you are there.

To calculate the z score for a given raw score, subtract the mean from the raw score and divide the difference by the standard deviation. The formula is:

$$z = \frac{\text{Raw Score} - \text{Mean}}{\text{Standard Deviation}}$$

Because it is often inconvenient to use negative numbers, other standard scores have been devised to eliminate this difficulty. The **T score** has a mean of 50 and uses a standard deviation of 10. Thus, a T score of 50 indicates average performance. If you multiply the z score by 10 (which eliminates the decimal) and add 50 (which gets rid of the negative number), you get the equivalent T score as the answer. The person whose z score was −1.5 would have a T score of 35.

First multiply the z score by 10: $-1.5 \times 10 = -15$
Then add 50: $-15 + 50 = 35$

As you saw, the scoring of the SAT test is based on a similar procedure, with a mean score set at 500, and a standard deviation of 100. Most IQ tests have a mean score of 100 and a standard deviation of 15. Different states have different ways of determining standards-based scores. For example, scale scores for each grade and subject on the California Standards Tests (CSTs) range from 150 to 600 (http://star.cde.ca.gov/star2009/help_scoreexplanations.asp).

Before we leave this section on types of scores, we should mention one other widely used method. **Stanine scores** (the name comes from "standard nine") are standard scores. There are only nine possible scores on the stanine scale, the whole numbers 1 through 9. The mean is 5, and the standard deviation is 2. Each unit from 2 to 8 is equal to half a standard deviation.

Stanine scores provide a method of considering a student's rank, because each of the nine scores includes a specific range of percentile scores in the normal distribution. For example, a stanine score of 1 is assigned to the bottom 4% of scores in a distribution. A stanine of 2 is assigned to the next 7%. Of course, some raw scores in this 7% range are better than others, but they all get a stanine score of 2.

Each stanine score represents a wide range of raw scores. This has the advantage of encouraging teachers and parents to view a student's score in more general terms instead of making fine distinctions based on a few points. Figure 12.4 on the next page compares the four types of standard scores we have considered, showing how each would fall on a normal distribution curve.

Interpreting Standardized Test Reports

STOP & THINK Look at the test printout in Figure 12.5. on page 579. What are this student's strengths and weaknesses? How do you know? •

What specific information can teachers expect from achievement test results? Test publishers usually provide individual profiles for each student, showing scores on each subtest. Figure 12.5 is an example of a Student Report for a 4th grader, Sally Valenzuela, on the *Stanford Achievement Test, 10th Edition*. Note that the Student Report has three sections.

Standard scores Scores based on the standard deviation.

z score Standard score indicating the number of standard deviations above or below the mean.

T score Standard score with a mean of 50 and a standard deviation of 10.

Stanine scores Whole number scores from 1 to 9, each representing a wide range of raw scores.

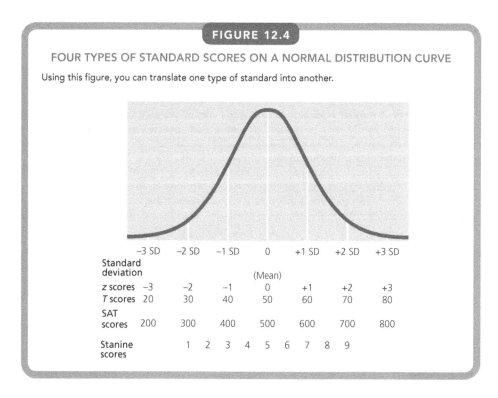

FIGURE 12.4

FOUR TYPES OF STANDARD SCORES ON A NORMAL DISTRIBUTION CURVE

Using this figure, you can translate one type of standard into another.

	−3 SD	−2 SD	−1 SD	0	+1 SD	+2 SD	+3 SD
Standard deviation				(Mean)			
z scores	−3	−2	−1	0	+1	+2	+3
T scores	20	30	40	50	60	70	80
SAT scores	200	300	400	500	600	700	800
Stanine scores		1 2	3	4 5 6	7	8 9	

Connect and Extend to PRAXIS II™

Interpreting Achievement Tests (II, C4)

Accurate information from the teacher is essential for students' academic progress. The ERIC Digest *Explaining Test Results to Parents* (http://www.ericdigests.org/pre-9210/parents.htm) will help with this task. See Chapter 6 for a discussion of how to use praise effectively. These guidelines apply to written feedback as well.

The first, (About This Student's Performance), is a brief narrative explanation that may include a Lexile Measure™, which is computed from the Reading Comprehension score and helps teachers identify Sally's reading level in order to select appropriate texts.

The second section (Subtests and Totals) attempts to paint a picture of the student's achievement in *Reading, Mathematics, Language, Spelling, Science, Social Science, Listening,* and *Thinking Skills*. That section also includes total scores on the battery of tests and scores on the Otis-Lennon School Ability test—a kind of group IQ or scholastic aptitude test. Some of the subtests are further divided into more specific assessments. For example, *Reading* is broken down into "word study skills," "reading vocabulary," and "reading comprehension." Next to each subtest are several different ways of reporting Sally's score. The school decides which scores are reported, based on a list of possible reporting formats. This school chose the following types of scores:

Number Correct: Under the second column is the number of items that Sally answered correctly for that subtest (the total number of items on the subtest is in the first column).

Scale Score: This is basic score used to derive all the other scores, sometimes called a *growth score* because it describes growth in achievement that typically occurs as students move through the grades. For example, the average score for 3rd graders might be 585, whereas the average score for 10th graders might be 714 on tests with possible scores that range from 0 to 1000 across the entire K–12 grades. Often, the difficulty of items is included in calculating scale scores. Schools are increasingly using this score because they can compare across years, classes, or schools in the district (Popham, 2005a).

National PR-S (National Percentile Rank and Stanine): This score tells us where Sally stands in relation to students at her grade level across the country in terms of percentile rank (percent with the same score or lower) and stanine.

National NCE (Normal Curve Equivalent): This is a standard score derived from the percentile rank, with a range of 1 to 99, a mean of 50, and a standard deviation of 21.

Grade Equivalent Score: This indicates that Sally's scaled score is the same as an average student in the indicated grade and month of school. Beware of the problems with grade-equivalent scores described earlier.

AAC (Achievement/Ability Comparison) Range: The ACC score compares Sally's achievement on each subtest to a norm group of other students who have her same ability as measured by the Otis-Lennon School Ability test. The ACC range categorizes Sally's ACC score as HIGH, MIDDLE, or LOW. You can see that Sally is in the middle on most of the subtests, so her achievement is in the middle compared to students with abilities similar to hers.

National Grade Percentile Bands: The range of national percentile scores in which Sally's true score is likely to fall. You may remember from our discussion of true scores that this range, or confidence interval, is determined by adding and subtracting the standard error of the test from Sally's actual score. Chances are high that Sally's true score is within this range. Bands that do not overlap indicate likely differences in achievement.

The bottom of Figure 12.5 (Clusters) breaks Sally's subtests down into even more specific skills. For each skill we see the number of questions possible to answer (NP), the number Sally attempted (NA), and the number she got correct (NC). The check marks beside the skills indicate if she is average, above average, or below average in each. Notice that some skills are assessed with only a few (3 to 8) questions. Remember that fewer items means less reliability.

FIGURE 12.5

A TYPICAL SCORE REPORT

A sample test score report, with no actual test data used.

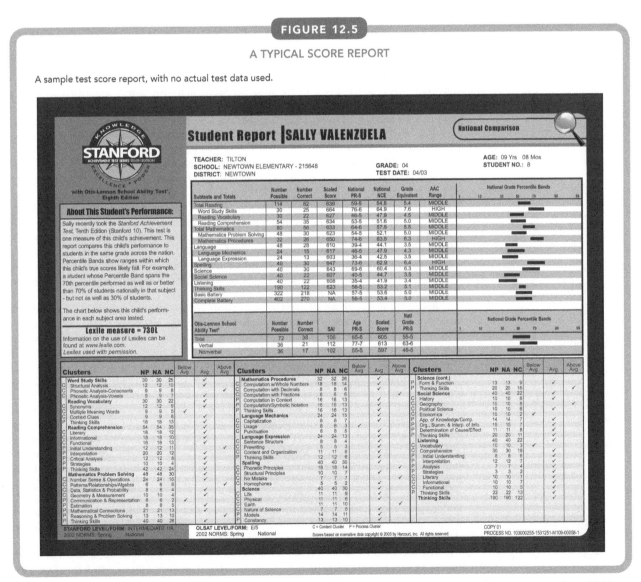

Source: Sample Stanford Student Report in Score Report Sampler: Guide-Teaching and Learning Toward High Academic Standards for the Stanford Achievement Test Series, 10th Edition (Stanford 10). Copyright © 2003 by NCS Pearson, Inc. Reproduced with permission. All rights reserved.

DISCUSSING TEST RESULTS WITH FAMILIES. Teachers often have formal conferences and informal talks with parents or caregivers. Often the topic is testing results. At times, you will be expected to explain or describe test results to your students' families. The *Family and Community Partnerships Guidelines* give some ideas.

Accountability and High-Stakes Testing

STOP & THINK How has standardized testing affected your life so far? What opportunities have been opened or closed to you based on test scores? Was the process fair? •

Every day, there are many decisions made about individuals that are based on the results of tests. Should Russell be issued a driver's license? How many and which students from the 8th grade would benefit from an accelerated program in science? Who needs extra tutoring? Who will be admitted to college or professional school? Test scores may affect "admission" to 1st grade, promotion from one grade to the next, high school graduation, access to special programs, placement in special education classes, teacher licensure and tenure, and school funding.

MAKING DECISIONS. In making these decisions, it is important to distinguish between the *quality* of the test itself and the way the test is *used*. Even the best assessments can be, and have been, misused. Years ago, for example, using otherwise valid and reliable individual intelligence tests, many students were inappropriately identified as having mental retardation, the term used at that time (Snapp & Woolfolk, 1973). The problem was not with the tests, but with the fact that the test score was the only information used to classify students. Much more information is always needed to make this type of placement decision.

Behind all the statistics and terminology are issues related to values and ethics. Who will be tested? What are the consequences of choosing one test over another for a particular purpose with a given group? What is the effect of the testing on the students? How will the test scores of minority-group students be interpreted? What do we really mean by *intelligence, competence,* and *scholastic aptitude*? Do our views agree with those implied by the tests we use to measure these constructs? How will test results be integrated with other information about the individual to make judgments? Answering these questions requires choices based on values, as well as accurate information about what tests can and cannot tell us. Keep these values issues in mind as we examine testing uses and decisions.

Because the decisions affected by test scores are so critical, many educators call this process **high-stakes testing**. One of the high-stakes uses for test results is to hold teachers, schools, and administrators **accountable** for student performance. For example, teacher bonuses might be tied to their students' achievement or schools' funding may be affected by testing results. One of the provisions in the No Child Left Behind Act is that states must develop **adequate yearly progress (AYP)** objectives for all students in general and also for specific groups such as students from major ethnic and racial groups, students with disabilities, students from low-income families, and students whose English is limited. These AYP objectives must be set with the goal that all students are proficient or better by the 2013–2014 school year. Schools that fail to meet their AYP objectives for two years will be identified as needing improvement (Linn, Baker, & Betebenner, 2002). The students in these "failing schools" can transfer. If a school's scores don't improve after three years, the school curriculum and/or staff can be replaced. In 2011 Arne Duncan, the Secretary of Education, waived the requirement to reach 100% proficiency for states that could demonstrate they have adopted their own testing and accountability programs and are making progress toward the goal of college or career readiness for all their high school graduates (Dillion, 2011).

The teachers I work with are frustrated that often test results come too late in the year to help them plan instruction or remediation for their current students. They also

Connect and Extend to PRAXIS II™

Standardized Testing: Major Issues (II, C5)
Since their inception, there have been controversies regarding the use of standardized tests in the schools. Familiarize yourself with the major issues that underlie these controversies. Explain the positions of the different camps in these controversies.

High-stakes testing Standardized tests whose results have powerful influences when used by school administrators, other officials, or employers to make decisions.

Accountable Making teachers and schools responsible for student learning, usually by monitoring learning with high-stakes tests.

Adequate yearly progress (AYP) Objectives for yearly improvement for all students and for specific groups such as students from major ethnic and racial groups, students with disabilities, students from low-income families, and students whose English is limited.

GUIDELINES — FAMILY AND COMMUNITY PARTNERSHIPS

Conferences and Explaining Test Results

GENERAL CONFERENCING GUIDELINES

Decide on a few clear goals for the conference.
Examples

Gathering information about the student to help in your instruction

Explaining grades or test results

Letting parents know what is coming during the next unit or marking period

Soliciting help from parents

Making suggestions for use at home

Begin and end with a positive statement.
Examples

"Jacob is a natural leader."

"Eve really enjoys the science center."

"Yesim is really supportive when other students are upset."

"Ashanti's sense of humor keeps the class positive."

Listen actively.
Examples

Accept the emotions of parents or caregivers. Don't try to talk them out of what they feel.

"You seem to feel frustrated when Lee doesn't do his homework."

Respect family members' time and their concern about their child—Establish a partnership.
Examples

Speak plainly, briefly, and avoid jargon.

Be tactful, but don't avoid talking about tough issues.

Ask families to follow through on class goals at home: "Ask Leona for her homework checklist and help her keep it up to date. I will do the same at school."

Learn from the family members.
Examples

What are the students' strengths as revealed in hobbies or extracurricular activities?

What are the students' interests?

Follow-up and follow through.
Examples

Send a brief note thanking the family members for attending.

Share student successes through notes or e-mail messages.

Keep families informed before problems develop.

EXPLAINING AND USING TEST RESULTS

Explain in nontechnical terms, what each type of score on the test report means and why tests are not "perfect."
Examples

1. If the test is norm-referenced, know what the comparison group was (National? State? Local district?). Explain that the child's score shows how he or she performed in relation to the other students in the comparison group.

2. If the test is criterion-referenced, explain that the scores show how well their child performs specific tasks such as word problems or reading comprehension.

3. Encourage parents to think of the score not as a single point, but as a range or band that includes the score.

4. Ignore small differences between scores.

For norm-referenced tests, use percentile scores. They are the easiest to understand.
Examples

1. Percentile scores tell what percent of students in the comparison group made the same score or lower—higher percentiles are better and 99 is as high as you can get: 50 is average.

2. Percentile scores do not tell the "percent correct," so scores that would be bad on a classroom test (say 65% to 75% or so) often are above average—even good—as percentile scores.

Avoid using grade-equivalent scores.
Examples

1. If parents want to focus on the "grade level" of their child, tell them that high grade-equivalent scores reflect a thorough understanding of the current grade level and NOT the capacity to do higher grade-level work.

2. Tell parents that the same grade-equivalent score has different meanings in different subjects—reading versus mathematics, for example.

Source: Based on ideas from The Successful Classroom: Management Strategies for Regular and Special Education Teachers by D. P. Fromberg & M. Driscoll. Published by Teachers College, Columbia University; Scholastic. (2011). Planning for parent conferences, http://www2.scholastic.com/browse/article.jsp?id=4194; and Kennedy, K. (2009). Teacher tips: Explaining achievement test results to parents, http://www.helium.com/items/1636565-parents-and-achievement-tests

For more help explaining tests to parents, see http://pareonline.net/getvn.asp?v=1&n=1

are troubled by the amount of time that testing takes—to prepare for the tests and to give them. They complain that the tests cover material that their curriculum does not include. Are they right?

DOCUMENTED PROBLEMS WITH HIGH-STAKES TESTING. When so much rides on the results of a test, you would assume that the test actually measured what had been taught. In the past, this match has been a problem. Recently, the overlap between what is taught and what is tested has been improving, but it still makes sense to be aware of possible mismatches.

What about time? Studies have found that in some states, 80% of the elementary schools spend about 20% of their instructional time preparing for the end-of-grade tests (Abrams & Madaus, 2003). Studies of the actual high-stakes tests in action show other troubling consequences. Testing narrows the curriculum. In fact, after examining the results of years of testing, Lisa Abrams and George Madaus (2003) concluded "In every setting where a high-stakes test operates, the exam content eventually defines the curriculum" (p. 32). For example, using the Texas Assessment of Academic Skills has led to curriculum changes that overemphasize what is tested and neglect other areas. In addition, it seems that the test of mathematics is also a test of reading. Students with poor reading ability have trouble with the math test, especially if their first language is not English.

Another unintended consequence of the early-warning testing in elementary school is to "push out" students who believe they are going to fail the high school graduation test. If they won't graduate anyway, they see no point in continuing to attend school (McNeil & Valenzuela, 2000). For example, in the 2000–2001 school year, about one-third of the English Language Learners dropped out of high school in New York. The main reason given was their inability to pass the required Regents Exam (Medina, 2002). No matter how good the test, some uses of high-stakes tests are not appropriate. Table 12.5 describes some of them.

USING HIGH-STAKES TESTING WELL. To be valuable, testing programs must have a number of characteristics. Of course, the tests used must be reliable, valid for the purposes used, and free of bias. In addition, the testing program must:

1. Match the content standards of the district—this is a vital part of validity.
2. Be part of the larger assessment plan. No individual test provides all the necessary information about student achievement. It is critical that schools avoid making pass/fail decisions based on a single test.
3. Test complex thinking, not just skills and factual knowledge.
4. Provide alternate assessment strategies for students with identifiable disabilities.
5. Provide opportunities for retesting when the stakes are high.
6. Include all students in the testing, but also provide informative reports of the results that make the students' situations clear if they have special challenges or circumstances such as disabilities.
7. Provide appropriate remediation when students fail.
8. Make sure all students taking the test have adequate opportunities to learn the material being tested.
9. Take into account the student's language. Students who have difficulty reading or writing in English will not perform well on tests that require English proficiency.
10. Use test results for children, not against them (Haladyna, 2002).

This is important, so I will repeat it: High-stakes standardized **achievement tests** must be chosen so that the items on the test actually measure knowledge gained in the classes. Also, students must have the necessary skills to take the test. If students score low on a science test not because they lack knowledge about science, but because they have difficulty reading the questions, don't speak English fluently, or have too little time to finish, then the test is not a valid measure of science achievement for those students.

Connect and Extend to PRAXIS II™

Alternatives to Standardized Testing (II, C1)
For an overview of the major forms of authentic testing, go to Teachervision.com (http://www.teachervision.com/lesson-plans/lesson-6385.html).

Achievement tests Standardized tests measuring how much students have learned in a given content area.

TABLE 12.5 • **Inappropriate Uses for High-Stakes Test Results**

Beware of some uses for standardized test results. Tests were not designed for these purposes.

Pass/Fail Decisions	In order to deny students graduation from any grade, there must be strong evidence that the test used is valid, reliable, and free of bias. Some tests, for example, the *Texas Assessment of Academic Skills* (TAAS), have been challenged in the courts and found to meet these standards, but not all tests are good enough to make pass/fail decisions.
State-to-State Comparisons	You cannot really compare states using standardized test scores. States do not have the same curriculum, tests, resources, or challenges. If comparisons are made, they usually tell us what we already know—some states have more funding for schools and families with higher incomes or education levels.
Evaluation of Teachers or Schools	Many influences on test scores—family and community resources—are outside the control of teachers and schools. Often students move from school to school, so many students taking a test in spring may have been in the school only for a few weeks.
Identifying Where to Buy a House	Generally speaking, the schools with the highest test scores are in the neighborhoods where families have the highest levels of education and income. They may not be the "best schools" in terms of teaching, programs, or leadership, but they are the schools lucky enough to have the "right" students.

Source: From Essentials of Standardized Achievement Testing: Validity and Accountability. T. H. Haladyna, Published by Allyn and Bacon, Boston, MA. Copyright © 2002 by Pearson Education. Adapted by permission of the publisher.

Reaching Every Student: Helping Students with Disabilities Prepare for High-Stakes Tests

Erik Carter and his colleagues (2005) tested a procedure for preparing students with learning disabilities, mild intellectual disabilities, and language impairments for a high-stakes state test The students were ages 15 to 19; over half were African American males and all had IEPs (Individual Educational Programs—see Chapter 4) to guide their education. None had passed the state-required achievement tests. Over six class periods, an instructor taught the students strategies such as filling in bubbles on answer sheets completely, sorting problems by difficulty and doing the easy ones first, using rounding to estimate answers in math, identifying exactly what the question is asking by underlining key words and phrases, and strategies for eliminating alternatives that have redundant information or extreme qualifiers.

The good news is that after completing the preparation program, students improved their scores significantly on the tests. But the bad news is that the increases were not large enough to bring most of the students to the passing level. The authors recommend that preparation for testing should occur much earlier for students with disabilities. At an average age of 16, the students in this study already were discouraged. The strategies taught should be closely aligned with the specific types of problems that the students will encounter on the test and should be embedded in good content instruction. Finally, these

GUIDELINES

Preparing Yourself and Your Students for Testing

ADVICE FOR TEACHERS

Make sure the test actually covers the content of the unit of study.
Examples

1. Compare test questions to course objectives. Make sure that there is good overlap.
2. Check to see if the test is long enough to cover all important topics.
3. Find out if there are any difficulties your students experience with the test, such as not enough time, too difficult a level of reading, and so on. If there are, discuss these problems with appropriate school personnel.

Make sure students know how to use all the test materials.
Examples

1. Several days before the testing, do a few practice questions with a similar format.
2. Demonstrate the use of the answer sheets, especially computer-scored answer sheets.
3. Check with new students, shy students, slower students, and students who have difficulty reading to make sure they understand the questions.
4. Make sure students know if and when guessing is appropriate.

Follow instructions for administering the test exactly.
Examples

1. Practice giving the test before you actually use it.
2. Follow the time limits exactly.

Make students as comfortable as possible during testing.
Examples

1. Do not create anxiety by making the test seem like the most important event of the year.
2. Help the class relax before beginning the test, perhaps by telling a joke or having everyone take a few deep breaths. Don't be tense yourself!
3. Make sure the room is quiet.
4. Discourage cheating by monitoring the room. Don't become absorbed in your own paperwork.

ADVICE FOR STUDENTS

Use the night before the test effectively.
Examples

1. Study the night before the exam, ending with a final look at a summary of the key points, concepts, and relationships.
2. Get a good night's sleep. If you know you generally have trouble sleeping the night before an exam, try getting extra sleep on several previous nights.

Set the situation so you can concentrate on the test.
Examples

1. Give yourself plenty of time to eat and get to the exam room.
2. Don't sit near a friend. It may make concentration difficult. If your friend leaves early, you may be tempted to do so, too.

Make sure you know what the test is asking.
Examples

1. Read the directions carefully. If you are unsure, ask the instructor or proctor for clarification.
2. Read each question carefully to spot tricky words, such as *not, except, all of the following but one*.
3. On an essay test, read every question first, so you know the size of the job ahead of you and can make informed decisions about how much time to spend on each question.
4. On a multiple-choice test, read every alternative, even if an early one seems right.

Use time effectively.
Examples

1. Begin working right away and move as rapidly as possible while your energy is high.
2. Do the easy questions first.
3. Don't get stuck on one question. If you are stumped, mark the question so you can return to it easily later, and go on to questions you can answer more quickly.
4. On a multiple-choice test, if you know you will not have time to finish, fill in all the remaining questions with the same letter if there is no penalty for guessing.
5. If you are running out of time on an essay test, do not leave any questions blank. Briefly outline a few key points to show the instructor you knew the answer but needed more time.

Know when to guess on multiple-choice or true-false tests.
Examples

1. Always guess when only right answers are scored.
2. Always guess when you can eliminate some of the alternatives.
3. Don't guess if there is a penalty for guessing, unless you can confidently eliminate at least one alternative.
4. Are correct answers always longer? shorter? in the middle? more likely to be one letter? more often true than false?
5. Does the grammar give the right answer away or eliminate any alternatives?

Check your work.
Examples

1. Even if you can't stand to look at the test another minute, reread each question to make sure you answered the way you intended.

2. If you are using a machine-scored answer sheet, check occasionally to be sure the number of the question you are answering corresponds to the number of the answer on the sheet.

On essay tests, answer as directly as possible.
Examples
1. Avoid flowery introductions. Answer the question in the first sentence and then elaborate.
2. Don't save your best ideas till last. Give them early in the answer.
3. Unless the instructor requires complete sentences, consider listing points, arguments, and so on by number in your answer. It will help you organize your thoughts and concentrate on the important aspects of the answer.

Learn from the testing experience.
Examples
1. Pay attention when the teacher reviews the answers. You can learn from your mistakes, and the same question may reappear in a later test.
2. Notice if you are having trouble with a particular kind of item; adjust your study approach next time to handle this type of item better.

For more test-taking strategies see
http://www.eop.mu.edu/study/ or
http://www.testtakingtips.com/

students often are anxious about the negative consequences of failing—not receiving a regular diploma, or no access to college or trade school. The best way to deal with this anxiety is to better equip the students with the academic skills they will need to succeed (Carter et al., 2005). The *Guidelines* should help you and all your students prepare for high-stakes testing.

Lessons for Teachers: Quality Assessment

Quality teaching and quality assessment share the same basic principles, and these principles hold for all students. Carol Tomlinson (2005b, pp. 265–266) suggests that good instruction and good grading both depend on a teacher who:

- Is aware of and responds to student differences.
- Specifies clear learning outcomes.
- Uses pretests and formative assessments to monitor student progress toward learning goals.
- Adapts instruction in a variety of ways to ensure, as much as possible, that each student continues to progress.
- Makes sure students know the criteria for success on summative assessments that are tightly aligned to the stated learning goals.
- Provides varied forms of assessment to ensure that students have an unobstructed opportunity to express what they have learned.

▼ SUMMARY

Basics of Assessment (pp. 444–450)

Distinguish between measurement and assessment. Measurement is the description of an event or characteristic using numbers. Assessment includes measurement, but is broader because it includes all kinds of ways to sample and observe students' skills, knowledge, and abilities.

Distinguish between formative and summative assessment. In the classroom, assessment may be formative (ungraded, diagnostic) or summative (graded). Formative assessment helps form instruction, and summative assessment summarizes students' accomplishments.

Distinguish between norm-referenced and criterion-referenced tests. In norm-referenced tests, a student's performance is compared to the average performance of others. In criterion-referenced tests, scores are compared to a pre-established standard. Norm-referenced tests cover a wide range of general objectives. However, results of norm-referenced tests do not tell whether students are ready for advanced material, and they are not appropriate for affective and psychomotor objectives. Criterion-referenced tests measure the mastery of very specific objectives.

What is test reliability? Some tests are more reliable than others; that is, they yield more stable and consistent estimates. Care must be taken in the interpretation of test results. Each test is only a sample of a student's performance on a given day. The score is only an estimate of a student's hypothetical true score. The standard error of measurement takes into account the possibility for error and is one index of test reliability.

What is test validity? The most important consideration about a test is the validity of the decisions and judgments that are based on the test results. Evidence of validity can be related to content, criterion, or construct. Construct-related evidence for validity is the broadest category and encompasses the other two categories of content and criterion. Tests must be reliable to be valid, but reliability does not guarantee validity.

What is absence of bias? Tests must be free of assessment bias. Bias occurs when tests include material that offends or unfairly penalizes a group of students because of the students' gender, SES, race, or ethnicity. Culture-fair tests have not proved to solve the problem of assessment bias.

Classroom Assessment: Testing (pp. 450–454)

How can testing support learning? Learning is supported by frequent testing using cumulative questions that ask students to apply and integrate knowledge. With the goals of assessment in mind, teachers are in a better position to design their own tests or evaluate the tests provided by textbook publishers.

Describe two kinds of traditional testing. Two traditional formats for testing are the objective test and the essay test. Objective tests, which can include multiple-choice, true/false, fill-in, and matching items, should be written with specific guidelines in mind. Writing and scoring essay questions requires careful planning, in addition to criteria to discourage bias in scoring.

Authentic Classroom Assessments (pp. 454–462)

What is authentic assessment? Critics of traditional testing believe that teachers should use authentic tests and other authentic assessment procedures. Authentic assessment requires students to perform tasks and solve problems that are similar to the real-life performances that will be expected of them outside of school.

Describe portfolios and exhibitions. Portfolios and exhibitions are two examples of authentic assessment. A portfolio is a collection of the student's work, sometimes chosen to represent growth or improvement or sometimes featuring "best work." Exhibitions are public performances of the student's understandings. With portfolios and exhibitions, there is an emphasis on performing real-life tasks in meaningful contexts.

What are the issues of reliability, validity, and equity with portfolios and performance assessment? Using authentic assessments does not guarantee reliability, validity, and equity (absence of bias). Using rubrics is one way to make assessment more reliable and valid. But the results from assessment based on rubrics may not predict performance on related tasks. Also, rater bias based on the appearance, speech, or behavior of minority-group students or a lack of resources may place minority-group students at a disadvantage in performance assessments or projects.

How can teachers use informal assessments? Informal assessments are ungraded (formative) assessments that gather information from multiple sources to help teachers make decisions. Some examples of informal assessment are student observations and checklists, questioning, and student self-assessment. Journals are very flexible and widely used informal assessments. Students usually have personal or group journals and write in them on a regular basis.

Grading (pp. 462–468)

Describe two kinds of grading. Grading can be either norm-referenced or criterion-referenced. One popular norm-referenced system is grading on the curve, based on a ranking of students in relation to the average performance level. This is not recommended. Criterion-referenced report cards usually indicate how well the individual student has met each of several objectives.

How can failure support learning? Students need experience in coping with failure, so standards must be high enough to encourage effort. Occasional failure can be positive if appropriate feedback is provided. Students who never learn how to cope with failure and still persist in learning may give up quickly when their first efforts are unsuccessful.

Which is better, "social promotion" or being "held back"? Simply retaining or promoting a student who is having difficulty will not guarantee that the student will learn. Unless the student is very young or emotionally immature compared to others in the class, the best approach may be to promote, but provide extra support such as tutoring or summer school sessions. Differentiated instruction could prevent problems.

Can grades promote learning and motivation? Written or oral feedback that includes specific comments on errors or faulty strategies, but that balances this criticism with suggestions about how to improve along with comments on the positive aspects of the work, increases learning. Grades can encourage students' motivation to learn if they are tied to meaningful learning.

How can communications with families support learning? Not every communication from the teacher needs to be tied to a grade. Communication with students and families can be important in helping a teacher understand students and present effective instruction by creating a consistent learning environment. Students and families have a legal right to see all the information in the students' records, so the contents of files must be appropriate, accurate, and supported by evidence.

Standardized Testing (pp. 468–479)

What are mean, median, mode, and standard deviation? The mean (arithmetical average), median (middle score), and mode (most common score) are all measures of central tendency. The standard deviation reveals how scores spread out around the mean. A normal distribution is a frequency distribution represented as a bell-shaped curve. Many scores cluster in the middle; the farther from the midpoint, the fewer the scores.

Describe different kinds of scores. There are several basic types of standardized test scores: percentile rankings, which indicate the percentage of others who scored at or below an individual's score; grade-equivalent scores, which indicate how closely a student's performance matches average scores for a given grade; and standard scores, which are based on the standard deviation. T and z scores are both common standard scores. A stanine score is a standard score that incorporates elements of percentile rankings.

What are some current issues in testing? Controversy over standardized testing has focused on the role and interpretation of tests, the widespread use of tests to evaluate schools, the problems with accountability based on test scores, and the testing of teachers. If the test matches important objectives of the curriculum, is given to students who actually studied the curriculum for a reasonable period of time, is free of bias, fits the students' language capabilities, and was administered properly, then test results provide some information about the effectiveness of the school. But studies of the actual tests in action show troubling consequences such as narrowing the curriculum and pushing some students out of school early. Teachers should use results to improve instruction, not to stereotype students or justify lowered expectations.

Can students become better test takers? How? Performance on standardized tests can be improved if students gain experience with this type of testing and are given training in study skills and problem solving. Many students can profit from direct instruction about how to prepare for and take tests. Involving students in designing these test preparation programs can be helpful. Students with learning challenges may benefit from intensive and ongoing preparation for taking tests, particularly if the test-taking strategies are tied to specific problems and content learned and tested.

▼ KEY TERMS

Accountable (474)
Achievement tests (476)
Adequate yearly progress (AYP) (474)
Assessment (445)
Assessment bias (449)
Authentic assessments (454)
Central tendency (468)
Classroom assessments (444)
Confidence interval (448)
Criterion-referenced grading (462)
Criterion-referenced testing (446)
Culture-fair/culture-free test (450)
Distractors (452)
Exhibition (456)
Formative assessment (445)
Grade-equivalent score (470)

Grading on the curve (462)
High-stakes testing (474)
Informal assessments (460)
Mean (468)
Measurement (445)
Median (468)
Mode (468)
Norm group (446)
Norm-referenced grading (462)
Norm-referenced testing (446)
Normal distribution (469)
Objective testing (450)
Percentile rank (470)
Performance assessments (455)
Portfolio (456)
Pretest (445)

Range (469)
Reliability (447)
Scoring rubrics (456)
Standard deviation (468)
Standard error of measurement (448)
Standard scores (471)
Standardized tests (444)
Stanine scores (471)
Stem (452)
Summative assessment (445)
T score (471)
True score (448)
Validity (448)
Variability (469)
z score (471)

▼ CONNECT AND EXTEND TO LICENSURE

MULTIPLE-CHOICE QUESTIONS

1. Which of the following assessment methods provides feedback that is nonevaluative, occurs before or during instruction, and guides teachers in planning and improving instruction?
   A. Summative
   B. Criterion referenced
   C. Formative
   D. Norm referenced

2. The yearly standardized test in Mr. Taylor's class is given in the spring. By the summer, Mr. Taylor's students received their scores in the mail. Many of the parents were upset and contacted Mr. Taylor regarding their children's 'low scores'. "Mr. Taylor, I don't understand how my daughter could be in Honors classes and have scores on her standardized test in the 70s?"

   "Your daughter's scores are above the average nationally. The average score would be a 50." What type of scoring is being utilized in the yearly tests Mr. Taylor's class must take?
   A. Criterion referenced
   B. Norm referenced
   C. Raw scores
   D. Authentic scoring

3. Maria had proven to be a very good student in Mr. Rhodes' class despite having just moved to the United States from another country. So, it came as a surprise when Maria performed poorly on her tests. When Mr. Rhodes consulted another teacher who also had Maria as a student, he learned that maybe his test questions had something to do with it. His colleague explained that Maria comes from a relatively primitive area which does not have television. Her exposure to concepts which draw upon a wide variety of cultural experiences was limited. This indicated to Mr. Rhodes that his tests unfairly penalized Maria. This type of assessment which unfairly penalizes a student for his or her lack of resources or culture is known as which one of the following?
   A. Attribution bias
   B. Assessment bias
   C. Reliability bias
   D. Validity bias

4. Which one of the follow types of assessments would be most beneficial for assessing a student's ability to debate?
   A. Formative assessment
   B. Portfolio assessment
   C. Summative assessment
   D. Performance assessment

CONSTRUCTED-RESPONSE QUESTIONS

Case

"How will you grade our oral book reports Miss Wren?"

"We are going to both grade them! We will develop what is called a rubric. It is a list of items on which you should focus while preparing and presenting your book report."

"How will we be involved?"

"You will help me make the rubric. What are some of the things you think should be included in your oral report?"

"I think we should have to have audience participation or else it gets too boring!"

"Good idea, Terry. What else?" The class continued to add to the rubric until there were six aspects on which to focus. "Class, you will also assist me in grading your performance by using the rubric. By making the rubric and using it to grade yourself, you should do very well."

"There are no surprises that way!" Lisa shouted.

5. In addition to listing the criteria for what constitutes quality work and having students self-assess, list some additional guidelines for Miss Wren to remember when developing a rubric.

6. Grades, a form of extrinsic reinforcement, can be a source of celebration for Miss Wren's students or a punishment. In order to make the most of grades and increase her students' chances for success, what should Miss Wren keep in mind when grading her students?

▼ WHAT WOULD THEY DO?

TEACHERS' CASEBOOK: Giving Meaningful Grades

Here is how some practicing teachers responded to the grading challenge at the beginning of the chapter.

KATIE CHURCHILL • 3rd Grade Teacher
Oriole Parke Elementary School, Chicago, IL

I would use a combination of assessment tools to evaluate my students. Using a rubric that students and parents alike are familiar with provides an easy-to-follow-and-understand grading system. The rubric needs to remain in a focal area in the classroom as a constant reminder to the students of what their expectations are.

By differentiating instruction consistently to cover all learning styles and modalities, the students would hopefully become more involved and invested in their own learning and, as a result, produce better quality work and exceed expectations.

Several factors would play a part in obtaining a particular letter grade. The letter grade would be earned through a combination of group work, completing objectives, and following the rubric guidelines for quality work.

MADYA AYALA • High School Teacher of Preperatoria
Eugenio Garza Lagüera, Campus Garza Sada, Monterrey, N. L. Mexico

I think it is important to assess a cross-section of student work. First, portfolios can be a useful way to gather various types of work throughout the year. Using a portfolio, a teacher can then attach a letter grade to student progress and achievement. It is important to grade children not only on progress, but also on their understanding of material. I would use meaningful, written assessments to test for retention and understanding of my students' knowledge. Finally, I would grade various projects and experiments so that the students who are better project-based learners will be graded fairly. I also like the idea of using a rubric system to grade students on writing or projects. Under a rubric system, a teacher allocates a certain number of points to each content area. It is then easy to attach a letter grade based on the number of points received.

KATIE PIEL • Kindergarten–6th Grade Teacher
West Park School, Moscow, ID

Students should be given the latitude to express achievement in different ways like group projects, daily class work, tests, and individual projects. All students would be held accountable for demonstrating their own learning. With each teacher grading on a different standard, the teachers must also take on the responsibility of collaborating with their peers. Communicating to other teachers the skills a student can be expected to bring with him or her to the next level is crucial.

AIMEE FREDETTE • 2nd Grade Teacher
Fisher Elementary School, Walpole, MA

I believe that students are not all smart in the same ways. I give the students a variety of ways to demonstrate their knowledge. I also focus on the students' ability to take their knowledge and integrate it into other subject areas across the curriculum.

I use a student portfolio for each child, compiled throughout the year and used to show growth and development. Each time I correct papers I choose a couple of pieces of work that each child has done. I put these papers in the portfolio folder. I try to choose a variety of work, not necessarily their "prize work." At the end of the year the children receive the entire folder to keep.

ALLAN OSBORNE • Assistant Principal
Snug Harbor Community School, Quincy, MA

Any grading system should consider a student's progress and effort. Grading systems also should be individualized to account for a student's unique strengths and weaknesses. Thus, a mainstreamed special education student should not be held to the same expectations as a gifted student.

The most critical aspect of any successful grading system is that it is fair. Fairness dictates that students and their parents be given information in advance about class requirements and expectations, along with a description of grading criteria. A system that is fair can be easily justified. It is also important to keep accurate and detailed records of student progress. In addition to recording grades on tests, quizzes, and projects, anecdotal records describing a student's typical performance should be kept. These records can be valuable if a report card grade is questioned.

Although group assignments can be an important learning experience, I would be reluctant to place too much emphasis on a group project grade. As we all know, each member of the group does not participate equally, and thus, a group grade does not reflect the contribution of each individual member.

chapter thirteen
CASE STUDIES

THE HATRED WITHIN

This writer wrestles with issues of family, ethnicity, and self-esteem. José, a twenty-year-old Latino junior, whose parents emigrated to the United States from Central America, explores his early experiences at school and his growing belief that his academic success made him not only "different" from other Latino/Latina students, but "better." Only when he reaches college does he come to understand this attitude and his disdain for his parents' relatively humble origins as a form of internalized racism. Drawn into the major Latino organization at his college and assuming a leadership role in student government, he comes painfully to name and eschew his self-hatred and embrace his developing Latino identity.

We were always horrible to the poor old man, Mr. Connors. He was the stereotypical high school substitute teacher—scolding us in a voice that echoed off the back wall and putting us to work with boring written exercises. We would respond by acting up, throwing papers, talking back, and pulling practical jokes—tormenting him in any way we could.

"Poor old guy," I thought. No more than five feet tall, he was bald except for the fringe of white hair that circled his bare dome. He wore rectangular eyeglasses and always came decked out in a full gray suit. I think it was the only suit he owned because he seemed to wear it whenever he substituted.

One morning, only a few minutes into the tormenting, the national anthem began over the P. A. system. As always, we stood up while the music played. Usually we did a good job of being quiet, but this time my friend Andrew and I kept joking and chatting as the music played.

When the song was over, Mr. Connors did exactly what I expected the typical "old-timer" would do. He began to yell at us for showing disrespect to the nation, but instead of focusing his obvious anger at both of us, he looked dead at me.

"Why don't you try that in your own country?" he barked.

Silence. I was in absolute shock. Did he really just say that? Without a second's pause I responded, "Why don't you try that in yours?" I took a step forward. There was no mirror there, so I have no sure idea what I looked like. But knowing how I get, I'm sure my face turned a bright red, my eyes became narrow and angry, my eyebrows crouched down. When I'm enraged, I make it very obvious. And it usually has the desired effect of intimidation because it's such a contrast to my usual jovial expression.

"This *is* my country," he answered back without a pause.

I took a few more steps forward. Not rushing to him, but with a slow threatening pace. "Well, this is *my* country, too."

"Well, how about your parents' country?" he asked, seeming not to realize that he was pushing me more and more and that with every comment he uttered, he was becoming more and more offensive.

"How about *your* parents' country?" I snapped back in the same mocking tone.

"My parents are indigenous," he said smugly.

The word at the time was unfamiliar to me. Although I was mad at myself for not knowing it (I wanted to step above this man as his intellectual and physical superior), I shot back, "What the fuck does that mean?" I didn't know what had come over me. I didn't swear at teachers, even substitute teachers. I joked, I kidded around, but I was always as respectful as my sense of humor allowed me to be.

He answered back by saying that the word meant his family had always lived here. Since he didn't look Native American, I had to assume he meant his ancestors came aboard the *Mayflower* or a similar absurdity. At that point I was at the foot of his desk, an arm's length away from his gleaming dome. I had no idea what I was doing. How can you ever be prepared for a confrontation like that? What did I hope to do when I reached him? Hit him? Spit in his face? I stood there barely a second before Andrew and my other pal Dave came from behind me and pulled me away, yelling, "Come on, José, back off! He's not worth it." And I knew he wasn't worth it. But what was it? What had happened to me? What did I think I was going to do? Why was I so enraged?

I wasn't the kind of student who turned violent so quickly, not with students and especially not with teachers. But something had come over me. My shock and disbelief at his words had drawn me magnetically toward him. Did he really say that? To this day, it remains the first situation that comes to mind whenever someone asks me if I have ever encountered outright racism. It was a slap in the face. But in hindsight, the incident reveals more about me than it does about Mr. Connors.

Why did he look at me and not see a student like any other, or even an annoying teenager who had little respect for his country? Why did he appear to view me as a brown-skinned foreigner who didn't belong and deserved to have his identity questioned by a high school substitute teacher? That day in my sophomore year I felt like a minority. I felt like a Latino student. I felt like I didn't belong. Every other day, however, I took pride when my friends told me, "José, you're so white."

I'm surprised that it isn't harder to admit. As I see it now, I was a sellout in high school. I was a box-checker. I was a coconut. Name the insult and I was the epitome of it. In college, a friend referred to Latino students who didn't recognize their background or culture as "those who didn't associate." That was me. I didn't associate.

My high school was pretty diverse. The students in the Honors and Advanced Placement courses I took, however, were almost entirely white. I was lost, along with a handful of other students of color, in a sea of white faces. Given the fact that my classes were full of white students, it's no surprise that my friends were all white as well. I occasionally hung out with the one other Latino student whom I had known since kindergarten, but he, too, didn't "associate." He dressed in khakis and corduroys, polo shirts and button-ups, clothes that most people considered "preppie." And in my high school, preppie was synonymous with smart, and smart was, with a few exceptions, white.

Daniel, my good friend from the fourth grade on, was white with blond hair and blue eyes. My two best friends at the time, Nelson and Sara, both had dirty blond hair and piercing blue eyes. The pack of a dozen or so girls I hung out with junior and senior year were, with few exceptions, white. All of them were upper middle class. Most of them owned cars when they turned 16. These were my friends, and I was proud of them.

But it was more than just the fact that they were white. I don't think there's a problem with having a lot of white friends, and I don't think I sought them out because of their skin color. They were just the people I saw every day. But what *did* matter was the attitude and thoughts that grew from this valuing of whiteness. Why did Mr. Connors's comments hit me so hard? Precisely because I was in denial of the fact that I was any different from my friends. I was like them. They were like me. It hurt me to be singled out as a Latino because, deep down, I really did believe that I was better than most Latinos. I was smart. I was hardworking. I was ambitious. I was successful. I was funny. These traits, I thought, were uncharacteristic of most Latinos. Mr. Connors brought me down, and I'm sad to say that that was the biggest reason he upset me so much all those years ago. He tore me away from my misconception that I was accepted and belonged in the white world, which I saw as the embodiment of the good, happy, and successful life. He forced me to confront my own racism.

I talked to my mom about this late in my senior year of high school. I actually complimented her on her parenting skills. I pondered how she had managed to raise us in a way that made us better than most Latinos. It never occurred to me how wrong this thinking was. I would never have dared to repeat my racist thoughts out loud. But at the time, I thought them. I saw other Latinos and would often assume the worst. It was easy to convince me that one was a drug dealer or a criminal, as I was already biased against them. And I always made that distinction clear: I, and for the most part my nuclear family, was not a part of *them.*

But these were all thoughts I kept buried deep down inside. I continued to check off "Hispanic" whenever forms asked for the optional race/ethnicity classification. I took pride in it then. With so few Latinos who aren't wastes, I figured I was helping myself. They would see me as an anomaly, I told myself. I was unique and that made me very happy.

So, besides the little box that I would check off from time to time, my culture and background meant nothing. In fact, I would treat it as a joke:

> "Quit stealing my money, spic."
> "Hey, don't look at me, I'm just a spic."
> "Ah, those spics just don't get it."
> "You're such a grubby, grubby spic."

These were words I spoke, phrases that sprung out of my mouth and the mouths of my closest friends. They were always said in jest and I always approved. I found it funny, because I thought being called a spic was pretty damned ironic. I recall a white friend telling me I was more white than he: I acted white, I dressed white, I talked white. In essence, to him I was normal, and normal was white. You're not part of a gang? You must be normal, you must be white. You don't shoot up every morning or carry a gun? You must be normal, you must be white. You don't speak Spanish in school, you don't know how to Latin dance? You must be normal, you must be white. And I laughed when he said I was a spic. How funny, I told myself, me…a spic? I thought I was anything and everything but that.

Besides these occasional insults, which I then thought were perfectly fine, my days at school had nothing to do with being Latino. I was normal, I told myself, therefore my ethnicity couldn't be my prime characteristic. I considered it a contradiction. This kind of thinking—this utter disdain for who I was—is something most people will never be able to understand. I think it's natural for adolescents to question their identity, but I did more than just question: I denied everything that was natural to me.

I would avoid the sun as much as possible late in high school. Why? Because I tan pretty easily and I didn't want to get too much darker than other students. A slight tan was okay, but I didn't want to get carried away. I didn't want to stick out. Sometimes I would actually fret over my darkening summer tan. How can I remain as white as possible? I would look in the mirror each morning and wish not just that my skin and features were different, but that my whole ethnicity could be washed away. My self-hatred lay at the core of my being. And that's where I kept it.

When I brought my friends home, I would be ashamed when my mom and dad, whose English was so bad, spoke to them. I would cringe when my dad tried to crack jokes because his thick accent made him sound like some teenager in a man's body. I would be embarrassed when my dad swore without pause and told them some anecdote. I would never bring my parents to school as other children did for events or programs. Worst of all, the superiority I felt over Latinos I also felt over my parents. They were older, and more experienced, but because they couldn't communicate on the phone with their mortgage bank as well as I could, or because I understood the seven o'clock news better than they did, I felt like I stood on a higher plane. I used to look at my best qualities as traits that were somehow incompatible with the language I spoke at home, the color of my skin, and the values my parents taught me.

My story, my struggle as a Latino student in a white community, is also the story of my parents. The two cannot be separated. I now realize that much of my journey is a continuation of what they began so many years ago. They emigrated illegally from Honduras to the United States several years before I was born. In Honduras, my father was on his way to becoming an engineer; my mother was a teacher in the school system. When they came here, they lost everything and were forced to take menial jobs in a country where the language confused them. Within months, they were caught and sent back by la migra. When they came to the United States the second time, they struggled constantly but they also thrived. My oldest brother Armando, who is nine years older than me, immigrated with my parents. My other brother Steve, five years older than I, was their first-born in America and therefore was given the most American name they could think of.

Until I was seven years old, we lived in the "poor" section of our city. Surrounded by black and Latino kids, the feeling I can most recall is fear. I was scared of riding the bus to school. I was scared of the other kids. I was much like the scared white boy in a black neighborhood. I was scared of the others because I saw myself as inherently different. Even in elementary school, I had begun to develop the self-hatred and racism I would carry with me throughout my adolescence. All I knew was that while I was home, I had to cover my head with my pillow to drown out the police sirens and gun shots. But when I went to school and sat with the "smart kids" in the reading and math courses, I was nestled in a peaceful, white community. When my parents were finally able to save enough money, we moved out of the poor section and into the white community I had held so dear.

My father was, and still is, a drunk. Drinking was more than just something he did; through the years it had become a part of the man. I cannot imagine him without a beer in his hand, just as I cannot separate the man from the violence he inflicted. I respected and looked up to my father when I was young, but perhaps most of that came from my fear of him; fear of what he would do if I misbehaved. He was a pretty intimidating man, with a big round beer belly and huge biceps and calves. Some of my earliest memories are of me hanging off his extended arms, like a skillful monkey swinging along the trees. He had a loud, booming voice. His Spanish was always rough and convoluted. It wasn't that he spoke poorly, it was just the slang or expressions he picked up and used like Standard English: "So I told him, 'Hey guy, fuck you, okay? Fuck you.' " He seemed always to be telling a story, always swearing, and, of course, always drinking. He was in his forties, but to me he sounded like a teenager trying to be cool. But as I grew up, I came to see him as a meaner, darker character. He wasn't just big anymore, he was scary. His resonant voice, which sounded like he was yelling even when he was in a good mood, often brought me to tears.

The last time my father hit me is still vivid in my mind. I was in seventh grade. I had a paper route all through middle school, and I usually delivered the papers right after school. One weekday after school I went to a friend's house instead of delivering my papers. We hung out the whole afternoon, playing cards and telling stories. I didn't get home until a little after five o'clock. I froze when I saw my dad standing on our front steps as I rode my bike into the driveway. He stared at me, clearly angry. My dad didn't even wait until I was inside the house to start yelling. "Que hora es esta para llegar?" He asked why I was late. Living in front of the high school, I was aware of the crowd of students staring at me as my father scolded me. I went inside, angry that my father would embarrass me like that. As soon as I was inside, he slammed the door and continued his abuse: "Donde estabas, babosada?" In Spanish he called me a little shit, irresponsible, no good for not calling and telling him where I was. His face was bright red as his words tore through me.

As he stormed upstairs, I knew where he was going and what he was getting. The door to my brother Steve's room, which is down the hall from the kitchen, opened up and I saw his face pop out. I clung to Steve as little brothers tend to do. "If he hits me, I'm running away." I whispered, "If he hits me, I swear, I don't care, I'm running away." Tears were already streaming down my face and I braced myself for what I knew was coming. I heard my father pound down the stairs. He swung a belt and I foolishly tried to block the blows with my hands as he screamed to me to put my hands down. Again and again he brought the belt down across my thighs. The pain spurted in quick stings. There's no pain worse to me, at least in my memory, than the feel of a belt against my skin. I just wanted him to stop. I screamed louder, begging him to stop.

Eventually he stopped, probably tired of my screaming and tears; he turned abruptly and went upstairs. I remained crying, curled up in a little ball on the kitchen floor. I wished that I had the guts to actually stand up, grab my things, and leave the house forever. I had imagined and planned it so many times before— what things I would take with me, where I would go. But it was never meant to be anything more than a product of my imagination. Instead of making my plan a reality, I cried, just as I had done so many times before.

I'm not sure if he had been drinking that day or if it was just a bad mood. I mean, why hit your son for being late? My father, and the way he made me feel that day, became the personification of Honduras and my cultural roots. He was exactly what I wanted to avoid becoming. When he drank, I saw him as a stupid, pitiful fool. And it didn't take long for me to project those feelings on to all minorities around me. Except my mother—whom I saw as different.

My mother is the sweetest woman in the world. She would do anything for me, including staying married to my father. She did it for me because she knew a divorce would hurt me. She did it for me because she didn't want us to have to move out of our nice home in front of my high school. She did it for me because she needed my father to help pay for college. I guess I take it for granted that it really was all for *me*. But there's no doubt in my mind that it was.

I was born with a heart murmur, which made me vulnerable as a child. My family took extra care of me, but more than anyone my mother was anxious for my safety. It was partially because of her personality but also due to the circumstances. The combination of my sickness at a very young age and the fact that I was her last child—forever her baby—meant I was bound to be treated differently. She poured the last of her motherly instincts and care into me. Well into high school, she would tuck me in at night and wake me up in the morning. Some nights I asked her to rub my back and, though she jokingly complained, she always did it. My closeness with my mother was a contrast to my father, whom I saw as the enemy.

As I grew up, my importance in the family and in her eyes grew. Armando never finished high school and failed my parents' dream of being the first son to graduate college in America. Steve failed similarly after only two terms away at the state university. I became their last chance. Out of 32 cousins on my father's side, I am the fourth youngest yet only the second to go to college. When Armando got into trouble, my dad unloaded on him in the only way he knew how. My father's mother had supposedly whipped my father into submission many years ago. A rope would have been a welcome change to some of the instruments he was beaten with as a boy in Honduras. Yet somehow he grew up loving and thanking his mother for every bit of punishment she handed to him. Similarly, my brother Armando has consistently defended my father for the pain he has inflicted on us. He, out of all of us, has stood by as my father's sole defender. For that reason, among others, my brother Armando and I did not often get along. Even though he knew my dad beat me, Armando felt he had gotten it much worse and viewed me as a spoiled brat.

My mother did not defend my father for most of their marriage, nor did she fight back. She quietly withstood his verbal abuse whenever he drank too much. Over time, however, whether it was the freedom she felt now that she was in the United States or her own personal growth, she began to speak up and assert herself. When he yelled, she would yell back. Usually, though, she was the voice of reason to his temper tantrums. Most of the time he didn't listen and kept on shouting, stalking off in anger and sleeping for the next few weeks in the basement, where he had a bed. Eventually, when I was in high school, my father moved most of his clothes down there and for months at a time would not sleep in his own bed with my mother. Through it all they stayed together...although *together* is a strange word to use for two people who never spoke, never stayed in the same room together for more than a moment, and were married, it seemed to me, in name only.

When they argued, my dad would say anything to interrupt her, to keep her quiet, to regain the peaceful life he remembered from Honduras. Her spirit took him by surprise. This wasn't the way it was in Honduras, he must have thought to himself. This wasn't the way it should be. The wife, he felt, was supposed to cook his food, serve him his drinks and meals, clean the house, stand by him always, and never talk back. But my mom, the wonderful woman that she is, would not stand for that. She knew that she was an American woman now and that things would have to change. Sometimes, crying to myself, I would hope that my mom would just give up and stop arguing back. I respect her now for being strong, but as a little boy I just wanted the shouting to stop. But no matter what, I always blamed my father. He was exactly what I didn't want to become and yet he was also the biggest male presence in my life. In my mind he represented Latino males, therefore I had no desire to grow up and become one.

As easy as it is to blame my father, another side of him, a gentler one, surfaces in my memory. He isn't always the man who beat me and yelled at my mother; sometimes he's the man who sacrificed so much for his family. During my sophomore year in college I was profiled in the college newspaper as a campus activist. The article described everything I'm involved in and all of my accomplishments. I referred to my mother as the "force in my life." A few days after it was published, I sent the clipping home. I was worried how my father would take it. When I finally spoke to my mom about it, she said they had read it together and they both had cried. He was not angry or jealous, as I would have expected him to be. She told me that my family had had a barbecue and invited all my family members. Sometime during the party, my father pulled out the article, which he had already taken to work to show his friends and translated the article into Spanish for my relatives. My mom told me that everyone was so proud of me, but my thoughts were with my father. This is the man I call my dad, this is the man who, along with my mother, I strive to prove myself to each day in spite of his harshness toward me. When I look back on my life, I won't see it as a success unless both of my parents see it that way as well. In the back of my mind is the knowledge that if things had gone differently 20-odd years ago—if my parents had made just a slightly different decision or if my father hadn't worked half as hard—my life would be completely different. I owe something to them, whether I like it or not, and that knowledge drives me to achieve, even when I feel that "I have too much to do."

That's why my narrative can't be separated from my parents' story. Their journey to the United States didn't end when they arrived for good or even when they finally became citizens. The two stories continue in tandem, and just as important is the extended family they left in Honduras and the extended family that traveled with them. Growing up, I was often surrounded by my many aunts and uncles, cousins and second cousins. Just as my father became the embodiment of the Latino man—everything I didn't want to grow to be—my extended family also represented my ethnicity, my culture, and the target of my racism.

I saw my nuclear family as different from their little clans, and as I grew up, *different* also meant *better*. We Garcias were somehow special. My aunts were either single, divorced, or remarried. My cousins were constantly being arrested, having children out of wedlock, causing their parents grief. My cousins were the only Latinos I had any close connection to, so, to me their behavior exemplified all Latinos. They got into trouble, broke the law, stole, cheated, lied, and were disobedient. Although my brothers and I occasionally exhibited some of these behaviors, I nevertheless saw us as above it all. My female cousins got pregnant, moved in with boyfriends, married and divorced early—all the kind of behavior that I considered "subwhite." To do the wrong thing, then, as I saw my cousins do the wrong things, was to be less than white, to be *not* succeeding in America.

It is true that my brothers and I were generally better behaved, and better educated, and better mannered than many of my cousins. But instead of leaving the comparison there, I took it a step further and said that this was because they were Latino and were acting it, while we were Latino but we had somehow overcome our heritage. Overcome our heritage! This idea disgusts me now, and yet there was a time I didn't even question it. I didn't think of my family as successful because we were Latino or in addition to being Latino, but *in spite* of that fact.

The notion of overcoming my heritage recalls a poignant incident that occurred during a family vacation to Honduras. On the road, a small child around my age came up to our van and asked for a ride. We told him we didn't have any room, but as we started to drive we noticed that he had climbed on the back of the van and was prepared to ride with us, at 50 or 60 miles per hour, holding onto a ladder. At the time I disliked the little brat; I couldn't believe he had the nerve to try and hitch a ride from us. A dozen years later I think of that kid and can't help but see myself. If circumstances had been different, I could have been him. That notion would occur to me again and again, but at the time, and even as I packed bags for college, I still looked at that boy—at so much of my identity—with disdain.

My parents didn't pressure me much to succeed; I put the pressure on myself: I was the one who had to bring respect to my family after Armando dropped out of high school and Steve dropped out of college. Armando and I constantly argued, and he refused to come to my high school graduation. I think my success only highlighted his failure. My parents' pride in me was a sharp stab at him. He had been expected to be the first one to do so many things that I was now doing. Steve was more complacent, always assuming he would return to school and catch up with me. And that's how I left for college—angry with most of my family, convinced that I was better than my family and my heritage, and bearing the burden of bringing home what my parents wanted to see: a good report card and a college diploma.

For the most part, college was everything it was supposed to be: I was having the time of my life and meeting so many amazing people. It wasn't until my first meeting of La Unidad, the Latino student organization, that I had my first confrontation with the hate inside me. I had gone to the meeting because I felt an obligation to go. Despite my belief that I was better than my background, I was also confronted by the feeling that my status as a so-called box-checking Latino was what got me into college. Why else would I have identified myself as such? *Associate, identify*—words like these meant the difference between being seen as an outsider to the Latino community or a link within it. If you identified, that basically meant you acknowledged your heritage, you went beyond your box-checking status.

I went to that first Unidad meeting because I felt an obligation, not because I felt I would gain anything from it. I didn't want to be seen as a Latino student by the mainstream but I also didn't want to be seen as a sellout by the Latino students. My self-hatred and hatred of my ethnicity was deeply buried, and I had no intention of making it known. I barely thought about it, and that's the way I liked it. But my first weeks at college were characterized by a sense of exclusion, a sense that I didn't fit in anymore. Dressed in Abercrombie and Fitch, attending their parents' alma mater, most students seemed so different from me. I was afraid someone would suddenly discover that I didn't really belong. I had an overwhelming feeling that I had to start my life over again, build myself back up, yet I didn't know who I was or how to go about it.

That first Unidad meeting we all sat in a stuffy room, the Latino students on display for one another. I was immediately hit by the feeling that I was very *unLatino*. The others somehow exuded more Latinoness. It was in their accents, the speed of their speech, the Spanish words they mixed into their English. They all talked about home cooking and dishes that they loved, and although I loved my mom's home cooking, I didn't know the correct names of the foods she prepared. But most important, they all seemed to know more about their individual cultures. They were more culturally, socially, and politically aware than I ever thought I could be. What did I know about Honduras? I couldn't even tell you what kind of government they have there, let alone how "my people" are doing. What did I know about Latino culture besides what I learned in school, which was nothing? My cultural ignorance had never even occurred to me as a problem; suddenly it became a very big one.

The worst moment was when we went around the room and introduced ourselves. One by one they spoke, pronouncing their names with a full Spanish accent. Some people I knew always did so, but a few caught me off guard. *Drew* became *Andres, John* became *Juan;* the speed at which people said their names increased, and as we quickly went around the circle, I didn't know what to do. Of course, I could easily have used an accent, but I never did and I didn't want to do so just to fit in. I even had a fear about doing that. What if it came out badly? What if I couldn't even say my own name right? I didn't want their eyes on me, them to snicker and know that I was only a fake. I just wanted to come to the meeting, sit back, and feel like I had made up for the fact that I checked *Hispanic/Latino* instead of *white*, which is what I wished I were, or *Other*, which is what I felt like.

When the introductions finally came around to me, I blurted out my name, *José García*, with a full accent. I felt like a sellout, not because I didn't want to be Latino, but because I was willing to hide my true self in order to be accepted as Latino. I was more confused than ever. Inside I knew that I thought poorly of Latinos and that my racism was deeply rooted, yet I was willing to act unlike myself in order to be accepted by my Latino peers. I didn't know who I was or what I wanted. I only knew that I wanted to be accepted. I wanted to please everyone, and was finding I couldn't please anyone.

My confusion got worse before it got better. I had gotten involved early freshman fall in my college's student government. Representing the student body, the organization constantly worried about whether or not they were truly being representative. So they would literally take a count based on gender and race/ ethnicity. I wasn't just a normal involved student, I was the token Latino, or so it seemed to me.

The word *token* was one that I would get to know well as time went on. Token Latino, token minority, people of color versus minority, ignorance versus racism, the relationship of power in racism, prejudice, institutional racism…these were all terms and phrases that I had never been acquainted with before my first year at college. I had a crash course in being nonwhite. I'm convinced that if you asked a white person, half of those terms would draw a blank response. It's not simply because they're white, but because they have had no contact with these issues. I'm a great example. I had never considered any of these issues, yet I was that person of color, I was that token minority. I was *supposed* to know. That lesson came to me during a student government meeting when I was asked to give my opinion as a Latino. I wasn't asked to give it as a student who happens to be Latino, but to give the official Latino opinion, as if all we Latinos got together one day and took a straw poll on a number of issues, all of which came out unanimous. There is diversity among races, but there is also diversity within races. I wanted my friends to be color blind. I didn't want to be seen as Latino or ethnic or other. In a short time, I went from hating my ethnicity to not minding it but still being grateful when people could ignore it. The inner hatred I had grown up with was gone, but something rotten remained. I still had a way to go before I would embrace and actually be proud of my culture, rather than just tolerating it.

I continued going to Unidad meetings, continued struggling through my ignorance. I heard other students of color talk about the racial issues they had confronted growing up. I began to find more and more aspects of my childhood that related to their childhoods—similarities in being the children of immigrants. Most of all, I was surrounded for the first time by students who shared my skin color and also shared my academic success. I was no longer the exception in a sea of white faces. The wall I had built up between myself and my ethnicity began to break down. Despite being 70 percent white, my college introduced me to diversity. So before I realized it was happening, that lifelong correlation between *white* and *successful* stopped making sense to me.

I recall a late-night conversation with my friend Jake who is half Latino and half white. He casually mentioned that he was against affirmative action, that he saw it as reverse discrimination against white students, and felt that it only served to emphasize racial lines more. As he put it, "Why should white people today have to suffer for what white people in the past have done?" This comment led to a passionate debate. I argued that, despite what he believed, there was a racial divide in this country. It was social, as evidenced by my high school substitute's behavior years before. It was economic, as evidenced by the poor section of my hometown that bussed me in and out when I was younger. It was educational, as shown by all the white faces in my upper-level classes from elementary school through high school. It was cultural, as witnessed by the isolation I felt at my first Unidad meeting. "You're right," I argued. "Most white people of today have nothing to do with what happened years before. But that doesn't erase the problem. That doesn't change the fact that minorities are still suffering because of what happened years before. Furthermore, whether whites are directly at fault or not, it doesn't change the fact that whites have benefited. Because others have lost, whites have gained. It's not a question of right or wrong—it's just the way things are. But that doesn't mean we shouldn't try to change things." Jake kept arguing that minorities just needed to "stop feeling sorry for themselves."

That night I developed my own theory on this subject: "Look Jake, it's like life is this one big long-distance race. Ever since the race began, the minority runners have been oppressed, kept back, slowed by slavery, by conquest, and so on. And all this time, the white runners have been getting ahead. Suddenly, all restrictions are dropped. No more slavery. No more segregation. Everything is made equal. But is it really equal, Jake? All that equalization under the law doesn't change the fact that all these white runners have had centuries' long head start. How does that translate to real life? In economics, in education, in social attitudes? These are all big problems, and they call for big solutions. I don't think affirmative action is the best long-term solution, but it is a temporary one until people are willing to make the bigger commitment."

Jake said that he used his Latino background to get him into college, just as he used his running talent (he was recruited by the college for cross-country). That was all his identity as a Latino meant to him. With my mind entrenched in issues of race and ethnicity, I was outraged at him for saying something like that. And yet just a few months before, I could have said the same thing.

At college, once I began to deal with the long-suppressed issues of my ethnic identity, the floodgates opened. Sometimes I got in serious arguments and found myself saying things I couldn't believe I was saying. In those moments, I claimed all white people were racists or the United States border should be completely open all the time. But that was part of my learning process, of pushing forward. I was in the process of testing, trying things out, seeing where thoughts would go, and then evaluating whether I still believed them or not. I was trying to find myself under years of buried ignorance, self-hate, and prejudice toward my own culture.

In another late-night conversation with friends, I recalled that small boy who had wanted to hitch a ride with us in Honduras, whom I had disliked so much. "What's so different from me and so many of the naked kids I see running around in Honduras, begging on the streets? Sure, I think my drive and my work ethic have been important, but I think the key difference has been the opportunities I have had—attending schools that are leaps and bounds above anything in Honduras and pursuing so many things that my parents never had the chance to. And yet it might have been completely different. It could be another kid sitting here today and me in Honduras. That's why I don't think I'll be happy in life unless I'm helping them realize their own potential. I want to give others all the opportunities that I had." And the minute I said it, I knew I believed it with all my being—I knew I would never look at my role or purpose in life in the same light again. I was never religious, and yet I felt I had found my calling. I knew then I could never be an investment banker or businessman. My place was in service, in education, in any field where I could use my skills to improve the lives of others and help them open doors.

In spite of my new insights, the same demons remained inside of me. When you look at yourself in the mirror for years and see someone who is unattractive because of his skin color, hair color, speech, and other characteristics, those negative feelings don't go away easily. I felt I had a big nose, that it was too round and not slim enough. I hated the fact that I would always be a good four inches below average height. I even came to dislike my boring brown eyes and black hair. My own insecurities about how I looked and fit in remained. Even though I was growing intellectually and emotionally, I had not yet purged many of the old thoughts that haunted me.

My self-hatred was also hatred of my background and my relatives. My perception of myself and others had been altered by all the new people I met at college. Generalizations I had held to—that all Latinos are lazy, all students of color are inferior to whites—were shattered while I was at school. My relationships with members of my family and their relationships with each other had also been forced to change as a result of my absence. My leaving home was exactly what my family needed.

Just how far the healing had progressed is evident in a radiant photo taken at Armando's new apartment, which he shared with his fiancée, Molly. In the photo, we're embracing each other tightly. My father has one arm extending far to his right to reach my brother and the other hand is tightly grasping my mother's shoulder. My mother is smiling beautifully; it's a genuine smile. She seems truly happy—happy to have her family all around her. You can almost read her thoughts: She has her family together again, different than before, but together. Caught in that photo is me kissing my brother. For no other reason than because I was feeling happy and wanted a funny picture, I embraced Armando's face and kissed him on his right cheek. He remained smiling while looking at the camera, his arm tightly around me. After the photo was taken, Armando wrapped his arms around me and pulled me in for a full hug. Steve came over as well. And right there, in the kitchen of my brother's new house, with my parents and his fiancée watching, Armando began to apologize to me for mistreating me for years and years. As we embraced, Armando sobbed, "I'm so sorry, José, I'm so sorry for everything I put you through. But you know I did it because I loved you and wanted only the best from you. You're my little brother, there's nothing I wouldn't do for you." He then opened his arms to Steve, and with the three of us wrapped in each other's arms, forming a little circle, Armando continued, with tears in his eyes, "You guys are my brothers, my little men. I love you two so much. So fucking much! I'm always going to be there for you guys, whatever you might need. You fucking come to me, all right? There's nothing I won't do for my brothers." The tears were coming down my cheeks now, and Steve, usually calm and reserved, also began to cry. Our coming together in love and reconciliation was the climax to what I had slowly been developing the whole year—my acceptance by and of my brothers after years of alienation. While we hugged, I remember hearing my mother tell my father to look over at us. I sensed her deep inner happiness. She was so proud to see her sons finally come together.

Several months later, I took another step forward in my journey. I interned in Washington, DC, working as a research assistant for a nonprofit organization focused on strengthening the Latino community. I found myself surrounded by people who had centered their lives around making a difference in the Latino community. Two men in particular, leaders in the organization, further altered my views on Latinos. Both had gone to Ivy League schools, and their résumés were packed with incredible experiences. They could have done anything they wanted to in life, but they chose to give back to their respective communities. I met many prominent Latinos through them, and my perceptions of Latinos, which had expanded exponentially since high school, was further improved. Any significant prejudices I had were eliminated by the success of these two men. I admired them *and* they were Latino. In the past, I would have joined these two facts by thinking, *in spite of* their being Latino. It's such a small detail and yet reveals so much about how I thought.

I was still working in DC when I flew home for the weekend to see the production of a musical in my high school. I saw the show with Dan, my friend since the fourth grade. I told him about my involvement in student government, my increased activism, and life in general at my small liberal arts college. But since I was in DC at the time, I also mentioned my internship and the great time I was having. With pride, I pulled out my business card. "Empowering the Latino community?" He read off the card, smiling at me and waving the card to a mutual friend from high school. "Look Chris, José is Latino now. Look at the card. Our little brown friend's creating community!" His tone was mocking, and they both began to laugh as they gazed at the card. "This is the biggest load of PC bullshit. I can't believe you're a part of this crap!" He laughed louder, staring at the card in disbelief.

I felt crushed. This had been my childhood friend? This had been the life that I had enjoyed so much? I was ashamed of who I had been and what I had believed, but I didn't think the shame ran so deep. Was there anything I could turn back to? Was there anything that didn't stink of my racism? It had been a while since I felt so uncomfortable, fidgeting in place, wanting to be anywhere but there. And right then I was struck with a realization that came just before I would have begun feeling sorry for myself. "Hey Dan, fuck you," I said. His mouth opened in disbelief, his laugh stopped in midbreath. I continued, "Just because you haven't grown up in the last two years, doesn't mean that I haven't."

"Hey Mr. Latino, don't take it personally. I just think that doing this sort of thing is very unlike the José I knew in high school," Dan said, handing the card back to me.

"A lot about me is unlike the José you once knew. People change, Dan, and ya know what? I'm happy with the changes I've made." I gave both of them one last look in the eye and then returned to my seat in the theater. I don't think I was particularly articulate or eloquent, but I got across what I wanted. I didn't back off.

As the show continued, I recalled that late-night conversation with Jake and the passion with which I spoke of privilege and racism. An image of that boy from Honduras came to mind and I again imagined myself living his life. I then remembered Mr. Connors, the substitute teacher, and the anger he had made me feel. I reflected on the dozens of conversations in which I called myself a spic and spat on my culture. Finally, I thought of my mother and father and all they had given me and continue to give me. Dan, who silently took his seat next to me, had accused me of being "very unlike the José he knew in school." I smiled, happy that he was right, proud that I didn't joke along with him and deny what I had spent two years forming, what is still forming, what I hope never stops forming.

FALLING FROM MY PEDESTAL

Living in a family characterized by disharmony and constant threat of divorce, this author traces her serious eating disorder to her attempts to compensate for her parents' unhappiness by being a perfect child. But no matter how hard she works or how perfect her grades, Chhaya's parents remain unhappy and even criticize her efforts. The emergence of adolescent sexuality creates a crisis in her sense of perfect self-control that is followed by the devastating news that despite her obsessive hard work, she will not be valedictorian. Drastically restricting her intake of food becomes a compensating obsession and means of asserting self-control and achieving perfection. Her health deteriorates and she is hospitalized. She learns that she must discover her own realistic goals and give up her "insane drive for perfection." Her recovery proves to be arduous and long, but by the end of her story she feels she has turned the corner.

So many people have asked me, "How did you become anorexic?" that I'm about ready to tape-record my life story and play it back the next time the question comes up. I try to explain using the analogy of a rainbow. The entire spectrum of colors comprises the rainbow, but no single color can be extracted—they all blend together to form a continuum. The same can be said of the illness. Anorexia wasn't something that just "happened" to me—I didn't one day suddenly decide to stop eating. My problems ran much deeper than simply "not eating." The disorder was my desperate attempt to maintain some semblance of control in my life. It was a cry to establish who I was, to pick up the pieces of my shattered identity. To make sense of this insidious disease, and ultimately of myself, I must confront and examine the issues that led to my using the eating disorder as a coping mechanism to deal with the turmoil that surrounded and threatened to suffocate me.

I am convinced that my childhood represents the beginning of much of what led to the anorexia. My identity problem goes back as far as the elementary school years and starts with my ethnic heritage. I come from what you might call a mixed background. My parents could not be more opposite in their histories if they tried—my father is East Indian and my mother is a typical WASP. As for me, I've gone through my entire life not knowing exactly what I was. I've always despised filling out standardized forms that ask for personal information, because I never know what box to check under "ethnic origin." The categories are neatly defined, literally black and white, and people who are "melting pots" like me present problems for this efficient form of classification. Technically, I'm more Indian than anything else, but I always feel deceptive saying I'm Indian when I'm really only a half-breed. Thus, I end up the perpetual "Other," an unclassifiable anomaly.

No one would guess merely by looking at me that I'm part Indian—my hair and eyes may be dark, but I'm quite fair skinned. The one thing that gives me away is my name—my horrible, terrible Sanskrit name which I'm convinced no one on this planet can pronounce correctly without help. I have lambasted my parents endlessly for sentencing me to a lifetime with this albatross around my neck. I can't even count how many times people have completely massacred my name, either in pronunciation, spelling, or both—the number is utterly unfathomable. I'm forever giving what I call my "name spiel," explaining the origin and meaning of my name. Since such an understanding requires knowledge of my background, the subject inevitably leads into a discussion of my family, one of my least favorite conversational topics.

Even though my parents' relationship was tenuous (to say the least), they never fought in public. No one would have guessed they were anything other than normal as far as married couples go. At home, though, the masks came off, the farce ended, and the boxing gloves were donned. The match would usually begin at the dinner table. Supper was the only time we all came together as a "family," if you can call it that. It typically started with something insignificant like, "Why didn't you fix mashed potatoes with the steak?" and escalated inevitably into the divorce fight. You could always tell when one was coming on. First, they'd bicker for a few minutes, then the voices would rise. The remark, "Why don't you just leave?" by either of them was the cue for my exit, for I could recite practically verbatim the arguments that would follow. Mom would snap, "You should go back to India. You haven't been happy since you left." Dad's bark ran along the lines of, "Why don't you move in with your parents?" In spite of all the fighting and all the threats of divorce that were made, though, it was always just words. Neither of the two ever acted upon their vow to end the marriage.

I think the instability and uncertainty of their relationship bothered me the most. The dark, intense fear always loomed in my mind—would this be the fight that leads to divorce? Is this fight going to be the straw that's going to break the camel's back? What if they're really serious this time? I'd be fraught with anxiety after every one of their quarrels. Within a few days, things usually returned to normal, meaning the usual strained relations in the absence of verbal brawls. Once I knew things were "safe," that divorce was not imminent and that we would remain a foursome, I could breathe a small sigh of relief, at least until the next argument.

When you're young, you think the world revolves around you. Given my egocentrism, I blamed myself as the cause of my parents' marital strife. I felt it was up to me to salvage their marriage, which I tried desperately to do. After each fight, I would ask myself what I had done wrong and how I could rectify the situation. Harboring intense feelings of guilt, I lambasted myself for not pleasing them and not living up to their expectations. Maybe if I'd cleaned my room like they'd asked ... I wondered. If I could just be good enough, I thought, they'd love each other and, in turn, love me. I erroneously believed I could bring my parents together by the sheer force of my will. Frustration over my inability to positively influence their relationship caused me to feel completely ineffective and inadequate. My solution was to be more perfect than anyone could expect a child to be, to hide all signs of anger and rebellion, in order to deserve and gain their love.

Being achievement oriented in school was my answer to many of the problems I faced. By making the grades, I was sure (or so I thought) to gain the love and attention I so desperately craved, not only from my parents but from my teachers as well. Because my family life was like an emotional roller-coaster ride over which I had no influence, I turned to school for comfort and security. I knew that by working hard, I could do well—in the classroom, I could exert complete control. As the perfect student, people would respect and admire me. Only if others saw worth in me could I be truly assured of my substance and value.

Unfortunately, my plan backfired on me. The more A's I received, the more my parents and classmates began to expect I would continue to do well. I strove endlessly (and fruitlessly) to impress my parents with my good grades. At the end of the marking period, I would rush home, report card clutched in hand, hoping to have glowing praise lavished upon me. Words can't begin to describe the crushing disappointment I felt when they merely remarked pointedly, "We knew that's what you'd get." Part of me was angry at having my hard work and accomplishment minimized. Whenever I mentioned my grades, all they did was preach about how "Grades aren't everything in life." Another common point they made was that "Common sense [which they felt I lacked] will get you farther in this world than will good grades." I felt I could never win with them. It seemed as though no matter what I did, no matter how hard I tried, there was always something lacking, something else I could and should have done better. I yearned for reassurance and affirmation of my worth, but because I felt that I could never be perfect in their eyes, I could never be truly convinced of gaining their love.

These traits I have described were present throughout my childhood, but no one ever recognized them as potential problems. On the contrary, my drive to be good, to achieve, to live by the rules, and to avoid disappointing or arousing the criticism of others was what made me a model child, even though I never felt like one. The severe misconceptions I held became dramatically apparent, however, with the onset of adolescence, for I was pitifully unprepared to meet the issues of this period.

As I entered high school, I became even more rigid in my interpretations. My self-doubt intensified, and my self-esteem plunged even lower. I was convinced everyone else was more capable, both socially and intellectually, than I. Never comfortable with myself, I constantly devalued my abilities, thinking I wasn't good enough for anything. Striving for perfection, for being the best (and then some), became my all-consuming goal, my purpose in life, to the point where I sacrificed all else. I studied all the time, believing that if I let up in the slightest bit, I would inevitably slip up and fail. All of my flaws would then be revealed, and I would be exposed for the imperfect person and the fraud that I was. To me, failure represented the loss of control, and once that happened, I feared I would never be able to regain it.

I became petrified of showing any signs that could possibly be interpreted as imperfection. I felt compelled to live up to and surpass the expectations of my parents, teachers, and peers in order to avoid arousing criticism, which I took as a personal attack. While others may have expected 100 percent from me, I pushed for 110 percent. So driven was I to succeed—or rather, to be seen as a success—that I imposed the strictest of standards on myself. Rather than creating a sense of pride, worth, and accomplishment, however, my role as the good, obedient, successful student—the girl who had it all together (at least on the outside)—caused me to feel increasingly empty inside. Paradoxically, the more "successful" I became, the more inadequate I felt. I began to lose control of my identity more and more as I fell victim to the Perfect Girl image in all areas of my life. I had no idea of who I *was*, only who I was *supposed* to be.

I denied myself pleasure throughout high school, never allowing myself to simply have fun. To do something for the sake of enjoyment brought forth incredible feelings of guilt and self-indulgence. I think part of this conflict arose from my parents' disagreement over issues regarding my (non)social life. My mother always had a tendency to be overprotective. She tells me that when I was an infant, she used to peek in on me, sleeping soundly in my crib, and pinch me ever so slightly, just to make sure I was still breathing. I think her reluctance to let me out of the house had to do with her overriding concern with shielding my brother and me from the dangerous outside world. At the time, though, I felt she was trying to suffocate me. I would vehemently protest against her fears; what reason had I ever given her not to trust me? "It's not you or your friends I don't trust," she would respond, "it's the rest of the world." My father, on the other hand, pushed to get me more involved with my peers. "Why don't you invite your friends over here?" he'd prod. I always found that suggestion rather amusing, given the nature of our household. If I asked to do something with friends, I was always bounced from one parent to the other to obtain permission, and usually they ended up arguing over the incident. As a result, I ended up feeling guilty for being the cause of their marital strife, a position that tore me up inside. Rather than jeopardize the family harmony (or rather, lack of discord), I often didn't even bother to ask to go out. I tried to avoid the conflict by removing myself from the situation.

I had friends throughout high school, but I always kept them at a distance, scared that if I let them get too close, they would see that I wasn't perfect and reject me. Relating to my peers was extremely difficult for me as a result, because rarely could I talk about my inner feelings. I equated the expression of emotion with weakness and vulnerability, so I always remained deadly serious and kept things on a strictly superficial level. To others, I must have seemed frigid, removed, and detached. I myself felt lonely and isolated. I desperately wanted to reveal the true me, but my intense fear of exposure silenced me.

Two specific events, both of which occurred during the spring of my junior year in high school, catalyzed the emergence of the eating disorder. One of these two major happenings involved my very first romantic encounter with a member of the opposite sex. Prior to meeting Kevin, I had had no experience whatsoever with guys. My self-confidence being what it was (practically nil), I thought no one could ever possibly be interested in me. An extensive "screening" process, with stringent standards that few guys could measure up to, was a way of protecting myself from unnecessary pain and hurt. If in every guy I met I found some fault that immediately made him undesirable as a mate, then I'd never have to worry about him rejecting me. I could remain in control and would therefore be safe.

My encounter with Kevin changed things dramatically. I met him in March at a two-day science symposium held at our state university. I had mixed emotions about Kevin—on the one hand, I found myself incredibly attracted to him and excited at the prospect of what might lie ahead, but at the same time, I didn't want to open myself up for fear of getting hurt. I wanted badly to be "swept away," to experience all the wonderful emotions described in romance novels, but reminded myself I should remain calm and levelheaded. After all, I was treading on completely foreign territory. My intelligence was of absolutely no use here, and since I couldn't rely on previous experience, I had to make sure I protected myself. Despite all of my hesitance, I was able to let my guard down long enough to experience my first kiss. Kevin and I, along with another couple, parked in his car in a secluded area of the campus. As the two in the back seat started going at it immediately, I sat uncomfortably in the front, eyes focused straight ahead. I was afraid to even look at Kevin, sure I'd flush with embarrassment. He would see right through me and realize how inexperienced with guys I really was. He was definitely the one in control here, as I had absolutely no idea how to behave.

We talked for a while (with his friends in the back continuing their dalliance), and then it happened. By "it," I am referring to one of the most monumental moments in a person's life—the first kiss. I had wanted mine to be as passionate and romantic as they come. After practicing on pillows for so long, I thought for sure I'd be ready when the time came. All of my rehearsing turned out to be in vain, though, for in no way did it prepare me for the intense emotions I felt. I remember the mixture of thrill and nervousness that jumped around in my stomach more than I do the actual physical interaction of our lips (which I simply recall as being warm and wet). Thinking back on the event, I have to laugh at how it came about. I had undone my seat belt while we were parked, and when we were getting ready to leave, I couldn't rebuckle it. As I fumbled with the strap, Kevin leaned over to lend a helping hand, but instead ended up giving me much more than just a hand.

I was exhilarated by the thought that this tall, intelligent, incredibly gorgeous guy actually saw something good in me, something more than just my grades.

He validated my sense of worth, and I began to think that perhaps I wasn't such a horrible person after all. Maybe there was something inside me other than the empty space that all the As in the world couldn't fill. Whereas my academic accomplishments gave me only a transient sense of self-satisfaction, the knowledge that Kevin liked me provided a warm feeling inside me that didn't fade away. For the first time in my life, I felt truly happy just to be alive.

In addition to the positive aspects of the relationship, there was, of course, a down side. I feared losing control of myself, a worry that was intensified by the fact that I was in completely new and unfamiliar territory. The incredible power of my feelings scared me immensely. In my family, I had learned the importance of always being rational and logical, of keeping my emotions in check and exhibiting self-discipline. Now here I was being "swept away," throwing all caution to the wind and acting purely on impulse and desire. The guilt I felt was extreme.

When I related the incident to my mother (the fear of telling my father loomed so large that I never talked about the relationship with him), I was thrown totally off guard by her reaction. I had pictured her throwing a fit and saying I shouldn't be getting involved with members of the opposite sex at my age. But just the opposite happened—she was glad I had met a "nice boy." Perhaps if he had lived in our town, she might have reacted differently. Given how far apart we lived, dating was never feasible, so she didn't have to worry about my going out late at night doing God knows what.

Kevin and I had been writing and calling each other on a fairly regular basis, and I began to entertain the thought of asking him to the junior prom. Though absolutely terrified at the prospect of rejection, the encouragement of my friends and mother (who actually offered to have him spend the night at our house!) finally convinced me to take the risk via the mail. At the post office, my hands shook and my stomach quivered as I took a deep breath, opened the mailbox, and dropped the letter down the chute. As soon as the deed was done, though, I thought, God, what the hell have I done?! I'm setting myself up for the biggest fall of my life! How stupid could I be to think Kevin would want to go with ME?!

I awaited his reply with nervous anticipation, checking the mail every day as soon as I got home to see if it was there. When the letter finally arrived, I was so nervous I could barely open it. My stomach was literally doing flip-flops as I began scanning the note for signs of his reply. When I read about how he would love to be my date, how he thought we'd have a great time together, and how he looked forward to seeing me again, I was euphoric. I was practically bouncing off the walls, so full of exuberance and utter joy that I thought I'd burst with energy.

Within a week's time, I found an outfit (gown, shoes, and a clutch purse—the whole set works), made dinner reservations and a hair appointment, and bought the tickets. Everything was in place when the big night finally arrived. After I finished getting ready, I decided to risk taking a look in the mirror. I was worried that I would find a brainy nerd who was trying hard to fit in where she didn't belong. The image that reflected back at me, though, caught me by surprise. With my hair pulled up and with flowers in it, my mother's pearl choker around my neck, the teal-colored gown flaring out around my waist, and the rosy glow of my cheeks (due more to my excitement, I think, than to the makeup I had applied), I was actually not half bad to look at. I felt as though I was looking at a stranger, for I knew the elegant young woman in the mirror couldn't possibly be me, the same person who always felt awkward and ugly. I truly felt like Cinderella, transformed if only for one night.

I was anxiety-ridden about seeing Kevin again—it would be the first time we had seen each other in some months. Everyone, both family and friends, loved him as soon as they met him. They all thought he was attractive, intelligent, and an all-around great guy. I floored everyone as I made my entry with him—not only had I myself been transformed, but here I was with a gorgeous date at my side. Finally, my feelings of inferiority melted away. I had always been recognized as smart, but now on top of that, people saw me as attractive. The culminating event that evening was my election to the junior prom court. Normally a popularity contest, I never dreamed of standing among the four couples who flocked the king and queen. When my name was announced, I arose from my seat, mouth agape, as everyone around me applauded. Again I had stunned everyone, especially myself—smart people simply did not make the court. Proving them all wrong gave me a sense of uniqueness that I cherished. I reveled in my now complete blossoming from a former ugly duckling into a beautiful swan.

In spite of all its magic, the prom experience stirred up the same mixed bag of emotions I had felt when I first met Kevin, only to a much greater degree than before. At the dance, Kevin's open display of affection bothered me tremendously. I felt uncomfortable expressing my emotions in public, especially since I wasn't even sure exactly what I was feeling. I had no idea how to behave, and so I distanced myself from Kevin. If he moved his chair closer to where I was sitting, I moved in the opposite direction. If he tried to hold my hand, I would fold my arms across my chest. I wouldn't even let him kiss me in front of everyone. He was probably totally baffled by my behavior—I know I myself was, but I couldn't help it. Since I felt out of control and didn't know what to do, I turned to the only defense mechanism that I knew from previous experience had worked—isolation.

After the weekend of the prom, Kevin and I stopped writing and calling each other. To add to my confusion, my mother and friends expressed their disdain for my handling of the situation. They reminded me that I had had the chance at a relationship with a wonderful person and had blown it, big time. My mother, who had thought Kevin was one of the nicest, most polite, handsome young men she'd ever met, laid the worst guilt trip of all on me. She made it seem as though he had done me this enormous favor, for which I should feel some sense of undying gratitude and obligation. "Here this nice boy drove all the way over here just to escort you to your dance, and how do you treat him? Like dirt." As a result of others' reactions to my behavior, I became even more miserable and disgusted with myself. This relationship represented the first time in my life that I had tested the wings of independence and trusted my own feelings, and I had failed. The incident reinforced my belief that I was worthless and incapable of making decisions on my own.

I mentioned before that the prom was one of two important events that helped catalyze the emergence of my eating disorder. The second event, which occurred within a month after the prom, was my guidance counselor informing me that I was not ranked as first in my class. My very first reaction was that some terrible mistake had been made. There was absolutely no way I could be anything but number one. I was the only person I knew who had maintained a 4.0 GPA, with nothing less than A's on all of my report cards. Becoming valedictorian had become my life; every aspect of my identity was in some way wrapped up in it.

When I expressed my disbelief to my guidance counselor, he assured me that no mistake had been made—I simply was not first. That's when the shock set in. I sat in his office thinking, "I have to get out of here NOW." The walls were closing in on me, and I felt as though I was suffocating. I quickly mumbled something about having to get back to class and practically ran out of his office and into the nearest bathroom, where I let the intense pain that had been welling inside me burst forth. My heavy sobs shook my entire body, and I was hyperventilating so badly I could barely breathe. I leaned up against the wall and slid slowly to the ground, clutching my knees to my chest and pressing my hot face against the cool wall tiles. "How could this be happening to me?" I screamed in my head. Why? What had I done wrong? Hadn't I sacrificed everything for the sake of the almighty grade? Wasn't I the perfect student? How could I pretend everything was normal when inside I was falling completely apart? Afterward I fought desperately to keep up my false image of control and stability, stuffing my pain down further and further inside me in the hopes it would somehow magically disappear. Everyone expected me to be number one—what would they think when they found out I wasn't? If only they knew…. I felt duplicitous and deceitful, as though I was projecting a false image that was just waiting to be debunked. I was falling from my pedestal, and I knew the fall would be a long and hard one from which I might never recover.

The fall was even more profound than I could have ever anticipated. It devastated my life to such an extent that now, five years later, I am still trying to put back the pieces and recover. An eating disorder, however, was the last thing I expected. In my mind, I had imagined people losing respect for me, devaluing my abilities, and seeing me for the incapable fool I felt I was. That didn't happen. The only person to turn her back on me was me. I was truly my own worst enemy, endlessly berating and cursing myself for being so stupid. Gone was the radiant, smiling teenager from prom night, so full of life and exuberance. In her place was an ugly, sullen person who could barely drag herself out of bed in the morning because she saw no purpose to her life. The change was dramatic, but no one ever commented on it, perhaps because I was so good at putting on a happy face, and perhaps because they felt (or maybe hoped) I was just going through one of the low points that characterize the average adolescent's life. What others didn't realize was that this was not simply a phase that would pass in time—it was to become a deadly disease that would grab me by the throat and nearly choke the life out of me.

I don't really know when the anorexia actually hit me. Thinking back, it seems to have been more a progression than an event whose full impact hits all at once. Why I turned to food as a means of establishing control in my life, I honestly have no idea. I had never been concerned with my weight prior to this time. I was always thin, but ate whatever I wanted—in fact, I was the ultimate junk food addict. Chocolate, candy, cookies, chips—if it was bad for you, I loved it. These items were, of course, the first to go when I started my downward spiral, and as time went on, the list of "forbidden" foods grew while my food intake gradually but steadily diminished.

The earliest recollection I have of anorectic behavior involves its isolation more than the self-starvation. During the spring of my junior year, I began skipping lunch. My friends and I usually sat together during the lunch period, eating and chatting. Instead of going to the cafeteria with them, I started holing myself up in the library, where I could be alone with my pain, as I felt I deserved to be. My friends immediately noticed my absence and commented on it. I told them I was simply doing my own research into the different colleges that interested me. I wasn't completely starving myself at this time, but what I now know were the early signs of my eating disorder went unnoticed at the time.

It wasn't until that summer that the disease began to intensify. With the school year over, I no longer had to deal with my teachers and peers on a daily basis. Thus, it became easier to isolate and confine myself to my own internal world, a jail cell out of which there was no escape. I felt I was divided into two separate personalities—one jailer and one prisoner, simultaneously beating myself up while begging for mercy. I would lie on my bed, behind the safety of my locked bedroom door, crying endlessly. One part of me was saying, "I hate you—you're stupid and worthless," while another part was pleading, "Please don't hate me—I'll work harder to make you like me." It was a no-win situation, though. There was no pleasing the jailer, no matter how hard the prisoner inside me tried.

As the prison walls began closing in on me, I fought desperately to hang on. I got a job waitressing at a nearby restaurant and tried to keep busy by working as much as I could. My work schedule made it easy to hide my eating patterns from others. Since Mom and Dad worked full-time, I was safe for most of the day. "I ate something before going to work and then had dinner on my break," I'd lie. If anyone at work asked about my eating habits, I'd say my mother was saving dinner for me when I got home. I was really clever about deceiving others, as most anorectics are, and delighted in the thought that I was able to pull the wool over everyone's eyes. No one would be able to figure me out, I vowed. By keeping to myself, I'd be safe and protected and could get back some of the security that I felt had been brutally snatched from me.

I started cutting back on my intake with the initial goal of becoming "healthier." I'll look and feel better if I get toned up and shed a few pounds, I told myself. After a period of restriction combined with exercise, I lost between 5 and 10 pounds, and did in fact feel better about myself. The source of my improved self-image wasn't so much being thinner as being able to accomplish something with tangible results as reinforcement. I could step on the scale and watch the number drop from day to day, just as I could feel my clothes getting baggier around my waist. Here was something I could do successfully! Maybe I wasn't good enough to be first in school, but I certainly seemed able to lose weight, a task that presents enormous difficulty for many American women.

I read every article on health, nutrition, and weight loss I could find. I sought the diets that offered the quickest route to losing weight, pulling together bits and pieces from each to develop an elaborately detailed plan of my own. I learned what foods were "good" and what foods were "bad," and became a careful label reader, comparing caloric and fat content for a wide variety of foods. Going to the grocery store was a big production—I would spend ages in each aisle, trying to hunt out the products that would give me the most food for the fewest calories. Almost paradoxically, food became my obsession, the center of my world. Pouring myself into losing weight became a substitute for pouring myself into my schoolwork.

As with all other areas of my life, I gave 110 percent to the illness (when I commit to something, I do a thorough job). My insane drive for perfection, however, once again turned on me, in the same way it had done with my schoolwork. Losing that first bit of weight left me feeling good about myself for a little while, but then I began to question the greatness of my accomplishment. After all, I told myself, 5 pounds really wasn't that much—anyone could lose that amount of weight in no time with minimal effort. Now, if I could lose 10 pounds, *that* would be something—shedding that much weight requires more commitment and dedication. If I could do that, I'd really feel capable of doing something important. Thus, longing desperately for that feeling of self-worth, I readjusted my target and continued in pursuit of my new goal.

Of course, once I reached this new weight, the same thing happened, and a vicious cycle developed. No sooner would I finish patting myself on the back than a little voice in the back of my head would squelch my pride, saying okay, maybe you achieved that goal, but I bet you can't meet this one…. I found myself getting caught in a cycle of self-destruction. Even though I craved success, I would go out of my way to ensure it eluded my grasp. As soon as I reached one goal, I'd set a new, higher standard. I was doing to myself the very thing I hated my parents for doing to me. Whereas I could detach myself from my parents, however, I couldn't escape myself. I internalized the frustration of not knowing how to please them, to the point that I was unable to recognize and meet my own needs and desires. Because I didn't even know how to satisfy myself, I was forced as a consequence to look to outside indicators of my value. My life became dominated by the numbers of the scale, which governed all of my feelings and emotions. If the number fell, I was secure and happy (for at least a little while). If it moved in the opposite direction or not at all, I panicked and tried frantically to think of a way to regain control of my body. I based my every mood on my weight, not realizing that in doing so I was setting myself up for failure—though I didn't realize it at the time, self-worth comes from within, and can't be found outside oneself.

As I continued my quest for a "wholeness," an identity I thought thinness would provide, I failed to recognize the self-destructive path I was following. My body became more emaciated, but all I saw in the mirror was excess flab that I had to be rid of. I rejoiced when the skirt of my waitressing uniform became so big I had to use safety pins to keep it up. One day while going through my clothes (which were becoming baggier with each passing day), my eye caught a glimpse of my prom gown, sheathed in plastic and hanging at the very back of the closet. I decided to try the dress on, just to see how it fit. As I removed it from the plastic, I thought about how far away the dance seemed—almost like another era, even though in actuality only a few months had passed. I pulled the dress on and zipped it up, only to have it fall past my bare and bony hips to the ground. Gone was the elegant gown that had transformed me into Cinderella. All that remained now was a mass of teal-colored satin lying in a pile around my feet. Though somewhat wistful over my inability to recapture the magical quality of prom night, I comforted myself with the thought that at least I wasn't fat like I had been then. Thinness was the one measure I could grasp hold of to convince myself I was better now than I had ever been.

I deluded myself into believing I really was doing fine. Though I experienced all the telltale symptoms of the eating disorder—constantly feeling cold (especially my hands and feet), hair falling out, problematic bowel movements, insomnia, amenorrhea, dizzy spells, skin discoloration, and the gnawing hunger that penetrated to the bottom of my stomach—I brushed them off in denial. I can recall only one instance that summer when I was forced to face the gravity of my illness. I remember getting out of bed and heading for the bathroom to take a shower. As I reached my bedroom door, I got a swift, overpowering head rush that nearly bowled me over. The room started spinning, and I had to clutch the door frame just to keep from collapsing. My heart started palpitating, and I felt as though my chest was going to explode. For the first time in my life, I truly thought I was facing death. I leaned against the door frame and let my body go limp as I slid to the ground. Stabbing pains pierced my heart so sharply that they blinded me. Oh my God, I thought, what have I done to myself? I prayed to God to please let me live. I'll eat, I promise I'll eat…. I won't try to lose any more weight…. I'll go back to eating normally…. Just please make the pain stop and don't let me die!

Being faced with the all-too-real prospect of death shook me up enough that I did fix myself something to eat. The frightening impact of the incident faded rapidly, however, and within a few days I was once again back to restricting. I passed off this danger signal, reassuring myself that since I survived the episode, I must be fine. When I tightened my grip over the food, I was in control—I was invincible, and no one could touch me. The eating disorder gave me an incredible feeling of power and superiority, a sense of independence. I could prove that I had control, that I could accomplish something on my own.

You may wonder where my family was in all of this mess. Didn't they see me slowly wasting away into nothing? I vaguely recall them nagging me from time to time to eat. I don't feel any resentment toward them for "letting" me become anorexic, for not catching me before I got as bad as I did. They were, I'm sure, in as much denial as I was. Acknowledging my disease would (and eventually did) open a Pandora's box full of problems, ones that went far beyond my not eating to include the entire family. My mother did get worried enough toward the end of the summer to call my pediatrician. When she explained my situation, his advice was to get me to take vitamins (just the solution to an anorectic's problems!). His failure to recognize the severity of my illness made it easier, I think, for my parents to gloss over the situation. Having a doctor's reassurance probably put their minds at ease. The family problems could stay safely locked away, at least for the time being.

I somehow managed to make it through that summer, and the beginning of my senior year in high school soon arrived. My mother tried to warn me of the reactions people at school would have to my emaciated appearance, but I could see no difference in how I looked now as opposed to how I looked at the end of junior year, when I was at least 20 pounds heavier. She was right on target in her assessment of the situation. I'll never forget the looks I received from my classmates and teachers that first day of school. Their eyes bulged and their mouths dropped in horror as they stared at the withered, drawn figure before them. Three months earlier, I had been a healthy teenager, and now all that remained was a skeleton covered with skin. I was incredibly self-conscious walking through the halls, certain all eyes were on me and that the topic on everyone's mind was my dramatic weight loss. Feeling like a queer anomaly, I tried desperately to cover my twig-like arms and hide my body under baggy clothes. My answer to the stunned looks was that I had been sick and was run-down as a result. Though I found it perfectly plausible, my explanation was met with skepticism. No one pushed the issue, though, probably due to my unwillingness to discuss the subject, evident by my curt responses to their questions.

Within the next few days, the nurse called me down to her office. Apparently, nearly all of my teachers had voiced their concerns regarding my health. I offered the same excuse to her as I had to everyone else—yes, I had lost some weight, but would be fine once I had a chance to recoup from being sick. She was skeptical at my insistence that everything was okay, but I promised to work hard to get back my health. I was, of course, lying through my teeth. I had absolutely no intention whatsoever of returning to what I considered my grossly fat previous weight. Did people think I was going to abandon my quest for thinness just like that, simply because that's what they wanted me to do? No way was I going to let all the hard work I had poured into this project over the past three months go to pot! I was annoyed with others meddling in my life. Rather than seeing their concern for its genuineness, I was convinced they were trying to undermine me. They just wanted to see me fail at something else so they could laugh in my face. Well, I wouldn't let that happen! I'd show them that I could achieve! They would marvel at how well I could shed those pounds and admire me at least for that, if nothing else. I thought that perhaps by being successful at losing weight, I could somehow make up for my intellectual flaw of not being valedictorian.

I was knocking myself out to impress others for no reason, though. The only one who cared that I wasn't first was me, but ironically, that was the one person I was unable to satisfy no matter how hard I tried.

I remember one key experience that clued me in to the severity of my problem. While going through candid photographs for the yearbook, I discovered two of myself. I picked them up to examine more closely and gasped in horror as I looked at the ghastly image captured on film. Her face was as white as a sheet, her eyes sunken, and her cheeks severely drawn. The blue veins bulged out of her stick-like arms, and her clothes hung limply on her fragile frame. She looked morbidly depressed, a pathetic creature who seemed ready to snap at any moment. Surely that person couldn't be me! Tears started welling in my eyes as I looked at that picture. What had happened to the smiling, vivacious teenager of the previous spring? She was like a rose that had bloomed and then withered away. I bawled uncontrollably as I realized I was falling apart. The life was being slowly sucked from me, and I was growing increasingly weak and helpless. Please God, help me get my life back together, I prayed. I don't want to die!

You may think that, having recognized myself as having this disorder, I would be well on my way to recovery. I know that's how I felt—now that I really *wanted* to get better, to get back to a normal life, I would. I tried to convince myself and everyone else that I could tackle and overcome this problem on my own. The solution was simple, I thought—all I have to do is eat and gain back the weight I had lost, and I would be fine. Unfortunately, it wasn't quite that easy. Anorexia nervosa had come to symbolize 17 years of emotional instability, psychological turmoil, shattered dreams, and bits and pieces of my fragmented identity. There was a lot more that needed fixing than simply my diet—all of the issues that permeated my entire life needed to be confronted and dealt with before recovery would be possible. It took everyone—my family, friends, teachers, and even myself—a long time to realize this and to recognize the full, devastating extent of the disease.

Though I really did want to get better, I was unable to regain the weight my body required. Having gone beyond the point of no return, so to speak, I continued to lose poundage. The nurse finally suggested my mother take me to a specialist, someone who might offer the assistance I needed to get better. I became absolutely irate at the very mention of the subject. "I am NOT crazy, and have no intention whatsoever of seeing a shrink!" I hollered at my mother. But she was adamant. The psychologist I went to see was unable to help me, though. My disease had progressed much too far by the time she intervened. About a month later, she told my parents there was nothing more she could do for me and recommended I be evaluated for admission into the Eating Disorders Service at a nearby children's hospital. Though I strenuously resisted the idea of hospitalization, my mother calmly but forcefully put her foot down: "We can commit you without your having any say in the matter." My parents were finally taking charge.

In terms of my treatment in the hospital, Mom and Dad focused more on the outer me—my body and its weight—than the evolution of my inner self.

Whenever I spoke with them on the phone or whenever they visited, the very first question was always, "How's the weight doing?" My recovery became framed in terms of numbers, the very thing I was trying so hard to get away from. I had based my entire identity on tangible indicators of my worth—grades, class rank, and weight—at the expense of my true inner being. As a result, I never established a self-directed identity. My work in therapy to evoke an awareness and understanding of the impulses, needs, and feelings that arose within myself was incredibly difficult and emotionally draining.

Before my admission, I had been closer to my mother. She was always the more reliable one. If I had a problem or needed something, I always went to her first. My father, on the other hand, was a lazy bum. I couldn't count on him for anything except for material objects. When I was in the hospital, this changed dramatically. Mom was like an ice woman. All the other parents felt guilty, thinking they were in some way responsible for their child's eating disorder. Not my mother. She staunchly and promptly informed me that she was not going to take the blame for my problem. At the time, I saw her as cold and heartless. I *wanted* her to feel sorry for everything she had ever said or done that caused me to be the way I was. She *deserved* to feel guilty for creating the sham of a family life I had to endure. My father, on the other hand, was easier to deal with when I was heavily dependent on him, as I was when in the hospital. I think he needed to feel needed by me, to feel in control of my life. He called me every night, just to find out how my day had gone. On his frequent visits, he would always bring fresh flowers, and we would sit and talk, watch TV, or take a walk. I remember on one occasion, we even made the bed together. It was times like these when I felt closest to him. I wanted to be taken care of, and he seemed willing to do the job. The combination of my not wanting to grow up and his wanting me to stay daddy's little girl helped to sustain this dependence. Though at the time I saw his behavior as a form of care and affection, I now recognize it for the power game it was.

Paradoxically, our weekly family therapy sessions failed to reflect these newly developed interactions. During that one hour, the family roles reverted to their usual prehospital form. At first, I actually looked forward to family therapy, thinking it would expose some of the important and volatile issues that had always been buried underground. Finally, we would be able to resolve our problems and, I hoped, become a loving, cohesive unit, the perfect family I longed to be a part of. Unfortunately, this miracle transformation didn't occur. Our problems ran much too deep for even a therapist to tackle. The sessions became as much of a sham as our family itself was. Every week it was the same thing. Everyone, with the exception of myself, shied away from the real issues, the potent problems we faced as a group of four individuals collectively termed a "family." My parents always wanted to discuss specific aspects of the Eating Disorders program, details that were "safe" for them—for example, "Why isn't she eating any red meat?" or "When is she going to get back to eating normal foods?" Getting them to recognize that food was not the main issue, that the eating disorder cut far deeper, to the very core of my identity (or lack thereof), was the most difficult task I faced. I would try to bring up a particular aspect of our home life—for example, my parents' marriage or my brother's attempt to shut himself off from the rest of the world. Before I could even finish my account, though, my father interjected, shaking his head and protesting, "She's making too much of this and blowing things way out of proportion."

The dismissal of my emotions as trivial wasn't nearly as bad as what came next. "Our family life may not have been wonderful," Dad admitted, "but it was relatively normal until she began this whole mess and disrupted all of our lives. She's the one with the problem, not us." I sat dumbfounded, not believing my ears. How could he possibly lay the entire blame on me? Did he honestly believe I had planned on becoming anorectic, that I set out on some mission to destroy our family? I refused to just sit back and let him heap any more blame on me. I had meekly taken all the denouncing for so long that I had internalized and turned it back on myself, resulting in incredible feelings of guilt and self-doubt. I couldn't stand the torture any longer. "You're wrong if you think I'm the cause of everyone's problems," I told my father point-blank. "We had problems long before I got sick." To my surprise, my mother then spoke on my behalf, saying to him, "You can't blame her for everything. We're part of the problem, too." Finally, someone was taking my side! I looked over to my mother with gratitude in my eyes, silently thanking her for saving me from drowning in a sea of guilt and self-worthlessness. At least she was beginning to recognize my problem encompassed much more than a simple decision to stop eating. Throughout this entire scene, my brother remained isolated and detached from the rest of us. When confronted, he would usually just shrug his shoulders. He had a grand total of two standard responses to the therapist's questions—"I don't know" or "I try not to think about it."

After six weeks in the Eating Disorders Service, I returned to the real world—back to my home and family and to my teachers and friends at school. Everything was pretty much the same, though. My parents still fought, and my brother still shut himself off in his room. I was still obsessed with food. Though I had gained weight and was now eating more, I still kept a meticulous log of every (measured) bit of food that entered my mouth. I refused to touch red meat, junk food, or any kind of fat whatsoever.

Eventually, I had to resign myself to the fact that I alone cannot repair the immense damage that exists within our family. Without the cooperation of others, my endeavor is doomed to failure. I have relinquished my role as the family savior, realizing I am unable to control the behavior of my parents and my brother. I can, however, change my own actions and reactions within the family structure. An important, and difficult, part of the recovery process has been extricating myself from the dynamics of the family in order to develop and accept my own independent sense of self.

I can't believe I'm almost through with my college career. So many things have changed since I was a clueless, teary-eyed freshman. Now I'm half through my senior year. Within the past year alone I have undergone a complete metamorphosis, beginning with my revealing my anorexia to the world. I had wondered for so long whether I would ever be able to overcome this wretched disorder, and finally, I have reached the point where I can eat when I'm hungry and stop when I'm full. My recovery has been due in large part to the drug Prozac, which has also made me less obsessive and less high strung. My recovery, however, has had its ups and downs. This past summer I fell into a deep depression. I felt like my life was spiraling out of my control, that everything I had worked so hard for was falling apart. I spent most of my days crying and mulling over things. I didn't even want to go back to school in September to finish my senior year, but everyone convinced me to do so. I got treated for the depression and finally decided to take medication for it. I had adamantly refused to do so in the past, though an antidepressant was recommended by two of my previous psychiatrists. When I think back to how bad I was this past summer, I'm so thankful that I got help in time and was able to turn things around before they got completely out of control. I'm finally starting to feel good about myself, comfortable with who I am, and actually happy!

A big part of the change in me is due to LOVE. Yes, I finally met someone who was as attracted to me as I was to him. He has stood by me through some of the worst times of my life, through fighting the eating disorder as well as depression. I started seeing him nearly a year ago. Things were rough at first, mainly because of my inexperience and the issues I was having to deal with about myself. I was freaked out about sex and mostly about opening myself up to someone. I had been so egocentric for so long that it's been hard to give some of that self-centeredness up. I also had my first sexual encounter with him. That was another issue I had a hard time dealing with at first, but now, after having lived with him for the summer, it seems pretty silly.

I thought for sure that we would spend the rest of our lives together, deliriously happy and in love. But this past summer really put our relationship through the wringer. We've been fighting a lot, but more than that, I think we've been starting to pull back from each other. We pretty much both know that June will bring with it not only graduation but the end of our relationship. It's been really hard for me to accept that what I thought was an infallible, perfect romance is actually not immune to problems. I really wish things had worked out the way we planned them, but I guess I should have learned by now that life doesn't always follow the plans you make for it.

So, you might ask, what happens next? Well, I have moved ahead, and after four long years, I have finally beaten this disease. I feel as though an enormous weight has been lifted off my shoulders (no pun intended), and that I am finally ready to move ahead with the rest of my life—to "live, laugh, and love," as they say. I'm optimistic about the future, for if there's one thing I've learned, it's that I'm a fighter…. And, more importantly, I'm a survivor.

BEYOND THE EUPHORIC BUZZ

This author, a college junior, describes her double life as a high school student—respected student leader and secret weekend drinker. Growing up in a permissive family in Florida, Sarah slips into a pattern of binge drinking, drunkenness, and promiscuity. With utmost skill, she manages to keep her high school responsibilities and her drinking compartmentalized and for a while sees no need to change her habits. However, finding "common ground" and romance with a Chinese American man at college compels her to reassess her life and to master her addiction. Now a wife and mother, she commits herself to "a whole new appreciation for the sober life" and to caring for her husband and infant child.

Someone go find Luke! His girlfriend is puking."

I'm lying on the bathroom floor of the hotel room. Luke and I had been going together for only a month, when he had asked me to be his date for his junior prom. We drank together plenty in those four weeks, but this was the first time I had gotten sick. In my excitement at the after-party, I had veered from my "Beer then liquor, never sicker" rule, and that's how I came to be in my present situation.

I wake up to see Luke walking through the hotel room's bathroom door. "Oh, hi." I try to smile, but the room is spinning wildly. I can't make it stop. I close my eyes. Oh, worse. I grab the toilet bowl to puke some more. I hate vomiting. It feels like my guts are being yanked out through my mouth for everyone to have a look at. But there's nothing I can do to stop it. I keep waking up, feeling the room spin, puking, then falling back asleep.

At some point Luke decides I need to get in the shower. I argue with him because I can't move without the entire room turning into a carousel gone mad, spinning and spinning. Eventually, he ignores my whimpers. As he stands me up, dizziness overwhelms me. I begin to fall in slow motion. The world is tipping, like a bottle of tequila, and I'm inside, sloshing back and forth sickeningly. . . .

I am lying in the bathtub. Every movement creates another current in the water around me and the bottle sways back and forth. I slosh from side to side, bumping my head on the glass side. Luke is trying to hold the small plastic trash bin for me to puke into. I stop throwing up as the waves die down. I move my arm to get comfortable. More waves. More vomiting. I knock the trash bin on its side and vomit spills into the bath water. For just a moment I'm watching the room from above. I see myself lying there pitifully; sopping clothes, stringy hair, unable to control my bodily functions, bits of vomit floating around me. Then I'm back inside me, inside the bottle that almost finds equilibrium to stand up straight, but then something sets it rocking again. After what seems like hours I drift back to sleep, with Luke holding my head above the water. I'm too exhausted to keep up the fight.

Luke says I need to change into some dry, clean clothes. I look at him. He's never seen me without clothes on. But there's no way I can argue. I obviously can't go to bed like this, and I can't even stand up by myself. My body is not my own. He pushes my pants down to my ankles and sits me on the toilet to pull them off and to put on dry ones. I relax into his arms as he carries me to the bed.

Looking back at that night, I marvel that I never apologized to Luke. I remember feeling awkward because I had never become so ill from drinking, and I wasn't sure how to act. But apologizing was not my instinctive response. Instead, as soon as I had the realization that I had ruined Luke's big night, I began making excuses for myself. "It was only his *junior* prom," I told myself. My philosophy had always been that when I make a mistake, I should resist guilt and invest my energy in learning from the experience instead. But learning from my mistakes assumes some logical cause—something solvable. When drinking became the source of my mistakes, my already formed habit of avoiding guilt became a perpetuating force for my mental addiction. If I didn't feel guilty about the negative consequences of my drinking, what would motivate me to quit?

Today I can answer that question easily. I am finishing my last year in college, I am a wife and mother, and I comfortably identify myself as a nondrinker. But I cannot pretend that the person I am today is unconnected to my past. Just two and a half years ago I was driving home drunk, with a six-pack on the seat next to me, and I cruised into a tree in my front yard, putting a sizeable dent in my mom's car hood. So I must ask, how did things get so bad? Are there aspects of my personality that allowed me to sink so low or was this a simple case of alcohol addiction? And what keeps me from having a drink tomorrow, starting the whole cycle over again? What I've found is that the more I uncover in the complex networks of my mind, the more I see how this will be a lifetime process of realization and readjustment.

I am the youngest of four girls in my family. So, I learned everything about growing up from watching my sisters go through it. School, boyfriends, adolescence, alcohol, high school, drugs . . . I saw it all—first through the eyes of a little girl, and then later as I experienced it myself.

Lilliana, my oldest sister by six years, was my idol growing up. She was a cheerleader. She was on Homecoming Court. She was popular. She drank, she partied. After a while she even did drugs. Pot. Acid. Probably more. But I knew her only as my beautiful, glamorous sister whom I wanted to be just like when I grew up.

Her teenage years were extremely hard on the family. Lilliana was anything but subtle in her disobedience. She would yell and scream at my mother at the slightest cause. It was not unusual to find my mother chasing her around the kitchen table, out the front door, and around the rickety old station wagon parked in the driveway. She wielded a wooden paddle and a fierce look—intent not on hurting her, but on disciplining her rebellious spirit by punishing her defiant acts.

My parents learned a lesson in dealing with Lilliana—you can't force a teenager to do what you want. So they never took an authoritarian approach with the rest of us. Whereas my parents would try to tell Lilliana to come home at one and she would purposely stay out all night, I never had a curfew. Their strategy with the rest of us was to persuade us to do what they thought was best by reasoning with us, discussing the issues, telling us about their experiences. But ultimately, the decision was ours. They understood that sometimes hearing about their mistakes wasn't enough. We needed to experience and learn for ourselves too.

And that was our relationship, for as long as I lived in that household. I respected my parents, obeyed their few rules, considered their abundant counsel, and made my own choices. I could say that not having a curfew was conducive to excessive partying. I could say that being allowed to drink at home was convenient for heavy drinking. But I don't. I never blame my parents for any position I found myself in. I made my own decisions and I dealt with the repercussions myself.

As the offspring of genuine hippies, drugs were never a taboo topic. Growing up, I knew that my parents had lived on a commune with a diet consisting mostly of tofu and pot for the majority of their young adult lives. I was raised on all the "psychedelic" music of the 1960s and by the time I was 12 knew all about the allusions to drugs in the Beatles' songs and many others. But drug use was not a subject that I took lightly.

A memory is imprinted on my mind not because it had great meaning or emotional impact, but from sheer repetition. My mother would be doing something around the house and talking to me at the same time. Suddenly she would stop—always midsentence, sometimes midword. It appeared that she was just pausing in order to concentrate better on what she was doing. I would wait for her to finish the task, expecting her to then complete the sentence, but she never would.

"Mom. What were you going to say?"

"What?"

"What were you going to say? You were just telling me to do something."

"Oh," she would say with surprise. "I was? I'm sorry, honey, I don't remember."

"But *Mom!*" I would reply, drawing out the "o" in exasperation. "You were *just* saying it."

"I'm sorry, sweetie." And the conversation was over. Now for that to happen once is understandable, twice is forgivable, three times a little trying. But over and over and over . . . it's something you can't forget. Later when I found out that this is a typical symptom of being "burnt out," this memory served as the greatest incentive I could ever ask for never to try pot.

By the time I was 13, both Lilliana and Rachel, eighteen months my elder, were heavily into drugs. Everyone knew it, but there wasn't much we could do about it. I resented the huge role that pot played in Rachel's and Lilliana's lives. They totally dropped out of family life. Not just by neglecting chores, but also by retracting all emotional investment. They couldn't stand to be around the family without the buffer of being high. They only valued smoking and people who smoked with them. They were always off in their fairy-tale land where everything was cool and chill and nothing really mattered.

High school was a wonderful time, filled with new experiences, new faces, new challenges. Our freshman class was composed of six hundred students. Wandering through the halls I saw many familiar faces from middle school, and many new ones. I smiled brightly and said hello to everyone, without hesitation. During the second week of school I was in the attendance office and I saw sign-up sheets for anyone who wanted to run for Freshmen Board. Instantly, my mind was flooded with memories of helping Lilliana run for student office. Late nights spent making stickers that read, "Vote for Lilliana Fox!" with little legs and a bushy tail drawn around the "Fox." It sounded like fun! I put my name down for treasurer, a notable title without a lot of work, I thought. The following week I made posters and stickers that looked like a sun and wrote "Vote for Sarah Sunshine!" To my surprise, I won.

The following week a freshmen student assembly was called to introduce the Freshmen Board. The four elected ones sat in four lonely chairs on the vast gymnasium floor. The kids who filled the seats in the towering bleachers were full of that first-week-of-school, fidgeting, bottled-up kind of energy. The assistant principal spoke (for too long) and then began introducing the board. Finally, it was my turn! "And here is your newly elected treasurer, Sarah Fox." Applause, stomping, yelling. Wow! Was that louder than they had cheered for the President? It sure sounded like it to me. But as I approached the microphone, the mob before me was still daunting.

"Thanks for electing us to Freshmen Board," I said with a smile. "Our goal is to make school a more enjoyable place. And I think we've done good so far. We got you out of class today, didn't we?" Hooting, hollering! I was beginning to blush. They hadn't cheered during anyone else's speeches. As it was getting quiet again, Ted Williams, hunk of the class, yelled out, "We love you, Sarah Sunshine!" That started another round of rowdiness. Realizing that I could control this great throng, I willed my bashfulness to disappear. "Okay, okay," I said, as if I was used to this, unimpressed. I continued with my speech, and glancing up, I saw it. People were actually listening to me! With this reassurance, I flashed smiles at faces I recognized. When I came to the end of my note cards, I headed to my seat. The compulsory applause followed. But I couldn't stand such a mediocre ending. Just before I reached my seat I dashed back to the podium. "Freshmen class rules!" I cried into the microphone. They exploded! They stood on their seats, they went wild! But I wasn't a participant in the excitement—I was the leader of it. Yes, that's right, follow my lead, I chuckled to myself, as I sat down.

Looking back I see that this experience had quite an impact on me. That feeling of power over the multitude was intoxicating. Until then I had lived like a little girl, without a care about the consequences of my words and actions. But in the course of that speech I lived my first calculated moments. I did not smile or speak as I always had, out of an impulsive, friendly instinct. I acted in order to produce a desired effect. I was rewarded for my calculation with instant popularity. As my high school career progressed, I treated every action as a political statement.

Being on class board was not just about popularity, for me. I quickly involved myself in every aspect of the school's inner workings. The principal of the school once introduced me saying, "This girl runs the school. She holds everything together around here with her sunshine smile." I once let a curse word slip out in class and was sent to the office. "Look," I said to the assistant principal. "I've heard you use that word how many times? How are you gonna punish me for it?" Not only did I have administrative immunity, but I was making honor roll without trying terribly hard and all my teachers loved me.

I seemed to spread the fairy-tale glitter of my life over everything and everyone that I came in contact with. And the better I became at playing to the crowd, the better my life seemed to get. I couldn't have asked for more. This was every girl's dream of high school. So why shouldn't I become totally immersed in it? Yes, it required some acting, putting up of façades, surrendering of my hopes to live life with childlike innocence. But it was worth it. Hell, it was more than worth it. What I had was better than innocence. It was perfection.

Throughout junior high and freshman year of high school I never drank. I had always been firm in my refusal to drink, to the point that I never had to mention it; it was known. I was confident in my role and I felt I was being wise. So when I decided to get drunk for the first time I could honestly say it was a choice that I made for myself when I felt I was ready. I wasn't just following the crowd. *I* wanted to try it. I set the date in my head and then I told everyone else. "Next Saturday I'm going to get drunk," I said.

"All right! We'll have to get some good stuff, then!" That was Frank. He was two years older than me and had this incredibly charismatic personality. He had an air of relaxed confidence about him, as if he were so cool he could just relax about it. We were part of a group that hung out on the beach every night. He lived near me so he often drove me home in his jeep.

All that week I looked forward to it. On Friday, Frank asked, "Why don't you just do it tonight?"

"Nope. Tomorrow. Don't worry, Frankie, it'll be just as fun!" And was it ever! I drank a beer and felt giddy. I was talking and laughing, which is not uncommon for me. Everything just seemed to have an extra sparkle. Then I drank another and I was off and running. Weighing one hundred pounds, I knew it wouldn't take much alcohol to affect me. "Let's go down to the water!" I said excitedly. I met with groans and sighs.

"It's too far."

"Aw come on, Sarah, just sit down and relax."

"Come on, come on! It'll be fun!" I urged. "Come *on!*" I said pulling on Frank's arm. Finally Diana, who had not yet tried drinking, decided to go down with me. And then I convinced Frank to come too. "I'll race ya," I said to Diana and set off running. I arrived at the water's edge out of breath. Diana was trailing behind me, laughing.

"Sarah, you're such a nut!" she cried happily.

"Oooh!" I said, as I had another thought, "Let's go swimming!" And before she could respond I was running toward the water. As soon as it was deep enough I collapsed into the water. I felt it close in around me, hugging my body, making me warm. I moved and turned, feeling the water swirl around me. And after a while I popped my head out of the water, took a gulp of air, then let the water envelop me again. I just lay there this time. Letting the lull of the waves move my body for me, relaxed completely. And then I felt arms around me. Real, human arms. Someone was dragging me out of the water.

"Oh, hi Frankie!"

"Diana thought you were drowning," he said flatly. He didn't sound amused.

"Oh. Well, I wasn't," I explained. I began thinking how unfortunate it was that he had pulled me out. It was so much warmer in the water! He set me on the ground. And then I caught sight of the sky. "Ooooh! Diana look at the stars!" I said. "Let's spin!" I stretched my arms out, let my head fall back, and spun around and around and around, looking at the stars in the heavens. I was a little girl again. Grinning so widely that my cheeks bulged out to twice their normal size. No cares outside of the here and now. Ah life! What joy! I sat down and pondered with amazement, while the world slowly stopped spinning around me.

This is the story of the first time I got drunk. But it is also the story of how I fell in love with the drunken state of mind, and still love it today. Being drunk is like being a kid again. When I was drunk I could experience careless bliss. Once I tasted the forbidden fruit, I couldn't give it up. When I discovered that being drunk was like artificial childlike innocence, I couldn't resist. And why should I? I could have my cake and eat it too.

Sophomore year I was elected class president. I was passionate about the work I was doing to improve the school. The people around me seemed to sense my dedication. It was the same with all the people I worked with: facilities managers, administrators, students, teachers. They worked extraordinarily well with me and for me because they respected me professionally, liked me personally, and thought that the final results of my work repaid their efforts. My products were inherently more valuable because I put so much of my self into my work. I wasn't just the president anymore; I became a public figure. As much depended on my personal integrity as on my capability.

Sophomore year I was partying with all the most popular kids on campus. Yes, I stood out from the crowd, but only because when I wanted to have fun, I *really* had fun. No inhibitions, no quiet reservations. Everyone had a "One time

Sarah was so drunk . . ." story to tell at school the following Monday and I thought it was great.

I always drank to get drunk. And I usually passed out sometime during the night. I knew people thought it was a big deal to black out but it didn't make much sense to me. Passing out to me was just like falling asleep. And when can anyone remember the exact circumstances of falling asleep? I remembered my nights in the form of a flash: action, feeling. And the emotion washes over me, in that flash, with an intensity that can hardly be paralleled when sober. Why dilute that memory with specifics and particulars? In my eyes, I was sucking the marrow out of life.

From the second or third time I got drunk I began to think about alcoholism. I still wonder, was my instinct warning me, from the very beginning? Could I have known somewhere deep within my subconscious that I was *too* in love with being drunk—that it could become a problem for me? I wanted to find out more about alcoholism, but I was scared my political career would be over if my secret concerns became known. In eleventh grade the opportunity I had been waiting for finally came. I had to do a documentary on a topic of my choice. I immediately knew I wanted to interview recovering alcoholics and counselors for substance abuse; then take what I learned from them and apply it to students who were known as fun partiers. I wanted to show that what most people thought of as harmless fun was truly dangerous. Looking back I realize that I wanted to increase social awareness so that people like me would be taken seriously. The best definition of alcoholism I heard from those interviews was, "When your alcohol use begins having a negative effect on more than one area of your life and you continue to drink." The only problem is that the more addicted one becomes, the more subjective one's judgment becomes. The definition of what's "bad enough" keeps sliding.

Going into the summer before senior year I had it all made. I was managing to keep my school responsibilities and my drinking compartmentalized, balanced. At that time I was involved in my most serious relationship yet, over one-and-a-half years long. His name was Luke. His family was moving to Orlando at the start of the summer, about six hours upstate, and he was leaving for the state university in the fall. Lately, I'd noticed myself looking at other guys. I was just hoping to stay faithful until he left, and then I'd be free. I had already convinced him it would be better not to attempt a long-distance relationship.

Two days before Luke's departure, we went to a party. When I had become sufficiently intoxicated, I pulled aside Steve, a friend of his that I had always thought was cute. "So, listen," I said. "Luke is leaving on Tuesday. Why don't you give me a call and we can go party or something?"

He looked at me quizzically, peering into my face to confirm the implications he thought he had just heard. His face broke into a broad smile. "Sure."

Tuesday came and Luke left. Thursday came and Steve called. We went to a kicking party. The end of the night found us skinny-dipping in the jacuzzi. We made out passionately in the steamy water. He pressed himself against me, and for the first time in my life I seriously considered not saving myself for marriage.

Luckily, I was too nervous about the whole situation (nude in a strange place with my recent ex-boyfriend's good friend) to do anything.

A few nights later I went to another party at the same girl's house. There was an attractive guy there who I had my eye on. He had graduated from my high school two years earlier. When I introduced myself, he said, "I know. I used to watch you during lunch when you sat outside." I was flattered. He used to watch me from afar! I always wanted an admirer! As the party cleared out, Christopher and I were left on the fold-out couch. We started making out and it got pretty intense pretty quickly. At some point he asked me whether I wanted to "do it." I said I never had and he dropped it. A while later he brought it up again and after a few minutes of pondering I said sure. Just like that. That night seemed like it never ended. I don't know what girls are talking about when they say the first time hurts. I thought it was terrific. Over and over. At times I would forget his name, then the next time I woke up I'd remember it.

I awoke the next morning and knew right away that everything had changed. Why had I decided to go for it? I asked myself. I had no answer. Saving myself for marriage was such an integral part of my self-identity as a moral, good person. Without my virginity, I was left devoid of any positive self-image.

It took less than one moment to decide my response. I would not regret losing my virginity to Christopher. No regrets! I would make it a meaningful experience by developing a real relationship with him. And if that worked, wouldn't it be fantastic if I actually ended up marrying my first?

For the next month, there was little time that we spent together when we weren't drunk or having sex. But we were getting to know each other a little more. For instance, I learned he was much more uptight than I was, he had been a complete loser at school, he had been kicked out of two state universities in the past year, and none of his friends or family thought highly of him. In fact, anyone who knew about us tried to convince me that I shouldn't be with him. Not many people knew, though. If any of my friends from school heard I was with him, they might also hear that I was sleeping with him. And that, I knew, would be the end of my perfect reputation at school.

Our relationship was a constant roller coaster. Every time something came up that put us on less than good terms, I panicked. I could sense that Guilt was just out of eyesight, impending, threatening, and if we didn't stay together it would come barreling down on me. It got to the point that the simplest interaction, like calling him up, required having at least a few drinks to calm my nerves and rally up my courage.

After about five weeks I stopped caring. I found what I needed in my drinking. I finally ended it by kissing another guy. While we had been together, I told myself that Christopher would be the only exception to my sexual abstinence. But once we broke up, Guilt again threatened to overcome me. I still did not want to surrender to it. The only alternative was to keep going without looking back. That's just what I did.

All summer I partied every night. Drinking was starting to lose its excitement. My new thrill was hooking up with whomever I wanted. There was a certain satisfaction in knowing that I could seduce anyone. My conquests were always one-night stands and I never became emotionally involved. Looking back it was as if I became a completely different person when I went out drinking. Never would I have done those things sober. I knew they were wrong, and I would have felt too ashamed. But as the summer went on I could plan who I was going to get that night, before I ever started drinking. By the end of the summer drinking was not a necessity. Although it was a large part of my lifestyle, I didn't have to be drunk to carry out my conquests.

I was drinking more and more during the day. Partying all night left me depleted of energy during the day. Drinking made the daylight hours bearable, made me feel physically better, more energetic and happier. Not only was my physical health failing, but my emotional health was also deteriorating. My sexual conquests required cutting off all emotions. Once I learned how to cut myself off, I found myself doing it all the time. Not only was it easier to live life without a conscience, but there was a convenient aftereffect: since I didn't care about anything, even when alcohol was having a negative effect on all areas of my life, in my mind things never became "bad enough" to quit.

When school started in the fall I hardly paused. I was president of student council, captain of the debate team, and treasurer of the National Honor Society. I was enrolled in two AP courses and three honors courses. I stayed two hours after school every day, and sometimes arrived an hour early, to take care of the official business of my various positions. I was dedicated to my academics, but somehow I still found the time to drink. On Wednesdays I arrived home from school at four o'clock. My church orchestra practice started at six. On my way home from church, I stopped by 7-Eleven and bought some brew with my fake ID. A few of my nonschool friends would be waiting for me when I got home.

I was able to keep my reputation and positions at school because no one there knew about my drinking. I never partied with people from school. At the time it was because I thought they were superficial and their mere presence annoyed me, inhibited me. In retrospect I see that I was successful in the various spheres of my life, and in order to maintain that success while continuing to drink, I had to preserve barriers that would never be crossed.

About halfway through the fall of my senior year I started getting a bit bored by my drinking routine. It had lost its excitement. I felt so old and tired. I could feel myself getting numb. I decided to clean up my act. I wanted to start a real relationship. My plan was to build up a relationship slowly, and at the same time cut down on my drinking and partying. Eventually we would spend all of our time together and I'd have no need to drink at all. It was a good plan.

I picked out a sweet, innocent underclassman, Ted. By the next week we were passing notes between classes. Already I felt like a normal teenager again, excited at the mere hope of being someone's girlfriend. I could almost feel the spiritual calluses softening up.

And then came the big football game that Friday. I hadn't gone to a game sober in ages. At first I tried to make plans with some of my old nondrinking friends. But I hadn't even called them in ages. They couldn't just drop their new friends and welcome me back with open arms. Friday came and I couldn't resist. My drinking buddies bought a bottle of tequila and we drank a good portion of it before walking over to the field.

Before I could get very far I ran into Ted. What terrific luck! I was actually hoping I'd see him here. We saw each other from a few yards away and we both burst into smiles. I ran into his open arms. He picked me up and he swung me around. This is the way it should be, I thought to myself. I stood with him for a bit, until I spotted my friends, looking impatient as ever. I gave Ted one last hug.

The night was still young, the halftime show had just ended. I was beginning to tire of putting on fake smiles for my superficial school friends. Then I ran into an old acquaintance. Not just anyone, mind you. Rick Marciano. Wow! What a hotty! He had graduated two years ago, and he was still known as a legend amongst the lady folk. I greeted him with an extra close hug and barely stepped away after the embrace. We talked for a few minutes about nothing and then he told me about a party after the game. I already had plans, so he gave me his number to meet up later. "You'd better not forget my number!" he said as we parted.

Don't forget his number? Who was he joking? Did he really think he was the pursuant here? Or that any girl in her right mind would give up such a golden opportunity? I walked away feeling even happier than the eight drinks had made me feel.

And what about Ted? Well, I did think about him for a moment, as I walked away from Rick. But this was such a once-in-a-lifetime opportunity that I couldn't give it up. By this time I was so good at making excuses for myself that I hardly had to think twice to defend my actions. Ted and I hardly have anything going, I told myself. I mean, it's not like we're going out or anything. Plus, maybe it was a bad idea to try to have a normal relationship. Maybe I'm not ready for it yet. And that was that.

That night one of my only true friends from school was throwing his first big party. When I arrived, all the popular kids from his grade were there. After a few drinks, I called Rick to invite him over.

The next thing I remember Rick and I were making out in the bushes in front of the house. Of course, everyone saw. Wilson persuaded me to at least find somewhere more discreet to do whatever I wanted to do. So Rick and I hopped in his car and drove away. That was all that people needed to start the rumors.

It wasn't long until Ted heard the stories. He called me on Sunday night. It was horrible. He told me I was the first person who ever made him feel like a real man. Why did I do this to *him?* Was he not fast enough for me? He was crying. There was nothing I could do to make amends for what I had done. Not just to Ted, but to myself, my family, my church, God. I could feel the weight of the world bearing down on me, about to collapse. In that moment the gates opened up. Feelings of worthlessness, guilt, shame, sadness—all the emotions that I had been refusing to feel, that I had intentionally dammed up inside me by drinking alcohol, alcohol, and more alcohol—it all came rushing out in a torrent. I felt like Jesus Christ, all the sins of the world cast upon me in a matter of moments. Except these weren't the sins of the world, these were *my* sins.

Do you know what a shock it is to the system to feel so many emotions all at once, after not feeling anything—nothing—for months on end? It's paralyzing, to say the least. He was sobbing. What could I do? I was bawling inside. But I had forgotten how to express those kinds of emotions. Or maybe I should say I had unlearned it.

I slept for only two hours that night. I dreaded Monday. I considered staying home from school, but that would be a cowardly public statement. At school I could feel the stares, hear the whispers as I walked by. By the end of the school day I felt extreme blackness cover my insides like a blanket. It was too much to bear. I had to shut myself off again or else I would have a nervous breakdown. I was sure of it.

The worst part was the Student Council meeting. Ted was a representative. He sat quietly in the back row, like the martyr that he was. The meeting was complete disorder. Everyone thought they had the right and the duty to condemn me. This was their way of showing their disrespect.

Eventually things at school died down. I didn't get back my ability to feel, but I didn't really expect to either. I had undergone a trauma. I would never be the same again. Sometimes I pitied myself. I'm still a kid, I would say to myself. I'm not supposed to have to grow up this fast. But I knew I had only myself to blame for it all.

It took this harrowing experience for me to realize I had become obsessed with the powerful feeling I obtained from controlling men. Through it all, I never thought to quit my drinking. I knew that my lack of self-control was worst when I was drunk. But quitting drinking would disrupt my whole life. And I just wasn't ready for that. I needed all the comfort I could get at that point.

In many ways college was just like high school. I quickly got a reputation that I was fun to party with, and everyone had a funny, "One time Sarah was so drunk that she . . ." story to tell. The most important difference was Dan. I met him my second day on campus. The moment I saw him my heart started racing. He wasn't just good-looking, he was strikingly so. This guy was *gorgeous*. And as we began to talk I saw that his beauty was not just skin deep. Our friendship was like love at first sight. From that first night and every day after, my amazement, admiration, and enjoyment of Dan just grew and grew.

We spent all our free time together. We could be found lying side-by-side on the lawn doing homework, meandering through town, and eating breakfast, lunch, and dinner together. Not only did we have a terrific time, but I was constantly in wonder of how alike we seemed, despite our apparent differences. He from the Northeast, me from the South; he from the big city of Boston, me from the midsized tourist town of Sarasota; he Chinese American, me white, Cuban American; he the oldest of his siblings, me the youngest. But we seemed to find common ground in everything. We were like two puzzle pieces made of different materials, by the hands of different craftsmen, who had spent their lives adjusting to the fact that we would never quite fit in with the rest. Then all of a sudden, by some twist of fate, we discovered that we fit—together, perfectly.

It was three months into our friendship before we confessed our romantic love for each other. The ensuing months were heavenly. We were so in love and happy about it that the most frequent comment we received from friends was, "You guys make me sick."

The only thing we didn't have in common was drinking. Dan wasn't a big drinker. His social scene in high school had never included drinking as a regular activity. Our freshman year he went to the frats, because that was the main social activity, but he didn't derive his pleasure from drinking, like I did. About four months into freshman year—we had been together as a couple for only a short time—my partying became a problem for us. Dan was getting tired of staying at frats until midmorning, when he wasn't even having a good time. But this was my way of having fun and I wasn't ready to give that up for any reason. I don't think it was a matter of being addicted to alcohol at that point. I just enjoyed that scene— the people, the noise, the drunk intellectual conversations, and, yes, the drinking. But maybe that lifestyle is part of the mental addiction.

Dan and I never discussed these issues. About three months into our romantic relationship I kissed another guy at a frat after Dan had left. It wasn't a long, passionate kiss. A quick peck. But the guilt was overwhelming. I confessed to Dan the next morning. We talked about why it had happened, how I needed to control myself when I drank, but we hardly scraped the surface. The real conversation started when I confessed to a much greater sin. Two weeks after we started dating we had a one-month vacation. On my trip back home I slept with my recent ex-boyfriend, Keith. Dan almost couldn't handle it. We practically broke up. But my begging and pleading finally convinced him that *he* was the one I wanted to be with, that I would never let it happen again.

Other than those incidents, our relationship was wonderful. It was the happiest, healthiest relationship I had ever been in. We never came out of the "in love" stage. We were affectionate and snuggly and passionate, but we also had stimulating intellectual discussions and challenged each others' perspectives.

At the end of our freshman year, we were faced with a summer apart. I had an internship in Miami, about five hours from my hometown, and he had an internship in Boston. I knew I'd be spending several weekends at home, and a part of me wanted the freedom to be able to hook up with people at parties, if the opportunity arose. I explained that I wanted to be with him. In fact, I wanted to marry him, eventually. But I needed this last chance to be free and irresponsible, before I grew up and settled down. He couldn't understand how we could be anything but monogamous and still stay together. Finally he put his foot down. Either we stayed exclusive or we broke up. I agreed. We would stay exclusive.

All summer we talked every day. We talked on the phone at night, we e-mailed each other from work during the day. All was going well. I had visited home a few times and I was confident in my ability to stay true to my promise.

Fourth of July is always a big celebration in my town, and it's a huge drinking affair. By the time the fireworks ended, I was very happily drunk. I had invited a few of my old drinking buddies over, for old times sake. While we were all hanging out on the front porch drinking, I began to notice how attracted I was to one of my old friends. When everyone else had left, we began to kiss. One thing led to another and we ended up in bed. I didn't really want to have sex with him. That wasn't at all what I had in mind. But that's what happened. I was so drunk that I didn't really care. All I could muster was a questioning, "Um, Rob?" As if to say, what are you doing? But I didn't feel strongly enough about it, at the time, to put up much of an argument. Needless to say, it was terribly unenjoyable.

The next morning came and I felt like shit. I knew I had to tell Dan. That had been his one request. "Sarah, if you care about me in the slightest, you'll give me the respect of telling me if anything happens over the summer." I boarded the bus back to Miami and thought about how I was going to tell him. How I was going to explain that it wasn't passionate, it wasn't meaningful, it had just happened. Most of all, how was I going to keep him from dumping me?

I called that night. I cried. He was silent. He had expected it, he explained. He had felt something, a certain foreboding, about me going home for the holiday. He called me late on the night of the fourth, hoping that if the thought of him was fresh on my mind, it would stop me from doing anything. But it hadn't. He broke up with me. I said everything I could to win him back. Finally I told him I would quit drinking.

"Good! You need to. But that's not going to make what you did any better. And it won't solve the problem, either. I want you to want *me*. No one else. Whether you're drunk or sober, I need to be the object of your love *and* your lust. You need me, but you don't want me." Maybe he was right. But I had to do something. I called AA that night and found out where the meetings were held.

For twenty-four hours Dan and I were in Hell, separately. I called him the next night. We were miserable. I don't think he even liked me, at that point. I could hear the distaste in his voice. I didn't deserve him. We both knew it. I had caused him so much awful pain. But we were even more miserable apart. So he took me back. It was going to take a long time to mend his broken heart and regain his trust. All I could do was hope—hope that our happiness together wasn't over for good.

Quitting was the only thing I could actively work on to improve things with Dan. I stopped drinking cold turkey. It was easy while I was in Miami. I barely had a social life there, so I rarely had the opportunity to drink. My visits home were the true test. My family had become so accustomed to my drinking habits, that they questioned my sudden abstinence. Over the next few months, my sisters and parents each took their turn explaining that I need not be so extreme. A little alcohol surely couldn't hurt, they implied. But I knew myself. I knew I couldn't drink without getting drunk. I never had experienced that mentality. My mind only worked a certain way. Once I have the first sip, my only goal is getting wasted. I knew that my craving wouldn't be quenched by one drink. It wasn't the taste that I desired, it was the feeling. That euphoric buzz that leads to a numb semiconsciousness. No, I couldn't even have a sip.

When I first quit drinking, I felt like I was missing out on the best of life. Who can go back to a normal lifestyle once they've experienced the passion and extreme highs of living for the moment, completely rid of the inhibitions of societal norms and personal conscience? The memory of my fast-paced, extravagant lifestyle was not enough. I wanted to experience more. Being at a college where drinking makes up the bulk of social interaction did not help. When I saw crowds of drunk people meandering through frat row I felt so much hostility. I wanted to be there, I wanted to join them. I didn't want to grow up yet. And, damn it, I shouldn't have to. I'm 18 and I deserve to be still having fun, I told myself. What I knew had been fun and exciting. How could something else be anything but dull and mediocre?

To Dan, my decision to quit drinking on July 5, 1998 was a statement that I had recognized, at last, all the pain and injury that my alcohol use had inflicted on myself and those around me. But that's not what it was to me. To me, it was admitting that keeping Dan was more important to me than continuing to drink. Realizing the myriad of ways that alcohol had affected my life would be a long process.

Before I could see that my alcohol use was the cause of many problems, I had to admit that I had problems. I needed to admit that *by my own standards* my life had gone to hell. I had to admit that I had slipped so far from where I wanted to be. I thought of myself as a failure. The first step is admitting to myself that I feel this way and then recognizing that the source of these feelings is me, my perspective, the way I think life ought to be.

I feel like I have done a lot of harm in my day, to myself and to others. I've broken the hearts of guys who were foolish enough to invest feelings in me, during my alcohol and sex binges. And I never to this day even thought about what I had done to them. I've seen sides of myself that I never wanted to believe I was capable of. God gave me the ability to influence people, to captivate them, and I desecrated these gifts by using them for sexual conquests and to further myself politically. This is not religious guilt, put on me by someone else. It's the way I feel inside.

It took me two years just to gain enough distance to be able to talk about drinking without wanting to be engaged in it, deep inside. I'm finally secure enough in my identity as a nondrinker to be able to look objectively at my experiences. I have just started this process. It seems like I'm rather late—two years and I haven't made much progress in all that time. But the way I look at it, at least the process has started. With the birth of my daughter six months ago I became responsible for a brand new life. Today, my desire to take care of my family gives me a whole new appreciation for the sober life.

LICENSURE APPENDIX

Part 1
Licensure Examination Study Guide

You probably will have to take a licensure examination in order to become a teacher in your state. In almost 40 states the Praxis II™ test is the required licensure examination. This section highlights the concepts from each chapter that may be on your licensure test.

Chapter 1

For Piagetian and Vygotskian theories of development, you should understand:

- Basic assumptions of each
- How students build their unique knowledge bases
- How students acquire skills
- Important terms and concepts related to each
- The key steps, mechanisms, or milestones related to each theory
- The limitations of each theory

Chapter 2

Understand the major concepts and progressions related to:

- Bronfenbrenner and the Social Context for Development
- Erikson's theory of psychosocial development
- Piaget's and Kohlberg's perspectives on moral development
- Gilligan's theory of caring

Design or choose strategies that:

- support optimal social and emotional development of students
- help students cope with major life transitions and challenges to safety, physical, and mental health
- help students build a sense of self-concept, self-esteem, and self-identity (including racial identity)

Recognize signs or behaviors that indicate sexual abuse or child abuse

Chapter 4

Explain the effects of legislation on public education:

- Americans with Disabilities Act
- Individuals with Disabilities Education Improvement Act
- Section 504
- Individualized Education Plans
- Inclusion, Mainstreaming and Least Restrictive Environment
- Inclusion, Mainstreaming and Least Restrictive Environment

Understand views of intelligence and describe its measurement:

- Types of intelligence tests and their uses
- Multiple intelligences
- Interpreting intelligence scores
- Modifications to testing

Accommodate the needs of students with exceptionalities:

- Attention-Deficit Hyperactivity Disorder
- Visual, speech, and physical difficulties
- Learning disabilities
- Intellectual disabilities/mental retardation

Chapter 5

For the development of language, you should understand:

- Basic assumptions of major theories
- The major accomplishments of language development of school-age children
- The relationship between language and literacy
- Basic steps that teachers can take to enhance literacy among their students
- Strategies that support English acquisition in non-English speaking students

Chapter 6

Recognize the influences that ethnicity, socioeconomic status, and community values may have on:

- Student–teacher relationships/parent–teacher relationships
- Student learning styles
- Academic achievement
- Attitudes, self-esteem, and expectations for success
- Opportunities for quality educational experiences

Understand the influences that gender may have on:

- Teachers' attention to students
- Differences in mental abilities

Devise strategies that:

- Eliminate sexist teaching practices
- Promote positive school–home relationships
- Reduce or eliminate racial and ethnic stereotypes and biases

Chapter 7

Explain the advantages and appropriate uses of major student-centered approaches to learning and instruction:

- Inquiry method
- Problem-based learning
- Cognitive apprenticeships
- Cooperative learning
- Service learning

Understand important concepts related to student-centered models of instruction:

- Situated learning
- Complex learning environments
- Authentic tasks
- Multiple representations of content
- Piaget and Vygotsky: Theories of constructivism

Chapter 8

Focus on these major topics:

- Bandura
- Modeling and Observational Learning
- Social Cognitive Theory
- Self Regulated Learning
- Self-Efficacy
- Teachers' Sense of Efficacy

Chapter 9

Describe the theoretical foundations of the major approaches to motivation.

- Identify and define important terms related to motivation including goals, attributions, intrinsic and extrinsic motivation, self-determination.
- Use your knowledge of motivation to:
  - identify situations and conditions that can enhance or diminish student motivation to learn.
  - design strategies to support individual and group work in the classroom.
  - implement practices that help students become self-motivated.

Chapter 10

Understand principles of classroom management that promote positive relationships by:

- Establishing daily procedures and routines
- Responding effectively to minor student misbehavior
- Implementing reasonable rules, penalties, and rewards
- Keeping students actively engaged in purposeful learning

Diagnose problems and prevent or reduce inappropriate behaviors by:

- Communicating with students and parents
- Addressing misbehaviors in the least intrusive way possible
- Confronting disruptive behaviors in an effective, efficient manner

Chapter 11

Develop plans for instruction and consider:

- The role of objectives in instruction
- Writing behavioral and cognitive objectives
- The use of educational taxonomies to design effective objectives
- The role of independent practice (i.e., seatwork and homework)
- Direct instruction and expository teaching
  - Basic assumptions
  - Inductive reasoning/deductive reasoning
  - Appropriate uses/principles of implementation

Understand the basic principles of teacher-centered and student-centered forms of instruction, including:

- Appropriate uses and limitations
- The role of the teacher
- Effective questioning techniques
- Whole group discussions
- Recitation
- Thematic/interdisciplinary instruction
- Differentiated instruction

Chapter 12

Describe the characteristics and purposes of major types of tests:

- Criterion-referenced and norm-referenced tests
- Achievement, aptitude, and diagnostic tests

Explain the major issues related to concerns about standardized testing, including:

- High-stakes testing
- Bias in testing
- Test-taking programs

Understand major concepts related to classroom assessment and grading:

- Formative and summative assessment
- Reliability and validity
- Criterion-referenced and norm-referenced grading

Describe the characteristics, uses, and limitations of major assessment techniques, including:

- Multiple-choice items
- Essays
- Portfolios
- Exhibitions

Design a scoring rubric for an authentic learning task that possesses:

- Validity
- Reliability
- Generalizability
- Equity

Part 2
Correlating Text Content to the PRAXIS II™ Principles of Learning and Teaching Tests and Intasc Standards

Each state in the country has its own set of licensure requirements that new teachers must meet in order to work in the classroom. An increasing number of states are basing their requirements on standards developed by INTASC (Interstate New Teacher Assessment and Support Consortium). These standards are based on ten principles of effective teaching that INTASC has identified as essential for optimal student learning. Many states assess new teachers' knowledge of those principles through the use of tests from the PRAXIS II™ series published by the Educational Testing Service. Within the PRAXIS II™ series are three *Principles of Learning and*

Teaching (PLT) tests, one each for grades K–6, 5–9, and 7–12. Each PLT test assesses students' knowledge of educational psychology and its application in the classroom.

The following table is designed to help you study for your PLT test and meet the Knowledge standards for each of INTASC's ten principles of effective teaching. The left-hand column of the table lists the topics assessed in a PLT test. The right-hand column contains INTASC's Knowledge standards. In the center column, you will find the chapters, sections, and page numbers in this textbook that correspond to the PLT tests and INTASC standards.

PRAXIS II™ Topics	Woolfolk Text Connections	INTASC Principles
I. Students as Learners **A. Student Development and the Learning Process**		
1. Theoretical foundations about how learning occurs: how students construct knowledge, acquire skills, and develop habits of mind	*Chapters 1, 7–12* (entire chapter)	1(d) The teacher understands how learning occurs—how students construct knowledge, acquire skills, and develop habits of mind—and knows how to use instructional strategies that promote student learning.
■ Examples of important theorists:		
• Jean Piaget	*Chapter 1*/Piaget's Theory of Cognitive Development (pp. 16-29)	
• Lev Vygotsky	*Chapter 1*/Vygotsky's Sociocultural Perspective (pp. 29-34)	
• Howard Gardner	*Chapter 4*/Multiple Intelligences (pp. 122-124)	
• Robert Sternberg	*Chapter 4*/Intelligence as a Process (pp. 125-126)	
• Urie Bronfenbrenner	*Chapter 2*/Bronfenbrenner: The Social Context for Development (pp. 49-61)	
■ Important terms that relate to learning theory:		
• Adaptation	*Chapter 1*/Basic Tendencies in Thinking (pp. 17-18)	
• Conservation	*Chapter 1*/Basic Tendencies in Thinking (pp. 20)	
• Constructivism	*Chapter 1*/Implications of Piaget's and Vygotsky's Theories for Teachers (pp. 60–64); *Chapter 7*/Constructivist Views of Learning (pp. 253-255)	
• Equilibration	*Chapter 1*/Basic Tendencies in Thinking (pp. 17-18)	
• Co-constructed process	*Chapter 1*/The Social Sources of Individual Thinking (pp. 29-30)	
• Private speech	*Chapter 1*/The Role of Language and Private Speech (pp. 32-33)	
• Scaffolding	*Chapter 1*/Assisted Learning (pp. 36-39); *Guidelines:* Applying Vygotsky's Ideas in Teaching (pp. 37); *Chapter 7*/Cognitive Apprenticeships and Reciprocal Teaching (pp. 259-262)	

PRAXIS II™ Topics	Woolfolk Text Connections	INTASC Principles
• Zone of proximal development	*Chapter 1*/The Zone of Proximal Development (pp. 33-34)	
• Learning	*Chapter 7*/Cognitive and Reciprocal Teaching (pp. 263-266) *Chapter 9*/Motivation in Teaching and Learning (pp. 234-360)	
• Knowledge	*Chapter 1*/The Social Sources of Individual Thinking (pp. 29-30); Activity and Constructing Knowledge (pp. 35-36) *Chapter 7*/How Is Knowledge Constructed? (p. 256); Knowledge: Situated or General? (p. 257)	
2. Human development in the physical, social, emotional, moral, and cognitive domains		1(f) The teacher is aware of expected developmental progressions and ranges of individual variation within each domain (physical, social, emotional, moral, and cognitive), can identify levels of readiness in learning, and understands how development in any one domain may affect performance in others.
■ Contributions of important theorists:		
• Jean Piaget	*Chapter 1*/Piaget's Theory of Cognitive Development (pp. 16-29)	
• Lev Vygotsky	*Chapter 1*/Vygotsky's Sociocultural Perspective (pp. 39-34)	
• Erik Erikson	*Chapter 2*/Erikson: Stages of Psychosocial Development (pp. 61-67)	
• Lawrence Kohlberg	*Chapter 2*/Kohlberg's Theories of Moral Development (pp. 74-75)	
• Carol Gilligan	*Chapter 2*/Gender Differences: The Morality of Caring (pp. 75-76)	
■ Major progressions in each developmental domain and the ranges of individual variation within each domain	*Chapter 1*/Four Stages of Cognitive Development (pp. 18-25); Some Limitations of Piaget's Theory (pp. 27-29); Information Processing, Neo-Piagetian, and Neuroscience Views of Cognitive Development (pp. 26-27); The Social Sources of Individual Thinking (pp. 29-30) *Chapter 2*/Physical Development (pp. 44-48); Young Children (p. 44); Elementary School (p. 44); Adolescence (p. 45); Moral Development (pp. 73-76) *Chapter 5*/The Development of Language (pp. 170-177)	1(e) The teacher understands that students' physical, social, emotional, moral and cognitive development influence learning and knows how to address these factors when making instructional decisions.

PRAXIS II™ Topics	**Woolfolk Text Connections**	**INTASC Principles**
■ Impact of students' physical, social, emotional, moral, and cognitive development on their learning and ways to address these factors when making decisions	*Chapter 1*/Four Stages of Cognitive Development (pp. 18-25); Some Limitations of Piaget's Theory (pp. 27-29); *Guidelines*: Helping Families Care for Preoperational Children (p. 21); *Guidelines*: Teaching the Concrete-Operational Child (p. 23); *Guidelines*: Helping Students to Use Formal Operations (p. 25); The Social Sources of Individual Thinking (pp. 29-30); Assisted Learning (pp. 36-37); The Zone of Proximal Development (pp. 33-34); *Chapter 2*/Physical Development (pp. 44-48); The Preschool Years: Trust, Autonomy, and Initiative (pp. 62-63); Elementary and Middle School Years: Industry versus Inferiority (pp. 63-64); Adolescence: The Search for Identity (pp. 64-65); Kohlberg's Stages of Moral Development (pp. 74-75); Self-Concept and Self-Esteem (pp. 69-71); School Life and Self-Esteem (p. 72); Diversity and Perception of Self (pp. 67-69); Theory of Mind and Intention (p. 73); Moral Judgment, Social Conventions, and Personal Choices (pp. 76-77) *Chapter 5*/The Development of Language (pp. 170-177) *Chapter 10*/Maintaining a Good Environment for Learning (pp. 380-384)	
■ How development in one domain, such as physical, may affect performance in another domain, such as social	*Chapter 1*/General Principles of Development (p. 6); The Brain and Cognitive Development (pp. 6-16); Influences on Development (p. 17) *Chapter 2*/Physical Development (pp. 44-48)	
B. Students as Diverse Learners		
1. Differences in the ways students learn and perform	*Chapter 4*/Learner Differences and Learning Needs (entire chapter) *Chapter 6*/Culture and Diversity (entire chapter)	2(g) The teacher understands and can identify differences in approaches to learning and performance, including different learning styles, multiple intelligences, and performance modes, and can design instruction that helps use students' strengths as the basis for growth.
• Learning styles	*Chapter 4*/Learning Styles/Preferences (pp. 130-132) *Chapter 6*/Diversity in Learning (pp. 236-239)	
• Multiple intelligences	*Chapter 4*/Multiple Intelligences (pp. 122-124)	
• Performance modes	*Chapter 1*/Later Elementary to the Middle-School Years: The Concrete-Operational Stage (pp. 21-24); *Guidelines*: Teaching the Concrete-Operational Child (p. 23)	
— Concrete operational thinking	*Chapter 4*/Learning and Thinking Styles (pp. 130-132)	
— Visual and aural learners	*Chapter 4*/Students with Learning Challenges (pp. 138-157)	
• Gender differences	*Chapter 2*/Gender Differences: The Morality of Caring (pp. 75-76) *Chapter 6*/Gender in Teaching and Learning (pp. 226-231); *Guidelines*: Avoiding Gender Bias in Teaching (p. 231)	
• Cultural expectations and styles	*Chapter 6*/Today's Diverse Classrooms (pp. 208-212); Ethnicity and Race in Teaching and Learning (pp. 218-226); *Guidelines*: Culturally Relevant Teaching (p. 241) *Chapter 11*/Teacher Expectations (pp. 433-437)	

PRAXIS II™ Topics	Woolfolk Text Connections	INTASC Principles
2. Areas of exceptionality in students' learning	*Chapter 4*/Learner Differences (Full chapter)	2(h) The teacher knows about areas of exceptionality in learning—including learning disabilities, visual and perceptual difficulties, and special physical or mental challenges.
• Special physical or sensory challenges	*Chapter 4*/Students with Communication Disorders (pp. 144-146); Students with Health and Sensory Impairments (pp. 152-155); Students Who Are Deaf (p. 155)	
• Learning disabilities	*Chapter 4*/Students with Learning Disabilities (pp. 138-141); Individual Education Programs (pp. 134-135); Section 504 (p. 137)	
• ADHD	*Chapter 4*/Students with Hyperactivity and Attention Disorders (pp. 141-143)	
• Functional and mental retardation	*Chapter 4*/Students with Intellectual Disabilities (pp. 151-152); *Guidelines*: Teaching Students with Intellectual Disabilities (p. 152)	
3. Legislation and institutional responsibilities relating to exceptional students	*Chapter 4*/Individual Differences and the Law (pp. 132-137); Section 504 (p. 137)	9(g) The teacher understands and implements laws related to students' rights and teacher responsibilities (e.g., for equal education, appropriate education for handicapped students, confidentiality, privacy, appropriate treatment of students, reporting in situations related to possible child abuse).
• Americans with Disabilities Act (ADA), Individuals with Disabilities Education Act (IDEA); Section 504 Protections for Students		
• Inclusion, mainstreaming, and "least restrictive environment"	*Chapter 4*/Individual Differences and the Law (pp. 132-137); Least Restrictive Environment (p. 134) *Chapter 11*/Reaching Every Student: Differentiated Instruction in Inclusive Classrooms (p. 430)	
4. Approaches for accommodating various learning styles and intelligences	*Chapter 4*/Learner Differences; focus on: Multiple Intelligences Go to School (p. 124); Teaching Gifted Students (pp. 160-162); Individual Differences and the Law (pp. 132-137)	2(g) The teacher understands and can identify differences in approaches to learning and performance, including different learning styles, multiple intelligences, and performance modes, and can design instruction that uses students' strengths as the basis for growth.
• Differentiated instruction	*Chapter 11*/Differentiated Instruction (pp. 427-433); Technology and Differentiation (pp. 430-433); Reaching Every Student: Effective Teaching in Inclusive Classrooms (pp. 430)	
• Alternative assessment	*Chapter 12*/Informal Assessment (pp. 460-462); Authentic Classroom Assessment (pp. 454-462); Portfolios and Exhibitions (pp. 455-456); *Guidelines*: Creating Portfolios (p. 458); *Guidelines*: Developing a Rubric (p. 458)	
• Testing modifications	*Chapter 12*/Reaching Every Student: Helping Students with Disabilities Prepare for High-Stakes Testing (pp. 477-479)	
5. Process of second language acquisition and strategies to support the learning of students	*Chapter 5*/Dialects (pp. 184-186); Bilingualism (pp. 177-180)	2(i) The teacher knows about the process of second language acquisition and about strategies to support the learning of students whose first language is not English.

PRAXIS II™ Topics	Woolfolk Text Connections	INTASC Principles
6. Understanding of influences of individual experiences, talents, and prior learning, as well as language, culture, family, and community values on students' learning		
• Multicultural backgrounds	*Chapter 6*/American Cultural Diversity (pp. 208-209); Ethnic and Racial Differences in School Achievement (pp. 219-221)	2(j) The teacher understands how students' learning is influenced by individual experiences, talents, and prior learning, as well as language, culture, family and community values. 2(k) The teacher has a well-grounded framework for understanding cultural and community diversity and knows how to learn about and incorporate students' experiences, cultures, and community resources into instruction.
• Age-appropriate knowledge and behaviors	*Chapter 1*/Four Stages of Cognitive Development (pp. 18-25); Vygotsky's Sociocultural Perspective (pp. 29-34); Implications of Piaget's and Vygotsky's Theories for Teachers (pp. 34-37) *Chapter 2*/entire Chapter—focus on: The Preschool Years: Trust, Autonomy, and Initiative (pp. 62-63); Elementary and Middle School Years: Industry versus Inferiority (pp. 63-64); Adolescence: The Search for Identity (pp. 64-65); Emotional and Moral Development (pp. 73-78)	
• The student culture at the school	*Chapter 2*/Bronfenbrenner: The Social Context for Development (pp. 49-61); Peers (pp. 54-57) *Chapter 9*/Learned Helplessness (p. 339-340)	
• Family backgrounds	*Chapter 2*/Families (pp. 51-54) *Family and Community Partnership Guidelines* (all chapters)	
• Linguistic patterns and differences	*Chapter 4*/Students with Language and Communication Disorders (pp. 144-146) *Chapter 5*/The Development of Language (pp. 170-177); Dialects (pp. 184-186); Bilingualism (pp. 177-180)	1(g). The teacher understands communication theory, language development, and the role of language in learning.
• Cognitive patterns and differences	*Chapter 4*/Learning and Thinking Styles (pp. 130-132)	
• Social and emotional issues	*Chapter 2*/Moral Behavior (pp. 78-82) *Chapter 4*/Students with Emotional or Behavioral Difficulties (pp. 146-151)	
C. Student Motivation and the Learning Environment		
1. Theoretical foundations about human motivation and behavior	*Chapter 9*/What Is Motivation? (pp. 324-328); Five General Approaches to Motivation (pp. 326-328)	3(i). The teacher can use knowledge about human motivation and behavior drawn from the foundational sciences of psychology, anthropology, and sociology to develop strategies for organizing and supporting individual and group work.
• Important terms that relate to motivation and behavior	*Chapter 9*/(entire chapter) *Chapter 11*/Teacher Expectations (pp. 433-437)	
2. How knowledge of human emotion and behavior should influence strategies for organizing and supporting individual and group work in the classroom	*Chapter 9*/Emotions and Anxiety (pp. 345-348); *Guidelines*: Coping with Anxiety (p. 349); *Guidelines*: Supporting Self-Determination and Autonomy (p. 331) *Chapter 11*/Teacher Expectations (pp. 433-437)	3(i) The teacher can use knowledge about human motivation and behavior drawn from the foundational sciences of psychology, anthropology, and sociology to develop strategies for organizing and supporting individual and group work.

PRAXIS II™ Topics	Woolfolk Text Connections	INTASC Principles
3. Factors and situations that are likely to promote or diminish students' motivation to learning, and how to help students to become self-motivated	*Chapter 9*/Needs: Lessons for Teachers (p. 331); Goals: Lessons for Teachers (pp. 335-336); Curiosity, Interests and Emotions: Lessons for Teachers (p. 348); Supporting Autonomy and Recognizing Accomplishment (pp. 352-353)	3(j). The teacher recognizes factors and situations that are likely to promote or diminish intrinsic motivation and knows how to help students become self-motivated.
4. Principles of effective management and strategies to promote positive relationships, cooperation, and purposeful learning		3(k) The teacher understands the principles of effective classroom management and can use a range of strategies to promote positive relationships, cooperation, and purposeful learning in the classroom.
• Establishing daily procedures and routines		
• Establishing classroom rules, punishments, and rewards	*Chapter 10*/Routines and Rules Required (pp. 372-376); *Guidelines*: Establishing Class Routines (p. 373); Prevention Is the Best Medicine (pp. 381-383); *Reaching Every Student*: Peer Mediation and Negotiation (pp. 394-395) *Chapter 11*/Teacher Expectations (pp. 433-437)	
• Giving timely feedback	*Chapter 10*/The Need for Communication (pp. 390-396) *Chapter 11*/Responding to Student Answers (pp. 424-425) *Chapter 12*/Effects of Grading on Students (p. 464)	
• Maintaining accurate records	*Chapter 12*/Portfolios and Exhibitions (pp. 455-456); *Guidelines*: Creating Portfolios (p. 458); Evaluating Portfolios and Performances (pp. 456-457)	
• Communicating with parents and caregivers	*Chapters 1–12*/Family and Community Partnerships	
• Responding to student misbehavior	*Chapter 10*/Dealing with Discipline Problems (pp. 384-389); Special Problems with High School Students (pp. 387-389); *Guidelines:* Imposing Penalties (p. 385); Counseling: The Students' Problem (p. 392); Confrontation and Assertive Discipline (pp. 392-394); Handling Potentially Explosive Situations (p. 390)	
• Arranging classroom space	*Chapter 10*/Planning Spaces for Learning (pp. 377-378); *Guidelines*: Designing Learning Spaces (p. 378)	
• Pacing and the structure of the lesson	*Chapter 10*/Encouraging Engagement (pp. 380-381); *Guidelines:* Keeping Students Engaged (p. 381); Withitness (pp. 381-382); Overlapping and Group Focus (p. 382); Movement Management (p. 382) *Chapter 11*/Clarity and Organization (p. 404); *Guidelines*: Teaching Effectively (p. 418)	

II. Instruction and Assessment

A. Instructional Strategies

1. Major cognitive processes associated with student learning		
• Critical thinking		8(j) The teacher understands the cognitive processes associated with various kinds of learning (e.g., critical and creative thinking, problem structuring and problem solving, invention, memorization and recall) and how these processes can be stimulated.
• Creative thinking		
• Inductive and deductive thinking		

PRAXIS II™ Topics	Woolfolk Text Connections	INTASC Principles
• Problem structuring and problem solving		
• Invention		
• Memorization and recall		
2. Major categories, advantages, and appropriate uses of instructional strategies		
• Cooperative learning	*Chapter 7*/Collaboration and Cooperation (pp. 266-268); *Guidelines*: Using Cooperative Learning (p. 276)	8(k) The teacher understands principles and techniques, along with advantages and limitations, associated with various instructional strategies (e.g., cooperative learning, direct instruction, discovery learning, whole-group discussion, independent study, interdisciplinary instruction).
• Direct instruction (often referred to as *teacher-centered instruction*)	*Chapter 11*/Direct Instruction (pp. 415-419)	
• Discovery learning	*Chapter 7*/Inquiry and Problem-Based Learning (pp. 260-263)	4(k). The teacher understands how students' conceptual frameworks and their misconceptions for an area of knowledge can influence their learning.
• Whole-group discussion	*Chapter 11*/Group Discussion (p. 425); *Guidelines*: Productive Group Discussions (p. 426)	
• Independent study	*Chapter 8*/Models of Self-Regulated Learning and Agency (pp. 306-307);	
• Interdisciplinary instruction (sometimes referred to as *thematic instruction*)	*Chapter 7*/Inquiry and Problem-Based Learning (pp. 260-263); *Chapter 11*/Planning from a Constructionist Perspective (p. 414)	
• Questioning	*Chapter 11* Questioning and Discussion (pp. 420-425)	
3. Principles, techniques, and methods associated with major instructional strategies		
• Direct instruction (*often referred to as teacher-centered instruction*)	*Chapter 11*/Direct Instruction (pp. 415-419); Questioning and Discussion (pp. 420-425); Rosenshine's Six Teaching Functions (p. 416)	8(k) The teacher understands principles and techniques, along with advantages and limitations, associated with various instructional strategies (e.g., cooperative learning, direct instruction, discovery learning, whole-group discussion, independent study, interdisciplinary instruction).
• Student-centered models	*Chapter 7*/Cognitive and Social Constructivism (pp. 252-259); Applying Constructivist Perspectives (pp. 259-277)	
4. Methods for enhancing student learning through the use of a variety of resources and materials	*Chapter 7*/Service Learning (pp. 277-279) *Chapter 11*/Technology and Differentiation (pp. 430-433)	8(n). The teacher knows how to enhance learning through the use of a wide variety of materials as well as human and technological resources (e.g., computers, audio-visual technologies, videotapes and discs, local experts, primary documents and artifacts, texts, reference books, literature, and other print resources).
B. Planning Instruction		
1. Techniques for planning instruction to meet curriculum goals, including the incorporation of learning theory, subject matter, curriculum development, and student development		
• National and state learning standards • State and local curriculum frameworks • State and local curriculum guides	*Chapter 12*/Issues in Standardized Testing (pp. 447-448)	7(g). The teacher understands learning theory, subject matter, curriculum development, and student development and knows how to use this knowledge in planning instruction to meet curriculum goals.

PRAXIS II™ Topics	Woolfolk Text Connections	INTASC Principles
• Scope and sequence in specific disciplines • Units and lessons	*Chapter 11*/The First Step: Planning (pp. 408-415); Planning from a Constructivist Perspective (pp. 414-415)	
• Behavioral objectives: affective, cognitive, and psychomotor • Learner objectives and outcomes	*Chapter 11*/Objectives for Learning (pp. 409–410); The Cognitive Domain (pp. 411-412); The Affective Domain (pp. 412-413); The Psychomotor Domain (p. 413); *Guidelines*: Using Instructional Objectives (p. 414)	
2. Techniques for creating effective bridges between curriculum goals and students' experiences • Modeling		7(j). The teacher knows how to take contextual considerations (instructional materials, individual student interests, needs, and aptitudes, and community resources) into account in planning instruction that creates an effective bridge between curriculum goals and students' experiences.
• Guided practice	*Chapter 1*/Assisted Learning (pp. 36-37) *Chapter 7*/Cognitive Apprenticeships and Reciprocal Teaching (pp. 263-266) *Chapter 11*/Rosenshine's Six Teaching Functions (p. 416)	
• Independent practice, including homework	*Chapter 8*/Models of Self-Regulated Learning and Agency (pp. 306-307); *Family and Community Partnerships*: Supporting Self-Regulation at Home and at School (p. 310) *Chapter 11*/Seatwork and Homework (pp. 419-420)	
• Transitions	*Chapter 10*/Overlapping and Group Focus (p. 382); Movement Management (p. 382); *Guidelines*: Keeping Students Engaged (p. 381)	
• Activating students' prior knowledge • Anticipating preconceptions • Encouraging exploration and problem solving	*Chapter 1*/Implications of Piaget's Theory for Teachers (pp. 34-37) *Chapter 8*/Models of Self-Regulated Learning and Agency (pp. 306-307)	
• Building new skills on those previously acquired	*Chapter 1*/Basic Tendencies in Thinking (pp. 17-18); *Chapter 4*/Students with Intellectual Disabilities (pp. 151-152); *Guidelines*: Teaching Students with Intellectual Disabilities (p. 152) *Chapter 8*/Observational Learning in Teaching (pp. 296-298);	
C. Assessment Strategies		
1. Types of assessments	*Chapter 12*/Norm-Referenced versus Criterion-Referenced Grading (pp. 462-463); Authentic Classroom Assessments (pp. 454-462); Formative and Summative Assessment (pp. 444-446); Objective Testing (pp. 450-452); Essay Tests (pp. 452-454); Portfolios and Exhibitions (pp. 455-456); Informal Assessments (pp. 460-462)	6(j). The teacher understands the characteristics, uses, advantages, and limitations of different types of assessments (e.g., criterion-referenced and norm-referenced instruments, traditional standardized and performance-based tests, observation systems, and assessments of student work) for evaluating how students learn, what they know and are able to do, and what kinds of experiences will support their further growth and development.
2. Characteristics of assessments	*Chapter 12*/Reliability (p. 447); Validity (pp. 448-449); Writing Multiple-Choice Questions (pp. 451-452); Constructing Essays (p. 453); Reliability, Variability, Generalizability, (pp. 459-460); *Guidelines*: Developing a Rubric (p. 458)	6(k) The teacher knows how to select, construct, and use assessment strategies and instruments appropriate to the learning outcomes being evaluated and to other diagnostic purposes.

PRAXIS II™ Topics	Woolfolk Text Connections	INTASC Principles
3. Scoring assessments	*Chapter 12*/Using Multiple-Choice Tests (p. 451); Evaluating Essays: (p. 453); Evaluating Essays: Methods (pp. 453-454); Evaluating Portfolios and Performances (pp. 456-460); Guidelines: Developing a Rubric (p. 458)	
4. Uses of assessments	*Chapter 12*/Norm-Referenced versus Criterion-Referenced Grading (pp. 462-463) Accountability and High Stakes (pp. 474-476); Formative and Summative Assessment (pp. 444-446); Alternatives to Traditional Assessment (pp. 454-462)	
5. Understanding of measurement theory and assessment-related issues	*Chapter 12*/Norm-Referenced versus Criterion-Referenced Grading (pp. 462-463)	6(k) The teacher understands measurement theory and assessment-related issues, such as validity, reliability, bias, and scoring concerns.
III. Communication Techniques		
A. Basic, effective verbal and nonverbal communication techniques	*Chapter 10*/The Need for Communication (pp. 390-396) *Chapter 10*/Teacher Expectations (pp. 433-437)	8(m). The teacher recognizes the importance of nonverbal as well as verbal communication. 6D. The teacher knows about and can use effective verbal, nonverbal, and media communication techniques.
B. Effect of cultural and gender differences on communications in the classroom	*Chapter 5*/Language Differences in the Classroom (pp. 184-186); Sociolinguistics (p. 239)	3(e). The teacher understands how cultural and gender differences can affect communication in the classroom.
C. Types of questions that can stimulate discussion in different ways for different purposes	*Chapter 11*/Questioning and Discussion (pp. 420-425)	5(n). The teacher knows about and can use effective verbal, nonverbal, and media communication techniques.
• Probing for learner understanding	*Chapter 11*/Questioning and Discussion (pp. 420-425)	
• Helping students articulate their ideas and thinking processes	*Chapter 11*/Group Discussion (pp. 425-426); Guidelines: Positive Group Discussions (p. 426);	
• Promoting risk-taking and problem solving		
• Facilitating factual recall	*Chapter 11*/Questioning and Discussion (pp. 420-425)	
• Encouraging convergent and divergent thinking	*Chapter 11*/Kinds of Questions (pp. 422-423)	
• Stimulating curiosity	*Chapter 9*/Tapping Interests (pp. 342-343); *Guidelines*: Building on Students' Interests (p. 345); Curiosity, Novelty and Complexity (pp. 343-345)	
• Helping students to question	*Chapter 11*/Fitting the Questions to the Students (pp. 423-424)	
IV. Profession and Community		
A. The Reflective Practitioner		
1. Ability to read and understand articles about current views, ideas, and debates regarding best teaching practices	*Chapters 1–12*/Teachers' Casebook (opening and closing sections of each chapter)	10(h). The teacher is aware of major areas of research on teaching and of resources available for professional learning (e.g., professional literature, colleagues, professional associations, professional development activities).
2. Why personal reflection on teaching practices is critical, and approaches that can be used to achieve this	*Chapters 1–12*/Point/Counterpoint (one per chapter)	10(h). The teacher is aware of major areas of research on teaching and of resources available for professional learning (e.g., professional literature, colleagues, professional associations, professional development activities).
	Chapters 1–12/Point/Counterpoint (one per chapter)	4(j). The teacher understands major concepts, assumptions, debates, processes of inquiry, and ways of knowing that are central to the discipline(s) s/he teaches.

PRAXIS II™ Topics	Woolfolk Text Connections	INTASC Principles
B. The Larger Community		
1. Role of the school as a resource to the larger community	*Chapter 6*/Culture and Diversity (entire chapter) *Chapter 10*/The Classroom Community (pp. 383-384)	10(i). The teacher understands schools as organizations within the larger community context and understands the operations of the relevant aspects of the system(s) within which s/he works.
2. Factors in the students' environment outside of school (family circumstances, community environments, health, and economic conditions) that may influence students' life and learning	*Chapter 2*/Families (pp. 51-54); Peers (pp. 54-57); *Chapter 4*/Children with Learning Challenges (pp. 151-156)	10(m). The teacher understands how factors in the students' environment outside of school (e.g., family circumstances, community environments, health and economic conditions) may influence students' life and learning.
3. Basic strategies for involving parents/ guardians and leaders in the community in the educational process	*Chapter 6*/Culture and Diversity (entire chapter) *Chapter 7*/ Service Learning *Chapters 1–11/Family and Community Partnerships*: (one in each chapter)	

4. Major laws related to students' rights and teacher responsibilities
  • Equal education
  • Appropriate education for handicapped children
  • Confidentiality and privacy
  • Appropriate treatment of students
Reporting situations related to possible child abuse
	Chapter 4/ Individual Differences and the Law (pp. 132-137)
	Chapter 4/The Rights of Students and Families (p. 135)
	Chapter 10/The Need for Communication (pp. 390-396)
	Chapter 2/Child Abuse (p. 59)
		9(j). The teacher understands and implements laws related to students' rights and teacher responsibilities (e.g., for equal education, appropriate education for handicapped students, confidentiality, privacy, appropriate treatment of students, reporting in situations related to possible child abuse).

The Interstate New Teacher Assessment and Support Consortium (INTASC) standards were developed by the Council of Chief State School Officers and member states. Copies may be downloaded from the Council's website at http://www.ccsso.org.

Council of Chief State School Officers. (1992). Model standards for beginning teacher licensing, assessment, and development: A resource for state dialogue. Washington, DC: Author. http://www.ccsso.org/content/pdfs/corestrd.pdf.

Glossary

Absence seizure A seizure involving only a small part of the brain that causes a child to lose contact briefly.

Academic language The entire range of language used in elementary, secondary, and university-level schools including words, concepts, strategies, and processes from academic subjects.

Academic learning time Time when students are actually succeeding at the learning task.

Academic tasks The work the student must accomplish, including the product expected, resources available, and the mental operations required.

Accommodation Altering existing schemes or creating new ones in response to new information.

Accountable Making teachers and schools responsible for student learning, usually by monitoring learning with high-stakes tests.

Achievement tests Standardized tests measuring how much students have learned in a given content area.

Acronym Technique for remembering by using the first letter of each word in a phrase to form a new, memorable word.

Action research Systematic observations or tests of methods conducted by teachers or schools to improve teaching and learning for their students.

Action zone Area of a classroom where the greatest amount of interaction takes place.

Active teaching Teaching characterized by high levels of teacher explanation, demonstration, and interaction with students.

Adaptation Adjustment to the environment.

Adaptive teaching Provides all students with challenging instruction and uses supports when needed, but removes these supports as students become able to handle more on their own.

Adequate yearly progress (AYP) Objectives for yearly improvement for all students and for specific groups such as students from major ethnic and racial groups, students with disabilities, students from low-income families, and students whose English is limited.

Adolescent egocentrism Assumption that everyone else shares one's thoughts, feelings, and concerns.

Advance organizer Statement of inclusive concepts to introduce and sum up material that follows.

Affective domain Objectives focusing on attitudes and feelings.

Algorithm Step-by-step procedure for solving a problem; prescription for solutions.

Allocated time Time set aside for learning.

Americans with Disabilities Act of 1990 (ADA) Federal legislation prohibiting discrimination against persons with disabilities in employment, transportation, public access, local government, and telecommunications.

Analogical thinking Heuristic in which one limits the search for solutions to situations that are similar to the one at hand.

Anorexia nervosa Eating disorder characterized by very limited food intake.

Antecedents Events that precede an action.

Anxiety General uneasiness, a feeling of tension.

Applied behavior analysis The application of behavioral learning principles to understand and change behavior.

Appropriating Being able to internalize or take for yourself knowledge and skills developed in interaction with others or with cultural tools.

Argumentation The process of debating a claim with someone else.

Arousal Physical and psychological reactions causing a person to feel alert, attentive, wide awake, excited, or tense.

Articulation disorders Any of a variety of pronunciation difficulties, such as the substitution, distortion, or omission of sounds.

Assertive discipline Clear, firm, unhostile response style.

Assessment Procedures used to obtain information about student performance.

Assessment bias Qualities of an assessment instrument that offend or unfairly penalize a group of students because of the students' gender, SES, race, ethnicity, etc.

Assimilation Fitting new information into existing schemes.

Assisted learning Providing strategic help in the initial stages of learning, gradually diminishing as students gain independence.

Assistive technology Devices, systems, and services that support and improve the capabilities of individuals with disabilities.

Attachment Forming an emotional bond with another person, initially a parent or family member.

Attention Focus on a stimulus.

Attention-deficit hyperactivity disorder (ADHD) Current term for disruptive behavior disorders marked by overactivity, excessive difficulty sustaining attention, or impulsiveness.

Attribution theories Descriptions of how individuals' explanations, justifications, and excuses influence their motivation and behavior.

Authentic assessments Assessment procedures that test skills and abilities as they would be applied in real-life situations.

Authentic task Tasks that have some connection to real-life problems the students will face outside the classroom.

Autism/Autism spectrum disorders Developmental disability significantly affecting verbal and nonverbal communication and social interaction, generally evident before age 3 and ranging from mild to major.

Automated basic skills Skills that are applied without conscious thought.

Automaticity The ability to perform thoroughly learned tasks without much mental effort. The result of learning to perform a behavior or thinking process so thoroughly that the performance is automatic and does not require effort.

Autonomy Independence.

Availability heuristic Judging the likelihood of an event based on what is available in your memory, assuming those easily remembered events are common.

Aversive Irritating or unpleasant.

Balanced bilingualism Adding a second language capability without losing your heritage language.

Basic skills Clearly structured knowledge that is needed for later learning and that can be taught step by step.

Behavior modification Systematic application of antecedents and consequences to change behavior.

Behavioral learning theories Explanations of learning that focus on external events as the cause of changes in observable behaviors.

Behavioral objectives Instructional objectives stated in terms of observable behaviors.

Being needs Maslow's three higher-level needs, sometimes called *growth needs*.

Belief perseverance The tendency to hold on to beliefs, even in the face of contradictory evidence.

Bilingual Speaking two languages and dealing appropriately with the two different cultures.

Bioecological model Bronfenbrenner's theory describing the nested social and cultural contexts that shape development. Every person develops within a *microsystem*, inside a *mesosystem*, embedded in an *exosystem*, all of which are a part of the *macrosystem* of the culture. All development occurs in and is influenced by the time period—the *chronosystem*.

Blended families Parents, children, and stepchildren merged into families through remarriages.

Body mass index (BMI) A measure of body fat that evaluates weight in relation to height.

Bottom-up processing Perceiving based on noticing separate defining features and assembling them into a recognizable pattern.

Brainstorming Generating ideas without stopping to evaluate them.

Bulimia Eating disorder characterized by overeating, then getting rid of the food by self-induced vomiting or laxatives.

CAPS A strategy that can be used in reading literature: *Characters, Aim* of story, *Problem, Solution.*

Case study Intensive study of one person or one situation.

Central executive The part of working memory that is responsible for monitoring and directing attention and other mental resources.

Central tendency Typical score for a group of scores.

Cerebral palsy Condition involving a range of motor or coordination difficulties due to brain damage.

Chain mnemonics Memory strategies that associate one element in a series with the next element.

Chunking Grouping individual bits of data into meaningful larger units.

Classical conditioning Association of automatic responses with new stimuli.

Classification Grouping objects into categories.

Classroom assessments Classroom assessments are selected and created by teachers and can take many different forms—unit tests, essays, portfolios, projects, performances, oral presentations, etc.

Classroom management Techniques used to maintain a healthy learning environment, relatively free of behavior problems.

Cloud computing Allows computer users to access applications, such as Google documents or Microsoft Web Mail, as well as computing assets such as network-accessible data storage and processing to use online applications.

Cmaps Tools for concept mapping developed by the Institute for Human and Machine Cognition that are connected to many knowledge maps and other resources on the Internet.

Coactions Joint actions of individual biology and the environment—each shapes and influences the other.

Co-constructed process A social process in which people interact and negotiate (usually verbally) to create an understanding or to solve a problem. The final product is shaped by all participants.

Code-switching Moving between two speech forms.

Cognitive apprenticeship A relationship in which a less experienced learner acquires knowledge and skills under the guidance of an expert.

Cognitive behavior modification Procedures based on both behavioral and cognitive learning principles for changing your own behavior by using self-talk and self-instruction.

Cognitive development Gradual orderly changes by which mental processes become more complex and sophisticated.

Cognitive domain In Bloom's taxonomy, memory and reasoning objectives.

Cognitive evaluation theory Suggests that events affect motivation through the individual's perception of the events as controlling behavior or providing information.

Cognitive load The volume of resources necessary to complete a task.

Cognitive objectives Instructional objectives stated in terms of higher-level thinking operations.

Cognitive science The interdisciplinary study of thinking, language, intelligence, knowledge creation, and the brain.

Cognitive view of learning A general approach that views learning as an active mental process of acquiring, remembering, and using knowledge.

Collaboration A philosophy about how to relate to others—how to learn and work.

Collective monologue Form of speech in which children in a group talk but do not really interact or communicate.

Commitment In Marcia's theory of identity statuses, individuals' choices concerning political and religious beliefs, for example, usually as a consequence of exploring the options.

Community of practice Social situation or context in which ideas are judged useful or true.

Compensation The principle that changes in one dimension can be offset by changes in another.

Complex learning environments Problems and learning situations that mimic the ill-structured nature of real life.

Concept A category used to group similar events, ideas, objects, or people.

Concept map A drawing that charts the relationships among ideas.

Concrete operations   Mental tasks tied to concrete objects and situations.

Conditioned response (CR)   Learned response to a previously neutral stimulus.

Conditioned stimulus (CS)   Stimulus that evokes an emotional or physiological response after conditioning.

Confidence interval   Range of scores within which an individual's true score is likely to fall.

Confirmation bias   Seeking information that confirms our choices and beliefs, while disconfirming evidence.

Consequences   Events that follow an action.

Conservation   Principle that some characteristics of an object remain the same despite changes in appearance.

Constructionism   How public knowledge in disciplines such as science, math, economics, or history is constructed.

Constructivism/Constructivist approach   View that emphasizes the active role of the learner in building understanding and making sense of information.

Context   Internal and external circumstances and situations that interact with the individual's thoughts, feelings, and actions to shape development and learning. The physical or emotional backdrop associated with an event.

Contiguity   Association of two events because of repeated pairing.

Contingency contract   A contract between the teacher and a student specifying what the student must do to earn a particular reward or privilege.

Continuous reinforcement schedule   Presenting a reinforcer after every appropriate response.

Convergent questions   Questions that have a single correct answer.

Convergent thinking   Narrowing possibilities to a single answer.

Cooperation   Way of working with others to attain a shared goal.

Cooperative learning   Situations in which elaboration, interpretation, explanation, and argumentation are integral to the activity of the group and where learning is supported by other individuals.

Co-regulation   A transitional phase during which students gradually appropriate self-regulated learning and skills through modeling, direct teaching, feedback, and coaching from teachers, parents, or peers.

Correlations   Statistical descriptions of how closely two variables are related.

Creativity   Imaginative, original thinking or problem solving.

Criterion-referenced grading   Assessment of each student's mastery of course objectives.

Criterion-referenced testing   Testing in which scores are compared to a set performance standard.

Critical periods   If learning doesn't happen during these periods, it never will.

Critical thinking   Evaluating conclusions by logically and systematically examining the problem, the evidence, and the solution.

Crystallized intelligence   Ability to apply culturally approved problem-solving methods.

Cueing   Providing a stimulus that "sets up" a desired behavior.

Cultural deficit model   A model that explains the school achievement problems of ethnic minority students by assuming that their culture is inadequate and does not prepare them to succeed in school.

Cultural tools   The real tools (computers, scales, etc.) and symbol systems (numbers, language, graphs) that allow people in a society to communicate, think, solve problems, and create knowledge.

Culturally relevant pedagogy   Excellent teaching for students of color that includes academic success, developing/maintaining cultural competence, and developing a critical consciousness to challenge the status quo.

Culturally responsive management   Taking cultural meanings and styles into account when developing management plans and responding to students.

Culture   The knowledge, values, attitudes, and traditions that guide the behavior of a group of people and allow them to solve the problems of living in their environment.

Culture-fair/culture-free test   A test without cultural bias.

Cyber aggression   Using e-mail, Twitter, Facebook, or other social media to spread rumors, make threats, or otherwise terrorize peers.

Decay   The weakening and fading of memories with the passage of time.

Decentering   Focusing on more than one aspect at a time.

Declarative knowledge   Verbal information; facts; "knowing that" something is the case.

Deficiency needs   Maslow's four lower-level needs, which must be satisfied first.

Defining attribute   Qualities that connect members of a group to a specific concept.

Descriptive studies   Studies that collect detailed information about specific situations, often using observation, surveys, interviews, recordings, or a combination of these methods.

Development   Orderly, adaptive changes we go through between conception and death and remain for a reasonably long period of time.

Developmental crisis   A specific conflict whose resolution prepares the way for the next stage.

Deviation IQ   Score based on a statistical comparison of an individual's performance with the average performance of others in that age group.

Dialect   Any variety of a language spoken by a particular group.

Differentiated instruction   A flexible approach to teaching that matches content, process, and product based on student differences in readiness, interests, and learning needs. Teaching that takes into account students' abilities, prior knowledge, and challenges so that instruction matches not only the subject being taught but also students' needs.

Direct instruction/Explicit teaching   Systematic instruction for mastery of basic skills, facts, and information.

Disability   The inability to do something specific such as walk or hear.

Discrimination   Treating or acting unfairly toward particular categories of people.

Disequilibrium   In Piaget's theory, the "out-of-balance" state that occurs when a person realizes that his or her current ways of thinking are not working to solve a problem or understand a situation.

Distractors   Wrong answers offered as choices in a multiple-choice item.

Distributed practice   Practice in brief periods with rest intervals.

Distributive justice   Beliefs about how to divide materials or privileges fairly among members of a group; follows a sequence of development from equality to merit to benevolence.

Divergent questions   Questions that have no single correct answer.

Divergent thinking   Coming up with many possible solutions.

Domain-specific knowledge   Information that is useful in a particular situation or that applies mainly to one specific topic.

Domain-specific strategies   Consciously applied skills to reach goals in a particular subject or problem.

Dual coding theory   Suggests that information is stored in long-term memory as either visual images or verbal units, or both.

Educational psychology   The discipline concerned with teaching and learning processes; applies the methods and theories of psychology and has its own as well.

Educationally blind   Individuals who have very little or no functionalal vision for learning and primarily use Braille, audio, and tactile aids, and other assistive technologies in their learning.

Effective instruction delivery   Instructions that are concise, clear, and specific, and that communicate an expected result. Statements work better than questions.

Egocentric   Assuming that others experience the world the way you do.

Elaboration   Adding and extending meaning by connecting new information to existing knowledge.

Elaborative rehearsal   Keeping information in working memory by associating it with something else you already know.

Embodied cognition   Theory stating that cognitive processes develop from real-time, goal-directed interactions between humans and their environment.

Emergent literacy   The skills and knowledge, usually developed in the preschool years, that are the foundation for the development of reading and writing.

Emotional and behavioral disorders   Behaviors or emotions that deviate so much from the norm that they interfere with the child's own growth and development and/or the lives of others—inappropriate behaviors, unhappiness or depression, fears and anxieties, and trouble with relationships.

Empathetic listening   Hearing the intent and emotions behind what another says and reflecting them back by paraphrasing.

Empirical   Based on systematically collected data.

Enactive learning   Learning by doing and experiencing the consequences of your actions.

Engaged time/Time on task   Time spent actively engaged in the learning task at hand.

English as a Second Language (ESL)   The classes devoted to teaching ELL students English.

English language learners (ELLs)   Students who are learning English when their primary or heritage language is not English.

Entity view of ability   Belief that ability is a fixed characteristic that cannot be changed.

Epilepsy   Disorder marked by seizures and caused by abnormal electrical discharges in the brain.

Episodic buffer   The process that brings together and integrates information from the phonological loop, visuospatial sketchpad, and long-term memory under the supervision of the central executive.

Episodic memory   Long-term memory for information tied to a particular time and place, especially memory of the events in a person's life.

Epistemological beliefs   Beliefs about the structure, stability, and certainty of knowledge, and how knowledge is best learned.

Equilibration   Search for mental balance between cognitive schemes and information from the environment.

Ethnicity   A cultural heritage shared by a group of people.

Ethnography   A descriptive approach to research that focuses on life within a group and tries to understand the meaning of events to the people involved.

Event-related potential (ERP)   Measurements that assess electrical activity of the brain through the skull or scalp.

Evidenced-based practice in psychology (EBPP)   Practices that integrate the best available research with the insights of expert practitioners and knowledge of the characteristics, culture, and preferences of the client.

Executive control processes   Processes such as selective attention, rehearsal, elaboration, and organization that influence encoding, storage, and retrieval of information in memory.

Exemplar   An actual memory of a specific object.

Exhibition   A performance test or demonstration of learning that is public and usually takes an extended time to prepare.

Expectancy X value theories   Explanations of motivation that emphasize individuals' expectations for success combined with their valuing of the goal.

Experimentation   Research method in which variables are manipulated and the effects recorded.

Expert teachers   Experienced, effective teachers who have developed solutions for classroom problems. Their knowledge of teaching process and content is extensive and well organized.

Explicit memory   Long-term memories that involve deliberate or conscious recall.

Exploration   In Marcia's theory of identity statuses, the process by which adolescents consider and try out alternative beliefs, values, and behaviors in an effort to determine which will give them the most satisfaction.

Expressive vocabulary   The words a person can use in speaking.

Extended families   Different family members—grandparents, aunts, uncles, cousins, etc.—living in the same household or at least in daily contact with the children in the family.

Extinction   The disappearance of a learned response.

Extraneous cognitive load   The resources required to process stimuli irrelevant to the task.

Extrinsic motivation   Motivation created by external factors such as rewards and punishments.

Failure-accepting students   Students who believe their failures are due to low ability and there is little they can do about it.

Failure-avoiding students   Students who avoid failure by sticking to what they know, by not taking risks, or by claiming not to care about their performance.

First wave constructivism   A focus on the individual and psychological sources of knowing, as in Piaget's theory.

Flashbulb memories   Clear, vivid memories of emotionally important events in your life.

Flexible grouping   Grouping and regrouping students based on learning needs.

Fluid intelligence   Mental efficiency, nonverbal abilities grounded in brain development.

Flynn effect   Because of better health, smaller families, increased complexity in the environment, and more and better schooling, IQ test scores are steadily rising.

Formal operations   Mental tasks involving abstract thinking and coordination of a number of variables.

Formative assessment   Ungraded testing used before or during instruction to aid in planning and diagnosis.

Free, appropriate public education (FAPE)   Public funding to support appropriate educational programs for all students, no matter what their needs.

Functional behavioral assessment (FBA)   Procedures used to obtain information about antecedents, behaviors, and consequences to determine the reason or function of the behavior.

Functional fixedness   Inability to use objects or tools in a new way.

Functional magnetic resonance imaging (fMRI)   An MRI is an imaging technique that uses a magnetic field along with radio waves and a computer to create detailed pictures of the inside of the body. A functional MRI uses the MRI to measure the tiny changes that take place in the brain during brain activity.

Funds of knowledge   Knowledge that families and community members have acquired in many areas of work, home, and religious life that can become the basis for teaching.

Gender biases   Different views of males and females, often favoring one gender over the other.

Gender identity   The sense of self as male or female as well as the beliefs one has about gender roles and attributes.

Gender schemas   Organized cognitive structures that include gender-related information that influences how children think and behave.

Genderlects   Different ways of talking for males and females.

General intelligence (*g*)   A general factor in cognitive ability that is related in varying degrees to performance on all mental tests.

General knowledge   Information that is useful in many different kinds of tasks; information that applies to many situations.

Generalized seizure   A seizure involving a large portion of the brain.

Generation 1.5   Students whose characteristics, educational experiences, and language fluencies are somewhere in between those of students born in the United States and students who are recent immigrants.

Generativity   Sense of concern for future generations.

Germane cognitive load   Deep processing of information related to the task, including the application of prior knowledge to a new task or problem.

Gestalt   German for *pattern* or *whole*. Gestalt theorists hold that people organize their perceptions into coherent wholes.

Gifted and talented students   Very bright, creative, and talented students.

Glial cells   The *white matter* of the brain. These cells greatly outnumber neurons and appear to have many functions such as fighting infections, controlling blood flow and communication among neurons, and providing the *myelin* coating around axon fibers.

Goal   What an individual strives to accomplish.

Goal orientations   Patterns of beliefs about goals related to achievement in school.

Goal structure   The way students relate to others who are also working toward a particular goal.

Goal-directed actions   Deliberate actions toward a goal.

Good behavior game   Arrangement where a class is divided into teams and each team receives demerit points for breaking agreed-upon rules of good behavior.

Grade-equivalent score   Measure of grade level based on comparison with norming samples from each grade.

Grading on the curve   Norm-referenced grading that compares students' performance to an average level.

Group consequences   Rewards or punishments given to a class as a whole for adhering to or violating rules of conduct.

Group discussion   Conversation in which the teacher does not have the dominant role; students pose and answer their own questions.

Group focus   The ability to keep as many students as possible involved in activities.

Handicap   A disadvantage in a particular situation, sometimes caused by a disability.

Heritage language   The language spoken in the student's home or by members of the family.

Heuristic   General strategy used in attempting to solve problems.

Hierarchy of needs   Maslow's model of seven levels of human needs, from basic physiological requirements to the need for self-actualization.

High-stakes testing   Standardized tests whose results have powerful influences when used by school administrators, other officials, or employers to make decisions.

Hostile aggression   Bold, direct action that is intended to hurt someone else; unprovoked attack.

Human agency   The capacity to coordinate learning skills, motivation, and emotions to reach your goals.

Humanistic interpretation   Approach to motivation that emphasizes personal freedom, choice, self-determination, and striving for personal growth.

Hypothesis/Hypotheses   A prediction of what will happen in a research study based on theory and previous research.

Hypothetico-deductive reasoning   A formal-operations problem-solving strategy in which an individual begins by identifying all the factors that might affect a problem and then deduces and systematically evaluates specific solutions.

"I" message   Clear, nonaccusatory statement of how something is affecting you.

Identity   Principle that a person or object remains the same over time. (Piaget) The complex answer to the question: "Who am I?" (Erikson)

Identity achievement   Strong sense of commitment to life choices after free consideration of alternatives.

Identity diffusion   Uncenteredness; confusion about who one is and what one wants.

Identity foreclosure   Acceptance of parental life choices without consideration of options.

Images   Representations based on the physical attributes—the appearance—of information.

Immersive Virtual Learning Environment (IVLE)   A simulation of a real-world environment that immerses students in tasks like those required in a professional practicum.

Immigrants People who voluntarily leave their country to become permanent residents in a new place.

Implicit memory Knowledge that we are not conscious of recalling, but that influences our behavior or thought without our awareness.

Importance/Attainment value The importance of doing well on a task; how success on the task meets personal needs.

Incentive An object or event that encourages or discourages behavior.

Inclusion The integration of all students, including those with severe disabilities, into regular classes.

Incremental view of ability Belief that ability is a set of skills that can be changed.

Individualized Education Program (IEP) Annually revised program for an exceptional student, detailing present achievement level, goals, and strategies, drawn up by teachers, parents, specialists, and (if possible) the student.

Individuals with Disabilities Education Improvement Act (IDEA) Latest amendment of PL 94-142; guarantees a free public education to all children regardless of disability.

Industry Eagerness to engage in productive work.

Informal assessments Ungraded (formative) assessments that gather information from multiple sources to help teachers make decisions.

Information processing The human mind's activity of taking in, storing, and using information.

Initiative Willingness to begin new activities and explore new directions.

Inquiry learning Approach in which the teacher presents a puzzling situation and students solve the problem by gathering data and testing their conclusions.

Inside-out skills The emergent literacy skills of knowledge of graphemes, phonological awareness, syntactic awareness, phoneme-grapheme correspondence, and emergent writing.

Insight In problem solving, the sudden realization of a solution. In the triarchic theory of intelligence, the ability to deal effectively with novel situations.

Instructional objectives Clear statement of what students are intended to learn through instruction.

Instrumental aggression Strong actions aimed at claiming an object, place, or privilege—not intended to harm, but may lead to harm.

Integration Fitting the child with special needs into existing class structures.

Integrity Sense of self-acceptance and fulfillment.

Intellectual disabilities/Mental retardation Significantly below-average intellectual and adaptive social behavior, evident before age 18.

Intelligence quotient (IQ) Score comparing mental and chronological ages.

Intelligence Ability or abilities to acquire and use knowledge for solving problems and adapting to the world.

Interest or intrinsic value The enjoyment a person gets from a task.

Interference The process that occurs when remembering certain information is hampered by the presence of other information.

Intermittent reinforcement schedule Presenting a reinforcer after some but not all responses.

Internalize Process whereby children adopt external standards as their own.

Intersubjective attitude A commitment to build shared meaning with others by finding common ground and exchanging interpretations.

Interval schedule Length of time between reinforcers.

Intimacy Forming close, enduring relationships with others.

Intrinsic cognitive load The resources required by the task itself, regardless of other stimuli.

Intrinsic motivation Motivation associated with activities that are their own reward.

Jigsaw Classroom A learning process in which each student is part of a group and each group member is given part of the material to be learned by the whole group. Students become "expert" on their piece and then teach it to the others in their group.

Keyword method System of associating new words or concepts with similar-sounding cue words and images.

KWL A strategy to guide reading and inquiry: Before—What do I already *know*? What do I *want* to know? After—What have I *learned*?

Lateralization The specialization of the two hemispheres (sides) of the brain cortex.

Learned helplessness The expectation, based on previous experiences with a lack of control, that all of one's efforts will lead to failure.

Learning Process through which experience causes permanent change in knowledge or behavior.

Learning disability Problem with acquisition and use of language; may show up as difficulty with reading, writing, reasoning, or math.

Learning Management System (LMS) Systems that deliver e-learning, provide tools and learning materials, keep records, administer assessments, and manage learning.

Learning preferences Preferred ways of studying and learning, such as using pictures instead of text, working with other people versus alone, learning in structured or in unstructured situations, and so on.

Learning sciences An interdisciplinary science of learning, based on research in psychology, education, computer science, philosophy, sociology, anthropology, neuroscience, and other fields that study learning.

Learning strategies A special kind of procedural knowledge— *knowing how* to approach learning tasks.

Learning styles Characteristic approaches to learning and studying.

Least restrictive environment (LRE) Educating each child with peers in the regular classroom to the greatest extent possible.

Legitimate peripheral participation Genuine involvement in the work of the group, even if your abilities are undeveloped and contributions are small.

Lesson study As a group, teachers develop, test, improve, and retest lessons until they are satisfied with the final version.

Levels of processing theory Theory that recall of information is based on how deeply it is processed.

Limited-English-proficient (LEP) A term also used for students who are learning English when their primary or heritage language is not English—not the preferred term because of the negative connotations.

LINCS Vocabulary Strategy A strategy that uses stories and imagery to help students learn how to identify, organize, define, and remember words and their meanings.

Loci method Technique of associating items with specific places.

Locus of causality The location—internal or external—of the cause of behavior.

Long-term memory Permanent store of knowledge.

Low vision Vision limited to close objects.

Mainstreaming Teaching children with disabilities in regular classes for part or all of their school day.

Maintenance rehearsal Keeping information in working memory by repeating it to yourself.

Massed practice Practice for a single extended period.

Massive Multi-player Online Games (MMOG) Interactive gaming environments constructed in virtual worlds where the learner assumes a character role or avatar.

Mastery experiences Our own direct experiences—the most powerful source of efficacy information.

Mastery goal A personal intention to improve abilities and learn, no matter how performance suffers.

Mastery-oriented students Students who focus on learning goals because they value achievement and see ability as improvable.

Maturation Genetically programmed, naturally occurring changes over time.

Mean Arithmetical average.

Means-ends analysis Heuristic in which a goal is divided into subgoals.

Measurement An evaluation expressed in quantitative (number) terms.

Median Middle score in a group of scores.

Melting pot A metaphor for the absorption and assimilation of immigrants into the mainstream of society so that ethnic differences vanish.

Menarche The first menstrual period in girls.

Mental age In intelligence testing, a performance that represents average abilities for that age group.

Metacognition Knowledge about our own thinking processes.

Metalinguistic awareness Understanding about one's own use of language.

Microgenetic studies Detailed observation and analysis of changes in a cognitive process as the process unfolds over a several-day or several-week period of time.

Minority group A group of people who have been socially disadvantaged—not always a minority in actual numbers.

Mirror systems Areas of the brain that fire both during perception of an action by someone else and when performing the action.

Mnemonics Techniques for remembering; the art of memory.

Mode Most frequently occurring score.

Modeling Changes in behavior, thinking, or emotions that happen through observing another person—a model.

Monolingual Speaking only one language.

Moral dilemma Situations in which no choice is clearly and indisputably right.

Moral realism Stage of development wherein children see rules as absolute.

Moral reasoning The thinking process involved in judgments about questions of right and wrong.

Morality of cooperation Stage of development wherein children realize that people make rules and people can change them.

Moratorium Identity crisis; suspension of choices because of struggle.

Motivation An internal state that arouses, directs, and maintains behavior.

Motivation to learn The tendency to find academic activities meaningful and worthwhile and to try to benefit from them.

Movement management Keeping lessons and the group moving at an appropriate (and flexible) pace, with smooth transitions and variety.

Multicultural education Education that promotes equity in the schooling of all students.

Multiple representations of content Considering problems using various analogies, examples, and metaphors.

Myelination The process by which neural fibers are coated with a fatty sheath called *myelin* that makes message transfer more efficient.

Natural/logical consequences Instead of punishing, have students redo, repair, or in some way face the consequences that naturally flow from their actions.

Need for autonomy The desire to have our own wishes, rather than external rewards or pressures, determine our actions.

Negative correlation A relationship between two variables in which a high value on one is associated with a low value on the other. Example: height and distance from top of head to the ceiling.

Negative reinforcement Strengthening behavior by removing an aversive stimulus when the behavior occurs.

Neo-Piagetian theories More recent theories that integrate findings about attention, memory, and strategy use with Piaget's insights about children's thinking and the construction of knowledge.

Neurogenesis The production of new neurons.

Neurons Nerve cells that store and transfer information.

Neutral stimulus Stimulus not connected to a response.

Nigrescence The process of developing a Black identity.

Norm group Large sample of students serving as a comparison group for scoring tests.

Normal distribution The most commonly occurring distribution, in which scores are distributed evenly around the mean.

Norm-referenced grading Assessment of students' achievement in relation to one another.

Norm-referenced testing Testing in which scores are compared with the average performance of others.

Object permanence The understanding that objects have a separate, permanent existence.

Objective testing Multiple-choice, matching, true/false, short-answer, and fill-in tests; scoring answers does not require interpretation.

Observational learning Learning by observation and imitation of others—vicarious learning.

Operant conditioning Learning in which voluntary behavior is strengthened or weakened by consequences or antecedents.

Operants Voluntary (and generally goal-directed) behaviors emitted by a person or an animal.

Operations Actions a person carries out by thinking them through instead of literally performing the actions.

Organization Ongoing process of arranging information and experiences into mental systems or categories. Ordered and logical network of relations.

Outside-in skills The emergent literacy skills of language, narrative, conventions of print, and emergent reading.

Overlapping Supervising several activities at once.

Overlearning Practicing a skill past the point of mastery.

Overregularize To apply a rule of syntax or grammar in situations where the rule does not apply, e.g., "the bike was broked."

Overt aggression A form of hostile aggression that involves physical attack.

Paraphrase rule Policy whereby listeners must accurately summarize what a speaker has said before being allowed to respond.

Parenting styles The ways of interacting with and disciplining children.

Part learning Breaking a list of items into shorter lists.

Participant observation A method for conducting descriptive research in which the researcher becomes a participant in the situation in order to better understand life in that group.

Participants/Subjects People or animals studied.

Participation structures The formal and informal rules for how to take part in a given activity.

Pedagogical content knowledge Teacher knowledge that combines mastery of *academic content* with knowing *how to teach* the content and how to match instruction to *student differences.*

Peer cultures Groups of children or adolescents with their own rules and norms, particularly about such things as dress, appearance, music, language, social values, and behavior.

Percentile rank Percentage of those in the norming sample who scored at or below an individual's score.

Perception Interpretation of sensory information.

Performance assessments Any form of assessment that requires students to carry out an activity or produce a product in order to demonstrate learning.

Performance goal A personal intention to seem competent or perform well in the eyes of others.

Personal development Changes in personality that take place as one grows.

Personal Learning Environment (PLE) Provides tools that support individualized learning in a variety of contexts and situations.

Personal Learning Network (PLN) Framework in which knowledge is constructed through online peer interactions.

Perspective-taking ability Understanding that others have different feelings and experiences.

Pervasive developmental disorder (PDD) A term favored by the medical community to describe autism spectrum disorders.

Phonological loop Part of working memory. A speech- and sound-related system for holding and rehearsing (refreshing) words and sounds in short-term memory for about 1.5 to 2 seconds.

Physical development Changes in body structure and function over time.

Plasticity The brain's tendency to remain somewhat adaptable or flexible.

Portfolio A collection of the student's work in an area, showing growth, self-reflection, and achievement.

Positive behavior supports (PBS) Interventions designed to replace problem behaviors with new actions that serve the same purpose for the student.

Positive correlation A relationship between two variables in which the two increase or decrease together. Example: calorie intake and weight gain.

Positive practice Practicing correct responses immediately after errors.

Positive reinforcement Strengthening behavior by presenting a desired stimulus after the behavior.

Positron emission tomography (PET) A method of localizing and measuring brain activity using computer-assisted motion pictures of the brain.

Pragmatics The rules for when and how to use language to be an effective communicator in a particular culture.

Precorrection A tool for positive behavior support that involves identifying the context for a student's misbehavior, clearly specifying the alternative expected behavior, modifying the situation to make the problem behavior less likely, then rehearsing the expected positive behaviors in the new context and providing powerful reinforcers.

Prejudice Prejudgment or irrational generalization about an entire category of people.

Premack principle Principle stating that a more-preferred activity can serve as a reinforcer for a less-preferred activity.

Preoperational The stage before a child masters logical mental operations.

Presentation punishment Decreasing the chances that a behavior will occur again by presenting an aversive stimulus following the behavior; also called *Type I punishment.*

Pretest Formative test for assessing students' knowledge, readiness, and abilities.

Priming Activating a concept in memory or the spread of activation from one concept to another.

Principle Established relationship between factors.

Private speech Children's self-talk, which guides their thinking and action. Eventually, these verbalizations are internalized as silent inner speech.

Problem Any situation in which you are trying to reach some goal and must find a means to do so.

Problem solving Creating new solutions for problems.

Problem-based learning Students are confronted with a problem that launches their inquiry as they collaborate to find solutions and learn valuable information and skills in the process.

Procedural knowledge Knowledge that is demonstrated when we perform a task; "knowing how."

Procedural memory Long-term memory for how to do things.

Procedures/routines Prescribed steps for an activity.

Production deficiency Students learn problem-solving strategies, but do not apply them when they could or should.

Productions The contents of procedural memory; rules about what actions to take, given certain conditions. Units of knowledge that combine conditions with actions in "if this happens, do that" relationships that often are automatic.

Prompt A reminder that follows a cue to make sure the person reacts to the cue.

Propositional network Set of interconnected concepts and relationships in which long-term knowledge is held.

Prototype A best example or best representative of a category.

Psychomotor domain Physical ability and coordination objectives.

Psychosocial Describing the relation of the individual's emotional needs to the social environment.

Puberty The physiological changes during adolescence that lead to the ability to reproduce.

Punishment Process that weakens or suppresses behavior.

Pygmalion effect Exceptional progress by a student as a result of high teacher expectations for that student; named for mythological king, Pygmalion, who made a statue, then caused it to be brought to life.

Quasi-experimental studies Studies that fit most of the criteria for true experiments, with the important exception that the participants are not assigned to groups at random. Instead, existing groups such as classes or schools participate in the experiments.

Race A socially constructed category based on appearances and ancestry.

Racial and ethnic pride A positive self-concept about one's racial or ethnic heritage.

Radical constructivism Knowledge is assumed to be the individual's construction; it cannot be judged right or wrong.

Random Without any definite pattern; following no rule.

Range Distance between the highest and the lowest scores in a group.

Ratio schedule Reinforcement based on the number of responses between reinforcers.

READS A five-step reading strategy: *Review* headings; *Examine* boldface words; *Ask,* "What do I expect to learn?"; *Do* it—Read; *Summarize* in your own words.

Receptive vocabulary The words a person can understand in spoken or written words.

Reciprocal questioning Students work in pairs or triads to ask and answer questions about lesson material.

Reciprocal teaching Learning to apply the strategies of questioning, summarizing, predicting, and clarifying; designed to help students understand and think deeply about what they read.

Reconstruction Recreating information by using memories, expectations, logic, and existing knowledge.

Reflective Thoughtful and inventive. Reflective teachers think back over situations to analyze what they did and why, and to consider how they might improve learning for their students.

Refugees A special group of immigrants who also relocate voluntarily, but who are fleeing their home country because it is not safe.

Reinforcement Use of consequences to strengthen behavior.

Reinforcer Any event that follows a behavior and increases the chances that the behavior will occur again.

Relational aggression A form of hostile aggression that involves verbal attacks and other actions meant to harm social relationships.

Reliability Consistency of test results.

Removal punishment Decreasing the chances that a behavior will occur again by removing a pleasant stimulus following the behavior; also called *Type II punishment.*

Representativeness heuristic Judging the likelihood of an event based on how well the events match your prototypes—what you think is representative of the category.

Reprimands Criticisms for misbehavior; rebukes.

Resilience The ability to adapt successfully in spite of difficult circumstances and threats to development.

Resistance culture Group values and beliefs about refusing to adopt the behaviors and attitudes of the majority culture.

Respondents Responses (generally automatic or involuntary) elicited by specific stimuli.

Response Observable reaction to a stimulus.

Response cost Punishment by loss of reinforcers.

Response set Rigidity; the tendency to respond in the most familiar way.

Response to intervention (RTI) A process to make sure students get appropriate research-based instruction and support as soon as possible and that teachers are systematic in documenting what interventions they have tried with these students so this information can be used in planning.

Restructuring Conceiving of a problem in a new or different way.

Retrieval Process of searching for and finding information in long-term memory.

Reversibility A characteristic of Piagetian logical operations—the ability to think through a series of steps, then mentally reverse the steps and return to the starting point; also called reversible thinking.

Reversible thinking Thinking backward, from the end to the beginning.

Reward An attractive object or event supplied as a consequence of a behavior.

Ripple effect "Contagious" spreading of behaviors through imitation.

Rote memorization Remembering information by repetition without necessarily understanding the meaning of the information.

Rules Statements specifying expected and forbidden behaviors; dos and don'ts.

Scaffolding Support for learning and problem solving. The support could be clues, reminders, encouragement, breaking the problem down into steps, providing an example or anything else that allows the student to grow in independence as a learner. Teachers and students make meaningful connections between what the teacher knows and what the students know and need in order to help the students learn more.

Schema-driven problem solving Recognizing a problem as a "disguised" version of an old problem for which one already has a solution.

Schemas (singular, *schema*) Basic structures for organizing information; concepts.

Schemes Mental systems or categories of perception and experience.

Scoring rubrics Rules that are used to determine the quality of a student's performance.

Script Schema or expected plan for the sequence of steps in a common event such as buying groceries or ordering pizza.

Scripted cooperation Learning strategy in which two students take turns summarizing material and criticizing the summaries.

Seatwork Independent classroom work.

Second wave constructivism A focus on the social and cultural sources of knowing, as in Vygotsky's theory.

Section 504 A part of civil rights law that prevents discrimination against people with disabilities in programs that receive federal funds, such as public schools.

Self-actualization Fulfilling one's potential.

Self-concept Individuals' knowledge and beliefs about themselves—their ideas, feelings, attitudes, and expectations.

Self-efficacy A person's sense of being able to deal effectively with a particular task. Beliefs about personal competence in a particular situation.

Self-esteem The value each of us places on our own characteristics, abilities, and behaviors.

Self-fulfilling prophecy A groundless expectation that is confirmed because it has been expected.

Self-handicapping Students may engage in behavior that blocks their own success in order to avoid testing their true ability.

Self-instruction Talking oneself through the steps of a task.

Self-management Management of your own behavior and acceptance of responsibility for your own actions. Also the use of behavioral learning principles to change your own behavior.

Self-regulated learning A view of learning as skills and will applied to analyzing learning tasks, setting goals and planning how to do the task, applying skills, and especially making adjustments about how learning is carried out.

Self-regulation Process of activating and sustaining thoughts, behaviors, and emotions in order to reach goals.

Self-regulatory knowledge Knowing how to manage your learning, or knowing how and when to use your declarative and procedural knowledge.

Self-reinforcement Controlling (selecting and administering) your own reinforcers.

Semantic memory Memory for meaning.

Semilingual A lack of proficiency in any language; speaking one or more languages inadequately.

Semiotic function The ability to use symbols—language, pictures, signs, or gestures—to represent actions or objects mentally.

Sensitive periods Times when a person is especially ready to learn certain things or responsive to certain experiences.

Sensorimotor Involving the senses and motor activity.

Sensory memory System that holds sensory information very briefly.

Serial-position effect The tendency to remember the beginning and the end, but not the middle of a list.

Seriation Arranging objects in sequential order according to one aspect, such as size, weight, or volume.

Service learning A teaching strategy that invites students to identify, research, and address real community challenges, using knowledge and skills learned in the classroom.

Sexual identity A complex combination of beliefs about gender roles and sexual orientation.

Shaping Reinforcing each small step of progress toward a desired goal or behavior.

Shared regulation Students working together to regulate each other through reminders, prompts, and other guidance.

Sheltered instruction Approach to teaching that improves English language skills while teaching content to ELL students by putting the words and concepts of the content into context to make the content more understandable.

Sheltered Instruction Observation Protocol or SIOP® An observational system to check that each element of sheltered instruction is present for a teacher.

Short-term memory Component of memory system that holds information for about 20 seconds.

Single-subject experimental studies Systematic interventions to study effects with one person, often by applying and then withdrawing a treatment.

Situated learning The idea that skills and knowledge are tied to the situation in which they were learned and that they are difficult to apply in new settings.

Social cognitive theory Theory that adds concern with cognitive factors such as beliefs, self-perceptions, and expectations to social learning theory.

Social conventions Agreed-upon rules and ways of doing things in a particular situation.

Social development Changes over time in the ways we relate to others.

Social goals A wide variety of needs and motives to be connected to others or part of a group.

Social isolation Removal of a disruptive student for 5 to 10 minutes.

Social learning theory Theory that emphasizes learning through observation of others.

Social negotiation Aspect of learning process that relies on collaboration with others and respect for different perspectives.

Social persuasion A "pep talk" or specific performance feedback—one source of self-efficacy.

Sociocultural theory Emphasizes role in development of cooperative dialogues between children and more knowledgeable members of society. Children learn the culture of their community (ways of thinking and behaving) through these interactions.

Sociocultural views of motivation Perspectives that emphasize participation, identities, and interpersonal relations within communities of practice.

Socioeconomic status (SES) Relative standing in the society based on income, power, background, and prestige.

Sociolinguistics The study of the formal and informal rules for how, when, about what, to whom, and how long to speak in conversations within cultural groups.

Spasticity Overly tight or tense muscles, characteristic of some forms of cerebral palsy.

Speech disorder Inability to produce sounds effectively for speaking.

Spermarche The first sperm ejaculation for boys.

Spiral curriculum Bruner's design for teaching that introduces the fundamental structure of all subjects early in the school years, then revisits the subjects in more and more complex forms over time.

Spreading activation Retrieval of pieces of information based on their relatedness to one another. Remembering one bit of information activates (stimulates) recall of associated information.

Standard deviation Measure of how widely scores vary from the mean.

Standard error of measurement Hypothetical estimate of variation in scores if testing were repeated.

Standard scores Scores based on the standard deviation.

Standardized tests Tests given, usually nationwide, under uniform conditions and scored according to uniform procedures.

Stanine scores Whole number scores from 1 to 9, each representing a wide range of raw scores.

Statistically significant Not likely to be a chance occurrence.

Stem The question part of a multiple-choice item.

Stereotype Schema that organizes knowledge or perceptions about a category.

Stereotype threat The extra emotional and cognitive burden that your performance in an academic situation might confirm a stereotype that others hold about you.

Stimulus Event that activates behavior.

Stimulus control Capacity for the presence or absence of antecedents to cause behaviors.

Story grammar Typical structure or organization for a category of stories.

Structured controversy Students work in pairs within their four-person cooperative groups to research a particular controversy.

Structured English immersion (SEI) An environment that teaches English rapidly by maximizing instruction in English and using English at a level appropriate to the abilities of the ELLs in the class.

Successive approximations Reinforcing small steps to reach a goal; the small component steps that make up a complex behavior.

Summative assessment Testing that follows instruction and assesses achievement.

Sustaining expectation effect Student performance is maintained at a certain level because teachers don't recognize improvements.

Synapses The tiny space between neurons—chemical messages are sent across these gaps.

Syntax The order of words in phrases or sentences.

_T_ score Standard score with a mean of 50 and a standard deviation of 10.

Task analysis System for breaking down a task hierarchically into basic skills and subskills.

Taxonomy Classification system.

Teachers' sense of efficacy A teacher's belief that he or she can reach even the most difficult students and help them learn.

Theory Integrated statement of principles that attempts to explain a phenomenon and make predictions.

Theory of mind An understanding that other people are people too, with their own minds, thoughts, feelings, beliefs, desires, and perceptions.

Theory of multiple intelligences In Gardner's theory of intelligence, a person's eight separate abilities: logical-mathematical, linguistic, musical, spatial, bodily-kinesthetic, interpersonal, intrapersonal, and naturalist.

Theory-based An explanation for concept formation that suggests our classifications are based on ideas about the world that we create to make sense of things.

Time out Technically, the removal of all reinforcement. In practice, isolation of a student from the rest of the class for a brief time.

Token reinforcement system System in which tokens earned for academic work and positive classroom behavior can be exchanged for some desired reward.

Top-down Making sense of information by using context and what we already know about the situation; sometimes called _conceptually driven perception_.

Tracking Assignment to different classes and academic experiences based on achievement.

Transfer Influence of previously learned material on new material; the productive (not reproductive) uses of cognitive tools and motivations.

Transition programming Gradual preparation of students with special needs to move from high school into further education or training, employment, or community involvement.

Triarchic reciprocal causality An explanation of behavior that emphasizes the mutual effects of the individual and the environment on each other.

Triarchic theory of successful intelligence A three-part description of the mental abilities (thinking processes, coping with new experiences, and adapting to context) that lead to more or less intelligent behavior.

True score The score the student would get if the measurement were completely accurate and error-free.

Unconditioned response (UR) Naturally occurring emotional or physiological response.

Unconditioned stimulus (US) Stimulus that automatically produces an emotional or physiological response.

Universal design Considering the needs of all users in the design of new tools, learning programs, or Web sites.

Utility value The contribution of a task to meeting one's goals.

Validity Degree to which a test measures what it is intended to measure.

Variability Degree of difference or deviation from mean.

Verbalization Putting your problem-solving plan and its logic into words.

Vicarious experiences Accomplishments that are modeled by someone else.

Vicarious reinforcement Increasing the chances that we will repeat a behavior by observing another person being reinforced for that behavior.

Virtual Learning Environments (VLE) A broad term that describes many ways of learning in virtual or online systems.

Visuospatial sketchpad Part of working memory. A holding system for visual and spatial information.

Voicing problems Inappropriate pitch, quality, loudness, or intonation.

Volition Will power; self-discipline; work styles that protect opportunities to reach goals by applying self-regulated learning.

Warm demanders Effective teachers with African American students who show both high expectations and great caring for their students.

Within-class ability grouping System of grouping in which students in a class are divided into two or three groups based on ability in an attempt to accommodate student differences.

Withitness According to Kounin, awareness of everything happening in a classroom.

Work-avoidant learners Students who don't want to learn or to look smart, but just want to avoid work.

Working memory The brain system that provides temporary holding and processing of information to accomplish complex cognitive tasks as language comprehension, learning, and reasoning; the information that you are focusing on at a given moment.

Working-backward strategy Heuristic in which one starts with the goal and moves backward to solve the problem.

z score Standard score indicating the number of standard deviations above or below the mean that a particular score falls.

Zero reject A basic principle of IDEA specifying that no student with a disability, no matter what kind or how severe, can be denied a free public education.

Zone of proximal development Phase at which a child can master a task if given appropriate help and support.

References

Aamodt, S., & Wang, S. (2008). *Welcome to your brain: Why you lose your car keys but never forget how to drive and other puzzles of everyday life*. New York, NY: Bloomsbury.

Aber, J. L., Brown, J. L., & Jones, S. M. (2003). Developmental trajectories toward violence in middle childhood: Course, demographic differences, and response to school-based intervention. *Developmental Psychology, 39*, 324–348.

Aboud, F. E. (2003). The formation of in-group favoritism and out-group prejudice in young children: Are they distinct attitudes? *Developmental Psychology, 39*, 48–60.

Abrams, I. M., & Madaus, G. F. (2003). The lessons of high stakes testing. *Educational Leadership, 61*(32), 31–35.

Ackerman, B. P., Brown, E. D., & Izard, C. E. (2004). The relations between contextual risk, earned income, and the school adjustment of children from economically disadvantaged families. *Developmental Psychology, 40*, 204–216.

Ackerman, P. L., Beier, M. E., & Boyle, M. O. (2005). Working memory and intelligence: The same or different constructs? *Psychological Bulletin, 131*, 30–60.

Adams, G. R., Berzonsky, M. D., & Keating, L. (2006). Psychosocial resources in first-year university students: The role of identity processes and social relationships. *Journal of Youth and Adolescence, 35*(1), 78–88.

Ainley, M., Hidi, S., & Berndorf, D. (2002). Interest, learning, and the psychological processes that mediate their relationship. *Journal of Educational Psychology, 94*, 545–561.

Airasian, P. W. (2005). *Classroom assessment: Concepts and applications* (5th ed.). New York, NY: McGraw-Hill.

Albanese, M. A., & Mitchell, S. A. (1993). Problem-based learning: A review of literature on its outcomes and implementation issues. *Academic Medicine, 68*, 52–81.

Alber, S. R., & Heward, W. L. (1997). Recruit it or lose it! Training students to recruit positive teacher attention. *Intervention in School and Clinic, 32*, 275–282.

Alber, S. R., & Heward, W. L. (2000). Teaching students to recruit positive attention: A review and recommendations. *Journal of Behavioral Education, 10*, 177–204.

Alberto, P. A., & Troutman, A. C. (2009). *Applied behavior analysis for teachers* (8th ed.). Boston, MA: Pearson.

Alderman, M. K. (2004). *Motivation for achievement: Possibilities for teaching and learning*. Mahwah, NJ: Erlbaum.

Alexander, P. A. (1992). Domain knowledge: Evolving themes and emerging concerns. *Educational Psychologist, 27*, 33–51.

Alexander, P. A. (1996). The past, present, and future of knowledge research: A reexamination of the role of knowledge in learning and instruction. *Educational Psychologist, 31*, 89–92.

Alexander, P. A. (1997). Mapping the multidimensional nature of domain learning: The interplay of cognitive, motivational, and strategic forces. *Advances in Motivation and Achievement, 10*, 213–250.

Alexander, P. A., Kulikowich, J. M., & Schulze, S. K. (1994). How subject-matter knowledge affects recall and interest. *American Educational Research Journal, 31*, 313–337.

Alexander, P. A., Schallert, D. L., & Reynolds, R. E. (2009). What is learning anyway? A topographical perspective considered. *Educational Psychologist, 44*, 176–192.

Alexander, P. A., & Winne, P. H. (2006). *Handbook of educational psychology* (2nd ed.). Mahwah, NJ: Erlbaum.

Alferink, L. A., & Farmer-Dougan, V. (2010). Brain-(not) based education: Dangers of misunderstanding and misapplication of neuroscience research. *Exceptionality, 18*, 42–52.

Alfieri, L., Brooks, P. J., Aldrich, N. J., & Tenenbaum, H. R. (2011). Does discovery-based instruction enhance learning? *Journal of Educational Psychology, 103*, 1–18.

Alliance for Service Learning in Education Reform. (1993). Standards of quality for school based service learning. *Equity and Excellence in Education, 26*(2), 71–77.

Allington, R. L., & McGill-Frazen, A. (2003). The impact of summer setback on the reading achievement gap. *Phi Delta Kappan, 85*(1), 68–75.

Allington, R. L., & McGill-Frazen, A. (2008). Got books? *Educational Leadership, 65*(7), 20–23.

Alloway, N. (1984). *Teacher expectations*. Paper presented at the meetings of the Australian Association for Research in Education, Perth, Australia.

Alloway, T. P., Banner, G. E., & Smith, P. (2010). Working memory and cognitive styles in adolescents' attainment. *British Journal of Educational Psychology, 80*, 567–581.

Alloway, T. P., Gathercole, S. E., & Pickering, S. J. (2006). Verbal and visuo-spatial short-term and working memory in children: Are they separable? *Child Development, 77*, 1698–1716.

Alloy, L. B., & Seligman, M. E. P. (1979). On the cognitive component of learned helplessness and depression. *The Journal of Learning and Motivation, 13*, 219–276.

Aloe, A. M., & Becker, B. J. (2009). Teacher verbal ability and school outcomes: Where is the evidence? *Educational Researcher, 38*, 612–624.

Alter, A. L., Aaronson, J., Darley, J. M., Rodriguez, C., & Ruble, D. N. (2009). Rising to the threat: Reducing stereotype threat by reframing the threat as a challenge. *Journal of Experimental Social Psychology, 46*, 166–171.

Altermatt, E. R., Pomerantz, E. M., Ruble, D. N., Frey, K. S., & Greulich, F. K. (2002). Predicting changes in children's self-perceptions of academic competence: A naturalistic examination of evaluative discourse among classmates. *Developmental Psychology, 38*, 903–917.

Alvidrez, J., & Weinstein, R. S. (1999). Early teacher perceptions and later student academic achievement. *Journal of Educational Psychology, 91*, 731–746.

Amabile, T. M. (1996). *Creativity in context*. Boulder, CO: Westview Press.

Amabile, T. M. (2001). Beyond talent: John Irving and the passionate craft of creativity. *American Psychologist, 56*, 333–336.

Amato, L. F., Loomis, L. S., & Booth, A. (1995). Parental divorce, marital conflict, and offspring well-being during early adulthood. *Social Forces, 73*, 895–915.

Amato, P. R. (2001). Children of divorce in the 1990s: An update of the Amato and Keith (1991) meta-analysis. *Journal of Family Psychology, 15*, 355–370.

Amato, P. R. (2006). Marital discord, divorce, and children's well-being. In A. Clarke-Stewart & J. Dunn (Eds.), *Families count: Effects on child and adolescent development* (pp. 179–202). New York, NY: Cambridge University Press.

American Association on Intellectual and Developmental Disabilities (AAIDD). (2010). Definition of intellectual disability. Available online at: http://www.aamr.org/content_100.cfm?navID_21

American Cancer Society. (2010). Child and teen tobacco use: Understanding the problem. Atlanta, GA: Author. Available online at: http://www.cancer.org/cancer/cancercauses/tobaccocancer/childandteentobaccouse/child-and-teen-tobacco-use

American Psychiatric Association. (2000). *Diagnostic and statistical manual of mental disorders* (4th ed., text revision) *DSM-IV-TR*. Washington, DC: Author.

American Psychological Association. (2001). Making stepfamilies work. Available online at: http://www.apa.org/helpcenter/stepfamily.aspx. APA Psychology Help Center.

American Psychological Association. (2004). An Overview of the psychological literature on the effects of divorce on children. Available online at: http://www.apa.org/about/gr/issues/cyf/divorce.aspx

American Psychological Association Task Force on Evidence-Based Practice for Children and Adolescents. (2008). *Disseminating evidence-based practice for children and adolescents: A systems approach to enhancing care*. Washington, DC: Author. Available online at: www.apa.org/pi/cyf/evidence.html

Ames, C. (1992). Classrooms: Goals, structures, and student motivation. *Journal of Educational Psychology, 84*, 261–271.

Anderman, E. M., & Anderman, L. H. (2009). *Motivating children and adolescents in schools*. Columbus, OH: Merrill/Prentice Hall.

Anderman, E. M., & Anderman, L. H. (2010). *Motivating children and adolescents in schools*. Columbus, OH: Merrill/Prentice Hall.

Anderman, E. M., Cupp, P. K., & Lane, D. (2009). Impulsivity and academic cheating. *Journal of Experimental Education, 78*, 135–150.

Anderman, E. M., & Maehr, M. L. (1994). Motivation and schooling in the middle grades. *Review of Educational Research, 64*, 287–310.

Anderman, E. M., & Midgley, C. (2004). Changes in self-reported academic cheating across the transition from middle school to high school. *Contemporary Educational Psychology, 29,* 499–517.

Anderman, E. M., & Patrick, H. (2012). Achievement goal theory, conceptualization of ability/intelligence, and classroom climate. In S. L. Christenson, A. L. Reschly, & C. Wylie (Eds.), *The handbook of research on student engagement.* New York, NY: Springer Science.

Anderson, C. A., Berkowitz, L., Donnerstein, E., Huesmann, L. R., Johnson, J. D., Linz, D., & Wartella, E. (2003). The influence of media violence on youth. *Psychological Science in the Public Interest, 4,* 81–110.

Anderson, C. A., Shibuya, Al, Ihori, N., Swing, E. L., Bushman, B. J., Sakamoto, A., ... Saleem, M. (2010). Violent video game effects on aggression, empathy, and prosocial behavior in eastern and western countries: A meta-analytic review. *Psychological Bulletin, 136,* 151–173.

Anderson, C. W., Holland, J. D., & Palincsar, A. S. (1997). Canonical and sociocultural approaches to research and reform in science education: The story of Juan and his group. *The Elementary School Journal, 97,* 359–384.

Anderson, J. R. (1993). Problem solving and learning. *American Psychologist, 48,* 35–44.

Anderson, J. R. (1995). Cognitive psychology and its implications (4th ed.). New York, NY: Freeman.

Anderson, J. R. (2010). *Cognitive psychology and its implications* (7th ed.). New York, NY: Worth.

Anderson, J. R., Reder, L. M., & Simon, H. A. (1995). *Applications and misapplication of cognitive psychology to mathematics education.* Unpublished manuscript. Available online at http://www.psy.cmu.edu/~mm4b/misapplied.html

Anderson, J. R., Reder, L. M., & Simon, H. A. (1996). Situated learning and education. *Educational Researcher, 25,* 5–11.

Anderson, L. W., & Krathwohl, D. R. (Eds.). (2001). *A taxonomy for learning, teaching, and assessing: A revision of Bloom's taxonomy of educational objectives.* New York, NY: Longman.

Anderson, L. W., & Sosniak, L. A. (Eds.). (1994). *Bloom's taxonomy: A forty-year retrospective.* Ninety-third yearbook for the National Society for the Study of Education: Part II. Chicago, IL: University of Chicago Press.

Anderson, P. J., & Graham, S. M. (1994). Issues in second-language phonological acquisition among children and adults. *Topics in Language Disorders, 14,* 84–100.

Anderson, R. C., Nguyen-Jahiel, K., McNurlen, B., Archodidou, A., Kim, S-Y., Reznitskaya, A., et al. (2001). The snowball phenomenon: Spread of ways of talking and ways of thinking across groups of children. *Cognition and Instruction, 19,* 1–46.

Anderson, S. M., Klatzky, R. L., & Murray, J. (1990). Traits and social stereotypes: Efficiency differences in social information processing. *Journal of Personality and Social Psychology, 59,* 192–201.

Angier, N., & Chang, K. (2005, January 24). Gray matter and the sexes: Still a scientific gray area. *The New York Times,* A1+.

Antonenko, P., Paas, F., Grabner, R., & van Gog, T. (2010). Using electroencephalography to measure cognitive load. *Educational Psychology Review, 22,* 425–438.

Anyon, J. (1980). Social class and the hidden curriculum of work. *Journal of Education, 162,* 67–92.

Archer, S. L., & Waterman, A. S. (1990). Varieties of identity diffusions and foreclosures: An exploration of the subcategories of the identity statuses. *Journal of Adolescent Research, 5,* 96–111.

Arends, R. I. (2001). *Learning to teach* (5th ed.). New York, NY: McGraw-Hill.

Arends, R. I. (2004). *Learning to teach* (6th ed.). New York, NY: McGraw-Hill.

Arends, R. I. (2007). *Learning to teach* (7th ed.). New York, NY: McGraw-Hill.

Arends, R. I., & Kilcher, A. (2010). *Teaching for student learning: Becoming an accomplished teacher.* New York, NY: Routeledge.

Armbruster, B. B. (2000). Taking notes from lectures. In R. F. Flippo & D. C. Caverly (Eds.), *Handbook of college reading and study strategy research* (pp. 175–200). Mahwah, NJ: Lawrence Erlbaum.

Arnold, M. L. (2000). Stage, sequence, and sequels: Changing conceptions of morality, post-Kohlberg. *Educational Psychology Review, 12,* 365–383.

Aronson, E. (2000). *Nobody left to hate: Teaching compassion after Columbine.* New York, NY: Worth.

Aronson, J. (2002). Stereotype threat: Contending and coping with unnerving expectations. In J. Aronson & D. Cordova (Eds.), *Improving education: Classic and contemporary lessons from psychology* (pp. 279–301). New York, NY: Academic Press.

Aronson, J., Fried, C. B., & Good, C. (2002). Reducing the effects of stereotype threat on African American college students: The role of theories of intelligence. *Journal of Experimental Social Psychology, 33,* 113–125.

Aronson, J., Lustina, M. J., Good, C., Keough, K., Steele, C. M., & Brown, J. (1999). When White men can't do math: Necessary and sufficient factors in stereotype threat. *Journal of Experimental Social Psychology, 35,* 29–46.

Aronson, J., & Steele, C. M. (2005). Stereotypes and the fragility of human competence, motivation, and self-concept. In C. Dweck & E. Elliot (Eds.), *Handbook of competence and motivation.* New York, NY: Guilford.

Aronson, J., Steele, C. M., Salinas, M. F., & Lustina, M. J. (1999). The effect of stereotype threat on the standardized test performance of college students. In E. Aronson (Ed.), *Readings about the social animal* (8th ed.). New York, NY: Freeman.

Ashcraft, M. H., & Radvansky, G. A. (2010). *Cognition* (5th ed.). Upper Saddle River, NJ: Prentice-Hall/Pearson.

Ashton, P. (2009). Learning in infant development: Promising paradigm shift or another swing of the pendulum? (2009). *PsycCRITIQUES, 54*(4): doi: 10.1037/a0014993

Associated Press. (2001, February 21). ABA recommends dropping zero-tolerance in schools. Available online at: http://www.cnn.com/2001/fyi/teachers.ednews/02/21/zero.tolerance.ap

Association for the Gifted. (2001). *Diversity and developing gifts and talents: A national action plan.* Arlington, VA: Author.

Astington, J. W., & Dack, L. A. (2008). Theory of mind. In M. M. Haith & J. B. Benson (Eds.), *Encyclopedia of infant and early childhood development* (Vol. 3, pp. 343–356). San Diego, CA: Academic Press.

Atkinson, R. C., & Shiffrin, R. M. (1968). Human memory: A proposed system and its control processes. In K. Spence & J. Spence (Eds.), *The psychology of learning and motivation* (Vol. 2, pp. 89–195). New York, NY: Academic Press.

Atkinson, R. K., Levin, J. R., Kiewra, K. A., Meyers, T., Atkinson, L. A., Renandya, W. A., & Hwang, Y. (1999). Matrix and mnemonic text-processing adjuncts: Comparing and combining their components. *Journal of Educational Psychology, 91,* 242–257.

Atkinson, R. K., & Renkl, A. (2007). Interactive example-based learning environments: Using interactive elements to encourage effective processing of worked examples. *Educational Psychology Review, 19,* 375–386.

Au, K. H. (1980). Participation structures in a reading lesson with Hawaiian children: Analysis of a culturally appropriate instructional event. *Anthropology and Education Quarterly, 11,* 91–115.

Au, T. K., Knightly, L. M., Jun, S., & Oh, J. S. (2002). Overhearing a language during childhood. *Psychological Science, 13,* 238–243.

Au, T. K., Oh, J. S., Knightly, L. M., Jun, S-A., & Romo, L. F. (2008). Salvaging a child language. *Journal of Memory and Language, 58,* 998–1011.

Aud, S., Hussar, W., Planty, M., Snyder, T., Bianco, K., Fox, M., Frohlich, L., Kemp, J., & Drake, L. (2010). *The condition of education 2010* (NCES 2010-028). National Center for Education Statistics, U.S. Department of Education. Washington, DC: U.S. Government Printing Office.

Aufderheide, P., & Firestone, C. (1993). *Media literacy: A report of the national leadership conference on media literacy.* Queenstown, MD: Aspen Institute.

Avramidis, E., Bayliss, P., & Burden, R. (2000). Student teachers' attitudes toward the inclusion of children with special education needs in the ordinary school. *Teaching and Teacher Education, 16,* 277–293.

Azevedo, R. (2005). Using hypermedia as a metacognitive tool for enhancing student learning? The role of self-regulated learning. *Educational Psychologist, 40,* 199–209.

Azevedo, R., Johnson, A., Chauncey, A. & Graesser, A. (2011). Use of hypermedia to assess and convey self-regulated learning. In B. Zimmerman & D. Schunk (Eds.), *Handbook of self-regulation of learning and performance* (pp. 102–121). New York, NY: Routledge.

Azzam, A. M. (2006, April). A generation immersed in media. *Educational Leadership,* 92–93.

Babad, E. Y., Inbar, J., & Rosenthal, R. (1982). Pygmalion, Galatea, and the Golem: Investigations of biased and unbiased teachers. *Journal of Educational Psychology, 74,* 459–474.

Baddeley, A. D. (1986). *Working memory.* Oxford, UK: Clarendon Books.

Baddeley, A. D. (2001). Is working memory still working? *American Psychologist, 56,* 851–864.

Baddeley, A. D.. (2007). *Working memory, thought, and action.* New York, NY: Oxford University Press.

Baddeley, A. D., Hitch, G. J., Allen, R. J. (2009). Working memory and binding in sentence recall. *Journal of Memory and Language, 61,* 438–456.

Baer, J. (1997). *Creative teachers, creative students.* Boston, MA: Allyn & Bacon.

Bagley, E., & Shaffer, D. W. (2009). When people get in the way: Promoting civic thinking through epistemic gameplay. *International Journal of Gaming and Computer-mediated Simulations, 1,* 36–52.

Bailey, U. L., Lorch, E. P., Milich, R., & Charnigo, R. (2009). Developmental changes in attention and comprehension among children with attention deficit hyperactivity disorder. *Child Development, 80*, 1842–1855.

Baillargeon, R. (1999). Young infants' expectations about hidden objects: A reply to three challenges. *Developmental Psychology, 2*, 115–132.

Baker, K. (1998). Structured English immersion breakthrough in teaching limited-English-proficient students. *Phi Delta Kappan, 80*(3), 199–204. Available online at: http://pdkintl.org/kappan/kbak9811.htm

Bakerman, R., Adamson, L. B., Koner, M., & Barr, R. G. (1990). !Kung infancy: The social context of object exploration. *Child Development, 61*, 794–809.

Balass, M., Nelson, J. R., & Perfetti, C. A. (2010). Word learning: An ERP investigation of word experience effects on recognition and word processing. *Contemporary Educational Psychology, 35*, 126–140.

Baldwin, J. M. (1895). *Mental development in the child and the race: Methods and processes*. New York, NY: Macmillan.

Ball, D. L. (1997). What do students know? Facing challenges of distance, context, and desire in trying to hear children. In B. J. Biddle, T. L. Good, & I. F. Goodson (Eds.), *The international handbook of teachers and teaching* (pp. 769–818). Dordrecht, the Netherlands: Kluwer.

Bandura, A. (1965). Influence of models' reinforcement contingencies on the acquisition of imitative responses. *Journal of Personality and Social Psychology, 1*, 589–595.

Bandura, A. (1977). *Social learning theory*. Englewood Cliffs, NJ: Prentice-Hall.

Bandura, A. (1982). Self-efficacy mechanisms in human agency. *American Psychologist, 37*, 122–147.

Bandura, A. (1986). *Social foundations of thought and action*. Englewood Cliffs, NJ: Prentice-Hall.

Bandura, A. (1993). Perceived self-efficacy in cognitive development and functioning. *Educational Psychologist, 28*, 117–148.

Bandura, A. (1994). Self-efficacy. In V. S. Ramachaudran (Ed.), *Encyclopedia of human behavior* (Vol. 4, pp. 71–81). New York, NY: Academic Press.

Bandura, A. (1997). *Self-efficacy: The exercise of control*. New York, NY: Freeman.

Bandura, A. (2001). Social cognitive theory: An agentic perspective. *Annual review of psychology* (Vol. 52, pp. 1–26). Palo Alto, CA: Annual Reviews, Inc.

Bandura, A. (2006). Adolescent development from an agentic perspective. In F. Pajares & T. Urdan (Eds.), *Self-efficacy beliefs of adolescents*. Greenwich, CT: Information Age.

Bandura, A. (2007). Albert Bandura. In L. Gardner & W. M. Runyan (Eds.). *A history of psychology in autobiography* (Vol. IX, pp. 43–75). Washington, DC: American Psychological Association.

Bandura, A., & Locke, E. (2003). Negative self-efficacy and goal effects revisited. *Journal of Applied Psychology, 88*, 87–99.

Bandura, A., Ross, D., & Ross, S. A. (1963). Vicarious reinforcement and imitative learning. *Journal of Abnormal and Social Psychology, 67*, 601–607.

Banks, J. A. (1997). *Teaching strategies for ethnic studies* (6th ed.). Boston, MA: Allyn & Bacon.

Banks, J. A. (2002). *An introduction to multicultural education* (3rd ed.). Boston, MA: Allyn & Bacon.

Banks, J. A. (2006). *Cultural diversity and education: Foundations, curriculum, and teaching* (5th ed.). Boston, MA: Allyn & Bacon.

Banks, S. R. (2005). *Classroom assessment: Issues and practice*. Boston, MA: Allyn & Bacon.

Barden, L. M. (1995). Effective questioning and the ever-elusive higher-order question. *American Biology Teacher, 57*, 423–426.

Barkley, R. A. (Ed.). (2006). *Attention-deficit hyperactivity disorder: A handbook for diagnosis and treatment* (3rd ed., pp. 547–588). New York, NY: Guilford.

Barnard-Brak, L. (2008). Academic red-shirting among children with learning disabilities. *Learning Disabilities: A Contemporary Journal, 6*, 43–54.

Barnett, M. S., & Ceci, S. J. (2002). When and where do we apply what we learn? A taxonomy for far transfer. *Psychological Bulletin, 128*, 612–637.

Barnhill, G. P. (2005). Functional behavioral assessment in schools. *Intervention in School and Clinic, 40*, 131–143.

Baron, R. A. (1998). *Psychology* (4th ed.). Boston, MA: Allyn & Bacon.

Baron, R. A., & Byrne, D. (2003). *Social psychology* (10th ed.). Boston, MA: Allyn & Bacon.

Barros, E., Silver, J., & Stein. R. E. K. (2009). School recess and group classroom behavior. *Pediatrics, 123*, 431–436.

Bartholomew, B. (2008). Sustaining the fire. *Educational Leadership, 65*(6), 55–60.

Bartlett, F. C. (1932). *Remembering: A study in experimental and social psychology*. New York, NY: Macmillan.

Bartlett, S. M., Rapp, J. T., Krueger, T. K., & Henrickson, M. L. (2011). The use of response cost to treat spitting by a child with autism. *Behavioral Interventions, 26*, 76–83.

Basow, S. A., & Rubin, L. R. (1999). Gender influences on adolescent development. In N. G. Johnson, M. C. Roberts, & J. Worell (Eds.), *Beyond appearance: A new look at adolescent girls* (pp. 25–52). Washington, DC: American Psychological Association.

Battistich, V., Solomon, D., & Delucci, K. (1993). Interaction processes and student outcomes in cooperative groups. *Elementary School Journal, 94*, 19–32.

Bauer, P. J. (2006). Event memory. In D. Kuhn & R. S. Siegler (Eds.), *Cognition, perception, and language* (6th ed., Vol. 2, pp. 373–425). New York, N Y: Wiley.

Baumeister, R. F., Campbell, J. D., Krueger, J. L., & Vohs, K. D. (2003). Does high self-esteem cause better performance, interpersonal success, happiness, or healthier lifestyles? *Psychological Science in the Public Interest, 4*, 1–44.

Baumeister, R. F., & Leary, M. R. (1995). The need to belong: Desire for interpersonal attachments as a fundamental human motivation. *Psychological Bulletin, 117*, 497–529.

Baumert, J., Kunter, M., Blum, W., Brunner, M., Voss, T., Jordan, A., Klusmann, U., Krauss, S., Neubrand, M., & Tsai, Y.-M. (2010). Teachers' mathematical knowledge, cognitive activation in the classroom, and student progress. *American Educational Research Journal, 47*(1), 133–180.

Baumrind, D. (1991). Effective parenting during early adolescent transitions. In P. A. Cowan & M. Hetherington (Eds.),. *Family transitions* (pp. 111–165). Hillsdale, NJ: Erlbaum.

Baumrind, D. (1996). The discipline controversy revisited. *Family Relations, 45*, 405–414.

Bayliss, D. M., Jarrold, C., Baddeley, A. D., Gunn, D., & Leigh, E. (2005). Mapping the developmental constraints on working memory span performance. *Developmental Psychology, 41*, 579–597.

Beane, J. A. (1991). Sorting out the self-esteem controversy. *Educational Leadership, 49*(1), 25–30.

Bear, G. G. (with Cavalier, A. R., & Manning, M. A.). (2005). *Developing self-discipline and preventing and correcting misbehavior*. Boston, MA: Allyn & Bacon.

Beck, I. L., McKeown, M. G., Worthy, J., Sandora, C. A., & Kucan, L. (1996). Questioning the author: A yearlong classroom implementation to engage students with text. *The Elementary School Journal, 96*, 385–414.

Beebe-Frankenberger, M., Bocian, K. L., MacMillan, D. L., & Gresham, F. M. (2004). Sorting second grade students with academic deficiencies: Characteristics differentiating those retained in grade from those promoted to third grade. *Journal of Educational Psychology, 96*, 204–215.

Beghetto, R. A. (2008). Prospective teachers' beliefs about imaginative thinking in K-12 schooling. *Thinking Skills and Creativity, 3*, 134–142.

Begley, S. (2007, October). The case for chutes and ladders. *Newsweek*. Available online at: http://www.newsweek.com/2007/10/13/the-case-for-chutes-and-ladders.html

Benenson, J. F. (1993). Greater preference among females than males for dyadic interaction in early childhood. *Child Development, 64*, 544–555.

Bennett, C. I. (2011). Comprehensive multicultural education: Theory and practice (7th ed.). Boston, MA: Allyn & Bacon.

Bereiter, C. (1995). A dispositional view of transfer. In A. McKeough, J. Lupart, & A. Marini (Eds.), *Teaching for mastery: Fostering generalization in learning* (pp. 21–34). Mahwah, NJ: Erlbaum.

Bereiter, C. (1997). Situated cognition and how I overcome it. In D. Kirshner & J. A. Whitson (Eds.), *Situated cognition: Social, semiotic, and psychological perspectives* (pp. 281–300). Mahwah, NJ: Erlbaum.

Berg, C. A., & Clough, M. (1991). Hunter lesson design: The wrong one for science teaching. *Educational Leadership, 48*(4), 73–78.

Berger, K. S. (2006). The developing person through childhood and adolescence (7th ed.). New York, NY: Worth.

Berger, K. S. (2012). The developing person through the life span (8th ed.). New York, NY: Worth.

Bergin, D. (1999). Influences on classroom interest. *Educational Psychologist, 34*, 87–98.

Berk, L. E. (2001). *Awakening children's minds: How parents and teachers can make a difference*. New York, NY: Oxford University Press.

Berk, L. E. (2005). *Infants, children, and adolescents* (5th ed.). Boston, MA: Allyn & Bacon.

Berk, L. E., & Spuhl, S. T. (1995). Maternal interaction, private speech, and task performance in preschool children. *Early Childhood Research Quarterly, 10*, 145–169.

Berko, J. (1958). The child's learning of English morphology. *Word, 14*, 150–177.

Berliner, D. C. (1983). Developing concepts of classroom environments: Some light on the T in studies of ATI. *Educational Psychologist, 18*, 1–13.

Berliner, D. C. (1987). But do they understand? In V. Richardson-Koehler (Ed.), *Educators' handbook: A research perspective* (pp. 259–293). New York, NY: Longman.

Berliner, D. C. (1988). Simple views of effective teaching and a simple theory of classroom instruction. In D. Berliner & B. Rosenshine (Eds.), *Talks to teachers* (pp. 93–110). New York, NY: Random House.

Berliner, D. C. (2002). Educational research: The hardest science of all. *Educational Researcher, 31*(8), 18–20.

Berliner, D. C. (2005). Our impoverished view of educational reform. *The Teachers College Record, 108*, 949–995.

Berliner, D. C. (2006). Educational psychology: Searching for essence throughout a century of influence. In P. A. Alexander & P. H. Winne (Eds.), *Handbook of educational psychology* (2nd ed., pp. 3–27). Mahwah, NJ: Erlbaum.

Berlyne, D. (1966). Curiosity and exploration. *Science, 153*, 25–33.

Berndt, T. J., & Keefe, K. (1995). Friends' influence on adolescents' adjustment to school. *Child Development, 66*, 1312–1329.

Bernstein, D. A., & Nash, P. W. (2008). *Essentials of psychology* (4th ed.). Boston, MA: Houghton-Mifflin.

Berry, R. Q., III. (2005). Voices of success: Descriptive portraits of two successful African American male middle school mathematics students. *Journal of African American Studies, 8*(4), 46–62.

Berthold, K., & Renkl, A. (2009). Instructional aids to support a conceptual understanding of multiple representations. *Journal of Educational Psychology, 101*, 70–87.

Bialystok, E. (2001). *Bilingualism in development: Language, literacy, and cognition.* New York, NY: Cambridge University Press.

Bialystok, E., Majumder, S., & Martin, M. M. (2003). Developing phonological awareness: Is there a bilingual advantage? *Applied Linguistics, 24*, 27–44.

Biggs, J. (2001). Enhancing learning: A matter of style of approach. In R. Sternberg & L. Zhang (Eds.), *Perspectives on cognitive, learning, and thinking styles* (pp. 73–102). Mahwah, NJ: Erlbaum.

Blair, C. (2002). School readiness: Integrating cognition and emotion in a neurobiological conceptualization of children's functioning at school entry. *American Psychologist, 57*, 111–127.

Blair, C. (2006). How similar are fluid cognition and general intelligence? A developmental neuroscience perspective on fluid cognition as an aspect of human cognition. Main article with commentaries. *Behavioral and Brain Sciences, 29*, 109–160.

Blakemore, S. K., & Frith, U. (2005). The learning brain: Lessons for education: a precis. *Developmental Science, 8*, 459–461.

Blatchford, P., Baines, E., Rubie-Davis, C., Bassett, P., & Chowne, A. (2006). The effect of a new approach to group work on pupil-pupil and teacher-interactions. *Journal of Educational Psychology, 98*, 750–765.

Bloom, B. S. (1981). *All our children learning: A primer for parents, teachers, and other educators.* New York, NY: McGraw-Hill.

Bloom, B. S. (1982). The role of gifts and markers in the development of talent. *Exceptional Children, 48*, 510–522.

Bloom, B. S., Engelhart, M. D., Frost, E. J., Hill, W. H., & Krathwohl, D. R. (1956). *Taxonomy of educational objectives. Handbook I: Cognitive domain.* New York, NY: David McKay.

Bloom, P. (2002). *How children learn the meanings of words.* Cambridge, MA: MIT Press.

Blumenfeld, P. C., Puro, P., & Mergendoller, J. R. (1992). Translating motivation into thoughtfulness. In H. Marshall (Ed.), *Redefining student learning: Roots of educational change* (pp. 207–240). Norwood, NJ: Ablex.

Bong, M. (2009). Age-related differences in achievement goal differentiation. *Journal of Educational Psychology, 101*, 879–896.

Boom, J., Brugman, D., & van der Heijden, P. G. (2001). Hierarchical structure of moral stages assessed by a sorting task. *Child Development, 72*, 535–548.

Borich, G. D. (2011). *Effective teaching methods: Research-based practice* (7th ed.). Columbus, OH: Pearson.

Borko, H., & Livingston, C. (1989). Cognition and improvisation: Differences in mathematics instruction by expert and novice teachers. *American Educational Research Journal, 26*, 473–498.

Borko, H., & Putnam, R. (1996). Learning to teach. In D. Berliner & R. Calfee (Eds.), *Handbook of educational psychology* (pp. 673–708). New York, NY: Macmillan.

Borman, G. D., & Overman, L. T. (2004). Academic resilience in mathematics among poor and minority students. *The Elementary School Journal, 104*, 177–195.

Borrero, N. E., & Yeh, C. J. (2010). Ecoogical English language learning among ethnic minority youth. *Educational Researcher, 39*, 571–581.

Bos, C. S., & Reyes, E. I. (1996). Conversations with a Latina teacher about education for language-minority students with special needs. *The Elementary School Journal, 96*, 344–351.

Bowlby, J. (1969). *Attachment and loss: Attachment.* New York, NY: Basic Books.

Boyd, D., Goldhaber, D., Lankford, H., & Wyckoff, J., (2008). The effect of certification and preparation on teacher quality. *The Future of Children, 17*(1), 45.

Boyle, J. R. (2010a). Note-taking skills of middle school students with and without learning disabilities. *Journal of Learning Disabilities, 43*, 530–540.

Boyle, J. R. (2010b). Strategic note-taking for middle school students with learning disabilities in science classes. *Learning Disabilities Quarterly, 33*, 93–109.

Boyle, J. R., & Weishaar, M. (2001). The effects of a strategic note-taking technique on the comprehension and long term recall of lecture information for high school students with LD. *Learning Disabilities Research and Practice, 16*, 125–133.

Braddock, J., II, & Slavin, R. E. (1993). Why ability grouping must end: Achieving excellence and equity in American education. *Journal of Intergroup Relations, 20*(2), 51–64.

Bradshaw, C. P., Zmuda, J. H., Kellam, S. G., & Ialongo, N. S. (2009). Longitudinal impact of two universal preventive interventions in first grade on educational outcomes in high school. *Journal of Educational Psychology, 101*, 926–937.

Brainerd, C. J. (2003). Jean Piaget, learning research, and American education. In B. J. Zimmerman & D. H. Schunk (Eds.), *Educational psychology: A century of contributions* (pp. 251–287). Mahwah, NJ: Erlbaum.

Brannon, L. (2002). *Gender: Psychological perspectives* (3rd ed.). Boston, MA: Allyn & Bacon.

Bransford, J. D., Brown, A. L., & Cocking, R. R. (2000). *How people learn: Brain, mind, experience, and school.* Washington, DC: National Academy Press.

Bransford, J. D., & Schwartz, D. (1999). Rethinking transfer: A simple proposal with multiple implications. In A. Iran-Nejad & P. D. Pearson (Eds.), *Review of research in education* (Vol. 24, pp. 61–100). Washington, DC: American Educational Research Association.

Bransford, J. D., & Stein, B. S. (1993). *The IDEAL problem solver: A guide for improving thinking, learning, and creativity* (2nd ed.). New York, NY: Freeman.

Brantlinger, E. (2004). Who wins and who loses? Social class and students' identities. In M. Sadowski (Ed.), *Adolescents at school: Perspectives on youth, identity, and education* (pp. 107–126). Cambridge, MA: Harvard University Press.

Branum-Martin, L., Foorman, B. R., Francis, D. J., & Mehta, P. D. (2010). Contextual effects of bilingual programs on beginning reading. *Journal of Educational Psychology, 102*, 341–355.

Bredekamp, S. (2011). *Effective practices in early childhood education: Building a foundation.* Columbus, OH: Merrill.

Bredekamp, S., & Copple, C. (1997). *Developmentally appropriate practice in early childhood programs.* Washington, DC: National Association for the Education of Young Children.

Briesch, A. M., & Chafouleas, S. M. (2009). Review and analysis of literature on self-management interventions to promote appropriate classroom behaviors (1988–2008). *School Psychology Quarterly, 24*, 106–118.

Broidy, L. M., Nagin, D. S., Tremblay, R. E., Bates, J. E., Brame, B., Dodge, K., . . . Vitaro, F. (2003). Developmental trajectories of childhood disruptive behaviors and adolescent delinquency: A six site, cross-national study. *Developmental Psychology, 39*, 222–245.

Bronfenbrenner, U. (1989). Ecological systems theory. In R. Vasta (Ed.), *Annals of child development* (Vol. 6, pp. 187–249). Boston, MA: JAI Press, Inc.

Bronfenbrenner, U., McClelland, P., Wethington, E., Moen, P., & Ceci, S. (1996). *The state of Americans: This generation and the next.* New York, NY: Free Press.

Bronfenbrenner, U., & Morris, P. A. (2006). The bioecological model of human development. In W. Damon & R. M. Lerner (Eds.), *Handbook of child psychology: Theoretical models of human development* (6th ed., Vol. 1, pp. 793–827). Hoboken, NJ: Wiley.

Brooks-Gunn, J. (1988). Antecedents and consequences of variations in girls' maturational timing. In M. D. Levin & E. R. McAnarney (Eds.), *Early adolescent transitions* (pp. 101–121). Lexington, MA: Lexington Books.

Brophy, J. E. (1981). Teacher praise: A functional analysis. *Review of Educational Research, 51*, 5–21.

Brophy, J. E. (1988). On motivating students. In D. Berliner & B. Rosenshine (Eds.), *Talks to teachers* (pp. 201–245). New York, NY: Random House.

Brophy, J. E. (1998). *Motivating students to learn.* New York, NY: McGraw-Hill.

Brophy, J. E. (2003). An interview with Jere Brophy by B. Gaedke, & M. Shaughnessy. *Educational Psychology Review, 15*, 199–211.

Brophy, J. E. (2005). Goal theorists should move on from performance goals. *Educational Psychologist, 40*, 167–176.

Brophy, J. E. (2008). Developing students' appreciation for what is taught in school, *Educational Psychologist, 43*, 132–141.

Brophy, J. E., & Everston, C. (1978). Context variables in teaching. *Educational Psychologist, 12*, 310–316.

Brophy, J. E., & Good, T. (1986). Teacher behavior and student achievement. In M. Wittrock (Ed.), *Handbook of research on teaching* (3rd ed.) (pp. 328–375). New York, NY: Macmillan.

Brophy, J. E., & Kher, N. (1986). Teacher socialization as a mechanism for developing student motivation to learn. In R. Feldman (Ed.), *Social psychology applied to education* (pp. 256–288). New York, NY: Cambridge University Press.

Brown, A. (1987). Metacognition, executive control, self-regulation, and other more mysterious mechanisms. In F. Weinert & R. Kluwe (Eds.), *Metacognition, motivation, and understanding* (pp. 65–116). Hillside, NJ: Erlbaum.

Brown, J. L., Jones, S. M., LaRusso, M. D., & Aber, J. L. (2010). Improving classroom quality: Teacher influences and experimental impacts of the 4Rs Program. *Journal of Educational Psychology, 102*, 153–167.

Bruer, J. T. (1999). In search of . . . brain-based education. *Phi Delta Kappan, 80*, 648–657.

Bruer, J. T. (2002). Avoiding the pediatrician's error: How neuroscientists can help educators (and themselves). *Nature Neuroscience, 5*, 1031–1033.

Bruner, J. S. (1966). *Toward a theory of instruction.* New York, NY: Norton.

Bruner, J. S. (1973). *Beyond the information given: Studies in the psychology of knowing.* New York, NY: Norton.

Brunner, M., Keller, U., Dierendinck, C., Reichert, M., Ugen, S., Fischbach, A., & Martin, R. (2010). The structure of academic self-concepts revisited: The nested Marsh/Shavelson model. *Journal of Educational Psychology, 102*, 964–981.

Bruning, R. H., Schraw, G. J., & Norby, M. M. (2011). *Cognitive psychology and instruction* (5th ed.). Boston, MA: Pearson.

Buffum, A., Mattos, M., & Weber, C. (2010). The why behind RTI. *Educational Leadership, 68*(2), 10–16.

Buhs, E. S., Ladd, G. W., & Herald, S. L. (2006). Peer exclusion and victimization: Processes that mediate the relation between peer group rejection and children's classroom engagement. *Journal of Educational Psychology, 98*, 1–13.

Burbules, N. C., & Bruce, B. C. (2001). Theory and research on teaching as dialogue. In V. Richardson (Ed.), *Handbook of research on teaching* (4th ed., pp. 1102–1121). Washington, DC: American Educational Research Association.

Burden, P. R. (1995). *Classroom management and discipline: Methods to facilitate cooperation and instruction.* White Plains, NY: Longman.

Burgess, S. R., Hecht, S. A., & Lonigan, C. J. (2002). Relations of the home literacy environment (HLE) to the development of reading-related abilities: A one-year longitudinal study. *Reading Research Quarterly, 37*, 408–426.

Burke-Spero, R. (1999). Toward a model of "civitas" through an ethic of care: A qualitative study of preservice teachers' perceptions about learning to teach diverse populations (Doctoral dissertation, The Ohio State University, 1999). *Dissertation Abstracts International, 60*, 11A, 3967.

Burke-Spero, R., & Woolfolk Hoy, A. (2002). *The need for thick description: A qualitative investigation of developing teacher efficacy.* Unpublished manuscript, University of Miami.

Burt, S. A. (2010). Are there shared environmental influences on attention-deficit/hyperactivity disorder? Reply to Wood, Buitelaar, Rijsdijk, Asherson, and Kuntsi (2010). *Psychological Bulletin, 136*, 341–343.

Buss, D. M. (1995). Psychological sex differences: Origin through sexual selection. *American Psychologist, 50*, 164–168.

Bussey, K. (2011). The influence of gender on students' self-regulated learning and performance. In B. Zimmerman & D. Schunk (Eds.), *Handbook of self-regulation of learning and performance* (pp. 426–441) New York, NY: Routledge.

Butcher, K. R. (2006). Learning from text with diagrams: Promoting mental model development and inference generation. *Journal of Educational Psychology, 98*, 182–197.

Butler, R. (1987). Task-involving and ego-involving properties of evaluation: Effects of different feedback conditions on motivational perceptions, interest, and performance. *Journal of Educational Psychology, 79*, 474–482.

Byrne, B. M. (2002). Validating the measurement and structure of self-concept: Snapshots of past, present, and future research. *American Psychologist, 57*, 897–909.

Byrnes, D. A. (1989). Attitudes of students, parents, and educators toward repeating a grade. In L. A. Shepard & M. L. Smith (Eds.), *Flunking grades: Research and policies on retention* (pp. 108–131). Philadelphia, PA: Falmer.

Byrnes, J. P. (1996). *Cognitive development and learning in instructional contexts.* Boston, MA: Allyn & Bacon.

Byrnes, J. P., & Fox, N. A. (1998). The educational relevance of research in cognitive neuroscience. *Educational Psychology Review, 10*, 297–342.

Cairns, R. B., & Cairns, B. D. (2006). The making of developmental psychology. In R. M. Lerner (Ed.), *Handbook of child psychology* (6th ed., Vol. 1: Theoretical models of human development, pp. 89–165). New York, NY: Wiley.

Calderhead, J. (1996). Teacher: Beliefs and knowledge. In D. Berliner & R. Calfee (Eds.), *Handbook of educational psychology* (pp. 709–725). New York, NY: Macmillan.

Callahan, C. M., Tomlinson, C. A., & Plucker, J. (1997). *Project STATR using a multiple intelligences model in identifying and promoting talent in high-risk students.* Storrs, CT: National Research Center for Gifted and Talented. University of Connecticut Technical Report.

Cameron, J., & Pierce, W. D. (1994). Reinforcement, reward, and intrinsic motivation: A meta-analysis. *Review of Educational Research, 64*, 363–423.

Cameron, J., & Pierce, W. D. (1996). The debate about rewards and intrinsic motivation: Protests and accusations do not alter the results. *Review of Educational Research, 66*, 39–52.

Cangelosi, J. S. (1990). *Designing tests for evaluating student achievement.* New York, NY: Longman.

Canter, L. (1996). First the rapport—then the rules. *Learning, 24*(5), 12+.

Canter, L., & Canter, M. (1992). *Lee Canter's Assertive Discipline: Positive behavior management for today's classroom.* Santa Monica, CA: Lee Canter and Associates.

Cantrell, S. C., Almasi, J. F., Carter, J. S., Rintamaa, M., & Madden, A. (2010). The impact of a strategy-based intervention on the comprehension and strategy use of struggling adolescent readers. *Journal of Educational Psychology, 102*, 257–280.

Capa, Y. (2005). *Novice teachers' sense of efficacy.* Doctoral dissertation, The Ohio State University, Columbus, OH.

Capon, N., & Kuhn, D. (2004). What's so good about problem-based learning? *Cognition and Instruction, 22*, 61–79.

Cariglia-Bull, T., & Pressley, M. (1990). Short-term memory differences between children predict imagery effects when sentences are read. *Journal of Experimental Child Psychology, 49*, 384–398.

Carnegie Council on Adolescent Development. (1995). *Great transitions: Preparing adolescents for a new century.* New York, NY: Carnegie Corporation of New York.

Carney, R. N., & Levin, J. R. (2000). Mnemonic instruction, with a focus on transfer. *Journal of Educational Psychology, 92*, 783–790.

Carney, R. N., & Levin, J. R. (2002). Pictorial illustrations *still* improve students' learning from text. *Educational Psychology Review, 14*, 5–26.

Carpendale, J. I. M. (2000). Kohlberg and Piaget on stages and moral reasoning. *Developmental Review, 20*, 181–205.

Carpenter, S. (2000). In the digital age experts pause to examine the effects on kids. *Monitor on Psychology, 31*(11), 48–49.

Carroll, J. B. (1997). The three-stratum theory of cognitive abilities. In D. P. Flanagan, J. L. Genshaft, & P. L. Harrison (Eds.), *Contemporary intellectual assessment: Theories, tests, and issues* (pp. 122–130). New York, NY: Guilford.

Carter, E. W., Wehby, J., Hughes, C., Johnson, S. M., Plank, D. R., Barton-Arwood, S. M., & Lunsford, L. B. (2005). Preparing adolescents with high-incidence disabilities for high-stakes testing with strategy instruction. *Preventing School Failure, 49*(2), 55–62.

Case, R. (1985). A developmentally-based approach to the problem of instructional design. In R. Glaser, S. Chipman, & J. Segal (Eds.), *Teaching thinking skills* (Vol. 2, pp. 545–562). Hillsdale, NJ: Erlbaum.

Case, R. (1992). *The mind's staircase: Exploring the conceptual underpinnings of children's thought and knowledge.* Mahwah, NJ: Erlbaum.

Case, R. (1998). The development of conceptual structures. In D. Kuhn & R. S. Siegler (Eds.), *Handbook of child psychology: Vol. 2: Cognition, perception, and language* (pp. 745–800). New York, NY: Wiley.

Casey, B. J., Getz, S., & Galvan, A. (2008). The adolescent brain. *Developmental Review, 28*, 62–77.

Cassady, J. C., & Johnson, R. E. (2002). Cognitive anxiety and academic performance. *Contemporary Educational Psychology 27*, 270–295.

Castellano, J. A., & Diaz, E. I. (Eds.). (2002). *Reaching new horizons. Gifted and talented education for culturally and linguistically diverse students.* Boston, MA: Allyn & Bacon.

Castle, S., Deniz, C. B., & Tortora, M. (2005). Flexible grouping and student learning in a high-needs school. *Education and Urban Society, 37,* 139–150.

Cattell, R. B. (1963). Theory of fluid and crystallized intelligence: A critical experiment. *Journal of Educational Psychology, 54,* 1–22.

Caughy, M. O., O'Campo, P. J., Randolph, S. M., & Nickerson, K. (2002). The influence of racial socialization practices on the cognitive and behavioral competence of African American preschoolers. *Child Development, 73,* 1611–1625.

Cazden, C. (2001). *Classroom discourse: The language of teaching and learning* (2nd ed.). Portsmouth, NH: Heinemann.

Ceci, S. J., & Roazzi, A. (1994). The effects of context on cognition: Postcards from Brazil. In R. J. Sternberg (Ed.), *Mind in context* (pp. 74–101). New York, NY: Cambridge University Press.

Center for American Progress. (2010, September 10). *Child poverty by the numbers: New data shows largest number of people in poverty on record.* Available online at: http://www.americanprogress.org/issues/2010/09/poverty_numbers.html

Centers for Disease Control. (2009). *Defining childhood overweight and obesity.* Retrieved from http://www.cdc.gov/obesity/childhood/defining.html

Centers for Disease Control. (2010). *Community report from the autism and developmental disabilities monitoring (ADDM) network.* Atlanta, GA: Author. Available online at: http://www.cdc.gov/ncbddd/autism/states/ADDMCommunityReport2009.pdf

Chamot, A. U., & O'Malley, J. M. (1996). The Cognitive Academic Language Learning Approach: A model for linguistically diverse classrooms. *The Elementary School Journal, 96,* 259–274.

Chan, C. K., & Sachs, J. (2001). Beliefs about learning in children's understanding of science texts. *Contemporary Educational Psychology, 26,* 192–210.

Chance, P. (1991). Backtalk: A gross injustice. *Phi Delta Kappan, 72,* 803.

Chance, P. (1992). The rewards of learning. *Phi Delta Kappan, 73,* 200–207.

Chance, P. (1993). Sticking up for rewards. *Phi Delta Kappan, 74,* 787–790.

Chang, L., Mak, M. C K., Li, T., Wu, B. P., Chen, B. B., & Lu, H. J. (2011). Cultural adaptations to environmental variability: An evolutionary account of East–West differences. *Educational Psychology Review, 23,* 99–129.

Chao, R. (2001). Extending research on the consequences of parenting style for Chinese Americans and European Americans. *Child Development, 72,* 1832–1843.

Chao, R., & Tseng, V. (2002). Parenting of Asians. In M. H. Bornstein (Ed.), *Handbook of parenting: Social conditions and applied parenting* (2nd ed., Vol. 4, pp. 59–93). Mahwah, NJ: Erlbaum.

Chapman, J. W., Tunmer, W. E., & Prochnow, J. E. (2000). Early reading-related skills and performance, reading self-concept, and the development of academic self-concept: A longitudinal study. *Journal of Educational Psychology, 92,* 703–708.

Charles, C. M. (2011). *Building classroom discipline* (10th ed.). Boston, MA: Allyn & Bacon.

Charmaraman, L., & Grossman, J. M. (2010). Importance of race and ethnicity: An exploration of Asian, Black, Latino, and multiracial adolescent identity. *Cultural Diversity and Ethnic Minority Psychology, 16,* 144–151.

Cheeseman Day, J., & Newburger, E. C. (2002). The big payoff: Educational attainment and synthetic estimates of work-life earnings. Washington DC: U.S. Bureau of the Census. Available online at: http://usgovinfo.about.com/od/moneymatters/a/edandearnings.htm

Chen, J. A., & Pajares, F. (2010). Implicit theories of ability of Grade 6 science students: Relation to epistemological beliefs and academic motivation and achievement in science. *Contemporary Educational Psychology, 35,* 75–87.

Chen, J.-Q. (2004) Theory of multiple intelligences: Is it a scientific theory? *Teachers College Record, 106,* 17–23.

Chen, L. H., Wu, C-H, Kee, Y. H., Lin, M-S., & Shui, S-H. (2009). Fear of failure, 2 × 2 achievement goal and self-handicapping: An examination of the hierarchical model of achievement motivation in physical education. *Contemporary Educational Psychology, 34,* 298–305.

Chen, Z., & Mo, L. (2004). Schema induction in problem solving: A multidimensional analysis. *Journal of Experimental Psychology: Learning, Memory, and Cognition, 30,* 583–600.

Chen, Z., Mo, L., & Honomichl, R. (2004). Having the memory of an elephant: Long-term retrieval and the use of analogues in problem solving. *Journal of Experimental Psychology: General, 133,* 415–433.

Chenoweth, K. (2010). Leaving nothing to chance. *Educational Leadership, 68*(3), 16–21.

Chi, M. T. H. (1978). Knowledge structures and memory development. In R. Siegler (Ed.), *Children's thinking: What develops?* (pp. 73–96). Hillsdale, NJ: Erlbaum.

Children's Defense Fund. (2005a). Child poverty. Washington, DC: Author.

Children's Defense Fund. (2005b, January). The minimum wage will not support a family of four. Washington, DC: Author.

Children's Defense Fund. (2008, June). Each day in America. Available online at: http://www.childrensdefense.org/site/PageServer?pagename=research_national_data_each_day.

Children's Defense Fund. (2010). *The state of America's children: 2010.* Washington DC: Author. Available online at: http://www.childrensdefense.org/child-research-data-publications/data/state-of-americas-children-2010-report.html

Chorzempa, B. F., & Graham, S. (2006). Primary-grade teachers' use of within-class ability grouping in reading. *Journal of Educational Psychology, 98,* 529–541.

Clark, C. M., & Peterson, P. L. (1986). Teachers' thought processes. In M. Wittrock (Ed.), *Handbook of research on teaching* (3rd ed.) (pp. 255–296). New York, NY: Macmillan.

Clark, D. B., Martin, C. S., & Cornelius, J. R. (2008). Adolescent-onset substance use disorders predict young adult mortality. *Journal of Adolescent Health, 42,* 637–639.

Clark, J. M., & Paivio, A. (1991). Dual coding theory and education. *Educational Psychology Review, 3,* 149–210.

Clark, K. (2009). The case for Structured English Immersion. *Educational Leadership, 66*(7), 42–46.

Clark, R., Anderson, N. B., Clark, V. R., & Williams, D. R. (1999). Racism as a stressor for African Americans. *American Psychologist, 54,* 805–816.

Clarke, J. H., & Agne, R. M. (1997). *Curriculum development; Interdisciplinary high school teaching.* Boston, MA: Allyn & Bacon.

Clifford, M. M. (1990). Students need challenge, not easy success. *Educational Leadership, 48*(1), 22–26.

Clifford, M. M. (1991). Risk taking: Empirical and educational considerations. *Educational Psychologist, 26,* 263–298.

Cobb, P., & Bowers, J. (1999). Cognitive and situated learning: Perspectives in theory and practice. *Educational Researcher, 28*(2), 4–15.

Cobley, S., McKenna, J., Baker, J., & Wattie, N. (2009). How pervasive are relative age effects in secondary school education? *Journal of Educational Psychology, 101,* 520–528.

Codell, E. R. (2001). *Educating Esme: Diary of a teacher's first year.* Chapel Hill, NC: Algonquin Books.

Coffield, F. J., Moseley, D. V., Hall, E., & Ecclestone, K. (2004). *Learning styles and pedagogy in post–16 learning: A systematic and critical review.* London, England: Learning and Skills Research Centre/University of Newcastle upon Tyne.

Cognition and Technology Group at Vanderbilt. (1996). Looking at technology in context: A framework for understanding technology and educational research. In D. Berliner & R. Calfee (Eds.), *Handbook of educational psychology* (pp. 807–840). New York, NY: Macmillan.

Cohen, A. B. (2009). Many forms of culture. *American Psychologist, 64,* 194–204.

Cohen, A. B. (2010). Just how many different forms of culture are there? *American Psychologist, 65,* 59–61.

Cohen, E. G. (1986). *Designing group work: Strategies for the heterogeneous classroom.* New York, NY: Teachers College Press.

Cohen, E. G. (1994). *Designing group work* (2nd ed.). New York, NY: Teachers College Press.

Cohen, M. R., & Graham, J. D. (2003). A revised economic analysis of restrictions on the use of cell phones while driving. *Risk Analysis, 23,* 5–17.

Coie, J. D., & Dodge, K. A. (1998). Aggression and antisocial behavior. In N. Eisenberg (Ed.), *Handbook of child psychology: Vol. 3. Social, emotional, and personality development* (5th ed., pp. 779–862). New York, NY: Wiley.

Cokley, K. O. (2002). Ethnicity, gender, and academic self-concept: A preliminary examination of academic disidentification and implications for psychologists. *Cultural Diversity and Ethnic Minority Psychology, 8,* 378–388.

Colangelo, N., Assouline, S. G. & Gross, M. U. M. (2004). *A nation deceived: How schools hold back America's brightest children* (Vols. 1& 2). The Connie Belin & Jacqueline N. Blank International Center for Gifted Education and Talent Development, College of Education, The University of Iowa, Ames, Iowa. Available online at: http://www.accelerationinstitute.org/Nation_Deceived/Get_Report.aspx

Cole, G. A., Montgomery, R. W., Wilson, K. M., & Milan, M. A. (2000). Parametric analysis of overcorrection duration effects: Is longer really better than shorter? *Behavior Modification, 24,* 359–378.

Cole, M. (1985). The zone of proximal development: Where culture and cognition create each other. In J. V. Wertsch (Ed.), *Culture, communication, and cognition: Vygotskian perspectives* (pp. 146–161). New York, NY: Cambridge University Press.

Coleman, J. S. (1966). *Equality of educational opportunity*. Washington, DC: U.S. Government Printing Office.

Colledge, E., Bishop, D. V. M., Koeppen-Schomerus, G., Price, T. S., Happe, F., Eley, T., … Plomin, R. (2002). The structure of language abilities at 4 Years: A twin study. *Developmental Psychology, 38*, 749–757.

Collins, A. (2006). Cognitive apprenticeship. In R. K. Sawyer (Ed.), *The Cambridge handbook of the learning sciences* (pp. 47–77). New York, NY: The Cambridge University Press.

Collins, A., Brown, J. S., & Newman, S. E. (1989). Cognitive apprenticeship: Teaching the crafts of reading, writing, and mathematics. In L. B. Resnick (Ed.), *Knowing, learning, and instruction: Essays in honor of Robert Galser* (pp. 453–494). Hillsdale, NJ: Erlbaum.

Collins, W. A., Maccoby, E. E., Steinberg, L., Hetherington, E. M., & Bornstein, M. H. (2000). Contemporary research on parenting: The case for nature and nurture. *American Psychologist, 55*, 218–232.

Colliver, J. A. (2000). Effectiveness of problem-based learning curricula: Research and theory. *Academic Medicine, 75*, 259–266.

Comadena, M. E., Hunt, S. K., & Simonds, C. J. (2007). The effects of teacher clarity, nonverbal immediacy, and caring on student motivation, affective and cognitive learning. *Communication Research Reports, 24*, 241–248.

Comer, J. P., Haynes, N. M., & Joyner, E. T. (1996). The School Development Program. In J. P. Comer, N. M. Haynes, E. T. Joyner, & M. Ben-Avie (Eds.), *Rallying the whole village: The Comer process for reforming education* (pp. 1–26). New York, NY: Teachers College Press.

Committee on Increasing High School Students' Engagement and Motivation to Learn. (2004). *Engaging schools: Fostering high school students' motivation to learn*. Washington, DC: The National Academies Press.

Confrey, J. (1990). A review of the research on students' conceptions in mathematics, science, and programming. *Review of Research in Education, 16*, 3–56.

Connell, R. W. (1996). Teaching the boys: New research on masculinity, and gender strategies for schools. *Teachers College Record, 98*, 206–235.

Conway, P. F., & Clark, C. M. (2003). The journey inward and outward: A re-examination of Fuller's concerns-based model of teacher development. *Teaching and Teacher Education 19*, 465–482.

Cook, C. R., Williams, K. R., Guerra, N. G., Kim, T. E., & Sadek, S. (2010). Predictors of bullying and victimization in childhood: A meta-analytic investigation. *School Psychology Quarterly, 25*, 65–83.

Cook, J. L., & Cook, G. (2009). *Child development: Principles and perspectives* (2nd ed.). Boston, MA: Allyn & Bacon.

Cooke, B. L., & Pang, K. C. (1991). Recent research on beginning teachers: Studies of trained and untrained novices. *Teaching and Teacher Education, 7*, 93–110.

Cooper, C. R. (1998). *The weaving of maturity: Cultural perspectives on adolescent development*. New York, NY: Oxford University Press.

Cooper, H. M. (2004). Special Issue: Homework. *Theory Into Practice, 43*(3).

Cooper, H. M., Robinson, J. C., Patall, E. A. (2006). Does homework improve academic achievement? A synthesis of research, 1987–2003. *Review of Educational Research, 76*, 1–62.

Cooper, H. M., & Valentine, J. C. (Eds.). (2001). Special Issue: Homework. *Educational Psychologist, 36*(3), Summer.

Cooper, H. M., Valentine, J. C., Nye, B., & Kindsay, J. J. (1999). Relationships between five after-school activities and academic achievement. *Journal of Educational Psychology, 91*, 369–378.

Copi, I. M. (1961). *Introduction to logic*. New York, NY: Macmillan.

Coplan, R. J., Prakash, K., O'Neil, K., & Armer, M. (2004). Do you "want" to play? Distinguishing between conflicted shyness and social disinterest in early childhood. *Developmental Psychology, 40*, 244–258.

Cordova, D. I., & Lepper, M. R. (1996). Intrinsic motivation and the process of learning: Beneficial effects of contextualization, personalization, and choice. *Journal of Educational Psychology, 88*, 715–730.

Cornelius-White, J. (2007). Learner-centered teacher–student relationships are effective: A meta-analysis. *Review of Educational Research, 77*, 113–143.

Corno, L. (2000). Looking at homework differently. *Elementary School Journal, 100*, 529–548.

Corno, L. (2008). On teaching adaptively. *Educational Psychologist, 43*, 161–173.

Corno, L. (2011). Studying self-regulation habits. In B. Zimmerman & D. Schunk (Eds.), *Handbook of self-regulation of learning and performance* (pp. 361–375) New York, NY: Routledge.

Corpus, J. H., McClintic-Gilbert, M. S., & Hayenga, A. O. (2009). Within-year changes in children's intrinsic and extrinsic motivational orientations: Contextual predictors and academic outcomes. *Contemporary Educational Psychology, 34*, 154–166.

Cota-Robles, S., Neiss, M., & Rowe, D. C. (2002). The role of puberty in violent and nonviolent delinquency among Anglo American, Mexican American and African American boys. *Journal of Adolescent Research*, 17, 364–376.

Cothran, D. J., & Ennis, C. D. (2000). Building bridges to student engagement: Communicating respect and care for students in urban high school. *Journal of Research and Development in Education, 33*(2), 106–117.

Covaleskie, J. F. (1992). Discipline and morality: Beyond rules and consequences. *The Educational Forum, 56*(2), 56–60.

Covington, M. V. (1992). Making the grade: A self-worth perspective on motivation and school reform. New York, NY: Holt, Rinehart, & Winston.

Covington, M. V., & Mueller, K. J. (2001). Intrinsic versus extrinsic motivation: An approach/avoidance reformulation. *Educational Psychology Review, 13*, 157–176.

Cowley, G., & Underwood, A. (1998, June 15). Memory. *Newsweek, 131*(24), 48–54.

Craik, F. I. M., & Lockhart, R. S. (1972). Levels of processing: A framework for memory research. *Journal of Verbal Learning and Verbal Behavior, 11*, 671–684.

Crawford, J. (1997). *Best evidence: Research foundations of the Bilingual Education Act*. Washington, DC: National Clearinghouse for Bilingual Education.

Creese, A. (2009). Building on young people's linguistic and cultural continuity: Complementary schools in the United Kingdom. *Theory Into Practice, 48*, 267–273.

Cremin, L. (1961). *The transformation of the school: Progressivism in American education, 1876–1957*. New York, NY: Vintage.

Crick, N. R., Casas, J. F., & Mosher M. (1997). Relational and overt aggression in preschool. *Developmental Psychology, 33*, 579–588.

Crisci, P. E. (1986). The Quest National Center: A focus on prevention of alienation. *Phi Delta Kappan, 67*, 440–442.

Crocker, J., & Park, L. E. (2004). Reaping the benefits of pursuing self-esteem without the costs. *Psychological Bulletin, 130*, 392–414.

Crone, D. A., & Horner, R. H. (2003). *Building positive behavior support systems in schools: Functional behavioral assessment*. New York, NY: The Guilford Press.

Crosnoe, R., Morrison, F., Burchinal, M., Pianta, R., Keating, D., Friedman, S. L., & Clarke-Stewart, K. A. (2010). Instruction, teacher–student relations, and math achievement trajectories in elementary school. *Journal of Educational Psychology, 102*, 407–417.

Cross, W. E. (1991). *Shades of black: Diversity in African-American identity*. Philadelphia, PA: Temple University Press.

Cross, W. E., Jr., & Cross, T. B. (2007). Theory, research, and models. In S. M. Quintana & C. McKown (Eds.), *Race, racism and developing child* (pp. 154–181). New York, NY: Wiley.

Crul, M., & Holdaway, J. (2009). Children of immigrants in schools in New York and Amsterdam: The factors shaping attainment. *Teachers College Record, 111*(6), 1476–1507.

Cummins, D. D. (1991). Children's interpretation of arithmetic word problems. *Cognition and Instruction, 8*, 261–289.

D'Agostino, J. V., & Powers, S. J. (2009). Predicting teacher performance with test scores and grade point average: A meta-analysis. *American Educational Research Journal, 46*(1), 146–182.

Daley, T. C., Whaley, S. E., Sigman, M. D., Espinosa, M. P., & Neumann, C. (2003). IQ on the rise: The Flynn Effect in rural Kenyan children. *Psychological Science, 14*(3), 215–219.

D'Amico, A., & Guarnera, M. (2005). Exploring working memory in children with low arithmetical achievement. *Learning and Individual Differences, 15*, 189–202.

Damon, W. (1994). Fair distribution and sharing: The development of positive justice. In B. Puka (Ed.), Fundamental research in moral development (pp. 189–254). *Moral development: A compendium, Vol. 2*. New York, NY: Garland Publishing.

Darcey, J. S., & Travers, J. F. (2006). *Human development across the lifespan* (6th ed.). New York, NY: McGraw-Hill.

Darling-Hammond, L., & Youngs, P. (2002). Defining "Highly Qualified Teachers": What does "Scientifically-Based Research" actually tell us? *Educational Researcher*, 13–25.

Darnon, C., Dompnier, B., Gillieron, O., & Butera, F. (2010). The interplay of mastery and performance goals in social comparison: A multiple-goal perspective. *Journal of Educational Psychology, 102*, 212–222.

Das, J. P. (1995). Some thoughts on two aspects of Vygotsky's work. *Educational Psychologist, 30*, 93–97.

DaSilva Idings, A. C. (2009). Bridging home and school literacy practices: Empowering families of recent immigrant children. *Theory Into Practice, 48*, 304–311.

Daunic, A. P., Smith. S. W., Brank, E. M., & Penfield, R. D. (2006). Classroom based cognitive-behavioral intervention to prevent aggression: Efficacy and social validity. *Journal of School Psychology, 44*, 123–139.

Davis, G. A., Rimm, S. B., & Siegle, D. (2011). *Education of the gifted and talented* (6th ed.). Boston, MA: Pearson.

Davis, H. A. (2003). Conceptualizing the role and influence of student–teacher relationships on children's social and cognitive development, *Educational Psychologist, 38*, 207–234.

Dawson-Tunik, T., Fischer, K. W., & Stein, Z. (2004). Do stages belong at the center of developmental theory? *New Ideas in Psychology, 22*, 255–263.

De Boer, H., Bosker, R. J., & van der Werf, M. P. C. (2010). Sustainability of teacher expectation bias effects on long-term student performance. *Journal of Educational Psychology, 102*, 168–179.

De Corte, E. (2003). Transfer as the productive use of acquired knowledge, skills, and motivations. *Current Directions in Psychological Research, 12*, 142–146.

De Corte, E., Greer, B., & Verschaffel, L. (1996). Mathematics learning and teaching. In D. Berliner & R. Calfee (Eds.), *Handbook of educational psychology* (pp. 491–549). New York, NY: Macmillan.

De Corte, E., & Verschaffel, L. (1985). Beginning first graders' initial representation of arithmetic word problems. *Journal of Mathematical Behavior, 4*, 3021.

De George, G. (2008). Is it language or is it special needs? Appropriately diagnosing English language learners having achievement difficulties. In L. S. Verplaetse & N. Migliacci (Eds.), *Inclusive pedagogy for English language learners: A handbook of research-informed practices* (pp. 277–303). New York, NY: Erlbaum.

de Kock, A., Sleegers, P., & Voeten, M. J. M. (2004). New learning and the classification of learning environments in secondary education. *Review of Educational Research, 74*(2), 141–170.

Dearing, E., Kreider, H., Simpkins, S., & Weiss, H. B. (2006). Family involvement in school and low-income children's literacy: Longitudinal associations between and within families. *Journal of Educational Psychology, 98*, 653–664.

Deaux, K. (1993). Commentary: Sorry, wrong number: A reply to Gentile's call. *Psychological Science, 4*, 125–126.

DeCecco, J., & Richards, A. (1974). *Growing pains: Uses of school conflicts*. New York, NY: Aberdeen.

deCharms, R. (1983). Intrinsic motivation, peer tutoring, and cooperative learning: Practical maxims. In J. Levine & M. Wang (Eds.), *Teacher and student perceptions: Implications for learning* (pp. 391–398). Hillsdale, NJ: Erlbaum.

Deci, E. L. (1975). *Intrinsic motivation*. New York, NY: Plenum.

Deci, E. L., Koestner, R., & Ryan, R. M. (1999). A meta-analytic review of experiments examining the effects of extrinsic rewards on intrinsic motivation. *Psychological Bulletin, 125*, 627–668.

Deci, E. L., & Ryan, R. M. (1985). *Intrinsic motivation and self-determination in human behavior*. New York, NY: Plenum.

Deci, E. L., & Ryan, R. M. (Eds.). (2002). *Handbook of self-determination research*. Rochester, NY: University of Rochester Press.

Deci, E. L., Vallerand, R. J., Pelletier, L. G., & Ryan, R. M. (1991). Motivation and education: The self-determination perspective. *Educational Psychologist, 26*, 325–346.

DeCuir-Gunby, J. T. (2009). A review of the racial identity development of African American adolescents: The role of education. *Review of Educational Research, 79*, 103–124.

Delazer, M., Ischebeck, A., Domahs, F., Zamarian, L., Koppelstaetter, F., Siednetoph, C. M., . . . Benke, T. (2005). Learning by strategies and learning by drill: Evidence from an fMRI study. *NeuroImage, 25*, 838–849.

Delpit, L. (1995). *Other people's children: Cultural conflict in the classroom*. New York, NY: The New York Press.

Delpit, L. (2003). Educators as "Seed People": Growing a new future. *Educational Researcher, 7*(32), 14–21.

Demetriou, A., Christou, C., Spanoudis, G., & Platsidou, M. (2002). The development of mental processing: Efficiency, working memory and thinking. *Monographs of the Society for Research in Child Development, 67*(1).

Demuth, K. (1990). Subject, topic, and Sesotho passive. *Journal of Child Language, 17*, 67–84.

Derry, S. J. (1992). Beyond symbolic processing: Expanding horizons for educational psychology. *Journal of Educational Psychology, 84*, 413–419.

Derry, S. J., Hmelo-Silver, C. E., Nagarajan, A., Chernobilsky, E., & Beitzel, B. (2006). Cognitive transfer revisited: Can we exploit new media to solve old problems on a large scale? *Journal of Educational Computing Research, 35*, 145–162.

Desautel, D, (2009). Becoming a thinking thinker: Metacognition, self-reflection, and classroom practice. *Teachers College Record, 111*, 1997–2020. http://www.tcrecord.org ID Number: 15504.

Deshler, D., & Schumaker, J. (2005). *Teaching adolescents to be strategic learners*. Thousand Oaks, CA: Corwin Press.

Dettmers, S., Trautwein, U, Lüdtke, O., Kunter, M., & Baumert, J. (2010). Homework works if homework quality is high: Using multilevel modeling to predict the development of achievement in mathematics. *Journal of Educational Psychology, 102*, 467–482.

Dewan, S. (2010, January 10). Southern schools mark two minorities. *New York Times*, p. A19+.

Dewey, J. (1896). The university school. *University Record (University of Chicago), 1*, 417–419.

Dewey, J. (1913). *Interest and effort in education*. Boston, MA: Houghton-Mifflin.

Diaz-Rico, L. T., & Weed, K. Z. (2002). *The cross-cultural, language, and academic development handbook* (2nd ed.). Boston, MA: Allyn & Bacon.

Dickinson, D., McCabe, A., Anastopoulos, L., Peisner-Feinberg, E., & Poe, M. (2003). The comprehensive language approach to early literacy: The interrelationships among vocabulary, phonological sensitivity, and print knowledge among preschool-aged children. *Journal of Educational Psychology, 95*, 465–481.

Dillon, S. (2011, August 8). Overriding a key education law: Waivers offered to sidestep a 100 percent proficiency rule. *New York Times*, A11.

Dingfelder, S. F. (2005). Closing the gap for Latino patients. *Monitor on Psychology, 36*(1), 58–61.

Dinnel, D., & Glover, J. A. (1985). Advance organizers: Encoding manipulations. *Journal of Educational Psychology, 77*, 514–522.

Dinsmore, D. L., Alexander, P. A., & Loughlin, S. M. (2008). Focusing the conceptual lens on metacognition, self-regulation, and self-regulated learning. *Educational Psychology Review, 20*, 391–409.

DiVesta, F. J., & Di Cintio, M. J. (1997). Interactive effects of working memory span and text comprehension on reading comprehension and retrieval. *Learning and Individual Differences, 9*, 215–231.

Dodge, K. A. (2011). Context matters in child and family policy. *Child Development, 82*, 433–442.

Dodge, K. A., & Pettit, G. S. (2003). A biopsychosocial model of the development of chronic conduct problems in adolescence. *Developmental Psychology, 39*, 349–371.

Doggett, A. M. (2004). ADHD and drug therapy: Is it still a valid treatment? *Child Health Care, 8*, 69–81.

Dolezal, S. E., Welsh, L. M., Pressley, M., & Vincent, M. (2003). How do nine third-grade teachers motivate their students? *Elementary School Journal, 103*, 239–267.

Doll, B., Zucker, S., & Brehm, K. (2005). *Resilient classrooms: Creating healthy environments for learning*. New York, NY: Guilford.

Domenech Rodriguez, M. M., Donovick, M. R., & Crowley, S. L. (2009). Parenting styles in a cultural context: Observations of protective parenting in first-generation Latinos. *Family Process, 48*(2), 195–210.

Dotterer, A. M., McHale, S. M., & Crouter, A. C. (2009). The development and correlates of academic interests from childhood through adolescence. *Journal of Educational Psychology, 101*, 509–519.

Doyle, W. (2006). Ecological approaches to classroom management. In C. Evertson & C. S. Weinstein (Eds.), *Handbook for classroom management: Research, practice, and contemporary issues*. Mahwah, NJ: Erlbaum.

Driscoll, MP. (2005). *Psychology of learning for instruction* (3rd ed.). Boston, MA: Allyn & Bacon.

Dubarry, M., & Alves de Lima, D. (2003). *Notes on Generation 1.5*. De Anza College, Cupertino, CA. Available online at: http://faculty.deanza.edu/alvesdelimadiana/stories/storyReader$438

DuBois, D. L., Burk-Braxton, C., Swenson, L. P., Tevendale, H. D., & Hardesty, J. L. (2002). Race and gender influences on adjustment in early adolescence: Investigation of an integrative model. *Child Development, 73*, 1573–1592.

Duell, O. K. (1994). Extended wait time and university student achievement. *American Educational Research Journal, 31*, 397–414.

Dufrene, B. A., Doggett, R. A., Henington, C., & Watson, T. S. (2007). Functional assessment and intervention for disruptive classroom behaviors in preschool and Head Start classrooms. *Journal of Behavioral Education, 16*, 368–388.

Duncan, G. J., & Brooks-Gunn, J. (2000). Family poverty, welfare reform, and child development. *Child Development, 71*, 188–196.

Duncan, R. M., & Cheyne, J. A. (1999). Incidence and functions of self-reported private speech in young adults: A self-verbalization questionnaire. *Canadian Journal of Behavioural Sciences, 31*, 133–136.

Duncker, K. (1945). On solving problems. *Psychological Monographs, 58*(5, Whole No. 270).

Dunn, K., & Dunn, R. (1978). *Teaching students through their individual learning styles*. Reston, VA: National Council of Principals.

Dunn, K., & Dunn, R. (1987). Dispelling outmoded beliefs about student learning. *Educational Leadership, 44*(6), 55–63.

Dunn, R., Dunn, K., & Price, G. E. (1989). *Learning Styles Inventory (LSI): An inventory for identification of how individuals in grades 3 through 12 prefer to learn.* Lawrence, KS: Price Systems.

Dunn, R., & Griggs, S. (2003). *Synthesis of the Dunn and Dunn Learning-Style Model Research: Who, what, when, where, and so what?* New York, NY: St. John's University.

Durbin, D. L., Darling, N., Steinberg, L., & Brown, B. B. (1993). Parenting style and peer group membership among European-American adolescents. *Journal of Research on Adolescence, 3,* 87–100.

Durik, A. M., & Harackiewicz, J. M. (2007). Different strokes for different folks: How individual interest moderates the effects of situational factors on task interest. *Journal of Educational Psychology, 99,* 597–610.

Durik, A. M., Vida, M., & Eccles, J. S. (2006). Task values and ability beliefs as predictors of high school literacy choices: A developmental analysis. *Journal of Educational Psychology, 98*(2), 382–393.

Dusenbury, L., & Falco, M. (1995). Eleven components of effective drug abuse prevention curricula. *Journal of School Health, 65,* 420–425.

Dweck, C. S. (2000). *Self-theories: Their role in motivation, personality, and development.* Philadelphia, PA: Routledge Press.

Dweck, C. S. (2002). The development of ability conceptions. In A. Wigfield & J. Eccles (Eds.), *The development of achievement motivation.* San Diego, CA: Academic Press.

Dweck, C. S. (2006). *Mindset: The new psychology of success.* New York, NY: Random House.

Dweck, C. S., & Bempechat, J. (1983). Children's theories on intelligence: Consequences for learning. In S. Paris, G. Olson, & W. Stevenson (Eds.), *Learning and motivation in the classroom* (pp. 239–256). Hillsdale, NJ: Erlbaum.

Dymond, S. K., Renzaglia, A., & Chun, E. (2007). Elements of effective high school service learning programs that include students with and without disabilities. *Remedial and Special Education, 28,* 227–243.

Ebbinghaus, H. (1964). *Memory* (H. A. Ruger & C. E. Bussenius, Trans.). New York, NY: Dover. (Original work published 1885)

Ebersbach, M. (2009). Achieving a new dimension: Children integrate three stimulus dimensions in volume estimations. *Developmental Psychology, 45,* 877–883.

Eccles, J. (2009) Who am I and what am I going to do with my life? Personal and collective identities as motivators of action. *Educational Psychologist, 44,* 78–89.

Eccles, J., & Wigfield, A. (1985). Teacher expectations and student motivation. In J. Dusek (Ed.), *Teacher expectancies* (pp. 185–226). Hillsdale, NJ: Erlbaum.

Eccles, J. & Wigfield, A. (2002). Motivational beliefs, values, goals. *Annual Review of Psychology, 53,* 109–132.

Eccles, J., Wigfield, A., & Schiefele, U. (1998). Motivation to succeed. In W. Damon (Series Ed.) & N. Eisenberg (Volume Ed.), *Handbook of child psychology: Vol. 3. Social, emotional, and personality development* (5th ed., pp. 1017–1095). New York, NY: Wiley.

Echevarria, J., & Graves, A. (2011). *Sheltered content instruction: Teaching English learners with diverse abilities* (4th ed.). Columbus, OH: Pearson.

Echevarria, M. (2003). Anomalies as a catalyst for middle school students' knowledge construction and scientific reasoning during science inquiry. *Journal of Educational Psychology, 95,* 357–374.

Egan, S. K., Monson, T. C., & Perry, D. G. (1998). Social-cognitive influences on change in aggression over time. *Developmental Psychology, 34,* 996–1006.

Ehrenfeld, T. (2001). Reflections on mirror neurons. *Observer: Association for Psychological Science, 24*(3), 11–13.

Eisenberg, N., & Fabes, R. A. (1998). Prosocial development. In W. Damon (Series Ed.) & N. Eisenberg (Vol. Ed.), *Handbook of child psychology: Vol. 3. Social, emotional, and personality development* (5th ed., pp. 701–778). New York, NY: Wiley.

Eisenberg, N., Shell, R., Pasernack, J., Lennon, R., Beller, R., & Mathy, R. M. (1987). Prosocial development in middle childhood: A longitudinal study. *Developmental Psychology, 23,* 712–718.

Eisenberg, R., Pierce, W. D., & Cameron, J. (1999). Effects of rewards on intrinsic motivation— Negative, neutral, and positive: Comment on Deci, Koestner, and Ryan (1999). *Psychological Bulletin, 125,* 677–691.

Eisner, E. W. (1999). The uses and limits of performance assessments. *Phi Delta Kappan, 80,* 658–660.

Elias, M. J., & Schwab, Y. (2006). From compliance to responsibility: Social and emotional learning and classroom management. In C. Evertson & C. S. Weinstein (Eds.), *Handbook for classroom management: Research, practice, and contemporary issues.* Mahwah, NJ: Erlbaum.

Elias, S. M., & MacDonald, S. (2007). Using past performance, proxy efficacy, and academic self-efficacy to predict college performance. *Journal of Applied Social Psychology, 37,* 2518–2531.

Elkind, D. (1981). Obituary—Jean Piaget (1896–1980). *American Psychologist, 36,* 911–913.

Ellerbrock, C. R., & Kiefer, S. M. (2010). Creating a ninth-grade community of care. *The Journal of Educational Research, 103,* 393–406.

Else-Quest, N. M., Hyde, J. S., & Linn, M. C. (2010). Cross-national patterns of gender differences in mathematics: A meta-analysis. *Psychological Bulletin, 136,* 103–127.

Embry, D. D. (2002). The Good Behavior Game: A best practice candidate as a universal behavior vaccine. *Clinical Child and Family Psychology Review, 5,* 273–297.

Emerson, M. J., & Miyake, A. (2003). The role of inner speech in task switching: A dual-task investigation. *Journal of Memory and Language, 48,* 148–168.

Emmer, E. T., & Aussiker, A. (1990). School and classroom discipline problems: How well do they work? In O. Moles (Ed.), *Student discipline strategies: Research and practice.* Albany, NY: SUNY Press.

Emmer, E. T., & Evertson, C. M. (1982). Effective classroom management at the beginning of the school year in junior high school classes. *Journal of Educational Psychology, 74,* 485–498.

Emmer, E. T., & Evertson, C. M., (2009). *Classroom management for middle and high school teachers* (8th ed.). Boston, MA: Allyn & Bacon.

Emmer, E. T., & Evertson, C. M., (2013). *Classroom management for middle and high school teachers* (9th ed.). Boston, MA: Allyn & Bacon.

Emmer, E. T., Evertson, C. M., & Anderson, L. M. (1980). Effective classroom management at the beginning of the school year. *Elementary School Journal, 80,* 219–231.

Emmer, E. T., & Gerwels, M. C. (2006). Classroom management in middle school and high school classrooms. In C. Evertson & C. S. Weinstein (Eds.), *Handbook for classroom management: Research, practice, and contemporary issues.* Mahwah, NJ: Erlbaum.

Emmer, E. T., & Stough, L. M. (2001). Classroom management: A critical part of educational psychology with implications for teacher education. *Educational Psychologist, 36,* 103–112.

Engle, R. W. (2001). What is working memory capacity? In H. Roediger, J. Nairne, I. Neath, & A. Suprenant (Eds.), *The nature of remembering: Essays in honor of Robert G. Crowder* (pp. 297–314). Washington, DC: American Psychological Association.

Entwistle, D. R., & Alexander, K. L. (1998). Facilitating the transition to first grade: The nature of transition and research on factors affecting it. *The Elementary School Journal, 98,* 351–364.

Epstein, J. L. (1989). Family structure and student motivation. In R. E. Ames & C. Ames (Eds.), *Research on motivation in education: Vol. 3. Goals and cognitions* (pp. 259–295). New York, NY: Academic Press.

Epstein, J. L. (1995). School/Family/Community partnerships: Caring for the children we share. *Phi Delta Kappan, 76,* 701–712.

Epstein, J. L., & MacIver, D. J. (1992). *Opportunities to learn: Effects on eighth graders of curriculum offerings and instructional approaches.* (Report No. 34). Baltimore, MD: Center for Research on Elementary and Middle Schools, Johns Hopkins University.

Epstein, J. L., & Van Voorhis, F. L. (2001). More than minutes: Teachers' roles in designing homework. *Educational Psychologist, 36,* 181–193.

Erdelyi, M. H. (2010). The ups and downs of memory. *American Psychologist, 65,* 623–633.

Ericsson, A. (2011, August). *Deliberate practice and the future of education and professional training.* Keynote address at the European Association for Research on Learning and Instruction, University of Exeter, UK.

Ericsson, K. A. (1999). Expertise. In R. Wilson & F. Keil (Eds.), *The MIT encyclopedia of the cognitive sciences* (pp. 298–300). Cambridge, MA: MIT Press.

Ericsson, K. A., & Charness, N. (1994). Expert performance: Its structure and acquisition. *American Psychologist, 49*(8), 725–747.

Ericsson, K. A., & Charness, N. (1999). Expert performance: Its structure and acquisition. In S. Ceci & W. Williams (Eds.), The nature-nurture debate: The essential readings. *Essential readings in developmental psychology.* Malden, MA: Blackwell.

Erikson, E. H. (1963). *Childhood and society* (2nd ed.). New York, NY: Norton.

Erikson, E. H. (1968). *Identity, youth, and crisis.* New York, NY: Norton.

Erikson, E. H. (1980). *Identity and the life cycle* (2nd ed.). New York, NY: Norton.

Evans, G. W. (2004). The environment of childhood poverty. *American Psychologist, 59,* 77–92.

Evans, L., & Davies, K. (2000). No sissy boys here: A content analysis of the representation of masculinity in elementary school reading texts. *Sex Roles, 42,* 255–270.

Evensen, D. H., Salisbury-Glennon, J. D., & Glenn, J. (2001). A qualitative study of six medical students in a problem-based curriculum: Toward a situated model of self-regulation. *Journal of Educational Psychology, 93*, 659–676.

Evertson, C. M., & Emmer, E. T. (2009). *Classroom management for elementary school teachers* (8th ed.). Boston, MA: Allyn & Bacon.

Evertson, C. M., & Emmer, E. T. (2013). *Classroom management for elementary school teachers* (9th ed.). Boston, MA: Allyn & Bacon.

Evertson, C. M., & Weinstein, C. S. (Eds.). (2006). *Handbook of classroom management: Research, practice, and contemporary issues.* Mahwah, NJ: Erlbaum.

Fabiano, G. A., Pelham, W. E., Coles, E. K., Gnagy, E. M., Chronis-Tuscano, A., & O'Connor, B. C. (2009). A meta-analysis of behavioral treatments for attention-deficit/hyperactivity disorder. *Clinical Psychology Review, 29*, 129–140.

Facione, P. A. (2011). *Think critically.* Boston, MA: Pearson.

Fantuzzo, J., Davis, G., & Ginsburg, M. (1995). Effects of parent involvement in isolation or in combination with peer tutoring on student self-concept and mathematics achievement. *Journal of Educational Psychology, 87*, 272–281.

Fast, L. A., Lewis, J. L., Bryant, M. J., Bocian, K. A., Cardullo, R. A., Rettig, M., & Hammond, K. A. (2010). Does math self-efficacy mediate the effect of the perceived classroom environment on standardized math test performance? *Journal of Educational Psychology, 102*, 729–740.

Feldman, J. (2003). The simplicity principle in human concept learning. *Current Directions in Psychological Science, 12*, 227–232.

Feldman, R. S. (2004). *Child development* (3rd ed.). Upper Saddle River, NJ: Prentice-Hall.

Fenton, D. F. (2007). The implications of research on expertise for curriculum and pedagogy. *Educational Psychology Review, 19*, 91–110.

Ferrer, E., & McArdle, J. J. (2004). An experimental analysis of dynamic hypotheses about cognitive abilities and achievement from childhood to early adulthood. *Developmental Psychology, 40*, 935–952.

Ferretti, R. P., Lewis, W. E., & Andrews-Weckerly, S. (2009). Do goals affect the structure of students' argumentative writing strategies? *Journal of Educational Psychology, 101*, 577–589.

Fillmore, L.W., & Snow, C. (2000). What teachers need to know about language. Available online at: http://citeseerx.ist.psu.edu/viewdoc/download?doi=10.1.1.92.9117&rep=rep1&type=pdf

Finkel, D., Reynolds, C. A., McArdle, J. J., Gatz, M., & Pedersen, N. L. (2003). Latent growth curve analyses of accelerating decline in cognitive abilities in adulthood. *Developmental Psychology, 39*, 535–550.

Fischer, K. W. (2009). Mind, brain, and education: Building a scientific groundwork for learning and teaching. *Mind, Brain, and Education, 3*, 2–16.

Fischer, M. A., & Gillespie, C. S. (2003). Computers and young children's development. *Young Children, 58*(4), 85–91.

Fiske, S. T. (1993). Social cognition and social perception. *Annual Review of Psychology, 44*, 155–194.

Fitts, P. M., & Posner, M. I. (1967). *Human performance.* Belmont, CA: Brooks Cole.

Fives, H. R., Hamman, D., & Olivarez, A. (2005, April). *Does burnout begin with student teaching? Analyzing efficacy, burnout, and*

support during the student-teaching semester. Paper presented at the Annual Meeting of the American Educational Research Association, Montreal, CA.

Flavell, J. H., Green, F. L., & Flavell, E. R. (1995). Young children's knowledge about thinking. *Monographs of the Society for Research in Child Development, 60*(1) (Serial No. 243).

Flavell, J. H., Miller, P. H., & Miller, S. A. (2002). *Cognitive development* (4th ed.). Upper Saddle River, NJ: Prentice-Hall.

Fleith, D. (2000). Teacher and student perceptions of creativity in the classroom environment. *Roeper Review, 22*, 148–153.

Fletcher, A., Bonell, C., & Hargreaves, J. (2008). School effects on young people's drug use: A systematic review of intervention and observational studies. *Journal of Adolescent Health, 42*, 209–220.

Floden, R. E. (2001). Research on effects of teaching: A continuing model for research on teaching. In V. Richardson (Ed.), *Handbook of research on teaching* (4th ed., pp. 3–16). Washington, DC: American Educational Research Association.

Flum, H., & Kaplan, A. (2006). Exploratory orientation as an educational goal. *Educational Psychologist, 41*, 99–110.

Ford, D. Y. (2000). *Infusing multicultural content into the curriculum for gifted students.* (ERIC EC Digest #E601). Arlington, VA: The ERIC Clearinghouse on Disabilities and Gifted Education.

Fox, E., & Riconscente, M. (2008). Metacognition and Self-Regulation in James, Piaget, and Vygotsky. *Educational Psychology Review, 20*, 373–389.

Francis, D. J., Lesaux, N., & August, D. (2006). Language of instruction. In D. August & T. Shanahan (Eds.), *Developing literacy in second language learners: Report of the national literacy panel on language-minority children and youth* (pp. 365–413). Mahwah, NJ: Erlbaum.

Frank, S. J., Pirsch, L. A., & Wright, V. C. (1990). Late adolescents' perceptions of their parents: Relationships among deidealization, autonomy, relatedness, and insecurity and implications for adolescent adjustment and ego identity status. *Journal of Youth and Adolescence, 19*, 571–588.

Franklin, J. (2007). Achieving with autism: Dispelling common misconceptions is essential for success. *Education Update, 49*(7), 1–9.

Fredricks, J. A., Blumenfeld, P. C., & Paris, A. H. (2004). School engagement: Potential of the concept, state of the evidence. *Review of Educational Research, 74*, 59–109.

Freeman, S. (2011). *Top 10 Myths About the Brain, How Stuff Works.* Available online at: http://health.howstuffworks.com/human-body/systems/nervous-system/10-brain-myths.htm

Freiberg, H. J., (in press). Classroom management and student achievement. In J. Hattie and E. Anderman (Eds.). *International Handbook of Student Achievement.* New York, NY: Routledge.

Freiberg, H. J., & Driscoll, A. (2005). *Universal teaching strategies* (4th ed.). Boston, MA: Allyn & Bacon.

Freiberg, H. J., & Lamb, S. M. (2009). Dimensions of person-centered classroom management. *Theory Into Practice, 48*, 99–105.

Freiberg, J. (2006). Research-based programs for preventing and solving discipline problems. In C. Evertson & C. S. Weinstein (Eds.), *Handbook for classroom management: Research,*

practice, and contemporary issues. Mahwah, NJ: Erlbaum.

Freisen, J. (2010, March 10). The hanging face of Canada: Booming minority populations by 2031. *The Globe and Mail: National.*

Frenzel, A. C., Goetz, T., Lüdtke, O., Pekrun, R., & Sutton, R. E. (2009). Emotional transmission in the classroom: Exploring the relationship between teacher and student enjoyment. *Journal of Educational Psychology, 101*, 705–716.

Frey, N., & Fisher, D. (2010). Reading and the brain: What early childhood educators need to know. *Early Childhood Education Journal, 38*, 103–110.

Frick, T. W. (1990). Analysis of patterns in time: A method of recording and quantifying temporal relations in education. *American Educational Research Journal, 27*, 180–204.

Friedman-Weieneth, J. L., Harvey, E. A., Young-swirth, S. D., & Goldstein, L. H. (2007). The relation between 3-year-old-children's skills and their hyperactivity, inattention, and aggression. *Journal of Educational Psychology, 99*, 671–681.

Friend, M. (2006). *Special education: Contemporary perspectives for school professionals.* Boston, MA: Allyn & Bacon.

Friend, M. (2011). *Special education: Contemporary perspectives for school professionals* (3rd ed.). Boston, MA: Allyn & Bacon/Pearson.

Friend, M., & Bursuck, W. D. (2002). *Including students with special needs* (3rd ed.). Boston, MA: Allyn & Bacon.

Friend, M., & Bursuck, W. D. (2009). *Including students with special needs: A practical guide for classroom teachers* (5th ed.). Boston, MA: Allyn & Bacon/Pearson.

Friend, M., & Bursuck, W. D. (2012). *Including students with special needs: A practical guide for classroom teachers* (6th ed.). Boston, MA: Allyn & Bacon/Pearson.

Frisbie, D. A. (2005). Measurement 101: Some fundamentals revisited. *Educational Measurement: Issues and Practices, 24*(2), 21–28.

Frost, J. L., Wortham, S. C., & Reifel, S. (2005). *Play and child development* (2nd ed.). Upper Saddle River, NJ: Prentice-Hall.

Fuchs, L. S., Fuchs, D., Compton, D. L., Rowell, S. R., Seethaler, P. M., Capizzi, A. M, … Fletcher, J. M. (2006). The cognitive correlates of third-grade skill in arithmetic, algorithmic, computation, and arithmetic work problems. *Journal of Educational Psychology, 98*, 29–43.

Fuchs, L. S., Fuchs, D., Hamlett, C. L., & Karns, K. (1998). High-achieving students' interactions and performance on complex mathematical tasks as a function of homogeneous and heterogeneous pairings. *American Educational Research Journal, 35*, 227–268.

Fulk, C. L., & Smith, P. J. (1995). Students' perceptions of teachers' instructional and management adaptations for students with learning or behavior problems. *The Elementary School Journal, 95*(5), 409–419.

Fuller, F. G. (1969). Concerns of teachers: A developmental conceptualization. *American Educational Research Journal, 6*, 207–226.

Fuller-Thomson, E., & Dalton, A. (2011, January 5) Suicidal ideation among individuals whose parents have divorced: Findings from a representative Canadian community survey. *Psychiatry Research.* Available online at: http://www.ncbi.nlm.nih.gov/pubmed/21251718

Furrer, C., & Skinner, E. (2003). Sense of relatedness as a factor in children's academic engagement and performance. *Journal of Educational Psychology, 95*(11), 148–161.

Gage, N. L. (1991). The obviousness of social and educational research results. *Educational Researcher, 20*(A), 10–16.

Gagné, E. D. (1985). *The cognitive psychology of school learning.* Boston, MA: Little, Brown.

Gagné, E. D., Yekovich, C. W., & Yekovich, F. R. (1993). *The cognitive psychology of school learning* (2nd ed.). New York, NY: Harper-Collins.

Galambos, S. J., & Goldin-Meadow, S. (1990). The effects of learning two languages on metalinguistic development. *Cognition, 34,* 1–56.

Gallagher, M. (2001, June 11). More on zero-tolerance in schools. *NewsMax.com.* Available online at: http://www.newsmax.com/archives/articles/2001/6/11/123253.shtml

Gallimore, R., & Goldenberg, C. (2001). Analyzing cultural models and settings to connect minority achievement and school improvement research. *Educational Psychologist, 36,* 45–56.

Galton, M., Hargreaves, L., & Pell, T. (2009). Group work and whole-class teaching with 11–14-year-olds compared. *Cambridge Journal of Education, 39,* 119–140.

Gamoran, A. (1987). The stratification of high school learning opportunities. *Sociology of Education, 60,* 135–155.

Gamoran, A., & Mare, R. D. (1989). Secondary school tracking and educational inequality: Compensation, reinforcement, or neutrality. *American Journal of Sociology, 94,* 146–183.

Ganis, G., Thompson, W. L., & Kosslyn, S. M. (2004). Brain areas underlying visual mental imagery and visual perception: An fMRI study. *Cognitive Brain Research, 20,* 226–241.

Garbarino, J., & deLara, E. (2002). *And words can hurt forever: How to protect adolescents from bullying, harassment, and emotional violence.* New York, NY: Free Press.

Garcia, E. E. (1992). "Hispanic" children: Theoretical, empirical and related policy issues. *Educational Psychology Review, 4,* 69–94.

Garcia, E. E. (2002). *Student cultural diversity: Understanding the meaning and meeting the challenge.* Boston, MA: Houghton Mifflin.

Garcia, S. B., & Tyler, B-J. (2010). Meeting the needs of English language learners with learning disabilities in the general curriculum. *Theory Into Practice, 49,* 113–120.

Gardner, H. (1975). *The shattered mind: The person after brain damage.* New York, NY: Knopf.

Gardner, H. (1983). *Frames of mind: The theory of multiple intelligences.* New York, NY: Basic Books.

Gardner, H. (1991). *The unschooled mind: How children think and how schools should teach.* New York, NY: Basic Books.

Gardner, H. (1993). *Creating minds: An anatomy of creativity seen through the lives of Freud, Einstein, Picasso, Stravinsky, Elliot, Graham, and Gandhi.* New York, NY: Basic Books.

Gardner, H. (1998). Reflections on multiple intelligences: Myths and messages. In A. Woolfolk (Ed.), *Readings in educational psychology* (2nd ed.) (pp. 61–67). Boston, MA: Allyn & Bacon.

Gardner, H. (2003, April 21). *Multiple intelligence after twenty years.* Paper presented at the American Educational Research Association, Chicago, IL.

Gardner, H. (2009). Birth and the spreading of a meme. In J-Q Chen, S. Moran, & H. Gardner (Eds.), *Multiple intelligences around the world* (pp. 3–16). San Francisco, CA: Wiley.

Gardner, H., & Moran, S. (2006). The science of multiple intelligences theory: A response to Lynn Waterhouse. *Educational Psychologist, 41,* 227–232.

Gardner, R., Brown, R., Sanders, S., & Menke, D. J. (1992). "Seductive details" in learning from text. In K. A. Renninger, S. Hidi, & A. Krapp (Eds.), *The role of interest in learning and development* (pp. 239–254). Hillsdale, NJ: Erlbaum.

Garmon, L. C., Basinger, K. S., Gregg, V. R., & Gibbs, J. C. (1996). Gender differences in stage and expression of moral judgment. *Merrill-Palmer Quarterly, 42,* 418–437.

Garner, P. W., & Spears, F. M. (2000). Emotion regulation in low-income preschool children. *Social Development, 9,* 246–264.

Garner, R. (1998). Choosing to learn and not-learn in school. *Educational Psychology Review, 10,* 227–238.

Garnets, L. (2002). Sexual orientations in perspective. *Cultural Diversity and Ethnic Minority Psychology, 8,* 115–129.

Garrison, J. (1995). Deweyan pragmatism and the epistemology of contemporary social constructivism. *American Educational Research Journal, 32,* 716–741.

Gathercole, S. E., Pickering, S. J., Ambridge, B., & Wearing, H. (2004). The structure of working memory from 4 to 15 years of age. *Developmental Psychology, 40,* 177–190.

Gay, G. (2000). *Culturally responsive teaching: Theory, research, and practice.* New York, NY: Teachers College Press.

Gay, G. (2006). Connections between classroom management and culturally responsive teaching. In C. Evertson & C. S. Weinstein (Eds.), *Handbook for classroom management: Research, practice, and contemporary issues.* Mahwah, NJ: Erlbaum.

Geary, D. C. (1995). Sexual selection and sex differences in spatial cognition. *Learning and Individual Differences, 7,* 289–303.

Geary, D. C. (1999). Evolution and developmental sex differences. *Current Directions in Psychological Science, 8,* 115–120.

Geary, D. C., & Bjorklund, D. F. (2000). Evolutionary developmental psychology. *Child Development, 7,* 57–65.

Gee, J. P., (2008). Learning and games. In K. Salen (Ed.), *The ecology of games: Connecting youth, games, and learning* (pp. 21–40). Cambridge, MA: The MIT Press, The John D. and Catherine T. MacArthur Foundation Series on Digital Media and Learning. doi:10.1162/dmal.9780262693646.021

Gehlbach, H. (2004). A new perspective on perspective taking: A multidimensional approach to conceptualizing an aptitude. *Educational Psychology Review, 16,* 207–234.

Geier, R., Blumenfeld, P., Marx, R., Krajcik, J., Fishman, B., & Soloway, E., & Clay-Chambers, J. (2008). Standardized test outcomes for students engaged in inquiry based science curriculum in the context of urban reform. *Journal of Research in Science Teaching, 45,* 922–939.

Gelman, R. (2000). The epigenesis of mathematical thinking. *Journal of Applied Developmental Psychology, 21,* 27–37.

Gelman, R., & Cordes, S. A. (2001). Counting in animals and humans. In E. Dupoux (Ed.), *Essay in honor of Jacques Mehler.* Cambridge, MA: MIT Press.

Gentner, D., Loewenstein, J., & Thompson, L. (2003). Learning and transfer: A general role for analogical encoding. *Journal of Educational Psychology, 95,* 393–408.

George, P. S. (2005). A rationale for differentiated instruction in the regular classroom. *Theory Into Practice, 44,* 185–193.

Gergen, K. J. (1997). Constructing constructivism: Pedagogical potentials. *Issues in Education: Contributions from Educational Psychology, 3,* 195–202.

Gersten, R. (1996a). The language-minority students in transition: Contemporary instructional research. *The Elementary School Journal, 96,* 217–220.

Gersten, R. (1996b). Literacy instruction for language-minority students: The transition years. *The Elementary School Journal, 96,* 217–220.

Gersten, R., Baker, S. K., Shanahan, T., Linan-Thompson, S., Collins, P., & Scarcella, R.. (2007). *Effective literacy and English language instruction for English learners in the elementary grades.* IES Practice Guide. Princeton, NJ: What Works Clearinghouse.

Gerwe, M., Stollhoff, K., Mossakowski, J., Kuehle, H-J., Goertz, U., Schaefer, C., . . . Heger, S. (2009). Tolerability and effects of OROS® MPH (Concerta ®) on functioning, severity of disease and quality of life in children and adolescents with ADHD: Results from a prospective, non-interventional trial. *Attention Deficit Hyperactive Disorder, 1,* 175–186.

Gess-Newsome, J. (2012). Pedagogical content knowledge. In J. Hattie & E. Anderman (Eds.), *International handbook of student achievement.* New York, NY: Routledge.

Gibson, D., Aldrich, C., & Prensky, M. (Eds.). (2006). *Games and simulations in online learning: Research and development frameworks.* Hershey, PA: Information Science Publishing.

Gillies, R. (2003). The behaviors, interactions, and perceptions of junior high school students during small-group learning. *Journal of Educational Psychology, 96,* 15–22.

Gillies, R. (2004). The effects of cooperative learning on junior high school students during small group learning. *Learning and Instruction, 14,* 197–213.

Gillies, R., & Boyle, M. (2011). Teachers' reflections of cooperative learning (CL): A two-year follow-up. *Teaching Education, 22,* 63–78.

Gilligan, C. (1982). *In a different voice: Psychological theory and women's development.* Cambridge, MA: Harvard University Press.

Gilligan, C., & Attanucci, J. (1988). Two moral orientations: Gender differences and similarities. *Merrill-Palmer Quarterly, 34,* 223–237.

Gini, G. (2008). Italian elementary and middle school students' blaming the victim of bullying and perception of school moral atmosphere. *The Elementary School Journal, 108,* 335–354.

Ginott, H. G. (1972). *Teacher and child: A book for parents and teachers.* New York, NY: Collier Books.

Ginsburg, K. R. (2007). The importance of play in promoting healthy child development and maintaining strong parent-child bonds. *Pediatrics, 119,* 182–191.

Glasgow, K. L., Dornbusch, S. M., Troyer, L., Steinberg, L., & Ritter, P. L. (1997). Parenting styles, adolescents' attributions, and educational outcomes in nine heterogeneous high schools. *Child Development, 68,* 507–523.

Glasser, W. (1969). *Schools without failure.* New York, NY: Harper & Row.

Glasser, W. (1990). *The quality school: Managing students without coercion.* New York, NY: Harper & Row.

Glassman, M. (2001). Dewey and Vygotsky: Society, experience, and inquiry in educational practice. *Educational Researcher, 30*(4), 3–14.

Gleitman, H., Fridlund, A. J., & Reisberg, D. (1999). *Psychology* (5th ed.). New York, NY: Norton.

Gluck, M. A., Mercado, E., & Myers, C. E. (2008). *Learning and memory: From brain to behavior.* New York, NY: Worth.

Godden, D. R., & Baddeley, A. D. (1975). Context-dependent memory in two natural environments: On land and underwater. *British Journal of Psychology, 66,* 325–331.

Goetz, T., Cronjaeger, H., Frenzel, A. C., Ludtke, O., & Hall, N. (2010). Academic self-concept and emotion relations: Domain specificity and age effects. *Contemporary Educational Psychology, 35,* 44–58.

Goetz, T., Frenzel, A. C., Hall, N. C., & Pekrun, R. (2008). Antecedents of academic emotions: Testing the internal/external frame of reference model for academic enjoyment. *Contemporary Educational Psychology, 33,* 9–33.

Goldenberg, C. (1996). The education of language-minority students: Where are we, and where do we need to go? *The Elementary School Journal, 96,* 353–361.

Goldman, S. R., Lawless, K., Pellegrino, J. W., & Plants, R. (2006). Technology for teaching and learning with understanding. In J. Cooper (Ed.), *Classroom teaching skills* (8th ed., pp. 104–150). Boston, MA: Houghton-Mifflin.

Goleman, D. (1995). *Emotional intelligence.* New York, NY: Bantam.

Golombok, S., Rust, J., Zervoulis, K., Croudace, T., Golding, J., & Hines, M. (2008). Developmental trajectories of sex-typed behavior in boys and girls: A longitudinal general population study of children aged 2.5–8 years. *Child Development, 79,* 1583–1593.

Gonzales, N., Moll, L. C., Floyd-Tenery, M., Rivera, A., Rendon, P., Gonzales, R., & Amanti, C. (1993). *Teacher research on funds of knowledge: Learning from households.* Washington, DC: The Georgetown University National Center for Research on Cultural Diversity and Second Language Learning. Available online at: http://www.ncela.gwu.edu/pubs/ncrcdsll/epr6.htm

Gonzalez, A. L. (2010, June). *Hispanics in the US: A new generation.* BBC News: US and Canada. Available online at: http://www.bbc.co.uk/news/10209099

Gonzalez, N., Moll, L. C., & Amanti, C. (2005). *Funds of knowledge: Theorizing practices in households and classrooms.* Mahwah, NJ: Erlbaum.

Gonzalez, V. (1999). *Language and cognitive development in second language learning: Educational implications for children and adults.* Boston, MA: Allyn & Bacon.

Gonzalez, V., Brusca-Vega, R., & Yawkey, T. (1997). *Assessment and instruction of culturally diverse students with or at-risk of learning problems: From research to practice.* Boston, MA: Allyn & Bacon.

Good, C., Aronson, J., & Inzlicht, M. (2003). Improving adolescents' standardized test performance: An intervention to reduce the effects of stereotype threat. *Journal of Applied Developmental Psychology, 24,* 645–662.

Good, T. L. (1983a). Classroom research: A decade of progress. *Educational Psychologist, 18,* 127–144.

Good, T. L. (1983b). Research on classroom teaching. In L. Shulman & G. Sykes (Eds.), *Handbook of teaching and policy* (pp. 42–80). New York, NY: Longman.

Good, T. L. (1988). Teacher expectations. In D. Berliner & B. Rosenshine (Eds.), *Talks to teachers* (pp. 159–200). New York, NY: Random House.

Good, T. L. (1996). Teaching effects and teacher evaluation. In J. Sikula (Ed.), *Handbook of research on teacher education* (pp. 617–665). New York, NY: Macmillan.

Good, T. L., & Brophy, J. E. (2008). *Looking in classrooms* (10th ed.). New York, NY: Longman.

Goodrich, H. (1997). Understanding rubrics. *Educational Leadership, 54*(4), 14–17.

Gordon, E. W. (1991). Human diversity and pluralism. *Educational Psychologist, 26,* 99–108.

Gordon, T. (1981). Crippling our children with discipline. *Journal of Education, 163,* 228–243.

Goswami, U. (2004). Neuroscience, education, and special education. *British Journal of Special Education, 31,* 175–183.

Gottlieb, G., Wahlsten, D., & Lickliter, R. (2006). The significance of biology for human development: A developmental psychobiological systems view. In R. M. Lerner (Ed.), *Handbook of child psychology* (6th ed., Vol. 1: Theoretical models of human development, pp. 210–257). New York, NY: Wiley.

Graham, S. (1991). A review of attribution theory in achievement contexts. *Educational Psychology Review, 3,* 5–39.

Graham, S. (1996). How causal beliefs influence the academic and social motivation of African-American children. In G. G. Brannigan (Ed.), *The enlightened educator: Research adventures in the schools* (pp. 111–126). New York, NY: McGraw-Hill.

Graham, S. (1998). Self-blame and peer victimization in middle school: An attributional analysis. *Developmental Psychology, 34,* 587–599.

Graham, S., & Weiner, B. (1996). Theories and principles of motivation. In D. Berliner & R. C. Calfee (Eds.), *Handbook of educational psychology* (pp. 63–84). New York, NY: Macmillan.

Gray, P. (2002). *Psychology* (4th ed.). New York, NY: Worth.

Gray, P. (2011). *Psychology* (6th ed.). New York, NY: Worth.

Gredler, M. E. (2005). *Learning and instruction: Theory into practice* (5th ed.). Boston, MA: Allyn & Bacon.

Gredler, M. E. (2009). Hiding in plain sight: The stages of mastery/self-regulation in Vygotsky's cultural-historical theory. *Educational Psychologist, 44,* 1–19.

Gredler, M. E. (2009). *Learning and instruction: Theory into practice* (6th ed.). Columbus, OH: Merrill.

Green, M., & Piel, J. A. (2010). *Theories of human development: A comparative approach* (2nd ed.). Boston, MA: Allyn & Bacon.

Greene, J. A., Muis, K. R., & Pieschl, S. (2010). The role of epistemic beliefs in students' self-regulated learning with computer-based learning environments: Conceptual and methodological issues. *Educational Psychologist, 45,* 245–257.

Greeno, J. G., Collins, A. M., & Resnick, L. B. (1996). Cognition and learning. In D. Berliner & R. Calfee (Eds.), *Handbook of educational psychology* (pp. 15–46). New York, NY: Macmillan.

Greenwald, A. G., Oakes, M. A., & Hoffman, H. G. (2003). Targets of discrimination: Effects of race on responses to weapons holders. *Journal of Experimental Social Psychology, 39,* 399–405.

Gregorc, A. F. (1982). *Gregorc Style Delineator: Development, technical, and administrative manual.* Maynard, MA: Gabriel Systems.

Griffins, P. E., & Gray, R. D. (2005). Discussion: Three ways to misunderstand developmental systems theory. *Biology and Philosophy, 20,* 417–425.

Grigorenko, E. L., Jarvin, L., Diffley III, R., Goodyear, J., Shanahan, E. J., & Sternberg, R. J. (2009). Are SSATs and GPA enough? A theory-based approach to predicting academic success in secondary school. *Journal of Educational Psychology, 101,* 964–981.

Grigorenko, E. L., & Sternberg, R. J. (2001). Analytical, creative, and practical intelligence as predictors of self-reported adaptive functioning: A case study in Russia. *Intelligence, 29,* 57–73.

Grolnick, W. S., Gurland, S. T., Jacob, K. F., & DeCourcey, W. (2002). The development of self-determination in middle childhood and adolescence. In A. Wigfield & J. Eccles (Eds.), *Development of achievement motivation* (pp. 147–171). New York, NY: Academic Press.

Gronlund, N. E., & Brookhart, S. M. (2009). *Gronlund's writing instructional objectives* (8th ed.). Columbus, OH: Pearson.

Gronlund, N. E., & Waugh, C. K. (2009). *Assessment of student achievement* (9th ed.). Columbus, OH: Pearson.

Gröschner, A., Seidel, T., & Shavelson, R. S. (2012). Methods for studying teacher and teaching effectiveness. In J. Hattie & E. Anderman (Eds.), *International handbook of student achievement.* New York, NY: Routledge.

Grossman, H., & Grossman, S. H. (1994). *Gender issues in education.* Boston, MA: Allyn & Bacon.

Grotevant, H. D. (1998). Adolescent development in family contexts. In N. Eisenberg (Ed.), *Handbook of child psychology: Vol 3. Social, emotional, and personality development* (5th ed.) (pp. 1097–1149). New York, NY: Wiley.

Guerra, N. G., Williams, K. R., & Sadek, S. (2011). Understanding bullying and victimization during childhood and adolescence: A mixed methods study. *Child Development, 82,* 295–310.

Guglielmi, R. S. (2008). Native language proficiency, English literacy, academic achievement, and occupational attainment in limited-English-proficient students: A latent growth modeling perspective. *Journal of Educational Psychology, 100,* 322–342.

Guilford, J. P. (1988). Some changes in the Structure-of-Intellect model. *Educational and Psychological Measurement, 48,* 1–4.

Gurian, M., & Henley, P. (2001). *Boys and girls learn differently: A guide for teachers and parents.* San Francisco, CA: Jossey-Bass.

Guskey, T. R. (1994). Making the grade: What benefits students? *Educational Leadership, 52*(2), 14–21.

Guskey, T. R. (2011). Five obstacles to grading reform. Educational Leadership, 69(3), 17-21.

Guskey, T. R., & Bailey, J. M. (2001). *Developing grading and reporting systems for student learning.* Thousand Oaks, CA: Corwin Press.

Guthrie, J. T., & Alao, S. (1997). Designing contexts to increase motivations of reading. *Educational Psychologist, 32,* 95–105.

Guthrie, J. T., Cox, K. E., Anderson, E., Harris, K., Mazzoni, S., & Rach, L. (1998). Principles of integrated instruction for engagement in reading. *Educational Psychology Review, 10,* 227–238.

Gutman, L. M., Sameroff, A., & Cole, R. (2003). Academic growth curve trajectories from 1st grade to 12th grade: Effects of multiple social risk factors and preschool child factors. *Developmental Psychology, 39*, 777–790.

Hacker, D. J., & Tenent, A. (2002). Implementing reciprocal teaching in the classroom: Overcoming obstacles and making modifications. *Journal of Educational Psychology, 94*, 699–718.

Haertel, E. H. (1999). Performance assessment and educational reform. *Phi Delta Kappan, 80*, 662–666.

Hagborg, W. J. (1993). Rosenberg Self-Esteem Scale and Harter's Self-Perception Profile for Adolescents: A concurrent validity study. *Psychology in Schools, 30*, 132–136.

Haier, R. J., & Jung, R. E. (2008). Brain imaging studies of intelligence and creativity: What is the picture for education? *Roeper Review, 30*, 171–180.

Hakuta, K. (1986). *Mirror of language: The debate on bilingualism.* New York, NY: Basic Books.

Hakuta, K., & Garcia, E. E. (1989). Bilingualism and education. *American Psychologist, 44*, 374–379.

Haladyna, T. H. (2002). *Essentials of standardized achievement testing: Validity and accountability.* Boston, MA: Allyn & Bacon.

Hall, L. J., Grundon, G. S., Pope, C., & Romero, A. B. (2010). Training paraprofessionals to use behavioral strategies when educating learners with autism spectrum disorders across environments. *Behavioral Interventions, 25*, 37–51.

Hall, V. C., Bailey, J., & Tillman, D. (1997). Can student-generated illustrations be worth ten thousand words? *Journal of Educational Psychology, 89*, 677–681.

Hallahan, D. P., & Kauffman, J. M. (2006). *Exceptional learners: Introduction to special education* (10th ed.). Boston, MA: Allyn & Bacon.

Hallahan, D. P., Kauffman, J. M., & Pullen, P. C. (2009). *Exceptional learners: Introduction to special education* (11th ed.). Boston, MA: Allyn & Bacon.

Hallahan, D. P., Lloyd, J. W., Kauffman, J. M., Weiss, M. P., & Martinez, E. A. (2005). *Introduction to learning disabilities* (5th ed.). Boston, MA: Allyn & Bacon.

Halpern, D. F., Benbow, C. P., Geary. D. C., Gur, R. C., Hyde, J. S., & Gernsbacher, M. A. (2007). The science of sex differences in science and mathematics. *Psychological Science in the Public Interest, 8*, 1–51.

Hamann, D. L., Baker, D. S., McAllister, P. A., & Bauer, W. I. (2000). Factors affecting university music students' perceptions of lesson quality and teaching effectiveness. *Journal of Research in Music Education, 48*, 102–113.

Hambrick, D. Z., Kane, M. J., & Engle, R. W. (2005). The role of working memory in higher-level cognition. In R. Sternberg & J. E. Pretz (Eds.), *Cognition and intelligence: Identifying the mechanisms of the mind* (pp. 104–121). New York, NY: Cambridge University Press.

Hamers, J. F., & Blanc, M. H. A. (2000). *Bilinguality and bilingualism* (2nd ed.). Cambridge, England: Cambridge University Press.

Hamilton, J. (2009). Multitasking teens may be muddling their brains. Available online at: http://www.npr.org/templates/story/story.php?storyId_95524385

Hamman, D., Berthelot, J., Saia, J., & Crowley, E. (2000). Teachers' coaching of learning and its relation to students' strategic learning. *Journal of Educational Psychology, 92*, 342–348.

Hammer, C. S., Lawrence, F. R., & Miccio, A. W. (2007). Bilingual children's language abilities and reading outcomes in Head Start and kindergarten. *Language, Speech and Hearing Services in Schools, 38*, 237–248.

Hamre, B. K., & Pianta, R. C. (2001). Early teacher–child relationships and the trajectory of children's school outcomes through eighth grade. *Child Development, 72*, 625–638.

Hanushek, E. A., Rivkin, S. G., & Kain, J. J. (2005). Teachers, schools and academic achievement, *Econometrica 73*, 417–458.

Hapgood, S., Magnusson, S. J., & Palincsar, A. S. (2004). Teacher, text, and experience: A case of young children's scientific inquiry. *The Journal of the Learning Sciences, 13*, 455–505.

Harackiewicz, J. M., Barron, K. E., Pintrich, P. R., Elliot, A. J., & Thrash, T. M. (2002). Revision of achievement goal theory: Necessary and illuminating. *Journal of Educational Psychology, 94*, 562–575.

Harackiewicz, J. M., & Linnenbrink, E. A. (2005). Multiple achievement goals and multiple pathways for learning: The agenda and impact of Paul R. Pintrich. *Educational Psychologist, 40*, 75–84.

Hardin, C. J. (2008). *Effective classroom management: Models and strategies for today's classrooms* (2nd ed.). Columbus, OH: Merrill/Prentice-Hall.

Hardman, M. L., Drew, C. J., & Egan, M. W. (2005). *Human exceptionality: Society, school, and family* (8th ed.). Boston, MA: Allyn & Bacon.

Harklau, L., Losey, K. M., & Siegal, M. (Eds.) (1999). *Generation 1.5 Meet college composition: Issues in the teaching of writing to U.S.-educated learners of ESL.* Mahwah, NJ: Lawrence Erlbaum Associates.

Harmer, C. S., Farkas, G., & Maczuga, S. (2010). The language and literacy development of Head Start children: A study using the family and child experiences survey database. *Language, Speech, and Hearing Services in Schools, 41*, 70–83.

Harp, S. F., & Mayer, R. E. (1998). How seductive details do their damage: A theory of cognitive interest in science learning. *Journal of Educational Psychology, 90*, 414–434.

Harris, J. R. (1998). *The nurture assumption: Why children turn out the way they do: Parents matter less than you think and peers matter more.* New York, NY: Free Press.

Harris, K. R., Alexander, P., & Graham, S. (2008). Michael Pressley's contributions to the history and future of strategies research. *Educational Psychologist, 43*, 86–96.

Harris, K. R., & Graham, S. (1996). Memo to constructivist: Skills count too. *Educational Leadership, 53*(5), 26–29.

Harris, M. A., Prior, J. C., & Koehoom, M. (2008). Age at menarche in the Canadian population: Secular trends and relationship to adulthood BMI. *Journal of Adolescent Health, 43*, 548–554.

Harris, P. L. (2006). Social cognition. In D. Kuhn & R. Siegler (Eds.), *Handbook of child psychology* (6th ed., Vol. 2). New York, NY: Wiley.

Harrow, A. J. (1972). *A taxonomy of the psychomotor domain: A guide for developing behavior objectives.* New York, NY: David McKay.

Harrower, J. K., & Dunlap, G. (2001). Including children with autism in general classrooms. *Behavior Modification, 25*, 762–784.

Harter, S. (1998). The development of self-representations. In N. Eisenberg (Ed.), *Handbook of child psychology: Vol. 3. Social, emotional, and personality development* (5th ed., pp. 553–618). New York, NY: Wiley.

Harter, S. (2003). The development of self-representation during childhood and adolescence. In M. R. Leary & J. P. Tangney (Eds.), *Handbook of self and identity* (pp. 610–642). New York, NY: Guilford.

Harter, S. (2006). The self. In W. Damon & R. M. Lerner (Series Eds.) *Social, emotional and personality development* (6th ed., pp. 646–718). New York, NY: Wiley.

Hartshore, J. K., & Ullman, M. T. (2006). Why girls say "holded" more than boys. *Developmental Science, 9*, 21–32.

Hartup, W. W., & Stevens, N. (1999). Friendships and adaptation across the lifespan. *Current Directions in Psychological Science, 8*, 76–79.

Hatfield, D. (2011). *The right kind of telling: An Analysis of feedback and learning in a journalism epistemic game.* Dissertation, University of Wisconsin-Madison.

Hattie, J., & Timperley, H. (2007). The power of feedback. *Review of Educational Research, 77*, 81–112.

Haugland, S. W., & Wright, J. L. (1997). *Young children and technology: A world of discovery.* Boston, MA: Allyn & Bacon.

Hawkins, M. R. (2004). Researching English language and literacy development in schools. *Educational Researcher, 33*(3), 14–25.

Hawley, W. D., & Nieto, S. (2010). Another inconvenient truth: Race and ethnicity matter. *Educational Leadership, 68*(3), 66–71.

Hayes, S. C., Rosenfarb, I., Wulfert, E., Munt, E. D., Korn, Z., & Zettle, R. D. (1985). Self-reinforcement effects: An artifact of social standard setting? *Journal of Applied Behavior Analysis, 18*, 201–214.

Heath, S. B. (1989). Oral and literate traditions among black Americans living in poverty. *American Psychologist, 44*, 367–373.

Hecht, S. A., & Vagi, K. J. (2010). Sources of group and individual differences in emerging fraction skills. *Journal of Educational Psychology, 102*, 843–859.

Helms, J. E. (1995). An update of Helms's White and People of Color racial identity models. In J. G. Ponterotto, J. M. Casas, L. A. Suzuki, & C. M. Alexander (Eds.), *Handbook of multicultural counseling* (pp. 181–198). Thousand Oaks, CA: Sage.

Helwig, C. C., Arnold, M. L., Tan, D., & Boyd, D. (2003). Chinese adolescents' reasoning about democratic and authority-based decision making in peer, family, and school contexts. *Child Development, 74*, 783–800.

Henderson, M. (1996). *Helping your students get the most of homework* [Brochure]. Chicago, IL: National Parent–Teacher Association.

Henry, B. (2011, May 2). Personal communication.

Herbert, E. A. (1998). Design matters: How school environment affects children. *Educational Leadership, 56*(1), 69–71.

Herman, J. (1997). Assessing new assessments: How do they measure up? *Theory Into Practice, 36*, 197–204.

Herman, J., & Winters. L. (1994). Portfolio research: A slim collection. *Educational Leadership, 52*(2), 48–55.

Herman, M. (2004). Forced to choose: Some determinants of racial identification in multiracial adolescents, *Child Development, 75*, 730–748.

Hetherington, E. M. (2006). The influence of conflict, marital problem solving and parenting on children's adjustment in nondivorced, divorced and remarried families. In A. Clarke-Stewart &

J. Dunn (Eds.), *Families count: Effects on child and adolescent development* (pp. 203–237). New York, NY: Cambridge University Press.

Hetherington, E. M., & Kelly, J. (2003). *For better or for worse: Divorce reconsidered*. New York, NY: W. W. Norton.

Hewstone, M. (1989). Changing stereotypes with disconfirming information. In D. Bar-Tal, C. Graumann, A. Kruglanski, & W. Stroebe (Eds.), *Stereotyping and prejudice: Changing conceptions* (pp. 207–223). New York, NY: Springer-Verlag.

Hickey, D. T. (2003). Engaged participation vs. marginal non-participation: A stridently sociocultural model of achievement motivation. *Elementary School Journal, 103*(4), 401–429.

Hickey, D. T., Kindfield, A. C. H., Horwitz, P., & Christie, M. A. (1999). Advancing educational theory by enhancing practice in a technology supported genetics learning environment. *Journal of Education, 181*, 25–55.

Hickey, D. T., Wolfe, E. W., & Kindfield, A. C. H. (2000). Assessing learning in a technology-supported genetics environment: Evidential and consequential validity issues. *Educational Assessment, 6*, 155–196.

Hidi, S., & Renninger, K. A. (2006). The four-phase model of interest development. *Educational Psychologist, 41*, 111–127.

Hidi, S., Renninger, K. A., & Krapp, A. (2004). Interest, a motivational variable that combines affective and cognitive functioning. In D. Y. Dai & R. J. Sternberg (Eds.), *Motivation, emotion, and cognition: Integrative perspectives on intellectual functioning and development* (pp. 89–115). Mahwah, NJ: Erlbaum.

Hilgard, E. R. (1996). History of educational psychology. In R. Calfee & D. Berliner (Eds.), *Handbook of educational psychology* (pp. 990–1004). New York, NY: Macmillan.

Hill, E. L., & Khanem, F. (2009). The development of hand preference in children: The effect of task demands and links with manual dexterity. *Brain and Cognition, 71*, 99–107. doi:10.1016/j.bandc.2009.04.006

Hill, H. C., Rowan, B., & Ball, D. L. (2005). Effects of teachers' mathematics knowledge for teaching on student achievement. *American Educational Research Journal, 42*, 371–406.

Hill, W. F. (2002). *Learning: A survey of psychological interpretations* (7th ed.). Boston, MA: Allyn & Bacon.

Hindi, E. R., & Perry, N. (2007). Elementary teachers' application of Jean Piaget's theories of cognitive development during social studies curriculum debates in Arizona. *The Elementary School Journal, 108*, 64–79.

Hines, C. V., Cruickshank, D. R., & Kennedy, J. J. (1985). Teacher clarity and its relation to student achievement and satisfaction. *American Educational Research Journal, 22*, 87–99.

Hines, M. (2004) *Brain gender*. New York, NY: Oxford University Press.

Hinnant, J. B., O'Brien, M, & Ghazarian, S. R. (2009). The longitudinal relations of teacher expectations to achievement in the early school years. *Journal of Educational Psychology, 101*, 662–670.

Hinton, C., Miyamoto, K., & Della-Chiesa, B. (2008). Brain research, learning and emotions: Implications for education research, policy and practice. *European Journal of Education, 43*, 87–103.

Hipsky, S. (2011). *Differentiated literacy and language arts strategies for the elementary classroom*. Columbus, OH: Merrill.

Hiroto, D. S., & Seligman, M. E. P. (1975). Generality of learned helplessness in man. *Journal of Personality and Social Psychology, 31*, 311–327.

Hirsch, E. D., Jr. (1996). *The schools we need: Why we don't have them*. New York, NY: Doubleday.

Hirvikoski, T., Waaler, E., Alfredsson, J., Pihlgren, C. Holmström, A., Johnson, A., . . . Nordström, A. L. (2011). Reduced ADHD symptoms in adults with ADHD after structured skills training group: Results from a randomized controlled trial. *Behavioural Research and Therapy, 49*, 175–185.

Hmelo, C. E. (1998). Problem-based learning: Effects on the early acquisition of cognitive skill in medicine. *Journal of the Learning Sciences, 7*, 173–208.

Hmelo-Silver, C. E. (2004). Problem-based learning: What and how do students learn? *Educational Psychology Review, 16*, 235–266.

Hmelo-Silver, C. E., Ravit, G. D., & Chinn, C. A. (2007). Scaffolding and achievement in problem-based and inquiry learning: A response to Kirschner, Sweller, and Clark (2006). *Educational Psychologist, 42*, 99–107.

Hobbs, R. (2004). A review of school-based initiatives in media literacy education. *American Behavioral Scientist, 48*, 42–59.

Hodges, E. V. E., & Perry, D. G. (1999). Personal and interpersonal antecedents and consequences of victimization by peers. *Journal of Personality and Social Psychology, 76*, 677–685.

Hoeffler, T. N., & Leutner, D. (2011). The role of spatial ability in learning from instructional animations – Evidence for an ability-as-compensator hypothesis. *Computers in Human Behavior, 27*, 209–216.

Hofer, M. (2010). Adolescents' development of individual interests: A product of multiple goal regulation? *Educational Psychologist, 45*(3), 149–166.

Hoff, E. (2006). How social contexts support and shape language development. *Developmental Review, 26*, 55–88.

Hofferth, S. L., & Sandberg, J. F. (2000). *Changes in American children's time, 1981–1997*. Ann Arbor, MI: University of Michigan Population Studies Center.

Hoffman, M. L. (2000). *Empathy and moral development*. New York, NY: Cambridge University Press.

Hoffman, M. L. (2001). A comprehensive theory of prosocial moral development. In A. Bohart & D. Stipek & (Eds.), *Constructive and destructive behavior* (pp. 61–86). Washington, DC: American Psychological Association.

Hogan, T., Rabinowitz, M., & Craven, J. A. III. (2003). Representation in teaching: Inferences from research of expert and novice teachers. *Educational Psychologist, 38*, 235–247.

Hoge, D. R., Smit, E. K., & Hanson, S. L. (1990). School experiences predicting changes in self-esteem of sixth- and seventh-grade students. *Journal of Educational Psychology, 82*, 117–126.

Holahan, C., & Sears, R. (1995). *The gifted group in later maturity*. Stanford, CA: Stanford University Press.

Hong, G., & Raudenbush, S. W. (2005). Effects of kindergarten retention policy on children's cognitive growth in reading and mathematics. *Educational Evaluation and Policy Analysis, 27*, 205–224.

Hoover-Dempsey, K. V., Battiato, A. C., Walker, J. M. T., Reed, R. P.,DeJong, J. M., & Jones, K. P. (2001). Parental involvement in homework. *Educational Psychologist, 36*, 195–209.

Horn, J. L. (1998). A basis for research on age differences in cognitive capabilities. In J. J. McArdle & R. W. Woodcock (Eds.), *Human cognitive theories in theory and practice* (pp. 57–87). Mahwah, NJ: Erlbaum.

Horovitz, B. (2002, April 22). Gen Y: A tough crowd to sell. *USA Today*, pp. B1–2.

Howe, M. J. A., Davidson, J. W., & Sloboda, J. A. (1998). Innate talents: Reality or myth? *Behavioral and Brain Sciences, 21*, 399–406.

Hoy, W. K., & Woolfolk, A. E. (1993). Teachers' sense of efficacy and the organizational health of schools. *Elementary School Journal, 93*, 355–372.

Hudley, C., & Novak, A. (2007). Environmental influences, the developing brain, and aggressive behavior. *Theory Into Practice, 46*, 121–129.

Hudley, C., Graham, S., & Taylor, A. (2007). Reducing aggressive behavior and increasing motivation in school: The evolution of an intervention to strengthen school adjustment. *Educational Psychologist, 42*, 251–260.

Huesmann, L. R., Moise-Titus, J., Podolski, C. P., & Eron, L. D. (2003). Longitudinal relations between children's exposure to TV violence and their aggressive and violent behavior in young adulthood: 1977–1992. *Developmental Psychology, 39*, 201–221.

Huguet, P., & Régner, I. (2007). Stereotype threat among schoolgirls in quasi-ordinary classroom circumstances. *Journal of Educational Psychology, 99*, 345–360.

Hulit, L., & Howard, M. (2006). *Born to talk: An introduction to speech and language development* (4th ed.). Boston, MA: Allyn & Bacon.

Hulleman, C. S., Godes, O., Hendricks, B. L., & Harackiewicz, J. M. (2010). Enhancing interest and performance with a utility value intervention. *Journal of Educational Psychology, 102*, 880–895.

Hung, D. W. L. (1999). Activity, apprenticeship, and epistemological appropriation: Implications from the writings of Michael Polanyi. *Educational Psychologist, 34*, 193–205.

Hunt, E. (2000). Let's hear it for crystallized intelligence. *Learning and Individual Differences, 12*, 123–129.

Hunt, J. McV. (1961). *Intelligence and experience*. New York, NY: Ronald.

Hunt, N., & Marshall, K. (2002). *Exceptional children and youth: An introduction to special education* (3rd ed.). Boston, MA: Houghton Mifflin.

Hunter, M. (1982). *Mastery teaching*. El Segundo, CA: TIP Publications.

Hurry, J., Nunes, T., Bryant, P., Pretzlik, U., Parker, M., Curno, C., & Midgley, L. (2005) Transforming research on morphology into teacher practice *Research Papers In Education, 20*(2), 187–206.

Hutchinson, N. L. (2009). *Inclusion of exceptional learners in Canadian classrooms: A practical handbook for teachers* (3rd ed.). Toronto, Canada: Prentice Hall.

Hyman, I., Kay, B., Tabori, A, Weber, M., Mahon, M., & Cohen, I. (2006). Bullying: Theory, research and interventions about student victimization. In C. Evertson & C. S. Weinstein (Eds.), *Handbook for classroom management: Research, practice, and contemporary issues*. Mahwah, NJ: Erlbaum.

IDEA. (1997). Available online at: http://www.ed.gov/policy/speced/guid/idea/idea2004.html

Idol, L. (2006). Toward inclusion of special education students in general education: A program evaluation of eight schools. *Remedial and Special Education, 27,* 77–94.

Iran-Nejad, A. (1990). Active and dynamic self-regulation of learning processes. *Review of Educational Research, 60,* 573–602.

Irvine, J. J. (1990). *Black students and school failure: Policies, practices, and prescriptions.* New York, NY: Praeger.

Irvine, J. J., & Armento, B. J. (2001). *Culturally responsive teaching: Lesson planning for elementary and middle grades.* New York, NY: McGraw-Hill.

Irvine, J. J., & Fraser, J. W. (1998, May). Warm demanders. *Education Week.* Available online at: http://www.edweek.org/ew/ewstory. cfm?slug=35irvine.h17&keywords=Irvine

Irving, O., & Martin, J. (1982). Withitness: The confusing variable. *American Educational Research Journal, 19,* 313–319.

Jackson, A., & Davis, G. (2000). *Turning points 2000: Educating adolescents in the 21st century.* New York, NY: Teachers College Press.

Jackson, L. A., von Eye, A., Biocca, F. A., Barbatsis, G., Zhao, Y., & Fitzgerald, H. E. (2006). Does home Internet use influence the academic performance of low-income children? *Developmental Psychology, 42,* 429–435.

Jacobs, J. E., Lanza, S., Osgood, D. W., Eccles, J. S., & Wigfield, A. (2002). Changes in children's self-competence and values: Gender and domain differences across grades one through twelve. *Child Development, 73,* 509–527.

Jaffee, S., & Hyde, J. S. (2000). Gender differences in moral orientation. *Psychological Bulletin, 126,* 703–726.

Jain, S., & Dowson, M. (2009), Mathematics anxiety as a function of multidimensional self-regulation and self-efficacy. *Contemporary Educational Psychology, 34,* 240–249.

James, W. (1890). *The principles of psychology* (Vol. 2). New York, NY: Holt.

James, W. (1912). *Talks to teachers on psychology: And to students on some of life's ideals.* New York, NY: Holt.

Jang, H., Reeve, J., & Deci, E. L. (2010). Engaging students in learning activities: It is not autonomy support or structure but autonomy support and structure. *Journal of Educational Psychology, 102,* 588–600.

Jang, H., Reeve, J., Ryan, R. M., & Kim. A. (2009). Can self-determination theory explain what underlies the productive, satisfying learning experiences of collectivistically oriented Korean students? *Journal of Educational Psychology, 101,* 644–661.

Jarrett, R. (1995). Growing up poor: The family experiences of socially mobile youth in low-income African American neighborhoods. *Journal of Adolescent Research, 10,* 111–135.

Jarrold, C., Tam, H., Baddeley, A. D., & Harvey, C. E. (2011). How does processing affect storage in working memory tasks? Evidence for both domain-general and domain-specific effects. *Journal of Experimental Psychology: Learning, Memory, and Cognition, 37,* 688–705.

Jaswal, V. K., & Markman, E. M. (2001). Learning proper and common names in inferential versus ostensive contexts. *Child Development, 72,* 787–802.

Jensen, E. (2009). *Teaching with poverty in mind: What being poor does to kids' brains and what schools can do about it.* Alexandria, VA: Association for Supervision and Curriculum Development.

Jensen, L. A., Arnett, J. J., Feldman, S. S., & Cauffman, E. (2002). It's wrong but everybody does it: Academic dishonesty among high school and college students. *Contemporary Educational Psychology, 27,* 209–228.

Jerome, E. M., Hamre, B. K., & Pianta, R. C. (2009). Teacher—child relationships from kindergarten to sixth grade: Early childhood predictors of teacher-perceived conflict and closeness. *Social Development, 18*(4), 915–945.

Jia, Y., Way, N., Ling, G., Yoshikawa, H., Chen, X., & Hughes, D. (2009). The influence of student perceptions of school climate on socioemotional and academic adjustment: A comparison of Chinese and American adolescents. *Child Development, 80,* 1514–1530.

Jimenez, R. (2000). Literacy and identity development of Latina/o students who are successful English readers: Opportunities and obstacles. *American Educational Research Journal, 37,* 971–1000.

Jimerson, S. R. (1999). On the failure of failure: Examining the association between early grade retention and education and employment outcomes during late adolescence. *Journal of School Psychology, 37,* 243–272.

Jimerson, S. R., Anderson, G. E., & Whipple, A. D. (2002). Winning the battle and losing the war: Examining the relation between grade retention and dropping out of high school. *Psychology in the Schools, 39,* 441–457.

Jimerson, S. R., & Ferguson, P. (2007). A longitudinal study of grade retention: Academic and behavioral outcomes of retained students through adolescence. *School Psychology Quarterly, 22,* 314–339.

Jitendra, A. K., Star, J. R., Starosta, K., Leh J. M., Sood, S., Caskie, G., … Mack, T. R. (2009). Improving seventh grade students' learning of ratio and proportion: The role of schema-based instruction. *Contemporary Educational Psychology, 34,* 250–264.

Johnson, A. (2003). Procedural memory and skill acquisition. In A. F. Healy & R. W. Proctor (Eds.), *Experimental psychology* (Vol. 4, pp. 499–523). New York, NY: Wiley.

Johnson, A. M., & Notah, D. J. (1999). Service learning: History, literature, review, and a pilot study of eighth graders. *The Elementary School Journal, 99,* 453–467.

Johnson, D. W., & Johnson, R. T. (1999). *Learning together and alone: Cooperation, competition, and individualization* (5th ed.). Boston, MA: Allyn & Bacon.

Johnson, D. W., & Johnson, R. T. (1999). The three Cs of school and classroom management. In H. J. Freiberg (Ed.), *Beyond behaviorism: Changing the classroom management paradigm* (pp. 119–144). Boston, MA: Allyn & Bacon.

Johnson, D. W., & Johnson, R. T. (2002). *Meaningful assessment: A meaningful and cooperative process.* Boston, MA: Allyn & Bacon.

Johnson, D. W., & Johnson, R. T. (2009a). An educational psychology success story: Social interdependence theory and cooperative learning. *Educational Researcher, 38,* 365–379.

Johnson, D. W., & Johnson, R. T. (2009b). Energizing learning: The instructional power of conflict. *Educational Researcher, 38,* 37–51.

Johnson, D. W., Johnson, R. T., Dudley, B., Ward, M., & Magnuson, D. (1995). The impact of peer mediation training on the management of school and home conflicts. *American Educational Research Journal, 32,* 829–844.

Johnson, M. H. (2003). Development of human brain functions. *Biological Psychiatry, 54,* 1312–1316.

Johnson, S. (2008, January 14). A childhood in poverty informs her teaching. *USA Today*, p. 7D.

John-Steiner, V., & Mahn, H. (1996). Sociocultural approaches to learning and development: A Vygotskian framework. *Educational Psychologist, 31,* 191–206.

Johnston, L. D., O'Malley, P. M., Bachman, J. G., & Schulenberg, J. E. (2011). *Monitoring the Future national results on adolescent drug use: Overview of key findings, 2010.* Ann Arbor, MI: Institute for Social Research, The University of Michigan.

Jonassen, D. H. (2003). Designing research-based instruction for story problems. *Educational Psychology Review, 15,* 267–296.

Jonassen, D. H. (2011). Ask systems: Interrrogative access to multiple ways of thinking. *Education Technology Research and Development, 59,* 159–175.

Jones, D. C. (2004). Body image among adolescent girls and boys: A longitudinal study. *Developmental Psychology, 40,* 823–835.

Jones, M. C. (1965). Psychological correlates of somatic development. *Child Development, 36,* 899–911.

Jones, M. G., & Gerig, T. M. (1994). Silent sixth-grade students: Characteristics, achievement, and teacher expectations. *Elementary School Journal, 95,* 169–182.

Jones, M. S., Levin, M. E., Levin, J. R., & Beitzel, B. D. (2000). Can vocabulary-learning strategies and pair-learning formats be profitably combined? *Journal of Educational Psychology, 92,* 256–262.

Jones, S. M., & Dindia, K. (2004). A meta-analytic perspective on sex equity in the classroom. *Review of Educational Research, 74,* 443–471.

Jurbergs, N., Palcic, J., & Kelly, M. L. (2007). School-home notes with and without response cost: Increasing attention and academic performance in low-income children with attention deficit/hyperactivity disorder. *School Psychology Quarterly, 22,* 358–379.

Jurden, F. H. (1995). Individual differences in working memory and complex cognition. *Journal of Educational Psychology, 87,* 93–102.

Jussim, L. (2012). Teachers' expectations. In J. Hattie & E. Anderman (Eds.), *International handbook of student achievement.* New York, NY: Routledge.

Jussim, L., & Harber, K. (2005). Teacher expectations and self-fulfilling prophecies: Knowns and unknowns; resolved and unresolved controversies. *Personality and Social Psychology Review, 9,* 131–135.

Jussim, L., Robustelli, S., & Cain, T. (2009). Teacher expectations and self-fulfilling prophecies. In A. Wigfield and K. Wentzel (Eds), *Handbook of motivation at school* (pp. 349–380). Mahwah, NJ: Erlbaum.

Kagan, J. (1976). Commentary on reflective and impulsive children: Strategies of information processing underlying differences in problem solving. *Monograph of the Society for Research in Child Development, 41*(5) (Ser. No. 168).

Kagan, J., & Herschkowitz, N. (2005). *A young mind in a growing brain.* Mahwah, NJ: Erlbaum.

Kagan, S. (1994). *Cooperative learning.* San Juan Capistrano, CA: Kagan Cooperative Learning.

Kail, R. (2000). Speed of processing: Developmental change and links to intelligence. *Journal of School Psychology, 38*, 51–61.

Kail, R., & Hall, L. K. (1999). Sources of developmental change in children's word-problem performance. *Journal of Educational Psychology, 91*, 600–668.

Kail, R., & Park, Y. (1994). Processing time, articulation time, and memory span. *Journal of Experimental Child Psychology, 57*, 281–291.

Kalyuga, S. (2011). Cognitive load theory: How many types of load does it really need? *Educational Psychology Review, 23*, 1–19.

Kalyuga, S., Chandler, P., Tuovinen, J., & Sweller, J. (2001). When problem solving is superior to studying worked examples. *Journal of Educational Psychology, 93*, 579–588.

Kalyuga, S., & Renkl, A. (2010). Expertise reversal effect and its instructional implications: Introduction to the special issue. *Instructional Science, 38*, 209–215.

Kanaya, T., Scullin, M. H., & Ceci, S. J. (2003). The Flynn effect and U.S. policies: The impact of rising IQ scores on American society via mental retardation diagnoses. *American Psychologist, 58*, 1–13.

Kanazawa, S. (2010). Evolutionary psychology and intelligence research. *American Psychologist, 65*(4), 279–289.

Kantor, H., & Lowe, R. (1995). Class, race, and the emergence of federal education policy: From the New Deal to the Great Society. *Educational Researcher, 24*(3), 4–11.

Kaplan, A., & Maehr, M. L. (2007). The contributions and prospects of goal orientation theory. *Educational Psychology Review, 19*, 141–184.

Kaplan, J. S. (1991). *Beyond behavior modification* (2nd ed.). Austin, TX: Pro-Ed.

Kardash, C. M., & Howell, K. L. (2000). Effects of epistemological beliefs and topic-specific beliefs on undergraduates' cognitive and strategic processing of dual-positional text. *Journal of Educational Psychology, 92*, 524–535.

Karpov, Y. V., & Bransford, J. D. (1995). L. S. Vygotsky and the doctrine of empirical and theoretical learning. *Educational Psychologist, 30*, 61–66.

Karpov, Y. V., & Haywood, H. C. (1998). Two ways to elaborate Vygotsky's concept of mediation implications for instruction. *American Psychologist, 53*, 27–36.

Katz, I., & Assor, A. (2007). When choice motivates and when it does not. *Educational Psychology Review, 19*, 429–442.

Katz, P. A. (2003). Racists or tolerant multiculturalists? How do they begin? *American Psychologist, 58*, 897–909.

Katz, S. R. (1999). Teaching in tensions: Latino immigrant youth, their teachers, and the structures of schooling. *Teachers College Record, 100*(4), 809–840.

Katzir, T., & Paré-Blagoev, J. (2006). Applying cognitive neuroscience research to education: The case of literacy. *Educational Psychologist, 4*, 53–74.

Kazdin, A. E. (2001). *Behavior modification in applied settings* (6th ed.). Belmont, CA: Wadsworth.

Kazdin, A. E. (2008). *The Kazdin method for parenting the defiant child*. Boston, MA: Houghton-Mifflin.

Keefe, J. W. (1982). Assessing student learning styles: An overview. In *Student learning styles and brain behavior*. Reston, VA: National Association of Secondary School Principals.

Keefe, J. W., & Monk, J. S. (1986). *Learning style profile examiner's manual*. Reston, VA: National Association of Secondary School Principals.

Keller, M., Neumann, K., & Fischer, H. E. (2012). Teacher enthusiasm and student learning. In J. Hattie & E. Anderman (Eds.), *International handbook of student achievement*. New York, NY: Routledge.

Keller, P., & El-Sheikh, M. (2011). Children's emotional security and sleep: Longitudinal relations and directions of effects. *Journal of Child Psychology and Psychiatry, 52*(1), 64–71. doi: 10.1111/j.1469-7610.2010.02263.x

Kemp, C., & Carter, M. (2006). The contribution of academic skills to the successful inclusion of children with disabilities. *Journal of Developmental and Physical Disabilities, 18*, 123–146.

Kerckhoff, A. C. (1986). Effects of ability grouping in British secondary schools. *American Sociological Review, 51*, 842–858.

Kiewra, K. A. (1985). Investigating notetaking and review: A depth of processing alternative. *Educational Psychologist, 20*, 23–32.

Kiewra, K. A. (1989). A review of note-taking: The encoding storage paradigm and beyond. *Educational Psychology Review, 1*, 147–172.

Kiewra, K. A. (2002). How classroom teachers can help students learn and teach them how to learn. *Theory Into Practice, 41*, 71–80.

Kim, J. S., & Guryan, J. (2010). The efficacy of a voluntary summer book reading intervention for low-income Latino children from language minority families. *Journal of Educational Psychology, 102*, 20–31.

Kim, K. M. (1998). Korean children's perceptions of adult and peer authority and moral reasoning. *Developmental Psychology, 5*, 310–329.

Kindsvatter, R., Wilen, W., & Ishler, M. (1992). *Dynamics of effective teaching* (2nd ed.). New York, NY: Longman.

King, A. (1990). Enhancing peer interaction and learning in the classroom through reciprocal questioning. *American Educational Research Journal, 27*, 664–687.

King, A. (1994). Guiding knowledge construction in the classroom: Effects of teaching children how to question and how to explain. *American Educational Research Journal, 31*, 338–368.

King, A. (2002). Structuring peer interactions to promote high-level cognitive processing. *Theory Into Practice, 41*, 31–39.

Kirk, S., Gallagher, J. J., & Anastasiow, N. J. (1993). *Educating exceptional children* (7th ed.). Boston, MA: Houghton Mifflin.

Kirk, S. A., Gallagher, J. J., Anastasiow, N. J., & Coleman, M. R. (2006). *Educating exceptional children* (11th ed.). Boston, MA: Houghton Mifflin.

Kirschner, P. A., Sweller, J., & Clark, R. E. (2006). Why minimal guidance during instruction does not work: An analysis of the failure of constructivist, discovery, problem-based, experiential, and inquiry-based teaching. *Educational Psychologist, 41*, 75–86.

Kirsh, S. J. (2005). Cartoon violence and aggression in youth. *Aggression and Violent Behavior, 11*, 547–557.

Kirst, M. (1991). Interview on assessment issues with James Popham. *Educational Researcher, 20*(2), 24–27.

Klahr, D., & Nigram, M. (2004). Equivalence of learning paths in early science instruction: Effects of direct instruction and discovery learning. *Psychological Science, 15*, 661–667.

Klassen, R. M. (2004). A cross-cultural investigation of the efficacy beliefs of South Asian immigrant and Anglo Canadian nonimmigrant early adolescents. *Journal of Educational Psychology, 96*, 731–742.

Klassen, R. M., & Chiu, M. M. (2010). Effects on teachers' self-efficacy and job satisfaction: Teacher gender, years of experience, and job stress. *Journal of Educational Psychology, 10*, 741–756. doi: 10.1037/a0019237

Klein, S. S., & Harris, A. H. (2007). A users guide to the Legacy Cycle. *Journal of Education and Human Development, 1*. Available online at: http://www.scientificjournals.org/journals2007/articles/1088.pdf

Kleinfeld, J. (2005). Culture fuels boys learning problems. *Alaska Daily News*, p. B6.

Kling, K. C., Hyde, J. S., Showers, C. J., & Buswell, B. N. (1999). Gender differences in self-esteem: A meta-analysis. *Psychological Bulletin, 125*, 470–500.

Klinger, J., & Orosco, M. J. (2010). This issue: Response to intervention. *Theory Into Practice, 49*, 247–249.

Knapp, M., Turnbull, B. J., & Shields, P. M. (1990). New directions for educating children of poverty. *Educational Leadership, 48*(1), 4–9.

Knapp, M. S., & Woolverton, S. (2003). Social class and schooling. In J. A. Banks & C. A. Banks (Eds.), *Handbook of research on multicultural education*. San Francisco, CA: Jossey-Bass.

Kohlberg, L. (1963). The development of children's orientations toward moral order: Sequence in the development of moral thought. *Vita Humana, 6*, 11–33.

Kohlberg, L. (1975). The cognitive-developmental approach to moral education. *Phi Delta Kappan, 56*, 670–677.

Kohlberg, L. (1981). *The philosophy of moral development*. New York, NY: Harper & Row.

Kohn, A. (1993). Rewards versus learning: A response to Paul Chance. *Phi Delta Kappan, 74*, 783–787.

Kohn, A. (1996a). *Beyond discipline: From compliance to community*. Alexandria, VA: Association for Supervision and Curriculum Development.

Kohn, A. (1996b). By all available means: Cameron and Pierce's defense of extrinsic motivators. *Review of Educational Research, 66*, 1–4.

Kohn, A. (2005). Unconditional teaching. *Educational Leadership, 62*, 12–17.

Kohn, A. (2006). *The homework myth: Why our kids get too much of a bad thing*. Cambridge, MA: Da Capo Press.

Kokko, K., & Pulkkinen, L. (2000). Aggression in childhood and long-term unemployment in adulthood: A cycle of maladaptation and some protective factors. *Developmental Psychology, 36*, 463–472.

Kolb, G., & Whishaw, I. Q. (1998). Brain plasticity and behavior. In J. T. Spence, J. M. Darley, & D. J. Foss (Eds.), *Annual review of psychology* (pp. 43–64). Palo Alto, CA: Annual Reviews.

Koppleman, K. L. (2011). *Understanding human differences: Multicultural education for a diverse America* (3rd ed.). Boston, MA: Pearson.

Korf, R. (1999). Heuristic search. In R. Wilson & F. Keil (Eds.), *The MIT encyclopedia of the cognitive sciences* (pp. 372–373). Cambridge, MA: MIT Press.

Koriat, A., Goldsmith, M., & Pansky, A. (2000). Toward a psychology of memory accuracy. In S. Fiske (Ed.), *Annual review of psychology* (pp. 481–537). Palo Alto, CA: Annual Reviews.

Kornhaber, M., Fierros, E., & Veenema, S. (2004). *Multiple intelligences: Best ideas for research and practice*. Boston, MA: Allyn & Bacon.

Kosslyn, S. M., & Koenig, O. (1992). *Wet mind: The new cognitive neuroscience*. New York, NY: Free Press.

Kounin, J. S. (1970). *Discipline and group management in classrooms*. New York, NY: Holt, Rinehart & Winston.

Kozulin, A. (1990). *Vygotsky's psychology: A biography of ideas*. Cambridge, MA: Harvard University Press.

Kozulin, A., (2003). Psychological tools and mediated learning. In A. Kouzlin, B. Gindis, V. Ageyev, & S. M. Miller (Eds.), *Vygotsky's educational theory in cultural context* (pp. 15–38). Cambridge, UK: Cambridge University Press.

Kozulin, A. (Ed.). (2003). *Vygotsky's educational theory in cultural context*. Cambridge, UK: Cambridge University Press.

Kozulin, A., & Presseisen, B. Z. (1995). Mediated learning experience and psychological tools: Vygotsky's and Feuerstein's perspectives in a study of student learning. *Educational Psychologist, 30*, 67–75.

Krajcik, J., & Czerniak, C. (2007). *Teaching science in elementary and middle school classrooms: A project-based approach* (3rd ed.). Mahwah, NJ: Erlbaum.

Kratchovil, C. J. (2009). Current pharmacotherapy for ADHD. 2nd International Congress on ADHD. From Childhood to Adult Disease. May 21-24, 2009, Vienna, Austria. *Attention Deficit and Hyperactivity Disorders, 1*: 61.

Krathwohl, D. R., Bloom, B. S., & Masia, B. B. (1964). *Taxonomy of educational objectives. Handbook II: Affective domain*. New York, NY: David McKay.

Kratzig, G. P., & Arbuthnott, K. D. (2006). Perceptual learning style and learning proficiency: A test of the hypothesis. *Journal of Educational Psychology, 98*, 238–246.

Krauss, M. (1992). Statement of Michael Krauss, representing the Linguistic Society of America. In U.S. Senate, *Native American Languages Act of 1991: Hearing before the Select Committee onIndian Affairs* (pp. 18–22). Washington, DC: U.S. Government Printing Office.

Kreitzer, A. E., & Madaus, G. F. (1994). Empirical investigations of the hierarchical structure of the taxonomy. In L. W. Anderson & L. A. Sosniak (Eds.), *Bloom's taxonomy: A forty-year retrospective*. Ninety-third yearbook for the National Society for the Study of Education: Part II (pp. 64–81). Chicago, IL: University of Chicago Press.

Kroger, J. (2000). *Identity development: Adolescence through adulthood*. Thousand Oaks, CA: Sage.

Kronholz, J. (2011), Challenging the gifted: Nuclear chemistry and Sartre draw the best and brightest to Reno. *Education Next, 11*(2), 1-8. Available online at: http://educationnext.org/challenging-the-gifted/

Krumboltz, J. D., & Yeh, C. J. (1996). Competitive grading sabotages good teaching. *Phi Delta Kappan, 78*, 324–326.

Kuhn, D. (2007). Is direct instruction an answer to the right question? *Educational Psychologist, 42*, 109–113.

Kuhn, D., & Dean, D. (2004). Connecting scientific reasoning with casual inference. *Journal of Cognition and Development, 5*, 261–288.

Kuhn, D., & Franklin, S. (2006). The second decade: What develops (and how). In D. Kuhn &

R. S. Siegler (Eds.), *Cognition, perception, and language* (6th ed., Vol. 2, pp. 953–993). New York, NY: Wiley.

Kuhn, D., Goh, W., Iordanou, K., & Shaenfield, D. (2008). Arguing on the computer: A microgenetic study of developing argument skills in a computer-supported environment. *Child Development, 79*, 1310–1328.

Kuklinski, M. R., & Weinstein, R. S. (2001). Classroom and developmental differences in a path model of teacher expectancy effects. *Child Development, 72*, 1554–1578.

Kulik, J. A., & Kulik, C. L. (1997). Ability grouping. In N. Colangelo & G. Davis (Eds.), *Handbook of gifted education* (2nd ed., pp. 230–242). Boston, MA: Allyn & Bacon.

Kumar, D. D., & Sherwood, R. D. (2007). Effect of problem-based simulation on the conceptual understanding of undergraduate science educational majors. *Journal of Science Education and Technology, 16*, 239–246.

Kuo, L., & Anderson, R. C. (2006). Morphological awareness and learning to read: A cross-language perspective. *Educational Psychologist, 41*, 161–180.

Lachter, J., Forster, K. I., & Ruthruff, K. I. (2004). Forty-five years after Broadbent (1958): Still no identification without attention. *Psychological Review, 111*, 880–913.

Ladson-Billings, G. (1990). Like lightning in a bottle: Attempting to capture the pedagogical excellence of successful teachers of Black students. *Qualitative Studies in Education, 3*, 335–344.

Ladson-Billings, G. (1992). Culturally relevant teaching: The key to making multicultural education work. In C. A. Grant (Ed.), *Research and multicultural education* (pp. 106–121). London: Falmer Press.

Ladson-Billings, G. (1994). *The dream keepers*. San Francisco, CA: Jossey-Bass.

Ladson-Billings, G. (1995). But that is just good teaching! The case for culturally relevant pedagogy. *Theory Into Practice, 34*, 161–165.

Ladson-Billings, G. (2004). Landing on the wrong note: The price we paid for Brown. *Educational Researcher, 33*(7), 3–13.

Lamb, M. E., & Lewis, C. (2005). The role of parent-child relationships in child development. In M. H. Bornstein & M. E. Lamb (Eds.), *Developmental science: An advanced textbook* (5th ed., pp. 429–468). Mahwah, NJ: Erlbaum.

Lambert, N. M. (1994). Seating arrangement in classrooms. *The International Encyclopedia of Education* (2nd ed.) 9, 5355–5359.

Landrum, T. J., & Kauffman, J. M. (2006). Behavioral approaches to classroom management. In C. M. Evertson & C. S. Weinstein (Eds.), *Handbook of classroom management: Research, practice, and contemporary issues*. Mahwah, NJ: Erlbaum.

Lane, K., Falk, K., & Wehby, J. (2006). Classroom management in special education classrooms and resource rooms. In C. M. Evertson & C. S. Weinstein (Eds.), *Handbook of classroom management: Research, practice, and contemporary issues*. Mahwah, NJ: Erlbaum.

Langan-Fox, J., Waycott, J. L., & Albert, K. (2000). Linear and graphic organizers: Properties and processing. *International Journal of Cognitive Ergonomics, 4*(1), 19–34.

Lashley, T. J., II, Matczynski, T. J., & Rowley, J. B. (2002). *Instructional models: Strategies for teaching in a diverse society* (2nd ed.). Belmont, CA: Wadsworth/ Thomson Learning.

Lather, P. (2004). Scientific research in education: A critical perspective. *Journal of Curriculum and Supervision, 20*, 14–30.

Lave, J. (1988). *Cognition in practice: Mind, mathematics, and culture in everyday life*. New York, NY: Cambridge University Press.

Lave, J. (1997). The culture of acquisition and the practice of understanding. In D. Kirshner & J. A. Whitson (Eds.), *Situated cognition: Social, semiotic, and psychological perspectives* (pp. 17–35). Mahwah, NJ: Erlbaum.

Lave, J., & Wenger, E. (1991). *Situated learning: Legitimate peripheral participation*. Cambridge, MA: Cambridge University Press.

Leaper, C. (2002). Parenting girls and boys. In M. H. Bornstein (Ed.), *Handbook of parenting, Vol. 1: Children and parenting* (2nd ed., pp. 127–152). Mahwah, NJ: Erlbaum.

Leaper, C., & Smith, T. S. (2004). A meta-analytic review of gender variations in children's language use: Talkativeness, affiliative speech, and assertive speech. *Developmental Psychology, 40*, 993–1027.

Lee, A. Y., & Hutchinson, L. (1998). Improving learning from examples through reflection. *Journal of Experimental Psychology: Applied, 4*, 187–210.

Lee, C. (2008). Synthesis of research on the role of culture in learning among African American youth: The contributions of Asa G. Hilliard, III. *Review of Educational Research, 78*, 797–827.

Lee, J., & Shute, V. J. (2010). Personal and social-contextual factors in K–12 academic performance: An integrative perspective on student learning, *Educational Psychologist, 45*, 185–202.

Lee, K., Ng, E. L., & Ng, S. F. (2009). The contributions of working memory and executive functioning to problem representation and solution generation in algebraic word problems. *Journal of Educational Psychology, 101*, 373–387.

Lee, R. M. (2005). Resilience against discrimination: Ethnic identity and other-group orientation as protective factors for Korean Americans. *Journal of Counseling Psychology, 52*, 36–44.

Lee, S. J. (2004). Model minorities and perpetual foreigners: The impact of stereotyping on Asian American students. In M. Sadowski (Ed.), *Adolescents at school: Perspectives on youth, identity, and education* (pp. 41–49). Cambridge, MA: Harvard University Press.

Lee, S. J., Wong, N-W. A., & Alvarez, A. N. (2008). The model minority and the perpetual foreigner: Stereotypes of Asian Americans. In N. Tewari & A. Alvarez (Eds.), *Asian American psychology: Current perspectives* (pp. 69–84). Boca Raton, FL: CRC Press.

Lefton, L. (1994). *Psychology* (5th ed.). Boston, MA: Allyn & Bacon.

Lehman, D. R., & Nisbett, R. E. (1990). A longitudinal study of the effects of undergraduate training on reasoning. *Developmental Psychology, 26*, 952–960.

Leinhardt, G. (2001). Instructional explanations: A commonplace for teaching and location for contrasts. In V. Richardson (Ed.), *Handbook of research on teaching* (4th ed., pp. 333–357). Washington, DC: American Educational Research Association.

LeMahieu, P., Gitomer, D. H., & Eresh, J. T. (1993). *Portfolios in large-scale assessment: Difficult but not impossible*. Unpublished manuscript, University of Delaware.

Lemelson, R. (2003). Obsessive-compulsive disorder in Bali. *Transcultural Psychiatry, 40*, 377–408.

Leming, J. S. (1981). Curriculum effectiveness in value/moral education. *Journal of Moral Education, 10,* 147–164.

Lenhart, A. (2010). *Teens, cell phones and /texting: Text messages become the centerpiece communication.* Washington, DC: Pew Research Center. Available online at: http://pewresearch.org/pubs/1572/teens-cell-phones-text-messages

Lepper, M. R., & Greene, D. (1978). *The hidden costs of rewards: New perspectives on the psychology of human motivation.* Hillsdale, NJ: Erlbaum.

Lepper, M. R., Keavney, M., & Drake, M. (1996). Intrinsic motivation and extrinsic reward: A commentary on Cameron and Pierce's meta-analysis. *Review of Educational Research, 66,* 5–32.

Lerner, R. M., Theokas, C., & Bobek, D. L. (2005). Concepts and theories of human development: Historical and contemporary dimensions. In M. H. Bornstein & M. E. Lamb (Eds.), *Developmental science: An advanced textbook* (5th ed., pp. 3–43). Mahwah, NJ: Erlbaum.

Lessow-Hurley, J. (2005). *The foundations of dual language development.* Boston, MA: Allyn & Bacon.

Leung, A. K-y., & Chiu, C-y. (2010). Multicultural experience, idea receptiveness, and creativity. *Journal of Cross-Cultural Psychology, 41,* 723–741.

Leung, A. K., Maddux, W. W., Galinsky, A. D., & Chiu, C. (2008). Multicultural experience enhances creativity: The when and how. *American Psychologist, 63,* 169–181.

Levin, J. R. (1994). Mnemonic strategies and classroom learning: A twenty-year report card. *Elementary School Journal, 94,* 235–254.

Levin, J. R., & Nolan, J. F. (2000). *Principles of classroom management: A professional decision-making model.* Boston, MA: Allyn & Bacon.

Lewinsohn, P. M., Rohde, P., & Seeley, J. R. (1994). Psychological risk factors for future attempts. *Journal of Consulting and Clinical Psychology, 62,* 297–305.

Lewis, R. (2001). Classroom discipline and student responsibility: The students' view. *Teaching and Teacher Education, 17,* 307–319.

Lewis, T. J., Sugai, G., & Colvin, G. (1998). Reducing problem behavior through a school-wide system of effective behavioral support: Investigation of a school-wide social skills training program and contextual interventions. *School Psychology Review, 27,* 446–459.

Liben, L. S., & Bigler, R. S. (2002). The developmental course of gender differentiation: Conceptualizing, measuring, and evaluating constructs and pathways. *Monographs of the Society for Research in Child Development, 67*(2), 1–187.

Liben, L. S., & Signorella, M. L. (1993). Gender-schematic processing in children: The role of initial interpretations of stimuli. *Developmental Psychology, 29,* 141–149.

Lindberg, S. M., Hyde, J. S., Peterson, J. L., & Linn, M. C. (2010). New trends in gender and mathematics performance: A meta-analysis. *Psychological Bulletin, 136,* 1123–1135.

Lindsay, P. H., & Norman, D. A. (1977). *Human information processing: An introduction to psychology* (2nd ed.). New York, NY: Academic Press.

Linn, M. C., & Eylon, B. S. (2006). Science education: Integrating views of learning and instruction. In P. A. Alexander & P. H. Winne (Eds.),

Handbook of educational psychology (2nd ed., pp. 511–544). Mahwah, NJ: Erlbaum.

Linn, R. L., Baker, E. L., & Betebenner, D. W. (2002). Accountability systems: Implications of requirements of the No Child Left Behind Act of 2001. *Educational Researcher, 31*(6), 3–16.

Linn, R. L., & Miller , M. D. (2005). *Measurement and assessment in teaching* (9th ed.). Upper Saddle River, NJ: Prentice-Hall/Merrill.

Linnenbrink-Garcia, L., & Pekrun, R. (2011). Students' emotions and academic engagement: Introduction to the special issue. *Contemporary Educational Psychology, 36,* 1–3.

Liu, W. M., Ali, S. R., Soleck, G., Hopps, J., Dunston, K., & Pickett, T., Jr. (2004). Using social class in counseling psychology research. *Journal of Counseling Psychology, 51,* 3–18.

Lochman, J. E., & Wells, K. C. (2003). The Coping Power program for preadolescent aggressive boys and their parents: Effects at the one-year follow-up. *Journal of Consulting and Clinical Psychology, 72,* 571–578.

Locke, E. A., & Latham, G. P. (2002). Building a practically useful theory of goal setting and task motivation: A 35-year odyssey. *American Psychologist, 57,* 705–717.

Lorch, R. F., Lorch, E. P., Ritchey, K., McGovern, L., & Coleman, D. (2001). Effects of headings on text summarization. *Contemporary Educational Psychology, 26,* 171–191.

Loveless, T. (1998). The tracking and ability grouping debate. *Fordham Report, 2*(88), 1–27.

Loveless, T. (1999). Will tracking reform promote social equity? *Educational Leadership, 56*(7), 28–32.

Lowenstein, G. (1994). The psychology of curiosity: A review and reinterpretation. *Psychological Bulletin, 117,* 75–98.

Luckner, A. E., & Pianta, R. C. (2011). Teacher student interactions in fifth grade classrooms: Relations with children's peer behavior. *Journal of Applied Developmental Psychology, 32,* 257–266. doi:10.1016/j.appdev.2011.02.010.

Lyon, G. R., Shaywitz, S. E., & Shaywitz, B. A. (2003). A definition of dyslexia. *Annals of Dyslexia, 53,* 1–14.

Ma, X. (2012). The relation of teacher characteristics to student achievement. In J. Hattie & E. Anderman (Eds.), *International handbook of student achievement.* New York, NY: Routledge.

Maag, J. W., & Kemp, S. E. (2003). Behavioral intent of power and affiliation: Implications for functional analysis. *Remedial and Special Education, 24,* 57–64.

Mabry, L. (1999). Writing to the rubrics: Lingering effects of traditional standardized testing on direct writing assessment. *Phi Delta Kappan, 80,* 673–679.

Maccoby, E. E. (1998). *The two sexes: Growing up apart, coming together.* Cambridge, MA: Harvard University Press.

Mace, F. C., Belfiore, P. J., & Hutchinson, J. M. (2001). Operant theory and research on self-regulation. In B. Zimmerman & D. Schunk (Eds.), *Self-regulated learning and academic achievement: Theoretical perspectives* (2nd ed.). Mahwah, NJ: Erlbaum.

Macionis, J. J. (2003). *Sociology* (9th ed.). Upper Saddle River, NJ: Prentice-Hall.

Macionis, J. J. (2010). *Sociology* (13th ed.). Upper Saddle River, NJ: Prentice-Hall.

Macrae, C. N., Milne, A. B., & Bodenhausen, C. V. (1994). Stereotypes as energy-saving devices: A peek inside the cognitive toolbox. *Journal of Personality and Social Psychology, 66,* 37–47.

Maddux, W. W., & Galinsky, A. D. (2009). Cultural borders and mental barriers: Living in and adapting to foreign cultures facilitates creativity. *Journal of Personality and Social Psychology, 96,* 1047–1061.

Madsen, C. H., Becker, W. C., Thomas, D. R., Koser, L., & Plager, E. (1968). An analysis of the reinforcing function of "sit down" commands. In R. K. Parker (Ed.), *Readings in educational psychology.* Boston, MA: Allyn & Bacon.

Madsen, K. (2003). The effect of accuracy of instruction, teacher delivery, and student attentiveness on musicians' evaluation of teacher effectiveness. *Journal of Research in Music Education, 51,* 38–51.

Mager, R. (1975). *Preparing instructional objectives* (2nd ed.). Palo Alto, CA: Fearon.

Mager, R. F. (1997). Preparing instructional objectives: A critical tool in the development of effective instruction (3rd Ed.). Atlanta, GA: Center for Effective Performance.

Magnusson, S. J., & Palincsar, A. S. (1995). The learning environment as a site of science reform. *Theory Into Practice, 34,* 43–50.

Maguire, E. A., Gadian, D. G., Johnsrude, I. S., Good, C. D., Ashburner, J., Frackowiak, R. S., & Frith, C. D. (2000). Navigation-related structural change in the hippocampi of taxi drivers. *Proceedings of the National Academy of Science, USA, 97*(8), 4398–4403.

Major, B., & Schmader, T. (1998). Coping with stigma through psychological disengagement. In J. Swim & C. Stangor (Eds.), *Stigma: The target's perspective* (pp. 219–241). New York, NY: Academic Press.

Manning, B. H., & Payne, B. D. (1996). *Self-talk for teachers and students: Metacognitive strategies for personal and classroom use.* Boston, MA: Allyn & Bacon.

Manning, M. L., & Baruth, L. G. (1996). *Multicultural education of children and adolescents* (2nd ed.). Boston, MA: Allyn & Bacon.

Mantzicopolos, P., & Morrison, D. (1992). Kindergarten retention: Academic and behavioral outcomes through the end of second grade. *American Educational Research Journal, 29,* 182–198.

Marchland, G., & Skinner, E. A. (2007). Motivational dynamics of children's academic help-seeking and concealment. *Journal of Educational Psychology, 99,* 65–82.

Marcia, J. E. (1991). Identity and self development. In R. Lerner, A. Peterson, & J. Brooks-Gunn (Eds.), *Encyclopedia of adolescence* (Vol. 1). New York, NY: Garland.

Marcia, J. E. (1994). The empirical study of ego identity. In H. Bosma, T. Graafsma, H. Grotebanc, & D. DeLivita (Eds.), *The identity and development.* Newbury Park, CA: Sage.

Marcia, J. E. (1999). Representational thought in ego identity, psychotherapy, and psychosocial development. In I. E. Sigel (Ed.), *Development of mental representation: Theories and applications.* Mahwah, NJ: Erlbaum.

Marcus, N., Cooper, M., & Sweller, J. (1996). Understanding instructions. *Journal of Educational Psychology, 88,* 49–63.

Marinova-Todd, S., Marshall, D., & Snow, C. (2000). Three misconceptions about age and L2 learning. *TESOL Quarterly, 34*(1), 9–34.

Markman, E. M. (1992). Constraints on word learning: Speculations about their nature, origins, and domain specificity. In M. Gunnar & M. Maratsos (Eds.), *Minnesota symposium on child psychology* (Vol. 25, pp. 59–101). Hillsdale, NJ: Erlbaum.

Marks, A. K, Patton, F., & Coll, C. G. (2011). Being bicultural: A mixed - methods study of adolescents' implicitly and explicitly measured multiethnic identities. *Developmental Psychology, 47,* 270–288.

Markstrom-Adams, C. (1992). A consideration of intervening factors in adolescent identity formation. In G. R. Adams, R. Montemayor, & T. Gullotta (Eds.), *Advances in adolescent development: Vol. 4. Adolescent identity formation* (pp. 173–192). Newbury Park, CA: Sage.

Marsh, H. W. (1990). Influences of internal and external frames of reference on the formation of math and English self-concepts. *Journal of Educational Psychology, 82,* 107–116.

Marsh, H. W., & Ayotte, V. (2003). Do multiple dimensions of self-concept become more differentiated with age? The differential distinctiveness hypothesis. *Journal of Educational Psychology, 95,* 687–706.

Marsh, H. W., & Craven, R. (2002). The pivotal role of frames of reference in academic self-concept formation: The Big Fish Little Pond Effect. In F. Pajares & T. Urdan (Eds.), *Adolescence and Education* (Volume II, pp. 83–123). Greenwich, CT: Information Age.

Marsh, H. W., Craven, R. G., & Martin, A. (2006). What is the nature of self-esteem: Unidimensional and multidimensional perspectives. In M. Kernis (Ed.), *Self-esteem: Issues and answers* (pp. 16–25). New York, NY: Psychology Press.

Marsh, H. W., & Hau, K-T. (2003). Big-Fish-Little-Pond effect on academic self-concept. *American Psychologist, 58,* 364–376.

Marsh, H. W., Seaton M., Trautwein, U., Lüdtke, O., Hau, K. T., O'Mara, A. J., & Craven, R. G. (2008). The Big-fish–little-pond-effect stands up to critical scrutiny: Implications for theory, methodology, and future research. *Educational Psychology Review, 20,* 319–350.

Marsh, H. W., Trautwein, U., Lüdtke, O., Köller, O., & Baumert, J. (2006). Integration of multidimensional self-concept and core personality constructs: Construct validation and relations to well-being and achievement. *Journal of Personality, 74,* 403–456.

Marsh, H. W., & Yeung, A. S. (1997). Coursework selection: Relation to academic self-concept and achievement. *American Educational Research Journal, 34,* 691–720.

Marshall, H. H. (Ed.). (1992). *Redefining student learning: Roots of educational change.* Norwood, NJ: Ablex.

Marshall, H. H. (1996). Implications of differentiating and understanding constructivist approaches. *Journal of Educational Psychology, 31,* 235–240.

Martin, J. (2006). Social cultural perspectives in educational psychology. In P. A. Alexander & P. H. Winne (Eds.), *Handbook of educational psychology* (2nd ed., pp. 595–614). Mahwah, NJ: Erlbaum.

Martinez-Pons, M. (2002). A social cognitive view of parental influence on student academic self-regulation. *Theory Into Practice, 61,* 126–131.

Marvin, K. L., Rapp, J. T., Stenske, M. T., Rojas, N. R., Swanson, G. J., & Bartlett, S. M. (2010). Response repetition as an error-correction procedure for sight-word reading: A replication and extension. *Behavioral Interventions, 25,* 109–127.

Marzano, R. J., & Marzano, J. S. (2003, September). The key to classroom management. *Educational Leadership, 61*(1), 6–13.

Mascolo, M. F., & Fischer, K. W. (2005). Constructivist theories. In B. Hopkins (Ed.), *The Cambridge encyclopedia of child development.* New York, NY: Cambridge University Press.

Maslow, A. H. (1968). *Toward a psychology of being* (2nd ed.). New York, NY: Van Nostrand.

Maslow, A. H. (1970). *Motivation and personality* (2nd ed.). New York, NY: Harper and Row.

Mason, D. A., & Good, T. L. (1993). Effects of two-group and whole-class teaching on regrouped elementary students' mathematics achievement. *American Educational Research Journal, 30,* 328–360.

Mason, L. (2007). Introduction: Bridging the cognitive and sociocultural approaches in research on conceptual change: Is it possible? *Educational Psychologist, 42,* 1–7.

Matson, J. L., Matson, M. L., & Rivet, T. T. (2007). Social-skills treatments for children with autism spectrum disorders. *Behavior Modification, 31,* 682–707.

Matsumara, L. C., & Crosson, A. (2008). Classroom climate, rigorous instruction and curriculum, and students' interactions in urban middle schools. *The Elementary School Journal, 108,* 293–312.

Matsumara, L. C., Slater, S. C., & Crosson, A. (2008). Classroom climate, rigorous instruction and curriculum, and students' interactions in urban middle schools. *The Elementary School Journal, 108,* 293–312.

Matthews, J. S., Kizzie, K. T., Rowley, S. J., & Cortina, K. (2010). African Americans and boys: Understanding the literacy gap, tracing academic trajectories, and evaluating the role of learning-related skills. *Journal of Educational Psychology, 102,* 757–771.

Matthews, J. S., Ponitz, C. C., & Morrison, F. J. (2009). Early gender differences in self-regulation and academic achievement. *Journal of Educational Psychology, 101,* 689–704.

Mayer, R. E. (1983). *Thinking, problem solving, cognition.* San Francisco, CA: Freeman.

Mayer, R. E. (1984). Twenty-five years of research on advance organizers. *Instructional Science, 8,* 133–169.

Mayer, R. E. (1996). Learners as information processors: Legacies and limitations of educational psychology's second metaphor. *Journal of Educational Psychology, 31,* 151–161.

Mayer, R. E. (2001). *Multimedia learning.* New York, NY: Cambridge University Press.

Mayer, R. E. (2005). Cognitive theory of multimedia learning. In R. E. Mayer (Ed.), *The Cambridge handbook of multimedia learning* (pp. 31–48). New York, NY: Cambridge University Press.

Mayer, R. E. (2008). *Learning and instruction* (2nd ed.). Columbus, OH: Merrill/Prentice-Hall.

Mayer, R. E. (2011). *Applying the science of learning.* Boston, MA: Pearson.

Mayer, R. E., & Gallini, J. K. (1990). When is an illustration worth ten thousand words? *Journal of Educational Psychology, 82,* 715–726.

Mayer, R. E., & Massa, L. J. (2003). Three facets of visual and verbal learners: Cognitive ability, cognitive style and learning preference. *Journal of Educational Psychology, 95*(4), 833–846.

Mayer, R. E., & Wittrock, M. C. (1996). Problem-solving transfer. In D. Berliner & R. Calfee (Eds.), *Handbook of educational psychology* (pp. 47–62). New York, NY: Macmillan.

Mayer, R. E., & Wittrock, M. C. (2006). Problem solving. In P. A. Alexander & P. H. Winne (Eds.), *Handbook of educational psychology* (2nd ed., pp. 287–303). Mahwah, NJ: Erlbaum.

Mayo Clinic. (2009). *Type 2 diabetes: Complications.* Available online at: http://www.mayo-clinic.com/health/type-2-diabetes/DS00585/DSECTION_complications

McAnarney, E. R. (2008). Adolescent brain development: Forging new links. *Journal of Adolescent Health, 42,* 321–323.

McCafferty, S. G. (2004). Introduction. *International Journal of Applied Linguistics, 14*(1), 1–6.

McCaslin, M., & Good, T. (1996). The informal curriculum. In D. Berliner & R. Calfee (Eds.), *Handbook of educational psychology* (pp. 622–670). New York, NY: Macmillan.

McCaslin, M., & Good, T. L. (1998). Moving beyond management as sheer compliance: Helping students to develop goal coordination strategies. *Educational Horizons, 76,* 169–176.

McCaslin, M., & Hickey, D. T. (2001). Self-regulated learning and academic achievement: A Vygotskian view. In B. Zimmerman & D. Schunk (Eds.), *Self-regulated learning and academic achievement: Theoretical perspectives* (2nd ed., pp. 227–252). Mahwah, NJ: Erlbaum.

McClelland, D. (1985). *Human motivation.* Glenview, IL: Scott, Foresman.

McCoach, D. B., Kehle, T. J., Bray, M. L., & Siegle, D. (2001). Best practices in the identification of gifted students with learning disabilities. *Psychology in the Schools, 38,* 403–411.

McCoy, A. R., & Reynolds, A. J. (1999). Grade retention and school performance: An extended investigation. *Journal of School Psychology, 37,* 273–298.

McDonald, J. P. (1993). Three pictures of an exhibition: Warm, cool, and hard. *Phi Delta Kappan, 6,* 480–485.

McGoey, K. E., & DuPaul, G. J. (2000). Token reinforcement and response cost procedures: Reducing disruptive behavior of children with attention-deficit/hyperactivity disorder. *School Psychology Quarterly, 15,* 330–343.

McHugh, J. R., & Barlow, D. H. (2010). The Dissemination and implementation of evidence-based psychological treatments: A review of current efforts. *American Psychologist, 65*(2), 73–84. DOI: 10.1037/a0018121.

McKenzie, T. L., & Kahan, D. (2008). Physical activity, public health, and elementary schools. *The Elementary School Journal, 108,* 171–180.

McKenzie, T. L., & Rushall, B. S. (1974). Effects of self-recording on attendance and performance in a competitive swimming training environment. *Journal of Applied Behavior Analysis, 7,* 199–206.

McKinley, J. C. (2011, January 24). Shot in the head, but getting back on his feet and on with his life. *New York Times,* A-16. Available online at: http://www.nytimes.com/2011/01/24/us/24rehab.html?scp=7&sq=Houston%20rehabilitation&st=cse.

McKown, C. (2005). Applying ecological theory to advance the science and practice of school-based prejudice reduction interventions. *Educational Psychologist, 40,* 177–189.

McLoyd, V. C. (1998). Economic disadvantage and child development. *American Psychologist, 53,* 185–204.

McMillan, J. H. (2004). *Classroom assessment: Principles and practice for effective instruction* (3rd ed.). Boston, MA: Allyn & Bacon.

McNeely, C. A., Nonnemaker, J. M., & Blum, R. W. (2002). Promoting school connectedness:

Evidence from the National Longitudinal Study of Adolescent Health. *Journal of School Health, 72*(4), 138–146.

McNeil, L. M., & Valenzuela, A. (2000). *The harmful impact of the TAAS system of testing in Texas: Beneath the accountability rhetoric.* Cambridge, MA: Harvard University Civil Rights Project. Available online at: www.law.harvard.edu/groups/civil-rights/testing.html

McTigue, E. M. (2009). Does multimedia learning theory extend to middle-school students? *Contemporary Educational Psychology, 34,* 143–153.

Mears, T. (1998). Saying 'Si' to Spanish. *Boston Globe,* April 12.

Mediascope. (1996). *National television violence study: Executive summary 1994–1995.* Studio City, CA: Author.

Medina, J. (2002, June 23). Groups say Regents Exam push immigrants to drop out. *The New York Times,* p. A28.

Meece, J. L., & Daniels, D. H. (2008). *Child and adolescent development for educators* (3rd ed.). New York, NY: McGraw-Hill.

Meece, J. L., & Kurtz-Costes, B. (2001). Introduction: The schooling of ethnic minority children and youth. *Educational Psychologist, 36,* 1–7.

Meijer, A. M., & Wittenboer, G. L. H. van den. (2004). The joint contribution of sleep, intelligence and motivation to school performance, *Personality and Individual Differences,37,* 95–106.

Melnick, S. A., & Meister, D. G. (2008). A comparison of beginning and experienced teacher concerns. *Education Research Quarterly, 31*(3), 39–56.

Mendle, J., Turkheimer, E., & Emery, R. E. (2007). Detrimental psychological outcomes associated with early pubertal timing in adolescent girls. *Developmental Review, 27,* 151–171.

Mendoza, E. M., & Johnson, K. O. (2000). Land of Plenty: Diversity as America's competitive edge in science, engineering, and technology. Washington DC: Congressional Commission on the Advancement of Women and Minorities in Science, Engineering and Technology Development.

Merrell, K. W., Isava, D. M., Gueldner, B. A., & Ross, S. W. (2008). How effective are school bullying intervention programs? A meta-analysis of intervention research. *School Psychology Quarterly, 23,* 26–42.

Mertler, C. A., & Charles, C. M. (2005). *Introduction to educational research* (5th ed.). Boston, MA: Allyn & Bacon.

Merton, R. K. (1948). The self-fulfilling prophecy. *Antioch Review, 8,* 193–210.

Messick, S. (1975). The standard problem: Meaning and values in measurement and evaluation. *American Psychologist, 35,* 1012–1027.

Metzler, C. W., Biglan, A., Rusby, J. C., & Sprague, J. R. (2001). Evaluation of a comprehensive behavior management program to improve school-wide positive behavior support. *Education and Treatment of Children, 24*(4), 448–470.

Midgley, C. (2001). A goal theory perspective on the current status of middle level schools. In T. Urdan & F. Pajares (Eds.), *Adolescence and education* (pp. 33–59). Volume I. Greenwich, CT: Information Age Publishing.

Midgley, C., Kaplan, A., & Middleton, M. (2001). Performance-approach goals: Good for what, for whom, under what circumstances, and at what cost? *Journal of Educational Psychology, 93,* 77–86.

Midgley, C., Kaplan, A., Middleton, M., Maehr, M. L., Urdan, T., Anderman, L. H., ... Roser, R. (1998). The development and validation of scales assessing students' achievement goal orientations. *Contemporary Educational Psychology, 23,* 113–131.

Miller, G. A. (1956). The magical number seven, plus or minus two: Some limits on our capacity for processing information. *Psychological Review, 63,* 81–97.

Miller, G. A., Galanter, E., & Pribram, K. H. (1960). *Plans and the structure of behavior.* New York, NY: Holt, Rinehart & Winston.

Miller, M. D., Linn, R. L., & Gronlund, N. E. (2009). *Measurement and assessment in education* (10th ed.) Boston, MA: Pearson.

Miller, N., & Harrington, H. J. (1993). Social categorization and intergroup acceptance: Principles for the development an design of cooperative learning teams. In R. Hertz-Lasarowitz & N. Miller (Eds.), *Interaction in cooperative groups: The theoretical anatomy of group learning* (pp. 203–227). New York, NY: Cambridge University Press.

Miller, P. H. (2011). *Theories of developmental psychology* (5th ed.). New York, NY: Worth.

Miller, R. B. (1962). Analysis and specification of behavior for training. In R. Glaser (Ed.), *Training research and education: Science edition.* New York, NY: Wiley.

Miller, S. A. (2005). Tips for getting children's attention. *Early Childhood Today,* 19.

Miller, S. A. (2009). Children's understanding of second-order mental statuses. *Psychological Bulletin, 135,* 749–773.

Milner, H.R. (2003). Teacher reflection and race in cultural contexts: History, meaning, and methods in teaching. *Theory into Practice 42*(3), 173–180.

Milner, H. R. (2006). Classroom management in urban classrooms. In C. M. Evertson & C. S. Weinstein, (Eds.), *Handbook of classroom management: Research, practice, and contemporary issues* (pp. 491–522). Mahwah, NJ: Erlbaum.

Milner, H. R. IV. (2010). *Start where you are but don't stay there: Understanding diversity, opportunity gaps, and teaching in today's schools.* Cambridge, MA: Harvard Education Press.

Miranda, T. Z. (2008). Bilingual education for all students: Still standing after all these years. In L. S. Verplaetse & N. Migliacci (Eds.), *Inclusive pedagogy for English language learners: A handbook of research-informed practices* (pp. 257–275). New York, NY: Erlbaum.

Mitchell, M. (1993). Situational interest: Its multifaceted structure in the secondary school mathematics classroom. *Journal of Educational Psychology. 85,* 424–436.

Moll, L. C., Amanti, C., Neff, D., & Gonzalez, N. (1992). Funds of knowledge for teaching: Using a qualitative approach to connect homes and classrooms. *Theory into Practice, 31,* 132–141.

Moller, A. C., Deci, E. L., & Ryan, R. M. (2006). Choice and ego-depletion: The moderating role of autonomy. *Personality and Social Psychology Bulletin, 32*(8), 1024–1036.

Möller, J., & Pohlmann, B. (2010). Achievement differences and self-concept differences: Stronger associations for above or below average students? *British Journal of Educational Psychology, 80,* 435–450.

Monroe, C. R., & Obidah, J. E. (2002, April). *The impact of cultural synchronization on a teacher's perceptions of disruption: A case study of an African American middle school classroom.* Paper presented at the American Educational Research Association, New Orleans, LA.

Montrul, S. (2010). Dominant language transfer in adult second language learners and heritage speakers. *Second Language Research, 26,* 293–327.

Moore, K. A., Redd, Z. Burkhauser, M., Mbwana, K., & Collins, A. (2009). *Children in poverty: Trends, consequences, and policy options.* Washington DC: Child Trends, #2009–11.

Moore, M. K., & Meltzoff, A. N. (2004). Object permanence after a 24-hr delay and leaving the locale of disappearance: the role of memory, space, and identity. *Developmental Psychology, 40,* 606–620.

Moreno, R., Ozogul, G., & Reisslein, M. (2011). Teaching with concrete and abstract visual representations: Effects on students' problem solving, problem representations, and learning perceptions. *Journal of Educational Psychology, 103,* 32–47.

Morin, V. A., & Miller, S. P. (1998). Teaching multiplication to middle school students with mental retardation. *Education & Treatment of Children, 21,* 22–36.

Morine-Dershimer, G. (2006). Instructional planning. In J. Cooper (Ed.), *Classroom teaching skills* (7th ed., pp. 20–54). Boston, MA: Houghton-Mifflin.

Morrow, L. M., & Weinstein, C. (1986). Encouraging voluntary reading: The impact of a literature program on children's use of library centers. *Reading Research Quarterly, 21,* 330–346.

Moshman, D. (1982). Exogenous, endogenous, and dialectical constructivism. *Developmental Review, 2,* 371–384.

Moshman, D. (1997). Pluralist rational constructivism. *Issues in Education: Contributions from Educational Psychology, 3,* 229–234.

Moskowitz, G., & Hayman, M. L. (1976). Successful strategies of inner-city teachers: A year-long study. *Journal of Educational Research, 69,* 283–289.

Mueller, C. M., & Dweck, C. S. (1998). Praise for intelligence can undermine children's motivation and performance. *Journal of Personality and Social Psychology, 75,* 33–52.

Muis, K. R., & Franco, G. M. (2009). Epistemic beliefs: Setting the standards for self-regulated learning. *Contemporary Educational Psychology, 34,* 306–318.

Mullis, I. V. S., Martin, M. O., Gonzalez, E., & Kennedy, A. M. (2003). *PIRLS 2001 International report: IEA's study of reading literacy achievement in primary schools.* Chestnut Hill, MA: Boston College. Available online at:. http://timss.bc.edu/pirls2001i/PIRLS2001_Pubs_IR.html

Mumford, M. D., Costanza, D. P., Baughman, W. A., Threlfall, V., & Fleishman, E. A. (1994). Influence of abilities on performance during practice: Effects of massed and distributed practice. *Journal of Educational Psychology, 86,* 134–144.

Murayama, K., & Elliot, A. J. (2009). The joint influence of personal achievement goals and classroom goal structures on achievement-relevant outcomes. *Journal of Educational Psychology, 101,* 432–447.

Murdock, S. G., O'Neill, R. E., & Cunningham, E. (2005). A comparison of results and acceptability of functional behavioral assessment procedures with a group of middle school students with emotional/behavioral disorders (E/BD). *Journal of Behavioral Education, 14*, 5–18.

Murdock, T. A., & Anderman, E. M. (2006). Motivational perspectives on student cheating: Toward an integrated model of academic dishonesty. *Educational Psychologist, 42*, 129–145.

Murdock, T. B., Hale, N. M., & Weber, M. J. (2001). Predictors of cheating among early adolescents: Academic and social motivations. *Contemporary Educational Psychology, 26*, 96–115.

Murdock, T. B., & Miller, A. (2003). Teachers as sources of middle school students' motivational identity: Variable-centered and person-centered analytic approaches. *Elementary School Journal, 103*, 383–399.

Murphy, P. K., & Alexander, P. A. (2000). A motivated exploration of motivation terminology. *Contemporary Educational Psychology, 25*, 3–53.

Murphy, P. K., & Benton, S. L. (2010).The new frontier of educational neuropsychology: Unknown opportunities and unfulfilled hopes. *Contemporary Educational Psychology, 35*, 153–155.

Murphy, P. K., Wilkinson, I. A. G., Soter, A. O., Hennessey, M. N., & Alexander, J. F. (2009). Examining the effects of classroom discussion on students' comprehension of text: A meta-analysis. *Journal of Educational Psychology, 101*, 740–764.

Myers, D. G. (2005). *Exploring psychology* (6th ed. in modules). New York, NY: Worth.

Myers, D. G. (2010). *Psychology* (9th ed.). New York, NY: Worth.

Myers, I. B., & McCaulley, M. H. (1988). *Manual: A guide to the development and use of the Myers-Briggs Type Indicator.* Palo Alto, CA: Consulting Psychologists.

National Alliance of Black School Educators. (2002). *Addressing over-representations of African American students in special education: The prereferral intervention process.* Arlington, VA: Council for Exceptional Education.

National Association for the Education of Young Children. (2006). *The value of recess and outdoor play.* Available online at: http://www.naeyc.org/ece/1998/08.asp.

National Center for Educational Statistics. (2003). *Indicators of school crime and safety 2002.* Available online at: http://nces.ed.gov/pubs2003/schoolcrime/6.asp?nav=1

National Center for Education Statistics. (2009). *Number and percentage distribution of 3- to 21-year-olds served under the Individuals with Disabilities Education Act (IDEA), Part B, and number served as a percentage of total public school enrollment, by type of disability: Selected school years, 1980–81 through 2008–09.* Washington, DC: U.S. Department of education. Available online at: http://nces.ed.gov/programs/coe/tables/table-cwd-1.asp

National Center for Education Statistics. (2009). *The nation's report card: Mathematics 2009 (NCES 2010–451).* Institute of Education Sciences, U.S. Department of Education, Washington, DC.

National Center for Education Statistics. (2010). *Condition of education 2010, indicator 23 (NCES 2010–028).* Institute of Education Sciences, U.S. Department of Education, Washington, DC.

National Center for Educational Statistics.(2011). *Characteristics of the 100 largest public elementary and secondary school districts in the United States: 2008–09.* Washington, DC: Author. Available online at: http://nces.ed.gov/pubs2010/100largest0809/how.asp

National Commission on Excellence in Education. (1983). *A nation at risk: The imperative for educational reform.* Washington, DC: Author. Available online at: http://www.ed.gov/pubs/NatAtRisk/index.html

National Commission on Teaching and America's Future. (2003). *No dream denied: A pledge to America's children.* Washington, DC: Author.

National Federation of the Blind (NFB). (2010). *NFB nonvisual accessibility web certification granted to Instructure Learning Management System.* Available online at: http://www.disabled-world.com/disability/accessibility/websitedesign/learning-management-system.php#ixzz1ZYiOqF56.

National Poverty Center. (2011). *Poverty in the United States: Frequently asked questions.* The University of Michigan, Gerald R. Ford School of Public Policy, Ann Arbor, MI. Available online at: http://npc.umich.edu/poverty/

National Science Foundation, Division of Science Resources Statistics. (2011). *Women, minorities, and persons with disabilities in science and engineering: 2011.* Special Report NSF 11-309. Arlington, VA. Available online at: http://www.nsf.gov/statistics/wmpd/

National Service Learning Clearinghouse. (n.d.). *Service learning is . . . .* Available online at: http://www.servicelearning.org/welcome_to_service-learning/service-learning_is/index.php

Navarro, R. L., Flores, L. Y., & Worthington, R. L. (2007). Mexican American middle school students' goal intentions in mathematics and science: A test of social cognitive career theory. *Journal of Counseling Psychology, 54*, 320–335.

Naveh-Benjamin, M. (1991). A comparison of training programs intended for different types of test-anxious students: Further support for an information-processing model. *Journal of Educational Psychology, 83*, 134–139.

Naveh-Benjamin, M., McKeachie, W. J., & Lin, Y. (1987). Two types of test-anxious students: Support for an information processing model. *Journal of Educational Psychology, 79*, 131–136.

Needles, M., & Knapp, M. (1994). Teaching writing to children who are underserved. *Journal of Educational Psychology, 86*, 339–349.

Neisser, U., Boodoo, G., Bouchard, A., Boykin, W., Brody, N., Ceci, . . . Urbina, S. (1996). Intelligence: Knowns and unknowns. *American Psychologist, 51*, 77–101.

Nelson, C.A. (2001). The development and neural bases of face recognition. *Infant and Child Development, 10*, 3–18.

Nelson, J. R., & Roberts, M. L. (2000). Ongoing reciprocal teacher-student interactions involving disruptive behaviors in general education classrooms. *Journal of Emotional and Behavioral Disorders, 4*, 147–161.

Nelson, K., & Fivush, R. (2004). The emergence of autobiographical memory: A social cultural developmental theory. *Psychological Review, 111*, 486–511.

Nelson, T. O. (1996). Consciousness and metacognition. *American Psychologist, 51*, 102–116.

Nesbit, J. C., & Adesope, O. O. (2006). Learning with concept and knowledge maps: A meta-analysis. *Review of Educational Research, 76*, 413–448.

Neumeister, K. L. S., & Cramond, B. (2004). E. Paul Torrance (1915–2003). *American Psychologist, 59*, 179.

Neville, H. (2007, March). *Experience shapes human brain development and function.* Paper presented at the biennial meeting of the Society for Research in Child Development, Boston.

Newcombe, N., & Baenninger, M. (1990). The role of expectations in spatial test performance: A meta-analysis. *Sex Roles, 16*, 25–37.

Newman, K. L., Samimy, K., & Romstedt, K. (2010). Developing a training program for secondary teachers of English language learners in Ohio. *Theory Into Practice, 49*, 152–161.

Nguyen, H.-H. D., & Ryan, A. M. (2008). Does stereotype threat affect test performance of minorities and women? A meta-analysis of experimental evidence. *Journal of Applied Psychology, 93*, 1314–1334.

NICHD Early Child Care Research Network. (2005a). *Child care and child development.* New York, NY: Guilford Press.

NICHD Early Child Care Research Network. (2005b). Pathways to reading: The role of oral language in the transition to reading. *Developmental Psychology, 41*(2), 428–442.

Nicholls, J., Cobb, P., Wood, T., Yackel, E., & Patashnick, M. (1990). Assessing student's theories of success in mathematics: Individual and classroom differences. *Journal for Research in Mathematics Education, 21*, 109–122.

Nicholls, J. G., & Miller, A. (1984). Conceptions of ability and achievement motivation. In R. Ames & C. Ames (Eds.), *Research on motivation in education. Vol. 1: Student Motivation* (pp. 39–73). New York, NY: Academic Press.

Nie, Y., & Lau, S. (2009). Complementary roles of care and behavioral control in classroom management: The self-determination theory perspective. *Contemporary Educational Psychology, 34*, 185–194.

Nielsen. (2010). *U.S. teen mobile report: Calling yesterday, texting today, using apps tomorrow.* New York, NY: The Nielsen Company. Available online at: http://blog.nielsen.com/nielsenwire/online_mobile/u-s-teen-mobile-report-calling-yesterday-texting-today-using-apps-tomorrow/

Nieto, S. (2004). *Affirming diversity: The sociopolitical context of multicultural education* (4th ed.). Boston, MA: Allyn & Bacon.

Nieto, S., & Bode, P. (2008). *Affirming diversity: The sociopolitical context of multicultural education* (5th ed.). Boston, MA: Allyn & Bacon.

Nitko, A. J., & Brookhart, S. M. (2011). *Educational assessment of students* (6th ed.). Boston, MA: Pearson.

No Child Left Behind Act. (2002). P. L. 107–110, Title IX, Part A, Section 9101 (22), pp. 544, 20 U.S. C. 7802.

Noddings, N. (1990). Constructivism in mathematics education. In R. Davis, C. Maher, & N. Noddings (Eds.), *Constructivist views on the teaching and learning of mathematics* (pp. 7–18). Monograph 4 of the National Council of Teachers of Mathematics, Reston, VA.

Noddings, N. (1995). Teaching themes of care. *Phi Delta Kappan, 76*, 675–679.

Noguera, P. (2005). The racial achievement gap: How can we assume an equity of outcomes. In L. Johnson, M. E. Finn, & R. Lewis (Eds.), *Urban education with an attitude.* Albany, NY: SUNY Press.

Nokes, J. D., Dole, J. A., & Hacker, D. J. (2007). Teaching high school students to use heuristics while reading historical texts. *Journal of Educational Psychology, 99*, 492–504.

Norbert, F. (2005). Research findings on early first language attrition: Implications for the discussion of critical periods in language acquisition. *Language Learning, 55*(3), 491–531.

Novotney, A. (2009). Dangerous distraction. *Monitor on Psychology, 40,* 32. Available online at: http://www.apa.org/monitor/2009/02/dangerous.aspx

Novotney, A. (2011). Coed versus single-sex schools. *Monitor on Psychology, 42*(2), 58–62.

Nucci, L. P. (2001). *Education in the moral domain.* New York, NY: Cambridge Press.

Nurmi, J. (2004). Socialization and self-development: Channeling, selection, adjustment, and reflection. In R. Lerner & L. Steinberg (Eds.), *Handbook of adolescent psychology.* New York, NY: Wiley.

Nylund, D. (2000). *Treating Huckleberry Finn: A new narrative approach to working with kids diagnosed ADD/ADHD.* San Francisco: Jossey-Bass.

O'Boyle, M. W., & Gill, H. S. (1998). On the relevance of research findings in cognitive neuroscience to educational practice. *Educational Psychology Review, 10,* 397–410.

O'Connor, C. (1997). Dispositions toward (collective) struggle and educational resilience in the inner city: A case analysis of six African American high school students. *American Educational Research Journal, 34,* 593–629.

O'Donnell, A. M. (Ed.). (2002, Winter). Promoting thinking through peer learning. Special issue of *Theory Into Practice, 61*(1).

O'Donnell, A. M. (2006). The role of peers and group learning. In P. A. Alexander & P. H. Winne (Eds.), *Handbook of educational psychology* (2nd ed., pp. 781–802). Mahwah, NJ: Erlbaum.

O'Donnell, A. M., & O'Kelly, J. (1994). Learning from peers: Beyond the rhetoric of positive results. *Educational Psychology Review, 6,* 321–350.

O'Leary, K. D., & O'Leary, S. (Eds.). (1977). *Classroom management: The successful use of behavior modification* (2nd ed.). Elmsford, NY: Pergamon.

O'Leary, S. (1995). Parental discipline mistakes. *Current Directions in Psychological Science, 4,* 11–13.

O'Mara, A. J., Marsh, H. W., Craven, R. G., & Debus, R. L. (2006). Do self-concept interventions make a difference? A synergistic blend of construct validation and meta-analysis. *Educational Psychologist, 41,* 181–206.

O'Neil, J. (1990). Link between style, culture proves divisive. *Educational Leadership, 48*(2), 8.

Oakes, J. (1985). *Keeping track.* New Haven, CT: Yale University Press.

Oakes, J. (1990a). Opportunities, achievement, and choice: Women and minority students in science and math. *Review of Research in Education, 16,* 153–222.

Oakes, J. (1990b). *Multiplying inequities: The effects of race, social class, and tracking on opportunities to learn mathematics and science.* Santa Monica, CA: Rand.

Oakes, J. (1999). Promotion or retention: Which one is social? *Harvard Education Letter, 15*(1), 8.

Oakes, J., & Wells, A. S. (2002). Detracking for high student achievement. In L. Abbeduto (Ed.), *Taking sides: Clashing views and controversial issues in educational psychology* (2nd ed., pp. 26–30). Guilford, CT: McGraw-Hill Duskin.

Ogbu, J. U. (1987). Variability in minority school performance: A problem in search of an explanation. *Anthropology and Education Quarterly, 18,* 312–334.

Ogbu, J. U. (1997). Understanding the school performance of urban blacks: Some essential background knowledge. In H. Walberg, O. Reyes, & R. P. Weissberg (Eds.), *Children and youth: Interdisciplinary perspectives* (pp. 190–240). Norwood, NJ: Ablex.

Ogden, C., & Carroll, M. (2010). Prevalence of obesity among children and adolescents: United States, trends 1963–1965 through 2007–2008. Washington, DC: Center for Disease Statistics. Available online at: http://www.cdc.gov/nchs/data/hestat/obesity_child_07_08/obesity_child_07_08.htm

Ogden, J. E., Brophy, J. E., & Evertson, C. M. (1977, April). *An experimental investigation of organization and management techniques in first-grade reading groups.* Paper presented at the annual meeting of the American Educational Research Association, New York.

Okagaki, L. (2001). Triarchic model of minority children's school achievement. *Educational Psychologist, 36,* 9–20.

Okagaki, L. (2006). Ethnicity, learning. In P. Alexander & P. Winne (Eds.), *Handbook of educational psychology* (2nd ed., pp. 615–634). Mahwah, NJ: Erlbaum.

Olsen, L. (1988). *Crossing the schoolhouse border: Immigrant students and the California public schools.* San Francisco, CA: California Tomorrow.

Olson, D. R. (2004). The triumph of hope over experience in the search for "what works": A response to Slavin. *Educational Researcher, 33*(1), 24–26.

Olson, K. (2008). The wounded student. *Educational Leadership, 65*(6), 46–48.

Omi, M., & Winant, H. (1994). *Racial formation in the United States: From the 1960s to the 1990s* (2nd ed.). New York, NY: Routledge.

Oosterhof, A. (2009). *Developing and using classroom assessments* (4th ed.). Columbus, OH: Pearson/Merrill.

Orange, C. (2000). *25 biggest mistakes teachers make and how to avoid them.* Thousand Oaks, CA: Corwin.

Orange, C. (2005). *44 smart strategies for avoiding classroom mistakes.* Thousand Oaks, CA: Corwin Press.

Orfield, G., & Frankenberg, E. (2005). Where are we now? In F. Shultz (Ed.), *Annual editions: Multicultural education* (pp. 10–12). Dubuque, IA: McGraw-Hill/Dushkin.

Orfield, G., Frankenberg, E., & Siegel-Hawley, G. (2010). Integrated schools: Finding a new path. *Educational Leadership, 68*(3), 22–27.

Organization for Economic Cooperation and Development. (2007). *Understanding the brain: The birth of a learning science.* Paris: Author OECD.

Orlando L., & Machado, A. (1996). In defense of Piaget's theory: A reply to 10 common criticisms. *Psychological Review, 103,* 143–164.

Ormrod, J. E. (2004). *Human learning* (4th ed.). Columbus, OH: Merrill/Prentice-Hall.

Ormrod, J. E. (2012). *Human learning* (6th ed.). Boston, MA: Pearson.

Ortony, A., Clore, G. L., & Collins, A. (1988). *The cognitive structure of emotions.* Cambridge, UK: Cambridge University Press.

Osborn, A. F. (1963). *Applied imagination* (3rd ed.). New York, NY: Scribner's.

Osterman, K. F. (2000). Students' need for belonging in the school community. *Review of Educational Research, 70,* 323–367.

Ostrov, J. M., & Godleski, S. A. (2010). Toward an integrated gender-linked model of aggression subtypes in early and middle childhood. *Psychological Bulletin, 117,* 233–242.

Otto, B. (2010). *Language development in early childhood* (5th ed.). Columbus, OH: Merrill.

Ovando, C. J., & Collier, V. P. (1998). *Bilingual and ESL classrooms: Teaching in multicultural contexts* (2nd ed.). Boston, MA: McGraw-Hill.

Overton, W. F. (2006). Developmental psychology: Philosophy, concepts, and methodology. In R. M. Lerner (Ed.), *Handbook of child psychology* (6th ed., Vol. 1: Theoretical models of human development, pp. 18–88). New York, NY: Wiley.

Owens, R. E. (2005). *Language development: An introduction* (6th ed.). Boston, MA: Allyn & Bacon.

Owens, R. E. (2010). *Language disorders: A functional approach to assessment and intervention* (5th ed.). Boston, MA: Allyn & Bacon.

Owens, R. E. (2012). *Language development: An introduction* (8th ed.). Boston, MA: Allyn & Bacon.

Pai, Y., & Adler, S. A. (2001). *Cultural foundations of education* (3rd ed.). Upper Saddle River, NJ: Merrill.

Paivio, A. (2006). *Mind and its evolution; A dual coding theoretical interpretation.* Mahwah, NJ: Lawrence Erlbaum Associates, Inc.

Pajares, F. (1997). Current directions in self-efficacy research. In M. L. Maehr & P. R. Pintrich (Eds.), *Advances in motivation and achievement* (Vol. 10, pp. 1–49). Greenwich, CT: JAI Press.

Pajares, F. (2000, April). *Seeking a culturally attentive educational psychology.* Paper presented at the annual meeting of the American Educational Research Association, New Orleans, LA. Available online at: http://www.emory.edu/EDUCATION/mfp/AERA2000Discussant.html

Pajares, F. (2003). William James: Our father who begot us. In B. J. Zimmerman & D. H. Schunk (Eds.), *Educational psychology: A century of contributions* (pp. 41–64). Mahwah, NJ: Erlbaum.

Pajares, F. (2008). Self-efficacy information. Retrieved from: http://www.des.emory.edu/mfp/banconversion.html

Pajares, F., & Schunk, D. H. (2001). Self-beliefs and school success: Self-efficacy, self-concept, and school achievement. In R. Riding & S. Rayner (Eds.), *Perception* (pp. 239–266). Westport, CT: Ablex Publishing.

Pajares, F., & Schunk, D. H. (2002). Self and self-belief in psychology and education: An historical perspective. In J. Aronson & D. Cordova (Eds.), *Psychology of education: Personal and interpersonal forces* (pp. 1–19). New York, NY: Academic Press.

Palincsar, A. S. (1986). The role of dialogue in providing scaffolded instruction. *Educational Psychologist, 26,* 73–98.

Palincsar, A. S. (1998). Social constructivist perspectives on teaching and learning. In J. T. Spence, J. M. Darley, & D. J. Foss (Eds.), *Annual Review of Psychology* (pp. 345–375). Palo Alto, CA: Annual Reviews.

Palincsar, A. S., & Brown, A. L. (1984). Reciprocal teaching of comprehension-fostering and monitoring activities. *Cognition and Instruction, 1,* 117–175.

Palincsar, A. S., & Brown, A. L. (1989). Classroom dialogues to promote self-regulated comprehension. In J. Brophy (Ed.), *Advances in research on teaching* (Vol. 1, pp. 35–67). Greenwich, CT: JAI Press.

Palincsar, A. S., & Herrenkohl, L. R. (2002). Designing collaborative learning contexts. *Theory Into Practice, 61*, 26–32.

Palincsar, A. S., Magnusson, S. J., Collins, K. M., & Cutter, J. (2001). Promoting deep understanding of science in students with disabilities in inclusion classrooms. *Learning Disabilities Quarterly, 24*(1), 15–32.

Palincsar, A. S., Magnuson, S. J., Marano, N., Ford, D., & Brown, N. (1998). Designing a community of practice: Principles and practices of the GIsML community. *Teaching and Teacher Education, 14*, 5–19.

Panitz, T. (1996). *A definition of collaborative vs cooperative learning.* Available online at: http://www.londonmet.ac.uk/deliberations/collaborative-learning/panitz-paper.cfm

Papanikolaou, K., & Boubouka, M. (2010-2011). Promoting collaboration in a project-based e-learning context. *Journal of Research on Technology in Education, 43*, 135–155.

Paris, S. G., Byrnes, J. P., & Paris, A. H. (2001). Constructing theories, identities, and actions of self-regulated learners. In B. J. Zimmerman & D. H. Schunk (Eds.), *Self-regulated learning and academic achievement: Theoretical perspectives* (2nd ed., pp. 253–287). Mahwah, NJ: Erlbaum.

Paris, S. G., & Cunningham, A. E. (1996). Children becoming students. In D. Berliner & R. Calfee (Eds.), *Handbook of educational psychology* (pp. 117–146). New York, NY: Macmillan.

Paris, S. G., Morrison, F. J., & Miller, K. F. (2006). Academic pathways from preschool through elementary school. In P. A. Alexander & P. H. Winne (Eds.), *Handbook of educational psychology* (2nd ed., pp. 61–85). Mahwah, NJ: Erlbaum.

Parker, W. C., & Hess, D. (2001). Teaching with and for discussion. *Teaching and Teacher Education, 17*, 273–289.

Pashler, H., McDaniel, M., Rohrer, D., & Bjork, R. (2009). Learning styles: Concepts and evidence. *Psychological Science in the Public Interest, 9*, 105–119.

Patall, E. A., Cooper, H., & Wynn, S. R. (2010). The effectiveness and relative importance of choice in the classroom. *Journal of Educational Psychology, 102*, 896–915.

Pate, P. E., McGinnis, K., & Homestead, E. (1995). Creating coherence through curriculum integration. In M. Harmin (1994), *Inspiring active learning: A handbook for teachers* (pp. 62–70). Alexandria, VA: Association for Supervision and Curriculum Development.

Patterson, C. (1995). Lesbian & gay parenting. Available online at: http://www.apa.org/pi/lgbt/resources/parenting.aspx

Patterson, G. R. (1997). Performance models for parenting: A social interactional perspective. In J. Grusec & L. Kuczynski (Eds.), *Parenting and the socialization of values: A handbook of contemporary theory* (pp. 193–235). New York, NY: Wiley.

Paul, A. M. (2011, September 10). The trouble with homework. *New York Times*, Sunday Review Section, p. 6.

Paulos, L. (2007). Multitasking madness. *Scholastic Choices, 23*(1), 10–13.

Pearl, R., Leung, M. C., Acker, R. V., Farmer, T. W., & Rodkin, P. C. (2007). Fourth- and fifth-grade teachers' awareness of their classrooms' social networks. *The Elementary School Journal, 108*, 25–39.

Pearson, B. Z., Fernandez, S. C., Lewedeg, V., & Oller, D. K. (1997). The relation of input factors to lexical learning by bilingual infants. *Applied Linguistics, 18*, 41–58.

Pekrun, R., Elliot, A. J., & Maier, M. A. (2006). Achievement goals and discrete achievement emotions: A theoretical model and prospective test. *Journal of Educational Psychology, 98*, 583–597.

Pekrun, R., Goetz, T., Daniels, L. M., Stupinisky, R. H., & Perry, R. P. (2010). Boredom in achievement settings: Exploring control–value antecedents and performance outcomes of a neglected emotion. *Journal of Educational Psychology, 102*, 531–549.

Pekrun, R., Goetz, T., Titz, W., & Perry, R. P. (2002). Academic emotions in students' self-regulated learning and achievement. A program of qualitative and quantitative research. *Educational Psychologist, 37*, 91–105.

Pellegrini, A. D., Bartini, M., & Brooks, F. (1999). School bullies, victims, and aggressive victims: Factors relating to group affiliation and victimization in early adolescence. *Journal of Educational Psychology, 91*, 216–224.

Pellegrini, A. D., & Bohn, C. M. (2005). The role of recess in children's cognitive performance and school adjustment. *Educational Researcher, 34*, 13–19.

Pellegrini, A. D., Dupuis, D., & Smith, P. K. (2007). Play in evolution and development. *Developmental Review, 27*, 261–276.

Pellegrino, L. (2002). Cerebral palsy. In M. L. Batshaw (Ed.), *Children with disabilities.* Baltimore, MD: Brookes.

Pellis, S. (2006). The effects of orbital frontal cortex damage on the modulation of defensive responses by rats in playful and nonplayful social contexts. *Behavioral Neuroscience, 120*, 72–84.

Peng, S., & Lee, R. (1992, April). *Home variables, parent–child activities, and academic achievement: A study of 1988 eighth graders.* Paper presented at the annual meeting of the American Educational Research Association, San Francisco, CA.

Penuel, W. R., & Wertsch, J. V. (1995). Vygotsky and identity formation: A sociocultural approach. *Educational Psychologist, 30*, 83–92.

Peregoy, S. F., & Boyle, O. F. (2009. *Reading, writing, and learning in ESL: A resource book for teaching K–12 English learners* (5th ed.). Boston, MA: Allyn & Bacon/Pearson.

Perkins, D. N., Jay, E., & Tishman, S. (1993). New conceptions of thinking: From ontology to education. *Educational Psychologist, 28*, 67–85.

Perner, J. (2000). Memory and theory of mind. In E. Tulving & F. I. M. Craik (Eds.), *The Oxford handbook of memory* (pp. 297–312). New York, NY: Oxford.

Perry, N. E., & Collie, R. J. (2011, April). School climate and social and emotional learning: Predictors of early career teacher well-being and efficacy. Paper presented at the annual meeting of the American Educational Research Association, New Orleans, LA.

Perry, N. E., & Drummond, L. (2002). Helping young students become self-regulated researchers and writers. *The Reading Teacher, 56*, 298–310.

Perry, N. E., Phillips, L., & Dowler, J. (2004). Examining features of tasks and their potential to promote self-regulated learning. *Teachers College Record, 106*, 1854–1878.

Perry, N. E., & Rahim, A. (2011) Studying self-regulated learning in classrooms. In B.

Zimmerman & D. Schunk (Eds.), *Handbook of self-regulation of learning and performance* (pp. 122–136) New York, NY: Routledge.

Perry, N. E., VandeKamp, K. O., & Mercer, L. K. (2000, April). *Investigating teacher-student interactions that foster self-regulated learning.* In N. E. Perry (Chair), Symposium conducted at the meeting of the American Educational Research Association, New Orleans, LA.

Perry, N. E., VandeKamp, K. O., Mercer, L. K., & Nordby, C. J. (2002). Investigating teacher-student interactions that foster self-regulated learning. *Educational Psychologist, 37*, 5–15.

Peter, M., Glück, J., & Beiglböck, W. (2010). Map understanding as a developmental marker in childhood. *Journal of Individual Differences, 31*, 64–67.

Petitclerc, A., Boivin, M., Dionne, G., Zoccolillo, M., & Tremblay, R. E. (2009). Disregard for rules: The early development and predictors of a specific dimension of disruptive behavior disorders. *Journal of Child Psychology and Psychiatry, 50*, 1477–1484.

Petitto, L. A. (2009). New discoveries from the bilingual brain and mind across the life span: Implications for education. *Brain, Mind, and Education, 3*, 185–197.

Petitto, L. A., & Kovelman, I. (2003). The bilingual paradox: How signing-speaking bilingual children help us resolve bilingual issues and teach us about the brain's mechanisms underlying all language acquisition. *Language Learning, 8*(3), 5–18.

Petrill, S. A., & Wilkerson, B. (2000). Intelligence and achievement: A behavioral genetic perspective. *Educational Psychology Review, 12*, 185–199.

Pettigrew, T. (1998). Intergroup contact theory. In J. T. Spence, J. M. Darley, & D. J. Foss (Eds.), *Annual review of psychology* (pp. 65–85). Palo Alto, CA: Annual Reviews.

Peverly, S. T., Brobst, K., Graham, M., & Shaw, R. (2003). College adults are not good at self-regulation: A study on the relationship of self-regulation, note-taking, and test-taking. *Journal of Educational Psychology, 95*, 335–346.

Peverly, S. T., Ramaswamy, V., Brown, C., Sumowski, J., & Alidoost, M., & Garner, J. (2007). What predicts skill in lecture note taking? *Journal of Educational Psychology, 99*, 167–180.

Pfiffner, L., Barkley, R. A., & DuPaul, G. J. (2006). Treatment of ADHD in school settings. In R. A. Barkley (Ed.), *Attention-deficit hyperactivity disorder: A handbook for diagnosis and treatment* (3rd ed., pp. 547–588). New York, NY: Guilford.

Pfiffner, L. J., & O'Leary, S. G. (1987). The efficacy of all positive management as a function of the prior use of negative consequences. *Journal of Applied Behavior Analysis, 20*, 265–271.

Phillips, D. (1997). How, why, what, when, and where: Perspectives on constructivism and education. *Issues in Education: Contributions from Educational Psychology, 3*, 151–194.

Phillips, D., & Zimmerman, M. (1990). The developmental course of perceived competence and incompetence among competent children. In R. Sternberg & J. Kolligian (Eds.), *Competence considered* (pp. 41–66). New Haven, CT: Yale University Press.

Phinney, J. S. (1990). Ethnic identity in adolescents and adults: Review of research. *Psychological Bulletin, 108*(3), 499–514.

Phinney, J. S. (2003). Ethnic identity and acculturation. In K. Chun, P. Ball, & Marin, G. (Eds.),

Acculturation: Advances in theory, measurement, and applied research (pp. 63–81). Washington, DC: American Psychological Association.

Phinney, J. S., & Devich-Navarro, M. (1997). Variations in bicultural identification among African American and Mexican American adolescents. *Journal of Research on Adolescence, 7,* 3–32.

Phye, G. D. (1992). Strategic transfer: A tool for academic problem solving. *Educational Psychology Review, 4,* 393–421.

Phye, G. D. (2001). Problem-solving instruction and problem-solving transfer: The correspondence issue. *Journal of Educational Psychology, 93,* 571–578.

Phye, G. D., & Sanders, C. E. (1994). Advice and feedback: Elements of practice for problem solving. *Contemporary Educational Psychology, 17,* 211–223.

Piaget, J. (1954). *The construction of reality in the child* (M. Cook, Trans.). New York, NY: Basic Books.

Piaget, J. (1962). *Comments on Vygotsky's critical remarks concerning "The language and thought of the child" and "Judgment and reasoning in the child."* Cambridge, MA: MIT Press.

Piaget, J. (1963). *Origins of intelligence in children.* New York, NY: Norton.

Piaget, J. (1964). Development and learning. In R. Ripple & V. Rockcastle (Eds.), *Piaget rediscovered* (pp. 7–20). Ithaca, NY: Cornell University Press.

Piaget, J. (1965). *The moral judgment of the child.* New York, NY: Free Press.

Piaget, J. (1965/1995). *Sociological studies.* New York, NY: Routledge. (Original work published in 1965.)

Piaget, J. (1969). *Science of education and the psychology of the child.* New York, NY: Viking.

Piaget, J. (1970a). Piaget's theory. In P. Mussen (Ed.), *Handbook of child psychology* (3rd ed.) (Vol. 1, pp. 703–732). New York, NY: Wiley.

Piaget, J. (1970b). *The science of education and the psychology of the child.* New York, NY: Orion Press.

Piaget, J. (1971). *Biology and knowledge.* Edinburgh, UK: Edinburgh Press.

Piaget, J. (1974). *Understanding causality* (D. Miles and M. Miles, Trans.). New York, NY: Norton.

Piaget, J. (1985). *The equilibrium of cognitive structures: The central problem of intellectual development* (T. Brown & K. L. Thampy, Trans.). Chicago, IL: University of Chicago Press.

Pianta, R. C., Belsky, J., Vandergrift, N., Houts, R., & Morrison, F. J. (2008). Classroom effects on children's achievement trajectories in elementary school. *American Educational Research Journal, 45,* 365–397.

Pianta, R. C., Howes, C., Burchinal, M., Bryant, D. M., Clifford, R. M., Early, D. M., & Barbarin, O. (2005). Features of pre-kindergarten programs, classrooms, and teachers: Do they predict observed classroom quality and child–teacher interactions? *Applied Developmental Science, 9*(3), 144–159.

Pigge, F. L., & Marso, R. N. (1997). A seven-year longitudinal multi-factor assessment of teaching concerns development through preparation and early teaching. *Teaching and Teacher Education, 13,* 225–235.

Pinker, S. (2002). *The blank slate: The modern denial of human nature.* New York, NY: Penguin.

Pintrich, P. R. (2000). Educational psychology at the millennium: A look back and a look forward. *Educational Psychologist, 35,* 221–226.

Pintrich, P. R. (2003). A motivational science perspective on the role of student motivation in learning and teaching. *Journal of Educational Psychology, 95,* 667–686.

Pintrich, P. R., Marx, R. W., & Boyle, R. A. (1993). Beyond cold conceptual change: The role of motivational beliefs and classroom contextual factors in the process of conceptual change. *Review of Educational Research, 63,* 167–199.

Pintrich, P. R., & Schunk, D. H. (2002). *Motivation in education: Research and applications* (2nd ed.). Boston, MA: Allyn and Bacon.

Pintrich, P. R., & Zusho, A. (2002). The development of academic self-regulation: The role of cognitive and motivational factors. In A. Wigfield & J. Eccles (Eds.), *Development of achievement motivation* (pp. 249–284). San Diego, CA: Academic Press.

Pinxten, M., De Fraine, B., Van Damme, J., & D'Haenens, E. (2010). Causal ordering of academic self-concept and achievement: Effects of type of achievement measure. *British Journal of Educational Psychology, 80,* 689–709.

Pisha, B., & Coyne, P. (2001). Smart for the start: The promise of universal design for learning. *Remedial and Special Education, 22,* 197–203.

Plant, E. A., & Peruche, B. M. (2005). The consequences of race for police officers' responses to criminal suspects. *Psychological Science, 16,* 180–183.

Plucker, J. A., Beghetto, R. A., & Dow, G. T. (2004). Why isn't creativity more important to educational psychologists? Potential pitfalls and future directions in creativity research. *Educational Psychology, 39*(2), 83–96.

Plummer, D. L, & Graziano, W. G. (1987). Impact of grade retention on the social development of elementary school children." *Developmental Psychology, 23,* 267–275.

Polson, P. G., & Jeffries, R. (1985). Instruction in general problem-solving skills: An analysis of four approaches. In J. Segal, S. Chipman, & R. Glaser (Eds.), *Thinking and learning skills* (Vol. 1, pp. 417–455). Mahwah, NJ: Erlbaum.

Ponitz, C. C., Rimm-Kaufman, S. E., Grimm, K. J., & Curby, T. W. (2009). Kindergarten classroom quality, behavioral engagement, and reading achievement. *School Psychology Review, 38,* 102–120.

Popham, W. J. (2005a). *Classroom assessment: What teachers need to know* (4th ed.). Boston, MA: Allyn & Bacon.

Popham, W. J. (2008). *Classroom assessment: What teachers need to know* (5th ed.). Boston, MA: Allyn & Bacon.

Popham, W. J. (2011). *Classroom assessment: What teachers need to know* (6th ed.). Boston, MA: Allyn & Bacon.

Portes, A., & Hao, L. (1998). E pluribus unum: Bilingualism and loss of language in the second generation. *Sociology of Education, 71:* 269–294.

Posada, G., Jacobs, A., Richmond, M., Carbonell, O. A., Alzate, G., Bustamante, M. R., & Quiceno, J. (2002). Maternal care giving and infant security in two cultures. *Developmental Psychology, 38,* 67–78.

Posner, M. I. (1973). *Cognition: An introduction.* Glenview, IL: Scott, Foresman.

Prat-Sala, M., & Redford, P. (2010). The interplay between motivation, self-efficacy, and approaches to studying. *British Journal of Educational Psychology, 80,* 283–305.

Prawat, R. S. (1992). Teachers beliefs about teaching and learning: A constructivist perspective. *American Journal of Education, 100,* 354–395.

Prawat, R. S. (1996). Constructivism, modern and postmodern. *Issues in Education: Contributions from Educational Psychology, 3,* 215–226.

Preckel, T., Goetz, T., & Frenzel, A. (2010). Ability grouping of gifted students: Effects on academic self-concept and boredom. *British Journal of Educational Psychology, 80,* 451–472.

Premack, D. (1965). Reinforcement theory. In D. Levine (Ed.), *Nebraska symposium on motivation* (Vol. 13, pp. 123–180). Lincoln, NE: University of Nebraska Press.

Pressley, M. (1995). More about the development of self-regulation: complex, long-term, and thoroughly social. *Educational Psychologist, 30,* 207–212.

Pressley, M. (1996, August). *Getting beyond whole language: Elementary reading instruction that makes sense in light of recent psychological research.* Paper presented at the annual meeting of the American Psychological Association, Toronto.

Pressley, M., & Harris, K. A. (2006). Cognitive strategies instruction: From basic research to classroom instruction. In P. A. Alexander & P. H. Winne (Eds.), *Handbook of educational psychology* (2nd ed., pp. 265–286). Mahwah, NJ: Erlbaum.

Pressley, M., Levin, J., & Delaney, H. D. (1982). The mnemonic keyword method. *Review of Research in Education, 52,* 61–91.

Pressley, M., Mohan, L., Raphael, L. M., & Fingeret, L. (2007). How does Bennett Woods Elementary School produce such high reading and writing achievement? *Journal of Educational Psychology, 99,* 221–240.

Pressley, M., Raphael, L., Gallagher, J. D., & DiBella, J. (2004). Providence St. Mel School: How a school that works for African American students works. *Journal of Educational Psychology, 96*(2), 216–235.

Pressley, M., & Roehrig, A. (2003). Educational psychology in the modern era: 1960 to the present. In B. J. Zimmerman & D. H. Schunk (Eds.), *Educational psychology: A century of contributions* (pp. 333–366). [A Project of Division 15 (Educational Psychology) of the American Psychological Association]. Mahwah, NJ: Erlbaum.

Pressley, M., & Woloshyn, V. (1995). *Cognitive strategy instruction that really improves children's academic performance.* Cambridge, MA: Brookline Books.

Price, L. F. (2005). The biology of risk taking. *Educational Leadership, 62*(7), 22–27.

Price, W. F., & Crapo, R. H. (2002). *Cross-cultural perspectives in introductory psychology* (4th ed.). Pacific Grove, CA: Wadsworth.

Proctor, C. P., August, D., Carlo, M. S., & Snow, C. (2006). The intriguing role of Spanish language vocabulary knowledge in predicting English reading comprehension. *Journal of Educational Psychology, 98,* 159–169.

Project Tomorrow. (2010). *The new 3 E's of education: Enabled, engaged, empowered. How today's students are leveraging emerging technologies for learning.* Irvine, CA: Project Tomorrow. Available online at: http://www.tomorrow.org/about/team.html

Public Agenda Foundation. (1994). *First things first: What Americans expect from public schools.* New York, NY: Author.

Pugh, K. J., & Bergin, D. A. (2006). Motivational influences on transfer. *Educational Psychologist, 41,* 147–160.

Pugh, K. J., & Phillips, M. M. (2011). Content appreciation: Why it matters and how you can foster it. *Theory Into Practice, 50.*

Puncochar, J., & Fox, P. W. (2004). Confidence in individual and group decision-making: When "Two Heads" are worse than one. *Journal of Educational Psychology, 96,* 582–591.

Puntambekar, S., & Hubscher, R. (2005). Tools for scaffolding students in a complex learning environment: What have we gained and what have we missed? *Educational Psychologist, 40,* 1–12.

Purdie, N., Hattie, J., & Carroll, A. (2002). A review of the research on interventions for Attention Deficit Hyperactivity Disorder: What works best? *Review of Educational Research, 72,* 61–99.

Puustinen, M., & Pulkkinen, L. (2001). Models of self-regulated learning: A review. *Scandinavian Journal of Educational Research, 45,* 269–286.

Rachlin, H. (1991). Introduction to modern behaviorism (3rd ed.). New York, NY: W. H. Freeman.

Rachlin, H. (2004). *The science of self-control.* Cambridge, MA: Harvard University Press.

Ramirez, J. D., Yuen, S. D., & Ramey, D. R. (1991). *Final report: Longitudinal study of structured immersion strategy, early-exit, and late-exit transitional bilingual education programs for language-minority children.* San Mateo, CA: Aguirre International.

Raudenbush, S. (1984). Magnitude of teacher expectancy effects on pupil IQ as a function of the credibility of expectancy induction: A synthesis of findings from 18 experiments. *Journal of Educational Psychology, 76,* 85–97.

Raudenbush, S.W. (2009). The *Brown* Legacy and the O'Connor Challenge: Transforming schools in the images of children's potential. *Educational Researcher, 38,* 169–180.

Raudsepp, E., & Haugh, G. P. (1977). *Creative growth games.* New York, NY: Harcourt Brace Jovanovich.

Rauscher, F. H., & Shaw, G. L. (1998). Key components of the Mozart effect. *Perceptual and Motor Skills, 86,* 835–841.

Reder, L. M. (1996). Different research programs on metacognition: Are the boundaries imaginary? *Learning and Individual Differences, 8,* 383–390.

Reder, L. M., Park, H., & Kieffaber, P. D. (2009). Memory systems do not divide on consciousness: reinterpreting memory in terms of activation and binding. *Psychological Bulletin, 135,* 23–49.

Reed, S. K. (2006). Cognitive architecture for multimedia learning. *Educational Psychologist, 41,* 87–98.

Reeve, J. (1996). *Motivating others: Nurturing inner motivational resources.* Boston, MA: Allyn & Bacon.

Reeve, J. (2002). Self-determination theory applied to educational settings. In E. L. Deci & R. M. Ryan (Eds.), *Handbook of self-determination research* (pp. 183–203). Rochester, NY: University of Rochester Press.

Reeve, J. (2009). Why teachers adopt a controlling motivating style toward students and how they can become more autonomy supportive. *Educational Psychologist, 44,* 159–175.

Reeve, J., Deci, E. L., & Ryan, R. M. (2004). *Self-determination theory: A dialectical framework for understanding the sociocultural influences on motivation and learning: Big theories revisited* (Vol. 4, pp. 31–59). Greenwich, CT: Information Age Press.

Reeve, J., & Jang, H. (2006a). Teachers as facilitators: What autonomy-supportive teachers do and why their students benefit. *Elementary School Journal, 106,* 225–236.

Reeve, J., & Jang, H. (2006b). What teachers say and do to support students' autonomy during a learning activity. *Journal of Educational Psychology, 98,* 209–218.

Reeve, J., Nix, G., & Hamm, D. (2003). The experience of self-determination in intrinsic motivation and the conundrum of choice. *Journal of Educational Psychology, 95,* 347–392.

Refugee Council USA. (2011). History of the U.S. refugee resettlement program. Washington DC: Refugee Council USA. Available online at: http://www.rcusa.org/index.php?page=history

Reid, J. M., & Byrd, P. (1998). *Grammar in the composition classroom.* New York, NY: Heinle & Heinle Publisher.

Reimann, P., & Chi, M. T. H. (1989). Human expertise. In K. J. Gilhooly (Ed.), *Human and machine problem solving* (pp. 161–191). New York, NY: Plenum Press.

Reinke, W. M., & Herman, K. C. (2002a). A research agenda for school violence prevention. *American Psychologist, 57,* 796–797.

Reinke, W. M., & Herman, K. C. (2002b). Creating school environments that deter antisocial behaviors in youth. *Psychology in the Schools, 39,* 549–560.

Reis, S. M., Kaplan, S. N., Tomlinson, C. A., Westberg, K. L., Callahan, C. M., & Cooper, C. R. (2002). Equal does not mean identical. In L. Abbeduto (Ed.), *Taking sides: Clashing on controversial issues in educational psychology* (pp. 31–35). Guilford, CT: McGraw-Hill/Duskin.

Reis, S. M., & Renzulli, J. S. (2004). Current research on the social and emotional development of gifted and talented students: Good news and future possibilities. *Psychology in the Schools, 41,* published online in Wiley InterScience (www.interscience.wiley.com).

Reisberg, D., & Heuer, F. (1992). Remembering the details of emotional events. In E. Winograd & U. Neisser (Eds.), *Affect and accuracy in recall: Studies of "flashbulb" memories.* Cambridge, UK: Cambridge University Press.

Reiss, S. (2004). Multifaceted nature of intrinsic motivation: The theory of 16 basic desires. *Review of General Psychology, 8,* 179–193.

Render, G. F., Padilla, J. N. M., & Krank, H. M. (1989). What research really shows about assertive discipline. *Educational Leadership, 46*(6), 72–75.

Renninger, K. A. (2009). Interest and identity development in instruction: An inductive model. *Educational Psychologist, 44,* 105–118.

Renzulli, J. S., & Reis, S. M. (2003). The schoolwide enrichment model: Developing creative and productive giftedness. In N. Colangelo & G. A. Davis (Eds.), *Handbook of gifted education* (pp. 184–203). Boston, MA: Allyn & Bacon.

Resnick, L. B. (1981). Instructional psychology. *Annual Review of Psychology, 32,* 659–704.

Reynolds, C. R., & Shaywitz, S. E. (2009). Response to Intervention: Ready or not? Or, from wait-to-fail to watch-them-fail. *School Psychology Quarterly, 24,* 130–145.

Rhodes, R. A. (1997). *Community service and higher learning: Explorations of the caring self.* Albany, NY: State University of New York Press.

Rice, F. P., & Dolgin, K. G. (2002). *The adolescent: Development, relationships, and culture* (10th ed.). Boston, MA: Allyn & Bacon.

Rice, M. L. (1989). Children's language acquisition. *American Psychologist, 44,* 149–156.

Richell, R., Deakin, J., & Anderson, I. (2005). Effect of acute tryptophan depletion on the response to controllable and uncontrollable noise stress. *Biological Psychiatry, 57,* 295–300.

Richtell, M. (2011, September 3). In classroom of the future, stagnant score. *New York Times,* A1.

Rideout, V. J., Foehr, U. G., & Roberts, D. F. (2010, January). Generation M: Media in the lives of 8–18 year-olds. Kaiser Family Foundation. Available online at: http://www.kff.org/entmedia/upload/8010.pdf

Rideout, V. J., Vandewater, E. A., & Wartella, E. A. (2003). *Zero to six: Electronic media in the lives of infants, toddlers, and preschoolers* (No. 3378). Menlo Park, CA: Henry J. Kaiser Family Foundation and the Children's Digital Media Centers (CDMC).

Riggs, N. R., Sakuma, K. K., & Pentz, M. A. (2007). Preventing risk for obesity by promoting self-regulation and decision-making skills: Pilot results from the PATHWAYS to health program (PATHWAYS). *Education Review, 31,* 287–310.

Rittle-Johnson, B., & Star, J. R. (2007). Does comparing solution methods facilitate conceptual and procedural knowledge? An experimental study on learning to solve equations. *Journal of Educational Psychology, 99,* 561–574.

Rivkin, S. G., Hanushek, E. A., & Kain, J. F. (2001). *Teachers, schools, and academic achievement.* Amherst, MA: Amherst College.

Rizzolatti, G., Fadiga, L., Gallese, V., & Fogassi, L. (1996). Premotor cortex and the recognition of motor actions. *Brain Research: Cognitive Brain Research, 3*(2), 131–141.

Robbins, S. B., Lauver, K., Davis, H. L., Davis, D., Langley, R., & Carlstrom, A. (2004). Psychosocial and study skill factors predict college outcomes? A meta-analysis. *Psychological Bulletin, 130,* 261–288.

Robbins, S. B., Le, L., & Lauver, K. (2005). Promoting successful college outcomes for all students: Reply to Weissberg and Owen (2005). *Psychological Bulletin, 131,* 410–411.

Roberge, M. M. (2002). California's Generation 1.5 immigrants: What experiences, characterisitcs, and needs do they bring to our English classes? *The CATESOL Journal, 14*(1), 107–129.

Roberson, D., Davidoff, J., Davies, I. R. L., & Shapiro, L. R. (2004). The development of color categories in two languages: A longitudinal study. *Journal of Experimental Psychology: General, 133,* 554–571.

Roberts, D. F., Foehr, U. G., & Rideout, V. (2005). *Generation M: Media in the lives of 8–18 year-olds.* Technical Reports 7250/7251. Menlo Park, CA: Kaiser Family foundation. Available online at: http://www.kff.org/entmedia/7251.cfm

Roberts, D. S., Tingstrom, D. H., Olmi, D. J., & Bellipanni, K. D. (2008). Positive antecedent and consequent components in child compliance training. *Behavior Modification, 32,* 21–38.

Roberts, G., Mohammed, S. S., & Vaughn, S. (2010). Reading achievement across three language groups: Growth estimates for overall reading and reading subskills obtained with the early childhood longitudinal survey. *Journal of Educational Psychology, 102,* 668–686.

Robinson, A., & Clinkenbeard, P. R. (1998). Giftedness: An exceptionality examined. In J. T. Spence, J. M. Darley, & D. J. Foss (Eds.), *Annual review of psychology* (pp. 117–139). Palo Alto, CA: Annual Reviews.

Robinson, D. H. (1998). Graphic organizers as aids to test learning. *Reading Research and Instruction, 37,* 85–105.

Robinson, D. H., & Kiewra, K. A. (1995). Visual argument: Graphic outlines are superior to outlines in improving learning from text. *Journal of Educational Psychology, 87,* 455–467.

Roediger, H. L., & Karpicke, J. D. (2006). The power of testing memory. *Perspectives on Psychological Science, 1,* 181–210.

Roeser, R. W., Peck, S. C., & Nasir, N. S. (2006). Self and identity processes in school motivation, learning, and achievement. In P. A. Alexander & P. H. Winne (Eds.), *Handbook of educational psychology* (2nd ed., pp. 391–424). Mahwah, NJ: Erlbaum.

Rogers, C. R., & Freiberg, H. J. (1994). *Freedom to learn* (3rd ed.). Columbus, OH: Merrill.

Rogoff, B. (1990). *Apprenticeship in thinking: Cognitive development in social context.* New York, NY: Oxford University Press.

Rogoff, B. (1995). Observing sociocultural activity on three planes: Participatory appropriation, guided participation, and apprenticeship. In J. Wertsch, P. del Rio, & A. Alverez (Eds.), *Sociocultural studies of mind* (pp. 139–164). Cambridge, UK: Cambridge University Press.

Rogoff, B. (1998). Cognition as a collaborative process. In W. Damon (Series Ed.) and D. Kuhn & R. S. Siegler (Vol. Eds.), *Handbook of child psychology: Vol. 2* (5th ed., pp. 679–744). New York, NY: Wiley.

Rogoff, B. (2003). *The cultural nature of human development.* New York, NY: Oxford University Press.

Rogoff, B., & Morelii, G. (1989). Perspectives on children's development from cultural psychology. *American Psychologist, 44,* 343–348.

Rogoff, B., Turkanis, C. G., & Bartlett, L. (2001). *Learning together: Children and adults in a school community.* New York, NY: Oxford.

Roid, G. H. (2003). *Stanford-Binet Intelligence Scales, Fifth Edition.* Itasca, IL: Riverside Publishing.

Rop, C. (1997/1998). Breaking the gender barrier in the physical sciences. *Educational Leadership, 55*(4), 58–60.

Rosch, E. H. (1973). On the internal structure of perceptual and semantic categories. In T. Moore (Ed.), *Cognitive development and the acquisition of language* (pp. 111–144). New York, NY: Academic Press.

Roschelle, J. M., Pea, R. D., Hoadiey, C. M., Gordon, D. N., & Means, B. M. (2000, Fall/Winter). Changing how and what children learn in school with computer-based technologies. *Children and Computer Technology, 10*(2), 76–101.

Rosen, L. (2010). *Rewired: Understanding the iGeneration and the way they learn.* New York, NY: Palgrave Macmillan.

Rosenberg, M. (1979). *Conceiving the self.* New York, NY: Basic Books.

Rosenberg, M. S., Westling, D. L., & McLeskey, J. (2011). *Special education for today's teachers: An introduction.* Boston, MA: Allyn & Bacon/Pearson.

Rosenfeld, M., & Rosenfeld, S. (2004). Developing teacher sensitivities to individual learning differences. *Educational Psychology, 24,* 465–486.

Rosenshine, B. (1988). Explicit teaching. In D. Berliner & B. Rosenshine (Eds.), *Talks to teachers* (pp. 75–92). New York, NY: Random House.

Rosenshine, B., & Furst, N. (1973). The use of direct observation to study teaching. In R. Travers (Ed.), *Second handbook of research on teaching.* Chicago, IL: Rand McNally.

Rosenshine, B., & Meister, C. (1992, April). *The uses of scaffolds for teaching less structured academic tasks.* Paper presented at the annual meeting of the American Educational Research Association, San Francisco, CA.

Rosenshine, B., & Meister, C. (1994). Reciprocal teaching: A review of the research. *Review of Educational Research, 64,* 479–530.

Rosenshine, B., & Stevens, R. (1986). Teaching functions. In M. Wittrock (Ed.), *Handbook of research on teaching* (3rd ed., pp. 376–391). New York, NY: Macmillan.

Rosenthal, R. (1995). Critiquing Pygmalion: A 25-year perspective. *Current Directions in Psychological Science, 4,* 171–172.

Rosenthal, R., & Jacobson, L. (1968). *Pygmalion in the classroom.* New York, NY: Holt, Rinehart, Winston.

Roskos, K., & Neuman, S. B. (1998). Play as an opportunity for literacy. In O. N. Saracho & B. Spodek (Eds.), *Multiple perspectives on play in early childhood education* (pp. 100–115). Albany, NY: State University of New York Press.

Ross, J. A., & Raphael, D. (1990). Communication and problem solving achievement in cooperative learning groups. *Journal of Curriculum Studies, 22,* 149–164.

Rotherham-Borus, M. J. (1994). Bicultural reference group orientations and adjustment. In M. Bernal & G. Knight (Eds.), *Ethnic identity.* Albany, NY: State University of New York Press.

Rowe, E. W., Kingsley, J. M., & Thompson, D. F. (2010). Predictive ability of the general ability index (GAI) versus the full scale IQ among gifted referrals. *School Psychology Quarterly, 25,* 119–128.

Rowe, M. B. (1974). Wait-time and rewards as instructional variables: Their influence on language, logic, and fate control. Part 1: Wait-time. *Journal of Research in Science Teaching, 11,* 81–94.

Rubie-Davies, C. M. (2010). Teacher expectations and perceptions of student attributes: Is there a relationship? *British Journal of Educational Psychology, 80,* 121–135.

Rubin, K. H., Coplan, R., Chen, X., Buskirk, A. A., & Wojslawowicz, J. C. (2005). Peer relationships in childhood. In M. H. Bornstein & M. E. Lamb (Eds.), *Developmental science: An advanced textbook* (pp. 469–512). Mahwah, NJ: Erlbaum.

Rubinsten, O., & Henik, A. (2006). Double dissociations of functions in developmental dyslexia and dyscalculia. *Journal of Educational Psychology, 98,* 854–867.

Ruble, D. N., Martin, C. L., & Berenbaum, S. A. (2006). Gender development. In *Handbook of child psychology* (Vol. 3, pp. 858–932). Hoboken, NJ: John Wiley & Sons.

Rudolph, K. D., Lambert, S. F., Clark, A. G., & Kurlakowsky, K. D. (2001). Negotiating the transition to middle school: The role of self-regulatory processes. *Child Development, 72,* 926–946.

Rueda, R., & Moll, L. C. (1994) A sociocultural perspective on motivation. In F. O'Neil Jr. & M. Drillings (Eds.), *Motivation: Theory and research* (pp. 117–137). Hillsdale, NJ: Erlbaum.

Rummel, N., Levin, J. R., & Woodward, M. M. (2003). Do pictorial mnemonic text-learning aids give students something worth writing about? *Journal of Educational Psychology, 95,* 327–334.

Ryan, A. (2001). The peer group as a context for development of young adolescents' motivation and achievement. *Child Development, 72,* 1135–1150.

Ryan, K. E., & Ryan, A. M. (2005). Psychological processes underlying stereotype threat and standardized math test performance. *Educational Psychologist, 40,* 53–63.

Ryan, R. M., & Deci, E. L. (1996). When paradigms clash: Comments on Cameron and Pierce's claim that rewards do not undermine intrinsic motivation. *Review of Educational Research, 66,* 33–38.

Ryan, R. M., & Deci, E. L. (2000). Intrinsic and extrinsic motivation: Classic definitions and new directions. *Contemporary Educational Psychology, 25,* 54–67.

Sackett, P. R., Hardison, C. M., & Cullen, M. J. (2004). On the value of correcting mischaracterizations of stereotype threat. *American Psychologist, 59,* 48–49.

Sackett, P. R., Kuncel, N. R., Arneson, J. J., Cooper, S. R., & Waters, S. D. (2009). Does socioeconomic status explain the relationship between admissions tests and post-secondary academic performance? *Psychological Bulletin, 135,* 1–22.

Sadker, M., & Sadker, D. (1986). Questioning skills. In J. Cooper (Ed.), *Classroom Teaching Skills: A Handbook* (3rd ed., pp. 143–160). Boston, MA: D. C. Heath.

Sadker, M., & Sadker, D. (2006). Questioning skills. In J. Cooper (Ed.), *Classroom teaching skills* (8th ed., pp. 104–150). Boston, MA: Houghton-Mifflin.

Sadker, M., Sadker, D., & Klein, S. (1991). The issue of gender in elementary and secondary education. *Review of Research in Education, 17,* 269–334.

Sagor, R. (2003). *Motivating students and teachers in an era of standards.* Alexandria, VA: Association for Supervision and Curriculum Development.

Sakiz, G., Pape, S., & Woolfolk Hoy, A. (2008, March). Does teacher affective support matter? The role of affective support in middle school mathematics classrooms. Paper presented at the annual meeting of the American Educational Research Association, New York, NY.

Salomon, G., & Perkins, D. N. (1989). Rocky roads to transfer: Re-thinking mechanisms of a neglected phenomenon. *Educational Psychologist, 24,* 113–142.

Sanchez, F., & Anderson, M. L. (1990, May). Gang mediation: A process that works. *Principal,* 54–56.

Sanders, W. L., & Rivers, J. C. (1996). *Cumulative and residual effects of teachers on student academic achievement.* Knoxville, TN: University of Tennessee Value-Added Research and Assessment Center.

Sattler, J. M. (2001). *Assessment of children: Cognitive applications* (4th ed.). San Diego, CA: Jerome M. Sattler, Inc.

Sattler, J. M., & Hoge, R. D. (2006). *Assessment of children: Behavioral, social, and clinical foundations.* La Mesa, CA: Jerome M. Sattler Publisher.

Savage, T. V. (1999). *Teaching self-control through management and discipline*. Boston, MA: Allyn & Bacon.

Savin-Williams, R. C. (2006). Who's gay? Does it matter? *Current Directions in Psychological Science, 15*(1), 40–44.

Sawyer, R. K. (2006). *Explaining creativity: The science of human motivation*. New York, NY: Oxford University Press.

Sawyer, R. K. (2006). Introduction: The new science of learning. In R. K. Sawyer (Ed.), *The Cambridge handbook of the learning sciences* (pp. 1–16). New York, NY: Cambridge.

Saxe, G. B. (1999). Source of concepts: A cross cultural-developmental perspective. In E. K. Scholnick, K. Nelson, S. A. Gelman, & P. H. Miller (Eds.), *Conceptual development: Piaget's legacy* (pp. 253–267). Mahwah, NJ: Erlbaum.

Schacter, D. L., Gilbert, D. T., & Wenger, D. M. (2009). *Psychology*. New York, NY: Worth.

Scheibe, C., & Rogow, F. (2004). *12 basic principles for incorporating media literacy and critical thinking into any curriculum* (2nd ed.). Ithaca, NY: Project Look Sharp—Ithaca College.

Scherer, M. (1993). On savage inequalities: A conversation with Jonathan Kozol. *Educational Leadership, 50*(4), 4–9.

Scherer, M. (1999). The discipline of hope: A conversation with Herb Kohl. *Educational Leadership, 56*(1), 8–13.

Schiefele, U. (1991). Interest, learning, and motivation. *Educational Psychologist, 26*, 299–324.

Schmidt, H. G., van der Molen, H. T., te Winkel, W. W. R., & Wijnen, W. H. F. W. (2009). Constructivist, problem-based learning does work: A meta-analysis of curricular comparisons involving a single medical school. *Educational Psychologist, 44*, 227–249.

Schneider, W., & Bjorklund, D. F. (1992). Expertise, aptitude, and strategic remembering. *Child Development, 63*, 416–473.

Schoen, R., & Canudas-Romo, V. (2006). Timing effects on divorce: 20th century experience in the United States. *Journal of Marriage and the Family, 68*, 749–758.

Schoenfeld, A. H. (1989). Teaching mathematical thinking and problem solving. In L. B. Resnick & L. E. Klopfer (Eds.), *Toward the thinking curriculum: Current cognitive research* (pp. 83–103). Alexandria, VA: ASCD.

Schoenfeld, A. H. (1994). *Mathematics thinking and problem solving*. Hillsdale, NJ: Erlbaum.

Schoenfeld, A. H. (2011). *How we think: The theory of goal-oriented decision making and its educational applications*. New York, NY: Routledge.

Scholastic. (2011). Planning for parent conferences. Available online at: http://www2.scholastic.com/browse/article.jsp?id=4194

Schommer, M. (1997). The development of epistemological beliefs among secondary students: A longitudinal study. *Journal of Educational Psychology, 89*, 37–40.

Schommer-Aikins, M. (2002). An evolving theoretical framework for an epistemological belief system. In B. K. Hofer & P. R. Pintrich (Eds.), *Personal epistemology: The psychology of beliefs about knowledge and knowing* (pp. 103–118). Mahwah, NJ: Erlbaum.

Schraw, G. (2006). Knowledge: Structures and processes. In P. A. Alexander & P. H. Winne (Eds.), *Handbook of educational psychology* (2nd ed., pp. 825–847). Mahwah, NJ: Erlbaum.

Schraw, G., & Olafson, L. (2002). Teachers' epistemological world views and educational practices. *Issues in Education, 8*, 99–148.

Schunk, D. H. (2000). *Learning theories: An educational perspective* (3rd ed.). Columbus, OH: Merrill.

Schunk, D. H. (2004). *Learning theories: An educational perspective* (4th ed.). Columbus, OH: Merrill.

Schunk, D. H. (2008). *Learning theories: An educational perspective* (5th ed.). Columbus, OH: Merrill.

Schunk, D. H. (2012). *Learning theories: An educational perspective* (6th ed.). Boston, MA: Allyn & Bacon/Pearson.

Schunk, D. H., & Hanson, A. R. (1985). Peer models: Influence on children's self-efficacy and achievement. *Journal of Educational Psychology, 77*, 313–322.

Schunk, D. H., Pintrich, P. R., & Meece, J. L. (2008). *Motivation in education: Theory, research, and applications* (3rd ed.). Columbus, OH: Merrill.

Schutz, P. A., & Davis, H. A. (2000). Emotions and self-regulations during test-taking. *Educational Psychologist, 35*, 243–256.

Schwab, J. J. (1973). The Practical 3: Translation into curriculum. *School Review, 81*, 501–522.

Schwartz, B., Wasserman, E. A., & Robbins, S. J. (2002). *Psychology of learning and behavior* (5th ed.). New York, NY: W. W. Norton.

Schwarz, B. B., Neuman, Y., & Biezuner, S. (2000). Two wrongs may make a right . . . if they argue together! *Cognition and Instruction, 18*, 461–494.

Schworm, S., & Renkl, A. (2007). Learning argumentation skills through the use of prompts for self-explaining examples. *Journal of Educational Psychology, 99*, 285–295.

Seaton M., Marsh, H. W., & Craven, R. G. (2009). Earning its place as a pan-human theory: Universality of the Big-Fish-Little-Pond effect across 41 culturally and economically diverse countries. *Journal of Educational Psychology, 101*, 403–419.

Seligman, M. E. P. (1975). *Helplessness: On depression, development, and death*. San Francisco, CA: Freeman.

Seligman, M. E. P. (2006). *Learned optimism: How to change your mind and your life* (2nd ed.). New York, NY: Pocket Books.

Selman, R. L. (1980). *The growth of interpersonal understanding*. New York, NY: Academic Press.

Sénéchal, M., & LeFevre, J. A. (2002). Parental involvement in the development of children's reading skills: A five-year longitudinal study. *Child Development, 73*, 445–460.

Senghas, A., & Coppola, M. (2001). Children creating language: How Nicaraguan Sign Language acquired a spatial grammar. *Psychological Review, 96*, 323–328.

Serpell, R. (1993). Interface between sociocultural and psychological aspects of cognition. In E. Forman, N. Minick, & C. A. Stone (Eds.), *Contexts for learning: Sociocultural dynamics in children's development* (pp. 357–368). New York, NY: Oxford University Press.

Shaffer, D. W. (2010). *The Bicycle Helmets of "Amsterdam": Computer games and the problem of transfer* (Epistemic Games Group Working Paper No. 2010-01). Madison, WI: University of Wisconsin-Madison.

Shaffer, D. W., Hatfield, D., Svarovsky, G. N., Nash, P., Nulty, A., Bagley, E., . . . Mislevy, R. J. (2009). Epistemic network analysis: A prototype for 21st century assessment of learning. *International Journal of Learning Media, 1*(2), 33–53.

Shavelson, R. J. (1987). Planning. In M. Dunkin (Ed.), *The international encyclopedia of teaching and teacher education* (pp. 483–486). New York, NY: Pergamon Press.

Shaywitz, B. A., Shaywitz, S. E., Blachman, B. A., Pugh, K. R., Fulbright, R. K., Skudlarski, P., . . . Gore, J. C. (2004). Development of left occipitotemporal systems for skilled reading in children after a phonologically-based intervention. *Biological Psychiatry, 55*, 926–933.

Sheets, R. H. (2005). *Diversity pedagogy: Examining the role of culture in the teaching-learning process*. Boston, MA: Allyn & Bacon.

Shepard, L. A., & Smith, M. L. (1988). Escalating academic demand in kindergarten: Counterproductive policies. *Elementary School Journal, 89*(2), 135–145.

Shepard, L. A., & Smith, M. L. (1989). Academic and emotional effects of kindergarten retention. In L. Shepard & M. Smith (Eds.), *Flunking grades: Research and policies on retention* (pp. 79–107). Philadelphia, PA: Falmer Press.

Sherwood, R. D. (2002). Problem-based multimedia software for middle grade science: Development issues and an initial field study. *Journal of Computers in Mathematics and Science Teaching, 21*, 147–165.

Shih, S. S. (2008). The relation of self-determination and achievement goals to Taiwanese eighth graders' behavioral and emotional engagement in schoolwork. *The Elementary School Journal, 108*, 313–334.

Shonkoff, J. P. (2006). A promising opportunity for developmental and behavioral pediatrics at the interface of neuroscience, psychology, and social policy: Remarks on receiving the 2005 C. Anderson Aldrich Award. *Pediatrics, 118*, 2187–2191.

Shu, H., McBride-Chang, C., Wu, S., & Liu, H. (2006). Understanding Chinese developmental dyslexia: Morphological awareness as a core cognitive construct. *Journal of Educational Psychology, 98*, 122–133.

Shuell, T. J. (1996). Teaching and learning in a classroom context. In D. Berliner & R. Calfee (Eds.), *Handbook of educational psychology* (pp. 726–764). New York, NY: Macmillan.

Shulman, L. S. (1987). Knowledge and teaching: Foundations of the new reform. *Harvard Educational Review, 19*(2), 4–14.

Shute, V. J. (2008). Focus on formative feedback. *Review of Educational Research, 78*, 153–189.

Siddle Walker, V. (2001). African American teaching in the South: 1940–1960. *Review of Educational Research, 38*, 751–779.

Siegel, J., & Shaughnessy, M. F. (1994). Educating for understanding: An interview with Howard Gardner. *Phi Delta Kappan, 75*, 536–566.

Siegel, L. S. (2003). Basic cognitive processes and reading disabilities. In H. L. Swanson, K. R. Harris, & S. Graham (Eds.), *Handbook of learning disabilities* (pp. 158–181). New York, NY: Guilford Press.

Siegler, R. S. (1993). Adaptive and non-adaptive characteristics of low-income children's mathematical strategy use. In B. Penner (Ed.), *The challenge in mathematics and science education: Psychology's response* (pp. 341–366). Washington, DC: American Psychological Association.

Siegler, R. S. (1998). *Children's thinking* (3rd ed.). Upper Saddle River, NJ: Prentice-Hall.

Siegler, R. S. (2000). The rebirth of children's learning. *Child Development, 71,* 26–35.

Siegler, R. S. (2004). Turning memory development inside out. *Developmental Review, 24,* 469–475.

Siegler, R. S., & Alibali, M. W. (2005). *Children's thinking* (4th ed.). Upper Saddle River, NJ: Prentice-Hall.

Siegler, R. S., & Crowley, K. (1991). The microgenetic method: A direct means for studying cognitive development. *American Psychologist, 56,* 606–620.

Silverman, S. K. (2008, April, 11). Personal communication, Columbus, Ohio.

Simon, D. P., & Chase, W. G. (1973). Skill in chess. *American Scientist, 61,* 394–403.

Simon, H. A. (1995). The information-processing view of mind. *American Psychologist, 50,* 507–508.

Simon, T. (2010). Rewards and challenges of cognitive neuroscience studies of persons with intellectual and developmental disabilities. Special Issue for the *American Journal on Intellectual and Developmental Disabilities, 115,* 79-82. doi: 10.1352/1944-7558-115.2.79

Simonton, D. K. (1999). Creativity from a historiometric perspective. In R. J. Sternberg (Ed.), *Handbook of creativity* (pp. 116–133). New York, NY: Cambridge University Press.

Simonton, D. K. (2000). Creativity: Cognitive, personal, developmental, and social aspects. *American Psychologist, 55,* 151–158.

Simos, P. G., Fletcher, J. M., Sarkari, S., Billingsley-Marshall, R., Denton, C. A., & Papanicolaou, A. C. (2007). Intensive instruction affects brain magnetic activity associated with oral word reading in children with persistent reading disabilities. *Journal of Learning Disabilities, 40* (1), 37–48.

Simpson, E. J. (1972). The classification of educational objectives in the psychomotor domain. *The Psychomotor Domain. Vol. 3.* Washington, DC: Gryphon House.

Sinatra, G. M., & Mason, L. (2008). Beyond knowledge: Learner characteristics influencing conceptual change. In S. Vosniadou (Ed.), *International handbook of research on conceptual change.* Mahwah, NJ: Erlbaum.

Sinatra, G. M., & Taasoobshirazi, G. (2011). Intentional conceptual change: The self-regulation of sciene learning. In B. Zimmerman & D. Schunk (Eds.), *Handbook of self-regulation of learning and performance* (pp. 203–216). New York, NY: Routledge.

Singley, K., & Anderson, J. R. (1989). *The transfer of cognitive skill.* Cambridge, MA: Harvard University Press.

Sio, U. N., & Ormerod, T. C. (2009). Does incubation enhance problem solving? A meta-analytic review. *Psychological Bulletin, 135,* 94–120.

Sirin, S. R. (2005). Socioeconomic status and academic achievement: A meta-analytic review of research. *Review of Educational Research, 75,* 417–453.

Skiba, R. J., Michael, R. S., Nardo, A. C., & Peterson, R. (2000). *The color of discipline: Sources of racial and gender disproportionality in school punishment* (Report #SRS1). Bloomington, IN: Indiana Education Policy Center.

Skinner, B. F. (1950). Are theories of learning necessary? *Psychological Review, 57,* 193–216.

Skinner, B. F. (1953). *Science and human behavior.* New York, NY: Macmillan.

Skinner, B. F. (1989). The origins of cognitive thought. *American Psychologist, 44,* 13–18.

Slaby, R. G., Roedell, W. C., Arezzo, D., & Hendrix, K. (1995). *Early violence prevention.* Washington, DC: National Association for the Education of Young Children.

Slater, L. (2002, February 3). The trouble with self-esteem. *The New York Times Magazine,* pp. 44–47.

Slavin, R. E. (1995). *Cooperative learning* (2nd ed.). Boston, MA: Allyn & Bacon.

Slavin, R. E. (2002). Evidence-based education policies: Transforming education practice and research. *Educational Researcher, 31*(7), 15–21.

Slavin, R. E., Lake, C., Chambers, B., Cheung, A., & Davis, S. (2009). Effective reading programs for elementary grades: A best–evidence synthesis. *Review of Educational Resaerch, 79,* 1391–1465.

Smetana, J. G. (2000). Middle-class African American adolescents' and parents' conceptions of parental authority and parenting practices: A longitudinal investigation. *Child Development, 71,* 1672–1686.

Smith, C. R. (2004). *Learning disabilities: The interaction of learner, task, and setting* (5th ed.). Boston, MA: Allyn & Bacon.

Smith, C. S., & Hung, L-C. (2008). Stereotype threat: Effects on education. *Social Psychology of Education, 11,* 243–257.

Smith, D. D. (2006). *Introduction to special education: Teaching in an age of opportunity* (5th ed.). Boston, MA: Allyn & Bacon.

Smith, D. D., & Tyler, N. C. (2010). *Introduction to special education: Making a difference* (7th ed.). Columbus, OH: Merrill.

Smith, E. E., & Kosslyn, S. M. (2007). *Cognitive psychology: Mind and brain.* Upper Saddle River, NJ: Pearson/Prentice-Hall.

Smith, F. (1975). *Comprehension and learning: A conceptual framework for teachers.* New York, NY: Holt, Rinehart & Winston.

Smith, J. K., Smith, L. F., & De Lisi, R. (2001). *Natural classroom assessment: Designing seamless instruction and assessment.* Thousand Oaks, CA: Corwin Press.

Smith, J. L., Sansone, C., & White, P. H. (2007). The stereotyped task process: The role of interest and achievement motivation. *Journal of Educational Psychology, 88,* 99–114.

Smith, S. M., Glenberg, A., & Bjork, R. A. (1978). Environmental context and human memory. *Memory and Cognition, 6,* 342–353.

Snapp, M., & Woolfolk, A. E. (1973, March). *An examination of children in special education over a thirteen-year period.* Paper presented at the National Association of School Psychologists, 5th Annual Meeting, New York, NY.

Snow, C. E. (1993). Families as social contexts for literacy development. In C. Daiute (Ed.), *New directions for child development* (No. 61, pp. 11–24). San Francisco, CA: Jossey-Bass.

Snow, R. E. (1995). Pygmalion and intelligence. *Current Directions in Psychological Science, 4,* 169–171.

Snow, R. E., Corno, L., & Jackson, D. (1996). Individual differences in affective and cognitive functions. In D. Berliner & R. Calfee (Eds.), *Handbook of educational psychology* (pp. 243–310). New York, NY: Macmillan.

Snowman, J. (1984). Learning tactics and strategies. In G. Phye & T. Andre (Eds.), *Cognitive instructional psychology* (pp. 243–275). Orlando, FL: Academic Press.

Soar, R. S., & Soar, R. M. (1979). Emotional climate and management. In P. Peterson & H. Walberg (Eds.), *Research on teaching: Concepts, findings,* *and implications* (pp. 97–119). Berkeley, CA: McCutchan.

Soares, D. A., Vannest, K. J., & Harrison, J. (2009). Computer aided self-monitoring to increase academic production and reduce self-injurious behavior in a child with autism. *Behavioral Interventions, 24,* 171–183.

Sobesky, W. E. (1983). The effects of situational factors on moral judgment. *Child Development, 54,* 575–584.

Society for Research in Child Development (SRCD). (2009). Young Hispanic children: Boosting opportunities for learning. *Society for Research in Child Development: Social Policy Report Briefs, 23*(2), 1–2.

Sokolove, S., Garrett, J., Sadker, D., & Sadker, M. (1986). Interpersonal communications skills. In J. Cooper (Ed.), *Classroom teaching skills: A handbook* (pp. 233–278). Lexington, MA: D. C. Heath.

Solomon, D., Watson, M. S., & Battistich, V. A. (2001). Teaching and schooling effects on moral/prosocial development. In V. Richardson (Ed.), *Handbook of research on teaching* (4th ed., pp. 566–603). Washington, DC: American Educational Research Association.

Soodak, L. C., & McCarthy, M. R. (2006). Classroom management in inclusive settings. In C. M. Evertson & C. S. Weinstein (Eds.), *Handbook of classroom management: Research, practice, and contemporary issues.* Mahwah, NJ: Erlbaum.

Sotillo, S. M. (2002). Finding our voices, finding ourselves: Becoming bilingual and bicultural. In G. S. Boutte (Ed.), *Resounding voices: School experiences of people from diverse ethnic backgrounds* (pp. 275–307). Boston, MA: Allyn & Bacon.

Spearman, C. (1927). *The abilities of man: Their nature and measurement.* New York, NY: Macmillan.

Spencer, M. B., & Markstrom-Adams, C. (1990). Identity processes among racial and ethnic-minority children in America. *Child Development, 61,* 290–310.

Spencer, M. B., Noll, E., Stoltzfus, J., & Harpalani, V. (2001). Identity and school adjustment: Questioning the "Acting White" assumption. *Educational Psychologist, 36*(1), 21–30.

Spera, C. (2005). A review of the relationship among parenting practices, parenting styles, and adolescent school achievement. *Educational Psychology Review, 17,* 125–146.

Spörer, N., & Brunstein, J. C. (2009). Fostering the reading comprehension of secondary school students through peer-assisted learning: Effects on strategy knowledge, strategy use, and task performance. *Contemporary Educational Psychology, 34,* 289–297.

Sprenger, M. (2005). Inside Amy's brain. *Educational Leadership, 62*(7), 28–32.

Sprenger, M. (2010). *Brain-based teaching in the digital age.* Alexandria, VA: Association for Supervision and Curriculum Development.

Stage, S. A., Jackson, H. G., Erickson M. J., Moscovitz, K. K., Bush, J. W., Violette, H. D., . . . Pious, C. (2008). A validity study of functionally-based behavioral consultation with students with emotional/behavioral disabilities. *School Psychology Quarterly, 23,* 327–353.

Stahl, S. A. (2002). Different strokes for different folks? In L. Abbeduto (Ed.), *Taking sides: Clashing on controversial issues in educational psychology* (pp. 98–107). Guilford, CT: McGraw-Hill/Duskin.

Stanovich, K. E. (1992). *How to think straight about psychology* (3rd ed.). Glenview, IL: Scott, Foresman.

Star, J. R., & Rittle-Johnson, B. (2009). It pays to compare: An experimental study on computational estimation. *Journal of Experimental Child Psychology, 102*, 408–426.

Steele, C. (1992). Race and the schooling of African-Americans. *Atlantic Monthly, 269*(4), 68–78.

Steele, K. M., Bass, K. E., & Crook, M. D. (1999). The mystery of the Mozart effect: Failure to replicate. *Psychological Science, 10*, 366–368.

Stefanou, C. R., Perencevich, K. C., DiCintio, M., & Turner, J. C. (2004). Supporting autonomy in the classroom: Ways teachers encourage student decision making and ownership. *Educational Psychologist, 39*, 97–110.

Steffens, M. C., Jelenec, P., & Noack, P. (2010). On the leaky math pipeline: Comparing implicit math-gender stereotypes and math withdrawal in female and male children and adolescents. *Journal of Educational Psychology, 102*, 947–963.

Steinberg, L. (1996). *Beyond the classroom: Why schools are failing and what parents need to do.* New York, NY: Simon & Schuster.

Steinberg, L. (1998). Standards outside the classroom. In D. Ravitch (Ed.), *Brookings papers on educational policy* (pp. 319–358). Washington, DC: Brookings Institute.

Steinberg, L. (2005). *Adolescence* (7th ed.). New York, NY: McGraw-Hill.

Steinberg, L. (2008). A social neuroscience perspective on adolescent risk-taking. *Developmental Review, 28*, 78–106.

Stemler, S. E., Sternberg, R. J., Grigorenko, E. L., Jarvin, L., & Sharpes, K. (2009). Using the theory of successful intelligence as a framework for developing assessments in AP physics. *Contemporary Educational Psychology, 34*, 195–209.

Sternberg, R. J. (1985). *Beyond IQ: A triarchic theory of human intelligence.* New York, NY: Cambridge University Press.

Sternberg, R. J. (1997). *Successful intelligence.* New York, NY: Plume.

Sternberg, R. J. (1999). A propulsion model of types of creative contribution. *Review of General Psychology, 3*, 83–100.

Sternberg, R. J. (2000). *Handbook of human intelligence.* New York, NY: Cambridge University Press.

Sternberg, R. J. (2004). Culture and intelligence. *American Psychologist, 59*, 325–338.

Sternberg, R. J., & Davidson, J. (1982, June). The mind of the puzzler. *Psychology Today*, 37–44.

Sternberg, R. J., & Sternberg, K. (2012). *Cognitive psychology* (6th ed.). Belmont, CA: Wadsworth.

Stevenson, H. W., & Stigler, J. (1992). *The learning gap.* New York, NY: Summit Books.

Stewart, L., Henson, R., Kampe, K., Walsh, V., Turner, R., & Frith, U. (2003). Brain changes after learning to read and play music. *NeuroImage, 20*(1), 71–83.

Stice, E., & Shaw, H. (2004). Eating disorder prevention programs: A meta-analytic review. *Psychological Bulletin, 130*, 206–227.

Stiggins, R. J., & Chappuis, J. (2005). Using student-involved classroom assessment to close achievement gaps. *Theory Into Practice, 44*, 11–18.

Stigler, J. W., Lee, S., & Stevenson, H. W. (1987). Mathematics classrooms in Japan, Taiwan, and the United States. *Child Development, 58*, 1272–1285.

Stinson, D. W. (2006). African American male adolescents, schooling, (an mathematics): Deficiency, rejection, and achievement. *Review of Educational Research, 76*, 477–506.

Stipek, D. J. (1981). Children's perceptions of their own and their peers' academic competence. *Journal of Educational Psychology, 73*, 404–410.

Stipek, D. J. (1993). *Motivation to learn* (2nd ed.). Boston, MA: Allyn & Bacon.

Stipek, D. J. (2002). *Motivation to learn: Integrating theory and practice* (4th ed.). Boston, MA: Allyn & Bacon.

Stipek, D. (2006). Relationships matter. *Educational Leadership, 64*(1), 46–49.

Stipek, D., de la Sota, A., & Weishaupt, L. (1999). Life lessons: An embedded classroom approach to preventing high-risk behaviors among preadolescents. *The Elementary School Journal, 99*, 433–451.

Stodolsky, S. S. (1988). *The subject matters: Classroom activity in math and social studies.* Chicago, IL: University of Chicago Press.

Stoeger, H., & Ziegler, A. (2011). Self-regulatory training through elementary-school students' homework completion. In B. Zimmerman & D. Schunk (Eds.), *Handbook of self-regulation of learning and performance* (pp. 87–101) New York, NY: Routledge.

Storch, S., & Whitehurst, G. (2002). Oral language and code-related precursors to reading: Evidence from a longitudinal structural model. *Developmental Psychology, 38*, 934–947.

Stormont, M., Stebbins, M. S., & Holliday, G. (2001). Characteristics and educational support needs of underrepresented gifted adolescents. *Psychology in the Schools, 38*, 413–423.

Stormshak, E. A., Bierman, K. L., Bruschi, C., Dodge, K. A., Coie, J. D., et al. (1999). The relation between behavior problems and peer preference in different classrooms. *Child Development, 70*, 169–182.

Story, M., & Stang, J. (2005). Nutrition needs of adolescents. In J. S. M. Story (Ed.), *Guidelines for adolescent nutritional services* (pp. 158–159). Minneapolis, MN: University of Minnesota Press.

Strayer, D. L., & Drews, F. A. (2007). Cell-phone induced driver distraction. *Current Directions in Psychological Science, 16*, 128–131.

Strom, P. S., & Strom, R. D. (2005). Cyberbullying by adolescents: A preliminary assessment. *The Educational Forum, 70*(1), 21–36.

Stumpf, H. (1995). Gender differences on test of cognitive abilities: Experimental design issues and empirical results. *Learning and Individual Differences, 7*, 275–288.

Subrahmanyam, K., Greenfield, P., Kraut, R., & Gross, E. (2001). The impact of computer use on children's and adolescents' development. *Applied Developmental Psychology, 22*, 7–30.

Suldo, S. M., Friedrich, A. A., White, T., Farmer, J., Minch, D., & Michalowski, J. (2009). Teacher support and adolescents' subjective well-being: A mixed-methods investigation. *School Psychology Review, 38*, 67–85.

Sullivan, M. A., & O'Leary, S. G. (1990). Maintenance following reward and cost token programs. *Behavior Therapy, 21*, 139–149.

Sulzer-Azaroff, B., & Mayer, G. R. (1986). *Achieving educational excellence using behavioral strategies.* New York, NY: Holt, Rinehart & Winston.

Sunburst Software. (1999). *A Field Trip to the Sea.*

Svoboda, J. S. (2001). Review of *Boys and girls learn differently.* The Men's Resource Network.

Available online at: http://mensightmagazine.com/reviews/Svoboda/boysandgirls.htm

Swanson, H. L. (1990). The influence of metacognitive knowledge and aptitude on problem solving. *Journal of Educational Psychology, 82*, 306–314.

Swanson, H. L. (2001). Research on interventions for adolescents with learning disabilities: A meta-analysis of outcomes related to higher-order processing. *The Elementary School Journal, 101*, 332–348.

Swanson H. L., & Saez, L. (2003). Memory difficulties in children and adults with learning disabilities. In H. L. Swanson, S. Graham, & K. R. Harris (Eds.), *Handbook of learning disabilities* (pp. 182–198). New York, NY: Guilford Press.

Swanson, T. C. (2005). Providing structure for children with learning and behavior problems. *Intervention in School and Clinic, 40*, 182–187.

Swearer, S. M., Espelage, D. L., Vaillancourt, T., & Hymel, S. (2010). What can be done about school bullying? Linking research to educational practice. *Educational Researcher, 39*, 38–47.

Sweeney, W. J., Salva, E., Cooper, J. O., & Talbert-Johnson, C. (1993). Using self-evaluation to improve difficult to read handwriting for secondary students. *Journal of Behavioral Education, 3*, 427–443.

Sweller, J., Kirschner, P. A., & Clark, R. E. (2007). Why minimally guided teaching techniques do not work: A reply to commentaries. *Educational Psychologist, 42*, 115–121.

Sweller, J., van Merrienboer, J. J. G., & Paas, F. G. W. C. (1998). Cognitive architecture and instructional design. *Educational Psychology Review, 10*, 251–296.

Sylvester, R. (2003). *A biological brain in a cultural classroom* (2nd ed.). Thousand Oaks, CA: Sage.

Tait, H., & Entwistle, N. J. (1998). Identifying students at risk through ineffective study strategies. *Higher Education, 31*, 97–116.

Talbot, M. (2002, February 24). Girls just want to be mean. *The New York Times Magazine*, pp. 24–29+.

Tallal, P., & Miller, S. L. (2003). How the brain learns to read. *Middle Matters, 12*(1), 7.

Tang, Y., Zhang, W., Chen, K., Feng, S., Ji, Y. Shen, J,. et al. (2006). Arithmetic processing in the brain shaped by culture. *Proceedings of the National Academy of Sciences USA, 103*, 10775–10780.

Taylor, E. (1998). Clinical foundation of hyperactivity research. *Behavioural Brain Research, 94*, 11–24.

Taylor, R. L., Richards, S. B., & Brady, M. P. (2005). *Mental retardation: Historical perspectives, current practices, and future directions.* Boston, MA: Allyn & Bacon.

TenBrink, T. D. (2003). Assessment. In J. Cooper (Ed.), *Classroom teaching skills* (7th ed., pp. 311–353). Boston, MA: Houghton-Mifflin.

TenBrink, T. D. (2006). Assessment. In J. Cooper (Ed.), *Classroom teaching skills* (8th ed., pp. 55–78). Boston, MA: Houghton-Mifflin.

Tenenbaum, H. R., & Ruck, M. D. (2007). Are teachers' expectations different for racial minority than for European American students? A meta-analysis. *Journal of Educational Psychology, 99*, 253–273.

Terman, L. M., Baldwin, B. T., & Bronson, E. (1925). Mental and physical traits of a thousand gifted children. In L. M. Terman (Ed.), *Genetic studies of genius* (Vol. 1). Stanford, CA: Stanford University Press.

Terman, L. M., & Oden, M. H. (1947). The gifted child grows up. In L. M. Terman (Ed.), *Genetic studies of genius* (Vol. 4). Stanford, CA: Stanford University Press.

Terman, L. M., & Oden, M. H. (1959). The gifted group in mid-life. In L. M. Terman (Ed.), *Genetic studies of genius* (Vol. 5). Stanford, CA: Stanford University Press.

Tesser, A., Stapel, D. A., & Wood, J. V. (2002). *Self and motivation:Emerging psychological perspectives*. Washington, DC: American Psychological Association.

Tharp, R. G. (1989). Psychocultural variables and constants: Effects on teaching and learning in schools. *American Psychologist, 44*, 349–359.

Tharp, R. G., & Gallimore, R. (1988). *Rousing minds to life: Teaching, learning, and schooling in social context*. New York, NY: Cambridge University Press.

Theodore, L. A., Bray, M. A., Kehle, T. J., & Jenson, W. R. (2001). Randomization of group contingencies and reinforcers to reduce classroom disruptive behavior. *Journal of School Psychology, 39*, 267–277.

Thomas, K. T., & Thomas, J. R. (2008). Principles of motor development for elementary school physical education. *The Elementary School Journal, 108*, 181–195.

Thome, J., & Reddy, D. P. (2009). The current status of research into attention deficit hyperactivity disorder: Proceedings of the 2nd International Congress on ADHD: From childhood to adult disease. *Attention Deficit Hyperactive Disorder, 1*, 165–174.

Thompson, G. (1991). *Teaching through themes*. New York, NY: Scholastic.

Thompson, G. (2008). Beneath the apathy. *Educational Leadership, 65*(6), 50–54.

Thompson, R. A., & Raikes, H. A. (2003). Toward the next quarter-century: Conceptual and methodological challenges for attachment theory. *Development and Psychopathology, 15*, 691–718.

Tierney, R. J., Readence, J. E., & Dishner, E. K. (1990). *Reading strategies and practices: A compendium* (3rd ed.). Boston, MA: Allyn & Bacon.

Tierney, W. G. (1993). *Building communities of difference: Higher education in the twenty-first century*. Westport, CT: Bergin and Garvey.

TIMSS. (1998). *Third International Mathematics and Science Study*. Washington, DC: National Center for Educational Statistics. Available online at: http://nces.ed.gov/timss/

TIMSS. (2008). Fourth International Mathematics and Science Study. Available online at: http://ncesed.gov/timss/

Tingstrom, D. H., Sterling-Turner, H. E., & Wilczynski, S. M. (2006). The Good Behavior Game: 1962–2002. *Behavior Modification, 30*, 225–253.

Tobias, S. (2010). Generative learning theory, paradigm shifts, and constructivism in educational psychology: A tribute to Merl Wittrock. *Educational Psychologist, 45*, 51–54.

Tobler, N., & Stratton, H. (1997). Effectiveness of school-based drug prevention programs: A metaanalysis of the research. *Journal of Primary Prevention, 18*, 71–128.

Tollefson, N. (2000). Classroom applications of cognitive theories of motivation. *Education Psychology Review, 12*, 63–83.

Tomasello, M. (2006). Acquiring linguistic constructions. In D. Kuhn & R. S. Siegler (Eds.), *Handbook of child psychology* (6th ed., Vol. 2: Cognition, language, and perception, pp. 255–298). New York, NY: Wiley.

Tomasello, M., Kruger, A. C., & Ratner, H. H. (1993). Cultural learning. *Behavioral and Brain Sciences, 16*, 495–552.

Tomlinson, C. A. (2003). *Fulfilling the promise of the differentiated classroom*. Alexandria, VA: Association for Supervision and Curriculum Development.

Tomlinson, C. A. (2005a). Grading and differentiation: Paradox or good practice? *Theory Into Practice, 44*, 262–269.

Tomlinson, C. A. (2005b, Summer). Differentiating instruction. *Theory Into Practice, 44*(3).

Tomlinson-Keasey, C. (1990). Developing our intellectual resources for the 21st century: Educating the gifted. *Journal of Educational Psychology, 82*, 399–403.

Tomporowski, P., Davis, C. L., Miller, P. H., & Naglieri, J. A. (2008). Exercise and children's intelligence, cognitive and academic achievement. *Educational Psychology Review, 20*, 111–131.

Toppo, G. (2003, January 13). School violence hits lower grades: Experts who see violent behavior in younger kids blame parents, prenatal medical problems and an angry society; educators search for ways to cope. *USA Today*. Available online at: http://www.usatoday.com/educate/college/education/articles/20030119.htm

Torrance, E. P. (1972). Predictive validity of the Torrance tests of creative thinking. *Journal of Creative Behavior, 6*, 236–262.

Torrance, E. P. (1986). Teaching creative and gifted learners. In M. Wittrock (Ed.), *Handbook of research on teaching* (3rd ed., pp. 630–647). New York, NY: Macmillan.

Torrance, E. P., & Hall, L. K. (1980). Assessing the future reaches of creative potential. *Journal of Creative Behavior, 14*, 1–19.

Toth, E., Klahr, D., & Chen, Z. (2000). Bridging research and practice: A cognitively based classroom intervention for teaching experimentation to elementary school children. *Cognition and Instruction, 18*, 423–459.

Trautwein, U. (2007). The homework–achievement relation reconsidered: Differentiating homework time, homework frequency, and homework effort. *Learning and Instruction, 17*, 372–388.

Trautwein, U., & Koller, O. (2003). The relationship between homework and achievement—Still a mystery. *Educatonal Psychology Review, 15*, 115–145.

Trautwein, U., & Lüdtke, O. (2007). Students' self-reported effort and time on homework in six school subjects: Between-students differences and within-student variation. *Journal of Educational Psychology, 99*, 232–234.

Trautwein, U., Schnyder, I., Niggli, A, Neuman, M., & Lüdtke, O. (2009). Chameleon effects in homework research: The homework–achievement association depends on the measures used and the level of analysis chosen. *Contemporary Educational Psychology, 34*, 77–88.

Trebaticka, J., Paduchova, Z., Suba, J. et al. (2009). Markers of oxidative stress in ADHD and their modulation by Polyhenolic extract, Pycnogenal. From Childhood to Adult Disease. May 21–24, 2009, Vienna, Austria. *Attention Deficit and Hyperactivity Disorders, 1*: 33.

Trouilloud, D., Sarrazin, P., Bressoux, P., & Bois, J. (2006). Relation between teachers' early expectations and students' later perceived competence in physical education classes: autonomy-supportive climate as a moderator. *Journal of Educational Psychology, 98*, 75–86.

Tsantis, L. A., Bewick, C. J., & Thouvenelle, S. (2003). Examining some common myths about computer use in the early years [Electronic Version]. *Beyond the Journal: Young Children on the Web*, 1-9. Available online at: http://journal.naeyc.org/btj/200311/CommonTechnoMyths.pdf

Tschannen-Moran, M., & Woolfolk Hoy, A. (2001). Teacher efficacy: Capturing an elusive construct. *Teaching and Teacher Education, 17*, 783–805.

Tschannen-Moran, M., Woolfolk Hoy, A., & Hoy, W. K. (1998). Teacher efficacy: Its meaning and measure. *Review of Educational Research, 68*, 202–248.

Turkle, S. (2011). *Alone together: Why we expect more from technology and less from ourselves*. New York, NY: Basic Books.

Turner, J., Patrick, H., & Meyer, D. (2011). Engaging students in learning: A Special Issue dedicated to Jere Brophy. *Theory Into Practice, 50*.

Twenge, J. M., & Campbell, W. K. (2001). Age and birth cohort differences in self-esteem: A cross temporal meta-analysis. *Journal of Personality and Social Psychology Review, 5*, 321–344.

Uline, C. L., & Johnson, J. F. (2005). Closing the achievement gap: What will it take? Special Issue of *Theory Into Practice, 44*(1), Winter.

Umbreit, J. (1995). Functional analysis of disruptive behavior in an inclusive classroom. *Journal of Early Intervention, 20*(1), 18–29.

Unsworth, N., & Engle, R. W. (2005). Working memory capacity and fluid abilities: Examining the correlation between Operation Span and Raven. *Intelligence, 33*, 67–81.

Urdan, T. C., & Maehr, M. L. (1995). Beyond a two-goal theory of motivation and achievement: A case for social goals. *Review of Educational Research, 65*, 213–243.

U.S. Bureau of the Census. (2010a). *State and country quick facts*. Available online at: http://quickfacts.census.gov/qfd/states/00000.html

U.S. Bureau of the Census. (2010b). *Hispanic population of the United States: Projections*. Available online at: http://www.census.gov/population/www/socdemo/hispanic/hispanic_pop_presetation.html

U.S Bureau of the Census. (2011). *Children below poverty level by race and Hispanic origin*. Available online at: http://www.census.gov/compendia/statab/2011/tables/11s0711.pdf

U.S. Bureau of the Census. (2011). U.S. population projections 2010–2050. Available online at: http://www.census.gov/population/www/projections/summarytables.html.

U.S. Citizenship and Immigration Services. (2011). Home page. Available online at: http://www.uscis.gov/portal/site/uscis.

U.S. Department of Education. (2004). *26th Annual report to Congress on the implementation of the Individuals with Disabilities Act, 2005*. Washington DC: Office of Special Education and Rehabilitative Services.

U.S. Department of Education. (2007). *27th Annual report to Congress on the implementation of the Individuals with Disabilities Act, 2005*. Washington DC: Office of Special Education and Rehabilitative Services.

U.S.Department of Education. (2009, November). *Race to the Top Program: Executive summary*. U. S. Department of Education, Washington, D. C. Available online at http://www2.ed.gov/programs/racetothetop/executive-summary.pdf

U.S. Department of Education. (2010, March). *ESEA Blueprint for Reform*. Washington, DC: USDE, Office of Planning, Evaluation and Policy

Development. http://www2.ed.gov/programs/racetothetop/index.html

U.S. Department of Health and Human Services. (2007). *Frequently asked questions: Administration for Children and Families.* Available online at: http://www.acf.hhs.gov/acf_services.html#caan

Usher, E. L., & Pajares, F. (2009). Sources of self-efficacy in mathematics: A validation study. *Contemporary Educational Psychology, 34,* 89–101.

Uttal, D. H., Hand, L. L., & Newcombe, N. S. (2009, April). *Malleability of spatial cognition: Results of a meta-analysis.* Paper presented at the biennial meeting of the Society for Research in Child Development, Denver, CO.

Valentine, J. C., DuBois, D. L., & Cooper, H. (2004). The relations between self-beliefs and academic achievement: A systematic review. *Educational Psychologist, 39,* 111–133.

Valenzuela, A. (1999). *Subtractive schooling: U.S.–Mexican youth and the politics of caring.* Albany, NY: SUNY Press.

Valiente, C., Lemery-Chalfant, K., & Swansos, J. (2010). Prediction of kindergartners' academic achievement from their effortful control and emotionality: Evidence for direct and moderated relations. *Journal of Educational Psychology, 102,* 550–560.

van den Broek, P., Lorch, E. P., & Thurlow, R. (1996). Children's and adults' memory for television stories: The role of causal factors, story-grammar categories, and hierarchical level. *Child Development, 67,* 3010–3028.

van de Pol, J., Volman, M., & Beishuizen, J. (2010). Scaffolding in teacher–student interaction: A decade of research. *Educational Psychology Review, 22,* 271–296.

van der Mass, H. L. J., Dolan, C. V., Grasman, R. P. P. P., Wicherts, J. M., Huizenga, H. M., & Raijmakers, M. E. J. (2006). A dynamic model of general intelligence: The positive manifold of intelligence by mutualism. *Psychological Review, 113,* 842–861.

Van Der Veer, R. (2007). Vygotsky in context: 1900–1935. In H. Daniels, M. Cole, & J. V. Wertsch (Eds.), *The Cambridge companion to Vygotsky* (pp. 21–49). New York, NY: Cambridge University Press.

Van de Walle, J. A., Karp, K. S., & Bay-Williams, J. M. (2010). *Elementary and middle school mathematics: Teaching developmentally* (7th ed.). Boston, MA: Pearson Education, Inc.

van Gelderen, A., Schoonen, R., Stoel, R. D., de Glopper, K., & Hulstijn, J. (2007). Development of adolescent reading comprehension in language 1 and language 2: A longitudinal analysis of constituent components. *Journal of Educational Psychology, 99,* 477–491.

van Gog, T., Pass, F., & Sweller, J. (2010). Cognitive load theory: Advances in research on worked examples, animations, and cognitive load measurement. *Educational Psychology Review, 22,* 375–378.

van Kraayenoord, C. E., Rice, D., Carroll, A., Fritz, E., Dillon, L., & Hill, A. (2001). *Attention deficit hyperactivity disorder: Impact and implications for Queensland.* Queensland, Australia: Queensland Disability Services. Available online at: www.families.qld.gov.au

van Laar, C. (2000). The paradox of low academic achievement but high self-esteem in African American students: An attributional account. *Educational Psychology Review, 12,* 33–61.

Van Matre, J. C., Valentine, J. C., & Cooper, H. (2000). Effect of students' after-school activities on teachers' academic expectations. *Contemporary Educational Psychology, 25,* 167–183.

Van Merriënboer, J. J. G., & Sweller, J. (2005). Cognitive load and complex learning: Recent developments and future directions. *Educational Psychology Review, 17,* 147–177.

Van Meter, P. (2001). Drawing construction as a strategy for learning from text. *Journal of Educational Psychology, 93,* 129–140.

Van Meter, P., Yokoi, L., & Pressley, M. (1994). College students' theory of note-taking derived from their perceptions of note-taking. *Journal of Educational Psychology, 86,* 323–338.

Vandell, D. L. (2004). Early child care: The known and the unknown. *Merrill-Palmer Quarterly, 50,* 387–414.

Vandewater, E. A., Bickham, D. S., Lee, J. H., Cummings, H. M., Wartella, E. A., & Rideout, V. J. (2005). When the television is always on: Heavy television exposure and young children's development. *American Behavioral Scientist, 48,* 562–567.

Vansteenkiste, M., Lens, W., & Deci, E. L. (2006). Intrinsic versus extrinsic goal contents in self-determination theory: Another look at the quality of academic motivation. *Educational Psychologist, 41,* 19-31.

Vansteenkiste, M., Simons, J., Lens, W., Sheldon, K. M., & Deci, E. L. (2004). Motivating learning, performance, and persistence: The synergistic role of intrinsic goals and autonomy-support. *Journal of Personality and Social Psychology, 87,* 246–260.

Varma, S., McCandliss, B. D., & Schwartz, D. L. (2008). Scientific and pragmatic challenges for bridging education and neuroscience. *Educational Researcher, 37,* 140–152.

Vasquez, J. A. (1990). Teaching to the distinctive traits of minority students. *The Clearing House, 63,* 299–304.

Vaughn, S., Levy, S., Coleman, M., & Bos, C. S. (2002). Reading instruction for students with LD and EBD: A synthesis of observation studies. *Journal of Special Education, 36*(1), 2–13.

Vecchio, G. M., Gerbino, M., Pastorelli, C., Del Bove, G., & Caprara, G. V. (2007). Multi-faceted self-efficacy beliefs as predictors of life satisfaction in late adolescence. *Personality and Individual Differences, 43,* 1807–1818.

Veenman, S. (1984). Perceived problems of beginning teachers. *Review of Educational Research, 54,* 143–178.

Veenman, S. (1997). Combination classes revisited. *Educational Research and Evaluation, 65*(4), 319–381.

Vélez, C. E., Wolchik, S. A., Tein, J Y., & Sandler, I. (2011). Protecting children from the consequences of divorce: A longitudinal study of the effects of parenting on children's coping processes. *Child Development, 82,* 244–257. doi: 10.1111/j.1467-8624.2010.01553.x

Vera, A. H., & Simon, H. A. (1993). Situated action: A symbolic interpretation. *Cognitive Science, 17,* 7–48.

Verhallen, M. J. A. J., Bus, A. G., & de Jong, M. T. (2006). The promise of multimedia stories for kindergarten children at risk. *Journal of Educational Psychology, 98,* 410–419.

Verplaetse, L. S., & Migliacci, N. (2008). Inclusive pedagogy: An introduction. In L. S. Verplaetse & N. Migliacci (Eds.), *Inclusive pedagogy for English language learners: A handbook of research-informed practices* (pp. 3–13). New York, NY: Erlbaum.

Vispoel, W. P., & Austin, J. R. (1995). Success and failure in junior high school: A critical incident approach to understanding students' attributional beliefs. *American Educational Research Journal, 32,* 377–412.

Vogt, M. E., Echevarria, J, & Short, D. J. (2010). *The SIOP® Model for teaching English-language arts to English learners.* Boston, MA: Pearson.

Volkow, N. D., Wang, G. J., Newcorn, J., Fowler, J. S., Telang, F., Solanto, M. V., . . . Pradhan, K. (2007). Brain dopamine transporter levels in treatment and drug naïve adults with ADHD. *NeuroImage, 34,* 1182–1190.

von Glaserfeld, E. (1997). Amplification of a constructivist perspective. *Issues in Education: Contributions from Educational Psychology, 3,* 203–210.

Vroom, V. (1964). *Work and motivation.* New York, NY: Wiley.

Vygotsky, L. S. (1978). *Mind in society: The development of higher mental process.* Cambridge, MA: Harvard University Press.

Vygotsky, L. S. (1986). *Thought and language.* Cambridge, MA: MIT Press.

Vygotsky, L. S. (1987a). The genetic roots of thinking and speech. In R. W. Rieber & A. S. Carton (Eds.), *Problems of general psychology, Vol. 1. Collected works* (pp. 101–120). New York, NY: Plenum. (Work originally published in 1934.)

Vygotsky, L. S. (1987b). *Problems of general psychology.* New York, NY: Plenum.

Vygotsky, L. S. (1987c). Thought and word. In R.W. Rieber & A. S. Carton (Eds.), *Collected works of L. S. Vygotsky: Vol. 1. Problems of general psychology* (pp. 243–285). New York, NY: Plenum. (Work originally published in 1934.)

Vygotsky, L. S. (1993). *The collected works of L. S. Vygotsky: Vol. 2* (J. Knox & C. Stevens, Trans.). New York, NY: Plenum.

Vygotsky, L. S. (1997). *Educational psychology* (R. Silverman, Trans.). Boca Raton, FL: St. Lucie.

Wade, S. E., Schraw, G., Buxton, W. M., & Hayes, M. T. (1993). Seduction of the strategic reader: Effects of interest on strategies and recall. *Reading Research Quarterly, 28,* 3–24.

Waits, B. K., & Demana, F. (2000). Calculators in mathematics teaching and learning: Past, present, future. In M. J. Burke & F. R. Curcio (Eds.), *Learning mathematics for a new century: NCTM 2000 Yearbook* (pp. 51–66). Reston, VA: National Council of Teachers of Mathematics.

Walberg, H. J. (1990). Productive teaching and instruction: Assessing the knowledge base. *Phi Delta Kappan, 72,* 470–478.

Wald, J. (2001, August 29). The failure of zero tolerance. *Salon Magazine.* Available online at: http://www.salon.com/mwt/feature/2001/08/29/zero_tolerance/index.html?sid=1046257

Walker, J. E., Shea, T. M., & Bauer, A. M. (2004). *Behavior management: A practical approach for educators.* Upper Saddle River, NJ: Merrill/Prentice Hall.

Walker, L. J., & Pitts, R. C. (1998). Naturalistic conceptions of moral maturity. *Developmental Psychology, 34,* 403–419.

Walker, V. S. (1996). *Their highest potential.* Chapel Hill: University of North Carolina Press.

Walqui, A. (2008). The development of teacher expertise to work with adolescent English learners: A model and a few priorities. In L. S. Verplaetse & N. Migliacci (Eds.), *Inclusive pedagogy for English language learners: A handbook of research-informed practices* (pp. 103–125). New York, NY: Lawrence Erlbaum.

Wang, A. Y., & Thomas, M. H. (1995). Effects of keywords on long-term retention: Help or hindrance? *Journal of Educational Psychology, 87,* 468–475.

Wang, A. Y., Thomas, M. H., & Ouellette, J. A. (1992). Keyword mnemonic and retention of second-language vocabulary words. *Journal of Educational Psychology, 84,* 520–528.

Ward, L. M. (2004). Wading through the stereotypes: Positive and negative associations between media use and Black adolescents' conception of self. *Developmental Psychology, 40,* 284–294.

Warren, J. S., Bohanon-Edmonson, H. M., Turnbull, A. P., Sailor, W., Wickham, D., Griggs, P., & Beech, S. E. (2006). School-wide positive behavior support: Addressing behavior problems that impede student learning. *Educational Psychology Review, 18,* 187–198.

Waterhouse, L. (2006). Multiple intelligences, the Mozart effect, and emotional intelligence: A critical review. *Educational Psychologist, 41,* 207–225.

Watt, H. M. G., & Richardson, P. W. (2012). Teacher motivation and student achievement outcomes. In J. A. C. Hattie & E. M. Anderman (Eds.), *The international handbook of student achievement.* New York, NY: Routledge.

Waxman, S. R., & Lidz, J. L. (2006). Early word learning. In D. Kuhn & R. S. Siegler (Eds.), *Handbook of child psychology* (6th ed., Vol. 2: Cognition, perception, and language, pp. 299–335). New York, NY: Wiley.

Wayne, A. J., & Youngs, P. (2003). Teacher characteristics and student achievement gains: A review. *Review of Educational Research, 73,* 89–122.

Webb, N. M., Farivar, S. H., & Mastergeorge, A. M. (2002). Productive helping in cooperative groups. *Theory Into Practice, 41,* 13–20.

Webb, N. M., & Mastergeorge, A. M. (2003). The development of students' helping behavior and learning in peer-directed small groups. *Cognition and Instruction, 21,* 361–428.

Webb, N. M., & Palincsar, A. (1996). Group processes in the classroom. In D. C. Berliner & R. C. Calfee (Eds.), *Handbook of educational psychology* (pp. 841–876). New York, NY: Macmillan.

Wechsler, P. (2010, November 12). ADHD diagnoses soar in 4 years. *Columbus Dispatch,* Columbus, OH. Available online at: http://www.dispatch.com/content/stories/national_world/2010/11/12/adhd-diagnoses-soar-in-4-years.html.

Weil, E. (2008, March 2). Should boys and girls be taught separately? *The New York Times Magazine,* pp. 33–45+.

Weiner, B. (1986). *An attributional theory of motivation and emotion.* New York, NY: Springer.

Weiner, B. (1994a). Ability versus effort revisited: The moral determinants of achievement evaluation an achievement as a moral system. *Educational Psychologist, 29,* 163–172.

Weiner, B. (1994b). Integrating social and persons theories of achievement striving. *Review of Educational Research, 64,* 557–575.

Weiner, B. (2000). Interpersonal and intrapersonal theories of motivation from an attributional perspective. *Educational Psychology Review, 12,* 1–14.

Weiner, B. (2010). The development of an attribution-based theory of motivation: A history of ideas. *Educational Psychologist, 45,* 28–36.

Weinert, F. E., & Helmke, A. (1995). Learning from wise mother nature or big brother instructor: The wrong choice as seen from an educational perspective. *Educational Psychologist, 30,* 135–143.

Weinstein, C. S. (1977). Modifying student behavior in an open classroom through changes in the physical design. *American Educational Research Journal, 14,* 249–262.

Weinstein, C. S. (1999). Reflections on best practices and promising programs: Beyond assertive classroom discipline. In H. J. Freiberg (Ed.), *Beyond behaviorism: Changing the classroom management paradigm* (pp. 147–163). Boston, MA: Allyn & Bacon.

Weinstein, C. S., & Mignano, A. (2007). *Elementary classroom management: Lessons from research and practice* (4th ed.). New York, NY: McGraw-Hill.

Weinstein, C. S., & Novodvorsky, I. (2011). *Middle and secondary classroom management: Lessons from research and practice* (5th ed.). New York, NY: McGraw-Hill.

Weinstein, C. S., Romano, M. E., & Mignano, A. J. (2011). *Elementary classroom management: Lessons from research and practice* (5th ed.). New York, NY: McGraw-Hill.

Weinstein, R. S., Madison, S. M., & Kuklinski, M. R. (1995). Raising expectations in schools: Obstacles and opportunities for change. *American Educational Research Journal, 32,* 121–159.

Weisberg, R. W. (1993). *Creativity: Beyond the myth of genius.* New York, NY: W. H. Freeman.

Welsh, J. A., Nix, R. L., Blair, C., Bierman, K. L., & Nelson, K. E. (2010). The development of cognitive skills and gains in academic school readiness for children from low-income families. *Journal of Educational Psychology, 102,* 43–53.

Wenger, E. (1998). *Communities of practice: learning, meaning, and identity.* New York, NY: Cambridge University Press.

Wentzel, K. R. (1999). Social-motivational processes and interpersonal relations: Implications for understanding motivation in school. *Journal of Educational Psychology, 91,* 76–97.

Wentzel, K. R. (2002). Are effective teachers like good parents? Teaching styles and student adjustment in early adolescence. *Child Development, 73,* 287–301.

Wentzel, K. R., Barry, C. M., & Caldwell, K. A. (2004). Friendships in middle school: Influences on motivation and school adjustment. *Journal of Educational Psychology, 96,* 195–203.

Werts, M. G., Culatta, A., & Tompkins, J. R. (2007). *Fundamentals of special education: What every teacher should know* (3rd ed.). Columbus, OH: Pearson/Allyn & Bacon-Merrill.

Wertsch, J. V. (1991). *Voices of the mind: A sociocultural approach to mediated action.* Cambridge, MA: Harvard University Press.

Wertsch, J. V. (2007). Mediation. In H. Daniels, M. Cole, & J. V. Wertsch (Eds.), *The Cambridge companion to Vygotsky* (pp. 178–192). New York, NY: Cambridge University Press.

Wertsch, J. V., & Tulviste, P. (1992). L. S. Vygotsky and contemporary developmental psychology. *Developmental Psychology, 28,* 548–557.

Westberg, K. L., Archambault, F. X., Dodyns, S. M., & Slavin, T. J. (1993). The classroom practices observation study. *Journal of the Education of the Gifted, 16*(2), 120–146.

Westling, E., Andrews, J. A., Hampson, S. E., & Peterson, M. (2008). Pubertal timing and substance use: The effects of gender, parental monitoring and deviant peers. *Journal of Adolescent Health, 42,* 555–563.

Wheatley, K. F. (2002). The potential benefits of teacher efficacy doubts for educational reform. *Teaching and Teacher Education, 18,* 5–22.

Wheatley, K. F. (2005). The case for reconceptualizing teacher efficacy research. *Teaching and Teacher Education, 21,* 747–766.

Wheelock, A. (1992). *Crossing the tracks: How untracking can save America's schools.* New York, NY: The New Press.

Whitehead, A. N. (1929). *The aims of education.* New York, NY: Macmillan.

Whitehurst, G. J., Epstein, J. N., Angell, A. L., Payne, A. C., Crone, D. A., & Fischel, J. E. (1994). Outcomes of an emergent literacy program in headstart. *Journal of Educational Psychology, 86,* 542–555.

Whitehurst, G. J., & Lonigan, C. J. (1998). Child development and emergent literacy. *Child Development, 69,* 845–872.

Wigfield, A., Byrnes, J. P., & Eccles, J. S. (2006). Development during early and middle adolescence. In P. A. Alexander & P. H. Winne (Eds.), *Handbook of educational psychology* (2nd ed., pp. 87–113). Mahwah, NJ: Erlbaum.

Wigfield, A., & Eccles, J. (1989). Test anxiety in elementary and secondary school students. *Educational Psychologist, 24,* 159–183.

Wigfield, A., & Eccles, J. (2002). The development of competence beliefs, expectancies of success, and achievement values from childhood through adolescence. In A. Wigfield & J. Eccles (Eds.), *Development of achievement motivation* (pp. 91–120). San Diego, CA: Academic Press.

Wigfield, A., Eccles, J., MacIver, D., Rueman, D., & Midgley, C. (1991). Transitions at early adolescence: Changes in children's domain-specific self-perceptions and general self-esteem across the transition to junior high school. *Developmental Psychology, 27,* 552–565.

Wigfield, A., Eccles, J. S., & Pintrich, P. R. (1996). Development between the ages of 11 and 25. In D. Berliner & R. Calfee (Eds.), *Handbook of educational psychology* (pp. 148–185). New York, NY: Macmillan.

Wigfield, A., & Wentzel, K. R. (2007). Introduction to motivation at school: Interventions that work. *Educational Psychologist, 42,* 191–196.

Wiggins, G. (1989). Teaching to the authentic test. *Educational Leadership, 46*(7), 41–47.

Wiggins, G. (1991). Standards, not standardization: Evoking quality student work. *Educational Leadership, 48*(5), 18–25.

Willcutt, E. G., Pennington, B. F., Boada, R., Ogline, J. S., Tunick, R. A., Chhabidas, N. A., & Olson, R. K. (2001). A comparison of the cognitive deficits in reading disability and attention-deficit/hyperactivity disorder. *Journal of Abnormal Psychology, 110,* 157–172.

William, D. (2010) Standardized testing and school accountability. *Educational Psychologist, 45,* 107–122.

Williams, C., & Bybee J. (1994). What do children feel guilty about? Developmental and gender differences. *Developmental Psychology, 30,* 617–623.

Williams, T., & Williams, K. (2010). Self-efficacy and performance in mathematics: Reciprocal feterminism in 33 nations. *Journal of Educational Psychology, 102,* 453–466.

Willingham, D. T. (2004). Reframing the mind. *Education Next, 4*(3), 19–24.

Willis, J. (2007). Which brain research can educators trust? *Phi Delta Kappan, 88,* 697–699.

Willis, J. (2009). What brain research suggests for teaching reading strategies. *Educational Forum, 73,* 333–346.

Willoughby, T., Porter, L., Belsito, L., & Yearsley, T. (1999). Use of elaboration strategies by grades two, four, and six. *Elementary School Journal, 99,* 221–231.

Wilson, M. (2001). The case for sensorimotor coding in working memory. *Psychonomic Bulletin and Review, 8,* 44–57.

Wilson, M. (2002). Six views of embodied cognition. *Psychonomic Bulletin and Review, 9,* 625–636.

Wilson M., & Trainin, G. (2007). First-grade students' motivation and achievement for reading, writing, and spelling. *Reading Psychology, 28,* 257–282.

Windschitl, M. (2002). Framing constructivism in practice as the negotiation of dilemmas: An analysis of the conceptual, pedagogical, cultural, and political challenges facing teachers. *Review of Educational Research, 72,* 131–175.

Winett, R. A., & Winkler, R. C. (1972). Current behavior modification in the classroom: Be still, be quiet, be docile. *Journal of Applied Behavior Analysis, 15,* 499–504.

Wink, J., & Putney, L. (2002). *A vision of Vygotsky.* Boston, MA: Allyn & Bacon.

Winne, P. H. (1995). Inherent details in self-regulated learning. *Educational Psychologist, 30,* 173–188.

Winne, P. H. (2001). Self-regulated learning viewed from models of information processing. In B. J. Zimmerman & D. H. Schunk (Eds.), *Self-regulated learning and academic achievement: Theoretical perspectives* (2nd ed., pp. 153–189). Mahwah, NJ: Erlbaum.

Winne, P. H. (2011). A cognitive and metacognitive analysis of self-regulated learning. In B. Zimmerman & D. Schunk, (Eds.) *Handbook of self-regulation of learning and performance* (pp. 15–32). New York, NY: Routledge.

Winne, P. H., & Hadwin, A. F. (1998). Studying as self-regulated learning. In D. J. Hacker, J. Dunlosky, & A. C. Graesser (Eds.), *Metacognition in educational theory and practice* (pp. 277–304). Mahwah, NJ: Erlbaum.

Winne, P. H., & Perry, N. E. (2000). Measuring self-regulated learning. In P. Pintrich, M. Boekaerts, & M. Zeidner (Eds.), *Handbook of self-regulation* (pp. 531–566). Orlando, FL: Academic Press.

Winner, E. (2000). The origins and ends of giftedness. *American Psychologist, 55,* 159–169.

Winner, E. (2003). Musical giftedness. *Bulletin of Psychology and the Arts, 4,* 1, 2–5.

Winsler, A., Carlton, M. P., & Barry, M. J. (2000). Age-related changes in preschool children's systematic use of private speech in a natural setting. *Journal of Child Language, 27,* 665–687.

Winsler, A., & Naglieri, J. A. (2003). Overt and covert verbal problem-solving strategies: Developmental trends in use, awareness, and relations with task performance in children age 5 to 17. *Child Development, 74,* 659–678.

Winters, F. I., Greene, J. A., & Costich, C. M. (2008). Self-regulation of learning within computer-based learning environments: A critical analysis. *Educational Psychology Review* doi:10.1007/s10648-008-9080-9.

Wittrock, M. C. (1982, March). *Educational implications of recent research on learning and memory.* Paper presented at the annual meeting of the American Educational Research Association, New York.

Wittrock, M. C. (Ed.). (1986). *Handbook of research on teaching* (3rd ed.). New York, NY: Macmillan.

Wittrock, M. C. (1992). An empowering conception of educational psychology. *Educational Psychologist, 27,* 129–142.

Wittwer, J., & Renkl, A. (2010). How effective are instructional explanations in example-based learning? A meta-analytic review. *Educational Psychology Review, 22,* 393–409.

Wolf, M., Barzillai, M., Gottwald, S., Miller, L., Spencer, K., Norton, E. , . . . Morris, R. (2009). The RAVE-O intervention: Connecting neuroscience to the classroom. *Mind, Brain, and Education, 3,* 84–93.

Wolfe, P. (2010). *Brain matters: Translating research into classroom practice* (2nd ed.). Alexandria, VA: Association for Supervision and Curriculum Development.

Wong, K. F., & Xiao, Y. (2010). Diversity and difference: Identity Issues of Chinese heritage language learners from dialect backgrounds. *Heritage Language Journal, 7,* 153–187.

Wong, L. (1987). Reaction to research findings: Is the feeling of obviousness warranted? *Dissertation Abstracts International, 48/12,* 3709B (University Microfilms #DA 8801059).

Wood, D., Bruner, J., & Ross, S. (1976). The role of tutoring in problem solving. *British Journal of Psychology, 66,* 181–191.

Woods, B. S., & Murphy, P. K. (2002). Thickening the discussion: What can William James tell us about constructivism? *Educational Theory, 52,* 443–449.

Woodward, A., & Needham, A. (Eds.) (2009). *Learning and the infant mind.* New York, NY: Oxford University Press.

Woolfolk, A. E., & Brooks, D. (1983). Nonverbal communication in teaching. In E. Gordon (Ed.), *Review of research in education* (Vol. 10, pp. 103–150). Washington, DC: American Educational Research Association.

Woolfolk, A. E., & Brooks, D. (1985). The influence of teachers' nonverbal behaviors on students' perceptions and performance. *Elementary School Journal, 85,* 514–528.

Woolfolk, A. E., & Hoy, W. K. (1990). Prospective teachers' sense of efficacy and beliefs about control. *Journal of Educational Psychology, 82,* 81–91.

Woolfolk, A., E. & Perry, N. E. (2012). *Child development.* Boston Allyn & Bacon/Pearson.

Woolfolk, A. E., Perry, N., & Winne, P. (2006). *Educational psychology: Third Canadian edition* (3rd ed.). Toronto, CA: Pearson.

Woolfolk, A. E., Rosoff, B., & Hoy, W. K. (1990). Teachers' sense of efficacy and their beliefs about managing students. *Teaching and Teacher Education, 6,* 137–148.

Woolfolk Hoy, A., & Burke-Spero, R. (2005). Changes in teacher efficacy during the early years of teaching: A comparison of four measures. *Teaching and Teacher Education, 21,* 343–356.

Woolfolk Hoy, A., Davis, H., & Pape, S. (2006). Teachers' knowledge, beliefs, and thinking. In P. A. Alexander & P. H, Winne (Eds.), *Handbook of educational psychology* (2nd ed., pp. 715–737). Mahwah, NJ: Erlbaum.

Woolfolk Hoy, A., Demerath, P., & Pape, S. (2002). Teaching adolescents: Engaging developing selves. In T. Urdan & F. Pajares (Eds.), *Adoles-cence and education* (pp. 119–169, Volume I). Greenwich, CT: Information Age Publishing.

Woolfolk Hoy, A., Hoy, W. K., & Davis, H. (2009). Teachers' self-efficacy beliefs. In K. Wentzel & A. Wigfield (Eds.), *Handbook of motivation in school.* Mahwah, NJ: Erlbaum.

Woolfolk Hoy, A., & Murphy, P. K. (2001). Teaching educational psychology to the implicit mind. In R. Sternberg & B. Torff (Eds.), *Understanding and teaching the implicit mind* (pp. 145–185). Mahwah, NJ: Erlbaum.

Woolfolk Hoy, A., Pape, S., & Davis, H. (2006). Teachers' knowledge, beliefs, and thinking. In P. A. Alexander & P. H, Winne (Eds.), *Handbook of educational psychology* (2nd ed.). Mahwah, NJ: Erlbaum.

Woolfolk Hoy, A., & Tschannen-Moran. M. (1999). Implications of cognitive approaches to peer learning for teacher education. In A. O'Donnell & A. King (Eds.), *Cognitive perspectives on peer learning* (pp. 257–284). Mahwah, NJ: Erlbaum.

Woolfolk Hoy, A., & Weinstein, C. S. (2006). Students' and teachers' perspectives about classroom management. In C. Evertson & C. S. Weinstein (Eds.), *Handbook for classroom management: Research, practice, and contemporary issues.* Mahwah, NJ: Erlbaum.

Wout, D., Dasco, H., Jackson, J., & Spencer, S. (2008). The many faces of stereotype threat: Group- and self-threat. *Journal of Experimental Social Psychology, 44,* 792–799.

Wu, W., West, S. G., & Hughes, J. N. (2010). Effect of grade retention in first grade on psychosocial outcomes. *Journal of Educational Psychology, 102,* 135–152.

Yang, L., Shuai, L., Du, Q., et al. (2009). Atomoxetine and executive functioning in Chinese ADHD children. From Childhood to Adult Disease. May 21–24, 2009, Vienna, Austria. *Attention Deficit and Hyperactivity Disorders, 1,* 135.

Yarhouse, M. A. (2001). Sexual identity development: The influence of valuative frameworks on identity synthesis. *Psychotherapy, 38*(3), 331–341.

Yell, M. L. (1990). The use of corporal punishment, suspension, expulsion, and timeout with behaviorally disordered students in public schools: Legal considerations. *Behavioral Disorders, 15,* 100–109.

Yerkes, R. M., & Dodson, J. D. (1908). The relation of strength of stimulus to rapidity of habit formation. *Journal of Comparative Neurology, 18,* 459–482.

Yough, M. (2010, August). *An intervention: Teaching candidates' beliefs and linguistic minority students.* Paper presented at the American Psychological Association Annual Convention, San Diego, CA.

Younger, M. R., & Warrington, M. (2006). Would Harry and Hermione have done better in single-sex teaching in coeducational secondary schools in the United Kingdom? *American Educational Research Journal, 43,* 579–620.

Youniss, J., & Yates, M. (1997). *Community service and social responsibility in youth.* Chicago, IL: University of Chicago Press.

Zeidner, M. (1995). Adaptive coping with test situations. *Educational Psychologist, 30,* 123–134.

Zeidner, M. (1998). *Test anxiety: The state of the art.* New York, NY: Plenum.

Zelli, A., Dodge, K. A., Lochman, J. E., & Laird, R. D. (1999). The distinction between beliefs legitimizing aggression and deviant processing of social cues: Testing measurement validity and the hypothesis that biased processing mediates the effects of beliefs on aggression. *Journal of Personality and Social Psychology, 77,* 150–166.

Zhang, L., & Sternberg, R. J. (2005). The threefold model of intellectual styles. *Educational Psychology Review, 17,* 1–53.

Zhou, Z., Peverly, S. T., Beohm, A. E., & Chongde, L. (2001). American and Chinese children's understanding of distance, time, and speed interrelations. *Cognitive Development, 15,* 215–240.

Zimmerman, B. (2011). Motivational sources and outcomes of self-regulated learning and performance. In B. Zimmerman & D. Schunk, (Eds.), *Handbook of self-regulation of learning and performance* (pp. 49–64). New York, NY: Routledge.

Zimmerman, B. J., & Schunk, D. H. (Eds.). (2001). *Self-regulated learning and academic achievement: Theoretical perspectives* (2nd ed.). Mahwah, NJ: Erlbaum.

Zimmerman, B. J., & Schunk, D. H. (2004). Self-regulating intellectual processes and outcomes: A social cognitive perspective. In D. Y. Dao & R. J. Sternberg (Eds.), *Motivation, emotion, and cognition: Integrative perspectives on intellectual functioning and development* (pp. 323–350). Mahwah, NJ: Erlbaum.

Zimmerman, B., & Schunk, D. (Eds.). (2011). *Handbook of self-regulation of learning and performance.* New York, NY: Routledge.

Photo Credits

Kelly Hoy / Kushch Dmitry / Shutterstock.com, pp. 11, 46; © Stephen McBrady / PhotoEdit, p. 8; Bill Anderson / Photo Researchers, Inc., p. 24; Family Circus © Bil Keane, Inc. King Features Syndicate, p. 20; ©Michael Newman/PhotoEdit, p. 25; ©Elena Rooraid/PhotoEdit, p. 28; ©Felicia Martinez/PhotoEdit, p. 37; Dibyangshu Sarkar / AFP / Getty Images, Inc., p. 35; ©John Birdsall / The Image Works, p. 44; Color Symphony / Shutterstock.com, pp. 43, 83; © Jeff Greenberg / The Image Works, p. 45; © Angela Hampton Picture Library / Alamy, 48; Monkey Business Images / Shutterstock.com, pp. 51 top left; H. Tuller / Shutterstock.com, p. 51 right; BananaStock / Thinkstock.com, p. 51 bottom left; Courtesy of Ruth Chao, p. 53; © Bubbles Photolibrary / Alamy, p. 56; © Ted Streshinsky/ Corbis, p. 61; Ryan McVay / Photodisc / Thinkstock.com, p. 63; Marc Dolphin / Getty Images Inc. – Stone Allstock, p. 65; Marili Forastieri / Digital Vision / Thinkstock.com, p. 68; © Jeff Greenberg / PhotoEdit, pp. 70, 279; © David Young-Wolff / PhotoEdit, pp. 78, 126, 281; Peter Byron / Photo Researchers, Inc., p. 80; svkv / Shutterstock.com, pp. 117, 163; © Ted Foxx / Alamy, p. 120; Jim Cummins / Getty Images, Inc. – Taxi, p. 125; © Dennis MacDonald / PhotoEdit, p. 134; © Robin Nelson / PhotoEdit, p. 153; GL Archive / Alamy, p. 156; Courtesy of the Library of Congress, p. 156; © SuperStock / SuperStock, 156; Hans Namuth / Photo Researchers, Inc., p. 156; Scott Cunningham/Merrill, p. 157; Toby Wales/Lebrecht Music & Arts, p. 159; DGDESIGN / Shutterstock. com, pp. 169, 201; © Bob Ebbesen / Alamy, p. 171; Copyright © 2000 Sidney Harris. Reprinted with permission of Sidney Harris, p. 172; Golden Pixels LLC / Shutterstock.com, p. 178; © Dennis Kitchen / PhotoEdit, p. 186; © Israel Images / Alamy, p. 187; uttam gurjar / Shutterstock.com, pp. 207, 242; Ryan McVey / Getty Images, Inc. – Photodisc / Royalty Free, p. 210; © Will Hart / PhotoEdit, pp. 215; © John Neubauer / PhotoEdit, p. 215; Michael J. Doolittle / The Image Works, p. 216; Patrick White / Merrill, pp. 217, 266, 267; Stephen VanHorn / Shutterstock.com, p. 217; Carl Iwasaki / Time & Life Pictures / Getty Images, p. 221; "Doonesbury." Copyright © G. B. Trudeau. Reprinted with the permission of Universal Uclick. All Rights Reserved, p. 222; Benis Arapovic / Shutterstock.com, p. 230; © Bill Aron / PhotoEdit, pp. 236; © Image Source / Alamy, p. 240; David Mager / Pearson Learning Photo Studio, pp. 333; © Juice Images / Alamy, pp. 302; Getty Images – Stockbyte, p. 293; Anthony Magnacca / Merrill, pp. 282; Kelia Neokow / Shutterstock.com, pp. 249, 285; © Gabbro / Alamy, p. 254; © Ian Shaw / Alamy, p. 258; Laurence Gough / Shutterstock. com , p. 265; echo3005 / Shutterstock.com, p. 291, 318; Jon Brenneis/Time & Life Pictures/Getty Images, p. 293; © imagebroker / Alamy, p. 297; © Mason Trullinger / Alamy, p. 299; © Corbis Premium RF / Alamy, p. 311; © Spencer Grant / Alamy, pp. 315; thrashem / Shutterstock.com, pp. 324, 359; © PCN Photography / Alamy, p. 326; © Michelle D. Bridwell / PhotoEdit, p. 330; © Lon C. Diehl / PhotoEdit, p. 339; © UpperCut Images / Alamy, p. 343; © AGStockUSA / Alamy, p. 369; © richard mittleman / Alamy, p. 375; Liz Moore / Merrill, p. 383; mxz / Shutterstock.com, pp. 403, 437; Krista Greco / Merrill, p. 408; Courtesy of Glen Dines, p. 409; Getty Images, Inc. – Image 100 Royalty Free, p. 417; © Blend Images / Alamy, p. 445; © Corbis, p. 447; Angela Waye / Shutterstock.com, pp. 443, 479; © RubberBall / Alamy, p. 454; © Mary Kate Denny / PhotoEdit, p. 464; Matthew Benoit / Shutterstock.com, 465; AP Photo / Mary Ann Chastain, p. 470.

CONTENT AREA READING: TEACHING AND LEARNING IN AN AGE OF MULTIPLE LITERACIES

Chapter 1-3 taken from chapter 1, 3, and 11 of *Creating Literacy Instruction: For All Students*, Eighth Edition by Thomas G. Gunning

Chapter 4-15, and appendices taken from chapter 2, 4-13, 15 and appendices of *Content Area Reading: Teaching and Learning in an Age of Multiple Literacies*, by Maureen McLaughlin

Preface

This book has been specifically created for teacher candidates in the New Pathways to Teaching In New Jersey alternate route program. The Curriculum Committee determined that we needed to create a new textbook that included all of the elements necessary for excellence in literacy. Since reading, writing, thinking, viewing and speaking are the key elements in literacy that are present in every subject you teach, this custom book reflects literacy in all subject areas and at all levels of development. Whether you are teaching first grade or high school biology, you must be able to teach the skills and strategies necessary for students to comprehend text, to be able to think critically, and to become effective, life-long learners.

Best of luck to you in your journey as you acquire the teaching skills, strategies and experiences that will improve the literacy of each student, thereby improving the educational opportunities and possibilities for all.

New Pathways Curriculum Committee

Dr. Fran Levin, Academic Director, NPTNJ

Ms. Brenda Fisher

Dr. Beth Godett

Ms. Ave Latte

Mr. Louis Panigrosso

Mr. Dennis Siddons

Dr. Cordelia Twomey

Ms. Cynthia Vazquez

Dr. Thomas Vona

Brief Contents

Creating Literacy
Instruction for
All Students

The Nature of Literacy

Anticipation Guide

Complete the anticipation guide below. It will help to activate your prior knowledge so that you interact more fully with the chapter. It is designed to probe your attitudes and beliefs about important and sometimes controversial topics. There are often no right or wrong answers; the statements will alert you to your attitudes about reading instruction and encourage you to become aware of areas where you might require additional information. After completing the chapter, you might respond to the anticipation guide again to see if your answers have changed in light of what you have read. For each of the following statements, put a check under "Agree" or "Disagree" to show how you feel. Discuss your responses with classmates before you read the chapter.

	Agree	Disagree
1. Before children learn to read, they should know the sounds of most letters.	_____	_____
2. Reading should not be fragmented into a series of subskills.	_____	_____
3. Oral reading should be accurate.	_____	_____
4. Phonics should be taught only when a need arises.	_____	_____
5. Reading short passages and answering questions about them provide excellent practice.	_____	_____
6. Mistakes in oral reading should be ignored unless they change the sense of the passage.	_____	_____

Using What You Know

This chapter provides a general introduction to literacy instruction in preschool and grades K–8. Before reading the chapter, examine your personal knowledge of the topic so that you will be better prepared to interact with the information. Sometimes, you may not realize what you know until you stop and think about it. What do you think reading is? What do you do when you read? What do you think the reader's role is? Is it simply to receive the author's message, or should it include some personal input? How about writing? What processes do you use when you write? How would you go about teaching reading and writing to today's students? What do you think the basic principles of a literacy program should be? What elements have worked especially well in programs with which you are familiar?

The Nature of Reading

"Awake! Awake!" These are the first words I remember reading. But the words were as magical as any that I have read since. Even after all these years, I still have vivid memories of that day long ago in first grade when reading came alive for me, and, indeed, awakened a lifetime of reading and a career as a reading teacher.

Reading is, first and foremost, magical, as those who recall learning to read or who have witnessed their students discover the process will attest. It opens the door to a vast world of information, fulfillment, and enjoyment. After having learned to read, a person is never quite the same.

FYI

Using What You Know is designed to activate your prior knowledge on the general topic of the chapter. Sometimes, we don't realize that we already know something about a topic until we stop and think about it. By activating your prior knowledge, you will be better prepared to make connections between new information contained in this chapter and what you already know.

Although magical, reading is complex. Becoming an effective teacher of reading requires a grounding in the theories behind reading acquisition and instruction. As Pinnell, a noted literacy researcher and practitioner, states:

> Understanding learning is the only true foundation for sound teaching. No matter how good the materials, the program, or the instructional approach, teaching will miss the mark if it is not based on a coherent theory of learning. The word *theory* simply refers to the set of understandings that a teacher holds and believes about how children learn. Everything teachers do in the classroom proceeds from this set of beliefs and understandings, whether they are conscious of it or not. (2006, p. 78)

Major Theories of Literacy Learning and Language Development

The first step, then, in understanding reading requires understanding how children learn and how language develops. There are a number of theories that describe how children learn. They fall into two broad areas: behaviorism and cognitivism.

Behaviorism

Behaviorism stresses observable responses to stimuli. In a behavioral approach, learning consists of the acquisition of new behaviors. Responses that are reinforced increase in frequency. Responses that are not reinforced are extinguished (do not occur again). A response that has been conditioned to a particular stimulus should be elicited if that stimulus is presented. Behaviors are learned or increased when a person receives reinforcers such as praise, privileges, gold stars, or monetary rewards or simply sees that the responses are correct. A basic principle of behaviorism is that we tend to repeat behaviors that are rewarding and avoid those that are not. According to behaviorism, we are passive receivers of knowledge rather than active constructors. Behavioral approaches tend to be teacher-centered.

Scripted programs, such as Reading Mastery, often take a behavioral approach. In Reading Mastery, students first learn individual letter sounds and then learn to blend the sounds to form words. The teacher points to a letter and says, "Here is a new sound." The teacher touches the letter and says the sound for the letter. Students are told to say the sound when the teacher touches the letter. Signals are used so that students respond in unison. Then individuals are called on to say the sound. One objective of this procedure is to obtain as many correct responses from each child as possible. Incorrect responses are quickly corrected so that they will be extinguished.

Using Technology

The Association for Direct Instruction provides information about Reading Mastery, which is a bottom-up approach. The site has film clips showing Reading Mastery lessons. Click on Support Services and then on Movie Clips.
http://www.adihome.org

Cognitivism

Behavioral approaches to learning, with their emphasis on external forces, dominated from about the 1890s until about the 1950s. Rejecting a strictly external view of learning, cognitive psychologists became interested in the inner workings of the mind. **Cognitivism** is based on the proposition that mental processes exist and can be studied. A related proposition is that humans are active participants in their learning rather than passive recipients. Reinforcement is seen as being important in learning, not just because it strengthens responses, but because it is a source of information or feedback (Woolfolk, 2001). Cognitive approaches tend to be student-centered.

Piaget's theories are examples of a cognitive approach to learning. Piaget is also known as a constructivist because of his emphasis on the ways in which children construct an understanding of the world.

Behaviorism is a philosophy of learning that describes all the activities of an organism in terms of observable actions or behaviors.

Cognitivism is a philosophy of learning that describes the activities of an organism in terms of observable actions or behaviors and internal or mental states.

Piaget's Theories

Jean Piaget, a Swiss psychologist, stressed stages of cognitive development and the unique nature of children's thinking. As an adherent of **constructivism**, he believed that children construct their own understanding of reality and do not simply reproduce what they see and hear. Children's thinking, according to Piaget, is qualitatively different from adults' thinking, and it evolves through a series of hierarchical stages. He also believed that children's thinking develops through direct experience with their environment. Through *adaptation*, or interaction with the environment, the child constructs psychological structures, or *schemes*, which are ways of making sense of the world. Adaptation includes two complementary processes: **assimilation** and **accommodation**. Through assimilation, the child interprets the world in terms of his or her schemes. Seeing a very small dog, the child calls it "doggie" and assimilates this in his or her dog scheme. Seeing a goat for the first time, the child might relate it to his or her dog scheme and call it "doggie." Later, realizing that there is something different about this creature, the child may accommodate the dog scheme and exclude the goat and all creatures with horns. Thus, the child has refined the dog scheme. To Piaget, direct experience rather than language was the key determiner of cognitive development.

Social Cognitive Views of Learning

According to social cognitive theories, people are an important element in the learning equation. We learn from and with others. L. S. Vygotsky, an adherent of **social constructivism**, stressed the importance of social factors in cognitive development (1962). Although both Piaget and Vygotsky believed that children need to interact with the world around them, Vygotsky thought that learning results from both direct experience and social interaction. If, in examining minerals, a teacher emphasizes the hardness of the minerals, that is what the students will learn. If another teacher emphasizes the value or usefulness of the minerals, that is what the students will learn. Vygotsky is best known for the concept of the **zone of proximal development (ZPD)**. He distinguished between actual and potential development. Actual development is a measure of the level at which a child is functioning. In a sense, it is a measure of what the child has learned up to that point. Potential development is a measure of what the child might be capable of achieving. The difference between the two levels is the zone of proximal development. As explained by Vygotsky (1978), the zone of proximal development is "the distance between the actual developmental level as determined by independent problem solving and the level of potential development as determined through problem solving under adult guidance or in collaboration with more capable peers" (p. 84). In other words, the zone of proximal development is the difference between what a child can do on his or her own and what the child can do with help.

Focusing on the importance of interaction with adults or knowledgeable peers, Vygotsky's theory is that children learn through expert guidance. In time, they internalize the concepts and strategies employed by their mentors and so, ultimately, are able to perform on a higher level. The support and guidance provided by an adult or more capable peer is known as **scaffolding** (Bruner, 1975, 1986). When parents

 FYI

Vygotsky differentiated between learning and development. According to him, learning can often cause qualitative changes in the nature of thought. Certain kinds of knowledge can lead to higher levels of thinking (Bodrova & Leong, 2007). Behaviorists assert that the child simply acquires more knowledge.

☐ **Constructionism (constructivism)** is a cognitive philosophy of learning that describes learning as an active process in which the learner constructs mental models of reality.

☐ **Assimilation** is the process of incorporating new ideas into existing ones.

☐ **Accommodation** is the process by which concepts or schemes are modified or new ones created to accommodate new knowledge.

☐ **Social constructivism** is a cognitive philosophy of learning that describes learning as an active process in which the learner constructs mental models of reality individually and in interaction with others.

☐ The **zone of proximal development (ZPD)** is the difference between independent performance and potential performance as determined through problem solving under the guidance of an adult or more capable peer.

☐ **Scaffolding** refers to the support and guidance provided by an adult or more capable peer that helps a student function on a higher level.

FYI

Vygotsky neglected the importance of other ways of learning. Children can and do learn through nonverbal imitation and self-discovery (Berk, 1997).

REFLECTION

How might you apply Vygotskyian principles in your classroom?

converse with a child acquiring language, they respond at a higher level of language use but one that is in the child's zone of proximal development. In their responses, they provide contextual support by restating, repeating key words, and/or focusing on meaning rather than form. Support at the beginning levels of language learning is extensive but is gradually decreased as the child progresses.

Ideally, instruction should be pitched somewhat above a child's current level of functioning. Instruction and collaboration with an adult or more capable peers will enable a child to reach a higher level and ultimately function on that level. Instruction and interaction are key elements. The overall theories of evaluation and instruction presented in this book are grounded in Vygotsky's concepts of actual and potential development and the zone of proximal development.

Implications for classroom instruction based on an integration of the theories of Piaget and Vygotsky are listed below:

- Provide students with hands-on experiences and opportunities to make discoveries.
- Be aware of and plan for individual differences. Because children have different experiences and come from different backgrounds, they develop at different rates.
- Children learn best when activities are developmentally appropriate. Careful observation of the processes a child uses provides insight into the child's level of development. According to Piaget, the child's current level of development determines what she or he will learn. Teaching needs to be adjusted to the child. According to Vygotsky, teaching should be directed to a child's emerging skills. It should be in the zone of proximal development.
- According to Vygotsky, classrooms should be rich in verbal guidance. Interactions with the teacher and peers foster learning. Modeling of strategies for improving comprehension and using context clues are examples of ways teachers foster social cognitive learning.

Cognitive Behavioral Approach

Behavioral and cognitive principles have been combined in an approach known as **cognitive behavioral modification**. Our behavior is affected by the set of rewards and punishments we have experienced in the past and by our beliefs, thoughts, and expectations (Westmont Psychology Department, 2008). Suppose that, based on your past experience of receiving low grades on tests, you believe that you are not very smart and therefore it won't make much difference if you study for a test; so you don't study, and you get a poor grade, thus reinforcing your lack of self-efficacy. A cognitive behavioral approach helps students change their attributions, so they see that effort is required for success. They also learn to see themselves as competent learners. Cognitive behavioral classroom management provides techniques for students to gain control of their learning. Students are taught to set goals, establish and follow a plan for reaching each goal, monitor their progress toward reaching that goal, and evaluate whether they have reached it. Along with learning strategies for improving reading and writing, students are taught self-regulation strategies. A student might set as a goal improving comprehension of text content. The student might then use a checklist or self-talk to prompt herself or himself to set a purpose for reading, survey the text, think about what she or he knows about the topic, make predictions, ask questions while reading, and summarize at the end of each section. The student monitors the use of the strategies to see if they are helping and evaluates whether she or he is reaching the goal of improved comprehension of the text. As Meichenbaum and Biemiller (1998) explain, practice usually involves "both physically performing the skill or skills involved in the task and verbally guiding oneself (thinking out loud—demonstrating self-regulation overtly) while carrying out the task" (p. 126).

Cognitive behavioral modification is an approach to learning in which self-talk and rewards are used to replace faulty learning habits and beliefs with effective habits and strategies and realistic beliefs.

Top-Down and Bottom-Up Approaches

Another way of looking at theories of literacy learning is to note where those who apply them fall on a continuum. On one end of this continuum are those who espouse a subskills, or bottom-up, approach; on the other end, there are those who advocate a holistic, or top-down, approach. In between are the interactionists.

Bottom-Uppers

In the **bottom-up approach**, children literally start at the bottom and work their way up. First, they learn the names and shapes of the letters of the alphabet. Next, they learn consonant sounds, followed by simple and then more complex vowel correspondences. As Carnine, Silbert, and Kame'enui (1990) explain, "Our position is that many students will not become successful readers unless teachers identify the essential reading skills, find out what skills students lack, and teach those skills directly" (p. 3).

Bottom-up procedures are intended to make learning to read easier by breaking complex tasks into their component skills. Instruction proceeds from the simple to the complex. In essence, there are probably no 100 percent bottom-uppers among reading teachers. Even those who strongly favor phonics recognize the importance of higher-level strategies.

Top-Downers

A **top-down approach**, as its name indicates, starts at the top and works downward. Learning to read is seen as being similar to learning to speak; it is holistic and progresses naturally through immersion. Subskills are not taught because it is felt that they fragment the process and make learning to read more abstract and difficult (Goodman, 1986). One of the most influential models of reading is that proposed by Ken Goodman (1994b). According to Goodman, readers use their background knowledge and knowledge of language to predict and infer the content of print. Readers "use their selection strategies to choose only the most useful information from all that is available" (Goodman, 1994b, p. 1125). When reading the sentence "The moon is full tonight," the reader can use his or her knowledge of the moon, context clues, and perhaps the initial consonants *f* and *t* to reconstruct *full* and *tonight*. According to Goodman's theory, it is not necessary for the reader to process all the letters of *full* and *tonight*. However, in order to make use of background knowledge, context clues, and initial consonant cues, the reader must consider the whole text. If the words *full* and *tonight* were read in isolation, the reader would have to depend more heavily on processing all or most of the letters of each word. As far as comprehension is concerned, the top-down view is that students build their understanding through discussions of high-quality literature or informational texts. There is generally no direct, explicit instruction of comprehension strategies.

> **FYI**
>
> In Goodman's model, students use three cueing systems: semantic, syntactic, and graphophonic. Semantic cues derive from past experiences, so students construct meaning by bringing their background of knowledge to a story. Syntactic cues derive from knowledge of how the structure of language works. Graphophonic cues refer to the ability to sound out words or recognize them holistically. Based on their use of these cues, students predict the content of the text, confirm or revise their predictions, and reread if necessary.

Interactionists

Most practitioners tend to be more pragmatic than either strict top-downers or dyed-in-the-wool bottom-uppers and borrow practices from both ends of the continuum. These **interactionists** teach skills directly and systematically—especially in the beginning—but they avoid overdoing it, as they do not want to fragment the process. They also provide plenty of opportunities for students to experience the holistic nature of reading and writing by having them read whole books and write for real purposes. In his study of highly effective teachers, Pressley (2006) found that most were inter-

---

▢ **Bottom-up approach** refers to a kind of processing in which meaning is derived from the accurate, sequential processing of words. The emphasis is on the text rather than the reader's background knowledge or language ability.

▢ **Top-down approach** refers to deriving meaning by using one's background knowledge, language ability, and expectations. The emphasis is on the reader rather than the text.

▢ **Interactionists** hold the theoretical position that reading involves processing text and using one's background knowledge and language ability.

REFLECTION

What is your position on the bottom-up, top-down continuum? How might your approach impact your instruction?

Using Technology

Controversies similar to "Is reading top-down or bottom-up?" are often explored on the Web sites of professional organizations, such as the International Reading Association's Web site:

http://www.reading.org/General/AboutIRA/PositionStatements.aspx □

actionists: "There is a great deal of skills instruction, with as many as 20 skills an hour covered, often in response to the needs of a reader or writer. Skills instruction is strongly balanced with holistic reading and writing, with students reading and experiencing substantial authentic literature and other texts that make sense for them to be reading given their needs" (p. 3). As cognitive psychologist M. H. Ashcroft (1994) notes, "Any significant mental task will involve both data-driven (bottom-up) and conceptually driven (top-down) processing" (p. 75).

In an interactive compensatory model, students use top-down processes to compensate for weakness in bottom-up processes or vice versa. For instance, students who have weak decoding skills make heavy use of context to make sense of a passage. On the other hand, when content is unfamiliar, readers get all they can out of the data. They read every word carefully, may reread it several times, and may even read it out loud. Think about how you read a set of directions for completing a complex, unfamiliar activity or a list of new tax regulations.

Where do you fit on the bottom-up, top-down continuum? Go back to the anticipation guide at the beginning of the chapter. Take a look at how you answered the six statements. If you agreed with only the odd-numbered ones, you are a bottom-up advocate. If you agreed with only the even-numbered statements, you are a top-downer. If your answers were mixed, you are probably an interactionist.

Reader Response Theory

Still another way of looking at reading is from a literary, or reader response, view. Literary theory explores the role of the reader. In the past, the reader's role was defined as being passive, getting the author's meaning. Today, reading requires a more active role—the reader must construct meaning from text. The model of transmission of information in which the reader was merely a recipient has given way to transactional theory, a two-way process involving a reader and a text:

> Every reading act is an event, or a **transaction**, involving a particular reader and a particular pattern of signs, a text, and occurring at a particular time in a particular context. Instead of two fixed entities acting on one another, the reader and the text are two aspects of a total dynamic situation. The "meaning" does not reside ready-made "in" the text or "in" the reader but happens or comes into being during the transaction between reader and text. (Rosenblatt, 1994, p. 1063)

In her study of how students read a poem, Rosenblatt (1978) noted that each reader was active:

> He was not a blank tape registering a ready-made message. He was actively involved in building up a poem for himself out of his responses to text. He had to draw on his past experiences with the verbal symbols. . . . The reader was not only paying attention to what the words pointed to in the external world, to their referents; he was also paying attention to the images, feelings, attitudes, associations, and ideas that the words and their referents evoked in him. (p. 10)

The type of reading, of course, has an effect on the transaction. The reader can take an efferent or an aesthetic **stance**. When reading a set of directions, a science text, or a math problem, the reader takes an **efferent** stance, the focus being on obtaining information that can be carried away (*efferent* is taken from the Latin verb *efferre*, "to carry away"). In the **aesthetic** stance, the reader pays attention to the associations, feelings, attitudes, and ideas that the words evoke.

□ **Transaction** refers to the relationship between the reader and the text in which meaning is created as the text is conditioned by the reader and the reader is conditioned by the text.
□ **Stance** refers to the position or attitude that the reader takes. The two stances are aesthetic and efferent.

□ **Efferent** refers to a kind of reading in which the focus is on obtaining or carrying away information from the reading.
□ **Aesthetic** refers to a type of reading in which the reader focuses on experiencing the piece: the rhythm of the words, the past experiences the words call up (Rosenblatt, 1978, p. 10).

Does it make any difference whether reading is viewed as being transmissional, transactional, or somewhere in between? Absolutely. If reading is viewed as transmissional, students are expected to stick close to the author's message. If reading is viewed as transactional, students are

TABLE 1.1   Theories of Learning and Reading Development

Theory	Features	Implementation
Behaviorism	Observable behavior is stressed. Responses to stimuli are reinforced or extinguished. Drills, guided practice, and acquisition of facts, skills, and concepts are emphasized.	Present and reinforce skills, such as phonics, in systematic fashion. Reinforce appropriate behavior.
Cognitivism	Mental processes are important. Students are active learners as they use strategies to acquire facts, skills, and concepts.	Teach strategies. Ask questions that help reveal students' thinking.
Constructivism	Through active experiences, children construct their understanding of the world.	Arrange for learning experiences and opportunities for problem solving. Gear instruction to students' stage of development. Focus on inquiry and discovery learning.
Social Constructivism	Thoughts and ideas of others are an essential element in constructing knowledge. Students learn through expert guidance from more knowledgeable others. Social interaction, the zone of proximal development, and scaffolding are key elements in learning.	Make sure students are in their zone of proximal development. Co-construct knowledge with students. Scaffold students' learning.
Cognitive Behavioral	Learning is affected by the learning task and situation and the ability, interests, and attitudes of the students. Students use self-regulation to acquire facts, skills, and concepts.	Build self-efficacy. Teach students to set goals and self-regulate. Walk students through the process of setting goals, working to reach goals, and monitoring progress.
Interactionist	Both top-down and bottom-up processes are used. Students are active learners as they employ strategies to acquire facts, skills, and concepts.	Teach students to use phonics skills and context. Encourage students to relate new learning to what they already know. Use compensatory mechanisms.
Reader Response	Reading is a transaction in which the reader affects the text and is affected by it.	Emphasize personal responses and interpretations. Encourage students to make personal connections to what they have read.

Source: Portions of the chart are adapted from Woolfolk (2001), Table 9.8, Four Views of Learning (p. 358).

expected to put their personal selves into their reading, especially when encountering literature. From a transactional perspective, building background becomes especially important because it enriches the transaction between reader and text. Personal response and interpretation are at the center of the reading process. The reader's role is enhanced when a transactional view prevails. See Table 1.1 for a summary of theories of learning and language development.

Importance of Literacy Theories

Why is it important to be aware of different theories of teaching reading? For one thing, it is important that you formulate your own personal beliefs about reading and writing instruction. These beliefs will then be the foundation for your instruction. They will determine the goals you set, the instructional techniques you use, the materials you choose, the organization of your classroom, the reading and writing behaviors you expect students to exhibit, and the criteria you use to evaluate students. For instance, whether you use children's books or a basal anthology, how you teach phonics, and whether you expect flawless oral reading or are satisfied if the student's rendition is faithful to the sense of the selection will depend on your theoretical orientation (DeFord, 1985).

Approach Taken by This Book

This book draws heavily on research in cognitive psychology, combines an interactionist point of view with a holistic orientation, and takes an integrated approach. Both the bottom-up and top-down approaches are step by step (Kamhi & Catts, 1999). In the bottom-up model, the reader progresses from letters to sounds to words. Seeing the word *moon*, the novice readers sounds it out as /m-/oo/-/n/ and then blends the sounds to compose the word *moon*. In the top-down process as Goodman explained above, the reader uses language cues to predict and to confirm the word. Seeing the sentence "The wolf howled at the moon," the reader uses her knowledge of language and wolves

FYI

- To clarify your philosophy of teaching, ask: "What are my instructional practices, and why am I doing what I'm doing?" Examining your practices should help you uncover your beliefs.
- This book takes the position that all sources of information—semantic, syntactic, background knowledge, and letter–sound relationships—are essential when processing text and emphasize the use of both context and phonics. However, the book also agrees with the view that even in mature reading, nearly all words are processed.

to predict that the word is *moon* because that makes sense in the sentence. She may decode the initial letter but doesn't have to decode all the sounds in the word to predict that the word is *moon*. However, in an integrated approach, the processes occur in parallel fashion. For instance, when students decode words, four processors are at work: orthographic, phonological, meaning, and context (Adams, 1990, 1994). The orthographic processor is responsible for perceiving the sequences of letters in text. The phonological processor is responsible for mapping the letters into their spoken equivalents. The meaning processor contains one's knowledge of word meanings, and the context processor is in charge of constructing a continuing understanding of the text (Stahl, Osborne, & Lehr, 1990). The processors work simultaneously, and they both receive information and send it to the other processors; however, the orthographic and phonological processors are always essential participants. Context may speed and/or assist the interpretation of orthographic and phonological information but does not take its place (see Figure 1.1). (Context would speed the decoding of *moon*.) When information from one processor is weak, another may be called on to give assistance. With a word such as *lead*, the context processor provides extra help to the meaning and phonological processors in assigning the correct meaning and pronunciation.

In an integrated model, both top-down and bottom-up processes are used. However, depending on circumstances, either bottom-up or top-down processes are emphasized. If one is reading a handwritten note in which some words are illegible, top-down processes are stressed as knowledge of language and knowledge of the world are used to fill in what is missing. If one is reading unfamiliar proper names or words in isolation, bottom-up processes are emphasized.

In an integrated approach, reading is considered an active, constructive process, with the focus on the reader, whose experiences, cultural background, and point of view will play a part in her or his comprehension of a written piece. The focus is on cognitive processes or strategies used to decode words and understand and remember

FIGURE 1.1   Modeling the Reading Systems: Four Processors

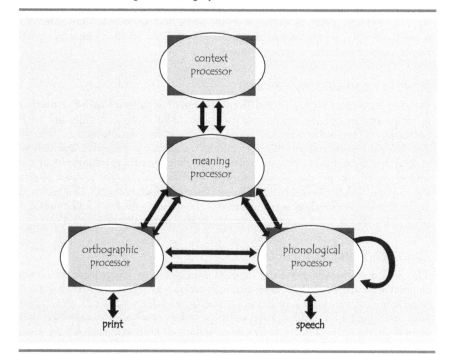

Source: Adams, M. J. (1990). *Beginning to read: Thinking and learning about print: A summary.* Prepared by S. A. Stahl, J. Osborne, & F. Lehr. Urbana-Champaign, IL: Center for the Study of Reading, University of Illinois.

text: using phonics and context to decipher unknown words, activating one's knowledge of a topic, predicting meaning, summarizing, and visualizing.

Stress is also placed on teaching strategies in context and holistically applying them to children's books, periodicals, ads and other real-world materials, and content-area textbooks. The integrated approach is a balanced approach in which systematic instruction and immersion in reading and writing play complementary roles.

The Status of Literacy

According to national testing results, some 67 percent of fourth-graders and 76 percent of eighth-graders can read at least on a basic level (National Center for Educational Statistics, 2011). Some 34 percent of fourth-graders and 34 percent of eighth-graders performed at or above the proficient level. Some 8 percent of fourth-graders and 3 percent of eighth-graders performed at the advanced level. Although there were more fourth- than eight-graders at the advanced level, there were more fourth-graders (33 percent) than eighth-graders (24 percent) at the below-basic level. What do the levels mean? Table 1.2 provides descriptions of the performance at each level. The basic level is a conservative estimate of grade level reading. Students at the below-basic level are reading below grade level. The proficient level is apparently above grade level (Pellegrino, Jones, & Mitchell, 1999). NAEP data provides an overview of the kinds of literacy instruction that students in the elementary grades and middle school will need. Students at the upper end will need to be challenged. Those at the lower end, especially those performing below the basic level, will need extra help and, in some cases, extensive intervention.

Impact of the Elementary and Secondary Act

The Elementary and Secondary Act plays a highly influential role in literacy instruction and assessment. The No Child Left Behind (NCLB) Act of 2001, a version of the Elementary and Secondary Act, had as its goal 100 percent of all students reaching proficiency at their grade level in state math and reading/language arts by the 2013–2014 school year, a provision that was waived in 2011. Although criticized because it led, in many instances, to teaching to the test and a narrowing of the curriculum, and demanded that English language learners be assessed before they have had adequate time to learn English, NCLB succeeded in drawing attention to the neediest students. It conveyed the idea that making provision for all students, including struggling learners, is every teacher's responsibility. The Elementary and Secondary Act (currently

TABLE 1.2 Description of National Assessment of Educational Progress (NAEP) Levels

Grade	Basic	Proficient	Advanced
4	Should be able to locate relevant information, make simple inferences, and use their understanding of the text to identify details that support a given interpretation or conclusion. Students should be able to interpret the meaning of a word as it is used in the text.	Should be able to integrate and interpret texts and apply their understanding of the texts to draw conclusions and make evaluations.	Should be able to make complex inferences and construct and support their inferential understanding of the text and apply their understanding of the texts to make and support a judgment.
8	Should be able to locate information; identify statements of main idea, theme, or author's purpose; and make simple inferences from texts. They should be able to interpret the meaning of a word as it is used in the text. Students performing at this level should also be able to state judgments and give some support about content and presentation of content.	Should be able to provide relevant information and summarize main ideas and themes. They should be able to make and support inferences about a text, connect parts of a text, and analyze text features. Students performing at this level should also be able to fully substantiate judgments about content and presentation of content.	Should be able to make connections with in and across texts and to explain causal relations. They should be able to evaluate and justify the strength of supporting evidence and the quality of an author's presentation. Students performing at this level should also be able to manage the processing demands of analysis and evaluation by stating, explaining, and justifying.

Source: Adapted from National Center for Education Statistics (2011). The Nation's Report Card: Reading 2011 (NCES 2012–458). Institute of Education Sciences, U.S. Department of Education, Washington, DC.

known as No Child Left Behind or NCLB) is up for renewal. Although its basic purpose will remain the same, emphasis will be on improving the effectiveness of teachers, using measures of students' performance as part of teacher evaluation systems, and using measures of growth rather than percentages of students passing a proficiency standard to assess the progress of schools. A key provision will be establishing standards that will prepare students to be college and career ready.

Common Core State Standards

One problem with NCLB was that each state set its own standards and used its own tests to determine proficiency. When individual state standards were translated into NAEP equivalent scores, most states had proficiency levels that were below NAEP's basic level (Bandeira de Mello, 2011). Current emphasis is now on having states adopt a challenging set of standards known as the Common Core State Standards and using an assessment system, now being constructed, that will be aligned with the standards so that every student will be college and career ready. The Common Core State Standards "define the knowledge and skills students should have to succeed in entry-level, credit-bearing, academic college courses and in workforce training programs" (National Governors Association and Council of Chief State School Officers, 2010). There are ten anchor standards for reading, writing, language, and content-area reading and content-area writing. The anchor standards are broad statements of objectives, which are further broken down into more specific grade-specific objectives. The anchor standards are listed on the inside front cover. To find specific standards by grade level, consult the Common Core State Standards at http://www.corestandards .org/assets/CCSSI_ELA%20Standards.pdf for English Language Arts and also Literacy in History/Social Studies, Science, & Technical Subjects.

The Common Core State Standards emphasize teaching for transfer. In other words, for teaching in such a way that the literacy skills presented can be used in other classes and in the world outside school. Emphasis is also placed on helping students see and understand the big ideas and answer essential questions. Higher-level thinking skills and reading informational text are given a more prominent role just as technology is (Kallick, & Troxell, 2011).

In a sense, the primary skill advocated by the Common Core State Standards is the ability to read complex text. ACT researchers (2006) found that "the clearest differentiator in reading between students who are college ready and students who are not is the ability to comprehend complex texts" (pp. 16-17). Since workplace text is equal in complexity to college-level text, the implication is that in order to prepare all students to be college and career ready, it is essential to prepare students to read complex texts. Learning to read complex text is a long-term objective that starts at the earliest levels and develops up through the elementary, middle school, and high school levels, as each level builds on skills and understandings established at earlier levels. Comprehending complex text requires vocabulary and background development, instruction in skills, and the development of higher-level discussion and writing skills. A key feature of the Common Core State Standards is the reading of a greater proportion of informational text. Reading additional informational text should not be interpreted as spending less time reading literary texts (Langer, 2011). It does mean, though, that students should be doing more reading in science and social studies and other content areas.

However, the most drastic change in the Common Core State Standards is the implementation of grade bands. There is an apparent gap between the reading skills possessed by today's students and those required for college and career readiness and also between the difficulty level of materials that students are reading at the end of high school and those that they will be required to read to become college and career ready (National Governors Association and Council of Chief State School Officers, 2010a). To close both gaps, the Common Core State Standards have incorporated a feature known as grade bands. The bands include grades 2–3, 4–5, 6–8, 9–10, and 11–12. The difficulty level at each band has been expanded so that by senior year students will be expected to be able to read at or close to college and career level. In other words, the standards call for students to be able to read more challenging material at every grade level beginning with grade 2. Even though Common Core Standards call for having students read more challenging materials, this does not mean that students should be given material that exceeds their reading ability. Giving students material that is too hard is virtually guaranteed to stunt their literacy growth.

Scientifically Based Literacy Instruction

Because large numbers of students are reading on a basic level or below and because the gap between the reading achievement of poor and middle-class students is substantial, there has been a call in federal regulations for programs that are scientifically based. In federal regulations, scientific evidence is interpreted as meaning studies in which Method A has been compared with Method B and/or a control group and found to be statistically superior. The International Reading Association (2002) uses the term *evidence-based* rather than scientifically based. *Evidence-based* is a broader term and includes qualitative studies as well as the more scientifically based studies that include comparison of experimental and control groups.

The most extensive study of research-based programs was conducted by John Hattie (2009), a New Zealand educator, who analyzed more than 800 meta-analyses. A meta-analysis is a study of studies that use statistical techniques to determine effect size. **Effect size** is the power of the element being tested to improve achievement or some other outcome. The effect size is the degree to which the experimental group did better than a matched group of students. Effect sizes are typically expressed in standard deviations. A **standard deviation** is a measure of the variability of performance and can be translated into percentiles or other units. One standard deviation at the average level is equal to 34 percentile points. For instance, summarizing and note taking have an effect size of 1 (Marzano, Gaddy, & Dean 2000). This is equal to a percentile gain of 34 points. If students were at the fiftieth percentile (an average rank) before the treatment, they would be at the eighty-fourth percentile after the treatment. In other words, instead of doing better than 50 percent of students, they would be doing better than 84 percent.

Average effect size is .4 (13.6 percentile points). An effect size of .2 (6.8 percentile points) is small, and one of .8 (27.2 percentile points) is high (Cohen, 1992). Effect sizes can also be negative. They can detract from progress. Negative effect sizes include summer vacation (–.09), retention (–.16), television (–.18), and mobility (–.34). Throughout the text, effect sizes, if available, will be noted in terms of percentiles so that you can better judge the value of teaching practices and techniques.

Back in the United States, researcher and educator Robert Marzano (2010) identified 41 instructional factors that have a positive impact on learning. In general, the factors he discovered mirror those uncovered by Hattie. Two of Marzano's highest factors are (1) setting goals and (2) tracking student progress and using scoring scales, which are similar to rubrics. These, of course, are key elements in visible teaching and learning. A third meta-analysis was conducted by the National Reading Panel (2000), which restricted its study to literacy. These three main sources and others have been used to help select the research-based strategies presented in this text. Table 1.3 shows the effect sizes of a number of instructional elements.

 FYI

Hattie (2009) considers an effect size of .6 to be large.

□ **Effect size** is the power of the element being tested to improve achievement or some other outcome. The effect size is the degree to which the experimental group did better than a matched group of students. Effect sizes are typically expressed in standard deviations. Average effect size is .4. An effect size of .2 is small, and one of .8 is high (Cohen, 1992).

□ **Standard deviation** is a measure of variance or how much dispersion there is from the average. A low standard deviation means there is little variance. Scores cluster around the mean or average. A high standard deviation means that there is a wide variance. Scores are more widely dispersed.

□ **Percentile rank** is the point on a scale of 1 to 99 that shows what percentage of students obtained an equal or lower score. A percentile rank of 75 means that 75 percent of those who took the test received an equal or lower score.

TABLE 1.3   Effect Size of Selected Instructional Elements

Element	Effect Size in Percentiles
Tracking progress	34
Intervention	28
Teacher clarity	27
Feedback	27
Teacher–student relationships	26
Setting goals	25
Professional development	23
Student engagement	21
Not labeling students	21
Teaching strategies	20
Direct instruction	20
Teaching vocabulary	20
Home environment	19
Socioeconomic status	19
Classroom cohesion	18
Peer influences	18
Classroom management	18
Parental involvement	17
Small-group learning	17
Concentration/persistence/engagement	16
Homework	15
Preschool program	15
Expectations	15
Practice	14
Recognition of students' efforts	14

Source: Based on Hattie, J. (2009). *Visible learning.* New York: Routledge; and Marzano, R. J. (2007). *The art and science of teaching.* Alexandria, VA: ASCD.

REFLECTION

What steps might you take to make sure that your teaching is research-based?

Visible Teaching and Learning

Based on his analyses, Hattie (2009) concluded that what is most effective is visible teaching.

> Visible teaching and learning occur when learning is the explicit goal, when it is appropriately challenging, when the teacher and the student both (in their various ways) seek to ascertain whether and to what degree the challenging goal is attained, when there is deliberate practice aimed at attaining mastery of the goal, when there is feedback given and sought, and when there are active, passionate, and engaging people (teacher, student, peers, and so on) participating in the act of learning. It is teachers seeing learning through the eyes of students, and students seeing teaching as the key to their ongoing learning. The remarkable feature of the evidence is that the biggest effects on student learning occur when teachers become learners of their own teaching, and when students become their own teachers. When students become their own teachers, they exhibit the self-regulatory attributes that seem most desirable for learners (self-monitoring, self-evaluation, self-assessment, self-teaching). (p. 22)

The theme of this text will be to make teaching and learning visible. To accomplish that purpose, the text will highlight key effective factors. Each chapter will conclude with a feature entitled "Extending and Applying," in which you will be asked to extend your knowledge of key effective practices and apply them, and also "Professional Reflection," in which you will be asked to reflect on your ability to implement key assessment and instructional practices. The Professional Reflection checklists are modeled on highly effective teacher evaluation systems in widespread use such as those constructed by Robert Marzano (2010), Charlotte Danielson (2010), and those used by charter schools such as Achievement First (2010), and those used by school districts such as the District of Columbia (2010) and also the IRA Standards for Reading

Professionals. The Professional Reflections only cover practices related to literacy instruction. Classroom management and routines are not addressed. The overall intent of this book is to equip you with the knowledge, understanding, and skills to become a highly effective literacy teacher. By focusing on key practices, you can develop the skills and practices needed to become a highly effective teacher.

As a teacher, you should become acquainted with the major findings of literacy research so that you can construct a literacy program that is based on research and so that you can assess whether new techniques or materials that you are thinking about trying are supported by research. You should also assess the research base to see if it is applicable to your students and your situation. A technique that works well on a one-to-one basis may not be effective with small groups. Of course, research doesn't answer all the instructional questions that arise. You need to become a teacher–researcher so that you can test methods and materials and have a better basis for selecting those that are most effective in your situation. You also need to assess all aspects of your program with a view to replacing or improving elements that aren't working and to adding elements that are missing.

As far as possible, the suggestions made in this text are evidence-based. However, in some instances they are based on personal experience or the experience of others. Teaching literacy is an art as well as a science.

Role of Language

As magical as it may be, reading is our second major intellectual accomplishment. Our first, and by far, most important, intellectual accomplishment is our acquisition of language. Without language, of course, there would be no reading. Reading is very much a language activity, and, ultimately, our ability to read is limited by our language skills. We can't read what we can't understand. Even if we can pronounce words we don't understand because of superior phonics skills, we are not reading. **Reading** is a process in which we construct meaning from print. Without meaning, there is no reading.

Components of Language

Language has a number of interacting components: **phonology** (speech sounds known as phonemes), **morphology** (word formation), **syntax** (sentence formation), **semantics** (word and sentence meaning), **prosody** (intonation and rhythm of speech), and **pragmatics** (effective use of language: knowing how to take turns in a conversation, using proper tone, using terms of politeness, etc.) (National Institute on Deafness and Other Communication Disorders, 2003).

Developing Language

Theories of language learning are similar to those of cognitive learning. From the behavioral standpoint, language is learned through reinforcement. As babies make sounds and toddlers say words, they are reinforced by their caregivers. Imitation is also a factor. The nativist viewpoint maintains that children are born with a language acquisition device (LAD) that predisposes them to learn and generate language structures (Chomsky, 1968). According to nativist theorists such as Noam Chomsky, syntax is too complex to be learned by imitation or instruction. The mental structures for syntax are activated by verbal input. Using words that they hear, children are able to understand and generate sentences that follow rules too complex for them to learn simply by imitation or instruction. Interactionists stress the interaction of children's

---

▫ **Reading** is a process in which we construct meaning from print.
▫ **Phonology** is the language component that consists of producing and understanding speech sounds.

▫ **Morphology** is the component of language that has to do with meaningful word parts, such as roots and affixes.
▫ **Syntax** is the language component that has to do with the way in which words are arranged in a sentence.

▫ **Semantics** is the component of language that has to do with word and sentence meaning.
▫ **Prosody** is the component of language that has to do with the intonation and rhythm of speech: pitch, stress, and juncture.

cognitive abilities and environmental factors, such as input from caregivers and others. Interactionists note that caregivers use a number of strategies, such as speaking slowly, repeating, and filling in missing words, to encourage and scaffold emerging speech. According to social interactionists, humans use these strategies naturally. We have an inborn need and desire to communicate.

Although young children learn many words through imitation, language learning is also a constructive process. If children were mere imitators, they would only be able to repeat what they hear. But they construct sentences such as "Mommy goed work," which is something that adults do not say. Creating a hypothesis about how language works, young children note that *-ed* is used to express past action and then overapply this generalization. With feedback and experience, they revise the hypothesis and ultimately learn that some action words have special past-tense forms.

Learning a Second Language

Large numbers of students learn English as a second or even a third language, so it's important to have some understanding of the acquisition of additional languages. Learning a second language is easier than learning a first language. Students who have a firm foundation in their first language have an easier time learning a second language. Concepts about language and its functions have already been formed. If English is similar to the first language, there may be a transfer of word and syntactical knowledge. Students are best able to learn a second language when their native language is accepted and they feel secure and confident. Input that is comprehensible is another key factor (Krashen, 2003). In reading, **English language learners (ELLs)** will acquire more language and comprehend better if they know 98 percent of the words in the text (Nation, 2001). Input can be enhanced through boldfaced vocabulary words and marginal glosses and illustrations. Speaking slowly, using gestures and visuals, and explaining new words help make oral input comprehensible. Motivation is also a key factor. The desire to make friends can be a powerful motivator (Lessow-Hurley, 2003). Initial success in acquiring language is also a motivator and leads to increased language acquisition.

Growth of Vocabulary

By age 3, children have a speaking vocabulary of about 1,000 words. By the time they enter kindergarten, they may know 5,000 words or more. The major influence on the size of children's vocabularies is the quantity and quality of the kind of talk they are exposed to. According to language expert Todd Risley (2003), the most important thing parents and other caregivers can do for their children is to talk to them. The amount of talk directed toward infants and toddlers is powerfully related to their verbal abilities and their success in school. Hart and Risley (1995) collected data on the quantity and quality of parent talk. They collected enough data on a sufficient number of families that they could reliably estimate the average amount of parent talk. They found that the sheer volume of talk that infants and toddlers hear varies greatly. Some children hear fewer than 500 words in an hour of family life. Others are exposed to 3,000 words in an hour. Some parents express approval or affirmation forty times an hour, whereas others, fewer than four times an hour. These differences add up. By age 4, some children have heard more than 50 million words, while others have heard just 10 million words. By age 4, some children have had 800,000 affirmations, while others have heard just 80,000. But there is more than just a quantitative difference between the most talkative and the least talkative families. The least talkative families use talk primarily to control and guide children. The most talkative families also use talk in this way, but they go beyond giving directions. Much of their extra talk consists of descriptions and explanations and contains a more complex vocabulary and structure and added positive reinforcement. The amount and quality of talk to which children are exposed are correlated with the size of their vocabularies and their later language and cognitive development.

Although studies show that the amount of talk is not strictly related to socioeconomic status, professionals talk the most, and parents on welfare talk the least. However, there is a great variability among the working class. Many of the most talkative parents, along with the quietest, are in the working class. And it is parental talkativeness rather than socioeconomic status that relates to later verbal ability. In other words, it isn't how much money parents have or how much education they have or whether they are members of a minority group that counts; it is how much and how well they talk to their children. As Risley (2003) hypothesized, "The accumulation of language experience is the major determiner of vocabulary growth and verbal intellectual development" (p. 2).

Children learn to read by reading.

In a longitudinal study of children in Bristol, England, Wells (1986) found that children's language was best developed in one-to-one situations in which an adult discussed matters that were of interest and concern to the child or the two talked over a shared activity. It is also essential that the adult adjust his or her language so as to take into consideration and to compensate for the child's limited linguistic ability, something parents seem to do intuitively.

In his extensive study, Wells (1986) found that some parents intuitively provided maximum development for their children's language. Far from being directors of what their children said, these parents were collaborative constructors of meaning. Careful listeners, they made genuine attempts to use both nonverbal and verbal clues to understand what their children were saying. Through careful listening and active involvement in the conversation, parents were able to help the children extend their responses so that both knowledge of the world and linguistic abilities were fostered.

As a teacher, you can't change the quality or quantity of language to which children have been exposed, but you can increase the quantity and quality of talk in your classroom and encourage parents and other caregivers to do the same. This book emphasizes high-quality, language-rich social interactions of the type conducted by the parents who best foster their children's language development.

Importance of the Students' Cultures

Living as we do in a multicultural, pluralistic society, it is important for us to explore and understand the literacy histories of our pupils. We have to ask such questions as these: In students' culture(s), how are reading and writing used? What values are placed on them? What are the ways in which the students have observed and participated in reading and writing? Is literacy in their environment primarily a group or an individual activity? Given this information, instruction should build on the students' experiences and develop and reinforce the skills and values important to their culture(s) as well as those important to the school.

 Using Technology

The Web site of the New Literacies Research Team offers videos and articles exploring the New Literacies.
http://www.newliteracies.uconn.edu/pubs.html □

Literacy and Technology: The New Literacies

The New Literacies are the reading, writing, and communication skills that are required for the successful use of information and communications technologies, especially the Internet. The Internet has a number of positive features that can be used to foster higher-level thinking and literacy, and it offers virtually unlimited content that is up-to-date and, in many instances, unavailable elsewhere. Students can work with real-life problems, such as global warming or hunger, and can interact with other students and publish their work on the Internet. However, because of its unlimited and unregulated content, the Internet demands critical thinking, including analysis and evaluation. A key feature of the Internet is the ease with which hyperlinks can be used to go from site to site. Students are able to direct their learning by deciding which links to click on. Again, this means that students must analyze, synthesize, and evaluate as they progress through sites via hyperlinks (Bradshaw, Bishop, Gens, Miller, & Rogers, 2002).

On the minus side, the Internet offers some unique challenges. As Bradshaw and colleagues (2002) warn, "The vast amount of information available can be overwhelming and lead to disorientation, information overload and devaluation of information" (p. 277). Students can suffer from "information fatigue" and simply give up. They might also experience navigational disorientation and have difficulty finding their way around the Internet. Knowledge of the topic and experience with effective search techniques can help overcome these problems. Another problem, and perhaps the most significant, is the danger of falling into shallow thinking patterns. Students might gather a lot of information but not process it. Seeing the amount of information they have collected may give them the false impression of having a greater understanding of the topic than they actually do have. A related issue is the uneven quality of online information. The accuracy, reliability, and depth of information on the Internet can vary dramatically, which calls for careful, critical reading.

"At its best the web offers opportunities that simply cannot be replicated via other media without the learning environment becoming ridiculously clumsy and inefficient. The web offers options and access that can change the way teachers teach and learners learn" (Bradshaw et al., 2002, p. 278). But making the most of the Internet and other technologies requires careful planning and teaching. "Successful searchers used the skills of thinking, acting, integrating, transforming and reaching resolution, but not all searchers are able on their own to use these skills" (p. 279). As researchers note, using the Internet is more complex than traditional inquiry. The New Literacies required for its use include the

> intricacies of rapidly integrating a *physical* process of clicking the mouse, dragging scroll bars, rolling over dynamic images, and navigating pop-up menus that intertwine with a *cognitive* process of planning, predicting, monitoring, and evaluating one's pathway through open Internet text spaces (as opposed to multiple printed texts or closed hypertext systems). In addition, this self-regulated cycle often occurred across much shorter and disparate units of Internet text than the continuous text passages typically included in printed text comprehension tasks. (Coiro & Dobbler, 2007, p. 242)

In addition, as Coiro (2010) notes, "Each online reading activity may require very different skill sets (e.g., informational websites, search engines, email, IM, blogs)." As teachers, we need to determine our students' current level of proficiency in these areas and build on that level.

Adapting Traditional Skills

A key reading skill for the era of the information superhighway is the ability to decide quickly and efficiently whether an article, study, or other document merits reading. With so much information available, it is essential that students not waste time reading texts that are not pertinent or worthwhile. Having more data to work with means that students must be better at organizing information, evaluating it, drawing conclusions from it, and conveying the essence of the information to others. They also need cognitive flexibility in order to utilize the vast amounts of information when proposing diverse solutions to increasingly complex problems. The more complex skills required to make the best use of technology will be addressed in subsequent chapters. Of course, these more complex skills build on traditional comprehension and

 Using Technology

Joan Ganz Cooney Center
Provides information on using media to advance learning.
http://www.joanganzcooneycenter.org

 Using Technology

The average 5- to 8-year-old spends more than 4 hours each day with recreational media. The average 8- to 10-year-old spends 5 hours and 29 minutes per day with recreational media, but that increases to 8 hours and 40 minutes a day for 11- to 14-year-olds. For 11- to 14-year-olds, much of the media usage occurs on cell phones and other handheld devices (Rideout, Foehr, & Roberts, 2010; Gutnick, Robb, Takeuchi, & Kotler, 2011).

study skills. Technology is also changing the way teachers present materials, make assignments, assess students, and manage pupil data. Technology as a teacher tool will be explored in upcoming chapters.

A Reading and Writing Program for Today's Students

What kind of program will help meet the literacy needs of today's students? That is a question that the remainder of this book will attempt to answer. However, when all is said and done, the ten principles discussed below, if followed faithfully, should make a difference in determining such a program.

The teacher is the key to effective reading instruction.

1. *Children learn to read by reading.* Learning to read is a little like learning to drive a car—instruction and guidance are required. In addition to instruction and guidance, novice readers, like novice motorists, require practice. They must read a variety of fiction and nonfiction books, newspapers, and magazines to become truly skilled. In a way, each book or article makes a child a better reader. As Hirsch (1987) pointed out, children must have a broad background in a variety of areas in order to be able to understand much of what is being written and said in today's world. For example, a child who has read the fable "The Boy Who Cried Wolf" will have the background necessary to understand a story that includes the sentence "Frank cried wolf once too often." Reading is not simply a matter of acquiring and perfecting skills; it also requires accumulating vocabulary, concepts, experiences, and background knowledge.

To provide the necessary practice and background, children's books are an essential component of a reading program. Unfortunately, large numbers of students are aliterate: They *can* read, but they *do* not, at least not on a regular basis. Only 56 percent of students ages 6 to 8 are frequent readers, which means they read at least five days a week. That percentage drops to 38 percent for 9- to 11-year-olds and 30 percent for 12- to 14-year-olds (Harrison Group, 2010). Lewis and Samuels (2003) found that additional reading was beneficial for all students. For average students, it added about 17 percentile points, a half-year's gain in reading skills, but it was especially beneficial for ELLs, struggling readers, and students just beginning to learn to read.

The case for including children's books in a reading program is a compelling one. First, as just noted, those who read more, read better. Second, research suggests that students who read widely and are given some choice in what they read have a more favorable attitude toward reading (Harrison Group, 2010). As a practical matter, wide reading builds the skills needed to do well on assessments for the Common Core Standards.

 Using Technology

PARCC

Provides assessment and instructional resources.

http://www.nationalreadingpanel .org ⬛

> To succeed on the . . . assessments, students need access to a wide range of materials on a variety of topics and genres, both in their classrooms and in their school libraries, to ensure that they have opportunities to independently read widely among texts of their own choosing during and outside of the school day in order to develop their knowledge and joy of reading. (PARCC, 2011, p. 6)

Using children's books in the reading program not only leads to greater enjoyment of reading but also builds skill in reading. In addition, allowing some self-selection should produce students who can and do read. To assist you in choosing or recommending books for your students, lists of appropriate books are presented throughout the text along with a description of several extensive lists of leveled books (see Chapter 2). Chapter 2 also describes a number of devices for leveling or assessing the difficulty level of books.

FYI

Although materials should be within students' zone of proximal development, instruction should include teaching students how to read complex text.

2. *Reading should be easy—but not too easy.*   Think about it this way: If children find reading difficult, they will acquire a distaste for it and will simply stop reading except when they have to. Because of inadequate practice, they will fall further behind, and their distaste for reading will grow. In addition, students will be unable to apply the strategies they have been taught, and learning will be hampered if the text is too difficult (Clay, 1993a). As Fry (1977a) put it years ago, make the match: Give students a book that they can handle with ease. Research by Berliner (1981), and Gambrell, Wilson, and Gantt (1981), and Nation (2001) suggested that students do best with reading materials in which no more than 2 to 5 percent of the words are difficult for them.

3. *Instruction should be functional and contextual.*   Do not teach skills or strategies in isolation—teach a word-attack skill because students must have it to decipher words. For example, teach the prefix *pre-* just before the class reads a selection about prehistoric dinosaurs. Students learn better when what they are being taught has immediate value. Suggestions for lessons that are both functional and contextual are presented throughout this book.

4. *Teachers should make connections.*   Build a bridge between children's experiences and what they are about to read. Help them see how what they know is related to the story or article. Students in Montana reading about an ice hockey game may have no experience either playing hockey or watching the sport. However, you could help create a bridge of understanding by discussing how hockey is similar to soccer, a sport with which they probably are familiar. You should also help students connect new concepts to old concepts. Relate reading, writing, listening, and speaking—they all build on each other. Reading and talking about humorous stories can expand students' concept of humor and remind them of funny things that have happened to them. They might then write about these events. Also build on what students know. This will make your teaching easier, since you will be starting at the students' level. It will also help students make a connection between what they know and what they are learning.

5. *Teachers should promote independence.*   Whenever you teach a skill or strategy, ask yourself: How can I teach this so that students will eventually use it on their own? How will students be called on to use this skill or strategy in school and in the outside world? When you teach students how to summarize, make predictions, or use context, phonics, or another skill or strategy, teach so that there is a gradual release of responsibility (Pearson & Gallagher, 1983). Gradually fade your instruction and guidance so that students are applying the skill or strategy on their own. Do the same with the selection of reading materials. Although you may discuss ways of choosing books with the class, you ultimately want students to reach a point where they select their own books.

6. *Teachers should believe that all children can learn to read and write.*   Given the right kind of instruction, virtually all children can learn to read. There is increasing evidence that the vast majority of children can learn to read at least on a basic level. Over the past two decades, research (Reading Recovery Council of North America, 2006) has shown that Reading Recovery, an intensive 12- to 20-week early intervention program, can raise the reading levels of about 76 percent of the lowest achievers to that of average achievers in a class. Reading Recovery uses an inclusive model:

> It has been one of the surprises of Reading Recovery that all kinds of children with all kinds of difficulties can be included, can learn, and can reach average-band performance for their class in both reading and writing achievement. Exceptions are not made for children of lower intelligence, for second-language children, for children with low language skills, for children with poor motor coordination, for children who seem immature, for children who score poorly on readiness measures, or for children who have already been categorized by someone else as learning disabled. (Clay, 1991, p. 60)

A number of intervention programs have succeeded with struggling readers (Hiebert & Taylor, 2000). An important aspect of these efforts is that supplementary assistance is complemented by a strong classroom program. These results demonstrate the power of effective instruction and the belief that all children can learn to read. Actually, a quality program will prevent most problems. A national committee charged with making recommendations to help prevent reading difficulties concluded, "Excellent instruction is the best intervention for children who demonstrate problems learning to read" (Snow, Burns, & Griffin, 1998, p. 33).

7. *The literacy program should be goal-oriented and systematic.* In keeping with the current concern for preparing all students to be college and career ready and the widespread adoption of the Common Core State Standards, this text has incorporated these standards throughout the text. The margin note "CCSS" designates places in the text where suggestions for implementing a particular standard are presented.

8. *Teachers should build students' motivation and sense of competence.* Students perform at their best when they feel competent, view a task as being challenging but doable, understand why they are undertaking a task, are given choices, feel part of the process, and have interesting materials and activities. For many students, working in a group fosters effort and persistence. Students also respond to knowledge of progress. They work harder when they see that they are improving, and they are also energized by praise from teachers, parents, and peers, especially when that praise is honest and specific (Schunk & Zimmerman, 1997; Sweet, 1997; Wigfield, 1997).

9. *Teachers should build students' language proficiency.* Reading and writing are language-based. Students' reading levels are ultimately limited by their language development. Students can't understand what they are reading if they don't know what the words mean or if they get tangled up in the syntax of the piece. One of the best ways to build reading and writing potential is to foster language development. In study after study, knowledge of vocabulary has been found to be the key element in comprehension. Students' listening level has also been found to be closely related to their reading level. The level of material that a student can understand orally is a good gauge of the level at which the student can read with understanding. While fostering language development is important for all students, it is absolutely essential for students who are learning English as a second language.

10. *Teachers need to know how students are progressing so that they can give them extra help or change the program, if necessary.* Assessment need not be formal. Observation can be a powerful assessment tool. However, assessment should be tied to the program's standards and should result in improvement in students' learning. In each chapter in which lessons are presented, suggestions are made for assessing those lessons. Suggestions for assessment can also be found in annotations in the margins and in Chapter 2. In addition, there are several assessment instruments in the Appendix.

Highly Effective Teachers

In the 1960s, the U.S. Department of Education spent millions of dollars in an attempt to find out which method of teaching reading was the best (Bond & Dykstra, 1967; Graves & Dykstra, 1997). More than a dozen approaches were studied. There was no clear winner. No method was superior. Although the research didn't directly prove it, many professionals concluded that the teacher was key. Teachers using the same methods got differing results. Some teachers were simply more effective than others. Hattie's (2009) research found that two of the most powerful factors in student achievement were the clarity of instruction and teacher–student relationships.

What are the characteristics of effective teachers? A number of top researchers have visited the classes of teachers judged to be highly effective. Their students read more books and wrote more stories. Virtually all read on or above grade level. Their writing skills were surprisingly advanced. They also enjoyed school. On many occasions, observers watched in surprise as students skipped recess so that they could continue working on an activity. Their work was more appealing to them than play.

FYI

Differentiated instruction has a powerful impact on achievement. Teachers typically direct most of their questions and reinforcement to the top third of the class. When teachers make successful attempts to direct instruction to all students, including the bottom third of the class, overall achievement improves. ⬚

Adapting Instruction for Struggling Readers and Writers

Classroom teachers are taking increased responsibility for helping struggling readers and writers. Suggestions for working with struggling readers and writers are made throughout this book. ⬚

FYI

Fostering student engagement involves proving effective classroom management and routines so that students sense that they are in a safe, productive environment. ⬚

FYI

In the past, emphasis was on instructional input. There was an assumption that given high-quality teaching, students would learn. However, in many teacher evaluation systems, the importance of learning has been added to the quality of instructional input. Increasingly, teachers are being assessed on how much their students learn. As a result, this text will emphasize assessing for learning to make sure students are learning what is being taught and are making adequate progress.

Caring and High Expectations

Perhaps the most outstanding characteristic of highly effective teachers is that they cared for their students and believed in them (Pressley, Allington, Wharton-McDonald, Block, & Morrow, 2001). They were genuinely convinced that their students could and would learn, and they acted accordingly. In writing, for instance, typical first-grade teachers believed that writing was difficult for young students and expected their students would only be able to produce pieces of writing composed of a sentence or two by year's end (Wharton-McDonald, 2001). Their expectations were discouragingly accurate. By year's end, most students in their classes were producing narratives that consisted of one to three loosely connected sentences with little attention to punctuation or capitalization.

Highly effective teachers had higher expectations. They believed that first-graders were capable of sustained writing. By year's end, they expected a coherent paragraph that consisted of five or even more sentences, each of which started with a capital letter and ended with a period. And that's the kind of writing their students produced. Students have a way of living up to or down to teachers' expectations.

However, the highly effective teachers realized that high expectations are in the same category as good intentions; they need to be acted upon. High expectations were accompanied by the kind of instruction that allowed students to live up to those expectations. Highly effective teachers were also superior motivators. The teachers created a feeling of excitement about the subject matter or skill areas they taught (Ruddell, 1995).

Balanced Instruction

As students evidenced a need for instruction, effective teachers were quick to conduct a mini-lesson. A student attempting to spell *boat*, for instance, would be given an on-the-spot lesson on the *oa* spelling of long *o*. However, essential skills were not relegated to opportunistic teaching. Key skills were taught directly and thoroughly but were related to the reading and writing that students were doing.

Extensive Instruction

Effective teachers used every opportunity to reinforce skills. Wherever possible, connections were made between reading and writing and between reading and writing and content-area concepts. Often, students would develop or apply science and social studies concepts in their writing.

Scaffolding

Exemplary teachers scaffolded students' responses. Instead of simply telling students answers, these teachers used prompts and other devices to help students reason their way to the correct response.

Classroom Management

Highly effective teachers were well organized. Routines were well established and highly effective. The core of their classroom management was building in students a sense of responsibility. Students learned to regulate their own behavior. One of the things that stood out in the rooms of highly effective teachers was the sense of purpose and orderliness. The greatest proportion of time was spent with high-payoff activities. When students composed illustrated booklets, for instance, the bulk of their time was spent researching and composing the booklets. Only a minimum of time was spent illustrating them.

Students learned how to work together. The classroom atmosphere was one of cooperation rather than competition. Effort was emphasized. Praise and reinforcement were used as appropriate. Students were also taught to be competent, independent learners.

They were taught strategies for selecting appropriate-level books, for decoding unfamiliar words, and for understanding difficult text. Their efforts were affirmed so that they would be encouraged to continue using strategies. "Jonathan, I liked the way you previewed that book before selecting it to read. Now you have a better idea of what it is about and whether it is a just-right book for you."

High-Quality Materials

The best teachers used the best materials. Students listened to and read classics as well as outstanding contemporary works from children's literature. There was a decided emphasis on reading. Classrooms were well stocked with materials, and time was set aside for various kinds of reading: shared, partner, and individual.

Matching of Materials and Tasks to Student Competence

Highly effective teachers gave students materials and tasks that were somewhat challenging but not overwhelming. Teachers carefully monitored students and made assignments on the basis of students' performance. If the book students were reading seemed to have too many difficult words and concepts, students were given an easier book. If they mastered writing a brief paragraph, they were encouraged to write a more fully developed piece. However, they were provided with the assistance and instruction needed to cope with more challenging tasks.

REFLECTION

What steps might you take to become a highly effective teacher? What step would you take first? Why?

Becoming a Highly Effective Teacher

Although a great variety of topics will be covered in later chapters, the ten primary principles discussed earlier are emphasized throughout. Teaching suggestions and activities are included for fostering wide reading, keeping reading reasonably easy, keeping reading and writing functional, making connections, setting goals and assessing progress, and, above all, building a sense of competence and promoting independence. This book is based on the premise that virtually all children can learn to read and write.

Essentials for an Effective Lesson

In order to translate the key concepts discussed so far into a practical instructional context, the basic components of an effective lesson are listed below. These components are based on research and incorporate the essential elements contained in widely used teacher evaluation systems, which means that when your lessons are being evaluated, these are the elements that will most likely be considered. A variety of sample lessons are provided in this text. The lessons will incorporate these essential elements.

Objectives: Objectives incorporate key skills or understanding that are based on national, state, or district standards and students' needs. They are clearly stated and shared with students. They might be posted. One way of checking on clarity of objectives would be to ask students to explain what they are learning and why.

Content/Texts/Activities: Content and activities are challenging but engaging. Texts/materials are of high quality and on students' instructional levels. Where appropriate, students are given a choice of activities or texts. Texts might be traditional print, digital, or online.

Instruction: Instruction includes an explanation of what is being taught and why. Skills, strategies, or understandings are presented explicitly through modeling, demonstration, simulation, and/or explanation. Students are provided with guided practice interspersed with additional instruction as needed. The teacher continuously checks for understanding and modifies instruction as necessary. Ultimately, students apply what they have learned. Emphasis is on lots of reading and writing.

Evaluation: Using observation, quizzes, and checks for understanding, and other means, teachers assess students' grasp of the skills, strategies, and understandings presented. Instruction is modified as needed. Teachers document progress and reflect on the effectiveness of the lesson. What went well? What might need improvement?

The following key elements are not specifically described in the sample lessons but are implied:

Differentiation: Students are grouped, as appropriate, and are also provided with additional instruction and practice, as required. Adjustments are made in instruction, activities, and materials to meet the needs of all students.

Classroom Atmosphere: The classroom is set up for maximum efficiency, management routines are established, and students are engaged in learning. Instructional time is maximized. A caring, supportive atmosphere is established, and there is a spirit of mutual cooperation and respect and a we-are-readers-and-writers attitude.

Summary

Reading is an active process in which the reader constructs meaning from text. Key elements in learning to read are cognitive development, language development, and background of experience. Reading development is also affected by one's culture. Approaches to teaching reading can be viewed as being bottom-up, top-down, or interactive. Behavioral theories of learning favor bottom-up approaches, focus on observable phenomena, describe the student as being a passive recipient, tend to be teacher-centered, and emphasize subskills and mastery learning. Cognitive theories tend to be top-down or interactive in their approach, emphasize the active role of the reader as a constructor of meaning, are often student-centered or teacher–student interactive, and stress mental activities. Social cognitive theories stress the social aspects of learning, scaffolding of instruction, and the zone of proximal development.

In their language theories, behaviorists emphasize imitation and reinforcement, nativists stress an inborn propensity for learning language, and interactionists stress the interaction of the learner with opportunities to learn. According to Vygotsky, language is key to the development of thinking.

Learning a second language is easier than learning an original language, but an accepting environment, self-confidence, and motivation foster second-language development.

Current trends in literacy instruction include research-based instruction, Common Core State Standards, educational legislation such as the renewal of the Elementary and Secondary Act, performance on national tests such as the NAEP, and New Literacies. New Literacies build on traditional literacy skills but are more complex.

Widespread reading and functional instruction commensurate with children's abilities are essentials of an effective reading program. Also necessary is instruction that helps students make connections and fosters independence. Believing that virtually every child can learn to read and building students' motivation and sense of competence are important factors in an effective literacy program, as are setting goals; systematic, direct instruction; managing classroom behavior; building language proficiency; building higher-level literacy; and ongoing assessment. These factors can be translated into effective literacy lessons. The ultimate key to a successful program is a highly effective teacher.

Extending and Applying

1. Analyze one or more of your lessons in terms of the Essentials of an Effective Lesson discussed earlier in the chapter. What changes might you need to make to your lessons?

2. Evaluate your literacy program in terms of the major characteristics listed earlier in the chapter. What are

the strengths of your program? What changes might you need to make? How would you go about making those changes?

3. Take another look at the characteristics of Highly Effective Teachers. What are your strengths and weaknesses in this area? What might you do to build on

your strengths and work on your weaknesses?

4. Many school systems require teacher applicants to submit a portfolio. Some require new teachers to complete portfolios as part of the evaluation process. Even if a portfolio is not required in your situation, creating and maintaining one provide you with the opportunity to reflect on your ideas about teaching and your teach-

ing practices. It will help you get to know yourself better as a teacher and so provide a basis for improvement. Set up a professional portfolio. The portfolio should highlight your professional preparation, relevant experience, and mastery of key teaching skills. Also, draw up a statement of your philosophy of teaching reading and writing.

Professional Reflection

Do I

___ Have an understanding of the nature of literacy?

___ Have an understanding of the key components of an effective literacy program and a plan for implementing them in my teaching situation?

___ Have a general understanding of the Common Core State Standards or other standards in the school district where I teach or plan to teach?

___ Have a personal philosophy for teaching literacy?

Reflection Question

In the past, teachers were evaluated on the quality of their presentations. Today, many school districts also evaluate teachers on the basis of how much their students learn. How might you prepare yourself for an evaluation system that combines quality of presentation with degree of student learning?

Building Competencies

To build competencies, consult the following sources for more detailed information:

Bodrova, E., & Leong, D. J. (2007). *Tools of the mind: The Vygotskian approach to early childhood education* (2nd ed.). Upper Saddle River, NJ: Merrill. Also reread the section on Vygotsky and Piaget in this chapter. Compare and contrast their main beliefs.

Hattie, J. (2009). *Visible learning: A synthesis of over 800 meta-analyses relating to achievement.* New York; Routledge.

The site of the New Literacies Research Team at the University of Connecticut, http://www.newliteracies.uconn.edu, has a wealth of information about the New Literacies.

MyEducationLab™

Go to the Topic "Media/Digital Literacy" in the MyEducationLab (www.myeducationlab.com) for your course, where you can:

- Find learning outcomes for "Media/Digital Literacy" along with the national standards that connect to these outcomes.
- Complete Assignments and Activities that can help you more deeply understand the chapter content.
- Apply and practice your understanding of the core teaching skills identified in the chapter with the Building Teaching Skills and Dispositions learning units.
- Examine challenging situations and cases presented in the IRIS Center Resources.
- Check your comprehension on the content covered in the chapter by going to the Study Plan in the Book

Resources for your text. Here you will be able to take a chapter quiz, receive feedback on your answers, and then access Review, Practice, and Enrichment activities to enhance your understanding of chapter content. (optional)

A+RISE A+RISE® Standards2Strategy™ is an innovative and interactive online resource that offers new teachers in grades K–12 just-in-time, research-based instructional strategies that meet the linguistic needs of ELLs as they learn content, differentiate instruction for all grades and abilities, and are aligned to Common Core Elementary Language Arts standards (for the literacy strategies) and to English language proficiency standards in WIDA, Texas, California, and Florida.

2 Assessing for Learning

Anticipation Guide

For each of the following statements related to the chapter you are about to read, put a check under "Agree" or "Disagree" to show how you feel. Discuss your responses with classmates before you read the chapter.

	Agree	Disagree
1. Nationwide achievement tests are essential for the assessment of literacy.	_____	_____
2. Setting high standards and assessing student achievement on those standards is a good way to improve the quality of reading and writing instruction.	_____	_____
3. Most writing assessments are too subjective.	_____	_____
4. Today's students take too many tests.	_____	_____
5. Teachers should be evaluated on the basis of how much their students learn.	_____	_____
6. Observation yields more information about a student's progress in reading and writing than a standardized test does.	_____	_____

Using What You Know

Evaluation is an essential part of literacy learning. It is a judgment by teachers, children, parents, administrators, and the wider community as to whether instructional goals have been met. Evaluation also helps teachers determine what is and what is not working so that they can plan better programs. Self-evaluation gives students more control over their own learning. Taking all of this into consideration, what kinds of experiences have you had with evaluation? How has your schoolwork been assessed? Do you agree with the assessments, or do you think they were off the mark? Keeping in mind the current emphasis on preparing every student to be college and career ready, what might be some appropriate ways to evaluate the literacy development of today's students?

The Nature of Evaluation

In evaluation, we ask, "How am I doing?" so that we can do better. **Evaluation** is a value judgment. We can also ask, "How is the education program doing?" and base our evaluation on tests, quizzes, records, work samples, observations, anecdotal records, portfolios, and similar information. The evaluation could be made by a student while reviewing her or his writing folder or by parents as they look over a report card. The evaluator could be a teacher, who, after examining a portfolio or collection of a student's work and thinking over recent observations of that student, concludes that the student has done well but could do better.

Evaluation should result in some kind of action. The evaluator must determine what that action should be, based on his or her judgment. The student may decide that he or she has been writing the same type of pieces and needs to branch out, the parents might decide that their child must study more, and the teacher might choose to add more silent reading time to the program.

The Starting Point

Evaluation starts with a set of goals or standards. You cannot tell if you have reached your destination if you do not know where you were headed. For example, a teacher may decide that one of her goals will be to instill in children a love of reading. This is a worthy goal, one that is lacking in many programs. How will the teacher decide whether the goal has been reached, and what will the teacher use as evidence? The goal has to be stated in terms of a specific objective that includes, if possible, observable behavior—for example, students will voluntarily read at least 20 minutes a day or at least one book a month. The objective then becomes measurable, and the teacher can collect information that will provide evidence as to whether it has been met.

Broad goals should be stated for the school year so that you have a map of where you are going. These goals might be stated in the school district's framework. Goals are then broken down into unit objectives and finally lesson objectives. Objectives are sometimes confused with activities. Activities are what students do to achieve a goal. They are the means rather than the end. For example, the statement "Read a story that contains short-*a* words" is an activity. "Be able to read short-*a* words" or "Be able to use short-*a* words to read a story" are objectives. Objectives are what you expect students to know or be able to do as a result of instruction. Learning expert Robert Marzano recommends using the following frames to state objectives:

Students will be able to _____ .

or

Students will understand _____ . (Marzano, 2007, p. 18)

The first objective represents the acquisition of a skill or strategy. In the parlance of cognitive psychology, it is "procedural knowledge"; the second represents "declarative knowledge." You might want to add to the frames a statement that tells how you will know that students have attained the objective or are on track for attaining it. If it's a skill, you might observe how well students use it in their everyday reading and writing, or you might note their performance on a quiz or worksheet. If it's a knowledge objective, you might see how well they do in a discussion or oral or written retelling of the new knowledge.

The Standards Movement

The centerpiece of the standards movement is the statement of goals or objectives. The standards movement grew out of concern for the quality of education in the United States. The basic idea behind standards is that establishing challenging, world-class standards and measuring whether those standards have been reached will lead to instruction geared to the standards and higher achievement. Standards "define our expectations for what's important for children to learn, serve as guideposts for curriculum and instruction, and should be the basis of all assessment" (American Federation of Teachers, 2008, p. 2).

The Common Core State Standards

Because standards vary from state to state, the National Governors Association (NGA) and Council of Chief State School Officers (CCSSO, 2010) have created a set of Common Core State Standards in English language arts and math. The standards are designed to prepare students to be college and career ready. Anchor Standards for Reading are listed on the inside front cover. Anchor standards are broad statements of standards. There are also anchor

Evaluation is the process of using the results of tests, observations, work samples, and other devices to judge the effectiveness of a program. A program is evaluated in terms of its objectives. The ultimate purpose of evaluation is to improve the program.

standards for writing, language, and speaking and listening. The anchor standards are broken down into more specific grade level standards, which are available at the Common Core State Standards Web site at http://www.corestandards.org.

The Standards' authors recommend holding English language learners (ELLs) to the same standards set for native speakers but more time, instruction, and support should be provided. Similarly, it is also recommended that instruction and assessment of students with disabilities be guided by the standards, the philosophy being that "[t]he common core state standards provide a historic opportunity to improve access to academic content standards for students with disabilities" (National Governors Association and Council of Chief State School Officers, 2010). As the report points out, adjustments, including supports and accommodations, need to be made based on the nature and severity of the disability.

The Key Standard

What is the key ability that predicts success in college? According to studies conducted by ACT (2006), "The clearest differentiator in reading between students who are college ready and students who are not is the ability to comprehend complex texts" (pp. 16–17). The ability to read complex text is a better predictor than gender, race, or socioeconomic status. Of course, what ACT is describing is the outcome goal. This is the kind of reading that students should be able to perform when they are high school juniors or seniors, but obviously, reaching that goal means working toward it in every grade. However, there is a gap between the reading skills of many high school seniors and the reading demands of college and the workplace (National Governors Association and Council of Chief State School Officers, 2010a). There is also a gap between the materials generally read in high school and those read in college and the workplace. To close both gaps, the Common Core Standards have incorporated a feature known as grade bands. The bands include grades 2–3, 4–5, 6–8, 9–10, and 11–12. As stated in the Standards, "Students in the first year(s) of a given band are expected by the end of the year to read and comprehend proficiently within the band, with scaffolding as needed at the high end of the range. Students in the last year of a band are expected by the end of the year to read and comprehend independently and proficiently within the band" (p. 10). However, because of the gaps between what students can read at the end of high school and the demands of college and career and the gap between the difficulty level of high school materials and college and workplace materials, beginning at grade 2 and at every grade level after that, the upper range of that band represents an increase in difficulty. For instance, end-of-third-grade materials will be somewhat more challenging than what has typically been end-of-third-grade material. The difficulty level at every band has been expanded so that by senior year students will be expected to be able to read at or close to college and career level. In other words, the standards call for students to be able to read more challenging material at every grade level beginning with grade 2.

Common Core assessments will be demanding. The ability to read both literary and informational texts will be assessed, and both basic and higher level skills will be evaluated. Students will be expected to demonstrate a "close reading of text." Particular emphasis will be placed on citing evidence to support a position or conclusion along with the ability to analyze that evidence. For some items, students will be expected to draw from two or more sources rather than just one. Vocabulary will be assessed through items that will be embedded in the context of the test selections. The ability to write about texts will be stressed.

FYI

Grade bands represent the most significant change called for in the Common Core State Standards and the most difficult standard to achieve. Beginning in grades 2–3, the bands call for an increase in the overall literacy growth of students and an increase in the difficulty level of materials that they will be expected to read.

FYI

Even though Common Core Standards call for having students read more challenging materials, this does not mean that students should be given material that exceeds their reading ability. Giving students material that is too hard, unless they are adequately prepared for it, is virtually guaranteed to stunt their literacy growth.

Using Technology

Center for K–12 Assessment & Performance Management at ETS Provides information on the development of assessments for Common Core State Standards. http://www.k12center.org/

| □ **Standards** are statements of what students should know and be able to do. □ A **high-stakes test** is one whose results are used to make an important decision such as passing | students, graduating students, or rating a school. □ **Assessment** is the process of gathering data about an area of learning through tests, observations, work samples, and other means. | □ **Authentic assessment** involves using tasks that are typical of the kinds of reading or writing that students perform in school and out. |

Common Core assessments will provide information that can be used for planning instruction. Formative, benchmark/interim, and summative assessment will be available. Curriculum frameworks, learning progressions based on the Common Core standards, and other resources will also be available.

Assessing for Learning: Summative and Formative Assessments

Assessment can be characterized as being summative or formative. **Summative assessment** summarizes students' progress at the end of a unit or a semester or at some other point in time. Summative assessment occurs after learning has taken place. Norm-referenced and high-stakes tests are generally summative. **Formative assessment** is ongoing and is used to inform instruction. Formative assessment takes place during learning. "Teachers need to know about their pupils' progress and difficulties with learning so that they can adapt their own work to meet pupils' needs—needs that are often unpredictable and that vary from one pupil to another" (Black & Wiliam, 1998). As Chappuis, Chappuis, and Stiggins (2009) explain, it is not the assessment that is formative. It is the way the information derived from the assessment is used. It is formative if it used to adjust instruction.

Combining characteristics of summative and formative tests is a type of test known as an "interim" test. Interim tests, which are sometimes labeled as through-course, benchmark, or short cycle tests, are often used to determine whether students are on track to reach key instructional goals or benchmarks or to predict how students will perform on the end-of-year state test or other high-stakes tests. They are given periodically: every quarter or month, for instance. Because they are given at intervals during the school year, they can be used to plan future instruction (Hamilton, Halverson, Jackson, Mandinach, Supovitz, & Wayman, 2009).

Assessing for Learning: Using Summative and Interim Assessments

One problem with summative assessments, especially state-mandated tests, is that by the time results are sent to the schools, it is too late to use them. To make summative assessments more useful, they need to occur more frequently so that changes can be made in the program or additional help can be given to students who are not meeting the standards. Many school systems give interim tests that are similar to the state high-stakes tests or are released copies of those tests. Students who do poorly on interim tests are generally provided with added instruction. Areas on which all or most students have difficulty are scheduled for instruction (Stiggins & Chappuis, 2005). Hence, summative assessments are used in formative ways. In another attempt to use summative assessment in a formative way, schools collect and analyze the test data more efficiently so that instructional decisions can be based on that data.

Assessing for Learning: Using Formative Assessments

The basic idea behind assessing for learning is to obtain enough information about students so that you can give them the help they need. Assessing for learning begins with a clear explanation of the standards that students are expected to meet. This means that the classroom teacher may need to break down the state standards into a curriculum map or series of steps that, if followed, will lead to meeting the standard. The standard is expressed in terms that the students can understand. For a writing standard, for example, students are shown writing samples that meet and don't meet the standard so that they have a clear idea of what is expected. As part of instruction, students are

Summative assessment occurs after learning has taken place and summarizes students' progress at the end of a unit or a semester or at some other point in time.

Formative assessment takes place during learning and is used to plan or modify instruction.

IRA POSITION STATEMENT ON KEY ISSUE
High-Stakes Testing

As its name suggests, a high-stakes test is one for which an important decision will be based on the outcome. Because of the role they play in decision making, high-stakes tests have the potential to dictate curriculum. Instead of teaching what their community has judged to be important, educators might teach what is tested. This has the effect of narrowing the curriculum. Knowing, for instance, that students will be tested on narrative writing in the fourth grade, teachers in the early grades overemphasize story writing and neglect expository writing. A great deal of time is also spent writing to a prompt because that is the way students will be assessed on the state tests. To combat the misuse of tests, the International Reading Association (1999a) has made the following recommendations:

Teachers should

- construct rigorous classroom assessments to help outside observers gain confidence in teacher techniques.
- educate parents, community members, and policymakers about classroom-based assessment.
- teach students how tests are structured, but not teach to the test.

---

assessed to see where they are in relation to the standard and also what they need to do to achieve the standard. Progress is monitored, and students are informed of their progress along the way. Results of the monitoring are used to inform instruction.

Clear feedback is an essential part of assessing for learning. Feedback should be expressed so that students fully understand what they need to do to improve. Self-assessment is also a key component of formative assessment or assessing for learning. For students to carry out self-assessment, they need to understand what it is they are supposed to know or be able to do (the objective), how they are progressing (status), and what they need to do to reach the goal (corrective action). Students can't work toward a goal if they don't know what it is, don't know what their current capabilities are, or don't know how to take corrective action. As Stiggins (2004) recommends, "We must build classroom environments in which students use assessments to understand what success looks like and how to do better the next time. In effect, we must help students use ongoing classroom assessment to take responsibility for their own academic success" (pp. 25–26).

Formative assessment emphasizes process rather than product. Process assessment seeks to find out how the student learns. Process measures include observing students to see what strategies they use to arrive at a particular answer, to compose a piece of writing, or to study for a test. Having this kind of insight, the teacher is able to redirect errant thought processes, correct poorly applied strategies, or teach needed strategies. Actually, both product and process measures provide useful information. Knowing where a child is and how he or she got there, the teacher is better prepared to map out a successful path toward improvement.

Checking for Understanding

Literacy experts, researchers, and former classroom teachers Douglas Fisher and Nancy Frey (2007) confess to having asked students the question, "Does everybody understand?" and when a lone voice answered "Yes," proceeding with the lesson, only to find out through a quiz or discussion that understanding was not universal. It is vitally important to find out whether students are following along or are lost—or are somewhere in between. However, most students typically don't respond to the "Does everybody understand?" question. To elicit that kind of information, there are a number of

 Using Technology

The Assessment Training Institute site features a number of articles and other resources for assessing for learning.
http://www.assessmentinst.com

 Assessing for Learning

Assessment measures should also be fair to all who take them. There should be no biased items; content should be such that all students have had an equal opportunity to learn it.

 **R E F L E C T I O N**

What is formative assessment and what is its role in instruction? What are some types of formative assessment you might use in your current or projected teaching situation?

 FYI

Checking for understanding is a key element in an effective lesson and is part of widely used teacher evaluation systems.

steps you might take. You might call on a number of students, including those who don't usually raise their hands, or probe incorrect or incomplete responses to determine the nature of the misunderstanding and figure out ways to correct it. You might ask for thumbs up to indicate understanding or thumbs down to signal a lack of understanding. You might use every-pupil response cards. Younger students might hold up letters that represent the sounds that the teacher says. Or students might write their responses on a white board and hold them up. A teacher displaying various examples of energy via a PowerPoint presentation had students hold up cards labeled "kinetic energy" or "potential energy" to indicate their responses. This action, along with having students explain their choices when there was disagreement, allowed him to see how well students were grasping the concept and to remedy confusions immediately (Fisher & Frey, 2007). Listening in on student discussions, using a quick write, and observing students as they write or complete a lab assignment are also helpful checks to gauge students' understanding. An electronic interactive response system used in conjunction with an interactive whiteboard enables teachers to administer quizzes via the whiteboard at any point during the lesson. Students use remotes known as "clickers" to respond to multiple-choice or true-false questions. Students can also respond with very brief responses of about 20 letters or fewer. The response can also be used to take a poll: How many ate breakfast this morning? Responses are checked and compiled immediately: 80 percent had breakfast. Quizzes or questions can be prepared by the teacher or can be purchased or obtained free from a learning community. Some measure of how well teachers check for understanding is a key characteristic assessed on a number of widely used evaluations of teacher effectiveness (iObservation, 2010).

Self-Evaluation

The ultimate evaluation is, of course, self-evaluation. Students should be involved in all phases of the evaluation process and, insofar as possible, take responsibility for assessing their own work. Questionnaires and self-report checklists are especially useful for this. Figure 2.11 shows a self-report checklist with which students in grade 3 and beyond can assess their use of strategies in learning from text.

Self-assessment should begin early. Ahlmann (1992) noted that by October, her first-graders are already evaluating their own work and that of authors they read. To self-assess, students reflect on their learning, assemble portfolios of their work, list their achievements, and, with the guidance of the teacher, put together a plan for what they hope to achieve.

In some classes, students complete exit slips on which they write about what they have learned that day or raise questions that they did not have time to raise in class or were reluctant to raise. Learning logs and journals might perform a similar function. As an alternative, the teacher and the class might design a form on which students write what they learned in a certain class and list questions that they still have. In reading and writing conferences, part of the discussion should center on skills mastered and goals for the future, and how those goals might be met. These conferences, of course, should be genuinely collaborative efforts so that students' input is shown to be valued.

As students engage in a literacy task, they should assess their performance. After reading a selection, they might ask themselves: "How well did I understand this selection? Do I need to reread or take other steps to improve my comprehension?" After completing a piece of writing, they should also evaluate their performance. If a rubric has been constructed for the piece of writing, they should assess their work in terms of the rubric.

Logs and Journals for Self-Evaluation   Reading logs and response journals can also be a part of students' self-evaluation, as well as a source of information for the teacher. Reading logs contain a list of books read and, perhaps, a brief summary or assessment. Response journals provide students with opportunities to record personal reactions to their reading. Both reading logs and response journals offer unique insights into students' growing ability to handle increasingly difficult books, their changing interests, and personal involvement with reading.

Judging Assessment Measures

Reliability

To be useful, tests and other assessment instruments must be both reliable and valid. **Reliability** is a measure of consistency, which means that if the same test were given to the same students a number of times, the results would be approximately the same. Reliability is usually reported as a coefficient of correlation and ranges from .00 to 1 or −.01 to −1. The higher the positive correlation, the more reliable the test. For tests on which individual decisions are being based, reliability should be in the .90s.

Reliability can also be thought of as generalizability. For observations and other informal approaches to assessment, it means that similar findings have been found by different judges and at different times (Johnston & Rogers, 2001). One way of increasing reliability is by training observers. Another is to have several observations.

A test that is not reliable is of no value. It is the equivalent of an elastic yardstick—the results of measurement would be different each time.

Validity

In general, **validity** means that a test measures what it says it measures: vocabulary knowledge or speed of reading, for instance. Ultimately, it is consequential and means that a particular test will provide the information needed to make a decision, such as placing a student with an appropriate level book or indicating specific strengths and weaknesses in comprehension (Farr & Carey, 1986). Johnston and Rogers (2001) contend that unless an assessment practice helps to improve students' learning, it should not occur. Reading tests need content validity, meaning that the skills and strategies tested must be the same as those taught. To check for **content validity**, list the objectives of the program and note how closely a particular test's objectives match them. The test selections should be examined, too, to see whether they reflect the type of material that the students read. Also, determine how reading is tested. If a test assesses skills or strategies that you do not cover or assesses them in a way that is not suitable, the test is not valid for your class.

Concurrent validity means that an assessment measure correlates with a similar test or other form of assessment occurring at about the same time. *Predictive validity* means that there is a correlation between the assessment measure and some future behavior. This could be a correlation between phonological awareness in kindergarten and reading comprehension in the third grade.

However, a number of assessment measures that have high statistical (concurrent and predictive) validity may be lacking in content validity. For instance, phonics tests that use nonsense words might correlate well with measures of current and future performance but distort the reading process and so have limited content validity and thus limited usefulness for teachers. If an assessment measure doesn't assess what you teach or assesses a skill in a way that differs from the way that students actually apply it, then the measure is lacking in content validity.

R E F L E C T I O N

What is content validity? What is consequential validity? What is the importance of content and consequential validity? Why should they be considered along with concurrent and predictive validity?

□ **Reliability** is the degree to which a test yields consistent results. In other words, if students took a reliable test again, their scores would be approximately the same.

□ **Validity** is the degree to which a test measures what it is supposed to measure, or the extent to which a test will provide information needed to make a decision. Validity should be considered in terms of the consequences of the test results and the use to which the results will be put.

□ **Content validity** means that the tasks of an assessment device are representative of the subject or area being assessed.

□ **Concurrent validity** means that an assessment measure correlates with a similar assessment occurring at about the same time.

□ **Predictive validity** means that there is a correlation between the assessment and some future behavior.

Closely tied to validity are the consequences or uses to which the assessment will be put. A useful assessment answers the following questions: What decision is to be made? By whom? What information will help them? At the classroom level, teachers and students need to know the answer to this question: What do students need to learn next on their way to achieving the standard? At the program support level, which might be the grade-level team or the school learning team, a key question is this: Who needs additional support? At the school and district level, administrators and the public want answers to these questions: How many students are meeting standards or demonstrating adequate growth? Are a sufficient number of students meeting standards? Is growth adequate?

At the classroom level, teachers need to go beyond identifying students who are or are not meeting standards and determine what needs to be learned so that standards are met. This entails obtaining information about foundational skills that might be needed to meet a standard. Summative assessment tools indicate which standards are being met but don't provide information about the steps needed to meet the standards. Observation, quizzes, discussions, and examination of students' work are needed to reveal why the standard isn't being met or growth is not adequate. The students might have difficulty understanding basic details, seeing how details are related, drawing a conclusion based on details, or formulating a response.

General Questions for Evaluation

Essentially, evaluation is the process of asking a series of questions. Specific questions depend on a program's particular goals and objectives. However, some general questions that should be asked about every literacy program include the following:

- Where are students in their literacy development? What might be done to enhance development?
- At what level are they reading?
- Are they reading up to their ability level? If not, what will help them do better?
- Are they making adequate, ongoing progress? If not, what can be done to accelerate progress?
- How well do they comprehend what they read? What will help them improve comprehension?
- How well do they read complex text?
- How adequate are students' reading vocabularies? What can be done to foster vocabulary growth?
- What comprehension and word-analysis strategies do students use? How can the use of such strategies be improved?
- What is the level of students' language development? What can be done to enhance language development?
- What are students' attitudes toward reading? How might their attitudes be improved?
- Do students enjoy a variety of genres? If not, what might be done to entice them to read in a greater number of genres?
- Do students read on their own? What will encourage them to read more?
- How well do students write? What will enable them to improve their writing?
- What kinds of writing tasks have students attempted?
- How well prepared are students for the writing tasks on which they will be assessed? How well do they do when asked to provide constructed responses?
- Which students seem to have special needs in reading and writing?
- Are these special needs being met? If not, what steps might be taken so that all needs are met?
- Are students on track to becoming career and college ready?

Answers to these essential questions help teachers plan, revise, and improve their reading and writing programs. The rest of this chapter explores a number of techniques for gathering the assessment information necessary to answer them. Both traditional and alternative means will be discussed.

Placement Information

The first question the classroom teacher of reading has to answer is "Where are the students in their literacy development?" If they are reading, assessment begins with determining the levels at which they are reading. One of the best placement devices is an informal reading inventory (IRI). In fact, if properly given, it will provide just about everything a teacher needs to know about a student's reading. It will also supply useful information about language development, work habits, interests, and personal development.

Informal Reading Inventory

An **informal reading inventory (IRI)** is a series of graded selections beginning at the very easiest level—pre-primer—and extending up to eighth grade or beyond. Each level has two selections; one is silent and the other oral. Starting at an easy level, the student continues to read until it is obvious that the material has become too difficult.

An IRI yields information about four reading levels: independent, instructional, frustration, and listening capacity. The **independent level**, or the free-reading level, is the point at which students can read on their own without teacher assistance. The **instructional level** refers to the point at which students need assistance because the material contains too many unknown words or concepts, or their background of experience is insufficient. This is also the level of materials used for teaching. Material at the **frustration level** is so difficult that students cannot read it even with teacher assistance. The fourth level is listening capacity, the highest level at which students can understand what has been read to them. **Listening capacity** is an informal measure of ability to comprehend spoken language. Theoretically, it is the level at which students should be able to read if they had all the necessary decoding skills. In practice, a small percentage of students have listening deficiencies, so a listening test might underestimate their true capacity. Younger students also tend to read below capacity because they are still acquiring basic reading skills. As students progress through the grades, listening and reading levels grow closer together (Sticht & James, 1984).

The first IRIs were constructed by teachers and were created using passages from basal readers. This was a good idea because it meant that there was an exact match between the material the student was tested on and the material the student would be reading. Because constructing IRIs is time-consuming, most teachers now use commercially produced ones. (See Table 2.1.) Unfortunately, most inventories are out of sync with the beginning levels of today's reading programs. Up until recently, the major reading programs used a high-frequency approach to teaching beginning reading. This meant that the words of the easiest selections consisted mainly of frequently occurring words. However, all of today's major programs use a decodable text approach. Beginning reading materials are made up primarily of words that incorporate the phonics patterns that students have been taught plus some high-frequency

FYI

Placing students at the appropriate level is more important than ever. Concern with preparing students to be college and career ready may lead to placing students in texts that are too difficult, which will stifle their growth. A key condition for accelerating progress is to make sure students are properly placed.

FYI

If students are not yet reading, they can be given an emergent literacy assessment, as explained in Chapter 4.

An **informal reading inventory (IRI)** is an assessment device in which a student reads a series of selections that gradually increase in difficulty. The teacher records oral reading errors and assesses comprehension in order to determine levels of materials that a student can read.

The **independent level** is the level at which a student can read without any assistance.

Comprehension is 90 percent or higher, and word recognition is 99 percent or higher.

The **instructional level** is the level at which a student needs a teacher's help. Comprehension is 75 percent or higher, and word recognition is 95 percent or higher.

The **frustration level** is the level at which reading material is so difficult that the

student can't read it even with help. Frustration is reached when either word recognition is 90 percent or lower, or comprehension is 50 percent or lower.

Listening capacity is the highest level of reading material that students can understand with 75 percent comprehension when it is read to them.

TABLE 2.1   Commercial Reading Inventories

Name	Publisher	Grades	Added Skill Areas
Analytical Reading Inventory	Merrill	1–9	
Bader Reading and Language Inventory	Merrill	1–12	phonics, language, emergent literacy
Basic Reading Inventory	Kendall/Hunt	1–8	emergent literacy
Burns and Roe Informal Inventory	Houghton Mifflin	1–12	
Classroom Reading Inventory	McGraw-Hill	1–8	spelling
Comprehensive Reading Inventory	Merrill	K–12	emergent literacy, phonics, reading attitude (Spanish version on CD)
Critical Reading Inventory: Assessing Students' Reading and Thinking	Prentice Hall	1–12	critical thinking
Ekwall/Shanker Reading Inventory	Allyn & Bacon	1–12	emergent literacy, word analysis
English-Español Reading Inventory for the Classroom	Prentice Hall	1–12	emergent literacy (has an English-only version)
Flynt-Cooter Reading Inventory for the Classroom	Merrill	1–12	emergent literacy
Informal Reading Thinking Inventory	Harcourt	1–11	
Phonological Awareness Literacy Screening (PALS)	University of Virginia	K–3	emergent literacy, spelling
Qualitative Reading Inventory 5	Allyn & Bacon	1–12	emergent literacy
Stieglitz Informal Reading Inventory	Allyn & Bacon	1–8	emergent literacy, phonics
Texas Primary Reading Inventory	Texas Education Agency	K–3	(has a Spanish version)

words (Gunning, 2008a). However, most commercial reading inventories still take a high-frequency approach and fail to incorporate phonics patterns. At the pre-primer and primer levels, students are not being assessed on what they have been taught. If you are assessing students on the beginning reading levels, obtain passages that are representative of those levels. At the easiest levels, the ninth and tenth editions of the Basic Reading Inventory and the fifth edition of the Qualitative Reading Inventory have passages containing decodable and high-frequency words. Most basal reading programs have IRIs that would be aligned with their instruction.

IRIs can also be based on children's books. If, for instance, your program emphasizes the reading of children's books, you might designate certain titles as benchmark books and construct questions or retelling activities based on these books. Benchmark books can be used to place students and check their progress. Sets of benchmark books and accompanying questions are also available from basal reader publishers, or you can construct your own. This chapter lists benchmark books that can be used to judge the difficulty level of children's books at the beginning levels. You might use these books as the beginning basis for an informal reading inventory.

Determining Placement Levels   Placement levels are determined by having students read two selections, one orally and one silently, at appropriate grade levels. The percentages of oral-reading errors and comprehension questions answered correctly at each level are calculated. This information is then used to determine placement levels. Quantitative criteria for determining levels are presented in Table 2.2.

To be at the independent level, a reader must have, at minimum, both 99 percent word recognition and 90 percent comprehension. At the instructional level, the reader must have at least 95 percent word recognition and at least 75 percent comprehension. The frustration level is reached when word recognition drops to 90 percent or below, or comprehension falls to 50 percent or below. Even with 80 percent comprehension and 90 percent word recognition, readers are at the frustration level because they are encountering too many words that they cannot decode. Listening capacity is the level at which students can understand 75 percent of the material that is read to them.

Level	Word Recognition in Context (%)	Average Comprehension (%)
Independent	99–100	90–100
Instructional	95–98	75–89
Frustration	≤90	≤50
Listening capacity		75

TABLE 2.2 Quantitative Criteria for IRI Placement Levels

Running records and some other placement devices use lower standards for the instructional level, such as 90 to 95 percent word recognition. It is strongly advised that you stick to the 95 to 98 percent word-recognition standard. Research indicates that students do best when they can read at least 95 to 98 percent of the words (Berliner, 1981; Biemiller, 1994; Gambrell, Wilson, & Gantt, 1981; Nation, 2001). It is also important that the examiner adhere to strict standards when marking word reading errors. Enz (1989) found that relaxing IRI standards resulted in a drop in both achievement and attitude. Students placed according to higher standards spent a greater proportion of time on task, had a higher success rate, and had a more positive attitude toward reading.

REFLECTION

What are the most effective procedures for placing students? Some sources say that 90 to 95 percent word recognition is the instructional level. Others say 95 to 98 percent. Which standard do you intend to use? Why?

Administering the Word-List Test Rather than guessing the grade level at which to begin the IRI, a teacher can administer a word-list test to locate an approximate starting point. This test consists of a series of ten to twenty words at each grade level. Students read the words in isolation, starting with the easiest and continuing until they reach a level where they get half or more of the words wrong. In a simplified administration of the test, students read the words from their copy of the list, and the teacher marks each response as being right or wrong on her or his copy.

In a diagnostic administration, the teacher uses three-by-five cards to flash the words for one second each. When students respond correctly, the teacher moves on to the next word. If the answer is incorrect or if students fail to respond, the teacher stops and lets them look at the word for as long as they wish (within reason). While students examine the missed word, the teacher writes down their response or marks a symbol in the flash (timed) column. If students make a second erroneous response, it is written in the second, or untimed, column. Symbols used to mark word-list tests are presented in Table 2.3. A corrected word-list test is shown in Figure 2.1.

Besides indicating the starting level for the IRI, a word-list test can yield valuable information about students' reading, especially if a diagnostic administration has been used. By comparing flash and untimed scores, teachers can assess the adequacy of students' sight vocabulary (their ability to recognize words immediately) and their proficiency with decoding. Teachers can note which decoding skills students are able to use and which must be taught. Looking at the performance depicted in Figure 2.1, it is clear that the student has a very limited sight vocabulary. The flash column shows that the student recognized few of the words immediately; the untimed column gives an overall picture of the student's ability to apply decoding skills. The student was able to use initial and final consonants and short vowels to decode words; for example, the student was able to read *wet, king, let,* and *bit* when given time to decode them. However,

Word	Teacher Mark	Meaning
the	☐'	Correct
was	☐'	Incorrect response or repeated error
have	*O*	No response
dog	*boy*	Mispronunciation
are	*Dk*	Don't know

TABLE 2.3 Word-List Marking Symbols

FIGURE 2.1   A Corrected
Word-List Test

	Flash	Untimed
1. their	*the*	✓
2. wet	*o*	✓
3. king	*o*	✓
4. off	*o*	*dk*
5. alone	*uh*	*along*
6. hurt	✓	
7. near	✓	
8. tiger	*tie*	✓
9. stick	*sick*	✓
10. move	*moo*	*more*
11. let	*o*	✓
12. men	✓	
13. shoe	*o*	✓
14. wish	✓	
15. apple	*o*	*dk*
16. on	*o*	✓
17. sign	*o*	*o*
18. bit	*o*	✓
19. smell	*sell*	✓
20. floor	*for*	✓
Percent correct	*20%*	*60%*

the student had difficulty with initial clusters; note how
the student read *sick* for *stick*, *sell* for *smell*, and *for* for *floor*.

Rechecking Responses   When students misread
words, the logical assumption is that they are lacking in
decoding or word-recognition skills. However, this is
not always so. In their analysis of errors made by struggling readers, Cohn and D'Alessandro (1978) found
that students were able to correct half their errors when
the examiner requested, "Please look at it carefully and
try it again" (p. 342). If the student still got the word
wrong, the examiner tried a series of prompts to direct
the student's attention to the misread word. Through
prompting, another 28 percent of errors were corrected.
Results of assessments need to be carefully analyzed to
make sure that misread words actually indicate difficulty
with decoding or word-recognition skills. This is especially true with older struggling readers, who are more
likely to be able to correct errors than struggling readers
in the first or second grade. To make sure you are getting an accurate picture of students' word reading ability,
recheck erroneous responses to any word-list test that
you administer. Note if students are able to read the word
correctly after you prompt them to look at it carefully and
try again. If they still get the word wrong, you might
use sounding out and/or pronounceable word prompts.
Note how the students do when provided with prompts.
This information could help you plan instruction.

Administering the Inventory   The IRI is started at
the level below the student's last perfect performance on
the flash portion of the word-list test. For example, if
that perfect performance was at the fourth-grade level, the inventory is started at the
third-grade level.

An IRI is like a guided reading lesson, except that its main purpose is to assess a
student's reading. To administer an IRI, first explain to the student that she or he will
be reading some stories and answering some questions so that you can get some information about her or his reading. Before each selection is read, have the student read
its title and predict what it will be about (Johns, 1997). Doing this will help the student
set a purpose for reading, and it will give you a sense of the student's prediction ability
and background of experience.

The student reads the first selection orally. This is one of the few times at which
reading orally without having first read the selection silently is valid. As the student
reads, use the symbols shown in Table 2.4 to record her or his performance. Although
many different kinds of misreadings are noted, only the following are counted as
errors or **miscues**: mispronunciations, omissions, insertions, and words supplied by
the examiner because the student asked the examiner to read them or apparently could
not read them on her or his own. Self-corrected errors are not counted. Hesitations,
repetitions, and other qualitative misreadings are noted but not counted as errors.
A corrected inventory selection is shown in Figure 2.2.

After the student finishes reading
aloud, ask the series of comprehension
questions that accompany the selection
or ask for an oral retelling (see pp. 63-64
for information on retelling). Then

⊡ A **miscue** is an oral reading response that differs from the expected (correct) response. The term
miscue is used because miscue theory holds that errors are not random but are the attempts of
the reader to make sense of the text.

TABLE 2.4　Oral-Reading Symbols

Item	Marking	Meaning
Quantitative errors	the big dog *(bad)*	Mispronounced
	the big dog	Omitted word
	the (ferocious) dog	Asked for word
	the big dog *(bad)*	Inserted word
Self-correction	the big dog *(bad)*	Self-corrected
Qualitative errors	I hit the ball, and George ran.	Omitted punctuation
	The ‖‖‖ ferocious dog	Hesitation
	the ferocious dog	Repetition
	Good morning!	Rising inflection
	Are you reading?	Falling inflection
	W × W	Word-by-word reading
	HM	Head movement
	FP	Finger pointing
	PC	Use of picture clue

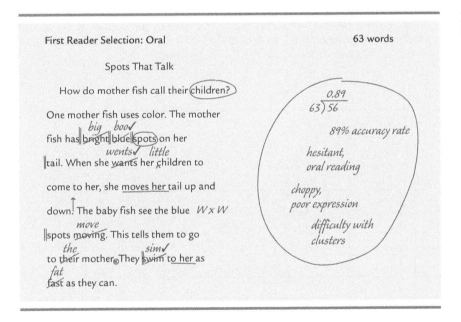

FIGURE 2.2　Corrected Inventory Selection

First Reader Selection: Oral　　　　　　　　　　63 words

Spots That Talk

How do mother fish call their (children?)

One mother fish uses color. The mother
fish has ‖bright‖blue‖(spots) on her *(big boo✓)*
‖tail. When she wants her children to *(wents✓ little)*

come to her, she moves her tail up and

down! The baby fish see the blue　W × W
‖spots moving. This tells them to go *(move)*
to their mother. They ‖swim to her as *(the sim✓)*
fast as they can. *(fat)*

0.89
63)56

89% accuracy rate

hesitant,
oral reading

choppy,
poor expression

difficulty with
clusters

introduce a silent selection on the same level. Just as with the oral selection, allow a very brief preparation phase and have the student make a prediction. During the silent reading, note finger pointing, head movement, lip movement, and subvocalizing. Symbols for these behaviors are given in Table 2.5. Ask comprehension questions when the student finishes reading. Proceeding level by level, continue to test until the student reaches a frustration level—that is, misreads 10 percent or more of the words or misses at least half the comprehension questions. Comprehension is calculated by averaging comprehension scores for the oral and silent selections at each level. Using the numbers on the summary sheet, determine the placement levels. Refer to the criteria in Table 2.2.

When the frustration level has been reached, read to the student the oral and silent selections at each level beyond the frustration level until the student reaches the highest level at which she or he can answer 75 percent of the comprehension questions.

 FYI

Some inventories recommend counting all miscues as errors. Others suggest counting only those that disrupt the meaning or flow of the passage. It is easier and quicker to count all misreadings but make note of whether they fit the sense of the passage. Deciding whether a miscue is significant is subjective. If standards are too lenient, the student being assessed may end up being paired with a text that is too difficult.

TABLE 2.5   Silent-Reading Symbols

Symbol	Meaning
HM	Head movement
FP	Finger pointing
LM	Lip movement
SV	Subvocalizing

This is the student's listening capacity, and it indicates how well the student would be able to read if she or he had the necessary word-recognition skills and related print-processing skills. For children who have limited language skills, limited background of experience, or deficient listening skills, you may have to backtrack and read selections at the frustration level and below. Because students will already have been exposed to the lower-level selections, you will have to use alternative selections to test listening comprehension.

Assessing Fluency   To assess reading rate, which is a key element in fluency, time the student's oral and silent reading for each passage. For oral reading, you can note how many words the student reads in the first minute of reading or time how long the student took to read the whole selection and divide that into the number of words read correctly. Silent reading rate is also assessed by dividing the number of words read by the time spent reading. Use timings from the instructional level, not the frustration level. If the student reads more than one passage at the instructional level, average the reading rates.

Tallying up Results   After administering the inventory, enter the scores from each level on the inventory's summary sheet (see Figure 2.3). Word-recognition scores are determined by calculating the percentage of words read correctly for each oral selection (the number of words read correctly divided by the number of words in the selection). For example, if the student made 5 miscues in a 103-word selection, the word-recognition score would be 98/103 = 95.1 percent.

FIGURE 2.3   IRI Summary Sheet

Word-List Scores			Inventory Scores						
			Word recognition (in context)	Comprehension (oral)	(silent)	(avg.)	Listening capacity	Reading rate (oral)	(silent)
Level	Flash	Untimed							
PP	80	95	100	100	90	95		20	15
P	70	80	96	100	80	90		20	20
1	30	55	89	60	60	60		15	20
2							90		
3							80		
4							50		
5									
6									
7									
8									

Levels

Independent	PP
Instructional	P
Frustration	1
Listening capacity	3

Strengths and weaknesses

Strong language development
Difficulty with high-frequency words and clusters

Interpreting the Inventory   After determining the student's levels, examine her or his performance on the inventory to determine word-recognition and comprehension strengths and weaknesses. What kinds of phonics skills can the student use? Is the student able to decode multisyllabic words? Could the student read words that have prefixes or suffixes? Did the student use context? Did the student integrate the use of decoding skills with context? How did the student's word recognition compare with her or his comprehension? How did the student handle literal and inferential questions? How did comprehension on oral passages compare with comprehension on silent passages? You can also note the quality of the student's responses as she or he answered questions and the way the student approached the tasks. What level of language did the student use to answer questions? What was the student's level of confidence and effort as she or he undertook each task? Through careful observation, you can gain insight into the student's reading processes. For example, you may observe the student decoding unfamiliar words sound by sound or using a combination of context and phonics to handle difficult words. Strengths and weaknesses as well as immediate needs can be noted on the IRI summary sheet.

Probing Comprehension Problems   Most students have difficulty comprehending because there are too many words in a selection that they don't know. However, occasionally there are students who are good decoders but poor comprehenders (see the Case Study). They sail through the word lists and read the oral passages flawlessly and with good expression. But they have difficulty answering the comprehension questions. To assess comprehension difficulties, probe responses so that you can gain some insight into the causes, which often have to do with the students' thinking processes. Some possible causes of poor comprehension are listed below, along with questions that might be asked to determine causes of difficulties (Dewitz & Dewitz, 2003).

- *Inadequate background knowledge.*   Ask questions about items that you believe the students might not know: "What can you tell me about planets? What is an asteroid? Have you ever seen a telescope?"
- *Difficulty with vocabulary.*   Go back to the passage, point to a key word that you believe may be unfamiliar to the student, and ask, "What does this word mean?"
- *Difficulty with syntax.*   Go back to the target sentence, and ask questions about it.
- *Overuse of background knowledge.*   Ask, "What makes you think that the sun is closer to Earth in the summertime? How did you know that? Is that in the article?"
- *Failure to recall or comprehend directly stated information.*   Ask, "Can you find the answer to that in the article?"
- *Failure to link ideas in a passage.*   Ask, "What happened because it rained? What else could have made Lee sad? Who else caused the team to lose?"
- *Failure to make inferences.*   Ask, "Why do you think the family decided to head west? What do you think the long, dry summer will cause to happen?"

Miscue Analysis of IRIS   Students use three cueing systems to decode printed words: syntactic, semantic, and phonic (graphophonic). In other words, they use their sense of how language sounds (syntax), the meaning of the sentence or passage (semantics), and phonics to read. To determine how they are using these systems, analyze their word-recognition errors, or miscues, with a modified **miscue analysis**. On a sheet similar to the one in Figure 2.4, list a student's miscues. Try to list at least ten miscues, but do not analyze any that are at or beyond the frustration level. Miscues can be chosen from the independent and instructional levels and from the buffer zone between the instructional and frustration levels (91 to 94 percent word recognition). Also list the correct version of each error. Put a check in the syntactic column if the miscue is syntactically correct—that is, if it is the same part of speech as

Building Language

When students are responding orally to IRI questions, note the level and quality of their language and use your observations to plan a program of language development.

Adapting Instruction for English Language Learners

ELLs may have particular difficulty with both vocabulary and syntax. Note difficulties and plan instruction, with the ESL teacher if possible, to help them overcome these difficulties.

FYI

Through analysis and probing, you can discover ways in which to foster students' thinking.

Miscue analysis is the process of analyzing miscues in order to determine which cueing systems or combination of cueing systems the student is using: semantic, syntactic, and/or phonic (graphophonic).

Case Study
Good Decoding, Poor Comprehending

Although he has excellent decoding skills and reads orally with fluency and expression, Mark has problems understanding what he reads. He also has difficulty answering questions about selections that have been read to him. On a reading inventory known as the QRI-3, Mark was able to read the sixth-grade word list with no difficulty. He was also able to read the words on the sixth-grade oral passage with no errors. However, his comprehension was below 50 percent on the sixth-grade passage and also on the fourth- and fifth-grade passages. Puzzled by Mark's performance, the reading consultant analyzed Mark's responses (Dewitz & Dewitz, 2003). The consultant wanted to get some insight into Mark's thinking processes. The correct responses didn't reveal much about Mark's thinking. They simply restated what was in the text. When erroneous responses were analyzed, patterns appeared. Mark could answer questions that required comprehending only a single sentence. However,

he had difficulty with questions that required linking ideas across sentences or passages. Putting ideas together posed problems for him. Mark could pick up information from one segment but couldn't integrate that with information from another segment.

Mark also overrelied on background knowledge. He made up answers. This happened when he was unable to recall a fact or put pieces of information together. Mark also had some minor difficulty with complex syntactical structures and vocabulary.

Based on an analysis of Mark's responses, the consultant created a program for Mark and other students who had similar difficulties. After instruction, Mark was able to comprehend sixth-grade material. He was no longer overrelying on background knowledge, and he was connecting and integrating ideas.

FYI

Generally, IRIs are given at the beginning of the school year to obtain placement information, when a new student enters the class, or whenever a student's placement is in doubt. They may also be given as pretests and posttests and are often more sensitive indicators of progress than norm-referenced tests.

the word in the text or could be used in that context. Put a check in the semantic column if the miscue makes sense in the sentence. In the graphic column, use a check to show whether the miscue is graphically and/or phonically similar to the text word. It is similar if it contains at least half the sounds in the text word. Also use a check to show whether the beginning, middle, and end of the miscue are similar to the text word. Put a check in the nonword column if the miscue is not a real word. Also indicate corrected miscues with a check in the self-correction column.

Tally each column (as shown in Figure 2.4), and convert tallies to percentages. After tallying the columns, examine the numbers to see whether the student is reading for meaning. Miscues that make sense in the context of the selection, self-corrections, and absence of nonwords are positive signs. They show that the student is reading for meaning. Conversely, the presence of nonwords is a negative sign, as are miscues that do not fit the sense of the passage or the syntax.

Also compare the tallies to see whether the cueing systems are being used in a balanced fashion or whether one is being overused or underused. The student could be overusing phonics and underusing semantic context, or vice versa. Draw tentative conclusions about the strategies that the student uses in his or her word recognition. Double-check those conclusions as you observe the student read in the classroom.

As you can see from Figure 2.4, fewer than half of this student's miscues fit the context either syntactically or semantically. Moreover, three of them

An informal inventory or running record yields a wealth of information.

FIGURE 2.4　Miscue Analysis

Name: _____　　Date: _____

Miscue	Text	Syntactic similarity	Semantic similarity	Graphic similarity	Beginning	Middle	End	Nonword	Self-correction
gots	gets	✓	✓	✓	✓	—	✓		
will	with	—	—	✓	✓	✓	—		
ran ✓	runs	✓	✓	✓	✓	—	✓		✓
balt	ball	—	—	✓	✓	✓	—	✓	
tricks	kicks	✓	—	✓	—	✓	✓		
my	me	—	✓	✓	✓		—		
trick	trust	✓	—	—	✓	—	—		
bell	ball	✓		✓	✓		✓		
frain	five	—	—	—	✓	—	—	✓	
grain	gray	—	—	✓	✓	✓	—		
there	that	—	—	—	✓	—	—		
eak	each	—	—	✓	✓		—	✓	
Totals		5	3	9	11	4	4	3	1
Numbers of miscues analyzed		12	12	12				12	12
Percentage		42	25	75				25	8

are nonwords, and the student had only one self-correction. All indications are that the student is failing to use context clues and is not reading for meaning. The student makes heavy use of phonics, especially at the beginning of words, but must better integrate the use of phonics with syntactic and semantic cues. The student also needs to improve the use of phonics skills with middle and ending elements.

IRIs require training and practice to administer and interpret. In the past, they were generally administered by the school's reading specialist. However, increasingly, classroom teachers are administering IRIs. To make the best possible use of time, classroom teachers might use a streamlined version of an IRI in which they give the full word-list test but administer only the oral passages of the inventory, without the listening portion. It will also save time if the inventory contains brief passages. Giving a shortened inventory reduces its reliability, so results should be regarded as tentative and should be verified by observation of the student's performance when reading books at the estimated instructional level.

Even if you, as a classroom teacher, never formally administer an IRI, it is still essential that you be familiar with the concept. Knowing the IRI standards for instructional and other levels, you have a basis for evaluating your students' reading performance. If students have difficulty orally reading more than five words out of a hundred, or if their oral and written comprehension seem closer to 50 percent than 75 percent, you may have to check the material they are reading to see whether it is too difficult. On the other hand, if both word recognition and comprehension in everyday reading tasks are close to perfect, you may want to try more challenging materials.

with difficult words, you may also want to conduct a mental

As children struggle with difficult words, you may also want to conduct a mental miscue analysis. By closely observing miscues, you can sense whether students might need added instruction in using context or phonics or in integrating the two.

Selecting an IRI   Although they share a common purpose, IRIs vary in length, types of passages included, ways in which comprehension is assessed, presence of supplementary assessments, and technical adequacy. In selecting an IRI, match the inventory with your needs. The Basic Inventory (Johns, 2008) or QRI-5 might be a good choice if you are assessing young children, since they have passages geared to materials being used at the easiest levels. Because none of its passages is more than 100 words long, the Basic Inventory can be administered fairly rapidly. For in-depth analysis of comprehension at higher levels, the QRI-5 might be a good choice since it includes lengthy content area passages and think-alouds. If you are working with Spanish-speaking students, you might want to consider the Comprehensive Reading Inventory, which contains assessments in Spanish. For a comparison of IRIs, see Nilsson (2008).

Running Records

Similar to the IRI and based on K. S. Goodman's (1974) theory of analyzing students' miscues to determine what strategies they are using to decode words, the **running record** has become a popular device for assessing students' progress. Like the IRI, the running record is administered individually. However, only an oral-reading sample is obtained. The running record has two major purposes: to determine whether students' reading materials are on the proper level and to obtain information about the word-recognition processes students are using. To get a fuller assessment of comprehension, some teachers supplement the administration of a running record by having students retell the selection. Teachers often take running records during guided reading, while other students are reading silently.

Although running records may be obtained from older readers, they are most often used to assess the performance of novice readers and are administered daily to Reading Recovery students. As used in Reading Recovery and recommended in *An Observation Survey of Early Literacy Achievement*, 2nd edition (Clay, 2005), running records are administered according to a standardized format in which students' errors and corrections are recorded on a separate sheet. As adapted for use by classroom teachers, running records may be recorded (as long as the fair-use provision of the copyright laws is adhered to or permission is obtained from the publisher) on a photocopy of the text that the student is using (Learning Media, 1991). To assess whether materials are on a suitable level of difficulty and to determine how well the child makes use of previously presented strategies, take a running record on a text that the student has recently read. To assess the student's ability to handle challenging materials and apply strategies independently, take a running record on material that the student has not previously read. If the book or article is very brief, take a running record of the whole piece. If the text is lengthy, select a sample of 100 to 200 words. As the student reads orally, record his or her performance with symbols such as those presented in Table 2.6. However, you may use the IRI symbols if you are more familiar with them. After taking a running record, record the number of words in the selection, number of errors made, error rate, number of self-corrections made, and the accuracy rate.

Clay (1993a) accepts 90 percent as an adequate accuracy rate; however, 95 percent seems more realistic. Word recognition is emphasized in a running record, so comprehension is

Quizzes and unit tests can be used as part of formative assessment.

The **running record is** an assessment device in which a student's oral reading errors are noted and classified in order to determine whether the material is on the appropriate level of difficulty and to see which reading strategies the student is using.

TABLE 2.6 Running Record Symbols

Symbol	Text	Example
Words read correctly are marked with a check.	Janice kicked the ball.	☐ ☐ ☐ ☐
Substitutions are written above the line.	A barn owl hooted.	☐ *big* ☐ ☐ *barn*
Self-corrections are marked *SC*.	A barn owl hooted.	☐ *big | Sc* ☐ ☐ *barn*
A dash is used to indicate no response.	I saw her yesterday.	☐ ☐ ☐ — *yesterday*
A dash is used to indicate the insertion of a word. The dash is placed beneath the inserted word.	We saw a big dog.	☐ ☐ ☐ ☐ *bad* ☐
A *T* is used to indicate that a child has been told a word.	Her cat ran away yesterday.	☐ ☐ ☐ ☐ *T* *yesterday*
The letter *A* indicates that the child has asked for help.	A large moose appeared.	☐☐☐ *A* *appeared*
At times, the student becomes so confused by a misreading that it is suggested that she or he "try that again" (coded *TTA*). Brackets are put around the section that has been misread, the whole misreading is counted as one error, and the student reads it again for a new score.	The deer leaped over the fence.	[☐ ☐ *landed* ☐ ☐ *field*] *TTA* *leaped* *fence*
A repetition is indicated with an *R*. Although not counted as errors, repetitions are often part of an attempt to puzzle out a difficult item. The point to which the student returns in the repetition is indicated with an arrow.	The deer leaped over the fence.	☐ ☐ *landed | Sc* ☐ ☐ *field | Sc* *R* *leaped* *fence*

not directly checked. However, you may ask the child to retell the story if you wish to obtain information about comprehension.

It is essential that you analyze a student's miscues in order to determine what strategies she or he is using. As you examine the student's miscues, ask the following questions:

- Is the student reading for meaning? Do the student's miscues make sense?
- Is the student self-correcting miscues, especially those that do not fit the meaning of the sentence? Is the student using meaning cues?
- Is the student using visual or sound-symbol cues (phonics)? Are the student's miscues similar in appearance and sound to the target word?
- Is the student using picture cues?
- Is the student integrating cues? Is the student balancing the use of meaning and sound-symbol cues?
- Based on the student's performance, what strategies does she or he need to work on?

For younger readers in the very early stages, note whether they read from left to right or top to bottom and whether there is a voice-print match (the word the child says matches the one she or he is looking at). For detailed information on analyzing and interpreting running records, see Clay (1993a, 2000, 2005) or Johnston (2000).

Commercial Running Records The Developmental Reading Assessment (DRA, 2nd edition) functions as an informal reading inventory or running record for students in grades K–3. It also assesses fluency and decoding skills. At its upper levels, students respond in writing to comprehension questions. DRA2 (2nd edition) is designed for grades 4–8. At the upper levels, note taking is assessed. The Fountas and Pinnell Benchmark Assessment System 1 (2nd edition), which is designed for grades K–2, has a format similar to that of DRA2. A word-list test is used to estimate students' reading level, and they read from a series of increasingly difficult booklets until their levels are established. Booklets are leveled according to the Fountas-Pinnell guided reading system. Accuracy, rate, fluency, and comprehension are assessed. A feature called Comprehension Conversation provides information about a reader's thinking. The Fountas and Pinnell Benchmark Assessment System 2 (2nd edition) is designed for grades 3–8. As an option, written responses to reading and note taking are assessed.

Group Inventories

Because of the time involved, it may be impractical to administer individual IRIs. However, you may choose to administer a group reading inventory. QRI-5 incorporates provisions for group administration at levels 3 and above. Students read a passage that is at their grade level. Those who have 70 to 75 percent comprehension or higher are tested with the next higher-level passage. Those who fail to meet the criteria are tested with passages at lower levels until they meet the criteria or they may be assessed with an individual administration of an IRI. Information about constructing and administering group reading inventories can be found in *Informal Reading Inventories* (2nd edition) by Johnson, Kress, and Pikulski (1987). Some reading series contain group reading inventories. There are also three tests that function as group inventories: Degrees of Reading Power, the Scholastic Reading Inventory, and STAR.

Degrees of Reading Power (DRP)   Composed of a series of passages that gradually increase in difficulty, Degrees of Reading Power (DRP) assesses overall reading ability by having students choose from among five options the one that best completes a portion of the passage from which words have been omitted (modified cloze). Each passage has nine deletions.

As in a traditional IRI, the passages gradually increase in difficulty and encompass a wide range of difficulty so that slow, average, and superior readers' ability may be appropriately assessed. Instead of yielding a grade-level score, the assessment provides a DRP score, which indicates what level of material the student should be able to read. A complementary readability formula is used to indicate the difficulty level of books in DRP units. Approximate grade equivalents of DRP units are presented in Table 2.7. The main purpose of DRP is to match students with books that are on their levels.

The Scholastic Reading Inventory   The Scholastic Reading Inventory, which also uses a modified cloze procedure and can be administered and scored manually or by

FYI

• Difficulty of questions varies on most tests. Students may give a wrong answer because the question was tricky or especially difficult. One advantage of the DRP is that there are no questions, so missing an item is an indication of failure of comprehension.
• The DRP measures the ability to comprehend text at a basic level; it doesn't measure the ability to summarize or draw inferences. However, without basic text comprehension, the student will not be able to summarize or make inferences based on the text.
• Degrees of Reading Power (DRP), the Scholastic Reading Inventory, STAR (Advantage Learning Systems), and Maze (http://www.aimsweb.com) all use modified cloze, which requires filling in the blanks when given a choice of words. See Chapter 8 for a discussion of cloze.

TABLE 2.7   Comparison of Readability Levels

Grade Equivalent	DRP	Lexile	Guided Reading	DRA	Reading Recovery
Emergent/Picture			A	A, 1	1–2
Frame/Caption (Early PP)			B	2	3
High Frequency PP–1			C	3	4
Pre-primer 2			D	4	5–6
Pre-primer 3			E	6, 8	7–8
Primer		200–300	F	10	9–10
First Reader		300–400	G–I	12, 16	11–17
Grade 2a	24–28	400–500	J–K	18, 20	18–20
Grade 2b	29–33	400–500	L–M	24, 28	
Grade 3	34–42	500–700	N–P	30, 34, 38	
Grade 4	43–49	700–800	Q–S	40	
Grade 5	50–55	800–900	T–V	50	
Grade 6	56–59	900–1000	W–X	60	
Grade 7	60–63	1000–1100	Y	70	
Grade 8	64–66	1000–1100	Z	80	

computer, yields lexile scores. Lexile scores range from about 70 to 1700+. A score of 70 to 200 indicates a reading level of about mid-first grade. A score of 1700 represents the level at which difficult scientific journals are written. Approximate grade equivalents of lexile scores are presented in Table 2.7.

Star   STAR (Advantage Learning Systems), which is administered and scored by computer and so doesn't require valuable teacher time, has a branching component: If students give correct answers, they are given higher-level passages, but if they respond incorrectly, they are given lower-level passages. STAR uses a modified cloze procedure and also assesses vocabulary. Students need a reading vocabulary of one hundred words in order to be able to take STAR. Testing time is 10 minutes or less.

Word-List Tests

To save time, teachers sometimes administer word-list tests instead of IRIs. Because they require only the ability to pronounce words, these tests neglect comprehension and may yield misleading levels for students who are superior decoders but poor comprehenders, or vice versa. One of the most popular word-list tests is the Slosson Oral Reading Test (SORT). SORT presents twenty words at each grade level from pre-primer through grade 12. The student is only required to pronounce the words and does not have to know their meanings.

Screening, Benchmark, and Progress-Monitoring Assessments

Screening measures range from those that assess alphabet knowledge and beginning sounds to those that assess comprehension. Younger readers need assessments that tap into phonological awareness, basic phonics skills, or ability to read high-frequency words. Older students need assessments that tap into comprehension or fluency or both. Screening tests are designed to identify students who are at risk or who are falling behind. Screening assessments are also frequently used to monitor progress and provide an overview of the effectiveness of instruction. If whole groups of students are not making expected progress, this is an indicator that the program might need to be adjusted. If some classes are not doing as well as others, this could be a sign that the teachers in those classes need assistance.

The screening tests that you select should assess the key skills that students need to be successful. In first grade, this might be phonics. In third grade, this might be word recognition, fluency, and/or comprehension. The most useful reading instruments are those that assess actual reading. An oral reading test can be used to assess word recognition, level of reading, fluency, decoding skills, and comprehension. Often the screening instrument is also used for benchmarking. **Benchmark** assessments are measures of expected level of performance *and* are typically based on grade-level performance standards. A benchmark might state that students should be able to read a grade-level passage with 75 percent accuracy or read grade-level material at a rate of 100 words a minute.

Informal reading inventories and running records have been widely used to place and screen students and can be used to monitor progress. Informal reading inventories can be created for children's books. Representative books can be designated as being benchmark books; questions or retelling activities based on these books are then used to assess students' comprehension. Benchmark books can be used to place students and track their progress. In Reading Recovery and a number of other intervention systems, students read books that gradually increase in difficulty. Students' progress from level

□ **Screening measures** are designed to indicate possible difficulties or problems.

□ A **benchmark** is an expected level of performance on a task. Benchmarks have also been defined as scores that can be used to predict later success.

to level is monitored by charting their progress in reading the texts. Failure to move to a higher level is a sign that the students aren't making adequate progress. Many programs also set achievement levels or benchmarks; in a 16-level program, for example, it is expected that students will be at level 4 by November, in level 8 by mid-year, level 12 by spring, and level 16 by year's end.

Curriculum-Based Measures

Curriculum-based measures (CBMs) are frequently recommended for screening and progress monitoring. These measures are actually curriculum-independent and not tied to a particular curriculum or program. CBMs have been described as general outcome assessments. They measure overall indicators of proficiency rather than mastery of specific skills. Thus, the ability to read lists of words or passages orally and to complete maze (fill-in-the-blank) passages are indicators of overall achievement in reading. CBMs are **standardized** and are quick, easy-to-administer probes of students' overall proficiency. They are designed in such a way that multiple but equivalent versions can be created, allowing progress to be monitored frequently, in some cases as often as once a week (Hosp, Hosp, & Howell, 2007). CBMs are most effective when used to measure lower-level skills. They don't do a very good job of measuring comprehension. As Fletcher, Lyon, Fuchs, and Barnes (2006) comment, CBMs

> . . . are best developed for word recognition, reading fluency, math, and spelling. It is possible to assess comprehension with CBM measures using cloze or maze tests, but the format provides a limited assessment of reading comprehension, which in itself is difficult to assess because it reflects so many underlying processes. (p. 67)

Emergent and Early Reading CBMS   Emergent and early literacy are typically assessed by measuring students' ability to name letters of the alphabet, give the sounds represented by letters of the alphabet, identify the first sound of a spoken word, segment spoken words, read nonwords, and read high-frequency (sight) words as in the following assessments.

Letter Name Fluency   Students name as many letters as they can within 1 minute. By timing the naming of the letters, the automaticity of the students' responses is being assessed. Students are asked to point to the letter as they say its name.

First Sound Fluency (DIBELS Next)   The assessor says a word, and the student is asked to say the first sound for the word: "What sound does *man* begin with?"

Phoneme Segmentation Fluency (DIBELS)   Given a spoken word, students are asked to say all the sounds in the word. The tester pronounces the word *stop*, and the student is expected to say "/s/, /t/, /o/, /p/."

Letter Sound Fluency   Letter Sound Fluency (Fuchs & Fuchs, n.d.) assesses students' ability to provide the sounds typically represented by letters shown in isolation. The letters *q* and *x* are not included. Except when used in proper names, *q* always appears with *u*. The letter *x* represents a blend or cluster of sounds or, in a few words, the sound /z/. The consonant digraphs *ch* and *sh* are included. For vowel letters, students are only given credit for giving the short sound of the letter. Limiting students to 1 minute indicates their automaticity, or fluency, and also their speed of processing. In a tryout with 1,500 kindergarten students and 1,500 first-graders, Fuchs and Fuchs judged students to be at risk if they could correctly sound

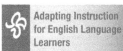

Adapting Instruction for English Language Learners

For additional information about screening and monitoring ELL, see *RTI for English Language Learners: Appropriately Using Screening and Progress Monitoring Tools to Improve Instructional Outcomes* (Brown & Sanford, 2011). http://www. rti4success.org/pdf/rtiforells.pdf

FYI

• Curriculum-based measures are not tied to a particular curriculum or program. Thus, the results are said to be more generalizable. Tasks deemed to be of universal importance are included in these measures.
• Many CBMs provide unofficial norms by supplying tables that indicate students' performance at a range of percentile levels. However, the cut scores or benchmarks can be regarded as criterion-referenced scores.

FYI

Multiple copies of the Letter Sound Fluency and the Word Identification Fluency Test are available from Lynn Fuchs, Vanderbilt University, Peabody #328, 230 Appleton Place, Nashville, TN 37203-5721.

A **curriculum-based measure** (CBM) is a brief, standardized assessment of a general outcome in reading, math, or some other content area.
Standardized means that a standard format is followed: standard set of directions, standard test items, and standard testing conditions. *Standardized* is often confused with *norm-referenced*. Not all standardized tests provide comparisons with a normative group.

fewer than 12 letters at the end of kindergarten and fewer than 19 at the beginning of first grade.

The results included a number of **false positives** and **false negatives**, so students' progress on this measure should be monitored closely.

Nonsense Word Fluency Reading nonsense words short-circuits the process of decoding words. When decoding words, students note whether the word they have decoded is a real word. If it is not a real word, then they are apt to try decoding again. When faced with reading nonsense words, many students try to make real words out of them (Moustafa, 1995). Reading nonsense words is a more difficult task than reading real words and so underestimates the reading ability of students (Cunningham et al., 1999; Walmsley, 1978–1979).

Word Reading Fluency Students are given a list of from 50 to 100 high-frequency words and are asked to read as many words as they can in 1 minute. Reading real words proved to be a more valid predictor of reading achievement than reading nonsense words (Fuchs, Fuchs, & Compton, 2004).

Fluency and Comprehension CBMs

Oral Reading Fluency The most widely used CBM is oral reading fluency, which measures how many words a student can accurately read in 1 minute. Many tests of oral reading fluency only measure the rate of reading. Oral reading fluency should also include accuracy, expression, and comprehension (Valencia, Smith, Reece, Li, Wixson, & Newman, 2010). A rubric for assessing fluency of expression is presented in Table 2.8. Oral reading fluency is a general outcome measure and is a rough indicator of a student's proficiency with lower-level reading skills. It has been compared to a thermometer in that it is an indicator of general reading health. However, in one study, 15 percent of students who had good oral reading fluency had poor comprehension. These students also tended to have low vocabulary scores (Riedel, 2007). Measures of oral reading fluency need to be complemented with measures of comprehension.

Screening and monitoring first-graders' oral reading fluency with passages are somewhat problematic. Because they

FYI

If you have any doubts about using real words as opposed to nonsense words, see Fuchs, Fuchs, & Compton, 2004.

Adapting Instruction for English Language Learners

A Spanish version of DIBELS is available: Indicadores Dinámicos del Éxito en la Lectura™.

False positive is an assessment that indicates a problem where none exists or predicts that a student will have difficulty, but the student does well.

False negative is an assessment that indicates there is no problem where one exists or predicts that students will do well but the student has difficulty.

Fluency Level	Description
4	Reads primarily in larger, meaningful phrase groups. Although some regressions, repetitions, and deviations from text may be present, these do not appear to detract from the overall structure of the story. Preservation of the author's syntax is consistent. Some or most of the story is read with expressive interpretation. Reads with at least 98 percent accuracy.
3	Reads primarily in three- or four-word phrase groups. Some small groupings may be present. However, the majority of phrasing seems appropriate and preserves the syntax of the author. Little or no expressive interpretation is present. Reads with at least 95 percent accuracy.
2	Reads primarily in two-word phrases with some three- or four-word groupings. Some word-by-word reading may be present. Word groupings may seem awkward and unrelated to larger context of sentence or passage. Reads with at least 90 percent accuracy.
1	Reads primarily word-by-word. Occasional two-word or three-word phrases may occur—but these are infrequent and/or they do not preserve meaningful syntax. Accuracy is below 90 percent.

TABLE 2.8 Adapted National Assessment of Educational Progress (NAEP) Oral Reading Fluency Scale

Note: Levels 4 and 3 are adequate. Levels 1 and 2 are not. The scale has been adapted to include reading accuracy, which was not included in the original.

Source: U.S. Department of Education, Institute of Education Sciences, National Center for Education Statistics, National Assessment of Educational Progress (NAEP), 2002 Oral Reading Study.

Using Technology

Maze Passage Generator
    Paste in a passage and a maze passage is generated. Also provides readability for the passage.
http://www.rti2.org/rti2/mazes ⬚

are still in the beginning stages of learning to read, first-graders aren't given passages to read until the winter of first grade. However, at that point the skills of many first-graders might still be too limited. For instance, the winter first-grade passage of the widely used DIBELS assessment contains words with long vowels, *r* vowels, and other vowels. However, in the winter of the school year, many first-graders would not have been taught these more complex vowel patterns.

The winter test passage would be more appropriate for spring administration. The passage would be overwhelming for struggling readers. A better assessment would be a word-list test.

Maze Passages   In grade 3 and beyond, **maze passages** are preferred to oral reading passages because they provide a measure of basic comprehension, can be administered to groups, and take very little time. Maze passages are 150 to 400 words in length. Every seventh word is deleted but no words are deleted from the first or last sentences. Answer options include the word from the selection, an option that is not the same part of speech and does not make sense in the selection, and another option that may or may not be the right part of speech but doesn't fit the sense of the selection. The two distracters are usually chosen from other parts of the selection (see the sample maze passage in Figure 2.5). Students read for 2.5 or 3 minutes.

Because they are group tests, mazes provide a quick and efficient way to screen a whole class. Students who score poorly on the mazes might be given individual tests, such as an IRI or oral reading test.

One problem with maze passages is that they are not very sensitive to growth. On average, students' scores increase by only half a word per month. AIMSweb has maze passages for grades 1–8. DIBELS Daze has passages for grades 3-6, which can be downloaded free of charge.

Mazes can also function as a group reading inventory. Students who have low scores might be given a maze assessment on a lower level; those with higher scores might be assessed on higher levels in order to obtain approximate reading levels. Assess until an instructional level is obtained. The highest level at which a student achieves a score of 70 to 80 percent is the estimated instructional level. These approximate levels might then be verified by observing students' performance or by administering additional assessments, such as an IRI or oral reading test.

When used for benchmarking or screening, maze and other tests are typically given on grade level. The idea is to see if the student has reached the benchmark. When used

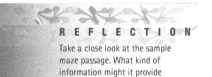

REFLECTION

Take a close look at the sample maze passage. What kind of information might it provide that could be used for planning instruction? What role might mazes play in an assessment program?

FIGURE 2.5   Sample Maze Passage: Kangaroos

Sample Maze Passage
Kangaroos

If you want to see one kind of kangaroo, you have to look up. One kind of kangaroo lives in (foods, trees, even). The tree kangaroo is small, but (it, that, from) has an extra-long tail. It (and, also, in) has long curved claws. The long (tail, fruit, move) and sharp claws help it to (climb, eat, to) trees. The tree kangaroo is a good (person, jumper, up). It can leap 30 feet from (good, one, is) tree branch to another or (even, faster, and) from one tree to another. It (look, can, small) also jump as much as 60 (claws, as, feet) to the ground. But on the (kind, another, ground) the tree kangaroo hops slowly. It (only, quickly, long) hops about as fast as a (person, bird, main) walks. Trees are good places for (see, which, the) tree kangaroo. They can move much (faster, smaller, it) in trees. Besides, their main food (is, want, also) tree leaves. But they also eat (branch, fruit, sharp) and sometimes will even eat small (places, birds, to). In addition, being in a tree helps (keep, jump, but) tree kangaroos safe from enemies.

Source: Gunning, T. (2011). *Success for All Readers: Using Formative Assessment Guide Instruction and Intervention.* San Francisco: Jossey-Bass.

for progress monitoring, tests are given on the students' reading level. The idea is to find out on what level the student is operating so that growth can be measured.

IRIs and Running Records.   Running records and informal reading inventories (IRIs) have been criticized for use as progress-monitoring devices because they focus on specific skills, whereas curriculum-based measures are indicators of overall reading proficiency. Actually, both inventories and oral reading fluency tests assess oral reading. Although some examiners skip this step, it is recommended that inventories be timed so that a rate of reading is obtained. In addition, through retelling and/or questioning, comprehension is assessed. Comprehension is the ultimate aim of reading, so IRIs and running records are better indicators of performance when retelling and/or questioning are included. IRIs and running records are time-consuming, but administration time can be reduced by assessing only oral reading and using brief passages. In addition, if students are tested several times a year, the examiner has a good idea of the level the student is on and so can arrange for the student to read passages on that level.

> **Using Technology**
>
> The University of Southern Maine Assessment Center has maze passages from books selected from the American Library Association's list of recommended books for students in grades 4–6.
> http://www.usm.maine.edu/cehd/assessment-center/CBM.htm

Setting Benchmarks

Many progress-monitoring measures have benchmarks, or expected levels of performance. Some benchmarks have been set because they are desired levels of performance. Others have been set by noting the relationship between students' performance on a benchmark and later performance on an outcome measure. For instance, according to the DIBELS, the benchmark for oral reading rate at the beginning of third grade is 70 words per minute (wpm). Students reading below that level scored below the 40th percentile on the GRADE, a standardized and norm-referenced reading test (Dynamic Measurement Group, 2010). Beginning third-graders reading below 70 wpm would be candidates for additional assessment or intervention. The benchmarks are less than perfect predictors, but they do provide helpful indicators. They need to be complemented with professional judgment and additional assessments.

> **REFLECTION**
>
> Why is progress monitoring such an essential element? Which progress-monitoring assessments do you think would provide the best information and be efficient in terms of the time needed to administer them?

Table 2.9 shows rates of letter naming and phonological awareness. Table 2.10 presents oral and silent reading rates of students at various percentiles. Note the variation of

Grade	Fall	Winter	Spring
K			
Letter Name Fluency	(1) 2–8 (8+)	(1–14) 15–26 (27+)	(1–28) 29–39 (40+)
Initial Sound Fluency	(1–3) 4–7 (8)	(1–9) 10–24 (25+)	NT
Phoneme Segmentation Fluency	NT	(1–6) 7–17 (18+)	(1–9) 10–34 (35+)
Letter Sound Fluency	5 (0)	17	27 (12)
Nonsense Word Fluency	NT	(1–4) 5–12 (13)	(1–14) 15–24 (25+)
Grade 1			
Letter Name Fluency	(1–24) 25–36 (37)		
Phoneme Segmentation Fluency	(1–9) 10–34 (35+)	(1–9) 10–34 (35+)	(1–9) 10–34 (35+)
Letter Sound Fluency	28 (19)	33	47
Nonsense Word Fluency	(1–12) 13–23 (24+)	(1–29) 30–49 (50+)	(1–29) 30–49 (50+)
Word Reading Fluency	6–10	20–25	40–45

TABLE 2.9   Rates of Letter Naming and Phonological Awareness

Scores are based on number of correct responses in 1 minute. Except for Letter Sound Fluency, the range of scores in the middle of the column indicates some risk. The range (or score) in parentheses to the left of the middle indicates at risk. The score in parentheses to the right of the middle indicates low risk. For Letter Sound Fluency, the score without parentheses indicates an average score; the score in parentheses indicates at risk. Scores for Word Reading Fluency are estimates of average performance. Adapted from Fuchs & Fuchs (n.d.), Good & Kaminski (2003), and AIMSweb (2006, as cited in Hosp, Hosp, & Howell, 2007).

TABLE 2.10　Rates of Oral and Silent Reading

Grade	Fall	Winter	Spring	Silent Reading
1		12 (23) 47	28 (53) 82	
2	(25) 51 (79)	(42) 72 (100)	(61) 89 (117)	121
3	(44) 71 (99)	(62) 100 (120)	(78) 107 (137)	135
4	(68) 94 (119)	(87) 112 (139)	(98) 123 (152)	149
5	(85) 110 (139)	(99) 127 (156)	(109) 139 (168)	163
6	(98) 127 (153)	(111) 140 (167)	(122) 150 (177)	177
7	128 (101) 156	136 (109) 165	(123) 150 (177)	191
8	(106) 133 (161)	146 (115) 173	(124) 151 (177)	205

Scores are based on number of words read in 1 minute. The score in the middle of the Fall, Winter, and Spring columns shows oral reading rate at the 50th percentile. The score in parentheses to the left of the middle shows oral reading rate at the 25th percentile. The score in parentheses to the right of the middle shows oral reading rate at the 75th percentile. The scores for oral reading are drawn from Tindal, Hasbrouck, & Jones (2005). The scores for silent reading are drawn from Carver (1990).

reading rate at each grade level. The table can be used to set benchmarks for students and cut points for determining which students are at risk. **Cut points** might be set at the 25th percentile or lower. Table 2.11 shows replacement rates for maze passages. Table 2.12 shows average growth rates for students on a variety of CBMs. In grade 1, students gain about 1.5 words a week and are able to read 1 additional word on a 50-word phonics inventory. In oral fluency, they gain about 1 word per week in grades 2 and 3, but only .5 word a week in grades 7 and 8. Using the tables, you can estimate whether students are making average progress.

The number and nature of monitoring assessments depend on the needs of the students. In Florida, for instance, Broad Screen/Progress Monitoring assessments are administered to all students (Florida Center for Reading Research, 2010). Those judged to be at risk are administered Broad Diagnostic Inventory assessments. If there is still a need for additional information, assessments from the Targeted Diagnostic Inventory are administered. Students judged to be at risk are given ongoing progress-monitoring assessments: Letter Name Knowledge (K), Letter Sound Knowledge (K), Phonemic Awareness (K & 1), Word Building (K & 1); (assembling letters to make words), Oral Reading Fluency (1 & 2), and Word Lists.

A key issue in screening and monitoring is the use of Curriculum-Based Measures versus Mastery Measures. **Mastery measures** assess what is being taught and so can be used to plan instruction. However, they may lack technical adequacy and might measure acquisition of skill rather than growth. Benchmark and screening instruments are often composed of grade-level material. However, monitoring instruments should be provided that are on the student's reading level. Otherwise, they may not be sensitive to growth (Deno, Fuchs, Marston, & Shin, 2001).

Creating Your Own Monitoring System

Because of the overemphasis on speed of responding and a possible lack of correspondence between what current progress-monitoring systems assess and what you teach, you might choose to construct your own system. First, decide what your key objectives are. Determine what it is that students should know and be able to do at the end of the year. These objectives should, of course, include school and district standards but might also include additional goals that you have set for your students. Translate these standards into language that students can

FYI

More frequent monitoring helps you to note which students aren't making adequate progress and so to intervene earlier with more intensive instruction or different materials. DIBELS provides materials for benchmark monitoring, designed to be administered three times a year, and also materials for progress monitoring, which may be given more frequently.

Cut points are the scores that are used to classify performance on a test, such as passing or failing. A cut score of 70 means that anyone who scores below 70 does not meet the benchmark.

A **mastery measure** assesses specific content or skills that have been taught to see whether students have learned the skills or content adequately: getting 100 percent on a list of spelling words or 8 percent on a comprehension test.

Grade	Fall	Winter	Spring
1	(0) 2 (6)	(2) 5 (10)	(3) 7 (13)
2	(2) 4 (8)	(6) 10 (15)	(9) 13 (18)
3	(8) 12 (17)	(10) 15 (19)	(10) 15 (21)
4	(9) 13 (17)	(13) 18 (25)	(14) 19 (25)
5	(12) 17 (22)	(15) 21 (27)	(18) 24 (30)
6	(10) 15 (22)	(13) 20 (28)	(14) 19 (27)
7	(13) 17 (22)	(13) 18 (24)	(15) 21 (28)
8	(14) 18 (23)	(14) 17 (22)	(17) 21 (28)

TABLE 2.11   Rates of Completion for Mazes

The score in the middle of each column shows the completion rate at the 50th percentile. The score in parentheses to the left of the middle shows the completion rate at the 25th percentile. The score in parentheses to the right of the middle shows the completion rate at the 75th percentile. Adapted from AIMSweb.

Grade									
CBM	K	1	2	3	4	5	6	7	8
Letter Name Fluency	1								
Letter Sound Fluency	1	1.2							
Word Reading Fluency		1.5							
Phonics Inventory		1							
Oral Reading Fluency			1	1	.75	.75	.75	.5	.5
Mazes					.25	.25	.25	.25	.25

TABLE 2.12   Average Growth Rates per Week on Various CBMs

Adapted from Good & Kaminski (2003); Gunning (2008); Hosp, Hosp, & Howell (2007); Fuchs & Fuchs (undated).

understand so that they have a clear idea of what is expected of them. You might also list the steps needed to meet the standards. Then create or adapt measures that assess those objectives. For instance, for phonics, you might use the Letter Sound Fluency test if students are at an early level of learning phonics or the Phonics Inventory if students are working with vowel patterns. For recognition of words in isolation, you might use the Word Reading Fluency test or word lists from an IRI. For reading rate, you could use the DIBELS oral fluency passages. For comprehension, you might use the maze passages from AIMSweb, DIBELS DAZE, IRI passages, or DIBELS Oral Reading Fluency passages with retellings or questions added.

The phonics and word-recognition tests can be administered rapidly since they only involve reading lists of words. The oral reading rate can also be assessed quickly since it entails reading a passage for just 1 minute. These measures could be given frequently. However, if given individually, comprehension passages are more time-consuming to administer. Because growth in comprehension is generally slower than growth in skills such as phonics and reading lists of words, comprehension tests might be given just three or four times a year. Other measures might be given monthly or even weekly.

Graph performances so that you can see whether students are on track. Mark where you believe students should be by the end of the year. Then mark where students are now. Draw an aimline from where students are to where it is expected they will be at year's end. The slope of the line gives you a sense of the rate of progress necessary for students to reach the end mark. Monitor students' progress at least three times a year and mark their progress. Monitor more frequently if students are struggling. If students fall below the aimline, provide added instruction and arrange for intervention, if necessary. If students are consistently scoring above the aimline, adjust the program

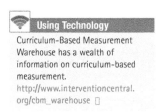

Using Technology

Curriculum-Based Measurement Warehouse has a wealth of information on curriculum-based measurement.
http://www.interventioncentral.org/cbm_warehouse

to make it more challenging. Monitoring progress is one of the most effective steps you can take to help all students reach their full literacy potential. Figure 2.6 shows a first-grader's progress on the Word Reading Fluency indicator. Note how the student's progress accelerated when he was provided intervention in November but was still below the aimline. The goal for the student was 40 words by the end of the year, which the student missed by 5 words. Summer sessions could help Roberto catch up.

Monitoring Progress and Assessing for Learning

Assessing for learning requires monitoring of progress. However, some CBMs don't do much more than provide a general indication of where students are. For instance, if a student has a low oral reading fluency, you need to determine why so that you can provide an effective intervention. If you analyze the student's miscues, you might find that the student is reading slowly because he or she is having difficulty with high-frequency words or with words containing complex vowels and so needs instruction in basic word recognition. Assessing for learning requires information that might not be provided by progress-monitoring assessments. Information from observations, discussions, work samples, and other sources is also required.

Norm-Referenced versus Criterion-Referenced Tests

Norm-Referenced Tests

Many traditional tests provide some sort of comparison. In a **norm-referenced test**, students are compared with a representative sample of others who are the same age or in the same grade. The scores indicate whether students did as well as the average, better than the average, or below the average. The norm group typically includes students from all sections of the country, from urban and nonurban areas, and from a variety of racial or ethnic and socioeconomic groups. The group is chosen to be representative of the nation's total school population. However, norm-referenced tests can result in unfair comparisons. Urban schools, for example, should only be compared with other urban schools.

Because norm-referenced tests yield comparative results that are generally used by school boards, school administrators, and the general public, they provide one source of information to assess the effectiveness of the school program. Classroom teachers can also make use of the data to complement information from quizzes, informal tests, and observations. Reading scores indicate an approximate level of achievement. If a measure of academic aptitude has been administered, results can be examined to see whether students are reading up to their expected or anticipated level of achievement. If they are not, the teacher can explore the problem.

The tests can also be used as a screening device. Very high-scoring students may be candidates for a gifted or enriched reading program. Low-scoring students may benefit from input from the reading or learning disabilities specialist, especially if there is a marked difference between capacity and performance. Subtest scores of individuals can also be analyzed for patterns of strengths and weaknesses. A high-vocabulary, low-comprehension score, for example, is often a sign that a student needs extra instruction in the use of comprehension strategies. A low-vocabulary, high-comprehension score might indicate the need for language development. Occasionally, norm-referenced tests yield surprises. Sometimes children, because of shyness or other factors, hide their talents. Norm-referenced tests occasionally spotlight a student whose abilities have gone unnoticed.

Some school districts have as a goal that all students will be reading on grade level according to the results of a norm-referenced test. This is the same thing as saying that everyone will be at least average. However, norm-referenced tests are created in such a way that half the students in

Norm-referenced tests are those in which students' performance is compared with a norm group, which is a representative sampling of students.

FIGURE 2.6 Progress-Monitoring Chart

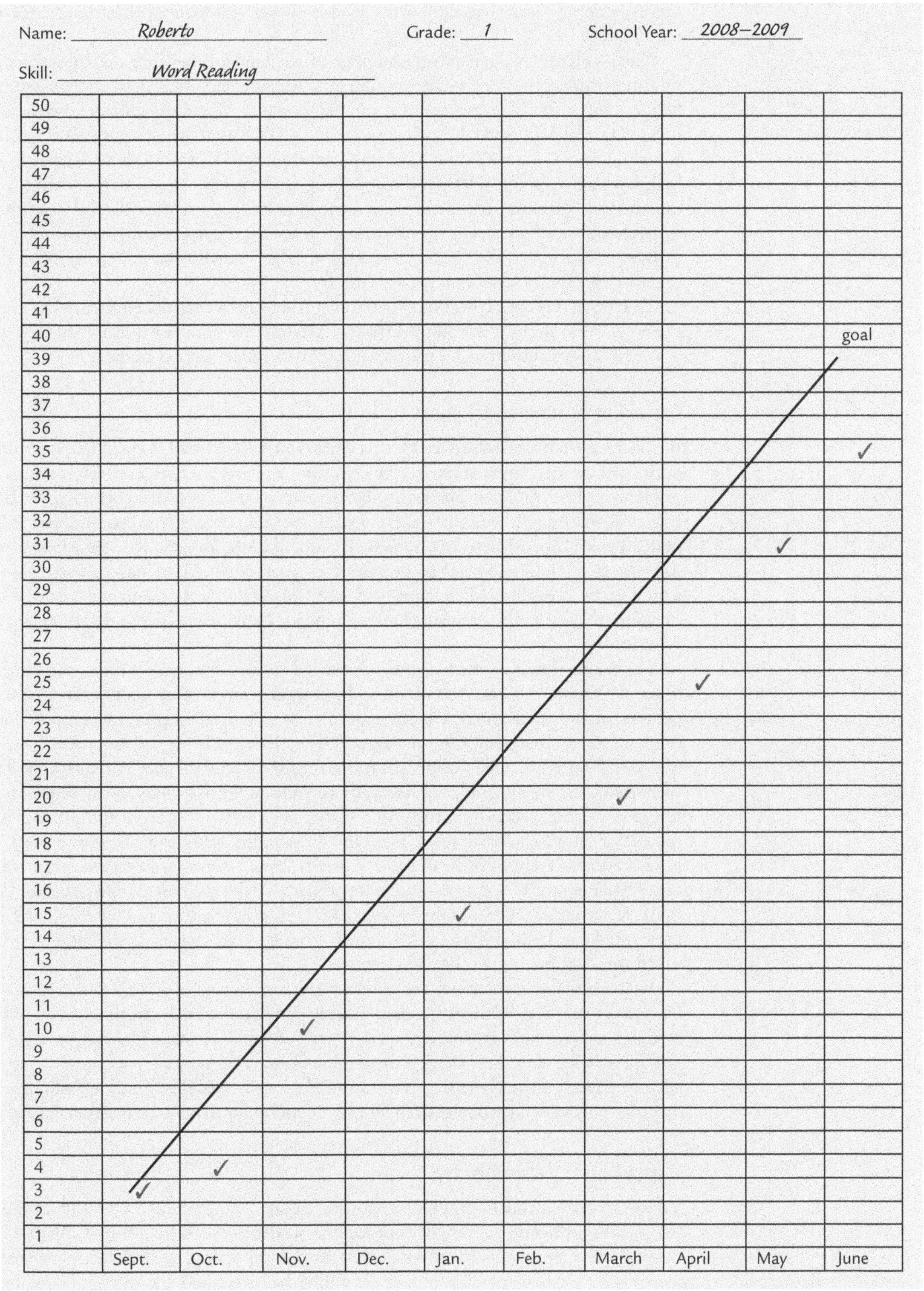

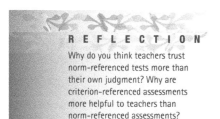

REFLECTION

Why do you think teachers trust norm-referenced tests more than their own judgment? Why are criterion-referenced assessments more helpful to teachers than norm-referenced assessments?

a typical group will score below average. Even if students' scores improve, this won't make the goal achievable. Test publishers periodically renorm their tests so that if scores generally improve, the norms are set higher (Harcourt Educational Measurement, 2000).

Norm-referenced tests have a number of weaknesses. Because their questions are multiple-choice, they don't assess reading the way it is taught or used, and guessing is a factor. They also invite competition and comparison. According to some theorists, the most serious problem with norm-referenced tests is that "they are often considered to be the single or at least the most important determinant of students' achievement" (Salinger, 2001, p. 394). When documenting students' progress, teachers tend to use information garnered from norm-referenced tests, even if they have data gathered through informal methods. It is as though teachers don't trust their own judgments (Johnston & Rogers, 2001). To offset this, teachers need to be more careful and systematic with their classroom assessments.

This book does not recommend administering norm-referenced tests. However, in many school systems, their administration is mandated. If information from these tests is available, you should make use of it along with other sources of data.

Criterion-Referenced Tests

In contrast to a norm-referenced test, a **criterion-referenced test** compares students' performance with some standard, or criterion. For instance, the criterion on a comprehension test might be answering 80 percent of the questions correctly. An IRI is criterion-referenced; a student must have at least 95 percent word recognition and 75 percent comprehension to be on the instructional level, for example. Tests that accompany basal readers also tend to be criterion-referenced. Many have a passing score, which is the criterion. Most state tests and the National Assessment of Educational Progress (NAEP) tests are criterion-referenced. Curriculum-based measures are also criterion-referenced.

The major weakness of criterion-referenced tests is that, all too often, the criterion is set arbitrarily. No one tests it to see whether average students usually answer 80 percent of the items correctly, for example, or whether 80 percent comprehension is adequate in most instances. Sometimes, the criterion is set too high. For instance, the NAEP tests have been criticized for having standards that are unrealistically high. Although U.S. fourth-graders outscored every country but Finland on an international test (Elley, 1992), according to NAEP test results, only 67 percent of fourth-graders read at or above the basic level, and only 33 percent read at or above the proficient level (National Center for Education Statistics, 2011). On a more recent international test, 68 percent of U.S. fourth-graders scored above the median (Mullis, Martin, Gonzalez, & Kennedy, 2003). Only Sweden, the Netherlands, England, and Bulgaria outperformed the United States. U.S. fourth-graders read as well as or better than the fourth-graders from the other 30 countries.

A second major shortcoming of criterion-referenced tests is that all too often they do not assess reading skills and strategies in the way students actually use them. For instance, comprehension might be assessed as in norm-referenced tests, with brief passages and multiple-choice questions. Despite these limitations, criterion-referenced tests are generally more useful to teachers than are norm-referenced tests. They indicate whether students have mastered particular skills and so are useful for making instructional decisions.

Reporting Performance

There are two primary ways of reporting scores: norm-referenced and criterion-referenced. In norm-referenced reporting, a student's performance is compared with that of other students. In criterion-referenced reporting, a student's performance might be described in terms of a standard or expected performance or in terms of the student's goals.

⬜ A **criterion-referenced test** is one in which the student's performance is compared to a criterion, or standard.

Norm-Referenced Reporting Tests and other assessment measures yield a number of possible scores. To interpret results correctly, it is important to know the significance of each score. Here are commonly used types of scores:

- A **raw score** represents the total number of correct answers. It has no meaning until it is changed into a percentile rank or other score.
- A **percentile rank** tells where a student's raw score falls on a scale of 1 to 99. A score at the first percentile means that the student did better than 1 percent of those who took the test. A score at the 50th percentile indicates that the student did better than half of those who took the test. A top score is the 99th percentile. Most norm-referenced test results are reported in percentiles; however, the ranks are not equal units and should not be added, subtracted, divided, or used for subtest comparison.
- The **grade-equivalent score** characterizes a student's performance as being equivalent to that of other students in a particular grade. A grade-equivalent score of 5.2 indicates that the student correctly answered the same number of items as the average fifth-grader in the second month of that grade. Note that the grade-equivalent score does not tell on what level the student is operating; that is, a score of 5.2 does not mean that a student is reading on a fifth-grade level. Grade-equivalent scores are more meaningful when the test students have taken is at the right level and when the score that the students achieve is not more than a year above or a year below the average for that grade. Because grade-equivalent scores are misleading and easily misunderstood, they should be used with great care or not at all.
- **Normal curve equivalents** (NCEs) rank scores on a scale of 1 through 99. The main difference between NCEs and percentile ranks is that NCEs represent equal units and so can be added and subtracted and used for comparing performance on subtests. NCEs can be used, for instance, to compare performance on vocabulary and comprehension subtests.
- **Stanine** is a combination of the words *standard* and *nine*. The stanines 4, 5, and 6 are average points, with 1, 2, and 3 being below average, and 7, 8, and 9 above average. Stanines are useful when making comparisons among the subtests of a norm-referenced test.
- **Scaled scores** are a continuous ranking of scores from the lowest levels of a series of norm-referenced tests—first grade, for example—through the highest levels—high school. They start at 000 and end at 999. They are useful for tracking long-term reading development through the grades. Lexiles, DRP units, and grade equivalents are examples of scaled scores.

Grade equivalents and other scaled scores rise over time. However, percentiles, stanines, and normal curve equivalents may stay the same from year to year. If they do, this means that the student is making average progress in comparison with others. For instance, if a student is at the 35th percentile in third grade and then tests again at the 35th percentile in fourth grade, that means that his or her relative standing is the same; the student continues to do better than 35 percent of the students who took the test. However, if the student moves to a higher percentile, this means that he or she outperformed students who started off with similar scores. If the student scores at the 40th percentile in fourth grade, it means that he or she is moving up in the relative standings. Now the student is doing better than 40 percent of those who took the test.

Criterion-Referenced Reporting Criterion-referenced results are reported in terms of a standard, or criterion. For example, the student answered 80 percent of the

FYI

Percentile ranks are not equal because test scores cluster in the middle so that scores in the middle of the range are closer together than are scores at the end of the range. It is easier to move from the 49th to the 59th percentile than it is to move from the 89th to the 99th.

FYI

Grade-equivalent scores, which have been opposed by the International Reading Association, are relatively valid when pupils are tested on their instructional level and when extrapolations are limited to a year or two beyond the target grade level.

FYI

- For additional information about tests, see the *Eighteenth Mental Measurements Yearbook*, (Spies, Carlson, & (Geisinger, 2010), or *Tests in Print VII* (Murphy, Spies, & Plake, 2006), which lists more than 4,000 tests. You might also consult the Buros Center for Testing, which specializes in test information: http://www.unl.edu/buros

Another source of information is the ERIC site for assessment: http://ericae.net

---

□ A **raw score** is the number of correct answers or points earned on a test.

□ The **percentile rank** is the point on a scale of 1 to 99 that shows what percentage of students obtained an equal or lower score. A percentile rank of 75 means that 75 percent of those who took the test received an equal or lower score.

□ A **grade-equivalent score** indicates the score that the average student at that grade level achieved.

□ A **normal curve equivalent** is the ranking of a score on a scale of 1 through 99.

□ A **stanine** is a point on a 9-point scale, with 5 being average.

□ A **scaled score** is a continuous ranking from 000 to 999 of scores from a series of norm-referenced tests, from the lowest- to the highest-level test. The first-grade test might have the lowest scores; the twelfth-grade test would have the highest.

REFLECTION

What role do rubrics play in assessment? What provision should be made in order to get the most out of rubrics?

comprehension questions correctly. Two types of standards now being used in authentic assessment are the benchmark, which is discussed on pp. 47 and 51, and the rubric, which is a descriptive form of criterion-referenced reporting.

Rubrics   A **rubric** is a written description of what is expected from students in order for them to meet a certain level of performance. It is usually accompanied by samples of several levels of performance. For example, for assessing a piece of writing, the characteristics of four to six levels of performance might be listed. Although rubrics are typically used in the assessment of writing tasks, they can also be used to assess combined reading and writing tasks, portfolios, and creation of Web sites, presentations, and projects. A writing rubric is presented in Table 2.13. A rubric for oral reading fluency was presented in Table 2.8.

In addition to their use as scoring guides, rubrics can be powerful teaching tools (Popham, 2000). Carefully constructed rubrics describe the key tasks that students must complete or the main elements that must be included in order to produce an excellent piece of work. This helps both the teacher and

> ▢ A **rubric** is a written description of the traits or characteristics of standards used to judge a process or product.

TABLE 2.13   Levels of Informational Writing in Primary Grades

	Expanding	Organizing	Elaborating	Expressing	Emerging
Content	Uses a variety of details and examples to develop a topic.	Expands on details by explaining how or why. May address a number of subtopics.	Begins to expand on details by explaining how or why.	Expresses several details related to topic.	Limited topic development. Topic might simply be stated and might be a label that identifies a person, place, or thing, but provides no information beyond a label.
Organization	Uses title, headings, connectives such as *and, also, for example, because,* and, *however* and sequencing to organize information. Has a beginning, middle, and end, but writing may be formulaic. Composes a conclusion that flows from the information provided.	Begins to organize details. Uses repetition of key ideas and connectives, such as *and* and *also* to show relationships among ideas. May use headings and subheadings. Provides a concluding sentence.	Information lacks overall organization. There are no headings or subheadings. Little or no use of connecting words or transitions.	Details follow a list-like structure and are not explained or elaborated upon.	Labels pictures with single words, phrases or sentences.
Writing/ Spelling	Spelling is accurate. May have one or two misspelled words.	Most words are spelled correctly.	Spelling is mostly conventional.	Uses invented and conventional spelling.	May draw, scribble, use random letters, or partial invented spelling.
Language	Uses technical vocabulary, more formal language, and may use some complex sentences.	Begins to use varied sentence patterns. Combines some ideas into compound sentences, but may string clauses together her with a series of *ands.*	Uses simple words and simple sentence patterns.	Uses simple words and brief sentences.	Uses simple words and brief phrases.
Mechanics	Few errors in mechanics. Makes some use of commas and quotation marks.	May have a few errors in capitalization and end punctuation. May use commas and quotation marks.	Increased use of capitalization and end punctuation.	Some use of capitalization and end punctuation.	Limited or lack of correct use of capitalization & punctuation.

Source: Adapted from Donovan, C.A., & Smolkin, L.B. (2011). Supporting informational writing in the elementary grades. *The Reading Teacher, 64,* 406–416. Georgia Department of Education (2000). *Developmental Stages/Scoring Guidelines for Writing.* Atlanta: Author. Resnick, L. B., & Hampton, S. (2009) *Reading and Writing Grade by Grade.* Newark, DE: International Reading Association & Washington, DC: National Center on Education and the Economy. Salahu-Din, D., Persky, H., and Miller, J. (2008). *The Nation's Report Card: Writing 2007*
(NCES 2008–468). National Center for Education Statistics, Institute of Education Sciences, U.S. Department of Education, Washington, D.C.

the student focus on key skills. To be effective, rubrics should contain only three to six evaluative criteria so that students and teachers do not get sidetracked by minor details. More important, each evaluative criterion must encompass a teachable skill. For instance, evaluative criteria for writing a story might call for an exciting plot, believable characters, an interesting setting, and the use of vivid language.

Creating a Rubric   To develop a rubric, first identify the key characteristics or traits of the performance or piece of work to be assessed. For example, for a rubric for a friendly letter, the key traits might include interesting content, chatty style, correct letter format, and correct mechanics. If available, examine finished products to see what their major traits are. Write a definition of each trait. What exactly is meant by "interesting content," "chatty style," "correct letter format," and "correct mechanics"? Develop a scale for the characteristics. It is usually easiest to start with the top performance. If you have examples of students' work, sort them into piles: best, worst, and middle. Look over the best pieces and decide what makes them the best. Look at the poorest and decide where they are deficient. Write a description of the best and poorest performances. Then fill in the middle levels. For the middle levels, divide the remaining papers into two or more piles from best to worst, depending on how many levels you wish to have. However, the more levels you create, the more difficult it becomes to discriminate between adjoining levels. You may find that four suffice. Evaluate your rubric, using the following checklist:

- Does the rubric measure the key traits in the student performance?
- Are differences in the levels clearly specified?
- Does the rubric clearly specify what students are required to do?
- Can the rubric be used as a learning guide by students?
- Can the rubric be used as an instructional guide by the teacher? (Chicago Public Schools, 2000)

Discuss the rubric with students, and invite feedback. Through helping with the creation of the rubric, students form a better idea of what is expected in the task being assessed and also feel more willing to use the rubric because they had a hand in its construction. When fourth-graders used cooperatively created rubrics to assess their writing (Boyle, 1996), their persuasive pieces showed a significant improvement.

Try out the rubric, revise it, and then use it. As you use the rubric with actual pieces of students' work, continue to revise it.

Teachers can align their rubrics with key state, local, or Common Core standards. To ease her students into using rubrics, Ferrell (Skillings & Ferrell, 2000) modeled the process. She also had students create rubrics for everyday activities such as picking the best restaurant. After students caught on to the idea of creating rubrics, she involved them in creating rubrics for basic writing tasks. To keep the rubrics simple, the class had just three levels: best, okay, not so good. Later, the class created rubrics for more complex tasks. Sample rubrics can be found at the following Web sites:

Discovery School Kathy Schrock's Guide for Educators lists sources for sample rubrics and information about rubrics.
http://school.discovery.com/schrockguide/assess.html

Rubistar has a library of rubrics and tools for creating rubrics.
http://rubistar.4teachers.org/

Rubrics for Constructed Responses   Along with rubrics for assessing stories and essays, create rubrics for assessing responses to open-ended questions of the type that your students will be asked to answer, if these are not already available (see Figure 2.7). These could be tests that you make up, tests from the reading program you are using, or state tests. Provide students with practice using the rubrics so that they understand what they are being asked to do. NAEP tests and some state tests supply rubrics and sample (or anchor) answers. Distribute sample answers and rubrics, and have students mark them. Begin with correct answers so that students have some guidance, and then have them assess answers that receive no credit or

FYI

Students should participate in the creation of rubrics. Through helping with the creation of rubrics, students form a clearer idea of what is expected in their writing. In one study, students used a rubric they helped create to assess their own writing. They also took part in peer evaluation sessions in which the rubric was used to judge their writing. As a result of creating and using the rubric, students' writing of persuasive pieces showed a significant improvement (Boyle, 1996).

FIGURE 2.7   Sample
Scoring Rubric

Score	3	2	1	0
Criterion	Names an important lesson. Gives evidence from the story to support answers.	Names an important lesson. Fails to give evidence from the story to support answer.	Names an unimportant lesson.	Does not state a lesson that could be learned from the story. No response.

partial credit. As a shared whole-group activity, compose responses to open-ended questions, and then assess the responses with a rubric. Once students have some sense of how to respond to open-ended questions, have them compose individual responses and check them.

Instructionally Supportive Assessment   Most high-stakes tests assess so many items that they fail to provide information that the teacher can use to plan instruction (Popham, 2004). What is more helpful is classroom assessment that tests a limited number of objectives—about six over the course of a year—and that can be used to plan instruction. To make assessment data instructionally useful, select or create a rubric that will help you and your students note the specific requirements for each objective.

Besides being used to support instruction, monitor students' progress, and identify students who need intervention, assessment data can be used in other essential ways. They can indicate what skills are needed and what skills have been mastered. At one urban public school where I worked as a literacy consultant, periodic assessment revealed the need for a strong program covering syllabic analysis, vocabulary instruction, and higher-level literacy skills—areas that were being neglected. However, it also revealed what didn't need to be taught. Most students had mastered phonological awareness and basic phonics, although teachers continued to teach these skills. The assessment data showed that instructional time could be more profitably spent in other areas.

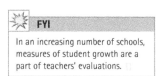

FYI

In an increasing number of schools, measures of student growth are a part of teachers' evaluations.

Measuring Growth

In the past, most states reported performance in terms of what percentage of students met the state's proficiency level. This is a threshold or status measures. Threshold testing might mask growth. Results tell what percentage of students have met a certain standard, but not how much students' scores have changed. For instance, students' scores might be increasing, bringing them closer to meeting the standard, but this is not indicated in the results. Unless growth is measured, schools that have large numbers of struggling students might be misjudged. Many urban schools have below-level achievement and might be classified as low-performing or in need of improvement. However, their students might be making better-than-average gains, but not enough to take them over the threshold. Measures of growth can be used to identify students who aren't making adequate progress and teachers whose classes are not making at least average progress.

Measuring growth also means that you need to make a comparison between where students were at the point of initial assessment and where they are at the end of assessment. You need to compare the same students at the beginning and end of the instructional period, not this year's students with last year's students, as most states do. The problem with this common comparison is that there might be significant differences between this year's students and last year's students.

A growth model fits in with the concept of meeting each student where he or she is and moving him or her upward. In addition to recognizing that there are certain key skills that are necessary for students to become college and career ready, such as being able to read and write effectively, it is also necessary to be aware of students' level of achievement. Additional efforts might be required so that all students, even those who are lagging behind, meet these standards (Tanner, 2010). Schools should be judged not just on the percentage of students who meet the standard, but on how much students improve.

Functional-Level Assessment

Measuring growth requires functional-level assessment. The typical elementary or middle school class will exhibit a wide range of reading ability. Just as students need appropriate levels of materials for instruction, they should have appropriate levels of materials for testing. Most literacy tests cover a limited range. For instance, a general reading test designed for fourth-graders will mostly have selections on a fourth-grade level, a selection or two on a third-grade level, and a few selections beyond the fourth-grade level. A fourth-grader reading on a second-grade level should not be given a fourth-grade reading test. It would be frustrating to the student and would yield misleading results. The student should take a test that includes material on her or his level of reading ability. This might mean giving the student a test designed for the third grade but that includes second-grade material. Similarly, a second-grade-level test would probably not be appropriate for a second-grader reading on a fifth-grade level. It would probably lack a high-enough ceiling and so would underestimate the student's true reading ability. With **functional-level testing**, students are tested at their functional level, which is not necessarily their grade level. Students reading significantly above or below grade level should be given out-of-level tests unless the tests they are taking cover a wide range of levels. As a rule of thumb, if a student answers more than 90 percent of the items on a test correctly, the student should be tested at a more difficult level (Touchstone Applied Science Associates, 2006). If a student answers less than 10 percent of the items correctly, she or he should be tested at an easier level. Giving students a test at the wrong level results in erroneous, invalid information. This is true whether a norm-referenced, criterion-referenced, or other type of assessment is being used. If teachers are being assessed on the basis of the progress that their students make, it is absolutely essential that accurate beginning and ending points be established. This requires functional-level assessment. For its assessments, Scholastic makes the following comments and suggestion:

> Traditional standardized grade-level reading tests are designed to measure grade-level standards. The scores' accuracy of these tests is not equal across all levels of ability. The further away from grade-level the student performs, the greater the degree of inaccuracy in the student's score. As a result, test scores of low- and high-ability students might not be accurate enough to be used instructionally or to monitor instructional growth from one year to the next. . . . In the case of Scholastic Reading Inventory (SRI), the accuracy of the test score can be substantially increased if the test is targeted by prior reading ability and grade level instead of by grade level only. (Scholastic Overview, n.d.)

To get a quick estimate of students' reading levels, you can use either your professional judgment or a test such as the GRADE Reading-Level Indicator and Spanish Companion (Pearson Assessments), a brief assessment designed to estimate the reading levels of students in grades 4 through 12. Although designed for students in grade 4 and above, the GRADE Locator Test has items on beginning reading levels as well as advanced reading levels. The test also has a Spanish component that provides an estimate of students' ability to read Spanish. Directions are provided in Spanish but

REFLECTION

How would you go about implementing functional-level testing? Why do you think most assessments incorporate a grade level rather than a functional-level approach? For which students would functional-level testing be especially effective?

⬥ **Functional-level testing** is the practice of assigning students to a test level on the basis of their reading ability rather than their grade level.

FYI

In some assessments, students are given materials on grade level to read and respond to. Because as many as one child in four or more will be reading significantly below grade level (Gunning, 1982), this practice is unfair to underachieving youngsters. Lower-achieving readers should be provided with at least some items that are on their instructional level. Test publishers support the concept of functional-level testing and offer guidelines for out-of-level assessment. A general practice is to use the teacher's estimate or a quick locator test provided by the publisher to obtain a rough estimate of the child's reading level and to test the child on that level.

may also be pantomimed. Florida, Massachusetts, and Oregon have locator tests for ELL. The Oregon Department of Education (2008) comments, "Using the locator items improves both the test experience for each student and the precision of the assessment" (p. B1). As the Florida Department of Education (2008) advises,

Administration of the Reading and Writing test at the appropriate functional level is important because it:

• Provides reliable results for all ELLs.
• Avoids student frustration during testing since administering the most appropriate level of Reading and Writing ensures that each student is given only test items that reflect his or her skill level (p. 10).

These benefits should be available to all students. Florida, Oregon, and Massachusetts have valuable suggestions for function level testing, suggestions that could be adapted to most tests.

Universal Design of Assessments   The idea behind universal design of assessments is to design assessments to make them accessible to as many students as possible and "to ensure that each student has a comparable opportunity to demonstrate achievement on the standards being tested" (Abedi, Leon, Kao, Bayley, Ewers, Herman, & Mundhenk, 2010, p. 2). Steps can be taken to make tests more accessible without changing the difficulty level of the test passages. These include making directions more explicit, breaking lengthy passages into shorter portions, allowing students to choose from passages of equivalent difficulty (Thurlow, Laitusis, Dillon, Cook, Moen, Abedi, & O'Brien., 2009) and changing the format of the test such as using a larger font size and putting fewer words on a page (Abedi et al., 2010). For instance, in a math test the directions might be changed from "A certain reference file contains approximately . . ." to, "Mack's company sold . . ." (Abedi, 2009). The simplified version is easier to read and understand but does not change the skill being assessed (Wolf, Herman, Dietel, 2010). Although these steps have the potential to increase the accessibility of assessment, they do not adequately address the needs of students reading significantly below grade level. Although the questions might be more understandable and the format more reader friendly, the grade level test passage would still have a high proportion of words that below-level readers would be unable to decode and/or whose meanings would be unfamiliar. One solution, would be to include some below-level passages in the assessment so that students reading below grade level would have the opportunity to demonstrate their reading skill or to use functional level or adaptive testing.

Adaptive Tests

Adaptive tests are usually taken on a computer. Based on the student's responses, the computer adapts to the student's level. If a student is getting all the questions correct, the computer presents higher-level questions. If the student is getting all or most of the items wrong, the computer switches to lower-level questions. Currently, there are two widely used adaptive tests: Measures of Academic Progress (MAP) and STAR. MAP tests consist of sentences or brief paragraphs and have a multiple-choice format. They can be given in grades 2 through 10 and four times a year to monitor progress. MAP tests, which are used as Idaho's high-stakes tests, can also be used to indicate students' reading level. STAR uses multiple choice and modified cloze.

A key step in assessing students is deciding on the level of material that will be used. Screening or benchmark tests are typically administered on grade level. If possible, select screening instruments that have items that are below level as well as on level so that all students will be able to respond. Progress-monitoring assessments should be on the students' reading levels. Struggling readers, by definition, are typically reading below grade level. If text that is too difficult is used, the assessment will probably not do a very good job of measuring growth or the effectiveness of the intervention. "As selections of text are made, however, one must be aware that using grade-appropriate text is not a simple solution to the question. Such text is certain to be very difficult for students with learning disabilities and that text might not be particularly sensitive to growth and intervention effects" (Deno, Fuchs, Marston, & Shin, 2001, p. 520).

Other Methods of Assessment

Performance Assessment

Performance assessment is just what its name suggests. Instead of showing what they know by answering multiple-choice questions or writing a brief response, students demonstrate knowledge through their performance (Popham, 2000). Students, after consulting several sources on a controversial topic, might write a persuasive essay or letter to the editor or they might compose an informational booklet for younger students. As Darling-Hammond and Pecheone (2010) point out, performance assessments provide opportunities for students to demonstrate "the ability to plan an inquiry and organize their time, develop self-discipline and perseverance as well as intellectual discipline, define problems and determine strategies for how to pursue answers, organize and display data, evaluate findings, draw conclusions, and express and defend their ideas according to standards of evidence" (p. 32).

Performance tasks potentially assess knowledge and skills in a more realistic way at the application level. Students who will be assessed on a performance measure need to be more active learners and must be able to apply knowledge, not merely recite facts. Despite its obvious value, performance assessment does have some limitations. Performance assessment can be more expensive and more time-consuming. However, performance assessments are expected to become part of the Common Core State Standards assessment.

Retelling

Retelling has the potential to supply more information about a student's comprehension than simply asking questions does. In a **retelling**, a student is asked to do what the name suggests: The student may retell a selection that has been read to her or him or one that the student has read independently. The student may do this orally or in writing. In addition to showing what the reader comprehended, retelling shows what she or he added to and inferred from the text (Irwin & Mitchell, 1983). Free from the influence of probes or questions, retelling demonstrates the student's construction of text and provides insight into her or his language and thought processes. It shows how the student organizes and shapes a response. The teacher can also assess the quality of language used by the student in the retelling. However, since retelling requires remembering the whole text, it places greater demands on memory and also communication skills (Caldwell & Leslie, 2010). There may also be cultural variation. Different cultural groups might emphasize different elements of a story. A cultural group might, for instance, emphasize setting and omit the actions in a story. As Leslie and Caldwell (2011), explain "Students who encounter a story structure different from what is familiar to them may retell the story according to their cultural format" (p. 9).

In addition, students typically do better with narrative retellings than they do with expository retellings. On the QRI 5 average narrative retellings ranged from 17 to 41 percent whereas average retellings for expository text ranged from 13 to 31 percent. The low scores on retellings indicate that the average student's ability to retell a story is limited. Correlations between

□ **Retelling** is the process of summarizing or describing a story that one has read. The purpose of retelling is to assess comprehension.

FYI

• Being less time-consuming, informal retellings are more practical for the classroom teacher. Of course, shy children may not perform up to their ability.

• Because the person assessing them obviously knows the story, students might provide a contextualized retelling. They may not give the characters' names, referring to them as *he* or *she* because they assume that the examiner is familiar with the characters. Knowing that the examiner is familiar with the story, they might omit or abbreviate crucial details (Benson & Cummins, 2000). When using a retelling as an assessment, stress that the students should pretend that they are telling the story to someone who has not read it or heard it.

Assessing for Learning

Students score higher on narrative (17 to 41 percent) passages than on expoitory passages (13 to 33 percent; Leslie & Calwell, 2011).

FIGURE 2.8 Evaluation of an Oral Retelling

retellings and question answering was relatively low (Leslie & Caldwell, 2011). This suggests that if retellings are used to assess comprehension, they need to be accompanied by questions. Otherwise, students' comprehension ability might be greatly underestimated.

To administer a retelling, explain to the student what she or he is supposed to do: Read a selection orally or silently or listen to one read aloud. It may be a narrative or expository piece. Tell the student that she or he will be asked to retell the story in her or his own words. Use neutral phrasing, such as "Tell me about the story that you read." For a young child, say, "Pretend I haven't read the story. Tell it to me in your own words." A shy younger child can use props—such as a puppet—to facilitate the retelling. If a student stops before retelling the whole selection, encourage her or him to continue or elaborate. When the student is finished, ask questions about any key elements that were not included in the retelling.

Evaluating Retellings   As the student retells the selection, record it and/or jot down brief notes on the major events or ideas in the order in which the child relates them. Note any recalls that were not spontaneous but were elicited by your questions. Tape recording provides a full and accurate rendition of the retelling but is time-consuming.

Retellings can be scored numerically by giving students credit for each major unit that they retell. However, this is a laborious process. Far less time-consuming, but still useful, is noting the major units in the retelling in one column, comments about it in a second column, and a summary and recommendations in a third. Because the main purpose of the retelling is to gain insight into students' reading processes, you should draw inferences about students' overall understanding of the selection and their ability to use strategies to construct the meaning of the piece. A sample evaluation of a retelling is presented in Figure 2.8.

Name of student: _Jamie S._

	Retelling	Comments	Summary and recommendations
Elves and the shoemaker	Shoemaker said had only one piece of leather left. Elves made shoes.	Drew inference. Started with story problem.	Good grasp of story.
	Man in hat came in. Woman came in. Many people bought shoes.	Told story in sequence.	Used structure of story to retell it.
	Shoemaker and wife waited up to see elves.		Didn't go beyond story to suggest why elves started or stopped helping.
	Elves had ragged clothes. Wife made new clothes.	Used picture to get information about elves. Misinterpreted passage.	
	Elves thought new clothes looked funny. Elves said would no longer be cobras. Never came back.	Missed _cobblers_.	Failed to use context to help with _cobblers_. Good average performance. Work on context and drawing conclusions.

Written Retellings   Written retellings allow the teacher to assess the class as a group. Using holistic scoring, the teacher can also assess the quality of the responses. It is important to keep in mind that, whether oral or written, the mode of expression will affect the information students convey. Students may have good knowledge of a selection but find it difficult to express their ideas orally and/or in writing. To obtain a better picture of that knowledge, the teacher might have a class discussion after students have completed their written retellings and compare impressions garnered from the discussion with those from the written versions.

Structured Written Retellings   In a structured written retelling, the teacher might ask students to read a whole selection and write answers to a series of broad questions. The questions are constructed to assess students' ability to understand major aspects of the text, such as characters, plot, and setting. The questions can also be framed to provide some insight into the strategies students are using. They are scored and analyzed by the teacher.

Think-Aloud Protocols

Think-alouds are used to show the thought processes students use as they attempt to construct meaning. During a think-aloud, the reader explains his or her thought processes while reading a text. These explanations might come after each sentence, at the end of each paragraph, or at the end of the whole selection. Students' thoughts might be expressed as "news bulletins or play-by-play accounts" of what students do mentally as they read (Brown & Lytle, 1988, p. 96).

Informal Think-Alouds   Whereas formal think-aloud procedures might be too time-consuming, informal think-alouds can be incorporated into individual and small-group reading conferences and classroom activities. For example, the teacher might simply ask students to share their thoughts on a difficult passage or question, or to tell what strategies they used. Think-aloud questions can include the following:

- Tell me how you figured out that hard word.
- Tell me how you got the answer to that question.
- What were you thinking about when you read that selection?
- Pretend that you are an announcer at a sports game. Tell me play by play what was going on in your mind as you read that sentence (or paragraph) (Brown & Lytle, 1988).
- What do you think will happen next in the selection? What makes you think that?
- How did you feel when you read that passage? What thoughts or pictures were going through your mind?

Think-alouds may also be expressed in writing. In their learning logs, students can note the difficulties they encountered in hard passages and describe the processes they used to comprehend the selections. In follow-up class discussions, they can compare their thought processes and strategies with those of other students (Brown & Lytle, 1988). A simple way for students to keep track of perplexing passages is to record comprehension problems on sticky notes and place them next to the passages.

Mystery Passages

Mystery Passages can be administered as an individual or group think-aloud. Mystery Passages are brief informational selections that have been inverted so that the main idea or topic is not revealed until the last segment has been read. Students read the Mystery Passages in segments and after each segment make a prediction as to what the paragraph is about. A Mystery Passage should be

 FYI

As an alternative to a strictly written response, you might invite students to use whatever form they want to retell a selection: semantic map or web, story map, outline, flowchart, diagram, or other graphic organizer. Students, especially those in the early grades, might also respond by drawing an illustration of the story.

R E F L E C T I O N

In addition to tests, what are some other useful sources of information about students' literacy development? Why do you think most experts recommend obtaining information from multiple assessments? What additional sources of information might you use? Why?

 FYI

- The Qualitative Reading Inventory–5 includes provision for think-alouds for grades 6 and beyond.
- Leslie and Caldwell (2006) recommend that you model the think-aloud process before asking students to engage in it. Read a passage or two and report on what is going on in your mind as you read.

 FYI

Having students think aloud as they read is an excellent way to gain insight into their thought processes so that needed guidance can be provided.

 FYI

Mystery Passages are an excellent source of information for determining students' comprehension needs.

Think-alouds are procedures in which students are asked to describe the processes they are using as they engage in reading or another cognitive activity.

on the student's instructional level and should be about a familiar topic. Otherwise, the student will not have the background knowledge needed to make predictions. For example, if a student has no knowledge of polar bears, a polar bear passage would not be appropriate.

Administering a Mystery Passage as a Diagnostic Instrument

In preparation for reading a Mystery Passage, students are told that they will be reading an article in parts and that after each part is read, they are to try to guess what the mystery animal is. After each part is read, the student is asked: "What do you think the mystery animal is?" The student is then asked to explain the reasoning for his or her response: "What makes you think that?" After the student has completed reading all the separate segments, the student is asked to reread the passage and then retell the entire selection. The student's responses are analyzed in light of the following questions:

- How well was the reader able to hypothesize the identity of the animal?
- How well did the reader support her or his hypotheses with reasons, inferences, or predictions?
- At what point did the reader guess the identity of the animal?
- What information from the text did the reader use?
- Did the reader integrate information from the current passage with information from previously read passages? Were clues used in additive fashion?
- Were the reader's inferences and predictions logical?
- How did the reader use her or his background knowledge?
- How well was the reader able to identify key information in the passage?
- What strategies did the reader use?
- How did the reader handle unfamiliar words or puzzling portions of the text? (Wade, 1990; Gunning, 2010)

Note in particular how much background knowledge students have and how well they make use of it. Note also how well students integrate information from succeeding segments and how logical their reasoning processes are.

Mystery Passages can be administered individually. Students' responses are recorded and then analyzed. Mystery Passages can also be administered to a group. In a group administration, ask the students to record their responses. After students have completed recording their responses, discuss them. This gives students the opportunity to expand on their responses. Give students one clue segment at a time. Otherwise, they may read down the page and locate the identity of the mystery animal.

Mystery Animal

- It is a very large animal. When fully grown, it might weigh up to 1,500 pounds or even more.
  My prediction: _____
  Reason(s) for my prediction:

  _____

  _____

- It is a powerful swimmer. It can swim for 10 hours or more.
  My prediction: _____
  Reason(s) for my prediction:

  _____

  _____

- It is a fast swimmer. It can swim 6 miles in an hour's time.
  My prediction: _____
  Reason(s) for my prediction:
  _____
  _____

- It doesn't mind the cold. It swims in icy water and sometimes floats on large sheets of ice.
  My prediction: _____
  Reason(s) for my prediction:
  _____
  _____

- It has a built-in life jacket. It has two coats of hair. The inner coat is made of fine white hair and keeps it warm. The outer coat is made up of longer hairs. These hairs are hollow. The hollow hairs are like tiny life jackets or tubes.
  My prediction: _____
  Reason(s) for my prediction:
  _____
  _____

- The two coats of hair help keep the polar bear floating on top of the water.
  What were the main things that you learned about the mystery animal?
  _____
  _____
  _____
  _____

Analyzing Students' Performance on Mystery Passages   Students to whom the think-aloud Mystery Passage was administered fell into five main categories.

Good Comprehenders: Use information from text and background knowledge to generate and support their hypotheses. They are flexible and change their hypotheses when this is called for by new information in the text.

Non-Risk-Takers: Stick closely to the text and are reluctant to offer a hypothesis. They fail to make adequate use of background knowledge. Nearly one in five students was a non-risk-taker. Most were younger readers or struggling readers.

Nonintegrators: Fail to put together information from various segments of the text. They might pose a new hypothesis based on the current segment of text without regard to previously read segments.

Schema Imposers: Hold onto their first hypothesis. The information in succeeding passages is changed to fit the readers' schema. About one in 10 students is a schema imposer. Schema imposers might overrely on background knowledge because of the difficulty they have processing the text.

Storytellers: Rely heavily on background knowledge to create a plausible scenario that might have little to do with the text. As with schema imposers, they may have difficulty processing the text and find it easier to create their own meaning rather than to construct meaning from the text. About one student in 12 is a storyteller (Wade, 1990; Gunning, 2010).

 Using Technology

Handheld computers can be used to record observational and other assessment data and generate reports. ☐

FYI

• Teachers may resist keeping anecdotal records because they believe they will remember the important things that the student does. Memories are fallible. Teachers may remember only the good things or not so good things that a student does, and thus fail to obtain a balanced view. For additional suggestions for taking and using anecdotal records, see the article by Boyd-Batstone (2004) and extensive coverage provided by Tierney & Readence (2005).

Observation

Teachers learn about children "by watching how they learn" (Goodman, 1985, p. 9). As "kidwatchers," teachers are better able to supply the necessary support or ask the kinds of questions that help students build on their evolving knowledge.

Opportunities for Observations   Observations can be made any time students are involved in reading and writing. Some especially fruitful opportunities for observation include shared reading (What emergent literacy behaviors are students evidencing?), reading and writing conferences (What are the students' strengths and weaknesses in these areas? What is their level of development? How might their progress in these areas be characterized?), and sustained silent reading (Do students enjoy reading? Are they able to select appropriate materials? What kinds of materials do they like to read?). Other valuable observation opportunities include author's circle, literature circle, and sharing periods in general (Australian Ministry of Education, 1990).

Teachers using a program known as Bookshop (Mondo) structure their observations. First, the teachers list from one to three focus areas for a lesson. Then they note whether students in the reading group master the focus area(s) or require added instruction. Each student in the group is listed, as shown in Figure 2.9.

Anecdotal Records

An **anecdotal record** is a field note or description of a significant bit of student behavior. It is an observational technique long used by both anthropologists and teachers. Almost any observation that can shed light on a student's literacy endeavors is a suitable entry for an anecdotal record, including notes on strategies, miscues, interests, interactions with others, and work habits (Rhodes, 1990). The anecdotal record should be "recordings of what the child said or did—not interpretations" (Bush & Huebner, 1979, p. 355). Interpretation comes later and is based on several records and other sources of information. It is important to keep in mind that when recording observations of strategy use, the way in which strategies are used may vary according to the nature of

> ◻ An **anecdotal record** is the recording of the description of a significant incident of student behavior; interpretation of the observation comes later.

FIGURE 2.9   Group Observation Sheet

Focuses	Alison	Matt	Stacey	Jesse	Emma
Uses headings to hypothesize main idea					
Locates supporting details					
Summarizes main idea and key details					

Key: S—satisfactory; N—needs additional instruction

Notes for future instruction:_____

_____

_____

the task—the type of story being read, its relative difficulty, and the purpose for reading it. Therefore, it would be helpful to record several observations before coming to a conclusion (Tierney and Readence, and Dishner, 2005). In going over anecdotal records, the teacher should ask what this information reveals about the student and how it can be used to plan her or his instructional program.

To keep track of observations and anecdotal records, you might keep a notebook that has a separate section for each student. Or you might use a handheld computer to record observations, which can then be downloaded into a database, classroom management system, or assessment management software, such as Learner Profile (Sunburst), which allows you to record and organize observations and other data in terms of standards or objectives. Sum up the anecdotal records periodically, and decide on the steps needed to assist each student (Boyd-Batstone, 2004). Observe five or six students a day. Have one sheet for each student.

By examining anecdotal records and other sources of information teachers can plan instruction that matches students' needs.

Ratings

A structured and efficient way to collect data is through the use of **ratings**. Ratings generally indicate the "degree to which the child possesses a given trait or skill" (Bush & Huebner, 1979, p. 353). The three kinds of ratings are checklists, questionnaires, and interviews.

Checklists   Checklists can use a present-absent scale (a student either has the trait or does not have it) or one that shows degrees of involvement. The present-absent scale might be used for traits for which there is no degree of possession, such as knowing one's home address and telephone number. The degree scale is appropriate for traits that vary in the extent to which they are manifested, such as joining in class discussions. Figure 2.10 shows a sample observation checklist designed to assess voluntary reading

 Ratings are an estimation of the degree to which a student possesses a given skill or trait.

FIGURE 2.10   Observation Checklist for Voluntary Reading

	Never	Seldom	Occasionally	Frequently
Name of student: _____ Date: _____				
Reads during free time	____	____	____	____
Visits the library	____	____	____	____
Reads books on a variety of topics	____	____	____	____
Recommends books to others in the class	____	____	____	____
Talks with others about books	____	____	____	____
Checks out books from the library	____	____	____	____

Exemplary Teaching
Ongoing Assessment

To make her instruction as fruitful as possible, Pat Loden, a first-grade teacher, bases it on ongoing assessment of students (Morrow & Asbury, 2001). Each day, she focuses on two students to assess. During the day, she carefully observes these students and records her observations. She keeps running records of their reading, assesses their story retellings, and notes their use of reading strategies. She also has a conference with them and goes over their reading logs. In their reading logs, they record titles and authors of books read and their reading goals for the week. During whole-class activities, Loden makes sure to direct questions to them and notes their responses. She also observes the two students as they work independently. She keeps a file on each student and uses the files when planning instruction, when making decisions about placing students in guided reading groups, and before holding conferences with students. Loden also keeps records of conferences she holds during writing workshop. During the conferences, she asks questions that help reveal students' thought processes as they write and the strategies they use. Emphasis throughout the assessment is on obtaining a deeper understanding of where students are and what processes and strategies they are using so that individual and group instructional activities can be planned to further foster their development.

Questionnaires

Questionnaires can provide information about reading interests, study habits, strategy use, and other areas in reading and writing. They can be forced-choice like ERAS or open-ended and requiring a written response. Questionnaires assessing study habits and skills might cover such topics as how students go about studying for a test, where they study, and how much time they spend doing homework each night.

A good example of a reading attitude questionnaire is the Elementary Reading Attitude Survey (ERAS; McKenna & Kerr, 1990). It includes twenty items designed to measure how students feel about recreational and school reading. ERAS can be read to younger, less-skilled readers; older, more-skilled students can read it themselves. The questionnaire addresses such areas as how children feel when they read a book on a rainy Saturday and how they feel about reading in school. Students respond by circling one of four illustrations of the cartoon cat Garfield, which range from very happy to very sad. Another questionnaire that might be used is the Reading Survey section of the Motivation to Read Profile (MRP), which can be found in the March 1996 issue of *The Reading Teacher*. The survey probes two aspects of reading motivation: self-concept as a reader and value of reading. For older students, administer the Adolescent Motivation to Reading Profile (Pitcher et al., 2007). The Adolescent MRP includes two parts. The first is a written questionnaire, which can be administered to groups. The second is a follow-up interview that is given individually. The questionnaire portion is designed to reveal students' attitudes about reading and common classroom literacy practices. The conversational interview probes the kinds of books the student likes to read, how reading material is chosen, and the kinds of literacy activities in which the student engages, and the kinds of activities that might motivate the student to read.

> **FYI**
>
> ERAS has not been copyrighted and was presented, ready to duplicate, in the May 1990 issue of *The Reading Teacher*.

Interviews **Interviews** are simply oral questionnaires. Their advantage is that the teacher can probe a student's replies, rephrase questions, and encourage extended answers, thereby obtaining a wide range of information. An interview can focus on such topics as a student's likes and dislikes about a reading

▢ A **questionnaire** is an instrument in which a subject is asked to respond to a series of questions on some topic.

▢ An **interview** is the process of asking a subject a series of questions on a topic.

group, preferences with respect to reading materials, and reasons for these attitudes. A good example of an interview is the Conversational Interview section of the Motivation to Read Profile (Gambrell, Codling, & Palmer, 1996). The Conversational Interview, which complements the Reading Survey, consists of a series of questions about a student's reading interests and habits and possible influences on those habits.

One kind of interview, the process interview, provides insight about the strategies students are using and also helps students become aware of their processes (Jett-Simpson, 1990). The process interview is best conducted informally on a one-to-one basis, but if time is limited, you might ask for written responses to your questions or hold sessions with small groups. Possible process interview questions include the following ones, which are adapted from Jett-Simpson (1990). Only one or two of these questions should be asked at one sitting.

1. If a young child asked you how to read, what would you tell him or her to do?
2. When you come to a word you don't know, what do you do?
3. How do you choose something to read?
4. How do you get ready for reading?
5. Where do you read or study at home?
6. When a paragraph is confusing, what do you do?
7. How do you check your reading?
8. What do you do to help you remember what you've read?

Conferences

Like interviews, conferences can be an excellent source of assessment information. During writing conferences, you might ask such questions as these: "What do you like best about writing? What kind of writing do you like to do? What is easy for you when you are writing? What is hard for you? What are some things that you might do to become an even better writer than you are now? What do you like best about reading? Do you have any favorite authors? Who are they? What is easy for you in reading? What is hard for you? What might you do to become a better reader?"

Checklists, questionnaires, interviews, and conferences have a common weakness. Their usefulness depends on students' ability and willingness to supply accurate information. Students may give answers that they think the teacher wants to hear. Information gathered from these sources, therefore, should be verified with other data.

In this era of mandated high-stakes assessment, informal measures are more important than ever. High-stakes tests tend to narrow the curriculum and lead to teaching to the test. What's more, they generally fail to yield information that is useful to teachers. Using observation, think-alouds, samples of students' work, and other informal measures can broaden the curriculum and yield useful information for teachers.

Basal Reader/Anthology Assessment Devices

Today's basal readers and literature anthologies offer a variety of assessment devices. One especially valuable assessment device is the theme-level test or unit test. These tests assess the strategies and skills taught in a theme or unit. Presenting open-ended as well as multiple-choice items, theme-level or unit tests provide an excellent opportunity to assess students' ability to cope with high-stakes tests. In a sense, there is a bit of a disconnection between daily and unit assessment. Students demonstrate a skill taught during a unit or theme primarily through discussion with the whole class or in small groups. However, the skill is assessed through open-ended questions. Students might do well when answering such questions orally, but have difficulty getting their thoughts down on paper. In discussion, you can provide prompts and ask additional questions to draw out students' responses. However, on written assessments, students are not given these aids. As with any other skill, students need to be taught how to deal with open-ended questions, especially if they have not previously been exposed to such questions.

 Using Technology

The National Center for Research on Evaluation, Standards, and Student Testing provides information on assessment:
http://www.cse.ucla.edu
The National Center on Educational Outcomes provides information on assessing students who have disabilities:
http://education.umn.edu/nceo ⬚

FIGURE 2.11   Student's Self-Report Checklist on Strategies for Learning from Text

	Usually	Often	Sometimes	Never
Before reading, do I				
1. Read the title, introductory paragraph, headings, and summary?	___	___	___	___
2. Look at photos, maps, charts, and graphs?	___	___	___	___
3. Think about what I know about the topic?	___	___	___	___
4. Predict what the text will be about or make up questions that the text might answer?	___	___	___	___
During reading, do I				
5. Read to answer questions that the teacher or I have made up?	___	___	___	___
6. Stop after each section and try to answer my questions?	___	___	___	___
7. Use headings, maps, charts, and graphs to help me understand the text?	___	___	___	___
8. Try to make pictures in my mind as I read?	___	___	___	___
9. Reread a sentence or get help if I don't understand what I am reading?	___	___	___	___
10. Use context or the glossary if I don't understand what I am reading?	___	___	___	___
After reading, do I				
11. Review the section to make sure that I know the most important information?	___	___	___	___
12. Try to organize the information in the text by creating a map, chart, time line, or summary?	___	___	___	___

 ## Evaluating Writing

Students' writing can be evaluated by holistic scoring, analytic scoring, or a combination of the two.

Holistic Scoring

What captures the essence of a piece of writing—its style, its theme, its development, its adherence to conventions, its originality? The answer is all of these elements and more. Because of the way the parts of the piece work together, it must be viewed as a whole. In **holistic scoring**, instead of noting specific strengths and weaknesses, a teacher evaluates a composition in terms of a limited number of general criteria. The criteria are used "only as a general guide . . . in reaching a holistic judgment" (Cooper & Odell, 1977, p. 4). The teacher does not stop to check the piece to see whether it meets each of the criteria but simply forms a general impression. The teacher can score a piece according to the presence or absence of key elements. There may be a scoring guide, which can be a checklist or a rubric. (A holistic scoring guide in the form of a rubric is shown in Table 2.14). The teacher should also use anchor pieces along with the rubric to assess compositions. Anchor pieces, which may be drawn from the work of past classes or from the compositions that are currently being assessed, are writing samples that provide examples of

Holistic scoring is a process for sorting or ranking students' written pieces on the basis of an overall impression of each piece. Sample pieces (anchors) or a description of standards (rubric) for rating the pieces might be used as guides.

TABLE 2.14   Rubric for Writing to Convey Experience, Real or Imagined

	Skillful	Sufficient	Developing	Needs Support
Re-creation of Experience	Effectively conveys experience. Uses well chosen examples, sensory details, and narrative techniques.	Conveys experience. Uses examples, sensory details, and narrative techniques, but some need more development.	Conveys elements of experience. Examples, sensory details, and narrative techniques are not sufficiently developed.	Details or examples are brief and undeveloped, or not relevant. Little or no use of narrative techniques.
Organization	Ideas are clearly focused on the topic. Logical progression of ideas. Transitions convey relationships.	Ideas are usually focused on the topic. Has an organizational structure. Elements are logically grouped.	Most ideas are focused on the topic. Uses a simple organizational structure.	Shows attempt to organize thoughts by grouping ideas, but groupings are illogical. Some ideas may not be focused on topic.
Sentence Structure	Sentence structure is well controlled and varied.	Sentence structure is adequately controlled and somewhat varied.	Sentence structure is usually correct but shows little variety.	Sentence structure is often incorrect. Little, if any, sentence variety.
Word Choice	Word choice is specific and precise.	Word choice is specific and adequate.	Word choice is not always clear or adequate.	Word choice is not adequate and rarely specific.
Mechanics	May be a few minor errors in mechanics.	Some distracting errors, but meaning is clear.	Some errors that may impede understanding.	Frequent errors that often impede understanding.

Source: Adapted from National Assessment Governing Board. (2010). *Writing Framework for the 2011 National Assessment of Educational Progress.* Washington, DC: Author and National Governors Association Center for Best Practices and Council of Chief State School Officers (2010). *Writing standards K–5, Common Core State Standards for English Language Arts & Literacy in History, Social Studies, Science, and Technical Subjects.*

deficient, fair, good, and superior pieces. The teacher decides which of the anchor pieces a student's composition most closely resembles.

Before scoring the pieces, the teacher should quickly read them all to get a sense of how well the class did overall. This prevents setting criteria that are too high or too low. After sorting the papers into four groups—beginning, developing, proficient, and advanced—the teacher rereads each work more carefully before confirming its placement. If possible, a second teacher should also evaluate the papers. This is especially important if the works are to be graded.

Analytic Scoring

Analytic scoring involves analyzing pieces and noting specific strengths and weaknesses. It requires the teacher to create a set of specific scoring criteria. (An analytic scoring guide for a friendly letter is presented in Figure 2.12.) Instead of overwhelming students with corrections, it is best to decide on a limited number of key features, such as those that have been emphasized for a particular writing activity. Spandel and Stiggins (1997) suggest the following six characteristics: ideas, organization, voice, word choice, sentence fluency, and conventions. Although more time-consuming than holistic scoring, analytic scoring allows the teacher to make constructive suggestions about students' writing.

Using a Combination of Techniques

In some cases, a combination of holistic and analytic scoring works best. Holistic scoring guards against the teacher's becoming overly caught up in mechanics or stylistics and neglecting the substance of the piece. Analytic scoring provides students with necessary direction for improving their work and becoming more proficient writers. Whichever approach is used,

> **Assessing for Learning**
>
> When students know why they are being assessed and when you share results with them and use results to plan reachable goals, they become more engaged in the learning process. Portfolio conferences are particularly effective for engaging students, especially when they can compare current with past work samples and see progress (Simmons, 1990). □

> □ **Analytic scoring** is a process for scoring that uses a description of major features to be considered when assessing a written piece.

FIGURE 2.12   Analytic
Scoring Guide for a Friendly
Letter

	Beginning	Developing	Proficient	Advanced
Content				
Has a natural but interesting beginning.	___	___	___	___
Includes several topics of interest.	___	___	___	___
Develops each topic in sufficient detail.	___	___	___	___
Shows an interest in what's happening to the reader.	___	___	___	___
Has a friendly way of ending the letter.	___	___	___	___
Style				
Has a friendly, natural tone.	___	___	___	___
Form				
Follows friendly letter form.	___	___	___	___
Indents paragraphs.	___	___	___	___
Is neat and legible.	___	___	___	___
Mechanics				
Begins each sentence with a capital.	___	___	___	___
Uses correct end punctuation.	___	___	___	___
Spells words correctly.	___	___	___	___

Name of student: _____   Date: _____

it is important that criteria for assessment be clearly understood. As Dahl and Farnan (1998) note, "When writers lack specific standards and intentions, their ability to reflect on and evaluate their writing is severely compromised. It is not surprising that if writers do not know what they want to accomplish with a particular writing, it will be difficult for them to judge whether they have created an effective composition" (p. 121).

Portfolios

Artists, photographers, designers, and others assemble their work in **portfolios** for assessment. Portfolios are now being used in a somewhat modified fashion to assess the literacy growth of elementary and middle school students. Portfolios have a number of advantages. First, they facilitate the assessment of growth over time. Because they provide the teacher with an opportunity to take a broad look at a student's literacy development, they are an appropriate method for assessing holistic approaches. Portfolio assessment can also lead to changes in the curriculum and teaching practices. In Au's (1994) study, for instance, teachers began emphasizing the revision phase of writing when portfolio assessment helped them see that they were neglecting that area. Teachers in Kentucky reported that portfolios were the key element in a program designed to improve writing (Stecher, Barron, Kaganoff, & Goodwin, 1998).

Types of Portfolios

There are five kinds of portfolios, each performing different functions and containing different kinds of materials: showcase, evaluation,

> ⬚ A **portfolio** is a collection of work samples, test results, checklists, and other data used to assess a student's performance.

documentation, process, and composite (Valencia & Place, 1994). Like the traditional portfolio used by artists to display their best works, the showcase portfolio is composed of works that students have selected as being their best. The focus in the evaluation portfolio is on collecting representative works from key areas. The samples included might be standardized—that is, based on a common text or a common topic—so that results are comparable across students. A documentation portfolio is designed to provide evidence of students' growth and so might contain the greatest number and variety of work samples. The process portfolio is designed to show how students work, so it includes samples from various stages of a project along with students' comments about how the project is progressing. A composite portfolio contains elements from two or more types of portfolios. For instance, a portfolio designed for district evaluation might contain showcase and process items.

Writing Samples

Collecting representative pieces from several types of writing assignments gives the teacher a broad view of a student's development. Including pieces written at different times of the year allows the teacher to trace the student's growth. Rough drafts as well as final copies illustrate the student's writing progress and indicate how well the student handles the various processes. Each student might include in her or his portfolio lists of pieces written, major writing skills learned, and current goals. Both student and teacher should have access to the portfolio and should agree on which pieces should be included. Teacher and student should also agree on how to choose what goes into the portfolio.

To help students reflect on their learning and make wise choices about the pieces they include, you might have them explain their choices by completing a self-evaluative statement. The statement can be a brief explanation with the heading "Why I Chose This Piece." Initially, reasons for inclusion and comments tend to be vague (Tierney, Carter, & Desai, 1991). However, through classroom discussions and conferences, you can help students explore criteria for including certain pieces rather than others—it tells a good story, it has a beginning that grabs the reader, it has many interesting examples, it seems to flow, and so on.

A portfolio can demonstrate the power of a reader and a writer. Unknown to the teacher, a student may read dozens or hundreds of books or be a budding author. A reading log or sampling of written pieces should reveal this (Tierney, Carter, & Desai, 1991). However, you might invite students to include in their portfolios pieces they have written on their own as nonschool literacy endeavors.

Reading Samples

Some teachers use portfolios primarily to assess writing. If you wish to use portfolios to assess reading, include samples of reading. Samples to be included depend on the goals of the program. Valencia (1990) cautioned, "If the goals of instruction are not specified, portfolios have the potential to become reinforced holding files for odds and ends" (p. 339). If a goal of reading instruction is to teach students to visualize, drawings of reading selections might be included. If you have been working on summaries, you may want to see sample summaries. A list of books read might be appropriate for a goal of wide reading. Running records or informal reading inventories might be included to demonstrate fluency, word recognition in context, comprehension, or overall reading development.

At certain points, reading and writing will converge—written summaries of selections and research reports using several sources might count toward both reading and writing goals. Other items that might be placed in the portfolio are checklists, quizzes, standardized and informal test results, learning logs, written reactions to selections, and graphic organizers.

Assessing for Learning

- Portfolios are most useful when goals are clearly stated and specific criteria are listed for their assessment. It is essential, that goals and criteria be understood by students (Snider, Lima, & DeVito, 1994).
- In Kentucky, teachers reported that the portfolio system was the most influential factor in determining their instructional practice (Stecher, Barron, Kaganoff, & Goodwin, 1998). They also credited the portfolio system with helping them become better teachers. ▯

Reviewing Portfolios

To check on students' progress, periodically review their portfolios. Farr and Farr (1990) suggested that this be done a minimum of four times a year. In order to make the best use of your time and to help students organize their work, you might have them prepare a list of the items included in the portfolio. The portfolio should also contain a list of students' learning objectives. Students might write a cover letter or fill out a form summarizing work they have done, explaining which goals they feel they have met, which areas might need improvement, and what their plans for the future are. A sample portfolio evaluation form is presented in Figure 2.13.

Before you start to review a portfolio, decide what you want to focus on. It could be number of books read, changes in writing, or effort put into revisions. Your evaluation should, of course, consider the student's stated goals; it is also important to emphasize the student's strengths. As you assess the portfolio, consider a variety of pieces and look at the work in terms of its changes over time. Ask yourself: "What does the student's work show about her or his progress over the time span covered? What might she or he do to make continued progress?"

To save time and help you organize your assessment of the portfolio, you may want to use a checklist or rubric that is supplemented with personal comments. A sample portfolio review checklist is presented in Figure 2.14. Because the objective of evaluation is to

FIGURE 2.13 Portfolio Evaluation by Student

Name: ______________________ Date: ____________

Portfolio Evaluation

What were my goals in reading for this period?

What progress toward meeting these goals does my portfolio show?

What are my strengths?

What are my weaknesses?

What are my goals for improving as a reader?

How do I plan to meet those goals?

What were my goals in writing for this period?

What progress toward meeting these goals does my portfolio show?

What are my strengths as a writer?

What are my weaknesses?

What are my goals for improving as a writer?

How do I plan to meet these goals?

What questions do I have about my writing or my reading?

FIGURE 2.14   Portfolio Review Checklist

Name of student: _____   Date: _____

Voluntary Reading
    Number of books read   _____
    Variety of books read   _____
    Strengths   _____
    Needs   _____

Reading Comprehension
    Construction of meaning   _____
    Extension of meaning   _____
    Use of strategies   _____
    Quality of responses   _____
    Strengths   _____
    Needs   _____

Writing
    Amount of writing   _____
    Variety of writing   _____
    Planning   _____
    Revising   _____
    Self-editing   _____
    Content   _____
    Organization   _____
    Style   _____
    Mechanics   _____
    Strengths   _____
    Needs   _____

Comments: _____
_____
_____

improve instruction, students should be active partners in the process. "It follows that . . . assessment activities in which students are engaged in evaluating their own learning help them reflect on and understand their own strengths and needs, and it instills responsibility for their own learning" (Tierney, Carter, & Desai, 1991, p. 7).

Alignment of Assessment and Data Analysis

A critical feature of assessment measures is alignment. Alignment means that the curriculum and instruction are based on agreed upon objectives and the tests are assessing what is being taught (Webb, 1999). This is especially important in view of the demands of making adequate yearly progress. Classroom and other assessments should be aligned with standards (objectives) and instruction. Alignment needs to be flexible. Based on a study of fourth-graders' performance on the comprehension section of a state proficiency test, Riddle, Buly, and Valencia (2002) warn:

> Alignment is certainly a centerpiece of standards-based reform and, most of the time, it makes good sense. However, sometimes it can be oversimplified and inadvertently lead to inappropriate instruction. More specifically, aligning instruction with state assessments

REFLECTION

What is the value of portfolios? What might be done to get the most out of portfolios? In what situation might portfolios be especially effective?

 FYI

Tests, observations, work samples, and other assessment devices can be used to verify and complement each other. A student's performance in phonics, for instance, might be assessed through a written quiz, an observation of oral reading, and an examination of his or her spelling. This triangulation of data might reveal that the student can read simple, short-vowel words (*top*, *pet*) but has difficulty with clusters (*stop*, *step*).

Adapting Instruction for English Language Learners

Obtaining a valid assessment of the ability and performance of English language learners is a problem. ELLs can obtain conversational proficiency in two years or less.

However, it may take five years or more for ELLs to learn enough academic English so that they can do as well on tests of academic proficiency as native speakers of English do (Cummins, 2001). ▢

may help teachers focus on what is tested. . . . It will not address the skills and strategies that underlie such competence. . . . A focus on comprehension would miss those who have difficulty in word identification or fluency, or those with specific second language issues. Similarly, requiring teachers to align their instruction with grade level content standards may also fall short. Assuring, for example, that 4th-grade teachers are teaching the 4th-grade content standards does not assure they are providing appropriate instruction for all students. To be sure, some students would benefit from instruction and practice reading material that is at a lower grade level and some would benefit from more advanced curriculum. It is not that grade level standards or expectations are unimportant or that aligning instruction, assessment, and standards is wrong. However, for many struggling students, grade level standards are goals rather than immediate needs. The teacher's challenge is to bring the students to the point where those grade level goals are within reach. (p. 234)

If you are using a commercial program, chances are that it is aligned. However, examine it closely to see if any revisions are needed. In addition, you might need to make some adjustment to ensure that the program aligns with state, district, and other outside assessments. If you are using a program that you or your school has created, you will need to construct or adopt an assessment system that aligns with your objectives and instruction.

Data Analysis

Adapting Instruction for English Language Learners

Students whose language is non-alphabetic or doesn't use the Roman alphabet will have a greater adjustment than those whose written language is more similar to English. ▢

Along with aligning assessment and instruction, it is essential that you analyze the data so that it can actually be used to plan instruction. Keep a record of students' performance on any assessments that are administered to them. Use that data to make instructional decisions. After an assessment has been administered, organize the results. Note especially students who did not perform adequately. What are some possible reasons for their poor performance? What might be done to assist them? If you have scores from the same or comparable assessments, note whether there has been an improvement and whether the improvement is such that the students are on track to reach the target benchmark by the end of the school year. Also analyze items that students responded to. On a phonics test, for instance, note the items that students got correct. Perhaps the students got most of the short-vowel items correct but had difficulty with clusters (blends). This is the kind of information that you can use to plan instruction. Consider other sources of data. You might have information from an IRI, running record, or personal observation that sheds additional light on students' skill levels and cognitive processes.

Adapting Instruction for English Language Learners

ELLs should not be given assessments that are so far beyond their English language capacity that they are overwhelmed. ▢

Assessing English Language Learners

Under the No Child Left Behind Act of 2001, the academic progress of every child in grades 3 through 8, including those learning English who have been enrolled in a U.S. school for at least a year, is tested in reading and math. English language learners (ELLs) are tested annually to measure how well they are learning English.

Apart from state and federal regulations, it is essential that you have information about ELLs' proficiency in literacy in their first language. Students who can read in another language will have learned basic concepts of reading. They will have developed phonological awareness, alphabetical knowledge, and knowledge of phonics, if their home language is an alphabetic one. You can build on this knowledge. It is also essential that you have information about the students' proficiency in oral and written English. If students are weak in understanding English, you can plan a literacy program that develops oral language.

Key questions include:

- What is the student's proficiency in speaking her or his first language?
- What is the student's proficiency in speaking English?
- What is the student's proficiency in reading in the first language?
- What is the student's proficiency in reading in English?
- What is the educational background of the student?

The ESL or bilingual specialist should be able to provide information about the students' proficiency in literacy in their first language and also their knowledge of English. If this information is not available, use informal techniques to assess the students' proficiency in reading and writing their first language. Ask students to bring in books in their first language and read them to you and then retell the selection in English. Also ask them to bring in a piece of writing that they have done in their first language and read it to you and then retell it in English. Based on the ease with which they read, you can judge whether they are literate in their first language, even if you don't know the language. You might also obtain or construct a list of common words in their language and ask students to read them. Figure 2.15 contains a list of twenty common Spanish words, phonetically respelled and with their English translations. You might use a list such as this one to get a very rough idea of the students' reading proficiency. (Spanish has a number of dialects. Pronunciations might vary somewhat from those provided.) If students can read all or most of these words, they can read at least at a basic level in Spanish. If you are fluent in Spanish, you might administer the Spanish Reading Inventory (Kendall/Hunt) or the English-Español Reading Inventory for the Classroom (Merrill).

A distinguished panel of experts on English language learners recommended administering measures of phonological awareness, letter knowledge, and word and text reading in English and using the results to identify ELLs who require additional instructional support:

> Research shows that early reading measures, administered in English, can be used to screen English learners for reading problems. This finding is important because until recently it was widely believed that an absence of oral proficiency in English prevented English learners from learning to read in English, thus limiting the utility of early screening measures. The common practice was to wait until English learners reached a reasonable level of oral English proficiency before assessing them on measures of beginning reading. (Gersten, Baker, Shanahan, Linan-Thompson, Collins, & Scarcella, 2007, p. 5)

The panel also recommended using the same early reading standards for ELLs as are used with native speakers of English:

> Schools with performance benchmarks in reading in the early grades can use the same standards for English learners and for native English speakers to make adjustments in instruction when progress is not sufficient. It is the opinion of the panel that schools should not consider below-grade-level performance in reading as "normal" or something that will resolve itself when oral language proficiency in English improves. (Gersten et al., 2007, p. 3)

This recommendation, which applies only to early reading, is somewhat controversial. While it is true that on-grade English reading tests administered to English learners will show whether they have reached a set benchmark or standard, it is easy to picture situations where the students' English is so limited that they are only able to respond to a few items or none at all. This seems to be a needlessly disheartening process. Teacher judgment needs to be exercised so that students are not overwhelmed with assessments that are far beyond their language capabilities. One solution would be to administer screening measures that include items on the lower end of the scale as well as on-grade items so that even students with limited English ability will be able to respond to some items and their performance will provide useful information for instructional planning. The CELLA (Comprehensive English Language Learning Assessment), for instance, is functionally based rather than grade-level based in reading and writing. Level A, which is designed for students in grades 1–2, ranges from

FIGURE 2.15 Spanish Word List

Spanish Word	Pronunciation	Meaning
no	no	no
mi	me	my
uno	OO-no	one
esta	ES-tah	this
ella	AY-yah	she
señor	sen-YOR	mister
leer	lay-AIR	read
libro	LEE-bro	book
amigo	ah-ME-go	friend
pelota	peh-LOH-tah	ball
vaca	BAH-kah	cow
musica	MYEW-see-kah	music
sorpressa	sor-PRES-ah	surprise
leopardo	lay-oh-PAR-doh	leopard
abuela	ah-BWEH-lah	grandmother
bicicleta	bee-see-KLAY-tah	bicycle
mañana	mon-YAH-nah	tomorrow
primavera	pre-mah-BEAR-ah	spring
zapatos	sah-PAH-toes	shoes
elefante	eh-leh-FAHN-teh	elephant
vaca	BAH-kah/VAH-kah	cow

Case Study
Lessons from 90/90/90 Schools

Assessment works best when it is connected to instruction and the attitude that all students can learn if given adequate instruction and whatever assistance they need. Assessment becomes a blueprint for instruction rather than a judgment. In 90/90/90 schools, there was frequent assessment of student progress with multiple opportunities for improvement. A 90/90/90 school was one in which 90 percent of the students were members of minority groups and lived in poverty but attained the proficient level on high-stakes tests. In many instances, assessments in these schools were weekly and were constructed by classroom teachers. Since many of the students in these schools were struggling readers and writers, they often did poorly on assessments. However, the consequence of a poor performance was not a low grade or a sense of failure but additional instruction and practice.

Another characteristic of assessment in 90/90/90 schools was an emphasis on students' written responses in performance assessments. Because the responses were written rather than oral, students were better able to elaborate on their thinking, and teachers were better able to judge the quality of the students' responses. Being better able to examine and analyze students'

responses, teachers had the information they needed to plan effective instructional activities. "By assessing student writing, teachers can discern whether the challenges faced by a student are the result of vocabulary issues, misunderstood directions, reasoning errors, or a host of other causes that are rarely revealed by typical tests" (Reeves, 2003, p. 5).

In 90/90/90 schools, teachers used a common rubric so that there were clear standards for writing and clear standards for assessing (Reeves, 2003). In addition, in many instances teachers would meet to assess papers or to exchange papers, so assessment was the result of applying the rubric rather than simply using highly subjective judgment. Disagreements about scoring generally arise when teachers use implicit criteria rather than stated criteria or when the criteria are not specific enough. For instance, a teacher might judge a paper partly on neatness, which isn't one of the stated criteria. Or a criterion such as "fully develops ideas," which lacks specificity, is interpreted in different ways by different teachers. By talking over standards and disagreements, teachers can clarify the criteria and refrain from adding criteria that are not stated.

---

identifying letters of the alphabet and reading high frequency words to reading brief passages. For grade 3 and beyond, a brief locator test is used to estimate the appropriate assessment level: Level A, B, C, or D. Another solution would be to gear assessment to the students' level of language development.

A second factor in the assessment of ELL is the use of cognitive resources, especially at higher levels. As compared to native speakers of English, ELL must draw on added cognitive resources to process English text (Francis, Rivera, Lesaux, Kieffer, & Rivera, 2006). This means that they may not be able to allocate a full measure of cognitive resources to process complex text, or it may take them longer. Providing them with accessible text and/or more time are possible accommodations. Even so, complex standardized tests may underestimate the abilities of ELL.

Assessing Language

To assess students' ability to understand language, request that they point to various objects: "Point to the book. Point to the red dot. Point to the square. Point to your knee, your foot, your ear" (Law & Eckes, 2002). Start with common objects, and progress to less common ones: "Point to the magnet. Point to the picture of the jet." Real objects work better, but you might also use magazine or other photos to assess students' receptive vocabulary. Also request that students follow a series of commands: "Stand. Sit. Open the book. Raise your hand. Write your name." To assess expressive vocabulary, have the students identify objects that you point to and ask, "What is this? What are those?" Also ask students a series of questions, and note how they respond: "What is your name? How old are you? Where do you live? Count to ten. Name the colors that I point to. Name the letters that I point to." For a copy of informal language tests for English language learners and additional suggestions for assessment, refer to the text by Law and Eckes (2002), which is listed in the References section.

REFLECTION

What are the main obstacles to obtaining valid and reliable information about the literacy development of English language learners? How might these obstacles be overcome?

Creating a Literacy Profile

Jiménez (2004) recommends that a literacy profile be created for English language learners. The profile provides information about the language the students speak at home. It is also important to determine whether there have been gaps in ELLs' schooling. Their schooling may have been fragmented, or they may have been moved from a regular class to an ESL class or to a special education class.

When looking at scores from an ELL student, compare them to the scores of other ELLs. Also consider such factors as when the student began learning English and how many years of exposure to English the student has had. Also find out if the student can read in his or her native language. If so, skills can be transferred. Get information, too, on the students' literacy activities. Some students act as translators for their parents, an activity known as *language brokering* (Lalas, Solomon, & Johannessen, 2006). Language brokering apparently strengthens students' academic achievement. These students might be translating medical forms, advertisements, and even income tax forms. Affirm students' native language, and help them see that their native language can be a source of help in understanding English.

Assessing Materials

Just about the most important instructional decision you will make is selecting the appropriate level of materials for your students. Choose a level that is too easy and students will be bored and unchallenged. Select material that is too difficult and they will be discouraged, have their academic self-concepts demolished, and fail to make progress. Perhaps, worst of all, they will learn to hate reading (Juel, 1994). As noted earlier, students should know at least 95 percent of the words in the materials they are asked to read and should have about 75 percent comprehension.

A three-part approach to estimating the readability of a text is recommended: quantitative measures of text difficulty, qualitative measures of text difficulty, and professional judgment in matching texts to reader and task (National Governors Association Center for Best Practices and Council of Chief State School Officers, 2010b). Quantitative measures consist of the use of formulas. Qualitative measures include leveling systems and checklists. Professional judgment involves considering reader factors in terms of the material to be read and the task to be performed.

Publishers of school materials generally provide reading levels for their texts. Using a formula or subjective leveling scale, they estimate that the material is at, for example, a second-, third-, or fourth-grade level, which means that the average second-, third-, or fourth-grader should be able to read it. Or they may use letters or numbers to indicate a level rather than a grade. Some publishers of children's books also supply **readability levels**. If no readability level is indicated for a book that you wish to use, you can can consult one of the following sources.

ATOS (Advantage-TASA Open Standard)

ATOS is a computerized formula that uses number of words per sentence, characters per word, and average grade level of words and analyzes the entire text to estimate the readability of a book and provide a grade-level equivalent. ATOS scores for more than 50,000 trade books are available from Renaissance Learning, the creators of Accelerated Reading, at http://www.arbookfind.com. Enter the title of the book for which you would like to have an ATOS score. ATOS scores appear in bold type after the abbreviation "BL" (for book level) and are expressed in grade equivalents. First grade is subdivided into a series of levels that are equated with Reading Recovery levels. If the text

□ **Readability level** indicates the difficulty of a selection. A formula may be used to estimate readability by measuring quantitative factors such as sentence length and number of difficult words in the selection. A leveling system may use a number of qualitative factors to estimate the difficulty of the text. Best results are obtained by assessing both qualitative and quantitative factors.

FYI

Lexiles are the most widely used readability estimate.

FYI

Common Core Standards allow lexiles, DRP units, and grade scores to be used to measure text difficulty.

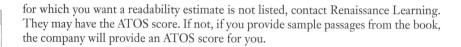
Using Technology

Titlewave provides extensive information about books and other media, including interest level, readability level, book reviews, and awards that books have won. You can search by author, title, topic, grade level, subject area, or curriculum standard.

http://www.flr.follett.com/login

for which you want a readability estimate is not listed, contact Renaissance Learning. They may have the ATOS score. If not, if you provide sample passages from the book, the company will provide an ATOS score for you.

Lexile Scale

The lexile scale is a two-factor computerized formula that consists of a measurement of sentence length and word frequency. Table 2.7 on page 46 provides approximate grade equivalents for lexile scores. A software program for obtaining readability estimates, the *Lexile Analyzer*, is available from MetaMetrics and can be used to calculate your own lexile scores. However, lexile scores for about 40,000 books are available online at http://www.lexile.com. ATOS and DRP seem to provide a more accurate estimate than does the lexile scale (Renaissance Learning, 2006, 2009). However, the lexile scale is more widely used.

Degrees of Reading Power

The Degrees of Reading Power test measures sentence length, number of words not on the Dale List of words known by fourth-graders, and average number of letters per word (Touchstone Applied Science Associates, 1994). Compilations of readability levels expressed in DRP units for some content-area textbooks can be found on the following Web site: http://www.questarai.com/readability.htm. DRP readabilities for trade books are available on easy-to-use software called *BookLink*. DRP units range from 15 for the easiest materials to 85 for the most difficult reading material. Table 2.7 provides approximate grade equivalents for DRP scores.

Other Readability Formulas

If you are unable to get a readability level from one of these sources, or if you prefer to assess the readability of the text yourself, there are a number of formulas you can apply. One of the easiest to use is the Fry Readability Graph, which bases its estimate on two factors: sentence length and number of syllables in a word. Number of syllables in a word is a measure of vocabulary difficulty. In general, the more syllables a word has, the harder it tends to be. The Fry Readability Graph (Fry, 1977b) is presented in Figure 2.16. A formula that counts the number of hard words but is relatively easy to use is the Primary Readability Formula (Gunning, 2002); it can be used to assess the difficulty level of materials in grades 1 to 4. The New Dale-Chall Readability Formula (Chall & Dale, 1995), which also counts the number of difficult words, is recommended for grade 3 and up.

One problem with readability formulas is that they are mechanical and so do not consider subjective factors, such as the density of concepts, use of illustrations, or background required to construct meaning from the text. Readability formulas should be complemented by the use of the subjective factors incorporated in a leveling system (Gunning, 2000b). A leveling system uses subjective or qualitative factors to estimate the difficulty level of materials.

FYI

The Primary Readability Formula, which is designed for grades 1–4, is available in the Instructor's Manual.

Qualitative Factors

In addition to failing to consider qualitative factors, traditional formulas do not work well at the very beginning levels. Formulas don't consider such factors as usefulness of illustrations and number of lines per page, which are major determinants of the difficulty level of beginning materials. Formulas do indicate with reasonable accuracy that materials are on a first-grade level. However, first-grade reading encompasses a wide range of material that includes counting or colorword books that have just one or two easy words per page as well as books, such as the Little Bear series, that contain brief chapters and may contain several hundred words. To make fine discriminations among the range of first-grade books, it is necessary to use a leveling system.

FIGURE 2.16 Fry's Graph
for Estimating Readability

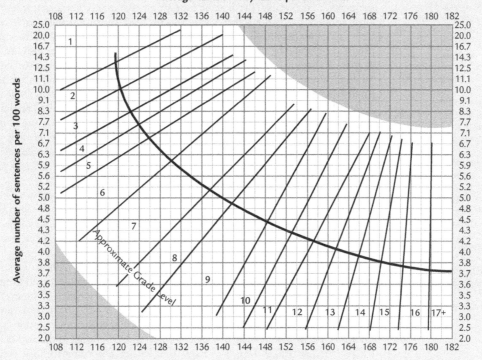

Average number of syllables per 100 words

Expanded Directions for Working Readability Graph

1. Randomly select three (3) sample passages and count out exactly 100 words each, beginning with the beginning of a sentence. Do not count proper nouns, initializations, and numerals.

2. Count the number of sentences in the 100 words, estimating length of the fraction of the last sentence to the nearest one-tenth.

3. Count the total number of syllables in the 100-word passage. If you don't have a hand counter available, an easy way is to simply put a mark above every syllable over one in each word, then when you get to the end of the passage, count the number of marks and add 100. Small calculators can also be used by pushing numeral 1, then the + sign for each word or syllable when counting.

4. Enter graph with *average* sentence length and *average* number of syllables; plot dot where the two lines

intersect. Area where dot is plotted will give you the approximate grade level.

5. If a great deal of variability is found in syllable count or sentence count, putting more samples into the average is desirable.

6. A word is defined as a group of symbols with space on either side; thus, *Joe, IRA, 1945,* and & are each one word.

7. A syllable is defined as a phonetic syllable. Generally, there are as many syllables as vowel sounds. For example, *stopped* is one syllable and *wanted* is two syllables. When counting syllables for numerals and initializations, count one syllable for each symbol. For example, *1945* is four syllables, *IRA* is three syllables, and & is one syllable.

FYI

- The classroom teacher must decide whether to arrange books by level. Books used for guided reading or by novice readers should be leveled. As students grow in reading skill and book selection ability, there is less need for leveling. It is a good idea to level books through third grade. When students have access to books on their level, there is a greater chance that they will read them. After third grade, you might have shelves of fast reads for students reading below grade level, or you might choose to maintain a leveling system.
- When matching books with students, leveling is just one factor. Students' interests, motivations, experience, knowledge, and sociocultural identities are also essential factors (Dzaldov & Peterson, 2005).
- Beginning reading texts can be leveled according to any or all of three criteria: frequency of occurrence of words, decodability of text, and predictability of text.

FYI

- Levels in the Basic Leveling Index correspond to those used by basal readers. Most basal reading systems divide materials into the following levels: three pre-primers, a primer, and a first-grade reader. Informal reading inventories typically feature a pre-primer, primer, and first-grade-level book.
- All the major reading programs now feature decodable texts in their beginning reading materials. If you are using a program that makes use of decodable text, it's a good idea to level your books according to the skills needed to read such text. See Chapter 5 for a guide for leveling decodable text.
- Reading Recovery levels should be double-checked. From a study of Reading Recovery books, Cunningham and others (2005) concluded that "books leveled for use in Reading Recovery do not consistently increase in word-level demands as their levels increase" (p. 425).

Leveling Systems

Although materials for beginning readers may look similar—large print and lots of illustrations—they incorporate different theories of teaching reading and have different uses (Hiebert, 1999). Early reading materials can be classified as being predictable, high-frequency, or decodable. Predictable texts are written in such a way that students can use illustrations or their knowledge of language to "read" the text. A predictable book might have the sentences "I can run. I can jump. I can sing. I can read," each on a separate page accompanied by an illustration showing the action. The reader gets heavy support from the illustrations and the repeated pattern. Predictable books are excellent for reinforcing concepts of print and giving students the feel of reading, and they can also help English language learners learn the patterns of English. Predictable books do a good job of introducing students to reading. Most students will pick up an initial reading vocabulary by repeatedly meeting words in print. However, some will continue to use picture and language clues, and the use of predictable text may actually hinder their progress.

Some texts emphasize high-frequency words. Words such as *of, and, the, was,* and *where* occur so often in print that they are said to be high-frequency. Most predictable books are composed primarily of high-frequency words.

Decodable texts contain phonics elements that have been taught. A story about a *bug* who lived in a *rug* would be decodable to students who have learned the *-ug* pattern. No text is totally decodable. High-frequency words such as *is, are,* and *the* need to be included, as do content words such as *bear* and *hungry* if the story is about a hungry bear.

The most widely used leveling system is based on the predictability of text. Adapting a system that was originally devised for Reading Recovery, Fountas and Pinnell (2009) have compiled a list of 18,000 leveled books for students in kindergarten through grade 8. Books are leveled from A through Z, with A being very beginning reading and Z being eighth-grade reading. Table 2.7 provides approximate grade equivalents. Books on the Graded Listing of Outstanding Children's Books at the author's Web site (http://www.wordbuilding.org) have been leveled according to both predictability and decodability, based on quantitative as well as qualitative factors.

However, you may wish to use books that have not been leveled, or you may not have access to a listing of leveled books. In that case, you need to be able to level books on your own. To level books, consider key subjective factors and compare passages from the book you are leveling to passages from benchmark books. *The Qualitative Assessment of Text Difficulty* (Chall, Bissex, Conard, & Harris-Sharples, 1996) provides benchmark passages and directions for leveling both fictional and informational books. For beginning books, use the Basic Leveling Index, which is explained below.

The Basic Leveling Index

Using the Basic Leveling System with Beginning Reading Books

Beginning reading books are more difficult to level than are upper-grade books because they encompass a very wide range of difficulty. The Basic Leveling System has seven beginning-reader through first-grade levels: picture, caption or frame (early pre-primer), pre-primer one, pre-primer two, pre-primer three, primer, and first. To determine the difficulty of an early reading text, compare the text being assessed with a benchmark book or benchmark passage. Ask: Which benchmark book or passage is this text most like? Also consider qualitative factors. Note especially the difficulty level of the words. Would your students be able to read them? Remember that they should be able to read about 95 percent of the words. At this level, most of the words will be in the students' listening vocabulary. Their major task is to pronounce or recognize the printed words. Words such as *the* and *are* appear with high frequency and so are easier to read. Some words such as *cat* and *hat* will be easy to decode. Consider, too, how helpful the illustrations are. Some of the words may be depicted by illustrations, which might also provide an overview of the text or portray significant portions of

Number of hard words depicted by illustrations:
　　　None _____　Some _____　Most _____　All _____

Number of words that would be easy to decode:
　　　None _____　Some _____　Most _____　All _____

Difficulty of vocabulary and concepts
_____ Familiar vocabulary and concepts
_____ One or two unfamiliar words or concepts
_____ Several unfamiliar words or concepts

Familiarity of topic or story line
　　　High _____　Medium _____　Low _____

When compared with benchmark passages or books, what level(s) do the sample passages from the text seem to be most like?
Passage 1 _____
Passage 2 _____
Passage 3 _____
Average　 _____

FIGURE 2.17 Worksheet for Estimating Difficulty of First-Grade Materials

it. Be attentive to the overall interest of the selection, familiarity of the topic and language, repetition of elements, use of rhyme, and such format factors as number of lines per page. Also consider the length of the text; short pieces are easier to read than longer ones. Above all, note whether the average beginning reader would have the background information necessary to read the text. A book about the Vietnam War, no matter how simply written, would be beyond most beginning readers. Watch out, too, for the use of figurative language and allusions that are beyond beginning readers. When estimating difficulty level, be conservative. If you are undecided whether a book is on a primer or first level, place it at the higher level. It's better to give a student a book that is on the easy side rather than one that is too difficult.

Consider both objective and subjective information to decide on a difficulty level. Use the worksheet in Figure 2.17 to note quantitative and qualitative factors. As you become familiar with leveling books, your estimates will become more accurate and there will be less need to rely on objective measures. However, objective measures provide a helpful check.

The next few pages provide a description of each level and a sample benchmark passage. Words that are judged to be difficult are boldfaced.

Picture Level　In books at the picture level, a single word or phrase is depicted with an illustration (see Figure 2.18). The word *lion*, for instance, is accompanied by a drawing of a lion; the word *three* is accompanied by the numeral 3 and three dots. The text is so fully and clearly depicted that no reading is required. In some books, the student might need to use the initial consonant to help identify the picture. For instance, the student might not know whether a wolf or a dog is being depicted. Seeing that the label for the picture starts with a *w*, the student uses knowledge of initial consonants to reason that a wolf is being depicted.

FIGURE 2.18

I see a lion.   I see a tiger.

FIGURE 2.19

Benchmark books:

Colors by John Burningham

Numbers by Guy Smalley

Caption or Frame Level   The text of caption-level books is illustrated so that the reader can use pictures to identify most but not all of the words (see Figure 2.19). These books feature frame sentences, which are easy sentences, such as: "I can _____," "I am _____," or "_____can swim," that are repeated throughout the text. The name of the object, animal, person, or action that completes the frame is depicted. The student would need to know initial consonants and the few high-frequency words that make up the frame.

Benchmark books:

Have You Seen My Cat? by Eric Carle

My Barn by Craig Brown

Cat on the Mat by Brian Wildsmith

Benchmark passage: I see _____.

Pre-primer 1 (Easy, High-Frequency Words)   Pre-primer 1 books are similar to caption-level books but there are a greater number of different words used and more reading is required. Illustrations usually depict some or much of the text. A pre-primer 1 book requires increased knowledge of high-frequency words and some beginning familiarity with short-vowel patterns, such as *-at* and *-am.*

Benchmark books:

Brown Bear, Brown Bear, What Do You See? by Bill Martin, Jr.

Bugs by Patricia and Fredrick McKissack

Benchmark passage: "The Bad Cat"

Matt is sad.

Matt had a hat.

Now **Pat** has **Matt's** hat.

Pat is a cat.

Matt ran after Pat.

But Pat ran away.

Pat ran away with Matt's hat.

Pat is a bad cat.

Pre-primer 2   Pre-primer 2 books are similar to pre-primer 1 books, but there are a greater number of different words used and more reading is required. Illustrations usually depict some of the text. This level requires increased knowledge of high-frequency words and some familiarity with most of the short-vowel patterns, such as *-at, -op,* and *-et.*

Benchmark books:

Cat Traps by Molly Coxe

The Carrot Seed by Ruth Krauss

Benchmark passage: "The Red Kangaroo"

Hop! Hop! Hop!

Kangaroos like to hop.

The red kangaroo can **hop** the best.

The red kangaroo can hop over you.

The red kangaroo can hop over the top of a **van**.

The red kangaroo is big.

The red kangaroo has big back legs.

Its back legs are very **strong**.

And it has a long **tail**.

The red kangaroo is bigger than a man.

The red kangaroo is the biggest kangaroo of all.

Pre-primer 3   The pre-primer 3 level is similar to pre-primer 2 but requires increased knowledge of high-frequency words and increased familiarity with short-vowel patterns that make use of consonant combinations such as *tr*, *st*, and *sch*.

Benchmark books:

The Foot Book by Dr. Seuss

Sleepy Dog by Harriet Ziefert

Benchmark passage: "Best Pet"

"I have the best pet," said Ted.

"My dog **barks** and **wags** his **tail** when I come home from school."

"No, I have the best pet," said **Robin**. "I have a cat. My cat **wakes** me up so that I can go to school."

"I have the best pet," said Will. "I have a pet pig.

My pig can do many **tricks**."

Then Ted said, "We all have the best pet.

I have the pet that is best for me.

Robin has the pet that is best for her.

And Will has the pet that is best for him."

Primer   At the primer level, vocabulary becomes more diverse, and illustrations are less helpful. Students need to know high-frequency words and short-vowel and long-vowel patterns (*-ake*, *-ike*, *-ope*). A primer-level book might also require some knowledge of r-vowel (*-ar*, *-er*) and other-vowel (*-our*, *-ought*) patterns.

Benchmark books:

And I Mean It Stanley by Crosby Bonsall

Jason's Bus Ride by Harriet Ziefert

Benchmark passage: The Little Red Hen

A little red hen lived on a farm with her **chickens**. One day she found a **grain** of **wheat** in the **barnyard**.

"Who will plant this wheat?" she said.

"Not I," said the Cat.

"Not I," said the Duck.

"I will do it **myself**," said the little Red Hen. And she planted the grain of wheat.

When the wheat was ripe she said, "Who will take this wheat to the **mill**?"

"Not I," said the Cat.

REFLECTION

What procedures might be used to assess the difficulty level of materials? Which formula would you use? Why? Why is it important to verify the difficulty level of a text by noting how well students can read the text?

Using Technology

Coh-Metrix Easability is a free text analysis system that uses five key language factors to assess text: word concreteness, narrativity, local cohesion, deep cohesion, and syntactic simplicity. Results can be used to plan instruction. See the Easibility site for more information.

"Not I," said the Duck.

"I will, then," said the little Red Hen, and she took the wheat to the mill.

When she **brought** the **flour** home, she said, "Who will bake some bread with this flour?"

First Grade   At the first-grade level, selections are becoming longer and more complex. Books may be divided into very brief chapters. Students need to know short-vowel, long-vowel, and some of the easier other-vowel (*-ow, -oy, -oo, -aw*), and *r*-vowel (*-ear, -or*) patterns. There may also be some easy two-syllable words. Illustrations support text and may depict a hard word or two.

Benchmark books:

The Cat in the Hat by Dr. Seuss

Little Bear's Visit by Else Minark

Benchmark passage: *Johnny Appleseed*

John Chapman wore a **tin pan** for a hat. And he was **dressed** in **rags**. But **people** liked John. He was kind to others, and he was kind to animals.

John loved **apples**. He left his home and headed **west** about 200 years ago. He wanted everyone to have apples. On his back he carried a **pack** of apple seeds. Walking from place to place, John planted his apple seeds. As the years **passed** the seeds **grew** into trees. After planting **hundreds** and hundreds of apple trees, John Chapman came to be called "**Johnny Appleseed.**"

Easability

Readability formulas measure surface factors such as word difficulty and sentence length. Using computer analysis, Coh-Metrix Easability attempts to go beyond the text base to the situation and mental model (McNamara, Graesser, Cai, & Kulikowich, 2011). Easability indices include narrativity, syntactic simplicity, word concreteness, referential cohesion, and deep cohesion and measure the degree to which segments in a text are tied together. The proportion of cohesive ties indicates the ease with which readers can go beyond understanding words and individual sentences and integrate ideas in the text and relate these to background knowledge and so form a situation or mental model. Using the Easability indices can shed light on the challenges posed by a text. Texts with the same overall readability level may have significant differences in their makeup. One might be more syntactically complex or less cohesive, or contain a smaller proportion of concrete words. Knowing the challenges posed by the text, it then becomes possible to plan lessons that will help students better understand the text. If referential and deep cohesion are low, you might pose questions that help students tie together ideas. Perhaps they will complete a graphic organizer. If syntactic simplicity is low, you might demonstrate a strategy for translating dense text into understandable English or provide instruction and practice in reading complex constructions. A low score on narrativity or word concreteness suggests the need to work both on vocabulary and background knowledge.

Reader and Task Factors

In addition to assessing the difficulty of the text, it is important to consider reader factors, such as motivation, interest, and background knowledge, and the knowledge of the reading task (National Governors Association and Council of Chief State School Officers, 2010a). The following question assesses the knowledge of the reading task: "Is the text being skimmed to get an overview or is it being read closely in order to learn how to carry out a complex procedure?" Reader factors are listed in

	Low			High		
Reader Factors	1	2	3	4	5	
Background knowledge						
Vocabulary						
Overall reading ability						
Interest						
Motivation						

TABLE 2.15   Reader Factors

Source: Adapted from Gunning, T. (2010), *Assessing and Correcting Reading and Writing Difficulties* (3rd ed.). Boston: Allyn & Bacon

	Narrative	Expository	Poetry
Purpose for Reading			
_____Following directions			
_____Learning a new procedure			
_____Reading for pleasure			
_____Evaluating a text			
_____Learning a new concept			
Complexity of Questions			
_____Locate & recall			
_____Integrate & interpret			

TABLE 2.16   Task Difficulty

Table 2.15. Task factors are presented in Table 2.16. Ultimately, the true measure of the difficulty level of a book is the proficiency with which students can read it. Note how well students are able to read books that have been leveled. Based on your observation of students' performance, be prepared to change the estimated difficulty level.

Summary

Evaluation entails making a subjective judgment about the effectiveness of instruction; it is based on data from tests, work samples, and observations. An evaluation is made in terms of standards or objectives and should result in the improvement of instruction.

The standards movement is an attempt to improve the quality of education by setting high, but clear, standards for all. A set of Common Core State Standards is now being emphasized. The purpose of these standards is to prepare all students to be college and career ready.

Assessment is categorized as being summative, formative, or interim. Summative assessment occurs after instruction and is used for grading or to evaluate students' progress or the effectiveness of a program. Formative assessment is administered during instruction and is used to plan and guide instruction. Interim assessment predicts performance on end-of-year summative measures and is used to plan instruction and schedule intervention. Assess-

ing for learning makes use of formative and interim assessment and involves students in the assessment process. This approach builds students' competence and confidence by clarifying standards and helping students see specifically what they need to do to meet standards.

Placement information is necessary to indicate where students are on the road to literacy. Continuous progress monitoring is used to track students' progress. Norm-referenced tests and criterion-referenced tests, as well as a variety of informal measures, are used to assess students' progress. Norm-referenced tests compare students with a norm group. Criterion-referenced assessments indicate whether students have reached a standard or objective. Benchmarks and rubrics are criterion-referenced assessment devices that offer ways of holistically indicating performance. Holistic evaluation of writing, observations, anecdotal records, checklists, and portfolios provide authentic information that complements data yielded by more formal measures. Formative assessment makes use of a variety of measures in order to improve instruction.

Students should be given tests designed for the level on which they are reading. Tests that are too easy or too hard are invalid and yield erroneous information.

A number of objective readability formulas and several subjective leveling systems and a computerized easability system can be used to assess the difficulty level of materials. Difficulty level is best assessed by using quantitative and qualitative measures and professional judgment.

Extending and Applying

1. Select a benchmark or progress-monitoring instrument described in this chapter. In terms of your theory of literacy instruction and/or research in the field, explain why you chose this particular instrument. Analyze the assessment instrument and make a judgment about its content validity. Obtain information on its concurrent and predictive validity and reliability. Make a judgment as to the usefulness and quality of the instrument. If possible, use the instrument with a student or group of students. Analyze the results, and explain what implications they have for instruction.

2. Administer an IRI, running record, or other placement device to one or more students. From the results of the assessment, estimate each student's independent, instructional, and frustration reading levels. Also list any strengths or needs that you noted. Discuss the results with the student and the student's teacher.

3. Create a portfolio system for literacy assessment for a class you are or might be teaching. Decide what kinds of items might be included in the portfolio. Also devise a checklist or summary sheet that can be used to keep track of and summarize the items and a rubric for assessing the portfolio.

4. In your professional portfolio, place any checklists, rubrics, or other assessment devices that you have devised and/or used. Reflect on the effectiveness and usefulness of these devices. If you used the devices, describe how you used the information they yielded to guide instruction.

5. Find out what the standards are for your state, how they are assessed, and how test results are used. Find out also if your state has recommendations for assessments that can be used to screen and monitor progress. Find out if your state has adopted the Common Core State Standards and, if so, how they are being implemented.

Professional Reflection

Do I
___ Have an understanding of the process of evaluation?
___ Have an understanding of test validity, reliability, and fairness?
___ Set realistic goals for instruction and communicate the goals to students?

___ Monitor progress and check for understanding?
___ Place students in the appropriate level of materials?
___ Evaluate progress and make changes as necessary?

Reflection Question

Data from summative tests indicate that Mr. Angelo's class has a general weakness in comprehension. He is in the process of planning an assessment program that he can use to monitor progress and provide information that will help him plan an effective program. What assessment instruments might Mr. Angelo use that would take a minimum of time but that would provide the information he needs?

Building Competencies

To build competencies, consult the following sources for more detailed information:

- Assessment Training Institute
  http://www.assessmentinst.com
  The institute advocates the kind of assessment that fosters students' competence and learning.

- National Center on Student Progress Monitoring
  http://www.studentprogress.org
  This site provides good coverage of CBMs but neglects other, more authentic ways of monitoring progress.

- The Lexile Framework® for Reading
  http://www.lexile.com
  The Lexile Framework is becoming the dominant system for estimating the difficulty level of books. This site offers a detailed explanation of the system and a number of resources.

- Colorín Colorado
  http://www.colorincolorado.org
  This site has a broad range of resources in both English and Spanish for teachers and parents of ELLs.

- Gersten, R., Baker, S. K., Shanahan, T., Linan-Thompson, S., Collins, P., & Scarcella, R. (2007). *Effective literacy and English language instruction for English learners in the elementary grades: IES practice guide* (NCEE 2007-4011). Washington, DC: National Cen-

ter for Education Evaluation and Regional Assistance, Institute of Education Sciences, U.S. Department of Education.
  http://www.ies.ed.gov/ncee/wwc/pdf/practiceguides/20074011.pdf

- This document makes research-based suggestions for assessing and instructing ELLs but includes some recommendations that are controversial.

- LD OnLine
  http://www.ldonline.org
  Excellent source of information and teaching resources regarding learning disabilities and ADHD.

- Brown, J. E., & Sanford, A. (2011). *RTI for English language learners: Appropriately using screening and progress-monitoring tools to improve instructional outcomes.* National Center on Response to Intervention.
  http://www.rti4success.org/pdf/rtiforells.pdf

- National Governors Association Center for Best Practices and the Council of Chief State School Officers (2010). *Common core state standards for English language arts & literacy in history/social studies, science, and technical subjects. Appendix A: Research supporting key elements of the standards. Glossary of key terms.*
  http://www.corestandards.org/assests/Appendix_A.pdf

MyEducationLab™

Go to the Topics "Assessment" and "Fluency" in the MyEducationLab (www.myeducationlab.com) for your course, where you can:

- Find learning outcomes for "Assessment" and "Fluency" along with the national standards that connect to these outcomes.
- Complete Assignments and Activities that can help you more deeply understand the chapter content.
- Apply and practice your understanding of the core teaching skills identified in the chapter with the Building Teaching Skills and Dispositions learning units.
- Examine challenging situations and cases presented in the IRIS Center Resources.
- Check your comprehension on the content covered in the chapter by going to the Study Plan in the Book

Resources for your text. Here you will be able to take a chapter quiz, receive feedback on your answers, and then access Review, Practice, and Enrichment activities to enhance your understanding of chapter content. (optional)

 A+RISE® Standards2Strategy™ is an innovative and interactive online resource that offers new teachers in grades K–12 just-in-time, research-based instructional strategies that meet the linguistic needs of ELLs as they learn content, differentiate instruction for all grades and abilities, and are aligned to Common Core Elementary Language Arts standards (for the literacy strategies) and to English language proficiency standards in WIDA, Texas, California, and Florida.

3

Approaches to Teaching Reading

Anticipation Guide

For each of the following statements related to the chapter you are about to read, put a check under "Agree" or "Disagree" to show how you feel. Discuss your responses with classmates before you read the chapter.

	Agree	Disagree
1. A structured approach to reading is most effective.	_____	_____
2. Extensive reading of children's books should be a part of every elementary and middle school reading program.	_____	_____
3. Teacher and method are equally important.	_____	_____
4. A writing approach to reading works best with young children.	_____	_____
5. An individualized reading program is hard to manage.	_____	_____
6. A commercial reading program, such as a basal series or literature anthology, is best for new teachers because it shows them step by step how to teach reading.	_____	_____
7. Teachers should combine the best parts of each reading approach.	_____	_____
8. Teachers should be free to choose the approach to reading that they feel works best.	_____	_____

Using What You Know

There are really just two main ways of learning to read: by reading and by writing, or some combination of the two. The approach that uses writing is known as language experience. Reading approaches use textbooks (including basal anthologies and linguistic reading series) and children's books. Children's books are used in the individualized and literature-based approaches. Of course, these approaches can also be combined in various ways. Teachers who use basals or literature anthologies often supplement their programs with language-experience stories and children's books. Which of these approaches are you familiar with? What are the characteristics of the approaches? What are their advantages? Their disadvantages?

Changing Approaches to Teaching Reading

Reading instruction is now undergoing a major change. With the goal of having every student college and career ready and the advent of the widely accepted Common Core State Standards, reading instruction is set to become more challenging. Because of an apparent gap between the demands made by college and career reading and the capabilities of high school seniors, students will be expected to read at higher levels beginning in grade two and extending up into high school so that the gap is eliminated. The Standards also call for increased reading of informational text. However, informational reading is more demanding than narrative fictional reading, so this also will make the literacy program more challenging. Because informational text requires its own specific set of skills and strategies or adaptations of general skills and strategies, it means that literacy instruction will need to be expanded. The Common Core Standards call for approaches to literacy instruction that are more rigorous and more effective but that consider the needs of all students.

FYI

Until recently, reading was considered a skills subject; it did not really matter what students read. Today, content is paramount, the idea being that students' minds and lives will be enriched if they read the best that has been written. ◼

 Using Technology

Information about the major basal series is available on the following sites:

Houghton Mifflin Harcourt
http://www.hmhschool.com

Macmillan/McGraw-Hill
http://www.mhschool.com/reading/index.html

Open Court (SRA/McGraw-Hill)
http://www.sraonline.com

Scott Foresman
http://www.pearsonschool.com/index.cfm?locator=PSZ14j ◼

Effective approaches incorporate the basic principles of teaching literacy that have been emphasized throughout this book:

Students become readers and writers by reading and writing.

- Literacy programs should include a rich variety of interesting, appropriate material and should stress a great deal of reading and writing.
- Strategies that promote independence in word recognition and comprehension should be taught.
- Literacy programs should be language-based. Provision should be made for developing speaking and listening as well as reading and writing skills.
- Because reading fosters writing development and writing fosters reading development, literacy programs should develop both.
- Provision should be made for individual differences. Because students differ in terms of interests, abilities, learning rate, experiential background, and culture, the approach used should take into consideration the needs of all students. Provision needs to be made for struggling readers and English language learners.
- Students' progress should be monitored, and provision should be made for helping students fully develop their potential.

This chapter examines the major approaches to teaching reading and writing. Each approach has its strengths and weaknesses. Suggestions are made for adapting each approach to take advantage of its strengths and compensate for its weaknesses. For instance, ways to make the basal approach more holistic are suggested. Thus, if it has been mandated that you use a basal series but you prefer a holistic approach, you can adapt your instruction to make the program more holistic and still keep within the guidelines of the school or school district that employs you.

Basal/Anthology Approach

How were you taught to read? Chances are you were taught through **a basal/anthology reading program**. Basal readers are the main approach to teaching reading in the United States. A complex package based on a relatively simple concept, the basal program includes a series of readers or anthologies and supplementary materials that gradually increase in difficulty, thus serving as stepping stones along a path that begins with emergent literacy and extends through sixth-grade reading. Accompanying teacher's manuals provide guidance so that the classroom teacher can lead students upward.

Designed to be integrated language arts programs, today's basals have comprehension, spelling, grammar, oral language, listening, and vocabulary components and, at the lower levels, systematic instruction in phonics. Created to meet the needs of most students, basals have materials for average, above average, and below-level readers and ELLs. They also have accompanying intervention programs. In addition to anthology selections, they include supplementary books and read-aloud anthologies. In some series, materials are written on the three difficulty levels but have the same topic, vocabulary, and strategies so that they can be used, at least in part, for whole-class instruction. In addition, basals have related workbooks, detailed teacher's manuals packed with teaching suggestions, big books, supplementary libraries of excellent children's books, read-aloud books, e-books, a wide array of games and manipulatives, audio recordings, digital versions of some text, computer software, video discs, inservice programs, home-school programs, posters, charts, unit, benchmark, and end-of-book tests, placement and diagnostic tests, observation guides, portfolio systems, Web sites, and more.

Some of the basal series have become partially digitized. Using a Web-based management system, teachers can plan lessons by consulting the online teacher's manual and noting which of the many resources they would like to use. Most of the basals have portions of the students' materials in

◼ A **basal/anthology reading program** is a comprehensive program for teaching reading that includes readers or anthologies that gradually increase in difficulty, teacher's manuals, workbooks, and assessment measures. In grades 7 and 8 and sometimes in grade 6, teachers use literature texts instead of basals.

digital format. Using the digital versions, students can highlight text and take notes as they read, and answer checkup questions by writing responses. They can also have words pronounced, and meanings provided. They can even have selections read aloud. One program has a dual speed for read-alouds: one for slower intensive reading and one at natural speed so as to model fluency. Another program allows ELL students to move back and forth between English and Spanish.

At one time, there were more than a dozen basal reading programs. Today, there are just four: Houghton Mifflin Harcourt, Macmillan/McGraw-Hill, Scott Foresman, and Open Court (SRA/McGraw-Hill). The programs from Houghton Mifflin Harcourt, Macmillan/McGraw-Hill, and Scott Foresman are more alike than different. However, each one has an area of relative strength. Houghton Mifflin Harcourt's basal reading program has a strong vocabulary component. Macmillan/McGraw-Hill's has a strong word study component that features sorting. Scott Foresman's has a focus on New Literacies. Open Court's basal reading program is somewhat different from the other three in that it is a scripted program. A scripted program is one in which the teacher is expected to closely follow the teacher's manual and even use the words indicated. Open Court also offers the most extensive word analysis component.

Today's basals are bigger and better than ever. But the real question is "Are today's basals good enough?" The answer is yes and no. Basals have many advantages, but they also have some shortcomings.

Advantages of Basals

Basals offer teachers a convenient package of materials, techniques, and assessment devices, as well as a plan for orchestrating the various components of a total literacy program. In their anthologies, which, for the most part, gradually increase in difficulty, basals offer students a steady progression from emergent literacy through a sixth-grade reading level. They also offer varied reading selections, an abundance of practice material, carefully planned units and lessons, and a wealth of follow-up and enrichment activities.

Disadvantages of Basals

Despite a major overhaul, basals are still driven by the same engine. The core of the basal reading program is the trio of anthology, workbook, and teacher's manual. Although the contents of the anthology are much improved, its function remains the same—to provide a base of materials for all students to move through. However, students have diverse interests and abilities and progress at different rates. Although basal selections are meant to be of high quality, they will not all be of interest to all students. The sports biography that delights one child is a total bore to another.

A second shortcoming has to do with the way basal readers are assembled: They are anthologies and often contain excerpts from whole books. For example, the fourth-grade reader from a typical series contains "The Diary of Leigh Botts," a delightful tale of a budding young writer that is excerpted from Beverly Cleary's 1983 Newbury Award winner, *Dear Mr. Henshaw*. If reading the excerpt is worthwhile, reading the whole book should be even better.

There is also the question of pacing and time spent with a selection. Students often move through basals in lockstep fashion. Part of the problem is the nature of the teacher's manuals; they offer too much of a good thing. Stories and even poems are overtaught. There are too many questions asked before a selection is read, too many asked after the piece has been read, and too many follow-up activities. A class might spend three days on a thousand-word story. To be fair, the manuals do present activities as choices. Teachers can choose those they wish to undertake and omit the others. Teachers may even be provided a choice of ways of presenting a story: interactively, with the teacher modeling strategies; independently, with the teacher providing a minimum of assistance; or with support, which means that students follow along as the

Using Technology

Programs, such as Reading Mastery (SRA), have been written specifically to reinforce phonic elements. Reading Mastery is a highly scripted program with a strict behaviorist approach. However, it has been used successfully with at risk learners. The National Institute for Direct Instruction provides more information on the theory behind Reading Mastery. http://nifdi.org ■

Teachers sometimes use minibooks in their guided reading lessons.

 FYI

In her comparison of students who were read *to* and students who read *with* her, Kuhn (2004) found that students showed more growth when they read rather than being read to.

teacher reads the story. All in all, the typical basal lesson has many fine suggestions, but the ideas are "canned," that is, created by someone in an editorial office far from the classroom. Designed to be all things to all teachers, the activities are not designed for a specific class of students with specific needs and interests.

Perhaps the biggest disadvantage of basals is the organizational pattern they suggest. Basal reading series have core selections in anthologies and also supplementary reading in libraries of leveled readers. The core basal selections are presented to the whole class. The selections are generally appropriate for average students but may not be challenging enough for the best readers and are too hard for as many as the one student out of four in the typical classroom who is reading below grade level. Suggestions are made for adapting instruction for all learners. This may mean reading selections to the poorest readers or providing them with an audio or digital version of the selection so that they can read along. Or, the teacher might simply read the selection to the whole class. Whatever your approach, you need to provide access for all students. If you do read the selection to students, have them follow along in their text. This provides them with exposure to print. To keep them involved, from time to time, call on the whole group to read a portion with you in choral reading style.

In addition to reading or listening to the core selection, students also read in guided reading groups. All basal series have sets of books on three levels—easy, average, and challenging—giving all students the opportunity to read books on their level. However, a key question remains: Which students do the least reading? Since the average and above-average students read the core selection and the least advanced group listens to the selection or reads along with it, those students most in need of reading practice do the least amount of reading. If you are using a basal, you need to make adjustments so that struggling readers are reading more, not less, than the other students. Some basals offer an alternative selection for struggling readers, which is related to the theme in the core selection but is easier to read. If available, you might use this option.

Unfortunately, even the use of both interactive read-alouds and guided reading groups does not quite solve the problem of meeting the needs of below-level readers. All of a theme's (or unit's) activities revolve around the core selection, including phonics or other decoding lessons and workbook exercises. However, these activities are on the same level as the core selection and so are too difficult and/or inappropriate for below-level readers. For instance, consider a basal core selection that is on a mid–first-grade level. The phonics lesson introduces the final-*e* long-*i* pattern, but the below-level readers haven't yet mastered short-vowel patterns. Long-vowel patterns are beyond their grasp. Workbook exercises reinforce the pattern. The core selection, *The Kite* by Alma Flor Ada, also provides practice with the pattern. Listening to the core selection would be useful for below-level readers, but taking part in the phonics lesson or attempting the workbook exercises would not be appropriate and, in fact, could undermine the confidence of the below-level readers, as noted in Chapter 5. What's the solution?

Above all, struggling readers need materials and instruction on their level. The "trickle-down" approach does not meet the needs of these readers. Instead of using the core on-level selection with struggling readers, obtain materials on their instructional level so that they are actually reading rather than simply listening to or reading along with selections too difficult for them to read on their own. They need decoding instruction and selections that reinforce the decoding skills they have been taught. The teacher might use texts and activities from the program that are on these students' level. For example, first-grade struggling readers might be placed in theme 2 (out of ten themes covered in a year's time) rather than theme 5, which is where the achieving readers are working. Second-graders who are below level might work in first-grade readers, perhaps starting with theme 6 or 7, depending on their reading level and the skills they have mastered. Using lower-level materials that match struggling readers' reading levels is generally the best solution, since it allows them to develop the skills needed to make progress in the program and provides coordination between the skills taught, the practice activities, and the key selections being read.

Another solution is to use the resources provided in the basal reading program. All basals include below-level books and phonics readers created for the series, as well as a listing of below-level trade books. These materials can be used with struggling readers, as long as they match those students' reading levels. Although these materials can provide much needed practice and application, they are not accompanied by essential decoding instruction. You will need to supply this.

A third solution is to use an intervention program. Most basal programs include an intervention program, or you can obtain a stand-alone program. Of course, you can combine these solutions. A good combination is to use the lower-level reader or anthology of the basal program that matches struggling readers' needs and an intervention program that provides added instruction and practice so that the struggling readers can catch up.

Adapting Basals

Despite the criticisms voiced here and elsewhere, there is nothing intrinsically wrong with basals. Over the years, thousands of teachers have successfully used basals to teach millions of children. However, in keeping with today's research and promising practices, basals should be adapted in the following ways.

Although basal manuals have been criticized as being too didactic (Goodman, 1994a), the fault may be with the professionals who use them. Manuals and, in fact, the entire basal program should be viewed as a resource. The manual is a treasure chest of ideas, and the anthologies are good, representative collections of children's literature. As professionals, we should feel free to use those selections that seem appropriate and to use the manual as a resource rather than a guide. Select only those suggestions and activities that seem appropriate and effective.

As a new teacher in a large urban school system, I had the good fortune to work for administrators who encouraged the integration of language arts and the use of themed units but frowned on the use of teacher's manuals and workbooks. In fact, a manual was not available for the basal that I used. Not having a teacher's manual, I planned my own units and my own lessons. In retrospect, I realize that some of my lessons fell flat. However, others worked extremely well. I still recall with pride being asked to present a model lesson for other new teachers at one of our monthly meetings. Good, bad, or indifferent, the lessons were my own, and so I had made a commitment to them. When I planned my lessons, I kept in mind the needs and interests of my students. I especially enjoyed building interest in a story so that they really wanted to read it. And I did not present any stories I disliked or thought the students would not like.

Other adaptations that might be made to make basals more effective include the following:

- *Use workbooks and other practice materials judiciously.* Workbooks and other practice materials have both management and instructional roles. Students can work in them independently while the teacher meets with a small group or individual children. Some workbook exercises provide valuable reinforcement. However, as Pincus (2005) comments, "Many workbook tasks are not interesting, do not provide rich instructional possibilities, lack clear objectives, allow false-positive feedback, consume teachers' time in scoring them, and, most importantly, occupy time that can be otherwise spent teaching students what they do not already know" (p. 79).

Adapting Instruction for Struggling Readers

To provide added reinforcement with phonics patterns, use the books listed on pp. 212–214. ∎

 FYI

Three of the four major basal series offer teachers a variety of instructional choices. However, the Open Court series is scripted. It tells teachers what to say and offers a tightly structured sequence of teaching activities. Although novice teachers might welcome the guidance, veteran teachers may desire more flexibility, despite the good results that this series often obtains. ∎

REFLECTION

What has been your experience with a basal/anthology program? Did you learn to read with a basal approach? Are you using one now? What do you see as the advantages and disadvantages of the basal/anthology approach? How might you deal with the issue of making sure that struggling readers were given more time reading on their level rather than less?

 FYI

Reading programs vary in the rate at which they introduce skills, the number of words they introduce, and the amount of practice they provide (Hiebert, Martin, & Menon, 2005; Dewitz, Jones, & Leahy, 2009). If your program does not offer enough practice or introduces skills too rapidly, use supplementary materials or children's books for added reinforcement or to bridge gaps. ∎

FYI

• Reading easy books independently provides students with much needed practice. "Clocking up reading mileage on easy materials is one of the most important aspects of independent reading" (Learning Media, 1991, p. 76).

• As Murray (2006d) notes, today's basal anthologies have high-quality selections and abundant resources. However, they differ in the quality and effectiveness of their lessons and the amount of reinforcement provided. Comprehension strategies—especially strategies as complex as summarizing—require extensive teaching and practice, probably more than a commercial reading program can offer. If you are using a commercial program, you will probably need to supplement it with comprehension instruction. ▪

Before using a workbook exercise, ask yourself these questions: Is the exercise worth doing? Does it reinforce a skill in which students need added practice? How should the exercise be completed? Should it be done independently, or does it require instruction? Also make sure that the exercise is on the appropriate level for your students. Especially valuable are workbook exercises that provide additional reading of paragraphs or other text, added experience with vocabulary words, or practice with graphic organizers. If a workbook exercise fails to measure up, it should be skipped. The teacher should provide alternative activities, such as having students read children's books or work in learning centers. Reading builds background and gives students an opportunity to integrate and apply skills. Instead of just practicing for the main event, they are taking part in it. In fact, students get far better practice reading children's books than they do completing workbook exercises. Writing, drawing, discussing, and preparing a presentation also provide superior alternatives to workbook exercises.

• *Emphasize wide reading of a variety of materials.*   No matter how well the basal program has been put together, students need to read a broader range of fiction and nonfiction materials, including books, magazines, newspapers, sets of directions, brochures, ads, menus, schedules, and other real-world materials. Make use of the extensive libraries of children's books offered by basal publishers to supplement the basal materials; excellent suggestions for additional reading are also provided in basal manuals.

• *Focus on a few key skills or strategies.*   Teach and use key skills and strategies in context. Today's basal series offer instruction in a wide variety of skills or strategies. In trying to cover so many areas, they typically spread themselves too thin and so fail to present crucial skills in sufficient depth. It may take twenty lessons or more before students are able to draw inferences or identify main ideas, but a basal program might present just two or three lessons on such skills. For instance, in one program the target strategy for the first week is summarizing; the next week, monitoring; the third week, visualizing. Although a summarizing question is in the selection read the second week, there is no review or extension of the strategy. Summarizing is not addressed in the third week. Make necessary adaptations so that skills and strategies are given the instruction and practice they require. In this instance, adapt instruction so that some summarizing activities are included, such as asking questions that require summarizing or provide practice in summarizing content-area reading in which students engage.

• *Provide opportunities for struggling readers to read appropriate-level material every day.*   Make use of the supplementary programs or leveled libraries designed for struggling readers. In this era of college and career readiness and RTI, struggling readers should be given added instruction and do more reading so that they can catch up.

• *Gradually take control of your literacy program.*   Decide what your philosophy of teaching literacy is. List the objectives you see as most important, aligning them, of course, with the standards set by your school and school district. If possible, work with other professionals to create a literacy program that makes sense for your situation. Consider basals as only one source of materials and teaching ideas. Basals are neither a method nor an approach to teaching reading. They are simply carefully crafted sets of materials. The core of any reading program is the teacher. It is the teacher who should decide how and when to use basals and whether to choose alternative materials. As Tyner (2004) recommends, "A basal reading program was never meant to provide a complete program, only a starting point. Basal readers are most effective when they are used flexibly and as part of a comprehensive, balanced program of instruction" (p. 2). Also use your professional expertise. For instance, if the basal your school district is using doesn't provide enough practice using strategies, arrange

▪ **Linguistic patterns** are regularities in the spelling of English words. A linguistic patterns approach presents patterns by comparing and contrasting words that have minimal differences (*pat–pan*) so that students can see how they differ. Although such an approach isn't used by many classroom teachers, it is frequently employed by remedial specialists.

for more practice. If the series fails to take advantage of regularities when teaching high-frequency words, adapt instructions so as to point out the regularities *wh* = /w/ and *t* =/t/ in a word such as *what* (Scott Foresman's Reading Street and Sidewalks follow this practice).

Basal readers extend only to grade 6. In grade 7 and beyond, students use literature anthologies or sets of texts that have literary value instead of basal readers. The main difference between basal readers and literature anthologies is the focus on literature. Literature anthologies also place emphasis on appreciation. However, the anthologies often provide some coverage of reading skills. Today's literature anthologies are very comprehensive. They typically feature a mix of contemporary works and classics. A full-length novel may accompany the anthology. The best of these anthologies provide a host of materials that teachers can use to prepare students to read the selections and to extend their appreciation and understanding. Well-designed literature anthologies also feature a program of skill development for struggling readers. In general, literature anthologies have the same advantages and disadvantages as basal series.

Minibook Series

A number of beginning-reading programs consist of series of minibooks of increasing difficulty. The series ease children into reading and move them from emergent to fluent reading. Books at the emergent stage are designed so that students can enjoy them before they can actually read them. Illustrations help children predict what the text might say. The text itself is brief, often consisting of a single sentence that contains a repetitive phrase. Each page of the book might contain the same repeated phrase. The books are read through shared reading, and eventually students can, with the help of illustrations, read the books on their own. At this point, students are primarily "reading" pictures rather than text. The intent is to emphasize reading for enjoyment and meaning. Of course, students are also picking up concepts about print.

After students have enjoyed a number of books and shown an interest in reading print, text-reading strategies are introduced. Difficulty and length of text are carefully controlled so that students gradually grow into reading. As students gain in skill, they move into more challenging stages. Some of the best-known kits include Story Box® (The Wright Group), Sunshine™ Series (The Wright Group), and Literacy by Design (Houghton Mifflin Harcourt). Literacy by Design provides instruction in phonemic-awareness, phonics, vocabulary, comprehension, fluency, and writing. One drawback of these series is that the texts at the early levels do not adequately reinforce decoding patterns. The series are not decodable. A minibook series that provides reinforcement for phonics patterns without resorting to tongue-twisting tales is Ready Readers (Modern Curriculum Press). Minibook series enjoy widespread use, especially in grade 1, and are often used as supplements to a basal or other approach. In fact, all of today's basal series have supplementary kits of easy-to-read booklets, which feature decodable texts at the early levels.

Closing the Gap: Providing Better Reinforcement

With the right kind of intervention, it is possible for struggling readers to catch up. In one study of first-graders, struggling readers caught up to average readers in just 15 weeks (Menon & Hiebert, 2003). The control group had a typical basal. The intervention group was given a series of 150 minibooks that were designed to reinforce the phonics patterns they had been taught but were not written in the sing-song fashion characteristic of some decodable texts. The minibooks were carefully sequenced so that in all instances easier books were presented before more difficult books. The books gradually became more challenging. In addition to reading books that were more carefully sequenced and did a better job of reinforcing patterns that had been

FYI

Programs such as Breakthrough to Literacy and Lightspan make heavy use of technology. In addition to computerized lessons, Breakthrough to Literacy includes big books, pupil books, and take-home books. Lightspan uses the Internet as well as traditional methods to provide ongoing assessment, professional development, and additional learning activities. ■

Using Technology

Titlewave offers lists of books to be used in conjunction with popular textbook programs (including basal anthologies), books for guided and leveled reading, and award-winning books.

Can search its database of 50,000 books by level, grade, genre, or general interest.

http://www.flr.follett.com/

See also Book Wizard

http://bookwizard.scholastic.com/tbw/homePage.do ■

taught, the intervention group read a greater variety of words. They read between 500 and 1,000 words a week. The basal group read an average of 250 words. The basal group, which devoted a full week to a selection, reread the same story several times, so they may have read as many words as the intervention group, but they did this by reading the same words over and over again. Reading several books seems to be more effective than reading the same book over and over again.

 Literature-Based Approach

More and more teachers are using literature as the core of their programs. Today's basal anthologies feature high-quality selections drawn from children's literature. Increasingly, basals are including children's books in their entirety as an integral part of the program or as a recommended component. Although there is some overlap between a basal program and a literature-based approach, the term **literature-based approach** is used here to describe a program that uses sets of children's books as a basis for providing instruction in literacy. A major advantage of this approach is that teachers, independently or in committees, choose the books they wish to use with their students; thus, the reading material is tailored to students' interests and needs.

A literature-based program may be organized in a variety of ways. Three popular models are core literature, text sets, and thematic units or transactional units. Transactional units are theme-based units that begin with an overall plan just as traditional thematic units do, but the plan is subject to modification depending on students' needs and interests. The unit becomes a "blend of preplanned lessons and response-centered teaching" (Serafini, 2006, p. 23).

Core Literature

Core literature is literature that has been selected for a careful, intensive reading. Core selections are often read by the whole class, but may be read by selected groups. Core literature pieces might include such children's classics as *The Little House* (Burton, 1942) and *Aesop's Fables* or more recent works such as *Shiloh* (Naylor, 1991), *Number the Stars* (Lowry, 1989), *Lunch Money* (Selznick, 2007), *Where the Mountain Meets the Moon* (Linn, 2009), or *Winn–Dixie* (DiCamillo, 2000).

Serafini (2006) uses what he calls *cornerstone texts* in his reading units. The cornerstone text introduces the unit and provides a foundation for discussing subsequent texts. For instance, for a unit on reading informational texts, the cornerstone text was *Volcano* (Magloff, 2003). *Volcano* has a rich array of access features: photos, charts, graphs, diagrams, headings, sidebars, glossary, and index. After being introduced to the use of these elements in *Volcano*, students were prepared to make use of them as they read other informational texts. *Volcano* was also used to demonstrate previewing and other key strategies for reading informational texts. After discussing *Volcano*, students selected topics of inquiry and read related high-quality informational texts.

In addition to providing students with a rich foundation in the best of children's literature, the use of core selections also builds community (Ford, 1994). It gives students a shared experience, thereby providing the class with common ground for conversations about selections and also a point of reference for comparing and contrasting a number of selections. The use of core literature should help boost the self-esteem of the poorer readers, who are often given less mature or less significant reading material. As Cox and Zarillo (1993) noted, in the core literature model, "no child is denied access to the best of children's literature" (p. 109).

However, there are some obvious problems with the core literature approach. Children have diverse interests and abilities. What is exciting to one child may be boring to another. An easy read for one child may be

CCSS

See Appendix B of Common Core State Standards.
for a listing of possible core literature texts.
http://www.corestandardsorg/assets/Appendix_B.pdf

 FYI

Provide students with choices in their reading. They might choose from a selection of three to five novels, for instance. ■

■ The **literature-based approach** is a way of teaching reading by using literary selections as the primary instructional materials.

■ **Core literature** is literature selected to be read and analyzed by a group or an entire class. In a core literature approach, students read the same book.

an overwhelming task for another. Careful selection of core books with universal appeal should take care of the interest factor. It is difficult, for instance, to imagine any child not being intrigued by Wilder's *Little House in the Big Woods* (1932). Selections can also be presented in such a way as to be accessible to all.

Core selections might also be overanalyzed. Move at a lively pace when working with a core book. Do not move so slowly that the book becomes boring—but do not rush through the book so that slower readers cannot keep up. Do allow students to read ahead if they want to. If they finish the text early, they might read related books or books of their own choosing. Also, avoid assigning too many activities. Activities should build reading and writing skills or background knowledge and should deepen or extend students' understanding of the text. In addition, if you do use core books, make sure that students are provided with some opportunities to select books, so that teacher-selected texts are balanced by student-selected ones. Also provide for individual differences in reading ability. If core books are too difficult for some students, provide additional assistance, or, if necessary, read the books to them or obtain audiotapes of the texts. If audiotapes are available for all to use, there will be no stigma attached to using them. However, make sure that low-achieving readers have ample opportunity to read books on their level. This may entail scheduling sessions in which books on their level are introduced and discussed.

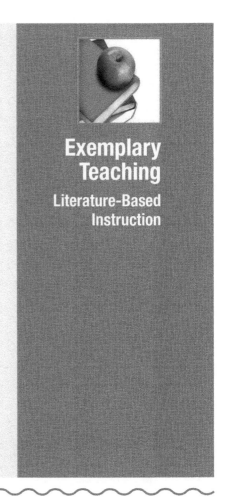

Exemplary Teaching
Literature-Based Instruction

Coming to a second-grade classroom composed primarily of poor children, many of whom were reading on a beginning reading level, researcher James Baumann set up a balanced literature-based program that reflected three principles: reading of high-quality children's books, explicit instruction in skills and strategies, and engaging in a significant amount of reading and writing each day.

The program was implemented through a series of routines that included reading aloud to students; intensive instruction in skills and strategies; providing students opportunities to read and discuss high-quality literature selections; providing time for self-selected, independent reading; and conducting writer's workshops. In addition, Baumann related reading and writing, used a variety of grouping patterns so that individual needs were met, and conducted a study buddies program with the fifth-grade class next door. In the study buddies program, half of Baumann's class went next door to meet their study buddies. The other half stayed where they were, and the study buddies came to them. During the 30-minute sessions, the second-graders worked on reading and writing with the help of their study buddies.

Baumann made use of a wide variety of techniques, including reading aloud, shared reading, choral reading, direct instruction, functional phonics lessons, and guided reading. Although explicit instruction was stressed, it was conducted within the context of real reading or writing. Baumann used an 80–20 rule, which meant that 80 percent of the time was spent reading and 20 percent was spent in skills/strategy instruction.

Working closely with parents, Baumann kept them informed about their children's progress and the work the class was doing. In notes sent home and in formal and informal conferences, parents were given suggestions for supporting their children's work. To foster reading at home, Baumann invited the children to take turns taking home Leo, the Read-With-Me Lion, or Molly, the Read-With-Me Monkey. Both stuffed animals had a pocket to hold a book and a parent card describing techniques that the parents might use to share the book with the child.

Assessment was conducted through observation, interviews, and examination of samples of the children's work. An abbreviated informal reading inventory was also administered. Inventory results showed that the children gained an average of two years. More importantly, they became avid readers. As Baumann commented, "They read up a storm" (Baumann & Duffy, 1997; Baumann & Ivey, 1997).

Text Sets

Text sets are groups of related books. Reading text sets fosters the making of connections. When students can make connections, their reading of all related texts is enriched (Harste, Short, & Burke, 1988). In addition to deepening readers' background, text sets broaden readers' framework for thinking about literature. Having read two or more related books, they can compare and contrast them. Discussions are also enlivened because students have more to talk about. If students read books on the same topic, understanding can be developed in greater depth.

Thematic Units

Another model of literature-based instruction is the **unit**, which has a theme or other unifying element. Its unifying element may be the study of a particular author, a genre—mystery or picture books, for example—or a theme. Possible themes include such diverse topics as heroes, distant places, sports and hobbies, animals, teddy bears, friendship, plants, or the Westward Movement. A unit's theme may involve only the language arts, or it may cut across the curriculum and include social studies, science, math, and the visual and performing arts.

Thematic organization has a number of advantages, the principal one being that it helps students make connections among reading, writing, listening, speaking, and viewing activities and among different pieces of literature. If the language arts are integrated with other subjects, even broader and more numerous connections can be constructed. However, Routman (1991) cautioned that before the language arts are integrated with content area subjects, they should first be integrated with each other.

Routman (1991) also warned that some thematic units lack depth and "are nothing more than suggested activities clustered around a central focus or topic" (p. 277). In her judgment, this is correlation rather than integration. In order for true integration to occur, the unit must develop some overall concepts or understandings, and activities must be designed to support those concepts or understandings. For instance, a unit may revolve around famous people, with students reading and writing about such people, but the unit is not truly integrated unless the reading and related activities developed a genuine theme or core idea. "Famous people" is a topic rather than a theme because it does not express a unifying idea. A unifying idea for a unit might be expressed as "Successful people have had to overcome obstacles on their way to success" or "Successful people have many characteristics in common." An excellent way to integrate such a unit is to create broad questions to be answered by students: "What are the secrets of success?" or "What are successful people like?" Ideally, these are questions that students have had a hand in creating. As part of the unit's activities, students read about successful people, then interview and write about them in order to integrate information from the unit and answer broad questions. They might look at successful people in science, social studies, and the arts.

A suggested procedure for creating and implementing a thematic unit follows:

1. *Select a topic or theme that you wish to explore.*   When deciding upon a theme, select one that encompasses concepts that are an important part of the curriculum and that will facilitate the development of essential language arts goals. The theme should be significant and interesting to students.

2. *Involve students in the planning.*   Determine through a modified KWL or similar technique what they know about the topic and what they would like to learn.

3. *State the overall ideas that you wish the unit to emphasize.*   Include questions that your students might have about the topic (Routman, 1991). Key reasons for a unit on the West-

▪ A **text set** is a group of related books. Because the books are related, reading and comparing them deepen readers' understanding of the unifying theme or topic.

▪ A **unit** is a way of organizing instruction around a central idea, topic, or focus.

ward Movement might include: reasons for moving west, problems encountered during the move, transportation in the west, and life in a frontier settlement (DiLuglio, Eaton, & de Tarnowsky, 1988). Also, compose a list of language arts objectives. What literary appreciations and comprehension, study, writing, or other skills and strategies will the unit develop? These objectives should tie in with the unit's overall ideas. They should help students understand the nature of the Westward Movement. Included in the list of skill/strategy objectives are reading skills, such as summarizing, and writing skills, such as report writing, that students need in order to investigate the Westward Movement. Because the unit is interdisciplinary, objectives are listed for each content area.

4. *Decide on the reading materials and activities that will be included in the unit.*   You may wish to focus on a core book that will become the center of the unit. Using a semantic map or web, show how you might integrate each of the language arts. Show, too, how you might integrate science, social studies, and other areas. Each activity should advance the theme of the unit. Activities should also promote skill/strategy development in the language arts and other areas. For instance, in the Westward Movement unit, students might simulate a journey west. As part of the simulation, they could write journal entries and track their progress on a map.

5. *List and gather resources, including materials to be read, centers to be set up, audiovisual aids, Web sites, and guest speakers or resource personnel.*   Be sure to work closely with school and town librarians if students will be doing outside reading or research. The "Westward Movement" unit might list *Sarah, Plain and Tall* (MacLachlan, 1985), *Caddie Woodlawn* (Brink, 1935), *A Gathering of Days* (Blos, 1979), and other high-quality selections (Di-Luglio, Eaton, & de Tarnowsky, 1988). These texts vary in difficulty level from grade 3 to grade 7, so all the students might have materials on an appropriate level of difficulty.

6. *Plan a unit opener that will set the stage for the unit.*   A unit opener might involve showing a film or video, reading a poem or the first chapter of the core book, or staging a simulation. The opener might involve brainstorming with students to decide which aspect of the topic they would like to explore. For the "Westward Movement" unit, students might imagine how it might feel if they were making a long, dangerous trip across the country.

7. *Evaluate.*   Evaluation should be broad-based and keyed to the objectives that you have set for your students or that they have set for themselves in collaboration with you. It should include the unit's major concepts or ideas as well as skills and strategies that were emphasized. For example, if the ability to visualize was emphasized, it needs to be assessed. If you emphasized the ability to take notes or to write journals, that might be assessed through holistic evaluation of students' written pieces. As part of the evaluation, you must decide whether students learned the concepts and skills or strategies listed in the objectives. If not, reteaching is in order. In addition, you should evaluate the unit itself and determine what might be done to improve it. You might eliminate activities or materials that proved boring or ineffective and revise other elements as necessary.

FYI

Units may encompass a single area, such as language arts or social studies, or they may be integrated and cut across subject matter areas. Integrated units apply the language arts to one or more content areas. The focus is on a theme topic, such as the essential role immigrants played in the development of the United States. Curriculum lines are dropped, and all activities are devoted to that topic. ▪

Self-Selection

Reading a chapter book, novel, or full-length biography is a major commitment of time. Students will be more willing to put forth the necessary effort if they enjoy the book and have some say in its selection. Even when working with groups, it is possible to allow some self-selection. Obtain several copies of a number of appropriate books. Give a brief overview of each, and have students list them in order of preference. Group students by their preferences into literature discussion groups or similar groups. You can even allow some self-selection when using a core literature approach with the entire class. Give the students a choice of two or three core books from

FYI

Self-selection of reading fosters engagement, as does taking part in a conference with a teacher. ▪

Case Study
Implementing a Thematic Approach

In a multiyear project with struggling readers and writers in grades 6 through 8, teachers in Memphis, Tennessee, implemented a thematic approach that involved cooperating across subject-matter boundaries. The idea behind the project was to "move curriculum from an unlinked catalog of texts, collection of superficially related works, or sequential or chronological structure to a more integrated whole of episodes echoing one another in support of ongoing curricular conversations" (Athanases, 2003, p. 110). In other words, teachers structured activities so as to make connections among key ideas to give students a broader perspective on major concepts and a deeper understanding of them. Ideas introduced in language arts class were reinforced and expanded in history and science classes. While the theme of community was being developed through reading literary works, the science teacher further developed the theme by exploring one of the theme's big ideas: interdependence. Family history was linked to science themes of nature versus nurture. Subthemes of discovery, motivation, and curiosity were developed through historical biographies of exploration and scientific experimentation.

As students were studying community, a tornado ripped through Memphis, causing enormous damage but also providing numerous opportunities for people of all economic, racial, and ethnic groups to come together and help each other out. Having studied interdependence in their community unit, students were able to arrive at a deeper understanding of what was happening in their city and do a better job writing about it.

At the outset, students' concepts of community were simplistic and tended to be limited to concepts of neighborhood. By year's end, students' concepts of community had grown considerably in breadth and depth. They were able to use analogies and metaphors in their discussions of community. They were also able to draw from the literature they had read. As their teacher commented:

> That was exciting to me to see that all of a sudden literature wasn't just born in books that sit on the shelf. It was "literature and my life." There is some connection there and I think the themes do that. . . . (Athanases, 2003, p. 116)

which to select. If it is necessary for the entire class to read a particular book, plan some activities in which students can select their own reading materials. You might also alternate teacher selection with self-selection: After teaching a unit that revolves around a teacher-selected book, plan a unit in which students select books.

Choosing Materials

One of the most important tasks in structuring a literature-based program is choosing the books. If the program is to be schoolwide or districtwide, teachers at each grade level should meet and decide which books might be offered at that level. Quality and appeal of the materials must be considered. Teachers also have to think about students' reading abilities, with easy, average, and challenging books provided for each grade. All genres should be included: novels, short stories, poems, plays, myths, and well-written informational books. And, of course, as noted above, students should have a voice in the selection of books to be read.

Advantages and Disadvantages of a Literature-Based Approach

The primary advantage of a literature-based approach is that books can be chosen to meet students' needs and interests. The major disadvantage of a literature-based program is that fine literature may be misused, by being made simply a means for developing reading skills rather than a basis for fostering personal response and an aesthetic sense. A second major disadvantage is that the books chosen may not be equally appealing to all students and may in some cases be too difficult for struggling readers.

Using Technology

Many authors and publishers of children's books maintain Internet sites. Some of the sites offer free teaching guides and other instructional resources. ■

Adapting a Literature-Based Approach

In a literature-based approach, selections can be read in one of three ways: whole-class, small-group, or individually. Whole-class reading creates a sense of community and builds a common background of knowledge but neglects individual differences in reading ability and interest. Working in small groups does not build a sense of larger community but can better provide for individual differences. Individualized reading, which is described in the next section, provides for individual differences and fosters self-selection but may be inefficient. If you do use whole-class reading, use it on a limited basis and complement it with small groups or an individualized approach and self-selection.

In an individualized approach, students might pursue a favorite author.

Individualized Reading/Reading Workshop

The **individualized reading** approach is designed to create readers who can and do read. As Serafini (2006) explains, "Reading workshop is a place for engaged reading." Each student chooses her or his own reading material and has periodic conferences with the teacher to discuss it. The most popular form of individualized reading is known as **reading workshop**. Reading workshop is similar to writing workshop, but the focus is on reading. Reading workshop has three major components: preparation time, self-selected reading and responding, and student sharing (Atwell, 1987; Cooper, 1997; Reutzel and Cooter, 1991).

Preparation Time

Reading workshop begins with preparation time, which includes a state-of-the-class conference and a minilesson. The state-of-the-class conference is a housekeeping procedure and can be as brief as a minute or two. During this time, the schedule for the workshop is set, and students note what they will be doing. In the minilesson, the teacher presents a skill or strategy lesson based on a need evidenced by the whole class. It could be a lesson on making inferences, predicting, using context clues, deciphering multisyllabic words, or interpreting metaphors. Or it could be a lesson on selecting a book, finding more time to read, or how to share a book with a partner (Calkins, 2001). The minilesson might be drawn from the basal series or a literature guide or might be created by the teacher (Cooper, 1997). It should be presented within the framework of a story or article that students have read or listened to, and it should be applicable to the reading that they will do that day. The minilesson should last approximately 10 minutes, but could be longer.

Although brief, minilessons should be memorable and effective. Calkins (2001) has found a five-part format to be effective. The parts are connection, teaching, active involvement, link, and follow-up. The connection explains why a particular strategy or topic was chosen. For instance, the teacher might say, "When I'm reading a book about a new topic, I use the pictures to help me. Yesterday, I was reading about robots. I don't know much about robots, but the illustrations really helped." The teaching is the actual instruction. The teacher shows specifically how the illustrations and diagrams added to his or her understanding of robots and clarified some ideas that weren't

■ **Individualized reading** is a system of teaching reading in which students select their own reading material, read at their own pace, and are instructed in individual conferences and whole-class or small-group lessons.

■ **Reading workshop** is a form of individualized reading in which students choose their own books and have individual or group conferences but may meet in groups to discuss books or work on projects. There may also be whole-class or small-group lessons.

clear. In the active involvement part of the minilesson, students try out the strategy or a portion of it for at least a few minutes. For example, the teacher gives students a handout that describes several unusual animals but contains no illustrations. The teacher then gives students the same handout with illustrations. The students briefly discuss how the second handout helped them better understand the selection. The link part connects the strategy with a story that the students are about to read. If students are reading informational books of their own choosing, the teacher could suggest that they use the illustrations to help them better understand the topics they are reading about. In the follow-up, students are asked to tell or demonstrate how they applied the strategy. The teacher asks students to tell how illustrations helped them better understand what they read.

Serafini (2006) uses read-alouds of literary selections to prepare his students for reading. Read-alouds are used to demonstrate fluent reading, key strategies, ways to respond to others in discussions, and ways to listen to and talk about literary selections. Read-alouds are also a way to introduce new authors, books, themes, and genres and to build a community of readers. After a book has been read aloud, a copy of its cover is posted so that the book may easily be referred to in subsequent sessions.

Self-Selected Reading and Responding

At the heart of the reading workshop is the time when students read self-selected books, respond to their reading, or engage in group or individual conferences. Self-selected reading may last approximately 30 minutes; if time is available, this period can be extended. If children have difficulty reading alone for that period of time, a portion of the period might be set aside for reading with a partner or in a small group. Because students will be reading their self-selected books independently, they should be encouraged to use appropriate strategies. Before reading, they should survey, predict, and set a purpose for reading. As they read, they should use summarizing, inferencing, questioning, and imaging strategies—if appropriate—and should monitor for meaning. As they read, students can use sticky notes to indicate a difficult word or puzzling passage. Or, as suggested by Atwell (1987), they can record difficult words and the page numbers of puzzling passages on a bookmark. A full bookmark could be a sign that a book is too difficult. After reading, students should evaluate their original prediction and judge whether they can retell the selection and relate it to their own experiences.

Response time may last from 15 to 30 minutes or longer. During response time, students may meet in a literature discussion group to discuss their reading, write in their journals, work on an extension activity, plan a reader's theater or other type of presentation, work at one of the classroom's centers, continue to read, or attend a conference. During response time, hold individual and/or group conferences. If time allows, circulate around the room, giving help and guidance as needed. Visiting literature discussion groups should be a priority.

Conferences Just as for writing workshop, conferences are a key part of reading workshop. Both individual and group conferences are recommended, each having distinct advantages.

Individual Conferences Although time-consuming, the individual conference allows each student to have the teacher's full attention and direct guidance and instruction for at least a brief period. It builds a warm relationship between teacher and student and provides the teacher with valuable insights into the needs of each child. While individual conferences are being held, other students are engaged in silent reading. No interruption of the conference is allowed, and those involved in silent reading are not to be disturbed.

An individual conference begins with some questions designed to put the student at ease and to get a general sense of the student's understanding of the book. Through questioning, the teacher also attempts to elicit the child's personal response to the text and encourages the child to relate the text to her or his own life. The teacher poses questions to clear up difficulties and to build comprehension—and concepts, if necessary—and reviews difficult vocabulary. If the teacher has taught a particular skill or strategy, such as analyzing characters, using context clues, or making personal connections, that might be the focus of a conference. In addition, the teacher assesses how well the student understood the book, whether she or he enjoyed it, and whether she or he is able to apply the strategies and skills that have been taught. The teacher notes any needs the student has and may provide spontaneous instruction or give help later.

As part of the conference, the teacher might conduct a brief running record that lasts just a minute or two (Reutzel, Jones, & Newman, 2010). The running record might be conducted at the beginning of the conference. Students' performance on the running record can be used to plan on-the-spot instruction as well as future lessons.

To prepare for individual conferences, students choose a favorite part of the book to read to the teacher and also give a personal assessment of the book, telling why they did or did not like it or what they learned from it. Students also bring words, ideas, or items they want clarified or questions that they have about the text. In addition, students may be asked to complete a generic response sheet or a specific response sheet geared to the book they have read. Figure 3.1 presents a generic response form designed to elicit a personal response from students. To avoid having students do an excessive amount of writing, you might focus on just a few of the personal response questions, or have students respond to the questions orally rather than in writing.

Another way that students can prepare for an individual conference is to keep track of their reading in journals. Students note the date, the title and author of the book, and their personal response to the piece, answering questions such as these: How does the selection make me feel? What will I most remember about it? Was there anything in it that bothered me (Gage, 1990)? Did it remind me of a person or event in my life? Do I have any questions about the piece (Parsons, 1990)? For an informational book, students answer such questions as these: What did I learn? Which details did I find most interesting? How might I use the information? What questions do I still have about the topic? Questions should not be so time-consuming or arduous to answer that children avoid reading so that they will not have to answer them. As an alternative, you might have students keep a dialogue journal, as described later in this chapter. Younger children may respond to a book by drawing a picture. Whatever form the response takes, it should be geared to the maturity level of the child and the nature of the text.

Students should keep a record of all books that they read. While helping the teacher keep track of students' reading, such records are also motivational. Students get a sense of accomplishment from seeing their list grow.

Individual conferences can last anywhere from 5 to 10 minutes. At least one individual or group conference should be held for each student each week. However, not every book needs a conference. A student who is reading two or three books a week should decide on one book to talk about. On the other hand, if the student is a slow reader, a conference may be held when she or he is halfway through the book. Conferences should be scheduled. A simple way to do this is to have students who are ready for conferences list their names on the chalkboard. The teacher can then fill in the times for the conferences.

After the conference is over, the teacher should make brief notes in the student's folder, including date, title of book read, assessment of student's understanding and satisfaction with the book, strategies or skills introduced or reinforced, student's present and future needs, and student's future plans. A sample conference report form is presented in Figure 3.2.

Group Conferences Group conferences are an efficient use of time and can be used along with or instead of individual conferences. The teacher has the opportunity to work with five or six students rather than just one. Conferences can be held to discuss books by the same author, those with a common theme, or those in the same genre.

 Assessing for Learning

After holding a conference, be sure to summarize it. Include date, selection read, and student's reaction to the text: Did the student enjoy it? Is she or he able to respond to it? Is the book too difficult or too easy? Does the student select books wisely? Did you note any needs? If so, how will these be provided for? Will she or he engage in an extension or enrichment activity? Will she or he read another book? ■

 FYI

Teachers might hold conferences during silent reading and during response time. A main reason that teachers found individualized reading unmanageable in the past was the demand that conferences made on their time. However, with group conferences, this should no longer be a major hindrance. ■

FIGURE 3.1   Response
Sheet for Fiction

Name: _____   Date: _____

Title of book: _____   Publisher: _____

Author: _____   Date of publication: _____

Plot

       Problem: _____

                _____

Main happenings: _____

                              _____

                              _____

                              _____

       Climax: _____

                              _____

       Outcome: _____

Answer any three of the following questions:

1. What did you like best about the book?

    _____

    _____

    _____

2. Is there anything in the book that you would like to change? If so, what? Also
    tell why you would like to make changes.

    _____

    _____

    _____

3. Is there anything in the book that puzzled you or bothered you?

    _____

    _____

    _____

4. Would you like to be friends with any of the characters in the book? Why or
    why not?

    _____

    _____

    _____

5. If other students your age asked whether you thought they might like to read
    this book, what would you tell them?

    _____

    _____

    _____

Group conferences work best when students have read the same book. If several copies of a book are available, they can be given to interested students, who then confer.

A group conference includes three types of questions: an opening question to get the discussion started, following questions to keep the discussion moving, and process questions to "help the children focus on particular elements of the text" (Hornsby, Sukarna, & Parry, 1986, p. 62). Process questions focus on comprehending and appreciating a piece and are similar to those asked in the discussion and rereading portions of a guided reading lesson. They are often related to reading strategies and might ask students to summarize a passage, compare characters, predict events, clarify difficult terms, or locate proof for an inference. Students should also have the

Name: *Althea S.*   Date: *10/19*

Title: *Owl at Home*   Author: *Arnold Lobel*

Understanding of text and personal response: *Discussion of Ch. 1 of text: Saw humor in story. Remembered time when furnace broke and apartment was cold but became cozy again.*

Oral reading: *Fairly smooth. Good interpretation. Some difficulty reading dialogue. 97% accuracy.*

Needs: *Read behav for behave. Needs to integrate context and phonics.*

Future plans: *Plans to finish book by end of week. Will join Arnold Lobel Literature Circle and compare Owl books with Frog and Toad books. Will share funniest incident with whole class.*

FIGURE 3.2   A Sample Conference Report Form

opportunity to respond personally to the text. Process and response questions might be interwoven. The teacher should lead the discussion, although students eventually may take on that role. Just as in individual conferences, the teacher evaluates students' performance, notes needs, and plans future activities based on those needs. Along with or instead of a group conference, students might take part in a literature discussion group.

Using Dialogue Journals   If you are working with older students, you might try **dialogue journals** as an alternative or supplement to conferences. In a dialogue journal a student responds freely to a piece of writing or to a prompt about the writing provided by the teacher. The teacher then responds to the student's response. Having the opportunity to write about their reading gives students time to reflect and leads to deeper insights (Atwell, 1987). The give and take of dialogue journals leads students to develop their thoughts and reconsider interpretations. In addition to providing students with an opportunity to respond, dialogue journals yield insight into students' growth as readers. Thus, they offer the teacher a rich source of ideas for teaching lessons. Because responding to each student's journal on a daily basis could be overwhelming, you might want to have one fifth of the class turn in their journals each day. That way you respond each day to just a few students, but you see each student's journal once a week.

Student Sharing

During the student-sharing portion of reading workshop, which should last from 10 to 20 minutes, students share their reading with the entire class. They might give the highlights of a book they especially enjoyed, read an exciting passage, share a poem, make a recommendation, enact a reader's theater performance, or share in some other way. "Sharing time advertises and promotes the excitement of literacy learning and helps to promote the class as a community of readers" (Cooper, 1997, p. 491). As an alternative to whole-class sharing, the teacher might arrange for small-group sharing with about four students in each group. The teacher can then visit with the groups as a participant or observer (Cooper, 1997).

 Building Language

To develop students' use of language, you can ask them to expand on responses. If a student said that he liked *Heads or Tails* (Gantos, 1994) because it was funny, ask him to tell what made it funny or to tell what the funniest part was. ■

 FYI

Through the use of dialogue journals, you can prompt students to look more deeply at characters and theme and to think more critically about their reading. ■

 FYI

Dialogue journals allow teachers to model and scaffold more mature expression (Atwell, 1987). Through comments and questions, they can elicit more elaborated responses and can direct students to look at essential aspects of the texts being discussed. Closed questions such as "Which character did you like best?" tend to elicit a limited response. Open questions such as "The story sounds interesting—tell me about it" tend to bring forth a fuller response. ■

■ A **dialogue journal** is a journal in which the student reacts to or makes observations about reading selections and the teacher responds by writing in the journal.

FYI

As a general rule, there should be at least seven times as many books as children in the class, with more books being added over time. School and local libraries might loan a classroom collection, children might bring in books from home, or the community might be asked to contribute. Old basals can be a part of the collection. ∎

R E F L E C T I O N

In what situations and with what students might a workshop approach work best? What would be the main challenges in implementing a workshop approach? How might a workshop approach be combined with other approaches?

Adapting Instruction for Struggling Readers and Writers

Because students select their own books and read at their own pace, individualized reading or a reading workshop works extremely well with students reading below grade level. No longer are they stigmatized by being put in the low group or forced to read material that is too difficult for them. ∎

Organizing the Program

The classroom must be organized carefully. Just as in a library, it should have an inviting browsing area where students can choose books and settle down comfortably to read. Routines should be established for selecting books, keeping track of books circulated, taking part in conferences, and completing independent activities. The nature of the activity should determine the types of rules and routines. Because they are expected to follow these procedures, students should have a role in formulating them. The teacher might describe the situation and have students suggest ways to make it work.

The following basic conditions must be met: (1) the teacher must be able to hold individual or group conferences with students without interruptions; (2) students must be able to work on their own without disturbing others; and (3) students must be responsible for choosing books on their own and reading them. Rules and routines might include the following:

- *Book selection.*   The number of students choosing books at one time is limited to five; students may select two books at one time; students may make one exchange. Some students, especially those who are struggling with their reading, may waste a great deal of time choosing books. Instead of having students select books during reading workshop, you might have students gather books from the school or classroom library prior to reading. Younger students might gather four or five books that they intend to read. Older students might gather two or three. These can be kept in book boxes or accordion folders or oversized envelopes along with students' reading logs and conference sheets and any other reading aids, such as a model words chart (Calkins, 2001).
- *Circulation.*   Students are responsible for the books they check out; a card, sign-out sheet, or computerized system is used to keep track of books; students are in charge of the circulation system; books may be taken home.
- *Conference time.*   No one may interrupt the teacher during conferences; students must come prepared to conferences; students (or the teacher) must arrange for periodic conferences.

Advantages and Disadvantages of Reading Workshop

Self-selection, moving at one's own pace, using group processes, and relating reading and writing are the major advantages of reading workshop. Disadvantages include potential neglect of skills and the possibility that the teacher might spread himself or herself too thin in an attempt to meet with a variety of groups and individuals and respond to students' journal entries. Also, reading workshop might be unsuitable for students who have a difficult time working independently or whose skills are so limited that there are few books they can read on their own.

Adapting Reading Workshop

Reading workshop can be used instead of a basal series or along with one. For instance, you might use a basal three days and reading workshop two days. Or you might use a basal for a part of the day and reading workshop for a portion. Use whole-class instruction as appropriate. For instance, teach book selection and strategies needed by all students to the whole class. Use small-group instruction for those children who evidence a specific need for additional help. Obtain multiple copies of selected titles, just as you might do for a literature-based approach, and periodically invite students to choose one of the titles and read it as part of a small-group guided reading lesson. Use efficient management techniques, and do not overextend yourself. If you use reading workshop with younger students whose writing skills are still rather limited, gradually lead them into the use of dialogue journals. They might begin by drawing pictures in response to selections they read.

It is essential that students be taught basic skills and strategies and be provided with adequate opportunities to apply them. Instructing students in the selection of books and regularly holding conferences are also essential elements (Hiebert & Reutzel, 2010).

Language-Experience Approach

The **language-experience approach** is very personal. Children's experiences, expressed in their own language and written down by the teacher or an aide, become their reading material. Because both the language and the experience are familiar, this method presents fewer difficulties for children who are learning to read. It also integrates thinking, listening, speaking, reading, and writing. Through discussion, the teacher can lead students to organize and reflect on their experiences. If time order is garbled, the teacher can ask, "What happened first? What happened next?" If details are scant, the teacher can request that the children tell more or can ask open-ended questions, such as "How do you think the dinosaur tracks got there? What do the tracks tell us about dinosaurs?" Through comments that show an interest in the children and the topic, the teacher affirms them and encourages them to elaborate.

Whereas the teacher should affirm, support, encourage, and scaffold, she or he needs to be careful not to take over. When recording students' stories, it is important to write their exact words. Rephrasing what they have dictated shows a lack of acceptance for the language used. In addition, if the story is expressed in words that the child does not normally use, the child may have difficulty reading it. However, when a group story is being written, the situation is somewhat different. The story and the way it is written reflect the language structures that the group typically uses. To record a nonstandard structure might confuse some members of the group and result in criticism of the child who volunteered the structure. Displaying group stories containing nonstandard structures might

 FYI
When initiating the language-experience approach, start with group stories so that the class becomes familiar with procedures. As students share experiences and learn about each other, they build a sense of community.

 Adapting Instruction for English Language Learners
Because it makes use of the student's language, the language experience approach can be used with ELL. The dictated story might be a combination of English and the student's native language.

■ The **language-experience approach** to teaching reading involves students dictating a story based on an experience they have had. The dictated story is written down by a teacher or aide and used to instruct the students in reading. Shared writing and interactive writing are language-experience activities.

 LESSON 3.1
Group Language-Experience Chart

Day 1

Step 1. Building experiential background for the story
The students have an experience that they share as a group and that they can write about. It might be a field trip, the acquisition of a pet for the classroom, the baking of bread, or another experience.

Step 2. Discussing the experience
Students reflect on their experience and talk about it. During the discussion, the teacher helps them organize the experience. In discussing a visit to the circus, the teacher might ask them to tell what they liked best so that they do not get lost in details. If they baked bread, the teacher would pose questions in such a way that the children would list in order the steps involved.

Step 3. Dictating the story
The children dictate the story. The teacher or aide writes it on large lined paper, an overhead transparency, or on the chalkboard or might type it on a computer that has an attachment to magnify the input and project it on a screen. The teacher reads aloud what she or he is writing so that children can see the spoken words being written. The teacher reads each sentence

 FYI
If, as part of composing an experience story, students talk about a field trip, planting a tree, or another experience, this provides the teacher with the opportunity to help them think about the experience and clarify and extend their understanding of it (Reutzel & Cooter, 1991).

 Adapting Instruction for Struggling Readers and Writers
The language-experience approach is most often used in the beginning stages of reading and is usually combined with another approach. However, it can be very useful when working with older students reading on a very low level. Instead of using books that are "babyish," students can read their language-experience stories.

to make sure it is what the child who volunteered the sentence wanted to say. The teacher sweeps her or his hand under the print being read so that students can see where each word begins and ends and that reading is done from left to right. For students just learning to read, each sentence is written on a separate line, when possible.

Step 4. Reviewing the story

After the whole story has been written, the teacher reads it aloud once more. Children listen to see that the story says what they want it to say. They are invited to make changes.

Step 5. Reading of story by teacher and students

The teacher reads the story, running her or his hand under each word as it is read. The children read along with the teacher.

Step 6. Reading of familiar parts by students

Volunteers are asked to read sentences or words that they know. The teacher notes those children who are learning words and phrases and those who are just getting a sense of what reading is all about.

Day 2

Step 1. Rereading of story

The story is reread by the teacher, who points to each word as it is read. The children read along. The story might then be read in unison by the teacher and students. The teacher continues to point to each word. Volunteers might be able to read some familiar words or phrases.

Step 2. Matching of story parts

The teacher has duplicated the story and cut it into strips. The teacher points to a line in the master story, and students find the duplicated strip that matches it. Individual words might also be matched. A volunteer reads the strip, with the teacher helping out as necessary. For students who can go beyond matching, the teacher plans activities that involve reading, asking questions such as the following: "Which strip tells where we went? Which strip tells what we saw?" Students identify and read the strips. On a still more advanced level, students assemble the strips in correct order. This works best with stories that have no more than four or five sentences. Individual sentences can also be cut up into words that students assemble into sentences. This can be done as a pocket chart activity. The scrambled words are displayed, and volunteers read each one. Then a volunteer reads the word that should come first, puts it in its place, and reads it once more. A second volunteer reads the word that should come next and places it after the first word. The teacher reads the two words that have been correctly placed or calls on a volunteer to do so. This continues until the sentence has been assembled correctly. Once the entire strip has been assembled, the teacher or a volunteer reads it. The class listens to see whether the sentence has been put together correctly. Once students agree that it has, they read it in unison. This technique works best with short sentences.

 FYI

Working with individual words helps both the least able and the most able readers. It helps poor readers see where words begin and end and more advanced readers learn to read words automatically. When words are looked at individually, students note their characteristics, such as which letter comes first. ▨

also result in protests from parents and administrators (Cunningham & Allington, 1999).

The language-experience approach can be used with individuals or groups. Lesson 3.1 describes the steps for a group language-experience story.

Personalizing Group Stories

One way to personalize group language-experience stories is to identify the name of each contributor. After a volunteer has supplied a sentence, the teacher writes the student's name and the sentence, as shown in Figure 3.3. When the story is reread, each student can read the sentence that she or he contributed originally. Seeing their names in print gives students a sense of ownership of the story. It also helps them remember the sentences that they supplied.

 FYI

If your students are creating individual language-experience stories, it's helpful to have an aide or volunteers assist with dictation. First, explain the process to your helpers, and let them observe you until they feel they can undertake it on their own. ▨

OUR PETS

Billy said, "I have a dog.

My dog's name is Ralph."

Amy said, "I have a cat.

My cat's name is Sam."

Julio said, "My pets are goldfish.

They don't have names.

They just swim and swim."

FIGURE 3.3 Personalized Group Language-Experience Story

An Individual Approach

Individual language-experience stories are similar to group stories, except that they are more personalized. Just as in the group approach, the child dictates a story and the teacher, an aide, or a volunteer writes it down and uses it as the basis for teaching reading. Often, an individual language-experience story starts out as a drawing. The child then dictates a story that tells about the drawing. A photo can also be used to illustrate a story or as a stimulus for dictating one.

When dictating a language-experience story, a child may bring up experiences that are highly personal or that reveal private family matters. Affirm the child's feelings, but suggest a more appropriate way for the child to relate the experience: "I'm pleased that you trusted me enough to share that with me, but I think maybe you should tell your mom or dad about it." If the child uses language that is unsuitable for the classroom, have her or him use more appropriate language: "Can you think of another way to say it?" (Tierney, Readence, & Dishner, 1995). Maintaining the child's dignity and self-concept is of primary importance. Handle delicate situations with sensitivity and careful professional judgment.

Other Uses for the Language-Experience Approach

The language-experience approach can be used to compose booklets on science and social studies topics, thank-you notes to a visiting author, a letter to a classmate who is hospitalized, an invitation to a guest speaker, recipes, a set of directions for the computer, class rules, charts, lists, captions, diaries, booklets, plays, and similar items that are suitable for the language-experience approach. When possible, the pieces should be written for real purposes.

Shared writing is another way in which the language-experience approach might be used. Shared writing is a cooperative venture involving teacher and students. In a regular language-experience story, the teacher records students' exact words. In shared writing, the teacher draws from the children the substance of what they want to say but may rephrase it (Cunningham & Allington, 1999). For instance, at the end of the day, the teacher may ask the students what they learned that day. Summarizing the contributions of many children, the teacher records the day's highlights. In doing so, the teacher is modeling how spoken language is transformed into written language.

 FYI

- Because the language-experience approach is based on students' individual backgrounds, it allows each student to share her or his culture, experience, and mode of self-expression. The approach has the power to promote understanding and community among students whose backgrounds may differ.
- How to handle dialect is a controversial issue. Shuy (1973) made the point that it is developmentally inappropriate to introduce another dialect to a young child. The child will be confused and will not pick up the second dialect. As students grow older, they may choose to use other dialects to be able to communicate more effectively with diverse groups. This does not mean that they will surrender their home dialect. ■

 Using Technology

Language experience stories can be composed on interactive white boards, computer words processing programs, PowerPoint or other electronic format and can be enlivened by importing photos, music, or filmclips. ■

FYI

• Group language-experience stories can be used beyond the beginning or early reading level to demonstrate writing techniques. One way of showing students how to write a letter to the editor or a persuasive essay is to have the class compose the item as a group.
• See the discussion of language-experience stories in Chapter 4. ◼

R E F L E C T I O N

What are some highly effective uses for the language experience approach? How might you adapt the language experience approach for use with your students?

Advantages and Disadvantages of the Language-Experience Approach

The language-experience approach is most frequently used as a supplement to other programs and is especially useful with children who are in the beginning stages of learning to read. The major advantage of the approach is that it builds on children's language and experience. A major disadvantage of using it as the sole approach to teaching reading is that the child's reading will be limited to his or her own experiences. However, in a sense this disadvantage is an advantage. By sharing experiences, students have the opportunity to learn about each other. As Landis, Umolu, and Mancha (2010) comment, "Teachers and students who participate in LEA reading and writing activities are introduced to the power of language to create opportunities for learning that bridge different language, cultural expectations, and values about diverse events and life experiences" (p. 588).

Adapting the Language-Experience Approach

Because it neglects published reading materials and limits children's reading experiences, language experience should not be the sole approach to reading instruction. However, it makes an excellent supplement to any of the other approaches presented in this chapter, especially at the emergent and early stages of reading.

 Guided Reading

Guided reading is a way of organizing reading instruction that uses grouping (see pp. 377–385 for a discussion of guided reading). In guided reading, students are grouped and instructed according to their level of development (Fountas & Pinnell, 1996, 2001c, 2006). The groups meet daily for 10 to 30 minutes or more. The teacher may organize as many groups as she believes are necessary, but the more groups assembled, the less time there is for each one. As a practical matter, three or four groups are the most that can be handled efficiently. Grouping, however, is flexible. When appropriate, students are moved into other groups.

What does the rest of the class do while the teacher is working with guided reading groups? Students can engage in a number of independent activities. These activities should provide students with the opportunity to apply and extend their skills. One of the best activities for developing reading skills is, of course, to read. Students can

- read independently in the reading corner,
- read with a buddy,
- read along with an audiotape or CD,
- read charts and stories posted around the room,
- meet with a literature discussion group,
- meet with a cooperative learning group,
- work on a piece of writing,
- research a project in the library or on the Internet,
- work on a carefully chosen Web site that fosters literacy, or
- work at one of the classroom learning centers.

Learning Centers

Learning centers can provide practice for skills, provide enrichment, or allow students to explore interests. Many of the reinforcement activities suggested throughout this text can be made into learning centers. For instance, word-analysis centers can be set up that include sorting activities. The nature of the centers should be dictated by learning outcomes.

FYI

• Not all teachers favor learning centers. Having students read independently or meet with a literature discussion group or a cooperative learning group can be more productive than working at learning centers, especially with students in grades 2 and above.
• Centers should contain puzzles, magnets, word games, magazines, and manipulatives that are appealing to children and allow them to make discoveries on their own. The best centers are those that children would want to work at even if they weren't assigned to do so (Cunningham & Allington, 2003). ◼

Adapting Instruction for Struggling Readers and Writers

Specialists in one elementary school helped teachers plan their learning centers and incorporate activities that would assist struggling learners (Guastello & Lenz, 2005). To check on the effectiveness of the centers, teachers had students take turns reporting what they learned. ◼

◼ A **dialect** is a variant of a language that may differ somewhat in pronunciation, grammar, and vocabulary.

Case Study
Guided Reading

After whole-group shared reading and writing, students in Pat Loden's first-grade class assemble for guided reading. Loden has four groups of four or five students. Students are grouped according to their levels and needs. While Loden is meeting with a group, other students read independently for 20 minutes. They reread books that were read during guided reading or select new books. A record is kept of books read, and each student responds to at least one book each week. After 20 minutes of silent reading, students engage in journal writing. After completing journal writing, they work in learning centers that focus on Internet penpals, science, literacy, poetry, writing, letter and word work, and read-the-room exercises. Reading-the-room consists of using

a pointer while reading signs, charts, and other materials posted around the room. Each center contains directions for completing the activity. Students also make a note of the work that they complete at a center.

Meanwhile, Loden conducts her guided reading lessons. Each lesson begins with a minilesson designed to teach a skill related to the reading of the day's text. Children read the text silently. While the group reads silently, Loden has each of the children in the group read a passage orally to her. After students finish reading the selection, they discuss it. Loden then signals another group to come to the guided reading table (Morrow & Asbury, 2001).

What do you want students to know or be able to do as a result of using the centers? Centers offer an almost infinite number of possibilities. However, most classrooms feature a reading center or book corner in which students choose and read books or periodicals; a listening center in which students listen to or view recorded stories; an Internet center in which students engage in Web-related activities; a writing center in which students compose messages, poems, or stories; a word-work center that might feature riddles, word games, or sorting activities; and a drama center that might feature books or scripts and puppets that can be used to dramatize selections or compose scripts. There might also be math, science, art, and social studies centers. For younger students, there might be a pretend play or role-playing center.

Connect the centers to the curriculum. The centers should extend skills and themes students are currently working on. Each center should have an objective. If your curriculum is standards-based, you might want to note the standard that a center addresses. This prevents having centers that are fun and interesting but don't really further any educational objective. Also, have a means for tracking students' performance at the centers. After working at a center, students might record the title of a book and the number of pages they read, or they might produce a piece of writing or note a story that they dramatized. Also, have students discuss with the class the kinds of things they are doing at the centers. This helps keep the work at the centers related to the overall objectives of the classroom. Components of a learning center include title, activities, directions, materials, and assessment. See Table 3.1 for a description of the activities in two typical centers.

Involve students in the creation of learning centers. Change the content of the centers frequently to keep them interesting. Although the nature of a center might stay the same, change the activities and materials periodically. Assess the centers. Which ones seem most popular? Which ones seem to result in the most learning?

Where possible, provide choices. Students might practice a phonics skill by reading a selection along with an ebook version, or they might complete a crossword puzzle or a sorting activity. The objective is the same in each case, but the means for getting there vary.

The Internet is an excellent resource for centers. The LiteracyCenter.net, for instance, offers a range of interactive alphabet-recognition, letter-formation, and word-creation activities for students in pre-K and kindergarten. The teacher needs to provide directions for logging on, select activities, and assess students' performance.

 Adapting Instruction for English Language Learners

Center activities should reinforce themes so that concepts are extended and vocabulary is reinforced. This added reinforcement is especially helpful to ELLs. ■

 Using Technology

A to Z Teacher Stuff offers links to a number of sites for creating literacy centers:
http://www.atozteacherstuff.com/Lesson_Plans/Learning_Centers/Literacy_Centers/index.shtml ■

 Using Technology

Examples of centers and resources.
Classroom Centers
http://www.mrsmcdowell.com/centers.htm
ABC Teach
http://www.abcteach.com/directory/learning_centers/ ■

TABLE 3.1   Two Sample
Learning Centers

Type	Objective	Sequence of Activities
Listening/ viewing post	Building fluency	1. Students listen to or view a brief recorded play. 2. Students read along with the recorded play. Each student reads a part. 3. Students listen to the recorded play again. 4. Students dramatize the play (Ford, 2004).
Word study	Building word recognition	1. Working in pairs, students sort words. 2. One student sorts as the other observes and makes corrections when necessary. The student sorting explains why each word is sorted: has the same sound as the headword or picture or follows the same pattern. 3. The second student sorts and explains. 4. Students sort several more times in order to obtain speed and accuracy. 5. Students fill out a response form, supplying their names, the title of their sort, and the number of sorts.

R E F L E C T I O N

How might guided reading be used with virtually any approach? What are some of the challenges of implementing guided reading? How might you meet these challenges in your teaching situation?

Managing Learning Centers   To manage the use of learning centers, a magnetic schedule board or pocket chart can be helpful. On the board or chart, list the possible activities, as in Figure 3.4.

Depending on the length of time students will be working independently, they may complete two or three activities. In Figure 3.4, students have each been assigned three activities. Students may be required to complete certain activities, or they might be given choices. Some teachers post a schedule so that students know exactly what they are to do. This allows visits to centers to be staggered so that the centers don't become too crowded.

Advantages and Disadvantages of Guided Reading

A key advantage of guided reading is that students are instructed on their level and are given the support and instruction they need. The approach works especially well if the grouping is flexible and if students not meeting in groups are provided with worthwhile activities. However, unless carefully planned, learning centers can deteriorate into busy-work. Tyner (2004, 2006) recommends integrating word study and writing into a guided reading approach. Word study prepares students for the text they will be

FIGURE 3.4   Pocket Chart
Schedule of Learning Centers

Wednesday, November 15			
Edna, Ashley, Kayla, Michael, Dylan	ABC	🎧	✏️
Luis, Juan, Alyssa, William	💻	✏️	📖
Jacob, Aaron, Maria, Marisol	🎧	📖	ABC
Rachel, Edith, Latasha, Carlos	📖	💻	🎧
Raymond, Nicole, Michael, Angel	✏️	ABC	💻

reading, and writing reinforces and extends the reading and the word study. As she points out, this integration is especially important for struggling readers.

An Integrated Approach

A large-scale comparison of approaches to teaching reading in the 1960s came up with no clear winner (Bond & Dykstra, 1967, 1997). All of the approaches evaluated were effective in some cases but ineffective in others. The study suggested that the teacher is more important than the method and that a method successful in one situation may not be successful in all. Combinations of approaches were recommended. Adding language experience to a basal program seemed to strengthen the program. A word-attack element also seemed to be an important component, a conclusion that was reached repeatedly in a number of studies and research reviews (Adams, 1990; Anderson, Hiebert, Scott, & Wilkinson, 1985; Chall, 1967, 1983a; Dykstra, 1974; Snow, Burns, & Griffin, 1998).

Another interpretation of the research strongly suggests that what is really most effective is using the best features of all approaches. Draw from holistic literature-based approaches the emphasis on functional–contextual instruction, the use of children's literature, and integration of language arts. From basal programs, adopt some of the structure built into the skills and strategies components. From individualized approaches, take the emphasis on self-selection of students' reading material. From the language-experience approach, adopt the practice of using writing to build and extend literacy skills.

Above all else, use your professional judgment. This book presents a core of essential skills and strategies in word recognition, comprehension, reading in the content areas, and study skills. Use this core of skills as a foundation when implementing your literacy program, regardless of which approach or approaches you use. If a skill or strategy is omitted or neglected in one approach, then add it or strengthen it. For instance, not all basals recommend the use of pronounceable word parts or analogy strategies. If you are using a basal and these elements are missing, add them.

At a computer center, students can follow a story in print as it is read to them.

REFLECTION

Considering all the approaches that have been discussed, which approach or combination of approaches would you adopt? How would that approach or combination fit in with your teaching style and teaching situation?

FYI

Reading programs vary in the rate at which they introduce skills, the number of words they introduce, and the amount of practice they provide (Hiebert, Martin, & Menon, 2005). If your program does not offer enough practice or introduces skills too rapidly, use supplementary materials or children's books for reinforcement. ■

IRA POSITION STATEMENT ON KEY ISSUE

Using Multiple Methods of Beginning Reading Instruction

Several large-scale studies of reading methods have shown that no one method is better than any other method in all settings and situations (International Reading Association, 1999a). For every method studied, some children learned to read very well while others had great difficulty. Perhaps the most important reason for a search for the best method is that there are a significant number of children who do not read as well as they must to function in a society that has increasing demands for literacy. Reading is not being taught as well as it should be. "Because there is no clearly documented best way to teach beginning reading, professionals who are closest to the children must be the ones to make the decisions about what reading methods to use, and they must have the flexibility to modify those methods when they determine that particular children are not learning" (International Reading Association, 1999a, p. 5).

 Using Technology

The Position Statement of the International Reading Association, "Using Multiple Methods of Beginning Reading Instruction," discusses in more depth why teachers need to be able to use more than one method to teach reading.
http://www.reading.org/resources/issues/positions_multiple_methods.html ■

Summary

A number of approaches are used to teach reading. The basal approach uses anthologies, which may be complemented by children's books. The literature-based approach and reading workshop use children's books. The language-experience approach uses writing to teach reading. Each approach has advantages and disadvantages and may be combined with other approaches and/or adapted to individual teaching goals.

Guided reading can be used along with most approaches to teaching reading. Guided reading is a way of grouping and instructing students according to their needs.

According to research, no single approach to teaching reading yields consistently superior results. A combination is probably best. Teachers should use their professional judgment and know-how to adapt programs to fit the needs of their students. Struggling readers need materials on their level and will benefit from additional instruction.

Extending and Applying

1. Plan a series of language-experience lessons, either for an individual or for a group of students, in which an experience story is written and used to present or reinforce appropriate literacy understandings or skills and strategies. Evaluate the effectiveness of your lessons.
2. Adapt a lesson in a basal/anthology reading program to fit the needs of a group of students you are teaching. Teach the lesson and assess its effectiveness. In what ways was the program's teacher's manual a helpful resource? What adaptations did you have to make?
3. Examine a current basal series. Look at a particular level and assess the interest of the selections, the kinds of strategies and teaching suggestions presented in the teacher's manual, and the usefulness of the workbook exercises. Summarize your findings. (You may be able to examine a series online. Some of the current series have their manuals and many of the reading and support materials available online.)
4. Examine your philosophy of teaching reading. Make a list of your beliefs and your teaching practices. Also note the approach that best fits in with your philosophy. Do your practices fit your beliefs? If not, what might you do to align the two?

Professional Reflection

Do I ...
___ Have an understanding of the major components of an effective reading program?
___ Have an understanding of the major approaches to teaching reading and the advantages and disadvantages of each?

Am I able to ...
___ Select the reading approach or combination that is most appropriate for my students?
___ Teach reading using a variety of approaches?
___ Adapt reading approaches to meet the needs of my students?

Reflection Question

Which of the approaches or combinations discussed in this chapter best suit your philosophy and style of teaching? How would you go about implementing your preferred approach? In many school, an approach or materials are chosen by the administration.

What adaptations might you make if you are working in a system that has chosen a basal? What adaptations might you make if you are working in a system that has chosen a workshop approach?

Building Competencies

To build competencies, consult the following source for more detailed information:

Serafini, F. (2006). *Around the reading workshop in 180 days: A month-by-month guide to effective instruction.* Portsmouth, NH: Heinemann.

Landis, D., Umolu, J., & Mancha, S. (2010). The power of language experience for cross-cultural reading and writing. *The Reading Teacher, 63,* 580–589.

MyEducationLab™

Go to the Topic "Organization and Management" MyEducationLab (www.myeducationlab.com) for your course, where you can:

- Find learning outcomes for "Organization and Management" along with the national standards that connect to these outcomes.
- Complete Assignments and Activities that can help you more deeply understand the chapter content.
- Apply and practice your understanding of the core teaching skills identified in the chapter with the Building Teaching Skills and Dispositions learning units.
- Examine challenging situations and cases presented in the IRIS Center Resources.
- Check your comprehension on the content covered in the chapter by going to the Study Plan in the Book

Resources for your text. Here you will be able to take a chapter quiz, receive feedback on your answers, and then access Review, Practice, and Enrichment activities to enhance your understanding of chapter content. (optional)

A+RISE A+RISE® Standards2Strategy™ is an innovative and interactive online resource that offers new teachers in grades K–12 just-in-time, research-based instructional strategies that meet the linguistic needs of ELLs as they learn content, differentiate instruction for all grades and abilities, and are aligned to Common Core Elementary Language Arts standards (for the literacy strategies) and to English language proficiency standards in WIDA, Texas, California, and Florida.

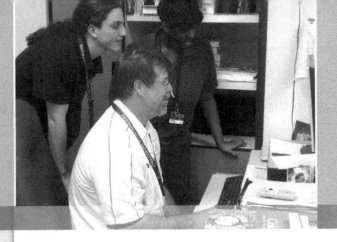

4

Teaching and Learning in an Age of Multiple Literacies

Whatever our discipline—mathematics, science, social science, foreign language, English, or other content area—literacies underpin everything we teach. In the past, being literate required only that we be able to read and write. In today's world, however, we need to be fluent in multiple literacies that require us not only to be able to read and write, but also to understand a variety of disciplines, navigate myriad information sources, examine the author's intent, and comprehend beyond the printed page.

Our ever-changing world has caused us to rethink literacy and the role it plays in our lives. We are living in an information age, one in which world news is readily available and access to friends on the other side of the world takes no longer than contacting the neighbor next door. We can shop, get the latest news, take university courses, or view the latest offerings in real estate in the privacy of our homes. The world is at our fingertips, and our resulting needs demand that we move beyond traditional views of literacy and embrace new perspectives.

In this chapter, we learn about multiple literacies and how we can integrate them into our teaching. We begin by questioning the nature of literacies. Next, we explore content literacies, which relate to the specific disciplines we teach. After that, we discuss adolescent literacy, which addresses the age category into which our students fall. Then we turn our focus to critical literacy. Finally, we learn about new literacies, such as information literacy, media literacy, and multicultural literacy. In each of these sections, we gain knowledge of a particular type of literacy and discover how we can integrate it into teaching.

What Do the Terms *Literacy, Multiple Literacies*, and *New Literacies* Mean?

In the past, *literacy* was typically defined as the ability to read and write. It was viewed as *functional literacy* and encompassed those literacy skills that were required for navigating satisfactorily in society. It referred to the ability to read words well enough to complete forms (such as job applications), follow directions (such as how to plug in a toaster or other appliance), or understand simple communications (such as a note from a child's teacher). Adults with a functional level of literacy were considered capable of being successful workers in their communities.

In recent years, the term *literacy* has expanded in meaning. The word itself has changed to *literacies*, reflecting the many different literacies that have emerged over time. These *multiple literacies* are diverse, multidimensional, and learned in different ways. For example, we still support adolescent literacy, but now each discipline also has its own literacy: Mathematics literacy, science literacy, and history literacy are just a few examples. There are technology-related literacies such as information literacy and media literacy. In addition, there is critical literacy, which has been in existence for decades and is now experiencing a wider range of acceptance. This widespread use has led to its inclusion in the list of literacies for the 21st century—the skills needed to flourish in today's society and in the future (Abilock, 2007). There is also multicultural literacy, which facilitates our understanding of our own cultures, as well as others.

New literacies are characterized by change and emerge from developments in technology (Reinking, 1998). We need to learn the new literacies to help our students learn how to use the emerging technologies. The new literacies "include the skills, strategies, and insights necessary to successfully exploit the rapidly changing information and communication technologies that continuously emerge in our world" (Leu, 2002, p. 313). Lonsdale and McCurry (2004) concur, observing that new literacies include the ability to "read" texts, master evolving technologies, manage information, and engage critically with texts. They further note that the boundaries of these literacies are not always clearly defined. For example, the term *information literacy* is often used interchangeably with *cyber, digital, electronic, computer, technological*, and *library literacy*. *Critical literacy* is thought to underpin all other literacies. Discipline-specific literacies, such as science, history, and mathematics literacy, are also viewed as new literacies.

According to Leu, Kinzer, Coiro, and Cammack (2004):

New literacies include the skills, strategies, and dispositions that allow us to use the Internet and other Information Communication Technologies (ICTs) effectively to identify important questions, locate information, critically evaluate the usefulness of that information, synthesize information to answer those questions, and then communicate the answers to others. We encounter new literacies nearly every time we try to read, write, and communicate with the Internet and other ICTs. In fact, when reviewing the following list, we can easily see how students completing a long-term project would need to engage in new literacies.

- Using a search engine to effectively locate information
- Evaluating the accuracy and utility of information located on a webpage relative to one's purpose
- Using a word processor effectively, including using functions such as checking spelling accuracy, inserting graphics, and formatting text
- Participating effectively in bulletin board or listserv discussions to get needed information
- Knowing how to use email to communicate effectively
- Inferring correctly the information that may be found at a hyperlink on a webpage. (p. 1590)

The emergence of new literacies can be linked to social, economic, and political change. Examples of these changes include learning being viewed as a lifelong process; individuals locating, managing, and evaluating a proliferation of information; teaching becoming more learner centered and inquiry based; a globalized economy demanding greater economic competition; intellectual capital replacing physical capital; and workers needing to be geographically mobile, adaptable, and multi-skilled (Lonsdale & McCurry, 2004). Leu (2002) notes that new literacies build on existing literacies and believes we can cautiously characterize these skills and strategies in the following ways:

- Change is a defining element.
- New kinds of strategic knowledge are required.
- Reading from a critical perspective is involved.
- They are socially constructed.
- Interest and motivation underpin them.
- Teachers thoughtfully guide learning within information environments.
- Governments around the world are investing in the new literacies monetarily and academically.

Because technology is changing so quickly and new literacies are constantly emerging, critics of the new literacies have expressed concerns about the need for greater teacher preparation, potentially higher costs, and inappropriate use of technology in the classroom (Leu, 2002). The new literacies are often described as including information literacy, media literacy, and multicultural literacy.

In the sections that follow, we examine content literacies, adolescent literacy, critical literacy, information literacy, media literacy, and multicultural literacy. We share current understandings about each topic and discuss how we can integrate these types of literacy into our teaching.

What Do We Know about Adolescent Literacy and Content Literacies?

We view *adolescent literacy* as,

> a set of socially organized practices which make use of a symbol system and a technology for producing and disseminating it. Literacy is not simply knowing how to read and write a particular script but applying this knowledge for specific purposes in specific contexts of use. The nature of these practices, including, of course, their technological aspects, will determine the kinds of skills associated with literacy (Scribner & Cole, 1981, p. 236). Moje (1996) supports this view and suggests that literacy involves the practices in which the processes of reading, writing, speaking, and listening are embedded. She views these processes "as tools for engaging in and making sense of social practice." (p. 175)

In other words, we and our students need to be able to read, write, speak, and listen to make sense of the world in which we live. One might assume that we would "be literate" by now, but over time literacy has evolved into an ongoing process. *Being literate* has become obsolete. *Becoming literate* is now the more relevant term (Leu & Kinzer, 2000).

Content literacies is a term that refers to how we use literacy in specific disciplines. Examples include mathematics literacy, science literacy, and social science literacy. Applications related to each of these literacies can be found in subsequent chapters of this book.

Content area courses often require the use of textbooks that many adolescents have difficulty reading. Some of these reading difficulties can be traced back to problems with decoding, which students should have learned when they were much younger. Other students' reading difficulties might be related to poorly developed vocabularies and a lack of background knowledge (Schoenbach, Greenleaf, Cziko, & Hurwitz, 1999). Schools continue to use content area textbooks, even though the average high school student is reading below the level of many of the texts (Allington, 2002). Biancarosa and Snow, the authors of *Reading Next—A Vision for Action and Research in Middle and High School Literacy* (2006), conclude that students "lack the strategies to help them comprehend what they read" (p. 8).

To address this issue, Biancarosa and Snow (2006) recommend the explicit teaching of reading comprehension and intensive writing across the curriculum, as well as instruction in how to learn from texts. They also advocate for greater student motivation and more opportunities for small-group instruction—factors that should work well for our Millennial students. Santa (2006) agrees with these suggestions and adds that the most influential factor in student achievement is the teacher. The International Reading Association's Commission on Adolescent Literacy (2001) has suggested that home-school literacy connections should also be developed.

So, although many people may believe that reading and writing are becoming less prevalent in an age of multiple literacies, just the opposite seems to be true. As Leu (2000) has reported:

> It is likely that reading and writing ability will become even more important in the future than they are today. This is due to the increasing need for acquiring and communicating information rapidly in a world of global competition and information economies. In this context, success will often be defined by one's ability to quickly locate useful information to solve important problems and then communicate the solution to others. Proficient readers can acquire many types of information more rapidly by reading than they can by listening to speech or viewing a video. In an age when speed of information access is central to success, reading will be even more critical to our children's futures. (p. 760)

Using What We Know about Adolescent Literacy and Content Literacies in Teaching

In *Reading Next—A Vision for Action and Research in Middle and High School Literacy*, Biancarosa and Snow (2006) encourage us to use what we know to teach adolescent literacy and content literacies. They remind us there are more than 8 million students in grades 4–12 who are struggling readers—students who cannot comprehend. These authors suggest that meeting the diverse literacy needs of such students will require a comprehensive approach. Although they note that the "optimal mix" of the elements will vary, they suggest that middle and high school literacy programs should focus on the following instructional improvements:

1. *Explicit teaching of comprehension strategies and processes.* We know that comprehension strategies can be taught. Within our districts, we need to work to ensure that such instruction begins in the primary grades, so students can develop a repertoire of strategies they can use as needed while they are reading. It is also critical that we and teachers throughout the grades and across content areas focus on students' strategy use. (See Chapters 5–8 for additional information about comprehension processes such as activating background knowledge and teaching reading comprehension strategies).

2. *Embedding effective instructional principles in content.* This improvement proposes that we, as content area teachers, infuse discipline-related reading and writing into our teaching and provide opportunities for application. Examples of this can be found in subsequent chapters in this text. (For further information about reading and writing, see Chapters 5–9 and 11–14)

3. *Motivating students.* As teachers, we know that student motivation is essential for learning in all subjects. We know many ways to motivate our students, including helping them make connections between their personal experiences and content, providing opportunities for self-selection of research/project topics, and encouraging students to represent their thinking in a variety of ways. (For more information about alternative ways to represent thinking, see Chapter 14.)

4. *Using text-based, collaborative learning.* This supports the Millennials' tendency to gravitate toward working in groups. This type of learning can promote student interaction related to the topic being studied. It can also advance other benefits of collaborative learning, such as shared ideas, respect for the thoughts of others, negotiated meaning, positive interdependence, individual accountability, interpersonal communication skills, and risk taking, as well as working with diverse types and levels of text (see instructional improvement 6).

5. *Strategic, intensive tutoring.* As noted earlier, there are millions of struggling readers, but few programs to help them read better during adolescence. This improvement would provide such tutoring for adolescents in reading, writing, and content knowledge.

6. *Using diverse types and levels of text.* Using multiple types and levels of text motivates students and provides access that they may not experience when reading the course textbook. Using theme-related trade books provides opportunities for students to learn from different perspectives. (See Chapter 9 for more information about types of texts.)

7. *Intensive writing.* Reading and writing are inextricably linked, and we know the more students engage in them, the better they perform. Courses infused with intensive writing will benefit students. (For more information about integrating writing in the content areas, see Chapter 11. For additional examples of integrating writing, see Chapters 13, 14, and 15.)

8. *Using technology as a tool for, and a topic of, literacy instruction.* Technology use is a great motivator for students. Most learners have an intrinsic interest in it. This improvement suggests that we use technology to motivate and to inform. (For more information about integrating technology in the content areas, see Chapter 12.)

9. *Assessing students through informal measures.* Informal measures are those that we use to assess our students every day. They include observation, students' strategy applications, discussion, and informal written responses.

In addition to the instructional improvements, *Reading Next* suggests that the educational infrastructure should be improved by providing extended time for literacy, long-term professional development, summative (more formal) assessment of students and programs, interdisciplinary teacher teams, and leadership in teaching reading and writing to all students. (For more information about professional development, see Chapter 15.)

According to *Reading Next*, the suggested improvements should not be viewed in isolation, but rather as elements of a group that have dynamic and powerful interrelations. Although professional development and formative and summative assessment are described as essential to effect change, Biancarosa and Snow (2006) suggest that the elements should be used in optimal mixes, dependent on contexts.

Regardless of technological developments that occur in the future, adolescent literacy and content literacies will continue to be important issues for our students. As their teachers, we need to ensure that they have the processes, strategies, knowledge, and opportunities they need to be successful. (For more detailed information about such strategies and the reading process, see Chapters 5–8.)

What Do We Know about Critical Literacy?

Current thinking about literacy suggests that we should help our students to comprehend at deeper levels—levels that require them to understand beyond the information on the printed page and critically analyze the author's message (Pearson, 2001). Reading from a critical literacy perspective encourages our students and us to examine the connections between language, power, and knowledge; to transform relationships; and to reason and act responsibly. It involves thinking beyond the text to understand issues such as why the author wrote about a particular topic, wrote from a particular perspective, and chose to include some ideas about the topic and exclude others.

For example, when we were in elementary school, content area text authors may have shared some information about a topic, but not all. Many of us may remember learning that Christopher Columbus sailed the ocean blue in 1492 and that he had three ships: the *Nina*, the *Pinta*, and the *Santa Maria*. We probably also learned that Italy—Columbus's homeland—would not provide funding for his explorations. The money came instead from Queen Isabella of Spain.

What we have just read about Columbus is what many believe to be the essential history of his explorations, but it is not the whole story. A textbook company decided that what we should learn about Columbus was what I have just recounted. The same company also decided what we should not learn about Columbus—that he is viewed as the person responsible for destroying the Tainos people. From a critical perspective, we would question why the textbook from which we learned did not include the whole truth, as current history textbooks do. We would also question what right the author and the textbook company had to withhold the whole story, to discount the perspective of the Tainos people. We would then reflect and try to take action that would provide justice for the Tainos, perhaps by ensuring that their story is told or by working to help other indigenous peoples.

Critical literacy is grounded in Freire's (1983) belief that reading is much more than decoding language or accepting text as true—it is preceded by and intertwined with knowledge of the world. Because language and reality are dynamically interwoven, the understanding attained by the critical reading of a text implies perceiving the relation between text and context.

Freire (1970) suggests that instead of passively accepting the information presented, readers should not only read and understand the word, but "read the world" and understand the text's purpose to avoid being manipulated by it. "Reading the world" enables critically aware readers to comprehend beyond the literal level and think about the function and the production of texts. Reading the world means trying to understand *what* authors are trying to convey in their messages and *how* they are communicating those messages. It requires that readers not accept only superficial responses to the text, but rather reflect on the text's purposes and the author's style. This reasoning is often expressed through dialogue with others who are seeking to understand the hidden forces at work. This kind of reflection takes time and requires constant monitoring of the text.

Reading from this perspective requires both the ability and the deliberate inclination to think critically about—to analyze and evaluate—texts, meaningfully question their origin and purpose, and take action by representing alternative perspectives. Questioning plays an important role in this process. Examples of the types of questions that facilitate thinking from a critical perspective are featured in Figure 4.1. These questions require readers to think at evaluative levels, to question what message the author is trying to convey and how that message relates to the truth. (For more information about generating questions at multiple levels of thinking, see Chapter 9.)

FIGURE 4.1

Questions That Promote Reading from a Critical Stance

Print (e.g., books, newspapers, magazines, song lyrics, hypertext)
- Whose viewpoint is expressed?
- What does the author want us to think?
- Whose voices are missing, silenced, or discounted?
- How might alternative perspectives be represented?
- How would that contribute to your understanding the text from a critical stance?
- What action might you take based on what you have learned?

Television/Photographs
- Who is in the video/photograph?
- Why are they there?
- What does the videographer/photographer want you to think?
- Who/what is missing from the video/photograph? (Silenced? Discounted?)
- What might an alternative video show?
- What might an alternative photograph look like?
- How would that contribute to your understanding the video or photograph from a critical stance?
- What action might you take based on what you have viewed?

Source: McLaughlin & DeVoogd, 2004a.

It is important to note that critical theorists' expanded notion of texts isn't limited to words from a novel or a song or a newscast. Texts can also be conditions (sociocultural influences, state assessment-driven curriculums, funding or lack of it) or relationships and situations in everyday life (analyzing an occurrence from another person's perspective).

Critical literacy views readers as active participants in the reading process and invites them to move beyond passively accepting the text's message to question, examine, or dispute the power relations that exist between readers and authors—to ponder what the author wants readers to believe, take action, and promote fairness between people. It focuses on issues of power and promotes reflection, action, and transformation (Freire, 1970).

The Principles of Critical Literacy developed by McLaughlin and DeVoogd (2004a) include a number of essential understandings and beliefs about the power relationship that exists between the reader and the author. The four principles and related examples are summarized next.

- Critical literacy focuses on issues of power and promotes reflection, transformation, and action.

Whenever readers commit to understanding a text—whether narrative or informational—they submit to the right of the author to select the topic and determine the treatment of the ideas.

- Critical literacy focuses on the problem and its complexity.

Situations that are fairly intricate are often viewed from an essentialist (very simplistic) perspective. In critical literacy, rather than accepting an essentialist view, we engage in *problematizing*—seeking to understand the problem and its complexity. In other words, we raise questions and seek alternative explanations as a way of more fully acknowledging and understanding the complexity of the situation.

- Critical literacy strategies are dynamic and adapt to the contexts in which they are used.

There is no list of methods in critical literacy that work the same way in all contexts at all times. No technique that promotes critical literacy can be exported to another setting without adapting it to that context. As Freire (1998, p. xi) has observed, "It is impossible to export pedagogical practices without reinventing them."

Comber (2001) has observed that when teachers and students are engaged in critical literacy, "They ask complicated questions about language and power, about people and lifestyle, about morality and ethics, about who is advantaged by the way things are and who is disadvantaged" (p. 271). To participate in such a classroom environment, readers must play not only the roles of code breakers, meaning makers, and text users, but also the role of text critics (Luke & Freebody, 1999). In other words, readers need to understand that they have the power to envision alternative ways of viewing the author's topic, and they exert that power when they read from a critical stance.

- Critical literacy disrupts the commonplace by examining it from multiple perspectives.

Examining the point of view from which a text is written and brainstorming other perspectives that may or may not be represented challenge students to expand their thinking and discover diverse beliefs, positions, and understandings (McLaughlin, 2001). These techniques help students to transition from accepting the text as it is presented to questioning the author's intent and the information presented in the text.

The principles of critical literacy provide insight into what critical literacy is and how it functions. This dynamic process examines power relationships, acknowledges that all texts are biased, and encourages readers to explore alternative perspectives and take action. It expands our thinking, and it enlightens our perceptions as we read both the word and the world from a critical stance.

Reading from a critical stance requires both the ability and the deliberate inclination to think critically about—to analyze and evaluate—texts (books, media, lyrics, electronic text, life relationships), meaningfully question their origin and purpose, and take action by representing alternative perspectives. The goal is for readers to become text critics in everyday life—to become active thinkers rather than passive recipients of knowledge.

Making Connections | Thinking about Critical Literacy

- Reflect on reading from a critical perspective. How could reading from a critical stance deepen your students' understanding of your content area?
- Share your thoughts with others in small-group discussion.

It is important to realize that critical literacy is more complex than other literacies. We cannot just "become" critically literate. Instead, this process requires learning, understanding, and changing over time. It includes developing theoretical, research, and pedagogical repertoires, changing with time and circumstance, engaging in self-critical practices, and remaining open to possibilities (Comber, 2001).

Integrating What We Know about Critical Literacy into Teaching

Teachers, students, and texts play important roles in creating a context that fosters critical literacy— one in which reading from a critical stance is a natural occurrence that extends beyond the classroom to everyday life experiences (McLaughlin & DeVoogd, 2004b). Our role in initiating and developing critical literacy is multifaceted. It begins with personal understanding and use of critical literacy and extends to teaching students about critical literacy, modeling reading from a critical stance in everyday teaching and learning experiences, and providing access to a variety of texts that represent critical literacy.

Once we become critically aware, teaching students to read from a critical stance should be a natural process. First, as in any other act of reading, the teacher should ensure that students have the background knowledge necessary to read from a critical stance. The teacher might then choose to scaffold learning by using a five-step instructional framework: explain, demonstrate, guide, practice, and reflect (McLaughlin & Allen, 2002). This scaffolding, or gradual release of responsibility to students, provides time and opportunity for them to become comfortable with reading from a critical stance. To begin, we can explain what it means to be critically aware and then demonstrate by using a read-aloud and a think-aloud. During this process, we provide a critical perspective that questions and challenges the text. We may use questions such as, Whose viewpoint is expressed? Whose voices are missing, silenced, or discounted? What action might you take based on what you have learned? We might also introduce strategies such as juxtapositioning or alternative texts. After we explain and demonstrate, students—working in pairs or small groups—can offer responses as we guide their reading and as they practice reading from a critical stance. As a final step, we and the students reflect on what they know about being critically aware and how it helped them to understand the text. This often results in their making connections (text–self, text–text, text–world) and leads to discussions of how students can apply what they have learned to the reading of other texts.

Students who engage in critical literacy become open-minded, active, strategic readers who are capable of viewing text from a critical perspective. They understand that the information presented in texts, magazines, newspapers, song lyrics, and websites has been authored from a particular perspective for a particular purpose. They know that meaning is "grounded in the social, political, cultural and historic contexts of the reading event" (Serafini, 2003).

Although methods are something most critical scholars shy away from, there are a variety of starting points that we can use to help students develop a critical stance. The following ideas and resources provide some direction for initial engagement. As noted earlier, we need to take these ideas, adapt them to our particular contexts, and scaffold students' learning.

JUXTAPOSITIONING TEXTS. Juxtapositioning is a technique that helps demonstrate multiple perspectives. It can occur in a variety of formats, using a number of informational sources. For example, in a high school history course in which World War II was being studied, juxtapositioning was used in theme-based focus groups. The students were reading excerpts from *The Greatest Generation,* a theme-related text that represented the Allies' perspective, in a whole-class setting. They were also reading theme-based books that represented different perspectives of World War II—those of Holocaust victims, German soldiers, American and Japanese survivors of the bombing of Pearl Harbor, various political leaders of the time, and victims of the Japanese American Internment—in small groups. After the books were read and discussed, the students regrouped, so that one student representing each book would be in each of the newly formed groups.

In this scenario, discussions focused on multiple perspectives. Students reported that they had not considered perspectives such as those of the Japanese American victims of internment, nor had they thought about the perspectives of women working on the homefront or of people who had worked to help save the victims of the Holocaust. An interesting discussion of the media during the 1940s also emerged. It focused on the immediacy of information we experience now as compared to the radio news and handwritten letters used to communicate military developments during World War II. The discussion then moved on to a critical analysis of the media, focusing on issues such as who decides what information is included in and excluded from the news we see and read. After in-depth small-group discussion, pairs of students created posters on which they juxtaposed visual representations of the World War II perspectives they had read about. The posters were then shared and discussed in a whole-class setting. Students took action by inviting Holocaust survivors and U.S. soldiers who had participated in World War II to school to share their perspectives on World War II. Figure 4.2 contains a list of sample texts used for the theme-based focus groups on World War II.

ALTERNATIVE TEXTS. We create alternative texts to represent perspectives that are different from those that are present in the texts we read. The text can be narrative or informational and can consist of oral, written, visual, or imagined representations—including, but not limited to, drawings, oral descriptions, dramatizations, and songs. By creating an alternative text, the reader perceives the information in a different way and begins to understand the complexity of the issue examined. When using this technique, students can examine the message conveyed by a text, photo, or song and then write an alternative text, take or find an alternative photo, or create alternative lyrics. For example, after seeing a billboard of happy people having dinner in their expensive house, a student might choose to create an alternative text—which might also have a billboard design—about a sad person who is alone, homeless, and dependent on shelters for food and a bed. The student might then take action by encouraging peers to actively participate in the school's food and clothing drive for the homeless or by organizing a group of friends to work for that effort.

Students have also created alternative texts in other curricular areas. For example, they have created alternative texts in science class after reading newspaper articles about the effects of medical waste pollution on the ocean and developments in the use of cloning. In music class, students have examined family relationships by creating alternative lyrics to a variety of songs including "Cat's in the Cradle." In social studies, students created alternative texts for texts expressing views on a variety of political issues.

Teaching ideas such as juxtapositioning, theme-based focus groups, and creating alternative texts are adaptable across curriculum areas. They provide opportunities to situate critical literacy in a variety of contexts and encourage both our students and us to view critical literacy as a natural part of learning.

Critical literacy permeates every other kind of literacy. Information literacy, media literacy, multicultural literacy, and discipline-specific literacies provide examples of its broad influence.

Allen, T. B. (2001). *Remember Pearl Harbor: American and Japanese survivors tell their stories*. Washington, DC: National Geographic Society.

Personal recollections of Pearl Harbor survivors, both American and Japanese, military and civilian, are presented in this book. Maps, pictures, and timelines to help readers follow the events of Pearl Harbor and World War II in general are included.

Appleman-Jurman, A. (1989). *Alicia: My story*. New York: Bantam Books.

This autobiography recounts Alicia Appleman-Jurman's triumph over the terrifying, unrelenting brutality of the Nazi regime. After managing to escape and witnessing her own mother's murder, she helps others escape with her to Palestine.

Elliott, L. M. (2001). *Under a war-torn sky*. New York: Hyperion.

Set in France during World War II, this book is based on recollections of the author's father. A young American pilot's plane is shot down in Nazi-occupied France, and the French Resistance works to get him safely out of enemy territory.

Friedman, I. R. (1990). *The other victims: Non-Jews persecuted by the Nazis*. Boston: Houghton Mifflin.

Personal narratives tell the stories of the many non-Jews persecuted by Hitler and the Nazis, both before and during World War II. Some of the groups discussed include gypsies, homosexuals, blacks, physically challenged individuals, and political and religious activists.

Gold, A. L. (2000). *A special fate: Chiune Sugihara: Hero of the Holocaust*. New York: Scholastic.

This biography tells the story of a Japanese diplomat working in Lithuania, who chooses to ignore his orders and listen to his conscience. Despite the risks to himself and his family, Sugihara writes thousands of transit visas and saves the lives of countless Jews.

Greene, B. (1973). *Summer of my German soldier*. New York: Puffin.

Patty, a young Jewish girl who is struggling to find herself, discovers Anton, a young German prisoner of war who has escaped. Patty takes incredible risks to conceal and protect Anton and learns a great deal about herself in the process.

Kuchler-Silberman, L. (1990). *My hundred children*. New York: Dell Laurel-Leaf.

A Holocaust survivor copes with the loss of her family by running an orphanage for 100 Jewish children who survived the Nazi occupation of Poland. The story recounts everyday victories like learning to laugh again as well as bigger issues such as leaving Poland for a safer home.

Lowry, L. (1989). *Number the stars*. Boston: Houghton Mifflin.

A ten-year-old Danish girl named Annemarie and her family risk their own safety to help Annemarie's best friend and her Jewish family escape to Sweden, where they will be safe from the Nazis.

Richter, H. P. (1987). *I was there*. New York: Viking Penguin/Puffin Books.

A young boy who is a member of the Hitler Youth Movement early in the Nazi era tells his story. The first-person account provides some insight into the people who were part of the Axis forces.

Talbott, H. (2000). *Forging freedom: A true story of heroism during the Holocaust*. New York: Putnam.

Jaap Penraat, a young Dutchman, helps save more than 400 Jews during World War II by using his father's printing press to forge identification papers for Jewish friends and neighbors. He then creates a bogus German construction company and smuggles his "construction workers" to phony job sites and safety.

Volavkova, H. (Ed.). (1971). *I never saw another butterfly*. New York: McGraw Hill.

Children of the Nazi concentration camp in Terezin, Czechoslovakia, created these haunting poems and drawings. Of the 15,000 children who went to Terezin, fewer than 100 survived.

Wiesel, E. (1982). *Night*. New York: Bantam Books.

This autobiography recounts the life of a young boy in a Nazi death camp. The book includes accounts of many tragic events, including the author witnessing the death of his own family.

FIGURE 4.2
Young-Adult Novels about World War II That Represent Critical Literacy

What Do We Know about Information Literacy?

Abilock (2007) defines *information literacy* as a "transformational process in which the learner needs to find, understand, evaluate, and use information in various forms to create for personal, social, or global purposes." The easiest way to think about information literacy may be to imagine a long-term, student performance–based research project. The students would utilize information literacy to use the Internet to develop important questions, locate information, synthesize the information to answer their questions, and communicate the information to others (Leu et al., 2004, p. 1572).

In Figure 4.3, Abilock (2007) presents information literacy as a problem-solving process in which students use certain skills and strategies to achieve particular outcomes in given contexts. Notice how inquiry pervades the performance-based nature of the process.

Using What We Know about Information Literacy in Teaching

In Figure 4.3, Abilock suggests that we can make connections among information literacy, students' skills and strategies, student outcomes, and curriculum and teaching design. This integration supports our use of information literacy across the curriculum. For example, students using information literacy in science might engage in research projects about scientific developments such as global warming or the viability of life on Mars, while students in foreign language class might research the various dimensions of the culture they are studying.

FIGURE 4.3
Overview of
Informational Literacy

Information Literacy	Student Skills and Strategies	Student Outcomes	Curriculum and Teaching Design
A problem-solving process for	The student uses habits of mind to	The student is a learner who is	The learning design provides
■ Exploring and questioning	■ Recognize problems	■ Independent	■ Authentic contexts
■ Defining an information need	■ Formulate hypotheses	■ Disciplined	■ Simulations, real applications, and problems
■ Creating a plan to locate relevant information	■ Make good predictions	■ Planful	■ Reiterative opportunities for unique performances
■ Reading the medium	■ Ask important questions	■ Self-motivated	
■ Synthesizing information to create knowledge	■ Locate, analyze, interpret, evaluate, and record information and ideas	■ Metacognitive	■ Ongoing assessments
■ Applying insight to personal, social, or global contexts to create wisdom	■ Assume multiple stances	■ Flexible	■ Longitudinal rubrics
■ Self-evaluating the process and the product	■ Apply heuristic strategies	■ Adventurous	■ Integration of information literacy
	■ Develop complex understanding		■ Creative roles for teachers
	■ Extend understanding through creative models		■ Collegiality
	■ Apply understanding to new problems		■ Culture of innovation

Source: Abilock, 2007.

Making Connections | Thinking about Information Literacy

■ Reflect on your content area and contemplate how your students might use information literacy.

■ Share your thoughts with others in a small-group discussion.

What Do We Know about Media Literacy?

According to Considine (1995), *media literacy* is "the ability to access, analyze, evaluate, and create information in a variety of media formats." Much like critical literacy, it moves beyond what we would generally consider as comprehension to analyzing and evaluating information. Media literacy applies critical perspectives to print and electronic media (Summers, 2000).

Media literacy fosters what Brown (1998) describes as "discriminating responsiveness" and what Singer and Singer (1998) term "critical viewers." In media literacy, viewers deconstruct media messages by analyzing the message, the product, and the influence (Scharrer, 2002–2003). We do this by raising questions similar to those we ask in critical literacy: Who chose the message that is being communicated? What does that person want us to believe? What perspectives may have been marginalized? What action might we take based on what we have viewed? Because media are pervasive in our lives and the lives of our students, questioning from a critical perspective is essential if we are to be able to interpret the messages we receive (Ivey, 2000).

Silverblatt (2000) suggests that we should use seven principles to guide the use of media literacy in our teaching:

1. Principle 1: Media literacy empowers individuals to make independent judgments about media consumption.
2. Principle 2: Media literacy focuses attention on the elements involved in the media communication process. Our online communication is both expressive and receptive, because we both impart and retrieve information.
3. Principle 3: Media literacy fosters an awareness of the impact of the media on the individual and on society as a whole.
4. Principle 4: Media literacy develops strategies with which to analyze and discuss media messages.
5. Principle 5: Media literacy promotes awareness of interactive media content as a "text" that provides insight into contemporary culture and ourselves.
6. Principle 6: Media literacy cultivates enhanced enjoyment, understanding, and appreciation of media content.
7. Principle 7: Media literacy challenges interactive media communicators to produce effective and responsible media messages.

Our goal is to teach our students to be active learners and to not passively accept media messages. Teaching media literacy will encourage our students to actively question the format, content, and intent of media communication.

Integrating Media Literacy into Teaching

Media literacy not only suggests that students learn from the media, resist media manipulation, and empower themselves in terms of media, but also promotes the development of skills that will motivate and empower students in everyday life. Critical discussions, analyses, and respect for inquiry play important roles in this process. When teaching our students about media literacy, Summers (2000) suggests that we use the three R's—*review, reflect,* and *react.* She describes these terms as follows:

- *Review:* examine, investigate, summarize, restate, describe, explain, analyze, deconstruct, and study
- *Reflect:* compare, contrast, personalize, apply, judge, debate, critique, defend, and evaluate
- *React:* support, subscribe to, reject, internalize, participate in, adopt, editorialize, and oppose

Our students can apply the three R's process to a variety of media, including news, controversial advertisements, and political message films. For example, science students might analyze messages about rainforests or cloning, while mathematics students might question the source and relevance of statistics about a particular issue. Because the media permeate our students' lives, it is increasingly important that the students know how to analyze messages from these sources.

What Do We Know about Multicultural Literacy?

Multicultural literacy is the ability to understand and appreciate the similarities and differences in the customs, values, and beliefs of one's own culture and the cultures of others (NCREL, 2003). Proponents of multicultural literacy

- *Value diversity.* They appreciate and accept similarities and differences in cultural beliefs, appearances, and lifestyles.
- *Exhibit an informed sensitivity.* They can take the perspectives of other cultural groups and can be sensitive to issues of bias, racism, prejudice, and stereotyping.
- *Actively engage in and with other cultures.* They communicate, interact, and work with individuals from other cultural groups, using technology where appropriate.

We live in a world in which communication with other cultures is instantaneous. To communicate cross-culturally in meaningful ways, we and our students not only need to understand and appreciate a variety of cultures, but also to develop the knowledge and skills necessary for positive interaction (Banks et al., 2001).

Integrating What We Know about Multicultural Literacy into Teaching

Communication seems to be the ultimate mode of engagement for multicultural literacy. We can communicate personally within our own communities or with cultures around the world through cyberspace. This includes classes using email, shared websites, or videoconferencing as formats for cultural exchange. For example, students in foreign language class can learn about particular cultures by communicating with students who actually live in those cultures. Students can also participate in shared class projects, such as animal extinction research with students in Greenland and Africa, or engage in moderated e-discussions of world issues, such as the economy or scientific discoveries.

FINAL THOUGHTS

Teaching in an age of multiple literacies is a complex, dynamic experience filled with challenges and rewards. Characterized by global innovation, evolving understandings of our content area subjects, and ever-emerging technologies, the time in which we live demands that we become critically aware and transition from passively accepting information to critiquing it, from relying on the author's intent to exploring multiple perspectives. Our goal: To make sense of the world in a time that is characterized by change.

In the next chapter we build upon what we have learned by examining standards-based teaching and learning. We explore national and state standards, situate them within a constructivist framework, and examine discipline-specific examples.

Teaching Connections

APPLYING WHAT WE HAVE LEARNED

E-Link

To gain a deeper understanding of the state of adolescent literacy, read *Reading Next—A Vision for Action and Research in Middle and High School Literacy*. In that report from the Alliance for Excellent Education, Biancarosa and Snow (2006) assess the state of adolescent literacy and make recommendations concerning how to address current challenges in the field. To find the document, visit www.all4ed.org/files/archive/publications/ReadingNext/ReadingNext.pdf.

Focus on the background information about struggling adolescent readers and the 15 suggestions to improve instruction and infrastructure. Remember that Snow and Biancarosa suggest that the 15 elements should be used in what they describe as an "optimal mix." Choose a school in which you have had a field experience or currently teach and develop what you perceive to be the optimal mix of elements that would benefit the adolescents in that school. Justify your thinking in a portfolio reflection.

Accountable Talk

Many of us grew up believing everything we read in a textbook. We never questioned who was writing the text, who was determining which topics would be included in it, or who was deciding what would be excluded from it. We never questioned if there was any perspective other than the one presented. As a result, we believed the information presented to us, which included that all inventors of importance were white men and excluded information about events such as the Japanese American Internment during World War II. Today's school students interact with many more information sources than we did at their age. They need to understand that critical literacy requires that we move beyond passively accepting information and question both the information and those who have created or compiled it. Consider critical literacy and explain how you would teach your students to think from a critical perspective. Choose a specific topic in your content area and offer an example of how you could use it to teach critical literacy. Discuss your ideas in small-group conversations and then share your group's thoughts in whole-class discussion.

Portfolio/Performance Opportunity

Integrating multiple literacies is essential for quality teaching and learning. Consider information literacy, media literacy, and multicultural literacy. Explain how you would integrate each when teaching in your content area. Choose a specific topic and create a lesson plan that incorporates two of these literacies. Include the lesson plan in your portfolio.

5

TEACHING IDEAS:

• ANTICIPATION/REACTION GUIDE• SEMANTIC MAP • PREREADING PLAN • BIO-IMPRESSIONS • CONNECTION STEMS • SAVE THE LAST WORD FOR ME • CODING THE TEXT • SKETCH AND LABEL CONNECTIONS

Comprehending Content Area Text

I magine trying to read a textbook, a novel, a newspaper, or a computer screen and not being able to understand it. Think about how frustrating it would be if you could not comprehend text and how that would affect your life—from everyday occurrences such as reading the newspaper or email to reading novels or textbooks. Then think about students who may find themselves in that same situation. As teachers, we want our students to be active, independent, strategic learners, but that is not possible if they cannot comprehend text. In this chapter, we examine ways to help students understand what they read in their content area classes. Our discussion focuses on three topics: what reading comprehension is, what contributes to successful reading experiences, and how we can help students use strategies to think through the reading process.

In this chapter, we explore these issues through theory and practice. We begin by focusing on what we know about reading comprehension. We examine reading from a social constructivist perspective and as a thinking process. Then we describe factors that contribute to successful reading experiences. Next, we investigate what we, as teachers, can do to contribute to students' understanding of content area text. After that, we take a closer look at reading comprehension strategies, paying particular attention to strategies for engaging student thinking.

What Do We Know about Reading Comprehension?

Every worthwhile educational practice has a strong theoretical foundation. So we begin our quest to understand reading's role in content area teaching by examining its roots—the theories and beliefs that support it. As Brian Cambourne (2002, p. 25) notes, "There is nothing so practical as a good theory."

Our theoretical investigation of the reading process focuses on two current beliefs: (1) that reading is a social constructivist process and (2) that readers think their way through the construction of meaning. We begin our discussion by noting that comprehension is an essential component of teaching and learning. One of our primary goals as content area teachers is to ensure that our students know how to comprehend text. This is a complex task, but as Duke and Pearson (2002) note, "Comprehension is a consuming, continuous, and complex activity, but one that, for good readers, is both satisfying and productive" (p. 206).

Comprehension of Text as a Social Constructivist Process

Savery and Duffy (1995, p. 31) suggest that constructivism is a "philosophical view on how we come to understand or know." Constructivists believe that students construct knowledge by linking what they already know to new information. In reading, this concept is reflected in schema-based learning development, which suggests that learning takes place when prior knowledge—what is already known—is integrated with new information—what is currently being read. The more knowledge and experience learners have with a particular topic, the easier it is for them to make connections between what they know and what they are learning (Anderson, 1994). Brian Cambourne suggests that knowledge and meaning are socially constructed through the processes of negotiation, evaluation, and transformation.

We refer to reading comprehension as a *social* constructivist process because readers often share ideas about what they are reading to negotiate meaning. Such discussions are "forums for collaboratively constructing meaning and for sharing responses" (Almasi, 1996, p. 2). Gambrell (1996) notes that these collaborations integrate listening, speaking, and thinking skills. Because of the dynamic nature of these discussions, the meanings that readers construct are continually transformed by their experiences, interactions with others, and information from the text (Almasi, 1996). This social interaction is another aspect of literacy that is underpinned by Vygotsky's (1978) theoretical framework. His work suggests that social interaction plays a fundamental role in the development of cognition. His beliefs support that students' thinking abilities develop more fully when students work with teachers or peers.

Multiple Literacies as Comprehension

In Chapter 4, Teaching and Learning in an Age of Multiple Literacies, we discussed the current focus on adolescent, content, critical, information, media, and multicultural literacies. These literacies are distinctive in nature, yet similar in that one of the outcomes of each is comprehension. For example, adolescent literacy involves understanding and applying knowledge in a variety of contexts, content literacy involves understanding through the uniqueness of each discipline, and critical literacy involves questioning the author and the message to move beyond everyday understanding to comprehend at deeper levels. (For more information about multiple literacies, see Chapter 4.)

Reading online, which is an integral part of today's literacies, is a constructivist process, just as reading offline is. Online reading comprehension is a problem-based, inquiry process (Coiro, Knoebel, Lankshear, & Leu, 2008; Leu, Kinzer, Coiro, & Cammack, 2004). Readers construct meaning based on their personal paths of inquiry and discovery (Schmar-Dobbler, 2003). (For more information about reading online and offline, see Chapter 12.)

Reading as a Thinking Process

Decades ago, Dolores Durkin (1978–1979) defined reading as comprehension, indicating that the focus of instruction should be the strategies readers use to make sense of text. Frank Smith (1997) extended this idea by defining reading as "thinking, cued by print." Suggesting that reading is a thinking process indicates that the focus of instruction should not be on the print, but rather on how readers connect with the print. Hiebert, Pearson, Taylor, Richardson, and Paris (1998) endorse this idea: "Teachers support their students' strategic reading through lessons that attend explicitly to how to think while reading" (p. 4). Harris and Hodge (1995) also support the idea of reading as a thinking process, noting that the meaning readers construct "resides in the intentional problem-solving, thinking processes of the interpreter during such an interchange" (p. 39).

Describing reading as a thinking process seems quite logical and natural if we examine a reader's interaction with text. To begin, the student contemplates text selection and uses a variety of thought processes to activate prior knowledge and make connections to the text. The reader previews the text by making predictions about the content and setting purposes for reading. During reading, the student may self-question, visualize, monitor, make connections, summarize the text read so far, and evaluate the author's purpose and the consistency of text. After reading, the learner may summarize, evaluate, and make connections, again engaging in cognitive processes. To successfully interact with text, students need to be thinkers. To effectively think through the reading process and interact with a variety of types and levels of text, students need to know how to use reading comprehension skills and strategies.

Although many factors appear to contribute to reader comprehension, three influences seem most prominent: influential teachers, good readers, and quality contexts. In the remainder of this section, we learn that influential teachers are described as knowledgeable—not only about content, but also about their students; good readers are represented as motivated and strategic; and contexts are viewed as meaningful teaching and learning environments.

Influential Reading Teachers Affect Students' Learning

As detailed in Chapter 1, researchers and professional organizations report that teachers are the single most influential factor in students' learning (International Reading Association, 2000; Ruddell, 2004). Characteristics of such teachers, who are commonly described as "influential" or "excellent," are featured in Figure 5.1.

As noted in the figure, these teachers know their content and how to teach it. They are aware of students' individual needs and the importance of motivation. They also use multiple grouping patterns and a variety of teaching and assessment methods.

What Good Readers Do

Reading researchers report that much of what we know about comprehension is based on studies of "good readers" (Duke & Pearson, 2002; Pearson, 2001; Pressley, 2000). They describe good readers as active participants in the reading process, who have clear goals and constantly monitor the relation between the goals they have set and the text they are reading. Good readers use a repertoire of comprehension strategies to facilitate the construction of meaning. These strategies include previewing, monitoring, making connections, self-questioning, visualizing, summarizing, and evaluating. Students should know how to use these strategies, so they can call upon them as needed when they are reading.

FIGURE 5.1
Characteristics of Influential Reading Teachers

- Believe all students can learn
- Motivate their students
- Teach in concept-rich environments
- Have in-depth knowledge of literacy
- Use diverse teaching methods
- Use multiple grouping patterns
- Are participants in the reading process

- Teach to the needs of individual learners
- Use multiple kinds and levels of text
- Have in-depth knowledge of content
- Teach for a variety of purposes
- Use a variety of materials
- Teach reading strategies
- Assess in multiple ways

Good readers read from aesthetic or efferent stances and have an awareness of the author's style and purpose (Rosenblatt, 1978). The aesthetic stance depicts a predominantly emotional perspective; the efferent stance, a predominantly factual one. Rosenblatt (2002) notes that no reading experience is purely aesthetic or purely efferent, but rather that readers continually make choices about their thinking, focusing on both stances, and sometimes more on one than the other. For example, if we were reading about the Holocaust and learned that 1.5 million Jewish children died in concentration camps during that time, we might choose an aesthetic stance in our emotional response to the deaths of the children and an efferent stance when noting the number of children who perished.

Making Connections
TO MULTIPLE LITERACIES

Reader stance is an issue of particular interest within multiple literacies, because in addition to reading from Rosenblatt's aesthetic and efferent stances, researchers suggest that we can read from a critical stance (McLaughlin & DeVoogd, 2004). When reading from a critical literacy perspective or critical stance, readers use their background knowledge to understand the power relationships between their ideas and the ideas presented by the author of the text. In this process, readers play the role of text critics (Luke & Freebody, 1999). In other words, readers have the power to question, to problematize, and to envision alternative ways of viewing the author's topic. Readers exert that power when they read from a critical stance. ■

The critical stance functions just as the aesthetic and efferent stances do during reading: Our reading experiences may involve one stance more than the others, but all three are represented during reading. For example, when reading about the Holocaust, we may respond aesthetically to the poetry and drawings the children created in the concentration camps, efferently to the number of children who died during the Holocaust, and critically to the issues of justice associated with this event.

Good readers read both narrative or story-based text and informational or fact-based text. They have ideas about how to figure out unfamiliar words. They often preview what they are about to read and use their knowledge of text structure to efficiently and strategically think through text. This knowledge develops from experiences with different genres and is correlated with age and time spent in school (Goldman & Rakestraw, 2000).

Making Connections
TO STRUGGLING READERS

When teaching struggling readers, we should check to ensure that the students know and can use the skills that underpin the reading comprehension strategies and the strategies themselves. For example, these students need to know the elements of narrative text and to recognize the various patterns associated with informational text. It is helpful for us to preteach struggling readers, so they will have some knowledge prior to the whole-class instruction. This often enables these students to gain a better understanding and participate in class discussions in more meaningful ways. For detailed information about how to teach skills such as text patterns and generating questions, see Chapter 9.■

Good readers also read widely. This helps them to understand a variety of genres and text formats, while accommodating their interests. It also provides opportunities for students to use reading strategies, increase their understanding of vocabulary, and engage in discussion and meaning negotiation.

FIGURE 5.2
Characteristics of Good Readers

- Use their prior knowledge
- Negotiate meaning
- Spontaneously generate questions
- Integrate reading, writing, speaking, and listening
- Read different kinds of text differently

- Set goals
- Are motivated and engaged
- Are problem solvers
- Use comprehension strategies
- Know text structures
- Make strategic decisions
- Adapt their thinking

Like influential teachers, good readers have numerous other characteristics (Block, Schaller, Joy, & Gaine, 2002; Duke & Pearson, 2002; Pressley & Afflerbach, 1995). Examples of those frequently cited are featured in Figure 5.2.

Making Connections | Thinking about Good Readers

- Think about when you were in high school. How would you have described a "good reader" then? At that time, did you consider yourself to be a good reader? Explain your response. Did you choose to read, or was your reading limited to your teachers' assignments? Did you think about reading as part of your learning in the content areas? Do you think today's middle and high school students are good readers? Justify your response.
- Share your thoughts in small-group discussions.

A Quality Context: An Integral Part of Meaningful Literacy Instruction

Context has been viewed as a broad concept that encompasses instructional settings, resources, approaches, and tasks (Lipson & Wixson, 2009). The instructional settings include facets such as teacher beliefs, literacy environment, classroom organization, classroom interaction, and grouping patterns. Instructional resources comprise elements such as text types and text structures. Instructional approaches include the curriculum, teaching methods, and assessment practices. Task type, content, form, and implementation are the elements of the instructional tasks. Duke (2001) has suggested that we expand our understanding of context and view curriculum, activity, classroom environment, teaching, discussion, text and society as context. Researchers and practitioners agree that both teaching and learning are greatly influenced by the contextual choices we make.

Making Connections | Thinking about the Contexts in Which We Teach

- Close your eyes and imagine the context in which you would like to teach. Open your eyes and sketch some of the ideas you visualized. Think about how you might create such a context while coping with influences such as pressure for your students to do well on state assessments.
- Share your sketches and ideas in small-group discussions.

What Can We Do to Foster Students' Comprehension of Content Area Text?

To help our students understand content area texts, we need to help them make connections between what they know and what they are reading. We must move beyond the traditional, "Read the next chapter" assignment and help students to become actively engaged in the text. To do so, we might provide a chapter overview and engage students in discussion about what they already know about the topic. We might motivate students by reading aloud, providing opportunities to view short videos, or sharing an array of related photos. We might also offer opportunities for self-selection of related readings or project topics.

Once our students are motivated, we need to continue to encourage them:

- *To activate and continue to expand their prior knowledge.* The constructivist view of reading focuses on the reader's prior knowledge interacting with the text that is being read. The more widely students read and the more they experience, the greater their prior knowledge will be and the better they will comprehend. To help students continue to increase their prior knowledge, we can provide them with a variety of content area experiences, types and levels of text, technology access, and opportunities for discussion.

- *To deepen their understanding of how language works.* Students often complain that they don't need to study grammar, because their computers will offer suggestions to correct it when they write. What they don't understand is that knowing how language works—parts of speech, word order, sentence structures—helps us to read more fluently, determine word meanings, and comprehend text.

- *To enhance their understanding of everyday and academic vocabularies.* Well-developed vocabularies help us to comprehend what we read. To help students increase their vocabularies, we can encourage them to read widely, teach them effective ways to learn new words, provide opportunities to use context clues, and support them while they use the terms while they read, write, and speak.

- *To read and respond to text.* The more our students read and respond to what they have read, the better they will comprehend. As teachers, we can provide students with frequent opportunities to read and communicate about what they have read. In the process, we should remain open to student thinking and offer access to multiple modes of presentation.

- *To develop and use a repertoire of comprehension strategies that they can call upon as needed to think through text.* We can explicitly teach these strategies; in the next section, we begin to focus on how to do that effectively.

Making Connections
TO ENGLISH LEARNERS

We expect all students to continually expand their knowledge, respond to what they read, and use strategies as needed, but these tasks can prove challenging for English learners. These students often need more support as they learn. We can provide this assistance in many ways, including (1) supplying text on tape or CD; (2) preteaching skills, strategies, and content as needed; and (3) simplifying or numbering graphic organizers. For more information on teaching English learners, see Chapter 10.■

How Can We Teach Students to Think through the Comprehension of Text?

To help students think through the comprehension process, we can teach them reading comprehension strategies. We use a repertoire of these strategies as needed when we read text. The comprehension strategies that we use include these:

- *Previewing.* This strategy includes activating prior knowledge (What do I already know about this topic?), setting purposes for reading (Why am I reading this text?), and predicting/inferring (Based on what I know and what I have read, what do I think will happen in this text?).

- *Making connections.* When reading, we make three kinds of connections: text–self, text–text, and text–world (connections to others).
- *Monitoring/clarifying.* This strategy involves asking ourselves, "Does this make sense?" as we read, and, if it doesn't, adapting strategic processes to make it clear.
- *Self-questioning.* This strategy comprises generating questions to guide reading.
- *Visualizing.* We visualize by creating mental pictures of the text while reading.
- *Summarizing.* This strategy involves synthesizing important ideas. When we read narrative text, such as novels or short stories, we focus on elements such as characters, setting, problem, attempts to resolve the problem, and resolution. This process changes when we read informational or factual text, which is based on different text patterns, such as cause and effect and comparison/contrast. (To learn more about text patterns, see. Chapter 9)
- *Evaluating.* We evaluate or make judgments about text as we read. Examples include questioning the author's purpose and the consistency of the author's message.

Later in this chapter and in Chapters 6 and 7, we discuss each of these strategies in detail and provide multiple examples of how we can teach our students to use them. We discuss the strategies in three categories: engaging, guiding, and extending thinking. When we use strategies to engage thinking, we motivate the students to read by activating background knowledge, setting purposes for reading, and making predictions about the text. We teach students to use these strategies *before* reading. When we use strategies to guide thinking, we help students to transact with the text to comprehend it. We teach students to use these strategies *during* reading. When we use strategies to extend thinking, we encourage students to synthesize their thoughts and transfer what they have learned to other subject areas. We teach students to use these strategies *after* reading. Of course, although we learn the strategies as before, during, or after reading or as engaging, guiding, and extending thinking, they can be used *throughout* the reading process. Our overall goal is to help students develop a repertoire of reading comprehension strategies that they can call upon as needed to think through text.

Teaching ideas that support these strategies are featured in the next section, as well as in Chapters 6 and 7. In each example, we explain and demonstrate each idea using content area text. Then we guide students as they (and a partner) try using the strategy. We offer support as requested when students practice using the strategies on their own. Finally, we join the students in reflecting about the strategy and how we will use it over time. Some ideas involve alternative modes of response such as sketching, dramatizing, and singing. Offering alternative modes of response provides variety and accommodates students' varying learning styles. For more comprehension-based teaching ideas and their related graphic organizers, see Chapters 6 and 7. For reproducible graphic organizers designed to support the strategies, see the Appendix.)

When we teach the reading comprehension strategies, we use the five-step explicit instruction process from the Guided Comprehension Model (McLaughlin & Allen, 2002a). The five steps in which we engage are explain, demonstrate, guide, practice, and reflect. When we use this Model, we can scaffold students' learning, gradually releasing responsibility from teacher to student (McLaughlin & Allen, 2002a). The Guided Comprehension Model is supported by Vygotsky's (1978) beliefs about scaffolding, the gradual relinquishing of support as the students become more competent in using the strategy. For example, when using the Guided Comprehension Model, we offer students full support when we explain and demonstrate the strategies. Then we gradually release responsibility for learning to the students. We guide their learning, offering support as needed when they practice the strategies with partners. Finally, we offer little or no support as students use the strategies on their own.

Strategies are more complex than skills, but they often integrate several skills. For example, we use skills such as questioning and sequencing when we engage in the comprehension strategy of summarizing. Linking skills and strategies facilitates comprehension. For a more detailed discussion of reading skills, including questioning, see Chapter 9.

How Can We Use Comprehension Strategies to Engage Thinking?

We use comprehension strategies throughout the reading process. We often describe this practice as using comprehension strategies before, during, and after reading. In this part of the chapter, we focus on strategies we can use *before* reading to engage student thinking. We use these strategies to activate background knowledge, make connections to text, and predict what may happen in the text based on what we already know or have read in the text.

In the examples that follow, we describe a variety of ways to support students' use of comprehension strategies before reading. Although we use previewing and making connections as examples of strategies that can be used to engage thinking, both strategies can also be used at other times during the reading process. In each step-by-step sequence, we begin by explaining the strategy and the teaching idea. Then we demonstrate it, using a think-aloud and a visual. Next, we guide students as they work with partners. Then the students attempt to use the strategy on their own. Finally, we reflect on what we have learned and how we can use the strategy in the content areas. Each sequence is followed by an example to support teaching in the content areas.

Making Connections
TO MULTIPLE LITERACIES

Although content literacy examples are featured in the sections that follow as well as in Chapters 6 and 7, the reading comprehension strategies we are learning how to teach are applicable in all literacies. In media literacy, examples of how we use the strategies include analyzing and evaluating information. Examples of how we use the strategies in information literacy include questioning to guide our inquiry and summarizing the information we locate. ■

Previewing

Previewing is a comprehension strategy that includes activating prior knowledge (What do I already know about this topic?), setting purposes for reading (I will read this text to learn . . .), and predicting and inferring (What can I hypothesize based on what I already know and what I am able to assume from the text?). Many teaching ideas support this strategy, including the seven featured in this section. For related graphic organizers, see Appendix A.

TEACHING IDEA ANTICIPATION/REACTION GUIDE. Students can use an Anticipation/Reaction Guide (Readence, Bean, & Baldwin, 2000) to preview what they are about to read and to monitor their thinking while reading. Specifically, this idea helps students activate their prior knowledge, make connections to text, set purposes for reading, and develop more accurate understandings of informational text. An Anticipation/Reaction Guide consists of several statements related to the text; the statements may or may not be true. Before reading, students indicate whether they agree or disagree with each statement and share their responses through partner, small-group, or whole-group discussion. After reading, students revisit the statements, decide whether their thinking has changed, and mark the statements accordingly. Then we discuss again and students explain any changes in their thinking that may have occurred. We use Anticipation/Reaction Guides before and after reading informational texts.

To teach students how to use an Anticipation/Reaction Guide, follow these steps:

1. **Explain:** Explain the strategy of previewing and how the Anticipation/Reaction Guide works. For example, you might say, "Previewing is a comprehension strategy that includes activating background knowledge, setting purposes for reading, and predicting what will come next, based on what has been read. Anticipation/Reaction Guides involve reading a

FIGURE 5.3 Biology Anticipation/Reaction Guide

Agree	Disagree	Statement
✓		1. An organ is a group of tissues that work together.
✓		2. There are ten organ systems in the human body.
✓	✗	3. Motor neurons are the only class of neurons in the body.
✓		4. An impulse is similar to the flow of an electrical current through a wire.

set of statements and determining whether we agree or disagree with them. After completing the guide, we discuss it. Then we read a text. Next, we revisit the Guide and record how our thinking may have changed based on what we have read (our reactions)."

2 Demonstrate: Demonstrate by using an Anticipation/Reaction Guide that you created prior to the lesson. The Guide should contain 3 to 5 statements that relate to the text. The statements may be facts or statements that are not accurate. Read the first statement in the Anticipation/Reaction Guide and think aloud about why you might agree or disagree with it. Put a check mark under the Agree or Disagree column at the start of the statement. For example, in the Anticipation/Reaction Guide shown in Figure 4.3, you might read the first statement, "An organ is a group of tissues that work together." Then you might say, "I will place a check mark in the Agree column, because we have already learned that organs are groups of tissues that work together."

3 Guide: Guide students to work with partners to read and respond to the next two statements, marking either Agree or Disagree, and discussing their reasoning.

4 Practice: Invite students to practice by working on their own to respond to the remaining statements. Discuss their responses. Introduce the text and read aloud the section of the text to which the statements relate. Discuss the text. Invite the students to revisit (react to) their original responses and place an "X" in the Agree or Disagree column to indicate their thinking has changed. Discuss students' responses.

5 Reflect: Encourage students to reflect on what they have learned about previewing and how they can use the Anticipation/Reaction Guides in other content areas.

In Figure 5.3, Michael Gress, a biology student, responded to an Anticipation/Reaction Guide based on a chapter in his biology textbook. As you can see, Michael originally agreed with all four statements, but, after listening to the text being read (or reading it on his own), he changed his thinking about the third statement and marked it with an "X." While reading, Michael discovered that statements 1, 3, and 4 were true, but statement 2 was not. He learned that there are three different classes of neurons in the body: sensory neurons, interneurons, and motor neurons.

 **TEACHING IDEA**   **SEMANTIC MAP.** We use Semantic Maps (Johnson & Pearson, 1984) to activate prior knowledge, introduce content specific vocabulary, and organize information about a topic. When teaching students how to use this map, we choose a focus word, engage students in brainstorming, and create and complete a graphic organizer that features categories and details. We can use completed Semantic Maps to create summaries. Because the design of the Semantic Map depends on students' responses, the structure of each map is different. We usually use Semantic Maps before and after reading either narrative or informational text.

To teach your students how to use Semantic Maps, follow these steps:

1. **Explain:** Begin by explaining the strategy of previewing and the use of a Semantic Map. For example, you might say, "Previewing is a comprehension strategy that includes activating background knowledge, setting purposes for reading, and predicting what will come next, based on what we have already read. Semantic Maps involve our brainstorming about a focus word and determining categories that emerge from our responses." We usually complete Semantic Maps before reading a text, and revisit them after reading.

2. **Demonstrate:** Begin the demonstration by choosing a focus word and writing it on a chart, chalkboard, or computer screen. Draw an oval around it. For example, if the focus word were *baseball*, we would write that word and draw an oval around it. Then think aloud about what word comes to mind when you read the focus word. For example, your response might be *pitcher*. Write that word on a different section of the chart paper, board, or computer screen where you will also list students' responses.

3. **Guide:** Guide students to work with a partner and think about what word comes to mind when they read the focus word. Write the students' responses beneath your response— *pitcher*—on the separate section of the board. Next, read the focus word and the list of responses. Think aloud about one category that you think emerges from the responses. For example, if the focus word were *baseball,* an emerging category might be *leagues.* Draw a line from the focus word oval to a satellite oval and write the category (*leagues*) within that oval. Underneath the oval, write the words from the list of responses that support that category. For example, in the *baseball* example, you might list *American League* and *National League.* Revisit the list of words on the separate board. Put a line through *American League* and *National League* to indicate that those responses have been used. Then invite the student partners to determine another category they think emerges from the list of responses. They might suggest *teams* as a category. Follow the same procedure of drawing a line through the student responses that have been used, adding a satellite oval, and listing the words beneath it.

4. **Practice:** Invite students to work on their own to determine other categories (e.g., *positions, players, stadiums*) and suggest which words should be listed beneath it. Add the students' suggestions to the Semantic Map about baseball. Continue this process until all of the words on the list of responses on the separate board have been used. Discuss the completed map and show students how the information on the map can be used to create a summary about the focus word. Then introduce the text, read it aloud, and discuss how the focus word relates to it. After the discussion, revisit the map to ensure it provides full and accurate information about the focus word. Revise as necessary. Use the completed map to summarize the topic.

5. **Reflect:** Encourage students to reflect on what they have learned about previewing and activating their background knowledge before reading. Engage them in discussion about how they can use Semantic Maps to preview text and learn vocabulary in other content areas.

Figure 5.4 shows a Semantic Map that Venetta Hurley and her students completed in geometry class. The figure focuses on the various types of triangles, which are classified by sides and angles. The map is simple in structure and was used to promote a class discussion of triangles. After the information contained on the map was verified through discussion, students worked with partners to illustrate each type of triangle.

For other examples of Semantic Maps as well as information about Semantic Question Maps and Concept of Definition Maps, see Chapter 8. For related reproducible graphic organizers, see the Appendix.

TEACHING IDEA

PREREADING PLAN. We use the Prereading Plan (PreP) (Langer, 1981) to activate prior knowledge about a topic, introduce new vocabulary, and make connections. When teaching students how to use PreP, we provide a cue word or idea and invite students to brainstorm related words or concepts. We record all ideas and then ask students why they suggested a particular word.

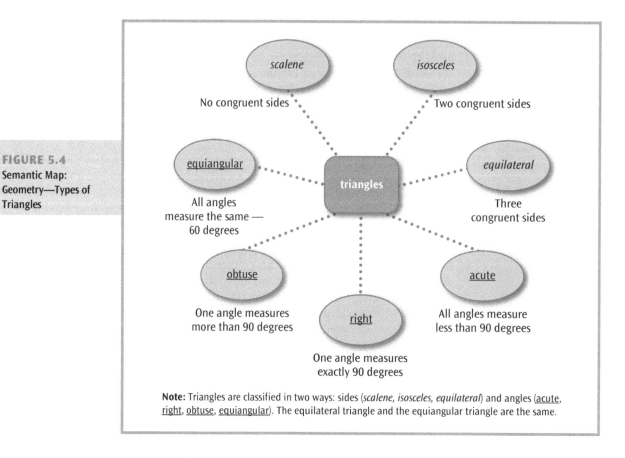

FIGURE 5.4
Semantic Map:
Geometry—Types of
Triangles

Note: Triangles are classified in two ways: sides (*scalene, isosceles, equilateral*) and angles (<u>acute</u>, <u>right</u>, <u>obtuse</u>, <u>equiangular</u>). The equilateral triangle and the equiangular triangle are the same.

Next, we read a text and revise the original list as necessary. We usually use PreP before and after reading informational text.

To teach your students how to use the Prereading Plan, follow these steps:

1 Explain: Begin by explaining that previewing is a comprehension strategy that includes activating background knowledge, setting purposes for reading, and predicting what will come next, based on what we have already read. Then explain how PreP works. For example, you might say, "PreP provides us with an opportunity to brainstorm words or ideas related to a topic and explain why we suggested particular words. After clarifying the words or ideas, we read a related text, revisit the terms, and revise as necessary."

2 Demonstrate: Begin the demonstration by providing a cue word or idea to stimulate thinking. Then think aloud about which related word comes to mind. Write the word or idea on the board or overhead screen. Then explain why you suggested it. For example, if the cue word or phrase is "U.S.S. *Maine*," the word that comes to mind might be *battleship*, and the reason might be "It was considered a floating tank."

3 Guide: Invite students to work with partners and brainstorm words or ideas related to the cue word and why they suggested them. Write down their responses.

4 Practice: Encourage students to practice by contributing other terms related to the cue word. Next, ask students to explain why they suggested them. Elaborate on the listed words. Then introduce the text and read it aloud. Join the students in reviewing the list of related words and the reasons they were offered. Revise as necessary.

5 Reflect: Encourage students to reflect on how PreP helps us to activate our background knowledge and predict what might appear in the text. Invite students to reflect on how they can use PreP in other content areas.

Cue Idea: U.S.S. *Maine*	
Brainstormed Responses	**Reasons**
battleship	It was considered a floating tank.
Spanish–American War	The sinking of the U.S.S. *Maine* was a cause of this war.
unknown cause of explosion	No one knows how the explosion was caused.
Alfonso XII	This is the ship that sent rescue crews to the U.S.S. *Maine*.

FIGURE 5.5
Excerpt from PreP about U.S.S. *Maine*

Figure 5.5 features an excerpt from a PreP about the U.S.S. *Maine*, that Jim Burke completed in history class. The sinking of the battleship was a cause of the Spanish-American War.

TEACHING IDEA

BIO-IMPRESSIONS. Bio-Impressions are adapted from the Story Impressions created by McGinley and Denner (1987). We use Bio-Impressions before reading to predict which information the text will contain. They provide a framework for biographical writing, encourage predictions about people's lives, and help us to make connections between vocabulary and biographical structure. To create Bio-Impressions, we choose a person and structure a list of clues about his life connected by downward arrows. Then we encourage pairs of students to use the clues in sequential order, as they write their Bio-Impressions—what they predict the content of the biography will be. The maximum number of clues is ten; the maximum number of words per clue is five. When students finish writing their Bio-Impressions, they share them with another pair of students. Next, each pair reads a biography about the person featured in their Bio-Impression. After reading, they revisit the Bio-Impression and revise it as necessary. Then the students add facts from their reading to their Bio-Impressions and share them with another pair of students.

We create Bio-Impressions before reading biographical (informational) text and insert additional facts after reading. We can also use this format to create Poem Impressions based on story poems or Story Impressions based on the narrative elements: characters, setting, problem, attempts to resolve and resolution.

To teach your students how to create Bio-Impressions, follow these steps:

1 Explain: Begin by explaining that previewing is a comprehension strategy that includes activating background knowledge, setting purposes for reading, and predicting what will come next, based on what we have already read.

Next, explain how Bio-Impressions work. For example, you might say, "We work with a partner and use a list of sequential clues to write Bio-Impressions. After writing the impressions, we share them with another pair of students. Next, we read a biography of the person whose life is the focus of the impression. Then we revisit the Bio-Impression and revise it as necessary. Finally, we either insert additional facts or sketch at least two ideas from the biography to enhance our Bio-Impressions."

2 Demonstrate: Model how to create a Bio-Impression by using a list of sequential clues connected by downward arrows (see Figure 5.6.). Include the sequential information as you write your Bio-Impression, beginning with the first clue. When the impression is complete, read it to the students. Then read a brief biography about the person who is the focus of the Bio-Impression. Revisit your impression and revise it as necessary. Include additional facts or a minimum of two sketches to represent ideas gleaned from reading. Discuss the process with your students.

3 Guide: Invite students to work with a partner to create Bio-Impressions using a new list of sequential clues. Encourage each pair to share and discuss their impressions with another pair of students.

4 Practice: Encourage students to practice by reading along silently as you read aloud a brief biography of the person who is the focus of the example Bio-Impression. Invite them to

Bio-Impression Clues

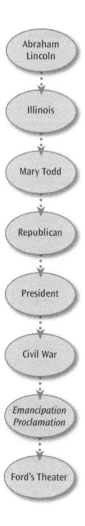

FIGURE 5.6
Bio-Impression
about Lincoln

Bio-Impression
(Before Reading)

Abraham Lincoln grew up in Illinois. He married
Mary Todd and they had several sons. Lincoln
was a member of the Republican Party. He was
elected President and supported the abolition of
slavery. The Union states fought the Confederacy
during the Civil War and won. Lincoln freed the
slaves by issuing the *Emancipation Proclamation*.
He was later assassinated by John Wilkes Booth
in Ford's Theater.

Bio-Impression with Additional Facts
(After Reading)

Abraham Lincoln grew up in Illinois. He married
Mary Todd and had four sons. In 1836, he began
to practice law. Twenty years later, he was known
as a distinguished and successful lawyer in Illinois. Andrew Jackson was president when Lincoln first entered politics. Lincoln was elected to
the Illinois State Legislature four times and to
Congress once. Lincoln became a member of the
Republican Party in 1856, the Republican presidential nominee in 1860, and President in 1861.
During his time in office, the Union states fought
the Confederacy during the Civil War. In 1864,
Lincoln put Ulysses S. Grant in command of all
federal armies, and that led to victory for the
Union. Lincoln freed the slaves by issuing the
Emancipation Proclamation. He was later assassi-
nated by John Wilkes Booth in Ford's Theater.

revise their Bio-Impression as necessary. Discuss the biography with the students and invite them to add facts to enhance their Impressions.

5 **Reflect:** Encourage students to reflect on how Bio-Impressions help us predict the information included in a biography. Ask them to think about how they could use Bio-Impressions in other content areas.

The Bio-Impression about Abraham Lincoln shown in Figure 5.6 was created by students studying American history. The teacher, James Phillips, prepared Bio-Impression clues about ten influential people during the time of the Civil War, and pairs of students chose one who interested them. The Bio-Impression featured in Figure 5.6 was created by Sonia Hernandez and Elizabeth Burke.

Making Connections | Thinking about Previewing

■ Previewing focuses on these essential processes: activating prior knowledge, setting purposes for reading, and predicting and inferring. Compare and contrast the value of teaching students how to preview with the past practice of simply assigning text for students to read. Consider specific examples.

■ Share your thoughts with others in small-group discussions.

Making Connections
TO STRUGGLING READERS

When teaching English learners or struggling readers in content areas, it is important to remember that prior knowledge plays a critical role in understanding text. There are many things we can do to help develop students' background knowledge, including (1) encouraging them to read widely and making available a variety of types and levels of content-related text; (2) creating cross-age partnerships between current students and those who have already completed the course; and (3) providing access to a variety of interactive websites that feature photographs and short video clips to support student learning. ■

Making Connections

Making connections is a reading comprehension strategy in which students activate their prior knowledge and make a variety of connections or associations to the text they are reading. There are three kinds of connections: text–self, text–text, and text–world (others). Connection Stems, Save the Last Word for Me, Coding the Text, and Sketch and Label Connections are the teaching ideas featured in this section. Details about how to teach them follow. Related graphic organizers can be found in the Appendix, along with other teaching ideas that will help students to make connections.

CONNECTION STEMS. Connection Stems (Harvey & Goudvis, 2000) provide a way for students to make connections or associations between the texts they are reading and themselves, other texts, and the world (others). The purpose of Connection Stems is to provide a structure to encourage students to make connections while reading and to encourage students to reflect on their reading. They can be used before, during, or after reading narrative or informational text.

To teach students how to use Connection Stems, follow these steps:

1 **Explain:** Begin by explaining making connections as a reading comprehension strategy in which students activate their prior knowledge and make a variety of connections or associations to the text they are reading. Note that there are three kinds of connections: text–self, text–text and text–world (others). Then explain Connection Stems, including a variety of stems. For example, you might say, "Connection Stems, such as 'That reminds me of . . .' or 'I remember when . . .', help us to make connections or associations between the texts we are reading and ourselves, other texts, and the world (others)."

Here are examples of Connection Stems:

- That reminds me of . . .
- I remember when . . .
- I have a connection . . .
- An experience I have that was similar to that . . .
- I felt like that person when . . .
- If I were that person, I would . . .

2 **Demonstrate:** After introducing a text, show students a sentence stem and think aloud about how to complete it. Use the text and personal experiences to explain the connection. For example, you might say, "I am going to use the Connection Stem 'That reminds me of . . .' So I will say, 'This text reminds me of my grandfather, because he was a soldier in World War II.' I have made a text-to-self connection, because I have related our text about World War II to my life."

3 **Guide:** Read a section of the text aloud or invite students to read a section silently. Then guide the students to work with a partner to complete one of the other connection stems. Invite partners to share their connections with the class, noting which type of connection they have made.

4 **Practice:** Encourage students to practice by reading a short text and completing Connection Stems. Discuss how they chose to complete the Connection Stems and which kinds of connections they made.

5 **Reflect:** Invite the students to think about how well they can use Connection Stems and how they might extend their use to other content areas.

Figure 5.7 shows two sets of connection stems, which were completed by students studying history and trigonometry.

 **TEACHING IDEA**   **SAVE THE LAST WORD FOR ME.** Save the Last Word for Me (Short, Harste, & Burke, 1996) is designed to help students make connections to the text, evaluate information in the text, and provide a structure for discussion of the text. When students use this technique, they select a quote, fact, or idea from the text and record it and the page number on which it is located on the front side of an index card. On the back of the card, they explain why they chose the information and which connections they can make to it. After reading, they gather in small groups and one at a time, students share the information on the front of their cards with the rest of the

---

FIGURE 5.7
Connection Stems Completed in History and Trigonometry Classes

These connection Stems were completed by students in history class while reading about World War II:

- That reminds me of . . . my grandmother, who was a nurse in World War II.
- I remember when . . . I saw *Schindler's List* and realized how horribly people were treated in the concentration camps during World War II.
- An experience I have had that was similar to soldiers being drafted into the Army was . . . when my brother enlisted in the Army.

These connection stems were completed by students beginning to study trigonometric functions in trigonometry class:

- The hypotenuse reminds me of . . . when we learned it was the side opposite a triangle's right angle in geometry.
- I remember when . . . we first learned about Pythagoras and now we are using his theorem.
- I have a connection . . . to SOH. I know it stands for "sine equals opposite over hypotenuse."

group. Each member of the group comments on the quote or idea. The student who wrote that card speaks last and shares the thoughts he/she has recorded on the back of the card (hence the title, Save the Last Word for Me). This technique is usually used after reading with either narrative or informational text.

To teach students how to use the Save the Last Word for Me strategy, follow these steps:

1 **Explain:** Begin by explaining making connections as a reading comprehension strategy in which students activate their prior knowledge and make a variety of connections or associations to the text they are reading. Then explain how Save the Last Word for Me works. For example, you might say, "Save the Last Word for Me is designed to help us make connections to the text, evaluate information in the text, and provide a structure for discussion of the text. We read a segment of text. Then we write a quote or idea from the text on one side on an index card (or at the top of the blackline) and the reason that we chose that quote or idea on the other side of the index card (or the bottom of the blackline). We share the quotes or ideas in small group, where each member comments on them. The last person to comment is the person who selected the quote or idea—hence the title, 'Save the Last Word for Me.'

2 **Demonstrate:** Use a short text, an index card or blackline, a pen, and a think-aloud to demonstrate how to use the Save the Last Word for Me strategy. Before beginning to read, think aloud about needing to find a quote, a fact, or an idea to write on the front of the index card. Read the text and then think aloud as you write the necessary information— including the page number on which the information is located— on the front of the card. Think aloud about why you chose the quote, fact, or idea, and which connection(s) you can make to it. Write that information on the back of the index card.

Next, model how to use Save the Last Word for Me by inviting three or four students to sit with you in a small group. Read the front of your card (or top of the blackline) and invite each of the students to respond to what you wrote. After each has had a chance to comment, read what you wrote on the back on the index card (or the bottom of the blackline) to make connections to the quote, fact, or idea that you selected. After the demonstration, discuss Save the Last Word for Me with the class.

3 **Guide:** Guide students to work with partners as they try Save the Last Word for Me. Provide students with index cards (or blacklines) and a copy of the short text. Read the short text aloud and provide time for the students to complete their index cards or blacklines. Remind students that what they write on the front of the index card may be something new, something that confirms previous ideas, something they disagree with, and so on. Also remind them to include the page number on which the information appears on the front of the card. Ask each pair of students to share with another pair, so each will have a group of four as they complete Save the Last Word for Me. Discuss the process.

4 **Practice:** Provide copies of a short text and invite students to practice by listening for a quote, fact, or idea to which they can make connections. When you have finished reading and they have completed their index cards or blacklines, ask students to meet in groups of four and participate in "Save the Last Word for Me." Discuss their efforts.

5 **Reflect:** Reflect on what the students know about making connections and how they can use Save the Last Word for Me when learning about other content area topics.

Figure 5.8 features Save the Last Word for Me information that John McGraw wrote while reading about global warming in science class.

TEACHING IDEA

CODING THE TEXT. Coding the Text (Harvey & Goudvis, 2000) was developed to help us actively engage in reading by make connections. During reading, we use small sticky notes to indicate the points in the text where we are able to make text–self, text–text, and text–world (others) connections. We use a code for each type of connection (T-S, T-T, and T-W, respectively) and include a few words to describe each connection. We can use Coding the Text while reading narrative and informational text.

FIGURE 5.8
Save the Last Word for
Me: Global Warming

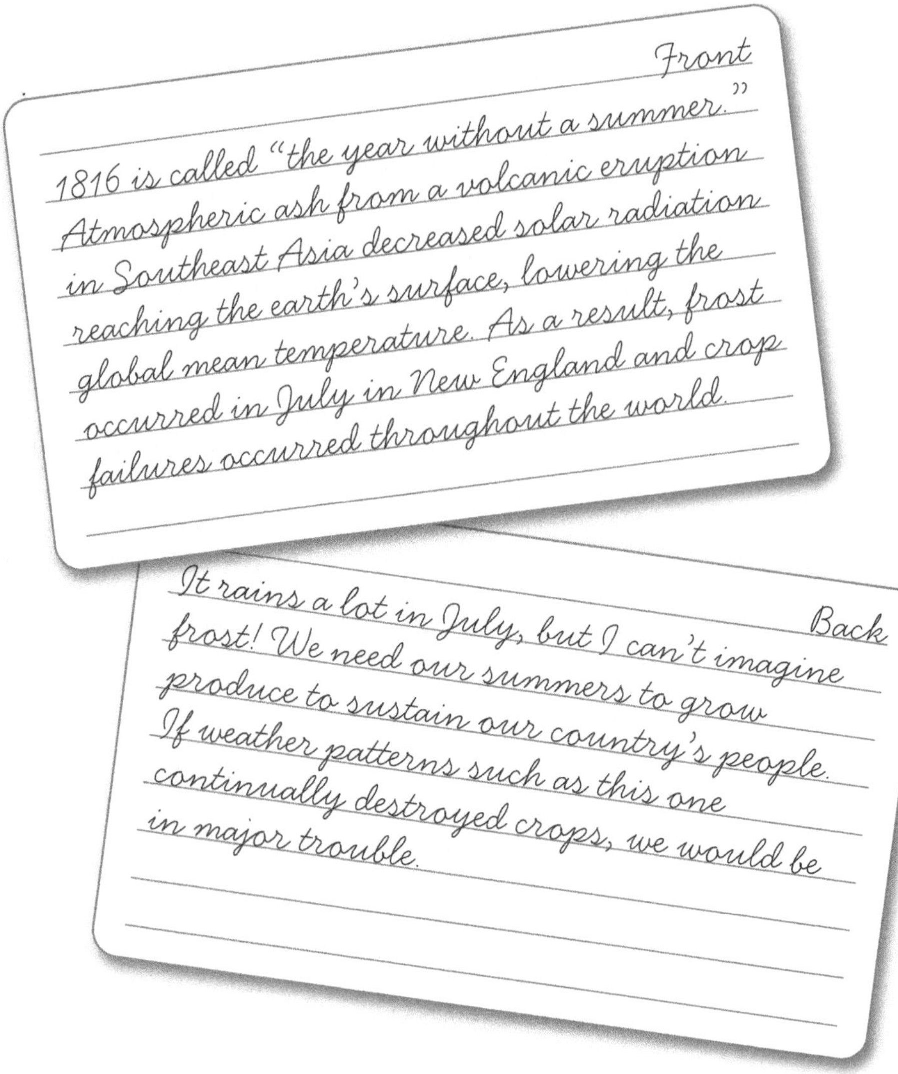

> *Front*
>
> 1816 is called "the year without a summer." Atmospheric ash from a volcanic eruption in Southeast Asia decreased solar radiation reaching the earth's surface, lowering the global mean temperature. As a result, frost occurred in July in New England and crop failures occurred throughout the world.

> *Back*
>
> It rains a lot in July, but I can't imagine frost! We need our summers to grow produce to sustain our country's people. If weather patterns such as this one continually destroyed crops, we would be in major trouble.

Source: The Woods Hole Research Center. (2008). Protecting the Integrity of the Global Environment.
http://www.whrc.org/resources/online_publications/warming_earth/potential_outcome.htm.

To teach students how to use Coding the Text, follow these steps:

1. **Explain:** Begin by explaining making connections as a reading comprehension strategy in which students activate their prior knowledge and make a variety of connections or associations to the text they are reading. Next, explain that Coding the Text provides us with a way to make connections while reading. For example, you might say, "We use Coding the Text to mark different points in our reading where we are able to make text–self, text–text, or text–world (others) connections. We write the code for a type of connection—T-S, T-T, or T-W—and a brief description of the connection on a small sticky note. Then we stick the sticky note in the section of the text where we are able to make the connection."

2. **Demonstrate:** Begin the demonstration by showing students how to label the different kinds of connections on sticky notes. Then read aloud a section of text and pause when you are able to make a connection. Think aloud about which kind of connection you are able to make. Code the sticky note, write a brief description, and stick it next to the section of text

where you were able to make the connection. Continue to read the section of text aloud and code your connections. Discuss the text and your connections with your students.

3 **Guide:** As students read a new section of text, encourage them to work in pairs, and guide them to make text–self, text–text, or text–world connections. Ask them to code the type of connections and brief descriptions on the sticky notes. Then guide them to insert the sticky notes at the correct points in the text. Discuss the text and the students' connections.

4 **Practice:** Invite students to practice on their own by continuing to read another segment and Coding the Text. Discuss the text and connections students made.

5 **Reflect:** Encourage students to reflect on how Coding the Text helps us to make connections while we are reading. Invite students to think about how they can use it when reading in other content areas.

Figure 5.9 shows sticky notes of text–text and text–self "Coding the Text" examples from Chapter 17, The History of Life, in *Biology* (Miller & Levine, 2008).

 **SKETCH AND LABEL CONNECTIONS.** Sketch and Label Connections (McLaughlin & Allen, 2002) is designed to help us use labeled visual representations to express connections. When using this approach, we read a section of text and think about a connection we can make. Then we sketch the connection, label it "text–self," "text–text," or "text–world," and write an explanation of why it is that type. We usually use "Sketch and Label Connections" before, during, and after reading narrative or informational text.

To teach students how to use Sketch and Label Connections, follow these steps:

1 **Explain:** Begin by explaining making connections as a reading comprehension strategy in which students activate their prior knowledge and make a variety of connections or associations to the text they are reading. Then explain Sketch and Label Connections as a way to use visual representations to express connections. For example, you might say, "When we use 'Sketch and Label Connections,' we use simple lines and shapes to represent our connections and then we label them. We indicate the type of connection and explain why it is that type."

2 **Demonstrate:** Begin demonstrating by introducing the text and thinking about connections you can make. Demonstrate how to sketch using simple lines and shapes. (This is a good time to remind students that we do not need to be talented artists to be able to sketch.) Think about the kind of connection you will make. Then think aloud as you sketch your connection. After you have sketched your connection, label the type of connection and explain why it is that type. Discuss your sketched and labeled connection with your students.

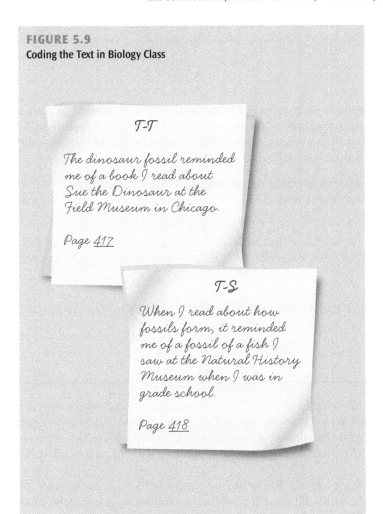

FIGURE 5.9
Coding the Text in Biology Class

T–T

The dinosaur fossil reminded me of a book I read about Sue the Dinosaur at the Field Museum in Chicago.

Page 417

T–S

When I read about how fossils form, it reminded me of a fossil of a fish I saw at the Natural History Museum when I was in grade school.

Page 418

FIGURE 5.10
Sketching Connections: "Because I Could Not Stop for Death"

I drew a picture of a clock after reading the first stanza, because to me the first stanza describes how we get so caught up in our lives that time passes without our knowing it. The narrator was so caught up in living her life that she didn't realize the end had come.

3 **Guide:** Provide the students with copies of the text and guide them to work in pairs to Sketch and Label Connections as you read a segment aloud. Encourage the students to discuss their connections with another pair. Then discuss the text and student responses with the class. Repeat this process with additional segments of text.

4 **Practice:** Encourage students to practice by working on their own to sketch their connections. Invite them to share their connections with a partner. Repeat this process using multiple segments of text.

5 **Reflect:** Encourage students to reflect on how Sketching and Labeling Connections helps us to understand what we read. Ask students how they can use it in other content areas.

In Figure 5.10, Rosario Pinto sketches and explains her connection to the opening stanza of Emily Dickinson's poem, "Because I Could Not Stop for Death."

FINAL THOUGHTS

When we engage students' thinking, we motivate them to make connections between what they already know and what they are learning. Activating background knowledge and setting purposes for reading are essential components of comprehension. Making connections between background knowledge and what we are learning supports our belief that reading is a constructivist process.

In the next chapter, we expand our discussion of strategies to those we use to guide our thinking during reading. Our focus shifts to approaches that are designed to help students transact with text and monitor their understanding.

Teaching Connections

APPLYING WHAT WE HAVE LEARNED

E-Links

Because we are mature, sophisticated readers, we use reading comprehension strategies unconsciously. Work with a partner and choose a website such as those listed to locate text related to your content area. As you read, consciously use comprehension strategies such as previewing and making connections. Discuss with your partner how using these strategies helped you understand the text. Record your thoughts as a reflective entry in your portfolio.

EXAMPLE WEBSITES

Absolute Shakespeare (English)
http://absoluteshakespeare.com

Biography
http://www.biography.com

Discovery Channel
http://dsc.discovery.com/news

Science Daily: Your Source for the Latest Research News
http://www.sciencedaily.com/articles

Accountable Talk

As content area teachers of the 21st century, we need to ensure that our students can read text effectively. Meet in small groups and discuss (1) how you will use reading comprehension strategies in your teaching and (2) how you will motivate your students to use reading strategies. Record your ideas and share what you believe to be the best suggestions in a class discussion.

Portfolio/Performance Opportunity

Work with a partner in your content area to develop a standards-based lesson plan that focuses on dual purposes: (1) to teach course content and (2) to help students use comprehension strategies as they read. Meet in small groups and teach your lesson to the group. Engage in peer feedback and revise the lesson plan as necessary. Discuss how including reading strategies and receiving peer feedback affected your lesson. Reflect on your work and include your lesson plan in your portfolio.

6

Chapter Overview

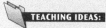
Using Comprehension Strategies to Guide Thinking

In this chapter, we continue to learn comprehension strategies we can use to think through text. Our specific focus is strategies to use *during* reading. Our goal is to help students develop a repertoire of strategies that they can use as needed while reading.

We begin by exploring how to use strategies such as self-questioning, monitoring, and visualizing to guide thinking. We learn how to teach the strategies by using a step-by-step model of explicit instruction. Student examples are featured throughout the chapter.

How Can We Use Comprehension Strategies to Guide Thinking?

We know that we use comprehension strategies to engage, guide, and extend thinking throughout the reading process. The strategies we use during reading help to guide our thinking—to monitor our understanding of text, make connections to text, clarify meaning, and respond actively. Although the strategies in this chapter are cited as examples to use during reading, we can also use them at other points during the reading process.

In the examples that follow, we describe a variety of ways to support students' use of comprehension strategies during reading. In each step-by-step sequence, we begin by explaining the strategy and the teaching idea. Next, we demonstrate it. Then, we guide students as they work with partners. After that, we provide support as requested as students attempt to use the strategies on their own. Finally, we reflect on what we have learned and how we can use the strategy in the content areas. Each teaching sequence is followed by a student example. Reproducible graphic organizers for these techniques can be found in the Appendix.

Self-Questioning

Self-questioning is a reading comprehension strategy that involves generating questions to guide thinking while reading. For example, if we are reading a science experiment, we may wonder what the next step will be, what the outcome of the previous step might be, what effect a particular action might cause, or what the result of the experiment might be. Many teaching ideas support this strategy, including those featured in this section. Descriptions of these ideas and step-by-step directions for teaching them follow. (For information about how to teach students the skill of generating questions at a variety of levels, see Chapter 9.)

 **TEACHING IDEA**

QUESTION–ANSWER RELATIONSHIPS. Question–Answer Relationships (Raphael, 1986) is a teaching idea that helps students understand how to self-question. Students learn that there are two information sources: text and prior knowledge. Within each information source, there are two question–answer relationships (QAR). This teaching idea helps students to develop self-questioning abilities by focusing on the information source needed to answer the question. QAR can be used when reading narrative and expository text.

To teach students how to use QAR, follow these steps:

1. **Explain:** Begin by explaining self-questioning as a reading comprehension strategy in which we generate questions to guide thinking. Then explain the QAR concept and terminology:
   - There are two kinds of information:
     In the book: Answers are found in the text (e.g., book, video, website).
     In my head: Answers require input from students' understandings and prior knowledge.
   - There are two kinds of QARs for each kind of information:
     In the Book:
     - Right There: The answer is stated in the passage.
     - Think and Search: The answer is derived from more than one sentence or paragraph but is stated in the text.

     In My Head:
     - On My Own: The answer is contingent on information the reader already possesses in his prior knowledge.
     - Author and Me: The answer is inferred in the text, but the reader must make the connections with his own prior knowledge.

2. **Demonstrate:** Think aloud as you demonstrate how to use QAR with a text. Model choosing the appropriate QAR strategy, answering from the designated source, and writing or saying the answer. Introduce a short passage and related questions.

3. **Guide:** Guide students to work with partners to use QAR with the passages and the questions. Encourage students to answer the questions and explain which QAR strategy they used. Any justifiable answer should be accepted.

4. **Practice:** Ask students to work on their own to use QAR. Discuss their responses.

5. **Reflect:** Invite students to reflect on what they have learned about self-questioning and how to use QAR in the content areas.

The question–answer relationships featured in Figure 6.1 were created by high school student Grace Fisher based on a chapter in her Spanish language and culture course text.

FIGURE 6.1 Question–Answer Relationships Created in a Spanish Language and Culture Course

In the Book:

Right There: What are some elements of Spanish culture?
Art, dance, music, writing, customs, and food are some elements of Spanish culture. (This information is directly stated in one sentence in the text.)

Think and Search: Which artists are considered to have made the greatest contributions to Spanish culture?
Artists who have contributed greatly to the Spanish culture have spanned several centuries and include El Greco, Velazquez, Goya, Picasso, Gris, Miró, and Dalí. (This information appears in the text, but is located in more than one sentence.)

In My Head:

On My Own: Which of the Spanish authors we have studied interests you the most? Justify your thinking.
Arturo Perez-Reverte is an author I would like to learn more about. He started out as a journalist but then became a novelist. He is also credited with motivating a lot of Spanish citizens to read. (This information was provided through the student's prior knowledge.)

Author and Me: Do you think Spanish culture has influenced American culture? Justify your response.
Spanish culture has influenced American culture. Evidence of this can be seen in the impact of Spanish architecture on American structures, the way we value the work of Spanish artists such as Picasso, and the increasing use of the Spanish language in our country. (This response was based on information in the text as well as the student's prior knowledge.)

TEACHING IDEA

"I WONDER . . ." STATEMENTS. "I Wonder . . ." Statements (Harvey & Goudvis, 2000) are designed to encourage students to generate questions and to provide a model for active thinking during the reading process. These statements can be used with either narrative or informational text, before, during, and after reading. "I Wonder . . ." Statements can be shared orally, through sketching, or in writing. In this section, the student example features "I Wonder . . ." Bookmarks that were created *during* reading.

To teach students how to use "I Wonder . . ." Statements, follow these steps:

1. **Explain:** Begin by explaining self-questioning as a reading comprehension strategy in which we generate questions to guide thinking. Then explain that we can use "I Wonder . . ." Statements to help us engage in active thinking and generate questions while reading.

2. **Demonstrate:** Think aloud about the text and the prior knowledge you have about the topic. Introduce the text and create "I Wonder . . ." Statements about the title, both orally and in writing. Read a segment of the text aloud and think aloud about whether your "I Wonder . . ." Statements were confirmed or disconfirmed.

3. **Guide:** Invite students to work with partners to create "I Wonder . . ." Statements. Ask selected students to share their "wonders." Ask students to listen to determine whether their statements are confirmed or disconfirmed as you read another segment of text. Discuss whether the students' statements were confirmed or disconfirmed.

4. **Practice:** Invite students to work on their own to create "I Wonder . . ." Statements in writing. Briefly discuss the students' wonders and then read another segment of text. Encourage the students to listen to determine whether their statements are confirmed or disconfirmed. Discuss this when you have finished reading the segment. Continue this process until you have finished reading the text.

5. **Reflect:** Encourage students to reflect on what they have learned about "I Wonder . . ." Statements and how they help us to engage in self-questioning while reading. Discuss how students can use "I Wonder . . ." Statements while reading texts in the content areas.

Maria Fernandez completed the "I Wonder . . ." Bookmarks featured in Figure 6.2 while reading "The Pedestrian" by Ray Bradbury in her literature anthology class.

TEACHING IDEA

REQUEST. When engaging in ReQuest (Manzo, 1969), students actively participate in the discussion of the text. After observing teacher modeling, they practice generating questions at multiple levels. Teachers and students also answer questions. This provides opportunities to engage in the social construction of knowledge and learn the content.

When teaching ReQuest, follow these steps:

1 Explain: Begin by explaining self-questioning as a reading comprehension strategy in which we generate questions to guide thinking. Focus on ReQuest as a type of reciprocal questioning that involves reading silently, generating questions at multiple levels, predicting, and discussing. Explain that the students and the teacher engage in ReQuest by reading silently and asking one another questions.

2 Demonstrate: Introduce the text, and then invite students to participate in the demonstration. Join them in reading a designated section of text (usually a few paragraphs) silently. Then ask the students to close their books while you ask them questions about the text they read. Comment on the quality of responses. Then close your book and encourage the students to ask you questions. Comment on the quality of the questions.

3 Guide: Guide students to engage in ReQuest by silently reading another section of text. Then question the students and encourage them to question you.

4 Practice: After students have read an appropriate amount of text, invite them to stop questioning and begin predicting. Provide prompts, such as "I think . . ." or "I wonder . . . ," to encourage predictions. Invite the students to read the remaining text silently. After they have finished reading the text, facilitate a discussion based on the text and students' predictions.

5 Reflect: Encourage students to think about how ReQuest helps us to use reciprocal questioning and prediction to understand text. Discuss other content areas in which students could use ReQuest.

When engaging in ReQuest, we may find that students ask too many memory-level questions. If we teach Ciardiello's (1998) four levels of questioning before we teach ReQuest, students will be able to use the signal words to generate questions at all levels of thinking. Although memory-level questions are certainly important, we should also encourage our students to think at higher levels. For example, if students are researching the biography of someone who is well respected in a content area—such as Churchill in history, Banneker in mathematics, Hemingway in literature, or

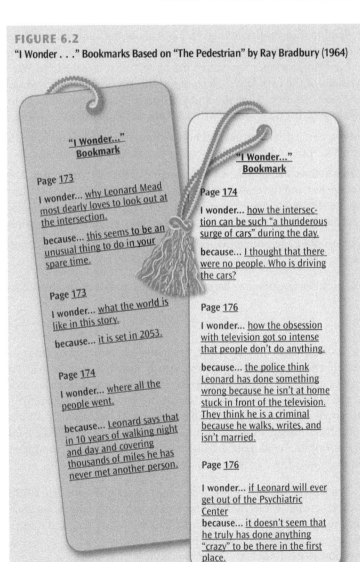

FIGURE 6.2
"I Wonder . . ." Bookmarks Based on "The Pedestrian" by Ray Bradbury (1964)

"I Wonder..."
Bookmark

Page 173
I wonder... why Leonard Mead most dearly loves to look out at the intersection.

because... this seems to be an unusual thing to do in your spare time.

Page 173
I wonder... what the world is like in this story.

because... it is set in 2053.

Page 174
I wonder... where all the people went.

because... Leonard says that in 10 years of walking night and day and covering thousands of miles he has never met another person.

"I Wonder..."
Bookmark

Page 174
I wonder... how the intersection can be such "a thunderous surge of cars" during the day.

because... I thought that there were no people. Who is driving the cars?

Page 176
I wonder... how the obsession with television got so intense that people don't do anything.

because... the police think Leonard has done something wrong because he isn't at home stuck in front of the television. They think he is a criminal because he walks, writes, and isn't married.

Page 176
I wonder... if Leonard will ever get out of the Psychiatric Center
because... it doesn't seem that he truly has done anything "crazy" to be there in the first place.

Einstein in science—memory levels questions about where and when the person was born provide some background information. We also want students to ask how that person's contribution to the field compared and contrasted to other contributions (convergent level), how students might imagine themselves making such a contribution (divergent thinking), and how students would defend or justify the person's contribution (evaluative level).

PAIRED QUESTIONING. In Paired Questioning (Vaughn & Estes, 1986), students engage in actively generating questions during reading. To teach students how to use Paired Questioning, follow these steps:

1 Explain: Begin by explaining self-questioning as a reading comprehension strategy in which we generate questions to guide thinking. Then explain that Paired Questioning involves students taking turns in generating text-related questions and responding to them. When the students have finished generating and responding to questions while reading segments of the text, one partner summarizes the important ideas in the text and the other agrees or disagrees and justifies his or her thinking.

2 Demonstrate: Arrange in advance to have a student volunteer to be your partner during the demonstration. Introduce the text and demonstrate how you and your partner read the title or subtitle of a section of text, set the text aside, and then respond to the questions each of you generate. Remind students that asking questions about the title or subtitle helps readers set purposes for reading. For example, if the title was *The Civil War* and the subtitle was *Causes of the Civil War,* the questions raised might be "What was the Civil War?" and "What were the causes of the Civil War?" Next, repeat this process, reading a section of text instead of the title or subtitle. After you and your partner have responded to the questions, discuss how generating questions as we read helps us to understand the text.

3 Guide: Invite students to work with a partner and new section of text to engage in Paired Questioning, first with a subtitle and then with a section of text. Encourage discussion.

4 Practice: Invite students to finish reading the text by engaging in Paired Questioning. Stop periodically to discuss the text and the questions that have been raised. When the students have finished reading the text, invite one partner to share the important ideas in the text with the other. Then encourage the other partner to agree or disagree and justify his response.

5 Reflect: Invite students to share their thoughts about Paired Questioning and how it can help us understand text.

Figure 6.3 features examples of Paired Questioning that students created in their earth science class.

Monitoring/Clarifying

Monitoring/clarifying is a reading comprehension strategy that involves constantly asking ourselves, "Does this make sense?", and adapting strategic processes to make the message clear. For example, if our reading makes sense, we continue reading. If our reading does not make sense, we might go back and reread the material, read that passage more slowly, examine a difficult vocabulary word more closely, or use other ideas that will help us clarify the meaning. A number of teaching ideas support this strategy. Information about how to teach several of them follows. We use this strategy during the reading of narrative or expository text. Reproducible graphic organizers related to monitoring/clarifying are found in the Appendix.

BOOKMARK TECHNIQUE. Readers can use Bookmark Technique (McLaughlin & Allen, 2002b) to help monitor their comprehension while reading and make evaluative judgments about aspects of the text. This technique can be used with narrative and expository text, and it works well with both in-class reading and homework assignments.

To teach your students how to use Bookmark Technique, follow these steps:

1 Explain: Begin by explaining that monitoring/clarifying is a reading comprehension strategy that involves constantly asking ourselves, "Does this make sense?", and adapting strategic processes to make the message clear. Begin by distributing the four Bookmarks (see the

FIGURE 6.3
Students' Paired
Questioning Example
about "Structure of the
Earth" in Earth Science

Student 1: How many layers of the earth are there?
Student 2: There are four layers of the earth.
Student 2: What is the outermost layer called?
Student 1: The outermost layer is called the crust.

After reading a selection:
Student 1: What is an example of the earth's crust?
Student 2: The continents are examples of the earth's crust.
Student 2: How thick is the earth's crust?
Student 1: The thickness of the earth's crust varies. It can be anywhere between 5 and 70 kilometers.
Student 1: The outermost layer of the earth is called the crust. This layer consists of the continents and
ocean basins. It varies in thickness.
Student 2: I agree, but I would add that the earth's crust is made up of mostly alumino-silicates.

Appendix for graphic organizers). Introduce the text and explain what monitoring is and how the Bookmark Technique can help us monitor our reading. Explain the four bookmarks, noting the information required for each:

- **Bookmark 1:** What was the most important part? Why?
- **Bookmark 2:** Which vocabulary word do you think the whole class should discuss? Why? Include predicted meaning of the word.
- **Bookmark 3:** What was confusing in this text? Why?
- **Bookmark 4:** Which chart, map, graph, or illustration helped you to understand what you read? Why?

There is a place for students to include page numbers on all Bookmarks. There is also a place for paragraph numbers on all Bookmarks except the fourth one. Providing page and paragraph numbers helps the class to locate the information during discussion.

2 Demonstrate: Read a short text to the students. Think aloud as you complete the first Bookmark. For example, if you are using the Bookmarks in biology class and the text was about DNA, you might say, "I think the double helix model was the most important part of the text, because it showed the structure of DNA."

3 Guide: Guide students to work with a partner to complete Bookmark 2 and 3. Discuss their vocabulary choices. Revisit the text to locate the words and assess whether the students' thoughts about the words' meanings are appropriate in the contexts. If needed, use a dictionary to clarify the meanings.

4 Practice: Ask students to work on their own to complete the fourth Bookmark. Discuss their choices.

5 Reflect: Invite students to reflect on what they know about monitoring and how they can use the Bookmark Technique in other aspects of their content area learning.

Bookmark Technique helps students focus on what they are reading and develop at least four points of information to contribute to class discussion. Figure 6.4 features Connor Watkins' responses using Bookmark Technique; Connor is a high school student who is studying biology.

TEACHING IDEA SAY SOMETHING. Readers can use Say Something (Short, Harste, & Burke, 1996) to help monitor their understanding. When using this technique, students work in pairs to read a text, stopping at designated points to turn and Say Something to their partners. Say Something can be used with narrative or informational text during and after reading. When participating in Say Something while reading informational text, students might make a comment, ask a question, make a prediction, clarify a point, or make a connection. When using the technique while reading narrative text, students might extend their comments to include narrative elements such as setting, characters, and theme.

FIGURE 6.4

Bookmark Technique: Biology—Student Responses When Reading about DNA

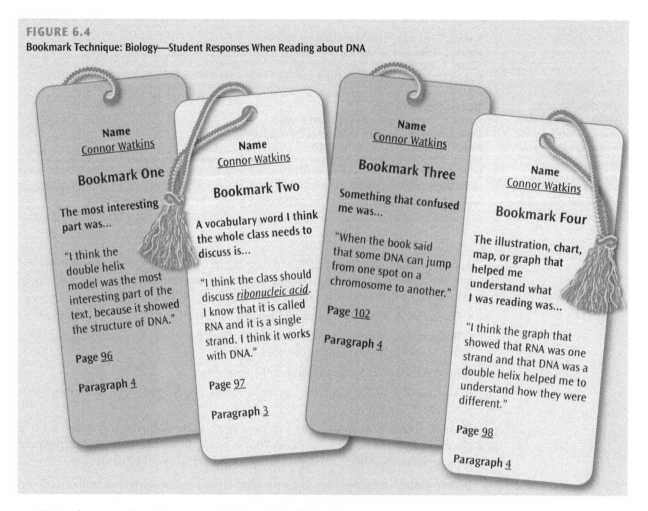

To teach your students how to use Say Something follow these steps:

1 **Explain:** Begin by explaining monitoring/clarifying as a comprehension strategy that involves constantly asking ourselves, "Does this make sense?" and adapting strategic processes to make the message clear. Then explain how Say Something helps students monitor their understanding. Next, introduce the text and invite a student to work with you to demonstrate this approach. (The designated stopping points in the text should have been labeled prior to the start of the lesson.)

2 **Demonstrate:** Read a designated segment of text, turn to your student partner, and Say Something. Next, your student partner should read a designated segment of text and Say Something to you. Model this with four segments of text. Remember to discuss the text periodically.

3 **Guide:** Ask students to work with a partner while using Say Something. Guide their practice by continuing to read aloud designated segments and inviting them to Say Something to their partners. Do this for four segments of text.

4 **Practice:** Encourage students to practice on their own by reading the remaining designated segments and continuing to Say Something to their partners. Remind students to discuss the text periodically. The students should continue this process until they come to the end of the text.

5 **Reflect:** Encourage students to reflect on what they know about monitoring their understanding and how they can use Say Something to help them do that. Discuss how the students can use Say Something as they study the content areas.

Stopping Point 1
Student 1: I didn't know *cryogenics* came from the Greek words for "frost" and "to produce."
Student 2: I knew cryogenics involved low temperatures, but I didn't know it referred to temperatures below −150 °C.

Stopping Point 2
Student 1: The lowest temperature that can be approached but not achieved is absolute zero.
Student 2: Absolute zero is equal to −273.15 °C.

Stopping Point 3
Student 1: I didn't know that normally mercury freezes and becomes useless at low temperatures.
Student 2: I didn't know some types of ceramics are high-temperature superconductors.

Stopping Point 4
Student 1: Cryogenics can be used for flash freezing some foods.
Student 2: It can also be used to treat cancers.

FIGURE 6.5
Examples of Say Something from Science Class

In Figure 6.5, Javier Martinez and Paul Romano engaged in "Say Something" while reading about cryogenics in science. The teacher had designated four stopping points and the students exchanged ideas at each point.

TEACHING IDEA

KWL AND KWLS. KWL supports multiple reading comprehension strategies. Its purposes include activating students' prior knowledge about a topic, setting purposes for reading, and confirming, revising, or expanding original understandings of a topic. In the traditional form of KWL, developed by Donna Ogle in 1986, readers ask themselves, "What do I know?" "What do I want to know?" and "What have I learned?". Sippola (1995) suggested that we add a fourth column to the KWL to create the KWLS. The first three questions are the same; the new question is "What do I still want to know?". The fourth column of the KWLS graphic organizer (see the Appendix) encourages students to examine whether they have found answers to all of the questions they raised in response to "What do I need to know?". If students have not found responses to all of these questions, they move the unanswered questions to the fourth column and research responses to them. Other adaptations to the KWL—such as KWDL ("What I know," "What I want to know," "What I did," and "What I learned"), which is often used in science and mathematics—can be found in Appendix A.

To teach your students how to use KWL, follow these guidelines and encourage discussion throughout the process:

Go to the Activities and Applications section under the topic *Activating Prior Knowledge and Interest* in the MyEducationLab for your course and complete the activity entitled *Using K-W-L in 8th Grade Math* to learn how to use this important graphic organizer to help build student interest.

1 **Explain:** Explain that the KWL supports the reading strategies of self-questioning, monitoring, and summarizing. Then focus on the three steps involved in KWL: What I Know, What I Want to Know, and What I Learned.

2 **Demonstrate:** Introduce the topic and a short text. Share the KWL graphic organizer with students (see the Appendix). Think aloud as you brainstorm what you know in the K column. Then move to the W column and list what you want to know. Discuss what you wrote in the K and W columns. Then read the text. After reading, record what you learned in the L column. Discuss what you learned with the class. Then revisit the K column to determine if what you knew was verified in the text and the W column to ensure that all of your questions were answered. Summarize what you learned.

3 **Guide:** Introduce a new text and guide students to work with a partner as each completes the K and W columns. Discuss the students' responses. Provide time for them to read the text and complete the L column. Discuss their responses. Then ask students to check the K and W columns to ensure that what they knew was verified by the text and that all of their questions were answered. Finally, encourage the pairs of students to summarize what they have learned.

4 **Practice:** Invite students to work on their own to complete a KWL for another short text. Monitor students as they complete each step, and discuss their work as noted earlier in the

K (What I know or think I know)	W (What I want to know)	L (What I learned)
Atoms have protons, neutrons, and electrons.	How do these work together?	Protons, neutrons, and electrons are subatomic particles. Each carries a charge. The proton is positive. The neutron is neutral. The electron is negative. The protons and neutrons together form the nucleus, which is in the middle of the atom.
A chemical compound is a combination of elements.	Can this be more than two elements combined?	A chemical compound is a substance formed by the combination of 2 *or more* elements.
There are two kinds of chemical bonds: covalent and ionic.	What is an ion?	An ion is either an atom that loses electrons (so it has a positive charge) or an atom that gains electrons (so it has a negative charge).
	How are they different?	If atoms are sharing electrons, then the bond between them is covalent. If an atom gives an electron to another atom, then they have an ionic bond.

FIGURE 6.6 KWL: Chemistry—The Nature of Matter

process. After the students have discussed the completed KWL chart, encourage them to revisit the K and L columns as noted in steps 2 and 3. Then invite students to share their oral summary of what they learned with a partner.

5 **Reflect:** Invite students to think about how the KWL helps us comprehend by providing opportunities to self-question, monitor, and summarize text.

Figure 6.6 features a KWL form that Melanie Younger completed when her chemistry class was studying matter.

Making Connections
TO MULTIPLE LITERACIES

Students can use ideas such as Say Something and KWLS to set purposes for reading, monitor understanding, and provide information for discussion. These approaches apply to multiple literacies. For example, when students engage in information literacy to research an issue, they can use these techniques to gain understanding of the facts presented on websites, which in turn may lead them to search for other sites and locate additional information. Students can also use the information gleaned from the strategy applications to interact with peers in small-group discussions or Internet Workshop (see Chapter 12).■

TEACHING IDEA

INTERACTIVE NOTATION SYSTEM TO EFFECTIVE READING AND THINKING (INSERT). The Interactive Notation System to Effective Reading and Thinking (INSERT) method was developed to encourage students to become active readers. When using this technique, students insert a number of symbols into the text. INSERT provides students with opportunities to reflect about what they know and encourages them to make some decisions about the ideas expressed in the text. We have adapted the original INSERT for our students' use; the revised version requires the reader to insert fewer symbols than does the original version.

To teach students how to use INSERT, follow these steps:

1 **Explain:** Begin by explaining that monitoring/clarifying is a reading comprehension strategy that involves our constantly asking ourselves, "Does this make sense?" and adapting strategic processes to make the message clear. Then explain that INSERT helps us to self-question, monitor, and summarize as we read. Focus on how INSERT begins with readers brainstorming a list of what they know about the topic, reading the text, and inserting four symbols as they read. Introduce the four symbols to be inserted into the text and explain what each means:

- Place a check mark (✓) in the margin if the information in the text verifies what is on the brainstormed list.
- Place a plus sign (+) in the margin if the information is new—that is, not on the reader's list.
- Place a minus sign (−) in the margin if the information contradicts or disproves information on the brainstormed list.
- Place a question mark (?) in the margin if there is something in the text that is confusing.

Explain that if the students are completing the INSERT Bookmarks, they will write information on each Bookmark, rather than in the margin of the text. Share the INSERT Bookmarks with the students and use the Bookmarks throughout the remainder of the lesson.

2 **Demonstrate:** Introduce a short text and think aloud as you brainstorm what you know about the topic. Write your brainstormed list on the board, on an overhead transparency, or on a computer. Then read the text and complete an INSERT Bookmark each time you insert a notation.

For example, in Figure 6.7, when David Bishop wanted to indicate that he read something that confirmed what he had brainstormed, he wrote the page and paragraph numbers and what was confirmed on the ✓ (check symbol) Bookmark. When he encountered information that was new to him, he wrote on the + (plus symbol) Bookmark. When he read something that did not support what appeared on his brainstormed list, he wrote it on the - (minus symbol) Bookmark. When he read something that confused him, he wrote it on the ? (question mark symbol) Bookmark.

After you have finished reading, discuss the notations you inserted and how they related to your brainstormed list. Then summarize the text.

3 **Guide:** Introduce another short text and invite students to work with a partner to brainstorm what they know about the topic. Then encourage the students to complete the INSERT Bookmarks, indicating when the text supported what they had brainstormed, when the text contained new information, when the text disconfirmed something that appeared on the brainstormed list, and when they found text information confusing. After the students complete the Bookmarks, invite them to discuss their ideas and summarize the text.

4 **Practice:** Invite students to work on their own to complete INSERT Method. Introduce another short text and encourage students to brainstorm what they know. Then monitor students, assisting as needed, as they read the text and complete the INSERT Bookmarks. Encourage them to discuss their completed Bookmarks and summarize the text.

5 **Reflect:** Invite students to reflect on how using INSERT helps us to self-question, monitor, and summarize as we read. Encourage students to think about other situations in which they can use INSERT.

In the following example, David Bishop, a high school history student, used INSERT while reading about the Louisiana Purchase. He began by brainstorming what he knew about the historic event before he began to read. David's brainstormed list included the following five statements:

1. The United States wanted the right to use the Mississippi River for shipping.
2. The United States purchased Louisiana.
3. The land was bought from France.
4. The land was bought for $15 million.
5. Napoleon, Monroe, and Livingston negotiated the deal.

FIGURE 6.7
INSERT Bookmarks about the Louisiana Purchase

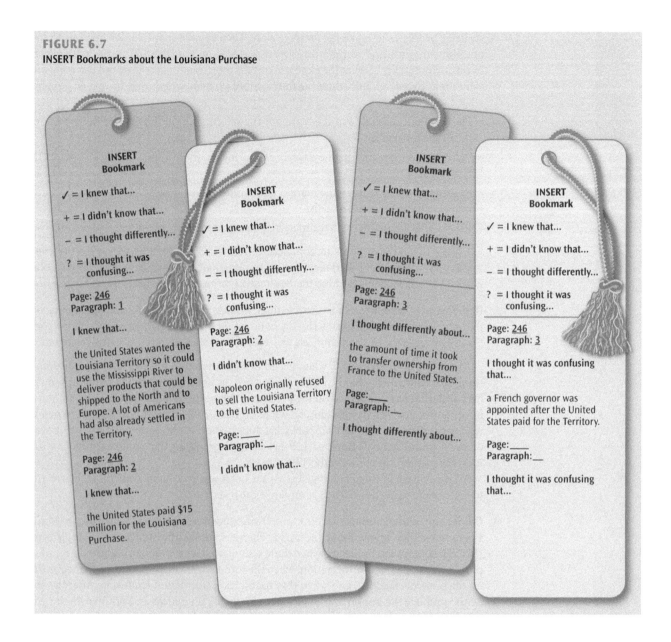

After brainstorming what he already knew, David read the section about the Louisiana Purchase in his history textbook. As he read, he completed the INSERT Bookmarks (McLaughlin & Allen, 2002b) as shown in Figure 6.7.

Visualizing

Visualizing is a reading comprehension strategy that involves creating mental images of the text as we read. When readers visualize, they often express their *mental pictures* through sketching. It is important that students understand that they do not need to be great artists to be able to sketch: They can use simple lines and shapes to communicate their thoughts. We can use this strategy while reading narrative or expository text. Detailed information about teaching ideas that help students to engage in visualization while reading follows.

PHOTOGRAPHS OF THE MIND. We can use Photographs of the Mind (Keene & Zimmerman, 1997) to help students to share the mental images they create while reading. While reading text, students stop at four designated points and sketch their visualizations. The graphic organizer we use with this teaching idea is divided into four sections, one for each time the students sketch their visualizations. Students can also use the organizer to create Photographs of the Mind during specific content area tasks, such as different steps used to conduct experiments in science.

To teach your students how to use Photographs of the Mind, follow these steps:

1 **Explain:** Explain visualizing as a comprehension strategy that involves creating mental images of text as we read. Then explain that when we use Photographs of the Mind, we can stop periodically while reading to express our visualizations through sketching.

2 **Demonstrate:** Before reading, divide a short selection into four sections. Read the first section and think aloud about the mental picture you have created. Then sketch the picture you have in your mind. Briefly discuss it with the students.

3 **Guide:** Read the next section and ask students to work with a partner to create and discuss their mental images and sketches. Briefly discuss the results as a class.

4 **Practice:** Read the third section. Invite students to create mental images and sketch on their own, and then share those images with a partner. Read the fourth section, and follow the same procedure.

5 **Reflect:** Ask students to reflect on what they know about visualizing and how they can use Photographs of the Mind when reading content area text.

Figure 6.8 shows Photographs of the Mind that Caitlin McLaughlin created in response to Margarita Engle's poem "Juan" about the life of Juan Francisco Manzano, the poet slave of Cuba, who was born in 1797 and died in 1854.

Making Connections
TO ENGLISH LEARNERS

Teaching English learners to create mental pictures and share them through sketching supports their ability to communicate their thoughts through an alternative mode of representation. Providing opportunities for English learners to use sketching, dramatizing, and singing to represent their ideas encourages these students to express themselves and their understandings. ■

TEACHING IDEA   **GUIDED IMAGERY.** Guided Imagery (Long, Winograd, & Bridge, 1989) helps readers to activate prior knowledge, create visualizations, solve problems, and use their imaginations. We can use this teaching idea with narrative or informational text that evokes images.

To teach students how to use Guided Imagery, follow these steps:

1 **Explain:** Begin by explaining visualizing as a comprehension strategy that involves creating mental images of the text as we read. Next, describe the process of Guided Imagery, noting that it helps readers to activate prior knowledge, create visualizations, solve problems, and use their imaginations. Then introduce the text. Remember to use a text that will evoke images.

2 **Demonstrate:** Ask a student to read a segment of text aloud as you demonstrate Guided Imagery. Close your eyes and create sensory images while listening to a segment of text. Stop periodically and use a think-aloud to describe what you are visualizing and sensing. At the end of the text, talk about the images you created, including how they helped you to understand the text.

3 **Guide:** Invite the students to work with partners as they close their eyes and listen to another segment of text. As you read aloud, stop periodically and ask the students to share what they are visualizing and sensing with their partners. When you finish reading, ask students to talk about the images they created and describe how their images helped them to understand the text. Record their thoughts on a chalkboard, overhead transparency, or computer.

4 **Practice:** Encourage students to create images on their own, as you continue to read the text aloud. Stop at designated points so that students can share the images they have

FIGURE 6.8 Photographs of the Mind: "Juan" (The Life of Juan Francisco Manzano)

created. When the students finish reading, ask them to discuss the images they created and describe how their visualizations helped them to comprehend the text. Discuss the importance of visualizing while we read.

5 **Reflect:** Ask students to reflect on what they learned about visualizing and discuss how they can use Guided Imagery throughout the content areas.

FIGURE 6.9
Holocaust Survivor
Guided Imagery
Example

I could see Eva's family gathered together as her parents decided who might survive if they jumped from the train. I felt afraid for them. When they jumped, I could see the bullets flying from the roof of the train as it continued to move. When Eva found her brother and sister dead, I saw a field of high brown grass dotted by dead bodies. I cringed. When she talked about pretending not to be Jewish and working on a farm during the rest of the war, I pictured a farm in the country where she waited to one day reclaim her identity. Creating images in my mind helped me to see what Eva experienced and to understand how horrible life was for all who were taken from their homes and sent to concentration camps during the Holocaust.

FIGURE 6.10
Poetry Guided
Imagery Example

While I listened to the poem being read, I could picture all of the people and things that Maya Angelou knows can be frightening. Then every time I heard the phrase, "Life doesn't frighten me at all," those images would disappear and I would start picturing the next items Maya Angelou included in the poem. For example, when I heard "Mean old Mother Goose, Lions on the loose," I pictured a book of fairy tales I had when I was in first grade and remembered how some of the stories like "Rumplestiltskin" did frighten me, but then the image disappeared when I was reminded it didn't frighten Maya Angelou. Creating images helped me to understand that none of the things mentioned frighten Maya Angelou and that we should all meet our fears and not let them frighten us anymore.

Figure 6.9 provides an example of Guided Imagery in which Tomas describes the images he created when he closed his eyes and listened as his European history teacher, Venetta Hurley, read Eva Galler's Holocaust survivor story to his class. Galler described how her parents encouraged her brother, her sister, and her to jump from a moving train as it transported her family and others to concentration camps. At predetermined stopping points, the students described their images to a partner. At the conclusion of the reading, they shared their images with the class.

In the example featured in Figure 6.10, Adelina describes the images she created while listening to her English teacher reading a poem. The poem was "Life Doesn't Frighten Me at All," by Maya Angelou.

Making Connections
TO STRUGGLING READERS

When teaching Guided Imagery to students who struggle with organizing, storing, and retrieving information, encourage them to activate all of their senses during reading—not just seeing. For example, encourage students to ask themselves what they are hearing, smelling, tasting, and touching. ■

TEACHING IDEA

GALLERY IMAGES. Gallery Images (Ogle, 2000) help us to create visualizations while reading and provide a format for sharing our mental images. This technique is usually used after reading informational text.

To teach your students how to create Gallery Images, follow these steps:

1 **Explain:** Begin by explaining that visualizing is a reading comprehension strategy that involves creating mental images of the text as we read. Then explain that we visualize when using Gallery Images, which provides us with a format for sharing our visualizations.

2 **Demonstrate:** Begin the demonstration by sharing a number of images that represent a variety of content area concepts. Next, visualize as you read a section of text. Think aloud about how to represent your mental pictures through sketching. Then use simple lines and shapes as you sketch on poster-size paper. Write a sentence or two below the sketches to explain the visualizations.

FIGURE 6.11 Gallery Images about the Water Cycle in Science Class

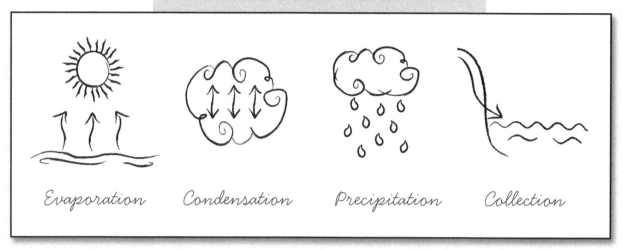

FIGURE 6.11 Gallery Images about the Water Cycle in Science Class

3 Guide: Ask students to work in pairs and visualize at least two images as you read another segment of text. Encourage the students to sketch their mental pictures on poster-size paper, write a description, and share their images with their partner. Then engage the students in a discussion about their visualizations.

4 Practice: Encourage students to practice by creating at least two more mental pictures as you read another segment of text. Then invite them to sketch and label their visualizations on the poster-size paper. Use the classroom wall to create Gallery Images, as the students display their sketches and discuss them with other students.

5 Reflect: Encourage students to reflect on how creating visualizations, and specifically Gallery Images, helps us to understand what we read. Ask students to reflect on how they can use Gallery Images in other content areas.

Figure 6.11 features examples of Gallery Images about the water cycle that were created in a science class.

Making Connections | Thinking about Engaging Students *during* Reading

■ Think about when you were in middle school or high school. Do you remember teachers activating background knowledge and making connections to engage you in reading? Do you remember their providing creative writing options or hands-on projects to extend thinking after reading? Engaging and extending thinking strategies are more commonly used than strategies such as monitoring, self-questioning, and visualizing, which guide our thinking during reading. Consider how you will integrate these strategies in your teaching and help your students think through the comprehension process.

■ Share your thoughts in small-group discussions.

FINAL THOUGHTS

Using reading comprehension strategies to guide our thinking helps us to focus on content and construct meaning. We use strategies such as self-questioning, monitoring, and visualizing during reading to help us engage with text and monitor our understanding.

In the next chapter, we focus on reading comprehension strategies we can use to extend our thinking. Summarizing and evaluating are examples of these. Of course, as noted earlier, we can use all of the strategies we have learned as needed while reading.

Teaching Connections

APPLYING WHAT WE HAVE LEARNED

E-Links

Work with a partner and choose a website such as those listed to locate text related to your content area. As you read, consciously use comprehension strategies such as monitoring and visualizing. Complete strategy-based ideas such as Bookmark Technique and Photographs of the Mind (see the Appendix for graphic organizers). Discuss with your partner how using these strategies helped you understand the text. Record your thoughts as a reflective entry in your portfolio.

EXAMPLE WEBSITES

American History: USA.gov
http://www.usa.gov/Citizen/Topics/History_American.shtml

Calculus—from Wolfram Math World
http://mathworld.wolfram.com/Calculus.html

Ernest Hemingway: His Life and Works
www.ernest.hemingway.com

Physics Central
www.physicscentral.com

Poets.org
http:www.poets.org

Profiles of Spanish Speaking Countries
http://www.donquijote.org/tourist/profiles

Smithsonian's History Explorer (National Museum of American History)
http://historyexplorer.americanhistory.si.edu

Accountable Talk

Consider why it is important to motivate students to engage with text during reading. Think about how strategies, such as those we learned in this chapter, support students' transaction with text and promote reader response. Consider how these strategies help students to construct meaning and what students' responses can tell us about their understanding of text. Record your ideas and share what you believe to be the best suggestions in the class discussion.

 ### Portfolio/Performance Opportunity

Work with a partner in your content area to develop a standards-based lesson plan that focuses on (1) teaching course content and (2) using reading comprehension strategies to engage and guide student thinking (before and during reading). Meet in small groups and teach your lesson to the group. Engage in peer feedback, and revise the lesson plan as necessary. Discuss how you can work with other content area teachers to support students' use of comprehension strategies to guide their thinking. Reflect on your work and include your lesson plan in your portfolio.

7

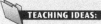

Using Comprehension Strategies to Extend Thinking

In this chapter, we continue our quest to help students learn a variety of comprehension strategies to use as needed while reading. Our focus is strategies to use *after* reading to extend student thinking. We use these strategies to elaborate on what we have learned, extend learning beyond the classroom, and clarify understandings.

We begin by discussing how we can use strategies to extend thinking. Then we focus on summarizing and evaluation—both strategies that help us to extend our understanding. Next, we consider which literacy professionals and school administrators will support us in our quest to teach students a repertoire of strategies they can use while reading.

How Can We Use Comprehension Strategies to Extend Thinking?

In the examples that follow, we describe a variety of ways to support students' use of comprehension strategies *after* reading. In each step-by-step sequence, we begin by explaining the strategy and the teaching idea. Next, we demonstrate it. Then, we guide students as they work with partners. After that, the students attempt to use the strategies on their own. Finally, we reflect on what we have learned, including how we can use the strategies in the content areas. Each teaching sequence is followed by a student example. Related reproducible graphic organizers can be found in the Appendix.

Summarizing

Summarizing is a reading comprehension strategy that involves extracting essential information from text. This strategy is often used formally after reading to provide students with the opportunity to gather important information about a topic, but as we read we often summarize informally—thinking about what the author has said to that point before we read on. Many teaching ideas support this strategy, including those featured in this section. Descriptions of these ideas and step-by step directions for teaching them follow. Detailed information about scaffolding students' writing of summaries can be found in Chapter 10. Strategy-based examples found in that chapter include the Concept of Definition Map Summary and Questions into Paragraphs (QuIP). In Chapter 13, Lyric Summaries and Rapping for Review—two ideas for summarizing that integrate singing—are featured. Reproducible copies of related graphic organizers can be found in the Appendix.

BIO-PYRAMID. The Bio-Pyramid (Macon, 1991) is a summary format for a person's life that requires particular information and a specific number of words per line. It involves a graphic organizer that appears as a pyramid. In addition to helping students learn how to summarize, the Bio-Pyramid helps them monitor and make connections to the text they are reading.

To teach your students how to complete a Bio-Pyramid, follow these guidelines:

1. **Explain:** Explain summarizing as a comprehension strategy that involves extracting essential information from text. Then describe how Bio-Pyramids work, noting that there are 8 lines and that each can accommodate only a certain number of words. Then explain that what we write on each line needs to accommodate the description that appears below the line. Finally, distribute copies of the graphic organizer (see the Appendix).

2. **Demonstrate:** Begin by distributing a short biography to the students. Introduce the text. Read the biography aloud to the students and briefly discuss the person's life. Then think aloud as you complete the first 2 lines of the Bio-Pyramid. For example, if you were creating a Bio-Pyramid about Dr. Martin Luther King, Jr., you might say, "I see that the first line requires the person's name. It provides only one space, so I will write 'King.' The second line asks for two words describing the person, so I will write 'educated' and 'dedicated,' because Dr. King was well educated and very dedicated to the Civil Rights Movement."

3. **Guide:** Ask the students to work with partners as they complete lines 3, 4, and 5 of the Bio-Pyramid. Encourage several partners to share their lines with the class. Then complete lines 3, 4, and 5 on the Bio-Pyramid you began about Dr. King. For example, you might write, "Brother, Son, Grandson" on line 3, "Prejudice in United States" on line 4, and "He was a Baptist minister" on line 5.

4. **Practice:** Invite the students to work on their own to complete lines 6, 7, and 8. Encourage several students to share their lines with the class. Then complete the remaining lines on the Bio-Pyramid about Dr. King. For example, you might write, "He worked for American civil rights" on line 6, "Gave the 'I Have a Dream' speech" on line 7, and "We learned to celebrate the equality of all" on line 8.

5. **Reflect:** Encourage students to reflect on how well they can summarize and how they can use Bio-Pyramids in other content areas.

Figure 7.1 shows a Bio-Pyramid about Pythagoras that was completed in mathematics class by Daisy Herrera.

NARRATIVE PYRAMID. The Narrative Pyramid (Waldo, 1991) is a retelling or summary format for texts such as short stories and novels. Much like the Bio-Pyramid, the graphic organizer requires particular information and a specific number of words per line. In this case, each line includes information linked to the narrative elements: characters, setting, problem, events, and solution. The Narrative Pyramid is used after reading.

Go to the Activities and Applications section under the topic *Writing* in the MyEducationLab for your course and complete the activity entitled Summarizing to better understand the importance of teaching students to summarize information.

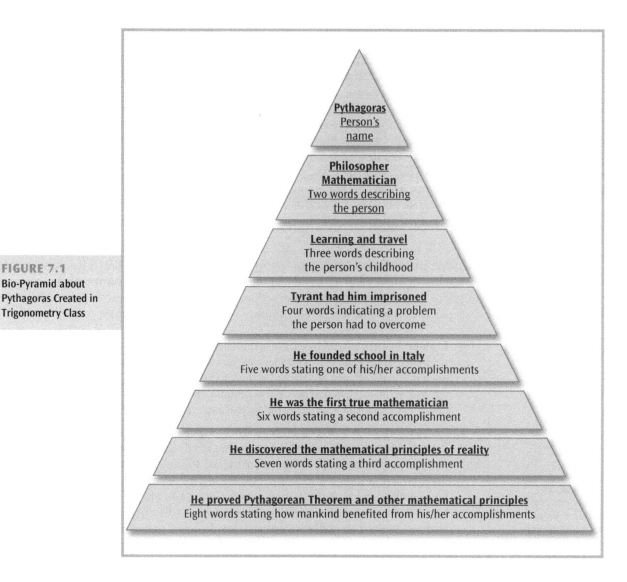

FIGURE 7.1
Bio-Pyramid about
Pythagoras Created in
Trigonometry Class

To teach your students how to complete a Narrative Pyramid, follow these guidelines:

1. **Explain:** Explain summarizing as a comprehension strategy that involves extracting essential information from text. Then explain how Narrative Pyramids help us to summarize stories. Note the number of lines, the number of words we can write per line, and the use of descriptions beneath each line to determine what we write. Distribute copies of the graphic organizer (see the Appendix).

2. **Demonstrate:** Engage students in completing a Narrative Pyramid after they have read a short story or novel. Briefly review the text. For example, you might say:

   > The text we will use while learning about the Narrative Pyramid is the novel we have just finished reading: *To Kill a Mockingbird*. I see that I will need to provide specific information about the narrative elements on the graphic organizer. So, I will think about the characters, setting, problem, attempts to resolve the problem, and resolution. Atticus, Scout, Jem, Boo Radley, and Tom Robinson are the characters that come to mind. I remember the story took place in a poor rural community in Alabama and that the people in the community supported white people when it came to justice. Atticus Finch defended Tom Robinson, a black man, against rape charges, and, as a result, Atticus's

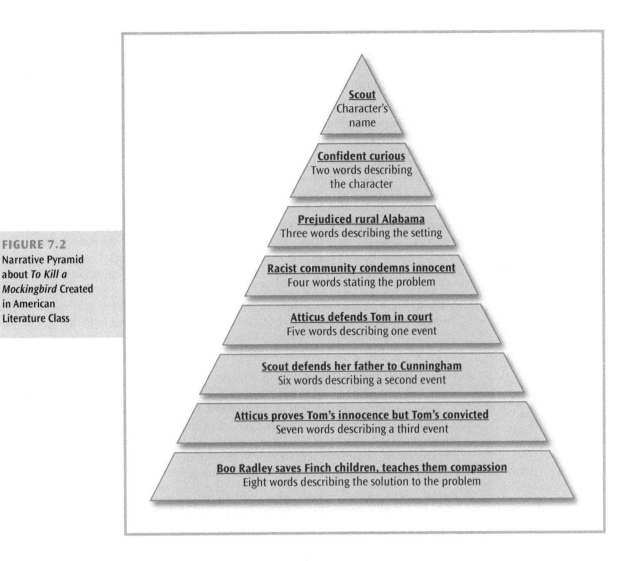

FIGURE 7.2
Narrative Pyramid about *To Kill a Mockingbird* Created in American Literature Class

children were harassed by Mr. Cunningham. Boo Radley came to the children's rescue, after Tom Robinson, who was innocent, was convicted.

Next, think aloud as you complete the first four lines of the Narrative Pyramid (Figure 7.2). For example, you might say, "I see that the first line requires the character's name. It provides only one space, so I will write <u>Scout</u>. The second line asks for two words that describe the character, and I know that Scout was <u>confident</u> and <u>curious</u>, so I will write those words in the two spaces in line 2." The setting needs to be described in line 3, so I might say, "The novel took place in rural Alabama during a time when prejudice was prevalent. I know I can use only three words, so I will write <u>prejudiced</u> <u>rural</u> <u>Alabama</u>." The problem needs to be stated in four words in line 4, so I might say, "<u>Racist</u> <u>community</u> <u>condemns</u> <u>innocent</u>."

3 Guide: Ask the students to work with partners to complete lines 5 and 6 of the Narrative Pyramid, each of which refers to an event in the novel. Encourage several partners to share their responses with the class. Then write responses on lines 5 and 6 on the Narrative Pyramid you have been completing. You may use student responses or create your own. For example, you might write "<u>Atticus</u> <u>defends</u> <u>Tom</u> <u>in</u> <u>court</u>" on line 5 and "<u>Scout</u> <u>defends</u> <u>her</u> <u>father</u> <u>to</u> <u>Cunningham</u>" on line 6.

4 Practice: Invite the students to work on their own to complete line 7, seven words describing another event, and line 8, eight words describing the solution to the problem. After a few students share their responses, complete the Narrative Pyramid you have been using for demonstration. For example, you might write, "<u>Atticus</u> <u>proves</u> <u>Tom's</u> <u>innocence</u> <u>but</u> <u>Tom's</u> <u>convicted</u>" on line 7 and "<u>Boo</u> <u>Radley</u> <u>saves</u> <u>Finch</u> <u>children</u>, <u>teaching</u> <u>them</u> <u>compassion</u>" on line 8. The completed demonstration Narrative Pyramid is featured in Figure 7.2.

5 **Reflect:** Encourage students to reflect on what they know about summarizing and how to use story elements to complete Narrative Pyramids. Discuss how the Narrative Pyramid can be used to summarize information when reading literature in the content areas.

PAIRED SUMMARIZING. Paired summarizing (Vaughn & Estes, 1986) provides a format for two students to work together to express their understandings and summarize narrative or informational text. After a text is selected and introduced, each student reads a segment and writes a summary of what she has read. Then the paired students read each other's summaries and summarize them. Next, students compare and contrast their summaries and share their ideas with a small group or the whole class. We engage in Paired Summarizing after reading.

To teach your students how to use Paired Summarizing, follow these guidelines:

1 **Explain:** Begin by explaining summarizing as a reading strategy that involves extracting essential information from text. Then explain that when we engage in Paired Summarizing, we have multiple opportunities to work with a partner to extract important information from text, determine what we understand, and generate questions we may have.

2 **Demonstrate:** Prior to demonstrating, arrange to have a student engage in Paired Summarizing with you. Think aloud as you follow each step in the process. To begin, you and your partner read a short text and write a summary of it. You may refer to the article, but you may not have the article in front of you while you are writing. When you finish writing, exchange summaries with your partner. Read that summary and write a summary of it. Then compare and contrast the summaries you wrote with those of your partner. Discuss what you do and do not understand. Create and respond to clarifying questions.

3 **Guide:** Invite students to work with a partner and guide them as they engage in Paired Questioning. Provide a short content area text they can read and summarize. Then observe as they exchange summaries and write summaries based on those they read. Encourage students to focus on what they understand and what questions they have. Guide them to discuss their summaries and questions in small groups. Contribute as requested. Repeat the process with another short text. Discuss Paired Summarizing with the students.

4 **Practice:** Encourage students to work with partners to independently engage in Paired Summarizing.

5 **Reflect:** Invite students to reflect on how Paired Summarizing helps us understand text. Encourage them to reflect on and discuss how they can use Paired Summarizing in other content area classes.

In the example featured in Figure 7.3, Brandon and Javier use Paired Summarizing as they are reading *Fields of Fury: The American Civil War* (McPherson, 2002), a content area trade book in American History class.

SKETCH TO STRETCH. Sketch to Stretch (Short, Harste, & Burke, 1996) involves using sketching to create, represent, and share personal understandings of text. Sketch to Stretch is usually used in small groups after reading narrative or informational text.

To teach your students how to use Sketch to Stretch, follow these steps:

1 **Explain:** Begin by explaining summarizing as a reading strategy that involves extracting essential information from text. Then explain Sketch to Stretch as a way to represent personal meaning through sketching after reading.

FIGURE 7.3
Brandon and Javier's
Examples of Paired
Summarizing

Brandon's Summary

March 4, 1865, began the Reconstruction period. After the Civil War, the South lay in ruins. President Lincoln asked that the high-ranking officials be pardoned because he wanted to create peace with the South. However, Lincoln never got to establish his Reconstruction ideas, because he was assassinated by John Wilkes Booth. His Vice-President, Andrew Johnson, took over. President Johnson was too lenient with the South, and Southerners reelected the same political parties and created black codes so they could almost use African Americans as slaves again. Congress got angry and took control of the Reconstruction. Southerners still resented African Americans and found new ways to keep them as second-class citizens. They enforced Jim Crow laws and segregation. Reconstruction ended in 1877.

Javier's Summary of Brandon's Summary

Reconstruction of the South began after the Civil War. The South was destroyed and President Lincoln was in charge of rebuilding it. Lincoln, however, was assassinated and so the job fell to his Vice-President, Andrew Johnson. Johnson attempted to bring order to the South, but he ran into problems. The South kept creating laws to keep African Americans in their control.

2 Demonstrate: Begin the demonstration by introducing and reading a short selection and thinking about what the text means to you. Next, express your thoughts through sketching. Share your sketch with a few students and ask them what they think it means. Then explain what you think it means.

3 Guide: Invite students to work in small groups of 3 to 5. Introduce another short text and either read the text aloud or encourage the students to read it. After reading, ask them to express what the text meant to them through a sketch. Then invite the students to engage in Sketch to Stretch, by sharing their sketches one at a time. After each group member comments on a sketch, the student who created it offers her interpretation.

4 Practice: Encourage students to practice by continuing to share and discuss their sketches, until everyone in the group has had a turn.

5 Reflect: Invite students to reflect on how expressing personal meaning of text through sketching helped them to comprehend. Encourage students to reflect on how they can use Sketch to Stretch in other content areas.

Figure 7.4 features the sketch Chrissy created in American story class when studying the *Brown v. Board of Education* decision. When it was her turn to share her interpretation, she said, "I drew a protest sign supporting the Fourteenth Amendment because *Brown v. Board of Education* was about ending segregation in places such as schools. Segregation violated the Fourteenth Amendment and needed to be abolished."

TEACHING IDEA   QUESTIONS INTO PARAGRAPHS (QuIP). Questions into Paragraphs (QuIP) (McLaughlin, 1987) provides a framework for initiating research, structuring writing, and summarizing. Students choose a topic and develop three related research questions. Then they respond to each question from two sources. When the graphic organizer is complete, students use the information to write a paragraph. We use QuIP before reading (generating questions), during reading (reading the information provided by the two sources), and after reading (writing the summary).

To teach your students how to use QuIP, follow these guidelines:

1 Explain: Begin by explaining summarizing as a reading strategy that involves extracting essential information from text. Then explain QuIP as a framework for questioning, researching, and summarizing that focuses on developing three questions and responding to them from two different sources.

FIGURE 7.4 Sketch to Stretch – *Brown v. the Board of Education*

The 14th Amendment means equal protection for all.

2 Demonstrate: Begin demonstrating by sharing the graphic organizer (see the Appendix) and selecting a topic. Then remind students about the importance of generating higher-level questions (see Chapter 9) and develop three research questions. For example, if the topic you chose was Mars, you would raise three questions about it. Question 1 might be "How did Mars get its name?"

3 Guide: Invite students to work with a partner and guide them as they generate two additional questions. For example, Question 2 might be "Why do scientists believe there could be life on Mars?" Question 3 might be "What do scientists predict we will learn about Mars in the future?" Continue to guide the students as they use bookmarked websites to respond to the three research questions from two sources. Encourage the students to continue to complete the graphic organizer and discuss their responses.

4 Practice: Encourage students to work on their own to write a paragraph based on the completed graphic organizers. Invite them to share their completed paragraphs with their partners. Discuss completed QuIPs with the class.

5 Reflect: Invite students to reflect on how QuIP helps us to summarize and comprehend. Encourage students to think of other ways they can use QuIP in the content areas.

Figure 7.5 shows the QuIP and paragraph about Mars that Earth Science teacher Edward Puchalski completed during the Guided Comprehension demonstration.

FIGURE 7.5 Questions into Paragraphs about Mars
QuIP Research Grid

Topic: Mars _____

Questions	Answers	
	Source 1: http://www.nineplanets.org/mars.html	Source 2: http://www.nasa.gov/worldbook/mars_worldbook.html
A. How did Mars get its name?	Mars was named after the god of war. It is also referred to as the red planet because of its coloring.	Mars was named after the Roman god of war. The Greeks and Romans named the planet after the god of war because the planet was blood colored.
B. Why do scientists believe there could be life on Mars?	In 1996, scientists discovered evidence of ancient Martian microorganisms in a meteorite.	Researchers found evidence of life in certain materials in meteorites found on Earth.
C. What do scientists predict we will learn about Mars in the future?	Scientists are still not convinced that there is/was life on Mars. Scientists will continue to search for answers.	Scientists are still attempting to prove that there is life on Mars through research.

QuIP Paragraph

Mars was named after the Roman god of war. The Romans named the planet after the god of war because the planet was red or blood colored. Scientists have discovered microorganisms in a meteorite that landed on Earth. Some researchers believe this indicates that there was life on Mars at one point, while others are skeptical. Scientists are still studying Mars today in hopes of proving that life does or did exist on Mars.

Making Connections
TO STRUGGLING READERS

Summarizing plays an essential role in student learning. Whether students are summarizing text as they read, creating summaries after reading, or representing summaries through alternative modes, students—and especially struggling learners—need to know how to summarize. For ideas about how to scaffold students' learning of how to summarize and, in particular, how to write summaries, see Chapter 11. For ideas about how to use music when summarizing, see the descriptions of Summary and Rapping for Review found in Chapter 14. ∎

Evaluating

Evaluating is a reading comprehension strategy that involves making judgments during and after reading. Issues we focus on include these questions: (1) Is the author's message consistent? and (2) Whose perspective is presented in the text? This strategy is used with narrative and expository text. A variety of teaching ideas support this strategy, including the four that are featured in this section. Related reproducible graphic organizers are located in the Appendix.

DISCUSSION WEB. The Discussion Web (Alvermann, 1991) provides students with a structure to discuss and evaluate given texts. To complete the Web, students investigate both sides of an issue and think critically about a topic with varying points of view. The Discussion Web begins with a question and ends when students come to consensus about the issue. Used with informational text, this technique is designed to spark discussion and debate in all content areas.

To teach your students how to complete a Discussion Web, follow these steps:

1. **Explain:** Begin by selecting a text—or two, if necessary—that provides information about two perspectives on a topic. Share the text(s) with the students. Explain evaluating as a reading comprehension strategy that involves making judgments while reading. Then explain how Discussion Webs focus on questions or statements that have pro and con perspectives and how pairs and ultimately the whole class come to consensus on such issues.

2. **Demonstrate:** Think aloud about the topic of the text(s) and a question that might be raised that would require readers to investigate pro and con perspectives. For example, if the topic was school violence, the question might be, "Do the media contribute to school violence?" Introduce each of the related texts and invite the students to take a few minutes to read the information. Continue demonstrating by writing the brainstormed question on the graphic organizer. Then take one fact from each perspective and write it in either the Pro (yes) or Con (no) column. For example, in the Pro column you might write, "The media report on many violent acts during the daily news," and in the Con column you might write, "People don't need to listen to the media. They can turn off or ignore the media outlets."

3. **Guide:** Ask students to work with a partner and add two more facts to each column. Discuss the information they add to the graphic.

4. **Practice:** Ask students to continue working with partners until they have exhausted the facts they would like to include. Then invite them to discuss the information they have compiled and come to an agreement on their position about the topic. Invite the partners to share their positions with the class and then engage in class discussion until consensus is reached. Record the class's perspective on the graphic organizer. Finally, ask students to provide a rationale and record that on the graphic organizer. For example, when discussing whether the media are responsible for school violence, the class might reach this conclusion: "Yes, the media are responsible for school violence." Then they might offer the

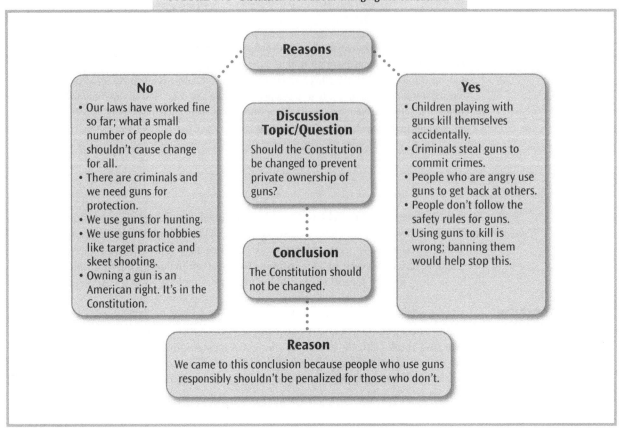

FIGURE 7.6 Discussion Web about Changing the Constitution

Reasons

No
- Our laws have worked fine so far; what a small number of people do shouldn't cause change for all.
- There are criminals and we need guns for protection.
- We use guns for hunting.
- We use guns for hobbies like target practice and skeet shooting.
- Owning a gun is an American right. It's in the Constitution.

Discussion Topic/Question
Should the Constitution be changed to prevent private ownership of guns?

Conclusion
The Constitution should not be changed.

Yes
- Children playing with guns kill themselves accidentally.
- Criminals steal guns to commit crimes.
- People who are angry use guns to get back at others.
- People don't follow the safety rules for guns.
- Using guns to kill is wrong; banning them would help stop this.

Reason
We came to this conclusion because people who use guns responsibly shouldn't be penalized for those who don't.

following rationale: "We came to this conclusion because students are exposed to so much violence in music, video games, and television, and on the Internet that when they react to real-life situations, they become violent just like the people they see in the media."

5 **Reflect:** Invite students to reflect on evaluating and how to use the Discussion Web in other content areas.

Figure 7.6 shows a Discussion Web focused on the following question: Should the Constitution be changed to prevent private ownership of guns? This Discussion Web was completed in Madeline Apfel's American History class.

TEACHING IDEA

MIND AND ALTERNATIVE MIND PORTRAITS. Mind and Alternative Mind Portraits (McLaughlin, 2001) is designed to help readers examine a topic from two viewpoints. This technique helps us to evaluate the perspectives that exist within a text. Mind and Alternative Mind Portraits, which are used with informational text, are usually completed after reading. Alternatives to Mind and Alternative Mind Portraits include Narratives and Alternative Narratives, Photographs and Alternative Photographs, and Videos and Alternative Videos.

To teach your students how to use Mind and Alternative Mind Portraits, follow these steps:

1 **Explain:** Begin by explaining evaluating as a reading comprehension strategy that involves making judgments while reading. Then explain how Mind and Alternative Mind Portraits represent two different perspectives. Introduce the text, noting that it contains multiple perspectives, and share the graphic organizer.

2 **Demonstrate:** Use a think-aloud and a read-aloud to demonstrate Mind and Alternative Mind Portraits. Read the text and think aloud about the ideas it presents. Choose the two

FIGURE 7.7   Mind and Alternative Mind Portraits

FIGURE 7.7   **Mind and Alternative Mind Portraits**

Mind Portrait	**Alternative Mind Portrait**
United States Government	Japanese Americans
Notice To All Japanese Persons AND Persons of Japanese Racial ORigin	
We put Japanese Americans into internment camps because of the attack on Pearl Harbor.	*We were removed from our homes and businesses. We are Americans. We should not be blamed for other people's mistakes.*

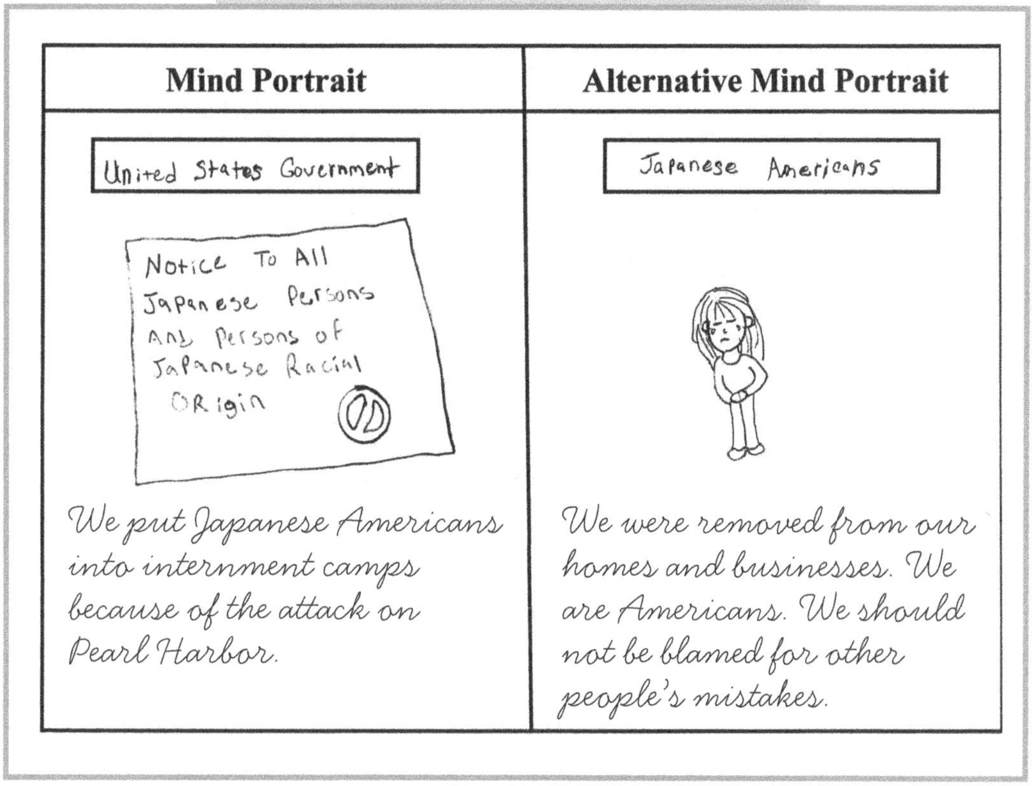

perspectives you will represent in Mind and Alternative Mind Portraits. For example, if the text is about the Japanese American internment during World War II, you might choose the predominant perspective of the U.S. government and the perspective of Japanese Americans living on the West Coast between 1942 and 1945, which may not be equally represented or may be missing in the text. Think aloud as you label the Mind Portrait on the graphic organizer. Inside the Mind Portrait, write or sketch ideas and experiences that describe the U.S. government's perspective. Next, label the Alternative Mind Portrait and think aloud as you write or sketch ideas inside that portrait that are characteristic of the Japanese Americans interned during World War II. (See the completed Portraits in Figure 7.7.) Think aloud as you contrast the Mind and Alternative Mind Portraits, noting which perspective is more predominant and pointing out that the Alternative Mind Portrait features a perspective that was not equally presented in the text.

3 **Guide:** Invite students to work with partners to begin Mind and Alternative Mind Portraits about another topic. Distribute copies of a short text in which multiple perspectives are represented. Introduce the text and read it aloud. After you have finished reading, encourage students to select two different perspectives on the topic and label the Portraits. Then invite the partners to discuss both perspectives and add two ideas each to the Mind Portrait and Alternative Mind Portraits. Invite the students to discuss their Portraits and share their reasoning.

4 **Practice:** Encourage students to work on their own to complete the Mind and Alternative Mind Portraits they began with their partners. After the graphic organizers are complete, encourage students to share their reasoning.

5 **Reflect:** Ask students to reflect on what they know about evaluating and how they can use Mind and Alternative Mind Portraits to help them evaluate as they read text in the content areas.

Figure 7.7 features the Mind and Alternative Mind Portraits that Jesse created in history class when they were studying the Japanese American internment.

EVALUATIVE QUESTIONING. Evaluative questioning (Ciardiello, 1998) provides a format for us to express ideas and to defend, judge, or justify our thinking. When using this approach, students work in small groups, read text, and generate and respond to evaluative questions. We can use Evaluative Questioning after reading, but we can also use it before and during the reading of narrative and informational text.

To teach your students how to use Evaluative Questioning, follow these guidelines:

1 **Explain:** Begin by explaining evaluating as a reading comprehension strategy that involves making judgments while reading. Then explain that Evaluative Questioning involves developing ideas and defending or justifying our thinking.

2 **Demonstrate:** Begin demonstrating by reminding students about Ciardiello's levels of questioning (see Chapter 9), noting that we will focus on the highest level—evaluating. Read a short text, and create an evaluative question. For example, if you were reading about the contributions Leonardo DaVinci and the Wright Brothers made to flight, a question you would generate might be, "In your opinion, who contributed more to flight, DaVinci or the Wright Brothers? Defend your response." Then you should continue the demonstration by responding to the question you raised. Discuss Evaluative Questioning with the students.

3 **Guide:** Introduce a short text to your students and read it aloud. Before reading, remind the students that they will be generating evaluative questions. After reading, guide students to work in pairs to generate and respond to evaluative questions. For example, if the text you read focused on the Japanese American internment, a question students would raise might be, "Was the U.S. government justified in mandating the Japanese American internment after the bombing of Pearl Harbor?" Defend your response. Encourage students to generate and respond to at least two evaluative questions.

4 **Practice:** Invite students to practice by reading a short text on their own and generating two evaluative questions. Then ask them to share their questions with their partners, who will respond to them. Reverse the process, so that both students have opportunities to generate and respond to evaluative questions. Discuss Evaluative Questioning with the students.

5 **Reflect:** Encourage students to reflect on how Evaluative Questioning helps us to understand text. Then ask students how they might use Evaluative Questioning in other content areas.

VENN DIAGRAM. The Venn Diagram is named for its creator, John Venn, who used it to express thoughts about logic. The diagram, which is represented by two interlocking circles, provides a format for us to note similarities and differences or two perspectives about a topic. The similarities appear in the overlapping sections of the circles; the differences appear in the outer sides of each circle.

To teach your students how to complete a Venn Diagram, follow these guidelines:

1 **Explain:** Begin by explaining evaluating as a comprehension strategy that involves making judgments while reading. Then explain that the Venn Diagram provides us with a format to express the similarities and differences associated with two topics.

2 **Demonstrate:** Read a short text that clearly represents two different perspectives or similarities and differences about a topic. For example, in Figure 7.8, the Venn Diagram focuses on two types of volcanoes. Demonstrate this technique by listing the topics to be compared and contrasted in the spaces provided on the graphic organizer. For example, in the Venn Diagram in Figure 7.8, the topics are cinder cones and composite volcanoes.

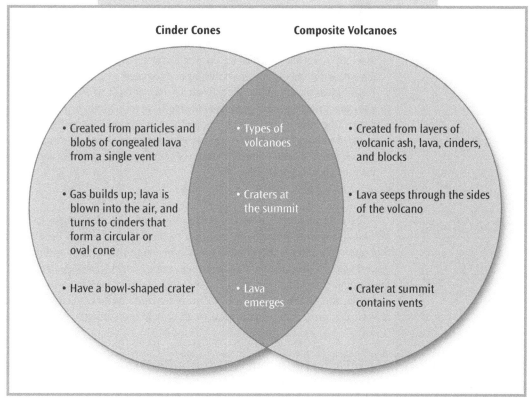

FIGURE 7.8 Venn Diagram about Two Types of Volcanoes

Cinder Cones   **Composite Volcanoes**

- Created from particles and blobs of congealed lava from a single vent
- Gas builds up; lava is blown into the air, and turns to cinders that form a circular or oval cone
- Have a bowl-shaped crater

- Types of volcanoes
- Craters at the summit
- Lava emerges

- Created from layers of volcanic ash, lava, cinders, and blocks
- Lava seeps through the sides of the volcano
- Crater at summit contains vents

Then think aloud as you list the common features in the overlapping section of the circles. In Figure 7.8, features the volcanoes have in common include that both are types of volcanos, both have craters at the summit, and lava emerges from both. Next, consider the descriptors that are unique to cinder cones. Write them in the outer section of the circle labeled "Cinder Cones." Then, consider the qualities that are unique to composite volcanoes and record them in the outer portion of that circle. Note the similarities and differences as they are represented on the graphic organizer. Discuss the completed Venn diagram with your students.

3 **Guide:** Encourage students to work in pairs to complete Venn Diagrams. Read a short text and provide copies for students. Then ask the students to revisit the text to determine which two topics they might use in their Venn Diagrams. Discuss the topics. Next, invite students to list qualities or characteristics that are common to both topics. Discuss the common qualities or similarities. Encourage students to determine which qualities are unique to each topic and list them in the outer portion of each circle. Discuss the unique qualities (contrasts).

4 **Practice:** Encourage students to practice by reading a short text that presents a topic from two different perspectives and completing a Venn Diagram. Discuss students' completed diagrams.

5 **Reflect:** Invite students to reflect on how Venn Diagrams help us to think through text. Encourage students to reflect on how they can use Venn Diagrams in other content areas and in everyday life to compare and contrast or present two perspectives.

Figure 7.8 shows Derek and Marianne's Venn Diagram about volcanoes.

Making Connections
TO MULTIPLE LITERACIES

We can use ideas such as Mind and Alternative Mind Portraits to examine multiple perspectives, an aspect of critical literacy. When we examine text and determine which position is represented as more powerful and which is either missing or discounted, we move beyond the text to understand issues such as why the author wrote about a particular topic, wrote from a particular perspective, and chose to include some ideas about the topic and exclude others. This is especially important for us as teachers in the content areas, because authors and publishers determine which content is included and which perspectives are represented in textbooks. As an example, consider what you learned about Columbus from textbooks when you were in grade school and what you know to be the truth about Columbus now. ■

Teaching students how to use reading comprehension strategies to think their way through text has numerous benefits. In addition to helping students to become strategic readers and thinkers, it illuminates the value of questioning at multiple levels and using alternative modes of representation. Using the Guided Comprehension Model's five steps of explicit instruction to teach the strategies provides opportunities for students to engage in scaffolded learning, application, and reflection. In the next section, we move beyond how to explicitly teach strategies and discuss how we can work with other professionals to help our students reach their reading potentials.

Who Will Work with Us to Help Our Students Become Strategic Readers?

Students begin learning to read at a very early age. Throughout their education, they are taught by knowledgeable teachers who are well acquainted with concepts such as the constructivist perspective and the importance of prior knowledge. Students begin learning the reading comprehension strategies in the primary grades, in the hope that they will use them as necessary from that time forward. But, as Biancarosa and Snow (2006) remind us, there are 8 million struggling adolescent readers who have not had that experience. They are not using reading comprehension strategies at the middle school and high school levels.

So, although we teach upper grades, one of our goals is for our students to understand and use a repertoire of comprehension strategies that will help them think through the reading process. The good news is we are not alone in this effort. In addition to our fellow content area teachers, other professionals—such as reading specialists, literacy coaches, and administrators—are among those who can help ensure that our students know and use such strategies. Figure 7.9 features excerpts from the International Reading Association's Standards for Reading Professionals that describe how such professionals can contribute to students' knowledge of reading.

We should add one more category to the list of professionals who work with us to help our students comprehend to their greatest potential: English as a Second Language (ESL) teachers. These educators can help us to make connections to our students who are English learners. For more information about teaching English learners in the content areas and working with ESL teachers, see Chapter 10.

Making Connections | Thinking about Those Who Will Help Students Reach Their Reading Potential

■ Think about who taught you to read and who continued to support your reading in the content areas when you were in middle school and high school. Did the answer to part one of this question come more easily than your response to part two? It often happens that way, because many of us can focus on the one person we think taught us to read but find it difficult to remember if anyone supported our reading in later years. Now consider all those who are currently available to support students' reading in the content areas: reading teachers, reading specialists, literacy coaches, school administrators, and ESL teachers. Think about how you envision your role as a member of this team of professionals and how you can make the most valuable contribution.

■ Share your thoughts in small-group discussions.

FINAL THOUGHTS

When we teach our students a repertoire of comprehension strategies, they become active, strategic readers. These students can then use the strategies as needed to think through text. This results in greater understanding. It also accommodates Biancarosa and Snow's (2006) recommendation in *Reading Next* that we explicitly teach reading comprehension strategies at the middle school and high school levels.

In the next chapter, we extend our discussion to teaching and learning vocabulary. As we know, vocabulary is an essential component of comprehension. Chapter 8 features a number of practical, classroom-based ideas to help our students expand their knowledge of words.

FIGURE 7.9
IRA Standards for
Reading Professionals:
Excerpts from the
Revised Role
Definitions, 2007

The Classroom Teacher
Teaches at the early childhood, elementary, middle, or high school and/or adult levels. Develops children's reading and related language arts; includes content area teachers who integrate literacy instruction with subject learning.

The Reading Specialist
Works at the early childhood, elementary, middle, secondary, and/or adult levels. Fulfills a number of responsibilities and many have a specific focus that further defines their duties. For example, a reading specialist can serve as a teacher for students experiencing reading difficulties; as a literacy or reading coach; or as a supervisor or coordinator of reading/literacy. The reading specialist must be prepared to fulfill the duties of all three of these:

■ **A reading intervention teacher** is a reading specialist who provides intensive instruction to struggling readers. Such instruction may be provided either within or outside the students' classrooms.
■ **A literacy coach** is a reading specialist who focuses on providing professional development for teachers by providing them with the additional support needed to implement various instructional programs and practices. They provide essential leadership for the school's entire literacy program by helping create and supervise a long-term staff development process that supports both the development and implementation of the literacy program over months and years. These individuals need to have experiences that enable them to provide effective professional development for the teachers in their schools.
■ **A reading supervisor or reading coordinator** is a reading specialist who is responsible for developing, leading, and evaluating a school reading program, from kindergarten through grade 12. They may assume some of the same responsibilities as the literacy coach, but in addition have responsibilities that require them to work more with systematic change at the school level. These individuals need to have experiences that enable them to work effectively as administrators and to be able to develop and lead effective professional development programs.

The Administrator
■ Includes principals and superintendents. Recognizes and supports reading professionals as they plan, implement, and evaluate effective reading instruction.

Source: International Reading Association. Reproduced with permission.

Teaching Connections
APPLYING WHAT WE HAVE LEARNED

E-Links

Work with a partner and choose a website such as those listed below to locate text related to your content area. As you read, consciously use summarizing as a comprehension strategy. Note how often you informally summarize text to a given point. After reading, complete strategy-based ideas such as Bio-Pyramids or Narrative Pyramids and Paired Summarizing. (See the Appendix for graphic organizers.) Discuss with your partner how using these techniques helped you understand the text. Record your thoughts as a reflective entry in your portfolio.

EXAMPLE WEBSITES

Poets.org
http:www.poets.org

Profiles of Spanish-Speaking Countries
http://www.donquijote.org/tourist/profiles

Smithsonian's History Explorer (National Museum of American History)
http://historyexplorer.americanhistory.si.edu

The Time 100: The Most Important People of the Century (Leaders and Revolutionaries, Scientists and Thinkers, Heroes and Icons—and More)
http://www.time.com/time/time100/scientist/profile/wright.html

Accountable Talk

We know that being active, strategic readers benefits students' learning. Meet in small groups and discuss (1) how middle school and high school teachers can help students to become strategic readers and (2) how middle and high school teachers can embed strategy instruction in standards-based lessons. Record your ideas and share what you believe to be the best suggestions in our class discussion.

 ### Portfolio/Performance Opportunity

Work with a partner in your content area to develop a standards-based lesson plan that focuses on the following: (1) teaching course content and (2) using reading comprehension strategies to engage, guide, and extend student thinking (before, during, and after reading). Meet in small groups and teach your lesson to the group. Engage in peer feedback and revise the lesson plan as necessary. Reflect on your work and include your lesson plan in your portfolio.

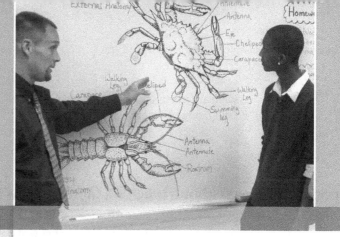

8

Chapter Overview

TEACHING IDEAS:

Teaching Vocabulary in the Content Areas

Our lives and the lives of our students are filled with words. We use words every day when we speak, write, read, and listen. We begin learning words when we are very young and continue to gain knowledge of them throughout our lives. Learning words is a lifelong pursuit, one in which we hope not only to participate, but also to engage our students.

Estimates of the number of words that students encounter in their reading at school range from 50,000 to 100,000 (Graves & Watts-Taffe, 2002). Researchers report that as students progress through school, their reading vocabulary increases by approximately 3,000 to 5,000 words each year. This results in a reading vocabulary of nearly 25,000 words by the eighth grade and more than 50,000 words by the end of high school (Graves & Watts-Taffe, 2002). Harris and Hodges (1995) describe this ever-growing knowledge of words and their meanings as *vocabulary development*. They note that vocabulary development also refers to the teaching–learning processes that lead to such growth.

Words fill our lives:

They may seem simple like simple entities, but they are not. Their surface simplicity belies a deeper complexity. For example, they connect with experience and knowledge, and their meanings vary depending on the linguistic contexts in which they can be found. (Pearson, Hiebert, & Kamil, 2007, p. 286)

In this chapter, we learn about vocabulary, including how to teach it to our students. We begin by discussing the theoretical framework. Next, we study a variety of practical instructional approaches, including context clues, graphic organizers, and structural analysis. Then we use several strategy-related ideas to teach vocabulary in our content areas. Finally, we discuss several essential points that will guide our development of vocabulary lessons.

What Do We Know about Teaching Content Area Vocabulary?

The most important information we know about vocabulary can be easily summarized: If our students do not know the vocabulary, they will have difficulty comprehending what they are reading (Dixon-Krauss, 2001/2002; Duke, 2007; McLaughlin & Allen, 2002; National Reading Panel, 2000; Richek, 2005). This is especially true at levels of education beyond the middle grades (Rupley, Logan, & Nicholas, 1998/1999). As teachers, our goal is to help our students to continue to develop their vocabularies. We want them to know lots of words, understand many different concepts, use context clues, and have in-depth understandings (Brabham & Villaume, 2002).

Many of us can probably remember learning lists of words and their definitions and taking the dreaded Friday vocabulary quizzes. Such practices seemed to permeate our middle school and high school years. What makes this traditional practice seem misguided is that researchers now believe that studying words one at a time by writing definitions is not an effective way to learn vocabulary. As Blachowicz (2007) has noted, "Very few people learn from definitions. Definitions may refine our knowledge, but they do not give us our knowledge." Students need to do much more than write a word's definition to make the word part of their working vocabulary. They need to talk about words; feel comfortable using them when reading, speaking, and writing; and use them in a variety of contexts.

If we want our students to actively use content-related words, we need to motivate them to understand how words work. Graves and Watts-Taffe (2002) describe this process as "word consciousness —the awareness of and interest in learning and using new words and becoming more skillful and precise in word usage" (p. 144). This is an essential point: If we expect students to learn content area vocabulary, we need them to be interested—to be engaged in learning. We need to ensure that they are well motivated and help them see the connections between what they are learning and their everyday experiences. We need to remember that most of our students have had long vocabulary lists given to them since they were in the primary grades and that many are probably still working with such lists in their content area classrooms today. We need to make our enthusiasm for vocabulary evident to our students. We need to help them get excited about words and view vocabulary in new and engaging ways.

Making Connections | Thinking about Vocabulary

- Think about your vocabulary. Reflect on how it developed through the years. Consider two sources that you believe helped you to increase your knowledge of words and their meanings.

- Share your thoughts with others in small-group discussion.

Making Connections
TO MULTIPLE LITERACIES

Because it contributes to our understanding of what we read, vocabulary is an essential component of every literacy. For example, when we are discussing critical literacy, we must have an in-depth understanding of that term as well as those terms associated with reading from a critical stance— such as *alternative perspectives, juxtapositioning,* and *transformations.* When using information literacy and media literacy, we need to understand both those ideas and the other terms associated with them. Vocabulary is essential to our thinking and our understanding. ■

How Can We Integrate What We Know into Our Teaching?

Go to the Activities and Applications section under the topic *Developing Vocabulary, Concepts, and Fluency* in the MyEducationLab for your course and complete the activity entitled Assessing Content Vocabulary Knowledge to examine reasons students must understand content vocabulary to apply the concepts they are learning.

To integrate what we know about vocabulary into our teaching, we should begin by putting theory into practice. Blachowicz and Fisher (2000) suggest four guidelines for vocabulary instruction that emerged from their review of the existing research. They note that students should

- Be actively engaged in understanding words and related strategies.
- Personalize their vocabulary learning.
- Be immersed in words.
- Develop their vocabularies through repeated exposures from multiple sources of information.

Of course, these four guidelines have strong implications for us as teachers.

In order for our students to be actively engaged in understanding words and related strategies, we need to motivate them and teach them how to use vocabulary strategies. We can begin by helping our students to develop an interest in and make connections to our content areas, including the related vocabulary. We should also make sure that our students are well aware of our enthusiasm for learning. Insights from students' previous learning experiences are helpful as well. We can learn about our students' perceptions of their previous content learning by inviting them to write their Literacy Histories and complete Content Inventories (see Chapter 9). We can also work to make our content areas appealing to the students by integrating creative and innovative practices as well as alternative modes of response, such as sketching.

When selecting vocabulary strategies to teach to our students, we can choose those that are interesting and work particularly well. We can also use a scaffolded approach when teaching such strategies. This means that we offer a great deal of support to our students when we begin teaching vocabulary strategies, but gradually decrease that level of support as students become more proficient in using the information we are teaching. For example, if we use the five-step Guided Comprehension explicit instruction process—explain, demonstrate, guide, practice, and reflect—we offer total support in the *explain* part of the process, as we provide the details of the strategy and how it works. When we *demonstrate*, we still offer a great deal of support, but we also use a think-aloud to share our thought processes with our students. Next, we *guide* students to work with partners as they attempt to use what we have just taught. In the *practice* part of the process, students use what we taught on their own. Finally, we and the students reflect on what we learned and how it will benefit our vocabulary development.

Making Connections
TO WRITING

Writing plays an important role in learning vocabulary. We use writing when we learn about words through strategies such as Semantic Maps and Concept of Definition Maps. We use the vocabulary we learn when we write for a variety of purposes, ranging from informal responses to long-term projects. Using the words in multiple formats and settings helps us to increase our vocabulary. ■

We know our students can learn vocabulary through explicit instruction and the use of context clues; but they can also learn vocabulary incidentally. When students learn new words and expand their understanding of words they already know by reading widely, having an extensive variety of experiences, engaging in discussion, and using technology, they are learning incidentally. As teachers, we can contribute to this incidental learning by creating informal opportunities to help students expand their vocabularies. For example, we can provide a rich context for learning, promote discussion, focus on multiple exposures to words, have a variety of reading materials available in the classroom, and use technology as an integral part of the teaching and learning process. Researchers acknowledge the importance of incidental word learning in students' general vocabulary development (Blachowicz, Fisher, Ogle, & Watts-Taffe, 2006).

Beyond opportunities for incidental learning, we can teach vocabulary through context clues and explicit instruction. Both of these approaches have been found to be effective, and research reports that using such strategies contributes to students' reading comprehension (Blachowicz & Fisher, 2000; National Reading Panel, 2000).

Making Connections
TO ENGLISH LEARNERS

When teaching vocabulary to English learners through explicit instruction, we can use pictures to scaffold students' learning. We should also encourage students to respond to the vocabulary words they are learning through alternative modes such as sketching. ■

Balancing Teaching And Context

When teaching vocabulary, explicit instruction and learning from context should be balanced. The instruction should be meaningful to students, include words from students' reading, and focus on a variety of strategies for determining the meanings of unfamiliar words. Two other important aspects of such teaching are making connections between the vocabulary and students' background knowledge and providing students with multiple exposures to words. In our study of approaches to teaching vocabulary, we will explore context clues, graphic organizers, structural analysis, and student self-selection.

CONTEXT CLUES. Context Clues help readers to become independent word learners. Readers use Context Clues to figure out the meaning of unknown words they encounter in text. For example, if we were to encounter the isolated word "pheffendorfer," we more than likely would not know what it means. If we encountered the word in context, however, we might easily determine its meaning. Consider the following scenario:

> *Before we started watching the movie at home, we decided to prepare some snacks. Bob poured the soda, while I put a popcorn packet in the <u>pheffendorfer</u> and waited for it to pop.*

At this point, we may guess that a pheffendorfer is a microwave oven, and in the context provided, we would be absolutely correct. In determining our response, we probably used the logic Context Clue. After reading the words surrounding the unknown word, we determined that the pheffendorfer provided a way to make popcorn. In our society, the appliance that usually performs this task is a microwave. So, even though "pheffendorfer" is not a real word, given the context, it means "microwave."

In our examination of "pheffendorfer," we used the logic clue. We often use more than one type of clue to determine a word's meaning. The types of Context Clues include the following:

■ **DEFINITION CLUE:** connects the unknown word to a known word or words.

Example: Mitosis is a process in which a cell's nucleus replicates and divides in preparation for division of the cell.

■ **EXAMPLE/ILLUSTRATION CLUE:** provides a model or picture that shows the meaning of the word.

Example: The distance around a circle is its circumference, but, as seen in the figure, the diameter is the measure across the midsection of the circle.

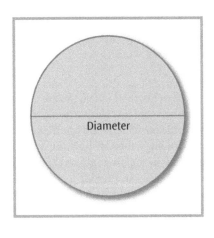

■ **COMPARISON/CONTRAST CLUE:** provides information about something similar or something different from the unknown word.

Example: The square and the right triangle are both geometric figures, but the square has four interior right (90-degree) angles and the right triangle has only one.

■ **LOGIC CLUE:** provides a common-sense/contextual connection to the unknown word.

Example: When Tim collapsed from cardiac arrest, we grabbed the defibrillator and used it to restore the heart to a regular rhythm.

■ **CAUSE/EFFECT CLUE:** the reason/result relation allows the reader to predict the word's meaning.

Example: When the rain got heavy, it caused the car to hydroplane.

■ **MOOD/TONE CLUE:** description of the mood related to the word allows readers to predict the word's meaning.

Example: A feeling of despondency *overwhelmed him as he floated alone in the dark sea and watched the search helicopters fly away.*

To teach your students how to use Context Clues, follow these steps:

1 **Explain:** When we use Context Clues, we use the words surrounding the unknown word to try to determine the word's meaning. Then explain the eight types of Context Clues and provide examples of each.

2 **Demonstrate:** Use a read-aloud and a think-aloud to determine the meaning of an unfamiliar word in the text. The think-aloud should demonstrate the most effective clues based on the context of the sentence. Remember that readers often need to use more than one type of clue to determine the meaning of the unknown word. When the word's meaning has been determined, refine the meaning by using a dictionary.

3 **Guide:** Support students as they work with partners to find unknown words in the texts they are reading and use context clues to figure out the meanings. Monitor as students search for words, making suggestions as they use Context Clues to discover the meanings of unknown words. Visit the pages on which the words appear in context and discuss the students' suggested meanings. Discuss the type of Context Clues the students used and verify with a dictionary as needed.

4 **Practice:** Encourage students to read and use selected segments of text and use Context Clues to determine the meanings of unknown words.

5 **Reflect:** Encourage students to reflect on how Context Clues help us understand what we read. Discuss using Context Clues with students. Remind the students that if the context does not provide enough information, there are other strategies for figuring out the meaning of the unknown word.

Go to the Activities and Applications section under the topic *Developing Vocabulary, Concepts, and Fluency* in the MyEducationLab for your course and complete the activity entitled Intentional Vocabulary Instruction to consider the benefit of introducing new words in context.

TEACHING IDEA   **GRAPHIC ORGANIZERS.** Graphic organizers are visual representations of ideas. Using graphic organizers to teach vocabulary has several benefits. First, the visual design helps students to better remember the types of information associated with the term. Second, completing the organizers in a whole-class or small-group setting promotes discussion of the word or concept. Third, completed organizers contain information about the word that students can use to create oral or written summaries.

Semantic Maps, Semantic Question Maps, Concept of Definition Maps, and Semantic Feature Analysis Charts are graphic organizers that were designed to help students learn vocabulary. Of course, before using these graphics, we need to be able to complete them on our own.

Making Connections
TO ENGLISH LEARNERS

When using graphic organizers to teach vocabulary to English learners, number the sections of the organizer to help students focus on the point of learning or discussion. As an alternative, sections of the organizer can be highlighted in different colors. See Appendix A for copies of the graphic organizers discussed in this section. ■

SEMANTIC MAP. The Semantic Map (Johnson & Pearson, 1984) was developed to help students activate prior knowledge and organize knowledge about a specific topic. This type of map has a free form in that its design depends on students' responses. It is often used before reading and revisited during and after reading. For a step-by-step approach to teaching Semantic Maps, see Chapter 5.

We usually use Semantic Maps before students read the text to introduce concepts and assess students' background knowledge. For example, if we were about to teach a concept in mathematics, science, or history, we might use a Semantic Map to gain an understanding of what students know—what background knowledge they have—about that topic. Because all students contribute to the map, it is easy to discern which students have previous understanding of the topic and which do not. The results can provide us with a starting point for our teaching. We often revisit Semantic Maps after reading to add more information and create summaries based on the maps.

When students in a world history class focused on the term *World War II*, they developed the Semantic Map in Figure 8.1. In science class, students reviewed their understanding of the focus word *biology* as they prepared for a test. See Figure 8.2 for the map these students created. For an example of a Semantic Map based on geometry, see Chapter 5.

SEMANTIC QUESTION MAP. The Semantic Question Map (McLaughlin, 2003) is a variation on the Semantic Map, but its general design is fixed (see Appendix A for a reproducible organizer). The focus word is placed in an oval, and then several questions about it are raised. The questions, which may be provided by the teacher or generated by the students, are placed inside the ovals that extend from the oval containing the focus word.

We use Semantic Question Maps when we want students to focus on particular aspects of a topic. Rather than leaving the shape of the map to be determined by student responses, we provide the structure, which usually includes three or four questions. To teach your students how to use Semantic Question Maps, follow these steps:

1 **Explain:** Begin by explaining the strategy of Previewing and describing how to use a Semantic Question Map. For example, you might say, "Previewing is a comprehension strategy that includes activating background knowledge, setting purposes for reading, and predicting what will come next, based on what we have already read. Completing these Maps involves brainstorming responses to three or four questions about a selected topic. We

Go to the Activities and Applications section under the topic *Developing Vocabulary, Concepts, and Fluency* in the MyEducationLab for your course and complete the activity entitled Vocabulary and Content Area Learning to examine steps teachers can take to help English learners understand content specific vocabulary.

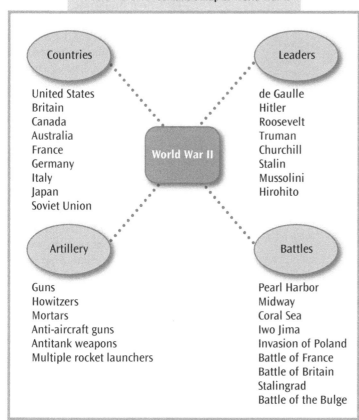

FIGURE 8.1 Semantic Map of World War II

Countries

United States
Britain
Canada
Australia
France
Germany
Italy
Japan
Soviet Union

World War II

Leaders

de Gaulle
Hitler
Roosevelt
Truman
Churchill
Stalin
Mussolini
Hirohito

Artillery

Guns
Howitzers
Mortars
Anti-aircraft guns
Antitank weapons
Multiple rocket launchers

Battles

Pearl Harbor
Midway
Coral Sea
Iwo Jima
Invasion of Poland
Battle of France
Battle of Britain
Stalingrad
Battle of the Bulge

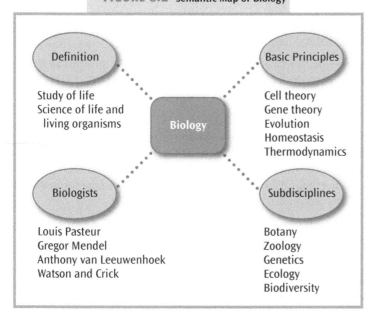

FIGURE 8.2 Semantic Map of Biology

Definition

Study of life
Science of life and
living organisms

Biology

Basic Principles

Cell theory
Gene theory
Evolution
Homeostasis
Thermodynamics

Biologists

Louis Pasteur
Gregor Mendel
Anthony van Leeuwenhoek
Watson and Crick

Subdisciplines

Botany
Zoology
Genetics
Ecology
Biodiversity

usually respond to the Semantic Question Map before reading a text, and revisit the map to verify our responses after reading."

2 **Demonstrate:** Begin the demonstration by choosing a focus word and writing it on a chart, chalkboard, or computer screen. Draw an oval around it. For example, in Figure 8.3, the focus word is *physics*. Then think aloud about that word. For example, you could say, "The focus word for this Semantic Question Map is 'physics,' so now I need to think of three or four questions about 'Physics' that need to be answered." Then you might say, "I have thought about the questions and I want them to relate to motion, velocity, acceleration, and speed. I think I will add these three questions to the map: *What are the rates that describe motion? In what ways can we describe relations such as velocity and acceleration? What is the difference between speed and velocity?*" Then write the questions on the map and use lines to attach the ovals containing the questions to the focus word. Next, offer a response to the first question. For example, you might say, "I know that speed is one of the rates that describes motion, so I am going to add *speed* under the first question." Next, ask students to brainstorm other rates that describe motion. If they suggest *velocity* and *acceleration*, add them underneath *speed* on the Semantic Question Map.

3 **Guide:** Guide students to work with partners to respond to the next two questions. In response to question 2, "In what ways can we describe relationships such as velocity and acceleration?", they might suggest *equations, tables,* and *graphs.* In response to question 3, "What is the difference between speed and velocity?", they might suggest that speed is *how fast an object moves* and velocity is *how fast AND in which direction an object moves.* Then read aloud the section of the text that addresses these topics and discuss it with the students. Make connections to the Semantic Question Map and confirm that the text verifies your responses.

4 **Practice:** Invite students to practice by responding individually to a Semantic Question Map about the next topic of study. Provide the Maps and ask students to write their responses, read the related text, and revise their answers as necessary. Then discuss the completed Semantic Question Maps.

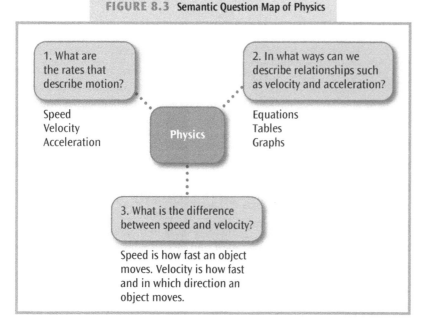

FIGURE 8.3 Semantic Question Map of Physics

1. What are the rates that describe motion?

Speed
Velocity
Acceleration

Physics

2. In what ways can we describe relationships such as velocity and acceleration?

Equations
Tables
Graphs

3. What is the difference between speed and velocity?

Speed is how fast an object moves. Velocity is how fast and in which direction an object moves.

5 **Reflect:** Reflect on how Semantic Question Maps are similar to Semantic Maps: Both help us preview the text, but the Semantic Question Maps raise specific issues. The Semantic Question Maps help to focus students' thinking. Also reflect on how we can use Semantic Question Maps when reading text in other content areas.

Semantic Question Maps help students to focus on responding to preset queries about the topic. Their responses provide information about their background knowledge and a starting point for teaching. After reading, we can revisit the Semantic Question Map and summarize the information. The questions also provide direction for that process.

TEACHING IDEA

CONCEPT OF DEFINITION MAP. The Concept of Definition Map (Schwartz & Raphael, 1985) is designed to help students construct meaning by making connections between their prior knowledge and new topics. It provides information such as a definition, a description, and examples. This graphic may be used before, during, and after reading. When the map is completed, the class should create a Concept of Definition Map Summary. When teaching summarizing, we usually ask students to extract important information from the text. Students, however, often struggle in determining which information is important. The completed Concept of Definition Map contains only important information. Therefore, creating a summary based on the Concept of Definition Map provides students with the opportunity to use the important information. In the process, students can learn that the important information includes the components of the Map: the definition, description, examples, and comparison.

To teach your students how to use Concept of Definition Maps, follow these steps:

1 **Explain:** Vocabulary helps us to understand what we read and the Concept of Definition Map is a graphic organizer that can help us to learn vocabulary.

2 **Demonstrate:** Use a think-aloud and a graphic organizer. Select or ask students to select a focus word to be explored. Write the focus word in the oval in the center of the Map. Think aloud to determine the broad category that best describes the word. Write the response in the "What is it?" box. Return to the focus word.

3 **Guide:** Guide students to work with partners to determine responses to the next question on the Concept of Definition Map: What's it like? Discuss the responses with the students and choose three to include on the map. Return to the focus word. Continue this process with the next question on the map: What are some examples? Return to the focus word. Then discuss possible comparisons for the focus word.

4 **Practice:** Encourage the students to read a related text and revisit and revise the Concept of Definition Map as necessary. Then invite the students to use the map to write Concept of Definition Map Summaries. Discuss the summaries.

5 **Reflect:** Encourage students to reflect on how Concept of Definition Maps help us to understand words and summarize our thinking. Discuss how we can use these maps in other content areas.

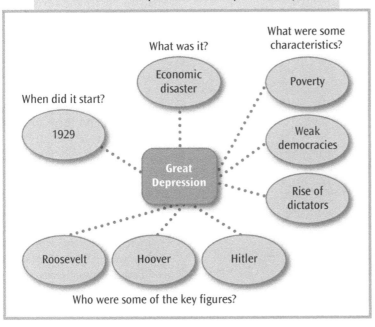

FIGURE 8.4 Concept of Definition Map of Great Depression

What was it?

What were some characteristics?

When did it start?

Economic disaster

Poverty

1929

Weak democracies

Great Depression

Rise of dictators

Roosevelt

Hoover

Hitler

Who were some of the key figures?

Note the following points:

- It is not always possible to determine a suitable comparison for the "A Comparison" section. If this is the case, eliminate that section of the graphic.

- Depending on the topic and the text being read, "What are some examples?" may not be the best question to ask in that section of the graphic. Changing the question to one that is more appropriate for the topic being studied is appropriate.

The Concept of Definition Map and Concept of Definition Map Summary shown in Figure 8.4 were created in a history class while studying the Great Depression.

A Concept of Definition Map about algebraic properties is featured in Figure 8.5. Notice that the comparison section is missing. As noted earlier, we can remove that section if there is no suitable comparison.

We can use the Concept of Definition Map for several purposes, including introducing a concept, sparking discussion, and summarizing. When a completed map is used as the basis of an oral or written summary, it is easier for students to summarize informational text. Instead of needing to extract essential information from the text, they simply use the information on the completed map. While using the Concept of Definition Map for this purpose, the students also learn what constitutes essential information from reading the categories on the map: What is it? How would you describe it? What are three examples? What is a comparison?

 **TEACHING IDEA**

SEMANTIC FEATURE ANALYSIS CHART. The Semantic Feature Analysis Chart (Johnson & Pearson, 1984) is a graphic organizer that helps students make predictions about attributes related to specific words, sort by characteristics, and set a purpose for reading or researching. It is often used before and after reading informational text, but it can also be adapted for use with narrative or story text by replacing the categories with characters' names and listing attributes that characters may or may not possess. We can also cross-match a variety of genres in the category section with various attributes of those genres in the characteristics section.

To teach students how to use the Semantic Feature Analysis Chart, follow these steps:

1 **Explain:** Describe how the Semantic Feature Analysis Chart helps us to monitor our thinking and learn about words. Then explain how the chart matches categories and characteristics to provide information.

2 **Demonstrate:** Use a read-aloud and a think-aloud. Select a topic and some words or categories that relate to that topic. List the words or categories in the far left column of the Semantic Feature Analysis Chart. Choose characteristics that relate to one or more of the related words. List those across the top row of the chart. Share the Chart with the students. Make predictions about which categories will have the first characteristic. Place a plus sign (+) in the box if the characteristic fits the category; place a minus sign (−) in the box if the characteristic does not fit the category. Place a question mark (?) in the space provided if you are not sure of the response.

3 **Guide:** Guide students to work with partners in completing the chart, using the symbols you demonstrated. Then read a text that contains information about the categories and characteristics. Discuss the text and the charts with the students. Guide the students

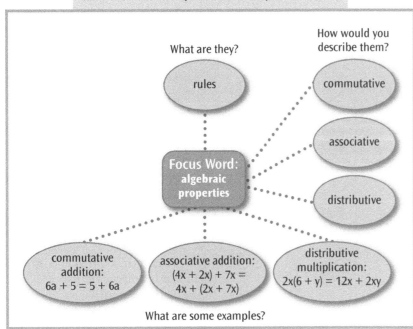

FIGURE 8.5 **Concept of Definition Map of Derivatives**

What are they?

How would you describe them?

rules

commutative

associative

distributive

Focus Word: **algebraic properties**

commutative addition:
$6a + 5 = 5 + 6a$

associative addition:
$(4x + 2x) + 7x = 4x + (2x + 7x)$

distributive multiplication:
$2x(6 + y) = 12x + 2xy$

What are some examples?

to revisit their Semantic Feature Analysis Charts and revise them as necessary.

4 **Practice:** Provide another Semantic Feature Analysis Chart and encourage students to complete it. Provide a related text for the students to read. Remind them to revise their charts as necessary based on what they read. Discuss the text and the revised charts.

5 **Reflect:** Encourage students to reflect on how Semantic Feature Analysis Charts help us to understand words and how we might use these charts in other content areas.

Students in science class used the Semantic Feature Analysis Chart featured in Figure 8.6 to analyze various life forms. As this example suggests, we use the Semantic Feature Analysis Chart when we want to compare and contrast the characteristics or qualities of multiple items or types of people. We use this chart before the students read to activate background knowledge and after they read to add information and/or draw conclusions.

Although research views graphic organizers as being highly effective in the teaching of vocabulary, there are other viable approaches. These techniques include structural analysis, which encourages the reader to examine small parts of a word to help determine its meaning.

Structural Analysis

When studying vocabulary, understanding the words and their meanings is our ultimate goal. Structural analysis contributes to that understanding. Knowing how to analyze a word's structure—its prefixes, roots, and suffixes—helps us to not only recognize the word, but also determine its meaning when we read.

Characteristics Categories	Hair/fur	Lay eggs	Warm-blooded	Care for young	Live in water	Breathe air	Have gills
Fish							
Birds							
Mammals							
Amphibians							
Reptiles							
Insects							

+ = yes   — = no   ? = don't know

FIGURE 8.6
Semantic Feature Analysis Chart

Prefixes, word roots, and suffixes are three types of word parts. *Pre* means "before" and *suf* means "after," so it makes sense that prefixes are added *before* the word root and suffixes are added *after* the root. Most words have at least one word root, and many have one or more prefix and suffix. Word roots are the main part of the word, so they are typically found after prefixes and before suffixes. Structural analysis refers to the process of examining each part of the word in an attempt to determine the word's meaning. The word root often provides the general meaning, while the prefixes and suffixes refine that meaning in that particular form of the word.

Knowing how to use structural analysis helps us determine words' meanings. For example, in the word "unhappiness," *happy* is the word root. We might define it as "joyful" or "glad", but when we add the prefix *un*, the word means the total opposite. When we add the suffix *ness*, the literal meaning of "unhappiness" becomes "the condition of not being happy." Similarly, *bio* is a word root that means "life"; *ology* is a suffix that means "study of." Therefore, *biology* is the "study of life." The better our students understand word roots, prefixes, and suffixes, the easier it will be for them to analyze the structure of words.

WORD ROOTS. The root is the main part of a word. There are usually many words derived from a single root. *Root mapping* provides an overview of a word root and the various words that are derived from it. In this technique, a root is selected to be the focus of the map. Then words containing that root are added at the end of branches that connect to the root. As the map is completed, it has the potential to continue growing, because as each new word is added, other words may branch from it. The following are examples of roots: *bio* (life), *chromo* (color), *psycho* (mind), *thermo* (heat), *zoo* (animal). A more extensive list of common word roots is presented in Figure 8.7.

FIGURE 8.7
Word Roots

Root	Meaning	Example
anthropo	*man*	anthropology
astro	*star*	astronaut
bio	*life*	biology
cardio	*heart*	cardiac
cede	*go*	precede
chromo	*color*	chromatology
demos	*people*	democracy
derma	*skin*	epidermis
dyna	*power*	dynamic
geo	*earth*	geology
helio	*sun*	heliocentric
hydro	*water*	hydroponics
hypno	*sleep*	hypnosis
ject	*throw*	eject
magni	*great, big*	magnify
man(u)	*hand*	manuscript
mono	*one*	monoplane
ortho	*straight*	orthodox
pod	*foot*	podiatrist
psycho	*mind*	psychology
pyro	*fire*	pyromania
script	*write*	manuscript
terra	*earth*	terrace
thermo	*heat*	thermometer
zoo	*animal*	zoology

PREFIXES. A prefix is a type of affix that involves adding a syllable or letter(s) to the beginning of a word to change its meaning or part of speech. According to *The Literacy Dictionary*, a prefix is "an affix attached before a base word or root, as *re-* in *reprint*" (Harris & Hodges, 1995, p. 192). Working with prefixes helps students to understand the structure of words. The following are examples of prefixes: *ad-* (to, toward), *ante-* (before), *anti-* (against), *extra-* (beyond), *micro-* (small). A more detailed list of prefixes appears in Figure 8.8.

FIGURE 8.8
Prefixes

Prefix	Meaning	Example
ab-, abs-, a-	*from, away*	abstain
ad-	*to, toward*	addict
ambi-	*both*	ambidextrous
ante-	*before*	antecedent
anti-	*against*	antifreeze
auto-	*self*	autobiography
be-	*near, about*	beside
bene-	*well, good*	benefactor
bi-	*two*	bimonthly
cata-	*below*	catacomb
centi-	*hundred*	centimeter
circum-	*around*	circumnavigate
con-	*with*	concert
contra-	*against*	contraband
de-	*from, down*	depress
deci-	*ten*	decimeter
di-	*two*	diameter
dia-	*through*	diagram
dis-	*opposite*	disrespect
dys-	*bad*	dysfunctional
en-, em-	*cause to*	encode
epi-	*upon*	epidermis
ex-	*out, from*	excavate
extra-	*beyond*	extracurricular
for-	*off, to the uttermost*	forward
fore-	*before*	forecast
hetero-	*different*	heterogeneous
hyper-	*beyond, excess*	hyperactive
hypo-	*too little, under*	hypoactive
in-, il-, im-, ir-	*not*	immature
in-, im-	*in*	infringe
inter-	*between*	interstate
intra-	*within*	intramurals
intro-	*within*	introspection
juxta-	*near*	juxtapose
macro-	*large*	macrobiology
meta-	*beyond, denoting change*	metamorphosis
micro-	*small*	microbiology
mid-	*middle*	midway
milli-	*thousand*	millipede

mis-	*bad*	misbehave
mono-	*single*	monotone
nano-	*billion*	nanosecond
neo-	*new*	neoclassical
non-	*not, opposite from*	nonviolent
omni-	*all*	omnipotent
out-	*beyond, more than*	outlaw
over-	*too much*	overcompensate
pan-	*all*	panoramic
para-	*side by side, near*	paraphrase
per-	*throughout*	pervade
peri-	*all around*	periscope
poly-	*many*	polygon
post-	*after*	postpone
pre-	*before*	predetermine
pro-	*forward*	progress
prot-	*first*	prototype
re-	*again*	reappear
retro-	*back*	retrograde
semi-	*half, partly*	semicircle
sub-	*under*	submarine
super-	*more than*	supermarket
syn-, sym-	*together*	symbol
trans-	*across*	transatlantic
ultra-	*beyond, extremely*	ultraconservative
un-	*not*	unwilling
with-	*against*	withhold

SUFFIXES. A suffix is a type of affix that involves adding a syllable or group of letters to the end of the word to change its meaning or part of speech. Specifically, according to *The Literacy Dictionary*, a suffix is "an affix attached to the end of a base, root, or stem that changes the meaning or grammatical function of the word" (Harris & Hodges, 1995, p. 246). Working with suffixes helps students to understand the structure of words. The following are examples of suffixes: *-able* (can be done), *-un* (not), *-ic* (relating to), *-ist* (one who practices), *-ology* (study of). Figure 8.9 contains a more extensive list of suffixes.

Making Connections
TO STRUGGLING READERS

When teaching prefixes, suffixes, and roots that pertain to our content areas, we should work with other teachers to develop a list of word parts that will benefit students across the curriculum. Once the list has been created, we can display the affixes and roots in a "word wall" format that includes meanings and example words. We can also color-code the affixes and roots that appear in the sample words. ■

Student Self-Selection

Using context clues, graphic organizers, and structural analysis will help students to develop their vocabularies, but using Vocabulary Bookmarks and the Vocabulary Self-Collection Strategy will

Suffix	Meaning	Example
-able, -ible	*can be done*	comfortable
-al, -ial	*relating to*	personal
-arium	*place of*	solarium
-ation, -ition, -ion, -tion	*act, process of*	animation
-dom	*quality/state*	freedom
-ed	*past tense for verbs*	voted
-en	*made of*	wooden
-er, est	*comparative*	harder
-er	*one who*	dancer
-ful	*full of*	hopeful
-ic	*relating to*	characteristic
-ile	*quality/state*	juvenile
-ing	*present participle*	hopping
-ism	*quality/state*	fanaticism
-ist	*one who practices*	zoologist
-ity, -ty	*state of*	infinity
-ive, -itive, -ative	*adjective form of a noun*	quantitative
-less	*without*	homeless
-ly	*characteristic of*	happily
-ment	*action or process*	excitement
-ness	*condition of*	sadness
-ology	*study of*	biology
-ous, -eous, -ious	*quality, state*	joyous
-s, -es	*more than one*	desks
-tion	*quality, state*	preservation
-ular	*relating to*	cellular
-y	*characterized by*	jumpy

FIGURE 8.9
Suffixes

help them take ownership of their learning. Both of these approaches invite students to select the vocabulary they would like to learn. This flexibility motivates students to choose meaningful, challenging words and promotes wonderfully rich discussion.

TEACHING IDEA

VOCABULARY BOOKMARK. Vocabulary Bookmarks (McLaughlin, 2003) are designed to motivate students to monitor their understanding and learn new words. When students use Vocabulary Bookmarks, they are able to choose a word from assigned class readings. This should be a word the student thinks the whole class needs to discuss.

When the student chooses such a word, she completes a Vocabulary Bookmark. The student writes three pieces of information on the Bookmark: (1) the word, (2) what she thinks the word means, and (3) the page number on which she found the word. Students enjoy choosing these vocabulary words, the resulting class discussion is rich and meaningful, and the whole class learns a wide variety of meaningful terms. During the class discussion, students introduce their words, explain what they think the word means, and tell the class where they found the word. Then they read the word in the context in which it appears and discuss the suggested meaning as well as their insights. A dictionary can be used after discussion to verify the meaning of the word. Finally, students discuss how they can use the new word and determine whether they want to add it to the word wall.

FIGURE 8.10
Vocabulary Bookmark Technique
Physics—Newton's First Law of Motion

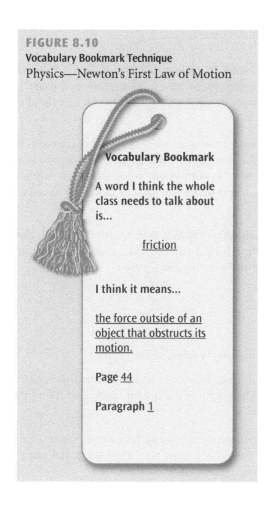

Vocabulary Bookmark

A word I think the whole class needs to talk about is...

friction

I think it means...

the force outside of an object that obstructs its motion.

Page 44

Paragraph 1

To teach your students how to use Vocabulary Bookmark Technique, follow these steps:

1 Explain: Begin by explaining that the Vocabulary Bookmark Technique helps us monitor our understanding of text. When using Vocabulary Bookmarks, students choose a word they think the whole class should discuss. Then they write three pieces of information on the Vocabulary Bookmark: (1) the word, (2) what they think the word means, and (3) the page number on which they found the word. Explain that the words are then used during class discussions of the reading.

2 Demonstrate: Begin demonstrating by distributing the blackline for Vocabulary Bookmark Technique (see the Appendix for the graphic organizer). Introduce the text and demonstrate what monitoring is and how Vocabulary Bookmark Technique can help us monitor our understanding. Think aloud as you complete the Vocabulary Bookmark. For example, you might say:

> Our assigned reading for homework last night was about whales. While I was reading, I came across a word I think we should all discuss. It is *echolocation.* So, I am going to write *echolocation* on my Vocabulary Bookmark. I noticed it is on page 243, so I will write that in the space for the page number. Next, I am supposed to write what I think *echolocation* means. I think it means that whales can locate things using echos from sounds they make, so I am going to write that on the bookmark. Then I am going to write that I think dolphins and bats can also use *echolocation.*

Then demonstrate how to use the page number to find the word in context. Discuss the term with the students, and verify your thinking by checking a dictionary.

3 Guide: Guide students to work with partners to find a vocabulary word in the assigned reading that they think the whole class should discuss. For example, some of their choices might be *migration, intimidating, hierarchy,* and *invertebrate.* Ask students to record the page numbers on which the words appear and what they think each word means. Then discuss their word choices and the related information provided. While discussing words such as *hierarchy* and *invertebrate* for example, you might consult a dictionary to verify detailed meanings students suggest. Similarly, if it seems students' definitions of words are not clear, you might also consult a dictionary to clarify.

4 Practice: Encourage students to practice the Vocabulary Bookmark Technique by working individually to find words in the next section of the text. After they have completed the Bookmarks, discuss the words and verify their thinking by checking with a dictionary.

5 Reflect: Invite students to reflect on what they know about monitoring and how they can use the Vocabulary Bookmark Technique in other aspects of their content area learning.

Figure 8.10 features a Vocabulary Bookmark about friction completed in physics class. Vocabulary Bookmarking is one aspect of the Bookmark Technique, detailed in Chapter 5.

 **TEACHING IDEA** VOCABULARY SELF-COLLECTION STRATEGY. The Vocabulary Self-Collection Strategy (VSS) (Haggard, 1986) was created to encourage students' interest in vocabulary. Although it is most often used with informational text, this technique can also be used with literature.

To teach your students how to use VSS, follow these steps:

1 **Explain:** The VSS is a process that motivates us to learn about words we think are important. Explain that when we are reading, we select a word that we would like to learn more about, provide information about it, and nominate it for a place on the class vocabulary list.

2 **Demonstrate:** Model the VSS by reading a selection and choosing a word you would like to learn more about. Share the word with the class by writing it on the board, an overhead transparency, or a chart. Then discuss the word in context, including where it was found in the text, what you think the word means, and where you think it should be placed on the class vocabulary list.

3 **Guide:** Guide students to read a text and engage in VSS. Ask students to select words they would like to learn more about from a previously read text. You should also choose a word. Invite the students to share the words and the following information:

- The word in context
- Where it was found in the text
- What they think the word means
- Why they think the word should be on the class vocabulary list

Accept all nominations and record them on a chart, overhead, or chalkboard. Encourage more discussion about each word. Then narrow the list for study and refine the definitions.

4 **Practice:** Encourage students to record their final word lists and definitions in their vocabulary journals or content area notebook. Remember when planning lessons and assignments to include the words to reinforce meanings and use.

5 **Reflect:** Invite students to reflect on how selecting vocabulary words motivates us to learn and to think about how this process is different from being assigned long lists of vocabulary words to define. Then reflect on how we can use the VSS in other content areas.

Whether using Vocabulary Bookmarks or the VSS, students never seem to tire of self-selecting vocabulary. They choose wonderfully exciting and complex words and enthusiastically vie to report the details of their selections. Following discussions, they are quick to use *their* words in all modes of communication. Self-selecting vocabulary is a highly motivational, vocabulary-enriching strategy.

Making Connections
TO STUDY SKILLS

To help students study and remember vocabulary they have self-selected or learned through other methods, we can encourage them to create personal word walls or vocabulary cards. A personal word wall can be as simple as an alphabetical list of words and their meanings on a manila folder that the students can transport to classes and home or a list maintained electronically on students' computers. Vocabulary cards usually have the word printed on one side and the definition and sentence using the word on the other side. Maintaining these study aides electronically is often highly motivational for students. ■

When Using These Ideas to Teach Vocabulary, What General Principles Should We Follow?

There are several general guidelines we can follow to ensure that our vocabulary instruction is effective:

1. *Our teaching should demonstrate that we have great interest in and excitement for vocabulary.* We know from experience that such enthusiasm is contagious and will motivate our students to expand their vocabularies.

2. *Our lessons should encourage students to make connections between their personal experiences and content area vocabulary.* For example, students may read about different legal cases that used DNA analyses to prove guilt or innocence before they encounter the detailed role of DNA in biology class.

3. *We should encourage students to understand that some words have multiple meanings in the content areas.* For example, students may know what the word "plot" means when they are reading a story, but they may not be aware of its meaning in mathematics when we "plot a point on a graph."

4. *Our teaching should incorporate multiple exposures to words, so students may become familiar with them and not view them as "words on a list" to be studied and forgotten, but rather as keys to engaging in higher-order thinking.*

5. *In our lessons, students should have opportunities to use content area vocabulary in multiple, meaningful ways.* This practice encourages students to take ownership of the vocabulary terms—to use them in conversation, in their writing, and in various performance projects.

6. *We should teach structural analysis as it relates to terms in our content area, so our students can learn how to analyze words they may encounter.*

7. *Our lessons should focus on **depth** rather than **coverage** of content area vocabulary.* This means that we should teach our students a reasonable number of terms in depth, rather than presenting a large number of words at a surface level. If we are required to teach a list of essential terms that appears to be somewhat extensive, we should consider using a vocabulary wall or having the students maintain electronic vocabulary notebooks to ensure that they have access to the words and their meanings as they engage in learning.

8. *We should use multiple texts in our teaching, so students will be aware of the multiple resources that address the topic they are studying.* Of course, these resources should include both print and electronic texts.

9. *Our lessons should reflect that although the vocabulary teaching ideas are effective, we may need to adapt them for our teaching.* For example, the Concept of Definition Map is a wonderfully effective graphic organizer, but we may want to use it to teach an idea that will not work well with the Concept of Definition Map's published format. For example, Figure 8.4 features a Concept of Definition Map about the Great Depression in which the teacher has kept the format of the Concept of Definition Map, but changed the labels on three of the categories. On the left side, where the original map asked for a comparison, this teacher asked when the Great Depression began. On the right side, where the map usually asks for three descriptive words, the teacher asked the students to list some of the characteristics of the Great Depression. Finally, at the bottom, where the original format asks for three examples, this history teacher asked the students to name some of the key players during the time of the Great Depression. In this example, the teacher adapted an effective teaching idea to the needs of his lesson, in which, of course, he was using a particular text.

10. *We should work with colleagues to ensure that we support students' use of vocabulary across the curriculum.*

FINAL THOUGHTS

As teachers, we have a lot to consider when we teach vocabulary. We want our students to increase their knowledge of words. We also want our students to actively engage with new vocabulary and use it freely when they read, write, speak, and listen.

In the end, it is important to remember that the most effective vocabulary instruction is the kind that improves comprehension. This relation or connection is especially important in the content areas, where the concepts students learn often become the basis for future learning. To accomplish this goal, our teaching must be motivational and our methods must be engaging.

Teaching Connections

APPLYING WHAT WE HAVE LEARNED

E-Links

Many websites provide lists of terms and definitions associated with the content areas. Examples are listed below. Visit two of these sites and complete the following tasks:

1. Note the website title and address. Reflect on all that you have learned about teaching vocabulary. Then critique the quality of the website's vocabulary list(s) and the suggestion(s) for teaching or learning it. Explain how you would teach such terms. Justify your response.
2. Choose 3 terms generally taught in your content area and demonstrate how you would use graphic organizers to teach them.

EXAMPLE WEBSITES

Languages
French Language
http://french.about.com/od/vocabulary/French_Vocabulary_Lessons_Lists.htm

Spanish Vocabulary
http://spanishvocabulary.ca

Mathematics
Mathword: Terms and Formulas from Beginning Algebra to Calculus
http://math.com/school/glossary/glossindex.html

Science
Science Academic Vocabulary—Biology I (also available for Chemistry, Physics, Ecology, and Anatomy/Physiology)
http://mnps.org/Page22565.aspx

Accountable Talk

As content area teachers of the 21st century, we have come a long way from the time when our learning consisted of writing long lists of vocabulary words and their definitions. Reflect on (1) how you will use more innovative practices, such as context clues, graphic organizers, structural analysis, and self-selection strategies in your subject area; and (2) how you will promote such teaching ideas among fellow faculty members, who may teach from a more traditional perspective. Share your thoughts in small groups.

 ## Portfolio/Performance Opportunity

When using the ideas presented in this chapter to teach vocabulary, we need to have models to share with our classes. Develop an electronic vocabulary resource file for your teaching by completing a model of each of the teaching ideas. Discuss your completed models in small groups. Provide feedback for peers and receive feedback for your work. Revise the models as necessary. Discuss how peer input influenced the final models. Email your completed project to your professor.

9

Organizing for Teaching and Learning

O rganizing for learning is an integral part of teaching. It demonstrates our understanding that teaching is about more than knowing the content. It involves a number of factors, including our understanding the concept of flexible grouping, our knowledge of multiple texts, ensuring that our students know and can use essential skills, and using a variety of methods to read texts.

Our organizational abilities greatly enrich our teaching. They help us to accommodate student needs and support learning in a variety of other ways. Our goal is to effectively structure our classrooms and our teaching so our students will be motivated to learn and be able to achieve to their greatest possible potentials. Questions we may have relating to organizing for teaching and learning include the following:

■ What lesson plan format will we use?

■ How can we differentiate instruction to accommodate students' needs?

■ How can we group students for learning?

■ How can we effectively use textbooks in the content areas?

■ How can we teach students to generate questions?

■ How can we teach students to recognize text patterns?

■ How can students read text without engaging in round-robin reading?

■ How can students learn to use textbook study strategies such as SQ4R?

In this chapter, we respond to each of these questions. We begin by discussing an effective lesson planning format. Then we focus on how we can adapt this format to differentiate instruction in the content areas. Next, we explore how to organize students in a variety of settings. Then we examine the use of textbooks in our teaching, and consider a variety of alternatives to students taking turns reading aloud in class. After that, we examine how to teach our students to generate questions and recognize text patterns. Finally, we focus on SQ4R, a study technique that students can use when reading content area texts independently.

What Lesson Planning Format Will We Use?

When creating lessons, we need to use a planning format that provides opportunities to address state standards, related lesson goals, authentic assessment, content, and multiple levels of student thinking. Although several different planning formats are used in our content areas, the one we will use integrates content and strategy use. In addition to the essential components, this lesson planning format provides opportunities for us to engage, guide, and extend student thinking.

As seen in Figure 9.1, we will need to include lesson goals and related state standards in our plans. Before reading, we will *engage* students' thinking by motivating our students, introducing the text, and encouraging students to activate their background knowledge, make connections, and set purposes for reading. During reading, we will *guide* student thinking by encouraging students to continue to make connections, self-question, monitor their understanding, visualize, summarize, and evaluate. After reading, we will help students to *extend* their student thinking by summarizing, evaluating, and discussing in the short term and applying what they have learned through inquiry-based projects in the long term. Discussion will permeate our lessons.

To engage students' thinking, we can use strategy-based teaching ideas such as Semantic Maps (Johnson & Pearson, 1984), Anticipation/Reaction Guides (Readence, Bean, & Baldwin, 2000), or Concept of Definition Maps (Schwartz & Raphael, 1985). When we guide students' thinking, we can engage students in using the Bookmark Technique (McLaughlin & Allen, 2002), KWL (Ogle, 1986), KWLS (Sippola, 1995), or Interactive Notation System to Effective Reading and Thinking (INSERT) (Vaughn, & Estes, 1986). To extend students' thinking, we can invite students to engage in summarizing techniques such as Summary Cubes (McLaughlin & Allen, 2002), Lyric Summaries (McLaughlin & Allen, 2002), or Bio-Pyramids (Macon, 1991). For examples of these strategy-based teaching ideas, see Chapters 5 through 7 and the Appendix. We can also encourage students to engage in inquiry-based projects (see Chapter 13), create alternative modes of representation (see Chapter 14), or participate in technology-based projects (see Chapter 12) to extend their thinking.

There are a number of ways in which we can adapt the lesson planning format of engaging, guiding, and extending student thinking to accommodate our students' needs. In the next section, we examine differentiated instruction, which provides for such adaptations.

How Can We Differentiate Instruction to Accommodate Students' Needs?

As teachers, we know that we have students of differing capabilities in our classes and we strive to help all students achieve to the best of their abilities. Differentiated instruction enables us to accommodate this diversity of student needs (Gibson & Hasbrouck, 2008; Tyner & Green, 2005).

FIGURE 9.1
Lesson Planning Format

I. Goals and Related State Standards

II. Bibliographic Information for Text(s) and Additional Materials

III. Engaging Students' Thinking (before reading)

IV. Guiding Students' Thinking (during reading)

V. Extending Students' Thinking (after reading)

VI. Assessments

To develop environments that promote differentiated instruction, Gibson and Hasbrouck (2008) suggest that we do the following:

- Embrace collaborative teaching and learning
- Use whole-class and small-group explicit strategy instruction
- Establish consistent routines and procedures
- Scaffold student learning
- Increase student engagement
- Teach students how to learn as well as what to learn
- Change the way teaching occurs

When we differentiate instruction, we create multiple pathways to learning. This practice supports our goal of helping students to perform to their maximum potential and motivates students to learn.

We can differentiate a number of instructional components to support students as they gain competence and confidence in learning. These include content—the information being taught; process—the way in which the information is taught; and product—how the students demonstrate their learning (Tomlinson, 1999). Details of each of these elements follow.

Differentiating Content

We can differentiate content by providing information about a topic or a group of related topics using a variety of sources. For example, there may be information in our textbook about the topic, but not all of our students may be able to read it. We can differentiate text by offering students alternative information sources such as informational articles, picture books, websites, video clips, or texts on tape or CD. These media would present the same or similar information in different ways and at different reading levels.

Differentiating Process

We can differentiate process by adapting our teaching methods. For example, we can preteach students who might be English learners or struggling readers; alternatively, we can teach these students in small groups, while other small groups work independently. We can also offer supports during teaching, such as including photos of essential vocabulary, numbering the components of graphic organizers, and providing students with opportunities to respond through multiple modalities such as sketching and labeling.

Differentiating Products

To differentiate products, we can provide a variety of ways for students to demonstrate what they have learned. For example, after learning about a new topic in a content area, some students might complete a research project requiring the use of multiple sources, some might write and illustrate form poems, and others might design informational posters. Students will show what they know through all three assessments, which vary in difficulty.

Making Connections
TO WRITING

When we differentiate instruction, we can use a variety of supports for student writing. For example, we can use photos or illustrations to support students' thinking as they write. We can also use paragraph frames (see Chapter 11) and study techniques such as text boxes and scaffolded outlines (see Chapter 11). ■

We can also use multiple grouping options when we differentiate instruction. In the next section we examine those possibilities.

How Can We Group Students for Learning?

Employing multiple instructional groupings helps us to accommodate student needs. There are several options for grouping students for learning, each of which is used for particular purposes. We call this practice *flexible grouping*, because the groups are not permanent and we have flexibility in using different kinds of groups at different points in our teaching. We can also use multiple grouping options within each lesson.

For group interactions to be effective, we need to align our reasons for grouping, the grouping formats we use, and materials we are using (Flood, Lapp, Flood, & Nagel, 1992). At this point the questions we may wish to explore about flexible grouping include the following:

- What are the possible grouping patterns?
- What are their purposes?
- When do we use them?
- What is our role in such groups?
- What are the students' roles?

Responses to these queries are provided in Figure 9.2. Details about each type of grouping follow.

Whole Group

All students are involved in this grouping option, which is used when we are teaching new information or any ideas that the whole class needs to learn. For example, if we were teaching mathematics and needed to introduce new information about different types of angles in geometry, we would use the whole-group format for our teaching. In this case, the teacher would be directly or explicitly teaching the information about angles; students would be participating and learning. If we were teaching new information and using the whole-group instructional pattern, however, we might also integrate other grouping patterns as the lesson progresses. For example, the teacher may at different points in the lesson ask students to draw a particular type of angle and then "turn to a partner" to share and explain the sketch. Similarly, we could integrate small groups by asking students to form them to practice drawing and discussing different kinds of angles. We can also use the whole-group option if we want to share a read-aloud with the class. (Learn more about read-alouds later in this chapter.)

Small Groups

Small groups may meet for several different purposes and often last about 20 minutes. As seen in Figure 9.2, the primary purposes of this grouping pattern are to preteach content, reteach the material, or reinforce learning. The focus of this kind of group will be students who did not have prior knowledge of the topic, did not demonstrate understanding after initial teaching, or seemed not to fully grasp the topic after it had been taught. For example, when teaching a new topic, we might survey the class and learn that most of the students already have some knowledge of the topic, but a few don't seem to have any knowledge of it. To ensure that the latter students gain initial understanding of the topic, we might meet with them in a small-group setting and preteach some information about the topic. Then, when we begin teaching the next level of the topic to the whole class, all of the students would be able to contribute to the discussion.

Enhancing students' learning is another reason we use small groups. The focus of this kind of small group might be students who are high-level thinkers and who easily become bored when learning is not consistently challenging or students who may have a great amount of knowledge about a particular topic we are teaching.

FIGURE 9.2
Content Area Grouping Options

Grouping	Purposes	When Used	Role(s) of Teacher	Role(s) of Students
Whole group	To teach new material	When everyone in the class needs to learn the material	Direct (explicit) instruction	Participating Learning
Small groups (approximately 5 students)	To preteach To reteach To reinforce learning	When some students need additional instruction or clarification	Guided instruction	Participating Clarifying Learning
	To enhance learning	When some students need to be challenged	Guided instruction	Participating Learning
Small Groups (3–5 students)	To work independently with peers	When the teacher is working with another small group	Monitoring students as they work	Participating Reinforcing Learning
Pairs/partners	To work in a guided context	During direct (explicit) instruction ("Work briefly with a partner" to apply . . . to discover)	Guided instruction	Participating Learning
	To work independently with peers	When the teacher is working with other students or the entire class is working in pairs	Monitoring students as they work	Participating Learning
Individuals	To work independently individually	When applying what has been learned or when reading silently	Monitoring students as they work	Engaging Learning

Another reason to use this type of organization is to invite students to work independently with peers in small groups while we are working with a particular group, such as English learners, advanced students, struggling readers, or special-needs students. For example, we might be involved in preteaching, reteaching, or enriching the learning of a small group of students, while the remaining students in the class also move into small groups for the purpose of working independently. The small groups may meet to continue to work cooperatively on a group project or as a discussion group. (For more information see the section about content area Discussion Circles.)

Making Connections
TO ENGLISH LEARNERS

Teaching in a small-group setting provides opportunities for us as teachers to work with students who may need extra support, such as English learners. While the other students work independently with peers in small groups, we can provide additional supports for students who are English learners by preteaching, teaching, or reteaching them in a small group. Examples of such supports include using visuals related to content vocabulary, offering students opportunities to respond through alternative modalities, providing a fluent oral language model, and encouraging students' learning by using scaffolded outlines. ■

Pairs or Partners

Students work with partners for a variety of reasons. First, students might work with partners as a grouping option. For example, everyone in the class might work with a partner to brainstorm what they know about a particular topic or to create a project, such as a content area alphabet book. Working with a partner can also occur within another organizational setting. For example, a teacher might be engaged in explicit instruction with the whole group, but, after teaching a concept, she might ask the students to "turn to a partner." This segment would be described as "guided instruction," because the teacher would guide the students through their task. In this situation, the teacher might offer a prompt, ask students to complete the next step in a strategy or process, or develop their application of an idea that was taught.

At other times, the students might work in pairs if the teacher is working with a small group and he invites the remainder of the class to work in pairs. In this setting, the teacher would not be able to walk around the room to directly monitor the partners' work, but the success of the pairs would be evident in their self-assessments as well as in the work they produced, which the teacher would review later in the day. Additionally, although the teacher would be busy teaching a pair or small group of students, the engagement of the pairs would be evident simply by quickly glancing around the room and listening to the low noise level.

As with small groups, the partner setting can accommodate the unique needs of English learners, advanced students, struggling readers, or special-needs students. For example, English learners can be partnered with English speakers who help provide a fluent language model, and struggling readers can be paired with students who have more background knowledge about the topic.

A paired setting also works well when students engage in peer assessment. In this case, students can exchange their work with partners, who would read it and provide feedback. In such situations, it is beneficial to ensure that the students understand that feedback should be constructive and generally involve providing a positive comment and a suggestion for improving the work.

Individuals

Students working individually is another option. For example, teachers might invite students to work individually to apply a concept that has already been taught and practiced with a partner. Students might also have some time in class to work on individual projects they may be creating. This is a good idea, because it allows us as teachers to observe how students engage in various steps of the project process. It also provides opportunities for students to ask us questions or to review their work to date. Of course, such occasions should conclude with the students developing new goals for the next step of their projects.

Making Connections | Thinking about Flexible Grouping

■ Think about a theme or topic in your content area. Reflect on how you would use the various types of grouping to teach it. Be sure to focus on which students will be participating and why you think the option you selected is the most beneficial.

■ Share your thoughts with others in small-group discussions.

How Can We Effectively Use Textbooks in the Content Areas?

Textbooks often serve as the foundation of content area instruction. For many teachers, they are the only texts used; for others, they are used in conjunction with a variety of other resources. In this section, we explore textbooks and examine how to select texts that are effective for our courses.

Content area textbooks are often used as the sole focus of instruction, but in today's educational contexts we have access to multiple text resources. We may choose to use a textbook, but we can easily supplement it with leveled texts, trade books, informational articles, websites, and DVDs. These supplemental types of text are rich sources of information and often have the ability to provide more up-to-date information than can be found in traditional textbooks.

Different levels of content area texts are available. From a reading perspective, texts are viewed as having three different levels. When texts are at the independent level, students can read them without any help. When texts are at the instructional level, students can read them with some help from the teacher. When texts are at the challenging level, students should not be asked to read them because attempting to do so could be a frustrating experience.

Using textbooks as the primary vehicle for instruction in content area learning has been a long-standing tradition. Textbooks designed for content area instruction can be traced as far back as the 1700s. The first geography text appeared in 1784, when Jedidiah Morse produced *Geography Made Easy* (McNergney & Herbert, 1998). As areas of study were added to school curricula, the use of texts to impart discipline-specific knowledge increased. Centuries later, textbooks continue to dominate content area instruction, with research suggesting that textbooks account for 75% to 90% of classroom instruction in the content areas (Palmer & Stewart, 1997; Tyson & Woodward, 1989) and that 95% of science teachers use a textbook 90% of the time. Despite these high percentages of use, textbooks often assume unrealistic levels of background knowledge (McKeown & Beck, 1993), cover a wide variety of topics at a surface level, fail to promote students' use of critical thinking (Morrow, Cunningham, & Murray-Olsen, 1994), and are written at levels that exceed students' reading abilities.

The readability level of textbooks should be a factor in their selection. We can determine approximate readability levels by using formulas, such as the Fry Readabilty Graph (1977), which consider length of text, length of sentences, and complexity of vocabulary. (To learn more about the Fry Readability Graph see school.discoveryeducation.com/schrockguide/fry/fry.html)

School districts may require their teachers to use textbooks, which we may or may not have a voice in selecting. If we are invited to review textbooks for our courses or to serve on a textbook selection committee, we should consider evaluating the texts based on elements such as the points presented in Figure 9.3.

Making Connections
TO MULTIPLE LITERACIES

What is included in or excluded from content area textbooks is decided by publishers. They also decide which voices are heard and which are silenced or discounted in texts. Consequently, the information that students learn from textbooks and the perspectives from which they are written are determined by those who publish the books. Decades ago, students would have been passive recipients of information, who were expected to believe that everything that appeared in textbooks was true. Today, critical literacy suggests that we comprehend text at deeper levels, question the author's message, examine the author's perspective, think about which perspectives may not be treated fairly, and take action to do what we can to ensure that all voices are heard. ■

Vardell, Hadaway, and Young (2006) suggest that we consider students' social and cultural backgrounds when selecting texts and planning instruction. This integration helps to create learning environments in which students feel engaged and successful. Holmes, Powell, Holmes, and Witt (2007) recommend using text that represents a variety of races and people to help students build awareness of and greater sensitivity toward one another.

As content area teachers, we need to do all we can to ensure that our students learn from multiple types and levels of text. This means that if we use a textbook, we should supplement it with a variety of resources. These sources should include, but not be limited to, informational articles from the Internet, newspapers, journals, magazines, primary sources, trade books, poetry, DVDs, leveled texts, and television segments.

1. Is the text well organized (contents, glossary, index, chapter structures)?

2. Is the text factually correct?

3. Is the text motivational?

4. What is the readability level of the text? For which grade was the textbook developed?

5. Does the textbook support state content standards? Is there evidence of standards-based learning?

6. Does the teacher's edition support teachers' use of a strategy-based lesson plan?

7. Is the content diverse?

8. Does the text require students to use skills and strategies?

9. Does the text integrate content literacy? Multiple literacies?

10. Does the text focus on meeting the needs of individual learners, such as English language learners, struggling readers, and special-needs students?

11. How are multiple types of assessment used throughout the text?

12. How are students asked to engage in higher-order thinking throughout the text?

13. How is technology integrated throughout the text? How are the students asked to use technology? Teachers?

14. Is a teacher's edition available? Are there special resources for English learners, struggling learners, and special needs students?

15. Are the charts, maps, graphs, tables, and illustrations accurate? Do they help to support students' thinking?

16. Are supplementary materials available (e.g., text on CD, leveled texts, videos)?

FIGURE 9.3
Questions to Consider When Evaluating a Content Area Textbook

How Can We Teach Students to Generate Questions?

The ability to generate questions is a skill that underpins many aspects of learning. Unfortunately, students more often think of themselves as those who answer questions than as those who ask questions. They are accustomed to responding to questions raised by teachers and textbooks, practices that have consistently been part of their learning experiences. They also view questions in terms of assessment and evaluation—items they respond to at the end of chapters and when taking tests—rather than as a learning skill.

We need to explicitly teach our students how to generate questions. We want them to understand that student-generated questions are an incredibly powerful tool for promoting student engagement, learning, and understanding (Busching & Slesinger, 1995). We want them to understand that questions are essential if we are to construct significant meaning. As Ciardiello notes, "To know how to question is to know how to become literate" (1998, p. 7).

Purposes of Questioning

When teaching students about questioning, we explain what questions are, discuss their purposes, and delineate their multiple levels. For example, we explain that there are many reasons for generating questions, including information seeking (Who was President in 1945?), connected understanding (How does the Holocaust relate to what we are learning about World War II?), psychological and moral reconstruction (What moral issues do you associate with the Holocaust and the Japanese American internment?), historical speculation (How would our world today be different if Hitler had never existed?), and imagination and research (If you had lived during that time, what contributions would you have made in the World War II era?). We also immerse students in topics from multiple perspectives by reading, writing, speaking, listening and viewing to foster their questioning abilities (Busching & Slesinger, 1995).

FIGURE 9.4
Ciardiello's Levels of
Questioning

Memory Questions
Signal words: who, what, where, when?
Cognitive operations: naming, defining, identifying, designating

Convergent Thinking Questions
Signal words: why, how, in what ways?
Cognitive operations: explaining, stating relationships, comparing, and contrasting

Divergent Thinking Questions
Signal words: imagine, suppose, predict, if/then
Cognitive operations: predicting, hypothesizing, inferring, reconstructing

Evaluative Thinking Questions
Signal words: defend, judge, justify/what do you think?
Cognitive operations: valuing, judging, defending, justifying

FIGURE 9.4
Ciardiello's Levels of
Questioning

Levels of Questioning

Ciardiello (1998) suggests that students generate questions at four levels: memory, convergent, divergent, and evaluative. As shown in Figure 9.4, he also provides signal words and describes cognitive (thinking) operations for each category. Figure 9.5 illustrates how Ciardiello's questioning levels are applicable across content areas.

When teaching students how to generate questions at multiple levels, we explain each question type and then model it. Next, students work with a partner in guided practice in a variety of settings. Finally, students engage in independent application and transfer. The effective teaching of skills, such as generating questions, creates links to reading comprehension strategies. For example, the skills of sequencing, noting details, making generalizations, and using text structure can be

FIGURE 9.5
Content Area Examples
of Ciardiello's Four
Levels of Questioning

Memory Level
History: Who was the first President of the United States?
Literature: Who is the author of the novel?
Algebra: What are algebraic equations?
Chemistry: What is the definition of liquid?
French: What is the French word for bread?

Convergent Level
History: How did the presidencies of Bill Clinton and George W. Bush differ?
Literature: How are the novel *Jane Eyre* and the current production of the movie the same? How are they different?
Algebra: How do the commutative property of multiplication and the distributive property differ?
Chemistry: How do liquids and gases differ?
French: How are French and English nouns similar? How are they different?

Divergent Level
History: If you were President, what would your top three priorities be?
Literature: Imagine that you were a character in the book. What would happen to you in a sequel to this novel?
Algebra: Create an algebraic equation and predict what the solution will be.
Chemistry: Oil-and-vinegar salad dressing contains two phases: an oil-rich liquid and a vinegar-rich liquid. What do you suppose will happen if you shake the bottle?
French: Imagine you were one of the great French authors. Who would you be and what would you consider to be your greatest work? Please respond in French.

Evaluative Level
History: Defend your position on paying taxes to the federal government.
Literature: What is your opinion of the author? Justify your response.
Algebra: Justify your prediction of the algebraic equation's solution.
Chemistry: Why should students study chemistry? Defend your response.
French: Why should students continue to learn French in today's global community? Justify your thinking.

FIGURE 9.6 Generating Questions: A Skill That Supports Comprehension Strategies

Comprehension Strategy	Informational Text	
	Example 1: World War II	**Example 2: Algebraic Equations**
Previewing	What do I already know about World War II?	What do I already know about algebraic equations?
Self-questioning	Why did World War II occur?	Why would I use an algebraic equation?
Making connections	What connections can I make between the text and the video we saw about World War II?	What connections can I make to the algebraic operations used in these equations?
Visualizing	How does my visualization of European concentration camps compare/contrast to the camps of the Japanese American internment?	How can my visualization of planning a party be expressed as an algebraic equation?
Knowing how words work	Which clues in the text can I use to figure out the word "draft"?	Which clues in the text can I use to figure out the word "polynomial"?
Monitoring	Does what I'm reading make sense? If not, what can I do to clarify my thinking?	Does what I am reading make sense? If not, what can I do to clarify my thinking?
Summarizing	What are the most important ideas in the text?	What is the most important information about algebraic equations?
Evaluating	Does the information presented support what I have learned from other sources?	Does the information in this section support what the author stated earlier in the chapter?

linked to summarizing, which is a comprehension strategy (Lipson, 2001). These and other skills, such as making inferences, distinguishing between important and less important ideas, and drawing conclusions, facilitate students' use of one or more comprehension strategies. The skill of generating questions, which underpins every comprehension strategy, is demonstrated in Figure 9.6, The figure features examples of questions at multiple levels using informational text.

Ideas for Teaching Question Generation

There are a variety of ways to teach students how to generate questions. ReQuest, Paired Questioning, and Thick and Thin Questions are three teaching ideas that work particularly well. Guidelines for teaching each of these strategies follow. The skills are presented here in order of "scaffolded" use. We begin with ReQuest, a process in which teachers and students actively engage. Next, we discuss Paired Questioning. The teacher does not have a role in this but the students work with partners. Finally, we explain Thick and Thin Questions; students may either work with a partner or generate questions individually when using this technique.

ReQUEST. When engaging in ReQuest (Manzo, 1969), students actively participate in the discussion of the text. After observing teacher modeling, students practice generating questions at multiple levels. Teachers and students also answer questions. This interaction provides opportunities to engage in the social construction of knowledge and learn the content.

When teaching ReQuest, follow these steps:

1. **Explain:** Focus on ReQuest as a type of *reciprocal questioning* that involves reading silently, generating questions at multiple levels, predicting, and discussing. Explain that the students and the teacher engage in ReQuest by reading silently and asking one another questions.

2. **Demonstrate:** Begin by introducing the text, and then invite students to participate in the demonstration. Join the students in reading a designated section of text (usually a few paragraphs) silently. Ask them to close their books when finished, while you ask them questions

about the text they read. Comment on the quality of responses. Then close your book and encourage the students to ask you questions. Comment on the quality of the questions.

3 Guide: Guide students to engage in ReQuest by silently reading another section of text. Then question the students and encourage them to question you.

4 Practice: After students have read an appropriate amount of text, invite them to stop questioning and begin predicting. Provide prompts, such as "I think . . ." or "I wonder . . ." to encourage predictions. Then invite the students to read the remaining text silently. After the students have finished reading the text, facilitate a discussion based on the text and students' predictions.

5 Reflect: Encourage students to think about how ReQuest helps us to use reciprocal questioning and prediction to understand text. Discuss other content areas in which students could use ReQuest.

When engaging in ReQuest, we may find that students ask too many memory-level questions. If we teach Ciardiello's four levels of questioning before we teach ReQuest, students will be able to use the signal words to generate questions at all levels. Although memory-level questions are certainly important, we are also trying to encourage our students to think at higher levels. For example, if students are researching the biography of someone who is well respected in a particular content area—for example, Winston Churchill in history, Banneker in mathematics, Hemingway in literature, or Einstein in science—memory-level questions about where and when the person was born provide some background information. Nevertheless, we also want students to ask how that person's contribution to the field compared and contrasted to other contributions (convergent level), how the students could imagine themselves making such a contribution (divergent thinking), and how the students would defend or justify the person's contribution (evaluative level).

 **TEACHING IDEA**

PAIRED QUESTIONING. In Paired Questioning (Vaughn & Estes, 1986), students engage in actively generating questions during reading. To teach Paired Questioning, follow these steps:

1 Explain: Explain that Paired Questioning involves students taking turns while generating text-related questions and responding to them. When the students have finished generating and responding to questions while reading segments of the text, one partner summarizes the important ideas in the text and the other agrees or disagrees and justifies his thinking.

2 Demonstrate: Arrange in advance to have a student volunteer be your partner during the demonstration. Introduce the text and demonstrate how you and your partner read the title or subtitle of a section of text, set the text aside, and then respond to the questions each of you generate. Remind students that asking questions about the title or subtitle helps the reader set purposes for reading. For example, if the title was *The Civil War* and the subtitle was *Causes of the Civil War*, the questions raised might be *What was the Civil War?* and *What were the causes of the Civil War?* Next, repeat this process, reading a section of text instead of the title or subtitle. After you and your partner have responded to the questions, discuss how generating questions as we read helps us to understand the text.

3 Guide: Invite students to work with a partner and a new section of text to engage in Paired Questioning, first with a subtitle and then with a section of text. Encourage discussion.

4 Practice: Invite students to finish reading the text by engaging in Paired Questioning. Stop periodically to discuss the text and the questions that have been raised. When the students have finished reading the text, invite one partner to share the important ideas in the text with the other. Then encourage the other partner to agree or disagree and justify her response.

5 Reflect: Invite students to share their thoughts about paired questioning, including how it can help us understand text.

THICK AND THIN QUESTIONS. Thick and Thin Questions (Lewin, 1998) encourages students to create questions pertaining to a text and helps students discern the depth of the questions they ask. Teachers often use sticky notes when teaching this technique. Smaller sticky notes are used to write thin questions (memory level) and noticeably larger notes are used to write thick questions (convergent, divergent, evaluative questions). We can also provide a blackline on which students can write Thick and Thin Questions (see Appendix A).

To teach Thick and Thin Questions, follow these steps:

1 Explain: Teach the students the difference between thick and thin questions. *Thick questions* deal with big pictures and large concepts. Answers to thick questions are involved, complex, and open ended (convergent, divergent, and evaluative questions). *Thin questions* deal with specific content. Answers to thin questions are short, close ended (memory-level questions), and usually clearly stated in the book.

2 Demonstrate: Model how to create thick and thin questions. Read a portion of text and think aloud about how to create a thick question and a thin question. Relate each type of question to Ciardiello's four levels of questioning. Discuss which signal words you used to create the questions and possible answers to them.

3 Guide: Guide students to work with partners to create Thick and Thin Questions as they read. Read another portion of text and prompt students with stems such as "Why . . ." or "What if . . ." for Thick Questions and "Who is . . ." and "Where . . ." for Thin Questions. Encourage students to respond to the questions their partners generate.

4 Practice: Invite students to work individually to generate Thick and Thin Questions as they continue to read the text. When they have finished reading the text, encourage students to share their questions with a partner, taking turns responding to them.

5 Reflect: Invite students to share their thoughts about Thick and Thin Questions and to describe how generating questions can help us understand text. Encourage the students to think about how they can use Thick and Thin Questions when reading in other content areas.

Generating questions is an essential skill. As Ciardiello notes, "Asking questions for the joy of discovery is the pathway to wandering and wondering" (2003, pp. 228–229). It is "wandering" in the sense of roaming or leisurely strolling through one's thoughts and reflections with no predetermined course to travel. The pathway is also filled with "wondering" in the sense of asking questions that express the object of curiosity or doubt. Ciardiello (2007) refers to this process as "question-finding" and notes that it strongly supports critical literacy (see Chapter 4) by helping students move beyond the surface message of text to actively question its deeper, more critical meanings.

Making Connections | Thinking about Generating Questions

■ Think about generating questions. Then choose a topic from your content area and use Ciardiello's signal words to develop one question at each level about that topic.

■ Share your thoughts with others in small-group discussions. Discuss how you will teach questioning to your students.

■ Save the questions you generated and use them as models when teaching your students about questioning.

How Can We Teach Students to Recognize Text Patterns?

Research tells us that students can find reading informational text challenging. Their knowledge of and experience with the text type and structure can influence the text's accessibility. For

Go to the Activities and Applications section under the topic *Text Structure* in the MyEducationLab for your course and complete the activity entitled Organization of Nonfiction to identify techniques teachers can use to guide their students to an understanding of text structures

example, many students have greater background knowledge of reading narrative text, which is generally based on characters, setting, problem, attempts to resolve the problem, and resolution. One reason they may find reading informational text more difficult is that they are not familiar with these text patterns (Dymock & Nicholson, 1999).

Researchers suggest that we should explicitly teach the informational text structure to our students (Pressley, 2002). Goldman and Rakestraw (2001) concur and note the following conclusions based on existing research on students' knowledge of text structure:

■ Readers use their knowledge of structure in processing text.

■ Knowledge of structural forms of text develops with experience with different genres, and is correlated with age and time in school.

■ Making readers more aware of genre and text structure improves learning. (p. 321)

Research reports that if students know the text patterns and understand how to generate questions, they will improve their comprehension of text. The following five text patterns appear most prevalent in informational text. Descriptions and examples of each follow.

Description

This pattern focuses on characteristics, facts, and features related to a topic, person, event, or object.

EXAMPLE:

Apple has introduced the world's slimmest laptop, the MacBook Air. The density of the laptop measures between 0.4 centimeter and 1.9 centimeters. The 13.3-inch display is lit by an energy-saving LED display. Equipped with a built-in camera, the MacBook Air also comes with an Intel Core-2-Duo processor and either a 1.6- or 1.8-gigahertz chip. The MacBook Air has 2 gigabytes of memory, comes with an 80-gigabyte hard drive, and is pre-equipped for an 802.11n Wi-Fi connection. Because it is so slim, the laptop has no built-in DVD drive. Buyers can also opt for a solid-state hard drive and a flash drive without moving parts, making the computer more resistant to shocks and letting it run faster.

Sequence

This pattern relates steps in a process or the order in which things happened.

EXAMPLE:

First, Martin Luther King, Jr., delivered his "I Have a Dream" speech during the March on Washington for Jobs and Freedom. Next, he became the youngest man to be awarded the Nobel Peace Prize. Then he took the Civil Rights Movement north and moved his family into the Chicago slums to demonstrate support for the poor. Finally, in 1968, King was assassinated in Memphis, Tennessee, where he went to support striking garbage workers.

Comparison and Contrast

This pattern illuminates similarities (comparisons) and differences (contrasts).

EXAMPLE:

When we examine the issues that Democrats and Republicans are supporting in the Presidential election, we can see that there are some issues on which they are clearly divided and others where their goals are similar, but their approaches are different. An example of the former is that their positions differ on the war in Iraq. The Democrats are in favor of ending the war in Iraq, while the Republicans support the war and have developed strategies for victory. As an example of the latter, both the Democratic and Republican candidates support changes in health care, reform of immigration laws, and improvements in education. Of course, their policies to promote these changes differ, and in some cases, differ dramatically.

Go to the Activities and Applications section under the topic *Comprehension Strategies* in the MyEducationLab for your course and complete the activity entitled Text Structure and Comprehension to examine ways in which content area textbook structure affects student comprehension.

Cause and Effect

This pattern shows how events or ideas (effects) come to be because of certain other ideas, acts, or events (causes).

EXAMPLE:

A number of factors contributed to the start of the Civil War. Economic and social differences between the North and the South laid a foundation for the conflict when the South became a single-crop economy and the North became more industrialized and diverse. As the South became more dependent on slaves to work the cotton plantations, the North focused on city life, where people of many different cultures worked together. In addition, the issue of state versus federal rights was hotly contested. When the states felt they were no longer respected, several seceded. The slave versus nonslave issue was complicated by the growth of the country through the Louisiana Purchase and the Mexican War. Concerns about whether the additional states would permit slave-holding were hotly debated. The abolition movement grew as Northerners became more opposed to slavery and the Fugitive Slave Act was passed. Finally, when Abraham Lincoln was elected president, the South viewed him as antislavery and a supporter of Northern interests. Seven Southern states had already seceded when Lincoln took office.

Problem and Solution

This pattern showcases a difficulty (problem) and provides an example of how it can be resolved (solution).

EXAMPLE:

Violent tornadoes are destructive. They can reduce homes to rubble and are responsible for 70 percent of all tornado-related deaths. To combat the devastating effects of this type of severe weather, the National Weather Service recommends that people who live in areas prone to tornadoes develop a disaster plan. Such a plan includes learning the community's warning signal and evacuation plan, having frequent drills, paying attention to weather conditions, mapping severe storm movements, and preparing a kit of disaster supplies. The value of such plans was demonstrated this past week when a college was severely damaged by tornadoes. Several buildings were destroyed, but no lives were lost.

Signal words for each pattern are presented in Figure 9.7. These words often offer readers clues about which pattern is prevalent in a particular section of text.

Recognizing the text structure can help readers understand the type of information included in the text and predict the types of questions that may be raised about it. For example, if students are reading a biography and realize that the text pattern is sequential, questions may focus on what happened when. When reading a section of text in which the pattern is comparison/contrast, questions may focus on similarities and differences.

FIGURE 9.7
Signal Words Commonly Associated with Text Patterns

Description: above, below, behind, down, across, under, such as, appears to be

Sequence: first, second, third, then, next, finally, during, until, preceding, initially, following

Comparison/contrast: although, but, compared to, however, on the other hand, either . . . or, not only . . . but also, similarly, different from

Cause/effect: because, as a result, since, accordingly, for this reason, in order to, if . . . then, therefore, consequently, nevertheless

Problem/solution: because, cause, since, therefore, consequently, as a result, this led to . . ., solve, resolve, conclude

In the next section, we describe a variety of ways to help students read content area text more effectively. Our goal is to eliminate round-robin reading and encourage students to actively engage with text.

How Can Students Read Content Area Text Without Engaging in Round-Robin Reading?

Many of us grew up engaging in what we call *round-robin reading*. Unfortunately, many students are still engaging in this practice at their content area teachers' requests. One of our primary goals as teachers is to eliminate this dated method of reading from education.

As you may recall, round-robin reading involves students taking turns reading aloud. Generally, each student reads a paragraph or other short segment of text. This process has several negative outcomes. First, students are usually reading the text *cold*—which means they have not had time to read or make connections to the text before they read it aloud. This is often complicated by teachers who do not encourage students to activate their prior knowledge prior to reading. The second difficulty is that not all students are comfortable reading aloud—especially when they might be corrected by teachers and/or peers if they mispronounce a word or read in a less than fluent fashion. The third problem is that it is very easy for students to read their segment and then ignore the rest of the students' reading. As a consequence, many students may not be comprehending the text. Finally, we are trying to encourage students to become lifelong readers. Round-robin reading interferes with that goal, because it presents an unrealistic view of reading. There is no other time in their lives when our students will ever be asked to read one paragraph aloud in front of an audience. Consequently, round-robin reading is not a meaningful process.

Better, more meaningful ways to enable students to understand text include the following:

- Students reading aloud when they engage in Patterned Partner Reading
- Students reading silently using the Bookmark Technique, INSERT or KWLS
- Students listening to books on tape
- Students interacting with peers in Discussion Circles
- Teachers engaging in read-alouds of selected texts

Active participation in these techniques helps to engage students and encourage them to stay focused and monitor their reading.

Students Reading with a Partner

Students can read text aloud with a partner when they engage in Patterned Partner Reading. Using patterns contributes to students' purpose for reading.

 **PATTERNED PARTNER READING.** Patterned Partner Reading (McLaughlin & Allen, 2002) promotes strategic reading, while providing a structure for reading interactively with a partner. A popular alternative to round-robin reading, this technique is used when two students read a text or section of a text together. The partners generally take turns reading, but this approach differs from the traditional partner or buddy reading in that it provides a particular pattern to help both students stay focused, whether they are the reader or the listener. The following is a list of possible patterns in which students can engage while partner reading:

> *Read–Pause–Question:* One student reads, the pair pauses, and the student that read asks the other student a question about the text.
> *Read–Pause–Make a Connection:* One student reads, the pair pauses, and each student makes a connection to self, to text, or to the world.

Read–Pause–Bookmark: One student reads, the pair pauses, and the students use the Bookmark Technique to mark the following information, so they can share it with the class:

- Most interesting
- Most confusing
- A word the whole class needs to know
- A chart, map, illustration, or graph that helped the readers understand what they read

Read–Pause–Sketch and Share: One student reads, the pair pauses, and each student visualizes and sketches. Then the students share and discuss their sketches.

Read–Pause–Say Something: One student reads, the pair pauses, and each student "says something" that he found interesting or didn't know before reading.

Read–Pause–Summarize: One student reads, the pair pauses, and the other student summarizes the segment that was read.

Students Reading Silently

When students read silently, ideas such as Bookmark Technique, KWL/KWLS, and INSERT help the students to interact with text. Bookmark Technique, which is detailed in Chapter 5, provides purposes for reading and helps students to focus. While they are reading, the students complete four Bookmarks: (1) the most important section of the text, (2) a vocabulary word the whole class needs to discuss, (3) something the reader found confusing, and (4) an illustration, chart, map, or graph that helped the reader to understand what she read. KWL/KWLS requires that the students brainstorm, raise questions, and think about responses as they read. INSERT asks students to brainstorm and then insert several symbols as they read.

 **TEACHING IDEA**

KWL AND KWLS. The KWL is a teaching idea that supports multiple reading comprehension strategies, including self-questioning, monitoring, and summarizing. Its purposes include activating students' prior knowledge about a topic, setting purposes for reading, and confirming, revising, or expanding original understandings of a topic. In the traditional form of KWL, developed by Donna Ogle in 1986, readers ask themselves, "What do I know?", "What do I want to know?", and "What have I learned?" In 1995, Sippola suggested that we add a fourth column to the KWL to create the KWLS. The fourth column accommodates the question, "What do I still want to know?" The final column of the KWLS encourages students to examine whether they have found answers to all of the questions they raised in response to "What do I need to know?" If students have not found responses to all of the questions they raised, they move the unanswered questions to the fourth column—or add new questions that may have arisen—and research responses to them. Graphic organizers for the KWL, KWLS, and the KWDL ("What I know," "What I want to know," "What I did," and "What I learned"), which is often used in science and mathematics—can be found in Appendix A. Guidelines for teaching the KWL and an example from a chemistry class can be found in Chapter 6. To teach your students how to use KWLS, follow these steps and encourage discussion throughout the process.

1. **Explain:** Explain that the KWLS supports the reading strategies of self-questioning, monitoring, and summarizing. Focus on the four steps involved in the KWLS: What I Know, What I Want to Know, and What I Learned, and What I Still Want to Know.

2. **Demonstrate:** Begin by introducing the topic and a short text. Share the KWLS graphic organizer with students (see the Appendix). Think aloud as you brainstorm what you know in the K column. Then move to the W column and list what you want to know. Discuss what you wrote in the K and W columns. Then read the text. After reading, record what you learned in the L column. Discuss what you learned with the class. Then revisit the K column to determine if what you knew was verified in the text and the W column to ensure

K What I <u>K</u>now	W What I <u>W</u>ant to Know	L What I <u>L</u>earned	S What I <u>S</u>till Want to Know
Founded in 1949 as a coalition of social classes	What were the social classes?	The workers, the peasants, the petite bourgeoisie, and the national-capitalists	How were social classes determined?
Involvement in Korean War	Who were "the enemies of the state"?	War criminals, traitors, capitalists, counter-revolutionaries	Who decided who was an enemy of the state?
	What was the next transition?	Transition to socialism in 1953–1957	What did this involve?
	What were China's needs at this time?	Food, funds, technology, equipment and military weapons.	Where did China get the technology and the weapons?

FIGURE 9.8
KWLS about the People's Republic of China 1949–1957

that all of your questions were answered. Include any remaining questions from the W (What I Want to Know) column and any new questions about the topic in the S column of the KWLS. Find responses to the questions in the S column. When the KWLS is complete, discuss it with the students and use it to summarize the information on the chart.

3 **Guide:** Introduce a new text and guide students to work with a partner as each completes the K and W columns. Discuss the students' responses. Provide time for them to read the text and complete the L column. Discuss their responses. Then ask students to check the K and W columns to ensure that what they knew was verified by the text and that all of their questions were answered. Then invite students to list any questions remaining from the W column or any new questions that may have arisen in the S column. Encourage the pairs of students to respond to the questions in the S column and to summarize what they have learned.

4 **Practice:** Invite students to work on their own to complete a KWLS chart about another short text. Monitor as they complete each step, and discuss as noted earlier in the process. After the students have discussed the completed K, W, and L columns, encourage them to revisit the K and L columns as noted earlier. Invite them to add and respond to questions in the S column. Finally, invite students to share an oral summary of what they learned with a partner.

5 **Reflect:** Invite students to think about how the KWLS helps us comprehend by providing opportunities to self-question, monitor, and summarize text.

Figure 9.8 features an excerpt from a KWLS about the People's Republic of China.

 **TEACHING IDEA**

INSERT (INTERACTIVE NOTATION SYSTEM TO EFFECTIVE READING AND THINKING). The INSERT method was developed to encourage students to become active readers. When using this technique, students insert a number of different symbols into the text. INSERT provides students with opportunities to reflect about what they know and encourages them to make some decisions about the ideas expressed in the text. It is important to note that we have adapted INSERT for our students' use. Our approach requires the reader to insert fewer symbols than the original version.

To teach students how to use INSERT, see the guidelines presented in Chapter 6. For examples of completed student INSERT Bookmarks, about the Louisiana Purchase, see Chapter 6. For examples of INSERT Bookmarks about marine life zones, see Figure 9.9

1 **Explain:** Begin by explaining that INSERT helps us to self-question, monitor, and summarize as we read. Focus on how INSERT begins with readers brainstorming a list of what

FIGURE 9.9 INSERT Bookmarks about Marine Life Zones from Tarbuck, E.J., & Lutgens, F.K. (2006). *Earth Science*. Needham, MA: Pearson.

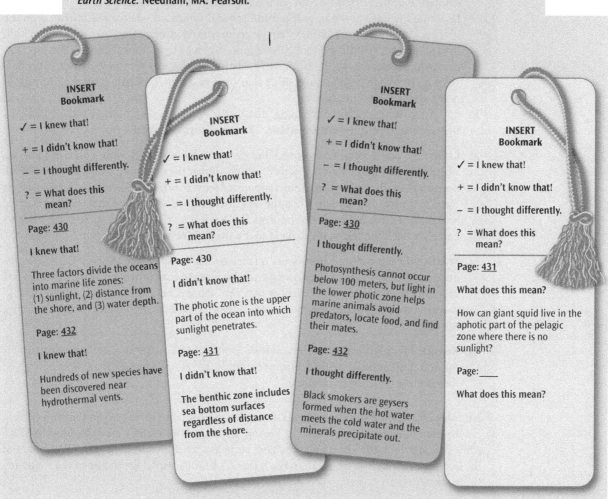

they know about the topic, reading the text, and inserting four symbols as they read. Introduce the four symbols to be inserted into the text and explain what each means:

- Place a check mark (✓) in the margin if the information in the text verifies what is on their brainstormed list.
- Place a plus sign (+) in the margin if the information is new to them—that is, not on their list.
- Place a minus sign (−) in the margin if the information contradicts or disproves information on the brainstormed list.
- Place a question mark (?) in the margin if there is something in the text that is confusing.

Explain that if the students are completing the INSERT Bookmarks, they will write information on each Bookmark, rather than in the margin of the text. Share the INSERT Bookmarks with the students and use them throughout the remainder of the lesson.

2 Demonstrate: Introduce a short text and think aloud as you brainstorm what you know about the topic. Write your brainstormed list on the board, on an overhead transparency, or on a computer. Then read the text and complete an INSERT Bookmark each time you insert a notation. For example, in Figure 9.8, when David Bishop wanted to indicate that he read something that confirmed what he had brainstormed, he wrote the page and paragraph numbers and indicated what was confirmed on the ✓ (check symbol) Bookmark. When he encountered information that was new to him, he wrote on the + (plus symbol) Bookmark. When he read something that did not support what appeared on his brainstormed list, he wrote it on the − (minus symbol) Bookmark. When he read something that confused him, he wrote it on the ? (question mark symbol) Bookmark.

After you have finished reading, discuss the notations you inserted and explain how they related to your brainstormed list. Then summarize the text.

3 **Guide:** Introduce another short text and invite students to work with a partner to brainstorm what they know about the topic. Then encourage the students to complete the INSERT Bookmarks, indicating when the text supported what they had brainstormed, when the text contained new information, when the text disconfirmed something that appeared on the brainstormed list, and when text information was found to be confusing. After the students complete the Bookmarks, invite them to discuss their responses and summarize the text.

4 **Practice:** Encourage students to work on their own to complete the INSERT Method. Introduce another short text and encourage the students to brainstorm what they know. Then monitor them, assisting as needed, as they read the text and complete the INSERT Bookmarks. Encourage the students to discuss their completed Bookmarks and summarize the text.

5 **Reflect:** Invite students to reflect on how using INSERT helps us to self-question, monitor, and summarize as we read. Encourage students to think abut other situations in which they can use the INSERT Method.

For more ideas to help students interact with text, see Chapters 4 through 6 and the Appendix.

In the following example, David Bishop, a high school history student, used INSERT while reading about the Louisiana Purchase. He began by brainstorming what he knew about the historic event before he began to read. David's brainstormed list included the following five statements:

1. The United States wanted the right to use the Mississippi River for shipping.
2. The United States purchased Louisiana.
3. The land was bought from France.
4. The land was bought for $15 million.
5. Napoleon, Monroe, and Livingston negotiated the deal.

After brainstorming what he already knew, David read the section about the Louisiana Purchase in his history textbook. As he read, he completed the INSERT Bookmarks (McLaughlin & Allen, 2002) shown in Figure 9.8.

Students Reading for Discussion Circles

Students can read on their own and share their insights, questions, and interpretations of texts in Discussion Circles. These small groups, which are similar to Literature Circles, provide students with an opportunity to discuss texts with peers in rich and meaningful ways. In our content area classes, we can use informational articles, sections of text, or theme-related novels as the focus of our Discussion Circles. Also, although Discussion Circles usually include just the students in our classrooms, we can arrange to have online Discussion Circles with students anywhere in the world.

To facilitate students' use of Discussion Circles, we need to explicitly teach the concept and engage in active demonstration. It is also important to review various aspects of cooperative learning before the students meet in their groups. Understanding that each person's opinion has value is an important idea to revisit.

The following guidelines facilitate the use of Discussion Circles:

1. Groups are temporary and are based on the texts students choose to read.
2. Each group may read a different text or all groups may read the same text.
3. Students take active roles in reading and discussing the texts.
4. Students' personal interpretations drive the discussion. There is not a list of questions to be answered, but rather a focus on students' inquiries, connections, and interpretations.
5. Groups meet regularly, according to predetermined schedules.
6. Students decide on topics for discussions and lead the conversations.
7. Sharing ideas in this format helps the students to broaden their interpretations and gain new perspectives from the other members of the group.
8. The teacher acts as a facilitator, not as an instructor or discussion leader.
9. Teachers assess students by observing conversations within groups and engaging students in self-assessment.

The time spent in Discussion Circles varies based on the length of the text, but usually 20 minutes is sufficient. It is important to allow enough time for each group's conversation to evolve on its own.

Some teachers prefer to use assigned roles and responsibilities as a way to guide the conversations. Roles adapted from their use in Literature Circles (Daniels, 1994) include the following:

- *Discussion Leader:* takes on the leadership of the group and guides the discussion. Responsibilities include choosing topics for discussion, generating questions, convening the meeting, and facilitating contributions from all members.
- *Passage Selector:* helps students revisit the text. Responsibilities include selecting memorable or important sections of the text and reading them aloud.
- *Connector:* guides students to make connections with the text. Responsibilities include sharing text–self, text–text, and text–world connections and encouraging others to do the same.
- *Illustrator:* creates a drawing or other symbolic response to text. Responsibilities include making the visual response and using it to encourage others to contribute to the conversation.
- *Word Finder:* selects one or two words from the reading that the whole class needs to discuss. Responsibilities include finding the words, noting where they are located in the text, and proposing definitions based on their use in context.

Students alternate roles each time a circle meets, so that eventually every student has a chance to take each role. Starting with clearly defined roles and then relaxing or relinquishing them as the students gain competence in Discussion Circles appears to be especially effective.

Books and Chapters on Compact Disc

Providing students with access to books and text chapters on compact discs or tapes is another way that students can learn what the text contains without engaging in round-robin reading. This approach simply requires that we or volunteer students record ourselves as we read a chapter or other segment of text. Students can then listen to the tapes or CDs individually or in pairs.

Making Connections
TO STRUGGLING READERS

Providing alternatives to round-robin reading is helpful for all students, but especially for students who struggle to read. Engaging struggling readers in Patterned Partner Reading, reading along with a tape or CD, reading leveled text, or reading in preparation for Discussion Circles and providing appropriate supports can increase student performance and motivation as well as self-esteem. Providing these students with alternative ways to respond to their reading is also beneficial. ■

Teacher Read-Alouds

Read-alouds play an important role in content area teaching and learning. They are used in the early grades and continue right through high school. As Albright (2002) notes, read-alouds and discussion engage adolescents, enrich content knowledge, and stimulate higher-order thinking.

When reading aloud to our content area classes, we may choose to read theme-related picture books or novel segments, but our options do not end there. We may also read excerpts from informational articles in magazines or newspapers, poetry, or various types of text from the Internet. It is important to remember that teacher read-alouds should include class discussions.

We begin this section by providing a rationale for using read-alouds in the content areas. Next, we explore how trade books can enhance our teaching. Finally, we discuss the role of informational articles in the read-aloud process.

RATIONALE. The rationale for using read-alouds in the content areas is multifaceted. They provide motivation; engage prior knowledge; furnish background information; introduce key concepts; can be used to teach strategies; incorporate a variety of genres, including biography and poetry; promote inquiry; and encourage students to view topics from different perspectives. Reading aloud also improves listening skills, builds vocabulary, aids reading comprehension, and positively influences students' attitudes toward reading (Fisher, Flood, Lapp, & Frey, 2004; Santoro, Chard, Howard, & Baker, 2008). Purposes for reading aloud in the content areas include stimulating interest in a topic, initiating discussions, posing dilemmas, stimulating debates, posing questions for research, and making interdisciplinary connections.

Teacher read-alouds can be narrative or informational text and include, but are not limited to, trade books, informational articles, poetry, lyrics, and primary sources, such as letters. For example, when teaching about DNA in biology, we can read articles about the role DNA plays in today's court cases. When studying about the Civil War, we can read aloud letters and examine photographs that family members sent home during the conflict. When studying great works of literature, we can read aloud a segment of the author's work. In mathematics, we can read aloud segments of biographies of famous mathematicians or informational articles about mathematics in everyday life. In foreign language classes, we can read aloud segments of poetry from a particular culture or informational articles written in that language.

TRADE BOOKS. Researchers who promote using trade books, such as picture books and novels, in the content areas report that these read-alouds expand students' knowledge base (Freeman & Person, 1998) and help them to develop richer understandings (Savage, 1998). They also explore topics in depth, enhance critical thinking, and help students to make connections to everyday life.

Trade books address a wide variety of content area topics. The diverse nature of such books is evident in the following examples in which content area topics are linked to particular trade book titles:

- If the Holocaust is the topic being studied, reading a segment from *The Diary of Anne Frank* will offer students a succinct understanding of her life, while selections from *I Never Saw Another Butterfly* will offer the perspectives of numerous Jewish children who were held in concentration camps during World War II.

- If Marie Curie or radium is the topic of study, consider reading aloud a section of *Something Out of Nothing: Marie Curie and Radium,* a text that chronicles the scientist's life.

- Another effective pairing uses *Baseball Saved Us* and excerpts from the novel *Snow Falling on Cedars* when the topic is the Japanese American internment during World War II.

- If any type of mathematics is the topic, we can share Jon Scieszka's *Math Curse,* a humorous look at mathematics for students of all ages. In science, read Scieszka's *Science Verse.*

- When teaching about African American contributions to our society, read *Martin's Big Words* or *Talkin' about Bessie* (Coleman).

For a more extensive list of trade books recommended for use as read-alouds in the content areas, see Figure 9.10.

INFORMATIONAL ARTICLES. Informational or factual articles are rich alternatives to traditional textbooks because the author's voice and point of view are obvious, making them more readable and more interesting. The high quality of pictures and graphics that accompany

---

FIGURE 9.10
Examples of Trade
Books to Use as

Content Area
Read-Alouds

Bunting, E. (1998). *So far from the sea.* New York: Clarion Books.

Frank, A. (1993). *Anne Frank: The diary of a young girl.* New York: Bantam Books.

Frazier, C. (1997). *Cold mountain.* New York: Atlantic Monthy Press.

Gibson, K. B. (2005). *The life and times of Catherine the Great.* Hockessin, DE: Mitchell Lane.

Gunderson, J. (2007). *Sacagawea: Journey into the west.* Mankato, MN: Capstone Press.

Guterson, D. (1994). *Snow falling on cedars.* New York: Harcourt.

Jacobs, F. (1992). *The Tainos: The people who welcomed Columbus.* New York: G. P. Putnam's Sons.

Keating, F. (2006). *Theodore.* New York: Simon and Schuster.

King, D.C. (2006). *Charles Darwin.* New York: DK Children.

McClafferty, C. K. (2006). *Something out of nothing: Marie Curie and radium.* New York: Farrar, Straus, Giroux.

McCollough, D. (2001). *John Adams.* New York: Simon & Schuster.

Mochizuki, K. (1995). *Baseball saved us.* New York: Lee and Low Books.

O'Connor, B. (2002). *Leonardo Da Vinci: Renaissance genius.* Minneapolis, MN: Carolrhoda Books.

Rappaport, D. (2001). *Martin's big words.* New York: Hyperion.

Scieszka, J. (1995). *Math curse.* New York: Viking.

Scieszka, J. (2004). *Science verse.* New York: Viking.

Volavkova, H. (1993). *I never saw another butterfly: Children's drawings and poems from Terezin Concentration Camp, 1942–1944.* New York: Schocken.

Whiting, J. (2006). *Aristotle.* Hockessin, DE: Mitchell Lane.

Wilkinson, P. (2007). *Gandhi: The young protester who founded a nation.* Washington, DC: National Geographic Children's Books.

Yolen, J. (1992). *Encounter.* New York: Harcourt Brace Jovanovich.

these selections add to the information they present and heighten their appeal to students. Informational articles are also more up-to-date in their coverage of topics than textbooks could ever be.

When selecting articles, we should remember to choose those that feature vivid descriptions and promote inquiry. Choosing articles that are reasonably short is also important. If we find longer articles that complement topics we are teaching, we can read selected segments of them. For example, we may choose to read the opening section and invite students to finish reading the article with a partner. Short, pertinent selections can be integrated seamlessly into the flow of our content area lessons. Sources of read-aloud articles include magazines and newspapers as well as a wide variety of websites such as Biography.com and Discovery.com.

Reading aloud can have many positive outcomes for students. For example, it may increase students' comprehension, enrich their vocabulary, help them become better writers, and motivate them to read on their own (Blessing, 2005).

How Can Students Learn to Use Textbook Study Strategies such as SQ4R?

We have already discussed the importance of students being able to generate questions and recognize text patterns while they are reading. We know it is essential for students to have background knowledge, to use a variety of reading comprehension strategies, and to discuss the meaning they construct. Textbook study strategies such as Survey, Question, Read, Record, Recite, and Reflect (SQ4R) can also help students when they are reading informational text independently.

SQ4R (Robinson, 1946) is a textbook reading study strategy that incorporates several of the strategies introduced in Chapter 4. It also accommodates learning styles by integrating multiple modes of learning. When using this study technique, students survey, question, read, record, recite, and reflect about the text. A detailed description of the process follows.

Step 1: Survey

Before you read, preview the text, activate prior knowledge, and make connections. When surveying, consider these suggestions:

- Read the text outline (title, headings, and subheadings) and the captions that accompany pictures, charts, graphs, or maps.
- Preview the introductory and concluding paragraphs.
- Read the summary.
- Review text-provided or teacher-created questions.

Step 2: Question

While you are reading, generate questions to help you think through the text and set purposes for reading; consider how to respond to text-provided or teacher-created questions. When questioning, consider these suggestions:

- Turn the title, headings, and subheadings into questions.
- Consider the questions provided in the text or by the teacher.

Note: If you believe you learn better by recording ideas while studying, you may wish to write the questions you are considering. This variation on the SQ4R study technique is called SQW4R.

Step 3: Read

Use the purpose questions you developed for each section to set purposes for reading. Read to respond to those questions. While reading, consider these suggestions:

- Set times to read and schedule regular breaks.
- Use your comprehension strategies as you read. If possible, use ideas such as Bookmark Technique or INSERT to help monitor your understanding.
- Think about possible responses to the questions you raised.

Step 4: Record

Recording information in writing, by taking notes or completing a text outline, can help to ingrain the ideas in our memory. When recording, consider these suggestions:

- Put the information in your own words to ensure understanding.
- Record information clearly, so that the written records can be used for review later.
- Record information after reading a section of text. (When we engage in writing or highlighting as we read, we often emphasize too much information.)
- Use marginal notes as another way to emphasize ideas.

Step 5: Recite

Reciting—saying and listening to information—helps us to remember it. When reciting, consider these suggestions:

- Recite aloud the major concepts of the section using your own words.
- Ask and answer questions relating to key terminology and important facts aloud.
- Study with a partner and orally explain the information to each other.

Step 6: Reflect

Reflecting helps us to remember information and become more self-aware of our learning. When reflecting, consider these suggestions:

- Make connections between new information you have learned and what you already knew.
- Think about how you can effectively use the new information.
- Review the information often to retain it.

SQ4R is an effective textbook reading strategy that includes strategies such as previewing, making connections, questioning, monitoring, and summarizing. It also incorporates reflection. Although SQ4R is only one of several textbook reading strategies, it is often viewed as the most effective.

FINAL THOUGHTS

Organizing for learning is an essential part of our teaching. Knowing how to group students, teaching them how to generate questions, understanding the roles of textbooks in teaching, and using alternatives to round-robin reading are everyday practices for us as teachers. The more we know about organizing for learning, the more likely our students are to be highly motivated, engaged learners who participate in high-quality, meaningful instruction.

In the next chapter, we investigate writing in the content areas. We explore the differences between informal and formal writing, and explain how we can integrate both in our content area teaching.

Teaching Connections

APPLYING WHAT WE HAVE LEARNED

E-Links

Work with a partner and visit a website that features standards-based lesson plans for your content area. Imagine that you are using that lesson to teach your students. Then consider how you could differentiate (1) the content, (2) the process, and (3) the product for English learners and special-needs students. For example, how would you group students for instruction? How could students use their ability to generate questions in the lesson? Will you choose more than one text? How will students show what they know and can do?

Discuss the possibilities in each category with your partner and record your thinking as a reflective entry in your portfolio.

EXAMPLE LESSON PLAN WEBSITES

Read–Write–Think: Literature, Content Areas
www.readwritethink.org

Teachnology: Lesson Plans—Math, Science, Social Studies
http://www.teach-nology.com/teachers/lesson_plans/math/

Accountable Talk

Think about the topics addressed in this chapter—lesson planning, grouping, skills instruction, alternatives to round-robin reading, and more—and explain how you will use them to create a foundation for your teaching. Focus on specific examples. Then share your ideas in a small group of students who are studying your discipline. Work together to complete a graphic organizer that represents your ideas. When your conversations in the small groups conclude, discuss this issue across subject areas.

 ### Portfolio/Performance Opportunity

As noted early in this chapter, textbook selection is a component of teaching. So, for your performance opportunity, you will work with a partner to complete a special project: the content area textbook evaluation. After the content area textbook evaluation is explained and modeled, you and your partner will complete one together. See the Evaluation of a Content Area Textbook form on the next page for details.

During this project, you and your partner will evaluate a discipline-specific content area textbook that you have brought to class. While evaluating the textbook, you will engage in several steps. First, you will review the questions included in the Evaluation of a Content Area Textbook form. Next, you and your partner will examine the textbook and respond to the questions that have been raised. When you have finished examining the text and responding to the questions, you and your partner will share what you have learned with another pair of students who are examining a text from the same discipline. You should then engage in a general class discussion about textbooks, including how teachers can use the textbook selection process to help them evaluate texts for their teaching. Finally, you will create a portfolio entry in which you summarize the information you learned about the text you examined and reflect on what you have learned about textbook selection.

Directions:

1. Work with a partner to evaluate a content area textbook.

2. Both of you should record your responses on separate copies of the Evaluation of a Content Area Textbook form.

3. When you and your partner have finished completing your forms and you have shared what you have learned with others, work on your own to write a summary of the information you recorded on your form and, based on what you have learned, explain whether you would use this textbook in your teaching. Justify your thinking.

4. When you have completed this project, remember to put your completed form and your "Summary and Explanation" into your portfolio.

Text Title: _____

Text Series: _____

Publisher: _____

Copyright Year: _____

Cost: _____

Authors: _____

_____

_____

In reviewing the textbook, your question is **Are the following qualities present in the text you are examining?** If your response is "yes," provide an example of it from the text along with the page number on which the example is located. If your answer is "no," explain whether you would be able to teach effectively if this quality were not present in the textbook.

1. Is the text well organized (contents, glossary, index, chapter structures)?

2. Is the text factually correct? (Review pages at the beginning, middle, and end of the text to determine if they are factually correct. Include examples of factual text from each page you review.)

3. Is the text motivational? (Is it the kind of text that you think would motivate students at that grade level to learn? Is it colorful? Does it have pictures? Does it include graphics? If you were a student, would you want to use this book?)

4. What is the readability level of the text? For which grade was the textbook developed?

5. Does the textbook support state content standards? Is there evidence of standards-based learning? (Does the text include state standards? Does the textbook indicate which standards the content addresses? What are three examples of standards that are included?)

6. Does the teacher's edition support teachers' use of a strategy-based lesson plan? (Does the text promote using a lesson format similar to the one we have learned—engaging, guiding, and extending student thinking? If so, provide examples.)

7. Is the content diverse? (Is there evidence of multiculturalism in the text? Are people with special needs represented? Are genders treated equally in the text?)

8. Does the text require students to use skills and strategies? [Skill examples would include generating questions and recognizing text patterns. Strategy examples would include previewing (Semantic Maps); monitoring (Bookmark Technique, Pattern Partner Reading); making connections (Connection Stems); knowing how words work (Concept of Definition Maps); summarizing (Lyric Summary, Concept of Definition Map Summary, Bio-Pyramid); and evaluating (Discussion Web).]

9. Does the text integrate content literacy? (Does it encourage reading, writing, speaking, listening, and viewing across the curriculum?) Multiple Literacies?

10. Does the text focus on meeting the needs of individual learners? (e.g., English language learners, students who struggle to read, special-needs students)?

11. Are multiple types of assessment used throughout the text (e.g., chapter questions, projects, research, tests, teacher observation)?

12. Are students asked to engage in higher-order thinking throughout the text?

13. How is technology represented throughout the text? How are the students asked to use technology? Teachers?

14. Is a teacher's edition available? Are there special resources for English learners, struggling learners, students with special needs?

15. Are the charts, maps, graphs, tables, and illustrations accurate? Do they help to support students' thinking?

16. Are supplementary materials available (e.g., text on CD, leveled texts, videos)?

Evaluation of a Content Area Textbook

10

TEACHING IDEAS:

• THINK-ALOUD • SEMANTIC QUESTION MAP • CONNECTION STEMS • SKETCH AND LABEL CONNECTIONS • PURPOSE QUESTIONS • BOOKMARK TECHNIQUE • CONCEPT OF DEFINITION MAP • INTERNET-RELATED PROJECTS

Teaching Culturally and Linguistically Diverse Students

As teachers in the 21st century, we find ourselves living in a time in which English learners are the fastest-growing portion of the U.S. population (Young & Hadaway, 2006). With more than 400 languages spoken in U.S. schools (Hadaway & Young, 2006), we are teaching increasingly high numbers of culturally and linguistically diverse students. "These students offer a rich resource of diversity that can enhance classroom dynamics" (Drucker, 2003, p. 22). Some are immigrants; others are U.S. citizens growing up in contexts in which English is not commonly spoken.

English learners are students who speak one or more languages and are learning English (Opitz & Harding-DeKarn, 2007). Pilgreen (2006) reminds us:

> Language is what enables students to communicate, language is what makes collaboration possible, and using language is a way of transmitting and negotiating knowledge. But language is precisely the barrier that English learners face when they sit in the classroom. (p. 41)

We want to help the English learners in our classes to move past the language barrier and learn content. To help our students learn how to use language more effectively, we will need to learn more about how to teach them (Fitzgerald & Graves, 2004/2005; Young & Hadaway, 2006).

That is why the focus of this chapter is teaching English learners. We begin by examining what we need to do to prepare to teach English learners at the middle and high school levels. Next, we explore the general instructional strategies that help us to teach these students. Then we discuss how we can teach reading comprehension strategies. After that, we examine ideas for teaching academic and functional vocabulary to English learners. Finally, we discuss some guidelines we can follow when teaching English learners.

How Can We Prepare to Teach English Learners?

Go to the Activities and Applications section under the topic *Diversity, Culture, and Literacy* in the MyEducationLab for your course and complete the activity entitled Cultural and Language Experiences to examine ways teachers can create a supportive environment for English learners.

Imagine how challenging it would be for us to learn about our content areas in a language we did not know. This is the challenge English learners face—except they are not just learning one content area, they are learning an entire grade's schedule of classes. As teachers, our goal is to do all we can to help these students be successful. Dong (2004/2005) reports that "Research in second-language acquisition has shown that adapting classroom discussion, textbook reading, and written activities to the language proficiencies of English language learners triggers English language acquisition in subject matter classrooms" (p. 14). Our challenge is to make this goal a reality.

Researchers report that the most important feature of English learners is their diversity (Peregoy & Boyle, 2005; Short & Echevarria, 2005). English learners have diverse backgrounds, languages, and educational experiences. Some are literate in their first languages; others are not. Some have had successful school experiences; others have had little schooling. Perkins-Gough (2007) describes the diversity of English language learners (ELLs) in this way:

> Adolescent ELLs differ from native English-speaking students in the dual challenge they face: They must learn to speak, read, and write in English and master complex academic content at the same time. Aside from this common characteristic, however, adolescent ELLs come to the classroom with widely diverse education backgrounds and socioeconomic circumstances. Some are recent immigrants who received effective schooling in their countries of origin, are literate in their native language, and have excellent content knowledge even though they lack English skills. Others came to the United States as refugees fleeing violence, have attended school only intermittently or not at all, and lack basic literacy skills. Some are undocumented, which can affect both their socioeconomic status and, in some states, their postsecondary education opportunities. The largest group of adolescent ELLs (57 percent) was born in the United States but has not developed academic literacy in English for various reasons, such as high mobility. (pp. 90–91)

Researchers tell us that appropriate professional development can help prepare us to teach English learners content and literacy skills (Short & Echevarria, 2004/2005). They suggest that we begin by accepting students from diverse cultural and linguistic backgrounds as capable learners. Figure 10.1 features a glossary of terms related to teaching English learners to help us get started.

To further promote our understanding of these students, researchers suggest that we do what is described in the following sections (Peregoy & Boyle, 2005; Short & Echevarria, 2004/2005; Villegas & Lucas, 2007).

Understand How Students Construct Meaning

As we learned in Chapter 1, constructivism is the process through which students create meaning. It involves the students using their background knowledge to make sense of the new information they are reading. The meaning that is constructed is personal, because each person's background knowledge is different. This is a crucial point for English learners. They may have a great deal of background knowledge in their first language, but it may differ significantly from the background knowledge of native English speakers. For example, there may be structural differences between English and their first language. In English, adjectives often come before nouns; in other languages, adjectives may come after the nouns.

Background knowledge is an essential ingredient in the construction of meaning. The more background knowledge we have, the better we can comprehend. Background knowledge is essential for all readers, but it is particularly important for English learners because it interacts with language proficiency during reading to alleviate comprehension difficulties (Aguilar, Fu, & Jago,

FIGURE 10.1
Glossary of Terms Related to Teaching English Learners

Comprehensible content Clear and understandable text. Teachers use a variety of methods to help make the text comprehensible for students.

Comprehensible input Language that students hear or read that is understandable enough for their brains to acquire and process (Krashen, 1982).

Culturally and linguistically responsive teachers Educators who take time to become knowledgeable about and open to students' cultures.

English as a Second Language (ESL) Term commonly used to refer to classes or programs in which English learners are taught.

English learners Students who are learning English in addition to their native language.

L1 Abbreviation that refers to a student's first or native language.

Native language A student's first language.

Scaffolded teaching and learning Providing varying degrees of support throughout the learning process from initial instruction to independent application.

Sheltered instruction Teaching content to English learners "in strategic ways that make the concepts comprehensible while promoting the students' academic language development" (Short & Echevarria, 2004/2005, p. 10).

2007). When teaching English learners, our goals concerning background knowledge are twofold: We need to ensure (1) that our students have background knowledge about a variety of topics and (2) that they are able to activate it. There are many different ways to assess whether students have and can activate background knowledge about a topic. These methods include discussion, engaging in informal writing, and completing activities such as Admit Slips and Tickets Out (see Chapter 11).

Using examples that relate to students' lives helps students build bridges between what they already know and what they are learning. Once again, it is important to remember the diversity of English learners. Knowledge acquired in their cultures may differ from that of native English speakers.

As culturally and linguistically responsive teachers, we need to help students make connections between what they already know and what they need to learn. Imagine the extent and type of background knowledge students might have if we were teaching about immigration in one of our courses. Students whose native language is English may have some background knowledge about immigration, particularly since immigration is a national political issue. By comparison, English learners may have much more to contribute to such a discussion, because they may have recently gone through the immigration process. Examples of books that can be used as read-alouds to facilitate discussions about immigration are listed in Figure 10.2. For more information about read-alouds and a more general list of books to read aloud in the content areas, see Chapter 9.

FIGURE 10.2
Read-Aloud Books about Immigration

Blohm, J. M., & Lapinsky, T. (2006). *Kids like me: Voices of the immigrant experience.* Boston, MA: Intercultural Press.

Bode, J. (1991). *New kids in town: Oral histories of immigrant teens.* New York: Scholastic.

Gallo, D. R. (Ed.) (2007). *First crossing: Stories of teen immigrants.* Somerville, MA: Candlewick Press.

Knight, M. B. (1993). *Who belongs here?* Gardiner, ME: Tilbury House.

Lai, H. M., Lim, G., & Yung, J. (1999). *Island: Poetry and history of Chinese immigrants on Angel Island, 1910–1940.* Seattle, WA: University of Washington Press.

Motomura, H. (2006). *Americans in waiting: The lost story of immigration and citizenship in the United States.* New York: Oxford University Press.

Making Connections
TO ENGLISH LEARNERS

Sharing a short text or a picture book through a teacher read-aloud contributes to student motivation and background knowledge. Teacher read-alouds, which are detailed in Chapter 9, are especially helpful to English learners because they eliminate the need for the students to read the text, provide information that supports the topic being studied, and promote discussion. In addition, read-alouds are often accompanied by photographs or illustrations that scaffold the students' understanding of language. ■

Learn about Students' Lives and Appreciate Their Cultures

As teachers, we need to know about our students' families, immigration histories, previous educational experiences, and information such as students' strengths, interests, and attitudes toward school. We can obtain this information in many ways, including learning about our students' backgrounds through conversations with them and their families. We can also use peer interviews, in which native English speakers and English learners can exchange information. Figure 10.3 features questions that can be used during peer interviews. Finally, we can integrate information about students' lives in class assignments and projects.

The information we gather will inform our teaching. For example, throughout this book, we have talked about ideas such as student-centered learning and discussion as natural components of teaching and learning. They are part of our culture, but there are other cultures in which teaching is very lecture based; in those classrooms, discussion and *sharing* ideas do not have an active role. In fact, there are languages in which the word "sharing" does not exist. If we learn that is the case for any of our students, we can incorporate that knowledge into our teaching and offer support as our students gradually become accustomed to student-centered learning and grow more comfortable with sharing their ideas through discussion.

Possess and Promote Positive Views about Diversity

When we are culturally responsive, we view ourselves and our students as participants in a learning community. We set high standards for all students and we inspire our students to gain confidence, participate in rigorous curriculums, use strategies to monitor their learning, strive to meet high standards, and contribute their personal and cultural backgrounds as resources for class learning. To accomplish these goals, we need to understand both ourselves and our students.

FIGURE 10.3
Peer Interview
Questions

Family
1. Please tell me about your family. Share photos, if possible.
2. When did your family come to the United States? What country did you come from? (Provide a world map, so both students can show the countries from which their families immigrated.)

Education
1. What do you like most about school? Why do you like it?
2. What was school like in the country in which you used to live?

Special Interests
1. How do you use technology in your life (computers, cell phones, digital cameras)? (Have a computer available.)
2. Do you like music? What is your favorite band? (Have CDs available.)
3. Do you watch television? What is your favorite television program?
4. What do you like to do when we are not in school?

We need to create ways to support English learners' abilities to learn content and acquire a new language. To do so, we will need to use supports such as welcoming the students' first languages into our classrooms, ensuring the prominence of vocabulary study, using cooperative learning, and incorporating culturally relevant materials into our lessons.

Work Collaboratively with Colleagues to Provide Support for English Learners

When we teach English learners, we can join or organize support teams. For example, schools often have ESL teachers whose focus is teaching the English language to students who are not native speakers. Developing positive relationships with these teachers can be helpful. This is especially true when we integrate students' native languages into our classes as a scaffold and when we need to know how much scaffolding particular students may need. Other members of such a support team may include, but are not limited to, literacy coaches and upper-grade students, as well as community volunteers, who speak students' first languages. When we partner with those who speak students' native languages, we can use those languages to help English learners access our curricula. Villegas and Lucas (2007) suggest that providing materials in students' native languages, such as informational articles, text adaptations, leveled text, or textbooks, can help them build background knowledge.

Making Connections | Thinking about Working with Other Professionals

■ Think about the value of working with a team of professionals to support students who are English learners. Reflect on how being a team member might enrich your teaching. Consider what you perceive to be the positive and negative points of such collaborative efforts. Focus on specific examples.

■ Share your thoughts with others in small-group discussions.

Understanding learning from a constructivist perspective, learning about our students' lives and appreciating their cultures, and having and promoting positive views about diversity will provide a sound foundation for teaching English learners. Of course, accomplishing each of these tasks should not be solely a personal effort or a team effort, but rather one in which entire school districts and communities engage.

Making Connections | Thinking about English Learners

■ Most of us are familiar with the phrase, "It takes a village to raise a child." Let's apply this idea to teaching English learners. It takes a community to make resources available to English learners, to teach them, and to provide them with full access to the community in which they and their families live. Consider how school administrators, community members, business leaders, and regional families can help these students reach their maximum potential. Focus on specific ideas. Then reflect on what you and fellow faculty members can do to enrich English learners' education.

■ Share your thoughts with others in small-group discussions.

What General Instructional Techniques Can We Use to Support Our Teaching of English Learners?

When we have established a solid foundation for teaching English learners, we will need to think about general approaches to instruction. We know that language acquisition involves the interplay of many factors (Hadaway & Young, 2006), and we want English learners to experience success in our content area courses. Researchers suggest that English learners need opportunities to gain knowledge, feel successful, acquire strategies, monitor learning, and be motivated to practice (Koskinen, Blum, Bisson, Phillips, Creamer, & Baker, 1999). In this section, we focus on general teaching techniques that will help ensure their success. These include scaffolded teaching and learning, sheltered instruction, and accessible text, among others.

Scaffolded Teaching and Learning

When we scaffold learning, we use supports to help students gain knowledge. For example, when we teach reading comprehension strategies, we provide the necessary supports, by explaining and modeling the strategies. This may include using think-alouds that provide a model for active thinking during the reading process.

TEACHING IDEA

THINK-ALOUD. Think-Alouds (Davey, 1983) help us to understand what we are reading. To teach your students how to use think-alouds, follow these steps:

Go to the Activities and Applications section under the topic *Comprehension Strategies* in the MyEducationLab for your course and complete the activity entitled Think Alouds to Model Comprehension to examine why this strategy can be effective with English learners.

1. **Explain:** Select a passage to read aloud to the students. The passage should require some strategic thinking to clarify understandings. Explain that we use Think-Alouds to model strategic behaviors and thoughts as we engage in the reading process. That is, we use Think-Alouds to help ourselves focus on strategically thinking our way through text. Then introduce the text.

2. **Demonstrate:** Before reading, demonstrate your connections to the text by thinking aloud. To make text-self connections, use prompts such as "I have a connection to this because . . ." and "This reminds me of . . ." To make text–text connections, use prompts such as "I read about this in an article and it said . . ." or "I read about this on the Internet and it said . . ." As you read, think aloud to demonstrate other reading comprehension strategies, including monitoring, visualizing, and summarizing. The following examples show how you might think aloud while using reading strategies.

   - Monitoring—ensuring that what we have read made sense: "I read this section about mitosis, but it does not make sense to me. I am going to go back and read it more slowly."
   - Visualizing—making mental pictures while reading: "When I read about mitosis and meiosis, I pictured how they were different in my mind. I am going to sketch my visualization so I can share what I am seeing in my mind with you."
   - Summarizing—synthesizing important ideas: "This part of the chapter is about meiosis. I know that I will be writing a summary about it when I finish reading, so I am going to take notes about the definition of meiosis, because I think that is important information to include in the summary."

3. **Guide:** After demonstrating the Think-Aloud several times, invite the English learners to practice with native English-speaking partners.

4. **Practice:** After sufficient practice, encourage students to try Think-Alouds on their own using text in which they have interest and about which they have background knowledge.

5. **Reflect:** Invite students to reflect on how thinking aloud helps them to focus on what they are reading. Encourage them to think about how they can use Think-Alouds in other subject areas.

Next, students can work with a partner as they attempt new tasks—in this case, using new strategies. Finally, students can apply the strategies independently. Throughout this process, we are gradually releasing responsibility for learning to the students, who learn about the strategies from the teacher, try them with a partner, and then try them on their own. There are a number of scaffolds we can use when teaching English learners, including using the student's native language.

Sheltered Instruction

Sheltered instruction involves teaching content to English learners "in strategic ways that make the concepts comprehensible while promoting the students' academic language development" (Short & Echevarria, 2004/2005, p. 10). One method for teaching sheltered instruction is to use the Sheltered Instruction Observation Protocol (SIOP). The SIOP Model is a "scientifically validated model of sheltered instruction designed to make grade-level academic content understandable for English learners while at the same time developing their English language" (Echevarria, Vogt, & Short, 2008, p. 246). The SIOP Model is a lesson planning and delivery system; the SIOP protocol is an instrument used to observe, rate, and provide feedback on lessons (Echevarria et al., 2008).

The following sheltered instruction techniques are recommended by a number of researchers (Genesee, 1999; Short & Echevarria, 2004/2005; Peregoy & Boyle, 2005). We can use these methods in our teaching.

USING COOPERATIVE LEARNING. Engaging English learners in cooperative learning supports them in a variety of ways. For example, students in the group who speak English can provide fluent language models. They can also listen to and support the English learners as they communicate their thoughts. In addition, learning in a peer setting is often motivational for students. Because valuing the ideas of others is a basic premise of cooperative learning, all students have opportunities to successfully participate in the learning process.

MAKING CONNECTIONS TO STUDENT EXPERIENCES. Students construct meaning by making connections between their background knowledge and experiences and the information that they are learning. The more background knowledge the students have, the better they comprehend. We also know that if students don't have background knowledge of or experiences with a topic, we can provide information in several ways, including through read-alouds, discussion, and sharing visuals.

USING SLOWER SPEECH AND FEWER IDIOMATIC EXPRESSIONS. As teachers, we should ensure that we not speak too quickly when teaching English learners so we can be fluent English language models and help students understand what we are saying. We should also try to avoid the use of idiomatic expressions, because they do not translate literally. Examples of idiomatic expressions include the following phrases:

- Actions speak louder than words
- Against the clock
- Dot all the i's and cross all the t's
- Lose face
- Take a raincheck
- Think outside the box
- Time flies
- Two heads are better than one

USING VISUAL SUPPORTS AND DEMONSTRATIONS WITH VERBAL INSTRUCTION. When we use visual supports such as pictures and demonstrations, we provide additional cues for English learners. For example, showing pictures of fruits and vegetables or the actual fruits may make it easier for English learners to understand the concept of nutritious foods. Demonstrating how to search for information about a topic on the Internet, in addition to providing directions, may help students to better understand how they should search.

USING ADAPTED TEXT AND SUPPLEMENTARY MATERIALS. When we paraphrase text, provide text on CD or tape, or make leveled text available, we support English learners' comprehension of text. Paraphrasing allows us to present the text in a less complex format.

Accessible Text

When teaching English learners, we must ensure that our students have accessible text—text they can read. This often means that we need to adapt texts and provide study aids. In this section, we examine several ways to help make text more accessible to our students. Examples include scaffolded outlines, study guides, rewritten texts, texts on tape or CD, and leveled texts. When reading about these processes, consider the benefits of working with English as a Second Language (ESL) teachers and fellow content area teachers.

SCAFFOLDED OUTLINES. Scaffolded outlines provide an opportunity for students to take limited notes. In a scaffolded outline, we provide part of the outline and students add to it. Students then use the outline to support their understanding of the content. Having a topic-based outline that uses key words and simplified language helps English learners comprehend.

The best way to introduce these outlines to English learners is to scaffold the process—beginning by providing a great deal of support and very gradually encouraging the learner to take more responsibility. For example, we would begin by providing outlines that are essentially complete. Over time, we would provide increasingly less information and require the students to add more. For example, when studying "the active sun" in earth science, a section of an outline we might usually provide for students would differ from a scaffolded outline that we would create for English learners. Figure 10.4 shows parallel sections of a traditional outline and a scaffolded outline with supports for English learners. The outlines are based on a section of text titled "The Active Sun" in Tarbuck and Lutgens' *Earth Science* (Prentice Hall, 2006).

STUDY GUIDES. Creating study guides in which we use simple language, key vocabulary, simple sentences, and meaningful questions is another way we can help English learners understand what they read. When structuring these guides, it is important to note the structure of the text for which the guide will be used. For example, many content area texts have subheadings, so study guides for those texts should have the same subheadings. Other texts have subheadings and a variety of tables and figures. If that is the case, we can create guides that loosely parallel the structure of the pages students will be reading. This consistency will help English learners to make connections between the information in the guide and the information that appears in the text. In addition, numbering each section of the page may help English learners to locate the area to which the teacher or partner may be referring.

Figure 10.5 shows an excerpt from a study guide for chemistry. The section to which the guide applies is primarily print (text), but does include one figure.

REWRITTEN TEXT. We can also rewrite text in simple sentences, focusing on text frames, the main idea, and supporting details. This approach works particularly well if we can share the task with peers. For example, if we teach chemistry and two other teachers teach the same course and use the same text, then each teacher can take responsibility for rewriting designated chapters. Copies of the rewritten text can be kept in three-ring notebooks that allow students to easily add or delete information.

FIGURE 10.4
Traditional and Scaffolded Outline Examples: Earth Science—"The Active Sun"

Traditional Outline Example	Scaffolded Outline Example
I. The active sun	1. Why is the sun described as "active"? (page 687)
A. Sunspots	2. What are sunspots? See Figure 15. (page 687)
B. Prominences	3. What are prominences? See Figure 16. (page 688)
C. Solar flares	4. What are solar flares? (page 688)
	• How do they impact solar wind?
	• What are auroras? What else are they called?
	• What happens following a strong solar flare? See Figure 17.

FIGURE 10.5
Excerpt from a
Study Guide for
Matter and
Measurement: The
Study of Chemistry

Chemistry: The Central Science (2008)

Making Connections to What We Know (Activating Background Knowledge)

We may think we do not know anything about chemistry, but we can see chemistry in our lives every day. The authors of our textbook tell us that when we light a match, that is chemistry. When drugs are developed to cure diseases, that is chemistry. So, even though we may not have studied chemistry before, we see it happening every day.

Chemistry is the study of properties of materials and the changes that materials undergo. Chemistry is how leaves change color in the fall and how batteries generate electricity. Chemistry is how our bodies use food. Chemistry is how our world works.

Key Vocabulary

1. What is matter? **Matter is the physical material of the universe.** It is anything that has mass and occupies space. Houses have mass and occupy space. Cars have mass and occupy space. Even our textbook has mass and occupies space.

2. What is a property? **A property is any trait or characteristic that allows us to know that one type of matter is different from another.**

3. What are atoms? **Atoms are the smallest building blocks of matter.**

4. What are molecules? **Two or more atoms can combine to form molecules.**

5. Sketch molecular models of oxygen, water, and carbon dioxide.

The **white spheres** represent **hydrogen.** When you sketch a hydrogen molecule, write an **H** on it.

The **dark gray spheres** represent **carbon.** When you sketch a carbon molecule, write a **C** on it.

The **red spheres** represent **oxygen.** When you sketch an oxygen molecule, write an **O** on it.

1. **Oxygen Molecular Model**

2. **Water Molecular Model**

3. **Carbon Dioxide Molecular Model**

TEXT ON TAPE OR CDS IN ENGLISH AND IN NATIVE LANGUAGES. Having texts on tape or CDs can support English learners in gaining knowledge of content and developing fluency as they read along. Having simultaneous access to the written text and the oral reading will provide students with opportunities to see, to listen, and to read along to improve their fluency. To enrich this process, invite students to work with partners who are fluent, native English speakers. Texts in native languages provide support and help students to learn content. Some publishers also provide texts in languages other than English and sectional summaries on CD-ROM. Miller and Levine's *Biology* (Prentice-Hall, 2008) is an example of a text for which such materials are available. Working with other teachers and with students who have already completed the course can also facilitate the development of a text on tape or CD library.

Go to the Activities and Applications section under the topic *Developing Vocabulary, Concepts, and Fluency* in the MyEducationLab for your course and complete the activity entitled Vocabulary and Content Area Learning to examine why it is helpful to work with English learners on content-specific vocabulary.

LEVELED TEXTS. We can also use texts about the topic being studied that have readability levels lower than that of the course textbook. English learners can read these texts while the other students are reading more complex texts, such as the course textbook. The information would focus on the same topic, but the leveled texts would be easier to read. These texts can be used to support English learners as they read about the topic in everyday settings, or they can be the texts that English learners read when the class engages in Discussion circles. (To learn more about Discussion Circles, see Chapter 9.) In the latter case, each student in the group would read a different title, and share the book they had read with the group. For the English learner, the book would be selected from leveled text.

All of these techniques will help us successfully face the challenges of planning instruction for this highly diverse group of learners. Of course, throughout our teaching, we also need to encourage English learners to use multiple modes of response, including speaking, writing, sketching, dramatizing, and music. For example, when students engage in the Say Something, they respond orally (see Chapter 6). When they complete a Scaffolded Outline, they respond in writing (see page 139). Sketching is a mode of response students use when they create Sketch and Label Connections (see Chapter 7) or complete adapted versions of teaching ideas such as the Bookmark Technique (see Chapter 6). To engage in activities such as Dinner Party and Living Newspaper Theatre (see Chapter 13), students dramatize. To respond through singing, students can create Lyric Summaries or participate in Rapping for Review (see Chapter 14).

Making Connections
TO STRUGGLING READERS

Although the scaffolding techniques discussed in this chapter are designed to benefit English learners, many of them also support the learning experiences of struggling readers. For example, struggling readers would benefit from the use of multiple modes of response, adapted graphic organizers, scaffolded outlines, and leveled texts. ■

Engaging, Guiding, and Extending Student Thinking

When teaching English learners, it is important that we use a structured approach. The SIOP Lesson Plan Design Template 1 provides a research-based lesson design for sheltered instruction (Echevarria et al., 2008, p. 230). In the SIOP Lesson Plan, there is a section labeled "Lesson Sequence", in which we can use the classic three-part lesson plan commonly known as *before*, *during*, and *after reading* that we use throughout this text. Viewing the stages of this plan as *engaging*, *guiding*, and *extending* student thinking helps us to make connections between our planning and our view of reading as a thinking process. This lesson format also provides the perfect opportunity to focus on reading comprehension strategies. Roit (2006) supports this approach and notes, "Teaching reading comprehension creates the perfect environment for English learners to not only learn how to derive meaning from text but also to learn how to talk about text and about what they are learning" (p. 80).

Each section of this plan has particular purposes. Figure 10.6 shows examples of what we can do during each stage.

As noted in the figure, *before* reading, we engage students' thinking by motivating them and helping them to make connections to their background knowledge. *During* reading, we provide a variety of ways to guide students' thinking by helping them monitor their understanding. *After* reading, we encourage students to engage in summarizing and completing a variety of projects to extend their thinking. Discussion permeates the plan. Details of each stage follow.

Engaging	Guiding	Extending
Activating or building background knowledge (read-alouds, films, photos, websites)	Teacher read-aloud of short section of text	Making connections to life experiences
	Reading along with text on CD	Summarizing
Making text–self connections	Patterned Partner Reading	Informal writing
Providing text overviews or scaffolded outlines	Cross-age reading experiences	Alternative modes of response
Explaining directions	Using purpose questions to guide reading	Inquiry-based projects/rubrics Discussion
Developing purpose questions	Bookmark Technique	
Preteaching vocabulary and essential concepts	Adapting text/accessible text	
	Discussion	
Obtaining assistance from native language speakers	Sketching	
	Informal writing	
Discussion		

FIGURE 10.6
Engaging, Guiding, and Extending Student Thinking

Engaging Students' Thinking (Before Reading)

Before reading, we engage students' thinking. Roit (2006) notes that motivation is key to reading comprehension for English learners. We motivate our students to read in a variety of different ways, including sharing pictures, visiting a website, or engaging in a read-aloud. We want to ensure that our students have background knowledge. If they don't have background knowledge, we engage in preteaching to provide it. We help them to activate this knowledge through discussion or use of a comprehension strategy. We also help students to set purposes for reading. Reading comprehension strategies, key vocabulary concepts, and discussion are prevalent in this stage.

If we know that the English learners in our classes do not have any background knowledge about a particular topic or strategy, we can preteach them. This involves a brief period of time away from the rest of the class in which we can (1) explain a concept we will be teaching later that day or (2) explain and demonstrate a graphic organizer the rest of the class already knows how to use. In the first case, preteaching content will help the students to feel more comfortable as they recognize related terminology while learning about the topic with the class. In the second case, preteaching the graphic organizer will help the English learners to feel comfortable using it with other class members. When we teach English learners about graphic organizers, we often number the sections of the organizer, so students can attend to them more readily. We can also simplify their structure if the model is too complex.

In the *before reading* stage of the lesson, there are many different ways to engage English learners (see Chapters 5 and 8). Two possibilities are discussed next.

SEMANTIC QUESTION MAP. Using a Semantic Question Map (McLaughlin, 2003) instead of the more common Semantic Map helps to focus students' thinking on predetermined questions and set purposes for reading. As presented in Figure 10.7, the components of the Semantic Question Map are determined before the students begin working with the map. The students' task is to contribute responses to the four questions that have been posed. This structure helps to focus student thinking, as do the numbers that appear before each question and in the corresponding numbered spaces where students can write their responses. In the traditional Semantic Map, responses are less structured and categories emerge from students' responses.

The Semantic Question Map featured in Figure 10.7 was used in a science class learning about the world environment. It provides examples of predetermined questions about the rainforests, which were one aspect of the discussion. This was an especially good choice of topic,

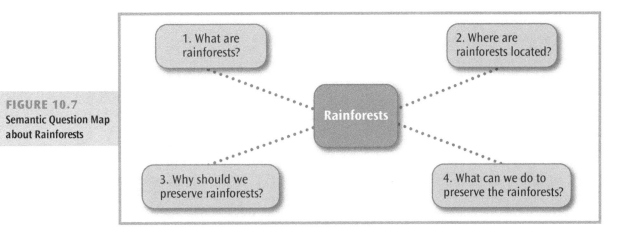

FIGURE 10.7
Semantic Question Map about Rainforests

because asking about the locations of rainforests may invite English learners to refer to their native lands.

For more information about the Semantic Question Map and the more traditional Semantic Map, see Chapters 5 and 8.

TEACHING IDEA

CONNECTION STEMS AND SKETCH AND LABEL CONNECTIONS. We can teach our students how to make text–self connections, text–text connections, and text–world connections (Harvey & Goudvis, 2000) to help them activate their background knowledge. See Chapter 5 for detailed descriptions of these teaching ideas and teaching examples; see Figure 5.10 for an example of Sketch and Label Visualizations. We can adapt the process of making connections for English learners by focusing on connections to their lives and changing the mode of response from only oral to sketch and label, followed by sharing with a peer.

Guiding Students' Thinking (During Reading)

During reading, we help to guide students' thinking, as they interact with text, construct meaning, and share ideas. Reading comprehension strategies, individual/partner perceptions, and discussion are evident in this stage.

TEACHING IDEA

PURPOSE QUESTIONS. To help students focus on particular sections of text, we can use Purpose Questions. These are easily constructed by turning text subheadings into questions to help guide students' reading. For example, in a geometry chapter about triangles, a subheading might read "Right Triangles." Our purpose question might be, "What are right triangles?" or "How do right triangles differ from other triangles?" English learners would then read to find the answer to that question. When they find it, they could sketch a right triangle to show that they understand what it is.

TEACHING IDEA

BOOKMARK TECHNIQUE. We use Bookmark Technique (McLaughlin, 2003) to help students set purposes for and monitor their reading. There are four types of Bookmarks, each of which seeks particular information. Bookmark 1 asks students what they thought was most interesting. Bookmark 2 asks them to find and attempt to define a vocabulary word they think everyone needs to learn. The third Bookmark asks students to share something they found confusing. The fourth Bookmark asks them to explain a chart, map, graph, or illustration that helped them to understand what they have read. We can adapt the Bookmark Technique by numbering the sections of the Bookmarks, simplifying the language, and offering students the option of sketching some of the responses instead of writing them. Figure 10.8 shows both the original Vocabulary Bookmark and a Bookmark adapted for use with English learners. For details about how to teach the Bookmark Technique and related student examples, see Chapters 6 and 9. For reproducible organizers, see the Appendix.

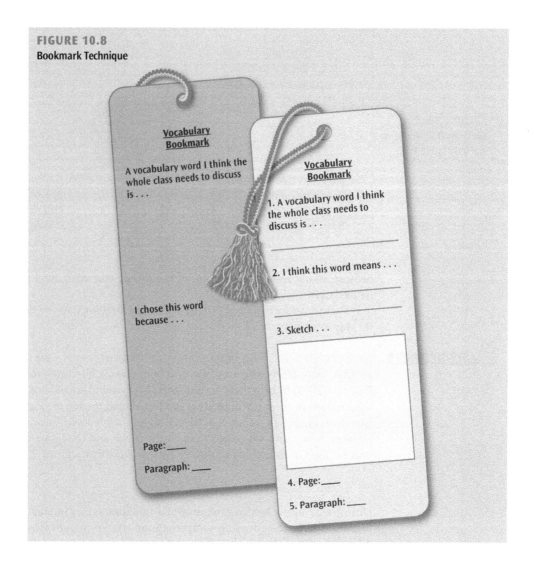

FIGURE 10.8
Bookmark Technique

Extending Students' Thinking (After Reading)

When students have finished reading the text, we help them to clarify their understandings and extend their thinking across the curriculum and beyond the classroom. This is also a time when we can reteach concepts students may not have thoroughly understood.

In this *after reading* stage of the lesson, there are a variety of ways to encourage English learners to extend their thinking. Two examples are discussed next.

 **CONCEPT OF DEFINITION MAP.** As we learned in Chapter 8, one of the easiest ways to learn how to summarize informational text is to write a summary based on a completed Concept of Definition Map (Schwartz & Raphael, 1985). See Chapters 8 and 11 for detailed information about and examples of the Concept of Definition Map Summary. Modifications we can make to this graphic organizer include numbering each section so that English learners can attend to sections as we refer to them, and providing the option of sketching in the sections labeled "Comparison" and "What are three examples?" Other ideas that help students summarize using alternative modes of response include Sketch to Stretch (see Chapter 7) and Lyric Summaries (see Chapter 14).

INTERNET-RELATED PROJECTS. Students engage with computers in school for a variety of purposes—from searching for information to participating in school projects that involve communicating with the global education community. Computers offer a number of supports for English learners. These include colored photos and graphics, access to a variety of sources, and opportunities to read about topics at text levels that may not be as challenging as the levels of class textbooks. As teachers, we can scaffold students' use of computers as an information source by bookmarking class-related websites, preparing scaffolded outlines for selected sites, and providing opportunities for students to engage in projects that we can scaffold. Internet Project (Leu, 2001) and Internet Workshop (Leu, 2002), are two examples of high-interest Internet projects in which students can engage. The first can be used with classrooms around the world, which may allow students who speak the English learner's native language to participate. The second is an individual research project that involves raising a question, using the Internet to seek responses, and analyzing the information. For details about and examples of these projects, see Chapter 12. For other inquiry-based projects, see Chapter 13.

Making Connections
TO MULTIPLE LITERACIES

When English learners use the Internet to participate in projects in which they generate search questions, locate information, synthesize the information, and communicate it to others, they are engaging in informational literacy (Leu, Kinzer, Coiro, & Cammack, 2004). Depending on their previous experiences, English learners may need to learn how to use, or require extra support when using, the Internet to engage in information literacy across the curriculum. This is a need that may be addressed through collaboration with other content area teachers, ESL teachers, computer specialists, and school administrators. ▪

The engaging, guiding, and extending students' thinking (before, during, and after) lesson structure contributes to the context for learning. It helps students to make connections to text and provides a variety of ways in which students can express their ideas. Haag and Williams (2004) support this thinking and remind us to encourage English learners to use these alternative formats to demonstrate what they know and can do. They also suggest that we should listen carefully to English learners' responses.

Figure 10.9 features a biology lesson plan that was created using the engaging–guiding–extending students' thinking format. Note how the teacher integrated supports for English learners throughout the lesson plan. The Pennsylvania State Standards are listed as the related standards in Part 1.

Making Connections
TO WRITING

Student writing is an integral part of the biology lesson shown in Figure 10.9. It is important to note that we can support English learners' writing in a variety of ways—for example, by providing illustrations and creating a word wall with photos that focuses on the current topic of study. We can also scaffold students' learning of summary writing (see Chapter 11). ▪

Aguilar, Fu, and Jabo (2007) note that in addition to well-structured lessons, we need to provide English learners with time to actually use the language. Offering access to a variety of texts, opportunities for choice, time for informal writing, fluent reading models, and social interaction with native English speakers will motivate students to become active language learners. Throughout these opportunities, we want our students to experience comprehensible text—language that students hear or read that is understandable enough for their brains to acquire and process (Krashen, 1982).

FIGURE 10.9 Biology Lesson Plan with Supports for English Learners

Content Area Reading Lesson Plan

Text: Chapter 3, "The Biosphere"; Section 3-2, "Energy Flow" in Miller, K. R., & Levine, S. J. (2008). *Biology.* Upper Saddle River, NJ: Prentice Hall.

I. Goals and Related Standards

Students will

- Use a Semantic Question Map. Standards: learning to read independently; quality of speaking and listening.
- Discuss. Standards: read, analyze and interpret text.
- Use Bookmark Technique. Standards: learning to read independently.
- Describe and discuss ecological pyramids. Standards: explain the structure and functional similarities and differences found among living things (biological sciences).
- Create six-slide PowerPoint presentations. Standards: learning to read independently; types and quality of writing, speaking, and listening; utilize computer software (technology).
- English Language Proficiency Standard 4: English language learners communicate information, ideas, and concepts necessary for academic success in the content area of science. Grade level Cluster: 9–12.

II. Engaging Students' Thinking

I will begin the lesson by reviewing what we have learned about food chains, food webs, and their trophic levels.* Then I will discuss *pyramids* with the students to help them activate their background knowledge about them. Next, I will explain the Semantic Question Map and model how it works. I will explain to the students that the focus words for the Map will be the *ecological pyramid*.

I will begin completing the Map by thinking aloud. I will ask myself, "What is it?" I will respond by saying, "An ecological pyramid is a diagram in a pyramid shape that shows the relative amounts of energy or matter contained within each trophic level in a food chain or food web." Then I will write my response on the Semantic Question Map.

Next, I will invite the students to work with a partner to explain the definition of *ecological pyramid* to each other and sketch the pyramid. I will monitor students' discussion and assist as necessary.

Then I will invite the students to help me respond to the remaining questions. When responding to question 2, we might say, "An energy pyramid shows that organisms pass on only small amounts of energy to the next level because they use much of the energy they store for respiration (breathing), movement, and reproduction." In response to question 3, we might say, "A biomass pyramid represents the amount of potential food available for each trophic level in an ecosystem." In response to question 4, we might say, "A pyramid of numbers refers to the number of individual organisms at each trophic level." When the Map is completed, we will discuss it and create a summary of the Semantic Question Map.

III. Guiding Students' Thinking

I will begin by introducing the section of the text on Ecological Pyramids. Next, we will make connections from the text to our completed Semantic Question Map. Then I will explain to the students that they will be using Patterned Partner Reading, using the pattern Read–Pause–Sketch-Share, to read the text.* I will explain that they will have 20 minutes to complete the reading. I will monitor as students engage in Patterned Partner Reading and assist as necessary. When the reading is completed, we will discuss what the students have read and the illustrations that appear as supports in that section of the chapter.

IV. Extending Students' Thinking

Students will extend their thinking by forming small groups and creating six-slide PowerPoint* presentations about ecological pyramids or a previously studied topic such as producers, consumers, and feeding relationships. Each group will address a different topic and share its presentation with the class. Before the students begin this project, I will provide them with a checklist to ensure that they include all of the necessary elements and present their work in a professional manner.

V. Assessment

I will

- Observe students as they contribute to the Semantic Question Map.
- Observe students' discussion to monitor participation and understanding.
- Observe students as they engage in Patterned Partner Reading and express their understandings through their sketches.
- Observe students as they work cooperatively in small groups.
- Use a checklist to assess students' PowerPoint presentations.

*I will meet with the English learner students to preteach the concepts in the section of text about ecological pyramids. I will use the illustrations of the various pyramids as visual supports. Preteaching using the text illustrations will provide the students with background knowledge about the topic before they participate in the lesson.

*I will pair students so that English learners will read with a more capable and fluent reader. I chose to use the Read–Pause–Sketch–Share) Pattern so English learners would be able to engage in sketching as an alternative mode of response.

*I will group students to ensure that English learners are supported. If needed, I will preteach English learners to create PowerPoint presentations.

Making Connections | Thinking about English Learners

■ Reflect on the need to provide English learners with opportunities to use the language. Consider what you can do to help these students become active language learners in your content area. Think about specific examples.

■ Share your thoughts with others in small-group discussions.

How Can We Teach Vocabulary to English Learners?

Discussions about teaching vocabulary to English learners generally focus on two types of language: functional and academic. Dong (2004/2005) notes that we should teach academic, discipline-specific language systematically and pay close attention to the functional use of language in our classrooms.

Teaching Academic Vocabulary

Gersten and Baker (2002) suggest the following guidelines for selecting and teaching academic vocabulary to English learners:

■ *Limit the number of new vocabulary words introduced in a lesson.* This is now a widely accepted idea in the teaching of vocabulary. Although some of us can recall times when teachers assigned twenty or more new words at the start of each chapter, today we are more likely to focus on five or six. These are generally terms that are critical to students' understanding of the material in the chapter.

■ *Teach the words in a variety of ways and ensure multiple exposures.* In the past, students were often told to look up words in a dictionary. Now, however, we teach terms in several different ways. For example, we might use (1) graphic organizers such as the Concept of Definition Map or Semantic Question Map; (2) the Vocabulary Bookmark from Bookmark Technique; (3) Context Clues; (4) Narrow Reading; and (5) teacher read-alouds to help students learn particular terms.

■ *Select words that convey key concepts, are widely used in content, and have meaning to the students' lives.* Although this practice specifically refers to words that are essential for students' understanding of our disciplines, words that are relevant across content areas would also be included. It is especially motivational if the terms students are learning relate to their lives. This link helps students to see beyond the classroom to their need to use the terms in their everyday lives.

■ *Use visuals such as graphic organizers to help students process and integrate word knowledge.* Using graphic organizers helps English learners remember the various aspects of a concept by identifying the information with a particular section of the graphic. Although this is certainly helpful, our teaching should not stop there. We need to move beyond promoting students' initial understanding of terms to ensure that the words become part of their speaking and writing vocabularies.

When teaching vocabulary to English learners, Echevarria and Graves (1998) suggest that we define words with the support of pictures, demonstrations, and examples familiar to students. Nagy (1988) proposes that we relate the words to familiar concepts, integrate new words by building prior knowledge, process words using new vocabulary to describe reality, and promote oral language development and listening comprehension. Dong (2004/2005) notes that extensive real-life examples help create a rich context in which students discover meaning for themselves.

Narrow reading and read-alouds are two effective methods for helping English learners to expand their vocabularies. Narrow reading focuses on students selecting texts from collections that either teachers or students and teachers have organized. Teachers select the texts they will use when reading aloud to the class. Details of these two techniques follow.

NARROW READING. Schmitt and Carter (2000) suggest that we engage students in narrow reading, which supports vocabulary acquisition. With this approach, students read authentic texts about a particular topic from many different sources. This helps the words to become part of the students' vocabularies. For example, students could read articles about global warming found in newspapers, in magazines, or on the Internet. Although the articles would come from different sources and would be written by different authors, they would feature common vocabulary. This would offer students multiple exposures to a variety of terms related to global warming.

READ-ALOUDS. Reading aloud to students every day promotes language development and vocabulary acquisition. We can read a wide variety of materials, ranging from theme-related picture books to articles found on the Internet, and from poetry to ongoing segments of theme-related biographies or novels. When we read aloud, students are free to relax and construct personal meaning. When reading aloud to English learners, it is a good idea to stop periodically to ensure understanding. Teaching ideas such as Photographs of the Mind (Keene & Zimmerman, 1997), and "Say Something" (Short, Harste, & Burke, 1996) work well when we are reading aloud to students.

- *Photographs of the Mind* is a simple graphic organizer that has four sections in which students can sketch their ideas in response to what teachers read. When we read aloud, we predetermine four stopping points—usually three during the reading of the text and one at the end. When we stop, students quickly sketch what they are thinking at that time. Then they share and discuss their sketches with their peers. This practice is especially beneficial because it offers students an opportunity to use sketching as an alternative mode of response. (See Chapter 6.)

- *Say Something* involves each student commenting to a peer when we stop at predetermined points. They literally Say Something to each other after short segments of the text are read. The exchanges are often supported by prompts such as "I did not know that . . ." or "I was surprised to learn that . . ." (see Chapter 6.)

Both Photographs of the Mind and Say Something create comfortable contexts for English learners because the students are only sharing their responses—either sketched or oral—with a peer. For details about these and other teaching ideas, see Chapters 5, 6, 7, and 8. (For more detailed information about using read-alouds in the content areas, see Chapter 9.)

When teaching vocabulary to English learners, Beck, McKeown, and Kucan (2002) suggest that we select an appropriate number of words for students to learn and create activities that provide multiple, diverse ways for students to practice. Approaches such as those listed next help us to scaffold and encourage students' learning of vocabulary:

- Provide numerous opportunities to say and write new words.

- Use word maps and word walls.

- Create sentence walls as a visual language scaffold (Carrier & Tatum, 2006).

- Use pictures or short video segments associated with keywords.

- Provide opportunities to practice language in an environment in which students feel safe.

- Encourage students to use their familiarity with the language of technology.

- Use the vocabulary during class.

Functional Vocabulary

When thinking about what functional terms we need to teach to English learners, it is a good idea to meet with other content area teachers as well as the English as a Second Language (ESL) teachers in our school. Together, we can brainstorm a meaningful list of functional vocabulary terms that our English learners will use across the curriculum. For example, we will all want the students to understand words such as *summary* and *concept*. We will also want the students to learn text pattern words such as *cause and effect*, *comparison and contrast*, and *problem and solution* and words that help us generate questions at multiple levels, including *imagine*, *predict*, and *justify*. (For more information about teaching text patterns and signal words for generating questions, see Chapter 9.) The ESL teachers can make suggestions about developing the list of functional vocabulary terms as well as ideas about how to teach them—especially about creating links from students' native languages to English. Learning a common list of functional terms will help our students to make connections across the curriculum. These terms can then be featured on word walls within each classroom.

When focusing on functional language, Dong (2004/2005) suggests we should promote English learners' participation. We can do this by checking on students' understanding during discussions ("What we are saying is . . ."), summarizing periodically ("The main point of our discussion is . . ."), and defining and discussing key vocabulary ("This means . . .").

Researchers note that poor vocabulary is a major cause of reading comprehension problems for English learners (Carlo et al., 2004). It is especially important that we help these students learn both functional and academic vocabulary. We can partner with other teachers to select functional vocabulary on which we will place a shared focus. We can also agree to teach students academic terms that extend beyond our discipline. Finally, we can ensure that we provide a wide range of authentic opportunities for students to use academic and functional vocabulary, teach a variety of effective vocabulary study techniques, and ensure that students learn words through a variety of modes, including seeing, hearing, and sketching.

When Using These Ideas for Teaching English Learners, What General Principles Should We Follow?

There are several general guidelines we can follow to help ensure that our teaching of English learners is effective:

1. We should teach from a culturally responsive perspective and establish high standards for English learners.
2. We should welcome diversity and teach all students from a constructivist perspective.
3. Working with peers, students, and families to learn about our students' cultural and linguistic backgrounds will help us to gain greater understanding of our students.
4. We need to scaffold teaching and learning to offer ongoing support for our English learners.
5. Sheltered instruction supports content learning.
6. Teaching English learners through explicit models, such as SIOP, provides structure for students' learning.
7. We should work with school administrators, peers, and current and former students to ensure that our English learners have accessible text—in a variety of formats.
8. Working with peers and students can help us provide the necessary supports for English learners in content classes.
9. Supporting English learners to ensure they are comfortable responding orally, in writing, and in other modes is essential.
10. Our teaching should reflect that we have in-depth knowledge of our content area and in-depth understanding of English learners.

FINAL THOUGHTS

Because the English learner population is ever-increasing, it is essential that we continue to learn all we can about how to teach these students effectively. From individual students' backgrounds to appropriate teaching methods and ways to adapt text, there is much we need to know. As Dong (2004/2005) notes, "Our classes are becoming increasingly linguistically and culturally diverse. It is imperative that subject-matter teachers sensitize their instruction to ELLs' backgrounds and needs and teach content knowledge through language" (p. 19).

In the next chapter, we explore writing in the content areas. We discuss a variety of purposes for writing and a number of engaging writing activities.

Teaching Connections
APPLYING WHAT WE HAVE LEARNED

E-Links

Many states have Language Proficiency Standards for English Learners. Visit the website for the Department of Education in the state in which you teach or plan to teach. Access the state's Language Proficiency Standards for English Learners. Consider how English learners in your classes can meet these standards. Examine a lesson plan that you have already written and think about how you can include the standards in that lesson. Discuss your ideas with a partner.

EXAMPLES OF WEBSITES FOR STATE LANGUAGE PROFICIENCY STANDARDS FOR ENGLISH LEARNERS

Guidelines for Implementing English Language Proficiency Standards in Iowa
www.iowa.gov/educate/archived/content/view/683/898

Pennsylvania Language Proficiency Standards for English Language Learners PreK–12
www.pde.state.pa.us/esl/lib/esl/Standards_Document_%28June_2007%29.doc

Accountable Talk

English learners are the fastest-growing student population in the United States. Reflect on what that trend means to you as a teacher. Consider how you will accommodate English learners' needs in your teaching. Focus on specific examples, including accessing textbooks, learning vocabulary, and using multiple modes of response. Think about how you can effectively prepare supports for these students. Discuss your thoughts with a partner.

Portfolio/Performance Opportunity

Develop a lesson plan that shows how you would teach English learners using the "engaging, guiding, and extending students' thinking" format.

Meet in small groups with others within your academic discipline. Discuss your lessons, focusing on the instructional and text adaptations you made for English learners. Adapt your lesson for teaching during your field experience. Include it in your portfolio.

11

TEACHING IDEAS:

• CONTENT AREA INVENTORY • CONTENT HISTORY • QUICKWRITES • ADMIT SLIPS • JOURNALS • DIALOGUE JOURNALS— PROMPTED AND UNPROMPTED • DOUBLE-ENTRY JOURNALS (LEARNING LOGS) • INVESTIGATIVE JOURNALS • WRITTEN CONVERSATIONS • TICKETS OUT • WRITE AND SKETCH IN MATH AND SCIENCE • BE A MATH OR SCIENCE AUTHOR • PARAGRAPH FRAMES • STRUCTURED NOTE TAKING • TEXT BOXES • EYEWITNESS ACCOUNT • DESCRIPTIVE TIMELINE • FIRST-PERSON EXPERIENCES • INQUIRING MINDS • LETTERS • ORAL HISTORY PROJECT • POETRY • STUDENT-AUTHORED ALPHABET BOOKS • TRANSMEDIATIONS • TRAVELOGUES

Writing in the Content Areas

At the beginning of this text, we learned that reading is a thinking process. Reif (2007) describes writing in the same way. Writing in the content areas is students' thinking in print. It enhances their learning and provides insights into how they think. It is not an add-on or something we use on rare occasions. Writing plays a dynamic, ongoing role in our teaching (Romano, 2007).

According to Tierney and Pearson (1983), reading and writing are inextricably linked—they cannot be separated. Brandenburg (2002) notes that learning integrates writing and reading to enhance students' comprehension. Duke and Pearson (2002) report that students who engage in writing in the content areas comprehend better than students who do not. Gammill (2006) agrees, noting, "Those teachers who do include writing components document more student involvement in their own learning and greater gains on test scores" (p. 754).

In this chapter, we explore writing in the content areas. We begin by presenting a rationale for writing in such contexts. Then we examine writing from two perspectives: informal and formal. Next, we investigate a variety of ideas for engaging our students in each type of writing. Following that, we discuss how to assess informal and formal writing. Finally, we consider the general principles we should follow when integrating writing into our content areas.

What Is "Writing to Learn"?

Like reading, writing is a constructivist process (Tierney & Pearson, 1983). Writers construct meaning when they make connections between prior knowledge and new information and then think through how they can best communicate their message. Research reports that writing promotes critical thinking, problem solving, and reading comprehension. Langer and Applebee (1985) see writing as helping students to make connections among what they read, what they understand, and what they think. Researchers agree that writing helps students to become better communicators and, consequently, better learners (Gammill, 2006).

According to Knipper and Duggan (2006), "Writing to learn helps students think about content and find the words to explain what they comprehend, reflect on how they understand the content, and consider what their own processes of learning involve" (p. 469). It engages students, encourages self-questioning, and deepens understanding, which leads to more student-centered classrooms and better test scores (Gammill, 2006; Knipper & Duggan, 2006). It also helps students to become active learners who reflect and think critically about content (Gammill, 2006).

Writing to learn requires that students question at higher thinking levels, analyze what they have learned, and synthesize their thoughts. This process allows us, as teachers, to gain insights into students' thinking processes as well as the products they create. Because it permeates our teaching, technology plays a prominent role in writing to learn. For more detailed information about the role of technology in writing, see Chapter 12.

In the following sections we investigate two types of writing: informal and formal. Informal writing naturally occurs in classroom situations when students write a short response to an open-ended question or create a journal entry. Informal writing is draft-stage writing. Formal writing is associated with long-term projects such as research papers or inquiry-based projects. These products are usually evaluated through the use of scoring guides called rubrics.

How Can We Use Informal Writing in Our Content Area Teaching?

Informal writing occurs in our classrooms every day. This is the type of writing in which students engage when they share their thoughts about content areas, discuss their prior experiences, respond to what they are learning, use reading comprehension strategies, and employ study skills. Figure 11.1 provides an overview of the desired student outcomes as well as corresponding types of informal writing.

Informal writing can usually be completed relatively quickly. For example, students often complete Tickets Out in five minutes at the end of class, and journal entries are often written in fewer than ten minutes. Of course, these times are approximations. We need to be aware of students' abilities and needs when estimating the amount of time they will need to engage in informal writing.

In the following sections, we explore how we can use informal writing in the content areas. We discuss the purposes of informal writing, including students sharing their thoughts about the content areas, the prior knowledge they may have, the ways they respond to learning, and the role of writing in reading strategy use. Then we describe examples of the writing activities that support each purpose.

Discovering Students' Prior Experiences with and Beliefs about Content Areas

To learn what students think about our content areas or about their previous experiences in our content areas, we can consider inviting students to create Content Inventories and Content Histories. These informal writing tasks are especially informative at the start of a course.

 **CONTENT AREA INVENTORY.** In Content Area Inventories, students record their thoughts about content-related topics. Content Area Inventories promote reflection and provide students with an opportunity to express their feelings about a content area they are studying.

To share information about previous experiences in this content area:
- Content histories
- Content inventories

To reveal the nature and depth of students' background knowledge:
- Quickwrites
- Admit slips

To communicate what students have learned and what they think about what they have learned:
- Dialogue journals (prompted and unprompted)
- Double-entry journals (learning logs)
- Investigative journals
- Written conversations
- Tickets out

To create and solve problems:
- Math problems/solutions
- Science experiments/outcomes

To use study skills:
- Paragraph frames
- Structured note taking
- Text boxes

To write summaries:
- Concept of Definition Maps
- Questions into Paragraphs (QuIP)
- Writing summaries independently

FIGURE 11.1
Student Learning Outcomes and Types of Informal Writing

Figure 11.2 contains a World Language Inventory that can be adapted for all subject areas. Richard completed this one when he was studying Spanish.

TEACHING IDEA

CONTENT HISTORY. A content history details a person's development in a particular content area from earliest memory to present day. Inviting students to contemplate their previous experiences in a content area has numerous benefits. For students, it promotes reflection,

1. **The best thing about the language I am studying is . . .** the culture. Spain has beautiful beaches and great guitar music. It has fascinating traditions like running with the bulls.

2. **The worst thing about the language I am studying is . . .** learning all the new vocabulary words and how to use them correctly when writing.

3. **One way that I use this language outside of school is . . .** at work. Sometimes people speak only Spanish and I can tell them what they owe for their purchase in Spanish.

4. **My favorite part of language class is . . .** speaking Spanish with my friends.

5. **In language class, I like to work in groups to . . .** practice my Spanish. I feel more confident speaking in a small group than in front of the class.

6. **In language class, I like to work . . .** alone to read and comprehend text. Working alone helps me concentrate better.

7. **When I speak the language I am studying, I feel . . .** accomplished. It makes me feel proud to know I can use what I have learned.

8. **My language journal helps me to . . .** keep track of my learning. It helps me know what I need to work on.

9. **When I am using this language, I am really proud of . . .** the way I have learned to understand and use it on my own.

10. **One thing about this language I wish I knew more about is . . .** how to speak with a better accent.

FIGURE 11.2
Richard's World-Language Inventory: Spanish

FIGURE 11.3
Mathematics History
Prompts

These prompts are offered to help you create your math history. A math history details a person's mathematical development from earliest memory to present day. Please note that these prompts are intended only to stimulate your thinking. You should feel free to include any information you would like to make your history viable.

1. What is your earliest math memory?

2. Can you recall how or if you used numbers before you entered school?

3. Can you recall any specific experiences from your math education in elementary school? Middle school? High school?

4. Do you remember any person or activity that helped you learn about math?

5. Do you recall any ways you used math outside of school in your elementary, middle, or high school years?

6. Did you enjoy math class at any particular grade level? Why? Why not?

7. Do you feel comfortable using math now? Why? Why not?

8. If you could change one thing about your experiences with math, what would it be? How would you change it?

9. If you could offer advice to students just beginning to study math, what would it be?

10. What are two ways you think you'll use math after you graduate from school?

FIGURE 11.3
Mathematics History Prompts

helps make connections between past and present-day experiences, and cultivates self-understanding. For teachers, it provides insights into students' previous learning experiences that can be used to foster motivation and inform planning. Figure 11.3 features prompts to facilitate this process in mathematics. The prompts are easily adaptable to all content areas. Figure 11.4 shows Lisa's Mathematics History, in which she shares memories from her engagement with math over the years.

Learning What Prior Knowledge Students Have

To learn what background knowledge our students already have about a topic, we often engage in discussion or complete a Semantic Map (see Chapters 5 and 8), but Quickwrites and Admit

FIGURE 11.4
Lisa's Mathematics History

My earliest math memory is playing "Heigh Ho! The Cherry O" game with my mother. It was one of my favorite games. In this game, the goal was to have the most cherries in your bucket. It taught preschoolers basic math. At home, my parents tried to make math fun. In school, however, I was never a good math student. In elementary school, the teachers always did timed problems. I could do the work, but I just couldn't do the work as fast as the teacher wanted it done. The goal was to see how many problems I could solve in a minute; unfortunately for me that wasn't many.

In middle school, we began learning algebra. I did well mostly due to the fact that my best friend took algebra with me and helped me along the way. In geometry, I was on my own, and I had a terrible teacher. He didn't seem to care whether we understood the problems. He just kept moving along. I was frustrated and couldn't wait for the class to end. I had this teacher two years in a row and didn't do well either time. I think the teacher really hindered my learning and made me fear math all the more. I am the kind of student who needs practice and he just moved on too quickly for me to keep up. He also made me feel dumb when I couldn't solve an equation and that kept me from asking questions that I really should have asked.

In high school, I had my best friend tutor me and I did better in math. I was able to ask her questions I feared that the teacher would laugh at. I have come to realize now that there is no stupid question. I am sure that there were other students just as lost as I was in those math classes. If I could give any advice to my younger self, I would say that it's okay to ask questions and admit when you need help. I'd also say that even though there are some terrible teachers, you shouldn't let one bad experience ruin a whole subject area. You never know what next year will bring. I am still not the world's greatest math student, but when I put my mind to it, I can do it.

When I finish high school, I will use math every day to ensure that I am being paid correctly. I will also use math to calculate my investments and do my taxes.

Slips also provide this information. Neither of these techniques requires more than five minutes of the students' time. We may or may not choose to ask students to include their names on the Quickwrites and Admit Slips, depending on our reason for using them. For example, if we want to know about the general prior knowledge of the entire class, we may not require student names. Conversely, if we want to know what prior knowledge each individual student has, we may require student names.

QUICKWRITES. This informal writing technique requires very little time and provides an effective way to learn what students know about a particular topic. In this reflective activity, students write what they know about a given topic. Depending on when this type of writing takes place, it can provide insight into students' prior knowledge, monitor students' understanding, or summarize what students have learned. This information can help us to determine a starting point for our teaching, assess student learning, and inform future planning. Once the purpose has been set, we should provide the students with a specified period of time— generally three to five minutes; offer them a topic or prompt about what they have just learned or what they know about a related topic; and ask them to write in response to the prompt for the specified amount of time. Figure 11.5 shows an example of a quickwrite about aqueducts.

ADMIT SLIPS. When completing this informal writing measure, students reflect on what they know about a particular topic. Students can write their responses on a graphic organizer (see the Appendix) or on an index card. On the first side, students write what they already know about a topic; on the second side, they write a question they have about that topic. Students need about five minutes to complete their Admit Slips.

This activity is called Admit Slips because teachers collect the slips before formally beginning class. It takes just a few minutes to read the Admit Slips. We should collect them with side one facing up. That way, we can quickly read all of the responses about what students know about the topic. As we read, we should be careful to set aside any responses that may need clarification. Then we can turn all of the Admit Slips over and read the questions students have about the topic. As we read, we should set aside questions that we think we will need to respond to in the next class. This is often just four or five questions, because several questions may be similar. Reading the slips will take only about five minutes.

Admit Slips can be used to assess prior knowledge when we are preparing to teach about a topic or assess student understanding of a topic as we teach it. In the first case, we can use what we learn from the Admit Slips (1) to assess how much—if any—prior knowledge the students already possess and (2) to determine the starting point for our teaching. In the latter case, we can use the information to understand how student learning is progressing. Figure 11.6 shows an Admit Slip that Shaquil wrote about triangles in his geometry class.

Gaining Insights into Students' Thoughts about Content

To learn what our students know about what we have been teaching or what they think about what we have been teaching, we can consider using journals, written conversations, or Tickets Out. These informal writing techniques provide insights into students' thinking about the content being taught.

JOURNALS. Traditional or electronic journals can be maintained in all content areas. Journals offer students a means to use writing to summarize, respond to, or extend their thinking

---

FIGURE 11.5
Quickwrite about
Aqueducts

Prompt: What do you know about aqueducts?

Quickwrite: Aqueducts carry water from one place to another. One of the most famous aqueducts was in Rome. It had underground pipes that carried water all over the city. You can still see the remains of the aqueducts today.

FIGURE 11.6
Shaquil's Admit Slip

I know what triangles are and that there are different kinds. I know that an equilateral triangle has equal sides. My questions are, "What are the other kinds of triangles and how are they different?"

about what they have read. Three types of journals frequently used in the content areas are dialogue, double entry, and investigative.

Journals have many positive outcomes. Students can use them to dialogue with us concerning their thoughts about a particular issue. They can summarize and comment on their thinking as they engage in course-related tasks such as conducting experiments. They can also use journals as a place to record their thoughts about topics for future research or other content investigations. Although journals can be used beneficially in a variety of ways, students often lose interest if journals are overused. For example, when keeping dialogue journals, students may view them as more motivational if used once or twice a week rather than every day.

 **TEACHING IDEA** DIALOGUE JOURNALS—PROMPTED AND UNPROMPTED. We can dialogue—converse in writing about a variety of topics—with our students in this type of journal. Students can also dialogue with peers. These entries may be prompted or unprompted.

Gordon and Macinnis (1993) suggest that when using prompts, we ask direct questions about learning, such as "What was the Renaissance?" "How do we form the future tense in Spanish?" "What are semiconductors?" or "What is a rhombus?" When using unprompted responses, students can write their reactions to learning, analyze their thinking, attempt to define new topics, or raise questions about what they have learned. Our responses validate students' ideas, offer new information, and/or pose new questions.

Figure 11.7 features mathematics journal prompts that can be adapted for all content areas. Figure 11.8 shows examples of Mary Ann's responses to selected math prompts. Figure 11.9 features an unprompted excerpt from a dialogue journal written by Jason and his English teacher while he was reading *Lord of the Flies*.

FIGURE 11.7
Mathematics Journal Prompts

When students are creating journal responses, they may self-select a topic to write about or they may respond to a prompt. Prompts may be particularly effective when introducing the concept of math journals or if you need specific feedback from the students. The following example prompts may be used as presented or adapted to facilitate such journal use.

1. Explain what you know about_____(a particular math concept).

2. (A) Create, solve, and explain a math problem using a math concept we studied in class this week. (B) Describe how you used technology to facilitate your work.

3. Explain how you could use_____ (fractions, algebraic equations, geometry, and so on) in another class or outside of school.

4. Use the newspaper to find an example of how a business in our community uses math. Respond to the article in your journal, citing the math concept(s) used and your thoughts on other ways math might benefit the company.

5. Create an acrostic poem about a particular math concept.

6. What are_____ (fractions, decimals, algebraic equations, geometric principles, and so on)?

7. Write questions about something in math you are having difficulty understanding or write questions about something we haven't studied yet that you would like to know about.

8. Draw a mathematician. How might he or she be employed in our community?

9. Describe a mathematically talented character from a book or television series.

10. Create a math problem based on a concept we are studying and explain how you would solve it.

FIGURE 11.8
Examples of Responses to Selected Math Prompts

1. Explain what you know about area.

Area is the space an object takes up. For example, if I were going to carpet a room, I would need to know the area of the room to buy the correct amount of carpet.

5. Create an acrostic poem about a particular math concept.

Angles

Angles are two rays that share the same endpoint.

Names for angles are right, obtuse, and acute.

Get the size of an angle by measuring degrees.

Let's use a protractor to create an angle.

Endpoint is called a vertex.

Supplementary angles have degree measurements that equal 180 degrees.

7. Write questions about something in math you have difficulty understanding or write questions about something we haven't studied yet that you would like to know about.

When solving an algebraic equation, I would like to know where to begin the equation. Do I start with the equation in the parentheses or do I start with the equation outside the parentheses?

TEACHING IDEA

DOUBLE-ENTRY JOURNALS (LEARNING LOGS). Double-Entry Journals, also known as learning logs, help us to monitor students' reading outside of class, promote reflection, and provide solid foundations for student interaction, class discussion, and conferencing. There are several ways to format double-entry journals; we should choose the approaches that best accommodate our students.

For example, we may choose to use the double-entry journal blackline that is available in the Appendix. The blackline is divided down the center. To the left of the divider line, students write summary statements or note important ideas from a chapter they have read. To the right of the divider line, students write their reflections or questions about the information they recorded on the left. Lealya's double-entry journal in this format is presented in Figure 11.10.

Making Connections
TO ENGLISH LEARNERS

When English learners use this Double-Entry Journal graphic organizer, we can structure it to include space for student sketching and include numbers to label spaces and provide focus points for students. For example, the Double-Entry Journal could be formatted as a Triple-Entry Journal that has three columns: Notes, Sketches, and Reflections/Questions. ■

FIGURE 11.9
Unprompted Dialogue Journal Excerpt

Student

I read the first chapter of *Lord of the Flies* and learned that the story is about a group of school boys who crash land on a deserted island. The boys create their own form of government because there are no adults on the island. Ralph is elected leader, and Jack is elected head of the hunters.

I do have one question about what I have read so far. The book talks about a scar on the island. I am confused about what that is.

Teacher

You seem to have a good understanding of what happens in Chapter 1. The scar on the island is a long trail that was created by the plane crash. I am looking forward to your thoughts about the next chapter.

FIGURE 11.10 Excerpt from Lealya's Double-Entry Journal: Three Civilizations in the Americas

Notes	Reflections and Questions
Civilization is an advanced culture in which people have developed cities, science, and industries.	I wonder how our civilization compares to those of the Mayas, Aztecs, and Incas.
Mayas lived in Mexico and Central America. Their greatest period was from 300 A.D. to 900 A.D.	I wonder if ruins of the Mayan civilization still exist.
The Mayas developed a government and a written language. They created the most accurate calendar known until modern times.	I wonder how the Mayan calendar differed from the one we use.
The Aztecs built Tenochtitlan in central Mexico. It was built on an island and they raised crops on floating platforms.	The Aztecs were inventive. I'd never think of planting crops on platforms that float.
By the early 1500s, the Aztecs had built an advanced civilization including cities, pyramids, and temples in Mexico.	
The Incas lived in South America. They were great engineers who built Forts, roads, and aqueducts.	
The Incas built using stones that carefully fit together.	I have seen some of the structures the Incas built. The way the stones fit together reminded me of the Pyramids.

In another approach to Double-Entry Journals, the first entry contains a summary of a chapter or informational article, and the second features students' reflections on what they have read. (See the Appendix for this blackline.) Figure 11.11 provides an excerpt from Lucia's "Summary and Reflection" Double-Entry Journal.

INVESTIGATIVE JOURNALS. Content area students maintain Investigative Journals to record ideas about topics they have interest in investigating at a future time or ideas about ongoing research. These journals promote inquiry, reflection, and critical thinking. Encourage students to begin their journal entries with the phrase "I wonder." Once ideas are recorded, students' "wonderings" can serve as the basis for written conversations or peer discussions. For example, students may be listening to other students or to a teacher present information to the class. If a topic in which they have interest is addressed, they would record an "I Wonder . . ." Statement about it in their Investigative Journals. Later, when selecting research topics of their own, students can review their Investigative Journals and revisit the topics in which they expressed interest. Figure 11.12 features an excerpt from Connor's Investigative Journal in biology.

WRITTEN CONVERSATIONS. Written Conversations offer an effective format for students to share their wonderings with peers. In this process, a student selects an "I wonder" section of his investigative journal and shares it in a Written Conversation with another class member. That student then reacts to the original idea and raises any questions he has, and the correspondence continues. This process both promotes student interaction and encourages reflection. Because it is a Written Conversation, it can occur without disturbing the rest of the class. The completed conversation then becomes the basis of further inquiry for the student who originated the dialogue. The "conversation" can be kept either in the investigative journal or in a class portfolio.

TICKETS OUT. This informal writing measure asks students to reflect on what they have learned and share two types of information: (1) What is the most important thing they

Summary

This article is about people during the time of the American Revolution. People who lived in our country at that time did not want to pay taxes to England when they had no say in the government. It was taxation without representation that motivated people to throw tea in the Boston Harbor. This event is now known as the Boston Tea Party.

The article also discusses leaders of importance in revolutionary times. George Washington and John Adams were two of the most important people in that category. George Washington was said to be indispensable in the war effort because he was such a well-respected leader. John Adams was described as a champion of independence. He was a diplomat who later served as Vice-President and President of the United States.

In 1776, the Declaration of Independence was approved by the Second Continental Congress. This document officially broke ties with England, although King George III wasn't willing to let that happen without a fight. It was not an easy war, but when Washington crossed the Delaware and won two battles in New Jersey, the people began to see the war as one the United States could win. The Treaty of Paris officially ended the war in 1783.

Reflection

This was a good article to read before we start studying the Revolutionary Era. As I read, I could make connections to events like the Boston Tea Party and to people such as George Washington and John Adams.

While reading, I was struck by the role individual citizens played in Revolutionary times. I thought about the townspeople who tossed the tea into Boston Harbor and those who fought in the military. These were everyday people doing what they could to help their lives by stopping taxation without representation and fighting for freedom.

Learning more about George Washington and John Adams helped me to see them not only as leaders, but also as citizens who greatly valued freedom. When I read that Washington and Adams were elected President and Vice-President by the Electoral College, I was surprised, but I was also able to make connections to how we vote today. I investigated the Electoral College on the Internet (www.archives.gov). I learned that during Washington's and Adams' first election, there were electors from 10 states. There were electors from 15 states in the election for their second term. In both cases, Washington had the highest amount of votes, followed by Adams.

FIGURE 11.11
An Excerpt from Lucia's "Summary and Reflection": Double-Entry Journal

learned during class that day? and (2) What questions do they have about what they learned that day? The student's response to what she has learned that day is usually recorded on the front of the graphic organizer, and any questions she may have are written on the back. The students need only about five minutes to complete their tickets.

This type of writing is called Tickets Out, because we collect the tickets as we stand at the door at the end of class. When the students hand us their tickets, they are able to leave the classroom. After the students have left, it takes just a few minutes to read their tickets. We collect the tickets with side one facing up, so we can quickly read all of the responses about the most important thing the students learned. As we read, we should be careful to set aside any responses that may need clarification. Then we can turn over the class tickets and read the questions students have about their learning. As we read these, we should set aside questions that we think we need to respond to in a whole-group setting. This is often just four or five questions, because several of them may be similar. Reading the tickets will only take about five minutes. The next day, we can begin class by clarifying any necessary information and responding to the students' questions.

FIGURE 11.12
Excerpt from Connor's Investigative Journal

In today's Press Conference, Kevin talked about DNA and people having DNA tests to find out if they might get heart disease or other illnesses. I would like to know more about this topic, so I might research it. I am wondering why people would want to know if they might get a disease when there isn't anything they can do to stop it. I am also wondering if these processes are private. I'm thinking about what would happen if an employer discovered that someone who works there might get heart disease, Alzheimer's disease, or some other serious disease.

FIGURE 11.13
Everene's Ticket Out

> **The most important think I learned today is:**
> The most important thing I learned today is the difference between inflation causing an economic slowdown and what a recession is.
>
> **One question I have is:**
> Is there any way to predict if a slowdown in the economy means that a recession is coming? If there is, are there ways to predict when the recession will happen?

This technique provides good transition from class to class, offers insights into students' learning, and lets students know that we value their thinking. (See Appendix C for a graphic organizer for Tickets Out.) In Figure 11.13, Everene shows how she completed her ticket in economics class.

Learning How Well Students Use Writing to Create and Solve Problems

To learn how well students use informal writing to create or solve problems, we may want to try some forms of informal writing that are used in mathematics and science to record problem creation and problem-solving efforts. Examples of these include Write and Sketch and Be a Math (or Science) Author.

 **WRITE AND SKETCH IN MATH AND SCIENCE.** This type of informal writing allows students to use both language and symbols to make their thinking about problem solving or conducting experiments visible to themselves and others. For example, in math a problem is posed. Students read or listen to the problem and paraphrase it. Then they record their thinking about how to solve the problem on a paper that has been divided in half vertically. On the left side of the paper, students sketch a picture to show how they solved a problem or completed an experiment. On the right side of the paper, students use words to describe how they solved or completed it.

 **BE A MATH OR SCIENCE AUTHOR.** When students create their own math problems or science experiments, they become more interested and engaged. Designing written problems or experiments is an effective way to tap into students' personal experiences and bridge the gap between existing and new knowledge. In addition, practice in interpreting problems or experiments invented by peers helps students better interpret more formal information presented in textbooks or by teachers. When engaging in the Be a Math or Science Author technique, students create problems to be solved by classmates. Problem topics may be left open to the imagination of the students, or may be directed by a topic currently being studied in math class.

Helping Students Engage in Note Taking and Using Study Skills

To help our students use writing when using note taking and study skills, we can scaffold their learning by using Paragraph Frames, Text Boxes, and Structured Note taking.

 PARAGRAPH FRAMES. When engaging in informal writing, students need to be able to write good summary paragraphs. If our students are new to writing in the content areas or if their content area writing is not strong, Paragraph Frames will help to scaffold their paragraph summary writing experiences. Scaffolding means that as teachers, we begin the process by providing a great deal of support and we gradually withdraw it over time. As our support dwindles, the students take on more and more responsibility until, in this case, they are writing paragraph summaries without using the frames. Paragraph Frames complement the text pattern (see Chapter 9) the students are reading. For example, if students are reading a section of the text that uses the comparison and contrast structure, they will focus on the similarities and differences in their paragraph.

This is the example of the comparison/contrast text pattern that was included in Chapter 8:

> *When we examine the issues that Democrats and Republicans are supporting in the Presidential election, we can see that there are some issues on which they are clearly divided and others where their goals are similar, but their approaches are different. An example of the former is that their positions differ on the war in Iraq. The Democrats are in favor of ending the war in Iraq, while the Republicans support the war and have developed strategies for victory. As an example of the latter, both the Democratic and Republican candidates support changes in health care, reforming immigration, and improving education. Of course, their policies to promote these changes differ, and in some cases, differ dramatically.*

Figure 11.14 features a comparison/contrast paragraph frame that students can use to write a one-paragraph summary as well as the summary itself. For Paragraph Frames based on the other informational text patterns, see Appendix C.

TEACHING IDEA

STRUCTURED NOTE TAKING. This informal writing technique provides a visual framework or organizer for students to use as they take notes. The visual framework looks like the layout of the page. This helps students to take notes more efficiently. Some frameworks focus only on text, while others include illustrations, charts, and graphs. Students can use the completed organizers when studying for tests. To ensure that students are proficient in note taking, we can scaffold students' learning. For example, when providing the graphic organizer the first time, we might complete most of the information, leaving just a few sections for students to complete. The next time we share the organizer, we would complete half of the information and ask the students to complete more sections. We should continue this process until we are not providing any details on the organizer and the students are completing all of the note-taking sections. Figure 11.15 features Jose's completed Structured Note Taking about the stages of food processing in biology class. Notice that the rectangles represent where text appears on the page and the oval represents an illustration.

To use Structured Note Taking in an alternative format, students can draw a line about two inches from the left margin of their notebook paper. Then, as they read or listen to the teacher, they record key words and phrases to the left of the line and details to the right. When they finish reading or listening, students use their notes to write a brief summary at the bottom of the page.

TEACHING IDEA

TEXT BOXES. Topping and McManus (2002) suggest that we can also use Text Boxes to promote successful note taking. In this approach, the design of the Text Boxes mirrors the

FIGURE 11.14
Comparison/Contrast Paragraph Frame and Paragraph

Comparison/Contrast Paragraph Frame

_____ and _____ agree on some topics and disagree on others. They both support _____ (comparison/similarities), but they differ on _____ _____ (contrast/differences).

The completed paragraph frame would read as follows:

<u>Democrats</u> and <u>Republicans</u> agree on some topics and disagree on others. They both support <u>health care, reforming immigration, and improving education</u> (comparisons/similarities), but they differ on <u>their positions about the war</u> (contrast/difference).

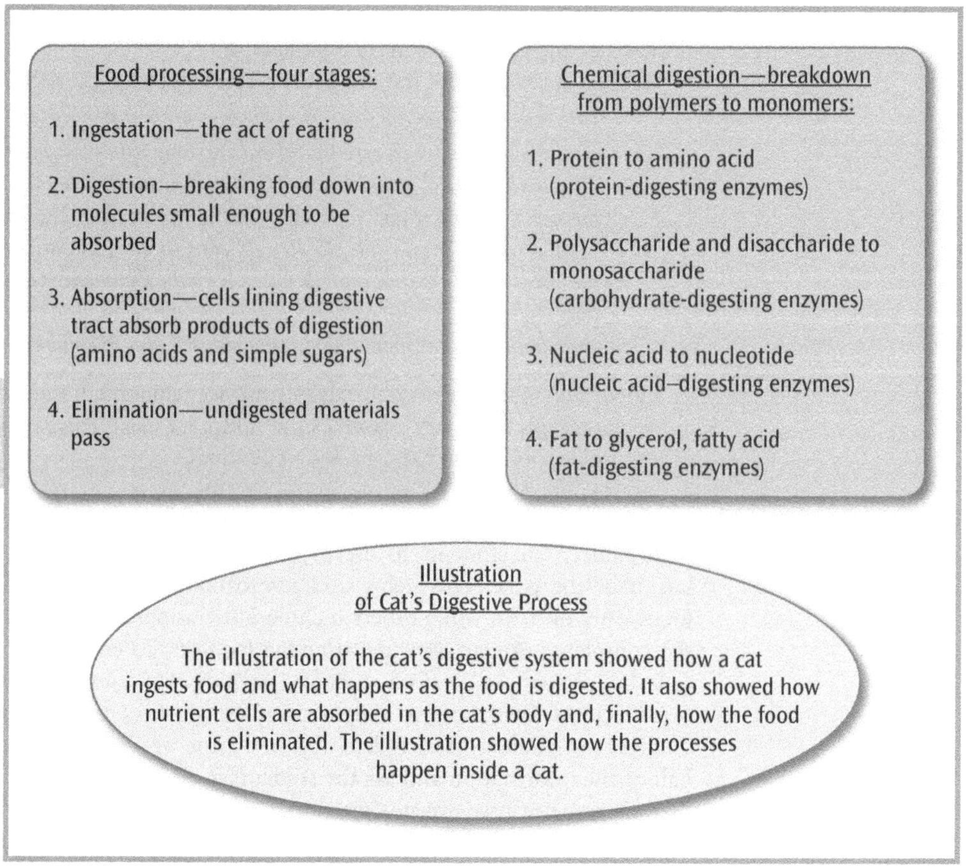

FIGURE 11.15
Structured Note
Taking in Biology

Food processing—four stages:

1. Ingestion—the act of eating

2. Digestion—breaking food down into molecules small enough to be absorbed

3. Absorption—cells lining digestive tract absorb products of digestion (amino acids and simple sugars)

4. Elimination—undigested materials pass

Chemical digestion—breakdown from polymers to monomers:

1. Protein to amino acid (protein-digesting enzymes)

2. Polysaccharide and disaccharide to monosaccharide (carbohydrate-digesting enzymes)

3. Nucleic acid to nucleotide (nucleic acid–digesting enzymes)

4. Fat to glycerol, fatty acid (fat-digesting enzymes)

Illustration of Cat's Digestive Process

The illustration of the cat's digestive system showed how a cat ingests food and what happens as the food is digested. It also showed how nutrient cells are absorbed in the cat's body and, finally, how the food is eliminated. The illustration showed how the processes happen inside a cat.

paragraphs, diagrams, and photos on a particular page of text. This is similar to the format used in Structured Note Taking, but the techniques differ significantly. Each Text Box contains *two* columns. The first column contains students' notes about important facts, much like in Structured Note Taking. The second column contains students' reflections about the text and any questions they may have about what they have read. The information required is similar to one of the options for creating double-entry journals, but the format is different.

Text Boxes help students to monitor their reading by focusing on text structure and important facts, as well as information provided by illustrations, charts, maps, and graphs. Todd's example of the Text Boxes he created while reading about the Rosetta Stone, including his reflections and questions, can be seen in Figure 11.16.

Scaffolding Students' Summary Writing

We usually teach our students to write summaries by pulling out the important facts in the text. So, if our students summarize a story, they include the narrative text pattern elements: the characters, setting, problem, attempts to resolve the problem, and resolution. As we learned in Chapter 8, however, informational text has several different patterns, so determining what the important facts are in this type of text can be more challenging.

We can eliminate this challenge if we scaffold our students' summary writing. We can support the class as members engage in completing a Concept of Definition Map. Then we can provide our total support as students write summaries based on the completed Concept of Definition Map (see Chapter 8). All of the information that appears on the map is essential, so when writing summaries students can use the categories as well as the responses.

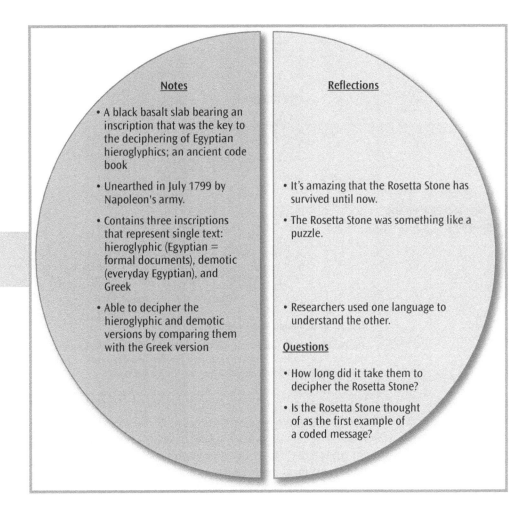

FIGURE 11.16
Text Boxes:
The Rosetta Stone

Consider Maria's completed Concept of Definition Map and Summary about the presidency of the United States, shown in Figure 11.17. All of the information in the summary appears in the completed map, so there is no need for students to determine which information may be important.

The resulting summary is brief, but includes all of the essential information. Teaching our students to write summaries using Concept of Definition Maps provides the necessary information to write a summary and also reminds students that the important information includes facts such as "What is it?", "How would you describe it?", "What are some examples?", and "What is a comparison?" Of course, as noted in Chapter 8, we can change the "What are some examples?" question to accommodate the text we are reading and we can choose to eliminate the comparison.

If we begin teaching summary writing with the Concept of Definition Map, we can then move on to teaching Questions into Paragraphs (QuIP), which will allow students to extend their thinking about a topic. When students use QuIP, we are still providing some teacher support, but we are gradually releasing responsibility to the students. We support student learning by teaching them how to use QuIP and the accompanying graphic organizer. Students then take responsibility for selecting a topic, generating three research questions, and using two different sources to respond to the questions. When the graphic organizer is complete, the students use the information to write a summary paragraph. Once again, we are not asking students to "pull out important facts." Students already provided the important facts when they completed the QuIP graphic organizer. Figure 11.18 features Ben's completed QuIP graphic organizer about hurricanes, as well as the paragraph he wrote based on his questions and responses.

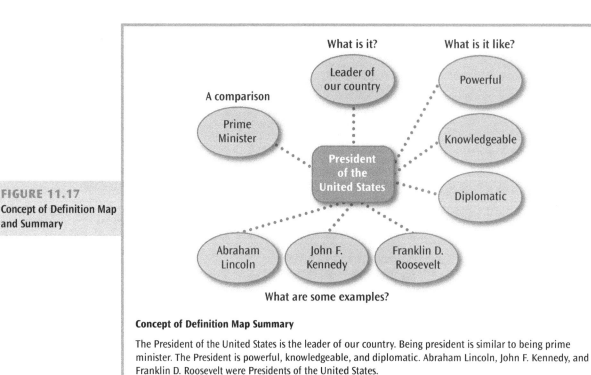

FIGURE 11.17
Concept of Definition Map
and Summary

Concept of Definition Map Summary

The President of the United States is the leader of our country. Being president is similar to being prime minister. The President is powerful, knowledgeable, and diplomatic. Abraham Lincoln, John F. Kennedy, and Franklin D. Roosevelt were Presidents of the United States.

After students have used Concept of Definition Maps and QuIP to write summaries several times, we can begin teaching other techniques for summary writing. These include Lyric Summaries (see Chapter 14), Biopyramid and Narrative Pyramid (see Chapter 7 and the Appendix), and form poems such as Acrostics and Definition Poems (see Chapter 14). After learning and practicing these summary techniques, students should be able to use them to write summaries independently.

FIGURE 11.18 QuIP Research Grid: Hurricanes

Questions	Answers	
	Source A: *Earth Science*, Tarbuck and Lutgens	**Source B:** www.nhc.noaa.gov
1. What are hurricanes?	Hurricanes are whirling tropical cyclones that produce winds of at least 74 miles per hour.	A hurricane is an intense tropical weather system with a well-defined circulation and *sustained* winds of 74 miles per hour (64 knots) or higher.
2. How do hurricanes develop?	A hurricane is a heat engine that is fueled by the energy given off when huge quantities of water vapor condense.	Hurricanes are products of a tropical ocean and a warm, moist atmosphere. They are powered by heat from the sea.
3. How are hurricanes classified?	The intensity of a hurricane is determined according to the *Saffir–Simpson Hurricane Scale*. It ranges from category 1, least powerful, to category 5, most powerful.	The *Saffir–Simpson Hurricane Scale* is a 1 to 5 rating based on the hurricane's sustained wind speed. This scale estimates potential property damage. Category 3 and higher/hurricanes are considered major. Katrina was a category 3.

QuIP Paragraph

Hurricanes are severe tropical weather systems that are usually described as whirling cyclones having sustained winds of 74 miles per hour or more. Hurricanes are powered by heat given off when massive quantities of water vapor condense. They often develop over tropical seas. The power of hurricanes is determined according to the *Saffir–Simpson Hurricane Scale*. The scale estimates property damage by designating hurricanes in categories from 1 (least powerful) to 5 (most powerful). Hurricanes in category 3 or higher are considered most dangerous. Katrina is an example of a category 3 hurricane.

Making Connections | Thinking about Summarizing

- Think about the importance of knowing how to summarize content area text. Consider your personal experience and determine how or if you were taught how to summarize. Focus on specific details, such as in which grade you began summarizing and how comfortable you felt doing it. Then think about how you will help to ensure that your students can summarize.
- Share your thoughts with others in small-group discussions.

Making Connections
TO STRUGGLING READERS

Scaffolding students' learning is especially important when we are teaching struggling learners. Using a completed Concept of Definition Map or QuIP offers support for these students when they engage in summary writing. Struggling students can use the graphic organizers, while other students may be able to write summaries independently. In the end, all of the students will write summaries. ■

There are many different ways for students to engage in informal writing. As teachers, our key tasks are to teach these ideas and demonstrate our enthusiasm for writing, so students can feel good about their writing and use it freely throughout the content areas.

How Can We Assess Informal Writing?

To assess our students' informal writing, we usually offer praise and suggestions based on the content. It is important to remember that we do not evaluate or grade informal writing because it is a draft and students have not had the opportunity to revise and edit.

Making Connections | Thinking about Informal Writing in the Content Areas

- Think about how you plan to use informal writing when teaching in your content area. Consider the teaching ideas presented in this section and explain how you would teach your students to take notes and write a summary. Justify your response.
- Share your thoughts with others in small-group discussions.

How Can We Use Formal Writing in Our Content Area Teaching?

Formal writing is most often associated with long-term, performance-based projects. These projects are usually evaluated with rubrics. Naturally, the types of projects we use depend on the content area we teach. Reasons for using formal writing in the content areas as well as suggested projects follow.

Persuasive Writing

When we want to learn our students' positions on particular topics, we need to provide them with ways to engage in persuasive writing. Students in the content areas can engage in this mode of writing in a variety of ways, including the following:

- Persuasive essays
- Newspaper editorials

- Political speeches (e.g., stem cell research, health care, the economy)
- Position statements
- Reviews of books, films, music, or websites
- Photo or illustration analysis
- Political cartoon analysis

When thinking about how our students can engage in this mode of writing, we can consider the following possibilities:

- Science students can argue their positions about Pluto being a planet.
- Mathematics students can write reviews of websites for their subject area.
- World-language students can write position statements about why that language should continue to be practiced when so much of the world is communicating in English.
- History students can write newspaper editorials about the impact of the past on present-day events.
- English students can write persuasive essays about their favorite authors.
- Science students can inquire about additional planets or life on Mars by studying photos of outer space.
- Mathematics students can create political cartoons about the state of the world as it relates to mathematics.
- World-language students can analyze the cultures of countries where the language they are studying is spoken by examining photos from different points in history.
- History students can analyze political perspectives by reviewing political cartoons.
- English students can speculate on the role of literature in a culture by analyzing photos and political cartoons of the period.

Inquiry-Based Writing

To determine how well our students can use writing to engage in inquiry-based learning, creative thinking, and research, we need to provide access to these types of projects. We should include projects such as the following on a list of possibilities and encourage student self-selection. Because these are examples of formal writing, we should also ensure that students have the project rubrics before they begin.

 **EYEWITNESS ACCOUNT.** In-depth research is essential for this project, which puts the writer in the moment. Excellent examples of published Eyewitness Accounts can be found in *The Century* by Peter Jennings and Todd Brewster (1998). In one of them, Mabel Griep, an eyewitness to the Wright brothers' first flight, details her experience. Of course, our students cannot be eyewitnesses to such events, but they can research and use this format to communicate their findings.

 **DESCRIPTIVE TIMELINE.** Chronological order is required in this project that extends the traditional timeline to a more detailed descriptive version. This encourages students to associate the sequence of dates with details about particular developments.

 **FIRST-PERSON EXPERIENCES.** In this inquiry-based project, individual students select a course-related topic, research it, and choose the mode in which they will present their findings. For details about First-Person Experiences and excerpts from students' projects, see Chapter 13.

 **INQUIRING MINDS.** This is a small-group, inquiry-based research project in which students work with others who have interest in particular topics. For details about Inquiring Minds, see Chapter 13.

 **LETTERS.** The power of using letters to communicate, to inform, and to persuade is well represented in recently published books. David McCullough's *John Adams* (2001) is based on letters exchanged between John and Abigail Adams, and Andrew Carroll's multiple volumes, including *War Letters: Extraordinary Correspondence from American Wars* (2001), feature authentic, soldier-authored letters. Students can choose to respond to these letters or use letter writing as a format when completing an inquiry-based project.

 **ORAL HISTORY PROJECT.** In this project, students choose a person to honor and document his life history in a variety of modes. For more details about the Oral History Project (Dickinson, Hyler, Reilly, & Romano, 2006), see Chapter 13.

 **POETRY.** This is an often-forgotten creative mode of communicating information. To learn about a variety of poetry formats and read student-authored poems, see Chapter 14.

 **STUDENT-AUTHORED ALPHABET BOOKS.** This project can be completed by individual students; alternatively, students can each contribute a page to a class book. For details about Student-Authored Alphabet Books, see Chapter 14.

 **TRANSMEDIATIONS.** When students create Transmediations, they change the medium of the original work. For example, a poem might be transmediated into a picture book, a novel might become a poem, or song lyrics might become a story. For more information about this project, see Chapter 14.

 **TRAVELOGUES.** When students engage in this project, they chronicle their virtual visits to countries that may be the origin of the language they are studying, the setting for a novel they are reading, or the location of a historic event. Travelogues can be formatted in many ways, including as a travel journal, a PowerPoint presentation, or a video.

When contemplating how our students can engage in inquiry-based writing, consider the following:

- Science students can write Eyewitness Accounts of significant scientific discoveries.
- Mathematics students can take on the identities of famous mathematicians when creating First-Person Experiences.
- World-language students can write in the language they are studying and create Travelogues through countries that speak that language.
- History students can engage in small-group research projects about multiple aspects of an historic event in Inquiring Minds.
- English students can create Descriptive Timelines of various periods of literature.

 Making Connections
TO MULTIPLE LITERACIES

When students engage in formal writing, they should be able to use information literacy to use the Internet to develop important questions, locate information, synthesize the information to answer their questions, and communicate the information to others. ■

Making Connections | Thinking about Formal Writing in the Content Areas

- Reflect on how you can incorporate formal writing into your content area. Describe the connections you can make between two formal writing activities and your subject area. Reflect on how you would motivate your students to engage in these activities.
- Share your thoughts with others in small-group discussions.

How Can We Evaluate Formal Writing?

We evaluate students' formal writing because it is usually a long-term project with multiple opportunities for revising and editing. We discuss information about how students use the writing process in formal writing in the next section.

To evaluate students' formal writing, we usually use rubrics or scoring guides. They include the criteria we will use to evaluate the project. We need to ensure that the students have copies of the rubric and are familiar with it before they begin their work. Knowing what they need to do to complete the project successfully helps to provide direction for students as they research and write.

When students engage in formal writing, they often use the writing process. This recursive process enables them to evolve their writing from their initial thoughts to the rubric-evaluated final copy. In the next section, we describe the writing process and consider how students can use it in the content areas.

How Can We Use the Writing Process in the Content Areas?

Although much of the writing in which our students engage is draft level, more formal writing requires them to revise and edit their work. The writing process provides guidelines to help students advance their ideas from draft stage to final copy. In this section, we discuss the writing process and consider how students can use it when writing in the content areas.

Students generally begin learning about the writing process when they are in the primary grades. By the time they reach middle school or high school, they have had many years of practice writing in this format. The writing process consists of several stages, including drafting, revising, editing, and publishing (final copy). For our purposes, we will add "making connections" as a first step. Figure 11.19 presents an overview of the stages for using the writing process in the content areas.

In the first stage, students select a topic and make connections between their topic and their prior knowledge. They also review the project rubric, think about their audience, develop questions to guide their writing, locate meaningful references, and develop a format for sharing the information. For example, if students in a mathematics class were investigating famous mathematicians, a student might ask himself, "Which mathematician interests me the most?"

Let's imagine that he chose Benjamin Banneker. During the *making connections* stage, he would also ask himself the following questions:

- What did I learn from reviewing the rubric? What am I required to do in this project?
- What do I already know about Benjamin Banneker?
- Who is the audience for this research?
- What do I want to know about Banneker? Which questions can I generate to guide my writing?
- What resources can I use to get the information I need?
- What format can I use that will allow me to present the information about Banneker in the most effective and engaging way?

FIGURE 11.19
The Writing Process in the Content Areas

I. Making connections

II. Drafting

III. Revising

IV. Editing

V. Publishing

Go to the Activities and Applications section under the topic *Writing* in the MyEducation-Lab for your course and complete the activity entitled Peer Editing to describe ways to group students for peer editing sessions.

In the *drafting* stage, students write their ideas. Informal writing such as journal entries, open-ended responses, and reading strategy applications stops at this stage, but formal writing such as research papers and projects continues through all stages of the writing process.

During the *revising* stage, students adapt or change the content based on suggestions offered by peers, teachers, or modifications in their own thinking. Peer revision, which is often used during this stage, involves students reading and commenting on the content of each other's writing. Peer revision can take place through peer conferencing or peers can provide written comments. Either way, it is important to teach students how to engage in peer revision. For example, students often offer one positive comment and one suggestion. In the case of the student researching Benjamin Banneker, the peer revisor might say:

- "I didn't know very much about Banneker until I read your paper. You did a good job of finding out information about him." (positive comment)
- "My idea is that you not use Banneker's name so often. Maybe you could use *he* or *this mathematician* instead." (suggestion)

In the *editing* stage, students focus on grammar and formatting. They can use a checklist or engage in a quick conference based on the checklist. Editing checklists often include the items featured in Figure 11.20. Students use such checklists to make sure that they have used correct grammar and formatting in their writing. For example, in this stage, the student researching Benjamin Banneker might decide to combine some simple sentences into compound or complex ones. He might also choose to use fewer quotations by paraphrasing some of the information.

Making Connections
TO ENGLISH LEARNERS

When English learners engage in peer revising or editing, we should partner them with students who speak English clearly at a comfortable rate. We should also ensure that the partners discuss their comments and suggestions to promote understanding. ■

In the *publishing* stage, students review what they have written, proofread carefully, and make final changes. After the students' writing has been through the publishing stage, it is submitted to the teacher to be evaluated using the rubric that was distributed at the start of the project.

We should note that although we have presented a series of stages, the writing process is recursive—not linear. This means that although there are several stages in the process, students do not just advance their writing from one stage to the next. For example, in the case of the student researching Benjamin Banneker, after suggestions for revision had been made, he would have reverted to the draft stage to revise the content of his writing.

FIGURE 11.20
Editing Checklist

1. Did the writer use complete sentences?
2. Do the sentences begin with capital letters and end with periods?
3. Is the other punctuation appropriate—apostrophe use, comma use?
4. Is the paper written in the active voice?
5. Is there subject–verb agreement?
6. Did the writer use correct verb tenses?
7. Are the paragraphs indented?
8. Are there simple, compound, and complex sentences?
9. Are tired words used—said, nice, good?
10. Do the pronouns correctly reference the people or items to which they refer?

Whether informal or formal in nature, writing is a mainstay in the content areas. Students can use informal writing to communicate their ideas every day and formal writing to demonstrate what they have learned over time. In the next section, we explore the general principles we should follow when integrating writing in the content areas.

When Integrating Writing in the Content Areas, What General Principles Should We Follow?

There are several general guidelines we can follow to ensure that our use of writing in the content areas is effective:

1. *We should integrate both informal and formal writing in our content area teaching.* Writing is not an add-on; it is a natural part of teaching and learning. As such, it should occur in everyday settings as well as in the form of long-term projects.

2. *Our teaching should encourage students to make connections between their previous writing experience and content area writing.* For example, most of our students—if not all—will have learned the writing process during their elementary school years. If this is the case, our students will probably have had better writing experiences than we did during our K–12 years. Although we may enjoy writing now, many of us grew up with "red ink syndrome." This occurred when teachers who were reading our writing covered our work with "red ink" negative comments and crossed out sections of our papers. We were usually told only what was wrong with our writing and we were not provided with opportunities to revise. Our students' experiences with the writing process, which includes positive comments, suggestions for improvement, and opportunities to revise and edit, probably differ greatly from the writing experiences most of us had.

3. *When asking our students to engage in informal writing, we should remember not to evaluate or grade the students' writing.* Informal writing is a draft. We should comment only on its content.

4. *When inviting our students to engage in formal writing, we should distribute the rubric we will be using when the assignment is introduced.* Rubrics provide content and format criteria for students, and they should have this information from the very beginning of the assignment.

5. *Our lessons should focus on **depth** rather than **coverage** of content area writing.* We don't need to use every idea to incorporate writing in the content areas. Rather, we need to choose topics and methods that are particularly meaningful.

6. *Our teaching should reflect our understanding that informal and formal writing enhance learning in the content areas and that both can be adapted to accommodate our students' needs.*

7. *When we invite our students to write in the content areas, we should demonstrate our enthusiasm for writing.* As Murray (2007) reminds us, teachers need to be writers. Our students need to know that we have positive feelings about writing. Although it involves a certain amount of risk taking on our part, sharing examples of our informal and formal writing will help our students see us as writers. We know from experience that our enthusiasm will motivate our students.

Making Connections | Thinking about Our Writing

- Think about yourself as a writer. Reflect on your K–12 writing experiences. Consider the following types of teachers you had: (1) teachers who did a great job of incorporating writing into their content areas; (2) teachers who did not include writing in their content areas; and (3) teachers who provided only negative comments about writing in the content areas. Think about what has changed over the years and how you will use your previous writing experiences to develop writing in your content area.

- Share your thoughts with others in small-group discussions.

FINAL THOUGHTS

Writing offers us insights into students' thinking and promotes communication in all content areas. It also enables students to share their knowledge, reveal their interests, contemplate connections, and engage in inquiry.

In the next chapter, we learn about technology in the content areas. We make connections to the literacies discussed in Chapter 4 and focus on how to integrate technology into teaching and learning.

Teaching Connections

APPLYING WHAT WE HAVE LEARNED

E-Links

We know that writing is a natural component of teaching and learning in the content areas. We also know that writing is another aspect of our teaching that relates to state standards. Consider the writing standards in the state in which you teach as well as state-assessment-based writing rubrics. Then (1) explain how you plan to address the standards in your teaching and (2) how you can use the state writing rubric to help students meet the criteria on which their state assessment writing sample will be evaluated.

SAMPLE WEBSITES

For examples of state writing rubrics, access the following websites:

Delaware State Writing Rubric
http://www.doe.k12.de.us/aab/files/GeneralRubricforWriting.pdf

Michigan Merit Exam (MME) Persuasive Writing Rubric Grade 11 (This assessment is evaluated separately for writing and for content.)
http://www.michigan.gov/documents/mde/MME_Persuasive_Writing_Rubric_174205_7.pdf

Pennsylvania State Writing Rubric—11th Grade PSSA Persuasive Writing Rubric
http://www.stsd.org/shs/staff/rj/Student%20Resources/
PSSA%20PERSUASIVE%20RUBRIC%202006.doc

Accountable Talk

Meet in discipline-specific small groups to discuss how you plan to integrate informal and formal writing in your content area teaching. Consider the following issues: (1) how you will make connections between writing and your content area; (2) how you will motivate your students to use writing to learn; and (3) how you will promote writing in the content areas among fellow faculty members who teach from more traditional perspectives.

Portfolio/Performance Opportunity

Choose a lesson plan you have already completed, and integrate informal writing into it. Then choose a formal writing project that could be meaningfully introduced at the conclusion of that lesson. Complete the informal writing activities and the formal writing project that you add to the lesson, and save them as models to be used in your future teaching. Share and discuss your revised plan and models with peers who teach your content area.

12

Using Technology in the Content Areas

Information and communication technologies provide exciting new ways to teach and learn. These technologies are ever-changing and, as new ones emerge, we must keep pace to ensure that we can provide our students with access to innovative practices. The possibilities for integrating technology into our teaching seem unlimited. We can use graphing calculators in mathematics to convert equations to graphic representations, and we can use calculator-based "laboratories"—hand-held devices that enable students to collect data, in science (Davis, 1997). We can take digital photos and compose digital movies in all of our classes (Brass, 2008). We can podcast Discussion Circles in any area of the curriculum. And, of course, we can use the Internet—perhaps our greatest technology—for extensive purposes throughout the content areas.

Researchers report that we are living in a technological revolution. Tierney (2008) observes that "the advent of digital spaces, especially the advent of hypertext, represents a revolution in communication of a magnitude exceeding the printing press" (p. 262). Leu, Coiro, Castek, Hartman, Henry, and Reinking (2008) agree, noting that the Internet has been adopted more quickly than any other technology for reading, writing, or communicating. These findings are corroborated by the fact that more than a billion people are already reading information online (de Argaez, 2006).

In this chapter, we explore the role of technology in the content areas. We begin by examining a rationale for using technology in our teaching. Next, we compare and contrast reading online and reading offline. Finally, we discuss a variety of Internet strategies and projects we can use in our content area classes.

How Does Using Technology in the Content Areas Enrich Our Teaching?

Technology permeates education, and incorporating it into our content area teaching provides a variety of benefits. These range from immediacy of response to increased socialization in learning. The benefits of using technology include the following:

- Making topics more real.
- Linking disciplines.
- Promoting collaboration.
- Lending immediacy to inquiry and data sharing.
- Promoting higher-level thinking.
- Deepening students' understanding of research.
- Helping students learn that content areas involve questions, not answers.
- Promoting inquiry.
- Encouraging learning in a social context.
- Promoting discussion at multiple levels (adapted from Lonergan, 1997; Mike, 1996).

Although a variety of technologies complement our teaching, we use the Internet most frequently for this purpose. Castek, Bevans-Mangelson, and Goldstone (2006) believe this approach is beneficial to our students. They note, "Providing opportunities for students to use the Internet at school helps them develop literacy skills that are important for their future participation in a digital world. Using computers increases students' motivation to read, write, and learn" (p. 715). Researchers report that many of our students also use the Internet at home. More than 90% of the adolescent students in the United States who have access to the Internet at home use this technology to do homework (Pew Internet & American Life Project, 2001). Mike (1996) notes that the Internet offers users "a natural blend of communication and information retrieval functions incorporated within a framework that literally encompasses the world" (p. 4). Figure 12.1 presents a glossary of Internet-specific terms that we frequently encounter in our teaching.

Making Connections
TO ENGLISH LEARNERS

Before inviting an English learner to participate in a technology-based project, use an informal assessment, such as an interest inventory or discussion, to learn about the student's previous experience using technology. The student may have a great deal of prior knowledge or very little. Knowing the degree of experience with technology will inform the teacher's understanding of whether the student needs support when using technology or will be able to complete the project on her own. ■

Making Connections | Thinking about Technology

- Consider technology-infused teaching. What do you think are the greatest challenges we, as teachers, face when trying to incorporate technology in our courses? The greatest benefits? Focus on specific examples.
- Share your thoughts with others in small-group discussions.

Blog (web log) An Internet journal that has dated entries. It provides opportunities for responses between the author and the readers. A blogosphere is the virtual community of blog writers and readers and the texts they create.

Discussion board An online venue for posting a comment or question that others can read and respond to over time. Those who respond do not need to be online at the same time as the person who posted the question. If one person *posts* a question and five others respond, those six *posts* form a *thread*.

Hypertext Digital print that allows for a variety of reading options in a single text. It contains hyperlinks that readers can click on to access other texts.

Key word search A search engine query (question) that contains carefully selected words to enable users to reach specific information.

New literacies The new skills, strategies, and dispositions that are required to successfully identify important questions, locate information, engage in critical evaluation, synthesize information, and communicate on the Internet.

Networked classroom The context in which teachers and students use the Internet for educational purposes.

Networked culture A geographical community connected to its members by the Internet.

Podcast A way to receive broadcasts through the Internet using an automatic *feed* in a process called *subscribing.* Podcast episodes can consist of audio files, video files, or documents, or any combination of the three.

Real time A descriptor for live interactions that occur online.

Search engine An online program that indexes the contents of registered websites and provides lists of responses to search queries.

WebQuest A scaffolded, inquiry-oriented activity in which motivated students use specific Web resources to investigate an open-ended question.

Wiki A collection of text that multiple users can revise and edit freely online. The wiki, which was inspired by the Hawaiian word for "quick," is a unique means of group communication because it allows not only the content to be revised and edited, but also the organization of the contributions.

FIGURE 12.1

Glossary of Selected Internet Terms

How Are Reading Online and Reading Offline Similar? How Are They Different?

When the Internet first emerged as a popular technology, it was generally accepted that reading offline skills and strategies were all that were required for successful online reading. Since then, however, researchers have determined that online readers need skills and strategies beyond those traditionally learned in school (Coiro, Knobel, Lankshear, & Leu, 2008). In this section, we explore the similarities and differences that exist between offline and online reading, particularly in terms of the nature of reading, the types of text encountered, and the appropriate skills and strategies.

Nature

Just like reading offline, reading online is constructivist in nature. Rather than having information transmitted into the learner by the Internet, knowledge is constructed by each individual. Students actively create meaning based on their personal paths to inquiry and discovery (El-Hindi, 1998; Schmar-Dobler, 2003). This approach is supported by researchers' beliefs that online reading comprehension is a problem-based, inquiry-focused process (Coiro et al., 2008; Leu, Kinzer, Coiro, & Cammack, 2004).

Text

Text is a critical factor in both offline and online reading. In Chapter 1, we discussed the expanding notion of text. In Chapter 4, we learned about the role of text in critical literacy. Now we compare and contrast offline and online text. Although they share several similarities, they also have marked differences. In Figure 12.2, which is presented in a Venn Diagram format, the overlapping circles in

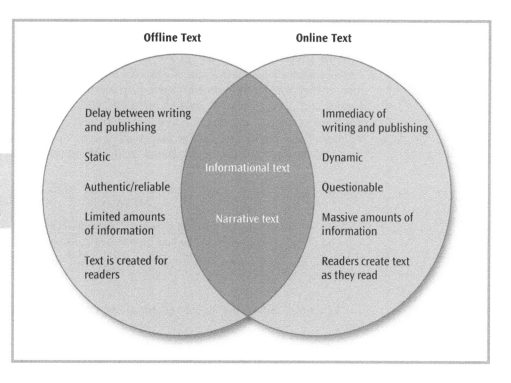

FIGURE 12.2
Comparing and Contrasting Offline and Online Content Area Text

the center feature the similarities. The information contained in the outer circles shows what is unique to offline and online reading, For example, we can see that narrative and informational text are common to both offline and online reading. We can also see that they differ in terms of immediacy of access and nature (Gilster, 1997), as well as in terms of the amount of information they provide.

Kamil and Lane (1998) report that reading on the Internet can be demanding. For example, although the Internet's bright colors, animation, audio, and video may be viewed as motivational by some users, they may be viewed as visually distracting by others. Kamil and Lane further note that the Internet provides access to massive amounts of text, which may be challenging to navigate.

Traditional print text is usually viewed as accurate and reliable, but anyone can post information on the Internet, whether it is accurate or not. For this reason, we must constantly question who has created a website and for what purpose.

Coiro and Dobler (2007) report that both offline and online reading involve purpose, task, and context, but only online reading features self-directed text construction. When reading online, self-directed text is constructed as readers navigate personal paths through massive amounts of information, creating their personal versions of the online texts they read. In essence, several students could be researching the same question online, but because of choices they make about key words, search engines, and site selection, each would construct unique, self-directed text. In contrast, although students reading traditional offline texts would also construct meaning as they read, they would not be constructing text.

Skills and Strategies

As we learned in Chapter 4, the nature of literacy and learning changes as new technologies emerge. A prime example of this can be seen in the increasing popularity of the Internet. In addition to an awareness of the variations in text found on the Internet, a variety of reading comprehension skills are required to navigate Internet-based text (Coiro & Dobler, 2007). As Coiro (2003) notes, "The Internet provides new text formats, new purposes for reading, and new ways to interact with information that can confuse and overwhelm people taught to extract meaning from only conventional print" (p. 458). The skills and strategies we use when reading online build upon those we use when reading offline (Coiro, 2003; Leu, 2000).

Researchers suggest that when we think about what we need to know and be able to do to use the Internet efficiently, we are focusing on what researchers refer to as *new literacies*. The term has several different meanings. We will focus on "new literacies" as the new skills, strategies, and dispositions that are required to successfully identify important questions, locate information, engage in critical evaluation, synthesize information, and communicate on the Internet (Castek et al., 2006; Leu et al., 2004). Kist (2000, 2002) suggests that students in new literacy classrooms construct meaning, understand different symbol systems, use creative forms of expression and representation, and evaluate and communicate information from multiple media. He further notes that such contexts are highly motivational.

Making Connections | Thinking about Technology as Motivation

- Consider the motivational nature of technology. Think specifically about how you can use technology to motivate students to learn in your content area. Focus on specific examples.
- Share your thoughts with others in small-group discussions.

When our students use the Internet for course-related projects, they generally follow these steps:

1. Select a topic of interest.
2. Generate a research question.
3. Think about key words.
4. Question search engines.
5. Evaluate the multiple sources provided by the search engine.
6. Synthesize information relevant to the research question.
7. Choose a mode to represent/communicate the findings.

While reading this list, we may notice that it is somewhat similar to the steps in a more traditional research process. The major difference, of course, is that rather than using reference books in the library, students research topics online. That distinction has implications for both reading and researching.

The good news is that when researching online, students use the traditional reading skills and strategies we have been learning to teach throughout this text. However, when using the Internet, students also need to be able to (1) identify important questions, (2) locate information, (3) evaluate information, (4) synthesize the information relevant to the question, and (5) communicate the answers to others (Leu et al., 2004, p. 1570; Leu, Zawilinski, Castek, Banerjee, Housand, Liu, & O'Neil, 2007). Bell (2001) reminds us that such skills are most productive when they are taught explicitly.

IDENTIFY IMPORTANT QUESTIONS. When we read online, we are usually seeking to answer a question or to solve a problem. This may be a key difference between online and offline reading (Leu et al., 2007). Of course, although our reading of traditional text doesn't necessarily begin with a question, questioning does play a vital role in offline reading. As we learned in Chapter 8, generating questions is an important offline reading skill; as we learned in Chapter 4, self-questioning is an important offline reading comprehension strategy. Our students' abilities to generate questions at a variety of levels and to self-question while reading offline strongly support this aspect of online reading.

In addition to developing an important question to direct our research, Burke (2002) suggests that when planning to access the Internet, we should consider the questions featured in Figure 12.3. Burke proposes that questioning should begin before we approach the Internet, continue as we search for information, and persist even when the search has concluded.

LOCATE INFORMATION. Leu et al. (2007) suggest there are at least four types of skills associated with locating information on the Internet: (1) knowing how to use a search

FIGURE 12.3
Questions to Raise
When Using the Internet
(Burke, 2002)

Before Using the Internet

- What is my goal?

- What kind of information do I need?

- What kinds of sources will provide that kind of information?

- How will I use the information?

- What are some key words that will help me locate the information?

During Use of the Internet

- Who is responsible for the website?

- What information is provided about the authors?

- When was it last updated?

- Who is the intended audience?

- Is the website clearly organized?

- Do the illustrations, charts, maps, graphs, and videos provide/clarify essential information?

- Is the information presented factually correct?

After Using the Internet

- How will I choose to communicate what I have learned?

engine effectively, (2) reading search engine results, (3) reading a webpage, and (4) making inferences when selecting a link at one site in an effort to find information at another site. Of course, all of these steps are dependent on the first skill: knowing how to use a search engine effectively.

When searching for information on the Internet, students are often content to type in a word or phrase and await the results. As teachers, we can help students make their searches more effective. For example, we can use search engine math—that is, simplified Boolean searching—to obtain more focused results. Ideas for using key words and symbols such as plus signs, minus signs, and quotation marks to search more effectively are presented in Figure 12.4.

FIGURE 12.4
Search Engine
Math

Guidelines for Using Search Engine Math (Simplified Boolean Search)

To focus your search on a specific topic, follow these guidelines:

1. Put a *plus sign* (+) in front of words that *must* be present on the webpage.

2. Put a *minus sign* (−) in front of a word to tell the search engine to *subtract* pages that contain that particular word.

3. A plus sign (+) is equivalent to the Boolean search term AND.

4. A minus sign (−) is equivalent to the Boolean search term NOT.

5. Avoid using a "−" term as the first term in your query. For example, if you are searching for information on horses and want to exclude information about ranches, write the query as "horses −ranches" rather than as "−ranches horses."

6. Use the minus sign (−) carefully. If you exclude topics with minus signs, you may also exclude pages that contain information about the topics you are trying to locate.

7. Plus and minus terms can be combined with quotation marks to focus searches.

8. There cannot be any space between the relevant sign and the word to which it refers. For example, write +"Pluto", not + " Pluto".

Source: Pandia Goalgetter Search Tutorial on Search Engine Math (http://www.pandia.com/goalgetter/10.html).

We can also teach our students to use search engines such as NetTrekker (http://www .nettrekker.com/) to locate quality educational information. An award-winning educational search engine that is aligned with state standards, NetTrekker connects users to educator-approved sites that are organized by subject area and readability levels. It also provides supports such as read-alouds and customized content for English learners. NetTrekker is frequently used by teachers, students, and parents of K–12 students.

Using informational search tools such as search engine math and NetTrekker not only saves time, but also helps the researcher to locate focused, quality, relevant information. We should note that the process of locating text contributes to the text that Internet readers construct as they read.

CRITICALLY EVALUATING INFORMATION. According to Coiro (2007) at least five different types of evaluation occur online:

- Evaluating understanding: Does it make sense to me?
- Evaluating relevancy: Does it meet my needs? Does it help me respond to my question?
- Evaluating accuracy: Can I verify it with another reliable source?
- Evaluating reliability: Can I trust it?
- Evaluating bias: How does the author shape it? Whose perspective is represented?

Although evaluation is especially important on the Internet, where anyone can post any type of information, we do engage in evaluating when reading offline. Evaluating is an essential factor in both reading and critical literacy. In the former, we evaluate elements such as the consistency of the author's message. In the latter, we question sources, authors' intent, and other issues (see Chapter 4). We should also note the importance of knowing how to generate questions at multiple levels when evaluating text (see Chapter 9).

SYNTHESIZING INFORMATION. As online readers seek answers to questions, they synthesize or integrate information in two ways (Leu et al., 2007). They pull relevant information from a variety of sources and combine it in terms of its relevance to the topic. Imagine that the research question was "What caused the Civil War?" Results of an Internet search would likely provide information about several issues that contributed to the Civil War. Students would then synthesize this information by organizing what they learned from different sites by topic. For example, there were economic causes of the Civil War, so students would synthesize or blend the information about that cause from all of the websites they choose to access. Synthesizing online text also means that students, "actively construct the texts that they read through the choices they make about which sites to visit, which links to follow, whom to communicate with, and whose messages to read as they seek answers to the questions that direct their online reading" (Leu, et al. 2007, p. 48.)

COMMUNICATING INFORMATION. After students synthesize information, they need to choose a way to communicate their findings. They may choose to use discussion, a PowerPoint presentation, or art forms such as dramatization or music to share what they have learned (see Chapter 13). Other options include blogs, wikis, discussion boards, and phone and video conferencing (Leu, et al. 2008).

Making Connections
TO WRITING

Writing plays a critical role in our use of technology. We use it—with immediacy—to communicate through e-mail and share ideas in blogs and wikis. As Leu (2000) has noted, we are living in a global society in which writing will become even more important than it is today. ■

Making Connections | Thinking about Technology

■ Don Leu and his colleagues suggest that knowing how to critically evaluate information is an impor- tant skill when reading online text. What are your thoughts on this topic? What connections can you make between critically evaluating text when reading online and being critically literate?

■ Share your thoughts with others in small-group discussions.

How Can We Use Technology as a Natural Part of Teaching and Learning?

When we use technology in our teaching, we need to be aware of how to incorporate it seam- lessly in meaningful ways. In this section, we share general ideas about how to do that. Next, we discuss specific Internet-based strategies including Internet Workshop, Internet Project, Inter- net Inquiry, and WebQuests. Then we discuss how to use podcasts, blogs, and wikis as resources to facilitate such projects.

Guidelines for Integrating Technology

Richardson (2004) suggests that we consider the following factors when designing content les- sons that incorporate technology:

1. *Think broadly.* Technology involves more than the Internet. Consider using presentation software, digital photography, e-mail, threaded discussions, podcasts, and wikibooks.
2. *Use an appropriate form of technology.* Consider the students, the materials you have to work with, the level of complexity, and the amount of preparation needed.
3. *Always have a backup plan.* Locate more than one website, in case the site is taken down before you teach the lesson. When using a digital camera, have an extra power extension and an extra battery at hand. If you need to transfer software or data, store it in two differ- ent ways (e.g., memory stick, CD).
4. *Incorporate technology as seamlessly as possible.* Technology is the means, not the content of the lesson. It should enhance the lesson, not overwhelm it. (p. 15)

Figure 12.5 features some examples of Internet resources we can use for teaching in the content areas.

 **TEACHING IDEA**

INTERNET WORKSHOP. Internet Workshop (Leu, 2002) is especially useful for introducing students to sites for an upcoming unit and developing background knowledge. During such a workshop, students can work individually, in collaboration with classmates, or in conjunction with international peers.

The workshop format is flexible, but it usually involves the following steps:

1. *Locate a central site, or several sites,* on the Internet with content related to a classroom unit of instruction and set a bookmark for the location(s). This limits random surfing on the Internet and helps ensure student safety on the Internet.
2. *Develop an activity related to class learning goals* that requires students to use the site(s). Internet Workshop works well before learning to help students build background knowl- edge, and during learning to enrich individual and class knowledge of the topic.
3. *Encourage students to record information in an electronic journal.* While students are using the Internet, we should be monitoring their work. Questions that might guide our obser- vations include these:

   ■ Did the student easily access the site?
   ■ Is the student focused on the task?

Annenberg Media Learner.Org
http://www.learner.org

Art at the Getty (J. Paul Getty Museum)
http://www.getty.edu

The History Channel
http://www.history.com

Language Learning Center
http://depts.washington.edu/llc/main/links/world.php

The Learning Page: Especially for Teachers (Library of Congress)
http://memory.loc.gov/learn

Mathworld
http://mathworld.wolfram.com/BolzaProblem.html

NASA's Online Interactive Projects
http://www.quest.arc.nasa.gov
(Students participate in scientific research.)

National Geographic Society Home Page
http://www.nationalgeographic.com

PBS
http://www.pbs.org

Smithsonian Museums
http://www.si.edu

Remember.Org: A Cybrary of the Holocaust
http://www.remember.org

FIGURE 12.5
Internet Teaching Resources for the Content Areas

- Does the student seem to be gathering quality information that will contribute to the class learning goals?
- If students are working in groups, are all members making valuable contributions?

4. *Hold periodic workshop sessions,* so students can share their work, raise questions, reveal new insights, and discuss the skills needed to function effectively online.

Internet Workshop is an effective way to help expand students' understanding of the topic being studied. For example, if we are beginning to teach a unit or topic about which students have little or no background knowledge, we can use Internet Workshop to increase their knowledge before reading text chapters or engaging in more formal projects. We can also use Internet Workshop when students are creating projects or after learning to extend their thinking.

The following is an example of how we can use Internet Workshop in literature class:

> *Literature Internet Workshop: Imagine that we are planning to begin teaching our students about Native American authors, but students have little or no background knowledge about the topic. We can research and locate several websites that offer quality information, bookmark the sites, and engage students in Internet Workshop. If necessary, we can also teach mini-lessons on topics ranging from ways to locate quality websites to the lives and publications of Native American authors. Students can then use the websites to gather information and report it to the class. During workshop sessions, they can also engage in conferencing, peer review, or idea exchanges.*

We can also use the Internet Workshop format when students are creating Internet Projects, undertaking Internet Inquiry, and engaging in WebQuests. This provides the students with regular access to mini-lessons as well as opportunities for sharing and peer feedback.

 **TEACHING IDEA**

INTERNET PROJECT. Internet Project (Leu, 2001) is a collaborative learning experience between two or more classrooms that takes place over the Internet. Internet projects may be either website-based or engaged in spontaneously.

Website Projects are coordinated through a website developed by the originator. They are usually precisely defined and include clear directions for participation. Because of their precise nature, website projects are sometimes more limited in scope and learning potential.

Spontaneous Projects include the following steps:

1. *Develop a collaborative project.* Be sure to include a summary of the project, a clear list of learning goals, expectations for the collaborating classrooms, and a projected timeline from beginning to completion.
2. *Post the project description and timeline on the Internet* several months in advance to seek collaborative class partners.
3. *Arrange collaboration details with teachers* of other classes who agree to participate.
4. *Exchange information* with your collaborating classrooms. Encourage discussion between and among classes as the project progresses.
5. *Complete the project.* Celebrate with the collaborating classrooms.

As teachers, we can engage our classes in Internet Projects that have been created by other teachers or experts in the field, such as those on the GLOBE Program and NASA Quest websites. In addition, we can create Internet Projects that provide opportunities for our students to interact with students throughout the United States or around the world. In the following example, we present specific steps to follow when creating an Internet Project.

When developing Internet Projects, we should choose a specific topic and post the following types of information on the Internet:

1. **Project title:** Choose a title that clearly relates to what the students will do. For example, if students will study African cultures, an appropriate title might be "Exploring Africa."
2. **Project summary:** Describe the project and its expected outcomes. For example, if our Internet Project is "Exploring Africa," we might summarize the project in this way:

   In *Exploring Africa,* students from the United States will investigate African culture, history, and geography. The project will be created collaboratively with other classes throughout the world. The components of the project will be discussed through e-mails, and each class will assume responsibility for a particular section. The components of the project will then be fused into a digital movie and shared with all participants.

3. **Dates:** Provide the dates on which the Internet project will begin and end.
4. **Ages:** List the student ages that would be appropriate for the project. Ages generally work better than grade levels, because many countries have school structures that differ from the U.S. system.
5. **Curriculum areas:** Indicate the subject areas involved in the Internet Project. For example, if the project is "Exploring Africa," areas such as the arts, history, language, and technology might be included.
6. **Types of technology:** Describe the types of technology that will be used. For example, in "Exploring Africa," the list might include audio files and CDs, student-created websites, e-mail, wikis, video clips, DVDs, and discussion forums.
7. **Types of collaboration:** Describe the nature of the collaboration. For example, in "Exploring Africa," the types of collaboration in which students engage might include information exchange, electronic publishing, intercultural exchange, peer feedback, and virtual meetings.
8. **Project registration:** Register the Internet Project online several months in advance, so other classes can access information about it. **Internet Projects Registry** (http://www.gsn.org/GSH/pr/) is the original clearinghouse for collaborative projects from around the world. This site features projects hosted by the Global SchoolNet Foundation, other well-respected organizations, and teachers around the globe.

 **INTERNET INQUIRY.** When students engage in Internet Inquiry (Leu & Kinzer, 1999; Leu & Leu, 1999) they use online sources to conduct research. During this discovery-based process, students identify important questions and then gather information as they seek answers to

those questions. Internet Inquiry is a student-centered activity in which students choose the issues they explore and take responsibility for completing the research. Students can work individually or in groups organized by interest.

Internet Inquiry includes five phases of student participation:

1. Generate research questions about a theme or topics being studied.
2. Search for responses to the research questions on the Internet.
3. Analyze the information found online.
4. Choose a mode to present the findings.
5. Share the results with the whole class.

For example, if we were planning to engage our students in Internet Inquiry about famous scientists, we might follow these guidelines:

INTERNET INQUIRY: FAMOUS SCIENTISTS

1. Create an Internet Inquiry about biographies of famous scientists.
2. Invite students to select a person to research from a list of possibilities.
3. Share and explain the rubric that will be used to evaluate Internet Inquiry.
4. Encourage students to choose how they will present the biographical information they locate about the person they chose.
5. Encourage students to generate questions to direct their research.

Example questions for a student who has chosen to investigate Albert Einstein:

- What scientific discoveries did Einstein make?
- What is Einstein's general theory of relativity?
- What role did Einstein play in the creation of the atomic bomb?

6. Monitor students' progress as they gather and analyze information.
7. Invite students to participate in periodic conferencing or workshops to ask questions, engage in peer review, and share ideas about the projects they are developing.
8. Use the rubric to evaluate students' Internet Inquiry projects.

Examples of how Internet Inquiry can be used in mathematics, history, and literature include the following:

- Mathematics Internet Inquiry: Students investigate famous women mathematicians.
- History Internet Inquiry: Students investigate the Spanish–American War.
- Literature Internet Inquiry: Students investigate the lives and achievements of F. Scott Fitzgerald and Ernest Hemingway.

Go to the Activities and Applications section under the topic *Technology* in the MyEducationLab for your course and complete the activity entitled Wireless WebQuests to explain ways in which WebQuests can enhance instruction in content area literacies.

TEACHING IDEA

WEBQUESTS. WebQuests are inquiry-oriented online tools for learning that are based on the teachers' preselected Internet resources (Dodge, 1995). There are six components to a WebQuest:

1. Introduction (activate background knowledge and motivate)
2. Task (formal description of what needs to be done)
3. Process (steps to accomplish the text)
4. Resources (list of bookmarked websites and other materials that will be used)
5. Evaluation (rubric)
6. Conclusion (summary and reflection).

March (2003/2004) notes that WebQuests are scaffolded and involve authentic tasks that respond to an open-ended question. Engaging in WebQuests helps students develop online expertise, promotes group participation, and cultivates critical thinking. To explore WebQuests such as *Genes: The Building Blocks of Life*, in which genetics-related issues are explored; *Artwork in Central Park: A WebQuest Integrating Geometry and Art,* in which students create art; and many others, visit the website entitled "Index of /academics/education/projects/webquests" (http://oncampus.richmond.edu/academics/education/projects/webquests).

Tools to Facilitate Online Learning: Podcasts, Blogs, and Wikis

Podcasts, blogs, and wikis are three technology tools that students can use to facilitate communication with their peers and with us during projects and other learning experiences. In the following section, we describe each and provide details about its use.

PODCASTS. Podcasting is a way to receive broadcasts through the Internet using an automatic *feed* in a process called *subscribing*. Podcast episodes can consist of audio files, video files, or documents, or any combination of the three. Kajder (2007) offers a classroom example. She notes that teachers can use podcasts to electronically review student conversations in Literature or Discussion Circles. For example, each small group can use an iPod paired with an iTalk microphone to digitally record their discussions and provide their teacher with access to their conversations. To learn more about podcasts, visit the Education Podcast Network at www.epnweb.org.

BLOGS. Blogs (more formally, "web logs") are websites that "allow individuals to create personal webpages of text, pictures, graphics, videos, and other multimedia with the same ease as creating a word processing document" (Boling, Castek, Zawilinski, Barton, & Nierlich, 2008, p. 504). According to Oravec (2002), blogs are similar to online journals. The format allows authors (known as "bloggers") to work individually or in teams, engage in personal expression, and interact with others who comment on their blogs.

There are numerous ways to use blogs in content area teaching. They include the following options (adapted from edublogs.org):

- Post materials and resources.
- Hold online discussions.
- Create a class publication.
- Replace your newsletter.
- Get your students blogging.
- Share your lesson plans.
- Integrate multimedia of all descriptions.
- Organize.
- Get feedback.
- Create a fully functional website.

To examine sites that promote blogging, visit Edublogs at edublogs.org or Word Press at wordpress.org.

WIKIS. As noted in Figure 12.1, *wiki* is the Hawaiian word for "quick." Wikis allow a number of people to freely revise and edit text online. Content area students can use wikis for a variety of purposes, including revising and editing small-group research projects and class-authored books.

Making Connections | Thinking about Technology

- Consider specific ways in which you could use podcasts, blogs, and wikis when teaching in your content area.
- Share your thoughts with others in small-group discussions.

Using technology in the content areas seems to have endless possibilities. The following list of ideas is designed to help us think about specific ways in which it can be integrated into our teaching. Students can:

- Become authors on the Web and share their self-authored poems and stories with other students.

- Collaborate with other students on a worldwide basis on Internet projects
- Conduct online Discussion Circles.
- Use web-based bookmarking (Forbes, 2004).
- Refine a search.
- Evaluate online sources in several ways, including learning who constructed the site and for what purposes, and comparing and contrasting the information posted on several sites.
- E-mail and chat with peers around the world.
- Experience virtual field trips ranging from a tour of the White House (www.whitehouse.gov) to a tour of the Egyptian pyramids (www.pbs.org/wgbh/nova/pyramid).
- Create virtual field trips.
- Use webcam sites on which they view exactly what is happening at the time—for example on safari (www.africam.com) or at the Eiffel Tower (www.abcparislive.com).
- Collaborate with other classes to publish electronic newspapers or literary magazines.
- Use digital photography to represent their thinking.
- Create a class website or create personal websites.
- Communicate with students who are native language speakers and practice speaking the language.
- Collect data about environmental issues.
- Compare and contrast historical events in the area in which students live with those in areas in which other students live (Mike, 1996).
- Create a network of classes to explore ecological issues.

There are myriad ways to integrate technology into our teaching—not as an add-on, but as a natural and beneficial component of teaching and learning. Encouraging our students to use technology to learn will motivate them and extend their understandings.

Making Connections
TO MULTIPLE LITERACIES

As Leu (2000) has reported, students write just as much in the age of technology as their counterparts did when curriculums were more traditionally based. This is especially true when students use information literacy to research. We need to ensure that our students know how to use the Internet as a research source and that they understand how to use informal and formal writing to record their thinking about these sites. For more information about these types of writing, see Chapter 11. ■

FINAL THOUGHTS

There is no doubt that technology has made, and will continue to make, important contributions to teaching and learning. It is certain that the future holds even greater possibilities. Clearly, traditional teaching and the technologies of the future will continue to be integrated. As Means (2000/2001) has observed:

> Schools that incorporate the technology of the future can offer the best combination of traditional face-to-face instruction—role modeling, socialization, and morale building—and projected benefits of learning with new technologies: increased participation in systems of distributed learning that engage broader communities, learning-enhancing representations of concepts and data, a restructuring of teaching and learning roles, and more meaningful assessment practices. (p. 61)

In the next chapter, we examine inquiry-based learning, a topic in which technology plays a significant role. Although inquiry can be traced back to early Greece, it has not always been valued in education. In Chapter 13, we explore it from a 21st century perspective.

Teaching Connections

APPLYING WHAT WE HAVE LEARNED

E-Links

The International Society for Technology in Education (ISTE) has developed National Educational Technology Standards and Performance Indicators for Students. Numerous Departments of Education have adapted these standards for use at the state level.

1. Review the ISTE Standards.
   (a) Consider how you plan to address selected standards in your teaching. Make specific connections between content and technology projects such as Internet Inquiry, Internet Project, Internet Workshop, or WebQuests. Record your thinking in a reflective portfolio entry.
   (b) Develop a standards-based lesson that integrates content and technology, including the use of resources such as podcasts, blogs, and wikis. Include your lesson in your portfolio as a resource for future teaching.

EXAMPLE WEBSITES

To review the National Educational Technology Standards and Performance Indicators for Students, visit this site:
http://www.iste.org/Content/NavigationMenu/NETS/ForStudents/2007Standards/NETS_for_Students_2007_Standards.pdf

Accountable Talk

Technology is an important facet of today's teaching. Meet in discipline-specific small groups to discuss how you will integrate technology into your teaching in your content area. Consider (1) what kind of technology access your students will need, (2) how you will motivate your students to participate in technology-based learning, and (3) how you will teach your students the skills needed to read online.

 ### Portfolio/Performance Opportunity

The Content Area Resource Anthology (CARA) is a project that is designed to align online resources with a variety of inquiry-based, creative teaching ideas. See Figure 12.6 for specifics of the project and Figure 12.7 for the CARA rubric. Create a CARA based on a specific topic related to your content area. The topic should be one you expect to teach, and one in which you have personal interest. (See Appendix F for sample excerpts from a CARA.) Include your CARA in your portfolio.

FIGURE 12.6
Content Area Resource Anthology

The Content Area Resource Anthology (CARA) is an Internet-based compilation of instructional resources that you can use in your teaching. Begin by selecting a topic that you would like to investigate—one that you believe will enhance your teaching and deepen students' understanding. After you discuss the topic with your professor, begin your investigation. The following guidelines will facilitate that process.

I. **Contents Page:** List each segment of the CARA and its corresponding starting page.

II. **Reflective Introduction:** Express your ideas about the topic, why you selected it, and how you think it will benefit your teaching.

III. **Poems:** Use the Internet to locate 3 topic-related poems. Include copies of the poems, APA references, and brief summaries in your CARA. Then describe a creative and innovative teaching idea for each poem. (See your notes and this text's chapters on technology, inquiry-based learning, and alternative modes of representation.)

IV. **Books (3 picture books, one chapter book):** Use the Internet, the library, and bookstores to locate 3 topic-related picture books and a chapter book. Include APA references and brief summaries of the books. Then describe a creative and innovative teaching idea you would use for each book. (See your notes and this text's chapters on technology, inquiry-based learning, and alternative modes of representation.)

V. **Informational Articles:** Use the Internet to locate 3 topic-related informational articles that are either short enough to be used as read-alouds or have segments that can effectively be used as read-alouds. Include copies of the articles, APA references, and brief summaries. Then describe a creative and innovative teaching idea you would use for each. (See your notes and the section on read-alouds in Chapter 8.)

VI. **Websites:** Use the Internet to locate 3 topic-related websites. Include APA references and brief summaries of the sites. Then describe a creative and innovative teaching idea you would use for each website. (See your notes and this text's chapters on technology, inquiry-based learning, and alternative modes of representation.)

VII. **Videos, DVDs, and CD-ROMs:** Use the Internet to locate 2 topic-related videos, DVDs, or CD-ROMs. Include APA references and brief summaries. Then describe a creative and innovative teaching idea you would use for each. (See your notes and this text's chapters on technology, inquiry-based learning, and alternative modes of representation.)

FIGURE 12.7 Content Area Resource Anthology Rubric

Reflection	4_____3_____2_____1
Connections to topic	4_____3_____2_____1
Teaching ideas	4_____3_____2_____1
Differentiated instruction	4_____3_____2_____1
Display of dispositions	4_____3_____2_____1
Use of technology	4_____3_____2_____1
Professional appearance	4_____3_____2_____1

4: Excellent reflection demonstrating depth of reasoning. Outstanding connections to the CARA topic. In-depth, resourceful use of a wide range of creative and innovative teaching ideas, methods, instructional grouping practices (whole class, small groups, pairs, individual, and computer based), and curriculum materials, including types and levels of text, technology-based information, and nonprint materials for students at differing stages of development and cultural and linguistic backgrounds. Differentiated instruction demonstrates exceptional knowledge of students' abilities, interests, and cultural and linguistic backgrounds. A wide variety of texts (books, articles, technology-based texts, and nonprint material) reflecting students' interests, cultures, and linguistic backgrounds are selected, reviewed, and used. Risk taking is evident. Advanced dispositions related to content area reading are displayed. Fully developed and detailed use of technology. Totally professional in appearance (design, presentation, APA format).

3: Thorough reflection demonstrating sound reasoning. Detailed connections to the CARA topic. Integration of a variety of creative and innovative teaching ideas, methods, grouping practices (whole class, small groups, pairs, individual, and computer based), and curriculum materials, including types and levels of text, technology-based information, and nonprint materials for learners at different stages of development and cultural and linguistic backgrounds. Differentiated instruction demonstrates thorough understanding of students' abilities, interests, and cultural and linguistic backgrounds. A variety of texts (books, articles, technology-based texts, and nonprint material) reflecting students' interests, cultures, and linguistic backgrounds are selected, reviewed, and used. Proficient dispositions related to content area reading are displayed. Appropriate use of technology. The paper is professional in appearance (design, presentation, APA format).

2: Adequate reflection demonstrates reasoning. Connections to the CARA topic are somewhat consistent. Teaching ideas, methods, grouping practices (whole class, small groups, pairs, individual, and computer based), curriculum materials, including types and levels of text, technology-based information, and nonprint materials for learners at different stages of development and cultural and linguistic backgrounds lack variety and creative and innovative perspectives. Differentiated instruction demonstrates adequate knowledge of students' abilities, interests, and cultural and linguistic backgrounds. A limited variety of texts (books, articles, technology-based texts, and nonprint material) reflecting students' interests, cultures, and linguistic backgrounds are selected, reviewed, and used. Developing dispositions related to content area reading are displayed. Limited use of technology. Lacking elements of professional appearance (design, presentation, use of APA format).

1: Inadequate reflection—lacks depth and logical reasoning. Connections to the CARA topic are nonexistent or illogical. Teaching ideas, methods, grouping practices (whole class, small groups, pairs, individual, and computer based), curriculum materials, including types and levels of text, technology-based information, and nonprint materials for learners at different stages of development and cultural and linguistic backgrounds are not creative or innovative. Differentiated instruction demonstrates insufficient knowledge of students' abilities, interests, and cultural and linguistic backgrounds. Texts (books, articles, technology-based texts, and nonprint material) have little or no variety and do not reflect students' interests, cultures, and linguistic backgrounds are selected, reviewed, and used. Unacceptable dispositions related to content area reading are displayed. Inadequate use of technology. Less than professional in appearance (design, presentation, APA format).

13

Inquiry: Key to Critical and Creative Thinking in the Content Areas

For many of us, content area learning experiences were passive situations in which we either copied information from the board or took notes while a teacher lectured. These activities were, of course, routinely interrupted by a written quiz or test. There were few opportunities for student interaction, and the questions raised came from either the teacher or the text. Clearly, opportunities for inquiry in these contexts were extremely limited. Bruce and Bishop (2002) acknowledge that such practices remain common:

> Traditional curricula in most countries have emphasized a delivery of content approach. Knowledge is assumed to exist or be encoded within texts. The role of the teacher is to manage the delivery of this knowledge, and the role of the learner is to absorb as much as possible. More specifically, students are expected to master certain basic learning skills such as solving problems, remembering textbooks, following directions, working alone, and "covering" the curriculum.

These teaching and learning practices were not adequate in the past, and they are not adequate now. Today we and our students need to be thinkers—critical thinkers who know how to raise meaningful questions, and creative thinkers who see multiple ways to engage in problem solving. Such thinkers see the world as their text. For these thinkers, classrooms are transitioning from the more traditional model to a student-centered paradigm that provides a solid foundation for inquiry-based learning.

In this chapter, we discuss the theory that underpins inquiry-based learning and present content area activities that promote inquiry in a variety of contexts. We begin by defining inquiry-based learning and linking it to constructivism. Next, we explain two types of inquiry: problem-based and project-based learning. We explore a variety of inquiry-based activities in each category, provide guidelines for engaging in them, and present student examples. Finally, we discuss how to assess and evaluate inquiry-based projects.

What Is Inquiry-Based Learning?

Inquiry-based learning (IBL) is a project-oriented teaching method that is constructivist in nature (Eick & Reed, 2002). It is a process in which students ask questions that lead to new understandings, which in turn lead to new questions (Flint & Bomer, 2002). Short and Burke (1996) suggest that inquiry should be viewed as a framework for learning, a context in which students are encouraged to understand at deeper levels.

Although inquiry-based learning can be traced back to Socrates, its most recent emergence is linked to the constructivist movement, which suggests that students link what is new to what is known to construct personal meaning. In constructivism, problem-solving approaches, project-based learning, and many other variations on the theme, inquiry is a student-centered process (UICU, 2008). Taking this active role in learning implies that students possess the skills needed to seek resolutions to issues, as new knowledge is constructed ("Concept to Classroom," 2008). Principles that guide the teacher's role in constructivism include emphasizing students' responsibility for learning and promoting connections between what students learn and the world in which they live.

Inquiry-based learning is viewed as a cyclical process that includes five steps: question, investigate, create, discuss, and reflect. This process begins with curiosity and reflection, which lead to question generation. This is followed by an investigation. When the research is complete, the student creates a solution or product. The creation is then presented and discussed. This leads to more reflection, which in turn leads to more questions—and the process begins anew. During this recursive inquiry process, the student makes a variety of decisions, including selecting a topic, generating questions, determining research methods, choosing resources, and deciding on a mode of presentation.

Making Connections
TO MULTIPLE LITERACIES

When students engage in inquiry-based learning, they use multiple literacies including content literacies, adolescent literacy, and critical literacy. In addition, students need to have a good understanding of information literacy to complete inquiry-based tasks. They need to be able to ask good research questions, conduct a viable search, use a variety of quality sources, understand the information they locate, synthesize what they learn, and communicate their findings. Before engaging students in inquiry-based learning, we should use discussion or an informal assessment such as Tickets Out to ensure that all of our students are comfortable using information literacy. ■

As noted in Figure 13.1, a number of motivational factors—including student self-selection of topics, accommodation of students' learning styles, and self-assessment and reflection—characterize inquiry-based learning. In addition, performance assessment provides students with opportunities to show what they know and can do through multiple modes. Inquiry-based learning also provides opportunities for students to use their strength modalities.

Inquiry-based learning benefits students in a variety of ways. It promotes collaborative learning and encourages students to understand at deeper levels. In the process, students become

FIGURE 13.1
Factors That Characterize Inquiry-Based Learning

Student centered	Self-selection of topics and research methods
Risk-taking context	Student ownership/responsibility for learning
Critical and creative thinking	Accommodation of students' learning styles
Research and exploration	Cross-curricular understandings
Social nature of learning	Self-assessment and reflection
Multiple modes of communication	Performance assessment
Learning at deeper levels	Teacher as facilitator

active, motivated participants. They generate questions and access and gather information. They engage in critical and creative thinking, and they analyze and synthesize information. They become problem solvers and understand questioning as a cyclical process.

Making Connections | Thinking about Inquiry-Based Learning

■ Teachers often recall their best teachers as those who engaged in inquiry-based learning. Reflect on your educational experiences. Did inquiry play a role? Contemplate how you would integrate inquiry into the curriculum you teach.

■ Share your reasoning with a partner and then join your partner in developing arguments to justify including inquiry-based learning in middle school and high school curriculums.

Making Connections
TO STRUGGLING READERS

When engaging struggling readers in inquiry-based learning, we can begin by reviewing Ciardiello's question generation techniques (see Chapter 9) and encourage use of presentation modes that accommodate students' differing learning styles. For example, some students might prefer to create a PowerPoint slideshow, use an electronic picture book format, or present what they have learned through songs or dramatizations. It is important that students choose a presentation mode that works well for them and that we, as teachers offer as much support as possible by scaffolding learning, arranging cross-age experiences, and ensuring students have a variety of accessible sources. ■

Which Instructional Techniques Promote Inquiry?

There are a variety of ways to integrate inquiry into content area teaching and learning. In this section, we address two frequently used approaches: problem-based and project-based learning. These methods naturally embed critical and creative thinking in inquiry-based experiences.

Problem-Based Learning

Problem-based learning challenges students to work collaboratively to reason their way to solutions of real-world problems. The problems are designed to motivate students to learn. The students work together and think critically and creatively to create solutions. As Checkley (1997) notes:

Problem-Based Learning is an instructional method that uses a real world problem as the context for an in-depth investigation of core content. The problems that students tackle are ill-structured; they include just enough information to suggest how students should proceed with an investigation, but never enough information to enable students to solve the problem without further inquiry. (p. 3)

Problem-based learning is generally characterized by four stages:

1. *Engaging students.* We motivate students by sharing general ideas about the problem-based scenario. We also leave gaps in the information. Students use questioning to fill in those gaps. This engages student interest in the problem-solving process.
2. *Inquiry and investigation.* Once students know some general information, they generate questions based upon it. Then they try to reason their way through the responses offered or derived from research.
3. *Solution products.* The products of problem-based learning are generally reasoned explanations. Students develop these solutions based on the information originally provided, responses to the questions they generated, and subsequent reasoning and additional questions.
4. *Debriefing.* This stage takes place after a solution has been proposed. Students revisit the clues derived from the responses, analyze the subsequent questions they generated, and discuss the paths each traveled to the solution.

These stages are linked because each progressive level builds a foundation for the subsequent phase (Stepien & Gallagher, 1997). Students become better problem solvers through problem-based learning because they refine their reasoning abilities, collaboration skills, and persistence as they engage in self-directed searches for solutions (Checkley, 1997).

GUIDELINES FOR STUDENTS ENGAGING IN PROBLEM-BASED LEARNING. When teaching this inquiry-based method to students, we can begin by explaining and demonstrating the process while emphasizing the importance of inquiry and reasoning. We can also share the following general guidelines, which provide direction for students engaging in problem-based learning:

1. *Understand the problem.* Listen carefully as your teacher explains what is known about the problem. Prepare to use your knowledge, skills, and other information as the solution progresses. Review the project rubric.
2. *Determine what you need to know.* Discuss what is known about the problem in small groups and brainstorm how it might be resolved. Revisit the rubric as necessary.
3. *Use collaborative skills when working in groups.* List each group member's strengths and consider how each might contribute to the solution.
4. *Communicate effectively.* Write the problem in your own words and revise as necessary throughout the process. Focus on meaningful questions and logical reasoning.
5. *Support thinking with evidence and sound reasoning.* List and discuss possible solutions. Write the group's solution and justify group members' thinking. Reflect on the reasoning process in which you engaged.

These guidelines provide support for students as they engage in problem-based learning and begin to structure problems on their own. As noted in these suggestions, questioning, collaboration, and reasoning are at the heart of this inquiry-based process.

Dramatized problem-based learning and Ripped from the Headlines: Real-Life Investigations are two examples of problem-based learning. In the former approach, students gather clues by interacting with those who have the problem; in the latter case, students work together to identify and resolve news-based problems.

 **TEACHING IDEA**

DRAMATIZED PROBLEM-BASED LEARNING. In dramatized problem-based learning, students use inquiry to identify the problem and work toward resolution, while interacting with people integrally involved in the problem (Stepien & Gallagher, 1997). The following scenario offers an example of dramatized problem-based learning:

> *Ask students to imagine that the classroom is actually their home. After a knock is heard on the door, students begin to respond to it. Before they open the door, the students begin brainstorming about what awaits them when the door is opened. Students ask questions of the visitors before opening the door. After the questions are raised and answered, the students choose to open the door. At this point, students know what the problem is. In this case, students determined that the problem was set in the 1850s and the people at the door were runaway slaves. The students chose to open the door and admit the visitors to their home.*
>
> *After the visitors have entered, students engage in conversation with them. As the scenario progresses, students learn that the runaway slaves were destined for a stop on the Underground Railroad when they noticed fugitive slave catchers, who would capture them and force them to return to their owners, near that house. To avoid apprehension, they journeyed on in the darkness to the students' door.*
>
> *At this point the students focused their questions on what they believed they needed to know to resolve the problem. They worked collaboratively and communicated with one another and with the runaway slaves. The students knew that letting the runaway slaves into their home was just the beginning. They reasoned that the real problem was how to hide the runaway slaves and avoid breaking the law.*

In this scenario, once all the information was discovered, the students realized that they must confront the situation and find a solution to the problem. This matter was, of course, complicated by the fact that it was illegal to hide runaway slaves in some states in the 1850s. This led to a number of fact-finding activities, including students' researching the issue using library and Internet sources, reviewing a journal kept by one of the runaway slaves, determining what they learned about the Underground Railroad that could help them resolve the problem, reading newspaper articles from the nineteenth century, and holding roundtable discussions about particular facts involved in the decision-making process. The inquiry-based process continued until the students came to a consensus of opinion about whether to hide the visitors in their home. After listing and debating possible solutions, the students decided to hide the runaway slaves in their home, find another home connected to the Underground Railroad, and send representatives there to determine how best to get the slaves back on the path to freedom.

TEACHING IDEA   **RIPPED FROM THE HEADLINES: REAL-LIFE INVESTIGATIONS.** Ripped from the Headlines is a long-term inquiry-based investigation that is often cross-curricular in nature. When using Ripped from the Headlines, teachers and students select an intriguing problem-based story from a news source as the basis for inquiry. Students clearly define the problem, and then they work to solve it. They decide which classes will investigate which aspect of the problem. They generate questions and use multiple research sources to gain and report information that will be used in the resolution of the case. Students brainstorm the types of information they need to know to make informed decisions and decide which research sources they will use. They meet regularly in workshop sessions, determine a solution to the problem, and often dramatize the outcome. In Ripped from the Headlines, the stories are always current, the basic information about the problem comes directly from a news source, and all of the known facts are released to the students at the start of the investigation.

The following application of this strategy was developed by Debi Stinner and her colleagues in the Bangor School District, Bangor, Pennsylvania. It focuses on integrating physics, history, and reading/language arts.

In this multiple-phase cross-curricular unit, students follow the events of an actual bus and train crash from reports of its occurrence to its closure in the judicial system. The unit incorporates reading/language arts, physics, and history classes and lasts for a period of approximately four weeks. All students work together, but each discipline does have some specific tasks. For example, physics students research the speed and impact of the train and bus, and history students investigate the state and town's train-crossing laws. The students' ultimate task is to decide who is responsible for the accident. Students clearly define the problem and research information about the accident through newspapers and the Internet. They carefully examine this information and participate in discussions with guest speakers, who include a defense attorney and a district attorney. Students also view the film *Twelve Angry Men*. As time progresses, the students develop courtroom evidence such as aerial scale drawings of the accident scene and calculations concerning momentum, stopping distance, speed, and force of impact.

The students then decide who they think caused the accident. They have determined that there are a variety of possibilities including the following:

- The bus driver, for not realizing the back of the bus was over the tracks
- The train engineer, for speeding
- The bus company, for improperly training substitute bus drivers
- The highway department, for widening the highway and not checking the timing on the trip switch
- The town council for insisting the highway be widened on the side toward the tracks

Next, the students participate in a mock trial. Prior to starting the unit, students have studied the judicial system, the roles it encompasses, and appropriate courtroom procedures. Students portray all roles including judge, jurors, prosecuting and defense attorneys, witnesses, and bailiff. Over the next several days, members of the court do a variety of things, including the following:

- Witnesses prepare their statements by researching their role and the comments they made in the newspaper articles.
- Lawyers prepare their cases, including interviewing the witnesses.
- Lawyers are provided with the National Transportation Safety Board report of the accident.
- The judge reviews the rules of the courtroom.
- The jurors review literature about types of evidence.

Then the actual trial takes place. After the verdict has been determined, members of the court engage in reflection about the roles they played. For example, the judge may ponder how she influenced the outcome of the trial and explain whether she agrees or disagrees with the verdict. Members of the jury may document why they felt the defendant was guilty or innocent. The lawyers may describe what the basis of their case was, who they think won or lost, and what they would do differently if the trial could be held again.

Ripped from the Headlines: Real-Life Investigations enhances students' learning and motivates them in a number of ways. First, it requires students to read the newspaper—a primary information source for our society. While students may have already been reading newspapers for sports, comics, advertisements, or advice columns, this activity helps them connect to actual news stories and raise their own questions. Students become attuned to the print medium and often continue reading the news after the project is complete, frequently suggesting topics for future investigations. In addition, the integrated nature of Ripped from the Headlines helps students see connections between and among subject areas. Further, students interact not only with classmates and teachers, but also with community members whose professions are linked to the topic of investigation. Finally, dramatizing the event accommodates individual learning styles and offers students an alternative way to demonstrate what they have learned.

Students are motivated to engage in problem-based learning because they find the real-life topics interesting and because they can contribute to the problem-solving process as independent thinkers. Students take an active role, raise questions, apply content area knowledge, use multiple sources, work cooperatively with others, and engage in decision making—all skills they will use throughout their lives.

Problem-based learning provides opportunities for students to take ownership of their learning, gain insights into their reasoning processes, and work with others to develop common understandings. In the next section, we focus on project-based learning, another type of inquiry-based experience.

Project-Based Learning

Project-based learning is a dynamic process that encourages students to learn at deeper levels. Students develop confidence in their ability to communicate, learn, and research when engaging in this project-centered approach. They create knowledge based on questions they have raised and information they have gathered. They can also choose to respond in modes that accommodate their learning styles.

Project-based learning generally involves long-term projects. After making several choices, students engage in inquiry about a self-selected topic. They research that topic using a variety of methods, including reference books and websites. The task usually ends in the creation of a product or performance that reflects what the students know and how they can use what they have learned.

GUIDELINES FOR STUDENTS ENGAGING IN PROJECT-BASED LEARNING. When teaching this type of inquiry-based learning to our students, we can begin by explaining how it works and encouraging students to make connections to previous knowledge and experiences. Then we can demonstrate it, emphasizing the critical roles that questioning and reasoning play. We can also share the following general guidelines, which provide direction for students engaging in project-based learning:

1. *Select an inquiry focus.* Choose a content-related topic to be the focus of your investigation. Be prepared to justify your choice. Review the project rubric.
2. *Consider what you want to know about the topic and develop a research plan.* Create meaningful questions and consider how you will navigate your route to responses, knowing that those questions may lead to other questions.
3. *Choose a presentation format.* Consider a variety of possibilities and choose one that accommodates your learning style preferences.
4. *Use multiple sources to research your topic.* Remember to include each in your list of references. Revisit the project rubric periodically to ensure you are addressing all of the criteria.
5. *Participate in class inquiry workshop sessions.* Discuss a variety of topics, including your research plan, questions, sources, and progress with peers. Provide feedback to others. Consider feedback you receive and revise your plan as necessary.
6. *Schedule progress conferences.* Meet with the teacher at least twice during the planning stages and after that as needed. Consider feedback and revise as necessary.
7. *Engage in self-evaluation by completing the project rubric.* Consider the outcome and revise as necessary.
8. *Practice and present the inquiry-based investigation.* Reflect on the inquiry processes in which you engaged.

These guidelines provide support and direction for students as they engage in project-based learning. As noted in these general suggestions, questioning, researching, revising, and reasoning play important roles in this inquiry-based process. Examples of project-based learning featured in this section include individual projects as well as small-group endeavors.

FIRST-PERSON EXPERIENCES. In First-Person Experiences, students assume the identities of people who played an active role in the event or time period they have chosen to investigate. This inquiry-based project is based on three student-directed decisions. First, students determine the topic they want to research and which person they will become to report their research. Second, they choose the format through which they will share their investigation. Third, they determine the information sources and inquiry techniques they will use to conduct their investigation.

Books, articles, newspapers, public documents, DVDs, interviews, correspondence, and the Internet are some of the information sources students have accessed when creating First-Person Experiences. Research techniques have included personal interviews, surveys, library and Internet searches, experiments, letters of inquiry, field trips, and e-mail. Figure 13.2 shows some of the formats students have chosen to use when presenting First-Person Experiences.

When teaching students how to create First-Person Experiences, we should explain and model the process, emphasizing the critical roles of student choice, reasoning, and

FIGURE 13.2
Examples of Formats for Presenting First-Person Experiences

Advertising campaigns	Alphabet books	Correspondence
Diaries	Digital films	Dramatizations
Historical documents	Interviews	Inventions
Journal entries	Messages in bottles	Newspaper articles
Personal narratives	Photo histories	Poetry
Radio scripts	Song lyrics	Travel brochures

planning. We should also share the following general guidelines, which provide direction for students:

1. Review the project rubric.
2. Choose the person that will be the focus of your First-Person Experience.
3. Discuss your choice and describe what you expect to learn from your research.
4. Create viable research questions.
5. Consider the sources you will use to research your topic.
6. Determine how you will present your First-Person Experience.
7. Meet in workshop sessions to review the project rubric, compile your information, discuss your progress, and plan your presentation.
8. When the research is complete, ensure that all of the important information and appropriate references are included in the presentation. Review the rubric. Practice the presentation.
9. Engage in self-evaluation by completing the project rubric. Revise as necessary.
10. Present your First-Person Experience.

The following is an excerpt from a First-Person Experience created in biology class. In this presentation, Yvonne Stoffey communicates what she learned about Robert Hooke, a scientist who discovered the cell, through a series of letters. She chose this mode of presentation because she learned that throughout his life Hooke had corresponded with Grace, a woman he loved but never married.

September, 1665

Dearest Grace,

This is perhaps the greatest day in my entire scientific career. I was looking through an instrument called a microscope. I was examining various objects and trying to figure out how the microscope can be helpful in applications to different aspects of sciences. I took a piece of cork and placed it under the scope. Alas! There were many small compartments. After studying them closer, I concluded they were pores. I also believe that they are passages to carry liquids for the plant's growth, and I am trying to locate the valves that must obviously be present.

I continued my investigation and examined materials from the mineral, vegetable, and animal kingdoms. I realized that they all consisted of the same tiny "cells." This is the term my fellow researchers and I have decided to label these small compartments. The cells have various shapes and sizes. I drew diagrams of my discovery. My work will now be published in a book I have written entitled Micrographia.

I miss you and wish you could be here to share these exciting times.

Robert

Students are motivated to create First-Person Experiences because they can self-select the topics and communicate factual information in creative ways. This inquiry-based process requires students to think in depth about their research topics and helps them feel as if they are participants in the times and events they are investigating.

First-Person Experiences offer students opportunities to present research in different modes. The Rest of the Story, another inquiry-based technique, encourages them to think more deeply about people and events about which they already have superficial knowledge.

THE REST OF THE STORY. Most of us can clearly recall particular facts we learned in science or social studies, such as lists of inventors and their inventions or explorers and their discoveries. Alexander Graham Bell is a great example. For most of us, his name was on an inventors list as the person who created the telephone. But what is The Rest of the Story? Did you know that Bell was very dedicated to helping the deaf and was, in fact, a mentor to Helen Keller? Did you know that he served as president of the National Geographic Society? Did you know that he filed his patent for the telephone hours before another man filed a similar patent? Did you know that Bell was very interested in airplanes and worked with a group that flew a plane they had developed in Canada in 1909? This is the type of information revealed when students choose to research The Rest of the Story.

The Rest of the Story is an inquiry-based investigation that encourages the researcher to go beyond the basic facts generally known about a person, discovery, invention, or event in content area study. When engaging in this project, students locate information by using reference books and websites as resources. Technology also plays a role in the way students choose to format their investigations to share them with the class; they often elect to design a home page or create software. CDs and DVDs are other popular formatting selections. When using DVDs, students may report their research as a news story or choose to dramatize the results of their investigation (for more information about drama in the content areas, see Chapter 14).

The following example of The Rest of the Story about Albert Einstein was researched by science student Sue Matol:

> Most people know that Albert Einstein is considered one of the greatest scientific minds the world has ever known. He is the physicist who discovered the theory of relativity. People quickly associate him with $E = mc^2$ because the formula is so closely linked to his name. Einstein's genius is legendary, but there is much more to know about him. The following is an excerpt from the Rest of the Story.
>
> Did you know that Einstein did not speak until he was four years old? Or that despite his high IQ, he failed his initial entrance exam to Zurich Polytechnic? Albert's favorite pastime was sailing, which he considered "the sport which demands the least energy." In 1905 Albert Einstein wrote his famous "Special Theory of Relativity" paper. It was published in a scientific journal that same year, but it took many years for Einstein's ideas to gain general acceptance. In fact, his theory was not verified by actual experiment until 25 years later. Einstein won the Nobel Prize for Physics and he was asked to be the president of Israel, but he declined.
>
> After his death, a pathologist removed Einstein's brain and preserved it for future study, hoping to one day learn the secret of Einstein's genius. Because Einstein feared his gravesite would attract curiosity seekers, he was cremated and his ashes were scattered over a river in New Jersey. In the year 2000, Time magazine named Einstein the "Person of the Century."

Students are motivated to engage in The Rest of the Story, because they are interested in learning more about people they know about only in passing. The research itself is motivational because students are interested in what they can learn and share that their classmates may not know. It is like successfully putting together the rest of a life puzzle.

When researching the rest of the story, students use their curiosity to learn more about a person's life. In Press Conference (another inquiry-based project), students use inquiry to learn more about topics—often current events—of interest to them. Then they present the information orally.

PRESS CONFERENCE. Press Conference is an inquiry-based activity that promotes oral communication. It is based on student interest in a particular content-related topic. Students peruse newspapers, magazines, or the Internet to find articles of interest to themselves and their peers. When they find a topic that intrigues them, they discuss it with their teacher and then begin their research.

Because a Press Conference lasts only a few minutes, it is the type of inquiry-based activity that each student might present once each marking period. To support students'

FIGURE 13.3 QuIP Research Grid: Tsunamis

Questions	Answers	
	Source A: The Tsunamis Story http://www.tsunami.noaa.gov/	**Source B: Tsunami** http://encarta.msn.com/encyclopedia_761559898/ Tsunami.html
1. What are tsunamis?	Tsunami is a Japanese word, represented by two characters: tsu, meaning, "harbor", and nami meaning, "wave".	Tsunami is a Japanese word meaning "harbor wave," used as the scientific term for a class of abnormal sea wave that can cause catastrophic damage when it hits a coastline.
2. What causes tsunamis?	Tsunamis are caused by any large, abrupt disturbance of the sea-surface, such as earthquakes.	Tsunamis can be generated by an undersea earthquake, an undersea landslide, the eruption of an undersea volcano, or by the force of an asteroid crashing into the ocean. The most frequent cause of tsunamis is an undersea earthquake.
3. How dangerous are tsunamis?	Since 1850 alone, tsunamis have been responsible for the deaths of more than 420,000 lives and billions of dollars of damage.	The worst tsunami disaster in history occurred in December 2004 when a tsunami that struck the coasts of 14 countries from Southeast Asia to northeastern Africa caused the deaths of 250,000 people.
4. How do tsunami warning systems work?	Since 1946, the tsunami warning system has provided warnings of potential tsunami danger in the pacific basin by monitoring earthquake activity and the passage of tsunami waves at tide gauges. But there is no instrument that accurately predicts the impact of a tsunami at a particular coastal location.	The Pacific Marine Environmental Laboratory developed the first reliable scientific instrument for detecting tsunamis and quickly alerting scientists when a tsunami occurs. The instrument, known as a tsunameter, is anchored on the ocean floor and measures changes in water pressure when a tsunami passes above. The early warning system is known as the Deep-ocean Assessment and Reporting of Tsunamis (DART).
5. What can people do to survive tsunamis	Listen to the tsunami warning system.	Listen to reports from DART.

preparation for Press Conference, teachers can encourage them to use an extended Questions into Paragraphs (QuIP) organizer to structure their research questions and responses. We can extend the QuIP to include five questions or three sources, or both. For example, the QuIP about tsunamis featured in Figure 13.3 has been extended by adding two additional research questions.

When preparing for Press Conference, students consult a minimum of two research sources. After reading the information they have searched, focusing on its essential points, synthesizing it, raising additional questions, and reflecting on personal insights, each student shares the information through an informal presentation to the class. Then members of the audience raise questions—just as if they were participating in an actual press conference. If the presenter cannot answer the question, he joins the questioner in researching a response and reporting back to the class.

To assess Press Conference, we can use a checklist that provides direction for students as they engage in this inquiry-based activity. Students can also use the checklist as a self-assessment after they have completed their Press Conference. Figure 13.4 features an example of such a checklist.

Press Conferences usually focus on content-related developments or current events. Students are motivated to engage in Press Conferences because they can choose the topics and engage in self-directed research.

Making Connections
TO ENGLISH LEARNERS

When English learners research and present Press Conferences, teachers can support them in several ways. To begin, students might choose a topic that relates to countries where their native language is spoken. Then they might choose to present the information with a native English speaker, with each partner reporting the research sentence by sentence first in one language, then in the other—a format similar to echo reading. Students can also choose to use a PowerPoint slideshow or record the Press Conference with a peer for presentation to the class. The presenter(s) could then become the press secretaries and ask preplanned questions. English learners can also use the Questions into Paragraphs graphic organizer when planning the presentation. To facilitate the organizer's use, we can color-code the various sections. The important point is that the English learners feel confident engaging in oral presentations that focus on self-selected content area topics. ■

Press Conference Checklist

The student

_____ Chose a topic.

_____ Conferenced with the teacher.

_____ Used the Questions into Paragraphs (QuIP) organizer.

_____ Developed at least 3 quality research questions.

_____ Conducted a viable search for sources.

_____ Used at least 2 quality sources.

_____ Demonstrated knowledge of the topic.

_____ Presented Press Conference effectively.

Student's comments:

_____

_____

_____

Teacher's comments:

_____

_____

_____

Name _____ Date _____

FIGURE 13.4
Press Conference Checklist

Making Connections | Thinking about Press Conferences

■ Peruse current newspapers and websites to locate a topic that relates to your content area. Research the topic, complete a QuIP, and prepare a 3-minute Press Conference.

■ Present your Press Conference to a partner. Save your research and completed QuIP as examples for when you teach Press Conference to your students.

Although students preparing Press Conferences work on their own when selecting topics and completing their research, they do have opportunities to conference with the teacher and workshop their ideas with peers. In Inquiring Minds, our next inquiry-based project, students work in small groups organized by topics of interest.

TEACHING IDEA

INQUIRING MINDS. Inquiring Minds is an inquiry-based, small-group research activity based on student-selected content area topics. When using Inquiring Minds, students form small groups based on their topic choices. The small groups brainstorm three to five questions about their topic that the group members would like to be able to answer through their research. This sets a purpose and offers direction to their investigation. Group members list their topic and the questions on a piece of chart paper. Each group in the class uses a different color marker to record this information.

After all groups have completed their questions, the charts are posted around the room. Each group then engages in a gallery walk, moving together from posted list to posted list reviewing the topics and questions each of the other groups has proposed. Each group in the class then adds any questions its members may have to the posted lists. Each group's contributions can either be labeled (e.g., "Group 3") or be indicated through the use of different colored markers. This allows the students who originated the list to see which groups made inquiries about their topics. It also provides a way to contact the contributors if any of the questions is unclear.

Next, the posted list about each topic is returned to the group that created it. At this point, the list contains both the original questions and the queries that have been added by other research groups. The group members then discuss the questions that have been proposed by their peers and seek clarification as necessary. This process helps the original group to broaden the scope of its research and creates great interest among those who added questions when the research is reported. They have interest in the results of all of the research, but they are especially motivated to learn how groups responded to the questions they raised. Figure 13.5 features a final research question list for Group 2 from a history class studying the American Presidents.

When teaching students how to engage in Inquiring Minds, we should explain and model the process, emphasizing the critical roles that reasoning, collaboration, and planning play in this project. We should also share the following general guidelines, which provide direction for students engaging in Inquiring Minds. To begin, students make a list of three research topics in which

FIGURE 13.5
Group 2's Original Research Question List and Final Research Question List

Group 2: Abraham Lincoln

Research Questions

1. What is known about Abraham Lincoln's early life?

2. How did Lincoln become interested in public service?

3. Why did Lincoln decide to write the Emancipation Proclamation? What was the message of this document?

4. How did Lincoln serve his country before becoming President? (Group 1)

5. Describe Lincoln's beliefs about our country at the end of the Civil War. (Group 3)

6. Compare and contrast the messages of Lincoln's first inaugural address and his second. (Group 5)

they have interest. Next, we review their lists and organize the students into groups of 4 or 5 members who have interest in researching the same topic. Then the students follow these guidelines:

1. Meet as a group and review the project rubric.
2. Discuss the group-selected topic and determine what the members would like to learn from researching it. Write the topic at the top of the chart paper provided.
3. Discuss how the group will share its research—PowerPoint slideshow, dramatization, alphabet book, and so on.
4. Create 3 to 5 research questions and write them on the chart paper using the color markers provided.
5. When the questions are complete, post the chart paper on the wall.
6. As a group, visit each posted list. Read the topic and the proposed research questions. Discuss these queries as a group. Then add one or two questions the group would like to have researched concerning the topic of each list. Be sure to label the questions your group adds with the group's number.
7. When all groups have visited all of the research lists, remove your group's list from the wall and discuss any additional questions with group members. Consider whether the questions would enhance the research goals and whether any of the questions can be combined. If necessary, contact the group that proposed the question for clarification.
8. Discuss how the group members will conduct the research. Develop a schedule to meet the Inquiring Minds project due date.
9. Meet in workshop sessions to review the project rubric, compile information, discuss progress, and plan the presentation.
10. When the research is complete, ensure that all of the important information is included in the presentation. Review the rubric. Practice the presentation.
11. Engage in self-evaluation by completing the rubric. Encourage all group members to share their completed rubrics. Discuss and revise the project as necessary.
12. Join the group in presenting Inquiring Minds.

Students are motivated to engage in Inquiring Minds because it is a student-centered activity. Group members enjoy working with peers who have expressed interest in researching the same topic and making the essential decisions about the project. They also take ownership of learning as they use the project rubric as a guide to research, workshop, plan, and present what they have learned.

The Oral History Project is another technique that captures students' interest. In this inquiry-based project, students choose an individual they know as the focus of their inquiry. The Oral History Project works because everyone has a life story to tell.

 **ORAL HISTORY PROJECT.** The Oral History Project is a long-term process in which students research the personal histories of other individuals (Dickson, Heyler, Reilly, & Romano, 2006). It is an authentic experience that often includes working with members of previous generations. This helps students to make connections to the past—times that they themselves did not experience—while researching another person's life story. During the project, students actively engage in interviewing the person they have selected and develop a presentation that will include research, artifacts, a feature article, a personal memoir, and a photograph.

When the project is complete, it is given to the person it is designed to honor during a class celebration. The Oral History Project has been purposefully designed to meet academic standards for reading, writing, speaking, and listening, as well as those related to information literacy and historical understanding. Formatting of oral histories can vary from traditional tri-folds to more creative methods. Figure 13.6 shows the completed history of Kevin Michael Gallagher.

Students find this project to be highly motivational for a number of reasons. First, the students choose the person they will honor in the oral history project. Next, even though they have a project outline and rubric to follow, the students are in charge of contacting the person, conducting the interview, and making the project work. Third, the students work with primary sources, which they often find more exciting than using secondary sources.

FIGURE 13.6
An Oral History Project

When students engage in inquiry-based learning, they create meaningful questions, use strategies, communicate effectively, think critically and creatively, and use technology. Detailed descriptions of resources students can use to facilitate these processes can be found in chapters throughout this text.

Making Connections
TO WRITING

Although students can use many creative ways to present what they learn through inquiry-based learning, writing is often part of the process and the product. For example, as they engage in the process of researching topics, students use writing to take notes and synthesize information about the inquiry-based topics. They also use writing when they choose to present what they have learned through writing-based products such as diary pages, PowerPoint slides, Inquiring Minds, and the Oral History Project. ■

How Can We Effectively Assess and Evaluate Inquiry-Based Learning?

When students engage in inquiry-based learning, they demonstrate what they know and can do. In most cases, we can assess how students engage in the process and evaluate the product they create.

To assess or gather information about how students engage in the process, we can use observation and a checklist. For example, if students were creating a First-Person Experience, we might include the items featured on the checklist in Figure 13.7. Then we could indicate that students have demonstrated each factor by placing a check mark in front of each statement.

Observation Checklist: First-Person Experience

The student

1. _____   Self-selected content-related topic to research.

2. _____   Determined which person to become.

3. _____   Selected, accessed, and used relevant information sources.

4. _____   Sought feedback from several peers during workshop sessions.

5. _____   Used feedback to revise project.

6. _____   Chose a meaningful format for presenting information.

7. _____   Presented First-Person Experience effectively

Comments on student performance:

_____

_____

_____

_____

_____

Name _____   Date _____

FIGURE 13.7
**Observation Checklist:
First-Person Experience**

We often use a checklist in conjunction with a rubric or scoring guide. We can use the checklist to assess students during the process and use the rubric to evaluate the final First-Person Experience. Rubrics are provided before students begin a project. This affords students the opportunity to view the rubric as a performance guide: In other words, they understand what they need to do to achieve at various levels.

Rubrics generally have multiple criteria, each of which is described at multiple levels. For example, a rubric for The Rest of the Story would include research sources. The sources would then be described at each level of the rubric. As seen in Figure 13.8, the research sources at the highest level (4.0) would be described as *outstanding* and at the lowest level (1.0) as *inadequate*. When creating rubrics, it is important to use language that clearly indicates the differences between and among performance levels.

FIGURE 13.8
First-Person
Experience Rubric

4.0 Made excellent decisions concerning topic selection. Used outstanding sources. Demonstrated exceptional knowledge of information literacy. Included excellent information. Demonstrated outstanding critical and creative thinking. Chose a superb presentation format. Used the workshop format to greatest benefit. Collaborated extremely well with others. Excellent reference list. Outstanding presentation.

3.0 Made very good decisions about topic selection. Used high-quality sources. Demonstrated proficient knowledge of information literacy. Included in-depth information. Demonstrated high levels of critical and creative thinking. Chose a very good presentation format. Used the workshop format to great benefit. Collaborated very well with others. Detailed reference list. Skillful presentation.

2.0 Made appropriate decisions concerning topic selection. Used satisfactory sources. Demonstrated adequate knowledge of information literacy. Included essential information. Demonstrated critical and creative thinking. Chose a viable presentation format. Used the workshop format to benefit. Collaborated with others. Sufficient reference list. Adequate presentation.

1.0 Made poor decisions about topic selection. Used inadequate sources. Demonstrated insufficient knowledge of information literacy. Included insufficient essential information. Demonstrated little critical and creative thinking. Chose a poor presentation format. Used the workshop format to little benefit. Did not collaborate well with others. Inadequate reference list. Poor presentation.

Comments: _____

_____

When we use a rubric to evaluate student work, it is essential that we provide it to the students when the project is first introduced. We should discuss the rubric at that point, noting that it provides a clear picture of what needs to be included and the quality of work it requires.

FINAL THOUGHTS

Inquiry-based learning experiences foster creativity, variety, and innovation. They also motivate and engage students. Inquiry-focused classrooms become places where ideas are born, valued, and nurtured. Students become problem seekers as well as problem solvers. Inquiry-based experiences and the resulting critical and creative thinking serve as the foundation of dynamic teaching and learning. These are, without question, the direct antithesis of the "read the chapter and answer the questions" contexts in which many students experience content area instruction. Rather, they are the classrooms of the 21st century in which teachers, students, and texts come together as active participants in learning communities.

In the next chapter, we discuss alternative representations of thinking. These modes provide students with a variety of ways to express their ideas and be creative in the process.

Teaching Connections
APPLYING WHAT WE HAVE LEARNED

E-Links

Consider how you will integrate project-based learning into your teaching. Then choose a topic related to your content area and develop an annotated list of 10 websites your students can use when engaging in inquiry-based learning. Share your choices with peers in small group discussions.

EXAMPLE WEBSITES

Use websites such as these to complete your project:

History: *The American Civil War Homepage*
http://sunsite.utk.edu/civil-war/warweb.html

Mathematics: *Biographies of Women Mathematicians*
http://www.agnesscott.edu/lriddle/women/alpha.htm

Biology: *The Biology Project*
http://www.biology.arizona.edu/

Accountable Talk

Inquiry is at the center of all learning. Think about the role inquiry has played in your learning process, and then reflect on how you might integrate it into your teaching. In particular, consider how you might teach your students to think from an inquiry-based perspective. Discuss your thoughts with others who teach in your content area. Include a summary of the discussion and your thoughts as a reflective entry in your portfolio.

 ## Portfolio/Performance Opportunity

Meet with peers in a small group and discuss how you can integrate the inquiry-based activities presented in this chapter into your teaching. Then (1) choose one of the project-based activities presented in this chapter, (2) select websites related to your content area to support your task, (3) choose a mode of presentation, and (4) complete the project. Share your completed project with peers and discuss your reflections on learning through inquiry. Include the completed project in your portfolio.

14

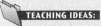
Poetry, Drama, Music, and Art: Alternative Representations of Thinking

In our teaching, traditional spoken and written responses may be the most common, but they are not the only modes of representation to which we and our students have access. Poetry, drama, music, and art permeate all subjects of content area study and may provide more meaningful and more creative ways for students to represent their ideas. These modes of representation, which are also known as symbol systems, can be used independently or in conjunction with other modes.

Elliot Eisner (1997) speaks about forms of representation as accommodating "the possibilities of the human mind." He notes:

> Each product humans create embodies the forms of thinking that led to its realization, each of them provides testimony to what humans can achieve, each one represents a silent but eloquent statement concerning the scope and possibilities of the human mind, and each one comes into being through the use of one or more forms of representation. (p. 350)

Eisner and others see forms of representation as culture based (Eisner, 1997; Greene, 1997; Salomon, 1997). Eisner (1993) also reminds us that using multiple modes of representation encourages students to construct meanings that they otherwise may not create. Understanding poses challenges to learners; using alternative modes of representation provides unique ways of expressing their understanding.

In this chapter, we provide information about the use of alternative modes of representation in content area study. We begin by presenting a rationale for using multiple modes of presentation. Next, we examine poetry, drama, music, and art individually. In each of these sections, we discuss rationales for using the formats, student motivation, teaching ideas, student examples, and assessment possibilities.

Why Should We Use Multiple Modes of Representation?

The goal of our teaching is student understanding, but our definition of understanding reaches beyond the usual comprehension of text. Mansilla and Gardner (1997) suggest that we consider understanding as "both the ability to use knowledge and the ability to engage in disciplinary modes of thinking" (p. 386). Eisner (1997) extends this thinking by proposing five principles that support our understanding of forms of representation:

1. The form we use to represent our ideas influences the processes and products of thinking.
2. Different forms of representation nurture different thinking skills.
3. The form of representation we choose influences what we are able to represent as well as what we are able to see.
4. Forms of representation can be combined to offer students a greater array of resources.
5. Each form can be used in different ways, each of which requires different skills and forms of thinking.

When we contemplate the prospect of students representing their content area thinking through a variety of modes, we should consider the possibilities provided by poetry, drama, music, and art. In poetry, students can share their thoughts by phrasing and organizing them in creative ways. In drama, students can use dialogue and actions to represent their thoughts. In music, students can represent their thoughts by writing song lyrics or by selecting instrumental music to support their thinking. Finally, in art, students can create transmediations, sketch, sculpt, paint, make collages, or integrate modes of representation by creating projects such as self-authored electronic books.

In the sections that follow we focus on poetry, drama, music, and art as modes students can use to represent their thoughts. These methods provide a variety of options beyond those commonly used in content area classrooms.

How Can We Teach Our Students to Use Poetry as a Mode of Representation?

Reading poetry offers a way to motivate students and help them acquire background knowledge. As teachers, it provides us with a means to capture students' attention, establish a focus, and encourage discussion. Using poetry as a mode of representation supports and enriches students' learning in the content areas. It also helps students to think critically and extend their understanding.

Using poetry in the content areas has benefits for both teachers and students. As noted in Figure 14.1, poetry offers us a variety of ways to motivate and encourage student learning in the content areas. Poetry also accommodates students' needs. As noted in Figure 14.2, it provides them with opportunities to engage in learning, use higher-level thinking, and communicate in alternative modes.

Poetry stimulates the use of mental imagery and critical thinking. Within that context, science and math concepts can more easily be visualized, social issues can be discussed or debated, people or events of historical significance can be made authentic, alternative viewpoints can be explored, and connections between personal experiences and new concepts can be made.

FIGURE 14.1
The Benefits of Using Poetry to Teach in the Content Areas

Teachers can use poetry for the following purposes:

- Motivating student learning
- Activating prior knowledge
- Providing prior knowledge
- Encouraging students to create personal meaning
- Encouraging students to engage socially
- Offering a different perspective
- Encouraging students to take an aesthetic stance
- Enriching and extending students' thinking
- Assessing student learning
- Providing an alternative mode to represent thinking

Using poetry as a form of representation expands the students' role from readers to authors and engages them in deeper thinking processes. It also offers multiple opportunities for student choice: They may self-select their writing topics; write in response to something they've read or reflect on personal content-related experiences; choose from a variety of formats to express their ideas; write collaboratively or individually; and express perspectives ranging from humorous observations to serious contemplations.

We can use discussion or simple informal measures such as quickwrites to determine what our students' past experiences with poetry have been. We can dispel misconceptions about poetry before teaching students how to use it to represent their thoughts. Among the most frequently encountered—and mistaken—beliefs are that poetry always needs to rhyme, poems have only one interpretation, and poetry is boring. Discussing these issues openly assures students that poetry has many formats, is open to personal interpretation, and is content related.

To assess the form poems in this section, we can use observation, use checklists that address components of the poems and students' work habits, or read and comment on the poems. These modes of representation are informal, so we should not use rubrics to evaluate them.

The following examples of form poems are appropriate for all content areas. We will need to explain and demonstrate the poetry formats, but because the formats guide students' thinking, they often feel comfortable writing form poems relatively quickly. Encouraging students to begin by working with a partner provides additional support during their initial endeavors.

 **TEACHING IDEA**   ACROSTIC POEMS. Using Acrostic Poems as forms of representation is motivational for students, because they have knowledge about the topic before they write. Acrostics are the easiest of the form poems to write and, consequently, serve as a good way to introduce content area students to using poetry to represent their thinking. This type of poem can be used for several purposes in the content areas. For example, students can use this format to share background knowledge about a topic, provide insights into their thinking, or summarize

FIGURE 14.2
The Benefits of Using Poetry to Learn in the Content Areas

Students can use poetry for the following purposes:

- Experiencing an alternative way of learning
- Developing communication skills, including active listening
- Thinking critically and creatively
- Summarizing their thinking
- Gaining new perspectives
- Exploring personal interpretations in social settings
- Visualizing abstract or challenging concepts
- Communicating in alternative modes

what they have learned. This form poem is appropriate for students at most grade levels, including those in middle and high school.

After explaining and demonstrating the format, we can invite students to use their first names to write Acrostics about themselves. This is a fun activity, because the students definitely have background knowledge of the subjects. Encouraging students to share their ideas with partners provides additional support.

When writing Acrostic Poems, students vertically write the word or phrase that is the focus of their poem. Then they use each letter of the word or phrase to start a line of the poem that refers to or describes the topic. This is an example John McGraw created to represent his thoughts about himself while learning about Acrostics in chemistry class:

Junior

Overworked

Happy

Never satisfied

Students can also use Acrostics to provide summaries about their content areas. Stephen Inghrim did just that when he wrote this Acrostic about geometry:

Graphs of points on a Cartesian plane

Endless calculations of areas

Oblique and right, obtuse and acute

Measures of angles

Endpoints, midpoints, bisectors

Three-dimensional or perhaps only two

Rectangles, squares, and circles abound

You are the mathematics of shapes

Once students have learned how to use this format, writing Acrostics takes only a portion of a class period. During the writing process, we should be available to support students as needed. When the Acrostics are completed, students should have the opportunity to share them in small groups. If they have written about their content area, they can also contribute their poems to a class book of Acrostic poems.

When creating Acrostics, the content of the poem is determined by the topic. When writing Cinquains, another type of form poetry, the content is also determined by the topic, but the number and types of words required in each line are determined by the format.

TEACHING IDEA

CINQUAINS. The Cinquain (pronounced "sin-kane") is another poetry format that can be used by middle and high school students to represent ideas in the content areas. The format of this 5-line poem focuses on a word and its synonym—a word that has the same meaning. (For a reproducible copy of the Cinquain poem format, see Appendix A.)

As when teaching all new ideas, we can begin by explaining how a Cinquain works and encouraging students to make connections. Then we can demonstrate the Cinquain by writing one. Students are motivated to use this format to represent their thoughts because following the Cinquain format is similar to completing a puzzle. Students may self-select topics, but they need to ensure that the topic they choose also has a synonym. When teaching students how to write Cinquains, it is a good idea to begin by completing the first line (the topic) and the last line (the synonym). Then write the remaining lines, which provide details about the topic. Encouraging students to write their first Cinquain with partners enables students to share ideas and provide support. When the Cinquains are completed, students can share them in small groups.

In the following example, Javier Martinez shares the Cinquain about Martin Luther King, Jr., in his American history class. Notice that the Cinquain format features a description of the words required directly below each line.

King
One-word noun

powerful intelligent
Two adjectives describing line 1

marching reasoning uniting
"Ing" words telling actions of line 1

inspirational civil rights defender
Four-word phrase describing a feeling related to line 1

leader
One-word synonym or reference to line 1

Once students are familiar with writing Cinquains, creating them should take only part of a class period. We can use Cinquains to make comparisons and to summarize ideas. When writing diamantes, the next poem format we will explore, we focus on antonyms instead of synonyms.

TEACHING IDEA

DIAMANTES. The Diamante is a poetry format in the shape of a diamond that encourages the writer to contrast a topic and its antonym or opposite. These 7-line poems can be used in all content areas. The first three and a half lines address the original word; the remaining three and a half lines address the antonym. The change in topic, which reveals a noticeable contrast, occurs midway through line 4. (For a reproducible copy of the Diamante poem format, see Appendix A.)

After explaining the diamante format and encouraging students to make connections to it, we can demonstrate how to write Diamantes. We can also encourage students to work with partners to write their first Diamante. We might suggest that the partners begin by writing the first line (the topic) and the last line (its opposite). This approach will help ensure that the topic they choose has a viable antonym. As teachers, we should be available to support students as needed as they write. When the Diamantes are completed, students can share their poem with another pair or in small groups.

In the following example, Beth Gress shares a Diamante about peace and war that she created after learning about World War II in history class.

Peace
Subject—one noun

Quiet Agreeable
Two adjectives describing the subject

Calming Nurturing Inspiring
Three participles ("ing" words) telling about the subject

Contentment Freedom Conflict Weapons
Four nouns: first two relate to subject; last two relate to the opposite

Crushing Storming Debilitating
Three participles ("ing" words) telling about the opposite

Harmful Dangerous
Two adjectives describing the opposite

War
Opposite of subject—one noun

We can encourage middle school and high school students to use Diamantes to summarize ideas about contrasting topics. Once students know how to write Diamantes, they should need only a portion of a class period to complete them. We can assess students' Diamantes by reading and commenting on them or by using an observational checklist.

Students can also use definition poems to represent their thoughts. These poems focus on our providing characteristics or details about the topic, rather than the antonyms required when writing diamantes.

 **DEFINITION POEMS.** Definition Poems provide a format for us to represent our ideas about a particular topic, including nine specific descriptors. The format, which can be used by middle and high school students, is easy to follow and concludes in an exclamation about the topic. (For a reproducible copy of the definition poem format, see the Appendix.)

We can begin teaching Definition Poems by explaining what they are and inviting students to make connections. Then we can write a poem to demonstrate how the format works. When students are comfortable with the format, we should encourage them to write a Definition Poem with a partner. As teachers, we should be available to provide support as needed when students are writing. When the poems are completed, students can share them in small groups.

In the following examples, Louis Pacchioli and Ken Gilbride share their Definition Poems about chemistry and history.

WHAT IS CHEMISTRY?

The central science

The study of all matter and all changes of matter

What our bodies do to survive

What industries do to make our lives easier

What industries may do to make our lives more dangerous

Research that helps to find cures for diseases

Baking cookies, shooting off fireworks, and burning wood in a fireplace

The only way plants can make their own food

The reason why you were able to drive your car today

That is chemistry!

WHAT IS HISTORY?

An attempt to explain past events

Where your ancestors came from

An exceptional tool used to help guide your future

What life was like long ago

The evolution of music, sports, and entertainment

A journey through many cultures

The key to understanding our world today

Not to be forgotten

The greatest story ever told

That is history!

We can use Definition Poems in all content areas to summarize or review what we know about a topic. Students often find this format motivational because it is open ended and they have control over the content. The format can easily be converted to a Biography Poem by changing the first and last lines. For example, the first line might say, "Who was George Washington?" and the last line could say, "That is who George Washington was!"

In the final type of poetry format, students have the opportunity to create Repeated-Phrase Collaborative Poems. These are class- or group-authored poems that have a unique structure.

TEACHING IDEA

REPEATED-PHRASE COLLABORATIVE POEMS. Repeated-Phrase Collaborative Poems are usually written by students working together in small groups. After reading a text chapter or a content-related novel, the students choose three passages of one to three lines that they found especially meaningful or powerful. Then they work in small groups, organizing the passages to evoke a mood. Next, they create the repeated phrase and insert it after each of the passages. For example, when writing about the Great Depression in the United States, the repeated phrase might be "We will survive." That phrase would appear after each passage. Repeated-Phrase Collaborative Poems rely on students' understanding of what they have read, their passage selections, the way they organize the ideas, and the repeated phrase.

The following is an excerpt from a Repeated-Phrase Collaborative Poem about Albert Einstein that was written by high school students in physics class. Prior to writing the poem, the students engaged in Discussion Circles (see Chapter 9). As a circle activity, six groups of students (approximately 5 students per group) read different chapters from *Einstein: His Life and Universe* (Isaacson, 2007) as well as a variety of articles about Einstein. As one of their extending activities, each group chose three passages (quotations or ideas) to share with the class through a Repeated-Phrase Poem. After organizing the passages about Einstein, the class created the repeated phrase. Here is an excerpt from the class's Repeated-Phrase Collaborative Poem:

ALBERT EINSTEIN

You can learn a lot of good things from me that no one else can offer you.

He had the greatest mind of the 20th century.

He to whom emotion is a stranger, who can no longer wonder and stand rapt in awe is as good as dead, a snuffed-out candle.

He had the greatest mind of the 20th century.

Logic will get you from A to B. Imagination will take you everywhere.

He had the greatest mind of the 20th century.

The only source of knowledge is experience.

He had the greatest mind of the 20th century.

We cannot solve our problems with the same thinking we used when we created them.

He had the greatest mind of the 20th century.

The important thing is not to stop questioning.

Middle and high school students find Repeated-Phrase Collaborative Poems to be motivational because the format provides them with opportunities to represent their shared thinking. Students can also use this format to demonstrate their understanding of multiple perspectives. To assess Repeated-Phrase Collaborative Poems, we can use a group observational checklist, such as the one shown in Figure 14.3.

Poetry provides an array of means for content area students to represent their thinking. These alternative modes of representation provide rich and stimulating ways for students to share their thoughts.

Making Connections | Thinking about Poetry in the Content Areas

- Reflect on your content area and choose one or more topics. Then use three different form poems to represent your thinking about the topic(s) you selected.

- Share and discuss your poems with a partner. Save the poems and use them as models for when you teach your students how to use poetry to represent their thinking.

Checklist for Repeated-Phrase Collaborative Poems

Group Members

1. _____ Selected a topic to address in the poem.
2. _____ Discussed the quotations from which selections would be made.
3. _____ Brainstormed, discussed, and chose a repeated phrase.
4. _____ Selected the quotations to include in the poem.
5. _____ Created a reference list.
6. _____ Formatted the poem correctly.
7. _____ Worked well together.
8. _____ Respected one another's ideas.

FIGURE 14.3
Checklist for Repeated-Phrase Collaborative Poems

Group Comments:

_____
_____
_____
_____

Teacher Comments:

_____
_____
_____
_____

Names:_____   Date _____

Making Connections
TO WRITING

The process of using multiple modes of representation often includes some form of writing. For example, students can represent their ideas through poetry, song lyrics, and electronic books. To effectively use many of these modes of representation, students need to know how to write in both informational and creative ways. From the simple act of summarizing to completing a project in which writing is a rubric criterion, students need to be able to effectively communicate their thoughts through writing. For more details about teaching writing in the content areas, see Chapter 11. ■

How Can We Teach Our Students to Use Drama as a Mode of Representation?

When we engage in drama, we use dialogue and actions to represent our thinking. Drama promotes active learning and accommodates a variety of learning styles. Students are motivated to engage in drama activities because they offer opportunities to interact with peers and to share thinking in unique ways.

Expressing ideas through drama can help students organize and clarify information. Such activities also enhance social and cognitive development and contribute to the development of learning communities (Wagner & Barnett, 1998).

Making Connections
TO ENGLISH LEARNERS

Working with peers and revisiting information during active learning can help scaffold learning and language acquisition for English learners (Richard-Amato, 1988). Representing ideas through drama also helps lessen the anxiety that English learners may experience when encountering new content, because students work in small groups and make choices about how ideas will be represented. Engaging in drama is motivational for English learners, and we should strive to ensure that it is included periodically as an option for representing students' ideas. ■

Drama helps students develop their strengths and foster their talents (Wagner & Barnett, 1998). Students who may be reluctant to speak out during content discussions can put aside their concerns and become a historic figure, an inventor, or a great mathematician during active learning.

Drama activities do not require large amounts of instructional time or theater expertise on our part. They do require that we plan appropriately, develop worthwhile applications, and use authentic assessments. In this section, we discuss several drama activities that are appropriate for middle and high school students. Some require less than a class period and can be assessed informally. Others are more long range in nature and should be evaluated through the use of a rubric.

TEACHING IDEA

DINNER PARTY. Dinner Party (Vogt, 2000) is a small-group drama activity that works well for middle and high school students in all content areas. When planning, the class raises questions about guests from the content area they are studying who might attend a dinner party. For example, if the class were studying English literature, the question might be, "Imagine you could have a dinner party for eight British authors or poets whom we have studied. Who would you invite? Why would you select them? What would be the seating arrangement of the guests at your table, and why would you place them in that order? What do you think the guests would talk about during dinner? Include specific references to the authors' lives and works in your response." This creative approach to assessing students' knowledge of English literature can serve as a springboard for dramatic play.

The purpose of the Dinner Party is for students to represent their thinking by assuming personas, such as those of authors or poets, historical figures, scientists, artists, or musicians. For example, Alexander the Great might be engaged in conversation with General George Patton and Hannibal, arguing the finer points of military strategies. Scripts can be written, but improvisation is often more interesting and fun. Of course, its success depends on the students' content knowledge. During each Dinner Party, specific content must be included, and the guests must respond to one another as realistically and accurately as possible. It is important to stress that in-depth knowledge of the figures' lives, accomplishments, flaws, and works must be used to inform the "performance."

To engage students in Dinner Party, we should begin by explaining how this activity works and inviting students to make connections. Then we can demonstrate the process and share a project rubric. We can also suggest they follow these guidelines when participating in Dinner Party :

1. Meet with a small group (approximately 6 students) that has interest in researching and dramatizing the question. Review the project rubric.
2. Decide who will attend the Dinner Party, what the participants might contribute to the conversation, and who will research and assume each role.
3. Develop a schedule to plan, research, and dramatize the Dinner Party.
4. Sign the schedule for the date you will present your Dinner Party.
5. Meet in workshop sessions to exchange ideas, review the rubric, and provide feedback periodically during the research process.
6. Practice Dinner Party, provide feedback to the group, and revise as necessary.
7. Invite the class to observe as you engage in your Dinner Party.

Dinner Party is an example of a long-range project that should be evaluated by using a rubric. Middle and high school students may need three to four weeks to prepare for this project, depending on the number of guests that will attend and how much time will be available for small-group meetings and class workshop sessions.

Students are highly motivated to engage in Dinner Party, because they are actively involved in every stage of production. They choose the topic, develop a plan, decide which research sources to use, and use drama to represent their thinking.

MEETING OF THE MINDS. Meeting of the Minds (Richard-Amato, 1998), a small-group drama activity, can be used in all content areas. In this active learning method, participants, who are usually well known in history, science, mathematics, or literature, are interviewed by a "host."

To begin, we can explain Meeting of the Minds and invite students to make connections. Then we can demonstrate the activity. When students are comfortable using the format, they can meet in small groups to engage in Meeting of the Minds. To begin, students take on the roles of individuals who have distinctly different viewpoints about a topic. The host is another student who directs questions to the participants, with the intent of pitting participants against one another in a debate about a particular topic. An interesting variation is an interview between a historical figure and a modern-day celebrity or expert with considerable knowledge of the same topic.

For example, in one world history class that was studying the 16th century and Henry VIII, students engaged in a discussion of the role of women. After additional reading and research, students participated in Meeting of the Minds. One student became Henry VIII, while another assumed the role of Anne Boleyn, the wife he executed in 1536. A third student served as the "host of the show," questioning the King and Queen about women's rights within the context of England in the early 1500s. Two more students entered the conversation as Eleanor Roosevelt and Hillary Clinton. Together, the women confronted Henry VIII about not only his beliefs, but also his methods for eliminating those who fell into his disfavor. The team enacting this Meeting of the Minds conducted in-depth research as they took on the identities involved.

Like the other drama activities, Meeting of the Minds can be used in science and mathematics as well as in history or literature. For example, the famous astronomer and physicist Galileo was imprisoned during the Inquisition because of his belief that the sun was at the center of the universe. Archimedes, the Greek mathematician, engineer, and physicist, also discovered the principle of buoyancy. The brilliant physicist and astronomer Stephen Hawking is a quadriplegic (he has amyotrophic lateral sclerosis, better known as "Lou Gehrig's disease") who has overcome more challenges as he explores the universe than most of us can imagine. The vivid tapestries of these lives provide enriching opportunities for students to represent their lives and beliefs in active learning.

Students are motivated to participate in Meeting of the Minds, because they can self-select the topic and view it from different perspectives. As teachers, we can use either a checklist or a rubric to assess or evaluate this project.

LIVING NEWSPAPER THEATER. The Living Newspaper Theater (Morrison & Chilcoat, 1998), a government-subsidized presentation of major current issues in a dramatic forum, was created in the 1930s. Its purpose was to educate the citizenry about socioeconomic problems of the times through drama. This same type of structure can be used in middle school and high school classrooms today.

To begin teaching the Living Newspaper Theater, we should explain how the process works and demonstrate it for students. Next, students can work in groups to select a historical topic of interest and research it. The topic should focus on some sociological, economic, or political issue, such as child labor laws, the role of women in the workforce, or economic and educational disparity. Students use what they have learned during the course of their research to write a script for a 15- to 20-minute dramatization involving people associated with the researched topic. The scripts should include an explanation of the problem (e.g., child labor in factories at the beginning of the 20th century), development of the problem (e.g., the government's role in protecting child laborers), and a solution to the problem (e.g., implementing legislation forbidding child labor despite protests from manufacturers). Students discuss and act out their scripts, revising their work as necessary. After sufficient rehearsal, each group presents its dramatization for the class. This includes involving class members in discussion about the problem and possible solutions.

In Living Newspaper Theater, authenticity is essential. Researching a topic from differing perspectives and including accurate facts are integral to the success of the project. The Living Newspaper Theater presents students with multiple challenges—researching, analyzing, designing, and presenting a dramatization of historical events, experiences, and lives. This project is designed to help students consider how their thinking informs their current experiences.

SNAPSHOTS OF HISTORY. In the mid-1800s, theatrical tableaux were frequently used to celebrate a striking historical scene such as the signing of the Declaration of Independence. Snapshots of History (Shurtz, 1998) combines theatrical tableaux and imaginative writing about historical events. We can begin by explaining and demonstrating how to create a tableau, a scene with groups of people who remain silent and motionless in appropriate postures. Then the students select a photograph or painting of an historical event that includes a fairly large group of people and make copies for all participants.

Begin creating the tableau by adding a few students at a time until approximately half the class is involved. Then, repeat this process with the other half of the class. Explain that students will make a "talking tableau" by adding dialogue that would lead up to the moment represented in the original picture. Rehearse what the figures might have been talking about prior to the scene being captured in the photo or painting. When we give the cue, "Begin," the scene comes alive. It continues to evolve until we say, "Freeze." At this point, the scene becomes the tableau. The other half of the class also practices until everyone understands the process

Next, divide the entire class into three to four groups. Let each group select a historical painting or photograph to depict. Then each class member should choose one person in the picture to represent. Next, each student writes a first-person narrative from the perspective of the person within the picture. These narratives are shared with other group members prior to creating the group's final tableaux. The members rehearse both their "frozen" and "talking" tableaux, prior to presenting the event for class members.

Drama enables students of all ages to personally experience the thoughts, motives, conflicts, ambitions, and emotions of other people. It can represent student thinking and encourage students to view content knowledge not as a series of abstract concepts, but rather as personally constructed understandings.

How Can We Teach Our Students to Use Music as a Mode of Representation?

Music is a mode of representation that provides a fun and creative way for students to express their thinking. Most of the teaching ideas related to music focus on either working with partners or working in small-group settings. These activities range from students performing songs for which they have written lyrics to rap songs they've created to review content.

LYRIC SUMMARIES. Students create Lyric Summaries (McLaughlin & Allen 2009) after learning and focusing on the topic of discussion or a unit of study. In this small-group activity (approximately 5 students per group), students meet and quickly brainstorm lists of what they perceive to be the most important information they have learned; then they use that information to write a Lyric Summary. First, the group members select a song that they all know. Students often choose television theme songs, classic children's songs, holiday songs, or current, popular songs. The selected song becomes the music for their Lyric Summary, and students use their list of important facts to write a summary as new lyrics to the song. Finally, the group sings its Lyric Summary for the class.

This is a great exercise in cooperative learning and a fun experience. Students remember the important facts because they are included in the lyrics they have written.

The following excerpt is from a Lyric Summary that students created about Edgar Allan Poe's short story, "The Tell-Tale Heart." They chose to write their Lyric Summary to the tune of the theme song from *The Addams Family*.

> *The young man and the old man*
> *As neighbors living they can,*
> *They didn't have a problem,*
> *Until the young man saw his eye.*
> *The eye was weird and creepy,*
> *It made him feel so freaky,*
> *He had to kill the old man,*
> *He was so very scared.*
> *Thumpety-thump-click, click,*
> *Thumpety-thump-click, click,*

Of course, in the theme from *The Addams Family*, the "click, click" phrases are not words to be read, but rather the sounds made when the performing students snap their fingers.

Lyric Summaries can be written and performed by students in all content areas. The song selections vary, but students always seem to enjoy singing their summaries. Lyric Summaries also help students to review essential facts about content area topics.

RAPPING FOR REVIEW. In this activity, students write rap songs to represent their thoughts about the content they have studied. Rapping for Review works best as an after-learning, small-group activity. (Each group should have approximately 5 members.) As teachers, we can create an extensive list of topics related to the content most recently studied and ask each group to choose a topic from the list or create one of its own. Then the group members focus on the most essential information connected to their topic and create a rap about it. Of course, the only way to share the rap is for each group to "rap" it to the class.

Rapping for Review is an engaging way to represent students' thinking and review content before an examination. The following is an excerpt from a rap created by a group of students in biology class:

THE BIO RAP

> *Lots of people think mitosis and meiosis are one and the same*
>
> *But each of these bio-terms has its own game.*
>
> *Mitosis results in the production of two*
>
> *Genetically identical diploid cells*
>
> *While meiosis produces four—not two—*
>
> *Genetically different haploid cells.*
>
> *They might look similar but they are different three ways.*
>
> *Mitosis produces two cells; meiosis four.*
>
> *Mitosis produces genetically identical; meiosis genetically different.*
>
> *Mitosis produces diploid; meiosis produces haploid.*
>
> *Now no one is thinking these terms are the same*
>
> *Everybody knows each has its own game.*

Rapping for Review is a motivational, small-group activity. Students will need at least half a class period to write their raps. To assess this activity, we can use an observation checklist. like the one shown in Figure 14.4.

How Can We Teach Our Students to Use Art as a Mode of Representation?

From sketching to painting to transmediating, art offers students many different options for sharing their ideas. In this section, we discuss four artistic modes students can use to represent their thinking.

IN MY MIND'S EYE. When working on this project, students represent their ideas through digital photography or movies. They choose a content-related topic, conference with us about their project, and then begin photographing or filming their ideas. As with other projects, students meet occasionally in workshop sessions to discuss the projects, share their progress, and review the project checklist or rubric.

When completing this project, students begin by choosing content-related topics. For example, mathematics students might select "geometry in everyday life" as a topic. Then they would outline the goals of their project. Next, they would digitally photograph or film everything from billboards to stop signs as examples of the use of geometry in the community. The students can also choose to narrate their presentations and integrate background music before sharing them with the class.

Students find In My Mind's Eye to be highly motivational, because they can self-select the topic and design a project to meet their goals. Middle and high school students also seem to enjoy representing their thinking in these digital formats.

Making Connections

Multiple literacies can both inspire thinking that can be represented in alternative modes and provide modes through which students may choose to represent their ideas. For example, if students read from a critical perspective, they can question the author's intent and why he chose to include some information and discount or ignore other ideas. To represent their thinking, students might create alternative texts or juxtaposition texts, photos, films, or sketches. If the topic the students were studying was the Boston Massacre, they might choose to represent their ideas by juxtapositioning sketches of the encounter from both military and civilian perspectives. ■

Checklist for Rapping for Review

Group Members

1. _____ Selected a recently studied content topic to review.
2. _____ Determined which information they would need.
3. _____ Used multiple sources to learn essential facts about the topic.
4. _____ Collaborated well.
5. _____ Used feedback to revise the rap.
6. _____ Effectively shared the rap.

Group Comments:

_____
_____
_____
_____

Teacher Comments:

_____
_____
_____
_____

Names:_____ Date _____

FIGURE 14.4
Checklist for Rapping for Review

TEACHING IDEA **STUDENT-CREATED ELECTRONIC PICTURE BOOKS.** Creating electronic picture books offers students opportunities to blend knowledge and creativity. The resulting project provides students with an alternative mode to represent their thinking and a variety of ways to format their content area research. The electronic nature of these books conserves paper and printer ink, while enabling students' to import illustrations and use LCD projectors to project the books when they are ready to be shared.

To teach students how to use an electronic book format, we can explain and demonstrate the process. We should also provide copies of the rubric we will use to evaluate the electronic books before the project begins. Figure 14.5 features an example of such a scoring guide, which focuses on criteria such as creativity, information, and technology use. The rubric can be adapted for use with particular types of books, such as biographies, fact/fiction, or alphabet.

Rubric for Student-Authored Electronic Books

Creativity	4 _____	3 _____	2 _____	1 _____
Quality of information	4 _____	3 _____	2 _____	1 _____
Content area connections	4 _____	3 _____	2 _____	1 _____
Relation of illustrations to text	4 _____	3 _____	2 _____	1 _____
Use of technology	4 _____	3 _____	2 _____	1 _____
Professional appearance	4 _____	3 _____	2 _____	1 _____

4 Outstanding creativity is evident. Excellent-quality information. Exceptional content area connections. Excellent relation of illustrations to text. Fully developed use of technology. Totally professional in appearance (e.g., format, conventions of writing, design, text, illustrations, and references).

3 In-depth creativity is evident. High-quality information is consistently used. Proficient content area connections. Skillful relation of illustrations to text. Consistent use of various types of technology. Very professional in appearance (e.g., format, conventions of writing, design, text, illustrations, and references).

2 Creativity is evident. Quality of information is adequate. Consistent connections to the content area. Illustrations and text are related. Use of technology is evident. Professional appearance (e.g., format, conventions of writing, design, text, illustrations, and references).

1 Creativity is lacking. Quality of information is inadequate. Inconsistent connections to the content. Illustration and text relations are inappropriate. Poor use of technology. Less than professional in appearance (e.g., format, conventions of writing, design, text, illustrations, and references).

Student Comments:_____

_____

_____

Teacher Comments:_____

_____

_____

FIGURE 14.5
Rubric for Student-Authored Electronic Books

Two types of electronic picture books that middle and high school students often use to represent their thinking are alphabet and informational books. Descriptions of each follow.

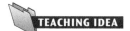

TEACHING IDEA

ELECTRONIC ALPHABET BOOKS. Alphabet picture books are currently enjoying a renaissance in the content areas. Books that were once characterized by "A is for apple, B is for boy" have emerged in recent years as themed volumes filled with in-depth research designed to inform students of all ages. *Jazz A-B-Z: An ABC Collection of Jazz Portraits* (Marsalis, 2005), *The Battle Alphabet Book* (Pallotta, 2004), *G Is for Googol: A Math Alphabet* (Schwartz, 1998), and *Q Is for Quark: A Science Alphabet Book* (Schwartz, 2001) are just a few examples of such published works.

Content area students can create alphabet books to share information about topics they choose to investigate. This format also affords opportunities for students to creatively illustrate their research. They learn early in the experience that although everyone may not be a gifted artist, everyone can be creative. The result is books that are informative, visually appealing, and inexpensive. Figure 14.6 features selected pages from *A Geometry Alphabet Book*, which was created by Stephen Ingram.

When they are creating alphabet books, students need to provide information about 26 aspects of a self-selected topic. These books also challenge students to develop illustrations that complement each topic discussed in the text. This activity incorporates student choice, research, writing, creativity, and technology and may be extended to other genres, including biography.

TEACHING IDEA   STUDENT-AUTHORED ELECTRONIC INFORMATIONAL BOOKS. Students can also create other types of books as alternative representations of their thinking. For example, they might investigate an aspect of the content they are studying and choose to report what they have learned in a self-authored book as opposed to a more traditional report.

While picture books were once enjoyed only by very young children, they are now widely used at all levels of education to stimulate students' engagement with the learning process. As a result, students often choose to create picture books to report their research. The books are then shared with classmates to stimulate their interest in the book's topic. They may also become part of the classroom library or be shared with younger learners.

Creating a picture book presents a number of challenges for the students. First, they must select a content-related topic for the book and research it. Second, they need to convey the essential elements of their research topic in a multiple-page narrative. Third, students need to develop illustrations to support the text. Fourth, the story they write needs to be creative and motivational, yet logical and informative. Students also need to choose the book style that best complements their story. Shape books, accordion books, pop-up books, television scrolls, and computer-animated books are among the styles most frequently selected. Finally, students need to use the appropriate conventions of writing. A rubric detailing these elements should be shared with students before the research project begins.

As mentioned earlier, students may use a variety of book formats to share their content knowledge, including shape books, accordion books, and slotted books, as well as PowerPoint files. In past projects, students have addressed topics ranging from outer space to Egyptian mummies. Examples of books they have created include the following: *John and Wayne's Excellent Outer Space Adventure, Geometry Is All Around Us, Man on the Moon,* and *Medieval Times.*

TEACHING IDEA   TRANSMEDIATIONS. Within a constructivist perspective, "teachers invite students to search for understanding, appreciate uncertainty, and inquire responsibly" (Brooks & Brooks, 1993, p. 6). These teaching practices help students internalize and shape new information, enabling them to make connections between what they know and what they are learning (McLaughlin & Allen, 2009; Wagner & Barnett, 1998). Understandings are further expanded through a process identified as transmediation (Harste, Burke, & Short, 1988; Hoyt, 1992). During this process, students transfer information and knowledge from one communication system to another.

When creating transmediations, students choose ideas in an existing medium and change its representation to another medium. For example, students might choose to take a poem and turn it into a picture book or they might choose song lyrics and turn them into a work of art. Maya Angelou's *Life Doesn't Frighten Me*, illustrated with the paintings of Jean-Michel Basquiat, is an example of a published transmediation. Angelou originally wrote "Life Doesn't Frighten Me" as a poem in 1978, but it was later published as text for a picture book illustrated by Basquiat.

Middle and high school students are motivated to create transmediations because they can self-select topics and choose the medium in which they will work. They also do not need to worry about content, because they are working with existing works (e.g., poems, song lyrics, paintings). Examples of excerpts from a transmediation created by a student can be found in the Appendix.

FIGURE 14.6 Excerpts from *A Geometry Alphabet Book*

A Geometry Alphabet Book

Stephen Inghrim

Angle

- The union of 2 rays that have the same endpoint
- Measured in degrees or radians
- The five types of angles are:
  - Zero
  - Acute
  - Right
  - Obtuse
  - Straight

FIGURE 14.6 *Continued*

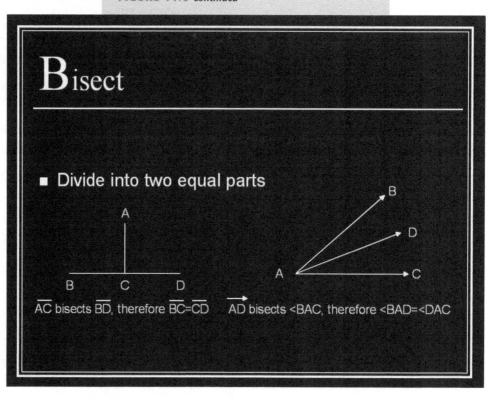

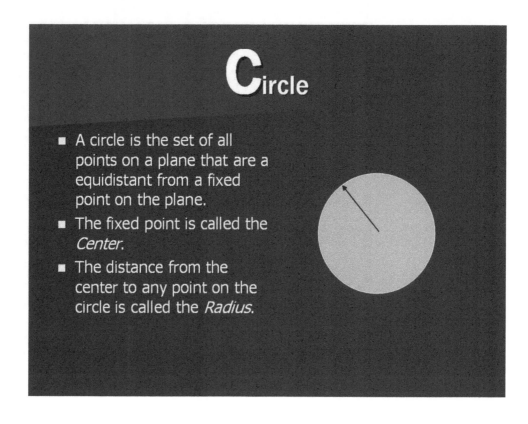

Making Connections

TO STRUGGLING READERS

Providing opportunities for students to represent their thinking in alternative modes often makes it possible for struggling students to show what they know and can do in ways that are more compatible with their learning styles. For example, when creating transmediations, struggling students may choose to read a poem, song lyrics, or a news article and change the original medium to a work of art. Having the option of creating a performance that does not involve writing may alleviate anxiety for students who may be less than confident about their writing abilities. ■

We and our students know that we are not all artists, but we can all express ourselves in artistic ways. Infusing art into our teaching encourages students to express their understandings in that mode of representation.

FINAL THOUGHTS

Our ultimate goal in teaching students multiple modes of representation is to ensure that they have the best possible means of communicating their thoughts. Each of us is an individual, capable of expressing thoughts in a variety of ways. Multiple forms of representation celebrate our unique natures and encourage us to share our ideas in the most meaningful ways. As Eisner (1997) has noted,

> Schools that cultivate the differences among us while escalating the mean for performance in each of these forms of representation provide for the richness of the full orchestra. We do better as a culture when we are not all violinists—even brilliant ones. (p. 352)

Teaching students to represent their thoughts in a variety of ways broadens their communication possibilities and strengthens their understanding. It also helps to engage their thinking and accommodate their learning styles.

In the next chapter, we discuss meaningful classroom assessment. We examine informal and formal assessments and explore how to use assessment and evaluation in our teaching.

Teaching Connections

APPLYING WHAT WE HAVE LEARNED

E-Links

Consider how you will integrate alternative forms of representation into your teaching. Meet with a small group of teachers from your content area and plan how each of you will help your students use music, drama, and art to represent their thinking. Each group member will (1) choose a topic; (2) select a specific mode of representation (e.g., Rapping for Review, Dinner Party, Transmediations); (3) develop an annotated list of at least 3 quality online sources; and (4) describe how he would use these sources to help represent his thinking. Provide feedback to each group member. Save the resources for use in your teaching.

EXAMPLE WEBSITES

Use websites such as these to complete the project:

Modern American Poetry
http://www.english.uiuc.edu/maps/poets.htm

Coolmath Algebra
http://www.coolmath.com/algebra/Algebra1/index.html#Algebra_1:_Absolute_Value_Inequalities

Cells Alive!
http://www.cellsalive.com/pen.htm

Accountable Talk

Consider the modes of representation you use most commonly and reflect on why you do so. Then consider a mode that you do not commonly employ. Reflect on how you might use this mode to expand representations of your thinking, using a specific project as an example. Record your thoughts as a reflective entry in your portfolio and share them in small-group discussion.

Portfolio/Performance Opportunity

Meet with your peers in a small group and discuss what you consider to be students' most common modes of representation in your area of study. Think about how you would integrate other modes into your teaching, and focus on a discipline-specific project you think could work well in at least two different modes. Complete the project in both modes. Share your work with the class by briefly discussing the project you chose. Include your work in your portfolio.

15

Meeting Challenges and Continuing to Learn through Professional Development

While enrolled in this course, we have learned a great deal about teaching reading in the content areas, but our learning does not end here. The next steps are to fully apply what we have learned in our teaching and to continue to discover the latest developments in education and in our content areas. In other words, our next step is to become lifelong learners. Because no one can predict what the next challenge or educational development will be, as teachers, we need to keep our minds open to the many possibilities that lie ahead.

And so, in this final chapter, we discuss three important topics: experiencing success in our teaching, participating in a mentoring program, and engaging in professional development. First, we examine the challenges often encountered during teaching. Next, we focus on the importance of partnering with a knowledgeable, experienced mentor. Finally, we explore the key components of professional development and discuss how to create meaningful professional development plans.

What Challenges Might We Encounter in Our Teaching?

As content area teachers, we face challenges every day. We teach a wide variety of students. We infuse critical and creative thinking,

325

inquiry-based learning, and technology into our work, and we do it all while accommodating federal programs, state standards, and individual students' needs. To become the best content area teachers we can be, we need to be able to meet any challenges that may arise. Ideas about how we might do that follow.

Time

To explore some of the obstacles and opportunities in a new teaching career, go to the Resources tab in the MyEducation-Lab for your course and click on Beginning Your Career

Most of us would agree that there simply is not enough time in the teaching day to do all that needs to be done. We need time to plan and teach, as well as to accommodate students' diverse academic, linguistic, and cultural needs.

Time will always be a concern for teachers, but we can take some steps to ensure that we use time to our best advantage. We might begin by considering how much time we need for planning and teaching. For example, rather than always teaching in a whole-group setting, we can use pairs and small groups when students are preparing presentations, creating projects, or applying what they are learning in other ways (see Chapter 9). This provides us with time to observe students, to interact with them about the projects they are creating, to provide suggestions about their research, or to conference about their progress.

There are many other things we can do to use time more efficiently. Consider the following examples:

- *Pre-assessing students' prior knowledge.* Before teaching a new topic, we can use techniques such as Admit Slips, Tickets Out, Semantic Maps, or Quickwrites for two purposes: to learn what students already know and to determine a starting point for our teaching that will accommodate students' needs.

- *Working with others who teach our content area.* Sharing ideas, resources, and planning with colleagues can help us to gain other perspectives and save time preparing materials and lessons.

- *Collaborating with teachers who do not teach our content area.* Certain skills, such as generating questions and using graphic organizers, benefit students across the curriculum. If we encourage all content teachers to focus on teaching and using such skills, individual teachers will need to spend less time teaching them. Of course, if we can persuade teachers across grade levels to teach and use these skills and strategies, we would only need to review them by the time the students reached the levels at which we teach.

Making Connections
TO ENGLISH LEARNERS

We can also engage the support of ESL teachers. Meeting with these teachers and learning how we can best help our English learners to succeed is often an invaluable experience. We can learn how to use supports such as visuals and a variety of response modes. Knowing how to explain and demonstrate these supports will save time that otherwise might be needed for reteaching. ■

Content Standards

National and state content standards have been developed in virtually every area of the curriculum. Most state assessments are based on those standards, which describe what students know and can do in the content areas. Sometimes we may feel pressure to "teach to the test" to help students perform at acceptable levels on high stakes tests, such as state assessments. This becomes complicated when students lack the prior knowledge and skills needed to successfully learn and apply content concepts.

We may be able to meet this challenge by remembering that our teaching is standards-based. We don't ignore the content when implementing innovative approaches, but rather support and enhance it. For example, we can invite students to engage in Inquiring Minds (see Chapter 13)—a small-group, inquiry-based, and standards-based research project in which students self-select topics—rather than writing individual traditional reports on the same subject. We can also help our students by teaching skills and strategies they may not know (see Chapters 5 through 11).

Texts and Other Resources

Some school districts may provide us with content texts and supplemental materials that are either outdated or overly demanding. Problems associated with this issue include inaccurate information, uninteresting text formats, few opportunities for student interaction, unnecessarily long texts, absence of critical and creative thinking, focus on literal meaning, and lack of strategy integration. As a result, we and our students may be unmotivated—a factor that influences not only the amount of learning that takes place, but also the quality of the experience for everyone involved.

In response to this challenge, we can use multiple types of text in our teaching (see Chapter 8). Informational text from magazines, newspapers, journals, and websites is up-to-date and readily available, so we should never feel limited to using textbooks (see Chapter 9). In addition, appropriate theme-related poetry or novels can significantly enhance students' understanding. For example, if we are teaching English/Spanish translation, we can access the works of poets such as Pablo Neruda in both English and Spanish. An example is Neruda's "Ode to a Chestnut on the Ground," which is entitled "Oda a Una Castaña En el Suelo" in Spanish; this poem is available in English and Spanish on the Internet. Another example would be integrating current information about a topic we are teaching. For example, if we are teaching DNA in biology, we might motivate students by sharing information about how DNA is now used in the search for justice; information about this topic is also available on the Internet. For an example of how to align young adult novels with a historical topic such as World War II, see Figure 4.3, which lists young adult novels about World War II that can be used to teach critical literacy.

Making Connections
TO MULTIPLE LITERACIES

The idea of alternative texts is virtually boundless when we engage in multiple literacies. In critical literacy, the nature of text includes books, articles, and lyrics, but also moves beyond traditional views of text to encompass conditions (e.g., sociocultural influences, state-assessment-driven curriculums funding or lack of it) or relationships and situations in everyday life (e.g., analyzing an occurrence from another person's perspective). Media literacy incorporates texts such as film and photography, and informational literacy provides access to the seemingly endless texts of the virtual world. ■

Creativity

Some content teachers believe that only "creative people" can teach students how to use methods such as inquiry-based learning and alternative representations. However, when creative teaching ideas are explained and demonstrated using classroom examples, these teachers often seem more willing to take the risk. Throughout this text, we have been encouraged to scaffold learning by explaining, demonstrating, guiding, practicing, and reflecting when teaching new methods or strategies to our students. These examples may include sketching or illustrating. Consider how teachers who doubt their creativity might feel after reviewing the rubric for student-authored electronic books (see Chapter 14). They would know that one of the criteria for that project is the relationship of illustrations to text. That might be an issue of concern if the teachers doubt their ability to illustrate the book, but in the case of electronic books we have choices. We—and our students—can download photos from the Internet or use computer clipart to illustrate such books. Utilizing these resources enables us to be creative without requiring us to be artists.

We can also choose to work through our "creative doubts" with colleagues in our content area. In fact, we can even invite them to work with us on examples we can share and use at different points during the school year.

Making Connections | Thinking about Our Creativity

■ Think about yourself as a creative person and about the role that creativity plays in teaching. (1) Consider how comfortable you would feel sketching, singing, or writing poetry when teaching through alternative representations. (2) Consider what you could do to help students feel comfortable in such situations.

■ Share your thoughts with others in small-group discussions.

Innovation Versus Reality

Another challenge we may experience is the contrast between what we have learned in our teacher education programs and what we see being practiced in the schools in which we teach. We have learned about new and interesting teaching methods such as student-centered, inquiry-based learning, yet when we go into the field we may see more traditional approaches, such as reading chapters and answering questions or round-robin reading, being used (see Chapter 9).

To meet this type of challenge, we need to consider the nature of each task and develop specific responses. For example, if we see content area teachers still asking students to silently read chapters and respond to questions or to take turns reading the chapter aloud (round-robin reading), we can invite them to consider multiple ways to respond to text (see Chapters 11, 13, and 14) and alternatives to round-robin reading (see Chapter 9). We can probably be most effective in sharing these techniques if we work with one or two teachers who demonstrate interest in engaging in more innovative practices. We can also serve as effective teaching models.

If it is difficult to find other teachers who choose to teach content subjects in creative and innovative ways, we shouldn't be discouraged. While some teachers enthusiastically endorse new approaches, others remain in a fixed position—teaching the way they've always taught. If we find ourselves surrounded by those for whom content teaching simply means lectures and test taking, we will need to act as the trailblazers. Of course, both we and our students will be the winners!

Making Connections | Thinking about Innovative Practice

■ Think about how you have integrated innovative practices into your teaching. Imagine that you were hired by a school district that supported very traditional methods of teaching. What would you do to introduce other teachers to alternatives to round-robin reading and other innovative approaches?

■ Share your thoughts with others in small-group discussions.

Student Diversity

Another common concern of content teachers at all levels is the challenge of meeting students' individual needs. Factors such as background knowledge and experience, language proficiency, learning styles, reading abilities, and culture all affect students' access to content. Classroom realities include large class sizes, increasing numbers of English learners, lack of materials to meet students' needs, unmotivated learners, and teachers who may feel unprepared to deal with these challenges.

We need to believe that our teaching methods can bridge these differences and help both teachers and students come together in a learning community. We know that we can differentiate our instruction (see Chapter 9). We also know that teaching that incorporates creative, strategy-based approaches benefits all students, including English learners and students with special needs. If we believe that "thinking" exists regardless of reading or language ability, then we can see that for many students, "other ways of knowing" may include drama, music, technology, hands-on manipulation, art, poetry, and physical movement. We have all taught students who can express their thoughts better in one mode than in others—students whose strength may not be written responses, but who share their thoughts freely through discussion; or students whose strength may not be discussion or writing, but can freely share their ideas through projects or dramatizations. Chapter 14 features information about alternative representations of student thinking, such as transmediations, in which students take content presented in one medium and change it into another, and Rapping for Review, in which students use essential information to create and sing a rap about the current topic of study.

Incorporating these ideas into content teaching provides opportunities for all students to share their thinking. In many ways, it levels the learning playing field.

Making Connections
TO STRUGGLING READERS

Knowing our students' needs helps us to differentiate instruction. For example, when working with struggling students, we can design projects that incorporate alternative modes of representation. Offering students choices about how to represent their thinking has dual benefits: It motivates students, and it provides opportunities for them to use their strength modalities. ■

Classroom Organization and Management

The challenge for today's teachers is to create student-centered classrooms in which students take ownership of learning. When we release some of the responsibility for learning to the students, classroom management issues change. A variety of grouping patterns, multiple texts, daily schedules, and classroom routines become prevalent, and management becomes more of a shared responsibility between teacher and students (see Chapter 9).

Keeping an open mind and being versatile with classroom organization enhances students' experiences in content area learning. We may wish to think about how we might organize our classrooms so that management issues are not paramount. We also need to think about how we might organize groups of students who will work together, plan for a system of accountability for students (such as daily group progress checks), and determine the degree to which we need to monitor each activity. Thinking through these issues carefully before we implement innovative approaches will help ensure success for everyone concerned.

Assessment and Evaluation

Tests, quizzes, and reports are the more traditional means of assessing student knowledge of content material. These methods of assessment are relatively quick to grade, the "correct answers" are easy to determine, and teachers, administrators, parents, and students all understand what the grades have meant.

When integrating creative and innovative teaching ideas, however, we use dynamic measures such as observation, discussion, strategy use, informal writing, and projects to document student progress. In this area, challenges may arise when assessment is viewed as separate from instruction, when the role of informal assessments is not understood, when the measures used do not accommodate students' strength modalities, and when criteria for performance assessments are not provided. As innovative strategies are integrated, assessment becomes a natural part of everyday teaching and learning. In such contexts, informal and formal assessments combine to offer a fuller, more meaningful picture of students' abilities. Another important benefit is that students can become more engaged in self-assessment, reflecting on their roles as active learners as well as their levels of understanding.

Students Working Independently

Because we want to ensure that our students continue to learn when they work independently, we may occasionally be concerned about whether they have the necessary skills and motivation to effectively work on their own. We can meet this challenge by teaching our students how to be active, independent learners who are motivated to engage in a variety of tasks. For example, Bookmark Technique, INSERT Method, Patterned Partner Reading and Say Something (see Chapters 5 through 9) require students to take an active role in learning by commenting on, questioning, making connections to, or summarizing what they are learning. We can also teach our students how to use techniques such as structured note taking and double-entry journals (see Chapter 9), which students can use as supports when working independently. Participating in interactive group tasks, such as Internet Workshops (see Chapter 12) or Discussion Circles (see Chapter 9), also foster student independence.

Making Connections
TO WRITING

Writing plays an important role when students are working independently. Although students also engage in discussion, the responses they write when using ideas such as structured notetaking, journaling, or Bookmark Technique provide informal assessments of student progress that we can read at a later time. Discussion does provide similar information, but we need to be able to observe that as it is occurring. ■

To ensure that our students are well-motivated, we can activate their prior knowledge and provide additional background information if necessary. For example, if we determine that students have little or no prior knowledge of a topic we will be teaching, we can use read-alouds of informational articles and trade books to enhance their knowledge (see Chapter 9). To engage our students in learning, we can also offer them choices, such as self-selecting topics and choosing formats when they are creating projects.

For example, when creating First-Person Experiences (see Chapter 13), students often choose unique ways to present their research. One student researched the Pilgrims' journey to America and presented her findings in a parchment travel journal rolled up and placed inside a bottle. She chose the "message in a bottle format" because the captain of the boat had announced that land had been sighted and, as a passenger approaching a new land, she feared what awaited her and her family. Another student researched Ben Franklin and came to class dressed as the inventor. "Franklin" presented his research by regaling the class with stories about "his" life. Still another student researched Edgar Allen Poe for his American poetry class. He came to class dressed as Poe, shared fascinating information about "his" life, and toward the end of the presentation noted that he was very pleased that he and his poetry remained so popular so long after his death. To support this premise, he shared a brief video clip about "The Raven" from an episode of *The Simpsons* television show. These three students self-selected their topics and chose distinctive presentation modes that embedded both the depth of their understanding and their engagement in learning.

Final Thoughts on Challenges We May Encounter in Our Teaching

Although we may encounter challenges during our teaching careers, we know that if we learn well, plan well, and teach well, we can meet them all. The essence of our success seems to involve our background knowledge: how well we know our students, how well we motivate them, how well we teach them, and how well we encourage them to apply what they learn in innovative and creative ways.

In the next section, we discuss mentoring, another process that can help us become better teachers. Early in our careers, we may be mentees. Later, we may become mentors.

How Can Mentoring Benefit Our Teaching?

As educators, we need to make our teaching all that it can be. We need to reflect on our efforts, and continually strive to enrich our teaching and learn more about our content areas. Mentors can help us achieve these goals.

The term "mentor" has a long-standing history. It dates back to Greek mythology and the story of Odysseus. When he left to fight the Trojan War, Odysseus entrusted his son, Telemachus, to his close friend, Mentor. Mentor was responsible for the protection, guidance, and education of Telemachus. Mentor taught Telemachus to think and to do things for himself with good judgment.

There are numerous definitions of mentoring. The descriptors that follow are drawn from a combination of resources (Allen, Cobb, & Danger, 2003; Holloway, 2001; Mtetwa & Kwari, 2003; Shank, 2005; Trubowitz & Robins, 2003). They agree that mentoring is:

- an active, evolving, one-on-one process.
- a reciprocal relationship in which an experienced, knowledgeable, and caring teacher invests time and knowledge to help a new teacher successfully acclimate to the real-life demands of experiences in the teaching profession.
- a professional partnership that successfully benefits both mentor and mentee.
- situationalized. The environment—which includes the school, the faculty, the administration, and the community—plays an integral role in the mentoring process.

Most novice teachers soon discover that while they are striving to address their goals, their school is focused on student success in federal programs and on state assessments. According to Mandel (2006), while school districts are focusing on state testing, new teachers are focusing on survival. Mentors, who understand the agenda needs to come from the first year teachers, can help those teachers meet the unique challenges they face during their first year. Mandel further notes that the concerns of the new teachers fall into five broad categories:

1. Setting up the classroom and preparing for the first weeks of class (physical arrangement, materials, bulletin boards, discipline problems, what to teach when, homework, and tests).
2. Covering the required curriculum without falling behind or losing student interest.
3. Grading fairly.
4. Dealing with parents. (Always have the student present for parent–teacher conferences.)
5. Maintaining personal sanity.

We may be somewhat surprised that the general category of "continuing professional development" was not included in Mandel's list. It is a topic we will add and explore as we examine the challenges that novice teachers face. First, however, we discuss those experienced educators who are available to guide first-year teachers as they strive to develop meaningful ways to meet the challenges described by Mandel. These teachers are the mentors.

Characteristics of Effective Mentors

Mentors are lifelong learners who understand and respect the mentoring process. They participate in special training and support mentees in all aspects of their teaching.

Mentors have patience, enthusiasm, and respect for their colleagues. They also have the respect of their colleagues. They have demonstrated expertise in their field and are willing to share it. Their goal is to provide less experienced teachers with guidance and support, while encouraging them to make their own decisions (Allen et al., 2003; Holloway, 2001; Mtetwa & Kwari, 2003; Shank, 2005; Trubowitz & Robins, 2003). Although mentors most often assist first-year teachers, they are also called upon to aid experienced teachers who may be beginning a new teaching assignment.

Mentors are dedicated educators who freely give their time to help others. They are respectful and nurturing in their quest to encourage mentees to reach their greatest potentials.

Characteristics of Mentees

Mentees are usually novice teachers who understand and respect the mentoring process. These lifelong learners appreciate their colleagues' willingness to be mentors. Mentees make their own decisions with the advice and encouragement of their mentors (Allen et al., 2003; Holloway, 2001; Mtetwa & Kwari, 2003; Shank, 2005; Trubowitz & Robins, 2003).

As noted earlier, mentees are most often first-year teachers. They are new to the full-time teaching experience, although their teacher education programs likely involved multiple professional experiences in addition to student teaching. Mentees may also be experienced teachers who become involved in mentoring when they begin a new teaching assignment. For example, if a teacher has taught seventh grade for ten years and is transferred to tenth grade, she might be offered the opportunity to work with a mentor from that grade level.

Good mentoring relationships are reciprocal in nature. Both the mentor and the mentee contribute to the relationship's success, which often depends on the context or situation in which the mentoring occurs. For example, when mentoring was introduced in the New York City Schools, the program in general was found to be helpful (Keller, 2006). In fact, mentoring participants were twice as likely to stay on their jobs compared to those who did not have mentors, but the mentors encountered a number of challenges including the number of mentees, the lack of a second year of mentoring, and poor communication between those in the mentoring program and building administrators.

When establishing a mentoring program, Northwest Regional Educational Laboratory (NWREL, 2001) suggests that we follow these general guidelines:

- *Provide support and training for mentors.* This should include program goals and purposes, district philosophies, and observational techniques and feedback methods (Halford, 1999).

- *Reward the mentors.* A reward system engenders positive feelings in both the mentor and the mentee (Halford, 1999).

- *Provide support, funding, and leadership to establish and maintain mentoring programs* (Halford, 1999). Mentors are not administrative representatives. Principals should take an active interest in the mentoring process.

- *Schedule mentor/mentee meetings on a regular basis.* Scheduling mentoring meetings can be a challenge. School districts should consider hiring one person who is a full-time mentor or retired teachers whose schedules may be more flexible.

Figure 15.1 lists selected books about mentoring. For additional resources, see the mentoring websites listed in the E-Links section at the conclusion of this chapter.

Final Thoughts on Mentoring

Mentoring is a valued component of teaching. As Halford (1998) notes, creating successful induction programs for novice teachers is an important goal of educational reform. Most districts that have mentoring partnerships have found that beginning teachers who participate in them are more likely to remain members of the teaching profession (Trubowitz, 2004). "As instructional leaders and master teachers, mentors can be a professional lifeline for their new colleagues" (Halford, 1998, p. 36). From our standpoint it is particularly important to note that mentoring

FIGURE 15.1
Books about Mentoring

Breaux, A. L. (2002). *101 "answers" for new teachers & their mentors: Effective teaching tips for daily classroom use.* Larchmont, NY: Eye on Education.

Hicks, C. D., Glasgow, N. A., & McNary, S. J. (2004). *What successful mentors do: 81 research-based strategies for new teacher induction, training, and support.* Thousand Oaks, CA: Corwin.

Jonson, K. F. (2008). *Being an effective mentor: How to help beginning teachers succeed* (2nd ed.). Thousand Oaks, CA: Corwin.

Niday, D., Boreen, J. Potts, J., & Johnson, M. K. (2009). *Mentoring beginning teachers: Guiding, reflecting, coaching* (2nd ed.). Portland, ME: Stenhouse.

Portner, H. (Ed.). (2008). *Mentoring new teachers.* Thousand Oaks, CA: Corwin.

works well in high school settings. Shank (2005, p. 81) draws these conclusions from her work in a secondary setting:

> New and veteran teachers alike can share their expertise and take responsibility for the learning of other teachers. They can develop a broader understanding of teaching approaches that are prevalent in their school. Through collegial support and challenge, novices and experienced teachers can learn to be open about their practices and grapple with the complexities of teaching. Together, teachers can develop and maintain a shared focus and a dynamic culture where collaborative and reciprocal mentoring can take place.

How Can We Make Professional Development a Meaningful Part of Our Teaching?

When thinking about professional development, we must begin by defining the term. Wiggins and McTighe (2006) suggest that four characteristics distinguish professionals in any field:

> Professionals (1) act on the most current knowledge that defines their field; (2) are client-centered and adapt to meet the needs of the individuals whom they serve; (3) are results-oriented; and (4) uphold the standards of the profession in their own practice and through peer review. (p. 27)

Kelleher (2003) extends these ideas to professional development in education, suggesting that the best programs "help teachers to think critically about their practice; to develop new instructional strategies, along with new techniques for creating curriculum and assessments; and to measure how new practices have affected student learning" (p. 754). Duffy (2004) extends the definition of professional development by addressing what kind of knowledge professional developers should be providing:

> As instructional situations change, teachers transform knowledge to fit the situation, often on a case-by-case basis. Consequently, our professional development goal should not be to simply disseminate knowledge to teachers; it should be to teach teachers to make judgments about how to modify or adapt professional knowledge to fit changing situations. (p. 11)

Greenleaf and Schoenbach (2004) classify professional development as high quality if teachers are involved in learning over time, necessary resources are accessible, opportunities for teachers to reflect on teaching and learning are created, and teachers' expertise is increased. Accountability is also a major factor. Because professional development emphasizes student learning, teachers need to be able to demonstrate measurable growth in terms of student learning.

In this section, we explore professional development. We begin by discussing how we can effectively engage in professional development. Then we examine a variety of professional development resources that can help us to reach our goals.

Becoming Lifelong Learners through Professional Development

Because we are lifelong learners, we engage in professional development throughout our teaching careers. Our goal is to increase our students' understanding and performance. Research suggests that professional development can help us to make profound changes in our practice and, consequently, provide learning opportunities that make a difference in student achievement (Greenleaf & Schoenbach, 2004).

The structure of professional development has changed over time. For example, its purpose was once viewed as increasing teachers' knowledge of various educational topics; now, however, its goals have moved beyond teacher knowledge to student learning. The focuses of professional development emerge from student learning, and the outcomes are measured through increased student performance. To ensure that the professional development in which we engage is meaningful, we should consider the following guidelines (Kelleher, 2003):

- Choose a goal that emerges from your students' learning and is related to school and district-wide goals.
- Set specific, measurable targets for student achievement.
- Create study groups, agree on how student work will be evaluated, or otherwise prepare for the professional development experience.
- Engage in a variety of settings and use a range of quality resources.
- Use meaningful measures to determine teacher and student growth.
- Self-reflect and share experiences with peers.
- Determine the changes you will make based on professional development and peer sharing.

Plans are often three years in duration and include learning through technology. Throughout the process, administrators, mentors, or peer coaches serve as guides and provide the participants with regular feedback.

Based on our understanding of professional development and guidelines such as those presented, we can develop an action plan by following these steps:

1. Consider topics such as integrating new literacies, content disciplines, or innovative teaching methods. Ultimately, however, the topic we choose should emerge from the needs of our students.
2. Consider the duration of our professional development and determine how we could measure change in students' performance that occurs as a result.
3. Consider settings, learning at some points in study groups and at other times with a peer.
4. Develop professional development goals based on students' needs.
5. Learn new information and integrate our learning into our teaching.
6. Measure student learning.
7. Reflect and share ideas throughout this process.

Although professional development is tied to district and school practices, we need to remember that it is always personal. Topics emerge from our students' learning, and we develop plans to address those needs. We make choices—the length of the plan, the settings in which we will learn, the formats we will use, and the resources we will integrate—throughout the process. When we engage in meaningful professional development experiences, such as these guidelines would provide, our learning informs students' learning, and we become "designers as well as implementers, informed professionals rather than mere conduits for other people's designs and agendas" (Greenleaf & Schoenbach, 2004, pp. 122–123).

Professional Development Resources

Resources for professional development range from more traditional graduate courses to online offerings. In fact, most resources are now accessible through electronic as well as traditional means. The types of resources we use relate directly to our professional development focus and the contexts in which we choose to learn. All are designed to help us discover new teaching methods, learn more about our content areas and other educational issues, and demonstrate our dedication to teaching.

The following professional development resources are easily accessible.

PROFESSIONAL ORGANIZATIONS. Most disciplines have professional organizations that are designed to help members learn about new advances in teaching and learning. Figure 15.2 lists some of these organizations, along with their website addresses.

PROFESSIONAL EDUCATION JOURNALS. Figure 15.3 features a list of some of the many journals published by professional educational organizations. Subscriptions are often available in hard copy as well as electronic formats. Most of these journals are peer reviewed.

PROFESSIONAL BOOKS. These publications are often available from professional organizations and groups dedicated to education in general. Of course, most titles are available from educational publishers, bookstores, and online booksellers, such as Amazon.com.

PROFESSIONAL STUDY GROUP MODULES/STUDY GROUPS. According to Baker (2004), study groups consist of literacy educators who share professional development interests. These educators meet on a regular basis to read and discuss materials about a topic they wish to study in depth. The composition of the group is determined by the participants; it may be organized formally within a school or school district, or informally by colleagues with comparable job responsibilities. The focus of the study group's work is often a study group module published by a professional organization. For examples of available modules, see the International Reading Association's website http://www.reading.org for literacy-related topics, such as adolescent literacy and reading comprehension, and the Association for Supervision and Curriculum Development's (ASCD) website http://www.ascd.org for general education topics, such as problem-based learning and differentiated instruction.

> *Making Connections* | Thinking about Professional Study Groups
>
> ■ Reflect on all that you have learned and (1) consider an educational topic that you would like to explore in a professional study group. Justify your choice. (2) Consider the value of such study groups within school districts.
>
> ■ Share your thoughts with others in small-group discussions.

GRADUATE COURSES. Offered by universities, these courses can be taken individually, based on interest, or as part of graduate degree programs. Many university courses are now offered both in the traditional manner and in electronic format through distance education. When taking distance education courses, we can remain in our homes and participate in class by using the Internet. These courses, which often are discussion and project based, eliminate the expenses associated with traveling to and from classes, as well as the time such a commute requires. Listings of traditional and distance education courses are usually posted on university websites.

IN-DISTRICT COURSES. School districts often offer courses to help teachers fulfill ongoing state certification requirements. These programs, which are usually provided at no cost, are taught by district teachers and administrators. The content focuses on developments in research and practice related to teaching in general or to specific content areas. Announcements about these courses are shared through district email, and the class meetings are generally held after school.

PROFESSIONAL WORKSHOPS, PRESENTATIONS, AND SEMINARS. Offered at the international, national, regional, and state levels, these meetings enable teachers to learn about specific

FIGURE 15.2
Professional
Organizations for
Teachers

English

National Council for Teachers of English (NCTE)
http://www.ncte.org/

ESL

National Association for Bilingual Education (NABE)
http://www.nabe.org/

Teachers of English Speakers of Other Languages (TESOL)
http://www.tesol.org/s_tesol/index.asp

Fine Arts

National Art Education Association (NAEA)
http://www.naea-reston.org

MENC: National Association for Music Education
http://www.menc.org

Foreign Language

American Council on the Teaching of Foreign Language (ACTFL)
http://www.actfl.org/i4a/pages/index.cfm?pageid=1

Modern Language Association (MLA)
http://www.mla.org/

Health

American Alliance for Health, Physical Education, Recreation, and Dance (AAHPERD)
http://www.aahperd.org/index.cfm

History

National Council for Social Studies (NCSS)
http://www.ncss.org

Math

National Council for Teachers of Mathematics (NCTM)
http://www.nctm.org/

Reading

International Reading Association (IRA)
http://www.reading.org

Science

American Association of Physics Teachers (AAPT)
http://www.aapt.org/

National Association of Biology Teachers (NABT)
http://www.nabt.org

National Science Teachers Association (NSTA)
http://www.nsta.org/

Special Education

Council for Exceptional Children (CEC)
http://www.cec.sped.org//AM/template.cfm?Section=Home

National Association of Special Education Teachers (NASET)
http://www.naset.org/

Technology

Association for Educational Communication and Technology (AECT)
http://www.aect.org/default.asp

International Society for Technology in Education (ISTE)
http://www.iste.org/

FIGURE 15.3
Educational Journals that Support Professional Development

English

National Council for Teachers of English (NCTE)
- *Voices from the Middle*
- *English Journal*

ESL

National Association for Bilingual Education (NABE)
- *Bilingual Research Journal NABE Journal of Research and Practice*

Teachers of English Speakers of Other Languages (TESOL)
- *TESOL Quarterly*

Fine Arts

National Art Education Association (NAEA)
- *Studies in Art Education*

MENC: National Association for Music Education
- *Music Educators Journal*
- *Journal of Music Teacher Education*
- *Journal of Research in Music Education*

Foreign Language

American Council on the Teaching of Foreign Language (ACTFL)
- *Foreign Language Annals*

Modern Language Association (MLA)
- *PMLA*

Health

American Alliance for Health, Physical Education, Recreation, and Dance (AAHPERD)
- *Journal of Physical Education, Recreation, & Dance (JOPERD)*
- *American Journal of Health Education (AJHE)*
- *STRATEGIES: A Journal for Physical and Sport Educators*
- *Research Quarterly for Exercise and Sport (RQES)*

History

National Council for Social Studies (NCSS)
- *Social Education*
- *Middle Level Learning*

Mathematics

National Council for Teachers of Mathematics (NCTM)
- *Journal for Research in Mathematics Education*
- *Mathematics Teaching in the Middle School*
- *Mathematics Teacher*
- *ON-Math*

Reading

International Reading Association (IRA)
- *Reading Research Quarterly*
- *Journal of Adolescent and Adult Literature*

Science

American Association of Physics Teachers (AAPT)
- *American Journal of Physics*
- *The Physics Teacher*

National Association of Biology Teachers (NABT)
- *The American Biology Teacher*

National Science Teachers Association (NSTA)
- *Science Scope*
- *The Science Teacher*

(continued)

FIGURE 15.3
(continued)

Special Education

Council for Exceptional Children (CEC)
- *TEACHING Exceptional Children*
- *Exceptional Children*

National Association of Special Education Teachers (NASET)
- *JAASEP: Research Based Journal in Special Education*
- *The Special Educator e-Journal*

Technology

Association for Educational Communication and Technology (AECT)
- *Instructional Science*
- *TechTrends*
- *Educational Technology Research and Development*

International Society for Technology in Education (ISTE)
- *Journal of Research on Technology in Education (JRTE)*
- *Journal of Computing in Teacher Education (JCTE)*

professional development topics by attending or presenting sessions at these meetings. They usually range in duration from one to four days. To learn about conferences offered in particular content areas, visit the websites for the professional organizations listed in Figure 15.2. Professional development workshops are also offered online through various publishers.

Although this list is not exhaustive, it does include the most common sources teachers use during professional development. As we work to attain the goals we set in our professional development plans, we will engage in a variety of professional readings, courses, and conferences.

Final Thoughts about Professional Development

Professional development is an integral part of content area teaching. It emerges from students' needs, is collaborative in nature, and helps us, as teachers, to continue to learn. Wiggins and McTighe (2006) support teachers' ongoing engagement in professional development, and suggest that teachers should be professional learners:

> Teachers should engage in deep, broad study of the learning they are charged to cause. What works? What doesn't? Where is student learning most successful, and why? How can we learn from that success? Where are students struggling to learn, and why? What can we do about it? Effectively tackling these questions is what the "professional" in "professional practice" means. (p. 26)

Professional development provides a means for us to create responses to these queries.

FINAL THOUGHTS

Although education is a social process, it is a unique journey for each of us—one fortified by ever-growing knowledge in an ever-changing world. As Mtetwa and Kwari (2003) note:

> The information age has resulted in a rapid turnover of knowledge, making lifelong learning increasingly important . . . For teachers, this means they have to perceive themselves as learners even after pre-service education and the period of induction into professional practice. The challenge in education . . . is to provide quality opportunities for people to continue learning throughout their professional and everyday lives. (p. 273)

We hope we and our teaching careers will echo their thoughts.

Teaching Connections:

APPLYING WHAT WE HAVE LEARNED

E-Links

Consider how engaging in mentoring could benefit your teaching. (1) Think about the roles of mentor and mentee. (2) Consider how being a mentee could benefit you as a novice teacher. (3) Consider how being a mentor after you have taught for more than five years could enrich your teaching experience. Share your thinking with peers in small-group discussions, and then write a reflective entry in your portfolio.

Use information from websites such as these to support your thinking.

SAMPLE WEBSITES

Resources for Teacher Leadership: Mentoring and Coaching (Center for Science Education)
http://cse.edc.org/products/teacherleadership/mentoring.asp

Some Teacher Mentoring Resources (Middle Web—Exploring Middle School Reform)
http://www.middleweb.com/mentoring.html

Survival Guide for New Teachers
http://www.ed.gov/teachers/become/about/survivalguide/index.html

Accountable Talk

Consider the "new teacher challenges" discussed in the first section of this chapter. Reflect on the three issues that you think may be most challenging for you. Think about how you will prepare to address them, including specific ideas to manage such challenges. Share your thoughts in small-group discussions, and then record your ideas as a reflective entry in your portfolio.

 ### Portfolio/Performance Opportunity

Professional development is an essential component of teaching. For our final performance opportunity, we will engage in a special professional development project. We will complete small-group projects after we have used individual reflection to provide direction for our thinking.

To begin, imagine your first three years of teaching and predict a literacy-related professional development topic that could emerge from your students' learning. Then join a "study group" of people who wish to focus on a similar topic. After we explain and model the project, use the professional development resource, planning, and demonstration project assignment sheet; project outline; and rubric as guides to complete your groupwork. As you will notice, the project culminates in demonstrations that you and your group members will present to the whole class.

PROFESSIONAL DEVELOPMENT RESOURCE, PLANNING, AND DEMONSTRATION PROJECT ASSIGNMENT SHEET

The professional development resource, planning, and demonstration project has three focuses: (1) study-group investigations of current literacy emphases; (2) development of a 3-year professional development plan; and (3) development, presentation, and evaluation of collaborative professional development sessions. Appropriate dispositions related to reading and the teaching of content must be displayed during all stages of this project.

Part 1: Professional Development Study Groups

Begin by brainstorming professional development topics in which you have interest. Collaborative groups will be formed according to topic selection. Then the groups will review a variety of study modules and current articles related to the chosen topics. We will explain the supportive materials and work with a focus group to demonstrate how study groups function successfully. Finally, the study groups will engage in planning and goal setting and will schedule specific electronic meeting times. Throughout this experience, electronic reflective journals will be maintained.

Part 2: Professional Development Plan

Begin by imagining you have completed your degree and are working as a content area teacher serving a particular grade or grade range. Next, consider what your students' needs might be. Contemplate your professional development needs in that context and create a 3-year professional development plan. Your plan should be based on your professional development goals and should feature a variety of types of professional development, including both events in which you are a participant and events in which you are the professional development provider. Examples of the former include, but are not limited to, participating in district study groups, taking additional courses, attending conferences, and reading articles from professional journals. Examples of the latter include teaching in-district professional development courses; presenting at local, state, or national conferences; and writing articles for state, regional, or national journals. Include your Professional Develpoment Plan in your portfolio.

Part 3: Professional Development Presentation and Evaluation

Use a variety of quality resources and technology to collaboratively develop and present a one-hour professional development session. Include appropriate follow-up information about your study group's topic and Professional Development Plans. Provide quality, informative feedback as you observe, participate in, and evaluate each group's professional development presentation.

PROFESSIONAL DEVELOPMENT RESOURCE, PLANNING, AND PRESENTATION
PROJECT OUTLINE

I. Contents Page

List each component of the professional development resource, planning, and presentation project and its corresponding starting page.

II. Reflective Introduction

Express your thoughts about (a) professional development, (b) your personal professional development interests, (c) your study group's investigation, and (d) your personal professional development plan.

III. Part 1: Study Groups

Begin by reflecting on your study group's topic, what you have learned, and how you plan to use that information in your teaching.

Next, detail your review of the resources that your group used.

Finally, include your study group reflective journal entries.

IV. Part 2: Professional Development Plan

Begin by reflecting on your students' needs and your professional development goals. Explain how you determined them and how what you will learn will affect your teaching.

Next, explain how you plan to achieve your professional development goals.

Finally, include your completed three-year professional development plan.

V. Part 3: Professional Development Presentation and Evaluation

Work collaboratively using a variety of quality resources and technology to plan, create, and present a one-hour professional development session. Include appropriate follow-up information about your study group's topic and Professional Development Plans.

OVERVIEW OF SELECTED MATERIALS

Materials we will use to facilitate our study groups will include but not be limited to the following: *IRA Literacy Study Groups*

- Adolescent Literacy Module (2003)
- English Language Learners Module (2004)
- Reading Comprehension (2003)
- Vocabulary (2003)

The IRA Literacy Study Groups modules offer materials that are representative of research and classroom-tested practices. The resources in the module address instructional issues and provide many suggestions for teachers to consider in developing sound pedagogical practices that will lead their students to success in reading. Each module contains an IRA-published text, a facilitator's guide to help candidates organize the study group, a journal for recording ideas and personal reflections, and a discussion guide that offers related journal articles and study group activities.

The *Discussion Guide and Related Journal Articles* includes information on related IRA resources; abstracts of 6 articles from *Reading Online*; abstracts from 4 ReadWriteThink lesson plans; full text of 11 articles from *The Reading Teacher, Journal of Adolescent & Adult Literacy, Reading Research Quarterly, Thinking Classroom*, and *Reading Today;* and one book chapter from *What Research Has to Say about Reading Instruction,* third edition.

The Common Sense of Differentiation: Meeting Specific Learner Needs in the Regular Classroom DVD and Facilitator's Guide

This module (ASCD, 2003) is designed to help candidates differentiate instruction to meet the needs of a wide range of exceptionalities—students with one or more learning problems, students with varying degrees of English language proficiency, students with different interests, students who are very advanced, and students without a "label" but whose learning needs are just as unique. The module includes a DVD and an accompanying *Facilitator's Guide* that shows teachers how a differentiated approach helps meet students' needs when they follow these steps:

- Identify the learning needs of their students
- Understand learner needs that affect students' achievement of learning goals
- Adapt instructional plans to maximize success for each learner
- Create classroom routines that support differentiation

PROFESSIONAL DEVELOPMENT RESOURCE, PLANNING, AND PRESENTATION PROJECT RUBRIC

	4	3	2	1
Resource Review				
Display of Dispositions				
Professional Development Plan				
Use of Technology				
Professional Presentation				
Evaluation of Peers				

4   Excellent review of quality resources. Display of advanced dispositions related to reading and the teaching of content during collaborative study groups and peer observation, evaluation, and feedback. Meaningful, detailed, knowledge-based, three-year professional development plan that continues to foster the acquisition of professional knowledge and advanced dispositions. Fully developed and detailed use of numerous types of technology. Totally professional presentation, including knowledge base, appropriate display of advanced dispositions, technology use, and presentation methods. Excellent quality contributions to collaborative study groups and peer observation, evaluation, and feedback.

3   Skillful review of quality resources. Display of proficient dispositions related to reading and the teaching of content during collaborative study groups and peer observation, evaluation, and feedback. Thorough knowledge-based, three-year professional development plan that continues to foster the acquisition of professional knowledge and proficient dispositions. Good use of technology. Very professional presentation, including knowledge base, display of proficient dispositions, technology use, and presentation methods. Quality contributions to collaborative study groups and peer observation, evaluation, and feedback.

2   Adequate review of quality resources. Display of developing dispositions related to reading and the teaching of content during collaborative study groups and peer observation, evaluation, and feedback. Knowledge-based, three-year professional development plan that continues to foster the acquisition of professional knowledge and advanced dispositions in limited ways. Adequate use of technology. Somewhat professional presentation, including limited knowledge base, display of developing dispositions, technology use, and presentation methods. Satisfactory contributions to collaborative study groups and peer observation, evaluation, and feedback.

1   Inadequate review of resources. Display of unacceptable dispositions related to reading and the teaching of content during collaborative study groups and peer observation, evaluation, and feedback. Poorly designed 3-year professional development plan, including insufficient knowledge base, display of unacceptable dispositions, improper technology use, and ineffective presentation methods. Unsatisfactory contributions to collaborative study groups and peer observation, evaluation, and feedback.

Comprehension Strategy-Based Teaching Ideas and Blackline Masters

Gallery Images

Students use Gallery Images (Ogle, 2000) to represent text information through sketches. Students work in small groups when creating these images. This teaching idea, which is used after reading, supports comprehension strategies such as making connections, visualizing, and summarizing. (See blackline master, page 290.)

To teach your students how to use gallery images, follow these steps:

1. **Explain:** Gallery Images support multiple comprehension strategies, including making connections, visualizing, and summarizing. Explain that Gallery Images involve sketching ideas to represent text. Remind students that when we sketch we use simple lines and shapes.

2. **Demonstrate:** Introduce a text and read a segment aloud. Discuss the text with a small group of students. Suggest an image that you think represents the text. Sketch it on the Gallery Images blackline in the section labeled Image One. Discuss your sketch with the students. Then encourage the other members of the group to suggest an image and sketch it as Image Two on the Gallery Images blackline. Discuss how the two images represent the text. Post the Gallery Images in a section of the classroom where the students' images will be displayed.

3. **Guide:** Organize students into small groups and guide them to engage in Gallery Images. Read a different text aloud and invite students to read along silently. Then encourage them to discuss the text and create an image. Discuss the image.

4. **Practice:** Invite students to work with group members to create and discuss a second image. When the Gallery Images are

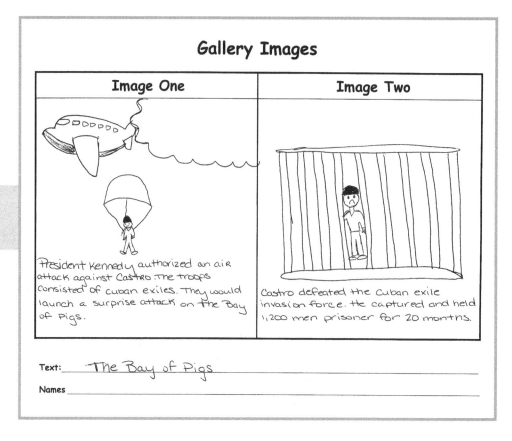

complete, encourage students to post them next to the images your group posted in the class gallery.

5 **Reflect:** Reflect on how we can make connections, visualize, and summarize when we use Gallery Images. Reflect on how using sketching to represent our thinking helps us to understand what we read.

Figure A.1 features an excerpt from Gallery Images about the Bay of Pigs incident. These Gallery Images were completed by students in a history class.

TEACHING IDEA

Genre Pyramids

Students use Genre Pyramids (Waldo, 1991) to summarize what happens in various types of literature, including mysteries. Students work with partners to create Genre Pyramids. This teaching idea, which is similar to the Narrative Pyramid and Bio-Pyramid, provides a structure for students to summarize what they have read. (See blackline master, page 435.)

To teach your students how to use Genre Pyramids, follow these steps:

1 **Explain:** Summarizing is a reading comprehension strategy that helps us to extract essential information from narrative text. When using the Genre Pyramid, we can include elements from a variety of genre. The Pyramid we will be completing today focuses on a mystery.

2 **Demonstrate:** Retell Edgar Allen Poe's "The Tell-Tale Heart." Invite students to contribute to the retelling. Distribute the Genre Pyramid blackline and demonstrate by completing

the first two lines. For example, you might say, "The first line asks us to identify the genre. I know that Poe's short story is a mystery, so I will write *mystery* on line 1. The information description for line 2 is 'victim,' so I will write *old man*, because I know he is the one who was murdered." Discuss the first two lines with the students.

3 **Guide:** Encourage students to work with partners to complete lines 3, 4, and 5. Discuss students' responses to each line as they are completed. After the students share their responses, continue to complete the demonstration Genre Pyramid.

4 **Practice:** Invite students to complete lines 6, 7, and 8. Discuss each line as it is completed. Then complete the remaining lines of the demonstration Genre Pyramid. Encourage each pair of students to share their completed Genre Pyramids with another pair of students. Invite a few students to share their pyramids with the class.

5 **Reflect:** Reflect on how we can summarize what we read using Genre Pyramids. Reflect on how completing Genre Pyramids helps us to understand what we read.

Figure A.2 features an example of a Genre Pyramid completed by students in their Short Story class. The genre is mystery and the Pyramid is about "The Tell-Tale Heart."

FIGURE A.2 Genre Pyramid: Mystery "The Tell-Tale Heart"

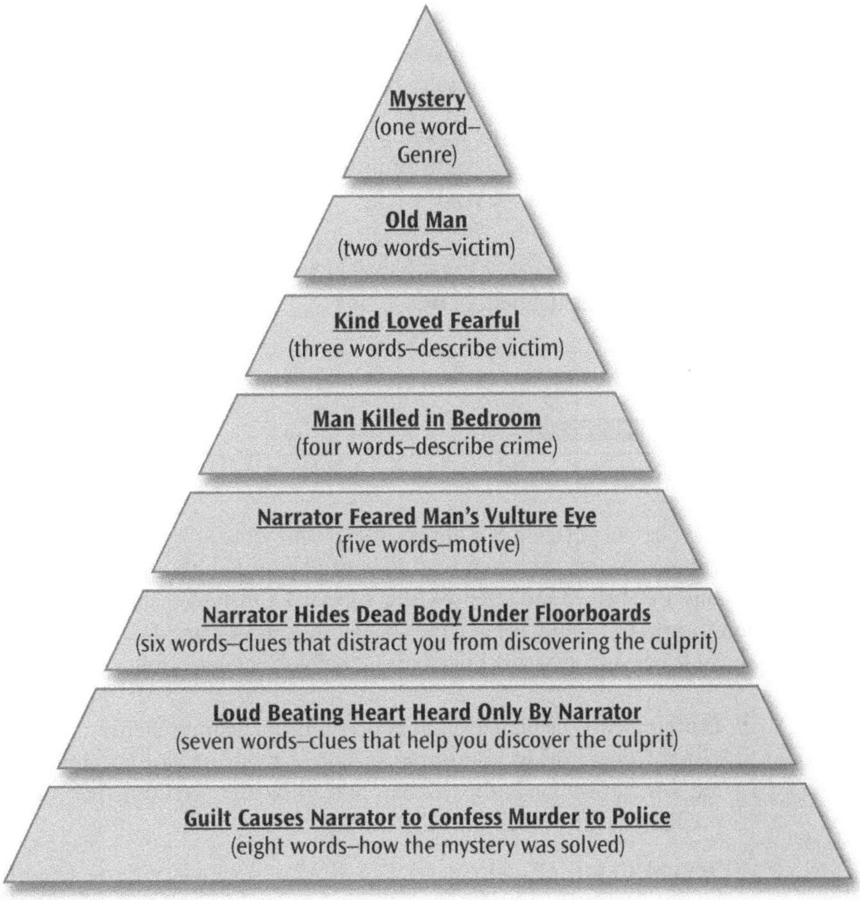

Mystery
(one word–Genre)

Old Man
(two words–victim)

Kind Loved Fearful
(three words–describe victim)

Man Killed in Bedroom
(four words–describe crime)

Narrator Feared Man's Vulture Eye
(five words–motive)

Narrator Hides Dead Body Under Floorboards
(six words–clues that distract you from discovering the culprit)

Loud Beating Heart Heard Only By Narrator
(seven words–clues that help you discover the culprit)

Guilt Causes Narrator to Confess Murder to Police
(eight words–how the mystery was solved)

TEACHING IDEA

List–Group–Label

Students use List–Group–Label (Maring, Furman, & Blum-Anderson, 1985) to preview and monitor information presented in informational text. This teaching idea is used before and after reading to activate background knowledge and to help students become familiar with how selected words relate to a concept and to other words.

To teach your students how to use List–Group–Label, follow these steps:

1 **Explain:** Explain that List–Group–Label relates to reading comprehension strategies, such as previewing and monitoring. Explain that List–Group–Label helps us refine our understanding of terms and their relation to other words.

2 **Demonstrate:** Provide a cue word or term and brainstorm examples of related words. Write your brainstormed examples on the chalkboard or overhead transparency. Think aloud about whether any of the brainstormed words should be deleted. Justify your changes. For example, if the cue term was *solar system*, you might brainstorm *Earth*, *Jupiter*, and *Sun*. You might decide the terms were appropriate and choose not to eliminate any of them.

3 **Guide:** Invite students to work with a partner to brainstorm additional words for the list. Add their responses to the master list. Then invite students to discuss whether any of the responses should be eliminated. Ask them to justify their thinking. Next, encourage the students to meet in groups of four to create clusters of words that relate to one another, and label each category with a descriptive term. Invite students to share their clusters and explain their thinking.

4 **Practice:** Invite students to read the text. Discuss the text and encourage students to revisit and revise their clusters as necessary. Discuss the final clusters with the students.

5 **Reflect:** Reflect on how we can use List–Group–Label to preview and monitor information. Reflect on how brainstorming, working with partners, and List–Group–Label help us to understand what we read.

Figure A.3 on page 374 features a List–Group–Label about the solar system that was completed in an earth science class.

TEACHING IDEA

Possible Sentences

Possible Sentences (Stahl & Kapinus, 1991) shows us how to use vocabulary to make predictions about content and then read to verify or modify those predictions. This teaching idea, which is used before and after reading, supports comprehension strategies such as previewing, monitoring, and summarizing. (See blackline master, page 377.)

To teach your students how to use Possible Sentences, follow these steps:

1 **Explain:** Possible Sentences supports multiple comprehension strategies, including previewing, monitoring, and summarizing. It involves using vocabulary to predict the information that will be in the text before reading and revisiting the words to verify or modify predictions after reading.

2 **Demonstrate:** Introduce several (6–8) new vocabulary terms from the text and several (4–6) words with which you think the students are already familiar. Think aloud as you discuss and define one word from each list. Then write a sentence using those two words.

Cue term: Solar system

Before reading: Brainstormed words and clusters

Stars	Planets	Dwarf Planets
Sun	Mercury	Pluto
	Venus	
	Earth	
	Mars	
	Jupiter	
	Saturn	
	Uranus	
	Neptune	

After reading: Revised class List–Group–Label

Stars	Planets	Dwarf Planets
Sun (Closest star to Earth)	Mercury	Pluto
	Venus	Ceres
	Earth	Eris
	Mars	Haumea
	Jupiter	Makemake
	Saturn	
	Uranus	
	Neptune	

FIGURE A.3
List–Group–Label about the Solar System

③ **Guide:** Invite students to work with partners to discuss and define the remaining words. Encourage students to work on their own to write sentences, using two vocabulary words in each sentence. Discuss their sentences.

④ **Practice:** Distribute a text and read it aloud to students. Invite them to read along silently. Then revisit the text, the definitions, and the sentences to verify that the words are defined and used correctly.

⑤ **Reflect:** Reflect on how we can preview, monitor, and summarize when we use Possible Sentences. Reflect on how predicting, verifying, and summarizing the information that will appear in text helps us understand what we read.

Figure A.4 on page 348 features Possible Sentences related to the Seneca Falls Convention about Women's Rights of 1848.

TEACHING IDEA

Story Impressions

In Story Impressions (McGinley & Denner, 1987), students use vocabulary to predict the content of a story and make connections between vocabulary and story structure. Story Impressions, which are usually used before reading, also provide a framework for narrative writing. They support reading comprehension strategies such as previewing and making connections. Each impression includes a maximum of ten clues, and each clue can be a maximum of five words. The clues are based on an existing story. As the teacher, it is your decision whether to share the title of the original story before reading the story later in the process. When using this teaching idea, students work in small groups and use a series of sequential clues based on the narrative elements to write a Story Impression—their prediction of the original story's content. (See blackline master, page 386.)

FIGURE A.4
Possible Sentences

> ### The Seneca Falls Convention about Women's Rights, 1848
>
> **I. New Words and Proposed Definitions**
>
> <u>Convention:</u> the summoning or convening of an assembly
> <u>Delegates:</u> a representative to a convention or conference
> <u>Quakers:</u> member of the Society of Friends
> <u>Legislation:</u> the exercise of the power and function of making rules
> <u>Sentiments:</u> attitudes, thoughts, or judgments prompted by feeling
> <u>Usurp:</u> to seize without right
>
> **II. Familiar Words and Proposed Definitions**
>
> <u>Antislavery:</u> opposition to slavery
> <u>Equality:</u> the state or quality of being equal
> <u>Declaration of Independence:</u> the public act by which the Second Continental Congress, on July 4, 1776, declared the Colonies to be free and independent of England
> <u>Resolution:</u> a formal expression of opinion or intention
>
> **III. Possible Sentences** (Use two vocabulary words in each sentence.)
>
> 1. The **delegates** discussed a **resolution** that had been introduced.
> 2. Those who attended the **convention** approved new **legislation**.
> 3. Many people believe in Martin Luther King, Jr.'s **antislavery sentiments**.
> 4. The **Quakers** supported **equality** for all.
> 5. We issued the **Declaration** of **Independence** so England could not usurp our rights.

To teach your students how to use Story Impressions, follow these steps:

1 **Explain:** Story Impressions support previewing and making connections. In this small-group activity, we use a list of sequential clues to write our impression of a story. Explain that it is important to use the clues in the order in which they appear and that after we write our impressions, we read them to the class and then listen to or read the original story. Later, we compare and contrast our story with the original.

2 **Demonstrate:** Share a sequential list of clues connected by downward arrows. Note that many of the clues represent narrative elements: characters, setting, problem, attempts to resolve, resolution. Remind students that these elements are present in every story. Then think aloud about how to include the first four clues in your Story Impression. For example, you might write, "A plane crashed, but Jack and Ralph survived."

3 **Guide:** Invite students to work in small groups as they continue to use the sequential clues to create their Story Impressions. Encourage them to use the next three clues to write the next part of the Story Impression.

4 **Practice:** Encourage students to use the remaining clues to write the rest of the story. Encourage them to share their completed Story Impressions with the class. Read the original story aloud, and ask students to compare and contrast their story with the original story.

5 **Reflect:** Reflect on how Story Impressions help us to predict text and make connections between the narrative elements and the story. Discuss how the sequential clues help to guide our writing.

Figure A.5 on page 349 features a Story Impression about *Lord of the Flies* that students completed in English class.

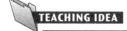 **TEACHING IDEA**

Summary Cubes

Students use Summary Cubes (McLaughlin & Allen, 2002b) to represent important information in text. Summary Cubes can easily be adapted for biography, mystery, or other genres.

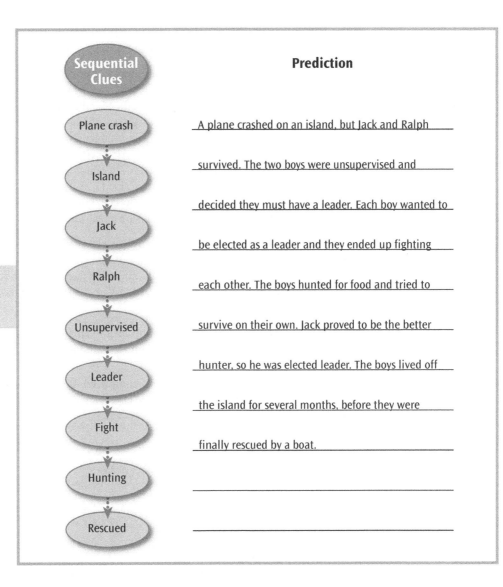

FIGURE A.5
Story Impression for
Lord of the Flies

Sequential Clues

- Plane crash
- Island
- Jack
- Ralph
- Unsupervised
- Leader
- Fight
- Hunting
- Rescued

Prediction

A plane crashed on an island, but Jack and Ralph

survived. The two boys were unsupervised and

decided they must have a leader. Each boy wanted to

be elected as a leader and they ended up fighting

each other. The boys hunted for food and tried to

survive on their own. Jack proved to be the better

hunter, so he was elected leader. The boys lived off

the island for several months, before they were

finally rescued by a boat.

Students select a topic and complete the cubes after reading by providing the information required on each side of the cube. They can use websites that you have bookmarked to confirm or gather further information. (See blackline master, page 387, or the electronic graphic found at www.readwritethink.org.)

To teach your students how to use Summary Cubes, follow these steps:

1. **Explain:** Summary Cubes help us to extract important information from narrative and informational text. The cubes can be adapted for use with a variety of genres, including biography (Bio-Cubes) and mystery (Mystery Cubes). Explain that today we will be completing a Bio-Cube and show the students one that has been completed. Explain that we will use the electronic graphic for Bio-Cubes and briefly explain how to complete it online.

2. **Demonstrate:** Read aloud a brief biography and think aloud about the information required for the Bio-Cube. For example, if you are creating a Bio-Cube about Dr. Martin Luther King, Jr., you might think aloud about Dr. King's name and note the years he lived and his place of birth as they were presented in the biography you read. Next, you might write, "M. L. King, Jr., 1929–1968, and Atlanta, Georgia," on the side labeled *Person's Name,*

Time Period, and Place of Birth. Then on the side labeled *Obstacle*, you might think of an obstacle Dr. King needed to overcome. For example, you might write "a segregated society."

3 Guide: Invite students to work with partners to complete the next side of the Bio-Cube. This side asks for information about Dr. King's background, so you would guide the students to locate background information in the biography. For example, they might suggest that Dr. King grew up during a time of segregation and his father taught him to stand up for what he believes. They might also suggest that Dr. King became a great speaker and civil rights leader. After a discussion, they could write their ideas on that section of the Bio-Cube. The next side requires information about Dr. King's personality. Invite the students to review the article and share words to describe Dr. King's personality. For example, they might say, "Dr. King was determined, passionate, kind, intelligent, and brave." Encourage students to write their responses on that side of the cube.

4 Practice: Encourage students to complete the remaining sides of the Bio-Cube, which include *Quotation* and *Significance*. When the students complete the Bio-Cube, invite them to construct their cube, glue it, and share it with another pair of students. Encourage students to discuss how their Bio-Cubes summarize the person's life. Display the completed cubes.

5 Reflect: Reflect on how extracting important information helps us understand what we read. Reflect on how Bio-Cubes help us understand biographies.

Figure A.6 features an example of a completed Bio-Cube about President Barack Obama that students completed in history class. They used the electronic organizer to complete their cube.

FIGURE A.6 Bio-Cube about Barack Obama

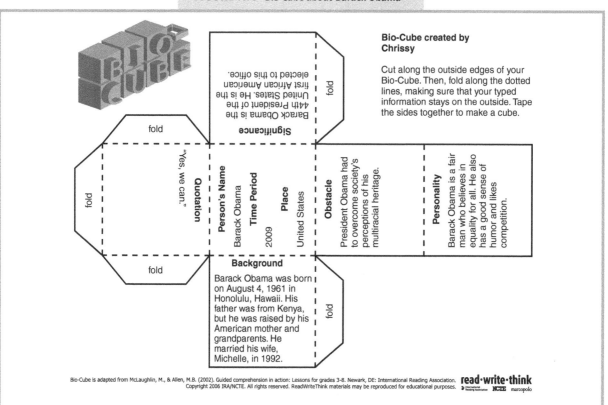

Bio-Cube created by Chrissy

Cut along the outside edges of your Bio-Cube. Then, fold along the dotted lines, making sure that your typed information stays on the outside. Tape the sides together to make a cube.

Significance
Barack Obama is the 44th President of the United States. He is the first African American elected to this office.

Quotation
"Yes, we can."

Person's Name
Barack Obama

Time Period
2009

Place
United States

Obstacle
President Obama had to overcome society's perceptions of his multiracial heritage.

Personality
Barack Obama is a fair man who believes in equality for all. He also has a good sense of humor and likes competition.

Background
Barack Obama was born on August 4, 1961 in Honolulu, Hawaii. His father was from Kenya, but he was raised by his American mother and grandparents. He married his wife, Michelle, in 1992.

That Was Then . . . This Is Now

That Was Then . . . This Is Now (McLaughlin & Allen, 2002b) provides a format for students to record their thinking before and after reading and compare and contrast their ideas. We can also use this teaching idea to activate background knowledge, create mental images before and after reading, and write summary statements. That Was Then . . . This Is Now can be used with narrative and informational text and supports comprehension strategies such as previewing, visualizing, and summarizing. (See blackline master, page 388.)

To teach your students how to use That Was Then . . . This Is Now, follow these steps:

1 Explain: Explain that when we use That Was Then . . . This Is Now, we sketch our thoughts about a specific topic prior to reading and write a summary statement. Next, explain that we read a text and then sketch our thoughts about what we have read and write a summary statement. Finally, we compare and contrast our thinking before and after reading.

2 Demonstrate: Self-select a topic related to the class's current studies. Think aloud as you sketch what you currently know about the topic. Create a sketch and write a summary statement. Discuss the sketch and the statement. Then introduce a brief new text, read it, and discuss it with the students. Next, create a sketch representative of your thoughts after reading and write a summary statement about it. Discuss it with the students, focusing on comparisons (similarities) and contrasts (differences) concerning your thoughts before and after reading.

3 Guide: Guide students to engage in That Was Then . . . This Is Now by self-selecting a current topic of study. Encourage them to create a sketch about what they know and write a summary statement. Invite them to share their sketches and statements with a peer. Then provide a brief new text for each student to read silently.

4 Practice: Encourage students to complete the This Is Now portion of the blackline by creating a sketch and writing a summary statement. Invite them to share their sketches and thoughts with a peer. Engage the students in discussion about comparisons and contrasts concerning their before and after reading sketches and summary statements.

5 Reflect: Encourage students to think about what they learned from their reading. Invite them to share their ideas about how That Was Then . . . This Is Now helps us to understand what we read.

Figure A.7 on page 352 features That Was Then . . . This Is Now about cloning completed by a student in science class.

Thinking Hats

Thinking Hats (DeBono, 1985) is a teaching idea that supports summarizing and evaluating. Students use Thinking Hats to represent multiple perspectives about a topic. Small groups of students engage in this teaching idea, which is completed after reading. (See blackline master, page 390.)

To teach your students how to use Thinking Hats, follow these steps:

1 Explain: Thinking Hats supports reading comprehension strategies such as summarizing and evaluating. It involves determining different perspectives that exist within a content area event, such as the Revolutionary War, the debate about whether the world was flat in the time of Columbus, the pursuit of flight by scientists such as DaVinci and the Wright brothers, or characters from a short story, novel, or play. Explain that once the event has been determined, we must select five roles that were meaningful in terms of the event.

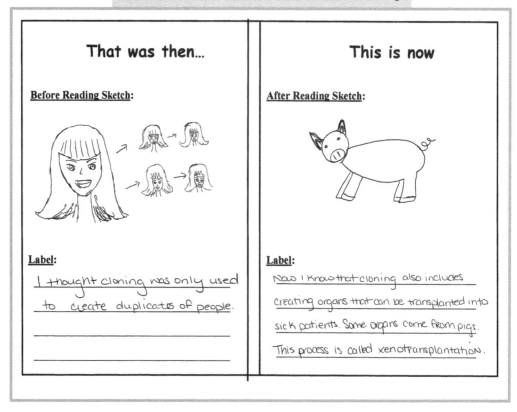

FIGURE A.7 That Was Then . . . This Is Now about Cloning

Finally, explain that this is a small-group activity and that each student is responsible for sharing a perspective.

2 **Demonstrate:** Model Thinking Hats with four students whom you have preselected. Discuss possible topics with the students and select one. Then brainstorm different perspectives that are associated with that topic. Record the different perspectives and indicate what each might say on the Thinking Hats graphic organizer. Provide sufficient time for each group member to choose a perspective and investigate it briefly to expand the knowledge she already has about the topic and the perspective. When the students are ready, gather them in a circle and engage in Thinking Hats by conducting a discussion in which each group member takes on the identity and perspective of one of the individuals associated with this topic.

3 **Guide:** Invite students to engage in Thinking Hats by choosing a topic and brainstorming perspectives. Encourage them to record their thoughts on the Thinking Hats graphic organizer. Invite each student to choose a perspective to represent and read additional information from that point of view. Then guide students to meet in small groups to discuss the event or work from multiple perspectives. The rest of the class should observe while one group is sharing ideas.

4 **Practice:** Encourage other groups to share their versions of Thinking Hats, while class members observe. Discuss Thinking Hats and the value of viewing events from multiple perspectives.

5 **Reflect:** Reflect on how we can engage in summarizing and evaluating when we use Thinking Hats. Discuss how viewing events from multiple perspectives helps us to understand what we read at deeper levels.

Figure A.8 features the Thinking Hats planner developed by a group of students who presented multiple perspectives from Shakespeare's *Romeo and Juliet*.

FIGURE A.8 Excerpt from Thinking Hats about *Romeo and Juliet*

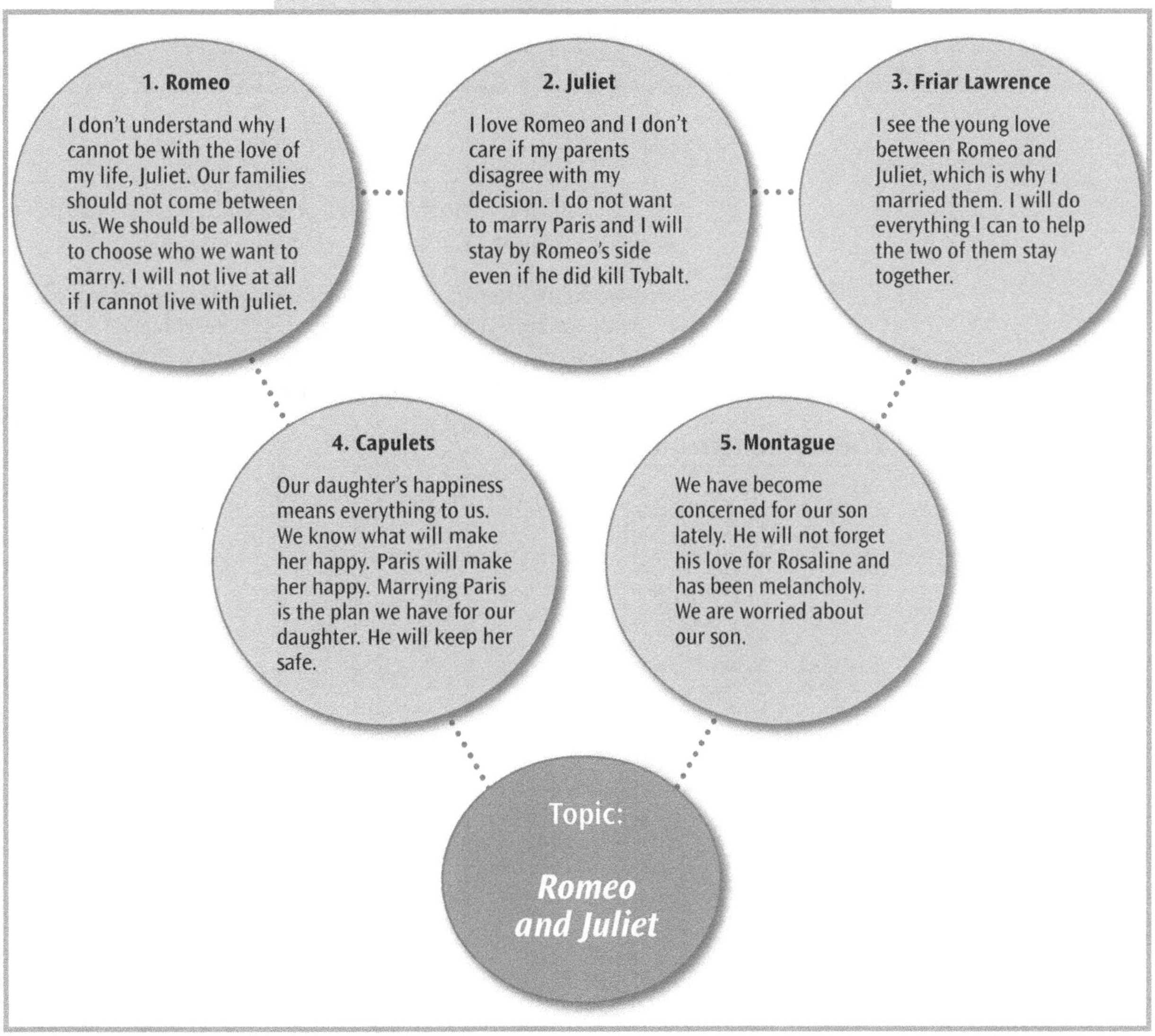

1. Romeo

I don't understand why I cannot be with the love of my life, Juliet. Our families should not come between us. We should be allowed to choose who we want to marry. I will not live at all if I cannot live with Juliet.

2. Juliet

I love Romeo and I don't care if my parents disagree with my decision. I do not want to marry Paris and I will stay by Romeo's side even if he did kill Tybalt.

3. Friar Lawrence

I see the young love between Romeo and Juliet, which is why I married them. I will do everything I can to help the two of them stay together.

4. Capulets

Our daughter's happiness means everything to us. We know what will make her happy. Paris will make her happy. Marrying Paris is the plan we have for our daughter. He will keep her safe.

5. Montague

We have become concerned for our son lately. He will not forget his love for Rosaline and has been melancholy. We are worried about our son.

Topic:

Romeo and Juliet

Blackline Masters for Comprehension-Based Teaching Ideas

Blackline masters for comprehension-based teaching ideas appear in this section. The blacklines support the teaching ideas featured in the book chapters, as well as those included at the start of this Appendix. These forms may be copied for classroom use.

BLACKLINE MASTERS FOR TEACHING IDEAS

Bio Pyramid

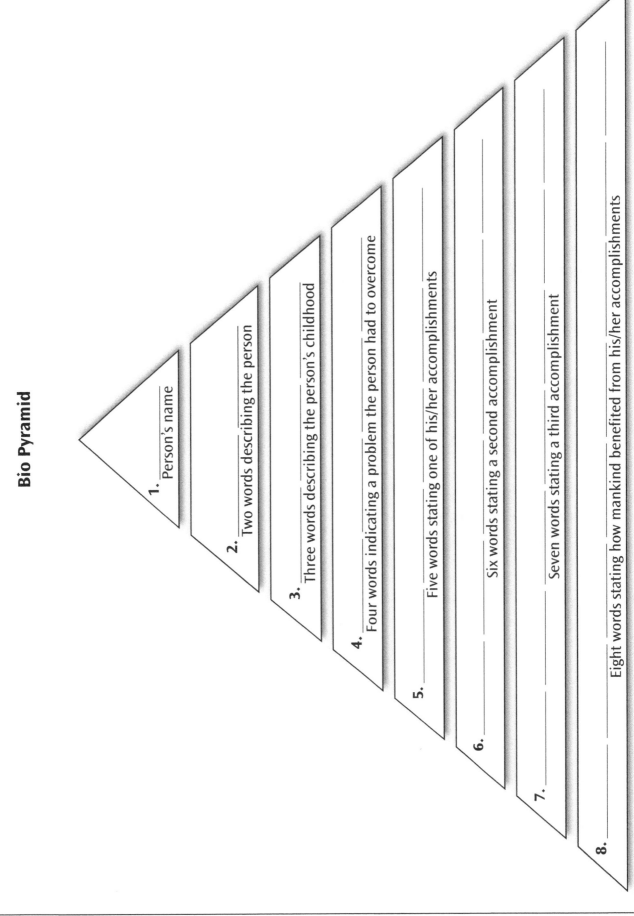

1. Person's name

2. Two words describing the person

3. Three words describing the person's childhood

4. Four words indicating a problem the person had to overcome

5. Five words stating one of his/her accomplishments

6. Six words stating a second accomplishment

7. Seven words stating a third accomplishment

8. Eight words stating how mankind benefited from his/her accomplishments

Bookmark One

Name _____

The part I found most interesting was

I thought it was interesting because

Page _____

Paragraph _____

Bookmark Two

Name _____

Something that confused me was

It confused me because

Page _____

Paragraph _____

Bookmark Three

Name _____

A word I think the whole class needs to talk about is

I think it means

Page _____

Paragraph _____

Bookmark Four

Name _____

The illustration, chart, map, or graph that helped me understand what I was reading was

It helped me to understand because

Page _____

Paragraph _____

Concept of Definition Map

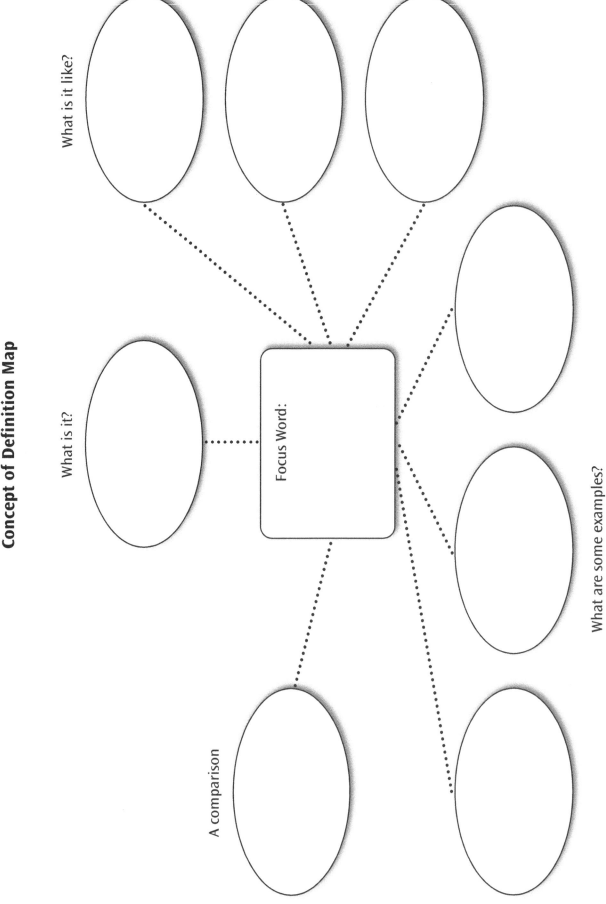

What is it like?

What is it?

Focus Word:

What are some examples?

A comparison

Concept of Definition Map Split Page with Summary Space
Concept of Definition Map

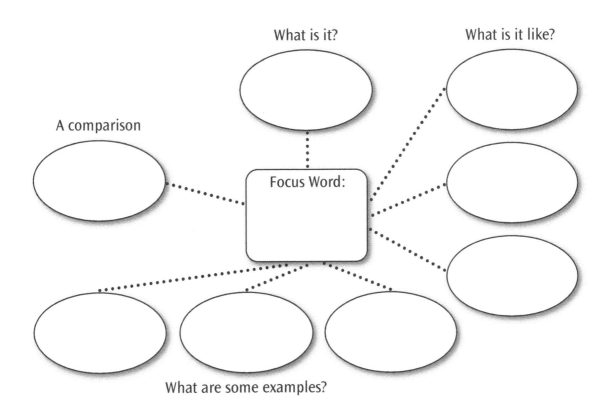

What is it?

What is it like?

A comparison

Focus Word:

What are some examples?

Concept of Definition Map Summary

_____

_____

_____

_____

_____

_____

_____

Contrast Chart

	1.	
	2.	
	3.	
	4.	
	5.	
	1.	
	2.	
	3.	
	4.	
	5.	

Discussion Web

Yes		
Reasons	**Discussion Topic/Question**	**Conclusion**
No		**Reason**

Gallery Images

Image One	Image Two

Text: _____

Name: _____

Genre Pyramid—Mystery

(one word—Genre)

(two words—victim)

(three words—describe victim)

(four words—describe crime)

(five words—motive)

(six words—clues that distract you from discovering the culprit)

(seven words—clues that help you discover the culprit)

(eight words—how the mystery was solved)

Guided Imagery

Name _____   **Date** _____

Describe image 1:

_____

_____

_____

_____

_____

_____

_____

Describe image 2:

_____

_____

_____

_____

_____

_____

_____

"I Wonder . . ." Bookmark

"I Wonder" Bookmark	"I Wonder" Bookmark
Page: _____	**Page:** _____
I wonder . . .	I wonder . . .
_____	_____
_____	_____
_____	_____
because . . .	because . . .
_____	_____
_____	_____
_____	_____
Page: _____	**Page:** _____
I wonder . . .	I wonder . . .
_____	_____
_____	_____
_____	_____
because . . .	because . . .
_____	_____
_____	_____
_____	_____

INSERT (Interactive Notation System to Effective Reading and Thinking) (Bookmarks)

INSERT Bookmark I

✓ = I knew that!

+ = I didn't know that!

− = I thought differently.

? = What does this mean?

_____

Page: _____

I knew that!

Page: _____

I knew that!

INSERT Bookmark II

✓ = I knew that!

+ = I didn't know that!

− = I thought differently.

? = What does this mean?

_____

Page: _____

I didn't know that!

Page: _____

I didn't know that!

INSERT Bookmark III

✓ = I knew that!

+ = I didn't know that!

– = I thought differently.

? = What does this mean?

_____

Page: _____

I thought differently.

Page: _____

I thought differently.

INSERT Bookmark IV

✓ = I knew that!

+ = I didn't know that!

– = I thought differently.

? = What does this mean?

_____

Page: _____

What does this mean?

Page: _____

What does this mean?

KWDL

Topic: _____

K (What I know)	W (What I want to know)	D (What I did)	L (What I learned)

KWL

Topic: _____

K (What I know or think I know)	W (What I want to know)	L (What I learned)

KWLS

Topic: _____

K (What I know or think I know)	W (What I want to know)	L (What I learned)	S (What I still want to know)

Mind and Alternative Mind Portraits

Mind Portrait

Reasoning:

Alternative Mind Portrait

Reasoning:

Narrative Pyramid

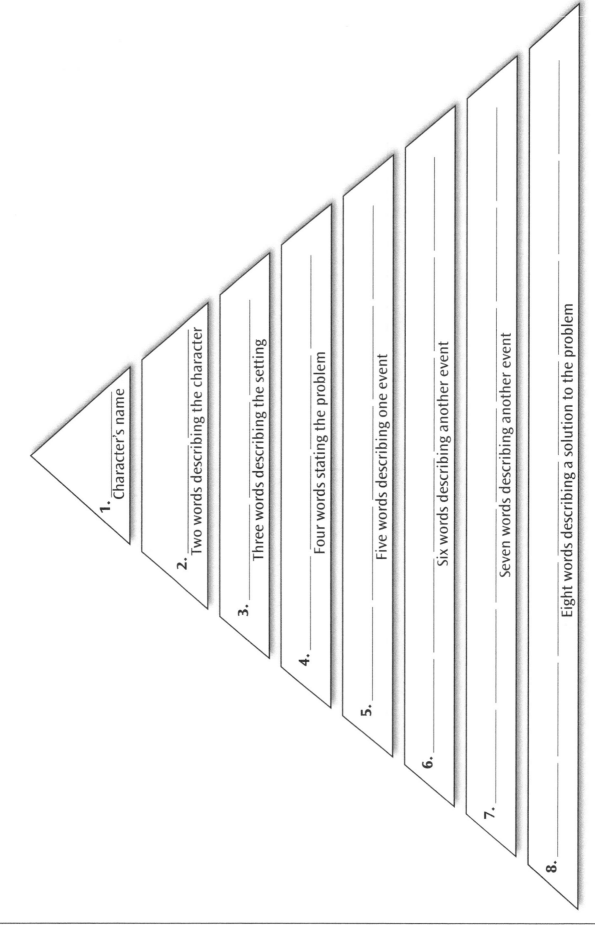

1. ___ Character's name

2. ___ Two words describing the character

3. ___ Three words describing the setting

4. ___ Four words stating the problem

5. ___ Five words describing one event

6. ___ Six words describing another event

7. ___ Seven words describing another event

8. ___ Eight words describing a solution to the problem

Narrative Pyramid: Adapted

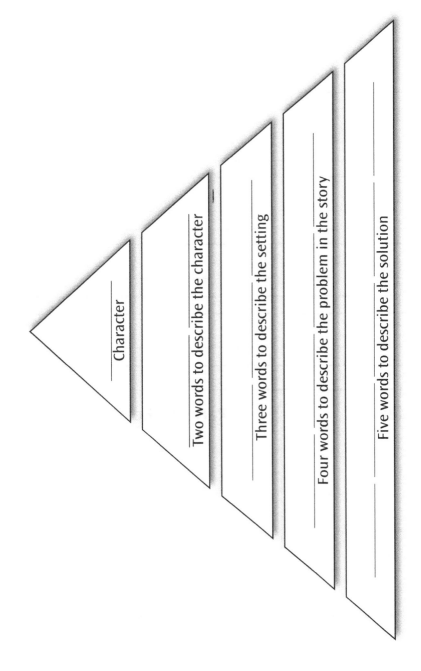

Character

_____ _____

Two words to describe the character

Three words to describe the setting

Four words to describe the problem in the story

Five words to describe the solution

Paired Questioning

Name: _____ **Date:** _____

Question 1: _____

Question 2: _____

Question 3: _____

Question 4: _____

Question 5: _____

Question 6: _____

Important Ideas	**Partner's Reasoning**
_____	_____
_____	_____
_____	_____
_____	_____

Paired Summarizing

Name: _____   **Date:** _____

My Summary	Summary of My Partner's Work
_____	_____
_____	_____
_____	_____
_____	_____
_____	_____
_____	_____
_____	_____
_____	_____
_____	_____
_____	_____
_____	_____

Photographs of the Mind

1	2
3	**4**

Possible Sentences

Name _____   Date _____

New Words	Proposed Definitions
1. _____	_____
2. _____	_____
3. _____	_____
4. _____	_____
5. _____	_____
6. _____	_____

Familiar Words	Proposed Definitions
1. _____	_____
2. _____	_____
3. _____	_____
4. _____	_____
5. _____	_____
6. _____	_____

Sentences (Use two vocabulary words—one from each list—in each sentence.)

1. _____

2. _____

3. _____

4. _____

5. _____

6. _____

Prereading Plan (PreP)

Name: _____   Date: _____

Cue Word(s): _____

Brainstormed Words/Concepts	Reasons for Choosing Words/Concepts
1. _____	1. _____ _____
2. _____	2. _____ _____
3. _____	3. _____ _____
4. _____	4. _____ _____
5. _____	5. _____ _____

Question-Answer Relationships (QAR)

- **In the text**

<u>Right There:</u> The answer is within one sentence in the text.

Example: _____

<u>Think and Search:</u> The answer is contained in more than one sentence in the text.

Example: _____

- **In my head**

<u>Author and You:</u> The answer is information from your background knowledge and the text.

Example: _____

<u>On Your Own:</u> The answer is information from only your background knowledge.

Example: _____

QuIP Research Grid

Topic: _____

Questions	Answers	
	Source 1:	Source 2:
A.		
B.		
C.		

QuIP (Split Page with Paragraph Space)

QuIP Research Grid

Topic: _____

Questions	Answers	
	Source 1:	Source 2:
A.		
B.		
C.		

QuIP Paragraph

_____

_____

_____

_____

_____

_____

_____

Save the Last Word for Me

Side 1: Choose an idea, phrase, quote, concept, word, or fact from the text that interests or intrigues you and write it below.

Name: _____	Date: _____

Side 2: Explain why you chose what you wrote on side 1 or share your reaction to it.

Name: _____	Date: _____

Semantic Feature Analysis

Characteristics

Categories							

Semantic Question Map

Name _____

Date _____

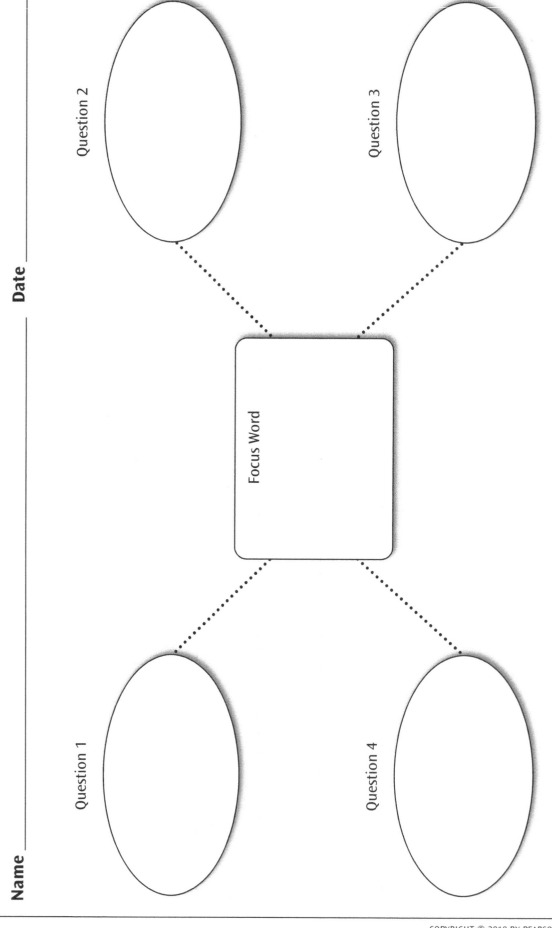

Question 1

Question 2

Question 3

Question 4

Focus Word

Sketch and Label Connections

Name: _____   **Date:** _____

Sketch

Label

_____

_____

_____

_____

Story Impression

Sequential Clues

Prediction

Summary Cube Model

This Is Now . . . .

After Reading Sketch:

Label: ____ ____ ____ ____

That Was Then . . . .

Before Reading Sketch:

Label: ____ ____ ____ ____

Thick and Thin Questions

Text: _____

Page	Thin Questions	**Thick Questions**

Thinking Hats

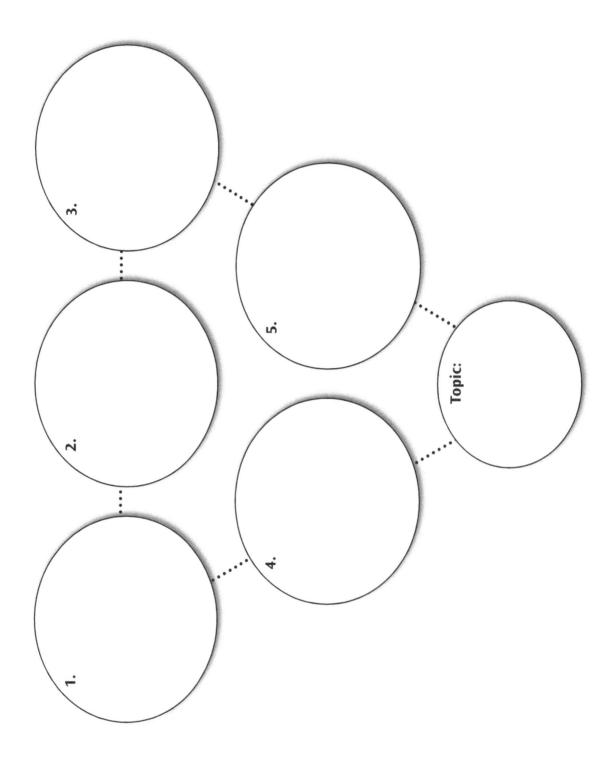

3.

2.

1.

5.

4.

Topic:

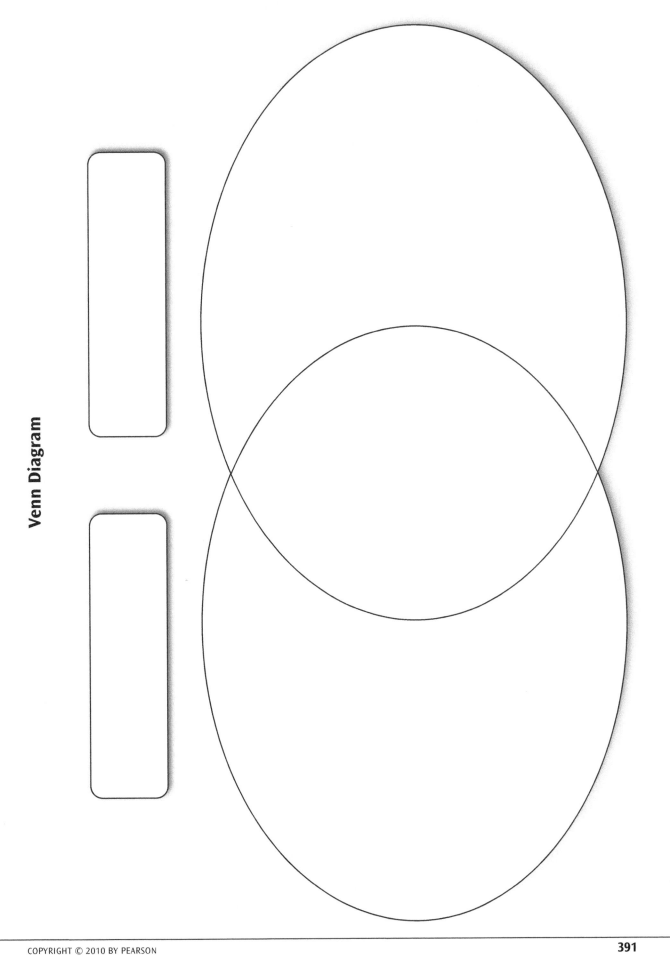

Venn Diagram

Vocabulary Bookmark

Name _____

Bookmark Three

A word I think the whole class needs to talk about is

I think it means

Page _____

Paragraph _____

Name _____

Bookmark Three

A word I think the whole class needs to talk about is

I think it means

Page _____

Paragraph _____

Appendix B

Skills

Discussion Circle Role Bookmarks

Discussion Director

- Choose topics for discussion.

- Ask questions.

- Convene the group meeting.

- Ensure that all members contribute.

Discussion Questions:

1. _____

   _____

   _____

2. _____

   _____

   _____

3. _____

   _____

   _____

4. _____

   _____

   _____

Passage Selector

- Select memorable or important sections of the text.

- Read them aloud for group.

Memorable Passages:

1. Page _____

   It is about _____

   _____

   _____

2. Page _____

   It is about _____

   _____

   _____

3. Page _____

   It is about _____

   _____

   _____

Connector

- Share text-self, text-text, and text-world connections.

- Encourage other group members to make connections.

Text-Self Connections:

Text-Text Connections:

Text-World Connections:

Illustrator

- Sketch visual response

- Use it to encourage others to contribute to the conversation.

Share Sketch

Explain how it relates to the text.

Invite group members to discuss it.

Word Finder

• Locate interesting words.

• Note where they are located in the text.

• Invite group to turn to the page where each word appears.

• Propose definitions based on their use in context.

Word: _____

Page: _____ Paragraph: _____

Proposed Definition: _____

_____

_____

Word: _____

Page: _____ Paragraph: _____

Proposed Definition: _____

_____

_____

Word: _____

Page: _____ Paragraph: _____

Proposed Definition: _____

_____

_____

Generating Questions

Directions: Revisit our text and create one question for each of Ciardiello's four levels:

> **Memory:** Who, what, where, when?
> **Convergent:** Why, how, in what ways?
> **Divergent:** Imagine, suppose, predict, if/then
> **Evaluative:** Defend, judge, justify/what do you think?

Memory Level

_____

_____

Convergent Level

_____

_____

Divergent Level

_____

_____

Evaluative Level

_____

_____

Standards-Based Lesson Plan:
Engaging, Guiding, and Extending Student Thinking

I.   **Goals and Related State Standards**

II. **Bibliographic Information for Text(s) and Additional Materials**

III. **Engaging Students' Thinking (Before Reading)**

IV. **Guiding Students' Thinking (During Reading)**

V.   **Extending Students' Thinking (After Reading)**

VI. **Assessments**

Roots

Root	Meaning	Example
anthropo	man	anthropology
astro	star	astronaut
bio	life	biology
cardio	heart	cardiac
cede	go	precede
chromo	color	chromatology
demos	people	democracy
derma	skin	epidermis
dyna	power	dynamic
geo	earth	geology
helio	sun	heliocentric
hydro	water	hydroponics
hypno	sleep	hypnosis
ject	throw	eject
magni	great, big	magnify
man(u)	hand	manuscript
mono	one	monoplane
ortho	straight	orthodox
pod	foot	podiatrist
psycho	mind	psychology
pyro	fire	pyromania
script	write	manuscript
terra	earth	terrace
thermo	heat	thermometer
zoo	animal	zoology

Prefixes

Prefix	Meaning(s)	Example
ab-, abs-, a-	from, away	abstain
ad-	to, toward	addict
ambi-	both	ambidextrous
ante-	before	antecedent
anti-	against	antifreeze
auto-	self	autobiography
be-	near, about	beside
bene-	well, good	benefactor
bi-	two	bimonthly
cata-	below	catacomb
centi-	hundred	centimeter
circum-	around	circumnavigate
con-	with	concert
contra-	against	contraband
de-	from, down	depress
deci-	ten	decimeter
di-	two	diameter
dia-	through	diagram
dis-	opposite	disrespect
dys-	bad	dysfunctional
en-, em-	cause to	encode
epi-	upon	epidermis
ex-	out, from	excavate
extra-	beyond	extracurricular
for-	off, to the utmost	forward
fore-	before	forecast
hetero-	different	heterogeneous
hyper-	beyond, excess	hyperactive
hypo-	too little, under	hypoactive
in-, il-, im-, ir-	not	immature
in-, im-	in	infringe
inter-	between	interstate
intra-	within	intramurals

intro-	within	introspection
juxta-	near	juxtapose
macro-	large	macrobiology
meta-	beyond, denoting change	metamorphosis
micro-	small	microbiology
mid-	middle	midway
milli-	thousand	millipede
mis-	bad	misbehave
mono-	single	monotone
nano-	billion	nanosecond
neo-	new	neoclassical
non-	not, opposite from	nonviolent
omni-	all	omnipotent
out-	beyond, more than	outlaw
over-	too much	overcompensate
pan-	all	panoramic
para-	side by side, near	paraphrase
per-	throughout	pervade
peri-	all around	periscope
poly-	many	polygon
post-	after	postpone
pre-	before	predetermine
pro-	forward	progress
prot-	first	prototype
re-	again	reappear
retro-	back	retrospect
semi-	half, partly	semicircle
sub-	under	submarine
super-	more than	supermarket
syn-, sym-	together	symbol
trans-	across	transatlantic
ultra-	beyond, extremely	ultraconservative
un-	not	unwilling
with-	against	withhold

Suffixes

Suffix	Meaning(s)	Example
-able, -ible	can be done	comfortable
-al, -ial	relating to	personal
-arium	place of	solarium
-ation, -ition, -ion, -tion	act, process of	animation
-dom	quality/state	freedom
-ed	past tense for verbs	voted
-en	made of	wooden
-er, -est	comparative	harder
-er	one who	dancer
-ful	full of	hopeful
-ic	relating to	characteristic
-ile	quality/state	juvenile
-ing	present participle	hopping
-ism	quality/state	pauperism
-ist	one who practices	zoologist
-ity, -ty	state of	infinity
-ive, -itive, -ative	adjective form of a noun	quantitative
-less	without	homeless
-ly	characteristic of	happily
-ment	action or process	excitement
-ness	condition of	sadness
-ology	study of	biology
-ous, -eous, -ious	quality, state	joyous
-s, -es	more than one	desks
-tion	quality, state	preservation
-ular	relating to	cellular
-y	characterized by	jumpy

Study Guide

I. Making Connections to What We Know (Activating Background Knowledge):

_____

_____

_____

_____

_____

II. Overview of Content

_____

_____

_____

_____

_____

III. Key Vocabulary

Word   Page   Predicted Meaning

1. _____   _____   _____

_____

2. _____   _____   _____

_____

3. _____ _____ _____

_____

IV. Sketch and Label Key Ideas.

Sketch	Sketch
Label	**Label**

V. Summary Statement

_____

_____

_____

VI. Questions about the Text

_____

_____

_____

Evaluation of a Content Area Textbook

Directions: 1. Please work with a partner to evaluate a content area textbook.

2. Both of you should record your responses on separate copies of the Evaluation of a Content Area Textbook form.

3. When you and your partner have finished completing your forms and you have shared what you have learned with others, please work on your own to write a summary of the information you recorded on your form and, based on what you have learned, explain whether you would use this textbook in your teaching. Justify your thinking.

4. When you have completed this project, remember to put your completed form and your "Summary and Explanation" into your portfolio.

Text Title: _____

Text Series: _____

Publisher: _____

Copyright Year: _____

Cost: _____

Authors: _____

_____

_____

In reviewing the textbook, your question is this: **Are the following qualities present in the text you are examining?** If your answer is "yes," provide an example of it from the text along with the page number on which the example is located. If your answer is "no," explain whether you would be able to teach effectively if this quality were not present in the textbook.

Evaluation of a Content Area Textbook (Continued)

1. Is the text well-organized (contents, glossary, index, chapter structures)?

2. Is the text factually correct? (Review pages at the beginning, middle, and end of the text to determine if they are factually correct. Include examples of factual text from each page you review.)

3. Is the text motivational? (Is it the kind of text that you think would motivate students at that grade level to learn? Is it colorful? Does it have pictures? Does it include graphics? If you were a student, would you want to use this book?)

4. What is the readability level of the text? For which grade was the textbook developed?

5. Does the textbook support state content standards? Is there evidence of standards-based learning? (Does the text include state standards? Does the textbook indicate which standards the content addresses? What are three examples of standards that are included?)

6. Does the teacher's edition support teachers' use of a strategy-based lesson plan? (Does the text promote using a lesson format similar to the one we have learned—engaging, guiding, and extending student thinking? If so, provide examples.)

7. Is the content diverse? (Is there evidence of multiculturalism in the text? Are people with special needs represented? Are genders treated equally in the text?)

8. Does the text require students to use skills and strategies? (Skill examples would include generating questions and recognizing text patterns. Strategy examples would include previewing—such as the Semantic Map; monitoring—such as Bookmark Technique and Patterned Partner Reading; making connections—such as Connection Stems; knowing how words work—such as the Concept of Definition Map; summarizing—such as the Lyric Summary, Concept of Definition Map Summary, and Bio-Pyramid; and evaluating—such as the Discussion Web.)

9. Does the text integrate content literacy? (Using reading, writing, speaking, listening, and viewing across the curriculum?)

10. Does the text focus on meeting the needs of individual learners? (English language learners, struggling readers, special needs students?)

11. Are multiple types of assessment used throughout the text? (Chapter questions, projects, research, tests, teacher observation?)

12. Are students asked to engage in higher-order thinking throughout the text?

Evaluation of a Content Area Textbook (Continued)

13. How is technology represented throughout the text? How are the students asked to use technology? Teachers?

14. Is a teacher's edition available? Are there special resources for English learners, struggling learners, special needs students?

15. Are the charts, maps, graphs, tables, and illustrations accurate? Do they help to support students' thinking?

16. Are supplementary materials available (text on CD, leveled texts, videos)?

BLACKLINE MASTERS

Writing

Admit Slip

What I already know about this topic:

_____

_____

_____

_____

_____

_____

_____

Questions I have about this topic:

1. _____

_____

2. _____

_____

3. _____

_____

4. _____

_____

Content Literacies History Prompts

These prompts have been developed to guide you in creating a history of your content literacies. This is not a definitive list of questions to which you should respond, but rather a sequence of ideas intended to stimulate your thinking about the development of your content literacies, starting with your earliest memories. As you listen to your professor's content literacies history, notice that while he or she may have chosen to include many of the ideas expressed in the prompts, they were not used to restrict your professor's thinking. Use the same creative freedom as you write about your experiences.

Early Memories

1. What are your earliest recollections of reading and writing?

2. Were you read to as a child?

3. Before you were able to read, did you pretend to read books? Can you remember the first time you read a book?

4. As a child, did you read and/or write with your siblings or friends?

5. Can you recall your early writing attempts (scribbling, labeling drawings, and so on)?

6. Was a newspaper delivered to your home? Do you recall seeing others read the newspaper? Did you read the newspaper?

7. Did you subscribe to children's magazines? Did your parents or siblings have magazine subscriptions?

8. Did your parents belong to a book club? Did they maintain a personal library? Did they read for pleasure?

9. Can you recall seeing family members making lists and receiving/sending mail?

10. Did you receive and send mail (such as birthday cards, thank-you notes, and letters) when you were a child?

11. Can you remember any other indications that reading and writing were valued in the environment in which you grew up?

12. What are your early memories of math?

13. What do you recall about using math while playing?

14. What do you remember about using money or seeing money used at this age?

15. What do you recall about historic events that may have occurred early in your life?

16. Do you remember how science may have impacted your life when you were very young?

Content Literacy Prompts (Continued)

School Memories

17. What can you recall about your first memories of reading/writing instruction? Materials used? Methods of teaching? Content?

18. What can you recall about reading for pleasure in elementary school?

19. What can you recall about writing for pleasure in elementary school?

20. What can you recall about the first book you chose to read in elementary school?

21. What can you recall about your first writing assignment in elementary school?

22. Did you write a report in elementary school? What do you remember about this experience?

23. Do you remember the purposes for your reading and writing in elementary school? Do you recall any particular type of instruction you received? Can you describe any instructional materials that were used?

24. What memories do you have of learning vocabulary?

25. When you were in school, what would you have described as the three most important things you learned in content area classes?

26. What do you remember about how you were taught in content area subjects?

27. What do you recall about how you used math and other subjects outside of school?

28. What specific experiences do you recall from your content area classes (math, science, history, English, foreign language) in elementary school? Middle school? High school?

29. Describe people or activities that helped you learn in the content areas.

30. Did you enjoy math class at any particular grade level? Why? Why not?

31. Do you feel comfortable using math now? Why? Why not?

32. If you could change one thing about your experiences in learning in the content areas, what would it be? How would you change it?

33. Did you have a library card when you were in elementary school? Did you use it then? In later school years?

34. Did you consider yourself to be a reader when you were in middle school?

35. Were you required to read certain books when you were in high school? How did you feel about that?

Content Literacy Prompts (Continued)

Reading for Pleasure and Social Purposes

36. Can you recall the first book you "couldn't put down"?

37. Have you ever read a book that has made a difference in your life?

38. Have you ever read a book that you knew had been challenged or censored? How did you feel about reading it?

39. Can you recall pleasurably sharing books with friends?

40. Did you read a certain type of book such as mysteries or biographies) at a particular age? Why do you think you made such choices?

41. When did you first visit a bookstore? What was it like?

42. What is your all-time favorite children's book? Novel? Nonfiction work?

43. Have you ever seen a book you've read turned into a film? Describe that experience.

44. Have there been times in your life when you have viewed reading as a pleasurable activity?

45. Have there been times in your life when you have not viewed reading as a pleasurable activity?

46. What contributions have your reading and writing abilities made to your life?

47. Are you a reader now?

48. Are you a writer now?

49. Do you feel comfortable modeling reading and writing in your content areas for your students?

50. What are you currently reading? Writing?

Information Literacy

51. How would you describe your first experience using a computer?

52. How do you use the Internet in your academic work?

53. How do you use a computer in your everyday life?

54. Why do you communicate through e-mail?

55. Which aspects of technology are you comfortable using?

Content Literacy Prompts (Continued)

Critical and Media Literacy

56. What can you recall about questioning the veracity of an information source?

57. Do you question an author's intent or a text's purpose? Provide an example.

58. When you are reading and writing, do you consider multiple perspectives? Provide an example.

59. What memories do you have of reading from a critical perspective?

60. What memories do you have of critically reading/listening to/viewing media?

Content Area Inventory

1. The best thing about the subject I am studying is _____

_____

2. The worst thing about the subject I am studying is _____

_____

3. One way that I use this subject outside of school is _____

_____

4. My favorite part of this class is _____

_____

5. In this class, I like to work in groups to _____

_____

6. In this class, I like to work alone to _____

_____

7. When I use what I am learning, I feel _____

_____

8. My class helps me to _____

_____

9. When I think about this class, I am really proud of _____

_____

10. One thing about this subject I wish I knew more about is _____

_____

Content Area Inventory: Language

1. The best thing about the language I am studying is _____

_____

2. The worst thing about the language I am studying is _____

_____

3. One way that I use this language outside of school is _____

_____

4. My favorite part of language class is _____

_____

5. In language class, I like to work in groups to _____

_____

6. In language class, I like to work alone to _____

_____

7. When I speak the language I am studying, I feel _____

_____

8. My language journal helps me to _____

_____

9. When I am using this language, I am really proud of _____

_____

10. One thing about this language I wish I knew more about is _____

_____

Double-Entry Journal

Name: _____   **Date:** _____

Quotes/Ideas from the Text	Reflections/Questions

Double-Entry Journal

Name: _____   **Date:** _____

Summary

Reflection

Editing Checklist

1. Did the writer use complete sentences?

2. Do the sentences begin with capital letters and end with periods?

3. Is the other punctuation appropriate—apostrophe use, comma use?

4. Is the paper written in the active voice?

5. Is there subject–verb agreement?

6. Did the writer use correct verb tenses?

7. Are the paragraphs indented?

8. Are there simple, compound, and complex sentences?

9. Are tired words used—said, nice, good?

10. Do the pronouns correctly reference the people or items to which they refer?

Journal Prompts

When students are creating journal responses, they may self-select a topic to write about or they may respond to a prompt. Prompts may be particularly effective when introducing the concept of content journals or if you need specific feedback from the students. The following example prompts may be used as presented or adapted to promote journal responses.

1. Explain what you know about _____ (a particular course concept).

2. Describe how you can use technology to facilitate your work in this course.

3. Explain how you can use what you learned in this course this week in another class or in your life outside of school.

4. Use the newspaper or news websites to find examples of how a business in our community uses the subject we are studying. Reflect in your journal about which concepts the business uses and how you think the company might benefit from using our subject in additional ways.

5. Create an acrostic poem or definition poem about a particular concept in our subject area.

6. What is/are_____ (include a particular concept taught in subject area)?

7. Write questions about something in our subject area you are having difficulty understanding or write questions about something we haven't studied yet that you would like to know about.

8. Sketch a _____ (person representing our subject area— mathematician, scientist, historian, writer). How might he or she be employed in our community?

9. Describe a _____ (mathematically, scientifically, historically, literarily) talented character from a book or television series.

10. Create a problem based on a concept we are studying and explain how you would solve it.

Paragraph Frame: Cause/Effect

Cause/Effect Paragraph Frame

As a result of the _____, several agencies took action. Because the

_____, federal agencies

responded. As a result of the _____, the

governor of the state directed the _____

_____. In order to

_____,

local authorities also took action.

Paragraph Frame: Comparison/Contrast

Comparison/Contrast Paragraph Frame

_____ and _____ agree on some topics and disagree

on others. They both support _____

_____ (comparison/similarities),

but they differ on _____

_____ (contrast/differences).

Paragraph Frame: Sequence

Sequence Paragraph Frame

When completing the science experiment, it is important to follow the steps. First,

I will _____. Next, I will _____.

Then I will _____. Following that, I will

_____. Finally, I will _____

_____.

Structured Note Taking

Directions: 1. Sketch the general shape of the sections that appear on the page.
2. Write a subheading and relevant notes in each section.
3. Sketch and describe illustrations that appear on the page.
4. Share and discuss with a partner.

Overview of Text Page: _____

Text Boxes

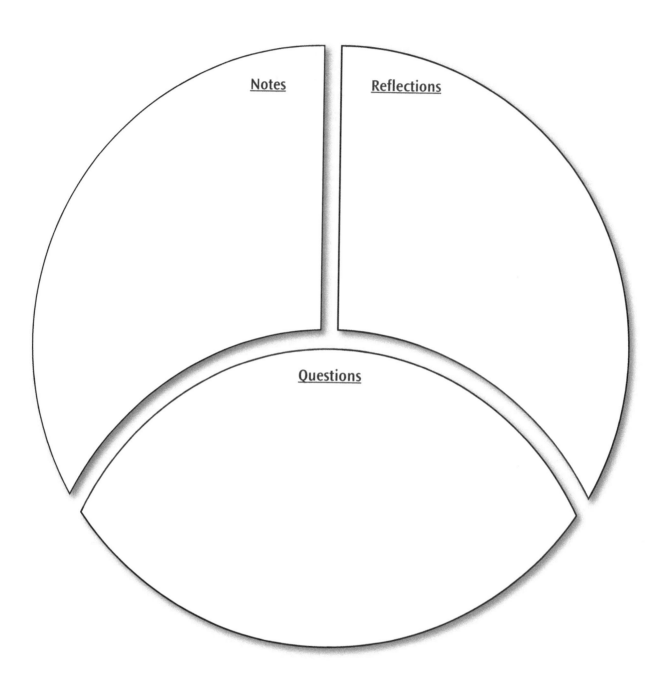

Ticket Out

The most important thing I learned today is

_____

_____

_____

_____

Ticket Out

One question I have about what I learned today is

_____

_____

_____

_____

Write and Sketch in Math and Science

Write

Sketch

Be a Math or Science Author

Choose a math or science concept and (1) create and solve a problem, (2) design an experiment, or (3) build on the existing concept to create a new math or science concept.

Topic: _____

Checklists and Rubrics

Group Checklist for Rapping for Review

The group

_____ 1. Selected a recently studied content topic to review.

_____ 2. Determined what information they would need.

_____ 3. Used multiple sources to learn essential facts about the topic.

_____ 4. Collaborated well.

_____ 5. Used feedback to revise the rap.

_____ 6. Effectively shared the rap.

Group Comments

_____

_____

_____

_____

Teacher Comments

_____

_____

_____

Names: _____

Date: _____

Internet Inquiry Student Checklist

Directions: Work individually or in small groups organized by interest. Check off each task as you complete it.

_____ 1. Generate research questions about a theme or topics being studied.

_____ 2. Search for responses to the research questions on the Internet.

_____ 3. Analyze the information found online.

_____ 4. Choose a mode to present the findings.

_____ 5. Share the results with the whole class.

Student Comments: _____

_____

_____

Teacher Comments: _____

_____

_____

Observation Checklist: First-Person Experience

The student

_____ 1. Self-selected content-related topic to research.

_____ 2. Determined which person to become.

_____ 3. Selected, accessed, and used relevant information sources.

_____ 4. Sought feedback from several peers during workshop sessions.

_____ 5. Used feedback to revise the project.

_____ 6. Chose a meaningful format for presenting the information.

Comments on Student Performance

_____

_____

_____

_____

_____

Name: _____

Date: _____

Press Conference Student Checklist

_____   1. I chose a topic.

_____   2. I conferenced with the teacher.

_____   3. I used the Questions into Paragraphs (QuIP) organizer.

_____   4. I developed at least three quality research questions.

_____   5. I conducted a viable search for sources.

_____   6. I used at least two quality sources.

_____   7. I demonstrated knowledge of the topic.

_____   8. I presented the Press Conference effectively.

Student's Comments

_____

_____

_____

Teacher's Comments

_____

_____

_____

Name:_____ **Date:**_____

Repeated-Phrase Collaborative Poem Checklist

Group Members

_____ 1. Selected a topic to address in the poem.

_____ 2. Discussed the quotations from which selections would be made.

_____ 3. Brainstormed, discussed, and chose a repeated phrase.

_____ 4. Selected the quotations to include in the poem.

_____ 5. Created a reference list.

_____ 6. Formatted the poem correctly.

_____ 7. Worked well together.

_____ 8. Respected one another's ideas.

Group Comments

_____

_____

_____

Teacher Comments

_____

_____

_____

_____

Names: _____

Date: _____

RUBRICS

Content Area Resource Anthology (CARA) Rubric

Reflection	4_____	3_____	2_____	1
Connections to topic	4_____	3_____	2_____	1
Teaching ideas	4_____	3_____	2_____	1
Differentiated instruction	4_____	3_____	2_____	1
Display of dispositions	4_____	3_____	2_____	1
Use of technology	4_____	3_____	2_____	1
Professional appearance	4_____	3_____	2_____	1

4. Excellent reflection demonstrating depth of reasoning. Outstanding connections to the CARA topic. In-depth, resourceful use of a wide range of creative and innovative teaching ideas, methods, instructional grouping practices (whole-class, small-group, pairs, individual, and computer-based practices), and curriculum materials, including types and levels of text, technology-based information, and nonprint materials for students at differing stages of development and cultural and linguistic backgrounds. Differentiated instruction demonstrates exceptional knowledge of students' abilities, interests, and cultural and linguistic backgrounds. A wide variety of texts (books, articles, technology-based, and nonprint) reflecting students' interests, cultures, and linguistic backgrounds are selected, reviewed, and used. Risk taking is evident. Advanced dispositions related to content area reading are displayed. Fully developed and detailed use of technology. Totally professional in appearance (design, presentation, APA format).

3. Thorough reflection demonstrating sound reasoning. Detailed connections to the CARA topic. Integration of a variety of creative and innovative teaching ideas, methods, grouping practices (whole-class, small-group, pairs, individual, and computer-based), and curriculum materials, including types and levels of text, technology-based information, and nonprint materials for learners at different stages of development and cultural and linguistic backgrounds. Differentiated instruction demonstrates thorough understanding of students' abilities, interests, and cultural and linguistic backgrounds. A variety of texts (books, articles, technology-based, and nonprint) reflecting students' interests, cultures, and linguistic backgrounds are selected, reviewed, and used. Proficient dispositions related to content area reading are displayed. Appropriate use of technology. The paper is professional in appearance (design, presentation, APA format).

2. Adequate reflection demonstrates reasoning. Connections to the CARA topic are somewhat consistent. Teaching ideas, methods, grouping practices (whole-class, small-group, pairs, individual, and computer-based), curriculum materials, including types and levels of text, technology-based information, and non-print materials for learners at different stages of development and cultural and linguistic backgrounds lack variety and creative and innovative perspectives. Differentiated instruction demonstrates adequate knowledge of students' abilities, interests, and cultural and linguistic backgrounds. A limited variety of texts (books, articles, technology-based, and nonprint) reflecting students' interests, cultures, and linguistic backgrounds are selected, reviewed, and used. Developing dispositions related to content area reading are displayed, Limited use of technology. Lacking elements of professional appearance (design, presentation, use of APA format).

1. Inadequate reflection; lacks depth and logical reasoning. Connections to the CARA topic are nonexistent or illogical. Teaching ideas, methods, grouping practices (whole-class, small-group, pairs, individual, and computer-based), curriculum materials, including types and levels of text, technology-based information, and nonprint materials for learners at different stages of development and cultural and linguistic backgrounds are not creative or innovative. Differentiated instruction demonstrates insufficient knowledge of students' abilities, interests, and cultural and linguistic backgrounds. Texts (books, articles, technology-based, and nonprint) have little or no variety and do not reflect students' interests, cultures, and linguistic backgrounds are selected, reviewed, and used. Unacceptable dispositions related to content area reading are displayed. Inadequate use of technology. Less than professional in appearance (design, presentation, APA format).

First-Person Experience Rubric

4.0 Made excellent decisions concerning topic selection. Used outstanding sources. Demonstrated exceptional knowledge of information literacy. Included excellent information. Demonstrated outstanding critical and creative thinking. Chose a superb presentation format. Used workshop format to greatest benefit. Collaborated extremely well with others. Excellent reference list. Outstanding presentation.

3.0 Made very good decisions about topic selection. Used high-quality sources. Demonstrated proficient knowledge of information literacy. Included in-depth information. Demonstrated high levels of critical and creative thinking. Chose a very good presentation format. Used workshop format to great benefit. Collaborated very well with others. Detailed reference list. Skillful presentation.

2.0 Made appropriate decisions concerning topic selection. Used satisfactory sources. Demonstrated adequate knowledge of information literacy. Included essential information. Demonstrated critical and creative thinking. Chose a viable presentation format. Used workshop format to benefit. Collaborated with others. Sufficient reference list. Adequate presentation.

1.0 Made poor decisions about topic selection. Used inadequate sources. Demonstrated insufficient knowledge of information literacy. Included too little information. Demonstrated little critical and creative thinking. Chose a poor presentation format. Used workshop format to little benefit. Did not collaborate well with others. Inadequate reference list. Poor presentation.

Comments: _____

_____

_____

Name:_____**Date:**_____

Oral History Presentation Rubric

4 Distinguished Project: The portrait is thoughtfully selected. Thorough research is evident after reading the news article and viewing the artifacts. Artifacts are present that directly relate to the person's life. The memoir* includes an anecdote. The news article shows a complete understanding of the news article format and is in published form with no major errors. The presenter demonstrates outstanding speaking skills (eye contact, volume, and clarity). Practice for the presentation is clearly evident. The triptych board shows effort and creativity, and the board goes beyond expectations. The board is handed in on time.

3 Proficient Project: The portrait is well chosen. Research is evident after reading the news article and viewing the artifacts. Artifacts relate to the person's life. The memoir* includes an anecdote. The news article shows an understanding of the news article format and has very few editing errors. The presenter demonstrates appropriate speaking skills (eye contact, volume, and clarity). Practice for the presentation is evident. The triptych board shows effort and some creativity. The board follows all guidelines given. The board is handed in on time:

2 Apprentice Project: The portrait shows some thought and planning and is mounted on the board. Only minimal research is evident after reading the news article and viewing the artifacts. Artifacts are present on the board that directly relate to the person's life. The memoir* is mounted on the board and is a narrative timeline. The news article does not demonstrate an understanding of the news article format and needs editing. The presenter needs to improve one or more of the following skills: eye contact, volume, or clarity. More practice is needed in preparing for the oral presentation. The triptych board shows some effort. The board does not follow all of the guidelines given. The board is handed in on time.

1 Novice Project: The portrait shows very little thought and planning. There is very little evidence of research after reading the news article and viewing the artifacts. It is not readily apparent how the artifacts on the board relate to the person's life. The memoir does not include an anecdote. The news article shows a limited understanding of the news article format and many editing errors are present. The presenter needs to improve two or more of the following skills: eye contact, volume, or clarity. Practice is needed in preparing for the oral presentation. The triptych board shows minimal effort and lacks creativity. The board does not follow the guidelines given. The board is not handed in on time.

Source: Diesinger & Kayser, 2000.

Professional Development Resource, Planning, and Presentation Project Rubric

Resource Review	4_____	3_____	2_____	1
Display of Dispositions	4_____	3_____	2_____	1
Professional Development Plan	4_____	3_____	2_____	1
Use of Technology	4_____	3_____	2_____	1
Professional Presentation	4_____	3_____	2_____	1
Evaluation of Peers	4_____	3_____	2_____	1

4 Excellent review of quality resources. Display of advanced dispositions related to reading and the teaching of content during collaborative study groups and peer observation, evaluation, and feedback. Meaningful, detailed, knowledge-based, three-year professional development plan that continues to foster the acquisition of professional knowledge and advanced dispositions. Fully developed and detailed use of numerous types of technology. Totally professional presentation, including knowledge base, appropriate display of advanced dispositions, technology use, and presentation methods. Excellent-quality contributions to collaborative study groups and peer observation, evaluation, and feedback.

3 Skillful review of quality resources. Display of proficient dispositions related to reading and the teaching of content during collaborative study groups and peer observation, evaluation, and feedback. Thorough knowledge-based, three-year professional development plan that continues to foster the acquisition of professional knowledge and proficient dispositions. Good use of technology. Very professional presentation, including knowledge base, display of proficient dispositions, technology use, and presentation methods. Quality contributions to collaborative study groups and peer observation, evaluation, and feedback.

2 Adequate review of quality resources. Display of developing dispositions related to reading and the teaching of content during collaborative study groups and peer observation, evaluation, and feedback. Knowledge-based, three-year professional development plan that continues to foster the acquisition of professional knowledge and advanced dispositions in limited ways. Adequate use of technology. Somewhat professional presentation, including limited knowledge base, display of developing dispositions, technology use, and presentation methods. Satisfactory contributions to collaborative study groups and peer observation, evaluation, and feedback.

1 Inadequate review of resources. Display of unacceptable dispositions related to reading and the teaching of content during collaborative study groups and peer observation, evaluation, and feedback. Poorly designed three-year professional development plan, including insufficient knowledge base, display of unacceptable dispositions, improper technology use, and ineffective presentation methods. Unsatisfactory contributions to collaborative study groups and peer observation, evaluation, and feedback.

Name:_____ Date:_____

Research Project Rubric

CATEGORY	4	3	2	1
Sources (quality, current)	Excellent sources	Very good sources	Adequate sources	Inadequate sources
Research	Outstanding research of topic	In-depth research of topic	Adequate research of topic	Inadequate research of topic
Organization (introduction, body, conclusion)	Excellent organization	Very good organization	Adequate organization	Inadequate organization
Style	Information flows perfectly sensibly and smoothly	Information flows sensibly and smoothly	Information flows somewhat sensibly and smoothly	Information does not flow sensibly and smoothly
APA formatting (citations, references)	APA format is consistently applied with no errors	APA format is consistently applied with a few errors	APA format is consistently applied with several errors	APA format is inconsistently or incorrectly applied
Presentation	Excellent presentation	Very good presentation	Good presentation	Poor presentation

Comments: _____

_____

_____

Name: _____ Date: _____

Restaurant Rubric

Criteria	4 (exceptional)	3 (very good)	2 (acceptable)	1 (poor)
Food	Delicious food	Tasty good food	Edible food	Inedible food
Service	Outstanding service	Attentive service	Adequate service	Inadequate service
Cleanliness	Exceptionally clean	Very clean	Adequately clean	Poor
Atmosphere	Extraordinarily welcoming	Inviting	Acceptable	Uninviting
Location	Excellent	Very good	Acceptable	Unacceptable
Parking	Excellent	Very good	Adequate	Poor

Comments: _____

_____

_____

Student-Authored Electronic Books Rubric

Creativity	4_____3_____2_____1
Quality of information	4_____3_____2_____1
Content area connections	4_____3_____2_____1
Relation of illustrations to text	4_____3_____2_____1
Use of technology	4_____3_____2_____1
Professional appearance	4_____3_____2_____1

4 Outstanding creativity is evident. Excellent-quality information. Exceptional content area connections. Excellent relation of illustrations to text. Fully developed use of technology, Totally professional in appearance (format, conventions of writing, design, text, illustrations, and references).

3 In-depth creativity is evident. High-quality information is consistently used. Proficient content area connections, Skillful relation of illustrations to text. Consistent use of various types of technology. Very professional in appearance (format, conventions of writing, design, text, illustrations, and references).

2 Creativity is evident. Quality of information is adequate. Consistent connections to the content areas. Illustrations and text are related. Use of technology is evident. Professional appearance (format, conventions of writing, design, text, illustrations, and references).

1 Creativity is lacking. Quality of information is inadequate. Inconsistent connections to the content. Illustration and text relations are inappropriate. Poor use of technology. Less than professional in appearance (format, conventions of writing, design, text, illustrations, and references).

Student Comments: _____

_____

_____

Teacher Comments: _____

_____

_____

Name: _____ **Date:** _____

E

BLACKLINE MASTERS

Alternative Modes of Representation

Bio-Poem

First name

Noun

Four adjectives

Lover of . . . three things

Who enjoys . . . three things

Who believes in . . .

Who wanted to . . . three things

Who uses . . . three things

Who gave us . . . three things

Who said . . .

Last name

Cinquain

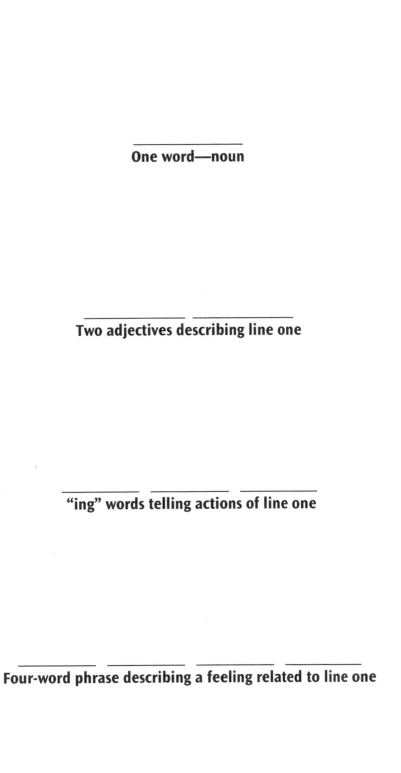

_____
One word—noun

_____ _____
Two adjectives describing line one

_____ _____ _____
"ing" words telling actions of line one

_____ _____ _____ _____
Four-word phrase describing a feeling related to line one

_____
**One word—synonym
or reference to line one**

Definition Poem

What is _____?

_____

_____

_____

_____

_____

_____

_____

_____

_____

_____

_____

That is _____!

Diamante

_____
Subject—one noun

_____ _____
Two adjectives describing the subject

_____ _____ _____
Three participles ("ing" words) telling about the subject

_____ _____ _____ _____
Four nouns—first two relate to the first noun, last two to opposite

_____ _____ _____
Three participles ("ing" words) telling about the opposite

_____ _____
Two adjectives describing the opposite

_____
Opposite of subject—one noun

Repeated-Phrase Collaborative Poem Group Planning Sheet

Names: _____

Topic: _____

Repeated Phrase: _____

_____

Three Passages

    Source: _____

Passage 1	

Passage 2	

Passage 3	

Lyric Summary

Directions

- Engage in small-group brainstorming of ideas about the topic or theme.
- Choose a song everyone knows.
- Work together as a group to write your summary as lyrics to the song.
- Sing the Lyric Summary for the whole class.

Brainstormed Ideas

Song Title: _____

Lyric Summary

_____

_____

_____

_____

_____

_____

_____

_____

_____

_____

_____

F

Project Examples

Content Area Resource Anthology Example

Reflective Introduction Example

Geometry is often thought of as the least-liked class among high school students. It has many abstract concepts that can be difficult to understand for students who are often used to concrete thinking. Until geometry is introduced, students have rarely been exposed to abstract thinking. Often students struggle with abstract thinking because it's a new concept, but sometimes students haven't developed cognitively enough to process abstract thought. Because it's often a difficult concept for students to understand, I chose geometry for my Content Area Resource Anthology (CARA). I believe that the more resources I have to help students comprehend, the more likely they are to understand what they are reading.

I wanted to find resources and innovative techniques for geometry. Using picture books, poems, informational articles, websites, and DVDs is a perfect way to help students grasp very abstract concepts. All students have different learning styles and, therefore, need teachers who use varied teaching styles. This CARA provides a broad range of resources that can be used during lessons to reach different learning styles. These resources also appeal to different intelligences. For example, students who have artistic intelligence will find that poetry helps them become comfortable with the concept.

This collection of resources is a starting point for me to build upon in the future. This anthology guides me in thinking outside the box when designing lesson plans. It serves as a reminder that utilizing resources can help me develop creative, innovative lessons that can intrigue and appeal to students who may have previously been bored with the topic.

Picture Book Example

Source: Micklethwait, L. (2004). *I spy shapes in art*. New York: Greenwillow.

Summary: In this seek-and-find book, students are asked to discover geometric shapes in famous paintings. This book depicts the work of many famous artists, including O'Keeffe, Matisse, Escher, and Warhol.

Teaching Idea: The Rest of the Story. I would incorporate The Rest of the Story teaching idea with *I Spy Shapes in Art*. The students would pick one of the artists whose work is featured in the book and research the artist and the specific piece that incorporated shapes. They would use technology such as a webpage, power point presentation, or exhibition to present their research findings to the class. The students could also present their research findings by creating their own artwork relevant to the era and genre of their artist. They would describe why their art depicts the genre of their artist, why (if known) the artist used those shapes, and the five most interesting facts they learned about the author.

Informational Article Example

Source: Hodara, S. (2007, March 4). From nature's geometry, healing art. *The New York Times*. Retrieved February 25, 2008, from nytimes.com.

Summary: This article, about an artist who paints using geometric shapes, tells of her experience with art and her inspiration from shapes in nature. Geometric shapes such as arcs, circles, and triangles are dominant in her work.

Teaching Idea: Press Conference. I would use this article to stimulate interest in discovering newspaper and magazine articles that relate to geometry. The class will discuss, analyze main points, and share our opinions of this article. I will encourage students to share their views on such issues as whether using shapes is really art. After our discussion, students will search online databases using the library's resources to find an article related to math that interests them. They will read the article using Bookmark Technique. Then they will analyze and critique the article. Finally, they will present Press Conferences in small groups. Group members will ask questions and offer comments regarding the article.

Student-Authored Electronic Alphabet Book Example

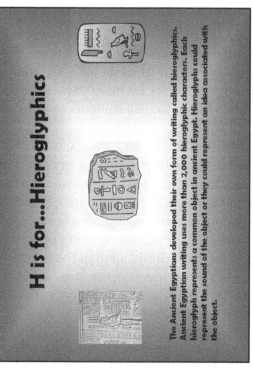

ANCIENT EGYPT

AN ALPHABET BOOK

Cali Roberts

H is for...Hieroglyphics

The Ancient Egyptians developed their own form of writing called hieroglyphics. Ancient Egyptian writing uses more than 2,000 hieroglyphic characters. Each hieroglyph represents a common object in ancient Egypt. Hieroglyphs could represent the sound of the object or they could represent an idea associated with the object.

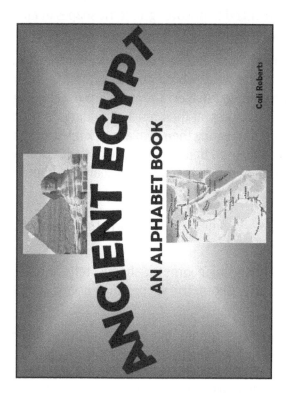

M is for... Mummification

The process of mummification was a method developed by the ancient Egyptians. They preserved the bodies of the dead in order for them to remain lifelike. The process included embalming the bodies and wrapping them in strips of linen and oils.

T is for...Tutankhamun

Tutankhamun was only eight or nine years old when he became pharaoh, and he ruled for approximately ten years. Due to his young age, he had a lot of help from advisors when making decisions. He was not a well-liked king and some scientists think that he was murdered. King Tutankhamun is the most famous king found in the Valley of the Kings because his tomb was in almost perfect condition when it was found. The mummy of King Tut was found in 1922 by Howard Carter and Lord Carnarvon.

**Student-Authored Electronic
Informational Book Example**

REAL WORLD MATH

A Comprehensive
Look at the Modern
Day World and the
Jobs That Need Math
to Function.

Joshua C. Miller

Industrial Engineer

◆ Industrial Engineers are extremely important to the industrial world because they use math to help increase the productivity and efficiency of companies. These engineers use math to analyze data to make managerial decisions, design effective work environments, and solve any industrial problems that may arise.

Architects

◆ Architects are the men and women behind the scenes of all buildings. These men and women use their knowledge of math to create scale model drawings of buildings and people's dream houses. They use math to help calculate the most efficient way to use the space provided and to create the illusion of buildings being bigger than they actually are.

Astronomers and Astrophysicists

◆ Astronomers and astrophysicists use math in their daily findings. These are men and women who study the stars, planets and galaxies that exist in our universe. These men and women often work in places such as NASA. Their discoveries help us to understand the worlds outside of our own.

Transmediation Example

Lyrics to Pink's "Family Portrait" Represented as a Picture Book

you fight about money
'bout me and my brother

and this

i come home to…

this is my shelter.

in our family portrait
we look pretty happy
let's play pretend, act
like it goes naturally

in our family portrait
we look pretty happy
we look pretty normal
let's go back to that

mama please stop cryin'.
i can't stand the sound.

your pain is painful,
and it's tearing me down.

can we work it out?
can we be a family?

i promise i'll be better.
mommy i'll do anything,
daddy please don't leave.

REFERENCES

Abilock, D. (2007). *Building blocks of research: Overview of design, process, and outcomes.* Retrieved May 15, 2009 http://www.noodletools.com/debbie/literacies/information/1over/infolit1.htm/

Afflerbach, P. (2002). Authentic assessment. In B. Guzzetti (Ed.), *Literacy in America: An encyclopedia of history, theory, and practice,* pp. 36–39 Santa Barbara, CA: ABC Publishing.

Aguilar, C. M., Fu, D., & Jabo, C. (2007). English language learners in the classroom. In K. Beers, R. E. Probst, & L. Reif (Eds.), *Adolescent literacy: Turning practice into promise* (pp. 105–125). Portsmouth, NH: Heinemann.

Albright, L. K. (2002). Bringing the Ice Maiden to life: Engaging adolescents in learning through picture book read-alouds in content areas. *Journal of Adolescent & Adult Literacy, 45*(5), 418–429.

Allen, D.D., Cobb, & Danger, S. (2003). Inservice teachers mentoring aspiring teachers. *Mentoring & Tutoring, 11*(2), 177–182.

Allington, R. L. (2002). You can't learn much from books you can't read. *Educational Leadership, 60*(3), 16–19.

Almasi, J. F. (1996). A new view of discussion. In L. B. Gambrell & J. F. Almasi (Eds.), *Lively discussions! Fostering engaged reading* (pp. 2–24). Newark, DE: International Reading Association.

Alvermann, D. (1991). The discussion web: A graphic aid for learning across the curriculum. *The Reading Teacher, 45,* 92–99.

Alvermann, D.E., & Nealy, A. (2004). Professional development content for reading educators at the middle and high school levels. In D. Strickland, & M. Kamil (Eds.) *Improving reading achievement through professional development* (pp. 85–94). Norwood, MA: Christopher Gordon.

Anderson, R. C. (1994). Role of reader's schema in comprehension, learning, and memory. In R. B. Ruddell, M. R. Ruddell, & H. Singer (Eds.), *Theoretical models and processes of reading* (4th ed., pp. 469–482). Newark, DE: International Reading Association.

Angaran, J. (1999). Reflection in an age of assessment. *Educational Leadership, 56*(6), 71–72.

Angelou, M. (1993). *Life doesn't frighten me.* New York: Stewart, Tabori, & Chang.

Arter, J. (1996). *Assessing student performance: A professional inquiry kit.* Alexandria, VA: Association for Supervision and Curriculum Development.

Baker, L., & Wigfield, A. (1999). Dimensions of children's motivation for reading and their relations to reading activity and reading achievement. *Reading Research Quarterly, 34*(4), 452–481.

Baker, L., Afflerbach, P., & Reinking, D. (1996). Developing engaged readers in school and home communities: An overview. In L. Baker, P. Afflerbach, & D. Reinking (Eds.), *Developing engaged readers in school and home communities* (pp. xiii–xxvii). Hillsdale, NJ: Lawrence Erlbaum Associates.

Baker, M. (2004). The International Reading Association's literacy study group initiative. In D. Strickland, & M. Kamil (Eds.) *Improving reading achievement through professional development* (pp. 236–237). Norwood, MA: Christopher Gordon.

Banks, J. A., Cookson, P., Gay, G., Hawley, W.D., Irvine, J. J., Nieto, S., Schofield, J. W., & Stephan, W. G. (2001). Diversity within unity: Essential principles for teaching and learning in a multicultural society. *Phi Delta Kappan, 82,* 196–203.

Barton, P. E. (2002). *Staying on course in education reform.* Princeton, NJ: Statistics & Research Division, Policy Information Center, Educational Testing Service.

Beck, I. L., McKeown, M. G., & Kucan, L. (2002). *Bringing words to life: Robust vocabulary instruction.* New York: Guilford Press.

Bell, R. (2001). Implicit instruction in technology integration and the nature of science: There's no such thing as a free lunch. *Contemporary Issues in Technology and Teacher Education, 1*(4), *Contemporary Issues in Technology and Teacher Education* [Online serial], *1*(4). Available: http://www.citejournal.org/vol1/iss4/currentissues/science/article1.htm

Biancarosa, G., & Snow, C. E. (2006). *Reading next—A vision for action and research in middle and high school literacy: A report from the Carnegie Corporation of New York* (2nd ed.). Washington, DC: Alliance for Excellent Education.

Blachowicz, C. L. (2007). *Vocabulary across the curriculum.* Paper presented at the Alaska State Literacy Conference, Anchorage, AK.

Blachowicz, C. L., & Fisher, P. (2000). Vocabulary instruction. In M. Kamil, P. D. Pearson, & R. Barr (Eds.), *Handbook of reading research* (Vol.3, pp. 503–523). Mahwah, NJ: Lawrence Erlbaum Associates.

Blachowicz, C. L., Fisher, P., Ogle, D. M., & Watts-Taffe, S. (2006). Vocabulary: Questions from the classroom. *Reading Research Quarterly, 41*(4), 524–539.

Blessing, C. (2005). Reading to kids who are old enough to shave. *School Library Journal, 51*(4), 44–45.

Block, C. C., Schaller, J. L., Joy, J. A., & Gaine, P. (2002). Process-based comprehension instruction. In C. C. Block & M. Pressley (Eds.), *Comprehension instruction: Research-based best practices* (pp. 42–61). New York: Guilford.

Boise State University. *A guide for mentor teachers, supervisors, and liaisons: Mentoring.* Available at: http://education.boisestate.edu/mentorteacher/Mentoring.htm

Boling, E., Castek, J., Zawilinski, L., Barton, K. & Nierlich, T. (2008). Collaborative literacy: Blogs and Internet projects. *The Reading Teacher, 61*(6), 504–506.

Brabham, E. G., & Villaume, S. K. (2002). Vocabulary instruction: Concerns and visions. *The Reading Teacher, 56*(3), 264–269.

Brandenburg, M.L. (2002). Advanced math? Write! *Educational Leadership, 30*(3), 67–68.

Brandt, R. (1991). Time for reflection. *Educational Leadership, 48*(6), 3.

Brass, J.J. (2008). Local knowledge and digital movie composing in an after-school literacy program. *Journal of Adolescent & Adult Literacy, 51*(6), 464–473.

Brooks, J. G., & Brooks, M. G. (1993). *In search of understanding: The case for constructivist classrooms.* Alexandria, VA: Association for Supervision and Curriculum Development.

Brown, J. A. (1998). Media literacy perspectives. *Journal of Communications, 48*(1), 44–57.

Bruce, B.C., & Bishop, A.P. (2002). Using the Web to support inquiry-based literacy development. *Journal of Adolescent & Adult Literacy, 45*(8), *Reading Online, 5*(7). Available: http://www.readingonline.org.

Burke, J. (2002). The Internet reader. *Educational Leadership, 60*(3), 38–42.

Burke, K., & Dunn, R. (2003). Learning style-based teaching to raise minority student test scores. *The Social Studies, 94,* 167–170.

Busching, B. A., & Slesinger, B. A. (1995). Authentic questions: What do they look like? Where do they lead? *Language Arts, 72*(5), 341–351.

California State Board of Education. (n.d.). *History–Social Science Content Standards—Grade 10.* Sacramento, CA: Author.

Cambourne, B. (1995). Toward an educationally relevant theory of literacy learning: Twenty years of inquiry. *The Reading Teacher, 49,* 182–192.

Cambourne, B. (2002). Holistic, integrated approaches to reading and language arts instruction: The constructivist framework on an instructional theory. In A.E. Farstrup & S.J. Samuels (Eds.), *What research has to say about reading instruction* (pp. 25–47). Newark, DE: International Reading Association.

Carlo, M. S., August, D., McLaughlin, B., Snow, C. E., Dressler, C., Lippman, D. N., Lively, T. J., & White, C. E. (2004). Closing the gap: Addressing the vocabulary need of English-language learners in bilingual and mainstream classrooms. *Reading Research Quarterly, 39*(2), 188–215.

Carrier, K. A., & Tatum, A. W. (2006). Creating sentence walls to help English-language learners develop content literacy. *The Reading Teacher, 60*(3), 285–288.

Carroll, A. (Ed.). (2001). *War letters: Extraordinary correspondence from American wars.* New York: Scribner.

Castek, J. Bevans-Mangelson, J, & Goldstone, B. (2006). Reading adventures online: Five ways to introduce the new literacies of the Internet through children's literature. *The ReadingTeacher, 59*(7), 714–728.

Checkley, K. (1997). Problem-based learning: The search for solutions to life's messy problems. *ASCD Curriculum Update,* 1–8.

Ciardiello, A. V. (1998). Did you ask a good question today? Alternative cognitive and metacognitive strategies. *Journal of Adolescent and Adult Literacy, 42*(3), 210–219.

Ciardiello, A. V. (2003). "To wander and wonder": Pathways to literacy and inquiry through question-finding. *Journal of Adolescent and Adult Literacy, 47*(3), 228–239.

Ciardiello, A. V. (2007). *Puzzle them first: Motivating adolescent readers with question-finding.* Newark, DE: International Reading Association.

Clinchy, E. (1995). Learning in and about the real world: Recontextualizing public schooling. *Phi Delta Kappan, 76* (5), 400–404.

Coiro, J. (2007). *Exploring changes to reading comprehension on the Internet: Paradoxes and possibilities for diverse adolescent readers.* Unpublished doctoral dissertation, University of Connecticut, Storrs. Available online at http://www.newliteracies.uconn.edu/coirodissertation/

Coiro, J., & Dobler, E. (2007). Exploring the online reading comprehension strategies used by sixth-grade skilled readers to search for and locate information on the Internet. *Reading Research Quarterly, 42,* 214–57.

Coiro, J., Knobel, M., Lankshear, C., & Leu, D.J. (2008). *Handbook of research on new literacies.* Mahwah, NJ: Erlbaum.

Comber, B. (2001). Critical literacies and local action: Teacher knowledge and a "new" research agenda. In B. Comber & A. Simpson (Eds.), *Negotiating critical literacies in classrooms* (pp. 271–282). Mahwah, NJ: Lawrence Erlbaum Associates.

Considine, D. (1995). An introduction to media literacy: The what, why, and how tos. Retrieved May 15, 2009. http://www.ced.Appstate.edu/departments/ci/programs/edmedia/media/it/article/htm/.

Daniels, H. (1994). *Literature circles: Voice and choice in the student-centered classroom.* York, ME: Stenhouse.

Darling-Hammond, L., & Falk, B. (1997). Using standards and assessments to support student learning. *Phi Delta Kappan, 79*(3), 190–199.

Davey, B. (1983). Think-aloud—modeling the cognitive processes of reading comprehension. *Journal of Reading, 27,* 44–47.

Davis, S.J.H. (1997). How mastering technology can transform math class. *Educational Leadership, 55*(3), 49–51.

de Argaez, E. (2006, January). One billion Internet users. *Internet world stats news, 14.* Retrieved February 1, 2006, from http://www.internetworldstats.com/pr/edi014.htm#3

DeBono, E. (1985). *Six thinking hats.* Boston: Little, Brown.

Dickinson, D., Hyler, D., Reilly, L., & Romano, S. (2006). *The oral history project: Connecting students to their community, grades 4–8* Portsmouth, NH: Heinemann.

Diesinger, J., & Kayser, A. (2000). *Oral history project CD-ROM.* BCD Interactive Productions.

Dixon-Krauss, L. (2001/2002). Using literature as a context for teaching vocabulary. *Journal of Adolescent & Adult Literacy, 45*(4), 310–318.

Dodge, B. (1995). *Meet Bernie Dodge: The Frank Lloyd Wright of learning environments.* Retrieved March 2, 2008 from http://www.educationworld.com

Dong, Y. R. (2004/2005). Getting at the content. *Educational Leadership, 62*(4), 14–19.

Douillard, K. (2002). Going past done: Creating time for reflection in the classroom. *Language Arts, 80,* 92–99.

Draper, R. J. (2002). School mathematics reform, constructivism, and literacy: A case for literacy instruction in the reform-oriented math classroom. *Journal of Adolescent and Adult Literacy, 45*(6), 520–529.

Drucker, M. J. (2003). What reading teachers should know about ESL learners. *The Reading Teacher, 57*(1), 22–29.

Duffy, G. (2004). Teachers who improve reading achievement: What research says about what they do and how to develop them. In D. Strickland, & M. Kamil (Eds.) *Improving reading achievement through professional development* (pp. 3–22). Norwood, MA: Christopher Gordon.

Duke, N. (2001). *A new generation of researchers looks at comprehension.* Paper presented at the 51st Annual Meeting of the National Reading Conference, San Antonio, TX.

Duke, N. (2007). *Comprehension throughout the day.* Paper presented at the Alaska State Literacy Conference, Anchorage, AK.

Duke, N., & Pearson, P. D. (2002). Effective practices for developing comprehension. In A. Farstrup & J. Samuels (Eds.), *What research has to say about reading instruction* (3rd ed., pp. 205–242). Newark, DE: International Reading Association.

Duke, N.K., & Pearson, P.D. (2002). Effective practices for developing reading comprehension. In A.E. Farstup & S.J. Samuels (Eds.), *What research has to say about reading instruction* (2nd ed., pp. 205–242). Newark, DE: International Reading Association.

Dunn, R., & Dunn, J. (1993). *Teaching secondary students through their individual learning styles: Practical approach for grades 7–12.* Boston: Allyn and Bacon.

Durkin, D. (1978–1979). What classroom observations reveal about reading comprehension instruction. *Reading Research Quarterly, 14,* 481–533.

Dymock, S. J., & Nicholson, T. (1999) *Reading comprehension: What is it? How do you teach it?* Wellington, New Zealand: New Zealand Council for Educational Research.

Echevarria, J., & Graves, A. (1998). *Sheltered content instruction: Teaching English language learners with diverse abilities.* Boston: Allyn & Bacon.

Echevarria, J., Vogt, M. E., & Short, D. J. (2008). *Making content comprehensible for English learners.* Boston: Allyn and Bacon.

Eick, C.J., & Reed, C.J. (2002). What makes an inquiry oriented science teacher? The influence of learning histories on student teacher role identity and practice. *Science Teacher Education, 86,* 401–416.

Eisner, E. (1999). The uses and limits of performance assessment. *Phi Delta Kappan, 80*(9), 658–660.

Eisner, E. (2006). The satisfactions of teaching. *Educational Leadership, 63*(6), 43–46.

Eisner, E.W. (1993). Forms of understanding and the future of educational research. *Educational Researcher, 22*(7), 5–11.

Eisner, E.W. (1997). Cognition and representation: A way to pursue the American dream? *Phi Delta Kappan, 78*(5), 348–353.

El-Hindi, A. E. (1998). Beyond classroom boundaries: Constructivist teaching with the Internet. *The Reading Teacher, 51*(8), 694–700.

Falk, B. (2002). Standards-based reforms: Problems and possibilities. *Phi Delta Kappan, 83*(8), 612–620.

Ferrara, S., & McTighe, J. (1992). A process for planning: More thoughtful classroom assessment. In A. Costa, J. Bellanca, & R. Fogarty (Eds.), *If minds matter: A forward to the future* (Vol. 2). Palantine, IL: Skylight.

Fisher, D., Flood, J., Lapp, D., & Frey, N. (2004). Interactive read-alouds: Is there a common set of implemention practices? *The Reading Teacher, 58*(1), 8–17.

Fitzgerald, J., & Graves, M. (2004/2005). Reading supports for all. *Educational Leadership, 62*(4), 68–71.

Flint, A. S., & Bomer, R. (2002). Inquiry-based instruction. In B. Guzzetti, Ed. *Literacy in America: An encyclopedia of history, theory, and practice,* (Vol . I, pp. 249–251. Santa Barbara, California: ABC-CLIO.

Flood, J., Lapp, D., Flood, S., & Nagel, G. (1992). Am I allowed to group? Using flexible patterns for effective instruction. *The Reading Teacher, 45*(8), 608–616.

Forbes, L. S. (2004). Using web-based bookmarks in K-8 settings: Linking the Internet to instruction. *The Reading Teacher, 58*(2), 148–153.

Frand, J. (2000). The information age mindset: Changes in students and implications for higher education. *EDUCAUSE Review, 35*(5), 15–24.

Freeman, E. B., & Person, D. G. (1998). *Connecting informational children's books with content area learning.* Boston, MA: Allyn and Bacon.

Freire, P. (1970). *Pedagogy of the oppressed.* New York: Continuum.

Freire, P. (1983). The importance of the act of reading. *Journal of Education, 165,* 5–11.

Freire, P. (1998). *Teachers as cultural workers: Letters to those who dare to teach.* Boulder, CO: Westview.

Fry, E. (1977). Fry's readability graph: Clarifications, validity, and extension to level 17. *Journal of Reading, 21,* 242 – 252.

Fulton, K., Burns, M., & Goldenberg, L. (2005). Teachers Learning in Networked Communities: The TLINC Strategy. *Phi Delta Kappan, 87*(4), 298–305.

Gambrell, L. B. (1996). Creating classroom cultures that foster reading motivation. *The Reading Teacher, 50*(1), 14–25.

Gambrell, L. B. (1996). What research reveals about discussion. In L. B. Gambrell & J. F. Almasi, *Lively discussions! Fostering engaged reading* (pp. 25–38). Newark, DE: International Reading Association.

Gambrell, L. B., Palmer, B. M., Codling, R. M., Mazzoni, S. A. (1996). Assessing motivation to read. *The Reading Teacher, 49(7),* 518–533.

Gamill, D. M. (2006). Learning the write way. *The Reading Teacher, 59(8),* 754–762.

Genesee, F. (Ed.). (1999). Program alternatives for linguistically diverse students. (Educational Practice Report I). Washington, DC: Center for Research on Education, Diversity & Excellence.

Gersten, R., & Baker, S. (2002). What we know effective instructional practices for English-language learners. *Exceptional Children, 55,* 451–471.

Gibson, V., & Hasbrouck, J. (2008). Differentiated instruction. New York: McGraw-Hill.

Gilster, P. (1997). Digital literacy. New York: John Wiley & Sons.

Goldman, S. R., & Rakestraw, J. A. (2000). Structural aspects of constructing meaning from text. In M. Kamil, P. D. Pearson, & R. Barr (Eds.), *Handbook of reading research* (Vol. 3, pp. 311–335). Mahwah, NJ: Lawrence Erlbaum Associates.

Goodrich, H. (1996–1997). Understanding rubrics. *Educational Leadership, 54*(4), 14–17.

Gordon, C. J., & Macinnis, D. (1993). Using journals as a window on students' thinking in mathematics. *Language Arts, 70*, 37–43.

Gratz, D. B. (2000). High standards for whom? *Phi Delta Kappan, 81*, 681–687.

Graves, M. F., & Watts-Taffe, S. M. (2002). The place of word consciousness in a research-based vocabulary program. In A. E. Farstrup & S. J. Samuels (Eds.), *What research has to say about reading instruction* (pp. 140–165). Newark, DE: International Reading Association.

Greene, M. (1997). Metphors and multiples: Representation, the arts, and history. *Phi Delta Kappan, 78*(5), 387–394.

Greenleaf, C.L., & Schoenbach, R. (2004). Building capacity for the responsive teaching of reading in the academic disciplines: Strategic inquiry designs for middle and high school teachers' professional development. In D. Strickland, & M. Kamil (Eds.) *Improving reading achievement through professional development* (pp. 97–128). Norwood, MA: Christopher Gordon.

Guskey, T. (2003). What makes professional development effective? *Phi Delta Kappan, 84*(10), 748–750.

Guthrie, J. (2005). Preparing students for high-stakes test taking in reading. In Z. Fang (Ed.), *Literacy teaching and learning: Current issues and trends* (pp. 285–295). Boston: Allyn and Bacon.

Guthrie, J. T., & Alvermann, D. (Eds.). (1999). *Engagement in reading: Processes, practices, and policy implications.* New York: Teachers College Press.

Guthrie, J. T., & Wigfield, A. (1997). *Reading engagement: Motivating readers through integrated curriculum.* Newark, DE: International Reading Association.

Guthrie, J. T., Wigfield, A., Metsala, J. L., & Cox, K. E. (1999). Motivational and cognitive predictors of text comprehension and reading amount. *Scientific Studies of Reading, 3*(3), 231–256.

Haag, C. C., & Williams, J. (2004). Classroom language: Inviting all students to participate. In F. B. Boyd, C. H. Brock, & M. S. Rozendal (Eds.), *Multicultural and multilingual literacy and language* (pp. 54–74). New York: Guilford.

Hadaway, N. L., & Young, T. (2006). Changing classrooms: Transforming instruction. In T. Young & N. L. Hadaway (Eds.), *Supporting the literacy development of English learners* (pp. 6–21). Newark, DE: International Reading Association.

Haertel, E. H. (1999). Performance assessment and educational reform. *Phi Delta Kappan, 80*(9), 662–666.

Haggard, M. R. (1986). The vocabulary self-collection strategy: Using student interest and world knowledge to enhance vocabulary growth. *Journal of Reading, 29*(7), 634–642.

Halford, J.M. (1998). Easing the way for new teachers. *Educational Leadership, 55*, 33–36.

Halford, J.M. (1999). Policies to support new teachers. *Educational Leadership, 56*(8), 85. Retrieved March 26, 2001, from the World Wide Web: http://www.ascd.org/

Harris, T. L., & Hodges, R. E. (Eds.). (1995). *The literacy dictionary: The vocabulary of reading and writing.* Newark, DE: International Reading Association.

Harste, J., Burke, C., & Short, K. (1988). *Creating classrooms for authors.* Portsmouth, NH: Heinemann.

Harvey, S., & Goudvis, A. (2000). *Strategies that work: Teaching comprehension to enhance understanding.* York, ME: Stenhouse.

Herman, J. L., & Winters, L. (1994). Portfolio research: A slim collection. *Educational Leadership, 52*(2), 48–55.

Herman, J. L., Ashbacher, P. R. & Winters, L. (1992). A practical guide to alternative assessment. Alexandria, VA: Association for Supervision and Curriculum Development.

Hiebert, E. (1994). Becoming literate through authentic tasks: Evidence and adaptations. In R. B. Ruddell, M. R. Ruddell, H. Singer (Eds.), *Theoretical models and processes of reading (4th ed.).* Newark, DE: International Reading Association.

Hiebert, E. H., Pearson, P. D., Taylor, B. M., Richardson, V., & Paris, S. G. (1998). *Every child a reader.* Ann Arbor, MI: Center for the Improvement of Early Reading Achievement.

Hoffman, J. V., Assaf, L. C., & Paris, S. G. (2001). High-stakes assessments in reading: Today in Texas, tomorrow? *The Reading Teacher 54*(5), 482–492.

Holloway, B. (2001). The benefits of mentoring. *Educational Leadership, 58*(8), 85–86.

Holmes, K., Powell, S., Holmes, S., & Witt, E. (2007). Readers and book characters: Does race matter? *The Journal of Educational Research, 100*(5), 276–282.

Hosking, N. J. (2000). *Student-centered literacy instruction in the middle years.* Dubuque, IA: Kendall/Hunt Publishing Company.

Howe, N. (2005). Harnessing the power of millennials: New education strategies for a confident, achieving youth generation. *School Administrator, 62*(8).

Howe, N., & Strauss, W. (2000). *Millennials rising: The next great generation.* New York: Vantage Books.

Howe, N., & Strauss, W. (2001). The rise of the millennials. *The Futurist, 7.*

Hoyt, L. (1992). Many ways of knowing: Using drama, oral interactions, and the visual arts to enhance reading comprehension. *The Reading Teacher, 45* (8), 580–584.

International Reading Association & National Council Teachers of English. (1996). *Standards for the English language arts.* Newark, DE: Authors.

International Reading Association, Commission on Adolescent Literacy. (August/September 2001). Adolescent literacy: Seven principles. *Reading Today, 18*(7), 23.

International Reading Association. (2000). *Excellent reading teachers: A position statement of the International Reading Association.* Newark, DE : IRA.

International Reading Association. (2007). IRA Standards for Reading Professionals – Excerpts from the Revised Role Definitions. Newark, DE: International Reading Association.

Isaacson, W. (2007). *Einstein: His life and universe.* New York: Simon & Schuster.

Ivey, G. (2000). Redesigning reading instruction *Educational Leadership, 58*(1), 42 – 45.

Jennings, P., & Brewster, T. (1998). *The century.* NewYork: Doubleday.

Johnson, C. C. (2006). Effective professional development and change in practice: Barriers science teachers encounter and implications for reform. *School Science & Mathematics, 106*(3), 150–161.

Johnson, D. D., & Pearson, P. D. (1984). *Teaching reading vocabulary* (2nd ed.). New York: Holt, Rinehart and Winston.

Johnson, D., & Zufall, L. (2004). Web watch not just for kids anymore: Webquests for professional development. *Reading Online, 26–30.*

Johnston, P. (1997). *Knowing literacy: Constructive literacy assessment.* York, Maine: Stenhouse Publishers.

Kadjer, S. B. (2007). Unleashing potential with emerging technologies. In K. Beers. R.E. Probst, & L. Reif (Eds.), *Adolescent reading: Turning promise into practice* (pp. 213 – 229). Portsmouth, NH: Heinemann.

Kamil, M., & Lane, D. (1998). Researching the relation between technology and literacy: An agenda for the 21st century. In D. Reinking, M.C. McKenna, L.D. Labbo, & R.D. Keiffer (Eds.), *Handbook of literacy and technology: Transformations in a post-typographic world* (pp. 323 – 341). Mahwah, NJ: Erlbaum.

Keene, E., & Zimmermann, S. (1997). *Mosaic of thought: Teaching comprehension in a reader's workshop.* Portsmouth, NH: Heinemann.

Kelleher, J. (2003). A model of assessment-driven professional development. *Phi Delta Kappan, 84*(10), 751–756.

Keller, B. (2003). Teachers travel the globe for professional development. *Education Week, 23*(14), 8. (12/3/2003)

Keller, B. (2006). New mentoring program found helpful for novice teachers in NYC. *Education Week, 25*(36), 7. (5/10/2006)

Kifer, E. (2001). *Large-scale assessment: Dimensions, dilemmas, and policies.* Thousand Oaks, CA: Corwin Press.

Kist, W. (2000). Beginning to create the new literacy classroom: What does the new literacy look like? *Journal of Adolescent & Adult Literacy, 43*(8), 710–718.

Kist, W. (2002). Finding 'new literacy' in action: An interdisciplinary high school western civilization class. *Journal of Adolescent & Adult Literacy, 45*(5), 368–377.

Knipper, K. J., & Duggan, T. J. (2006). Writing to learn across the curriculum: Tools for comprehension in content area classes. *The Reading Teacher, 59(5),* 462–470.

Koskinen, P., Blum, I., Bisson, S., Phillips, S., Creamer, T., & Baker, T. (1999). Shared reading, books, and audiotapes: Supporting diverse students in school and at home. *The Reading Teacher, 52*(5), 430–444.

Kramer, M. C. (2001). Triumph out of the wilderness: A reflection on the importance of mentoring. *Phi Delta Kappan, 82*(5), 411–412.

Krashen, S. (1982). *Principles and practice in second language acquisition.* Oxford, UK: Pergamon.

Langer, J. & Applebee, A. (1985). Learning to write: Learning to think, *Educational Horizons, 64,* 1, 36–39.

Langer, J. (1981). From theory to practice: A prereading plan. *Journal of Reading, 25,* 152–156.

Lasear, D. (1991). *Seven ways of teaching: The artistry of teaching with multiple intelligences.* Palatine, IL: Skylight Publishing, Inc.

Leahy, S., Lyon, C., Thompson, M., & Wiliam, D. (2005). Classroom assessment: Minute by minute, day by day. *Educational Leadership, 63*(3), 19–24.

Lefkowits, L., & Miller, K. (2006). Fulfilling the promise of the standards movement. *Phi Delta Kappan, 87*(5), 403–407.

Lester, J. H. (2003). Planning effective secondary professional development programs. *American Secondary Educations, 32*(1), 49–61.

Leu, D. J. (2000). Our children's future: Changing the focus of literacy and literacy instruction. *The Reading Teacher, 53*(5), 424–429.

Leu, D. J. (2001). Internet project: Preparing students for new literacies in a global village. *The Reading Teacher, 54,* 568–572.

Leu, D. J. (2002). Internet workshop: Making time for literacy. *The Reading Teacher, 55,* 466–472.

Leu, D. J. (2002). The new literacies: Research on reading instruction with the Internet. In A. E. Farstrup & S. J. Samuels (Eds.), *What research has to say about reading* (3rd ed., pp. 310–336). Newark, DE: International Reading Association.

Leu, D. J., Coiro, J., Castek, J., Hartman, D. K., Henry, L. A., & Reinking, D. (2008). Research on instruction and assessment in the new literacies of online reading Comprehension. In C. C. Block and S. Parris (Eds.) (pp. 321–347). *Comprehension instruction: Research-based best practices.* New York: Guilford Press.

Leu, D. J., Jr., & Kinzer, C. K. (1999). Effective reading instruction K-8 (4th ed.). Englewood Cliffs, NJ: Merrill.

Leu, D.J., Jr., & Kinzer, C.K. (2000). The convergence of literacy instruction and networked technologies for information and communication. *Reading Research Quarterly, 35,* 108–127.

Leu, D. J., Kinzer, C. K., Coiro, J. L., & Cammack, D. W. (2004). Toward a theory of new literacies emerging from the Internet and other information and communication technologies. In R. B. Ruddell & N. J. Unrau (Eds.), *Theoretical Models and Processes of Reading* (5th ed., pp. 1570–1613). Newark, DE: International Reading Association.

Leu, D.J., & Leu, D.D. (1999). *Teaching with the Internet: Lessons from the classroom* (2nd ed.) Norwood MA: Christopher-Gordon Publishers.

Leu, D.J., Zawilinski, L., Castek, J., Banerjee, M., Housand, B.C., Liu, Y., & O'Neil, M. (2007). What is new about the new literacies of online reading comprehension? In L. S. Rush, A. J. Eakle, & A. Berger (Eds.) (pp. 37–68). *Secondary School Literacy: What Research Reveals for Classroom Practice.* Urbana, IL: National Council Teachers of English.

Lewin, L. (1998). *Great performances: Creating classroom-based assessment tasks.* Alexandria, VA: ASCD.

Lewis, J., & Day, G. (2004). Continuing professional development for teachers. *Journal of Biological Education, 38*(3), 144–146.

Lidz, C. S. (1995). Dynamic assessment and the legacy of L. S. Vygotsky. *School Psychology International, 16,* 143–153.

Lipson, M. Y. (2001). A fresh look at comprehension. Paper presented at the Reading Language Arts Symposium, Chicago, Illinois.

Lipson, M. Y., & Wixson, K. (2009). *Assessment and instruction of reading and writing difficulties: An interactive approach* (4th ed.). Boston: Allyn & Bacon.

Littman, C. B., & Stodolsky, S. S. (1998). The professional reading of high school academic teachers. *Journal of Educational Research, 92*(2), 75–85.

Lonergan, D. (1997). Network science: Bats, birds, and trees. *Educational Leadership, 55*(3), 34–36.

Long, S. A., Winograd, P. N., & Bridge, C. A. (1989). The effects of reader and text characteristics on imagery reported during and after reading. *Reading Research Quarterly, 24*(3), 353–372.

Long, S.A., Winograd, P.A., & Bridge, C.A. (1989). The effects of reader and text characteristics on reports of imagery during and after reading. *Reading Research Quarterly, 24,* 353–372.

Lonsdale, M., & McCurry, D. (2004). *Literacy in the new millennium.* Formal report: National Centre for Vocational Education Research. Retrieved May 15, 2009. http://www.ncver.edu.au/research/proj/nr2.pdf

Luke, A., & Freebody, P. (1999). Further notes on the four resources model. *Reading Online.* Retrieved May 15, 2009, from http://www.reading.org/publications/ROL/.

Macon, J.M. (1991). Bio-Pyramid. In J.M. Macon, D. Bewell, & M.E.Vogt (Eds). *Responses to literature: Grades K-8.* Newark, DE: International Reading Association.

Madaus, G. F., & Kellaghan, T. (1993). Testing as a mechanism of public policy: A brief history and description. *Measurement and Evaluation in Counseling and Development, 26,* 6–10.

Madaus, G. F., & O'Dwyer, L. M. (1999). A short history of performance assessment. *Phi Delta Kappan, 80*(9), 688–695.

Mandel, S. (2006). What new teachers really need. *Educational Leadership, 63*(6), 66–69.

Mansilla, V.B., & Gardner, H. (1997). Of kinds of disciplines and kinds of understanding. *Phi Delta Kappan, 78*(5), 381–386.

Manzo, A. V. (1969). The ReQuest procedure. *The Journal of Reading, 13*(2), 123–126.

March, T. (2003/2004). The learning power of WebQuests. *Educational Leadership, 61*(4), 42–46.

Maring, G., Furman, G., & Blum-Anderson, J. (1985). Five cooperative learning strategies for mainstreamed youngsters in content area classrooms. *The Reading Teacher, 39*(3), 310–313.

Marsalis, W. (2005). *Jazz A-B-Z: An ABC collection of jazz portraits.* Cambridge, MA: Candlewick Press.

McCullough, D. (2001). *John Adams.* New York: Simon & Schuster.

McGinley, W. & Denner, P. (1987). Story impressions: A pre-reading/prewriting activity. *Journal of Reading, 31,* 248–253.

McKeown, M. G., & Beck, I. L. (1993). Grappling with text ideas: Questioning the author. *The Reading Teacher, 46*(7), 16–21.

McLaughlin, E.M. (1987). QuIP: A writing strategy to improve comprehension of expository structure. *The Reading Teacher, 40*(7), 650–654.

McLaughlin, M. (1995). *Performance assessment: A practical guide to implementation.* Boston, MA: Houghton Mifflin.

McLaughlin, M. (2001). Sociocultural influences on content literacy teachers' beliefs and innovative practices. Paper presented at the 51st Annual Meeting of the National Reading Conference, San Antonio, TX.

McLaughlin, M. (2003). *Guided Comprehension in the primary grades.* Newark, DE: International Reading Association.

McLaughlin, M., & Allen, M. B. (2002a). *Guided Comprehension: A teaching model for grades 3–8.* Newark, DE: International Reading Association.

McLaughlin, M., & Allen, M. B. (2002b). Guided Comprehension in action. Newark, DE: International Reading Association.

McLaughlin, M., & Allen, M. B. (2009). *Guided Comprehension in grades 3–8* (2nd ed.). Newark, DE: International Reading Association.

McLaughlin, M., & DeVoogd, G. (2004a). Critical literacy as comprehension: Expanding reader response. *Journal of Adolescent and Adult Literacy, 48*(1), 42–52.

McLaughlin, M., & DeVoogd, G. (2004b). *Critical literacy: Enhancing students' comprehension of text.* New York: Scholastic.

McLaughlin, M., & Kennedy, A. (1993). A classroom guide to performance-based assessment. Princeton, NJ: Houghton Mifflin.

McLaughlin, M., & Vogt, M. E. (1996). *Portfolios in teacher education.* Newark, DE: International Reading Association.

McLaughlin, M., & Vogt, M.E. (1998) Portfolio assessment for inservice teachers: A collaborative model. In M. McLaughlin, M. E. Vogt, J. Anderson, J. Dumez, M. G. Peter, & A. Hunter *Professional portfolio models: Applications in education,* (pp. 1–70) Norwood, MA: Christopher-Gordon.

McNergney, R. F., & Herbert, J. M. (1998). *Foundations of education: The challenge of professional practice* (2nd ed.). Boston, MA: Allyn and Bacon.

McPherson, J.M. (2002). *Field of Fury: The American Civil War.* New York: Atheneum.

McTighe, J., & O'Connor, J. (2005). Seven keys to effective learning. *Educational Leadership, 63*(3), 10–17.

Means, B. (2000/2001). Technology use in tomorrow's schools. *Educational Leadership, 58*(4), 57–61.

Mike, D. G. (1996). Internet in the schools: A literacy perspective. *Journal of Adolescent and Adult Literacy, 40*(1), 4–13.

Miller, K.R. & Levine, S.J. (2008). *Biology.* Upper Saddle River, NJ: Prentice Hall.

Minick, N. (1987). Implications of Vygotsky's theories for dynamic assessment. In C. S. Lidz (Ed.) *Dynamic assessment: An interactional approach for evaluating learning potential* (pp. 116–140). New York: Guilford.

Moje, E. B. (1996). "I teach students, not subjects": Teacher–student relationships as contexts for secondary literacy. *Reading Research Quarterly, 31*(2), 172–195.

Moorman, G., & Horton, J. (2007). Millennials and how to teach them. In J. Lewis & G. Moorman (Eds.), *Adolescent literacy instruction: Policies and promising practices* (pp. 263–285). Newark, DE: International Reading Association.

Morrison, T.G., & Chilcoat, G.W. (1998). The "Living Newspaper Theatre" in the language arts classroom. *Journal of Adolescent and Adult Literacy, 42* (2), 104–115.

Morrow, L. M., Cunningham, K., & Murray-Olsen, M. (1994). *Current strategies for literacy development in early childhood science texts* (Reading Research Report, No. 11). College Park, MD: Reading Research Center.

Mtetwa, D. K. J., & Kwari, R. (2003). Peer mentoring by resource teachers in Zimbabwean schools. *Mentoring & Tutoring: Partnership in Learning, 11*(3), 273–283.

Murray, D. M. (2007). Teach writing your way. In K. Beers, R . E. Probst, & L. Reif (Eds.), *Adolescent reading: Turning promise into practice* (pp. 179–187). Portsmouth, NH: Heinemann.

Nagy, W. (1988). *Teaching vocabulary to improve reading comprehension*. Newark, DE: International Reading Association.

National Commission on Excellence in Education. (1983). *A nation at risk: The imperative for educational reform*. Washington, DC: U.S. Department of Education.

National Commission on Teaching and America's Future. (1997). *Doing what matters most: Investing in quality teaching*. Available at http://www.tc.columbia.edu/-teachingcomm.

National Council of Teachers of Mathematics. (1989). *Curriculum and evaluation standards for school mathematics*. Reston, VA: Author.

National Reading Panel. (2000). *Teaching children to read: An evidence-based assessment of the scientific research literature on reading and its implications for reading instruction*. Washington, DC: National Institutes of Health.

Noddings, N. (1997). Thinking about standards. *Phi Delta Kappan, 79*(3), 184–189.

Northwest Central Regional Educational Laboratory (NCREL) & Metiri Group. (2003). *21st century skills: Literacy in the digital age*. http://www.metiri.com/features.html Downloaded May 15, 2009.

Northwest Regional Educational Laboratory (NWREL). (2001). Teacher Mentoring Programs. Available at http://www.nwrel.org/request/may01/mentoring.html

Oblinger, D. (2003). Boomers, Gen-Xers & Millennials: Understanding the new students. Educase Review, 37–47.

Ogle, D. (1986). K-W-L: A teaching model that develops active reading of expository text. *The Reading Teacher, 39*, 564–570.

Ogle, D. (2000). Making it visual: A picture is worth a thousand words. In M. McLaughlin & M.E. Vogt (Eds.), *Creativity and innovation in content area teaching* (pp. 55–71). Norwood, MA: Christopher-Gordon.

Opitz, M. F., & Harding-DeKam, J. L. (2007). Understanding and teaching English-language learners. *The Reading Teacher, 60*(6), 590–593.

Oravec, J. A. (2002). Bookmarking the world: Weblog applications in education. *Journal of Adolescent & Adult Literacy, 45*(7), 616–621.

Pallotta, J. (2004). *The battle alphabet book*. Watertown, MA: Charlesbbridge Publishing.

Palmer, R. G., & Stewart, R. A. (1997). Nonfiction trade books in content area instruction. *Journal of Adolescent and Adult Literacy, 40*, 630–641.

Patrick, H., & Yoon, C. (2004) Early adolescents' motivation during science investigation. *Journal of Educational Research, 97*(6), 319–328.

Pearson, P. D. (2001). What we have learned in 30 years. Paper presented at the 51st Annual Meeting of the National Reading Conference, San Antonio, TX.

Pearson, P. D., Hiebert, E. H., & Kamil, M. L. (2007). Vocabulary assessment: What we know and what we need to learn. *Reading Research Quarterly, 42*(2), 282–296.

Peregoy, S. F., & Boyle, O. F. (2005). English learners reading English: What we know, what we need to know. In Z. Fang (Ed.), *Literacy teaching and learning: Current issues and trends* (pp. 18–27). Upper Saddle River, NJ: Pearson/Merrill/Prentice Hall.

Perkins-Gough, D. (2007). Focus on adolescent English language learners. *Educational Leadership, 64*(6), 90–91.

Pew Internet & American Life Project (2001). The Internet and education: Findings of the Pew Internet & American Life Project. Retrieved May 15, 2009 from http://www.pewInternet.org/reports <http://www.pewinternet.org/reports>.

Pilgreen, J. (2006). Supporting English learners: Developing academic language in the content area classroom. In T. Young & N. L. Hadaway (Eds.), *Supporting the literacy development of English learners* (pp. 41–60). Newark, DE: International Reading Association.

Pressley, M. (2000). What should comprehension instruction be the instruction of? In M. Kamil, P. Mosenthal, P. D. Pearson, & R. Barr (Eds.), *Handbook of reading research* (Vol. 3, pp. 545–561). Mahwah, NJ: Lawrence Erlbaum Associates.

Pressley, M. (2002). *Reading instruction that works: The case for balanced teaching* (2nd ed.). New York: Guilford.

Pressley, M., & Afflerbach, P. (1995). *Verbal protocols of reading: The nature of constructively responsive reading*. Hillsdale, NJ: Lawrence Erlbaum Associates.

Raphael, T. (1986). Teaching children question–answer relationships, revisited. *The Reading Teacher, 39*, 516–522.

Ravitch, D. (1995). *National standards in American education*. Washington, DC: Brookings Institute.

Readence, J., Bean, T., & Baldwin, R. (2000). *Content area reading: An integrated approach* (7th ed.). Dubuque, IA: Kendall Hunt.

Reif, L. (2007). Writing: Commonsense matters. In K. Beers, R.E. Probst, & L. Reif (Eds.), *Adolescent reading: Turning promise into practice* (pp. 189–208). Portsmouth, NH: Heinemann.

Reigeluth, C. M. (1997). Educational standards: To standardize or to customize learning? *Phi Delta Kappan, 79*(3), 202–206.

Reinking, D. (1998). Introduction: Synthesizing technological transformations of literacy in a post-typographic world. In D. Reinking, M. McKenna, L. Labbo, & R. Kieffer (Eds.), *Handbook of literacy and technology* (pp. xi–xxx). Mahwah, NJ: Lawrence Erlbaum Associates.

Richard-Amato, P.A. (1988). *Making it happen: Interaction in the second language classroom*. New York: Longman.

Richardson, J. (2004). Content area literacy lessons go high tech. *Reading Online, 8*(1), 6–16.

Richek, M. A. (2005). Words are wonderful: Interactive, time-efficient strategies to teach meaning vocabulary. *The Reading Teacher, 58*(5), 414–423.

Robinson, F. P. (1946). *Effective study* (2nd ed.). New York: Harper & Row.

Roit, M. L. (2006). Essential comprehension strategies for English learners. In T. Young & N. L. Hadaway (Eds.), *Supporting the literacy development of English learners* (pp. 80–95). Newark, DE: International Reading Association.

Romano, T. (2007). Teaching writing from the inside. In K. Beers. R.E. Probst, & L. Reif (Eds.), *Adolescent reading: Turning promise into practice* (pp. 167–178). Portsmouth, NH: Heinemann.

Rosenblatt, L. (2002, December). *A pragmatist theoretician looks at research: Implications and questions calling for answers*. Paper presented at the 52nd annual meeting of the National Reading Conference, Miami, Florida.

Rosenblatt, L. M. (1978). *The reader, the text, and the poem: The transactional theory of the literary work.* Carbondale, IL: Southern Illinois University Press.

Ruddell, R. B. (1995). Those influential reading teachers: Meaning negotiators and motivation builders. *The Reading Teacher, 48,* 454–463.

Ruddell, R. B. (2004). Researching the influential literacy teacher: Characteristics, beliefs, strategies, and new research directions. In R. B. Ruddell & N. J. Unrau (Eds.), *Theoretical models and processes of reading* (5th ed., pp. 979–997). Newark, DE: International Reading Association.

Rupley, W. H., Logan, J. W., & Nicholas, W. D. (1998/1999). Vocabulary instruction in a balanced reading program. *The Reading Teacher, 52*(4), 336–346.

Salomon, G. (1997). Of mind and media: How culture's symbolic forms affect learning and thinking. *Phi Delta Kappan, 78*(5), 375–380.

Santa, C. M. (2006). A vision for adolescent literacy: Ours or theirs? *Journal of Adolescent and Adult Literacy, 49*(6), 466–476.

Santoro, L. E., Chard, D. J., Howard, L., & Baker, S. K. (2008). Making the very most of classroom read-alouds to promote comprehension and vocabulary. *The Reading Teacher, 61*(5), 396–408.

Savage, J. (1998). *Teaching reading and writing: Combining skills, strategies, and literature* (2nd ed.). Boston, MA: McGraw-Hill.

Savery, J. R., & Duffy., T. M. (1995). Problem-based learning: An instructional model and its constructivist framework. *Educational Technology, 35,* 31–38.

Scharrer, E. (2002–2003). Making a case for media literacy in the curriculum: Outcomes and assessment. *Journal of Adolescent & Adult Literacy, 46*(4), 354–358.

Schmar-Dobler, E. (2003). Reading on the Internet: The link between literacy and technology. *Journal of Adolescent and Adult Literacy, 47*(1), 80–85.

Schmitt, N., & Carter, R. (2000). The lexical advantages of narrow reading for second language learners. *TESOL Journal, 9*(1), 4–9.

Schmoker, M., & Marzano, R. J. (1999) Realizing the promise of standards-based education. *Educational Leadership, 56*(6), 17–21.

Schoenbach, R., Greenleaf, C., Cziko, C., & Hurwitz, L. (1999). *Reading for understanding.* San Francisco: Jossey-Bass.

Schon, D. (1987). *Educating the reflective practitioner.* San Francisco, CA: Jossey-Bass.

Schwartz, D. M. (2001). *Q is for quark: A science alphabet book.* Berkeley, California: Tricycle Press.

Schwartz, R., & Raphael, T. (1985). Concept of definition: A key to improving students' vocabulary. *The Reading Teacher, 39*(2), 198–205.

Scribner, S., & Cole, M. (1981). *The psychology of literacy.* Cambridge, MA: Harvard University Press.

Serafini, F. (2003, February). Informing our practice: Modernist, transactional, and critical perspectives on children's literature and reading instruction. *Reading Online, 6*(6). Available: http://www.readingonline.org/articles/art_index.asp?HREF=serafini/index.html. Downloaded May 15, 2009.

Shank, M.J. (2005). Mentoring among high school teachers: A dynamic and reciprocal group process. *Mentoring and Tutoring, 13*(1) 73–82.

Shepard, L.A. (2005). Linking formative assessment to scaffolding. *Educational Leadership, 63*(3), 66–70.

Short, D., & Echevarria, J. (2004/2005). Teacher skills to support English language learners. *Educational Leadership, 62*(4), 8–13.

Short, K. G., & Burke, C. (1996). Examining our beliefs and practices through inquiry. *Language Arts, 73,* 97–103.

Short, K., Harste, J., & Burke, C. (1996). *Creating classrooms for authors and inquirers.* Portsmouth, NH: Heinemann.

Shurtz, J. (November, 1998). *. . . and YOU are there! Helping your students write about history.* Unpublished workshop handout. Springfield, MO: Drury College Reading Conference.

Silverblatt, A. (2000, September). Media literacy in the digital age. *Reading Online, 4*(3). http://www.readingonline.org/newliteracies/lit_index.asp?HREF=/newliteracies/silverblatt/index.html.

Singer, D. G., & Singer, J. L. (1998). Developing critical viewing skills and media literacy in children. *Annals of the American Academy of Political and Social Science, 557,* 164–180.

Sippola, A. E. (1995). K-W-L-S. *The Reading Teacher, 48*(6), 542–543.

Sippola, A. E. (1995). K-W-L-S. *The Reading Teacher, 48,* 542–543.

Smith, F. (1997). *Reading without nonsense.* New York: Teachers College Press.

Stahl, S., & Kapinus, B. (1991). Possible sentences: Predicting word meaning to teach content area vocabulary. *The Reading Teacher, 45,* 36–43.

Stepien, B. & Gallagher, S. A. (1993). Problem-based learning: As authentic as it gets. *Educational Leadership, 50*(7), 25–28.

Stepien, B., & Gallagher, S. A. (1997). Infusing critical thinking skills into the problem-based learning process. A paper presented at the Assessment-Instruction Connection: ASCD Conference on Teaching and Learning, Orlando, Florida.

Stiggins, R., & DuFour, R. (2009) Maximizing the power of formative assessments. *Phi Delta Kappan, 90*(9), 640–644.

Strickland, D., & Kamil, M. (2004). *Improving reading achievement through professional development.* Norwood, MA: Christopher Gordon.

Summers, S. L. (2000, October). Get 'em thinking! Using the "3 Rs" of media literacy. *Reading Online, 4*(4). http://www.readingonline.org/newliteracies/lit_index.asp?HREF=/newlitera-cies/summers/index.html.

Teachers of English to Speakers of Other Languages (TESOL). (2006). *PreK – 12 English Language Proficiency Standards in the core content areas.* http://dcsd.k12.nv.us/pdc/2006_ tesol_proficiency_stds.htm Downloaded May 15, 2009.

Thompson, S. (2001). The authentic standards movement and its evil twin. *Phi Delta Kappan, 82,* 358–362.

Tierney, R. (1998). Literacy assessment reform: Shifting beliefs, principled possibilities, and emerging practices. *The Reading Teacher, 51*(5), 374–389.

Tierney, R. (2008). The agency and artistry of meaning makers within and across digital spaces. In S.E. Israel, & G.G. Duffy (Eds.) (pp. 261–288) *Handbook of Research on Reading Comprehension.* Lawrence Erlbaum Associates.

Tierney, R.J., & Pearson, P.D. (1983). Toward a composing model of reading. *Language Arts, 60,* 569–580.

Tomlinson, C. A. (2000). Reconcilable differences? Standards-based teaching and differentiation. *Educational Leadership, 58*(1), 6–11.

Tomlinson, C.A. (1999). *The differentiated classroom: Responding to the needs of all learners.* Alexandria, VA: Association for Supervision and Curriculum Development

Tomlinson, C.A., & Doubet, K. (2005). Reach them to teach them. *Educational Leadership, 62*(7), 8–15.

Topping, D.H., & McManus, R.A. (2002). A culture of literacy in science. *Educational Leadership, 60*(3), 30–33.

Trubowitz, S. (2004). The why, how, and what of mentoring. *Phi Delta Kappan, 85*(1), 59–62.

Trubowitz, S., & Robins, M. (2003). *The good teacher mentor: Setting the standard for support and* success. New York: Teachers College Press.

Tyner, B., & Green, S. E. (2005). *Small-group reading instruction: A differentiated model for intermediate readers, grades 3–8.* Newark, DE: International Reading Association.

Tyson, H., & Woodward, A. (1989). Why students aren't learning very much from textbooks. *Educational Leadership, 47*(3), 14–17.

Valencia, S. W. (1998). *Literacy portfolios in action.* Fort Worth, Texas: Harcourt Brace.

Vardell, S. M., Hadaway, N. L., & Young, T. A. (2006). Matching books and readers: Selecting literature for English learners. *The Reading Teacher, 59*(8), 734–741.

Vaughn, J., & Estes, T. (1986). *Reading and reasoning beyond the primary grades.* Boston: Allyn and Bacon.

Villegas, A. M., & Lucas, T. (2007). The culturally responsive teacher. *Educational Leadership, 64*(6), 28–33.

Vogt, M.E. (2000). Active learning: Dramatic play in the content areas. In M. McLaughlin and M.E. Vogt (Eds.), *Creativity and innovation in content area teaching* (pp. 73–90). Norwood, MA: Christopher Gordon Publishers.

Vogt, M. E., & McLaughlin, M. (2004). Teaching and learning in a global society: Examining changing definitions of literacy. In M. Pandis, A. Ward, & S. R. Mathews (Eds.), *Reading, writing, thinking: Proceedings of the 13th European Conference on Reading.* Newark, DE: International Reading Association.

Vygotsky, L. (1978). *Mind in society.* Cambridge, MA: Harvard University Press.

Vygotsky, L. S. (1987). The development of scientific concepts in childhood. In R. W. Rieber & A. S. Carton (Eds.) *The collected works of L. S. Vygotsky. Vol.1.* New York: Plenum.

Wagner, B.J., & Barnett, L.A. (1998). *Educational drama and language arts: What research shows.* Portsmouth, NH: Heinemann.

Waldo, B. (1991). Story pyramid. In J.M. Macon, D. Bewell, & M.E.Vogt (Eds). *Responses to literature: Grades K-8* (pp. 23–24). Newark, DE: International Reading Association.

Weber, E. (1999). *Student assessment that works. A practical approach.* Boston: Allyn Bacon.

Wiggins, G., & McTighe, J. (1998). *Understanding by design.* Alexandria, VA: Association for Supervision and Curriculum Development.

Wiggins, G., & McTighe, J. (2006). Examining the teaching life. *Educational Leadership, 63*(6), 26–29.

Wiggins, G., & McTighe, J. (2008). Put understanding first. *Educational Leadership, 65*(8), 36–41.

Willis, S. (1996). Student exhibitions put higher-order skills to the test. *Education Update, 38* (2), 1, 3. Alexandria, VA: Association for Supervision and Curriculum Development.

Young, T. A., & Hadaway, N. L. (2006). *Supporting the literacy development of English learners.* Newark, DE: International Reading Association.

Zemelman, S., Daniels, H., & Hyde, A. (2005). *Best practice: New standards for teaching and learning in America's schools,* (3rd ed.). Portsmouth, NH: Heinemann.

Richek, M. A., 94
Robins, M., 259, 260
Robinson, F. P., 134
Roit, M. L., 147, 148
Romano, P., 69
Romano, S., 173
Romano, T., 157
Rosenblatt, L. M., 45
Ruddell, R. B., 3, 4, 44
Rupley, W. H., 94

Salomon, G., 211
Santa, C. M., 16
Santoro, L. E., 132
Savage, J., 132
Savery, J. R., 7, 43
Schaller, J. L., 46
Schmar-Dobler, E., 43, 180
Schmitt, N., 154
Schmoker, M., 33, 236
Schoenbach, R., 15, 261, 262
Schon, D., 233
Schwartz, D. M., 225
Schwartz, R., 100, 113, 150
Scieszka, J., 133
Scribner, S., 15
Serafini, F., 20
Shank, M. J., 259–261
Shepard, L. A., 239, 251
Short, D. J., 67, 139, 140, 144, 147
Short, K. G., 7, 56, 82, 154, 226

Shurtz, J., 221
Silverblatt, A., 24
Singer, D. G., 24
Singer, J. L., 24
Sippola, A. E., 69, 113, 127
Slesinger, B. A., 119
Smith, F., 43–44
Snow, C. E., 7, 15–17, 26, 90, 91, 155
Sou, A., 244
Stepien, B., 197, 198
Stewart, R. A., 118
Stiggins, R., 239
Strauss, W., 4–5
Streightiff, K., 37–38
Summers, S. L., 24–25

Tatum, A. W., 154
Taylor, B. M., 43–44
Thompson, M., 235
Thompson, S., 38, 39
Tierney, R. J., 157, 178, 234
Tomlinson, C. A., 33, 34, 114
Topping, D. H., 167–168
Trubowitz, S., 259, 260
Tyner, B., 113
Tyson, H., 118

Valencia, S. W., 234
Vardell, S. M., 118
Vaughn, J., 66, 82, 113, 122
Venn, J., 88

Vergara, E., 35–37
Villaume, S. K., 94
Villegas, A. M., 139, 142
Vogt, M. E., 10, 144, 147, 219, 232, 235
Vygotsky, L., 43, 48, 232, 234

Wagner, B. J., 219, 226
Waldo, B., 79–82
Watkins, C., 67
Watkins, E., 233–234
Watts-Taffe, S. M., 93–95
Weber, E., 239
Wigfield, A., 9
Wiggins, G., 33, 251, 261, 266
William, D., 235
Williams, J., 151
Willis, S., 244
Winograd, P. A., 73
Winters, L., 238, 250
Witt, E., 118
Wixson, K., 46
Woodward, A., 118

Yoon, C., 9
Young, T. A., 118, 138, 142
Younger, M., 70

Zawilinski, L., 182–184, 189
Zemelman, S., 33
Zimmerman, S., 72, 154

SUBJECT INDEX